Adult Development and Aging

Ninth Edition

John C. Cavanaugh
Senior Consultant, Pathseekers II, Inc.

Cengage

Australia • Brazil • Canada • Mexico • Singapore • United Kingdom • United States

Cengage

Adult Development and Aging, **Ninth Edition**
John C. Cavanaugh

SVP, Cengage Academic Product Management: Erin Joyner

VP, Product Management, Learning Experiences: Thais Alencar

Portfolio Product Director: Laura Ross

Portfolio Product Manager: Cazzie Reyes

Vendor Content Manager: Manoj Kumar, Lumina Datamatics Limited

Product Assistant: Fantasia Mejia

Digital Project Manager: Scott Diggins

Content Acquisition Analyst: Deanna Ettinger

Content Acquisition Project Manager: Haneef Abrar, Lumina Datamatics Limited

Production Service: Lumina Datamatics Limited

Cover Designer: Sara Greenwood

Interior Designer: Leslie Kell

Cover Images Sources: Illustration
151926923 © Mtlapcevic | Dreamstime.com
Jupiterimages/Getty Images
Leland Bobbe/Getty Images
Inti St Clair/Getty Images
Bob Thomas/Getty Images
Ariel Skelley/DigitalVision/Getty Images

Library of Congress Control Number: 2022915221

ISBN: 978-0-357-79627-6

Cengage
200 Pier 4 Boulevard
Boston, MA 02210
USA

Printed in the United States of America
Print Number: 01 Print Year: 2023

To Chris

Contents

Brief Contents

Preface

People's experiences of growing older in the 21st century differ dramatically from their grandparents' and great-grandparents' experiences. The complex issues confronting individuals and societies resulting from populations that are becoming older on average are the reason a solid grounding in research and theory about adult development and aging is essential even for understanding news events. The debates about how to provide and prioritize aspects of health care, such as who should receive the COVID-19 vaccines in what order, bring many issues to the forefront. Increasingly, issues such as Medicare, end-of-life issues, and longevity and the possibility of significant intergenerational policy issues will receive more attention as important public policy issues. Other news stories about genetic breakthroughs, stem cell research, brain-imaging techniques, and the latest breakthroughs in treating dementia and cancer happen regularly. To understand why these issues are so critical, one must understand aging in a broader, rapidly changing context. That is why *Adult Development and Aging* is now in its ninth edition.

The next few decades of this century will witness a fundamental change in the face of the population—literally. Along with most other countries in the developed world, the United States will experience a rapid growth in the older adult population due to the continued aging of the baby-boom generation, soon to be followed by generation X. Additionally, the proportion of older adults who are Black, Latino/a, Asian, and Native American will increase even more rapidly. To address these changes effectively, new approaches need to be created through the combined efforts of people in many occupations—academics, gerontologists, social workers, healthcare professionals, financial experts, marketing professionals, teachers, factory workers, technologists, information technology workers, government elected officials and staff, human service providers, exercise professionals, and nutritionists, to mention just a few. Every reader of this book, regardless of their area of expertise, needs to understand older adults to master the art of living.

This ninth edition of *Adult Development and Aging* continues to provide in-depth coverage of the major issues in the psychology of adult development and aging. The ninth edition adds numerous topics and provides expanded coverage of many of the ones discussed in earlier editions. Each chapter was thoroughly reviewed and updated. Throughout the text, particular attention was paid to the effects of COVID-19 and on the effects of various types of discrimination and bias on the experience of adult development and aging. Among the numerous changes in the ninth edition are the following.

Chapter 1

- New **Controversies** feature on the importance of lenses in understanding issues related to gender, ethnicity, and race
- Introduces the concept of intersectionality as an important concept in understanding how different demographic categories interact in their influence on people
- New subsection on Tools for Doing Developmental Research that discusses online research skills training, tools for constructing surveys, and various data libraries and repositories
- Reframed discussion on sociocultural forces now includes gender and biological sex as key aspects
- Introduces COVID-19 as a major event that has had a pervasive influence on all aspects of adult development and aging

Chapter 2

- Updates throughout regarding neuroscience discoveries and effects on COVID-19 on brain functioning
- New **How Do We Know?** feature on relation between white matter hyperintensities and risk of falling

- Expanded discussion of neuroethics, including new **Social Policy Implications** feature
- Additional discussion of white matter hyperintensities and their relation to cognitive changes
- Additional discussion of brain processes and emotion, and more focused discussion on theories and models of brain–behavior changes

Chapter 3

- Additional discussion of herbal and plant-based foods that have positive effects on biological processes related to aging
- New discussion of effects of trauma, post-traumatic stress, and discrimination on DNA methylation, a measure of biological age
- New **Real People** feature on Marlee Matlin and Chella Man
- New **How Do We Know?** feature on sociodemographic factors in using telemedicine for cardiovascular disease
- New **Controversies** feature on the search for never-ending youth
- More information on medications to treat bone loss

Chapter 4

- New **Controversies** feature on what it would take to live to 200
- New **How Do We Know?** feature on older Samoans' concepts of age, aging, and wellness
- New discussion of COVID-19 and the immune system
- New discussion on the opioid crisis and pain management
- Additional coverage throughout the chapter of the impact of healthcare disparities on longevity and health

Chapter 5

- New **Discover Development** feature on age-friendly communities
- New **How Do We Know?** feature on disparities in quality of life among nursing home residents
- New **Social Policy Implications** feature on Evidence-based design of healthcare facilities
- New discussion of age-friendly communities
- Additional discussions of special care facilities

Chapter 6

- New discussion on heuristics as types of automatic processes to minimize cognitive effort
- New discussion of binding deficit as an explanation of age-related decline on episodic memory tasks
- More extensive discussion of neuroscience underpinnings of age-related differences in memory performance
- Discussion of the use of virtual reality and other technology-based interventions to improve memory performance in older adults, even those experiencing dementia
- New **Social Policy Implications** on COVID-19 effects on memory

Chapter 7

- New **Discovering Development** feature on sociocultural approaches to intelligence and intelligent behavior
- Expanded discussion of neuroscience research on decision making in daily life, with a focus on vulnerability to financial scams
- Expanded discussion of the cultural contexts of wisdom and the 6P model of wisdom
- Expanded **Social Policy Implications** feature on pseudomedicine for dementia and brain health
- New **Real People** feature on Thích Nhất Hạnh as an example of the highest level of thinking in the reflective judgment model

Chapter 8

- Reorganized chapter modules
- New subsection on stereotype embodiment theory
- New section on neuroscience evidence for social knowledge structures and beliefs
- New **How Do We Know?** feature on cross-cultural aspects of perceptions of aging
- Expanded discussion of collaborative cognition and sociocultural contexts of cognition

Chapter 9

- New **Controversies** feature on alternatives to the five-factor trait model
- New **Real People** feature on generativity through mentoring
- Expanded discussion on generativity in terms of its stability and its generalizability across sociodemographic groups
- New section on gender identity
- New **Social Policy Implications** feature on adult personality and the curated world of social media

Chapter 10

- New discussion of the definitions of mental health and psychopathology that includes cultural factors
- New section on post-traumatic stress disorder (based on DSM-5-TR)
- New **Controversies** feature on the impact of COVID-19 on mental health globally
- New **How Do We Know?** feature on Montessori-based activities delivered by family carers to nursing home residents with dementia

- Reorganized modules to bring additional focus on dementia and added more discussion of genetic research and neuroscience evidence

Chapter 11

- Added discussion of the effects of COVID-19 on various aspects of relationships throughout the chapter as appropriate
- Additional discussion of the decision process to have a first child and implications for relationships
- Additional discussion of the impact of the declining birth rate overall in the United States
- New **Controversies** feature on the lack of mandated paid family leave in the United States
- New **Social Policy Implications** feature on legal and social program support for grandfamilies

Chapter 12

- Added discussion of the effects of COVID-19 on the workplace and workers throughout the chapter as appropriate
- New **Real People** feature on burnout among healthcare workers
- New **Controversies** feature on creating an inclusive workplace
- Updated discussions regarding DEI in the workplace to reflect #MeToo, #BlackLivesMatter, and other movements, as well as LGBTQIA+ concerns
- New **Social Policy Implications** feature on the Great Resignation

Chapter 13

- Added discussions regarding the effects of COVID-19 on grieving, saying goodbye to loved ones, as well as other topics, and a new **Social Policy Implications** feature on COVID-19 and end-of-life issues
- New **Discovering Development** feature regarding burial options in one's community
- New updated section on prolonged grief and prolonged grief disorder based on DSM-5-TR
- New sections on what people of various ages understand about death and how they tend to view it
- New **How Do We Know?** feature on the impacts of child death and stillbirth on northern Indian parents

Chapter 14

- New **Real People** feature on how millennials and Gen-Z individuals view the future
- New section on salutogenesis and healthy aging
- New section on positive psychology and healthy aging
- New section on technology and healthy aging
- New **How Do We Know?** feature on the reliability between telemedicine and in-person assessments of cognitive functioning

Writing Style

Although **Adult Development and Aging, Ninth Edition** covers complex issues and difficult topics, clear, concise, and understandable language is used throughout. All terms were examined to ensure their use is essential; otherwise, they were eliminated.

The text is aimed at upper-division undergraduate students. Although it will be helpful if students have completed an introductory psychology or life-span human development course, the text does not assume this background.

Instructional Aids

The many pedagogical aids in previous editions have been retained and enhanced in the ninth edition.

- **Learning Aids in the Chapter Text.** Each chapter begins with a chapter outline and a set of Learning Objectives. At the start of each new module, Key Questions are presented that are keyed to each primary subsection that follows, and they direct the students' attention to the main points to be discussed. At the conclusion of each module are Review Questions, one for each primary subsection, that help students spot-check their learning. Key terms are defined in context; the term itself is printed in boldface, with the sentence containing the term's definition in color.
- **End-of-Chapter Learning Aids.** At the end of each chapter are In Review guides to help students create their own summaries of the chapter material. Because research over many decades has repeatedly showed that students learn information better when they put it in their own words, this approach was adopted to facilitate that process. Additionally, Integrating Concepts in Development questions are included as a way for students to link concepts and theories across modules within and across chapters to provide deeper understanding of how information is connected. Key terms are listed in alphabetical order with definitions and the page numbers where the term first appears.
- **Feature Boxes.** Five types of feature boxes are included. Those titled **How Do We Know?** draw attention to specific research studies that were discussed briefly in the

main body of the text. Details about the study's design, participants, and outcomes are presented as a way for students to connect the information about these issues in Chapter 1 with specific research throughout the text. **Controversies** boxes raise controversial and provocative issues about topics discussed in the chapter. These boxes encourage students to think about the implications of research or policy issues and may be used effectively as points of departure for class discussions. **Discovering Development** boxes give students a way to connect developmental principles and concepts to their and others' experiences and to resources and programs in the local community that connect with concepts and issues in the text. **Real People** provides examples of aspects of aging and how individuals or groups of people chose to handle them. These boxes provide a starting point for understanding such things as career opportunities, how to become an advocate for an issue, and so forth. Each chapter concludes with a **Social Policy Implications** feature that raises critical social policies issues connected directly to a topic discussed in the chapter; several of them also identify specific action steps that are necessary to address a social issue.

Instructor Resources

Additional instructor resources for this product are available online. Instructor assets include an Instructor's Manual, PowerPoint® slides, and a test bank powered by Cognero®. Sign up or sign in at **www.cengage.com** to search for and access this product and its online resources.

Acknowledgments

We'd like to thank several instructors who reviewed the prior edition:

- Maegan Jones, Ph.D., St. Cloud State University
- James R. Houston, Middle Tennessee State University
- Jocelyn Chen, Ph.D., Western Connecticut State University
- Julie Blaskewicz Boron, University of Nebraska, Omaha
- Nelly L. Sta. Maria, Suffolk County Community College
- Susan L. O'Donnell, George Fox University
- Erica Goddard, University at Buffalo
- Dannelle Larsen-Rife, Ph.D., Dixie State University
- Dr. Meredith McGinley, University of Wisconsin-Parkside
- Diane Cook, University of North Georgia
- Lauren Kleitz, Thomas More University
- Mary Shuttlesworth, La Roche University
- Geri M. Lotze, Virginia Commonwealth University
- Susan E. Mason, Niagara University
- Dr. Robert Hoople, SUNY Oneonta
- Gloria J. Jones, Ph.D., University of Maine at Farmington
- Nan Statton, Union County College
- Carol LaLiberte, M.Ed., Asnuntuck Community College
- Melissa Atkins, Marshall University
- Stephanie Bell, Briar Cliff University

As usual, it takes many people to produce a textbook; such is the case with the ninth edition. The editorial group at Cengage is excellent.

Thanks to Cazzie Reyes, Fantasia Mejia, Abigail J. DeVeuve, Manoj Kumar, Scott Diggins, Deanna Ettinger, Haneef Abrar, Dan'el Nighting, and Sara Greenwood for their valuable contributions.

Also, to a group too often overlooked—the sales representatives and marketing personnel. Without you, none of this would get to students to help them learn. You are an extension of us and the whole Cengage editorial and production team. What a great group of hardworking folks you are!

I also extend my deepest appreciation to Dr. Cindy Bergeman, chair, and Rhonda Singleton, department administrator, in the Department of Psychology at the University of Notre Dame for supporting my access to the Hesburgh Libraries. Without those outstanding holdings, the research base in the text would not be nearly as thorough.

My highest and sincerest thanks go to my wife, Dr. Christine Cavanaugh, who has always provided me with unconditional love and support for my work on this project. It's great fun to share with her what I continue to learn, and to get her wisdom and insights about it.

Thanks to you all. Live long and prosper!

John C. Cavanaugh

About the Author

Source: Courtesy of John C. Cavanaugh

John C. Cavanaugh is Senior Consultant at Pathseekers II, Inc. He is former president and CEO of the Consortium of Universities of the Washington Metropolitan Area, Chancellor Emeritus of the Pennsylvania State System of Higher Education, and former president of the University of West Florida. A researcher and teacher of adult development and aging for more four decades, he has published about 100 articles and chapters and authored, coauthored, or coedited 24 books on aging, information technology, and higher education policy. He is a past president of Division 20 (Adult Development and Aging) of the American Psychological Association (APA) and is a fellow of APA (Divisions 1, 2, 3, and 20) and the Gerontological Society of America, and a charter fellow of the Association for Psychological Science. He has held numerous leadership positions in these associations, including chair of the Committee on Aging for APA. He has served on numerous state and national committees for aging-related and higher education organizations. He also serves on the Yellowstone Forever National Advisory Council. John is a devoted fan of "Star Trek" and a serious traveler, photographer, backpacker, cook, and chocoholic. He is married to Dr. Christine K. Cavanaugh, with whom he writes, co-teaches, and learns something new each day.

Studying Adult Development and Aging

Chapter 1

Chapter Outline

Learning Objectives

After studying this chapter, you will be able to...

1.1. Describe the life-span perspective and the characteristics of the adult population.

1.2. Identify the basic forces of human development and the concept of age.

1.3. Describe the scientific methods used to conduct research in adult development and aging.

When the finish line came into view, Sister Madonna Buder, S.F.C.C. (who is a Catholic nun) knew her prayers had been answered. She would complete the Ironman triathlon competition—widely considered one of the most difficult athletic feats that encompasses a grueling combination of a 2.4-mile swim, 110-mile bike ride, and a 26.2 mile run (a marathon), all done in one day—and set a world record in the process. Her record? Sister Madonna was 82 years old, the oldest person ever to complete an Ironman competition within the 17-hour time limit. Even at age 90, Sister Madonna continued to compete in regular triathlons (she finished third as the oldest competitor at age 89 in the USA Triathlon national championships in the 85+ category).

Sister Madonna is only one of many older adults who have shattered our stereotypes of older adults and what they are capable of accomplishing. Consider that Jorge Mario Bergoglio was 76 when he became Pope Francis. Janet Yellen became U.S. Secretary of the Treasury at 74. The 14th Dalai Lama still inspired people in his 80s. John Lewis continued to work for social justice after turning 80. Anthony Hopkins won an Oscar for acting at 83. Whoopi Goldberg, still acting and entertaining as she nears age 70, is one of 16 entertainers to win an Emmy Award, a Grammy Award, an Academy Award, and a Tony Award. And *Rolling Stones* singer Mick Jagger still wowed audiences in his late 70s. Older adulthood is certainly not what it was once thought to be.

Sister Madonna Buder, John Lewis, and the Dalai Lama are great examples of how older adults are pushing and redefining boundaries. They demonstrate that adults are capable of doing things thought unimaginable or inappropriate not very long ago. They also illustrate how the normal changes people experience as they age vary across individuals and why we need to rethink common stereotypes about age.

There is also an entire generation actively redefining what growing older really means. The baby-boom generation, consisting of people born between 1946 and 1964, are on average the healthiest and most active generation to reach old age in history. They are not content with playing traditional roles assigned to older adults and are doing their best to change the way older adults are perceived and treated.

In this chapter, we examine a seemingly simple question: Who are older people? We will discover that the answer is more complicated than you might think. We also consider the ways in which gerontologists study adults and how adults develop.

Kyodo News/Getty Images

Even in his 80s, Dalai Lama still inspires.

Alex Wong/Getty Images News/Getty Images

John Lewis was a role model throughout his life.

Dpa Picture Alliance/Alamy Stock Photo

Sister Madonna Buder, S.F.C.C., competed in triathlons at age 90.

1.1 Perspectives on Adult Development and Aging

Key Questions

- What is gerontology? How does ageism relate to stereotypes of aging?
- What is the life-span perspective?
- What are the characteristics of the older adult population?
- How are they likely to change?

Roberto's great-grandmother Maria is 89 years old. Maria tells Roberto that when she was a young girl in El Paso, there were very few older women in either her family or the neighborhood. Roberto knows there are many older people, mostly women, in his own neighborhood, and wonders when and why this changed over her lifetime.

Before you read any more, take a minute and think about your own grandparents or great-grandparents. How would you and other people describe them? Do you want to be like them when you are their age? Would you trade places with them now?

There is one thing we all have in common—we are all headed toward older adulthood. How do you want to be thought of and treated when you get there? Do you look forward to becoming old, or are you afraid about what may lie ahead? Most of us want to enjoy a long life like Maria's but don't think much about growing old in our daily lives.

Reading this book will give you the basic facts about growing older. You will learn how to organize these facts by putting them into two contexts: the biopsychosocial framework and the life-span approach. By the time you are finished, you should have a new, different way of thinking about aging.

You already enjoy a major advantage compared with Maria. She and other people her age did not have the opportunity as students to learn much about what is typical and what is not typical about aging. Until the late 20th century, very little information was available about old age, which people generally thought to be characterized mainly by decline. **Gerontology**, the scientific study of aging from maturity through old age, has changed our understanding of aging and the aging process. As you can imagine from reading about famous older adults at the beginning of the chapter, and as you will encounter throughout this book, aging reflects both the total lived individual experiences people have as well as common experiences that define the contexts in which we live, such that the story of aging in one that has certain things in common across us all as well as our unique journey.

Despite the fact that much has changed about the image of a typical older adult since the mid-1900s, many myths about older people persist. These myths of aging lead to negative stereotypes of older people, which may result in **ageism**, a form of discrimination against older adults based on their age. Ageism has its foundations in myths and beliefs people take for granted, as well as in intergenerational relations (Nelson, 2016a, b; North & Fiske, 2012, 2016). It may be as blatant as believing that all older people should get out of the way for younger generations, are likely senile and are incapable of making decisions about their lives, and probably contribute little to society. It may occur when people show microaggressions toward older adults when they are impatient with older adults in a grocery store checkout line. Or it may be as subtle as dismissing an older person's physical complaints with the question, "What do you expect for someone your age?" As you will learn by doing the activities in the Discovering Development feature, such stereotypes surround us.

Discovering Development
Myths and Stereotypes About Aging

We are surrounded by misconceptions of older adults. We may have encountered cartoons or video segments making jokes about older adults whose memories are poor or whose physical abilities have declined. Most damaging are the ideas portrayed in the media that older adults are incapable of leading productive lives and making a difference. For example, many greeting cards portray older people as having little memory, no teeth, and no desire for sex. To discover something about adult development and aging, try to find several examples of myths or stereotypes about growing older. Explore content on YouTube and other social media sites, advertisements, articles in popular blogs, greeting cards, television shows, movies, and music. Gather as many examples as you can, and then fact check them against the research on the topic discussed in this text. By the end of the course, consider how many myths and stereotypes you can show to be busted.

This book rebuts these erroneous ideas, but it does not replace them with idealized views of adulthood and old age. Rather, it paints an accurate picture of what it means to grow old today, recognizing that development across adulthood brings growth and opportunities as well as loss and decline, and that the process of aging reflects the same systemic aspects of society that we find in other aspects of life. To begin, we consider the life-span perspective, which helps place adult development and aging into the context of the whole human experience. Afterward, we consider the fundamental developmental forces, controversies, and models that form the foundation for studying adult development and aging. In particular, we examine the biological, psychological, sociocultural, and life-cycle forces, and the nature–nurture and continuity–discontinuity controversies. We consider some basic definitions of age, making it clear that age is a truly complicated concept. Finally, by examining various research methods, we learn how the information presented in this book was obtained.

The Life-Span Perspective

Imagine trying to understand, without knowing anything about their life, what your best adult friend is like. We cannot understand adults' experiences without appreciating what came before in childhood, adolescence, and the portion of adulthood they have experienced thus far. Placing adulthood in this broader context is what the life-span perspective is all about. The **life-span perspective** divides human development into two phases: an early phase (childhood and adolescence) and a later phase (young adulthood, middle age, and old age). The early phase is characterized by rapid age-related increases in people's size and abilities. During the later phase, changes in size are slow, but abilities, perspectives, knowledge, and other characteristics continue to develop as people continue adapting to the environment (Baltes et al., 2006).

Viewed from the life-span perspective, adult development and aging are complex phenomena that cannot be understood within the scope of a single disciplinary approach. Moreover, aging is a lifelong process, so understanding how the experiences we had prior to this moment will shape those we have yet to have requires input from a wide variety of perspectives.

One of the most important perspectives on life-span development is that of Paul Baltes (1987; Baltes et al., 2006), who identified four key features of the life-span perspective:

1. **Multidirectionality.** Development involves both growth and decline; as people grow in one area, they may lose in another and at different rates. For example, people's vocabulary ability tends to increase throughout life, but reaction time tends to slow down.
2. **Plasticity.** One's capacity is not predetermined or set in concrete. Many skills can be trained or improved with practice, even in late life. There are limits to the degree of potential improvement, however, as described in later chapters.
3. **Historical context.** Each of us develops within a particular set of circumstances determined by the historical time in which we are born, the culture in which we grow up, and the opportunities and structural barriers we encounter. Maria's experiences were shaped by living in the 20th century in a Chicano neighborhood in southwest Texas.
4. **Multiple causation.** How people develop results from a wide variety of forces, which we consider later in this chapter. You will come to understand that development is shaped by biological, psychological, sociocultural, and life-cycle forces.

The life-span perspective emphasizes that human development takes a lifetime to complete. It sets the stage for understanding the many influences we experience and points out that no one part of life is any more or less important than another.

Basing their framing of the process of aging on these principles, Baltes and colleagues (2006) argue that life-span development consists of the dynamic interactions among growth, maintenance, and loss regulation. In their view, four factors are critical:

1. As people grow older, they show an age-related reduction in the amount and quality of biologically based resources.
2. There is an age-related increase in the amount and quality of culture needed to generate continuously higher growth. Usually this results in a net slowing of growth as people age.
3. People show an age-related decline in the efficiency with which they use cultural resources.
4. There is a lack of cultural, "old-age-friendly" support structures.

Taken together, these four factors create the need to shift more and more resources to maintain function and deal with biologically related losses as we grow older, leaving fewer resources to be devoted to continued growth. This shift holds true regardless of the circumstances of one's life. What does matter a great deal is whether a person has access to the support structures and processes that can help mitigate these changes. As we see throughout this book, this intersection of the shift in internal resources with the external realities of systemic factors in society paves very different paths for those who have access and those who do not. This fact has profound implications for experiencing aging and for pointing out different ways to age successfully.

These views led to Baltes and colleagues' (2006) proposing the model of selective optimization with compensation (SOC) to account for the developmental process experienced in adult development and aging. Their model posits that as people age, they naturally begin to focus on fewer areas in order to devote more of their resources to compensating for any losses they may have experienced. For example, a professional musician may play a smaller repertoire of pieces more expressively than the broader collection of pieces they previously played with more emphasis on technical skill (e.g., speed and dexterity). We will encounter the SOC model often throughout the text as a possible explanation for the behaviors we observe in adult development and aging.

Characteristics of the Older Adult Population

Did you ever stop to think about how many older adults you encounter in your day-to-day life? Did you ever wonder whether your great-grandparents had the same experience? Actually, you are privileged—there have never been as many older adults alive as there are now, so you encounter many more older people than your great-grandparents (or even your parents) did when they were entering adulthood. The proportion of older adults in the population of developed countries has increased tremendously, mainly due to better health care since the early 1900s (e.g., the elimination or prevention of previously fatal acute diseases, especially during childhood; the discovery of antibiotics and antiviral medications; better treatment for chronic diseases) and to lowering the mortality rate during childbirth. (We'll consider how this relates to how long we live in Chapter 4.)

People who study population trends, called **demographers**, use a graphic technique called a **population pyramid** to illustrate these changes. Figure 1.1 presents typical population pyramids for the most economically advantaged and least economically advantaged countries around the world. Let's consider the most economically advantaged countries first (they're the pyramids down the left side); we'll use the United States as an example. Notice the shape of the population pyramid in 1950 in the top panel. In the middle of the 20th century, there were fewer people over age 60 than under age 60, so the pyramid tapers toward the top. Compare this to projections for 2050; a dramatic change will occur in the number of people over 65.

These changes are also happening in less economically advantaged countries (the pyramids down the right side). The figures for both 1950 and 2015 resemble pyramids when you look at both the male and female halves together because there are substantially fewer older adults than younger people. But by 2050, the number of older adults even in these countries will have increased dramatically, substantially changing the shape of the figure.

Because the fertility rate in the United States has dropped from a post–World War II high of 3.6 children per woman in 1960 to a low of 1.8 in 2020 (Statista, 2021), the average age of Americans will continue to rise. By 2030, all of the baby boomers (people born between 1946 and 1964) will have reached at least age 65, meaning that 1 in 5 Americans will be 65 or older; by 2061, this ratio will increase to 1 in every 4 when members of the millennial generation (those born between 1981 and 1996) will have reached age 65 (Population Reference Bureau, 2020).

The sheer number of older Americans will place enormous pressure on federal income support systems (especially Social Security), health care (especially Medicare, Medicaid, and long-term care), and other human services. (We explore the future financing of Social Security and Medicare in Chapter 14.) The growing strain on social service systems will intensify because the most rapidly growing segment of the U.S. population is the group of people over age 85. The number of such people in the United States will increase nearly 500% between 2000 and 2050, compared with about a 50% increase in the number of 20- to 29-year-olds during the same period. Individuals over age 85 generally need more assistance with the tasks they have to accomplish in daily living than do people under 85. To meet the increasing need for support, substantially more people who have skills in working with older adults are needed. These changing ratios will also be felt in political debates over which age group deserves more federal support, creating a potential for intergenerational conflict over resources.

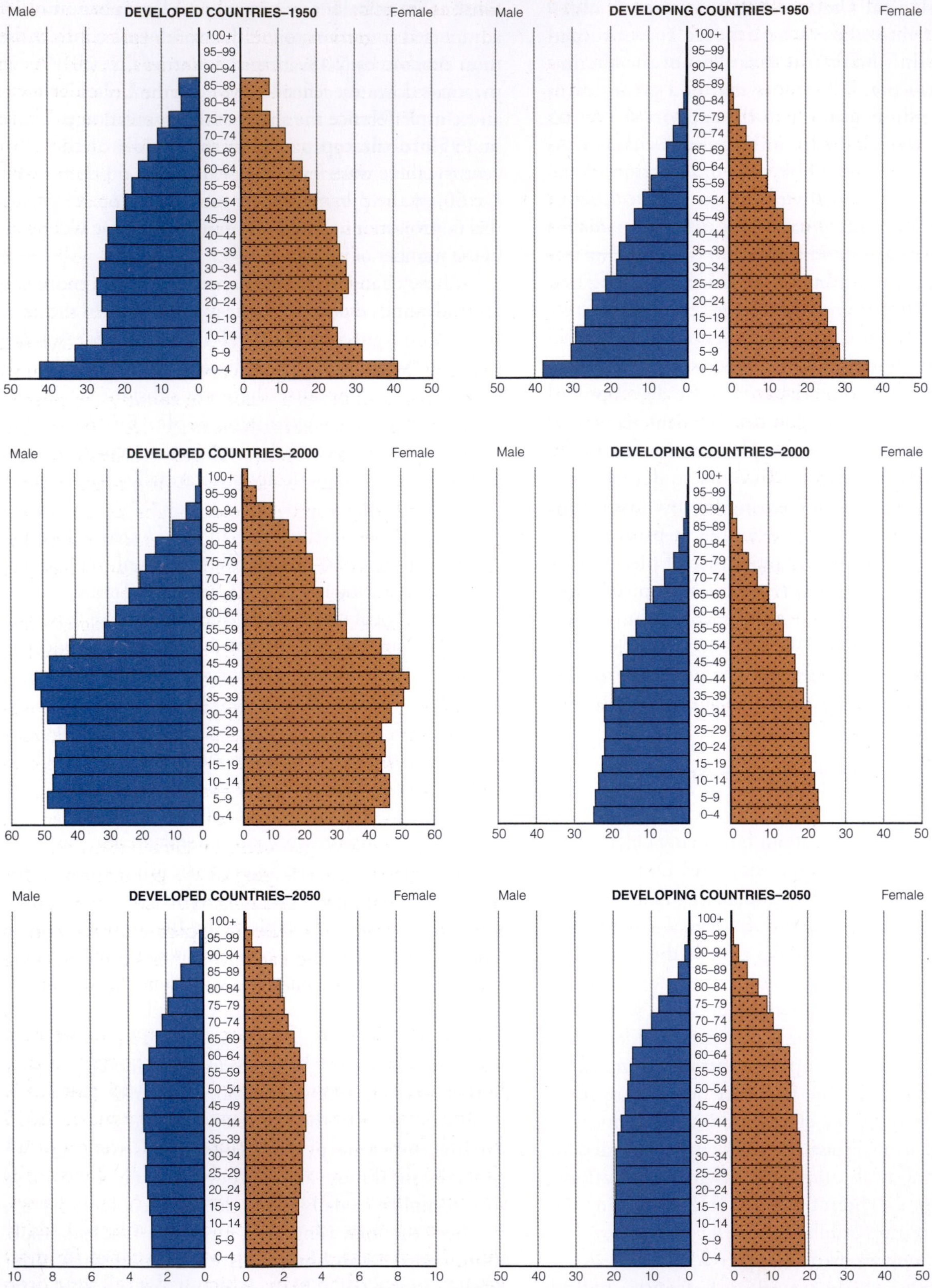

Figure 1.1 Population pyramids for developed and developing countries 1950–2050.

Sources: U.S. Data: For 1950, https://www.census.gov/dataviz/visualizations/055/. Data for 2020 and 2050, https://www2.census.gov/programs-surveys/popproj/tables/2017/2017-summary-tables/np2017-t2.xlsx. International data: For 1950, https://images.populationpyramid.net/capture/?selector=%23pyramid-share-container&url=https%3A%2F%2Fwww.populationpyramid.net%2Fworld%2F1950%2F%3Fshare%3Dtrue. For 2020, https://images.populationpyramid.net/capture/?selector=%23pyramid-share-container&url=https%3A%2F%2Fwww.populationpyramid.net%2Fworld%2F2020%2F%3Fshare%3Dtrue. For 2050, https://images.populationpyramid.net/capture/?selector=%23pyramid-share-container&url=https%3A%2F%2Fwww.populationpyramid.net%2Fworld%2F2050%2F%3Fshare%3Dtrue.

The Diversity of Older Adults in the United States. The characteristics of the older adult population in the United States are also changing rapidly—it is becoming increasingly diverse. In terms of racial and ethnic group percentages of the over-65 population, non-Hispanic White individuals comprise about 77%, non-Hispanic Black or African Americans about 9%, non-Hispanic Asians about 4.5%, non-Hispanic American Indians and Alaska Natives about 0.5%, non-Hispanic Native Hawaiians and Other Pacific Islanders about 0.1%, and Hispanic or Latino/as about 8%, with "some other race" or "two or more races" about 1% combined. Future trends will be that people of color will continue to increase in numbers and the non-Hispanic White group will continue to decrease. As you can conclude from the population pyramids, older women outnumber older men overall (Census Bureau, 2020e).

Older adults in the future will be better educated, too. By 2030, it is estimated that 85% will have a high-school diploma and about 75% will have a postsecondary credential (Census Bureau, 2021a). Better-educated people tend to live longer—mostly because they have higher incomes, which give them better access to good health care and a chance to follow healthier lifestyles (e.g., have access to and afford healthier food choices).

Blend Images - John Lund/Sam Diephuis/Getty Images

This Latina older woman represents the changing face of older adults in the United States.

Global Trends. Internationally, the number of older adults is also growing rapidly and is expected to more than double by 2050 (United Nations, 2020). As in the United States, older women outnumber older men, and this difference increases with advanced age. These rapid global changes are due mostly to improved health care overall, lower rates of death among people who give birth, and lower infant mortality. (These points will be explored in more detail in Chapter 4.) Nearly all countries are facing the need to adapt social policies to incorporate these changing demographics and resulting societal needs, especially for housing and social support.

Economically powerful countries around the world, such as China, are trying to cope with increased numbers of older adults that strain the country's resources. By 2025, China expects to have more than 300 million people over age 65. China is already addressing issues related to providing services and living arrangements for the increasing number of older adults, as the historic custom of children caring for aging parents confronts the reality of China's former one-child policy and changing lifestyles of younger generations (Xu, 2020).

China and the United States are not alone in facing increased numbers of older adults. As reported in Figure 1.2, the percentage of older adults in major geographic regions has changed since 1950 and will include many more older adults over the next few decades (United Nations, 2019). All of these regions will need to deal with an increased demand for services to older adults and, in some cases, competing demands with children and younger and middle-aged adults for limited resources.

The global general aging of the population is due mainly to two factors: a declining birth rate in many countries, often related to increases in opportunities for women (such as education and careers), and especially to more people living longer (which we examine in Chapter 4).

The COVID Caveat. The population trends we have just considered are based on data collected mostly before the full impact of the COVID-19 pandemic became clear. For example, data collection on the 2020 Federal Census ended before some of the most transmissible and deadly variants of the SARS-CoV-2 virus (the one that causes COVID-19) emerged. As time passes, it becomes clear that the pandemic affected many things, from average longevity, which declined for most groups, to Social Security, which had a full year drop in its underlying trust fund balance. The long-term effects of the pandemic on global population trends and the specific needs such as health care will continue to emerge. As a result, countries will need to be flexible in

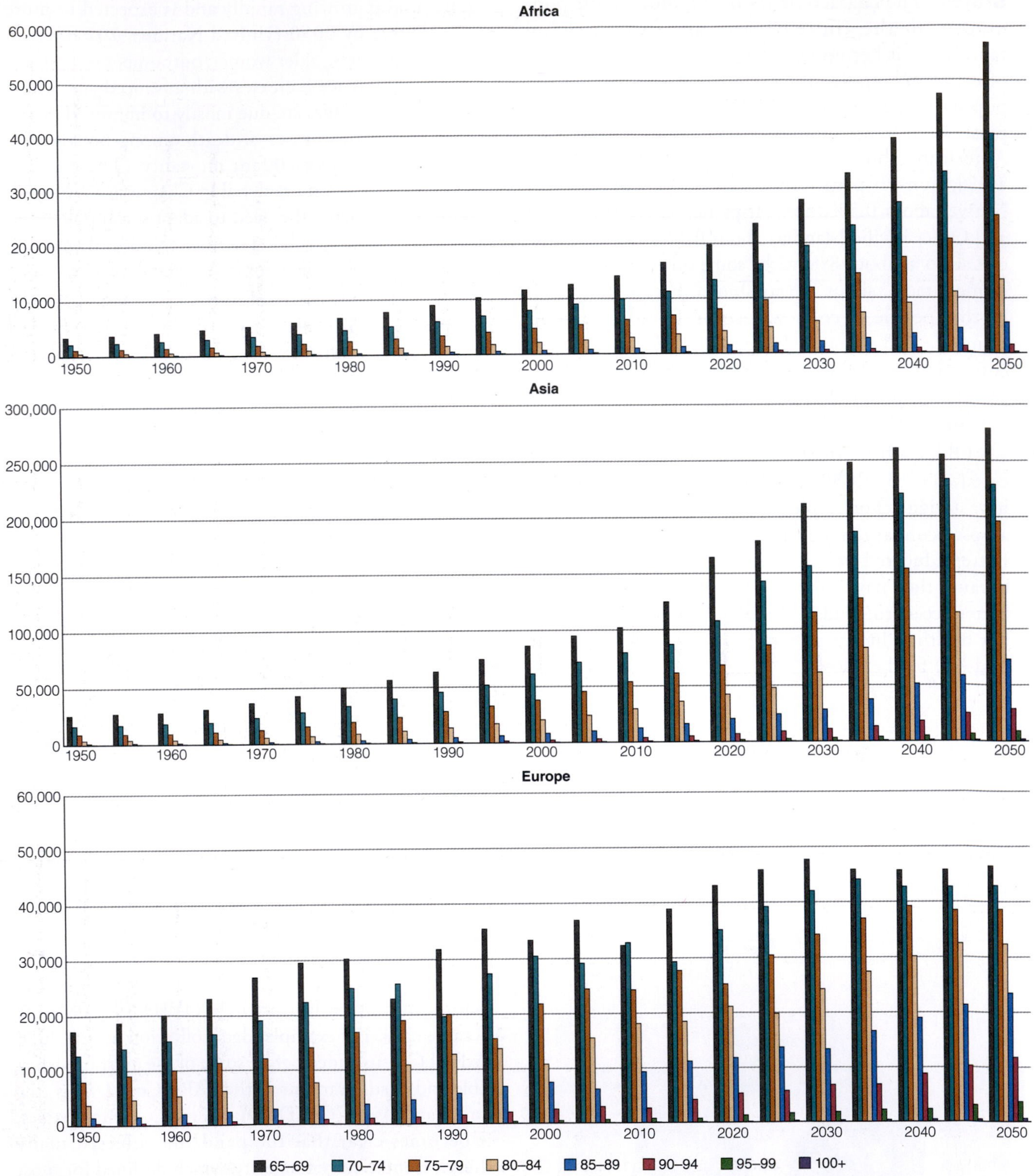

Figure 1.2 The proportion of older adults (65 years and older) is increasing globally and will continue to do so.

Source: United Nations, Department of Economic and Social Affairs Population Dynamics. World population prospects 2019. https://population.un.org/wpp/DataQuery/

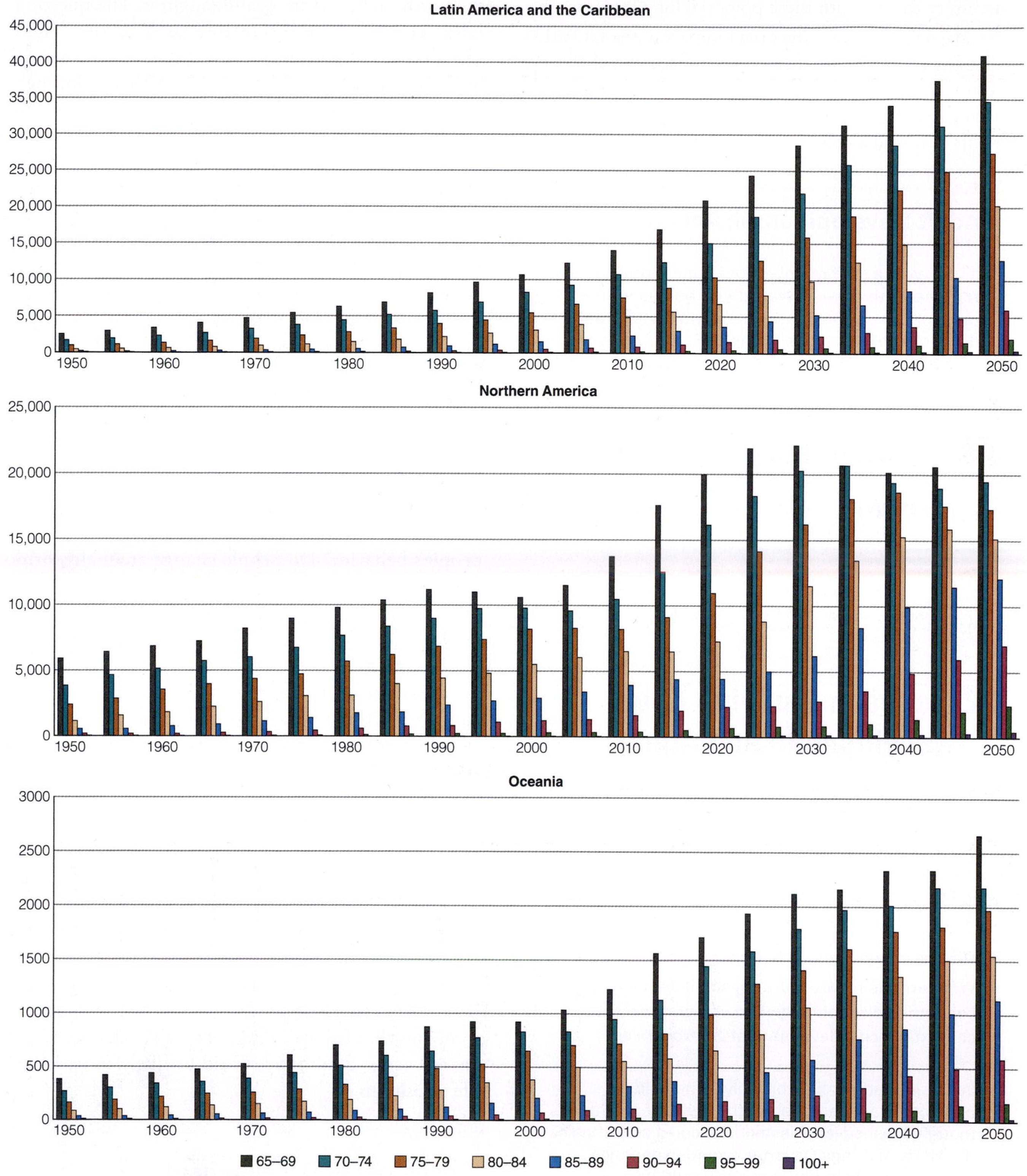

Figure 1.2 *(continued)*

their projections and ensure they will have the resources necessary to deal with these potential long-term issues.

We will encounter the broad impact of the COVID-19 pandemic and its differential effects on differing groups of people throughout the rest of the text. It will be apparent by the time you reach Chapter 14 that few events have had an equivalent impact on global aging.

Adult Development in Action

If you were a staff member for your congressional representative, what would you advise with respect to economic and social policy given the demographic changes in the U.S. population?

Review Questions

1.1 Perspectives on Adult Development and Aging

- What are the premises of the life-span perspective?
- How are population demographics changing around the world, and what difference does it make?

1.2 Issues in Studying Adult Development and Aging

Key Questions

- What four main forces shape development?
- What are normative age-graded influences, normative history-graded influences, and nonnormative influences?
- How do cultural, ethnic, and racial factors influence aging?
- What is the meaning of age?
- What are the nature–nurture, stability–change, continuity–discontinuity, and universal versus context-specific development controversies?

Levar Johnson smiled broadly as he held his newborn granddaughter for the first time. So many thoughts rushed into his mind. He could only imagine the kinds of things Devonna would experience growing up. He hoped that she would have a good neighborhood in which to play and explore her world. He hoped that she inherited the family genes for good health. He wondered how Devonna's life growing up as Black girl/woman in the United States would be different from his experiences.

Like many grandparents, Levar wonders what the future holds for his granddaughter. The questions Levar considers are interesting in their own right, but they are important for another reason: They get to the heart of general issues of human development that have intrigued philosophers and scientists for centuries. You have probably asked these or similar questions yourself. How do some people manage to remain thin, whereas other people seem to gain weight more easily? Why do some people remain very active and mentally well into later life? How does growing up in a Spanish-speaking culture affect one's views of family caregiving? Answering these questions requires us to consider the various forces that shape us as we mature. Developmentalists place special emphasis on four forces: biological, psychological, sociocultural, and life cycle. These forces direct our development much as an artist's hands direct the course of a painting or sculpture.

Following from the forces that shape adult development and aging are questions such as, What is the relative importance of genetics and environment on people's behavior? Do people change gradually, or do they change more abruptly? Do all people change in the same way? These questions reflect controversies that historically underlie the study of human development (Newman & Newman, 2016): the nature–nurture controversy, the change–stability controversy, the continuity–discontinuity controversy, and the universal versus context-specific development controversy.

Having a firm grasp on the forces and controversies of development is important because it provides a context for understanding why researchers and theorists believe certain things about aging or why some topics have been researched a great deal and others have been hardly studied at all. For example, someone who believes that a decline in intellectual ability is an innate and inevitable part of aging is unlikely to search for intervention techniques to raise performance. Similarly, someone who believes that personality characteristics change across adulthood would be likely to search for life transitions.

The Forces of Development

Gray hair, remembering, personality, friendship networks, activity levels—Why do adults differ so much on these and other things? The answer lies in understanding the basic forces that shape us and how they interact. Developmentalists typically consider four interactive forces (shown in Figure 1.3):

1. **Biological forces** include all genetic and health-related factors that affect development. Examples of biological forces such as genetics strongly influence certain physiological processes including menopause, facial wrinkling, and changes in the major organ systems.
2. **Psychological forces** include all internal perceptual, cognitive, emotional, and personality factors that affect development. Collectively, psychological forces such as cognitive abilities and personality shape the characteristics we notice about people that make them individuals.
3. **Sociocultural forces** include interpersonal, societal, cultural, and ethnic factors that affect development. Sociocultural forces such as financial assets, structural racism, and other society-wide factors provide the overall contexts in which we develop.
4. **Life-cycle forces** reflect differences in how the same event or combination of biological, psychological, and sociocultural forces affects people at different points in their lives. Life-cycle forces provide the role of timing that affects the impact of events and circumstances experienced during one's life.

One useful way to organize the biological, psychological, and sociocultural forces on human development is with the **biopsychosocial framework**. Together with life-cycle forces, the biopsychosocial framework provides a complete overview of the shapers of human development. Each of us is a product of a unique combination of these forces. Even identical twins growing up in the same family eventually have their own unique friends, partners, occupations, and so on because they each experience the combination of forces differently.

To understand why all these forces are important, imagine that we want to know how people feel about forgetting. We would need to consider biological factors, such as whether the forgetting was caused by an underlying disease. We would want to know about such psychological factors as what the person's memory ability has been throughout their life and about their beliefs about what happens to memory with increasing age. We would need to know about sociocultural factors, such as the influence of social stereotypes about forgetting on actual memory performance, whether they had access to good medical care and healthy food, or were under the continual stress of structural inequities. Finally, we would need to know about the age of the person and other historical timing issues surrounding when a forgetting experience occurs. Focusing on only one (or even two or three) of the forces would provide an incomplete understanding of how the person feels. The biopsychosocial framework, along with life-cycle forces, will provide a way to understand all the developmental outcomes you will encounter in this text.

Interrelations Among the Forces: Developmental Influences

All the forces combine to create people's unique sets of developmental experiences. One way to explore these combinations is to consider the degree to which they are common or are unique to people of specific ages. An important concept in this approach is cohort.

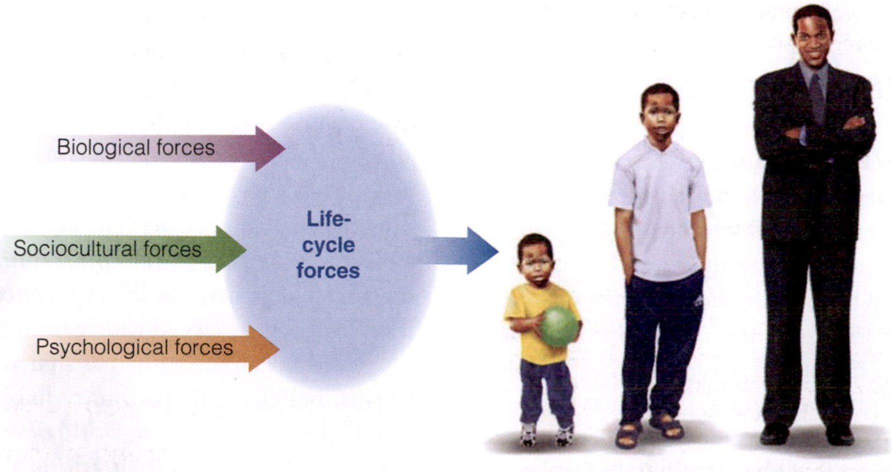

Figure 1.3 The biopsychosocial framework shows that human development results from interacting forces.

A **cohort** is a group of people born at the same point in time or within a specific time span. For example, everyone born in 1995 would be the 1995 cohort; similarly, those born between 1981 and 1996 represent the millennium cohort (or millennium generation). Based on this notion of cohort, Baltes (1987; Baltes et al., 2006) identifies three sets of influences that interact to produce developmental change over the life span: normative age-graded influences, normative history-graded influences, and nonnormative influences.

Normative age-graded influences are experiences caused by biological, psychological, and sociocultural forces that occur to most people of a particular age. Some of these, such as puberty, menarche, and menopause, are mainly biologically driven, although they can be influenced by certain other factors as well. These normative biological events usually indicate a major change in a person's life; for example, menopause is an indicator that a person can no longer bear children without medical intervention. Normative psychological events include focusing on certain concerns at different points in adulthood, such as a young adult's concern with establishing themselves as independent. Other normative age-graded influences involve sociocultural forces, such as the average age when first marriage occurs or when a person becomes eligible for Social Security payments. Normative age-graded influences typically correspond to major time-marked or age-marked events, which are often ritualized. For example, many emerging adults in the United States formally celebrate turning 21 as the official transition to adulthood, and getting married, having a child, and other events are typically surrounded with much celebration. These events provide the most convenient way to judge where we are on our social clock, an implicit marker of major life milestones and when they are supposed to be achieved.

Normative history-graded influences are events that most people in a specific culture experience at the same time. These events may be biologically caused (such as the COVID-19 pandemic), psychological (such as being subjected to particular stereotypes), or sociocultural (such as systemic discrimination). Normative history-graded influences often give a generation its unique identity, such as the baby-boom generation (born between 1946 and 1964), generation X (born between 1965 and 1980), the millennial generation (born between 1981 and 1996), and generation Z (born between 1997 and 2012). Normative history-graded influences can have a profound effect across all generations. For example, the attacks on the World Trade Center on September 11, 2001, and the COVID-19 pandemic had profound effects on people alive at the time.

Nonnormative influences are random or rare events that may be important for a specific individual but are not experienced by most people. These may be favorable events, such as winning the lottery or an election, or unfavorable ones, such as an accident or layoff. The relative unpredictability of when these events occur makes them different and can increase their effects on the individual. Such events can change one's life overnight.

Life-cycle forces are especially key in understanding the importance of normative age-graded, normative history-graded, and nonnormative influences. For example, history-graded influences may produce generational differences and conflict; parents' and grandparents' experiences as young adults in the 1960s and 1970s (before AIDS, smartphones, and global terrorism) may have little in common with the complex issues faced by today's young adults. In turn, these interactions have important implications for understanding differences that appear to be age-related. That is, differences may be explained in terms of different life experiences (normative history-graded influences) rather than as an integral part of aging itself (normative age-graded influences). We will return to this issue when we discuss age, cohort, and time-of-measurement effects in research on adult development and aging in this chapter, and also throughout the text as we unpack the meaning of each person's unique set of life experiences.

Cultural, Ethnic, Racial, Biological Sex, Gender, and Socioeconomic Factors

Several aspects of sociocultural forces are important to consider more closely. People do not grow up and live in a vacuum. Rather, they do so in specific contexts that enrich and define them in many core ways.

Culture, ethnicity, race, biological sex, gender, and socioeconomic factors jointly provide status, social settings, opportunities (or their systematic blockage), and other frameworks for personal experiences for people of all ages, and they influence and are influenced by biological, psychological, and life-cycle developmental forces. Together, culture, ethnicity, race, and gender form the bases for extremely important framings for understanding why people have the life experiences they do, and why these experiences vary so widely from person to person.

Culture can be defined as shared value orientations, norms, beliefs, and customary habits and ways of living. Culture provides the worldview of a society in that it gives it the basic explanations about the meanings and goals of everyday life (Matsumoto & Juang, 2017). Culture is such a powerful influence because it usually connects to biological forces through family lineage, which is often the way in which members of a particular culture are defined. Psychologically, culture shapes people's core beliefs; in some cases, this can result in ethnocentrism, or the belief that one's own culture is superior to others. Being socialized as a child within a culture usually has a more profound effect on a person than when one adopts a culture later in life, resulting in significant life-cycle timing effects. Culture is extremely important in gerontology because how people define basic concepts such as *person*, *age*, and *life course* varies a great deal across cultures.

Equally important is the concept of ethnicity, which is an individual and collective sense of identity based on historical and cultural group membership and related behaviors and beliefs (Matsumoto & Juang, 2017). Compared with culture, ethnic group identities have both solid and fluid properties, reflecting the fact that there are both unchanging and situation-specific aspects to ethnic identity, resulting in somewhat fluid definitions of ethnic membership and heritage (Jaspal, 2015; Jaspal & Cinnirella, 2012). Ethnic identity is first influenced by biology through one's parents. How that identity evolves over one's life depends on the unique interplay of psychological, other sociocultural, and life-cycle factors, as we will discover throughout the text.

Race matters. Aging in the United States is not the same experience for White individuals and persons of color. Nearly every aspect of aging that we will examine differs as a function of race. We will discover in Chapter 4 how racial disparities in health care and access to healthy food options, for instance, lower average longevity and affect health. The results of systematic race-based disparities and discrimination play out in long-term effects from access to education and certain types of occupations, to the average wealth (and what wealth provides) that these disparities create.

Similarly, gender plays a crucial role not only in self-identification but also in the opportunities (or lack thereof) that are the result of different stereotypes and behaviors toward different genders. As cultures come to terms with gender identities beyond the traditional binary categories of women and men, rifts have appeared reflected in disparate treatment and laws barring certain types of activities based on gender identities. In future chapters, we will explore how gender influences such things as employment (and employment law), interpersonal relationships, health, thinking, and numerous other topics.

Socioeconomic factors play another major role in determining the level of resources to which a person has access. Socioeconomic factors most often have to do with the financial assets a person has, and that is then used to categorize people into various "classes," such as middle or upper class. These terms are then used as proxy, or stand-in, labels that reflect the kinds and amounts of other resources (such as consumer goods, health care, jobs, etc.) that a person purchases, uses, or occupies.

The sociocultural forces of culture, ethnicity, race, gender, and socioeconomic factors are complex and interact with each other. An important construct in this regard is intersectionality. **Intersectionality refers to experiences that reflect combinations of race, ethnicity, gender, ability, or sexual orientation.** For example, Black women often point to their lived experiences as representing more than the sum of being a Black person and being a woman. Instead, their experiences are unique to being both Black and a woman (Collins & Bilge, 2020). Similarly, the intersection of race, ethnicity, and socioeconomic factors results in persons of color being less likely to occupy the very top socioeconomic classes.

Sociocultural forces provide the basis for the aspects of diversity that are often used to define us. Understanding the impact of diversity is particularly important in the United States, one of the most culturally diverse countries. Hundreds of different languages are spoken, and in many states, no single racial or ethnic group constitutes a majority of the population. The many customs of people from different cultures offer insights into the broad spectrum of the human experience and attest to the diversity of the U.S. population.

Barriers created by the use of various demographic categories such as culture, ethnicity, race, and gender are often confronted by social movements created to eliminate those barriers and effect change. The rapid rise of the Black Lives Matter (BLM) movement is an example of how centuries of systemic discriminatory treatment of Black individuals can become a global movement for justice. Although BLM began in 2013, it became a unifying global movement in 2020 following the murder of George Floyd. As a result, BLM became a potent example of a sociocultural force that has already influenced human behavior and development.

One way that the influence of culture, ethnicity, race, gender, and socioeconomic factors affect us in our lives is reflected in passionate arguments about how to refer to people with certain characteristics and histories. There is a song in the musical *Hamilton*—"Who Lives, Who Dies, Who Tells Your Story"—that reminds us that the lens through which even our own story is told depends on who is doing the telling and what they themselves have experienced. The lenses we use in telling the story

Each of these adults experiences the developmental process differently due to differences in culture, ethnicity, race, gender, and socioeconomic factors.

of adult development and aging are not all equivalent; for example, there is a youth-preferred lens used quite a lot in marketing cosmetics. The Controversies feature explores this notion in more detail. We will need to keep in mind that different lenses result in different stories as we proceed through this book.

Controversies

Lenses Matter

By the early 2020s, several social movements regarding individual rights, freedom, and dignity had not only emerged but had several major public and legal "wins" from their point of view. These movements included LGBTQIA+ rights (e.g., same-sex marriage, inclusion of personal pronouns on one's videochat namebar, increased availability of gender-neutral restrooms), the BLM movement (discussed in the text), and so on. Other movements also flourished, with members holding very different views (e.g., white supremacist groups, trans-exclusionary groups).

Ostensibly, debates among these groups reflect deeply held positions on "culture wars" issues. For example, this is the case with groups holding very different positions on the issue of transgender rights in which one group supports rights based on the gender claimed by the person and another group supports rights based on the gender assigned at birth.

Occasionally, different lenses get applied to the telling of the story even within groups that are usually on the same side of an issue. One example of this is how different forces relating to gender and the lenses of history are applied to the situation of how one describes the group of individuals who are pregnant—as "pregnant women" or as "pregnant persons" (Lewis, 2021). Those who strive to be inclusive of all individuals (that is, nonbinary individuals or trans men who are pregnant) urge the use of the term "pregnant persons." In contrast, those who aim to emphasize the historical fact of oppression of women, often through rape, barring from the workplace due to pregnancy, and the like, prefer "pregnant women" to drive home the gender-based subjugation targeting women (and not some generic "people"). Lewis (2021) adds that this distinction also underlies debates regarding Black Lives Matter as opposed to "All" Lives Matter, with the deliberate point being made regarding historical issues between police and the Black community, even though non-Black individuals are also shot and killed by police.

The key point in these debates is not an absolute judgment about who is "right" and who is "wrong." As the song in *Hamilton* reminds us, and as we will discover in Chapter 7 in our discussion of cognitive development across adulthood, there are multiple ways of approaching issues, and whether one of them is "correct" in an absolute sense may depend on the lens through which the issue is viewed.

Although the U.S. population is changing rapidly, much of the research we describe in this text was conducted on mostly middle- and upper-middle class White Americans. Accordingly, we must be careful *not* to assume that findings from this group necessarily apply to people in other groups. Indeed, we desperately need more research that includes diverse groups. Perhaps as a result of taking this course, you will help fill this need by becoming a developmental researcher yourself.

The Meaning of Age

When you are asked the question "How old are you?" what crosses your mind? Is it the number of years since the day of your birth? Is it how old you feel at that time? Is it defined more in terms of where you are biologically, psychologically, or socially than in terms of calendar time? You may not have thought about it, but age is not a simple construct (and in the case of the !Kung people living in the Kalahari Desert in southwest Africa, it has no meaning at all).

Likewise, aging is not a single process. Rather, it consists of at least three distinct processes: primary, secondary, and tertiary aging (Birren & Cunningham, 1985). **Primary aging** is normative, disease-free development during adulthood. Changes in biological, psychological, sociocultural, or life-cycle processes in primary aging are an inevitable part of the developmental process; examples include menopause, decline in reaction time, and the loss of family and friends. Much of the information in this book represents primary aging. **Secondary aging** is developmental changes that are related to disease, lifestyle, and other environmentally induced changes that are not inevitable (e.g., pollution). The progressive loss of intellectual abilities due to Alzheimer's disease and related forms of dementia, or that are caused by systemic disparities in access to core human services, are examples of secondary aging. Finally, **tertiary aging** is the rapid losses that occur shortly before death. An example of tertiary aging is a phenomenon known as terminal drop, in which intellectual abilities show a marked decline in the last few months or years before death.

Everyone does not grow old in the same way. Whereas most people tend to show similar patterns of aging that reflect the typical, or normative, changes with age, other people show highly successful aging in which few signs of change occur. For example, although most people tend to get chronic diseases as they get older, some people never do. What makes people who age without ever experiencing chronic disease different? At this point, we do not know for sure. It may be a unique combination of genetics, optimal environment, access to resources, flexibility in dealing with life situations, a strong sense of personal control, and maybe a bit of luck. For our present discussion, the main point to keep in mind is that everyone's experience of growing old is somewhat different. Although many people develop arthritis, how each person learns to cope is unique.

When most of us think about age, we usually think of how long we have been around since our birth; this way of defining age is known as chronological age. **Chronological age** is a shorthand way to index time and organize events and data by using a commonly understood standard: calendar time. Chronological age is not the only shorthand index variable used in adult development and aging. Gender, biological sex, race, ethnicity, and socioeconomic status are others. No index variable itself actually causes behavior.

This point is often forgotten when age is the index variable, perhaps because it is so familiar to us and so widely used. However, age (or time) does not directly cause things to happen, either. Iron left out in the rain will rust, but rust is not caused by time. Rather, rust is a time-dependent process involving oxidation in which time is a measure of the rate at which rust is created. Similarly, human behavior is affected by experiences that occur with the passage of time, not by time itself. What we study in adult development and aging is the result of time- or age-dependent processes, not the result of age (time) itself.

Whereas chronological age represents your age in elapsed time, *perceived age* refers to the age you think of yourself as. The saying "You're only as old as you feel" captures perceived age. Still another way of describing age is in terms of *biological age*, assessed by measuring the functioning of the various vital, or life-limiting, organ systems, such as the cardiovascular system.

Psychological age refers to the functional level of the psychological abilities people use to adapt to changing environmental demands. These abilities include memory, intelligence, feelings, motivation, and other skills that foster and maintain self-esteem and personal control.

Finally, **sociocultural age** refers to the specific set of roles individuals adopt in relation to other members of the society and culture to which they belong. Sociocultural age is judged on the basis of many behaviors and habits, such as style of dress, customs, language, and interpersonal style. Sociocultural age is especially important in understanding many of the family and work roles we adopt. When to get married, have children, make career moves, retire, and so on often are influenced by what we think our sociocultural age

Image Source/Photodisc/Getty Images

The "age" of these individuals depends on whether you are focusing on chronological, psychological, or sociocultural definitions.

is. Such decisions also play a role in determining our self-esteem and other aspects of personality. Many of the most damaging stereotypes about aging (e.g., that older people should not have sex) are based on faulty assumptions about sociocultural age.

A good example of the complexities of age are the concepts of emerging adulthood, established adulthood, and middle adulthood. Some human developmentalists view the period from the late teens to the mid- to late 20s as distinctive. They refer to it as **emerging adulthood**, a period when individuals are not adolescents but are not yet fully adults (Arnett, 2015, 2016; Arnett & Mitra, 2020). Five personal characteristics are especially prominent (Arnett, 2015; Arnett & Mitra, 2020): identity explorations, instability, self-focus, feeling in-between, and a sense of possibilities/optimism. It is also a time when certain biological and physiological developmental trends peak and brain development continues in different ways.

Similarly, theorists and researchers are coming to understand that emerging adulthood gives way to a separate developmental period prior to reaching middle age. **Established adulthood** is the period between roughly ages 30 and 45 when life is most intense, demanding, and perhaps rewarding (Mehta et al., 2020). Established adulthood is generally marked by a growing commitment to a chosen career path, a specific form of intimate relationships, and family formation.

Middle adulthood is different still, a time when many people are at the peak of their careers, children are leaving home, parents are aging, and one's priorities change. The distinguishing features among emerging adulthood, established adulthood, and middle age are described in Table 1.1.

In sum, a person's age turns out to be quite complex. Think about yourself. You probably have days when even though the calendar says you're a certain age, your exploits the day before resulted in your feeling much younger at the time and much older the next morning—or perhaps the other way around. How "old" anyone is can (and does) change from one moment to the next. A great example of these points can be found in the life of Pope Francis, as discussed in the Real People feature.

Core Issues in Development

Is it your genes or experiences that determine how intelligent you are? If a young adult person is outgoing, does this mean they will be outgoing in later life? If people change, is it more gradual or sporadic? Is aging the same around the world? These and similar questions have occupied some of the greatest thinkers throughout history. Four main issues occupy most of the discussion: nature versus nurture, stability versus change, continuity versus discontinuity, and universal versus context-specific development. Because each of these issues cuts across the topics we discuss in this book, let's consider each briefly.

The Nature–Nurture Issue. Think for a minute about a particular characteristic that you and several people in your family have. Why is this trait so prevalent? Is it because

Table 1.1 Distinctive Features of Emerging Adulthood, Established Adulthood, and Midlife

Educational Opportunities Country SES **Contextual Factors** Political Climate Culture Neighborhood

Ethnicity Birth Assigned Gender Category Nationality **Individual Factors** Gender Identity Sexual Orientation Race

Religious beliefs

Traits/personality characteristics

Internalized cultural beliefs/values

Immigrant status

Domain	Emerging Adulthood	Established Adulthood	Midlife
Romantic Relationships	Transient into long term	Long term committed	Long term committed
		Divorce/Separation—second relationship—long term—committed —	
Career	Information gathering about careers Occupational experimentation Frequent job changes	Committing to field Building expertise Increasing responsibility Greater occupational stability	Seniority in field Acquired expertise Mentoring next generation
Caregiving/ Family	Child free Living independently from parents Living parents who may still be providing emotional or instrumental support	Decision making about childbearing Birth of first child Young children at home Aging parents who may require care	Older children Helping to mentor and support adult children's independence Caring for aging parents or adjusting to loss of deceased parents
Physical	Risky behaviors Unhealthy eating Unstable sleep patterns High energy Strong immunity Overall high self-rated health	Reduction in risky behaviors Healthy eating Unstable sleep patterns for new parents Strong immunity Overall high self-rated health Declines in metabolism	Higher risk of heart disease and cancer Higher risk of obesity
Cognitive	Acquiring broad knowledge base High fluid intelligence Fast processing speed Developing crystalized intelligence Problem solving	Narrowing of knowledge base Developing expertise Declines in processing speed Increasing crystalized intelligence Problem finding	Domain specific deep knowledge Expertise Continued declines in processing speed Increasing crystalized intelligence Problem anticipation Development of wisdom
Well being	Lower positive affect		Higher positive affect

Other individual characteristics

Other contextual factors

HISTORICAL PERIOD

Source: Mehta, C. M., Arnett, J. J., Palmer, C. G., & Nelson, L. J. (2020). Established adulthood: A new conception of ages 30 to 45. *American Psychologist*, 75, 431–444. https://doi.org/10.1037/amp0000600, Table 1, p. 436

you inherited the trait from your parents? Or is it because of where and how you and other members of your family were brought up? Answers to these questions illustrate different positions on the **nature–nurture issue**, which involves the degree to which genetic or hereditary influences (nature) and experiential or environmental influences (nurture) determine the kind of person you are.

Scientists once hoped to answer these questions by identifying either heredity or environment as the only cause of a particular aspect of development. The goal was to be able to say, for example, that intelligence was due to heredity or that personality was due to experience. Today, however, we know that virtually no features of life-span development are due exclusively to either heredity or environment. Instead, development is always shaped by both: Nature and nurture are mutually interactive influences.

For example, it is known that some forms of Alzheimer's disease are genetically linked. However, whether one develops Alzheimer's disease, and possibly

Real People

Pope Francis Sets Many New Examples

History was made on March 13, 2013. For the first time since the year 741, when Pope Gregory II from Syria died, the Roman Catholic Church elected a non-European as its leader. Jorge Mario Bergoglio, who took the name of Pope Francis, became the first South American (he is from Argentina) and first Jesuit to be elected pope. He was 76 years old. It is likely that the Catholic Church will never be the same.

Pope Francis set out immediately to change the dynamic of the role of the pope. In doing so, he also showed that he held deep personal values and could not be stereotyped based on his age. For example, he refused to wear the traditional red shoes or to live in the posh Vatican apartment. He used his long-lived experience to focus on what he saw as essential central traits for a leader: mercy, humility, and compassion. He also defied our stereotypes of an older person—he was always on the go, full of energy, with a very sharp wit and intellect.

Pope Francis set out quickly to establish his values as central to the way people should live, especially in terms of sustainability in response to climate change, and in the need to provide adequate wages and living conditions for all. He embraced all religions and has emphasized the need to treat all people with respect.

Pope Francis

Pope Francis redefined what it means to be a church leader. He also redefined what it means to be an older adult through his upending of centuries of tradition, relentless schedule, and activity in service of others.

even how the disease progresses, may be influenced by the environment. Specifically, an environmental trigger may be needed for the disease to occur. Moreover, evidence indicates that providing a supportive environment for people with Alzheimer's disease improves their performance on cognitive tasks (De Witt-Hoblit et al., 2016).

To understand a person's future we must simultaneously consider their inborn, hereditary characteristics and the environment in which they live. Both factors must be considered together to yield an adequate account of why people behave the way they do. To explain a person's behavior and discover where to focus intervention, we must consider the unique interaction for that person between nature and nurture.

The Stability–Change Issue. Ask yourself the following question: Are you pretty much the same as you were 10 years ago, or are you different? How so? Depending on what aspects of yourself you considered, you may have concluded that you are pretty much the same (perhaps in terms of food preferences) or that you are different (perhaps in some physical feature such as hair color). The **stability–change issue** concerns the degree to which people remain the same over time. Stability at some basic level is essential for us (and others) to recognize that one is the same individual as time goes on. But we also like to believe that our characteristics are not set in concrete, that we can change ourselves if we so desire. (Imagine not being able to do anything to rid yourself of some habit that annoys others.)

Although there is little controversy about whether children change in some ways from birth through age 18, there is much controversy about whether people continue to change across adulthood. Much of the controversy over stability and change across adulthood stems from how specific characteristics are defined and measured. How much we remain the same and how much we change, then, turns out to be a difficult issue to resolve in an objective way. For many gerontologists, whether stability or change is the rule depends on what personal aspect is being considered and what theoretical perspective one is adopting. For example, we will find out in Chapter 9 that this distinction underlies what we conclude regarding personality.

The Continuity–Discontinuity Controversy. The third major issue in developmental psychology is a derivative of the stability–change controversy. The **continuity–discontinuity controversy** concerns whether a particular developmental phenomenon represents a smooth progression over time (continuity) or a series of abrupt shifts (discontinuity). Continuity approaches usually focus on the amount of a characteristic a person has, whereas discontinuity approaches usually focus on the kinds of characteristics a person has. Of course, on a day-to-day basis, behaviors often look nearly identical, or continuous. But when viewed over the course of many months or years, the same behaviors may have changed dramatically, reflecting discontinuous change. Throughout this book, you will find examples of developmental changes that appear to be more on the continuities side and ones that appear to be more on the discontinuities side.

An example of continuity is discussed in Chapter 6: reaction time. As people grow older, the speed with which they can respond slows down. But in Chapter 7 you will read about an example of discontinuity: How people approach problems, especially ones with complex and ambiguous features, undergoes fundamental shifts from young adulthood through middle age.

Within the discontinuity view lies the issue of how adaptable people are in situations as they age. Baltes and colleagues (1998; Baltes et al., 1999) use the term *plasticity* to describe this in relation to people's capacity. **Plasticity** refers to the belief that capacity is not fixed but can be learned or improved with practice. For example, people can learn ways to help themselves remember information, which in turn may help them deal with declining short-term memory ability with age. Although plasticity can be demonstrated in many arenas, there are limits to the degree of potential improvement, as we will discover in later chapters.

The Universal Versus Context-Specific Development Controversy. The **universal versus context-specific development controversy** concerns whether there is just one path of development or several. Consider the !Kung people, who live in the Kalahari Desert in southwest Africa (Bonvillain, 2021; Lee et al., 2002). If you were to ask an older !Kung, "How old are you?" you would quickly learn that the question has no meaning. !Kung also do not keep track of the number of years they have been alive, the number of children they have, or how often they move. To the !Kung, age per se is unimportant; when asked to describe people who are "younger" or "older," they give the names of specific people. Social roles among the !Kung also do not differ by age; for example, women in their 20s and 60s traditionally tend gardens, draw water from wells, and take care of children; men traditionally hunt.

Life among !Kung adults contrasts sharply with life among adults in the United States, where age

Akg-Images/Jürgen Sorges

Members of the !Kung experience development in ways very different from the ways most Americans do.

matters a great deal and prescribed social roles differ accordingly. Can one theory explain development in both groups? Maybe. Some theorists argue that such differences are more apparent than real, and that development worldwide reflects one basic process for everyone. According to this view, differences in development are simply variations on a fundamental developmental process, much as Hershey, Chocolopolis, Lore's, and Godiva chocolates are all products of the same basic manufacturing process.

The opposing view is that differences among people may not be just variations on a theme. Advocates of this view argue that adult development and aging are inextricably intertwined with the context in which they occur. A person's development is a product of complex interactions with the environment, and these interactions are not fundamentally the same in all environments. Each environment has its own set of unique procedures that shape development.

The view adopted in this book is that adult development and aging must be understood within the contexts in which they occur. In some cases, this means that contexts are sufficiently similar that general trends can be identified. In others, such as the !Kung and in U.S. societies, these differences prevent many general statements. In Levar's case with his granddaughter, it may be a blend of the two.

Adult Development in Action

How would understanding the forces and issues that shape human development help you be a better healthcare worker at a neighborhood clinic in a very diverse neighborhood?

Review Questions

1.2 Issues in Studying Adult Development and Aging

- What are the four basic forces in human development?
- What are the major characteristics of normative age-graded, normative history-graded, and nonnormative influences?
- How do nature and nurture interact?
- What are the impacts of culture, ethnicity, race, biological sex, gender, and socioeconomic factors on development?
- What is intersectionality?
- In what ways can age be defined? What are the advantages and disadvantages of each definition?
- What is the stability–change issue? What is the continuity–discontinuity issue? What kinds of theories derive from each view?
- What is the universal versus context-specific development issue, and how does it relate to sociocultural forces?

1.3 Research Methods in Adult Development and Aging

Key Questions

- What approaches do scientists use to measure behavior in adult development and aging research?
- What are the general designs for doing research?
- What specific designs are unique to adult development and aging research?
- What are some tools for doing and archiving developmental research?
- What are some ways to integrate findings from different studies?
- What ethical procedures must researchers follow?

Leah and Sarah are both 75 years old and are in fairly good health. They want their memory to remain sharp, so they both use various memory aids: Leah tries to think of images in her mind to remember her grocery list, whereas Sarah writes them down. Leah and Sarah got into a discussion recently about which technique works better.

You might be asking yourself why you need to know about research methods when you could just search the web on the topic and find out all sorts of things about it. Here's why—there is good research and bad research and everything in between. A web search does not help you tell the difference. The only way to differentiate good versus poor research is by knowing the principles of good research that result in trustworthy information.

Just as in any profession, gerontology has certain tools of the trade that are used to ensure good research. That's what we will be considering in this section—the tools that gerontologists have used for decades in discovering the secrets of adult development and aging.

So, suppose Leah and Sarah know that you're taking a course in adult development and aging, and they ask you to settle the matter. You know research could show whose approach is better under what circumstances, but how? Gerontologists must make several key decisions as they prepare to study any topic. They need to decide how to measure the topic of interest, they must design the study, they must choose a way to study development, and they must respect the rights of the people who will participate in the study.

What makes the study of adult development and aging different from other areas of social science is the need to consider multiple influences on behavior. Explanations of development entail consideration of all the forces we listed earlier. This makes research on adult development and aging more difficult, if for no other reason than it involves examining more variables.

Measurement in Adult Development and Aging Research

Researchers typically begin by deciding how to measure the topic of interest. For example, the first step toward resolving Leah and Sarah's discussion about remembering grocery items would be to decide how to measure remembering. Gerontologists usually use one of three approaches: observing systematically, using tasks to sample behavior, and asking people for self-reports. In addition, researchers need to be concerned with how representative the participants in the study are of the larger group of people in question.

Regardless of the kind of method chosen, researchers must show it is both reliable and valid. The **reliability** of a measure is the extent to which it provides a consistent index of the behavior or topic of interest. A measure of memory is reliable to the extent that it gives a consistent estimate of performance each time you administer it. All measures used in gerontological research must be shown to be reliable, or they cannot be used. The **validity** of a measure is the extent to which it measures what researchers think it measures. For example, a measure of memory is valid only if it can be shown to actually measure memory (and not vocabulary ability, for example). Validity often is established by showing that the measure in question is closely related to another measure known to be valid. Because it is possible to have a measure that is reliable but not valid (a ruler is a reliable measure of length but not a valid measure of memory), researchers must ensure that measures are both reliable and valid.

Systematic Observation. As the name implies, **systematic observation** involves watching people and carefully recording what they say or do. Two forms of systematic observation are common. In naturalistic observation, people are observed as they behave spontaneously in some real-life situation. For example, Leah and Sarah could be observed in the grocery store purchasing their items as a way to test how well they remember.

Two types of systematic observations are structured observations and naturalistic observations. Structured observations differ from naturalistic observations in that the researcher creates a specific, often artificial setting that is particularly likely to elicit the behavior of interest. Structured observations are especially useful for studying behaviors that are difficult to observe naturally (that is, in the normal course of people's routines and experiences). For example, how people react to emergencies is hard to study naturally because emergencies generally are rare and unpredictable events. For a structured observation study, a researcher could stage an emergency and watch how people react. However, whether the behaviors observed in staged situations are the same as would happen naturally often is hard to determine, making it difficult to generalize from staged settings to the real world.

Sampling Behavior with Tasks. When investigators can't observe a behavior directly, another popular alternative is to create tasks that are thought to sample the behavior of interest. For example, one way to test older adults' memory is to give them a grocery list to learn and remember, often in a laboratory setting, rather than testing them in the grocery store by looking at their shopping carts. This approach is popular with gerontological researchers because it is so convenient. The main question with this approach is its validity: Does the task provide a realistic sample of the behavior of interest? For example, asking people to learn grocery lists would have good validity to the extent it matched the kinds of lists they actually use.

Self-Reports. The last approach, self-reports, is a special case of using tasks to sample people's behavior. **Self-reports** are simply people's answers to questions about the topic of interest. When questions are posed in written form, it is a questionnaire or survey; when they are posed verbally, it is an interview. Either way, questions are created that probe different aspects of the topic of interest. For example, if you think imagery and lists are common ways people use to remember grocery items, you could devise a questionnaire and administer it to several people to find out.

Although self-reports are very convenient and provide information on the topic of interest, they are not always good measures of people's behavior, because they are inaccurate. Why? People may not remember accurately what they did in the past, or they may simply report what they think the researcher wants them to say.

Representative Sampling. Researchers usually are interested in broad groups of people called populations. Examples of populations are all the students taking a course on adult development and aging or all Asian American widows. Since accessing the whole population is usually difficult, the vast majority of studies are based on only a sample of people, which is a subset of the population. Researchers must be careful, though, to ensure that their sample is truly representative (i.e., has the same characteristics) of the population of interest. An unrepresentative sample can result in invalid research. For example, what would you think of a study of middle-aged parents if you learned that the sample consisted entirely of heterosexual two-parent households? You would, quite correctly, decide that this sample is not representative of all middle-aged parents and question whether its results apply to single middle-aged parents, for instance.

As you read on, you'll soon discover that most of the research we consider in this text has been conducted on middle-class, well-educated White Americans. That's because historically, people of color were largely not included in developmental research, and in some fields (e.g., medical research) were sometimes included unethically. Are these nondiverse samples representative of all people in the United States? In the world? No. Be careful not to assume that findings from this group apply to people of other groups. In addition, some developmental issues have not been studied in all racial and ethnic groups and cultures. For example, the U.S. government does not always report statistics for all racial and ethnic groups on every conceivable topic. To change this, some U.S. government agencies, such as the National Institutes of Health, require samples to be representative. Thus, in the future we may gain a broader understanding of aging.

General Designs for Research

Having selected the way we want to measure the topic of interest, researchers must embed this measure in a research design that yields useful, relevant results. Gerontologists rely on primary designs in planning their work: experimental studies, correlational studies, and case studies. The specific design chosen for research depends in large part on the questions the researchers are trying to address.

Experiments. To find out whether Leah's or Sarah's approach to remembering works better, we could gather representative samples of older adults and try the following. We could randomly assign the participants into three groups: those who are taught to use imagery, those who are taught to use lists, and those who are not taught to use anything. After giving all the groups time to learn the new technique (where appropriate), we could test each group on a new grocery list to see who does better.

What we have done is an example of an **experiment**, which involves manipulating a key factor that the researcher believes is responsible for a particular behavior and randomly assigning participants to the experimental and control groups. In our case, the key variable being manipulated (termed the **independent variable**) is the instructions for how to study. In a study of memory, a typical behavior that is observed (termed the **dependent variable**) is the amount of information actually remembered.

More generally, in an experiment the researcher is most interested in identifying differences between groups of people. One group, the experimental group, receives the manipulation, in this case training on a memory strategy; another group, the control group, does not. This sets up a situation in which the presence and/or type or amount of the key variable of interest differs across groups. In addition, the investigator exerts precise control over all important aspects of the study, including choosing the variable of interest, how it will be included in the study, the setting of the study, and the participants. Because the key variable is systematically manipulated in an experiment (e.g., some participants experience it, some do not), researchers can infer cause-and-effect relations about that variable. In our example, we can conclude that type of memory strategy instruction (how people study) causes better or worse performance on a memory test. Discovering such cause-and-effect relations is important if we are to understand the underlying processes of adult development and aging.

Finally, we must note that age cannot be an independent variable, because we cannot manipulate it and because, as we noted earlier, time per se does not cause anything. At best, we can find and discuss age-related effects of an independent variable on the behavior represented by the dependent variables.

Correlational Studies. Given that true experiments cannot be done to understand the effects of time-dependent developmental processes per se, what do scientists do to gain insights into how things change over time? The best way is to examine how different aspects of people's behavior vary in relation to each other, accomplished by using a correlational study. In a **correlational study**, investigators examine relations between variables as they exist naturally in the world. In the simplest correlational study, a researcher measures two variables, and then sees how they are related.

Suppose we wanted to know whether the amount of time spent studying a grocery list such as one that Sarah might create was related to how many items people remember at the store. To find out, the researcher would measure two things for each person in the study: the length of study time and the number of items purchased correctly.

The results of a correlational study usually are measured by computing a correlation coefficient, abbreviated r. Correlations can range from -1.0 to 1.0, reflecting three different types of relations between study time and number of groceries remembered.

1. When $r = 0$, the two variables are unrelated: study time has no relation to remembering groceries.
2. When $r > 0$, the variables are positively related: as study time increases (or decreases), the number of grocery items remembered also increases (or decreases).
3. When $r < 0$, the variables are inversely related: when study time increases (or decreases), the number of groceries remembered decreases (or increases).

Correlational studies do not give definitive information about cause and effect; for example, the correlation between study time and the number of groceries remembered does not mean that one variable caused the other, regardless of how large the relation was. However, correlational studies do provide important information about the strength of the relation between variables, which is reflected in the absolute value of the correlation coefficient. Moreover, because developmental researchers are interested in how variables are related to other factors besides age that are difficult, if not impossible, to manipulate, correlational techniques are used a great deal. In fact, most developmental research is correlational at some level because age cannot be manipulated within an individual, and many variables of interest cannot be manipulated for ethical reasons. Ultimately, this means that although we can describe a great many developmental phenomena and talk about how they interrelate, we cannot explain very many of them.

Case Studies. Sometimes researchers cannot obtain measures directly from multiple people and are able only to study one or very few of them carefully. Situations in which researchers may be able to study a single individual or very few individuals in great detail constitute a **case study**. This technique is especially useful when researchers want to investigate rare phenomena, such as people who have new or extremely rare diseases, or people with extremely high skill levels in some area. Identifying new diseases, for example, often begins with a case study of one individual who has a pattern of symptoms that differs from any known disorder. Case studies are also valuable for opening new areas of research, which can be followed by larger studies using other methods (e.g., experiments). However, their primary limitation is figuring out whether the information gleaned from one or very few individual(s) holds for others as well.

Designs for Studying Development

Once the general design is chosen, most gerontologists must decide how to measure possible changes or age differences that emerge as people develop. For example, if we want to know how people continue (or fail) to use imagery or lists in remembering grocery items as they get older, we will want to use a design that is particularly sensitive to developmental differences. Such designs are based on three key building blocks: age effects, cohort effects, and time of measurement effects. Once we have considered these, we will examine the specific designs for studying development.

Age, Cohort, and Time of Measurement. Every study of adult development and aging is built on the combination of three building blocks: age effects, cohort effects, and time of measurement effects (Cavanaugh & Whitbourne, 2003).

Age effects reflect differences caused by underlying processes, such as biological, psychological, or sociocultural changes that are time related. Although usually represented in research by chronological age,

age effects are inherent changes within the person and are not caused by the passage of time per se but are time-related.

Cohort effects are differences caused by experiences and circumstances unique to the generation to which one belongs. In general, cohort effects correspond to the normative history-graded influences discussed earlier. However, defining a cohort may not be easy. Cohorts can be specific, as in all people born in one particular year, or general, such as the millennial cohort. As described earlier, each generation is exposed to different sets of historical and personal events (such as World War II, tablet computers, social justice movements, or pandemics). Later in this section we consider evidence of how profound cohort effects can be.

Time-of-measurement effects reflect differences stemming from sociocultural, environmental, historical, or other events at the time the data are obtained from the participants. For example, data about wage increases given in a particular year may be influenced by the economic conditions of that year. If the economy is in a serious recession, pay increases probably would be small. In contrast, if the economy is booming, pay increases could be large. Clearly, whether a study is conducted during a recession or a boom affects what is learned about pay changes. In short, the point in time in which a researcher decides to do research could lead them to different conclusions about the phenomenon being studied.

The three building-block effects (age, cohort, and time of measurement) can be represented in a single chart, such as the one in Table 1.2. Cohort is represented by the years in the first column, time of measurement is represented by the years across the top, and age is represented by the numbers in the individual cells in the table. Note that age can be computed by subtracting the cohort year from the time of measurement year.

In conducting adult development and aging research, investigators have attempted to identify and separate the three effects. This has not been easy, because all three influences are interrelated. If one is interested in studying 40-year-olds, one must necessarily select the cohort that was born 40 years ago. In this case age and cohort are confounded, because one cannot know whether the behaviors observed occur because the participants are 40 years old or because of the specific life experiences they have had as a result of being born in a particular historical year. In general, **confounding** is any situation in which one cannot determine which of two or more effects is responsible for the behaviors being observed. Confounding among pairs of the three effects we are considering here is the most serious problem in adult development and aging research.

What distinguishes developmental researchers from their colleagues in other areas of psychology is a fundamental interest in understanding how people change. Developmental researchers must look at the ways in which people differ across time. Doing so necessarily requires that researchers understand the distinction between age change and age difference. An age change occurs in an individual's behavior over time. Leah's or Sarah's memory performance at age 75 may be different than it was at age 40. To discover an age change, one must examine the same person (in this case, Leah or Sarah) at more than one point in time. An age difference is obtained when at least two different people of different ages are compared. Leah and Sarah may not remember the same number of grocery items as a different person of age 40 does. Even though we may be able to document substantial age differences, we cannot assume they imply an age change. We do not know whether Leah or Sarah has changed since they were 40 (because we did not follow them over time), and of course we do not know whether the 40-year-old will be any different at age 75. In some cases, age differences reflect age changes; in other cases, they do not.

If what we really want to understand in developmental research is age change (what happens as people grow older), we should design our research with this goal in mind to the extent it is possible. However, different research questions necessitate different research designs. As we will explore next, settling for understanding age differences rather than identifying age changes may be necessary because that is the best we can do under the circumstances. We next consider the most common ways in which researchers gather data about age differences and age changes: cross-sectional, longitudinal, time lag, and sequential designs.

Table 1.2 Three Basic Building Blocks of Developmental Research Time of Measurement

Cohort	2020	2030	2040	2050
1970	50	60	70	80
1980	40	50	60	70
1990	30	40	50	60
2000	20	30	40	50

Cohort is represented by the years in the first column, time of measurement by the years across the top, and age by the values in the cells.

Table 1.3 Cross-Sectional Design

	Time of Measurement			
Cohort	**2020**	**2030**	**2040**	**2050**
1970	50	60	70	80
1980	40	50	60	70
1990	30	40	50	60
2000	20	30	40	50

Cohort is represented by the years in the first column, time of measurement by the years across the top, and age by the values in the cells.

Cross-Sectional Designs. Suppose we design a study to compare a group of 40-year-old people with a group of 75-year-old people (including Leah and Sarah) on remembering items from a grocery list. This approach would be known as a cross-sectional study because we have taken a cross-section, or time-slice, of different groups of people of different ages. In a **cross-sectional study**, developmental differences are identified by testing people of different ages at the same time. Any single column, such as the one highlighted in bold red font in Table 1.3, represents a cross-sectional design.

Cross-sectional research has several weaknesses. Because people are tested at only one point in their development, we learn nothing about the continuity of development. Consequently, we cannot tell whether someone born in 1970 who remembers grocery items well at age 50 (in 2020) is still able to do so at age 80 (in 2050), because the person would be tested at age 50 or 80, but not both. Cross-sectional studies also are affected by cohort effects, meaning that differences between age groups (cohorts) may result as easily from environmental factors as from developmental processes. Why? Cross-sectional studies assume that when the older participants were younger, they resembled the people in the younger age groups who actually participate in the study. This isn't always true, of course, which makes it difficult to know how to explain age differences found in a cross-sectional study. In short, age and cohort effects are confounded in cross-sectional research.

Despite the confounding of age and cohort and the limitation of being able to identify only age differences, cross-sectional designs dominate the research literature in gerontology. Why? The reason is a pragmatic one: because all the measurements are obtained at one time, cross-sectional research can be conducted more quickly and inexpensively than research using other designs.

In addition, one particular variation of cross-sectional designs is used the most: the extreme age groups design. Suppose you want to investigate whether people's ability to remember items at the grocery store differs with age. Your first impulse may be to gather a group of younger adults and compare their performance with that of a group of older adults. Typically, such studies compare samples obtained in convenient ways; younger adults usually are college students, and older adults often are volunteers from senior centers or other organizations.

Although the extreme age groups design is very common (most of the studies cited in this book used this design), it has several problems (Hertzog & Dixon, 1996). Three concerns are key. First, the samples, as convenient as they are to obtain, are rarely racially and ethnically representative of the whole population, so we must be careful not to read too much into the results; findings from studies using extreme age groups may not generalize to people other than ones like those who participated. Second, age should be treated as a continuous variable, not as a category ("young" and "old"). Viewing age as a continuous variable allows researchers to gain a better understanding of how age relates to any observed age differences. Finally, extreme age group designs assume the measures used mean the same thing to both age groups. They often do not. Measures may tap somewhat different constructs, so the reliability and validity of each measure should be checked in each age group.

Despite the problems with cross-sectional designs in general and with extreme age groups designs in particular, such studies can provide useful information if used carefully. Most importantly, they can point out issues that may provide fruitful avenues for subsequent longitudinal or sequential studies, in which case we can uncover information about age changes.

Longitudinal Designs. As noted in the previous section, one way to explore age changes is to follow people and measure the same behaviors over time. When a researcher wants to do that, they use a longitudinal design. In a **longitudinal study**, the same individuals are observed or tested repeatedly at different points in their lives. As the name implies, a longitudinal study involves a lengthwise (over time) account of

Table 1.4 Longitudinal Design

	Time of Measurement			
Cohort	**2020**	**2030**	**2040**	**2050**
1970	50	60	70	80
1980	40	50	60	70
1990	30	40	50	60
2000	20	30	40	50

Cohort is represented by the years in the first column, time of measurement by the years across the top, and age by the values in the cells.

development and is the most direct way to watch and measure growth. A longitudinal design is represented by any horizontal row, such as the one highlighted in bold red font in Table 1.4. A major advantage of longitudinal designs is that age changes are identified because we are studying the same people over time.

Usually, the repeated testing of longitudinal studies extends over years, but not always. In a **microgenetic study**, a special type of longitudinal design, participants are tested repeatedly over a span of days or weeks, typically with the aim of observing change directly as it occurs. For example, researchers might test people every week during a training program in how to use social media, for instance, starting on the first day of the course and continuing until a few weeks after the end of formal instruction. Microgenetic studies are particularly useful when investigators have hypotheses about a specific period when developmental change should occur, or in order to intensively document a behavior over time (Flynn et al., 2006).

Microgenetic studies are particularly useful in tracking change as a result of intervention. For example, adults could be given a health assessment on physiological indicators and diet. A series of educational sessions about how to improve health through exercise and eating habits could be introduced including additional assessments, followed by a posttest to find out how well the participants learned and remembered the information a few weeks later. The microgenetic method would look in detail at the performance of those who learned and improved after training compared to those who did not, and search for differences in the pattern of findings in the assessments given during the program. This would provide a vivid portrait of change over the period of the intervention. If you think about it, this course is an example of a microgenetic study, as you are given repeated assessments of what you are learning and may have the opportunity to pull all that learning together at the end of the course in a project or comprehensive exam.

If age changes are found in longitudinal studies, can we say why they occurred? Because only one cohort is studied, cohort effects are eliminated as an explanation of change. However, the other two potential explanations, age and time of measurement, are confounded. For example, suppose we wanted to follow the 1990 cohort over time. If we wanted to test these individuals when they were 30 years old, we would have had to do so in 2020. Consequently, any changes we identify could result from changes in underlying processes or factors related to the time we choose to conduct our measurement. For instance, if we conducted a longitudinal study of salary growth, the amount of salary change in any comparison could stem from real change in the skills and worth of the person to the company or from the economic conditions of the times, namely, the COVID-19 pandemic. In a longitudinal study we cannot tell which of these factors is more important in understanding the outcomes for the participants in the study.

Longitudinal studies present three additional challenges. First, if the research measure requires some type of performance by the participants, we may have the potential issue of practice effects. Practice effects result from the fact that performance may improve over time simply because people are tested over and over again with the same measures. If people improve over the course of the study, we won't know whether it as a genuine improvement or just due to their growing familiarity with the assessments.

Second, we may have a challenge with participant dropout because it is difficult to keep a group of research participants intact over the course of a longitudinal study. Participants may relocate, lose interest, become unavailable for some other reason (e.g., health), or die. Participant dropout can result in two different outcomes. We can end up with positive selective survival if the participants at the end of the study tend to be the ones who were initially higher on some variable (e.g., the surviving participants are the ones who were the healthiest at the beginning of the study). In contrast, we could have negative selective survival if the participants at the conclusion of the study were initially lower on an important variable (e.g., the surviving participants may have been those who performed least well). Either way, the group of participants at the end of the study do not reflect the characteristics of the entire group that began the study, making any conclusions very risky.

The third challenge with longitudinal designs is that our ability to apply the results to other groups is limited. The difficulty is that only one cohort is followed. Whether the pattern of results that is observed in one cohort can be generalized to another cohort is questionable. Thus, researchers using longitudinal designs run the risk of uncovering a developmental process that is unique to that cohort. For instance, a longitudinal study of using computers in daily life that included members of generation X (born between 1965 and 1980) may not discover findings of much use to understanding how members of Gen Z (born between 1997 and 2012) use computers.

Because longitudinal designs that extend over years necessarily take more time and usually are very expensive, they have not been used very often. Microgenetic studies, due to the typically shorter duration, are easier to conduct, so we have more of them. However, researchers recognize that we badly need to follow individuals over long periods of time to further our understanding of the aging process, and some funding sources (e.g., the National Institutes of Health) invest in larger scale longitudinal research. We will encounter some of these throughout the book.

Sequential Designs. Thus far, we have considered two developmental designs, each of which has challenges involving the confounding of two of the three building block effects. These confounds are age and cohort in cross-sectional designs, and age and time of measurement in longitudinal designs. These confounds create difficulties in interpreting behavioral differences between and within individuals. Some of these interpretive dilemmas can be alleviated by using more complex designs called sequential designs, which are shown in Table 1.5. Keep in mind, though, that sequential designs do not cure the confounding problems in the three basic designs, but they do provide ways to home in on better understanding of age change and age difference.

Sequential designs represent different combinations of cross-sectional or longitudinal studies. In Table 1.5, a cross-sequential design consists of two or more cross-sectional studies conducted at two or more times of measurement; an example is noted in the cells highlighted in bold red font. These multiple cross-sectional designs include the same age ranges; however, the participants are different in each wave of testing. For example, we might compare performances on personality tests for people between ages 30 and 40 in 2020 and then repeat the study in 2030 with a different group of people aged 30 and 40.

Table 1.5 Sequential Design

	Time of Measurement			
Cohort	**2020**	**2030**	**2040**	**2050**
1970	50	60	70	80
1980	**40**	**50**	**60**	**70**
1990	**30**	**40**	**50**	**60**
2000	20	30	40	50

Cohort is represented by the years in the first column, time of measurement by the years across the top, and age by the values in the cells.

Table 1.5 also depicts the longitudinal sequential design. A longitudinal sequential design consists of two or more longitudinal designs that represent two or more cohorts. Each longitudinal design in the sequence begins with the same age range and follows people for the same length of time. For example, we may want to begin a longitudinal study of intellectual development with a group of 40-year-olds in 2020 using the 1980 cohort. We would then follow this cohort for a period of years. In 2030, we would begin a second longitudinal study on 40-year-olds, using the 1990 cohort, and follow them for the same length of time as we follow the first cohort. This design helps clarify whether the longitudinal effects found in a single longitudinal study are cohort-specific or are more general findings.

Although sequential designs are powerful and provide by far the richest source of information about developmental issues, few researchers use them, because they are extremely costly. Trying to follow many people over long periods of time, generating new samples, and conducting complex data analyses are expensive and time consuming. Clearly, this type of commitment to one project is not possible for most researchers.

The How Do We Know? feature provides one of the best examples of a complex sequential study. The Seattle Longitudinal Study is one of the most comprehensive investigations of human aging ever conducted and has included over 6,000 participants. The feature introduces the study here; we will return to various aspects of the findings in later chapters.

How Do We Know?

Conflicts Between Cross-Sectional and Longitudinal Data

Who was the investigator, and what was the aim of the study? In the 1950s, little information was available concerning longitudinal changes in adults' intellectual abilities. What there was showed a developmental pattern of relative stability or slight decline, quite different from the picture of substantial across-the-board decline obtained in cross-sectional studies. To provide a more thorough picture of intellectual change, K. Warner Schaie began the Seattle Longitudinal Study in 1956. Over the years, a host of other colleagues joined Schaie in conducting the study. The Seattle Longitudinal Study is widely regarded as one of the most extensive investigations in gerontology of how adults develop and change across adulthood.

How did the investigator measure the topic of interest? Schaie used standardized tests of primary mental abilities to assess a wide range of abilities such as logical reasoning and spatial ability.

Who were the participants in the study? Over the course of the study, more than 5,000 individuals have been tested at eight testing cycles (1956, 1963, 1970, 1977, 1984, 1991, 1998, and 2005). The participants were representative of the upper 75% of the socioeconomic spectrum and were recruited through a very large health maintenance organization in Seattle. Extensions of the study include longitudinal data on second-generation family members and on the grandchildren of some of the original participants. Over 6,000 adults have participated in total.

What was the design of the study? To provide a thorough view of intellectual change over time, Schaie invented a new type of design—the sequential design. Participants were tested every seven years. Like most longitudinal studies, Schaie's sequential study encountered selectivity effects—that is, people who return over the years for retesting tend to do better initially than those who fail to return (in other words, those who don't perform well initially tend to drop out of the study). However, an advantage of Schaie's sequential design is that by bringing in new groups of participants, he was able to estimate the importance of selection effects, a major improvement over previous research.

Were there ethical concerns with the study? The most serious issue in any study in which participants are followed over time is confidentiality. Because people's names must be retained for future contact, the researchers were very careful about keeping personal information secure.

What were the results? Among the many important findings from the study are differential changes in abilities over time and cohort effects. Figure 1.4 indicates that scores on tests of primary mental abilities (discussed in Chapter 7) improve gradually until the late 30s or early 40s. Small declines begin in the 50s, increase as people age into their 60s, and become increasingly large in the 70s (Schaie & Zanjani, 2006).

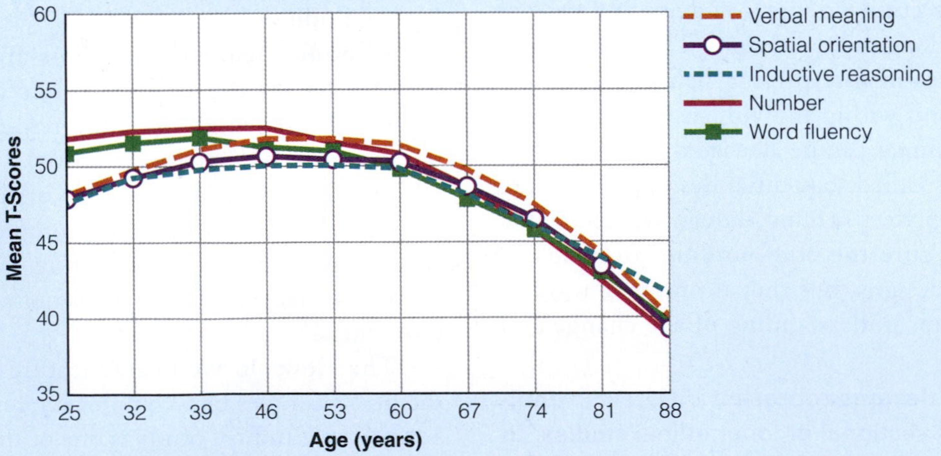

Figure 1.4 Longitudinal changes in intellectual functions from age 25 to 88.

Source: From "Intellectual Development Across Adulthood" by K. Warner Schaie and Faika A. K. Zanjani, in *Handbook of Adult Development and Learning*, ed. C. Hoare, p. 102. Copyright © 2006 by Oxford University Press.

(Continued)

Cohort differences were also found. Figure 1.5 indicates that on some skills, such as inductive reasoning ability, but not others, more recently born younger and middle-aged cohorts performed better than cohorts born earlier. An example of the latter is that older cohorts outperformed younger ones on number skills (Schaie & Zanjani, 2006). These cohort effects probably reflect differences in educational experiences; younger groups' education emphasized figuring things out on one's own, whereas older groups' education emphasized rote learning. Additionally, older groups (those born earlier) did not have calculators or computers, so they had to do mathematical problems by hand.

Schaie uncovered many individual differences as well; some people showed developmental patterns closely approximating the overall trends, but others showed unusual patterns. For example, some individuals showed steady declines in most abilities beginning in their 40s and 50s; others showed declines in some abilities but not others; but some people showed little change in most abilities over a 14-year period. Such individual variation in developmental patterns means that average trends, like those depicted in the figures, must be interpreted cautiously; they reflect group averages and do not represent the patterns shown by each person in the group.

Another key finding is that how intellectual abilities are organized in people does not change over time (Schaie et al., 1998). This finding is important because it means that the tests, which presuppose a particular organizational structure of intellectual abilities, can be used across different ages. Additionally, Schaie (1994) identified several variables that appear to reduce the risk of cognitive decline in old age:

- Absence of cardiovascular and other chronic diseases
- Living in favorable environmental conditions (such as good housing)
- Remaining cognitively active through reading and lifelong learning
- Having a flexible personality style in middle age
- Being married to a person with high cognitive status
- Being satisfied with one's life achievements in middle age

What did the investigator conclude? Three points are clear. First, intellectual development during adulthood is marked by a gradual leveling off of gains, followed by a period of relative stability, and then a time of gradual decline in most abilities. Second, these trends vary from one cohort to another. Third, individual patterns of change vary considerably from person to person.

Overall, Schaie and colleagues' findings indicate that intellectual development in adulthood is influenced by a wide variety of health, environmental, personality, and relationship factors. By attending to these influences throughout adulthood, we can at least stack the deck in favor of maintaining good intellectual functioning in late life.

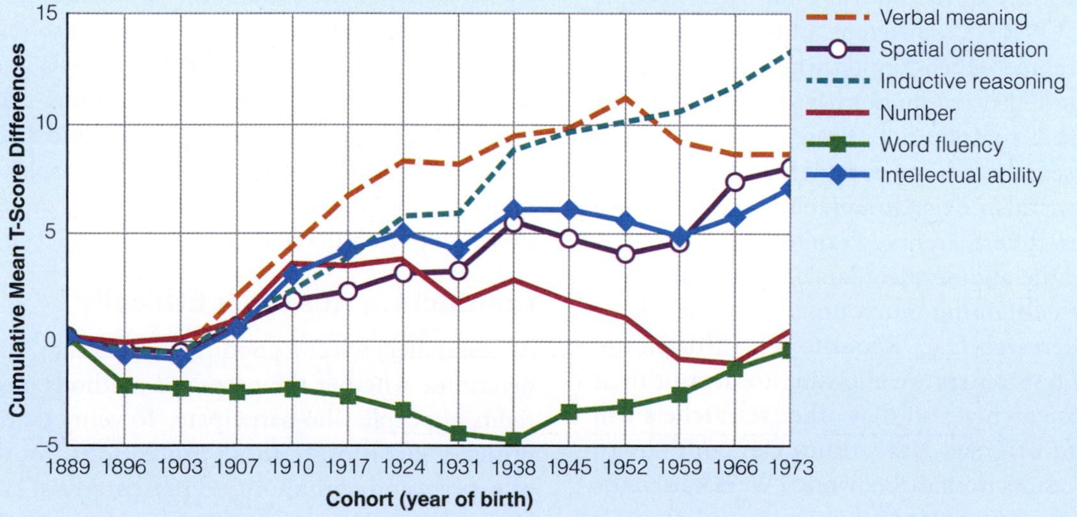

Figure 1.5 Cohort differences in intellectual functions from birth cohorts between 1889 and 1973.

Source: From "Intellectual Development Across Adulthood" by K. Warner Schaie and Faika A. K. Zanjani, *in Handbook of Adult Development and Learning*, ed. C. Hoare, p. 106. Copyright © 2006 by Oxford University Press.

Tools for Doing and Archiving Developmental Research

Designing and conducting good developmental research has been helped by the availability of a range of online tools for measurement, data collection, data analysis, and data archiving. You may already be familiar with some of these if you have, for instance, responded to online surveys.

Several online platforms have been created that allow researchers to conduct entire studies online, complete with remote data collection; among the most popular in psychology are E-Prime, PsychoPy, and PsyToolkit. These platforms provide libraries of common research studies that are customizable for different types of data collection strategies, including neuroscience and physiological measurements.

Because smartphones and webcams are so widely available, apps have been developed to turn these devices into research tools. For instance, apps have been developed to help older adults remember to take medication and to record whether they do. Such data collection tools have provided more insights into aspects of human development.

Similarly, several tools exist for the creation of self-report measures. The most well-known of these is SurveyMonkey, a platform that enables researchers to build and present surveys and questionnaires. These platforms are sufficiently flexible to permit different sets of questions to be presented depending on how respondents answer key questions. For example, if the survey is a measure of the kinds of knowledge people have about COVID-19, different follow-up questions could be presented depending on whether the respondent indicates they do or do not have friends who were hospitalized with complications caused by COVID-19.

Once researchers have completed their studies, online options also exist for placing the data into data archives. These archives range from the fairly specific (e.g., the audio/video data archive Databrary.org) to those containing much broader datasets (e.g., Registry of Research Data Repositories, re3data.org). Increasingly, researchers are choosing to deposit their data into these archives so that other researchers will have access to original data so they can continue to build on the results from earlier work. (We'll learn more about this in the next section.)

Overall, tech tools and data archives have increased our ability to piece together the puzzle of human development in far more sophisticated and complete ways.

Integrating Findings from Different Studies

Several times in the past few pages, we've emphasized the value of using different methods to study the same phenomenon and pooling results in data archives. The advantage is that conclusions are most convincing when the results are consistent regardless of method.

Meta-analysis allows researchers to synthesize the results of many quantitative studies to estimate actual relations between variables (Schmidt & Hunter, 2015; Sharpe & Poets, 2020). In conducting a meta-analysis, investigators find all studies published on a topic over a substantial period of time (e.g., 10 to 20 years) and then record and analyze the results and important methodological variables.

The usefulness of meta-analysis is illustrated in a study by Kojima and colleagues (2016). After identifying 5,145 potential studies on the association between frailty and the quality of life of older adults living in the community, only four studies could be included because of a lack of comparable measures of quality of life. This meta-analysis showed that people classified as frail or as likely to soon become frail had significantly lower mental health and quality of life scores. The meta-analysis also pointed out the challenges in comparing findings from different studies because researchers do not use the same measures to assess constructs such as frailty or quality of life.

Meta-analysis is a particularly powerful tool because it allows scientists to determine whether a finding generalizes across many studies. As Kojima and colleagues' (2016) research showed, meta-analysis also reveals the challenges of comparing different methods in examining the underlying developmental relations. The failure of researchers to use the same measures and assessments makes it extremely difficult to compare results, thereby creating a major barrier to understanding the processes underlying adult development and aging.

Conducting Research Ethically

As researchers select a good research design, they must determine whether the proposed methods protect the rights of people who participate. To verify that research projects incorporate these protections, local panels of experts and community representatives, called the Institutional Review Board, evaluate proposed studies before any data are collected. Only with the approval of this panel can scientists begin their study. If the review panel objects to some aspects of the proposed study,

Informed consent is a necessary aspect of any research effort in human development.

then the researcher must revise those aspects and present them anew for the panel's approval.

To guide review panels, professional organizations (e.g., the American Psychological Association) and government agencies (e.g., U.S. Department of Health and Human Services, National Institutes of Health; European Union Ethics Policy under the Horizons 2020 legislation) have codes of ethical conduct that specify the rights of research participants as well as procedures to protect these participants. The following essential guidelines are included in all of these codes:

- **Minimize risks to research participants.** Use methods that have the least potential for causing harm or stress for research participants. During the research, monitor the procedures to ensure avoidance of any unforeseen stress or harm.
- **Describe the research to potential participants so that they can determine whether they want to participate.** Prospective participants must be told the purpose of the project, what they will be asked to do, whether there are any risks or potential harm or any benefits they may receive, that they are free to discontinue participation at any time without penalty, and that, after they have participated, the project will be described. After the study has been explained, each participant signs a document stating that they understand what they will do in the study. When participants are children or adolescents, a parent, a legal guardian, or another responsible person must provide consent. When adult participants have conditions that affect intellectual functioning (e.g., dementia, severe head injury), the situation is more complex. To ensure that the rights of such adults are protected, another responsible adult (e.g., spouse/partner, adult child caregiver) must provide assent in addition to the consent provided by the participant.
- **Avoid deception; if participants must be deceived, provide a thorough explanation of the true nature of the experiment as soon as possible.** Providing complete information about a study in advance sometimes biases or distorts a person's responses. Consequently, investigators may provide participants with partial information about the study or even mislead them about its true purpose. As soon as it is feasible—typically, just after the experiment—any false information that was given to research participants must be corrected and the reasons for the deception must be provided.
- **Results should be anonymous or confidential.** Research results should be anonymous, which means that people's data cannot be linked to their name. When anonymity is not possible, research results should be confidential, which means that the identity of participants is known only to the investigator(s) conducting the study.

Conducting research ethically is an obligation of every investigator. If you conduct a project, you should submit your procedures for review. If you are a participant in someone else's project, make sure you are given complete information and read it thoroughly.

Adult Development in Action

If you were responsible for making grants at your local United Way organization, how might you determine through research whether the programs you fund actually have the outcomes they claim?

Review Questions

1.3 Research Methods

- What are the reliability and validity of a measure?
- What are the three main approaches scientists use to measure behavior in adult development and aging research? What are the strengths and weaknesses of each?
- How do we know whether a sample is representative?
- What is an experiment? What information does it provide?
- What is a correlational design? What information does it provide?
- What is a case study? What information does it provide?
- What are age, cohort, and time-of-measurement effects? How and why are they important for developmental research?
- What is a cross-sectional design? What are its advantages and disadvantages?
- What is a longitudinal design? What are its advantages and disadvantages?
- What differences are there between cross-sectional and longitudinal designs in terms of uncovering age differences and age changes?
- What are sequential designs? What different types are there? What are their advantages and disadvantages?
- What are the limitations of the extreme age groups design?
- What steps must researchers take to protect the rights of participants?

Social Policy Implications

Moving from Lab to Life

Creating sound social policy requires good information. Elected officials and others who create policy rely on research findings to provide the basis for policy. In terms of social policies affecting adults, the data obtained through the use of the research designs discussed earlier is critical.

The most important social policy implication from this chapter is the rapidly changing demographics of the United States' and the world's populations. In most countries, the population is aging overall. That means changes are necessary in the kinds of social support, health, and income support programs countries design. With millions more older adults needing specialized care, we can no longer focus only on providing child care for families; rather, any form of support program will have to address the need for care of older adult parents, for instance, as well. This is why elected officials the world over are putting more emphasis on issues of importance to older adults and their families.

Consequently, policy makers are paying a lot more attention to research on older adults for clues on how to respond. For example, research such as the Seattle Longitudinal Study described in the How Do We Know? feature had a major impact on the elimination of nearly all mandatory retirement rules in the United States in the 1980s. Research on older workers influenced decisions in corporations to hire older adults, who are highly reliable employees. The buying power of older adults has resulted in major advertising campaigns for everything from calcium replacement medications to adult diapers to treatments for erectile dysfunction to vacations for active older adults.

In each of the remaining chapters, we will be highlighting a particular social policy and how it relates to research. By making these ties, you will be able to understand better how research findings can be applied to address social issues.

In Review

Instead of a chapter summary, we've provided some ideas for how you can review and reflect upon your own learning. One suggestion is for you to create a summary explaining or describing major concepts, theories, researchers, studies, and controversies or unanswered questions covered in the chapter. Consider organizing your summary in paragraphs, with one paragraph (or more) for each of the modules in the chapter. Based on your reading of Chapter 1, you should be able to write a paragraph about the life-span perspective and how the world's population is changing with regard to age. In a second paragraph, you should be able to describe the major forces that shape human development and how they interact; the influences of gender, culture, ethnicity, and race; and how all of this plays out in the core issues in adult development and aging. Finally, you should be able to take an issue in adult development and aging, such as the ability to do two things at once, and design various types of research projects that address that issue.

In addition to writing summary paragraphs, some types of information are best summarized in a table or chart. For example, you could build a table of the major forces in development or the different types of development research designs. Each row would be a different force or research design, and each column would reflect a characteristic of it, such as the definition, pros/cons, and so forth. This approach might help you visualize the concepts better than a paragraph.

You might be thinking to yourself that you already have Review Questions and Integrating Concepts in Development, and perhaps more, to complete, so why bother with a summary? It turns out that the more you check what you've learned, the better you will remember it! We also know from research that the study techniques that work best are the ones you actually use, so always start with the technique or method that you like most, and add other techniques if you have the time. Some people find that switching techniques along the way works as well; reviewing your notes may work well for weekly quizzes, and more formal reviews might work better for major exams if you have any of those in your course. Remember that making notes isn't the only way to reflect what you've learned. You could make a short video of your verbal explanation of a concept or section of the chapter. Or you could make a graphic summary (in the style of a graphic novel). The point is to be as creative as possible in figuring out the study techniques that work best for you.

There's an important point about study techniques—the easiest ones don't always result in the best learning. Try several, with the goal of identifying the one(s) that result in the best retention of the material. Learning can be enjoyable, but it's also hard work. Your performance will be better in the long run when you put in the time to learn along the way. Also, tailor your approaches based on the type(s) of tests and exams you will encounter in the course. Tests that require you to recognize the correct answer (multiple choice and true/false questions) are easier than tests that require you to recall information (short answer and essay questions).

In the end, only you can create a set of study techniques that works best for you. The more you can focus on learning how to learn, the better you will master the material and go on to be better prepared for future situations that require you to master new information.

Integrating Concepts in Development

- Analyze each of the four major controversies in development in terms of the four developmental forces. What real-world examples can you think of that are examples of each combination of controversy and force?
- Using yourself as an example, figure out your age using chronological, perceived, biological, psychological, and sociocultural definitions. How do they differ? Why?
- Using the Leah and Sarah vignette as an example, design cross-sectional, longitudinal, and sequential studies of two different styles of caring for people with Alzheimer's disease. What will you learn from each of the studies?

Key Terms

age effects One of the three fundamental effects examined in developmental research, along with cohort and time-of-measurement effects, which reflects the influence of time-dependent processes on development. 23

ageism The untrue assumption that chronological age is the main determinant of human characteristics and that one age is better than another. 3

biological forces One of four basic forces of development that includes all genetic and health-related factors. 11

biopsychosocial framework Way of organizing the biological, psychological, and sociocultural forces on human development. 11

case study An intensive investigation of individual people. 23

cohort A group of people born at the same point in time or within a specific time span. 12

cohort effects One of the three basic influences examined in developmental research, along with age and time-of-measurement effects, which reflects differences caused by experiences and circumstances unique to the historical time in which one lives. 24

confounding Any situation in which one cannot determine which of two or more effects is responsible for the behaviors being observed. 24

continuity–discontinuity controversy The debate over whether a particular developmental phenomenon represents smooth progression over time (continuity) or a series of abrupt shifts (discontinuity). 19

correlational study An investigation in which the strength of association between variables is examined. 23

cross-sectional study A developmental research design in which people of different ages and cohorts are observed at one time of measurement to obtain information about age differences. 25

demographers People who study population trends. 5

dependent variable Behaviors or outcomes measured in an experiment. 22

emerging adulthood Period between late teens and mid- to late 20s when individuals are not adolescents but are not yet fully adults. 16

established adulthood Period between roughly ages 30 and 45 when life is most intense, demanding, and perhaps rewarding. 16

experiment A study in which participants are randomly assigned to experimental and control groups and in which an independent variable is manipulated to observe its effects on a dependent variable so that cause-and-effect relations can be established. 22

gerontology The study of aging from maturity through old age. 3

independent variable The variable manipulated in an experiment. 22

intersectionality Refers to experiences that reflect combinations of race, ethnicity, biological sex, gender, ability, or sexual orientation. 13

life-cycle forces One of the four basic forces of development that reflects differences in how the same event or combination of biological, psychological, and sociocultural forces affects people at different points in their lives. 11

life-span perspective A view of the human life span that divides it into two phases: childhood/adolescence and young/middle/late adulthood. 4

longitudinal study A developmental research design that measures one cohort over two or more times of measurement to examine age changes. 25

meta-analysis A tool that allows researchers to synthesize the results of many studies to estimate relations between variables. 30

microgenetic study A special type of longitudinal design in which participants are tested repeatedly over a span of days or weeks, typically with the aim of observing change directly as it occurs. 26

nature–nurture issue A debate over the relative influence of genetics and the environment on development. 17

nonnormative influences Random events that are important to an individual but do not happen to most people. 12

normative age-graded influences Experiences caused by biological, psychological, and sociocultural forces that are closely related to a person's age. 12

normative history-graded influences Events that most people in a specific culture experience at the same time. 12

plasticity The belief that capacity is not fixed, but can be learned or improved with practice. 19

population pyramid Graphic technique for illustrating population trends. 5

primary aging Normative, disease-free development during adulthood. 15

psychological forces One of the four basic forces of development that includes all internal perceptual, cognitive, emotional, and personality factors. 11

reliability The ability of a measure to produce the same value when used repeatedly to measure the identical phenomenon over time. 21

secondary aging Developmental changes that are related to disease, lifestyle, and other environmental changes that are not inevitable. 15

self-reports People's answers to questions about a topic of interest. 21

sequential designs Types of developmental research designs involving combinations of cross-sectional and longitudinal designs. 27

sociocultural forces One of the four basic forces of development that include interpersonal, societal, cultural, and ethnic factors. 11

stability–change issue A debate over the degree to which people remain the same over time as opposed to being different. 18

systematic observation A type of measurement involving watching people and carefully recording what they say or do. 21

tertiary aging Rapid losses occurring shortly before death. 15

time-of-measurement effects One of the three fundamental effects examined in developmental research, along with age and cohort effects, which result from the time at which the data are collected. 24

Universal versus context-specific development controversy A debate over whether there is a single pathway of development, or several. 19

Validity The degree to which an instrument measures what it is supposed to measure. 21

Neuroscience as a Basis for Adult Development and Aging

Chapter 2

Chapter Outline

Learning Objectives

After studying this chapter, you will be able to...

2.1. Describe the major imaging and other techniques used in neuroscience.

2.2. Identify and describe the major structures of the brain and their main functions.

2.3. Describe the major theories of age-related changes in the brain and how older adults compensate for these changes.

The most complex, flexible, and adaptive system that has ever been discovered sits inside our skull—our brain, depicted in Figure 2.1. Tripling in size during the first year after birth, our brain reaches 80% of full size by age 2 and typically weighs about 3 pounds by the time we are an adult of about 25 years of age. The cerebral cortex (the outer layer involved in higher level thinking) accounts for about 85 percent of the total weight, keeping in mind that over 75 percent of that weight is water. (That's why even being a little dehydrated is really bad for your brain.)

Our brain contains about 100 billion brain cells, called neurons; interestingly, this is about the same number of cells as there are stars in the Milky Way galaxy. Everything we associate with "being human" happens here—our thoughts, memories, emotions, personality, quirks, and so on. So, it's fitting that we begin our consideration of the adult development and aging process here. Changes in the brain are often involved in the changes in behavior and bodily processes we observe over time.

Figure 2.1 shows the major structures of the brain that are the focus of neuroscience research in adult development and aging. The study of the structure of the brain, called **neuroanatomy**, is fundamental to neuroscience. We will refer to a number of brain regions that exhibit age-related changes in both structure and function.

For much of human history, the brain wasn't considered very important. For instance, the ancient Egyptians thought that the heart was the source of human wisdom and the center of emotions and memory, so that was the only organ they kept in a mummified body. Even after people figured out the brain's importance, it kept its secrets well-guarded. Only recently have we had the tools to study the brain in detail, especially in living people engaged in various behaviors and activities.

As we will discover, the invention of ways to take pictures of the working brain "doing its thing" has fundamentally changed our knowledge and understanding of brain processes and functions. This development has coincided with the rapid surge of research in **neuroscience** or the study of the brain—in particular, typical and atypical changes, along with the adaptability of the aging brain. Neuroscience enables us to observe, measure, and understand what is going on in a person's brain (Nunes, 2021). Images such as the one in the photo are one way that researchers and clinicians

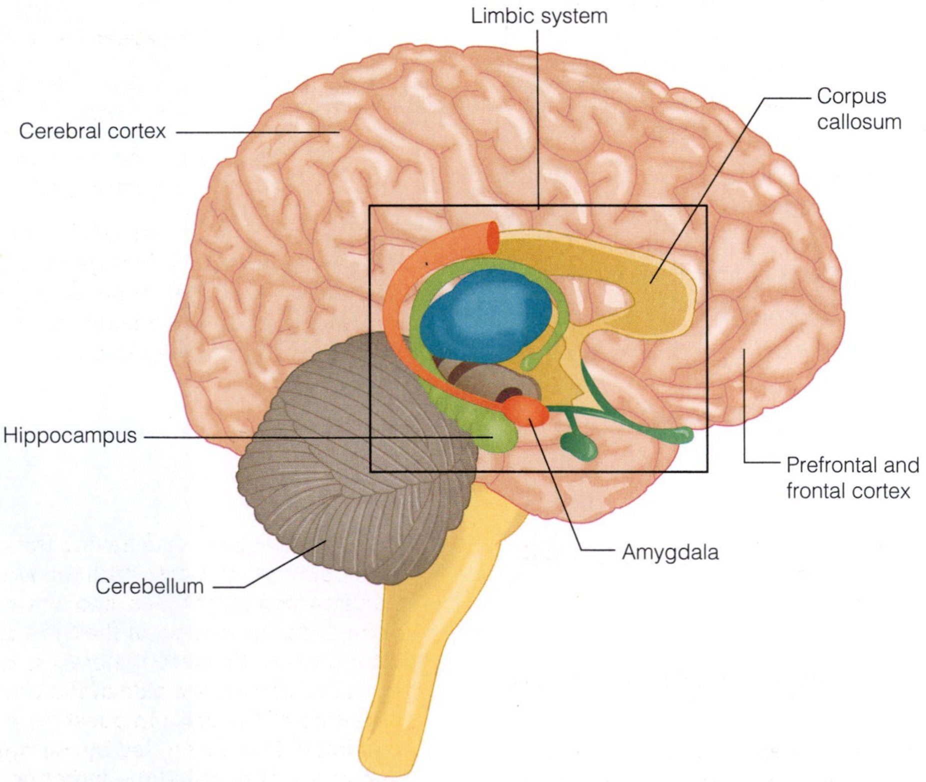

Figure 2.1 Major structures of the human brain depicting cerebral cortex, corpus callosum, prefrontal and frontal cortex, cerebellum, hippocampus, limbic system, and amygdala.

measure brain activity; we will focus on how they do this and what it means as we proceed through the chapter.

Our understanding of how the brain works is expanding exponentially. We now know through the Human Connectome Project, which uses sophisticated studies of brain imagery and computer analyses, what the brain's wiring essentially entails—each hemisphere of the brain (that is, the left and right halves) contains at least 180 distinct functional areas that differ in their structure, function, and connections with other brain areas (Elam et al., 2021; Glasser et al., 2016). As you might imagine, this translates into an extremely complicated wiring diagram with billions upon billions of interconnections.

Perhaps the most important insight from neuroscience research is the evidence that the brain can change for the better as we grow older. These findings send an intriguing message to our aging population. However, there is danger in this. As in any relatively new field, descriptions in the media, especially the internet, may extend well beyond the actual scope of our scientific understanding of the brain and misrepresent or exaggerate what was actually discovered, and provide false hope for miracle achievements.

In this chapter we explore our understanding of the aging brain by examining contemporary theories and recent empirical findings of neuroscience and aging. First, we briefly review the various neuroscience theories underlying and the research techniques used in studying the brain. Next, we focus on cognitive neuroscience and aging including age-related change in brain structures, neurochemical properties, and brain function. Although few studies have examined the possible effects that culture may have on the aging of brain structures and their functions per se, what data exist reveal no significant differences across culture (Chee, 2011; Gutchess et al., 2021). We will then examine the evidence for neural plasticity in later adulthood. Finally, we explore more developments in the area of social neuroscience and aging—in particular, intriguing findings that reveal the neurological underpinnings of enhanced emotional processing in older adulthood in contrast to declines in cognitive processing such as the ability to control information in the conscious mind.

Before we explore some of the scientific research on age-related changes in the brain, complete the Discovering Development exercise. Compare your findings with the evidence described in the text that follows. What similarities and differences are revealed?

Discovering Development
Adults' Views About Brain Aging

In Chapter 1, we briefly considered the existence and effect of stereotypes about aging. In this activity, we'll focus specifically on what adults think happens to our brains as we age. In order to get a sense of this, talk to some people of different ages you know and ask them the following questions:

- What happens to the brain as we grow older?
- What do you think causes these changes?
- How can we tell that there may be something changing in a person's brain?
- Do you think there is anything that a person can do to change the usual path of change?

Compile the results from each member of the class. As you proceed through the chapter, compare them with what neuroscience research has uncovered. How do people's beliefs match (or not) with the underlying science?

2.1 Unlocking the Brain's Secrets

Key Questions

- What brain imaging techniques are used in neuroscience research?
- What are the main research methods used and issues studied in neuroscience research in adult development and aging?

At age 70, Margaret was having trouble moving the left side of her body. With the aid of accurate brain imaging techniques, she was diagnosed as having a tumor located at the front of the right motor cortex. (Because the brain is wired in general to control the side of the body opposite of the side of the brain in question, movement on one's left side is controlled by the right side of the brain in the area called the motor cortex.) With image-guided surgery, the tumor was removed, and Margaret recovered comfortably.

How did Margaret's physicians figure out what was wrong with her? We are learning a great deal about the relations between changes in the brain and changes in behavior through technological advances in noninvasive imaging and in assessing psychological functioning (Henderson et al., 2020; Sugiura, 2016). **Neuroimaging** is a set of techniques in which pictures of the brain are taken in various ways to provide understanding of both normal and abnormal cognitive aging. Let's explore the different types and applications of neuroimaging in more detail.

Capturing Images of the Brain at Work

Neuroimaging allows us to see inside the brain of a living person to examine the various structures and functions of the brain even in a person engaged in a task. Neuroimaging has revolutionized our understanding of the relations between our brain and our behavior, and it is responsible for an explosion of knowledge over the past few decades. Advances in neuroimaging have led to much of our understanding of such diseases as dementia (which we will consider in detail in Chapter 10) and to other key insights into age-related changes that occur to everyone and those changes that reflect disease or other atypical changes.

But neuroimaging must be used carefully and ethically. For one thing, we are still figuring out which changes in the brain are normative and which ones are not. We need to know what a "healthy" brain looks like at different points in the human life span. So just because we observe a change does not mean anything in and of itself unless additional research is done to place it in context.

Two neuroimaging techniques are used most often:

1. **Structural neuroimaging** provides highly detailed images of anatomical features in the brain. The most commonly used structural neuroimaging methods are X-rays, computerized tomography (CT) scans, and magnetic resonance imaging (MRI). Images from structural neuroimaging techniques are like photographs in that they document what a specific brain structure looks like at a specific point in time. Structural neuroimaging is usually effective at identifying such things as bone fractures, tumors, and other conditions that cause structural damage in the brain, such as strokes.
2. **Functional neuroimaging** provides an indication of brain activity but not high anatomical detail. The most commonly used functional neuroimaging techniques are single photon emission computerized tomography (SPECT), positron emission tomography (PET), functional magnetic resonance imaging (fMRI), magnetoencephalograpy (or multichannel encephalography), and near infrared spectroscopic imaging (NIRSI). Functional neuroimaging provides researchers with information about what parts of the brain are active when people are doing specific tasks. A typical image will show different levels of brain activity as different colors; for example, red on an image might indicate high levels of brain activity in that region, whereas blue might indicate low levels of activity.

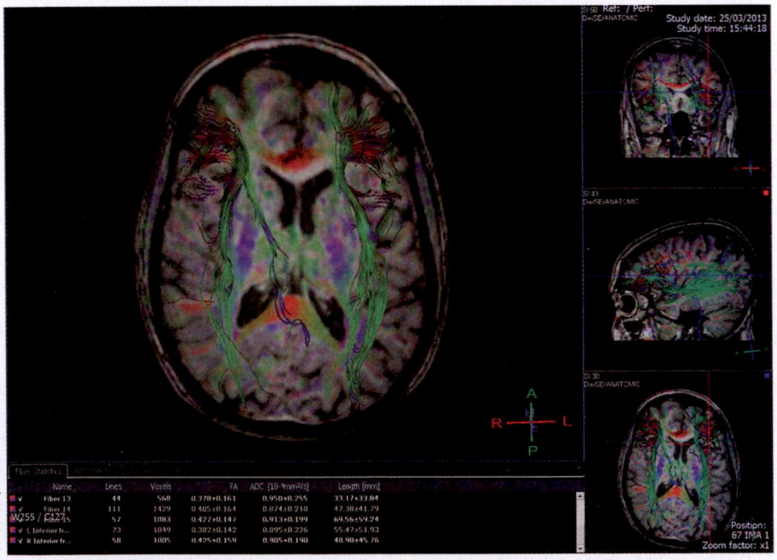

iStock.com/Wenht

Images such as this help us understand how the brain operates.

These techniques, coupled with tests of behavior such as specific cognitive processing tasks (e.g., recognizing which pictures you studied from a deck containing pictures you saw and pictures you did not), have shown quite convincingly that age-related brain changes are responsible for age-related changes in performance (Betzel, 2022).

In Margaret's case, an MRI scan was conducted. This identified areas of the brain associated with specific functions. The scan produced an image showing the brain location of interest and the outline of a tumor in the area of the brain involved in controlling movement.

In addition to using MRIs to locate brain tumors, we are interested in how neuroimaging techniques advance our understanding of how the brain changes structurally and functionally as we grow older. Do the changes reflect decline, stability, or perhaps improvement and compensation? Is there plasticity or growth in the aging brain? These are important questions that researchers in the field of contemporary neuroscience and aging are exploring.

A neuroscientific approach to the study of aging has several advantages. For example, the neuroscience approach has resulted in the development of new, effective interventions that are enhancing the quality of life of older adults (Levitin, 2020). It even has a very practical side. For instance, neuroscience research can be applied to protecting older adults from financial exploitation through understanding the connection between cognitive decline and the ability to understand financial transactions (Lamar et al., 2020; Sunderaraman et al., 2021).

These techniques can test models of cognitive aging. Neuroscience has become increasingly more relevant to cognitive aging research as the focus has expanded beyond studying pathologies of the aging brain, such as Alzheimer's or Parkinson's diseases, toward investigating normative and healthy aging (Aron et al., 2022). In addition, neuroscientific data are more informative for models of cognitive aging and usher in increased progress in the field by testing established theories using cutting-edge methods. Furthermore, examination of the structure and function of the brain has become even more informative for cognitive aging research as the focus has shifted from describing brain activation patterns toward explaining them and designing effective interventions where appropriate (Marcotte et al., 2022).

Doing Neuroscience

You might wonder if doing studies on the brain would require a special set of designs for research. Certainly, there are special ways to measure brain activity, and, as we noted in the previous section special ways of taking images of a working brain. But the basic research designs used in neuroscience are actually the same ones we encountered in Chapter 1 with minor modifications.

Researchers take three main methodological perspectives in studying the neuroscience of aging: the neuropsychological, the neurocorrelational, and the activation imaging approaches (Cabeza, 2004). The **neuropsychological approach** compares brain functioning of healthy older adults with adults displaying various pathologies and disorders of the brain. In this approach researchers are interested in whether persons of any age with damage in specific regions of the brain exhibit similar cognitive deficits to those shown by healthy older adults as documented in other research. If this is the case, then researchers can conclude that decline in cognitive functioning as we grow older may be related to underlying changes in the same specific regions of the brain observed in the persons with diagnosed and identified pathologies or disorders.

Let's suppose this type of comparison is made between healthy older adults and persons with diagnosed frontal lobe damage (noted in Figure 2.1). People with damage in the frontal lobe display lower levels of dopamine (a neurochemical substance we will consider a bit later in detail), which results in a decrease in how quickly mental processing occurs, termed speed of processing (discussed in more detail in Chapter 6). Interestingly, this pattern of slowing resembles what is observed in the typical aging trajectory of healthy older adults.

Another important objective of research using this approach is to isolate the neural or brain mechanisms that are associated with both normative and atypical decline in cognitive functions. These findings stimulate the creation of theories by identifying factors that explain how and why these factors may cause cognitive changes as we age.

Just as we considered in Chapter 1 in relation to adult development and aging research in general, neuroscience researchers use certain research designs to study changes in brain structures and processes, which brings us to the two remaining methodological perspectives.

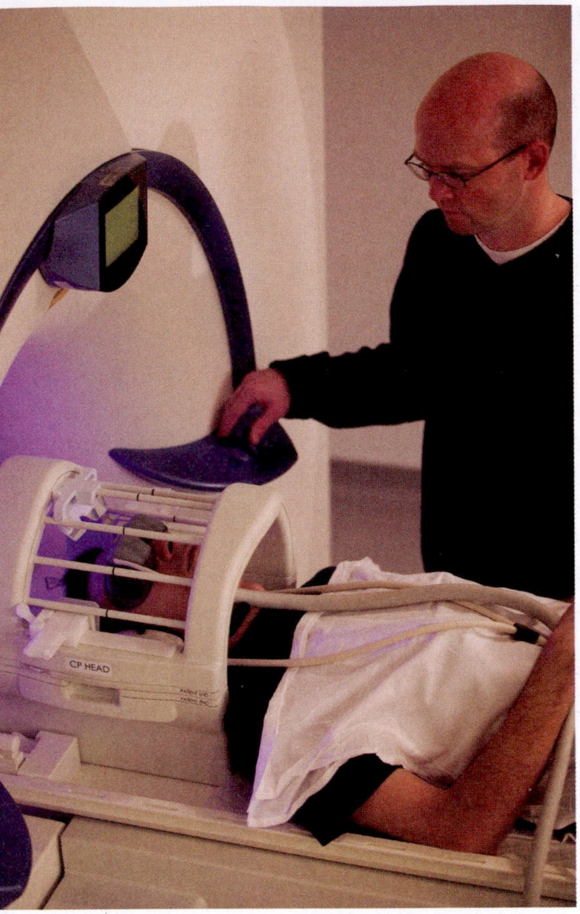

Mark Harmel/Science Source

A research participant being readied for an fMRI neuroimaging study.

The **neurocorrelational approach** relates measures of cognitive performance to measures of brain structure or functioning. For example, a researcher may be interested in the correlation between cognitive behavior, such as the ability to remember information over short periods of time, and neural structural measures, such as the volume of the brain or activity in specific areas of the brain (Cabeza & Dennis, 2013; Aron et al., 2022). Instead of direct measures of brain structure or functioning, some researchers investigate the correlation between medical assessments that are associated with the function of specific brain regions (e.g., tests of frontal lobe functioning) with the behavior of interest (such as decision making). This approach is useful especially when direct measures of brain functioning are unavailable or impractical. However, this approach is speculative, in that we cannot be certain whether the assessment tests of brain functioning accurately reflect the actual anatomical and functional activity of the specific brain region under investigation.

The best solution available to this shortcoming of the neurocorrelational approach is to watch the brain in action while a person is performing a particular behavior. The **activation imaging approach** attempts to directly link functional brain activity with cognitive behavioral data. This approach allows real-time investigation of changes in brain function as they affect cognitive performance in older adults. As you may have surmised, this approach relies on the functional neuroimaging techniques discussed earlier in this chapter, such as fMRI. For example, studies using this approach have found that younger adults' brains show unilateral activation (i.e., activation in only one hemisphere of the brain) when they perform specific cognitive tasks, but older adults' brains tend to have higher activation in both brain hemispheres when performing the same tasks (Aron et al., 2022). As we will discuss later, this difference in activation in younger and older adult brains may provide neurological evidence that older adults' brains actively compensate for age-related changes. **Compensatory changes** are changes that allow older adults to adapt to the inevitable behavioral decline resulting from changes in specific areas of the brain. We will encounter many examples of compensatory changes in older adults' behavior throughout the rest of this book.

Overall, neuroscience has brought an important perspective to studying cognitive aging, influencing theories of adulthood in several ways (Betzel, 2022; Marcotte et al., 2022; Neubeck et al., 2022). First, theories of brain–behavior relations can be tested using these approaches. For instance, age-related changes in how we selectively direct our attention to specific characteristics of our environment, as when we drive a car, can be validated by examining how age-related changes in performance are associated with both functional and structural changes in the brain. In other words, we can explain how changes in performance, like driving, map to changes in the brain.

Second, research methods that focus on age-related changes in the structure and functioning of the brain can help explain why certain cognitive functions, such as well-practiced tasks, vocabulary, and wisdom, can be preserved into old age while other functions, such as processing speed, decline rapidly as people age. By carefully tracking which brain structures and functions change in which direction—or in some cases remain the same—we can differentiate and explain seemingly contradictory patterns of behavior over time.

As powerful and useful as they are, neuroscientific methods, such as fMRI, SPECT, and PET scans, have limitations (Hurley et al., 2020). Like any set of tools, neuroscience techniques must be used appropriately and ethically, and research employing them needs to include participants that reflect the diversity of the whole population. Nevertheless, advances in the field of neuroscience have had a major impact on our understanding of cognitive aging because they have forced a rethinking of the typical aging process and under what conditions an atypical trajectory may occur.

Adult Development in Action

How would a physician decide whether to use structural neuroimaging or functional neuroimaging to aid in a clinical diagnosis?

Review Questions

2.1 The Neuroscience Approach

- Describe the major structural and functional neuroimaging techniques. How do they differ? What do they measure?
- Describe the neuroscience methodological perspectives used to study the aging brain. What are their strengths and their limitations?

2.2 Neuroscience and the Aging Brain

Key Questions

- How is the brain organized structurally?
- What are the basic changes in neurons as we age?
- What changes occur in neurotransmitters with age?
- How do age-related structural brain changes map to behavior?

Antonio is 73, and he is worried about contracting Alzheimer's disease. He remembers that his father became disoriented at this age and had trouble remembering things that he had just been told. How can Antonio find out if his brain is aging normatively or atypically?

Much adult development and aging research in neuroscience has focused on cognitive aging, examining both normative/typical and nonnormative/atypical patterns of change. Historically, this research was based mostly on behavioral data, coupled with findings from brain autopsies, which together gave rise to the classic theories of cognitive aging (discussed in Chapters 6 and 7). The rise of neuroscientific methods has stimulated research that allows us to study cognitive processes—and changes in these processes—in the living brain using the noninvasive brain imaging techniques discussed earlier. Knowing what is going on inside a living person's brain gives us enormous insights into both normative and nonnormative activity. It provides us with a map of which behaviors are based in which location(s) of the brain (Nunes, 2021). For instance, brain activity involved in the identification of faces occurs in areas of the brain that are among the first affected by Alzheimer's disease (Yamasaki, 2021). So changes in brain activity in these regions may signal the onset of the disease before other, more noticeable behavioral changes occur.

This is exactly the type of information in which Antonio, the man in the vignette, would be interested. To make these types of discoveries, we must first have a large knowledge base of how the brain ages. That is what we will consider in this module.

We will start with an overview of major brain structures essential to know with respect to age-related changes. Then we will focus on one area in particular, the prefrontal cortex, that is involved in many key cognitive processes as a prime example of the complex patterns of age-related changes that occur. We'll consider the breadth of involvement of the prefrontal cortex and several age-related changes in that involvement. All along, we will be sure to identify how age changes in specific parts of the brain are linked to everyday behaviors.

How Is the Brain Organized?

The human brain is an amazingly complex organ. It still remains more flexible and capable than any computer, handling billions of computations very rapidly and providing us with the wide range of emotions we experience. Needless to say, the structure of such a complex organ is, well, complex. At the most basic level, the brain is made up of cells called **neurons**, an example of which is shown in Figure 2.2. Key structural features of the neuron are the **dendrites**, which act like antennas

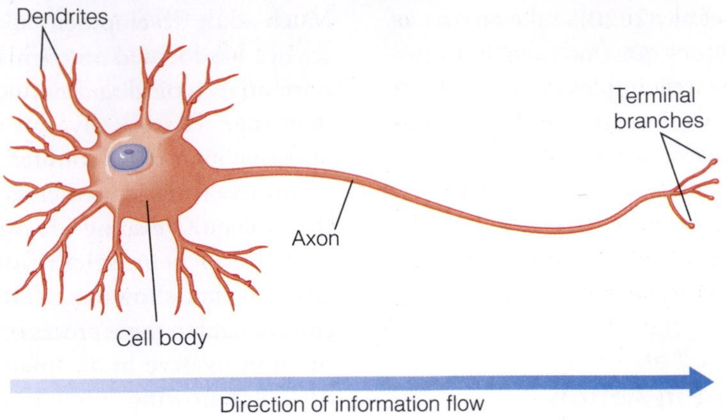

Figure 2.2 A typical neuron showing dendrites, axon, and terminal branches.

to receive signals from other nearby neurons, and the **axon**, which is part of the neuron containing the **neurofibers**, which are the structures that carry information inside the neuron from the dendrites to the **terminal branches**, which are the endpoints of the neuron. Neurons do not physically touch each other. In order for information to be passed from one neuron to another, the terminal branches release chemicals called **neurotransmitters** that travel across the space between neurons, called the **synapse**, where they are received by the dendrites of the next neuron.

Refer back to Figure 2.1 on page 36. The **cerebral cortex** is the outermost part of the brain. It consists of two hemispheres (left and right) that are connected by a thick bundle of neurons called the **corpus callosum**. Much of neuroscience research focuses on the cerebral cortex, mainly because it is in the cerebral cortex that the functions most people consider as defining what it means to be human reside.

Each region of the brain has distinguishing features that relate to the specific functions those regions control. For example, in most right-handed people, language processing is associated primarily with the left hemisphere, whereas recognizing nonspeech sounds, emotions, and faces is associated with the right hemisphere. For the study of adult development and aging, the following are key regions to recognize and understand:

- The **prefrontal and frontal cortex** is intimately involved in higher-order **executive functions** such as the ability to make and carry out plans, switch between tasks, and maintain attention and focus, and it connects with other key brain structures that are involved with emotion.
- The **cerebellum**, at the back of the brain, controls equilibrium and the coordination of fine motor movements, and it may be involved in some cognitive functions.
- The **hippocampus**, located in the middle of the brain, is a key structure associated with memory.
- The **limbic system** is a set of brain structures involved with emotion, motivation, and long-term memory, among other functions. For adult development and aging research, the most important components of the limbic system include the **amygdala** and the hippocampus.

Additional brain structures and their functional aspects will be pointed out when necessary as we move through this chapter. Next, we will briefly consider some of the basics of how the brain works, and the age changes that occur.

What Age-Related Changes Occur in Neurons?

Several changes occur with age in neurons that interfere with their ability to transmit information throughout the brain (Whalley, 2015). For one thing, as we age the number of neurons in the brain declines. More important, though, are the structural changes that occur normatively: decreases in the complexity, size, and number of dendrites (so less information gets passed along from neuron to neuron); the development of tangles in the fibers that make up the axon (greatly affecting how easily information is transmitted within each neuron); and increases in the deposit of certain proteins in and around neurons (also interfering with the transmission of information from neuron to neuron).

The number of potential connections also declines, as measured by the number of synapses among neurons.

Interestingly, these same changes occur but in much greater numbers in diseases such as Alzheimer's disease, leading some researchers to speculate that there may be a link between normative brain aging and nonnormative brain aging having to do with the speed and the number of changes, not in the kind of changes that occur. In other words, the same changes occur in normative and nonnormative brain aging; there are just many more of them in atypical brain aging.

Importantly, even though much of the age change in neurons reflects decrease and decrement, this does not mean that change is only negative. On the contrary, we will encounter evidence later in the chapter for the generation of new and complex neuronal connections, with increased complexity of dendrites. These positive changes occur in response to new learning and the development of more efficient ways of processing. As a result, the full story of age-related changes in neurons is one of both decline and improvement.

White Matter Hyperintensities. One of the most important structural changes relating to neurons overall is the declining health of the brain's white matter, termed white matter hyperintensities (WMH). **White matter** refers to neurons that are covered by myelin, an insulating sheath, that transmit information from one part of the cerebral cortex to another or from the cerebral cortex to other parts of the brain. **White matter hyperintensities** are determined by the observation of high signal intensity or a bright, spotty appearance on MRI images, which indicate brain pathologies (Habes et al., 2016; Tubi et al., 2020).

White matter hyperintensities were once thought to be simply generic indicators of aging. That's not the view anymore (Tubi et al., 2020). Much research has shown that WMH are clearly associated with progressive cognitive impairment, a two-fold increase in the risk of dementia, and a three-fold increase in the risk of stroke. The prevalence of WMH increases with increasing circulatory system risk factors, such as hypertension, diabetes, and smoking. Risk factor exposure appears particularly detrimental if it occurs in middle age.

White matter does show some normative deterioration with increasing age. A neuroimaging method called **diffusion tensor imaging (DTI)** is a type of magnetic resonance imaging (MRI) that assesses the rate and direction that water diffuses through the white matter. This results in an index of the structural health of the white matter (Emsell et al., 2016). By using DTI, studies examining WMH have demonstrated that deterioration of white matter may represent a cause of increased dysfunction in the prefrontal cortex in older adults. (DTI is also used to differentiate between neurological effects of Lyme disease [a disease transmitted by deer ticks] and multiple sclerosis.) As we will learn later, deterioration of the prefrontal cortex has important implications for cognitive functioning in late adulthood.

Of equal importance is the fact that WMH are linked to cerebrovascular diseases (e.g., stroke resulting from hypertension) that in turn are associated with the progression of dementia. WMH is also associated with increased risk for falling (Crockett et al., 2022). How these connections are discerned is the focus of the How Do We Know? feature.

The good news is that WMH may be preventable and be treated through medication and changes in lifestyle. For instance, Crockett and colleagues (2022) found that physical activity may hold promise in mitigating the effects of WMH on falling, as noted in the How Do We Know? feature.

These studies provide a key example of how DTI is used in diagnosing serious diseases in order to start treatment earlier than would occur otherwise. Researchers and clinicians alike urge caution, though, in not overinterpreting the correlational data between the sheer number of WMH and behaviors, as it remains to be seen whether WMH actually cause disease or behavioral change, or merely reflect a different underlying cause (Yassi & Campbell, 2021).

What Age-Related Changes Occur in Neurotransmitters?

As noted earlier, because neurons do not touch each other, information transmission from one neuron to another occurs mainly chemically via neurotransmitters. Advances have been made in measuring changes in neurotransmitters in the aging brain. Let's explore some of the key findings.

Dopamine. One neurotransmitter that has received a great deal of attention is dopamine. **Dopamine** is a neurotransmitter associated with higher-level cognitive functioning like inhibiting thoughts, attention, and planning, as well as emotion, movement, and pleasure and pain. Collectively, the neurons that use dopamine are called the **dopaminergic system**. For example, high dopamine levels are linked to cognitive processing that is effortful and deliberate, but not to the

How Do We Know?

The Risk of Falling and White Matter Hyperintensities

Who were the investigators, and what was the aim of the study? Previous research has indicated that WMH are associated with greater risk of falls and slow walking speed in older adults with cerebral small vessel disease. Whether these problems are caused by the disruption of large-scale functional neural networks is uncertain, though. Rachel Crockett and a large team of researchers (2022) wanted to find out.

Who were the participants in the study? A total of 164 older adults with cerebral small vessel disease who live in metropolitan Vancouver, Canada, participated. All of them were screened for dementia, and all lived independently. Cerebral small vessel disease is the most common type of blood vessel disease in the brain, in which blood flow to the brain is disrupted in the small blood vessels (arterioles and capillaries). The disease can occur in any organ; in the brain it causes memory and other cognitive impairment, as well as falls.

How did the investigators measure the topic of interest? All participants were given (1) the Physiological Profile Assessment (PPA), a five-component measure of the risk of falling; (2) two additional measures of body swaying (one with eyes open, and one standing on a foam cushion termed "foam sway"); (3) measures of a person's usual speed of walking; (4) a questionnaire about overall physical activity; and (5) a MRI to measure WMH as well as lesions in specific neural networks. The neural networks in question were the dorsal attention network and the ventral attention network; their location in the brain is noted in Figure 2.3. These attention networks are involved in a wide variety of cognitive process, including the noticing of pain.

What was the design of the study? The researchers used a cross-sectional design, and it was a correlational study.

Were there ethical concerns with the study? All participants were provided informed consent documents in writing.

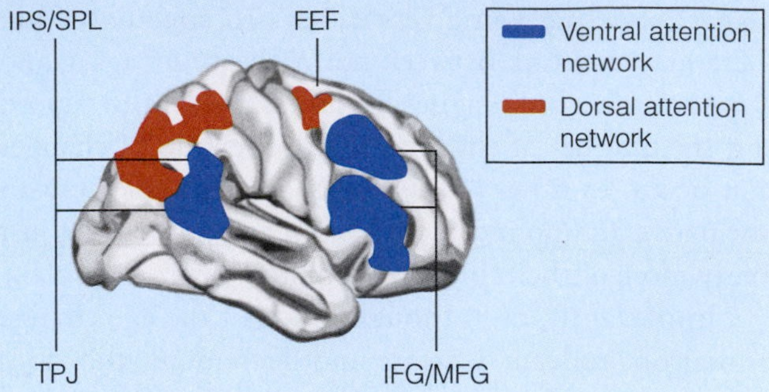

Figure 2.3 Dorsal and ventral attention networks

Anatomy of the ventral and dorsal attention networks. FEF: Frontal eye field, IPS/SPL: Intra parietal sulcus/superior parietal lobe, TPJ: Temporo-parietal junction, IFG/MFG: Inferior frontal gyrus/medial frontal gyrus.

Source: Torta, D. M., Legrain, V., Mouraux, A., & Valentini, E. (2017). Attention to pain! A neurocognitive perspective on attentional modulation of pain in neuroimaging studies. *Cortex, 89,* 120–134. https://doi.org/10.1016/j.cortex.2017.01.010, Figure 2, p. 123.

What were the results? Based on mapping of lesions in neural networks, significant correlations were found between the percentage of WMH-related disruption of the dorsal attention network and the PPA score and between disruption of the sensorimotor and ventral attention networks with foam sway. There were no significant associations with eyes open sway or walking speed. Physical activity moderated the association between the dorsal (top) attention network and PPA score. This intriguing finding is noted in Figure 2.4.

What did the investigators conclude? In older adults with cerebral small vessel disease the disruption to the sensorimotor, dorsal attention, and ventral attention networks as a result of WMH may underlie the greater fall risk evident in this population. However, physical activity may be an important lifestyle factor by which to moderate these relationships, because certain types of physical activity are known to lower the risk of falling. Future research should investigate whether physical activity should be recommended in the clinical management of older adults with cerebral small vessel disease.

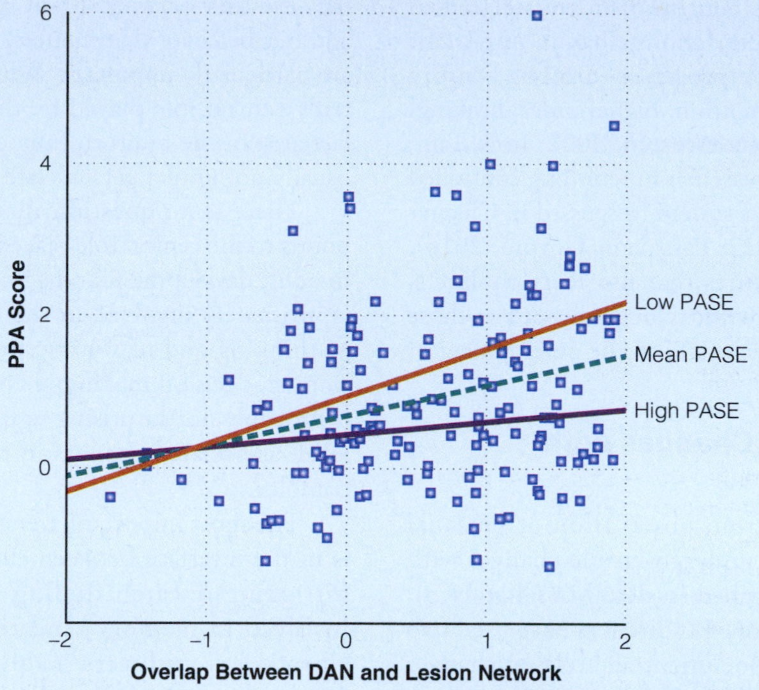

Figure 2.4 Association between the disruption to the dorsal attention network (DAN) and falls risk (PPA score) as a function of activity level

The association between the disruption to the dorsal attention network (DAN) and falls risk (PPA score) is moderated by physical activity level. Higher physical activity score for the elderly (PASE) lowered the association between greater disruption to the DAN and higher PPA score.

Source: Crockett, R. A., Hsu, C. L., Dao, E., Tam, R., Alkeridy, A., Eng, J. J., Handy, T. C., & Liu-Ambrose, T. (2022). Mind the gaps: Functional networks disrupted by white matter hyperintensities are associated with greater falls risk. *Neurobiology of Aging, 109*, 166–175. https://doi.org/10.1016/j.neurobiolaging.2021.09.023. Figure 4.

processes that are more automatic and less effortful. (The distinctions between these are explored in more detail in Chapter 6.) To investigate dopamine, most studies have used postmortem analyses (i.e., analyses during autopsies), results from neuropsychological tests, simulated modeling, and the imaging of dopamine activity. Researchers (Karalija et al., 2021; Mather, 2016; Park & Festini, 2017) have concluded that there is clear evidence that effective functioning of the dopaminergic system is critical for cognitive processes, and that it declines in typical aging. Exactly what does this mean?

Declines in the dopaminergic system are related to declines in several different aspects of memory (Karalija et al., 2021; Nevalainen et al., 2015; Yin & Wang, 2016), such as episodic memory and memory for information acquired in tasks that must be performed quickly, and the amount of information that can be held in mind at any given moment (called working memory). As we will explore in Chapter 6, these are cognitive tasks that require cognitive effort. In contrast, fewer age differences are observed in more automatic tasks, like judging the familiarity of information. Overall, the studies using neuroscience methods to examine changes in the dopaminergic system with increasing age suggest that changes in dopamine levels play a major role in cognitive aging and may explain why effortful and not automatic processes show more age-related change.

Other Neurotransmitters. The neurotransmitter serotonin is involved in several types of brain processes, including memory, mood, appetite, and sleep. Abnormal processing of serotonin has been shown to be related to cognitive decline both in normative aging and in dementia (such as Alzheimer's disease), as well as other disorders such as sleep problems and schizophrenia (McCarthy, 2021; Rodriguez et al., 2012; Štrac et al., 2016). Increasing the functional level of serotonin has beneficial effects for certain problems (McCarthy, 2021; Štrac et al., 2016). In Chapter 10, we will return to the role of serotonin in mental disorders.

Another important neurotransmitter related to aging is *acetylcholine*. Acetylcholine has an important role in general cognitive processes (arousal, sensory perception, sustaining attention, higher order thinking) and in dementia (Cools & Arnsten, 2022; Ju & Tam, 2022) as well as in cardiovascular functioning controlled by the autonomic nervous system (discussed in Chapter 3; Cools & Arnsten, 2022; Pascale & Govoni, 2016). Damage to brain structures that use acetylcholine is associated with serious memory declines such as those found in Alzheimer's disease and in the development of cardiovascular disease.

Linking Structural Changes with Behavior

As you already know from observation or personal experience, our bodies undergo visible changes with age (such as those described in detail in Chapter 3). The brain is no exception. Researchers have used two general approaches to document age-related changes in brain structures: a correlational approach employing postmortem and imaging analyses of adults' brains, and cross-sectional and longitudinal designs using brain imaging techniques. In either approach, different regions of the brain are examined in terms of various structural changes and deficiencies, such as thinning and shrinkage in volume and density, and other changes.

Postmortem and neuroimaging studies verify that many changes occur with age. One important change is that the brain shrinks, or atrophies, by late life, generally shrinking about 5% per decade starting around age 40 and perhaps increasing after age 70 in most people. The cerebral cortex gets thinner over this same time span. The ventricles (structures that look like open spaces) increase in size.

However, these structural changes are not uniform across the whole brain (Pini et al., 2016). For example, the prefrontal cortex, the hippocampus, and the cerebellum show more significant atrophy. In contrast, the areas of the brain related to sensory functions, such as the visual cortex, show relatively little atrophy. These differential patterns map to different rates of change in behavior and underlying abilities and can be used to track the difference between normative changes and changes associated with disease.

It is easy enough to focus on the structural, anatomical changes that occur in people's brains as they age through adulthood. But what do these changes really imply in a person's everyday life? For most of us, it is the link between brain structures and functions and our behavior that matters. Let's consider a few that are particularly important. What we will discover is the truly central role played by the prefrontal cortex, the last area in the brain to fully develop chronologically, usually not until a person's late 20s.

There is no question that neuroscience research points to the central role played by the prefrontal cortex in adult development and aging. This part of the brain is intimately involved in the most important aspects of thinking and reasoning, including executive functioning, decision making, memory, and emotion. So it is probably not surprising to discover that at a detailed level, age-related changes in the prefrontal cortex are complex.

The most important arena in this complex pattern is in the interface between emotion and memory. An intriguing research finding is that brain pathways involved in memory tend to deteriorate with age, whereas key pathways involved in emotion do not. How is this explained?

Let's start by focusing on a well-documented effect called the positivity effect. The **positivity effect** refers to the fact that older adults are often more motivated to derive emotional meaning from life and to maintain positive feelings (Isaacowitz & Blanchard-Fields, 2012; Kensinger & Gutchess, 2017; Petro et al., 2021). As a result, older adults are more likely than younger adults to attend to the emotional meaning of information.

Some of the brain pathways for processing both positive and negative emotion are the same for all adults

Eggeegg/Shutterstock.com

What each person in this couple eventually remembers about their relationship is likely to include more positive than negative memories due to the positivity effect.

regardless of age. Specifically, the common pathways in emotion processing for adults of all ages include the amygdala and the part of the prefrontal cortex right behind the eyes (the lateral orbitofrontal cortex). The prefrontal cortex is especially involved in regulating emotions (e.g., making sure that our emotional reaction is appropriate and fits the situation). The connections between the prefrontal cortex and the amygdala matter a great deal for emotion regulation. It turns out that how active the amygdala is during emotion processing appears particularly important. In certain people who have intermittent explosive disorder (i.e., become extremely angry when shown angry faces, for instance), the amygdala shows hyperactivation (McCloskey et al., 2016), which may be the cause of the disorder.

Research also indicates that in addition to some common brain areas that process all emotion, there are also some unique pathways. For instance, positive emotional processing occurs in the front section of the prefrontal cortex. For negative emotion processing, the temporal (side) region is brought into action instead.

But there are some important age-related differences in brain pathways, too, that help us understand age-related differences in emotion-related behaviors. When older adults process information that is emotionally positive, they have increased activity in the middle portion of the prefrontal cortex, the amygdala, and the cingulate cortex (a structure that forms a "collar" around the corpus callosum). Younger adults do not have this pattern. Bringing additional areas of the brain into play during emotion processing is an age-related phenomenon that matters and explains much about why older and young adults differ in how they react to emotional content and situations, a point we will return to a bit later.

These age-related changes in how the brain processes positive and negative emotional information indicate both that there are probably underlying structural changes in the brain that result in age-related differences in behavior, and that these structural changes can be quite nuanced and complex. Additionally, neuroimaging research has drawn attention to the truly central and critical role played by the prefrontal cortex in understanding why people are the way they are and process information in the ways they do (Grady et al., 2016). Changes in how the prefrontal cortex is connected with other parts of the brain have important implications for behavior, as we will encounter at several other points in this book. Because it is so important, let's make a closer examination of the role of the prefrontal cortex, in combination with other key brain structures, and find out what's going on as people age.

Structural Changes, Theory of Mind, and Executive Functions. One of the most important abilities we have is to interpret one's own and others' mental and emotional states. This ability, termed **theory of mind (ToM)**, helps us understand that other people have beliefs, desires, ideas, feelings, intentions, and viewpoints that are different from our own. One's ToM develops across the life span and is a crucial aspect of social cognition, as we will consider in Chapter 8. Because of its central role in everyday life, ToM is one benchmark by which to determine whether an individual demonstrates a developmental or cognitive impairment (Healey & Grossman, 2016; Lagattuta et al., 2016; Rosi et al., 2016).

In brief, ToM matters a great deal in everyday life. For instance, ToM is involved in people's sense of empathy and in emotional intelligence, characteristics that help us understand another person's experience and point of view. Research indicates that ToM abilities increase during childhood and show some age-related decline in adults over age 75. Let's go a bit deeper to consider the underlying changes in the brain that might explain the ToM changes in later life.

Understanding how changes in brain structures affect behavior involves careful linking of specific brain structures to specific behaviors, as we have discovered. First, it is necessary to carefully describe the behavior that interests us. Second, careful documentation of structural changes in the brain is necessary. Third, the two sets of data need to be connected to establish the link between structural brain changes and behavior.

Knowing what another person is thinking and feeling reflects a theory of mind.

One area in which this type of careful research has been done concerns executive functioning, the set of skills that underlies ToM (Roca, 2016). Executive function skills are the mental processes that enable us to plan, focus attention, remember instructions, and juggle multiple tasks successfully. They rely on three important brain functions: working memory (our ability to retain and manipulate distinct pieces of information over short periods of time), mental flexibility (our ability to sustain or shift attention in response to different demands or to apply different rules in different settings), and self-control (our ability to set priorities and resist impulsive actions or responses). Executive function skills develop from childhood through emerging adulthood (the late 20s) as the brain continues to mature and completes its creation of major interconnections.

Evidence indicates that some executive function skills decline in later life. Executive functioning failures in older adults can result in such behaviors as the erroneous selection of irrelevant information as relevant, the inability to divert attention away from irrelevant information to the task at hand, and inefficiency in switching tasks, among others. These changes matter; mortality rates are higher in those showing the most decline (Aron et al., 2022; Baggetta & Alexander, 2016; Wu et al., 2020). For example, consider a task in which one must distinguish true and false information, such as identifying an actual email from a phishing email. When older adults are reading an email that is filled with information, some of which is true and some of which is false, even if they are told which information is false, they still have a difficult time ignoring the false information in their understanding of the email.

How is this connected to changes in the brain? Poor performance on executive functioning tasks has been linked to decreased volume of the prefrontal cortex (McEwen et al., 2016; Reuter-Lorenz et al., 2021). Evidence also suggests that WMH in healthy older adults who show no signs of serious cognitive disease (such as dementia) have been linked to lower cognitive performance and decreased executive functioning (Coelho et al., 2021). Age-related decline in the functioning of blood vessels in the brain may affect white matter structures that underlie all the areas important to executive functioning.

Whatever the cause, evidence is mounting that decline in executive functioning with age is related to the degeneration and disruption of connections among various regions and structures of the brain (Reuter-Lorenz et al., 2021). This "disconnected brain" hypothesis (Coelho et al., 2021; Fjell et al., 2017) underlies contemporary theories explaining much of the cognitive decline in older adults.

Structural Changes and Memory. A great deal of research has examined links between memory and specific structural changes in the brain (Rudy, 2020). Many areas in the brain are intimately involved in the creation, storage, and retrieval of memories. Among the most important are the frontal, temporal, and parietal lobes; hippocampus; amygdala; and cerebellum. In this section, we'll focus on the temporal lobe and one of its key structures, the hippocampus.

The temporal lobe, highlighted in Figure 2.5, is the heart of memory processing, having involvement with

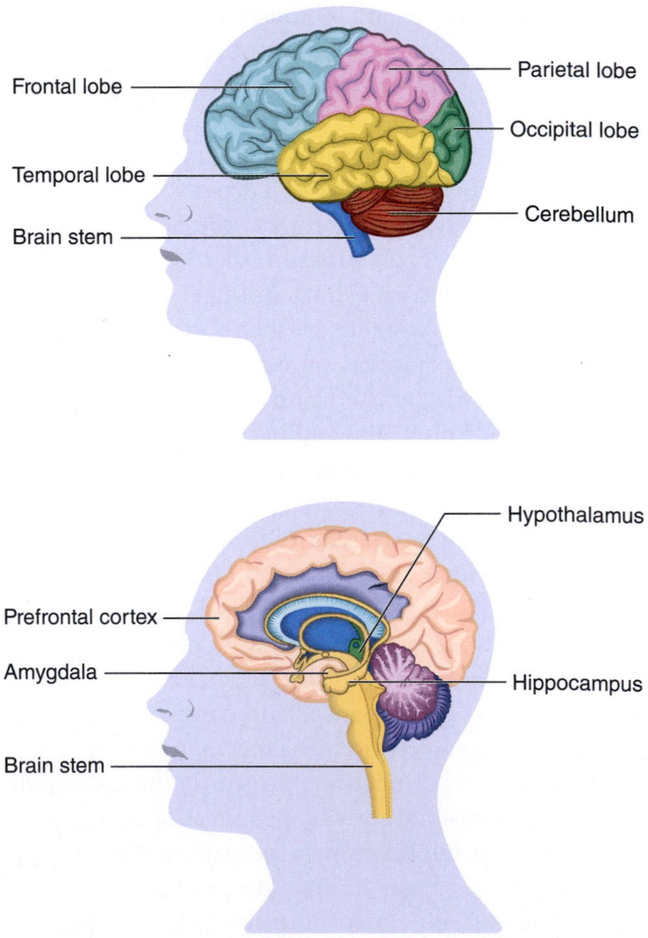

Figure 2.5 The structures in the temporal lobe play key roles in the creation of memory

each step of getting information in (encoding), consolidating it, and getting it back out (retrieval). The medial temporal lobe includes the hippocampus, amygdala, and nearby support structures and is crucial for episodic (time-stamped) and spatial memory, as well as the memory–emotion connection. Damage to the medial temporal lobe can result in serious and permanent loss of event-based and time-stamped memories, including aspects of a person's autobiography. As individuals age, the medial temporal lobe shrinks normatively, but this shrinkage is markedly increased in certain disease, such as Alzheimer's disease, which helps explain why severe memory loss is one hallmark of this disorder.

Considerable research has focused on the central involvement of the hippocampus in memory (Brunec et al., 2020). For example, the hippocampus is believed to be the brain location where related experiences or incoming information are integrated into a person's existing knowledge base. Several lines of inquiry have supported this notion. One involves the basic neuroscience understanding of how the hippocampus is involved in (creates) memory. From this approach, we know, for example, that the hippocampus is intimately involved in such types of memory as autobiographical memory (remembering aspects of our lives; Gurguryan et al., 2021; Sheldon & Levine, 2016) and recognizing patterns (Brunec et al., 2020).

A second approach involves examining structural changes to the hippocampus in diseases such as mild cognitive impairment and Alzheimer's disease (Goukasian et al., 2019) and chronic high levels of stress (McEwen, 2017; Woo et al., 2018) that produce negative impacts on memory. The stress connection is crucial—as discussed in Chapter 4, stress comes from many sources, including sociocultural factors such as system disparities and discrimination. Intriguingly, evidence suggests that intellectual stimulation in earlier adulthood (such as reading) helps increase the size of the hippocampus, which may provide some protection against memory decline associated with certain diseases (Sumowski et al., 2016).

In each of these cases, deterioration of the specific brain structure(s) due to normative age-related processes, disease, or injury results in a significant deficit in memory and related cognitive abilities (Rudy, 2020). In order to understand how these complex systems work and are connected and integrated, we will return to the case of memory and emotion as one key system that shows marked age-related changes.

Structural Changes in Emotional Memory. As we have noted earlier, the age-related changes observed in executive functioning and memory map onto age-related deterioration in specific brain structures. Let's now go deeper to consider a very important aspect of the human experience—emotion and memory—and explore how structural brain changes affect it.

To begin, let's consider an example of how neuroimaging research helps establish linkages between brain structures (the prefrontal cortex and the amygdala) and behavior relating to emotion. An excellent example of how this research is done is a groundbreaking study by Winecoff and colleagues (2011). They administered a large battery of tests to measure cognitive performance and emotional behavior to younger adults (average age = 23 years, range = 19–33 years) and older adults (average age = 69 years; range = 59–73 years). After these measures were obtained, participants were given a cognitive reappraisal task. During the experiment, participants learned a reappraisal strategy that involved thinking of themselves as an emotionally detached and objective third party. During the training session, they told the experimenter how they were thinking about the image to ensure task compliance, but they were instructed not to speak during the fMRI scanning session that provided images of ongoing brain activity.

Younger and older adults performed the reappraisal tasks similarly; that is, in the reappraisal condition, positive images were reported as less positive and negative images were reported as less negative. However, older adults' reports of negative emotion were higher than those of younger adults in the negative reappraisal situation.

Winecoff and colleagues' (2011) breakthrough was that examination of the fMRI results showed that reappraisals involved significant activation of specific areas in the prefrontal cortex for both positive and negative emotions. For both age groups, activity in the prefrontal area increased, and activity in the amygdala decreased during the reappraisal phase. These patterns are noted in Figure 2.6. As documented in the top figure, certain areas in the prefrontal cortex showed a pattern of activation that followed participants' self-reports of emotion regulation. Depicted here are activation patterns in the contrast between "Reappraise-Negative" and "Experience-Negative" conditions. The graph notes that for both positive and negative stimuli, and for both younger and older adults, prefrontal activation increased in "Reappraise" (reap) trials compared to "Experience" (exp) trials. In contrast,

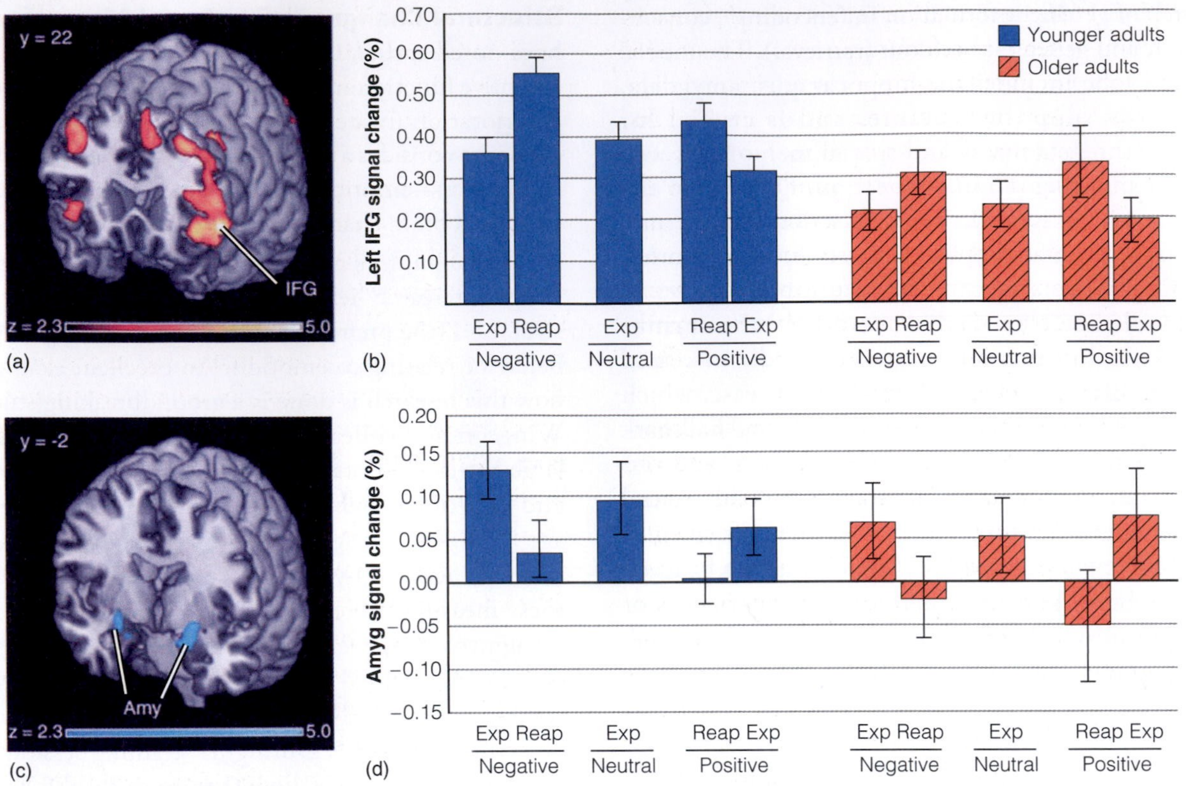

Figure 2.6 Modulation of prefrontal and amygdalar activation by emotion regulation

Source: Winecoff, A., LaBar, K. S., Madden, D. J., Cabeza, R., & Huettel, S. A. (2011). Cognitive and neural contributions to emotion regulation in aging. Social Cognitive and Affective Neuroscience, 6.

the lower graph notes that in the amygdala (amy) there was a systematic decrease in activation during emotion regulation between "Experience-Negative" and "Reappraise-Negative" conditions.

Additional analyses of the fMRI data indicate that emotion regulation modulates the functional interaction between the prefrontal cortex and the amygdala. Younger adults had more activity in the prefrontal cortex during "Reappraise" trials for negative pictures than older adults did. Cognitive abilities were related to the degree of decrease in amygdala activation, independent of age.

From these data, Winecoff and colleagues concluded that the prefrontal cortex plays a major role in emotional regulation, especially for older adults. The takeaway is the prefrontal cortex may help suppress (regulate) emotions in the same way as that area of the brain is involved in inhibiting other behaviors. Importantly, the degree of emotional regulation was predicted by cognitive ability, with higher cognitive ability associated with higher emotional regulation. This may mean that as cognitive abilities decline, people may be less able to regulate their emotions, a pattern typical in diseases such as dementia. Thus, not only is there evidence of underlying brain structures playing critical roles in emotion regulation, but there may be a neurological explanation for the kinds of emotional behavior outbursts that occur in dementia and related disorders.

Subsequent research has supported these conclusions regarding the dynamic nature of prefrontal–amygdala connections and their role in the modulation of emotion (Berboth & Morawetz, 2021; Lemaire, 2022). Moreover, the ability of people with dementia to correctly recognize emotions in other people (their ToM) is impaired relatively early in the disease (Fernández-Ríos et al., 2021); because the prefrontal cortex is one of the areas of the brain that shows the earliest deterioration in Alzheimer's disease, these data also point out the crucial role of prefrontal–amygdala connections.

How does the way that the brain processes emotions change across adulthood? The quick answer is that it's complicated (Mather, 2016; Ziaei & Fisher, 2016). In general, research shows that adults of all ages report about the same range and experience of emotion. But there is also evidence that changes in brain activity in the prefrontal cortex and the amygdala with age may be related to a differential decrease in processing of negative emotional information and an increase in processing of positive emotional information (Halfmann et al., 2021). These differences tend to be interpreted as reflecting increased emotional regulation with age; in other words, older adults tend to be able to regulate their emotions better than younger adults. It may be the reason that older adults seemed to fare better emotionally during the COVID-19 pandemic than did younger adults (Ford et al., 2021). Part of the reason may be due to a desire as people age to develop closer, more meaningful relationships that generate positive emotions, while avoiding people and situations that generate negative ones. We will return to this issue of the "positivity effect" later in this chapter and in Chapters 8 and 9.

Considered together, the results indicate that cognition and emotion interact in complex ways, and the prefrontal cortex and amygdala are the key brain structures involved. Kensinger and colleagues (Kensinger, 2012; Kensinger & Ford, 2020, 2021) propose that a specific area in the prefrontal cortex controls behaviors ranging from actions to emotions to social cognition—extracting meaning from events and the control of memories, particularly emotional memories. Its role begins during the encoding of emotional experiences, continues through their stabilization, and endures during the retrieval of memory content. At each phase, this area of the prefrontal cortex participates in the integration of emotional and cognitive components of memories, setting up networks and framings that either emphasize or de-emphasize emotional content.

Additionally, two distinct cognitive and neural processes contribute to emotional processing and memory. The difference depends upon how emotionally arousing the information is. Processing of negative high-arousal information for memory is relatively automatic in nature and is linked to activation of the amygdala as it interacts with the hippocampus to support memory performance. For memory processing of negative low-arousal stimuli, more activation of the prefrontal cortex–hippocampus network is necessary.

Kensinger (2012; Kensinger & Ford, 2020, 2021) argues that whether emotional arousal enhances memory depends on the engagement in emotion-specific processes that are linked to these distinct neural processes. So when a person accurately remembers negative high-arousal items, this corresponds to increased activation of the amygdala and prefrontal cortex. Other studies support this conclusion. For instance, if the amygdala is damaged, individuals do not attend to arousing stimuli. Additionally, the central role that the prefrontal cortex plays in processing emotion has also become a focus of research on the causes of emotion-related mental disorders, such as depression (Pizzagalli & Roberts, 2022). We will consider these issues in more detail in Chapter 10.

How do age-related structural and functional changes in the brain affect processing of emotion? The short answer is that it depends (Fossati, 2012; McEwen et al., 2016; Lemaire, 2022; Ziaei & Fisher, 2016). Older adults exhibit more brain activity between the prefrontal cortex and the medial temporal lobe than younger adults do, regardless of whether the content is emotionally positive or negative. These increases in connections may be due to age-related changes that occur in the prefrontal cortex that make it necessary for older adults to use more connections to process the information (Kensinger & Ford, 2020, 2022). When disorders such as mild cognitive impairment (MCI) occur, these connection patterns are disrupted and begin to exhibit loss (Hampstead et al., 2016). More important, fMRI evidence suggests that different memory retrieval pathways are invoked in older adults with MCI, perhaps indicating that the brain is attempting a way around the structural changes, but one that is much less effective (Weigard et al., 2020). We'll return to this need for and roles of extra connections a bit later when we consider whether older adults compensate for brain changes.

Linking Structural Changes with Social-Emotional Cognition. What happens in the brain when things get even more complicated, such as when we have to process complex situations that involve social judgments, when memory, emotion, and previously learned information come together? The story begins in the early 2000s, when researchers first suggested a social cognitive neuroscience approach to attributional inferences, that is, how people make causal judgments about why social situations occur (Lieberman et al., 2002). That work identified a social judgment process that involves a relatively automatic system in which people read cues in the environment quickly and easily, without deliberation, and then make social judgments.

For example, if someone is staggering down a hallway, we may automatically assume the person may be intoxicated without taking into consideration many other factors that might cause someone to stagger (e.g., the person is injured or is experiencing a medical emergency). In other words, we have a tendency to automatically put the person into a preexisting sociocultural category. We base this judgment on easily activated, well-practiced categories of information based on our past experiences and current goals, and we do this most prominently when the situation is ambiguous.

StaceStock/Shutterstock.com

The categories into which we tend to place the person driving this car reflect automatic processing.

In such situations, we are unlikely to consider alternative explanations.

What's intriguing is that researchers have presented compelling evidence that drawing these kinds of quick conclusions in ambiguous situations is probably a result of how our brains are wired. It turns out we have specialized areas in the brain, such as the orbitofrontal cortex, lateral temporal cortex, amygdala, and basal ganglia, that are associated with automatic social cognition (Platt et al., 2016; Testard et al., 2021). Humans are hard-wired to quick-process certain social cognitive information in particular ways that reflect well-rehearsed prior learning, so attempting to do it in other ways takes tremendous focusing and effort. As we will consider in Chapter 6, this is how bias operates.

But suppose we need to be more deliberate in our processing. Researchers also have identified another system that underlies a form of social cognitive judgments that employs symbolic logic and reflective awareness. The neural basis of these more reflective judgments appears to reside in the prefrontal cortex, the anterior cingulate cortex, and the hippocampus (Lee & Siegle, 2012).

How do these different brain pathways change with age, and what difference does that make? The brain structures involved in more automatic processing (e.g., the amygdala) have less age-related deterioration, whereas those involved in more reflective processing (e.g., the prefrontal cortex) have more severe deterioration. Based on these findings, we would expect that older adults might tend to rely more on automatic processes. We'll find out in Chapters 6, 7, and 8 whether they do.

Age-Related Change and Evidence of Compensation. We have noted that there is substantial evidence for age-related changes in patterns of brain activity. There are additional, and interesting, nuances to these findings. For example, it turns out that it is not simply that older adults show reduced activation in regions associated with a particular cognitive task. Rather, studies focusing on verbal working memory and long-term memory, for instance, show focused, unilateral activity in the left prefrontal region in younger adults but activation in both the left and right prefrontal areas in older adults when performing the same tasks, and connection patterns are reconfigured (Reuter-Lorenz & Park, 2014; Reuter-Lorenz et al., 2021; Rieck et al., 2021).

These findings surprised researchers and ushered in much discussion and research as to what this meant for the aging brain. Is the older brain working to compensate for deterioration in these focal regions related to the cognitive task? Is the older brain working harder and recruiting more brain structures? Or is the activation merely the ineffective attempt to inhibit irrelevant information that results in the interference of optimal functioning (Andrews-Hanna et al., 2019; Marcotte et al., 2022)?

The answer appears to be that older adults are compensating. Researchers concluded that this additional activation in older adults may serve a functional and supportive role in their cognitive functioning (Reuter-Lorenz et al., 2021). Supportive evidence comes from the association between additional activation in older adults and higher performance, evidence not found in younger adults, across several different tasks, including category learning, visual field, and various memory tasks.

Figure 2.7 indicates that there is greater prefrontal bilateral activity in older adults during working memory tasks than in younger adults. (We delve into working memory, a limited capacity aspect of memory processing, in detail in Chapter 6.) On the top left side of the figure is the typical left-lateralized prefrontal activation pattern observed in younger adults. On the bottom left side is the typical pattern found in older adults—notice how they engage both left and right prefrontal areas. The right side demonstrates that younger adults and low-performing older adults show right-lateralized activation during a long-term memory task. In contrast, high-performing older adults still show bilateral prefrontal engagement. It may be that high-functioning older adults are more adept at compensating for normative deterioration in the brain by figuring out how to utilize other related and available areas of the brain.

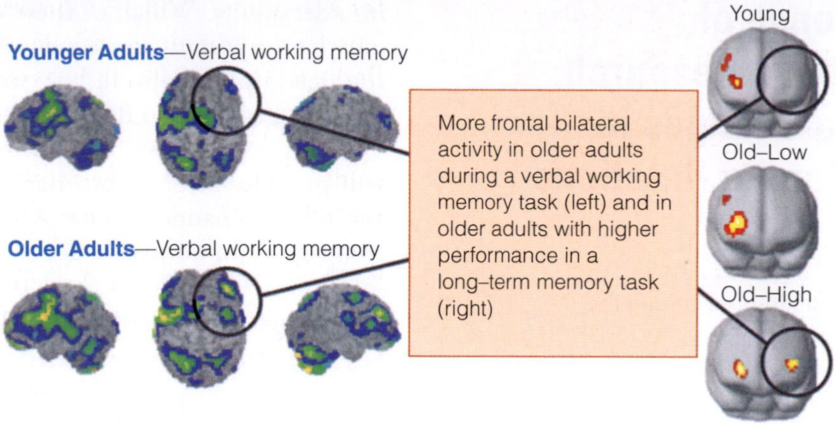
Younger Adults—Verbal working memory
Older Adults—Verbal working memory
More frontal bilateral activity in older adults during a verbal working memory task (left) and in older adults with higher performance in a long-term memory task (right)
Young
Old-Low
Old-High

Figure 2.7 Prefrontal bilateral activation increases with age

Source: Park, D. C., & Reuter-Lorenz, P. (2009). The adaptive brain: Aging and neurocognitive scaffolding. Annual Review of Psychology, 60, 173–196. www.annualreviews.org/URL.

To make matters even more interesting, there is evidence that under some circumstances researchers fail to find evidence of either reduced specialization of functions in the brain or of compensation. When Campbell and colleagues (2016) separated the different processes needed to complete a task (e.g., attention, decision making), they found consistent patterns of brain activity in both younger and older adults. The question is whether these results are simply a matter of which task was examined or evidence that challenges the conventional view of broader activation as compensation in older adults.

It appears that it's both. Ferré and colleagues (2020) reported that older adults are actually more efficient than younger adults in processing on certain picture naming tasks because they have developed a more efficient strategy, relying on a more experienced, specialized, and segregated, naming pathway. More frontal lobe activity was not seen in all situations, leading researchers to conclude that task factors probably led to the development of the more effective and efficient processing. In this case at least, older adults appear to apply the repeated experiences of picture naming to reconfigure their brains to operate better. Contrary to stereotype, older adults' brains do have the ability to improve. We'll explore this further in the final section of this chapter.

Adult Development in Action

You are a healthcare worker and a specialist in geriatric medicine. One of your clients exhibits significant declines in memory and executive functioning. What brain structures and processes might you want to examine closely for evidence of age-related change?

Review Questions

2.2 Neuroscience and the Aging Brain

- Describe the basic structures in the brain. What age-related changes are observed in neurons? What happens to dopamine functioning in the aging brain? What age-related changes occur in other neurotransmitters?
- What age-related changes occur in brain structures? What structures play major roles in the aging process?
- What are the differences in brain activation during cognitive tasks for younger and older adults? What key differences have been identified in activity in the prefrontal cortex between younger and older adults?
- What age-related differences have been documented in executive processing?
- What evidence is there that older adults compensate for age-related changes in the brain?
- What differences are there in memory with age as they relate to brain activation?
- How do younger and older adults process emotionally related material?

2.3 Making Sense of Neuroscience Research: Explaining Changes in Brain–Behavior Relations

Key Questions

- What are the major differences among the parieto-frontal integration theory, the CRUNCH model, and the STAC-r model of brain activation and aging?
- How does the concept of brain plasticity help explain age-related changes in brain activation and behavior?

Recently, Barbara read an article on a major news website describing research on brain aging. The article described in detail several aspects of negative changes in the brain that made Barbara wonder. Approaching 90, Barbara wondered whether all of the changes happening reflected potential problems.

We have considered evidence that structural and neurochemical changes occur in the brain as we grow older, and that these changes in the brain relate to changes in cognitive and emotional functioning. With that as background, let's now reconsider research that is based on functional brain imaging techniques, such as fMRI, that we noted earlier. In this module we will consider ways to organize these data into theories and models that help explain what is going on, and consider what these theories and findings mean in terms of normative and nonnormative change. These models and theories draw attention to how the brain develops into adulthood, organizes itself, operates at maximum efficiency and effectiveness, and deals with age-related change.

A second aim of this work, and the other main focus of this module, is to identify ways that the brain is sometimes able to compensate for negative age-related changes by activating different or additional regions under certain circumstances. This research is based on age differences in the structures and regions of the brain that are involved in processing the same information. In other words, older and younger adults may differ in terms of which regions of the brain are used in order to perform cognitive tasks more effectively. On one hand, these compensation strategies could result in roughly equivalent performance despite other differences in age. On the other hand, these compensation strategies could be ineffective and could reveal the neurological underpinnings of certain forms of cognitive decline observed in older adults. Which of these outcomes occurs not only has important consequences for performance on research tasks but also in how well older adults might adapt to challenges in their daily lives.

The research we will consider in this section will provide insights into Barbara's concerns. What age-related changes occur? Are older adults able to compensate for normative declines that occur?

Theories and Models of Brain–Behavior Changes Across Adulthood

As noted previously, several studies have shown evidence for age-related differences in patterns of brain activity in specific brain regions, especially in the prefrontal area, across numerous cognitive tasks (Betzel, 2022; Gallen et al., 2016; Grady et al., 2016; Marcotte et al., 2022). Researchers wanted to figure out whether additional age-related neural activation (especially in prefrontal areas) may be adaptive and improve performance as people grow older. What they learned, as we discovered in earlier sections, suggests that these activation patterns may reflect an adaptive brain that functionally reorganizes and compensates for age-related changes (Aron et al., 2022; Betzel, 2022; Marcotte et al., 2022). This possibility relates to the principle of plasticity that we encountered in Chapter 1.

One of the most important people who dedicated their life to understanding and documenting the mapping of behaviors to specific areas of the brain was Oliver Sacks. In addition to being a brilliant scientist, Sacks had another gift—the ability to explain very complicated research to the public. He accomplished this through a series of books and a regular column in the *New York Times* newspaper, including a set of articles documenting his own struggles with brain and liver cancer. The Real People feature provides more information about Sacks's insightful contributions.

Several theories and models have been proposed to organize and explain the research findings. Three of the most prominent are the parieto-frontal integration theory (P-FIT; Haier & Jung, 2018; Jung & Haier, 2007), the CRUNCH model (Reuter-Lorenz, 2002; Reuter-Lorenz & Mikels, 2006), and the STAC-r model (Reuter-Lorenz & Park, 2014). These models make a common assumption: The primary reason for greater activation in different brain regions, such as the different patterns within the prefrontal cortex, is the need for the recruitment and involvement of additional brain structures and processes in order to successfully execute cognitive functions as one grows older.

Real People

Oliver Sacks, Brain Mapper

It was the interesting cases that attracted and intrigued Oliver Sacks (1933–2015), a man who the *New York Times* called "the poet laureate of contemporary medicine" (Marshall, 1986). One such case involved a man who had visual agnosia (an inability to recognize visual objects due to damage in the parietal lobes) who mistook his wife for a hat. This recognition error became the title of one of his most popular books.

Sacks explored numerous aspects of brain–behavior relations in individuals who had brain disorders, such as Tourette syndrome, achromatopsia (total colorblindness), dementia, Parkinson's disease, and amyotrophic lateral sclerosis (Lou Gehrig's disease). His successful work with a group of survivors of the 1920s sleeping sickness epidemic *encephalitis lethargica* became the basis of the book and Oscar-nominated movie *Awakenings* that starred Robert DeNiro and Robin Williams.

Sacks's contribution to neuroscience was not through research, or even through his clinical practice. It was his ability to tell stories, to translate the complex world of neuroscience into language that even the casual reader could not only understand but find fascinating. Sacks was able to bring attention to a wide range of conditions and to provide outlets for people to share what it is like to experience them.

But Sacks's interests were much broader than neuroscience, too. He was insatiably curious about many things, and he brought a scientist's mind to each. He looked at music and music therapy in his book *Musicophilia: Tales of Music and the Brain*. He wrote of his own personal experience with prosopagnosia (the inability to recognize faces), his recovery from a serious muscle tear in his leg, and ocular melanoma and his loss of stereoscopic vision as a result of the treatment.

Chris McGrath/Getty Images News/Getty Images

Oliver Sacks

When he was diagnosed with metastatic cancer in December 2014 (the melanoma tumor in his eye had spread to his liver and brain), he wrote a series of deeply personal articles that expressed his intent to "live in the richest, deepest, most productive way I can" (Sacks, 2015). Sacks came out in 2015 when he first revealed that he was gay and in a committed relationship. His legacy will be his determination to shine a light on the many conditions that result in people having different patterns of activity in their brains that result in different life experiences and normalizing them. When he died in 2015, the man who could not recognize his own face had become one of the most recognized medical figures in history.

The Parieto-Frontal Integration Theory. As noted earlier in this chapter, the frontal and parietal lobes are involved in a wide variety of cognitive and emotional processes. A typical finding is age-related changes in activity in specific areas of the prefrontal cortex and related brain regions (e.g., the parietal lobe) during certain tasks, specifically memory for emotional material. There's more, though. Grady (2012) points out that on certain tasks older adults show reduced prefrontal activity in specific areas of the prefrontal cortex and increased activity in other areas. Grady's research noted that these patterns are context dependent. That is, older adults sometimes exhibit reduced activation or recruitment of the appropriate prefrontal regions, and sometimes exhibit the same or more recruitment compared to younger adults depending on the tasks they are doing at the time, meaning that the brain somehow reconfigures the connection pathways with age (Deng et al., 2021; Gallen et al., 2016).

Given the pivotal role played by the prefrontal cortex and parietal lobe in such a wide range of cognitive tasks, and the evidence for age-related reconfigurations of connections, researchers got excited. The wide range of tasks appeared quite similar to the kinds of tasks that are represented on intelligence tests (described in Chapter 7). Because of this, researchers began searching for ways to link basic understandings of intelligence with the patterns of brain changes they observed as a way to explain intelligence at a holistic level (Haier & Jung, 2018).

Based on large number of studies using various types of neuroimaging techniques, Jung and Haier (2007; Haier & Jung, 2018) offered such a theory: the parieto-frontal integration theory. The **parieto-frontal integration theory (P-FIT)** proposes that intelligence comes from a distributed and integrated network of neurons in the parietal and frontal areas of the brain. Figure 2.8 depicts these key brain areas. In general, P-FIT accounts for individual differences in intelligence as having their origins in individual differences in brain structure and function. For example, research indicates that the P-FIT predicts a type of intelligence termed *fluid intelligence* (discussed in Chapter 7) that includes such skills as spatial and matrix reasoning (Fraenz et al., 2021; Nikolaidis et al., 2017; Pineda-Pardo et al., 2016).

The P-FIT model is an example of theories based on neuroscience research and has been tested and supported in several studies. It is clear that performance on specific measures of intelligence, including many of those that we will consider in detail in Chapter 7, as well as how efficiently such information is processed, are quite likely related to connections in the prefrontal cortex and parietal lobe (Haier & Jung, 2018; Pineda-Pardo et al., 2016). Evidence also points to reconfiguration of these connections as people age, which accounts for changes in performance and behavior (Deng et al., 2021; Gallen et al., 2016). Clearly, any impairment in frontal lobe processing would likely cause challenges. Because such changes occur normatively with age, we would expect to find some degree of predictable patterns of change in cognition. We will pursue this idea in detail in Chapters 6 and 7. We will also consider more serious changes, such as those in dementia, in Chapter 10.

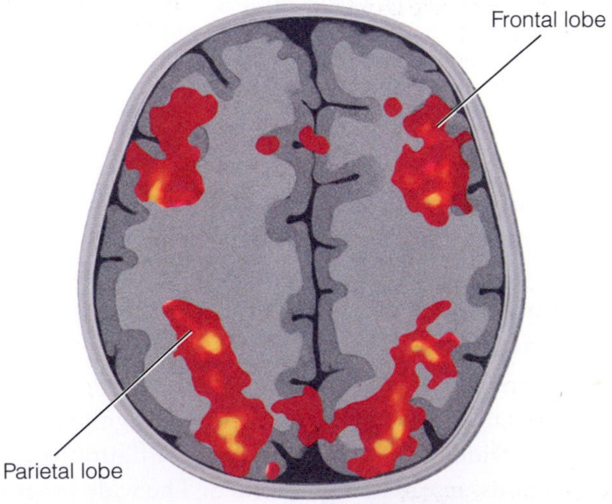

Figure 2.8 The P-FIT model indicates that integration of the parietal and frontal lobes underlies intelligence

The CRUNCH Model. The **CRUNCH model** stands for **compensation-related utilization of neural circuits hypothesis** and describes how the aging brain adapts to neurological decline by recruiting additional neural circuits (in comparison to younger adults) to perform tasks adequately (Cabeza et al., 2018; Reuter-Lorenz & Cappell, 2008). The CRUNCH model incorporates the fact that the brain has activation happening in both the left and right hemispheres, and that brain functions that cause behavior are controlled in both. This notion is referred to as bilaterality of activation. The fact that we have two hemispheres opens the possibility that older adults might compensate for age-related changes by recruiting brain power from the other hemisphere. The CRUNCH model goes further by noting that bilaterality is not the only possible form of compensation. According to the CRUNCH model, for example, the amount of task-related brain activity directly parallels task demands (i.e., the harder the task, the more brain activity) until a person's cognitive resource limit is reached, at which point (termed the "crunch point") the activity cannot increase and so will plateau or drop off, and task performance will suffer. The CRUNCH model predicts that older adults will reach this "crunch point" limit on resources at lower levels of task demand than will young adults.

Going a bit deeper, we can understand better what exactly the CRUNCH model is proposing. CRUNCH suggests that the older brain has two options to perform tasks: *more of the same* and *supplementary processes. More of the same* means that when task demands are increased, more activation can be found in the same brain region that is activated for processing easier tasks. This option is the one younger adults use most of the time, as do older adults, to a point. However, because older adults' neural efficiency declines, these additional neuronal circuits in the same area are recruited earlier than they are in younger adults. This is what pushes older adults to the "crunch point" more quickly.

Supplementary processes take place when different brain regions are activated to compensate for lacking or insufficient processing resources. The first choice is to recruit additional resources that mirror those already being used in the other hemisphere, taking advantage of the fact that in several cases the brain has some built-in redundancy by having similar areas in both hemispheres perform the same functions, creating a brain backup system of sorts. In addition, however, compared to younger adults' brains, older adults' brains also go into overdrive and show overactivation in different brain regions that may not usually be used for performing the tasks that are currently in play. This is reflected in brain scans when the picture of activation level in older adults' brains occurs in the same regions as in younger adults' brains, but at a significantly higher level, or in different regions altogether. These patterns suggest that compensation can take different forms in the aging brain.

The CRUNCH model has considerable support (Cabeza et al., 2018; Park & Festini, 2017). However, the point at which older adults are no longer able to compensate is not well established (Horne et al., 2021; Jamadar, 2020).

The STAC-r Model. How do we explain the specific patterns of age-related changes in prefrontal activity and resolve interpretive dilemmas? To answer that question, Reuter-Lorenz and Park (2014) proposed the STAC-r model, shown in Figure 2.9. The **scaffolding theory of cognitive aging–revised (STAC-r) model** is based on the idea that age-related changes in one's ability to function reflect a life-long process

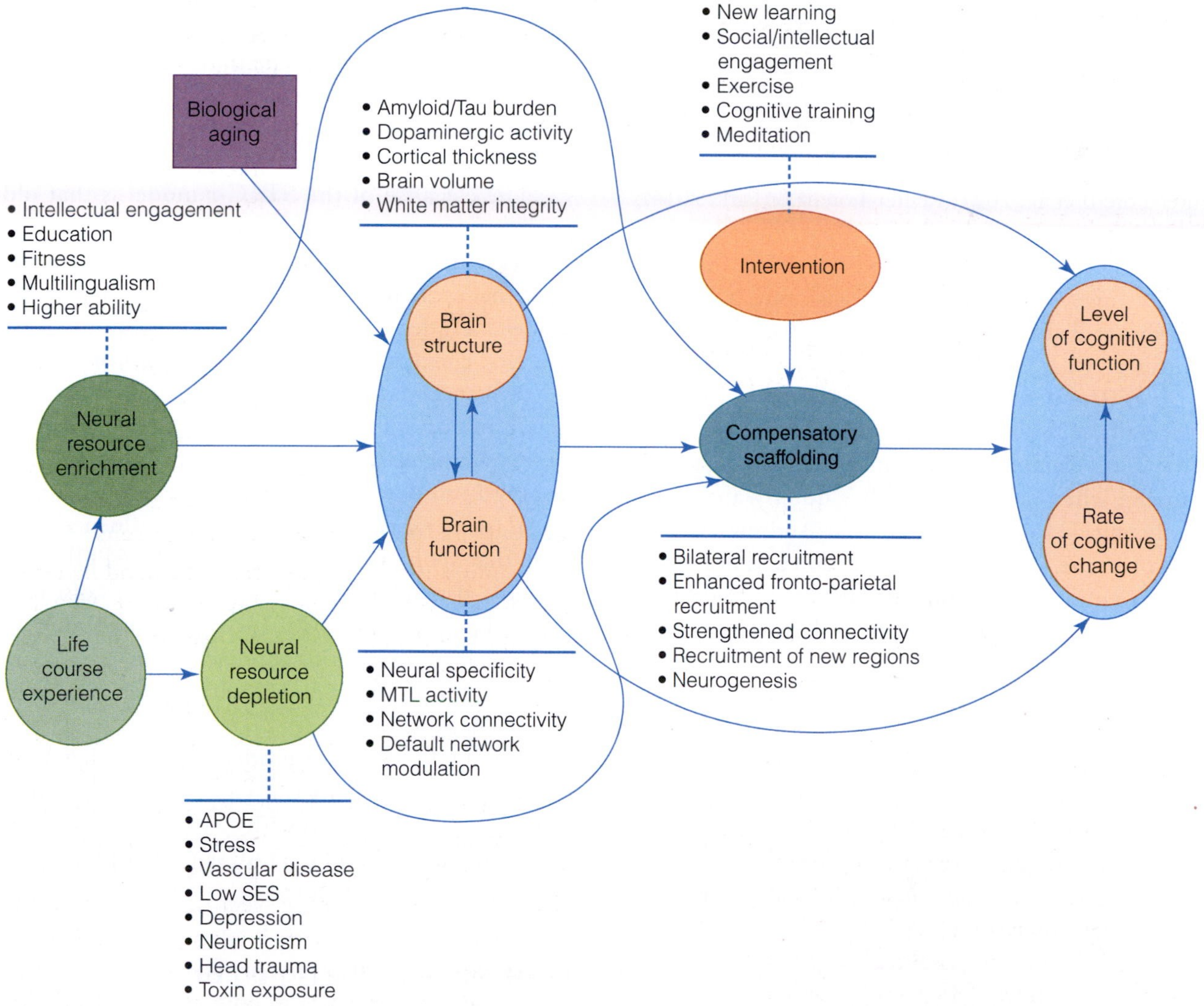

Figure 2.9 A life course model of the scaffolding theory of aging and cognition (STAC-r)

Source: Reuter-Lorenz, P. A., & Park, D. C. (2014). How does it STAC up? Revisiting the scaffolding theory of aging and cognition. *Neuropsychology Review, 24,* 355–370. https://doi.org/10.1007/s11065-014-9270-9, Figure 2.

of compensating for cognitive decline by recruiting additional brain areas, and takes life-course factors that enhance or deplete neural resources into account. It is based on an earlier version of the model (Park & Reuter-Lorenz, 2009) that did not include the life course variables.

As we will consider in Chapters 6 and 7, aging is associated with both decline as well as preservation of various cognitive abilities. The STAC-r model explains neuroimaging studies that note selective changes in the aging brain that reflect neural decline as well as compensatory neural recruitment, especially in the prefrontal cortex. Taking this life-span view makes STAC-r unique among the models of cognitive aging based on neuroscience (Reuter-Lorenz et al., 2021).

From the perspective of the STAC-r model, what's the purpose of the compensation in the brain? For one thing, there is growing evidence that the increase in prefrontal cortex activity in older adults may be a response to decreased efficiency of neural processing in the perceptual areas of the brain and normative neurophysiological deterioration (Liem et al., 2021; Reuter-Lorenz et al., 2021; Reuter-Lorenz & Park, 2014).

There's another reason, too. Remember how the prefrontal region helps suppress irrelevant information that may interfere with the task one is actually performing? It turns out that older adults have trouble suppressing what's referred to as the default network of the brain. **The default network of the brain refers to regions of the brain that are most active when one is at rest.** One example of this would be the brain activity occurring when an individual lies quietly and is not directly engaged in a cognitive task (Andrews-Hanna, 2012) or in the spontaneous generation and evaluation of creative ideas (Beaty et al., 2016).

When a younger adult begins a demanding cognitive task, this default network is suppressed. But older adults display less suppression of this default network, resulting in poorer performance (Andrews-Hanna, 2012; Andrews-Hanna et al., 2019). Thus, this failure to shift from a resting state to a more active state to engage in cognitive processing may be another reason for increased frontal activity in older adults as a way to "work around" the lack of suppression (Aron et al., 2022; Reuter-Lorenz et al., 2021).

The STAC-r model (Reuter-Lorenz & Park, 2014) suggests that the reason older adults continue to perform at high levels despite neuronal deterioration is because they create and rely on a backup neural pathway. It works like this. When you learn a new task, learning moves from effortful processing (new learning is hard work!) to overlearning (more automatic, less effortful processing). The result of overlearning is that your brain operates, essentially, on autopilot. The neurological shift from effortful processing to overlearning that happens in a young adult results from a temporary broader dispersed network (which Reuter-Lorenz and Park call the *scaffold*) used while learning something new to a more focal, efficient, and optimal neural circuit that is the outcome of overlearning. In older adults, though, the initial scaffolding remains available as a secondary, backup circuit that can be counted on when necessary. It is never dismantled. Scaffolded networks are less efficient than the honed, focal ones they used as young adults, so on average poorer (and slower) performance is the result. But enough of the time, information is remembered eventually, so in everyday life this is not usually a major problem. The trade-off is that without the scaffolding, performance would be even worse because older adults would have to rely on the more focal areas that may not be fully developed.

The elegance of the STAC-r model is that older adults' performance can be understood in terms of factors that explain both decline in performance and those that explain compensatory processes. The STAC-r model includes two concepts that accomplish this. The first concept, *neural resource enrichment*, refers to any influence that serves to enhance brain structure or function. For example, as we will explore in Chapter 14, remaining active is related to better cognitive functioning in middle and old age. The second concept, *neural resource depletion*, refers to those influences on the brain that are harmful. For example, the APOE-4 gene puts one at much higher risk of Alzheimer's disease. As Reuter-Lorenz and Park (2014) argue, combining both concepts in an integrative approach embraces a lifelong potential for plasticity and the ability to adapt to age-related changes.

Finally, the STAC-r model indicates that Barbara's concerns, noted in the vignette that began this section, can be countered with evidence of both decline and compensation. The STAC-r model predicts and accounts for both outcomes.

Plasticity and the Aging Brain

In Chapter 1, we encountered the concept of *plasticity*, which in that context related to the belief that capacity is not fixed but can be learned or improved with practice. We noted there that, for example, people can learn ways to help themselves remember information, which in turn may help them deal with declining short-term memory ability with age.

As discussed earlier in this chapter, there are certain situations in which the brain compensates for age-related changes in processing by reconfiguring neural pathways and enlisting additional brain structures in processing. These changes reflect another aspect of plasticity—in this case focused on changes in the brain that are mapped to behavioral change across the adult life span.

When these notions of plasticity are considered together, plasticity becomes a defining notion in adult development and aging that underlies the process by which people (and their brains) live in the world and accumulate information and knowledge from experiences over time.

Plasticity, then, provides a way to understand compensatory changes in both the more observable behavior and the less observable (without neuroimaging, anyway) reorganization of neural circuitry in the brain. Many attempts have been made to assess the potential for plasticity in cognitive functioning by focusing on ways to improve cognitive performance through training.

Baltes and colleagues' now classic research set the standard for documenting the range of plasticity in older adults' cognitive performance (Baltes & Kliegl, 1992; Willis et al., 1981). They found that whereas older adults are able to improve cognitive ability in memory tasks through tailored strategy training beyond the level of untrained younger adults, this is highly task-specific, and the ability-level gains are very narrow in focus.

Since these groundbreaking findings, research demonstrates that basic cognitive processes affected by aging can indeed be improved through training under certain conditions, and that they transfer to multiple other kinds of functioning as long as the tasks are based on the same basic underlying functioning. Training has also been shown to increase the level of activity in the prefrontal cortex, the strength of connections between the prefrontal and parietal cortex, and structural changes in neuronal dendritic connections (Constantinidis & Klingberg, 2016; Schmidt et al., 2021). Because we have already considered aspects of plasticity as exemplified by compensation processes at the level of brain structures (e.g., the "work arounds" created in the brain, additional brain regions recruited for dealing with cognitive tasks), we close this chapter at the level of the brain where we began—we focus here on plasticity at the level of neurons.

From a neural plasticity perspective, research on neural stem cells has revealed compelling evidence that the brain is capable of generating new neurons and related cells when needed (Ho et al., 2018; Pardal & Barneo, 2016). **Neural stem cells** (also known as neural progenitors or neural precursor cells) are cells in the brain and spinal cord (the central nervous system, CNS) that are thought to give rise to the broad array of specialized cells of the CNS, including both neurons and glial cells. The discovery of neural stem cells proved wrong the long-standing belief that neurogenesis (i.e., the development of new neurons) stops at the end of embryonic development during pregnancy. In practical terms, it means that you not only *can* teach a person "new tricks," they are capable of growing new neurons in order to do them. Not only that, but neural stem cells are the focus of much research relating to potential cures for various brain diseases, such as Parkinson's disease (Faour & Ashok, 2021) and Alzheimer's disease (Pinto et al., 2021).

All of this research adds a new level of understanding to what happens to individuals as they grow older. For example, even though aging is associated with an overall decrease in the number of new neurons (in fact, neurons are continually pruned throughout most of life), this differs a lot across regions of the brain, and alteration and expansion of neural connections may continue as long as the person lives.

The big question, of course, is whether the discovery of neural stem cells and the fact that neurons can regenerate even in late life means that neuroscience research could be used to cure brain diseases and essentially create "new brains" (Kazanis, 2012). Perhaps that may be possible years from now. In the meantime, what we do know is that brain cells can regenerate on their own, even in late life, under the right circumstances, and that the brain has considerable plasticity to create ways for people to compensate with age-related declines in functioning. But just because we *could* perfect neurogenesis to cure disease, *should* we? This is a very controversial question, as discussed in the Controversies feature.

Controversies

The Neuroethics of Interventions to Address Brain Aging

Imagine if you could replace brain cells that had either died or had been damaged through an accident or disease? That's a goal of researchers who study neural stem cells. Clearly, this research would fundamentally change our understanding of aging, brain injury, and brain disease.

Research on the potential of neural stem cells took a major leap forward in 2007 with the founding of the Neural Stem Cell Institute by Dr. Sally Temple and Dr. Jeffrey Stern. The Institute's mission is "developing regenerative stem cell therapies for diseases of the central nervous system (CNS): the brain, spinal cord and retina." Ongoing research programs include identifying potential uses of neural stem cells in treating such diseases as Alzheimer's disease, brain injury and stroke, macular degeneration, autism, Parkinson's disease, retinitis pigmentosa, and spinal cord injury, among others.

The National Human Neural Stem Cell Resource supplies researchers with reliable sources of neural stem cells obtained from the postnatal, postmortem human brain. They encourage research to study the cells "as potential transplantable tissue for addressing damage from stroke or brain injury, and for curing diseases."

These and other similar research centers play a critical role in brain research. Despite the great promise of this research to, for instance, offer potential cures for fatal and degenerative diseases, this work is controversial. A basic question some ask is whether this research should be done at all. Several key ethical questions arise that many argue need to be addressed before the results of this research are implemented (Ramos-Zúñiga, 2015; Wexler & Sullivan, 2021).

The field of neuroethics encompasses the many ways in which developments in basic and clinical neuroscience intersect with social and ethical issues. Neuroethics focuses on two general categories of issues: those emerging from what we can do and those emerging from what we know. In the first category are the ethical problems raised by advances in functional neuroimaging, psychopharmacology, brain implants, and brain–machine interfaces in the service of "treating" or "curing" diseases. In the second category are the ethical problems raised by our growing understanding of the neural bases of behavior, personality, consciousness, and states of spiritual transcendence that lead to interventions to "improve" humans.

Monkey Business Images/Shutterstock.com

Should neural stem cells be used to potentially cure this person who has dementia?

The questions raised by neuroethical analyses of various situations are many and far-ranging. How should incidental clinical findings be handled when a presumed healthy research participant is scanned for neuroscience research and the scan reveals a tumor, for instance? How safe are the drugs used to enhance normal brain function?

Neuroethics reminds us that the research considered in this chapter requires that the human brain be used as an experimental object of study and be manipulated in specific ways. Certainly, any such intervention, whether it is a treatment for a disease or a replacement of malfunctioning or nonfunctioning brain cells, requires the highest level of ethical principles. Perhaps the most difficult issue is that just because an intervention *can* be done, does not necessarily mean that it *should* be done.

But who gets to make these decisions?

The public policy that flows from neuroscience research must go to great lengths to analyze the ethical implications of every research project involving neural stem cells, along with any potential clinical applications and outcomes. The usual medical standard of "causing no harm" is especially important in neuroscience research and the interventions that derive from it, as is a very careful assessment of the risk–benefit balance. But most important is keeping in the forefront of everything the fact that the research involves a human and a human brain.

Adult Development in Action

You are an activity therapist at a senior center and want to design activities for the members that will help them compensate for typical age-related cognitive changes. Using the theories described in this section, what would an example of a good activity be?

Review Questions

2.3 Making Sense of Neuroscience Research: Explaining Changes in Brain-Behavior Relations

- Compare and contrast the P-FIT theory, CRUNCH model, and STAC-r model. What does each explain?
- What is neural plasticity? How might neural stem cells be used to increase neural plasticity?

Social Policy Implications

Neuroscience Influences on Social Policy

In Chapter 1, we faced the reality of a global aging human population and the fundamental social changes that will bring about. In this chapter, we faced the complexities of the aging of the human brain, and the fact that under some conditions those changes are beneficial and compensatory and under others they result in diseases such as dementia. As the world's population of older adults continues to rise, both outcomes will be more visible. Consequently, social policies will need to respond.

Many have made much of the possibility that the increased numbers of people with brain-based disorders could result in a massive challenge to global health care, not to mention presenting an enormous financial challenge to families and governments alike. But is that opinion realistic? The good news is that advanced research in neuroscience tells us that researchers are identifying ways in which such brain disorders can be reduced or perhaps even reversed. In addition, researchers have identified areas of the brain that are relatively preserved and may even show growth, and that certain activities, such as exercise, may at least delay decreases in performance. Thus, it is important for policy makers to obtain a more complete and accurate picture of aging. Why?

Research in neuroscience and aging is extremely important for a wide range of social policies from what sorts of coverage are included in basic healthcare insurance to laws pertaining to renewing drivers' licenses and the age at which people should be eligible for retirement benefits, among others. Some have already been put into place, such as increasing the age at which a person becomes fully eligible for Social Security benefits (a point we will examine in Chapter 14). Federal agencies such as the National Institutes of Health have shifted funding priorities to focus much of their efforts onto better ways to assess and understand changes in the brain and other key issues in aging. As we will explore in Chapter 12, organizations are adapting to having more older workers, and to take advantage of their special skills and knowledge.

What's at stake regarding policy? We are now working on extending the vitality of older adulthood. Evidence from neuroimaging research provides a platform from which new interventions might be developed to make this a reality.

In Review

Your summary of Chapter 2 could be organized into three paragraphs, each one corresponding to one of the chapter modules. The first paragraph should provide descriptions of the basic tools and techniques used in neuroscience, such as the different types of brain imaging. You should also describe what is unique about the neuroscience perspective.

Paragraph two should describe the main structures of the brain and what functions and processes they are most involved in. Describe also the basic age-related changes that brain structures, neurons, and neurotransmitters undergo. Provide descriptions of the various examples of brain–behavior mapping, such as theory of mind, memory, and emotion.

Your third paragraph should describe the three major theories and models explaining brain processes and age-related change. Describe the evidence for compensation in the brains of older adults. Describe the evidence for brain plasticity across adulthood. Discuss how neuroethics provides an interpretive lens for neuroscience research and intervention.

Integrating Concepts in Development

- Which of the theories or models of brain processes makes the most sense to you? Why?
- What would you say about the stereotypes of aging now that you understand the plasticity of brain functioning?
- What does the work on brain plasticity imply for therapies to address brain disorders?
- How would you plan a cognitive training program to take advantage of age-related changes in brain structures and plasticity?

Key Terms

activation imaging approach Attempts to directly link functional brain activity with cognitive behavioral data. 40

amygdala The region of the brain, located in the medial-temporal lobe, believed to play a key role in emotion. 42

axon A structure of the neuron that contains neurofibers. 42

cerebellum The part of the brain that is associated with motor functioning and balance equilibrium. 42

cerebral cortex The outermost part of the brain consisting of two hemispheres (left and right). 42

compensation-related utilization of neural circuits hypothesis (CRUNCH) model A model that describes how the aging brain adapts to neurological decline by recruiting additional neural circuits (in comparison to younger adults) to perform tasks adequately. 56

compensatory changes Changes that allow older adults to adapt to the inevitable behavioral decline resulting from changes in specific areas of the brain. 40

corpus callosum A thick bundle of neurons that connects the left and right hemispheres of the cerebral cortex. 42

default network of the brain The regions of the brain that are most active at rest. 58

dendrites A structural feature of a neuron that acts like antennas to receive signals from other nearby neurons. 41

diffusion tensor imaging (DTI) A type of magnetic resonance imaging that measures the diffusion of water molecules in tissue to study connections of neural pathways in the brain. 43

dopamine A neurotransmitter associated with higher-level cognitive functioning. 43

dopaminergic system Neuronal systems that use dopamine as their major neurotransmitter. 43

executive functions Include the ability to make and carry out plans, switch between tasks, and maintain attention and focus. 42

functional neuroimaging Provides an indication of brain activity but not high anatomical detail. 38

hippocampus Located in the medial-temporal lobe, this part of the brain plays a major role in memory and learning. 42

limbic system A set of brain structures involved with emotion, motivation, and long-term memory, among other functions. 42

neural stem cells (Also known as neural progenitors or neural precursor cells) Cells in the brain and spinal cord (the central nervous system, CNS) that are thought to give rise to the broad array of specialized cells of the CNS, including both neurons and glial cells. 59

neuroanatomy The study of the structure of the brain. 36

neurocorrelational approach An approach that attempts to relate measures of cognitive performance to measures of brain structure or functioning. 40

neurofibers Structures in the neuron that carry information inside the neuron from the dendrites to the terminal branches. 42

neuroimaging A set of techniques in which pictures of the brain are taken in various ways to provide understanding of both normal and abnormal cognitive aging. 38

neuron A brain cell. 41

neuropsychological approach Compares brain functioning of healthy older adults with adults displaying various pathological disorders in the brain. 39

neuroscience The study of the brain. 36

neurotransmitters Chemicals that carry information signals between neurons across the synapse. 42

parieto-frontal integration theory (P-FIT) A theory that proposes that intelligence comes from a distributed and integrated network of neurons in the parietal and frontal areas of the brain. 56

positivity effect When an individual remembers more positive information relative to negative information. 46

prefrontal and frontal cortex Part of the frontal lobe that is involved in executive functioning. 42

scaffolding theory of cognitive aging–revised (STAC-r) model A model based on the idea that age-related changes in one's ability to function reflect a life-long process of compensating for cognitive decline by recruiting additional brain areas and takes life-course factors that enhance or deplete neural resources into account. 57

structural neuroimaging A set of techniques that provides highly detailed images of anatomical features in the brain. 38

synapse The gap between neurons across which neurotransmitters travel. 42

terminal branches The endpoints in a neuron that help transmit signals across the synapse. 42

theory of mind (ToM) The ability that helps us understand that other people have beliefs, desires, ideas, feelings, intentions, and viewpoints that are different from our own. 47

white matter Neurons that are covered by myelin that serve to transmit information from one part of the cerebral cortex to another or from the cerebral cortex to other parts of the brain. 43

white matter hyperintensities (WMH) Abnormalities in white matter determined by the observation of high signal intensity or a bright, spotty appearance on MRI images which indicate brain pathologies. 43

Chapter

3

Learning Objectives

After reading this chapter, you will be able to...

3.1. Describe the major theories of biological aging.

3.2. Describe the typical age-related changes in the body affecting appearance and mobility.

3.3. Describe the main age-related changes in sensory systems.

3.4. Describe the major age-related changes in the cardiovascular and respiratory systems.

3.5. Describe the main age-related changes in the reproductive system.

3.6. Describe the main age-related changes in the autonomic nervous system.

Physical Changes Across Adulthood

Chapter Outline

Could you run 100 miles over two days? Not on flat ground, mind you, but along a trail in the California mountains such that by the time you have finished you will have climbed more than 18,000 feet overall and descended almost 23,000 feet along an up-and-down trail that also has ice-cold river crossings. The 2015 running of the Western States 100-Mile Endurance Run across this rugged terrain had its most thrilling moment a mere 6 seconds before the time clock was set to turn off. That's when 71-year-old Gunhild Swanson of Spokane Valley, Washington, crossed the finish line to become the first woman over age 70 to finish the race with a time of 29:59:54.

Older adult ultra-marathoners are shattering old beliefs about physical performance and age. To be sure, athletic success is a combination of years of intense training and excellent genes. But who would have thought that Gunhild could do it?

Certainly, Gunhild performs well beyond the level that most of us could attain even at much younger ages. But each of us can attain impressive levels of physical exertion when we work at it. In this chapter, we will discover how physical abilities typically change across adulthood, and why such things as race times lengthen with age. First, though, we will confront a very basic question: Why do living things age and die?

Inlander Health & Home/inlander.com

At age 71, Gunhild Swanson became the first woman over age 70 to complete the two-day Western States 100-Mile Endurance Run in 2015.

3.1 Why Do We Age? Biological Theories of Aging

Key Questions

- How do metabolic theories explain aging?
- What are the major hypotheses in cellular theories of aging?
- How do genetic programming theories propose that we age?
- How do the basic developmental forces interact in biological and physiological aging?

Olandan read that eating certain things in one's diet, such as blueberries, is really good for you and may have many positive effects. Some of Olandan's friends have warned him that you can't always believe what you read. Olandan thinks that the research he's read sounds credible, but he's not sure. He's wondering if he should eat his blueberries, as he likes them on his oatmeal.

Why is it that some people, like Dara Torres, who at age 41 became the oldest woman to win an Olympic medal in swimming, or Tom Brady, who quarterbacked two different NFL teams to Super Bowl victories after he turned age 40, or Kazuyoshi Miura, who in his mid-50s was the world's oldest soccer (football) player from Japan, manage to stay competitive in their sports into middle age and others of us experience significant physical decline?

Why do we age at all? After all, some creatures, such as lobsters, do not age as humans do. (As far as scientists can tell, lobsters never exhibit measurable signs of aging, such as changes in metabolism or declines in strength or health.) For millennia, scientists and philosophers have pondered this question. Their answers have spurred researchers to create a collection of theories based on basic biological and physiological processes. The search has included many hypotheses, such as metabolic rates and brain sizes, that haven't proved useful. But as scientists continue unlocking the keys to our genetic code, hope is rising that we may eventually have an

Discovering Development

Why Do Most People Think We Age?

What does the average person believe about how and why we age physiologically? To find out, do the following. First, list some of the explanations of why living things age and die that you have heard. Next, ask some people you encounter the same thing. Compile the results from your own ideas and your interviews, share them with your classmates to create a larger database, and then compare them with what you discover in this chapter. To what extent were your interviewees correct in their descriptions? Where were they off base? Does any of the misinformation match up with the stereotypes of aging we considered in Chapter 1? Why do you think this might be the case?

answer. To date, though, none of the more than 300 existing theories provides a complete explanation of all the normative changes humans experience (Candore & Caruso, 2021; Yin, 2016). Some of them involve considering things we eat more closely, such as the blueberries that Olandan is wondering about, as a way to slow aging.

Before we explore some of the partial explanations from scientific research, complete the Discovering Development exercise. Compare your results for this project with some of the theories described next. What similarities and differences did you uncover?

Metabolic Theories

One commonsense theory of aging speculates that organisms have only so much energy to expend in a lifetime. The basic idea is that the rate of an organism's metabolism is related to how long it lives (Adav & Wang, 2021). Despite considerable data indicating significant changes in energy usage and a host of other measures with increasing age, no useful biomarker of aging based on metabolism has ever been discovered.

Nevertheless, the search continues. One interesting avenue hints that significantly reducing the number of calories animals and people eat may increase longevity, but research focusing on nonhuman primates demonstrates that longer lives do not always result from restricting calories alone. For instance, research indicates that our circadian rhythms (the sleep–wake cycle) interact with caloric restriction in such a way that it matters when during the awake cycle feeding occurs, and the quantities and what exactly is eaten are major factors in whether the caloric restriction results in longer life, and the extreme reductions in calories needed to affect longevity usually lower quality of life (Chaudhari et al., 2017). Most people would be unwilling to make that trade.

Cellular Theories

A second family of ideas points to causes of aging at the cellular level. Because many cells in the body reproduce themselves, one notion focuses on the number of times cells can divide, which presumably limits the life span of a complex organism. Cells grown in laboratory culture dishes undergo only a fixed number of divisions before dying, and the number of possible divisions they make depend on the age of the donor organism. This upper limit is called the *Hayflick limit*, after its discoverer, Leonard Hayflick (Hayflick, 1996). For example, cells from human fetal tissue are capable of 40 to 60 divisions; cells from a human adult are capable of only about 20. It turns out that the Hayflick limit sets an upper bound on the number of cell divisions possible even in the absence of other factors, such as telomere damage, discussed next (Ogrodnik, 2021).

What causes cells to limit their number of divisions? Evidence suggests that the tips of the chromosomes, called **telomeres**, play a major role in aging by adjusting the cell's response to stress and growth stimulation based on cell divisions and DNA damage and by typically shortening with each cell replication. Healthy, normal telomeres help regulate the cell division and reproduction process.

An enzyme called **telomerase** is needed in DNA replication to fully reproduce the telomeres when cells divide. But telomerase normally is not present in somatic cells, so with each replication the telomeres become shorter. Eventually, the chromosomes become unstable and cannot replicate because the telomeres become too short. This process is illustrated in Figure 3.1. Many researchers believe that telomere shortening is a primary cause of aging (Razgonova et al., 2020).

Researchers believe that in some cases cancer cells proliferate so quickly because telomeres are not able to regulate cell growth and reproduction (Akincilar, et al., 2016). The culprit appears to be telomerase. Two processes are involved (Minasi et al., 2021). The most common, involving at least 85% of human cancers, involves the activation of telomerase and the unregulated reproduction of cells. The second involves a way that cancer cells work

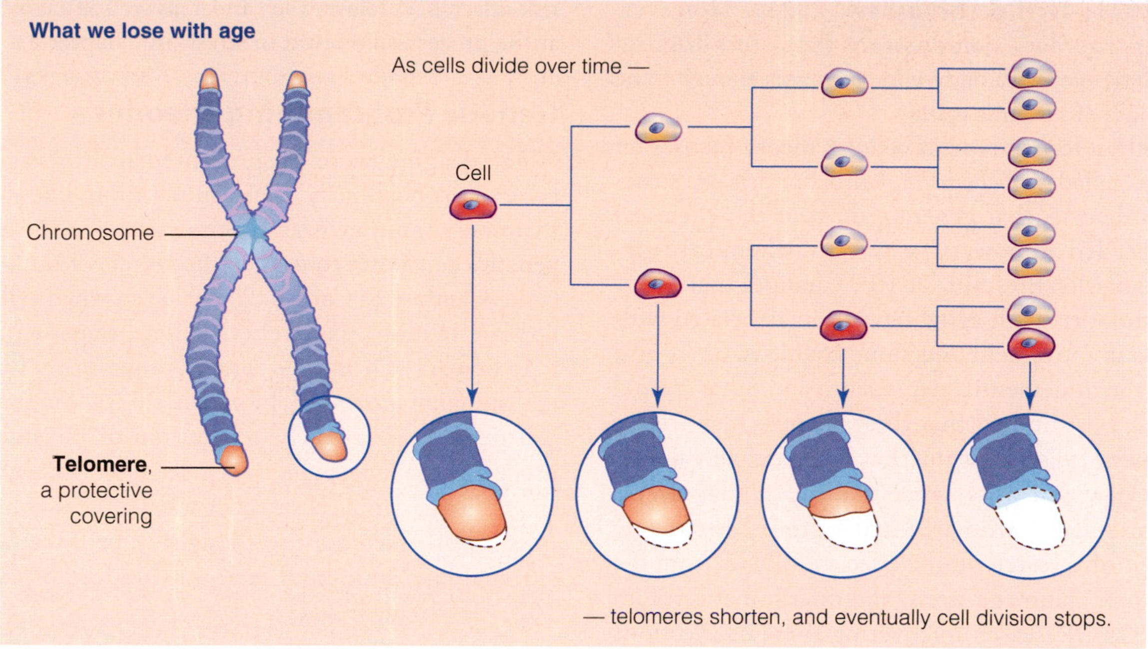

Figure 3.1 The process by which telomeres shorten as we age.
Source: telomeres-aging.com/images/shorteningdna.jpg.

around telomerase to keep telomeres longer but rather unbalanced in length. Based on this work, effective cancer treatments may involve targeting telomerase production.

Chronic stress (discussed in detail in Chapter 4) may accelerate the changes that occur in telomeres and thereby shorten one's life span (Oliveira et al., 2016; Razgonova et al., 2020). In contrast, research also indicates that physical activity and exercise are associated with maintaining telomere length, which may help slow the aging process itself (Denham & Sellami, 2021).

A second type of cellular theory proposes that aging is caused by a process called **oxidative stress**, an imbalance between free radicals and antioxidants in your body. **Free radicals** are highly reactive molecules produced randomly in normal metabolism that easily react with other molecules. **Antioxidants** are molecules that stabilize free radicals to become less reactive. When there are more free radicals present than can be kept in balance by antioxidants, the free radicals can start doing damage to DNA and proteins in your body. This oxidative stress process can lead to a vast number of diseases over time, such as cardiovascular disease and Alzheimer's disease (Babaei et al., 2021; Yan et al., 2021).

The most important evidence that oxidative stress may be involved in aging comes from research with antioxidants, the substances that neutralize the harmful effects of free radicals. Common antioxidants include vitamins A, C, and E, and coenzyme Q. A growing body of evidence documents that ingesting antioxidants postpones the appearance of age-related diseases such as cancer, cardiovascular disease, and immune system dysfunction (Suja et al., 2016; Yan et al., 2021). Examples of foods high in antioxidants include red/purple/blue grapes, blueberries, red berries, nuts, dark green vegetables, sweet potatoes and orange vegetables, tea, whole grains, beans, and fish. Eating a diet high in antioxidants improves health, but the direct effects on longevity remain to be seen (Cömert & Gökmen, 2020). So, Olandan, the person we met in the vignette, would be well advised to enjoy having blueberries with his oatmeal.

A third cellular theory is based on a process called **cross-linking**, in which certain proteins in human cells interact randomly and produce molecules that are linked in such a way as to make the body stiffer (Cavanaugh, 1999b). The proteins in question, which make up roughly one-third of the protein in the body, are called collagen. Collagen in soft body tissue acts much like reinforcing rods in concrete. The more cross-links there are, the stiffer the tissue. For example, leather tanning involves using chemicals that create many cross-links to make the leather stiff enough for use in shoes and other products. As we age, the number of cross-links increases. This process may explain why the heart and arteries become stiffer with age and cause cardiovascular disease (Adeva-Andany et al., 2021; Neff & Bradshaw, 2021). However, few scientific data demonstrate that cross-linking broadly interferes with body-wide processes enough to be a basic cause of systemic aging.

Finally, a fourth type of cellular theory focuses on structures called *mitochondria*. Mitochondria are structures inside cells that generate most of the chemical energy needed to power the cell's biochemical reactions (Rango & Bresolin, 2018). Changes that occur in mitochondria with aging have been associated with problems in movement and some cognitive functions, as well as with dementia, depression, and other mental disorders. It is thought that these changes may trigger more general cellular dysfunction and eventually death.

The view that what happens at the cellular level is crucial in understanding the aging process is strongly supported by research on the effects on DNA from life trauma, post-traumatic stress, and discrimination (Lim et al., 2022). Research uncovering these connections relies on measures of biological age and aging (discussed in Chapter 1). The measure frequently used is DNA methylation, a complex chemical process that involves changing how DNA works, especially in the manufacturing of proteins necessary in cell functioning. Essentially what happens is that the protein manufacturing is disrupted, even though the DNA structure itself remains intact. Scientists can measure how much DNA methylation has occurred to determine the biological age of any person (He et al., 2021).

It turns out that the rate at which DNA methylation occurs is sensitive to the amount of life trauma, post-traumatic stress, and discrimination a person experiences, along with other environmental and lifestyle factors, a result that is documented across numerous studies (Lim et al., 2022). This finding is groundbreaking for understanding health risks and why they vary systematically across different groups of people. As noted in Chapter 1, how cultures and societies treat people in various sociocultural groups can create vastly different levels of stress and trauma.

What does this mean? Measures of DNA methylation can correspond to ages that are higher or lower than the person's chronological age. In many cases, the age-related aspect of disease is best understood as that between biological age and risk. That means that people whose biological age diverges from their chronological age would be at greater risk. An emerging understanding is that much of the disparities in risk of cancer, for example, among various racial and ethnic groups can be traced to atypical DNA methylation processes (Wang et al., 2020). We will examine these risk differences relating to cancer, as well as a closer look at the processes involved in stress, in Chapter 4.

Genetic Programming Theories

What if aging were programmed into our genetic code? This possibility seems much more likely as the extremely rapid growth of knowledge about human genetics continues to unlock the secrets of our genetic code (Candore & Caruso, 2021). Even when cell death appears random, researchers believe that such losses may be part of a master genetic program that underlies the aging process (Tabibzadeh, 2021). Programmed cell death appears to be a function of physiological processes, the innate ability of cells to self-destruct, and the ability of dying cells to trigger key processes in other cells, all of which are also thought to be influenced by external environmental factors (Candore & Caruso, 2021; Tabibzadeh, 2021).

The circumstantial evidence that aging is programmed in our genetic code is substantial—one only has to consider the many diseases for which we have proof of genetic links (e.g., Alzheimer's disease, several types of cancer) to understand that this idea makes sense. It is quite likely that the other explanations we have considered in this section and the changes we examine throughout this text are the result of various genetic programs. Despite these insights, many mysteries remain. We do not yet know how this genetic self-destruct program is activated, nor exactly how it works. But there is a general consensus that we are undoubtedly on the right track to answering the big question: Why and how do we age?

Implications of the Developmental Forces

Although scientists do not yet have one unified theory of biological and physiological aging, the picture is becoming clearer. We know that there are genetic components, that the body's replicator sometimes produces incorrect copies, and that those errors mater in the long run (Candore & Caruso, 2021; Ogrodnik, 2021; Tabibzadeh, 2021). From the perspective of the basic developmental forces (discussed in Chapter 1), the biological theories provide ways to describe the biological forces. As we examine specific body systems in this chapter and health-related processes in Chapter 4, we will begin to integrate the biological forces with the psychological, sociocultural, and life-cycle forces. In those discussions, notice how changes in body systems and diseases are influenced by these other factors. Note especially how sociocultural forces can actually impact basic biological (e.g., genetic and cellular) functioning.

The implication of these dynamic, interactive processes is that the diagnosis and treatment of health-related concerns must include many perspectives. It is not enough to have your physical functioning checked to establish whether you are healthy. Rather, in addition to a bodily physical, one should have a checkup of psychological and sociocultural functioning. Finally, the results of all these examinations must be placed in the context of one's overall life span. Of course, many people do not have access to even the most basic of these checkups.

A unified theory of aging would have to account for a wide array of changes relating not only to biological forces but to other forces as well. Perhaps then we'll discover why Dara Torres was winning medals in the pool, Tom Brady was taking home Super Bowl rings, Kazuyoshi Miura was still on the pitch, and Gunhild Swanson was running 100 miles when most of their peers only watched from the stands or on a screen.

Or we just might discover how to reverse or stop aging. Much is being learned about how herbs and other plants have antiaging effects that have been known for centuries in certain Asian traditional medicine practices and in Indigenous cultures (Banerjee et al., 2021; Ling et al., 2016). For example, research on the Chinese herb Sanchi (or San Qi; *Panax notoginsengs*) holds promise in reducing wrinkles. Extracts of *Momordica charantia*, basil plant, can delay aging process and alleviate age-related diseases. Leaf and root extracts of *Tinospora cordifolia* and *Withania somnifera* delay aging in mesenchymal stem cells (MSCs) efficiently. Herbal extracts of *Curcumin Longa L.*, *Salvia miltiorrhiza*, and naringin from citrus fruits and grapes have strong potential in inducing cumulative growth of stem cells at precise concentrations. Western science is just now learning about these connections.

A word of caution, though. People who have known about and used plant-based supplements for millennia understand their limits. Beware of overhyped claims that any dietary supplement "cures" aging or can provide the "Fountain of Youth." They don't.

Adult Development in Action

If you were a geriatric nurse, what advice would you give to your patients about living longer based on existing biological theories of aging?

Review Questions

3.1 Why Do We Age? Biological Theories of Aging

- What biological theories have been proposed to explain aging? What are their similarities and differences?
- What are some dietary elements that may prolong life?
- How do the developmental forces influence the biological theories? What are some examples of these forces at work?

3.2 Appearance and Mobility

Key Questions

- How do our skin, hair, and voices change with age?
- What happens to our body build with age?
- What age-related changes occur in our ability to move around?

By all accounts, Katrina is extremely successful. She was a famous fashion model in her late teens and 20s, and by the time she was 36 she had learned enough about the business to start her own multinational modeling agency. The other day Katrina smiled wryly when she looked in the mirror and saw a wrinkle. "Well," she sighed, "I guess now I'll look like a mature corporate executive."

Katrina's experience isn't unique. We often recognize the outward signs of aging first in the mirror: gray hair, wrinkled skin, and an expanding waistline or hips. These changes occur gradually and at different rates; some of us experience all these changes in young adulthood, whereas others don't have them until late middle or old age. How we perceive the person staring back at us in the mirror says a great deal about how we feel about aging; positive feelings about the signs of aging are related to positive self-esteem. Katrina is an example of that.

In this section, we focus on these external signs of aging that are inevitable: what we look like and how we get around in our environment. Let's discover how people usually handle them.

Changes in Skin, Hair, and Voice

When we, like Katrina, notice the first visible signs of aging, it makes no difference that these changes are universal and inevitable. Nor does it matter that our wrinkles are caused by a combination of changes in the structure of the skin and its connective and supportive tissue and the cumulative effects of exposure to sunlight. As normal as the loss of hair pigmentation is, we may still want to hide the gray (Aldwin et al., 2018). What matters on that day is that we have seen our first wrinkle and gray hair.

Changes in the Skin. Why does our skin wrinkle? Wrinkling is actually a complex, four-step process (Letsiou, 2021; Tobin, 2017). First, the outer layer of skin becomes thinner through cell loss, causing the skin to become more fragile. Second, the collagen fibers that make up the connective tissue lose much of their flexibility, making the skin less able to regain its shape after a pinch. Third, elastin fibers in the middle layer of skin lose their ability to keep the skin stretched out, resulting in sagging. Finally, the underlying layer of fat, which helps provide padding to smooth out the contours, diminishes.

It may surprise you to learn that how quickly the face ages is largely under your control. Two major environmental causes of wrinkles are (1) exposure to ultraviolet rays from the sun, which breaks down the skin's connective tissue; and (2) smoking, which restricts the flow of blood to the skin around the lips. But diets lacking in fresh fruits and vegetables, and that include excessive alcohol, as well as sweating and making repetitive facial expressions also help create wrinkles (American Academy of Dermatology, 2021a; Tobin, 2017). There are several steps you can take to protect your skin throughout adulthood, including staying out of the sun, using moisturizer daily, not smoking, and avoiding repetitive facial movements (American Academy of Dermatology, 2021b, 2021c).

Much of the emphasis on skin aging and skin care is aimed at preventing the three types of skin cancer: basal cell, squamous cell, and melanoma. Decades of research indicate the overall health benefits of sunscreens in preventing skin cancers and slowing skin aging significantly outweigh criticism that they also interfere with the formation of vitamin D by the skin (Nash & Tanner, 2016). In fact, the Cancer Council of Australia (2021) created a public messaging campaign in the early 1980s to remind people what to do—the Slip Slop Slap Seek Slide campaign. It consists of:

- Slip on a shirt
- Slop on sunscreen
- Slap on a hat
- Seek shade
- Slide on some sunglasses that meet protection standards

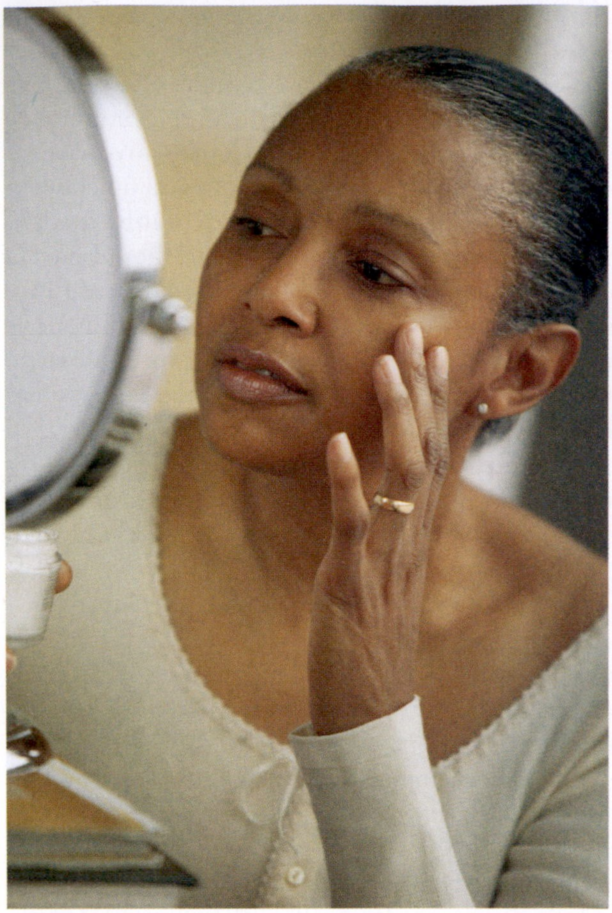

Ariel Skelley/Getty Images Entertainment/Getty Images

Getting wrinkles is part of the normative aging process.

In addition, age spots (areas of dark pigmentation that look like freckles) and moles (pigmented outgrowths) appear more often as we age (Tobin, 2017). It is important to distinguish between moles, which are benign, and melanoma, a deadly form of skin cancer than can resemble moles, as well as from other types of skin lesions (Skin Cancer Foundation, 2021; Wakelin, 2021). Most melanomas can be differentiated from moles based on the "ABCDEs" and the "Ugly Duckling" signs:

- A for Asymmetry in shape,
- B for irregular Borders,
- C for Color,
- D for Diameter of more than ¼ inch, and
- E for Evolving over time.
- The Ugly Duckling sign is that most moles on your body appear about the same, whereas a melanoma generally appears different.

Skin aging involves more than just protecting it from the sun. Older adults' skin is naturally thinner and drier, giving it a leathery texture, making it less effective at regulating heat or cold, and making it more susceptible to cuts, bruises, and blisters. To counteract these problems, people should use skin moisturizers, vitamin E, and facial massages (American Academy of Dermatology, 2021c).

The coloring of light-skinned people undergoes additional changes with age. The number of pigment-containing cells in the outer layer of skin decreases, and those that remain have less pigment, resulting in lighter skin.

Some of the blood vessels in the skin may become dilated and create small, irregular red lines. Varicose veins may appear as knotty, bluish irregularities in blood vessels, especially on the legs; various treatment methods are available (Aldwin et al., 2018; Gawas, 2022).

Although it is the case that all people's skin undergoes age-related change, it is certainly not the case that these signs of aging are held in high social regard. Youthful-looking skin has long been considered the ultimate standard of beauty, certainly for women, in many cultures, particularly in the developed world. Consequently, people spend many billions of dollars on cosmetics and other products, as well as surgeries, in hopes of meeting this standard. The Controversies feature considers at this issue in more detail.

Controversies

In Search of Never-Ending Youth

Throughout recorded history, cultures have set standards and expectations for appearance (Cutler, 2021). These standards cover everything from the clothes and hair styles one is supposed to wear to how one's face and body should look. All one has to do is look at art across the ages (or family photos if the collection extends across many decades) to see clear evidence of how fashion and "the look" changes over time. Although the clothes may look different across decades and generations, certain biases that underlie these trends may not. One that has withstood many superficial changes is the attitude that the way young adults' skin appears represents the epitome of beauty, especially for people who identify as women. The power of this belief is such that many tens of billions of dollars are spent to achieve that look.

The antiaging industry is an enormously profitable economic sector. Global Industry Analysts (2021) estimate that the worldwide market for antiaging products (estimated at $34.2 billion in 2020) is projected to reach $47.8 billion by 2027. Three of the biggest components of this market, antiwrinkle, antipigmentation, and hair care products, are each expected to increase at rates between 4% and 6% annually.

To be sure, much of the expenditure on the search to maintain the illusive standard of youthful beauty is money not well spent, but some of it is a good investment. For example, the American Academy of Dermatology Association (AADA, 2021) provides a six-step set of guidelines for selecting antiaging skin care products: (1) Start with sunscreen; (2) treat your number 1 aging-skin concern; (3) buy a product formulated for your skin type; (4) read product labels and select a product that is hypoallergenic, does not block pores or cause acne, and has a consumer hotline; (5) have realistic expectations, and (6) select a product within your price range. The AADA is clear that none of these products will eliminate or even reduce all the signs of aging, and that they cannot create the same outcomes as surgery (e.g., a facelift). Every major cosmetics company has antiaging products (or products that are claimed to be antiaging), resulting in markets that are crowded with a dizzying array of options.

It is easy to dismiss antiaging products as merely a way for people to chase an elusive (and ultimately unattainable) goal. However, it is the case that many of the products that are sold as "antiaging" are actually important in maintaining healthy skin and addressing a number of skin diseases (e.g., psoriasis, eczema, etc.). For example, as discussed in the text, sunscreens are critical in preventing skin cancer due to overexposure to the sun. However, as Bodner and colleagues (2021) point out, people who have high aging anxiety may take any number of steps to attempt to lower their anxiety and stress levels. So, it is possible that some find antiaging products to be ways to achieve those outcomes.

The rapid increase in the number of older adults could have an impact on the traditional views regarding youthful appearance. On one hand, there may be some change regarding hair color, with gray hair becoming somewhat more "acceptable" and as a sign of maturity and wisdom for all. Still, it seems unlikely that a wholesale change in the push toward staying youthful looking will disappear anytime soon.

What do you think?

Changes in the Hair. Gradual thinning and graying of the hair of both men and women occur inevitably with age, although there are large individual differences in the rate of these changes. Hair loss is caused by destruction of the germ centers that produce the hair follicles. Males usually do not lose facial hair as they age; you probably have encountered many balding males with thick, bushy beards. In addition, males often develop bushy eyebrows and hair growth inside the ears. In contrast, females often develop patches of hair on the face, especially on the chin (Aldwin et al., 2018). This hair growth is related to the hormonal changes of the climacteric, discussed later in this chapter.

Graying of the hair is also a widespread experience of most people as they age, although when the change occurs is subject to wide individual differences. Graying results from a cessation of pigment production in the hair follicle. Research has uncovered both genetic and lifestyle bases for graying hair, especially prematurely (Mahendiratta et al., 2020). Cultural variations, sometimes tied to gender, are evident in whether people let their hair turn gray or whether they color it.

Changes in the Voice. The next time you're in a crowd of people of different ages, close your eyes and listen to the way they sound. You probably will be fairly accurate in guessing how old the speakers are just from the sound of the voices you hear. Younger adults' voices tend to be fuller and resonant, whereas older adults' voices tend to be thinner or weaker.

Age-related changes in one's voice include lowering of pitch, increased breathlessness and trembling, slower and less precise pronunciation, and decreased volume (Howe, 2020; Whited et al., 2016). A longitudinal study of Japanese adults revealed that females have more changes in their fundamental frequency, and shimmer (i.e., frequent change from soft to loud volume) and glottal noise is characteristic of older voices (Kasuya et al., 2008). Most researchers report that these changes are due to changes in the larynx (voice box), the respiratory system, and the muscles controlling speech.

Changes in Body Build

If you have been around the same older people, such as your grandparents, for many years, you undoubtedly have noticed that the way their bodies look is likely to have changed over time. Two changes are especially visible: a decrease in height and fluctuations in weight. Height remains fairly stable in adults until the 50s and is a good indicator of overall health (Perkins et al., 2016). The tendency to become shorter occurs in all races, ethnicities, and genders. People typically lose about 1 centimeter (about 0.4 inches) every 10 years after age 40, and the loss is even more rapid after age 70. In all, you may lose a total of 2.5 to 7.5 centimeters (1 to 3 inches) in height as you age.

Height loss usually is caused by compression of the spine from loss of bone strength (often from osteoporosis, a disease we will consider a bit later), changes in the discs between the vertebrae in the spine, and changes in posture. Importantly, height loss of more than 3 centimeters (about 1.2 inches) is associated with increased risk of dying from cardiovascular (Klingberg et al., 2021; Perkins et al., 2016) and respiratory diseases (Jain & Ma, 2020; Masunari et al., 2012). These findings are consistent across race and ethnicity; for example, older Indonesians with significant height loss had lower lung functioning, higher risk of cardiovascular disease, and higher overall mortality (Jain & Ma, 2020). We consider some specific aspects of changes in bone structure a bit later.

Weight gain in middle age followed by weight loss in later life is common. Typically, people gain weight between their 20s and their mid-50s but lose weight throughout old age. In part, the weight gain is caused by reduced levels of exercise, which in turn reduces the number of calories needed daily (Pontzer, 2021). Unfortunately, many people do not adjust their food intake to match these changes and continue consuming the same number of calories, which is the main reason for midlife weight gain. The result of these age-related changes is often noticed first when one's clothes become tighter in midlife—or looser in later life.

For males, weight gain tends to be around the abdomen. For females, weight gain tends to be around the hips. By later life, though, the body loses both muscle and bone, which weigh more than fat, in addition to some fat, resulting in overall weight loss (Van Wicklin, 2020; Yang et al., 2008). Research on the relations among body weight, health, and survival supports the hypothesis that older adults who have normal body weight at age 65 have longer life expectancy and lower rates of disability than 65-year-olds in other weight categories. Additionally, greater weight loss per decade from middle age to late life is correlated with increased risk of mild cognitive impairment overall (Alhurani et al., 2016) and to specific biomarkers for Alzheimer's disease (Grau-Rivera et al., 2021).

Changes in Mobility

Being able to get around on one's own is an important part of remaining independent. We all experience some normative changes that can affect our ability to remain mobile, but most of these changes do not inevitably result in serious limitations.

Muscles and Balance. Although the amount of muscle tissue in our bodies declines with age, this loss is usually not noticeable in terms of strength and endurance up to age 70, as the loss is no more than 20% for most people up to that point. After that, however, the rate of loss increases. By age 80 the loss in strength is typically up to 40%, and it appears to be more severe in the legs than in the arms and hands. Additional evidence suggests that muscle endurance also diminishes with age but at a slower rate. There are no substantive systematic gender, race, or ethnic differences in the rate of muscle change. Research has begun to identify the genetic program underpinnings of these typical changes (Tumasian et al., 2021). However, some people don't experience the usual pattern and retain their strength well into old age for reasons that are not yet understood, as it is not due to exercise alone (Seene & Kaasik, 2015).

This loss of muscle strength is especially important in the lower body, as those muscles help control posture and our ability to walk without difficulty. As lower body strength declines, the likelihood of balance problems and falls increases, as do problems with walking (Michalska et al., 2021). Later-life balance and walking problems can also result from wearing high-heeled shoes regularly across adulthood (Michalska et al., 2021). That's because high heels change the way people stand and walk, as well as the location of one's center of gravity. Over time, this results in changes in muscle strength and overuse, including a decrease in an individual's balance including worsened postural balance, and less stability, thereby increasing the risk of falling. Fortunately, research evidence indicates that resistance-type exercise can rebuild muscle fitness and mass, and may help delay these changes (Seene & Kaasik, 2015).

Bones. You may have seen commercials and advertisements aimed at middle-aged and older adults for products that help maintain bone mass. If you surmise that such products reflect a serious and real health concern, you are correct. Normative aging is accompanied by the loss of bone tissue throughout the body in all adults to some degree.

Skeletal maturity, the point at which bone mass is greatest and the skeleton is at peak development, occurs at around 18 for people who are genetically female and 20 in people who are genetically male (Chevalley & Rizzoli, 2022). Bone mass is determined mostly by genetics (as high as 80% in some studies); effects due to environmental factors generally have their effects before puberty.

Loss of bone mass begins in the late 30s, accelerates in the 50s, and slows by the 70s (Pignolo et al., 2021). However, these changes differ significantly as a function of hormones, as evidenced by research comparing cisgender men and women and trans men and women who use gender-affirming hormone treatment (Wiepjes et al., 2020). In research comparing people younger than or older than 50, fracture risk was higher in older trans women who used hormone treatment compared with age-matched cisgender men, and about the same as in cisgender women. In young trans women, though, fracture risk tended to be increased compared with age-matched cisgender women and lower than for cisgender men. Fracture risk was not increased in young trans men. Much more research in this area is needed, though, before any firm conclusions can be drawn about the long-term effects of gender-affirming hormone treatment on bones.

Most of what we know about age-related bone loss comes from research on cisgender women and has focused on two main reasons for their more significant bone loss in later life. First, cisgender women have less bone mass than cisgender men in young adulthood, meaning that they start out with less ability to withstand bone loss before it causes problems. Second, the depletion of estrogen after menopause speeds up bone loss. Research examining bone mass loss in women and men of all races and ethnicities indicates that bone loss and bone diseases are lower in non-Hispanic Black individuals than in other racial and ethnic groups, due mainly to initial higher levels of bone density in non-Hispanic Black individuals (Noel et al., 2021).

What specifically are the age-related changes in bones? The process involves a loss of bone mass inside the bone, which makes bones more hollow. In addition, bones tend to become porous. The changes result from body weight, genetics, and lifestyle factors such as smoking, alcohol use, and diet (National Osteoporosis Foundation, 2021a; Noel et al., 2021; Pignolo et al., 2021). All these bone changes cause an age-related increase in the likelihood of fractures, because hollow, porous bones are easier to break. Furthermore, broken bones in older people present more serious problems than in younger adults, because they are more likely to be clean fractures that are difficult to heal. Younger adults' bones fracture in such a way that there are many cracks and splinters to aid in healing. This is analogous to the difference between breaking a young, green tree branch (which is harder to do) and snapping an old, dry twig.

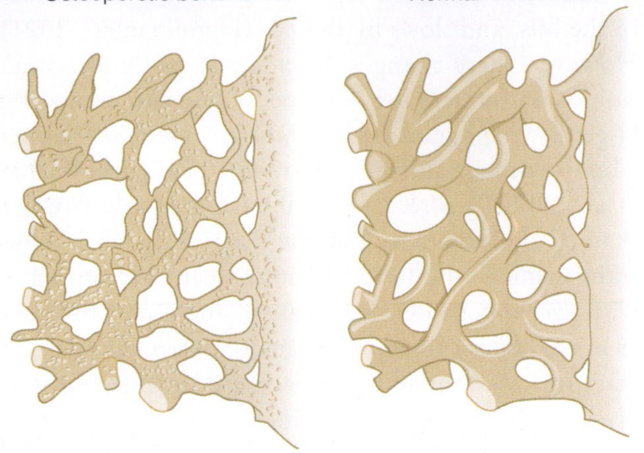

Figure 3.2 Osteoporotic and normal bone structures. Notice how much mass the osteoporotic bone has lost.

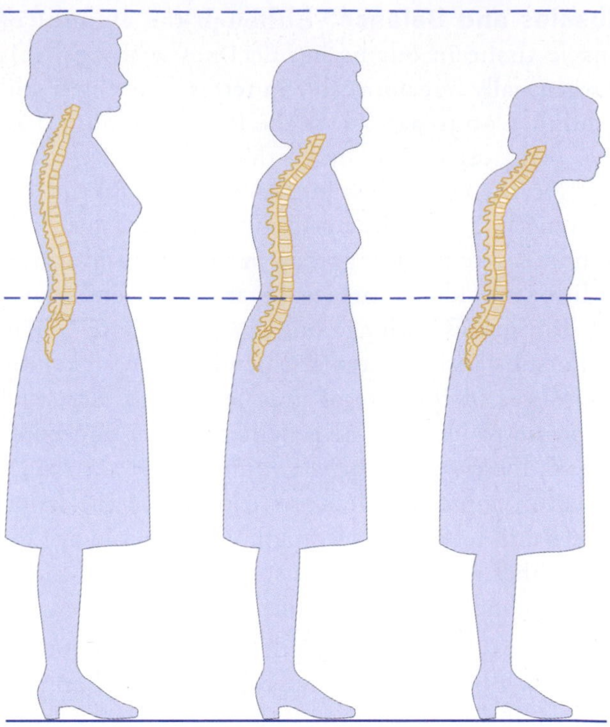

Figure 3.3 Changes in the curvature of the spine as a result of osteoporosis. These changes create the stooping posture common to older people with advanced osteoporosis.
Source: Based on Ebersole, P.,& Hess, P. (1998). *Toward Healthy Aging,* 5th ed., (p. 395). St. Louis, MO: Mosby.

Cisgender women and trans women who undergo gender-affirming hormonal treatment are especially susceptible to severe bone degeneration, a disease called **osteoporosis**, in which the severe loss of bone mass creates bones that resemble laced honeycombs. This process is depicted in Figure 3.2. Eventually, people with osteoporosis tend to develop a distinct curvature in their spines, as shown in Figure 3.3.

Osteoporosis is the leading cause of broken bones in all older women (National Osteoporosis Foundation, 2021a). Although it is most common overall in older adults, osteoporosis can occur in people in their 50s. Osteoporosis is more common in women than in men.

Osteoporosis is caused in part by having low bone mass at skeletal maturity (the point at which your bones reach peak development), deficiencies in calcium and vitamin D, estrogen depletion, and lack of weight-bearing exercise that builds up bone mass. Other risk factors include smoking; high-protein diets; excessive intake of alcohol, caffeine, and sodium; and lack of access to adequate medical care. People who are being treated for asthma, cancer, rheumatoid arthritis, thyroid problems, or epilepsy are also at increased risk because the medications used can lead to the loss of bone mass.

The National Osteoporosis Foundation (2021b, 2021c) recommends getting enough vitamin D and dietary calcium as ways to prevent osteoporosis. There is evidence that calcium supplements after menopause may slow the rate of bone loss and delay the onset of osteoporosis, but benefits appear to be greater when the supplements are provided before menopause. People should consume foods (such as milk, sardines, collard greens, broccoli, or kale) that are high in calcium and should also take calcium supplements if necessary. Recommended calcium intake for people of various ages is depicted in Table 3.1. Although sunlight is a good source for vitamin D, due to the risk of skin cancer from overexposure to the sun, most people get their recommended amounts of vitamin D from dietary sources.

Because of their higher risk, women who are late middle-aged or over age 65 are encouraged to have their bone mineral density (BMD) tested by having a **dual-energy X-ray absorptiometry (DXA) test**, which measures bone density at the hip and spine. The DXA test results are usually compared with the ideal or peak bone mineral density of a healthy 30-year-old adult, and DXA results are given as a "T-score." A score of 0 means that your bone mineral density is equal to the norm for a healthy young adult. A T-score between +1 and –1 is considered normative or healthy. The greater the negative number, the more severe the osteoporosis (National Institute of Arthritis and Musculoskeletal and Skin Diseases, 2019b).

Lowering the risk of osteoporosis involves dietary, medication, and activity approaches, all of which are

Table 3.1 Recommended Calcium and Vitamin D Intakes

Age	Calcium (Milligrams/ Daily)	Vitamin D (International Units/Daily)
Adult females		
Age 50 and younger	1,000	400–800
Age 51 and older	1,200	800–1,000
Adult males		
Age 70 and younger	1,000	
Age 71 and older	1,200	
Age 50 and younger		400–800
Age 51 and older		800–1,000

Source: Bone Health and Osteoporosis Foundation (2018). Calcium /Vitamin D. https://www.bonehealthandosteoporosis.org/patients /treatment/calciumvitamin-d/

affected by disparities in access (National Osteoporosis Foundation, 2021a, 2021b). Some evidence also supports the view that taking supplemental magnesium, zinc, vitamin K, and special forms of fluoride may be effective. Estrogen replacement is effective in preventing women's bone loss after menopause but is controversial because of potential side effects (as discussed later). There is also evidence that regular weight-bearing exercise (e.g., weightlifting, jogging, or other exercise that forces you to work against gravity) is beneficial. Slowing bone loss, or, even better, stimulating bone growth, is extremely important to minimize the risk of serious, potentially life-threatening fractures later in life.

In terms of medication interventions, bisphosphonates (e.g., Actonel®, Boniva®, Fosamax®, Reclast®) are commonly used and are highly effective but can have serious side effects if used over a long time (Diab et al., 2021; Palacios, 2022). Bisphosphonates slow the bone breakdown process by helping to maintain bone density during menopause. Research indicates that using bisphosphonates for up to five years appears relatively safe if followed by stopping the medication (called a "drug holiday"); there is evidence for protective effects lasting up to five years more. Periodic reevaluation of people taking medications to assess whether continued medication treatment is needed is crucial to appropriate and effective use of these drugs (Diab et al., 2021; Palacios, 2022).

Raloxifene (e.g., Evista®) is also approved for the treatment and prevention of osteoporosis. It is one of a group of medications known as selective estrogen receptor modulators (Jiang et al., 2021). **Selective estrogen receptor modulators (SERMs)** are not estrogens but are compounds that have estrogen-like effects on some tissues and estrogen-blocking effects on other tissues.

The newest classes of medications for osteoporosis are the RANK ligand inhibitors, such as denosumab (e.g., Prolia®, Xgeva®) that are considered "bone-modifying agents" because they work through proteins to decrease bone resorption (McClung, 2021; Tsourdi et al., 2019). Other research indicates that romosozumab (Evenity®), a monoclonal antibody, is also effective in stimulating bone growth in postmenopausal women (Cosman & Saag, 2021; Papapoulos, 2019).

Joints. Many middle-aged and older adults have good reason to complain of aching joints. Beginning in the 20s, the protective cartilage in and around joints starts to deteriorate, thinning and becoming cracked and frayed. Two types of arthritis can result: osteoarthritis and rheumatoid arthritis. These diseases are illustrated in Figure 3.4.

Over time and repeated use, the bones underneath the cartilage become damaged, which can result in **osteoarthritis**, a disease marked by gradual onset and progression of pain and disability, with minor signs of inflammation (National Institute of Arthritis and Musculoskeletal and Skin Diseases, 2019a). The disease usually becomes noticeable in late middle age or early old age, and it is especially common in people whose joints are subjected to routine overuse and abuse, such as athletes and manual laborers. Because it is caused by overuse and abuse of joints, osteoarthritis is considered a wear-and-tear disease. Pain from osteoarthritis typically is worse when the joint is used, but skin redness, heat, and swelling are minimal or absent. Osteoarthritis usually affects the hands, spine, hips, and knees, sparing the wrists, elbows, shoulders, and ankles. Effective management consists mainly of certain steroids and anti-inflammatory drugs, rest, nonstressful exercises that focus on range of motion, diet, and a variety of homeopathic remedies.

A second form of arthritis is **rheumatoid arthritis**, a more destructive disease of the joints that also develops slowly and typically affects different joints and causes other types of pain and more inflammation than osteoarthritis (National Institute of Arthritis and Musculoskeletal and Skin Diseases, 2019b). Most often, a pattern of morning stiffness and aching develops in the fingers, wrists, and ankles on both sides of the body. Joints appear swollen.

The American College of Rheumatology (2021) has adopted guidelines for treating rheumatoid arthritis.

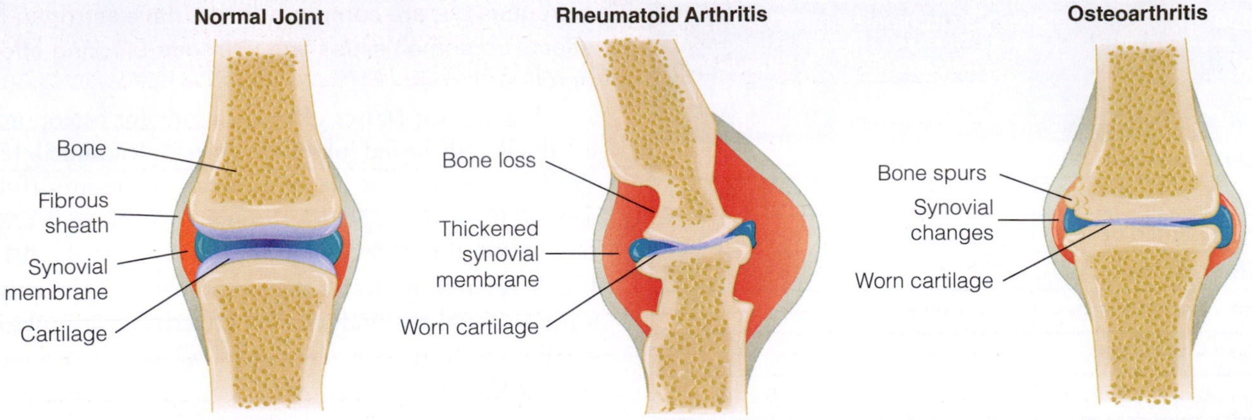

Figure 3.4 Rheumatoid arthritis versus osteoarthritis. Osteoarthritis, the most common form of arthritis, involves the wearing away of the cartilage that caps the bones in your joints. With rheumatoid arthritis, the synovial membrane that protects and lubricates joints becomes inflamed, causing pain and swelling. Joint erosion may follow.
Source: Adapted from the MayoClinic.com article, "Arthritis," https://www.mayoclinic.com/health/arthritis/DS01122

The typical low-level therapy consists of aspirin or other nonsteroidal anti-inflammatory drugs, such as Advil® or Aleve®. Newer treatments include disease-modifying antirheumatic drugs (DMARDs), such as hydroxychloroquine (e.g., Plaquenil®) and methotrexate (e.g., Trexall®) that limit the damage occurring in the joints, glucocorticoids, and TNF-alpha inhibitors that act as an anti-inflammatory agent and stop the disease's progression in some patients. Rest and passive range-of-motion exercises are also helpful. DMARDS can cause serious interactions with alcohol, so drinking should be avoided if one is taking these medications.

Both osteoarthritis (Reynard & Barter, 2020; Warner & Valdes, 2016) and rheumatoid arthritis (Onuora, 2021; Yarwood et al., 2016) have genetic components. Although the exact nature of these inheritance factors is unknown, several potential chromosome locations have been identified as possible markers. Further advances in our knowledge of these genetic links could result in more effective and more individualized treatments.

If a person has access to quality medical care, surgical interventions may be an option if medications do not provide relief. For example, arthroplasty, or the total replacement of joints damaged by arthritis, continues to improve as new materials help artificial joints last longer. Hip and knee replacement surgery is becoming both more common and more effective as less invasive surgical techniques are developed that dramatically reduce recovery time. When joints become inflamed, surgeons may be able to remove enough affected tissue to provide relief. In some cases, cartilage may be transplanted into a damaged joint. These latter two approaches help people avoid full joint replacement, generally viewed as the method of last resort.

Osteoporosis, osteoarthritis, and rheumatoid arthritis can appear similar and cause similar symptoms. As we have learned, though, they are different diseases requiring different treatment approaches. Comparisons among osteoporosis, osteoarthritis, and rheumatoid arthritis are listed in Table 3.2. As noted in our discussion of each condition, all three may result in pain that can become quite severe. One family of medications that may be prescribed are opioids, powerful pain-reducing medications that include oxycodone, hydrocodone, and morphine, among others (U.S. Food and Drug Administration, 2021a). These drugs have both benefits as well as potentially serious risks, including addiction (discussed in Chapter 4).

Psychological Implications

The appearance of wrinkles, gray hair, weight, and the like can have major effects on a person's self-concept (Aldwin et al., 2018) and reflect ageism in society (Levy & Macdonald, 2016). Older adults may still think of themselves as productive members of society and rebel against being made invisible by others who act on ageist beliefs. Because U.S. society places high value on looking young, middle-aged and older adults, especially women, may be stereotypically regarded as inferior on a number of dimensions, including intellectual ability, simply because they do not conform to an unrealistic image of "beauty." This is clearly an example of ageism.

Table 3.2 Similarities and Differences Among Osteoporosis, Osteoarthritis, and Rheumatoid Arthritis

	Osteoporosis	Osteoarthritis	Rheumatoid Arthritis
Risk factors			
Age-related	x	x	
Menopause	x		
Family history	x	x	x
Use of certain medications such as glucocorticoids or seizure medications	x		
Calcium deficiency or inadequate vitamin D	x		
Inactivity	x		
Overuse of joints		x	
Smoking	x		
Excessive alcohol	x		
Anorexia nervosa	x		
Excessive weight		x	
Physical effects			
Affects entire skeleton	x		
Affects joints		x	x
Is an autoimmune disease			x
Bony spurs		x	x
Enlarged or malformed joints	x	x	
Height loss	x		

Source: National Institute of Arthritis and Musculoskeletal and Skin Diseases (2006), www.niams.nih.gov/Health_Info/Bone/Osteoporosis/Conditions_Behaviors/osteoporosis_arthritis.asp

Consequently, women, especially, report higher levels of social pressure to engage in "beauty work" (dyeing their hair, cosmetic surgery, and the like) to remain visible in society. In contrast, parallel stereotypes describe aging men with some gray hair as distinguished, more experienced, and more knowledgeable than their younger counterparts. At the same time, there is pressure on men to look and act athletic, so they, too, feel pressure to conform.

Given the social stereotypes and ageism we examined in Chapter 1, many people engage in various behaviors to compensate for these changes. Some age-related changes in facial appearance can be disguised with cosmetics. Hair dyes can restore color. Surgical procedures such as face-lifts and tummy-tucks can tighten sagging and wrinkled skin. But even plastic surgery only hides or delays the inevitable; at some point everyone takes on a distinctly old appearance.

Losses in strength and endurance in old age can have much the same psychological effects as changes in appearance (Aldwin et al., 2018). In particular, these changes can be interpreted by the person that they are not as capable of adapting effectively to the environment. Loss of muscle coordination (which may lead to walking more slowly, for example) can prove embarrassing and stressful in social settings when others practice ageist attitudes and behaviors.

The changes in joints, especially in arthritis, have significant psychological effects, including depression (Aundhia et al., 2020). These changes can severely limit movement, thereby reducing mobility and the ability to complete normal daily routines. Moreover, joint pain is difficult to ignore or disguise, unlike changes in appearance. Older adults who suffer bone fractures face several other consequences in addition to discomfort. For example, a hip fracture may force hospitalization or even an extended stay in a rehabilitation facility. For all bone fractures experienced by older adults, the recovery period is much longer than for a younger adult. In addition, older people who witness friends or relatives struggling during rehabilitation may reduce their own activities as a precaution.

Adult Development in Action

If you were a personal exercise trainer, what regimen would you recommend for your older clients to help them maintain maximum health?

Review Questions

3.2 Appearance and Mobility

- What age-related changes occur in appearance?
- How does body build change with age?
- How do muscle and bone tissue change with age? What are common age-related diseases related to bones and joints?

3.3 Sensory Systems

Key Questions

- What age-related changes happen in vision?
- How does hearing change as people age?
- What age-related changes occur with age in people's somatosensory system?
- What happens to taste and smell with increasing age?

Bertha has attended Sunday services in her local African Methodist Episcopal (AME) church for 82 years. Over the past few years, though, she has experienced greater difficulty in keeping her balance as she walks down the steps from her row house to the sidewalk. Bertha is noticing that her balance problems occur even when she is walking on level ground. Bertha is concerned that she will have to stop attending her beloved church because she is afraid of falling and breaking a bone.

You have probably encountered people like Bertha walking slowly and tentatively along the sidewalk or in a store. Why do older people have these problems more often? If you said it is because people's sense of balance declines in later life, you would be in the right ballpark. It turns out that keeping one's balance is a complex process in which we integrate input from several sources, such as vision and touch (which we'll explore in this section), as well as muscles, bones, and joints (which we just discovered deteriorate with age). In this section we examine the changes that occur in our five primary sensory systems (vision, hearing, taste, smell, and the somatosensory system). These changes can challenge our ability to interact with the world and communicate with others. Let's explore them.

Vision

Have you ever watched middle-aged people try to read something that is right in front of them? If they do not already wear glasses or contact lenses, they typically move the material farther away so that they can see it clearly. On occasion, they may joke that "their arms are too short" to make the material come into focus. This change in vision is one of the first noticeable signs of aging, along with the wrinkles and gray hair we considered earlier. A major study of 10 European countries revealed that because we rely extensively on sight in almost every aspect of our waking life, its normative, age-related changes have profound and pervasive effects on people's everyday lives, especially feelings of sadness and loss of enjoyment of life (Mojon-Azzi et al., 2008).

How does eyesight change with age? The major changes are best understood by grouping them into two classes: changes in the structures of the eye, which begin in the 40s, and changes in the retina, which begin in the 50s (Alavi, 2016; Someya & Ikeda, 2021).

Structural Changes in the Eye. Two major kinds of age-related structural changes occur in the eye. One is a decrease in the amount of light that passes through the eye, resulting in the need for more light to do tasks such as reading (Alavi, 2016; Someya & Ikeda, 2021). As you might suspect, this change is one reason why older adults do not see as well in the dark, which may account in part for their reluctance to go places at night. One possible logical response to the need for more light would be to increase illumination levels in general. However, this solution does not work in all situations because we also become increasingly sensitive to glare as we age. So, turning up the lights will help, but only if it does not increase glare.

In addition, our ability to adjust to changes in illumination, called adaptation, declines. Going from a sunny day outside into a darkened movie theater involves dark adaptation; going back outside involves light adaptation. Research indicates that the time it takes for both types of adaptation increases with age (Alavi, 2016). These changes are especially important for older drivers, who have more difficulty seeing after confronting the headlights of an oncoming car while driving at night in switching quickly from dark to bright to dark conditions.

The second key structural changes involve the lens (Alavi, 2016). As we grow older, the lens becomes more yellow, causing poorer color discrimination in the green–blue–violet end of the spectrum. Also, the lens's ability to adjust and focus declines as the muscles around it stiffen. This is what causes difficulty in seeing close objects clearly, called **presbyopia**, necessitating either longer arms or corrective lenses. To complicate matters further, the time our eyes need to change focus from near to far (or vice versa) increases. This also poses a major problem in driving. Because drivers are constantly changing their focus from the instrument panel to other autos and signs on the highway, older drivers may miss important information because of their slower refocusing time.

Besides these normative structural changes, some people experience diseases caused by atypical structural changes. First, opaque spots called **cataracts** may develop on the lens, which limits the amount of light transmitted. Cataracts are usually treated by laser surgical removal of the original lens and the insertion of new lenses into the eye.

Second, the fluid in the eye may not drain properly, causing very high pressure; this condition, called **glaucoma**, can cause internal damage and progressive loss of vision. Glaucoma, a fairly common disease in middle and late adulthood, is usually treated with eye drops, though surgical intervention to improve fluid drainage may be necessary in some cases (Someya & Ikeda, 2021).

Retinal Changes. Another major family of changes in vision result from changes in the retina (Alavi, 2016; Someya & Ikeda, 2021). The retina sits along approximately two-thirds of the interior of the eye. It has specialized receptor cells, the rods and the cones. They are most densely packed toward the rear and especially at the focal point of vision, a region called the macula. At the center of the macula is the fovea, where incoming light is focused for maximum acuity, as when you are reading.

With increasing age, the probability of degeneration of the macula increases (Alavi, 2016). Age-related macular degeneration (AMD) involves the progressive and irreversible destruction of receptors from a combination of genetic predisposition, natural age-related changes in the eye, and lifestyle factors (such as smoking or nutritional intake) (Armento et al., 2021). This disease results in the loss of the central field of vision, which dramatically affects the ability to see details; for example, reading becomes extremely difficult. It is the leading cause of functional blindness in older adults. There are two forms of AMD: wet and dry. The wet form is usually treated by injection of drugs that stop the abnormal growth of blood vessels under the retina that are a cause of the disease. Unfortunately, there is still no effective treatment for the dry form, so physicians recommend a nutrient supplement as a preventive strategy (Armento et al., 2021).

A second age-related retinal disease is a by-product of diabetes, a chronic disease described in detail in Chapter 4. Diabetes is accompanied by accelerated aging of the arteries in the eye, with blindness being one of the more serious side effects. Diabetic retinopathy, as this condition is called, can involve fluid retention in the macula, detachment of the retina, hemorrhage, and aneurysms, and is the most common cause of blindness among younger and middle-aged people (National Eye Institute, 2022). Because it takes many years to develop, diabetic retinopathy is more common among people who developed diabetes early in life.

The combined effects of the changes in the eye reduce the ability to see detail and to discriminate different visual patterns, called visual acuity. Declines in visual acuity occur steadily between ages 20 and 60, with a more rapid decline thereafter. Loss of acuity is especially noticeable at low light levels (Alavi, 2016; Someya & Ikeda, 2021).

Psychological Effects of Visual Changes. Clearly, age-related changes in vision affect older adults' daily life and their well-being (Hajek et al., 2021; Mojon-Azzi et al., 2008). Some of the typical changes, such as presbyopia and cataracts, can be corrected easily through glasses or contacts, or by laser surgery. But treatment for other

Fizkes/Shutterstock.com

Due to presbyopia, middle-aged adults typically have trouble reading without glasses.

conditions, such as dry macular degeneration, remains elusive. It is the adjustment to these untreatable changes that impair vision and interfere with long-held routines, and it may take time to adapt to the changes in routine they bring.

If you want to provide environmental support for older adults, taking their normative vision changes into account, the strategies that will be most effective must be chosen carefully. For example, simply making the environment brighter may not be the answer; for increased illumination to be beneficial, surrounding surfaces must not increase glare. Using flat latex paint rather than glossy enamel and avoiding highly polished floors are two ways to make environments older adult friendly. There should be high contrast between the background and operational information on dials and controls, such as on stoves and remote controls. Older adults may also have trouble seeing some fine facial details, which may lead them to decrease their social contacts for concern of not recognizing someone. Small fonts on smartphones may make them harder to use.

Visual impairments with age change the relations between certain personality traits and emotion (Swenor et al., 2020). Visual impairment in older adults is primarily associated with emotional aspects of depression (Cosh et al., 2019). A reduction in social connectedness and in the ability to engage in pleasurable activities may underlie the depression–vision relationship. Deliberately providing more positive events that are sensitive to visual changes can help.

Visual problems also increase the risk of falling because the person may be unable to see hazards in their path or to judge distance very well. Thus, part of Bertha's concern about falling may be caused by changes in her ability to tell where the next step is or to see hazards along the sidewalk.

Hearing

Experiencing hearing loss is one of the most well-known normative changes with age globally (World Health Organization, 2021). A visit to any housing complex for older adults will easily verify this point; you will quickly notice that television sets and sound systems are turned up fairly loud in many of the apartments. Yet you don't have to be old to experience significant hearing problems. When he began to find it difficult to hear what was being said to him, former president Bill Clinton obtained two hearing aids. He was 51 years old at the time, and he attributed his hearing loss to too many high school bands and rock concerts when he was young. His situation is far from unique. Among many other celebrities, Oscar winner Halle Berry and Stephen Colbert both have significant hearing loss. In fact, nearly 20 percent of adults between ages 60 and 69 have a moderate or worse hearing loss (World Health Organization, 2021).

Loud noise is the chief enemy of hearing at any age. You may have seen people who work in noisy environments, such as construction workers and musicians during concerts, wearing protective headsets so that they are not exposed to loud noise over extended periods of time.

You don't need to be at a concert to damage your hearing, either. Using headphones or earbuds, especially at high volume, can cause the same serious damage and should be avoided (Jiang et al., 2016; Pienkowski, 2021). It is especially easy to cause hearing loss with headphones or earbuds if you wear them while exercising; the increased blood flow to the ear during exercise makes hearing receptors more vulnerable to damage. Interestingly, young adults tend not to consider their listening behavior as a risk (Gilliver et al., 2012), yet they do think that public music venues (e.g., dance clubs) are too loud (Beach & Gilliver, 2019). Due to the broad use of personal listening devices, hearing loss from these and other sources of loud noise is on the rise. In fact, a systematic review of research indicates that nearly 60% of adolescents and young adults listen to music on personal listening devices at levels that are unsafe, and significant losses in hearing ability result (Jiang et al., 2016). The worse news is that because of these behaviors, hearing loss is likely to increase (World Health Organization, 2021). Based on these findings, some researchers have proposed standards for personal listening devices that would limit the volume based on the length of time they are worn (Pienkowski, 2021).

The cumulative effects of noise and normative age-related changes create the most common age-related hearing problem: reduced sensitivity to high-pitched tones, called **presbycusis**, which occurs earlier and more severely than the loss of sensitivity to low-pitched tones (Davis et al., 2016). Research indicates that by the late 70s, roughly half of older adults have presbycusis. Males typically have greater loss than females, but this may be because of differential exposure to noisy environments. Hearing loss usually is gradual at first but accelerates during the 40s, a pattern that is evident in Figure 3.5.

Presbycusis results from four types of changes in the inner ear (Nagaratnam et al., 2016): *sensory*, consisting of atrophy and degeneration of receptor cells; *neural*, consisting of a loss of neurons in the auditory pathway in the brain; *metabolic*, consisting of a diminished supply of nutrients to the cells in the receptor area; and *mechanical*, consisting of atrophy and stiffening of the vibrating structures in the receptor area. Knowing the cause of a person's presbycusis is important, because the different causes have different implications for treatment and for other aspects of hearing (Nagaratnam et al., 2016). Sensory presbycusis has little effect on other hearing abilities. Neural presbycusis seriously affects the ability to understand speech. Metabolic presbycusis produces severe loss of sensitivity to all pitches. Finally, mechanical presbycusis also produces loss across all pitches, but the loss is greatest for high pitches.

Because hearing plays a major role in social communication, its progressive loss could have an equally important effect on people's quality of life (Davis et al., 2016; Liu et al., 2022). Tsimpida and colleagues (2022) found that people with hearing loss were significantly more likely to experience

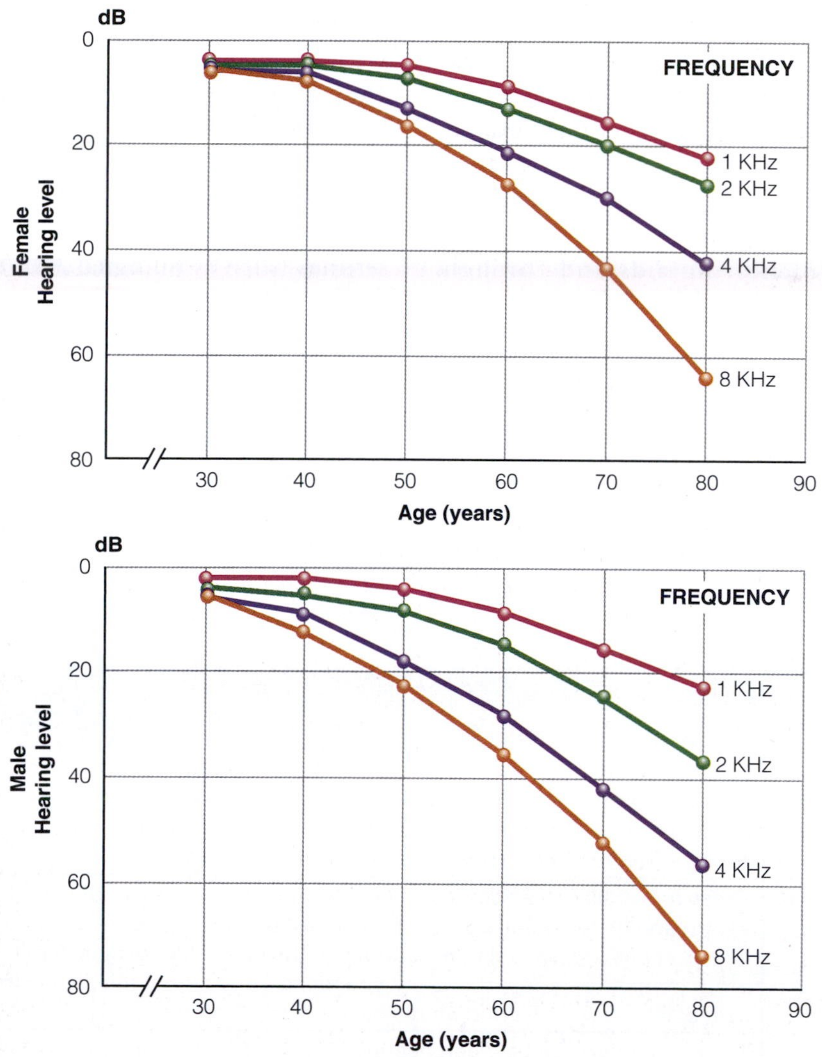

Figure 3.5 Gender differences in hearing loss. Notice that the changes in men are greater.

Source: Ordy, J. M., Brizzee, K. R., Beavers, T. & Medart, P. (1979). Age differences in the functional and structural organization of the auditory system in man. In J. M. Ordy & K. R. Brizzee (eds.), *Sensory Systems and Communication in the Elderly*. Raven Press.

symptoms of depression, especially if they face socio-economic inequalities. People with hearing loss are also more likely to show symptoms of cognitive decline and impairments with daily functioning (Liu et al., 2022).

Loss of hearing in later life can also cause numerous adverse emotional reactions, such as loss of independence, social isolation, irritation, paranoia, and depression (Cherko et al., 2016; Liu et al., 2022; Tsimpida et al., 2022), and is a global problem (World Health Organization, 2021). For example, research notes that people who report significant hearing loss are about 40% more likely to have limited social activity in the last month (Shukla et al., 2021). Much research indicates hearing loss per se does not cause social maladjustment or emotional disturbance.

Friends and relatives of an older person with undiagnosed or untreated hearing loss may think the person in question is demonstrating emotional changes instead of hearing loss, which strains the quality of interpersonal relationships (Li-Korotky, 2012).

Many people with hearing loss can be helped through two types of hearing aids and through cochlear implants. Table 3.3 describes some of the most popular options. Analog hearing aids are the most common and least expensive, but they provide the lowest-quality sound. Digital hearing aids are based on microchips that can be programmed for different hearing situations. Cochlear implants do not amplify sound; rather, a microphone transmits sound to a receiver, which stimulates auditory nerve fibers directly. Although technology continues to improve, none of these devices can duplicate our original equipment, so be kind to your ears. A study in Guatemala documents the power of treating hearing loss; people who were provided with hearing aids reported that their quality of life improved and the number of mental health issues declined significantly (Spreckley et al., 2020). By understanding hearing loss, the problems it causes, and ways to diagnose and treat them, we have a better chance of minimizing the effects of hearing loss on older people's lives.

Individuals who experience total or profound hearing loss earlier in life and who identify as part of the deaf community have much to share with those who experience hearing loss later in life. The deaf community view themselves as a unique cultural and linguistic minority who use sign language as their primary language (National Deaf Center on Postsecondary Outcomes, 2019). Among the values espoused by the deaf community are reliance on eyesight and a visual language and architectural design that facilitates that, use of the sign language of the region and supporting sign language use in educational settings (such as bilingual ASL/English programs in the United States), and the use of technology to overcome traditional communications barriers. Applying these values to situations involving late-life hearing loss go a long way to improving the quality of life for many older adults.

Members of the deaf community have changed the way we think about individuals who are deaf and hard of hearing. The Real People feature highlights two of them: Marlee Matlin and Chella Man.

Table 3.3 Helping People with Hearing Loss

Type of Device	How It Works
Analog hearing aid	Although there are various styles, the basic design is always the same. A mold is placed in the outer ear to pick up sound and send it through a tube to a microphone. The microphone sends the sound to an amplifier. The amplifier enhances the sound and sends it to the receiver. The receiver sends the amplified sound to the ear.
Digital hearing aid	These are similar to analog hearing aids, but digital aids use directional microphones to control the flow of sound. Compression technology allows the sound to be increased or decreased as it rises and falls naturally in the room. Microchips allow hearing aids to be programmed for different hearing situations. This technology also uses multiple channels to deliver sound with varying amplification characteristics.
Cochlear implant	The main difference between hearing aids and cochlear implants is that implants do not make the sound louder. Rather, the implant is a series of components. A microphone, usually mounted behind the ear on the scalp, picks up sound. The sound is digitized by microchips and turned into coded signals, which are broadcast via FM radio signals to electrodes that have been inserted into the inner ear during surgery. The electrodes stimulate the auditory nerve fibers directly.

Real People

Marlee Matlin and Chella Man—Cultural Transformers

Throughout history, deaf individuals have made several of the most important contributions to society. Consider how much different the world would be without Ludwig van Beethoven's music, Helen Keller's writings, or Thomas Edison's inventions. Such contributions continue. Two examples of members of the deaf community who are making a difference are Marlee Matlin and Chella Man.

Marlee Matlin (born 1965) is an actor, writer, and activist who was the first (and still the only) person from the deaf community to win an Academy Award as best actress for her role in *Children of a Lesser God*. She lost all hearing in her right ear and 80% of the hearing in her left ear at the age of 18 months. Marlee began her acting career at age 7 in a production of *The Wizard of Oz* at the International Center on Deafness and the Arts. In addition to her Oscar-winning role, Marlee has appeared in a wide range of productions, from *Sesame Street* to serious drama to interpreting the "Star Spangled Banner" at two Super Bowls. As a leading advocate for actors and others who are deaf, Marlee has testified before the U.S. Senate and promotes accessibility of video and communication devices for people who are deaf. She has received several major awards for her work on inclusion.

Reuters/Alamy Stock Photo

Marlee Matlin

Chella Man (born 1998) is an actor, model, artist, YouTuber, and LGBTQIA+ activist known for sharing his experiences as a trans-masculine, deaf, genderqueer, and Chinese–Jewish person of color. Man began to lose his hearing at four years old; he had cochlear implants placed in both ears by age 16. He is a widely sought speaker on the intersections of art, disability, queerness, race, and healing. Among his many "firsts" are his work as a columnist for Condé Nast's first queer publication *Them*, the launch of a truly inclusive clothing line in collaboration with Opening Ceremony, being signed as the first deaf and trans-masculine model with IMG Models, and being cast as a superhero in DC Universe's digital series *Titans*. Man's creative work and activism keep him at the forefront of several issues relating to inclusion and serve as an example to others.

Y.L. Johns/Prima Fotos/Newscom

Chella Man

Somatosensory System

Imagine that you are locked in an embrace with a romantic partner right now. Think about how good it feels when you are caressed and the tingly sensations you get. The way your lips feel during a passionate kiss.

You can thank your somatosensory system for that; without it, you probably wouldn't bother acting romantic. Remember Bertha, the older woman worried about falling? To maintain her balance and avoid falling, her somatosensory system integrates a great deal of information about her body position.

The somatosensory system is complex. It involves the conscious perception of touch, pressure, pain, temperature, body position, movement, and vibration, which arise from the muscles, joints, skin, and fascia (a thin casing of connective tissue that surrounds and holds every organ, blood vessel, bone, nerve fiber and muscle in place and is as sensitive as skin). It also combines input from many of these sources in order for us to make complex movements, such as maintain our balance. Let's consider some of these in more detail and discover what happens as we age.

As you've probably discovered, a lover's touch feels different on various parts of your body. That's because our skin is a very complicated system of receptors and nerves (Handler & Ginty, 2021). The distribution of touch receptors is not consistent throughout the body; the greatest concentrations are in the lips, tongue, and fingertips—as you likely already had figured out. Also, the skin contains an array of different types of receptors that enable us to sense different types of stimuli (e.g., distinguish a lover's touch from a hot stove). Although it takes more pressure with age to feel a touch on the smooth (nonhairy) skin on the hand, such as the fingertips, touch sensitivity in the hair-covered parts of the body is maintained into later life (Tremblay & Master, 2016).

Accurately determining whether you are too hot, too cold, or just right can be a life-or-death matter, such as when households lose power after a major storm. More older adults die from excessive heat and cold, in part related to their increased trouble regulating body temperature so that they feel comfortable (Guergova & Dufour, 2011). Changes in the perception of temperature are likely caused by aging of the skin and reduction in the number of temperature receptors, as well as possible changes in the peripheral nerves. These changes are greater in the extremities (arms and legs). We will consider other aspects of temperature regulation later in this chapter in our discussion of the autonomic nervous system.

Sensations from the skin, internal organs, joints, and fascia serve additional critical functions. They keep us in contact with our environment, help us keep our balance and avoid falling, help us communicate, keep us safe, and factor into our perception of pain. In terms of self-esteem, how well our body is functioning tells us something about how well we are doing. Losing bodily sensations can have major implications; loss of sexual sensitivity and changes in the ability to regulate one's body temperature affect the quality of life. How a person interprets these changes is critical for maintaining self-esteem. We can help by providing supportive environments that lead to successful compensatory behaviors. Despite years of research, we do not understand how or even whether our ability to perceive these sensations changes with age. Part of the problem has to do with how such sensations are measured and how individual differences in tolerance affects people's reports.

Chronic pain is a condition that affects roughly 50% of all older adults and over 80% of older adults who live in long-term care facilities (Tinnirello et al., 2021). Older adults appear to be more susceptible to prolonged pain development, and medications to address pain are less effective for them. Data indicate that deterioration in the nervous system is likely responsible for these changes, but the lack of age-appropriate standards for measuring pain is a barrier to treatment. In any case, older adults who experience chronic pain show lower scores on tests of cognitive function (Cardoso et al., 2021). This effect of chronic pain could impair the ability to live independently. We will return to the issue of managing pain in Chapter 4.

Bertha, the older woman we met in the vignette, is like many older adults—she is worried about losing her balance and falling. She has good reason to be concerned. Each year, about one in four older adults over age 65 falls (National Council on Aging, 2021). Falls are the leading cause of fatal injury and of nonfatal injuries requiring hospitalization in older adults. Why do so many older adults fall?

Bertha (and each of us) gets information about balance mainly from the vestibular system, housed deep in the inner ear, but vision also provides important cues, as do our muscles and joints (Johnson et al., 2020). All of this information gets integrated in our brain. Importantly, changes in the brain are associated with falling. Changes in white matter in the frontal cortex and in the occipital cortex that occur with age have been shown to be related to difficulty in maintaining proper balance (Nicolini et al., 2021). The importance of white matter in aging was discussed in Chapter 2. Similarly, lower amounts of gray matter at any age are associated with increased risk of falling, leading researchers to conclude that gray matter protects adults from falling (Boisgontier et al., 2016; DiSalvio et al., 2020).

Dizziness (the vague feeling of being unsteady, floating, and light-headed) and vertigo (the sensation that one or one's surroundings are spinning) are common experiences for older adults. Although age-related structural changes in the vestibular system account for some of the problems, they do not entirely account for increases in dizziness and vertigo. Another likely source for dizziness and vertigo is that it takes older adults longer to integrate all the other sensory information coming to the brain to control posture (Aldwin et al., 2018). There are nonphysiological reasons, too—dizziness can be a side effect of certain medications and physical illnesses.

Because of these changes, much research has focused on teaching older adults how to avoid falls (Nicolini et al., 2021). In 2015, the National Council on Aging (2015) revised its program *Falls Free® National Falls Prevention Action Plan* that provides an overview of numerous strategies to lower the risk of falling, such as home modifications and exercise programs. For example, environmental hazards such as loose rugs and slippery floors can be made safer.

Because fear of falling has a real basis, it is important that concerns not be taken lightly (Granacher et al., 2012). Careful assessment of balance is important in understanding the nature and precise source of older adults' problems and should be a part of any comprehensive health screening (Khanal et al., 2021). Indeed, balance training is the most common form of fall prevention intervention and is effective even when implemented at home (Ambrens et al., 2021; Halvarsson et al., 2021). Such training can even be successful using virtual reality (Sadeghi et al., 2021). One of the most popular exercise-based programs that has years of evidence for success is based on tai chi (Holmes et al., 2016; Wang, L-C., et al., 2021).

Taste and Smell

One of the worst side effects of the COVID-19 virus was that many people who became ill from it lost their ability to taste and smell (Maiorano et al., 2022). Not only was this incredibly annoying to affected persons who could no longer enjoy the smells and tastes of foods, but it presented safety threats as well, such as the inability to smell a natural gas leak in their home. Often given short shrift compared with vision and hearing, taste and smell provide some of the strongest associations for memories—consider your favorite holiday foods growing up—and for keeping us safe—consider knowing from the smell whether food is safe or should be discarded. In fact, these two senses, known together as the *chemical senses*, work together, as you have no doubt experienced. For example, if your nose gets stuffy from a cold, you may have noticed that food doesn't taste the same.

Taste. There is an expression "too old to cut the mustard," which dates to when people made mustard at home by grinding mustard seed and adding just the right amount of vinegar ("cutting the mustard") to balance the taste. If too much vinegar was added, the concoction tasted terrible, so the balance was critical. Many families found that older members tended to add too much vinegar.

Despite the everyday belief (and stories like cutting mustard) that taste ability changes with age, we do not have much data documenting what actually happens. We do know that the ability to detect different tastes declines gradually and that these declines vary a great deal from flavor to flavor and person to person (Doets & Kremer, 2016; Spence & Youssef, 2021). This may result in older adults wanting to add more salt or sugar to food and drinks to achieve the flavors they remember. Food preferences also change, influenced mainly by social and psychological factors, such as what others are eating and what is currently fashionable, making it difficult to draw firm conclusions about age-related change. Whatever age differences we observe are not caused by a decline in the sheer number of taste buds (Imoscopi et al., 2012). There is evidence that the ability to taste sour and bitter tastes changes most (thus, the trouble with cutting the mustard), but the physiological reasons for this are not yet understood due to the negative effects on taste from medications and chronic diseases (Sergi et al., 2017).

The influence of disease and medication, combined with the psychosocial aspects of eating, may underlie older adults' complaints about boring food, that in turn may underlie increased risk of malnutrition (Roigk & Graeb, 2021). Due to the serious consequences of malnutrition, numerous programs have been implemented to reduce the risk in older adults (Cederholm & Barazzoni, 2021; Roigk & Graeb, 2021). The Global Leadership Initiative on Malnutrition (GLIM; Cederholm et al., 2019) is a widely implemented set of criteria to diagnose malnutrition in clinical settings. Some key outcomes from research on malnutrition are that we are much more likely to eat a balanced diet and to enjoy our food when we feel well enough to cook, when we do not eat alone, and when we get a whiff of the enticing aromas from the kitchen. Speaking of enticing aromas…

How food tastes is a complex interaction among smell, psychological, and social factors in addition to the basic ability to taste.

Smell

"Those cookies smell delicious!" "Stop and smell the roses." "Ooh! What's that perfume you're wearing?" "Yuck! What's that smell?" There is a great deal of truth in the saying "The nose knows." Smell is a major part of our everyday lives—as those who lost it due to COVID-19 can attest. How something smells can alert us that dinner is cooking, warn of a gas leak or a fire, let us know that we are clean, or indicate that we have stopped to smell the roses. Many of our social interactions involve smell (or the lack of it). We spend billions of dollars making our bodies smell appealing to others. For all of these and thousands of other reasons, it is easy to understand that any age-related change in sense of smell would have far-reaching consequences.

Researchers agree that the ability to detect odors remains fairly intact until the 60s, when it begins to decline, but there are wide variations across people and types of odors (Croy et al., 2014). These variations could have important diagnostic and practical implications. For example, Dan and colleagues (2021) point out that some loss of smell occurs normally with aging, but decline is most prevalent and severe in certain neurogenerative diseases, such as in 90% of people with early-stage Parkinson's disease and 85% of persons with early-stage Alzheimer's disease (both are discussed in Chapter 10). Mastrangelo and colleagues (2021) report loss of smell as one of the key symptoms of COVID-19 infection. These connections to disease have made loss of smell an accepted biomarker for these and other conditions, and testing for loss of smell is now widely used in diagnosing them. Decreases in the ability to smell smoke or the chemicals put in natural gas for this purpose create personal safety risks.

The major psychological consequences of changes in smell concern eating, safety, and pleasurable experiences. Odors play an important role in enjoying food and protecting us from harm. Socially, decreases in our ability to detect unpleasant odors may lead to a risk of consuming spoiled food. Smells also play a key role in remembering life experiences, as noted at the beginning of this discussion. Who can forget the smell of one's favorite cookies baking in the oven? Loss of odor cues may mean that our sense of the past suffers as well.

Adult Development in Action

If you were a consultant asked to design the optimal home environment for older adults, what specific design features would you include that would provide support for normative age-related sensory changes? (Keep your answer and refer to it in Chapter 5.)

Review Questions

3.3 Sensory Systems

- What age-related changes occur in vision? What are the psychological effects of these changes?
- What age-related changes occur in hearing? What are the psychological effects of these changes?
- What age-related changes occur in somesthesia (perception of bodily sensations) and balance? What are the psychological effects of these changes?
- What age-related changes occur in taste and smell? What are the psychological effects of these changes?

3.4 Vital Functions

Key Questions

- What age-related changes occur in the cardiovascular system? What types of cardiovascular disease are common in adult development and aging? What are the psychological effects of age-related changes in the cardiovascular system?
- What structural and functional changes occur with age in the respiratory system? What are the most common types of respiratory diseases in older adults? What are the psychological effects of age-related changes in the respiratory system?

Steve is an active 73-year-old who walks and plays golf regularly. They smoked earlier in life but quit years ago. Healthy eating is not something that occurs consistently; they enjoy red meat and ice cream too much. Steve recently experienced some chest pains and sweating after playing nine holes but dismissed it as simply age related. However, Steve's husband, George, is concerned Steve may have a more serious problem.

It's quite simple—you cannot live without your cardiovascular (heart and blood vessels) and your respiratory (lungs and air passageways) systems; that's why they are called vital functions. Each needs tending to, and undergoes important normative changes with age that can affect the quality of life. In this section, we'll find out whether George has reason to worry about Steve's symptoms. We'll also discover why figuring out the pattern of age-related changes in the respiratory system is very difficult (spoiler alert—it has to do with biological–psychological–environmental interactions).

Overall, the age-related changes in the cardiovascular and respiratory systems are excellent examples of how the forces of development interact. On the biological front, we know that some cardiovascular and respiratory diseases have important genetic links and are grounded in specific physiological changes. Psychologically, certain personality traits have been linked with increased risk of disease. Socioculturally, some cardiovascular and respiratory diseases are clearly tied to lifestyle. The impacts of both cardiovascular and respiratory diseases also differ as a function of age. Let's explore in more detail how these various forces come together.

Cardiovascular System

Tune into your pulse. The beating of your heart is the work of an amazing organ. In an average lifetime, the heart beats more than 3 billion times, pumping the equivalent of more than 900 million gallons of blood. Two important age-related structural changes in the heart are the accumulation of fat deposits and the stiffening of the heart muscle caused by tissue changes. By the late 40s and early 50s, the fat deposits in the lining around the heart may form a continuous sheet. Meanwhile, healthy muscle tissue is being replaced by connective tissue, which causes a thickening and stiffening of the heart muscle and valves. These changes reduce the amount of muscle tissue available to contract the heart. The net effects are that the remaining muscle must work harder. As evidence of this, the amount of blood that the heart can pump declines from roughly 5 liters per minute at age 20 to about 3.5 liters per minute at age 70. Another outcome of age-related change in heart muscle is that the heart cannot beat as fast during times of physical stress as it did when people were younger (but resting pulse rates remain unchanged; National Institute on Aging, 2018). The heart muscle itself becomes discolored with a brown-yellow pigment (called lipofuscin) from the accumulation of oxidized proteins over time; the degree of accumulation of lipofuscin is a good indicator of chronological age but does not cause age-related cardiac disease (Kakimoto et al., 2019).

The most important age-related change in the circulatory system involves the stiffening (hardening) of the walls of the arteries. These changes are caused by calcification of the arterial walls and by replacement of elastic fibers with less elastic ones.

The combination of changes in the heart and the circulatory system results in a significant decrease in a person's ability to cope with physical exertion, especially aerobic exercise. By age 65, the average adult who does not regularly exercise will have experienced a 60 to 70% decline in the aerobic capacity since young adulthood. However, if you stay in good shape throughout adulthood, the decline is much less (National Institute on Aging, 2018). This decline in aerobic capacity, essentially one's reserve for use under exertion, is one reason why older adults who are not in good physical shape are more likely to have heart attacks while performing moderately exerting tasks such as shoveling snow or mowing the lawn. The changes that occur with aging in the heart at rest and when exercising are described in Figure 3.6.

Cardiovascular Diseases. In the United States, nearly half of adults over age 20 currently have some form of cardiovascular disease (defined as coronary heart disease, heart failure, stroke, or hypertension); this rate increases with age in all demographic groups (Virani et al., 2016). It is the leading cause of nonaccidental (and non–COVID-19 related during the pandemic) death in all demographic groups in the United States and in many other countries. The incidence of cardiovascular disease increases dramatically with age, with the rates for males higher for coronary heart disease and for females higher for stroke. The rate of cardiovascular disease in cisgender women and trans women who take hormone treatment before menopause is lower than that for cisgender men and trans men who take hormone treatment; rates for all women increase after menopause and converge with those of men over age 75. Overall, these are deadly

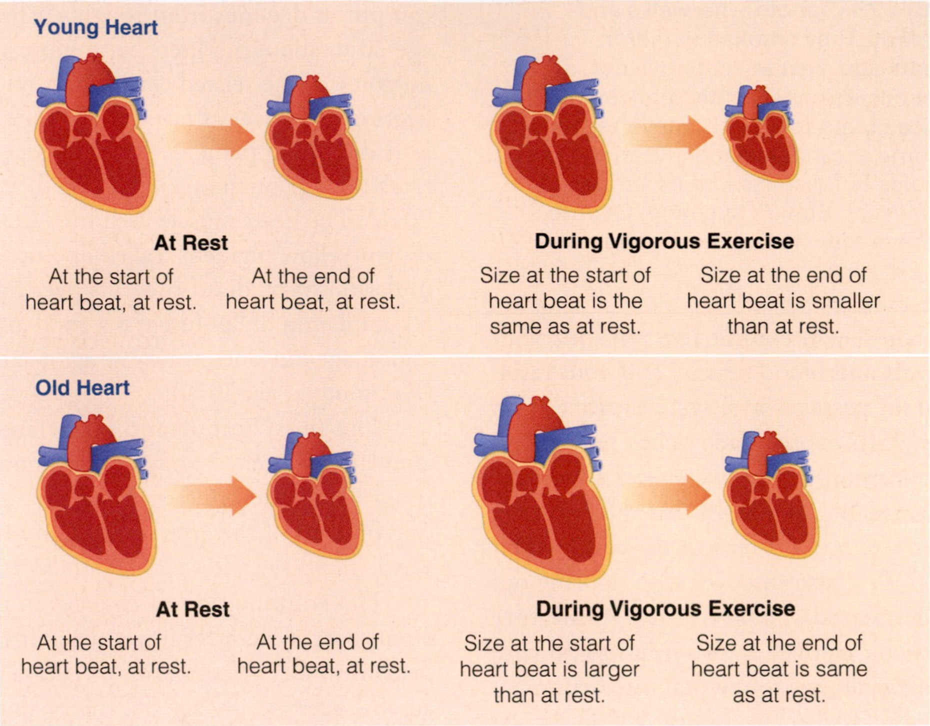
Young Heart
At Rest
At the start of heart beat, at rest.
At the end of heart beat, at rest.
During Vigorous Exercise
Size at the start of heart beat is the same as at rest.
Size at the end of heart beat is smaller than at rest.
Old Heart
At Rest
At the start of heart beat, at rest.
At the end of heart beat, at rest.
During Vigorous Exercise
Size at the start of heart beat is larger than at rest.
Size at the end of heart beat is same as at rest.

Figure 3.6 The Heart: Young and old.

Source: National Institute on Aging. (2008). *Aging Hearts and Arteries: A Scientific Quest*. Design by Levine and Associates, Washington, DC. https://www.nia.nih.gov/health/publication/aging-hearts-and-arteries/preface

statistics. One in every three deaths in the United States is caused by cardiovascular disease.

In terms of racial and ethnic differences in various types of cardiovascular disease, Black individuals, Native Americans, and Native Hawaiians have the highest rates of hypertension (high blood pressure; we will consider this condition a bit later), and Asian Americans have the lowest rate of heart disease (Virani et al., 2021). In part these differences are due to genetics, and in large part they are due to sociocultural effects such as inadequate access to and disparities in health care that impact lifestyle.

The good news is that rates of cardiovascular disease have been declining in the United States, especially among males, since the 1980s (Virani et al., 2021). In part this is due to lower rates of smoking and better nutrition. However, these declines may be deceiving because key risk factors are actually increasing (Virani et al., 2021); for example, roughly 40 percent of adults over age 40 in the United States are classified as obese, and rates of diabetes are increasing as well, both of which are associated with higher risk of cardiovascular disease.

Several types of cardiovascular disease are noteworthy in relation to age. **Congestive heart failure** occurs when cardiac output and the ability of the heart to contract severely decline, making the heart enlarge, pressure in the veins increase, and the body swell. Congestive heart failure is the most common cause of hospitalization for people over age 65. **Angina pectoris** occurs when the oxygen supply to the heart muscle becomes insufficient, resulting in chest pain. Angina may feel like chest pressure, a burning pain, or a squeezing that radiates from the chest to the back, neck, and arms (Mayo Clinic, 2021a). In most cases the pain is induced by physical exertion and is relieved within 5 to 10 minutes by rest. The most common treatment of angina is nitroglycerine, although in some cases coronary arteries may need to be cleared through surgical procedures or replaced through coronary bypass surgery.

Heart attack, called **myocardial infarction (MI)**, occurs when blood supply to the heart is severely reduced or cut off. Mortality after a heart attack is much higher for older adults (Virani et al., 2021). The initial symptoms of an MI may be identical to those of angina but typically are more severe and prolonged; there may also be nausea, vomiting, numbness or severe weakness, back or jaw pain, and sweating, which Steve experienced in the vignette. Thus, George is right to be concerned about Steve's symptoms.

For all people, the most common symptom of MI is chest pain. However, females are more likely to experience other symptoms, such as unusual fatigue; sudden sweating and shortness of breath without exertion; or neck, jaw, or back pain. (Cleveland Clinic, 2019). Treating heart attack victims of all ages includes careful evaluation and a prescribed rehabilitation program consisting of lifestyle changes in diet and exercise.

Atherosclerosis is an age-related disease caused by the buildup of fat deposits on and the calcification of the arterial walls (National Heart, Lung, and Blood Institute, 2021a). A diagram describing how atherosclerosis develops is shown in Figure 3.7. Much like sandbars in a river or mineral deposits in pipes, the fat deposits that develop inside arteries interfere with and restrict blood flow. These deposits begin very early in life and continue throughout the life span. Some amount of fat deposit inevitably occurs and is considered a normal part of aging. However, excess deposits may develop from poor nutrition, smoking, and other lifestyle factors.

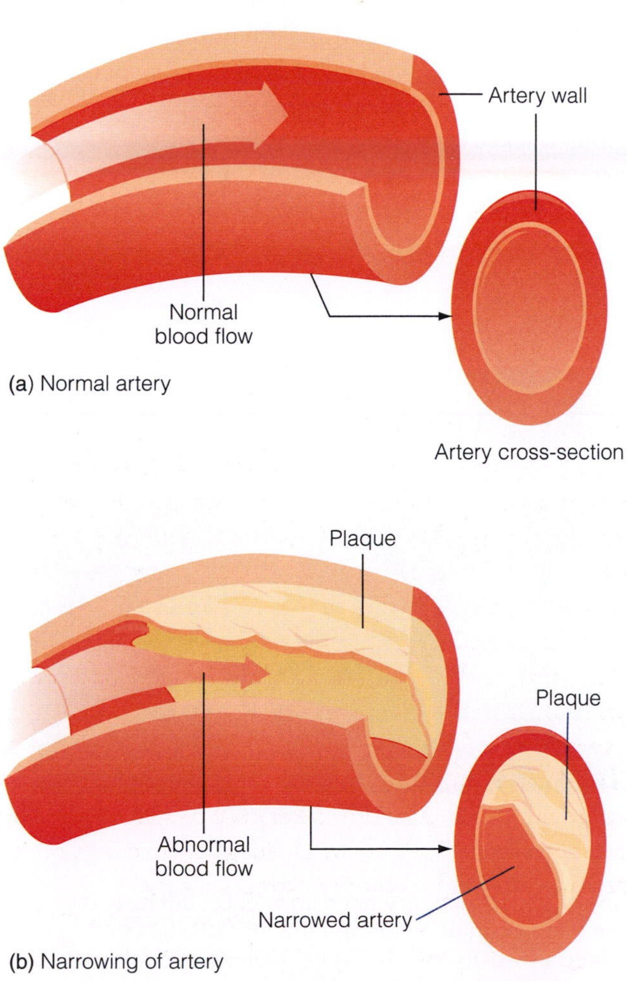

Figure 3.7 Normal artery and atherosclerosis. (A) shows a normal artery with normal blood flow. (B) shows an artery with plaque buildup.

Source: National Heart, Lung, and Blood Institute (2011). https://www.nhlbi.nih.gov/health/health-topics/topics/atherosclerosis/

When severe atherosclerosis occurs in blood vessels that supply the brain, neurons may not receive proper nourishment, causing them to malfunction or die, a condition called cerebrovascular disease. When the blood flow to a portion of the brain is completely cut off, a **cerebrovascular accident (CVA)**, or stroke, results. Estimates are that someone in the United States dies from a CVA every four minutes, making stroke one of the most common forms of cardiovascular disease (Centers for Disease Control and Prevention, 2021a). Causes of CVAs include clots that block blood flow in an artery or the actual breaking of a blood vessel, which creates a cerebral hemorrhage.

The severity of a CVA and likelihood of recovery depend on the specific area of the brain involved, the extent of disruption in blood flow, and the duration of the disruption. Consequently, a CVA may affect such a small area that it goes almost unnoticed, or it may be so severe as to cause immediate death. Two common problems following a CVA are *aphasia* (problems with speech) and *hemiplegia* (paralysis on one side of the body).

The risk of a CVA increases with age and is much more common among Black individuals, Native Americans, and Alaska Natives than for other groups (Centers for Disease Control and Prevention, 2021a). The higher risk among these three groups appears to be caused by a greater prevalence of hypertension in this population compounded by disparities in access to health care in general and disparities in the quality of treatment (Centers for Disease Control and Prevention, 2021a).

Medical treatment of CVA caused by clots has advanced significantly. The most important advance in pharmacological treatment is the clot-dissolving drug tissue plasminogen activator (r-tPA, known as alteplase) (American Stroke Association, 2018). Currently, r-tPA is the only approved pharmacological treatment for CVAs caused by blood clots, which constitute 80% of all CVAs. Not every patient should receive r-tPA treatment, and r-tPA is effective only if given promptly, which is vitally important. So if you or a person you know thinks they are experiencing a CVA, get medical attention immediately, because r-tPA therapy must be started within 3 hours after the onset of a stroke to be most effective.

A second treatment for stroke caused by a clot blocking a large blood vessel is surgical removal of the clot, a procedure called mechanical thrombectomy (Shakir & Levy, 2022). However, this technique is very difficult under the best circumstances and works best when performed within six hours of initial symptoms. It should also include use of r-tPA.

CVAs caused by hemorrhages may be treatable depending on the extent of the bleeding and cause (e.g., an aneurism (a ballooning and weakening of a vessel) or an abnormal growth of blood vessels). In some cases, surgery may be possible (American Stroke Association, 2021).

Recovery from CVA depends on the severity of the stroke, area and extent of the brain affected, and patient age. It can be a long, difficult process, as described in the Real People feature about Dr. Jill Bolte Taylor.

High blood pressure is the most common form of cardiovascular disease, and is a major factor in other types (Virani et al., 2021). Blood pressure consists of measuring two types of pressure: the pressure during the heart's contraction phase when it is pumping blood through the body, called the *systolic pressure*, and the pressure during the heart's relaxation phase between beats, called the *diastolic pressure*. The systolic pressure is always given first. On average, a blood pressure of 120 over 80 mm Hg (millimeters of mercury, the scale on which the pressure is measured) or a bit lower is considered optimal for adults. Do you know what yours is?

As we grow older, blood pressure tends to increase, mostly because of structural changes in the cardiovascular system, especially the stiffening of blood vessels. **When blood pressure increases become severe, defined as 130 mm Hg or more systolic pressure (the top number in a blood pressure reading) or 80 mm Hg or more diastolic pressure (the lower number in the reading), the disease hypertension results** (National Heart, Lung, and Blood Institute, 2020). Under these criteria, about 52 percent of males and 43 percent of females aged 20 and older have hypertension (Virani et al., 2021). These rates vary by race and ethnicity. Black Americans have one of the highest prevalence rates of hypertension in the world at about 56% for Black males and females. In contrast, the rates for Mexican America females is the lowest of any group tracked by the federal government.

Real People

Dr. Jill Bolte Taylor: *My Stroke of Insight*

Dr. Jill Bolte Taylor had a goal—to understand why she was able to distinguish her dreams during sleep, for instance, from reality whereas her brother could not (so experienced delusions). So she studied and specialized in neuroanatomy. On December 10, 1996, at age 37, she was working in a research lab in Boston focusing on how brain cells communicate when a blood vessel on the left side of her brain burst, causing a hemorrhage. She had the knowledge and experience of her brain beginning to shut down. Four hours later, she could not speak, read, walk, write, or remember anything from her past.

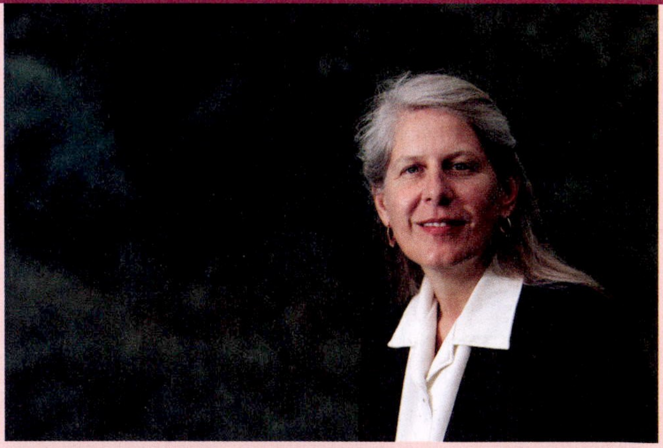

AJ Mast/The New York Times/Redux

Dr. Jill Bolte Taylor

Over the next eight years, Dr. Jill worked diligently through a very difficult rehabilitation program. Over that period, she was able to completely and successfully rebuild and reprogram her brain to recover all her thinking, emotional, and physical abilities. She describes what this entailed in her 2008 best-selling memoir *My Stroke of Insight: A Brain Scientist's Personal Journey*, which remains one of the best books about recovery from stroke. Dr. Jill has the distinction of delivering the first TED talk to ever go viral; to date, it has been viewed roughly 30 million times. As a result of her experience, Dr. Jill has continued to dedicate her career to helping people better understand their brain and recover from neurological trauma.

Hypertension is a disease you ignore at the risk of greatly increasing your chances of dying. Older adults with hypertension have three times the risk of dying from cardiovascular disease, and it has important negative effects on cognitive abilities and a host of other organs including kidney function (National Heart, Lung, and Blood Institute, 2020). Because hypertension is a disease with no clear symptoms, most people with undiagnosed hypertension are not aware they have a problem until they are diagnosed with it. This means, of course, that part of the issue with racial and ethnic differences in hypertension derives from healthcare disparities and the lack of access to care. This disparity matters. Regular blood pressure monitoring is the only sure way to find out whether you have and can control hypertension. It could save your life.

Another chronic cardiovascular condition that is discussed less often is *hypotension*, or low blood pressure (National Heart, Lung, and Blood Institute, 2021b). Hypotension is defined as blood pressure lower than 90/60. Symptoms of hypotension include dizziness or light-headedness that is caused most commonly when you stand up quickly after lying down or sitting, or sometimes after. Hypotension often is related to anemia and is more common in older adults. Although hypotension per se is not a dangerous condition, the resulting dizziness and other symptoms can increase the likelihood of fainting and falls, which may result in more serious injury.

Before we leave the topic of cardiovascular disease, it is important to note that diagnosing and treating these disorders is increasingly considering telemedicine, rather than visits to health centers, as a method of choice. Telemedicine involves a range of technology-mediated processes from videoconference to remote data collection to apps on one's phone or watch. The COVID-19 pandemic provided a good opportunity to study the relative merits and challenges of telemedicine. As reported in the How Do We Know? feature, Brown and colleagues (2021) note that the success of telemedicine varies significantly across sociodemographic groups, so we must be careful about how technology-based medical diagnostics and treatment are implemented.

Respiratory System

You probably don't pay much attention to your breathing unless you're gasping for breath after vigorous exercise or you have a respiratory disease—or you're an older adult. Older adults tend to notice their breathing a great deal more. Why? With increasing age, the rib cage and the air passageways become stiffer, making it harder to breathe.

Lots of changes also occur in the lungs to cause shortness of breath (American Lung Association, 2021a; Schneider et al., 2021). They change color over time, going gradually from their youthful pinkish to a dreary gray, caused mainly by breathing in carbon particles (from air pollution). Inside each lung are roughly 2,400 kilometers (about 1,491 miles) of airway and between 300 and 500 million air sacs where oxygen is taken in and carbon dioxide is exhaled. With increasing age, the air sacs deteriorate (American Lung Association, 2020a; Schneider et al., 2021). The maximum amount of air we can take into the lungs in a single breath begins to decline in the 20s, decreasing by 40% by age 85. The rate at which we can exchange oxygen for carbon dioxide also drops significantly as the membranes of the air sacs in the lungs deteriorate.

One of the difficulties in understanding age-related changes in the respiratory system is that it is hard to know how much of the change is caused specifically by normative developmental factors and how much is caused by environmental factors. For example, it is difficult to determine how much age-related change in respiratory function is due to air pollution and how much is due to the processes underlying aging. As a result, the significant sociocultural disparities in lung health are highly correlated with the conditions in which people live, making it the case that until these differences are addressed, people who live in environmentally stressed neighborhoods (e.g., with high levels of poor air quality) will have significantly higher rates of respiratory difficulties.

Respiratory Diseases. The most common and incapacitating respiratory disorder in older adults is **chronic obstructive pulmonary disease (COPD)**, a family of diseases that includes chronic bronchitis and emphysema. COPD is the third-leading cause of death by disease in the United States. Over 16 million people have been diagnosed with COPD, but millions more may have it and not know it. Both the rates of COPD and deaths from it are higher in females than in males; in part this is due to females' lungs being smaller and more susceptible to damage from smoking and pollutants, possibly due in turn to estrogen playing a role in lung disease. Smoking is the most important cause of COPD, but secondhand smoke, air pollution, and industrial dusts and chemicals can also cause it (American Lung Association, 2021b).

Emphysema is the most serious type of COPD and is characterized by the destruction of the membranes around the air sacs in the lungs (Schneider et al., 2021).

How Do We Know?

Sociodemographic Factors in Using Telemedicine for Cardiovascular Disease

Who were the investigators, and what were the aims of the studies? The use of telemedicine increased rapidly during the COVID-19 pandemic due to the changing protocols for in-person visits relating to COVID-19 spread. As potentially useful as phone apps and remote sensing software are, however, concern over access to telemedicine raised questions about possible disparities based on sociodemographic factors such as age, financial status, race, and ethnicity. To investigate this concern, Kemar Brown and several colleagues (2021) systematically tracked ambulatory cardiovascular patients' use of in-person and telemedicine options for a specified period during the COVID-19 pandemic.

How did the investigators measure the topic of interest? Sociodemographic characteristics measured included age, gender, race, ethnicity, preferred language, insurance type/primary payor (private insurance or public insurance [Medicare, Medicaid]), enrollment in the online patient portal, and zip-code-linked median household income (MHI). Cardiovascular conditions noted from patient records included atrial fibrillation/atrial flutter, coronary artery disease (CAD), congenital heart disease, diabetes, hyperlipidaemia, hypertension, systolic and diastolic heart failure (HF), obesity, history of COVID-19 infection, substance use disorder, alcohol use disorder, and tobacco use.

Who were the participants in the study? Participants were all adult ambulatory patients (aged 18 years or older) who completed at least one outpatient cardiology encounter, either in-person, by video telemedicine, or by phone telemedicine, at the Massachusetts General Hospital (MGH) in Boston, Massachusetts, during the initial peak of the COVID-19 pandemic between March 16 and June 19, 2020. Patients who missed or cancelled visits during this period were excluded.

What was the design of the study? This period was defined as coinciding with the Commonwealth of Massachusetts State of Emergency declaration on March 10, 2020, local stay-at-home orders, and the transition of routine healthcare services to telemedicine starting on March 15, 2020. For baseline comparison purposes, the researchers also identified all outpatient cardiovascular visits performed during an identical timeframe 1 year prior (March 16, 2019, to June 19, 2019) to determine whether there were significant changes in the demographics of the patients encountered and to establish a baseline comparator.

Were there ethical concerns with the study? Healthcare providers are required by law to obtain permission to examine, assess, and treat people who present themselves for evaluation. Those procedures were followed here. Additionally, any identifying information was removed from records prior to their review for inclusion in the study.

What were the results? A total of 8,446 ambulatory cardiology patient encounters were assessed during the height of the COVID-19 pandemic in Massachusetts state (March 16–June 19, 2020). Of the 8,446 patients, 86% were non-Hispanic (NH) Whites, 58% of all participants were male, and the overall median age was 66.9. A majority engaged through phone telemedicine ($n = 4{,}981$, 61.5%) and video telemedicine ($n = 2{,}693$, 33.2%). There was a substantial increase in telemedicine encounters (60% phone, 35% video, 5% in-person visit) in 2020 compared to a similar time frame in 2019. By comparison, between March 16 and June 19, 2019 there were 14,428 ambulatory cardiology patient encounters with more than 99% of patients seen in-person and only 48 total telemedicine visits. Of all patients seen in 2020, there were no differences in the sex, age, racial/ethnic demographics, primary language, or insurance type/primary payor when compared with those who engaged in traditional in-person ambulatory cardiovascular care in 2019.

Use of telemedicine video visits were significantly lower among NH Black patients and Hispanic patients than among NH-White patients, and among those on public insurance (Medicare or Medicaid). The likelihood of a telemedicine video encounter in patients over age 85 years was significantly lower when compared with patients less than 65 years of age; overall, video use increased with lower patient age. Video telemedicine use increased with median household income. Additionally, patients over age 85 (regardless of race and ethnicity), patients of Hispanic ethnicity, non-Hispanic Black race, non-English preferred language, holders of Medicare insurance, holders of Medicaid insurance, and those with median household income under $75,000 were less likely to be enrolled in the patient portal.

Finally, patients with heart failure were less likely to use video telemedicine.

What did the investigators conclude? Results show that structural inequities in access to telemedicine care disparately impacts cardiovascular patients based on socioeconomic, demographic, and clinical factors. The researchers found that older people (particularly those over age 85), non-Hispanic Blacks, Hispanics, those with low median household income, and those with public insurance were less likely to use video telemedicine. Older adult patients were found to have decreased access to telemedicine video visits during the COVID-19 pandemic but increased likelihood of telemedicine phone visits in patients older than 75 years. Although socioeconomic status may contribute to lack of device ownership and broadband access, lack of digital literacy and hesitancy to adopt new health technology due to insufficient dexterity in the hands and fingers, visual impairment, and cognitive impairment may also contribute to decreased telemedicine utilization among older adults. Because a high percentage of cardiovascular patients fall in this age range and among Black and Hispanic adults, these barriers raise much concern. Furthermore, the association between healthcare disparities and social determinants of health have been heightened by the disproportionate impact of COVID-19 on Black and Hispanic communities. To this end, socioeconomic status may serve as a more significant driver of reduced access to health technology, reduced engagement in telemedicine, and poor adoption of digital health among non-Hispanic Black and Hispanic patients.

This irreversible destruction creates holes in the lung, drastically reducing the ability to exchange oxygen and carbon dioxide. To make matters worse, the bronchial tubes collapse prematurely when the person exhales, thereby preventing the lungs from emptying completely.

Clearly, emphysema is a very debilitating disease. In its later stages, even the smallest physical exertion causes a struggle for air. People with emphysema may have such poorly oxygenated blood that they become confused and disoriented. Many cases of emphysema are self-induced by smoking or caused by other forms of pollution; the remaining cases are caused by a genetic deficiency of a protein known as a 1-antitrypsin (Schneider et al., 2021). This protein, a natural lung protector, is made by the liver; when it is missing, emphysema is inevitable. Although some medications are available to help ease breathing and prevent additional damage, lung transplantation remains the primary treatment for people with emphysema, especially in the genetic form of the disease. Research on alternatives regarding the genetic type of emphysema is focusing on gene therapy, but much work remains to be done (Schneider et al., 2021).

Chronic bronchitis, another form of COPD, can occur at any age, but it is more common in people over age 45, especially among people who are exposed to high concentrations of dust, irritating fumes, and air pollution. Treatment usually consists of medication (called bronchodilators) to open bronchial passages and a change of work environment. Similarly, asthma is another very common respiratory disease that is increasing in prevalence. Treatment for asthma also involves the use of bronchodilators.

Researchers are gathering evidence that e-cigarettes can at least damage the lungs and possibly result in COPD. Research at Johns Hopkins (2020) indicates that vaping increases the risk of asthma and COPD. Far from being benign, vaping is turning out to be a harmful habit.

Overall, treatment for COPD needs to begin as soon as a problem is diagnosed. Thus, a major problem for many is that the lack of access to health care means respiratory diseases remain undiagnosed and untreated. Separately, the most important step is to stop smoking if you are a smoker. In some cases, supplemental oxygen or glucocorticosteroid medications may provide some relief. The thing to remember, though, is that the damage to the lungs caused by COPD is irreversible.

Adult Development in Action

If you ran a training program for personal exercise trainers, what age-related changes in vital functions would you emphasize?

Review Questions

3.4 Vital Functions

- What changes occur with age in the cardiovascular system?
- What gender differences have been noted?
- Which cardiovascular diseases increase in frequency with age?
- What changes occur with age in the respiratory system?
- What are common respiratory diseases, and how are they related to age?

3.5 The Reproductive System

Key Questions

- What reproductive changes occur in women?
- What reproductive changes occur in men?
- What are the psychological effects of reproductive changes?

Helen woke up in the middle of the night drenched in sweat. She'd been feeling fine when she went to bed after her 48th birthday party, so she wasn't sure what was the matter. She thought she was too young to experience menopause. Helen wonders what other things she'll experience.

As you probably surmised, Helen has begun going through a time of life that some look forward to, some experience as loss, and some consider the beginning of old age. For women like Helen and transgender males who have not undergone gender-affirming interventions, this time is considered the defining physiological (and perhaps psychological) event in middle age. Men and transgender women who have not undergone gender-affirming interventions do not endure such sweeping biological changes, but rather experience several gradual changes instead. Beyond the physiological effects, these changes related to reproduction have important psychological implications because many people use them as a trigger for redefining themselves. Let's learn how the experiences unfold.

Biological Female Reproductive System

As Helen is beginning to experience, the major reproductive change in women and transgender males who have not undergone gender-affirming interventions during adulthood is the loss of the natural ability to bear children. This is obviously not the same as engaging in an active sex life. If you watched any television recently, you undoubtedly saw programs and advertisements showing middle-aged and older couples who clearly have active sex lives. Couples can and often do have sexual relationships that are thriving and based on a newfound or re-found respect and love for each other, and that are good for mental and physical health (Belsky, 2007; Gianotten, 2021).

Middle age brings changes to the reproductive system (Fisher et al., 2020) that affect sexual activity and childbearing. These changes are more significant for women and transgender males who have not undergone gender-affirming interventions, but males and transgender women who have not undergone gender-affirming interventions also experience certain changes. Let's discover what they are and how people learn to cope with them.

As biological females (cisgender women or trans men who have not undergone gender-confirming interventions) enter midlife, they experience a major biological process called the **climacteric**, during which they pass from their reproductive to nonreproductive years. **Menopause** is the point during the climacteric at which menstruation stops and is officially determined after periods have stopped for 12 consecutive months (Mayo Clinic, 2020a). Biological males (either cisgender men or trans women who have not undergone gender confirming interventions) do not have such sweeping biological changes but instead experience several gradual ones. These changes have important psychological implications because midlife is thought by many to be a key time for people to redefine themselves, an issue we will examine in Chapter 9. For example, some females view the climacteric as marking the loss of the ability to have children, whereas others view it as a liberating change because they no longer need to worry about getting pregnant.

The major reproductive change in biological females during adulthood is the loss of the natural ability to bear children. (Pregnancy and childbirth are still possible, though, through medical intervention, such as in vitro fertilization and implantation in the uterus.) This change typically begins in the 40s as menstrual cycles become irregular, and by age 50 to 55 it is usually complete; in the United States, the average age at menopause is 51 (Mayo Clinic, 2020a). This time of transition from regular menstruation to menopause is called **perimenopause**, and how long it lasts varies considerably. The gradual loss and eventual end of monthly menstruation is accompanied by decreases in estrogen and progesterone levels, changes in the reproductive organs, and changes in sexual functioning.

A variety of physical and psychological symptoms may accompany perimenopause and menopause with decreases in hormonal levels (WomensHealth.gov, 2019): hot flashes, night sweats, headaches, sleep problems, mood changes, more urinary infections, pain during sex, difficulty concentrating, vaginal dryness, less interest in sex, and an increase in body fat around the waist. Many individuals report no symptoms at all, but most experience at least some, and there are large differences across social, ethnic, and cultural groups in how they are expressed (Olajubu et al., 2017; Yazdkhasti et al., 2019). For example, females in the Mayan culture of Mexico and Central America welcome menopause and its changes as a natural phenomenon and do not attach any stigma to aging (Mahady et al., 2008). In the United States, Latina and African American biological females tend to view menopause more positively, whereas White biological females tend to describe it more negatively (Dillaway et al., 2008; Espinola et al., 2017). Individuals in South American countries report a variety of symptoms that impair quality of life, many of which persisted five years beyond menopause (Blümel et al., 2012).

The decline in estrogen that people experience after menopause is important. Estrogen loss is related to risk of numerous health conditions, including osteoporosis, cardiovascular disease, weight gain, and memory loss, in short, affecting almost every major body system. Consider cardiovascular disease, discussed earlier in this chapter (Mayo Clinic, 2020a). Prior to menopause, biological females have three times less risk of heart attacks than biological males on average. Ten years after menopause, when biological females are about 60, their risk equals that of biological males. Clearly, estrogen depletion has certain negative effects on health.

Estrogen depletion has been the focus of considerable research related to disruptions in cognitive function, colloquially called "brain fog," that is similar to the cognitive complaints from people being treated for breast cancer or prostate cancer (Brody, 2018), and in some cases in long-term aftereffects from having COVID-19. Complaints from menopausal individuals include problems with memory, organizing tasks, keeping track of things, goal setting, and making and implementing plans (Gayatri, 2018). Fortunately, longitudinal research indicates that these cognitive effects usually dissipate within a year or so after menopause (Santoro et al., 2021).

In response to these increased risks and to the estrogen-depletion-related postmenopausal symptoms, one approach is the use of **menopausal hormone therapy (MHT)**, low doses of estrogen that are often combined with progestin (synthetic form of progesterone). MHT has been controversial and the focus of many research studies with conflicting results over decades (Manson et al., 2017). However, there is consensus from the North American Menopausal Society, the American Society for Reproductive Medicine, and the Endocrine Society that MHT can be used effectively to alleviate menopausal symptoms (North American Menopause Society, 2021).

Rido/Shutterstock.com

Many middle-aged and older adults continue to enjoy active sex lives.

The genital organs undergo progressive changes after menopause. The vaginal walls shrink and become thinner, the size of the vagina decreases, vaginal lubrication is reduced and delayed, and the external genitalia shrink somewhat. These changes can have important effects on sexual activity, such as an increased possibility of painful intercourse and the need for more time and more stimulation to reach orgasm. Failure to achieve orgasm becomes more common in midlife and beyond. However, maintaining an active sex life throughout adulthood lowers the degree to which these changes are encountered. Even with these changes, there is no physiological reason not to continue having an active and enjoyable sex life from middle age through late life. The vaginal dryness that occurs, for example, can be countered by using personal lubricants, such as K-Y.

Whether people continue to have an active sex life is not related to desire for sexual relations. This is especially true for older biological females. Surveys consistently show that older married heterosexual females, for instance, are far more likely to have an active sex life than their unmarried counterparts; the difference is the availability (or lack thereof) of a consensual and willing partner, not a lack of physical ability or desire (AARP, 1999, 2005, 2010, 2015, 2018).

Biological Male Reproductive System

Unlike biological females, biological males (cisgender men and trans women who have not undergone gender-affirming interventions) do not have a major physiological (or cultural) event to mark reproductive changes (Fisher et al., 2020). Biological males experience a gradual decline in testosterone levels that can occur to a greater extent in those who are obese or have diabetes. Most do not experience a complete loss of fertility, as this varies widely from individual to individual, but do experience a normative decline in the quantity of sperm. However, even at age 80 fertility on average is still half of what it was at age 25. A concerning note, though, is that a significant overall decline in the quality of sperm has been found in both humans and other animals over the past several decades (Kristof, 2021). Additionally, researchers have documented a roughly 60% decline in human sperm count since the early 1970s. Although many scientists suspect that the rapid increase in now-ubiquitous chemicals called endocrine disruptors that mimic our body's hormones and thus fool our cells are to blame, much still needs to be learned. To be sure, the decline in sperm quality has clear negative implications for fertility and reproduction.

With increasing age, the prostate gland enlarges, becomes stiffer, and may obstruct the urinary tract and create difficulties with urination. Prostate cancer becomes a real threat during middle age; annual screenings are often recommended for those over age 50 (American Cancer Society, 2021a).

Biological males experience some physiological changes in sexual performance. By old age, they report a need for longer time and more stimulation to achieve erection and orgasm, less perceived demand to ejaculate, and a much longer resolution phase during which erection is impossible (Fisher et al., 2020). They also report more frequent failures to achieve orgasm and loss of erection during intercourse. However, the advent of medications to treat erectile dysfunction has provided easy-to-use treatments and the possibility of an active sex life well into later life.

Many biological males experience Peyronie's disease, an age-related condition in which scar tissue that develops in the penis causes it to become bent during an erection (Mayo Clinic, 2020b). The cause of Peyronie's disease is usually unknown, although individuals with Dupuytren's contracture (a cord-like thickening across the palm of the hand that causes the fingers to pull inward) have a higher risk. Peyronie's disease can cause painful erections and difficulty with intercourse.

As with biological females, the most important ingredients for an active and enjoyable sex life is the availability of a consensual and willing partner (AARP, 1999, 2005, 2010, 2015, 2018). Practicing safe sex is equally important for older adults, as sexually transmitted disease remains a major concern.

Adult Development in Action

As a gerontologist, what do you think should be done to create a more realistic view of reproductive changes and interest in sex across the adult lifespan?

Review Questions

3.5 The Reproductive System

- What age-related changes occur in females' reproductive system?
- What age-related changes occur in males' reproductive system?
- How does interest in sexual activity change with age? What forces operate in this domain?

3.6 The Autonomic Nervous System

Key Questions

- What major changes occur in the autonomic nervous system?
- What are the psychological effects of changes in the autonomic nervous system?

Jorge is an active 83-year-old former factory worker who lives with his wife, Olivia, in a crowded apartment in Phoenix. Over the past few years, Jorge has had increasing difficulty handling the heat of Arizona summers. Olivia has noticed that Jorge takes more naps during the day and sleeps poorly at night. Jorge and Olivia wonder whether there is something wrong with him.

Olivia is noticing that Jorge is having increasing difficulty dealing with extreme heat as he ages. Sensing and reacting to temperature shifts changes, as we noted earlier in the chapter. In this module, we explore why this and other changes happen in the first place. We build in the changes in the brain and central nervous system we explored in Chapter 2 and turn our attention to the autonomic nervous system. The **autonomic nervous system** consists of the nerves in the body outside the brain and spinal column. Jorge's experiences are related to changes in the autonomic nervous system; we'll discover whether Jorge's problems are normative.

Autonomic Nervous System

Do you feel hot or cold right now? Do your palms sweat when you get nervous? What happens when you get frightened? These and other regulation functions in your body are controlled by the autonomic nervous system. Fortunately, few changes occur in the autonomic nervous system as we age, but two changes that do occur matter to health and quality of life: disruptions in body temperature control and sleep. Jorge, whom we met in the vignette, is experiencing both of these changes.

Regulating Body Temperature. Every year, newscasts around the world report that during very cold or very hot spells more older adults die than people in other age groups. Why does this happen? We considered evidence earlier in this chapter that cold and warm temperature thresholds may change little with age. If older people can feel cold and warm stimuli placed against them about as well as people of other age groups, what accounts for these deaths?

It turns out that older adults have difficulty determining that their core body temperature is low (Blatteis, 2012). In other words, older people are much less likely to notice that they are cold. Regulating body temperature involves nearly all body systems, most of which undergo declines with age. Because some of them respond to training (e.g., fitness training can help with declines in the musculoskeletal system), some causes of the declines can be addressed. However, changes in the skin and metabolic systems are inevitable. To make matters worse, older adults also have slower vasoconstrictor response, which is the ability to raise core body temperature (i.e., warm up) when the body's peripheral temperature drops (Blatteis, 2012; Liao & Jan, 2016).

Similarly, older adults have trouble responding to high heat because they do not sweat as much, especially in their lower extremities (Coull et al., 2021). These changes mean that older adults have less ability to lower their body temperature, resulting in higher risk of heat-related health issues (e.g., heat stroke).

Lisa F. Young/Shutterstock.com

Older people are less able to regulate their core body temperature because they have more difficulty noticing they are too cold or too hot.

Taken together, the difficulties older adults have in regulating body temperature in extreme cold and heat are the primary reason why older adults are much more susceptible to hypothermia (body temperature below 95°F over a long period) and hyperthermia (body temperature above 98.6°F that cannot be relieved by sweating) (Blatteis, 2012; Coull et al., 2021; Liao & Jan, 2016). This is why social service agencies are especially mindful of older adults during major weather events due to their higher mortality rates at such times.

Sleep and Aging

How did you sleep last night? If you are older, chances are that you had some trouble. In fact, sleep complaints and problems are common in all adult age groups, but older adults report them the most (Steele et al., 2021). These complaints usually concern difficulty in falling asleep, frequent or prolonged awakenings during the night, frequently feeling the need to go to the bathroom, early morning awakenings, and a feeling of not sleeping very well. Effects of poor sleep are experienced the next day; moodiness, poorer performance on tasks involving sustained concentration, fatigue, and lack of motivation are some of the telltale signs.

Nearly every aspect of sleep undergoes age-related changes (Gorgoni & De Gennaro, 2021). It takes older adults longer to fall asleep, they are awake more at night, they are more easily awakened, and they experience major shifts in their sleep–wake cycles, called circadian rhythms. Across adulthood, circadian rhythms move from a two-phase pattern of sleep (awake during the day and asleep at night for most people) to a multiphase rhythm reminiscent of that of infants (daytime napping and shorter sleep cycles at night). These changes are related to the changes in regulating core body temperature discussed in the previous section. Other major causes of sleep disturbance include sleep apnea (stopping breathing for 5 to 10 seconds), periodic leg jerks, heartburn, frequent need to urinate, poor physical health, and depression.

Older adults try lots of things to help themselves, such as taking daytime naps. In a study of older adults living in the Mediterranean region who took midday naps, Foscolou and colleagues (2021) reported that nappers had higher scores on the Successful Aging Index and were more physically active overall; these findings were especially prominent for male nappers over age 80.

Many older adults are prescribed sleeping pills or hypnotic sedatives to help them sleep. But these medications must be used with great caution with older adults, and often do not help alleviate the problem in any case. Among the most effective treatments of sleep problems are increasing physical exercise, reducing caffeine intake, avoiding daytime naps, and making sure that the sleeping environment is as quiet and dark as possible (Boswell et al., 2015).

Research evidence also points to difficulties in regulating the optimal body temperature for good sleep that may also be part of the issue for older adults (Gorgoni & De Gennaro, 2021). Interestingly, this problem may in turn be related to changes in the frontal cortex, a key part of the brain that is involved in evaluating comfort. As we noted in Chapter 2, this part of the brain is involved in numerous age-related changes. Whether interventions that are aimed at helping insomniacs find their optimal body temperature for sleeping will alleviate sleep difficulties remains to be seen.

As we now know, Jorge's difficulty with heat and sleep reflect normative changes that occur with age. Olivia should be informed of these changes and encouraged to make sure Jorge drinks plenty of water and adopts good sleep habits.

Psychological Implications

Being able to maintain proper body temperature can literally be a matter of life and death. So the increased difficulty in doing that poses a real threat to older adults. Being in an environment that provides external means of temperature regulation (i.e., heating and air conditioning) and that has back-up systems in the event of emergency (e.g., generators in the event of power failures) is much more important for older adults.

Because thermoregulation involves so many of the body's systems, and because many of the age-related changes that occur are inevitable, it is important to focus on those systems that respond to intervention. By doing whatever is possible to keep those systems functioning as well as possible, people can lessen the overall problem of regulating body temperature.

A good night's sleep is also important for maintaining good overall health. By ensuring that the sleep environment is maximally conducive to sleeping and providing whatever environmental supports possible, we can increase the odds of improving sleep.

Adult Development in Action

What would be the best questions to ask an older adult client if you, as a social worker, were establishing whether the client had any problems with tolerating heat/cold or sleeping?

Review Questions

3.6 The Autonomic Nervous System

- What changes occur in people's ability to regulate body temperature?
- How does sleep change with age?

Social Policy Implications

Preventing Falls

No one wants to fall and get hurt. That's true in any age group, but especially so with older adults, particularly older adults who live alone. The fear of falling is real and even has been used as the basis for ads for emergency alert systems: An older woman is shown falling and saying, "I've fallen, and I can't get up."

Because of normative age-related changes in vision, hearing, balance, musculoskeletal system, and other aspects of functioning, the risk of falling increases with age. As noted in Figure 3.8, risk of falling varies by gender, race, and ethnicity and increases significantly with age.

Falls can result in serious injuries or even death to older adults. People with osteoporosis are especially vulnerable to breaking their hip or pelvis or may suffer a traumatic brain injury, any of which may necessitate a long rehabilitation. As a result, much attention has been paid to preventing falls. Some of these interventions are simple (such as removing loose floor rugs and ensuring that there is sufficient light and reduced glare). Others involve lifestyle changes or technology.

The Centers for Disease Control and Prevention (2021b) translated the research findings about increased risk and consequences of falls in older adults, as well as studies on successful intervention programs, and created the **Stopping Elderly Accidents, Deaths, and Injuries (STEADI)** program. STEADI is aimed at healthcare workers, especially physicians, nurses, and pharmacists, and has numerous resources available for professional training and patient information. Among the recommendations in STEADI for the public are

- Get exercise to strengthen muscles. Programs such as tai chi and qigong, among others, are effective.
- Be careful of medication side effects. Some medications may cause dizziness or drowsiness, which can increase the risk for falling.

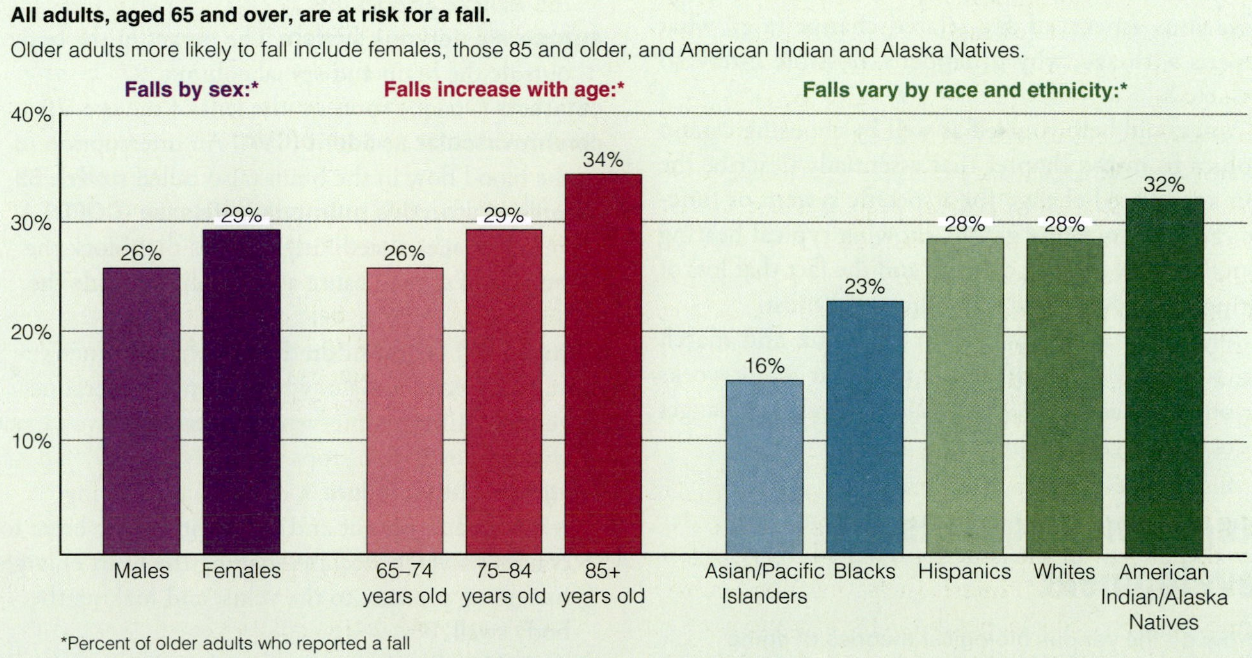

Figure 3.8 Risk of falling as related to gender, age, race, and ethnicity.

Source: Centers for Disease Control and Prevention. (2021b). *STEADI: Stopping Elderly Accidents, Deaths, & Injuries.* https://www.cdc.gov/steadi/index.html

(Continued)

- Correct any visual impairments to the extent possible.
- Remove hazards at home. Remove clutter you can trip over (books, clothes, and other materials on the floor). Install handrails on stairways. Use nonslip mats and grab bars in showers and bath tubs.

The materials compiled in STEADI and by the Centers for Disease Control and Prevention more generally include posters and brochures in English, Spanish, and other languages, as well as more formal booklets for community-based programs. These recommendations, if followed, would result in a safer environment for older adults.

In Review

This chapter covers a lot of topics. It may be more helpful in this case to really break down your summary into six parts, corresponding to the different modules. Within your summary, it may be especially useful to use tables and graphics as the best ways to condense and capture the main points.

A good example is the first module. Using a table to summarize the major biological theories of aging would help you remember the main points of each. Use the rows for the theories and the column for major aspects of each theory (e.g., what the theory claims is the cause of aging, what are the main components of each, etc.).

Similarly, all of the other modules could be set up the same way. You could list the various body parts or systems in the rows, then set up the columns to cover the various aspects of age-related change (e.g., what happens with age, why it happens, possible interventions, etc.).

You could help yourself as well by choosing certain graphics from the chapter that essentially describe the main age-related change for a specific system or function. For instance, the graphs showing typical hearing loss reflect how hearing declines and the fact that loss of hearing for high-pitched tones drops the most.

The most important point is to mix and match your summary techniques in a way that really works for you and that captures the major age-related changes that occur in typical aging.

Integrating Concepts in Development

- How do the various biological theories of aging match with the major age-related changes in body systems? Which theories do the best job? Why?
- Given what you now know about normative changes in appearance, what would you say about the stereotypes of aging you identified in the Discovering Development exercise you did in Chapter 1 ?
- Why do you think the rates of death from cardiovascular disease are so much higher in industrialized countries than elsewhere?
- How might the age-related changes in the respiratory system be linked with societal policies on the environment?

Key Terms

angina pectoris A painful condition caused by temporary constriction of blood flow to the heart. 88

antioxidants Molecules that stabilize free radicals to become less reactive. 67

atherosclerosis A process by which fat is deposited on the walls of arteries. 89

autonomic nervous system The nerves in the body outside the brain and spinal column. 97

cataracts Opaque spots on the lens of the eye. 79

cerebrovascular accident (CVA) An interruption of the blood flow in the brain (also called *stroke*). 89

chronic obstructive pulmonary disease (COPD) A family of age-related lung diseases that block the passage of air and cause abnormalities inside the lungs. 91

climacteric The transition during which women's and transgender males who have not undergone gender-affirming interventions reproductive capacity ends and ovulation stops. 94

congestive heart failure A condition occurring when cardiac output and the ability of the heart to contract severely decline, making the heart enlarge, increasing pressure to the veins, and making the body swell. 88

cross-linking Random interaction between proteins that produce molecules that make the body stiffer. 67

dual-energy X-ray absorptiometry (DXA) test Test of bone mineral density (BMD) at the hip and spine. 74

emphysema Most serious form of COPD characterized by the destruction of the membranes around the air sacs in the lungs. 91

free radicals Highly reactive chemicals produced randomly in normal metabolism. 67

glaucoma A disease in the eye caused by improper drainage of fluid in the eye resulting in internal damage and progressive loss of vision. 79

hypertension A disease in which one's blood pressure is too high. 90

menopausal hormone therapy (MHT) Low doses of estrogen, which are often combined with progestin (synthetic form of progesterone) taken to counter the effects of declining estrogen levels. 95

menopause The cessation of the release of eggs by the ovaries. 94

myocardial infarction (MI) Also called heart attack, a result of a blockage in blood supply to the heart. 88

osteoarthritis A form of arthritis marked by gradual onset and progression of pain and swelling, caused primarily by overuse of a joint. 75

osteoporosis A degenerative bone disease more common in women in which bone tissue deteriorates severely to produce honeycomb-like bone tissue. 74

oxidative stress An imbalance between free radicals and antioxidants in your body. 67

perimenopause The time of transition from regular menstruation to menopause. 94

presbycusis A normative age-related loss of the ability to hear high-pitched tones. 80

presbyopia The normative age-related loss of the ability to focus on nearby objects, usually resulting in the need for corrective lenses. 79

rheumatoid arthritis A destructive form of arthritis that develops slowly and involves different joints and more swelling than osteoarthritis. 75

selective estrogen receptor modulators (SERMs) Compounds that are not estrogens but have estrogen-like effects on some tissues and estrogen-blocking effects on other tissues. 75

telomerase An enzyme needed in DNA replication to fully reproduce the telomeres when cells divide. 66

telomeres Tips of the chromosomes that shorten with each cell replication. 66

Chapter

4

Longevity, Health, and Functioning

Learning Objectives

After studying this chapter, you will be able to...

4.1. Describe the different types of longevity measures and how biological sex, race, and ethnicity influence them.

4.2. Differentiate health and illness, and describe how changes in the immune system, acute and chronic disease, and stress affect the quality of life.

4.3. Describe cancer and diabetes as examples of common chronic diseases, and discuss how pain is managed.

4.4. Describe how adults manage their medication regimens.

4.5. Identify and describe models of disablement and how functional health status is determined.

Chapter Outline

Jeanne Calment was one of the most important people to have ever lived. Her amazing achievement was not made in sports, government, or any other profession. When she died in 1996 at age 122 years and 164 days, she set the world record that still stands for the longest verified human life. Jeanne lived her whole life in Arles, France. She met Vincent Van Gogh and experienced the invention of the lightbulb, automobiles, airplanes, space travel, computers, and all sorts of everyday conveniences. She survived two world wars. Longevity ran in her family: her older brother, François, lived to 97, her father to 93, and her mother to 86. Jeanne was extraordinarily healthy her whole life, rarely being ill. She was also active; she learned fencing when she was 85, and she was still riding a bicycle at age 100. She lived on her own until she was 110, when she moved to a nursing home. Her life was documented in the 1995 film **"Beyond 120 Years with Jeanne Calment."** Shortly before her 121st birthday, Musicdisc released **"Time's Mistress,"** a CD of Jeanne speaking over a background of rap and hip-hop music.

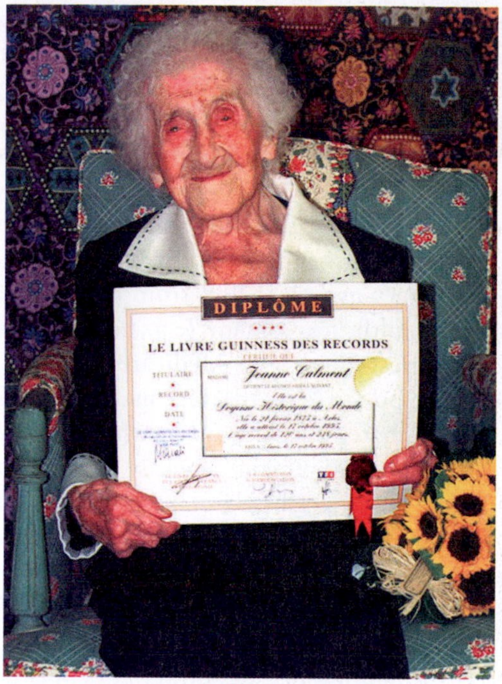

George Gobet/AFP/Getty Images

Jeanne Calment lived more than 122 years.

Do you ever wonder how long you will live? Would you like to break Jeanne Calment's longevity record? How might your life experiences and other factors (race, ethnicity, biological sex, class, where you live, and so forth) influence your decision? What if you come from a family that is known for living long lives—does that matter? What about your overall health and access to health care?

In this chapter, we will find out why longevity is a multifaceted, nuanced concept that embraces much more than the sheer number of years, months, and days we live. We will uncover different ways of thinking about longevity, and the various influences on it. Next, we will examine the meanings of health and illness. By examining certain chronic diseases and our ability to prevent and control them, we will consider the continuum of functional abilities that help frame our functional health status. Throughout these discussions we will examine differences among racial and ethnic groups, and highlight the reality of disparities in access to quality health care and lifestyle and the effects those disparities have on people's lives.

4.1 How Long Will We Live?

Key Questions

- What is the average and the maximum longevity for humans?
- What genetic and environmental factors influence longevity?
- What racial, ethnic, and gender factors influence average longevity?
- What international differences are there in average longevity?

Susie is a 51-year-old Chinese American living in San Francisco. Susie's mother (age 76), father (age 77), and grandmother (age 103), who are all in good health, live with Susie and her wife. Susie knows that several of her other relatives have lived long lives, but she wonders whether this has any bearing on her own life expectancy.

As we considered in Chapter 3, many more people are living to old age than ever before. Like Susie, people born since the mid-20th century have already seen (and perhaps lived with) far more older adults than their great-great-grandparents did. The tremendous increase in the number of older adults has focused renewed interest in how long you may live and what to expect in later life. Susie's wonderings about her own longevity exemplify this interest. Knowing how long we are likely to live is important not only for us but also for government agencies, service programs, the business world, and insurance companies, among many others. Why?

The length of life has an enormous impact on just about every aspect of life, from decisions about government healthcare programs (e.g., how much money should Congress allocate to Medicare and Medicaid) to retirement policy (e.g., the very meaning of "retirement," and debates over the age at which people may collect maximum retirement benefits) to life insurance premiums (e.g., longer lives on average mean cheaper rates for young adults because they are now healthier for longer periods of their lives on average). Longer lives are also partly responsible for the increase in the average age of the American and many other countries' populations over the past few decades (lower rates of childbirth is another factor). The impact on everyday life of more longer-lived people will continue for at least the next several decades.

Longevity is a great example of how of the basic developmental forces we examined in Chapter 1 actually operate, because how long we live depends on complex interactions among biological, psychological, sociocultural, and life-cycle forces. For example, some people, like Susie, know that they have many direct relatives who lived to very old age, whereas others may know they have relatives who tended to die young from certain diseases that are known to be inherited. Tendencies toward long lives (or short ones, for that matter) run in families, as you might discover by tracing your known and discoverable ancestral heritage (e.g., on Ancestry.com). As will be explained later in this module, our "longevity genes" play a major role in governing how long we are likely to live.

But the world in which we live also affects how long we live. Environmental factors such as diseases caused by pollution and toxic chemicals modify our genetic heritage and shorten our lifetime, sometimes drastically. By the same token, environmental factors such as disparities in access to high-quality health care can offset genetic advantages that would otherwise have been a positive influence on longevity, thereby reducing our life span. Such disparities reflect systemic effects of sociocultural forces such as racism and income inequity.

In short, no single developmental force can account for the length of one's life. Let's begin by exploring the complexities of longevity in more detail. To get started, complete the exercise in the Discovering Development feature and see a research-based prediction of how long you might live, all unexpected things (e.g., experiencing accidents, global pandemics) aside. When you have finished, continue reading to discover the evidence underlying longevity in its various forms.

Discovering Development

Take the Longevity Test

Are you curious about how long you might live? If so, and you'd like a preview of how several of the key influences on how long we live might affect you, take a few minutes and complete the survey at www.livingto100.com. This survey is based on the New England Centenarian Study and other related research on factors explaining why people who live to very old age do so, and what factors may significantly shorten life. Take notes about why you think each question is being asked. Once you're finished, submit your form. Take time to read about each of the topics, then read more about them in the text. How long might you live? Only time will really tell!

Average and Maximum Longevity

How long you live, called longevity, can be considered in two main ways: average longevity and maximum longevity. **Average longevity** is commonly called average life expectancy and refers to the age at which half of the individuals who are born in a particular year will have died. Average longevity is affected by many factors.

Average longevity can be computed for people at any point in their life span. The most common method is to compute average longevity at birth, which is the projected age at which half of the people born in that year will have died. This computation takes into account people who die at any age, from infancy onward. In 2021, average longevity at birth was about 77.3 years for people in the United States in general, a decline of 1.5 years from 2019, the last full year prior to the COVID-19 pandemic (Arias et al., 2021). This means that of all the people born in 2021, half of them will still be alive when the group reaches age 77.3. However, the decline noted due to COVID-19 did not affect all demographic groups equally. For example, the overall disparity in average longevity between all biological females (those born with an XX pair of chromosomes) and all biological males (those born with an XY pair of chromosomes), in favor of biological females, increased from 5.1 years in 2019 to 5.7 years in 2020. Digging deeper into average longevity at birth in 2020, we find other disparities: Black individuals' average longevity dropped 2.9 years, Latinas/os' average longevity dropped 3.0 years, and White individuals' average longevity dropped 1.2 years. We will explore the reasons for these disparities a bit later.

Average longevity is computed at other points in the life span in similar ways—the calculations are based on all the people who are alive at a specific age; people who died earlier are not included. For example, computing the average longevity for people currently 65 years old would provide a predicted age at which half of those people will have died. People who were born into the same birth cohort but who died before age 65 are not counted. Eliminating those who die at earlier ages from the computation makes projected average longevity at age 65 longer than it was at birth. In the United States, biological females in general aged 65 in 2020 can expect to live on average about 20 more years; biological males in general about 18 more years (Arias & Xu, 2020). Later in this section, we will examine whether these additional years are accompanied by good quality of life.

Average longevity is just that—an average. Another way to consider longevity is **maximum longevity**, the oldest age to which any individual of a species lives. Although mythical figures and persons in various sacred texts are sometimes claimed to have been extremely long-lived (for instance, the biblical character Methuselah is said to have lived to the ripe old age of 969 years), modern scientists are more conservative in their estimates of a human's maximum longevity. Even if we were able to eliminate all diseases and other environmental influences, researchers examining blood indicators estimate the absolute limit to be somewhere between 120 to 150 years (Pyrkov et al., 2021). Genetic theories and research also place the human limit around 120 years (Chmielewski, 2020; Rattan, 2020). As we noted at the beginning of the chapter, the world record for longevity that can be verified by birth records is held by Jeanne Calment of France, who died in 1997 at age 122 years.

It remains to be seen whether maximum longevity will change as new technologies produce better artificial organs and health care continues to advance. An important issue is whether extending the life span indefinitely would be a good idea. Because maximum longevity of different animal species varies widely (Chmielewski, 2020; Pyrkov et al., 2021; Rattan, 2020), scientists have tried to understand these differences by considering important biological functions that we noted in Chapter 3 when we examined biological theories of aging. But despite all this effort, no one has figured out how to predict species longevity accurately. For example, why the giant tortoises of the Galapagos Islands typically live longer than humans do remains a mystery.

Oher ways of considering longevity take a functional perspective rather than emphasizing the sheer number of years lived until death. A functional approach emphasizes the distinction between **active life expectancy** (living to advanced old age while remaining healthy and living largely independently) and **dependent life expectancy** (living a long time while depending on others or the healthcare system for significant assistance). Said another way, it is the difference between adding life to years (active life expectancy) and adding years to life (dependent life expectancy). One's active life expectancy ends at the point when one loses independence or must rely on others for most activities of daily living (e.g., cooking meals, bathing). The switch from active to dependent life expectancy can be temporary (e.g., needing assistance to recover during a period of rehabilitation after a hip fracture) or permanent (e.g., needing assistance due to advanced dementia). The dynamic nature of these states emphasizes that they reflect a continuum, again highlighting the complexity of understanding longevity in its many facets, and how all of these facets result from the interaction of genetic and environmental factors, to which we now turn.

Genetic and Environmental Factors in Average Longevity

Let's return to Susie, who wonders whether she can expect to live a long life. What influences how long she (and we) will live on average? Our average longevity is influenced most by genetic, environmental, racial, ethnic, gender, and sociocultural factors. Clearly, these factors interact; being from a particular racial group or economic class, for example, often means that, for example, one has a higher or lower risk of exposure to a harmful environment and less or more access to high-quality health care. For ease of understanding, though, we will examine each of these factors separately and learn how they influence our longevity. We'll consider the interactions afterwards.

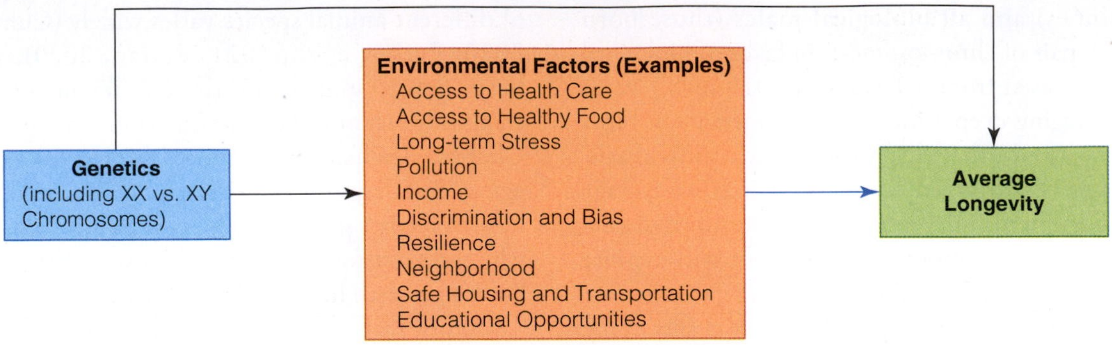

Figure 4.1 Example of genetic and environmental effects on average longevity.

Let's begin with the overview in Figure 4.1. This graphic provides a roadmap of the kinds of influences we will be considering in this section. As indicated, we start with a certain genetic heritage that does have a direct effect on how long we might live. However, many other factors come into play, as noted under the Environmental Factors box, that attenuate our genetic heritage. Let's find out how this works.

Genetic Factors. Living a long life has a clear, but complex, genetic link. We have known for a long time that a good way to have a greater chance of a long life is to come from a family with a history of long-lived individuals. Alexander Graham Bell (the same person who received credit for inventing the telephone) was one of the first people to systematically demonstrate the benefits of coming from a long-lived family (Bell, 1918). Bell considered 8,797 of William Hyde's descendants and found that children of parents who had lived beyond age 80 survived about 20 years longer than children whose parents had both died before they were age 60. Thus, Susie's long-lived family sets the stage for Susie to potentially have a long life herself.

Similar research indicates that about 25% of the variation in human longevity is due to a person's genetics (Caruso & Puca, 2021; Passarino et al., 2016). So people like Susie who are born into families with many long-lived members tend also to have longer average longevity.

One exciting line of research, the Human Genome Project, initially reported in 2003, mapped our genes. All of the gaps in the original mapping were closed in 2022 with the first reporting of the entire human genome (Nurk et al., 2022). This research and its spinoffs in microbiology and behavior genetics are continuing to produce astounding results in terms of genetic linkages to disease and aging (you can track these through the main website of the project: https://www.genome.gov/).

Based on this gene mapping work, ongoing research is revolutionizing how we treat diseases by tailoring medications based on a specific person's genes, such as through personalized medicine or targeted medicine to treat specific forms of cancer (National Cancer Institute, 2021a). Some research even focuses on implanting "corrected" genes into people in the hope that the good genes will reproduce and eventually wipe out the defective genes, and in other cases prevent the shortening of telomeres (discussed in Chapter 3). For instance, gene editing is being researched as a treatment to stop the growth of specific cancer cells, in which the genetic code of the tumor in each patient is individually targeted (Martinez-Lage et al., 2020).

Payoffs from such research are helping us understand the role of genetics in exceptional longevity, such as living to 100 or older (Caruso & Puca, 2021; Santos-Lozano et al., 2020). For example, research on people over age 100 (termed centenarians) in Sicily showed a connection between genetics and the immune system (Balistreri et al., 2012). The oldest-old, such as Susie's grandmother, are healthy because they have highly effective genetically based immune systems, and they show slower rates of disease progression than their peers who develop chronic diseases at younger ages and die earlier after controlling for other factors.

Environmental Factors. It turns out that where one lives is extremely important in understanding nongenetic factors in human longevity. In a study of 20 developed and developing countries, Chen and colleagues (2021) reported that the primary environmental influences on longevity have some commonality across countries and some important differences. Specifically, the urbanization rate has a significant positive impact, and carbon dioxide emissions have a significant negative impact on longevity in both developed countries and developing

Coming from a family with many long-lived members increases your chances of having a long life yourself.

countries. What are the most important influences in each case? In developed countries, gross domestic product (GDP; the total of all the goods and services produced within a country) per capita has the greatest positive impact on longevity, whereas fertilizer usage has the greatest negative impact. In developing countries, though, the urbanization rate has the greatest positive impact on longevity, while the Gini coefficient (a measure of the income disparity in a country) has the greatest negative impact.

Going a bit deeper, some environmental factors are more obvious; diseases, toxins, lifestyle, and socioeconomic status are among the most important. Diseases, such as cardiovascular disease and Alzheimer's disease, and lifestyle issues, such as smoking and exercise, receive a great deal of attention from researchers. Environmental toxins, encountered mainly as air and water pollution, are a continuing problem. For example, toxins in fish, bacteria and cancer-causing chemicals in drinking water, lead in pipes and paint, and airborne pollutants such as soot are major agents in shortening longevity.

Living in poverty significantly shortens longevity. The impact of socioeconomic status on longevity results from reduced access to goods and services, especially quality medical care and healthy affordable food, as clearly demonstrated in a very large study (566,402 participants) of premature mortality in community-dwelling adults (Doubeni et al., 2012). The structural inequities creating barriers to health care and nutrition are compounded by air pollution, poor drinking water, and lead poisoning from old water pipes and paint. The income disparities that are endemic in many locations means that residents do not have the resources to relocate. The income disparity problem is so acute that differences between high and low socioeconomic groups in access to quality health care, which had been improving during the latter part of the 20th century in the United States, have remained either unchanged or have worsened since 1990 (Swanson & Sanford, 2012). A subsequent analysis of 159 developed and developing countries found a constant longevity advantage of about 19 years in developed countries between 1970 and 2010, with income inequality the major factor creating this difference (Swanson & Tedrow, 2018).

How environmental factors influence average life expectancy changes over time. For example, acquired immunodeficiency syndrome (AIDS; Kinsella & Phillips, 2005) and diseases from bushmeat-related activities (Kurpiers et al., 2016) have had a devastating effect on life expectancy in sub-Saharan Africa since the 1980s. In contrast, negative effects of cardiovascular diseases on average longevity are lessening as the rates of those diseases decline due to lower rates of smoking (National Center for Health Statistics, 2021a).

The sad part about most environmental factors is that human activity is largely responsible. Denying adequate health care to everyone, continuing to pollute the environment, and failing to address the underlying causes of poverty have undeniable consequences: these causes needlessly shorten lives.

Racial, Ethnic, and Biological Sex Differences in Average Longevity

People in different racial, ethnic, and biological sex groups do not have the same average longevity at birth. For example, although Black individuals' average life

Controversies

Can We Live to 200? (And Would You if You Could?)

Over the course of the 20th century, average longevity doubled. The reason this happened had little to do with actual improvement in our DNA, and almost all to do with advances in health care, healthier lifestyles, and technological innovation. Suppose for a moment that we could continue this rate of life extension throughout this century, such that average longevity increases to 200 years. Fantasy? Or possibility?

In an interesting thought experiment in 2021, Nicholas St. Fleur, Chloe Williams, and Charlie Wood of the **New York Times** compiled a list of things that would need to occur to make living to 200 a real possibility. Here are some of their "must do" list:

Possible in 0–5 Years

- **Life-extending supplements.** A compound known as alpha-ketoglutarate (used by cells during growth and in healing from injuries and other wounds, especially in the healing of muscle tissue) is in human clinical trials to examine its effects on markers of aging.
- **Treat obesity more effectively.** Obesity reduces average longevity by 10 years. Semaglutide (Wegovy®), a drug that is FDA approved to treat obesity, is roughly twice as effective as current alternatives.
- **Immune system and mRNA vaccine cancer treatments.** Immunotherapy and mRNA vaccines become the standard treatments for cancer.

Possible in 5–10 Years

- **CRISPR-based tools.** Gene editing through CRISPR technology becomes the best option for preventing and treating blood disorders and cardiovascular disease.
- **Exercise in a pill.** Medications that mimic the benefits of exercise are under development to treat various diseases and possibly extend the life span.
- **A diabetes drug to slow aging.** Metformin, used widely to treat type-2 diabetes (discussed later in this chapter), is being studied for its anti-aging properties.

Possible in 10–20 Years

- **Designer genes.** Gene therapies may enable us to treat genetic diseases such as cancer, cardiovascular disease, and dementia, as well as stop certain disease and function-impairing genes from "turning on."
- **Empowering midwives.** Broadening the services midwives provide could help avoid 41% of deaths of individuals who give birth, 39% of neonatal deaths, and 26% of stillbirths in developing countries.
- **Lab-grown organs.** Being able to create human organs in labs rather than using animals for this purpose would be a major advance. Lab-grown bladders are already being implanted in humans. Improved techniques could expand this to kidneys, livers, and hearts.

Possible in 20–50 Years

- **Self-driving cars.** Not only would these cars nearly eliminate deaths in auto accidents, but they would also expand the number of people who can age in place.
- **Clean the air.** Meeting global climate change goals would extend average longevity simply by lowering pollution and temperature.
- **Eradicate malaria.** Effective vaccines and better treatments would save over 400,000 deaths annually worldwide.

Possible in 50–100 Years

- **Nanobots.** Micro-sized robots would inhabit our bodies and be an army of medical screeners and interventionists to detect and cure most diseases.
- **Cellular reprogramming.** Problematic genes or genes that are wearing out could be replaced or reprogrammed into well-functioning versions, perhaps even their "younger" selves.

These are some pretty amazing possibilities, all based on research and experimental trials. But—and this is the real question—would you actually want to live in this kind of world and expect to live 200 years (or more)? Or is there a point at which the life span becomes too long? What do you think?

expectancy at birth is about 4 years less for biological males and about 3 years less for biological females than it is for White individuals, by age 65 this gap has narrowed to about 2 and 1 years, respectively, for biological males and biological females. By age 85, Black individuals tend to outlive White individuals. Why the shift over time?

Genetics do not have an obvious role. Some researchers speculate that Black adults who survive to very old age may have better genetic protection against disease because they have, on average, much less access to quality health care. But this does not explain why Latinos/as have higher average life expectancies than either White or Black individuals at all ages despite having, on average, less access to quality health care (Arias & Xu, 2020). The full explanation for these racial and ethnic group differences remains to be discovered, as do the long-term effects of the COVID-19 pandemic on these differences in longevity. We will have more to explore regarding the effects of structural disparities in access to quality health care and affordable healthy food at several points in the remainder of this chapter.

With respect to biological sex, you may already be aware of basic differences between biological males and biological females. For instance, have you ever visited a senior center or a nursing home? If so, you may have asked yourself, "Where are all the very old males?" The answer is that biological females live longer, on average, than do males. Overall, biological females' average longevity is about 5 years more than males' at birth, narrowing to roughly 1 year by age 85 (Arias & Xu, 2020).

These biological sex differences are fairly typical of most developed countries but not of developing countries. In fact, the biological female advantage in average longevity in the United States became apparent only in the early 20th century (Hayflick, 1996). Why? Until then, so many people who bore children died in childbirth that their average longevity as a group was no more than that of biological males. Death in childbirth still helps explain the lack of a biological female advantage in developing countries today; however, other aspects include gender-based disparities in health care and infanticide of baby girls. In developed countries, factors such as access to health care and improved lifestyle factors also help account for the emergence of the female advantage.

Many ideas have been offered to explain the significant advantage biological females have over biological males in average longevity in both humans and in 101 other mammal species (Lemaître et al., 2020b). One obvious factor for humans is that biological males' rates of dying from the top 15 causes of death are significantly higher than biological females' rates at nearly every age, and biological males are also more susceptible to infectious diseases. These differences have led some to speculate that perhaps it is not just a biological sex-related difference at work in longevity, but a more complex interaction of environmental factors (lifestyle, health care), combined with genetic ones.

Other researchers disagree; they argue that there are potential biological explanations (Lemaître et al., 2020a). These include the fact that biological females have two X chromosomes, compared with one in males; biological males have a higher metabolic rate; biological females have a higher brain-to-body weight ratio; and biological females have lower natural testosterone levels. Some research points to older biological females' more effective natural killer (NK) cells, a key aspect of human immune systems, as another reason (Al-Attar et al., 2016; Oh et al., 2021). (We consider the role of NK cells later in this chapter.) However, no single explanation has sufficient scientific support to explain why most biological females in developed countries can expect, on average, to outlive most biological men (Lemaître et al., 2020a).

It is clear that many factors influence how long people live on average. But what if we decided to do something about them, especially those that create gender, racial, and ethnic disparities? What if we even went further, and applied technological innovations that could extend the life span? Could we push the limit on maximum longevity to 200? The Controversies feature explains what it would take—and raises a crucial question. Even if we could live to 200, would we actually want to?

International Differences in Average Longevity

Countries around the world differ dramatically in how long their populations live on average (World Bank, 2021). These differences are apparent in Figure 4.2. What do you notice in these data?

Some developing countries, such as Sierra Leone in Africa, have an overall average longevity at birth of 54 years, compared with developed countries such as Japan and Switzerland at 84. Such a wide divergence in life expectancy reflects vast discrepancies in the role of environmental factors. Sociocultural and socioeconomic conditions, access to health care and affordable healthy food, disease, and the like between developed and developing nations are the primary reasons for such large differences. The differences also mean that populations in countries such as Sierra Leone are very much

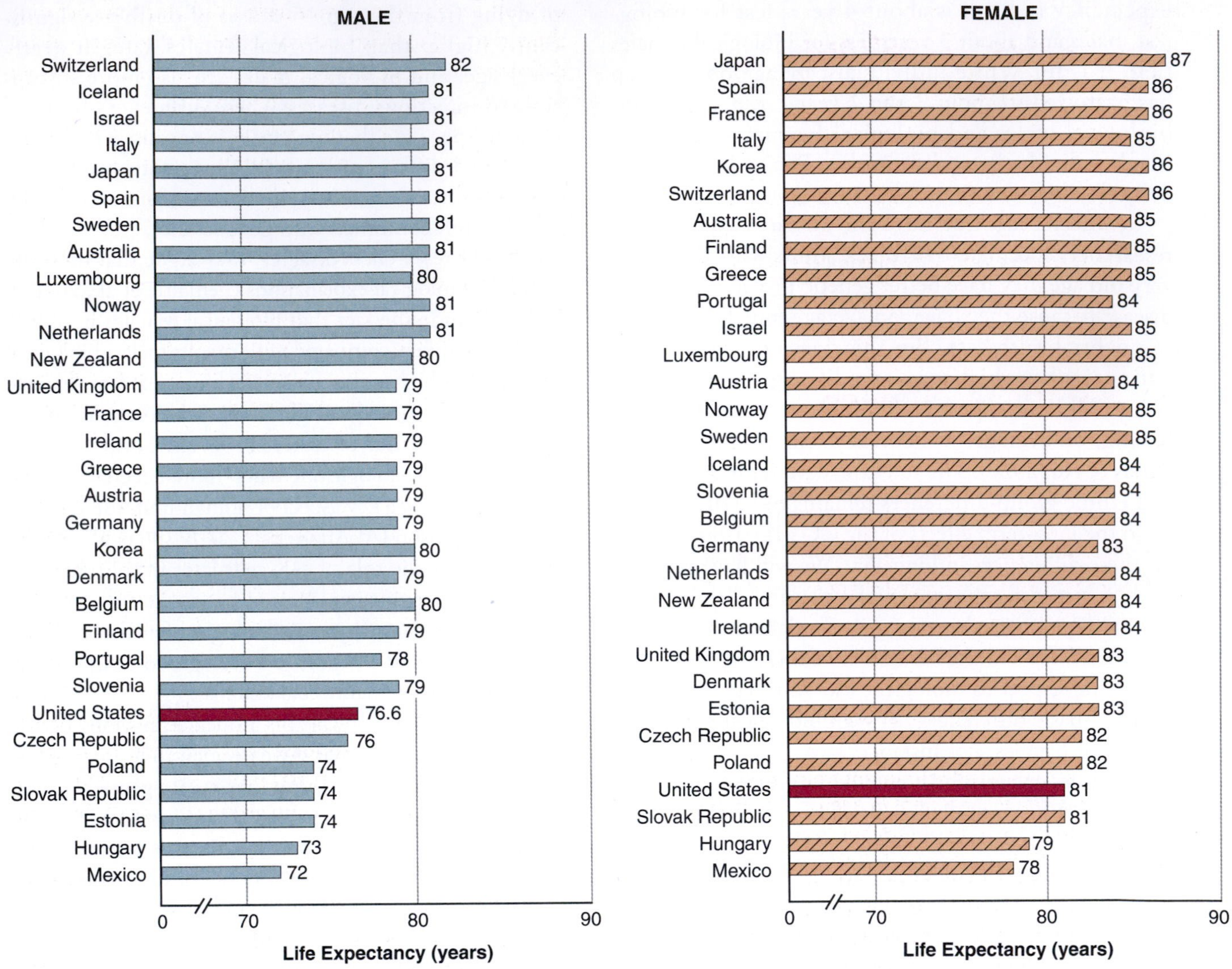

Figure 4.2 Average longevity at birth, selected countries.
Source: World Bank. (2021). *Life expectancy at birth, total (years).* https://data.worldbank.org/indicator/SP.DYN.LE00.IN?most_recent_value_desc=true

younger, on average, than they are in countries such as Japan or Switzerland, where the population average age is significantly older.

As we noted in Chapter 1, though, things are changing fairly rapidly in developing countries. First, more people in those countries are aging, due to such factors as improving health care and lower infant mortality and deaths in childbirth. But the pressures on those countries from the impact of climate change could reverse these trends as more people succumb to increased temperatures, scarcer food resources, and increased income disparities. The World Bank, among other global organizations, has had a long-standing emphasis on eliminating poverty and raising the quality of living conditions.

Adult Development in Action

Suppose you are a financial planner whose job is to create programs for people to be financially secure in later life. Given what you have learned about longevity, how would you design such programs?

Review Questions

4.1 How Long Will We Live?

- What is the difference between average longevity and maximum longevity?
- What genetic and environmental factors influence average longevity?
- What racial, ethnic, and biological sex differences have been found?

4.2 Health and Illness

Key Questions

- What are the key issues in defining health and illness?
- How is quality of life assessed?
- What normative age-related changes occur in the immune system?
- What are the developmental trends in chronic and acute diseases?
- What are the key issues in stress across adulthood?

Rosa is a 72-year-old immigrant from Mexico, living in a small apartment in a large city in the southwestern United States. For most of her life she has been very healthy, but lately she has noticed it is getting harder to get up every morning. In addition, when she gets a cold, she takes longer to recover than when she was younger. Rosa wonders whether these problems are typical or whether she is experiencing something unusual.

Each of us has had periods of health and of illness. Many people are like Rosa—healthy for nearly all their lives. In this section, we will tackle the difficult issue of defining health and illness. We will consider quality of life, an increasingly important notion as medical technology keeps people alive longer. We will learn how the differences between acute and chronic disease become more important with age. Because our immune system plays such a central role in health and illness, we will examine key age-related changes in it. Finally, we will consider how stress can affect our health.

Defining Health and Illness

What does the term health mean to you? A total lack of disease? Complete physical, mental, and social well-being? What about illness? Is it more than just not feeling healthy or well? Don't worry if you have a difficult time defining these terms. Scientists cannot agree on a comprehensive definition either, largely because the term has been used in so many different contexts (Brannon et al., 2022).

Most researchers and theorists now include biological, psychological, sociocultural, spiritual, and environmental components in their definitions; as Davies (2007) puts it, health is an ongoing outcome from the processes of a life lived well, and illness constitutes disruptions in those processes. The World Health Organization (WHO) defines **health** as a state of complete physical, mental, and social well-being, and not merely the absence of disease or infirmity; **illness** is the presence of a physical or mental disease or impairment (World Health Organization, 1946).

Think for a moment about your health in the context of the WHO definition. How would you rate it? Can people accurately self-report various health issues or diseases they have had? Although this all seems straightforward, it isn't. How people answer self-report surveys about their health is influenced by a variety of factors, from the accuracy of their memory to understanding the terms used in the survey to being skeptical of the motives of the person doing the asking (Sanchez et al., 2021). In some cases, self-reports are quite accurate (Cristina et al., 2016; Shafrir et al., 2021). In other cases, especially those involving surveys of different racial, ethnic, or cultural groups, self-reports tend not to provide accurate information because of previous historical or personal events that destroyed trust.

How could self-reports of health status be used appropriately? There are several possibilities. On one hand, self-rated health has a long history of use and relatively good accuracy in general; a meta-analysis of more than 30 years of research and large longitudinal studies have shown that self-ratings of health are typically very predictive of future health outcomes (Blazer, 2008; Doornenbal & Bakx, 2021). Longitudinal research further notes that self-reported health generally stays stable over time (Doornenbal & Bakx, 2021). On the other hand, historical misuse of data, lack of cultural sensitivity regarding asking questions about certain personal health matters, and lack of understanding unfamiliar terms referring to medical conditions significantly lowers the validity of self-report measures and points out the need for care and caution in the use of such measures (Sanchez et al., 2021). A good example of the need for cultural sensitivity is described in the How Do We Know? feature focusing on older Samoans' conceptualization of health and wellness.

How Do We Know?

Older Samoans' Perceptions of Age, Aging, and Wellness

Who was the investigator, and what was the aim of the study? Although the study of health and wellness in older adults is a popular topic for research, very little of this work has focused on Indigenous populations, especially among the Pacific peoples. Falegau Melanie Lilomaiava Silulu (2021) sought to learn how older Samoans define age, aging, and wellness.

How did the investigator measure the topic of interest? Silulu adopted a qualitative phenomenological approach through a Samoan lens using *talanoa* methodology. In this way, Silulu was able to gain understanding of how older Samoans conceive of age and aging as processes in their unique worldview, and how health fits within that.

Who were the participants in the study? Silulu studied eight Samoans between the ages of 63 and 84 in small groups and individually.

What was the design of the study? The design of the study used a *talanoa* process. Talanoa, in Fiji, means to hold a conversation in an inclusive, receptive space and reflects a process of inclusive, participatory, and transparent dialogue. Such an approach is crucial for understanding Indigenous people's experiences. Silulu carefully constructed interviews that would provide the opportunity for the participants to use their own terms of age, aging, health, and other key concepts, thereby providing additional insights into how these ideas fit within the Samoan spiritually based understanding of the world.

Were there ethical concerns in the study? All participants were provided informed consent and could withdraw from participation at any point in the study.

What were the results? Analysis of the data using descriptive phenomenology revealed the following. Samoan older adults used their own words and terms to describe age, aging, and wellness that related to *fa'a Samoa* ("the Samoan way"). These words were spiritually imbued and respectful signaling of different age stages (*matua, sinasina, tofa*) and wellness references (*soifua manuia/maua/lelei*). Older Samoans had a positive outlook despite having significant health conditions. God, church, and responsibilities to family influenced group talanoa views and impacted their experience of wellness. Individual *talanoa* conversations reinforced group findings and added new social connections, technology, and other factors, such as physical health, diet, and regular medical check-ups, as essential factors in maintaining older Samoans' wellness. Children and family were their most crucial concerns for the future as their focus was on the continuity and sustaining of *fa'amatai, 'āiga,* and family systems.

What did the investigator conclude? The qualitative approach through *talanoa* was most effective in capturing elders' perceptions and experiences. The views and understandings expressed by the older Samoans did not fit neatly within the models of health care and aging adopted by the New Zealand government, thus raising the important point that for services to be maximally effective they must be culturally appropriate. Thus, it is important to conduct more population-specific aging research on Indigenous groups globally and locally.

Among middle-aged and older adults, self-rated health is a powerful predictor of health conditions and mortality across cultures as long as trust and cultural sensitivity are addressed; for example, a two-year study in China showed that self-rated health still predicted mortality even after socioeconomic status and health conditions had been accounted for (Chen & Wu, 2008). Similar results were obtained for biological males in India (Hirve et al., 2012). Middle-aged biological females in Japan accurately self-reported gynecological and breast diseases (Takamatsu et al., 2021).

Self-ratings of health and illness reflect differences in sociocultural background in terms of how healthy people say they are. For example, Indigenous Australians rate their health as significantly poorer than non-Indigenous Australians, mainly due to differences in structural economic variables (e.g., access to health care) (Booth & Carroll, 2008). In the United States, Black Americans are twice as likely, and Mexican Americans and Puerto Rican Americans are three times more likely, to self-report their health as fair or poor than are White Americans (Benjamins et al., 2012; Landrine et al., 2016). Further research comparing nine racial and ethnic groups (non-Latina/o White, Mexican, Puerto Rican, Cuban, African American, Afro-Caribbean, Chinese, Filipino, and Vietnamese Americans) revealed serious concerns about the validity of comparing self-reports of health across these groups (Erving & Zajdel, 2022). Additionally, little research has been conducted on how individuals with multiracial backgrounds may differ in self-reports of health (Miller et al., 2019).

What can we conclude from research on self-reported health? First, structural differences in sociocultural factors affect what people say about their health in general. Second, if culturally sensitive measures are used to build trust, self-ratings can accurately predict current and future health conditions. The challenge is that self-reports of health are used so widely that it is difficult to know whether the conditions that improve accuracy by addressing known structural factors have been taken.

Quality of Life

A closely related concept to health and illness is quality of life. People often say something about a good quality of life in describing what they want in life. But what does that mean? Precise definitions are hard to find. Sometimes people find it easier to say what quality of life is not, for them, such as being dependent on a respirator while in a permanent vegetative state. Researchers, though, like to be more specific. When researchers ask focused questions, people identify two important aspects of quality of life: health-related quality of life and non-health-related quality of life. **Health-related quality of life** includes all of the aspects of life that are affected by changes in one's health status. **Non-health-related quality of life** refers to things in the environment, such as entertainment, economic resources, arts, and so on, that can affect our overall experience and enjoyment in life.

Most research on quality of life has focused on three specific areas: quality of life in the context of specific diseases or conditions, quality of life relating to end-of-life issues, and quality of life as an indicator of aging well from one's own perspective. We briefly lay out the issues here. We will return to them as we discuss specific situations in this chapter and in Chapters 5 (environmental interventions that increase quality of life), 13 (end-of-life issues), and 14 (aging well).

Rawpixel.com/Shutterstock.com

Having a high quality of life is a goal for most people.

In many respects, quality of life is a subjective judgment that can be understood in the context of broader models of adult development and aging. One such model describes ways in which people select domains of relative strength, optimize their use of these strengths, and compensate for age-related changes, the selective optimization with compensation (SOC) approach discussed in Chapters 1 and 14 (Baltes et al., 2006). In addition, one must also consider not only the physical health aspects but also mental health and the person's life situation in assessing quality of life (Brett et al., 2012).

From this perspective, quality of life is a successful use of the SOC approach to manage one's life, resulting in aging well from one's own perspective. Most important, the SOC approach is applicable in any situation, as it is individual-focused. Applying this approach to research in health care, quality of life refers to people's perceptions of their position in life in the context of their culture (Karim et al., 2008) and in relation to their goals, expectations, values, and concerns (Brett et al., 2012). This is especially important when studying cultures, such as Indigenous populations in Australia and New Zealand, that have very different perspectives on concepts such as health (Kite & Davy, 2015; Lilomaiava Silulu, 2021).

In general, research on health-related quality of life addresses a critical question (Lawton et al., 1999): to what extent does distress from illness or side effects associated with treatment reduce a person's wish to live? Lawton and colleagues (1999) set the standard for answering this question by showing that it depends a great deal on a person's valuation of life, or the degree to which a person is attached to their present life. How much one enjoys life, has hope about the future, and finds meaning in everyday events, for example, has a great deal of impact on how long that person would like to live. Assessing a person's valuation of life helps clinicians develop better strategies to maximize quality of life (Gitlin et al., 2016).

Narrowing the focus of the quality-of-life concept as it relates to specific conditions brings us to the domains of physical impairment or disability, and of dementia. Quality of life in the former context includes issues of environmental design that improve people's functioning and well-being, such as bathrooms and facilities that are accessible to all, as we explore in Chapter 5 (Pynoos et al., 2010).

Quality of life is more difficult to assess in people with dementia and chronic diseases, although assessment instruments have been developed (Ciarmoli, 2022; Gitlin et al., 2016). We consider this issue in more detail in Chapter 10 when we focus on Alzheimer's disease and other types of dementia.

Developmental Changes in the Immune System

As everyone learned firsthand after the arrival of the COVID-19 virus, our bodies are constantly threatened by invaders: bacterial, viral, and parasitic infections (as well as their toxic by-products), and atypical cells such as precancerous and tumor cells. Fortunately, we have a highly advanced defense system that is always on the lookout for these microscopic invaders: the immune system. To get an idea of how truly sophisticated our immune system actually is, refer to the National Institute of Allergy and Infectious Diseases' online overviews of how our immune system works (https://www.niaid.nih.gov/research/immune-system-research).

Although extremely sophisticated research has rapidly advanced our understanding of how our immune system works, many details remain unknown. For instance, one great mystery is how the immune system learns to differentiate your own cells from invaders. Researchers think the mechanism involves recognizing certain substances, called antigens, on the surface of invading bacteria and cells that have been taken over by viruses. Regardless of how this actually happens, once the immune system has learned to recognize the invader, it creates a defense against it. These defenses against certain bacteria and viruses (such as the ones causing COVID-19, measles, mumps, and yellow fever) can be jump started and boosted by vaccines by teaching the immune system to recognize these (future) invaders before they actually attack.

How does this defense system work? It's an amazing process that is based essentially on only three major types of cells that form an interacting network (Murphy & Weaver, 2022):

1. Cell-mediated immunity (consisting of cells originating in the thymus gland, or T-lymphocytes),
2. Immunity based on the release of antibodies in the blood, such as those manufactured in bone marrow or acquired from immunization or previous infection (B-lymphocytes), and
3. Nonspecific immunity (monocytes and polymorphonuclear neutrophil leukocytes).

Together, they work as specialized forces in the war against invaders.

The primary job of the T- and B-lymphocytes is to defend against malignant (cancerous) cells, viral infection, fungal infection, and some bacteria. The previously mentioned NK cells are another special type of lymphocytes that monitor our bodies to prevent tumor growth. They are our primary defense against cancer, although how this happens is not fully understood. These NK cells also help fight viral infections and parasites. In addition, there are five major types of specialized antibodies called immunoglobulins (IgA, IgD, IgE, IgG, and IgM). For example, IgM includes the "first responders" in the immune system, IgE is involved in allergies and asthma, and IgG (also called g-globulin) helps fight hepatitis.

How does aging affect the immune system? Researchers are only beginning to understand this process, and there are large gaps in knowledge, especially across racial, ethnic, and gender groups (Murphy & Weaver, 2022). Moreover, the immune system is sensitive to a wide variety of lifestyle and environmental factors, such as diet, stress, exercise, and disease, making it very difficult to isolate changes caused by aging alone (Valiathan et al., 2016).

Changes in health with age provide insights into immune functioning. Older adults are more susceptible to certain infections and have a much higher risk of cancer (both of which are discussed in more detail later in this chapter), so most researchers believe that the immune system changes with age. This idea was supported in the COVID-19 pandemic, as older adults were among the hardest hit early in the pandemic during the period prior to vaccines.

Although the number of NK cells appears to increase with age after midlife, this and several other aspects of the immune system decrease in effectiveness with age (Ligotti et al., 2021; Sharma, 2021; Vicente et al., 2016). For one thing, older adults' immune systems take longer to build up defenses against specific diseases, even after an immunization injection. This is probably caused by the changing balance in T-lymphocytes, which decline later in life, and may partially explain why older adults need to be immunized earlier, and may need stronger doses or boosters, against specific diseases such as influenza, pneumonia, and coronavirus (Sharma, 2021).

Similarly, B-lymphocytes decrease in functioning. Research examining the administration of substances such as growth hormones to older adults to stimulate lymphocyte functioning indicates that some specific lymphocyte functioning returns to normal with treatment and can regenerate the thymus gland, both of which are important in ensuring good immune system functioning (Feehan et al., 2021). However, growth hormone deficiency, which happens naturally with aging, appears favorable for a longer life span. Clearly, use of growth hormone presents a trade-off of improved immune function versus longer life. This process for T- and B-lymphocytes is described in Figure 4.3.

Changes in immune system function have important implications (Feehan et al., 2021; Murphy & Weaver, 2022; Sharma, 2021). Older adults become more prone to serious consequences from illnesses—such as those caused by viruses such as influenza and coronavirus—that are easily defeated by younger adults. Older adults also benefit less from immunizations, so they tend to need stronger doses or boosters. Again, we find everyday evidence of this declining effectiveness. For example, adults over age 65 are given stronger versions of flu vaccines, and the COVID-19 boosters were especially necessary for older adults to develop levels of immunity needed to decrease the severity of the infection. In addition, various forms of leukemia, which are cancers of the immune cells, increase with age, along with other forms of cancer. Finally, the immune system can begin attacking the body itself in a process called **autoimmunity**. Autoimmunity results from an imbalance of B- and T-lymphocytes, giving rise to autoantibodies, and is responsible for several disorders, such as rheumatoid arthritis (Mälzer et al., 2016). For reasons not fully understood, biological females have a higher rate of autoimmune disorders even after taking numerous other factors, such as sociocultural factors, into account (Murphy & Weaver, 2022). Whether there are systematic racial and ethnic differences remains a matter of debate, as sociocultural structural factors (e.g., access to health care) mean that individuals presenting with autoimmune diseases are often in more serious condition and later in the disease process due to a lack of or inaccurate diagnosis (B. T. Lee et al., 2021).

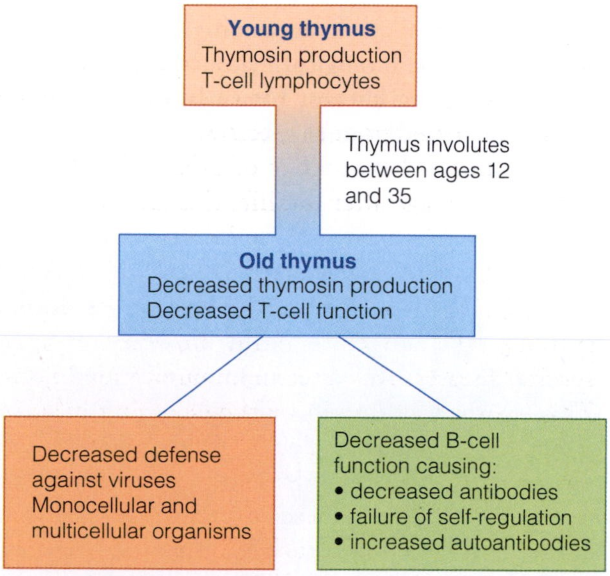

Figure 4.3 Process of aging of the immune system.

Source: Reprinted with permission from Ebersole, P., & Hess, P., *Toward Healthy Aging* (5th ed., p. 41). Copyright © 1998 Mosby St. Louis: with permission from Elsevier.

A growing body of evidence is pointing to key connections between our immune system and our psychological state. Decades of research show how our psychological state, or a characteristic such as our attitude, creates neurological, hormonal, and behavioral responses that directly change the immune system and make us more likely to become ill. This is especially the case in terms of the negative effects of stress on our immune system (Reed & Raison, 2016).

From this discussion, it should be clear that the immune system is affected by many other body systems. **Psychoneuroimmunology** is the study of the relations among psychological, neurological, and immunological systems that raise or lower our susceptibility to and ability to recover from disease. Psychoneuroimmunology is increasingly being used as a framework to understand health outcomes in predicting how people cope with and survive the stress of illness as a function of their personality (Mengelkoch et al., 2022; Reed & Raison, 2016). By considering the various factors influencing disease, such as life situations, financial resources, availability of care providers, and so on, interventions that optimally combine medication, diet, and mind–body strategies (e.g., mindful meditation) with the person's realities of everyday life can be devised.

COVID-19, HIV/AIDS, and Older Adults. Two examples of viral infections that are of increased concern for older adults are COVID-19 and HIV/AIDS. In the case of COVID-19, awareness of both the disease and one's vulnerability to it were very high. It was clear early in the pandemic that older adults and people of color were especially vulnerable to the disease and had a much higher hospitalization and death rate than did middle-aged and young adults and White individuals. Thus, much of the early discussions about COVID-19 focused on the vulnerability of older adult populations, particularly older adults of color, especially those in congregate living situations (e.g., assisted living, long-term care facilities).

In contrast, many older adults do not consider themselves at risk for HIV/AIDS, especially given the lower levels of public discussion of this disease since the early 2000s. However, older adults in particular remain vulnerable, in part because of a lack of attention to the disease. Let's dig a little deeper into each.

COVID-19. From the initial reports in late 2019 of a virus that caused a different form of respiratory infection and appeared quite serious, it was clear that humans would have no previously established immune system defenses against what was eventually identified as severe acute respiratory syndrome coronavirus 2 (SARS-CoV-2, the official name for COVID-19). As noted earlier in our discussion, the effectiveness of the human immune system depends critically on the learning it does from prior exposures to pathogens. Although people had been exposed to many coronaviruses (including the ones that cause the common cold), their defenses had never experienced anything like COVID-19. Thus, people were quite vulnerable to the ravages of the disease.

So what does COVID-19 stir up in the immune system, and why did the pandemic have such a worse effect on older adults, especially older adults of color? Why does COVID-19 infection lead to a wide spectrum of clinical diseases, from asymptomatic infection to an acute respiratory disease with acute lung injury, along with multisystemic failure leading to death? Why does the immune system behave erratically from person to person in how it responds?

Answers to these questions are complicated (Cedillo-Barrón et al., 2022; Ciarambino et al., 2021). As discussed in this section, there are age-related changes in the immune system that make older adults more susceptible to COVID-19 infection. Aging of the immune system is strongly linked with a less-than-ideal innate immune response to viral pathogens. Physiological aging is accompanied by a subclinical chronic low-grade state of systemic inflammation, sometimes referred to as "inflamm-aging," characterized by elevated serum levels of certain proteins (e.g., C-reactive protein) and pro-inflammatory cytokines (e.g., TNF-α, IL-6, and IL-8). Inflamm-aging predisposes older adults to severe COVID-19 by suppressing the immune response to SARS-CoV-2. This is a crucial aspect of why older adults are at greater risk.

There's more to the inflammation story. It has also been reported that an age-related increase in viral-induced inflammation may trigger an exaggerated response that results in significant lung damage, leading to the increased morbidity and mortality rates in older adults. Research during the first two years of the COVID-19 outbreak indicates that how the immune system behaves plays a crucial role in setting the severity of the disease. To prevent progression of the severe forms of the disease, the immune system needs to be targeted in its response. Moreover, higher levels of anti-S and anti-N IgG and IgM correlate with worse clinical symptoms and older age, suggesting potentially detrimental effects of antibodies in some patients.

Interestingly, similar patterns of inflammation have been observed in both COVID-19 and in certain forms of systemic cancer (Cha, 2022; Hervey-Jumper & Monje, 2021). Researchers have noted very similar reports of cognitive impairments, labeled as brain fog, in both. Moreover, there are similar patterns of structural changes in the brain as well. Whether the cause(s) of these changes related to the underlying changes in the immune system related to inflammation remain to be discovered.

For older people of color, immune system changes are exacerbated by the sociocultural systemic disparities in environmental quality and the access to health care and affordable healthy food. These disparities increase the risk for developing health conditions, such as diabetes, that greatly increase the consequences of serious complications from COVID-19 infection.

Finally, there are crucial differences between biological females and biological males, as well as trans men and trans women, in immune response. For example, estrogen has wide stimulatory effects on immune system cells and regulates cytokines; androgens have a suppressive effect. Thus, biological males and trans men who undergo hormonal therapy have a greater susceptibility to COVID-19 and poorer response to vaccines because

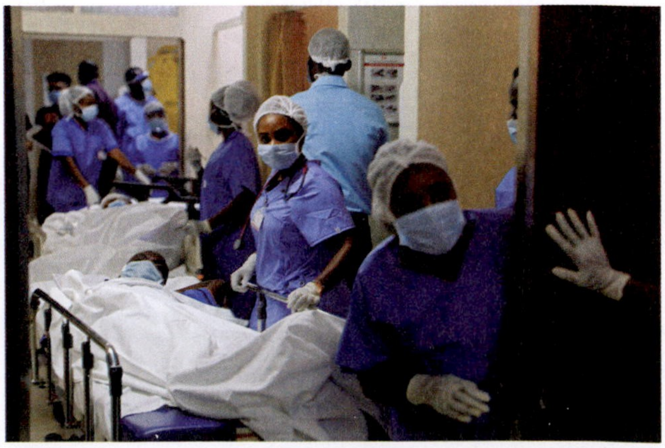

Reuters/Alamy Stock Photo

COVID-19 had a disproportionate impact on communities of color.

of their higher levels of testosterone on average. Biological females and trans women who undergo hormonal therapy have the opposite outcome because of estrogens. As the levels of these hormones change with age in later life, the effects may also diminish somewhat, but the degree that this is the case is largely unknown. We will encounter additional aspects of the disparities of COVID-19 in other contexts throughout the text.

HIV/AIDS. It may surprise you to learn that the Centers for Disease Control and Prevention (2021c) estimate that over half of the people in the United States living with diagnosed HIV are over age 50. Although 1 in every 6 new cases of HIV in the United States occurs in someone over age 50, social stereotypes that older adults are not sexually active result in many physicians not testing their older patients. This, combined with older adults confusing the symptoms of HIV/AIDS with other age-related issues, means that diagnosis occurs later in the course of the disease. Racial and ethnic differences in the stigmatization and attitudes toward people with HIV/AIDS result in differential levels of mental health difficulties and mortality (Benjamins et al., 2021). These disparities present treatment challenges, though most older adults with HIV are living longer and better lives because of advances in treatment, and mortality disparities between White and Black individuals with HIV/AIDS decreased between 2010 and 2019 (Benjamins et al., 2021).

Inequity in HIV outcomes traces to unequal HIV incidence and prevalence among Black and White populations in the United States. In 2019, the prevalence of HIV was six times higher in the Black population compared to the White population, but overall rates of infection continue to decline in all groups (Centers for Disease Control and Prevention, 2021g). Inequities are further exacerbated by disparities in HIV care, encompassing both primary and secondary prevention.

Although older men are at higher risk for HIV/AIDS, older women also are at significant risk. For men, the most common risk factor is male-to-male sexual behavior. In contrast, HIV/AIDS usually is transmitted to older women through female-to-male sexual contact with infected partners. Older adults may be more susceptible to HIV infection because of the changes in the immune system discussed earlier. For women, the thinning of the vaginal wall with age makes it more likely that it will tear, making it easier for HIV to enter the bloodstream. Older adults are the least likely group to practice safe sex through such things as condom usage, which also raises the risk (Silva, 2016).

Because AIDS/HIV is not a major focus of media stories about older adult sexual activity, older adults may mistakenly believe they have nothing to worry about. They are less likely to raise the issue with a physician, less likely to be tested, and, if diagnosed, less likely to seek support groups. Stereotypes about sexuality differ across racial and ethnic groups, and also across age groups, resulting in considerable pressure to not discuss the topic. In short, we need to change outmoded beliefs about older adults and sexuality and focus on health and prevention.

Chronic and Acute Diseases

You probably have had several encounters with illnesses that come on quickly, may range from mild to very severe, last a few days, and then go away. Illnesses such as influenza and the common cold are examples. You also may have experienced conditions that come on more slowly, last much longer, and have long-term consequences. Kidney disease, diabetes, and arthritis are examples. Some diseases, such as COVID-19 in certain people, can have aspects of both—the main symptoms come on quickly and then diminish, but certain symptoms, such as loss of taste and smell, linger indefinitely. These experiences reflect the difference between acute and chronic diseases. There are age-related differences in how people experiences these different types of illnesses.

Acute diseases are conditions that develop over a short period of time and cause a rapid change in health. We are all familiar with acute diseases, such as colds, influenza, food poisoning, and COVID-19. Many acute diseases are treated with medications (such as antibiotics for acute infections caused by bacteria, or antiviral agents and monoclonal antibodies for certain infections caused by viruses) or are monitored and allowed to run their course (the case with most viral infections such as the common cold or influenza).

In contrast, **chronic diseases** are conditions that last a longer period of time (at least three months) and may be accompanied by residual functional impairment that necessitates long-term management. Chronic diseases are often incurable, so interventions focus on disease management. Examples of chronic diseases are cardiovascular disease, cancer, COPD, arthritis, and diabetes mellitus.

What do you think happens to the incidence of acute diseases as people age? The rates decline. Contrary to what you might think, older adults have fewer colds, for example, than younger adults. That is because the human immune system learns from fighting invaders over the life span and creates an increasing catalog of different viruses, for instance. But keep in mind the age-related changes in the immune system discussed earlier. Those changes mean that when older adults do get an acute disease, they tend to get sicker, recovery takes longer, and death from acute disease occurs more often (National Center for Health Statistics, 2021a). Thus, although they get fewer acute infections, older people may actually spend more days feeling sick than their younger counterparts.

This is probably why many people mistakenly believe that the rates of acute disease increase with age. Because they have more problems fighting acute infections, older adults are more at risk from dying of an acute condition than are emerging, established, and middle-aged adults. This was certainly the case in the early phase of the COVID-19 pandemic, which was in line with data regarding other respiratory-type infections—the rate of these infections may decline for younger and older adults, but people over age 65 account for nearly all deaths from pneumonia and influenza. For these reasons, health professionals strongly recommend that older adults be vaccinated against acute diseases such as pneumonia (Pneumococcal Polysaccharide Vaccine [PPSV23] and perhaps Pneumococcal Conjugate Vaccine [PCV13]), and influenza (the quadrivalent or high dose annually) (Centers for Disease Control and Prevention, 2021d, 2021e). This is also why, after mRNA vaccines and boosters against COVID-19 became available, the rates of hospitalization for older adults, who as a group had relatively higher rates of vaccination, dropped dramatically; by early 2022, rates were higher among 18–49 year-olds (Centers for Disease Control and Prevention, 2022a).

No vaccine for any disease in modern times has been more controversial than that for COVID-19. These vaccines were developed much more quickly than previous vaccines, mainly because a great deal of the preliminary research and some testing had already been done in connection with previous outbreaks of related diseases. However, the rapid implementation of COVID-19 vaccines led some to question their reliability and safety. Research showed, though, that the vaccines were safe (Health and Human Services, 2021). Indeed, fewer side effects and deaths were related to these vaccines than occurred in the implementation of other vaccines (Sandalu, 2020). And they worked—in December 2021, the hospitalization rate for adults aged 65 or higher was 52 times higher in unvaccinated people than for those who had received the three-shot regimen (Centers for Disease Control and Prevention, 2022b).

The Role of Stress

You know what it feels like to be stressed. Whether it's from the upcoming exam in this course, the traffic jam you sat in on your way home yesterday, the demands your family or your job place on you, or the increasing cost of basic food and fuel without an increase in income, stress seems to come from everywhere.

There is plenty of scientific evidence that over the long term, stress is very bad for your health. But despite thousands of scientific studies that result in our certainty about what stress does to us, scientists still cannot agree on a formal definition of what stress is. What is clear is that stress involves both physiological and psychological aspects (Levy & Bavishi, 2018).

The most widely applied approaches to stress involve (1) focusing on the physiological responses the body makes through the nervous and endocrine systems, and (2) the idea that stress is what people define as stressful. Let's consider each in more detail.

Stress as a Physiological Response. There is widespread agreement across many research studies that people differ in their physiological responses to stress (Laurent et al., 2016; Rab & Admon, 2021). Prolonged exposure to stress results in damaging influences from the sympathetic nervous system (which controls such things as heart rate, respiration, perspiration, blood flow, muscle strength, and mental activity) and a weakening of the immune system. As Cohen and colleagues (2012) discussed in their model of these effects, prolonged stress has a direct causative effect on susceptibility to a wide range of diseases, from the common cold to cardiovascular disease to cancer. At the cellular level, stress plays a role in shortening telomeres, which in turn change the expression of genes and may be a biological cause of both aging and death (discussed in Chapter 3; Etzel & Shalev, 2021).

Biological sex differences in physiological stress responses have also been documented. For example, there is some evidence that the hormone oxytocin plays a different role in biological females than in biological males. Oxytocin is the hormone important in biological females' reproductive activities and for establishing strong bonds with one's children (Kim et al., 2016). Additional research indicates that the hormone oxytocin plays an important role in attachment (Cacioppo & Cacioppo, 2020). In biological males, it enhances their partner's attractiveness compared to other biological females (Lieberz et al., 2020). In biological females, it enhances their orgasms, among other things (Cacioppo & Cacioppo, 2013), which has earned it the nickname of the "cuddle hormone" (Lee et al., 2009).

The Stress and Coping Paradigm. Suppose you are stuck in a traffic jam. Depending on whether you are late for an important appointment or have plenty of time on your hands, you will probably feel very different about your situation. The **stress and coping paradigm** views stress not as an environmental stimulus or as a response but as the interaction of a thinking person and an event (Lazarus, 1984; Lazarus et al., 1985; Lazarus & Folkman, 1984). How we interpret an event such as being stuck in traffic is what matters, not the event itself or what we do in response to it. Put more formally, stress is "a particular relationship between the person and the environment that is appraised by the person as taxing or exceeding their resources and endangering their well-being" (Lazarus & Folkman, 1984, p. 19). Note that this definition states that stress is a transactional process between a person and the environment, that it considers personal resources, that the person's appraisal of the situation is key, and that unless the situation is considered to be threatening, challenging, or harmful, stress does not result. A diagram of the transactional model is shown in Figure 4.4.

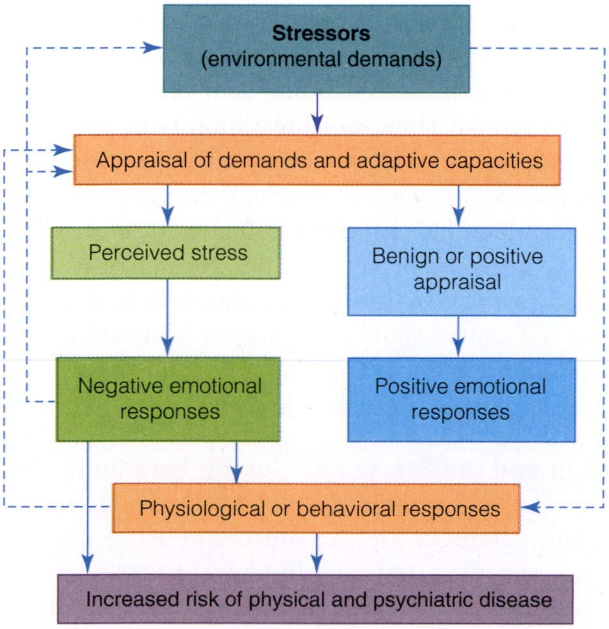

Figure 4.4 An example of a transactional model of stress.
Source: From Cohen, S., Kessler, R. & Gordon, L. (Eds.), *Measuring Stress: A Guide for Health and Social Scientists.*

Appraisal. Lazarus and Folkman (1984) describe three types of appraisals of stress. **Primary appraisal** categorizes events into three groups based on the significance they have for our well-being: irrelevant, benign or positive, and stressful. Primary appraisals filter the events we experience. Specifically, any event that is appraised as either irrelevant (things that do not affect us) or as benign or positive (things that are good or at least neutral) is not stressful. So, we literally decide which events are potentially stressful and which ones are not. This is an important point for two reasons. First, it means we can effectively sort out the events that may be problems and those that are not, allowing us to concentrate on dealing with life's difficulties more effectively. Second, it means that we could be wrong about our reading of an event. A situation that may appear at first to be irrelevant, for example, may actually be very important, or a situation deemed stressful initially may turn out not to be. Such mistakes in primary appraisal could set the stage for real (or imagined) crises later on.

If a person believes that an event is stressful, a second set of decisions, called secondary appraisal, is made. **Secondary appraisal** evaluates our perceived ability to cope with harm, threat, or challenge. Secondary appraisal is the equivalent of asking three questions: "What can I do?" "How likely is it that I can use one of my options successfully?" and "Will this option reduce my stress?" How we answer these questions sets the stage for addressing them effectively. For example, if you believe there is something you can do in a situation that will make a difference, then your perceived stress may be reduced, and you may be able to deal with the event successfully. In contrast, if you believe there is little that you can do to address the situation successfully or reduce your feelings of stress, then you may feel powerless and ineffective, even if others around you believe there are steps you could take.

Sometimes, you learn additional information or experience another situation that indicates you should reappraise the original event. **Reappraisal** involves making a new primary or secondary appraisal resulting from changes in the situation. For example, you may initially dismiss an accusation that your partner is cheating on you (i.e., make a primary appraisal that the event is irrelevant), but after being shown pictures of your partner in a romantic situation with another person, you reappraise the event as stressful. Reappraisal can either increase stress (if your partner had initially denied the encounter) or lower stress (if you discovered that the photographs were fakes).

The three types of appraisals demonstrate that determining whether an event is stressful is a dynamic process. Initial decisions about events may be upheld over time, or they may change in light of new information or personal experience. Different events may be appraised in the same way, and the same event may be appraised differently at any two points in time. This dynamic process helps explain why people react the way they do over the life span. For example, as our physiological abilities change with increasing age, we may have fewer physical resources to handle particular events. As a result, events that were appraised as not stressful in young adulthood may be appraised as stressful in late life.

Coping. During the secondary appraisal of an event labeled stressful in primary appraisal, we may believe there is something we can do to deal with the event effectively. Collectively, these attempts to deal with stressful events are called **coping**. Lazarus and Folkman (1984) view coping more formally as a complex, evolving process of dealing with stress that is learned. Much like appraisals, coping is seen as a dynamic, evolving process that is fine-tuned over time. Our first attempt might fail, but if we try again in a slightly different way we may succeed. Coping is learned, not automatic. That is why we often do not cope very well with stressful situations we are facing for the first time (such as the end of our first love relationship). The saying "practice makes perfect" applies to coping, too. Also, coping takes time and effort. Finally, coping entails only managing the situation; we need not overcome or control it. Indeed, many stressful events cannot be fixed or undone; many times the best we can do is to learn to live with the situation. It is in this sense that we may cope with the death of a partner.

People cope in different ways. At a general level we can distinguish between problem-focused coping and emotion-focused coping. **Problem-focused coping** involves attempts to tackle the problem head-on. Taking medication to treat a disease and spending more time studying for an examination are examples of problem-focused coping with the stress of illness or failing a prior test. In general, problem-focused coping entails doing something directly about the problem at hand. **Emotion-focused coping** involves dealing with one's feelings about the stressful event. Allowing oneself to express anger or frustration over becoming ill or failing an exam is an example of this approach. The goal here is not necessarily to eliminate the problem, although this may happen. Rather, the purpose may be to help oneself deal with situations that are difficult or impossible to tackle head-on.

Several other behaviors can also be viewed in the context of coping. Many people use their relationship with God as the basis for their coping (Kinney et al., 2003). For believers, using religious coping strategies usually results in positive outcomes when faced with negative events. International data show that this outcome is cross-cultural. For example, a study of Palestinian adults showed significant negative correlations between religious coping and stress, and with symptoms of depression (Mahamid & Bdier, 2021). Malaysian healthcare workers who used religious coping had lower levels of anxiety during the COVID-19 pandemic (Chow et al., 2021).

How well we cope depends on several factors. For example, healthy, energetic people are better able to cope with an infection than frail, sick people. Psychologically, a positive attitude about oneself and one's abilities is also important. Good problem-solving skills put one at an advantage by creating several options with which to manage the stress. Social skills and social support are important in helping one solicit suggestions and assistance from others. Finally, resources are important; having access to a place to exercise can help alleviate stress.

The most effective ways to deal with stress are through various relaxation techniques. Whether you prefer yoga, visualization, progressive muscle relaxation, meditation or contemplative prayer, or massage does not really matter. All good relaxation methods have a similar effect in that they slow your pulse, lower blood pressure, slow your breathing, reduce tension, focus concentration, lower anger and fatigue, and boost confidence.

Keep in mind that the number of stressful events, per se, is less important than one's appraisal of them and whether the person has effective skills to deal with them. Of course, should the number of stressful issues exceed one's ability to cope, then the number of issues being confronted would be a key issue.

Aging and the Stress and Coping Paradigm. Two important age-related differences in the stress and coping paradigm are the sources of stress and the choice of coping strategies. In terms of stress, national data in the United States show that younger adults, people of color, and those with lower levels of education or income report higher stress (National Center for Health Statistics, 2021a). The COVID-19 pandemic

Religiosity and spirituality are important aspects of a person's lifestyle that must be considered in holistic approaches to health and wellness.

exacerbated these outcomes. For example, in a global survey of 20,842 respondents from 24 universities in nine countries, college students reported that they felt increased stress in six major areas (financial situation, health, love life, relationships with family, relationships at work/school, problems experienced by loved ones) that were all related to increases in six types of mental disorders (major depressive disorder, bipolar disorder, generalized anxiety disorder, panic disorder, alcohol use disorder, and drug use disorder; Karyotaki et al., 2020).

Age differences in the choice of coping strategies across the life span are consistent (Rubio et al., 2016). One key difference is that older adults are less likely to use active coping strategies and are more likely to use past experience, emotion-focused, and religious coping strategies. It turns out that these strategies chosen by older adults are quite effective. During the COVID-19 pandemic, older adults showed significantly more resilience than did their younger counterparts in terms of dealing with the psychological consequences of the challenge (Fuller & Huseth-Zosel, 2021).

Effects of Stress on Health. How does stress affect us? If the stress is short, such as being stuck in a traffic jam for an hour when we're already late in an otherwise relaxed day, the answer is that it probably will have little effect other than on our temper. But if the stress is continuous, or chronic, then the picture changes dramatically.

There is ample evidence that perceived stress is related to brain structures; for instance, the size of the hippocampus, a brain structure intimately involved in cognition (discussed in Chapter 2) is smaller in people who report moderate to high levels of chronic stress (Goldfarb et al., 2020; Lindgren et al., 2016). Likewise, chronic stress has been clearly shown to have very significant negative effects on health, including pervasive negative effects on the immune system that cause increased susceptibility to viral infections (such as COVID-19), increased risk of atherosclerosis and hypertension, impaired memory and cognition, as well as mental health disorders (M. G. Frank et al., 2016; Karanikas et al., 2021). Effects of stress can last for decades; severe stress experienced in childhood has effects that last well into adulthood (Morton et al., 2019; Tan et al., 2020).

Research indicates that different types of appraisals that are interpreted as stressful create different physiological outcomes (M. G. Frank et al., 2016; Karanikas et al., 2021). This may mean that how the body reacts to stress depends on the appraisal process; the reaction to different types of stress is not the same. In turn, this implies that changing people's appraisal may also be a way to lower the impact of stress on the body.

One of the most serious consequences of chronic stress is that it increases the level of LDL cholesterol, which has significant negative consequences (covered in Chapter 14; McKay, 2016). LDL cholesterol levels rise because of chronic stress for several reasons: people stop exercising, eat more unhealthy foods, and have higher levels of cortisol and adrenaline (which stimulate the production of triglycerides and free fatty acids, which in turn increase LDL cholesterol levels over time). High levels of LDL cholesterol are associated with cardiovascular disease and stroke. These effects are one reason for differences across sociocultural groups in rates of cardiovascular disease as discussed in Chapter 3.

The COVID-19 pandemic really highlighted the interconnectedness between stress and health and their interaction with race, ethnicity, gender, and socioeconomic class (Qureshi, 2022). From greater susceptibility to COVID-19 infection (discussed earlier in relation to the immune system) to increased mental health issues in students and parents, and in people of color (explored in more detail in Chapter 10), burnout in the workplace (considered in Chapter 12), and memory and other cognitive function impairments (discussed in Chapters 6, 7, and 10), this interplay could be seen in every aspect of adults' experiences and behaviors.

Adult Development in Action

Design an education program for adults regarding health and the immune system, with special focus on stress and coping.

Review Questions

4.2 Health and Illness

- How are the definitions of health and illness linked? How is quality of life defined generally, especially in relation to health?
- What are the major age-related changes in the immune system? How do they affect health and illness?
- What is the difference between acute and chronic diseases? How do the rates of each change with age?
- How does the stress and coping paradigm explain the experience of stress? What age-related changes occur in the process?

4.3 Common Chronic Conditions and Their Management

Key Questions

- What are the most important issues in chronic disease?
- What are some common chronic conditions across adulthood?
- How can people manage chronic conditions?

Moses is a 75-year-old Black man who worked as a lawyer all his life. Recently, he was diagnosed as having prostate cancer. Moses has heard about several treatment options, such as surgery and radiation therapy, and he is concerned about potential side effects, such as impotence. Moses wonders what he should do.

Every day, millions of older adults get up and face another day of dealing with chronic diseases such as diabetes and arthritis. Although medical advances are made every year, true cures for these conditions probably are not imminent. We considered some chronic diseases in Chapter 3 in the context of discussing age-related changes in major body systems, including arthritis and cardiovascular disease. In this section, we will consider other very common chronic conditions, such as diabetes and cancer. As Moses will discover, in many situations there is no one clear-cut "right" way to proceed regarding treatment for chronic diseases. We will also examine some ways to help alleviate the effects of some chronic conditions and consider some ways in which we may be able to prevent such diseases or at least reduce our chances of getting them.

General Issues in Chronic Conditions

Having a chronic disease does not mean that one immediately becomes incapacitated. Even though the type and severity of chronic conditions vary across people, most older adults manage to accomplish the necessary tasks of daily living despite having a chronic condition.

Chronic conditions can make life unpleasant and, in some cases, can increase susceptibility to other diseases. Understanding chronic conditions requires understanding how the four developmental forces (biological, psychological, sociocultural, and life cycle) interact. We learned in Chapter 3 that researchers are beginning to understand these interactions in cardiovascular disease, for instance. In the case of other chronic conditions, key biological aspects include genetics and the changes in physical systems with age (such as the immune system), which can set the stage for chronic conditions. Major psychological aspects of chronic disease include the personality characteristics (described in Chapter 9) or coping skills (described in the previous section) people bring to bear on their conditions. Sociocultural factors include systemic social factors (e.g., racism, income disparities), access to or the lack of adequate health care, and other barriers to prevention, diagnosis, and treatment. Finally, life-cycle factors help us understand why reactions to the same chronic condition vary with the age of onset. Moreover, some conditions, such as rheumatoid arthritis, can occur at any point in adulthood, whereas others, such as prostate cancer, tend to occur mostly after midlife.

As the number of older adults increases rapidly, so will the extent of chronic conditions as health problems. This will necessitate a fundamental change in health care, reflecting a shift from a predominantly acute care focus to one that focuses much more on managing chronic conditions.

Common Chronic Conditions: Diabetes, Cancer, and Incontinence

Roughly half of adults in the United States have at least one chronic health condition (National Center for Health Statistics, 2016a). Some of the most common, such as cardiovascular disease and arthritis, were considered in Chapter 3. We will consider three other common conditions, diabetes mellitus, cancer, and incontinence, in this section.

Diabetes Mellitus. The disease **diabetes mellitus** occurs when the pancreas produces insufficient insulin.

The primary characteristic of diabetes mellitus is above-normal sugar (glucose) in the blood and urine caused by problems in metabolizing carbohydrates. People with diabetes mellitus can go into a coma if the level of sugar gets too high, and they may lapse into unconsciousness if it gets too low.

There are two general types of diabetes (American Diabetes Association, 2021a). **Type 1 diabetes** usually develops earlier in life and requires the use of insulin; hence it is sometimes called insulin-dependent diabetes. **Type 2 diabetes** typically develops in adulthood and is often effectively managed through diet. Considering how type 2 diabetes develops across adulthood, there are three patterns: those who develop diabetes as children, adolescents, or young adults; those who develop diabetes in late middle age and simultaneously typically develop cardiovascular problems; and those who develop diabetes in late life and usually experience only mild problems. This last group includes the majority of older adults with diabetes mellitus.

The symptoms of diabetes seen in younger people (excessive thirst, increased appetite and urination, fatigue, weakness, weight loss, blurry vision, impaired wound healing, and tingling numbness or pain in the hands or feet) may be far less prominent or absent in older adults. As a result, diabetes mellitus in older adults often is diagnosed during other medical procedures or screenings, such as regular annual examinations or hospitalizations for other conditions. Additionally, in adults, diabetes mellitus is often associated with obesity.

Overall, diabetes is more common among older adults, males, and persons of color (Centers for Disease Control and Prevention, 2022c). Overall, nearly 30 million people (about 10% of the U.S. population) have diagnosed diabetes. Many more millions of people have undiagnosed diabetes. As noted in Figure 4.5, rates differ across racial, ethnic, and gender groups. These disparities are caused mostly by unequal access to health care (prevention, diagnosis, treatment) and to affordable healthy food. The disparities are also exacerbated by higher average experiences of stress in persons of color, as noted earlier in this chapter. As will be noted in several places in this and later chapters, having diabetes is one of the most important risk factors for susceptibility to other diseases and in the outcome of dealing with those diseases. For example, individuals with diabetes were at much higher risk for hospitalization and death from COVID-19 (Centers for Disease Control and Prevention, 2022a).

For people with diabetes, the chronic effects of increased glucose levels may result in serious complications. The most common long-term effects include nerve damage, diabetic retinopathy (discussed in Chapter 3), kidney disorders, cerebrovascular accidents (CVAs; covered in Chapter 3), cognitive dysfunction, damage to the coronary arteries, skin problems, and poor circulation in the arms and legs, which may lead to gangrene. These potential complications emphasize the need for careful monitoring

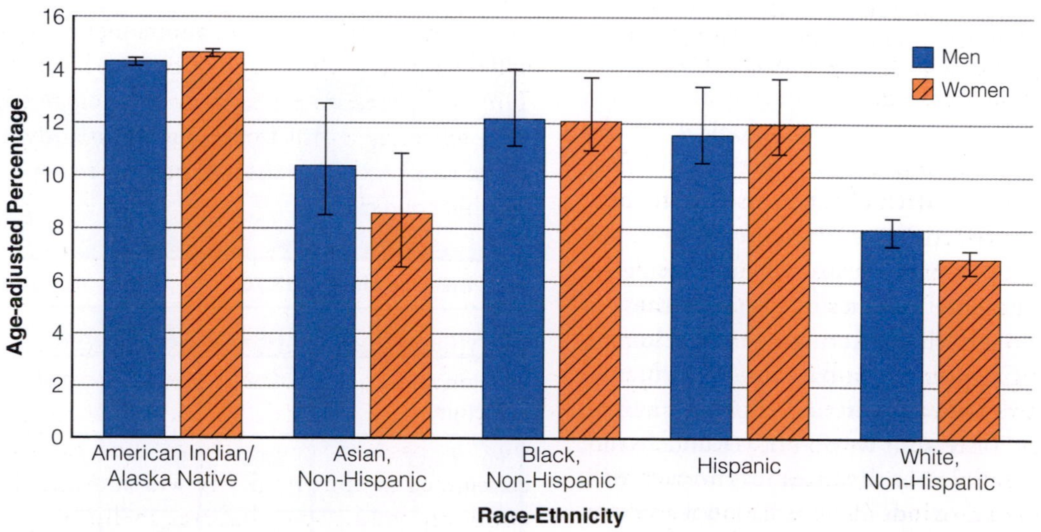

Figure 4.5 Age-adjusted estimated prevalence of diagnosed diabetes by race/ethnicity group and sex for adults aged 18 years or older, United States.

Source: Centers for Disease Control and Prevention. (2022). Prevalence of diagnosed diabetes. (Figure 2). https://www.cdc.gov/diabetes/data/statistics-report/diagnosed-diabetes.html

and management of the disease, and they highlight the consequences of inadequate access to health care.

Although it cannot be cured, diabetes can be managed effectively through a low-carbohydrate and low-calorie diet; exercise; proper care of skin, gums, teeth, and feet; and medication (insulin) if necessary (American Diabetes Association, 2021b). For older adults, it is important to address potential memory difficulties that can interfere with the daily testing and various management regimens. Following the appropriate management strategy is key to avoiding or minimizing the risks of the complications noted earlier. Education about diabetes is included in Medicare coverage, making it easier for older adults to learn how to manage their condition effectively. Taking the appropriate steps to avoid diabetes in the first place is the best strategy, of course, so monitoring weight is very important, as are blood pressure and blood glucose (sugar) levels. Exercise and good nutrition are important aspects of an overall wellness-based lifestyle. All of these treatment approaches depend, of course, on having access to them in the first place. Many people of color and adults who lack adequate financial resources do not.

Cancer. Cancer is the second leading cause of death in the United States, behind cardiovascular disease (Ortaliza et al., 2021). (It should be noted that during certain periods of 2020 and 2021, COVID-19 temporarily ranked higher.) However, given the twin factors of an aging population and declining rates of cardiovascular disease, it is likely that cancer will become the leading cause by the early 2030s.

Over the life span, American biological males have about a 40% chance, and American biological females have about a 39% chance of developing some form of cancer. The risk of dying from cancer is about 21% for biological males and 18% for biological females (American Cancer Society, 2020). The risk of getting cancer increases markedly with age, in part because of declines in the effectiveness of the immune system (discussed earlier), in part because of the cumulative effects of environmental pollutants, in part because of changes in our genetic structures (e.g., telomere shortening; see Chapter 3), in part due to structural disparities in access to health care and affordable healthy food, and in part for reasons we do not yet understand. Because of the remarkable advances in interventions, especially those based on advanced radiation techniques and designer genetic treatments, death rates for most types of cancer have been falling since the 1990s.

Many forms of cancer are preventable (American Cancer Society, 2021b). For example, some forms of cancer, such as lung and skin cancer, are caused in large part by lifestyle factors. Smoking causes more preventable health conditions, including cancer, than any other lifestyle issue. As noted in Chapter 3, most skin cancers can be prevented by limiting exposure to the sun's ultraviolet rays.

The incidence and mortality rates of some common forms of cancer in biological males and biological females are noted in Table 4.1. Prostate cancer is the second most common form of cancer in biological males, and breast cancer is the second most common form in biological females (the three types of skin cancers together are the most common for both groups), and that the death rates differ across types of cancer (American Cancer Society, 2020).

Table 4.1 Lifetime Risk of Developing or Dying from Selected Types of Cancer

	Risk of Developing		Risk of Dying from	
Males	%	1 in	%	1 in
All invasive sites	**40.14**	**2**	**21.34**	**5**
Bladder (includes in situ)	3.86	26	0.93	108
Colon and ractum	4.41	23	1.83	55
Lung and bronchus	6.70	15	5.49	18
Melanoma of the skin	2.77	36	0.39	256
Prostate	11.60	9	2.44	41
Females	%	1 in	%	1 in
All invasive sites	**38.70**	**3**	**18.33**	**5**
Breast	12.83	8	2.57	39
Colon and rectum	4.08	25	1.68	60
Lung and bronchus	6.05	17	4.50	22
Thyroid	1.93	52	0.07	1,429
Uterus	3.07	33	0.63	159

Source: American Cancer Society. https://www.cancer.org/cancer/cancer-basics/lifetime-probability-of-developing-or-dying-from-cancer.html

Racial and ethnic disparities are found in most types of cancer, but none are as large as those found in prostate cancer (Chowdhury-Paulino et al., 2022; Mahal et al., 2022). In the United States, Black biological males have an incidence rate 60% higher than that of White biological males, a disparity that has remained consistent even though the overall incidence of prostate cancer has declined for both groups. Black biological males tend to be diagnosed at a more advanced stage and have more health challenges overall. Multiple studies and reviews of the research demonstrate repeatedly that much of this disparity results from a combination of structural barriers to health care; historical concerns about medical diagnoses, treatment, and research abuses of the Black community; and other socioeconomic factors. As a result, Black biological males with high-risk disease are 40% less likely than White biological males to receive curative treatment. However, research also shows that if equity in treatment is provided, survival rates are comparable, providing additional evidence of the deadly effects of the structural racial disparities.

In terms of cancer treatment in general, research in molecular biology and microbiology points to genetic links, likely in combination with environmental factors (Battista et al., 2012). Genetics-based research, especially in precision medicine, is responsible for tremendous advances in detecting and treating cancer, and in understanding how cancer cells operate and reproduce. The National Cancer Institute initiated the Office of Cancer Genomics (OCG; https://ocg.cancer.gov/about-ocg). The mission of the OCG is both to understand the dynamics of cancer and to rapidly translate research findings into effective treatments.

Understanding the genetic underpinnings of cancer is key to understanding personal likelihood of having certain forms of cancer. For example, three breast cancer susceptibility genes that have been identified are *BRCA1* on chromosome 17 and *BRCA2* on chromosome 13, as well as *PALB2*, which works in conjunction with *BRCA2*. These genes produce proteins that suppress tumors; the proteins help repair damaged DNA and help ensure the stability of the cell's genetic material. When any of these genes is mutated, or altered, such that its protein product either is not made or does not function correctly, DNA damage may not be repaired properly. As a result, cells are more likely to develop additional genetic alterations that can lead to cancer. That is why a person who carries a mutation in *BRCA1*, *BRCA2*, or *PALB2* is at a greater risk of being diagnosed with breast or ovarian cancer at some point. A complete list, frequently updated, of all known genes that increase risk of breast cancer is provided by BreastCancer.org (2021).

Similarly, a number of genes related to susceptibility to prostate cancer have been identified (National Cancer Institute, 2021b). These include the *BRCA1* and *BRCA2* genes discussed in relation to breast cancer, as well as *HPC1* on chromosome 1, and *HOXB13* on chromosome 17. Over 150 other genes may have some relation to prostate cancer, but firm conclusions have not emerged from ongoing research (National Cancer Institute, 2021b).

Although routine genetic screening tests for breast and prostate cancer for the general population are not yet done routinely, people who are at risk for the diseases (e.g., have a family history of cancer) may get screened providing they have adequate access to health care. Should the results be positive for known-risk genetic mutations, a key question is what to do next. For people facing an increased risk of breast cancer, for instance, this may involve decisions about prophylactic mastectomy or other surgical or treatment procedures. One thing is certain, though. When famous people face these decisions, what they decide can have profound effects on what those in the general population do. The Real People feature explores how one famous woman, Angelina Jolie, made her decision and the broader societal effects of it.

Genetics research is also the basis for most new insights into possible treatments by discovering new ways to fight cancer (National Cancer Institute, 2021a). Age-related tissue changes have been associated with the development of tumors, some of which become cancerous; these may be genetically linked as well. The discovery that the presence of telomerase causes cells to grow rapidly and without limits on the number of divisions they can undergo provides additional insights into how cancer develops (Nenclares & Harrington, 2020; discussed in Chapter 3). What remains to be understood is how these genetic events interact with environmental factors, such as pollutants, and sociocultural factors, such as lifelong stress from a lack of adequate financial resources, discrimination, and so forth. Understanding these interaction processes, predicted by the basic developmental forces, could explain why there are great differences among individuals in when and

Real People

The "Angelina Jolie Effect"

Angelina Jolie is one of the most famous actresses in the world. Because of her fame, many people watch her behavior carefully and base their own actions on what she does. In 2013, Angelina learned that she carried the *BRCA1* gene, which, considered in the context of the rest of her family health history and other tests that detected protein abnormalities, gave her an estimated 87% risk of breast cancer and 50% chance of ovarian cancer. What she did next created both a media sensation and greatly increased awareness of the challenges and decisions that confront thousands of people each year.

Luigi De Pompeis/Alamy Stock Photo

Angelina Jolie

Angelina decided to have a double mastectomy and reconstructive surgery, and subsequently had her ovaries and fallopian tubes removed. After her mastectomies, she had reconstructive surgery using her own tissue. She decided to be public about her situation in order to raise awareness of breast cancer and ovarian cancer risks and the options people have. She wrote two op-eds in the *New York Times* (Jolie, 2013, 2015) to explain her decision making. Her decision, and her fame, made a very big difference.

It became clear that an "Angelina Jolie effect" resulted. Research in the United Kingdom indicated that following the announcement of her breast cancer risk and surgery in May 2013, referrals for genetic screening for breast cancer more than doubled (Evans et al., 2014). Such increases were found globally (Lebo et al., 2015). In general, people expressed increased knowledge of breast cancer screening, techniques of reconstructive surgery, and genetic testing and risk.

Angelina Jolie's public discussion of her learning of her cancer risk, how and why she made the decisions she did, and her recovery process caused controversy. Some argued that she should have monitored her health and not undergone surgery. Others argued that she provided additional support for the stereotype of beauty. Still others thought her decision was a brave one. What is indisputable is that her fame raised the issues much higher in public awareness, resulting in many more people consulting their physicians about potential genetic risk and health screening. And that is a very good and important outcome.

how cancer develops, even when they have identical genetic predispositions.

Additionally, genetics research has resulted in a therapeutic approach using monoclonal antibodies (mAbs; also used to treat COVID-19, for example), adaptive cellular therapy to treat cancer by modulating the immune response (Khalil et al., 2016), metabolic reprogramming of cancer cells (Chen & Li, 2022), and targeted therapy designed for a specific individual's unique form of cancer (National Cancer Institute, 2021a). Additionally, advancements in radiation therapy, such as proton therapy and brachytherapy, provide treatments implemented separately or in combination with genetic-based therapies (Johns Hopkins, 2021). These interventions have shown dramatic results, including the remission of advanced stage tumors. It is highly likely that most future cancer treatments will be based on these approaches. An obvious key task is to ensure equitable access to them.

Of course, prevention is the preferred way to address the problem of cancer. The appropriate use of screening techniques and preventive lifestyle changes can lower the rates of most cancers, as well as deaths. The American Cancer Society (2021b) strongly recommends these steps for people of all ages, but older adults need to be especially aware of what to do. Table 4.2 provides guidelines for the early detection of some common forms of cancer.

Table 4.2 American Cancer Society Guidelines for the Early Detection of Cancer

The American Cancer Society Recommends These Screening Guidelines for Most Adults	
Breast cancer	**Women** • **Women ages 40 to 44** should have the choice to start annual breast cancer screening with mammograms (x-rays of the breast) if they wish to do so. • **Women age 45 to 54** should get mammograms every year. • **Women 55 and older** should switch to mammograms every 2 years, or can continue yearly screening. • Screening should continue as long as a woman is in good health and is expected to live 10 more years or longer. • **All women** should be familiar with the known benefits, limitations, and potential harms linked to breast cancer screening. **Men** • **Men over age 35** who have a **BRCA2** or **BRCA1** inherited gene mutation should have a clinical breast exam annually. Adults should also know how their breasts normally look and feel, perform breast self-exams, and report any breast changes to a healthcare provider right away. Some people—because of their family history, a genetic tendency, or certain other factors—should be screened with MRIs along with mammograms. (The number of women who fall into this category is very small.) Talk with a healthcare provider about your risk for breast cancer and the best screening plan for you.
Colorectal cancer and polyps	For people at average risk for colorectal cancer, the American Cancer Society recommends starting regular screening at **age 45.** This can be done either with a sensitive test that looks for signs of cancer in a person's stool (a stool-based test) or with an exam that looks at the colon and rectum (a visual exam). Talk to your healthcare provider about which tests might be good options for you, and to your insurance provider about your coverage. No matter which test you choose, the most important thing is to get screened. If you're in good health, you should continue regular screening through **age 75.** For people **ages 76 through 85,** talk with your healthcare provider about whether continuing to get screened is right for you. When deciding, take into account your own preferences, overall health, and past screening history. People **over 85** should no longer get colorectal cancer screening.
Cervical cancer	• **Cervical cancer screening should start at age 25.** People under age 25 should not be tested because cervical cancer is rare in this age group. • **People between the ages of 25 and 65** should get a primary HPV (human papillomavirus) test* done every 5 years. If a primary HPV test is not available, a co-test (an HPV test with a Pap test) every 5 years or a Pap test every 3 years are still good options. • (*A primary HPV test is an HPV test that is done by itself for screening. The US Food and Drug Administration has approved certain tests to be primary HPV tests.) ***The most important thing to remember is to get screened regularly, no matter which test you get.*** • **People over age 65** who have had regular cervical cancer testing in the past 10 years with normal results should not be tested for cervical cancer. Once testing is stopped, it should not be started again. Those with a history of a serious cervical precancer should continue to be tested for at least 25 years after that diagnosis, even if testing goes past age 65. • **People whose cervix has been removed by surgery** for reasons not related to cervical cancer or serious precancer should not be tested. • **People who have been vaccinated against HPV** should still follow the screening recommendations for their age groups. Some individuals—because of their health history (HIV infection, organ transplant, DES exposure, etc.)—may need a different screening schedule for cervical cancer. Talk to a healthcare provider about your history.

(Continued)

Lung cancer	The most recent version of the American Cancer Society (ACS) lung cancer screening guideline [from 2018] is being taken down while we review new scientific evidence to be included in the next update. While this important update is being completed, the ACS advises that healthcare providers, and people at increased risk for lung cancer, follow the recently updated recommendations for annual lung cancer screening from the US Preventive Services Task Force (USPSTF), the American Academy of Family Physicians (AAFP), or the American College of Chest Physicians. These organizations recommend yearly lung cancer screening with LDCT scans for people who: • Are 50 to 80 years old and in fairly good health, **and** • Currently smoke or have quit in the past 15 years, **and** • Have at least a 20 pack-year smoking history. (This is the number of packs of cigarettes per day multiplied by the number of years smoked. For example, someone who smoked 2 packs a day for 10 years [2 × 10 = 20] has 20 pack-years of smoking, as does a person who smoked 1 pack a day for 20 years [1 × 20 = 20].) In addition, it's important that people who are going to be screened: • Receive counseling to quit smoking if they currently smoke, **and** • Have been told by their doctor about the possible benefits, limits, and harms of screening with LDCT scans, **and** • Can go to a center that has experience in lung cancer screening and treatment.
Prostate cancer (Men)	The American Cancer Society recommends that men make an informed decision with a healthcare provider about whether to be tested for prostate cancer. Research has not yet proven that the potential benefits of testing outweigh the harms of testing and treatment. We believe that men should not be tested without first learning about what we know and don't know about the risks and possible benefits of testing and treatment. Starting at age 50, men should talk to a healthcare provider about the pros and cons of testing so they can decide if testing is the right choice for them. If you are African American or have a father or brother who had prostate cancer before age 65, you should have this talk with a healthcare provider starting at age 45. If you decide to be tested, you should get a PSA blood test with or without a rectal exam. How often you're tested will depend on your PSA level.
Take control of your health, and reduce your cancer risk	• Stay away from all forms of tobacco. • Get to and stay at a healthy weight. • Get moving with regular physical activity. • Eat healthy with plenty of fruits and vegetables. • It's best not to drink alcohol. If you do drink, have no more than 1 drink per day for women or 2 per day for men. • Protect your skin. • Know yourself, your family history, and your risks. • Get regular check-ups and cancer screening tests.

Source: https://www.cancer.org/healthy/find-cancer-early/american-cancer-society-guidelines-for-the-early-detection-of-cancer.html and https ://www.komen.org/breast-cancer/screening/when-to-screen/high-risk-men/

Incontinence. For many people, the loss of the ability to control the elimination of urine and feces on an occasional or consistent basis, called **incontinence**, is a source of great concern and embarrassment. As you can imagine, incontinence can result in social isolation and lower quality of life if no steps are taken to address the problem.

Among community-dwelling older adults, roughly 60% of women and 40% of men have ever experienced urinary (the more common type) or bowel leakage

(National Center for Health Statistics, 2021a). Rates of both tend to increase with age.

Urinary incontinence occurs most often for four major reasons (Mayo Clinic, 2021b). **Stress incontinence** happens when pressure in the abdomen exceeds the ability to resist urinary flow. This may occur when a person coughs, sneezes, laughs, exercises, or lifts a heavy object. **Urge incontinence** usually is caused by a central nervous system problem after a stroke or urinary tract infection. People feel the urge to urinate but cannot get to a toilet quickly enough. **Overflow incontinence** results from improper contraction of the kidneys, causing the bladder to become overdistended. Certain drugs, tumors, and prostate enlargement are common causes of overflow incontinence. **Functional incontinence** occurs when the urinary tract is intact but because of physical disability or cognitive impairment the person is unaware of the need to urinate. This is the most common form in people with dementia, Parkinson's disease, or certain forms of nerve damage.

Most types of incontinence can be treated. Among the most effective treatments are behavioral interventions, which include diet changes, relearning to recognize the need to toilet, and pelvic floor muscle training for stress incontinence (Hsu et al., 2016). Certain medications and surgical intervention may be needed in some cases. Numerous products such as protective undergarments and padding also are available to help absorb leaks. All these options help alleviate the psychological and social effects of incontinence and help people have higher quality of life (Markland et al., 2012).

Managing Pain

People do not like to be in pain, and they fear pain more than almost any other aspect of disease. Perhaps that is because pain is one of the most unpleasant aspects of many chronic diseases. Pain is disruptive, saps energy, negatively affects quality of life, and can lead to an ever-intensifying cycle of pain, anxiety, and anguish. Pain is also one of the most common complaints of older adults, affecting more than 40% of community-dwelling older adults on a regular basis (Jones et al., 2016; Malec & Shega, 2015). Pain for older adults does not necessarily reflect the same things as pain in younger adults; for older adults it is not only an indication that something is wrong but can also be responsible for depression, sleep disorders, decreased social interaction, impaired mobility, and increased healthcare costs (Jones et al., 2016).

Unfortunately, many myths exist about pain in older adults, such as that older adults should simply accept the physical pain they experience as part of growing older. Failure to understand the real causes and nature of pain in older adults can lead to a failure to relieve it and to appropriately and accurately diagnose any underlying conditions that cause it.

There are two general pain management techniques: pharmacological and nonpharmacological (Jones et al., 2016). These approaches often are used together for maximum pain relief. Pharmacological approaches to pain management include nonnarcotic and narcotic medications. Nonnarcotic medications are best for mild to moderate pain, while narcotic medications are best for severe pain. Nonnarcotic medications include NSAIDs (nonsteroidal anti-inflammatory drugs), such as ibuprofen and acetaminophen, and are commonly used for conditions causing pain such as arthritis. However, these drugs must be used with caution because they may cause toxic side effects in older adults.

One family of medications prescribed for severe pain are opioids, powerful pain-reducing medications that include oxycodone, hydrocodone, and morphine, among others (U.S. Food and Drug Administration, 2021a). Narcotic or opioid drugs that work well in older adults include morphine and codeine; other commonly used drugs, such as meperidine and pentazocine, should be avoided because of age-related changes in metabolism. Patients taking any of these medications must be monitored very closely, as there is a significant risk of addiction or abuse of these medications.

In the early 2020s, roughly 100,000 people in the United States died each year from opioid-related overdoses, including prescription opioids, heroin, and illicitly manufactured fentanyl, a powerful synthetic opioid (National Center for Health Statistics, 2021b; National Institute on Drug Abuse, 2021). Roughly 1.7 million people had substance use disorders related to prescription opioid pain relievers, many of whom were also using heroin. In people under age 50, drug overdoses in general are the most common cause of accidental death, which is the leading cause of death in this age group. Data indicate that the COVID-19 pandemic actually resulted in an *increase* in the conditions for which opioids are prescribed, as well as the rate of substance abuse overall (McGonigle, 2021).

Due to the fact that nearly all the people who became dependent on opioids first received them from a physician and the fact that the U.S. healthcare system has documented racial and ethnic disparities in treating pain (people of color are prescribed pain medication at a lower rate), the opioid crisis is much more common among White, non-Hispanic adults than any other racial or ethnic group (Kaiser Family Foundation, 2021; Salmond & Allread, 2019). Moreover, rural populations were hit disproportionately harder than urban areas (American Farm Bureau Federation and National Farmers Union, 2021). Surveys indicate that nearly 50% of all rural residents and 75% of farm families specifically have been directly affected by the opioid crisis.

Beginning in the late 2010s, public education campaigns and wider availability of emergency treatments for overdose such as naloxone (NarCan®), a nasal spray that may counteract the life-threatening effects of an overdose, have saved lives. Additionally, a treatment for substance use disorder is available—buprenorphine—that has been shown to be effective for individuals diagnosed with opioid use disorder. Research for many years has shown that there is very little evidence for the long-term effectiveness of opioids in treating chronic pain from conditions other than cancer (Chou et al., 2014). Still, the prescriptions continue.

Although substance use disorder is a widespread problem and help for it is provided by the Affordable Care Act (Obamacare), relatively few other resources are provided for intervention, treatment, and recovery programs in the United States. Medical education is changing the way physicians approach treatments for chronic pain (Association of American Medical Colleges, 2021). Still, much remains to be done to stop these unnecessary deaths.

Because of the problems with opioids, including the fact that they lose potency over time even aside from their addictive side effects, several alternative techniques for pain management have become available, mostly through research. Most of these were designed to address pain that seems to originate in the spine, from such conditions as muscle or ligament strain, bulging or ruptured discs between vertebrae, osteoporosis, and arthritis.

Hanson L/Shutterstock.com

The massive opioid crisis led to efforts to make emergency treatments for overdose such as naloxone (NarCan®) more widely available.

Medical treatments for chronic back pain include a range of approaches, such as cortisone injections, radiofrequency neurotomy (in which a needle is inserted near the source of the pain and radio waves are used to damage nearby nerves, which serves to interfere with the transmission of pain signals to the brain), implanted nerve stimulators (devices that send electrical impulses to certain nerves to block pain signals), and surgery (trimming or removing bulging disks, fusing unstable portions of the spine together, and removing part or all of a vertebrae to relieve pressure on nerves) (Mayo Clinic, 2020c). On the horizon are custom-made implants created on 3D printers to match a patient's exact needs, as well as nanotechnology to stimulate growth of new tissue to heal or correct problems in order to avoid the need for implants.

Nonpharmacological and noninvasive pain control includes a variety of approaches, all of which are effective with some people; the trick is to keep trying until the best approach is found. Common techniques include the following:

- Physical therapy
- Deep and superficial stimulation of the skin through therapeutic touch, massage, vibration, heat, cold, and various ointments
- Electrical stimulation over the pain site or to the spine
- Acupuncture and acupressure
- Biofeedback, in which a person learns to control and change the body processes responsible for the pain
- Distraction techniques such as soft music that draw a person's attention away from the pain
- Relaxation, meditation, and imagery approaches that rid the mind of tension and anxiety
- Hypnosis, either self-induced or induced by another person

The most important point is that pain is not a necessary part of growing old or having a disease. Pain relief is an important part of recovery and should be included in any treatment regimen for adults of all ages.

Adult Development in Action

If you were a home health aide, what would you do to help your clients remember to take their medications? (Write down your answer and then check if you came up with similar ideas as you will read about in Chapter 7.)

Review Questions

4.3 Common Chronic Conditions and Their Management

- What are the general issues to consider in managing chronic disease?
- What are some common chronic diseases experienced by older adults?
- What are examples of emerging treatment options for chronic diseases?
- How is pain managed?

4.4 Pharmacology and Medication Adherence

Key Questions

- What are the developmental trends in using medication?
- How does aging affect the way the medications work?
- What are the consequences of medication interactions?
- What are the important medication adherence issues?

Lucy is an 80-year-old woman who has several chronic health problems. As a result, she takes 12 medications every day. She must follow the regimen very carefully; some of her medications must be taken with food, some on an empty stomach, and some at bedtime. Lucy's daughter is concerned that Lucy may experience serious problems if she fails to take her medications properly.

One of the most important health issues for older adults is the use of both prescription and over-the-counter medications. In fact, older adults take more medications on average than any other age group, totaling roughly half of all drugs prescribed in the United States. When over-the-counter drugs are included, this translates into about six or seven medications per older adult; Lucy takes more than the average. Like Lucy, most people take these drugs to relieve symptoms or other issues resulting from chronic conditions.

Patterns of Medication Use

The rapid increase of prescription and over-the-counter medications has created many options for physicians in treating disease, especially chronic conditions. Although advances in medication are highly desirable, there are hidden dangers for older adults (U.S. Food and Drug Administration, 2021b).

Only since the late 1990s have clinical trials of new medications been required to include older adults at all, and only more recently have they been required to have participants from racially and ethnically diverse backgrounds as well as all genders. Thus, for many medications currently on the market, we do not know whether they are as effective for older adults in general or for various racial, ethnic, or gender groups as they are for younger or middle-aged adults. Equally important, because of normative changes in metabolism with age, the effective dosage of medications may change as people get older, which can mean either a greater risk of overdose with potentially serious consequences, including death, or the need to increase the dose in order to get the desired effect. This lack of knowledge may result in physicians being more cautious in prescribing certain medications for older people.

In the United States, the cost of prescription drugs is both controversial and a barrier for many older adults with low incomes even with insurance through Medicare Part D because of premiums and co-payments. Additionally, figuring out which option is best can be quite complex, serving as a further barrier. You can get much more information from the official Medicare prescription drug coverage website (Medicare.gov, 2021a).

The age-related increase in chronic diseases typically results in related increases in the number of medications people take to help manage those diseases and help maintain health and quality of life. When multiple medications are used, interaction effects must be carefully understood and monitored. As we will discover, in many cases the need to take multiple medications results in complicated regimens that may also create memory challenges. Understanding how medications work, how these processes change with age, and the challenges of complicated medication regimens is extremely important.

Developmental Changes in How Medications Work

When Lucy takes her medications every day, what happens? Understanding how medications work involves knowing the developmental changes in absorption, distribution, metabolism, and excretion of medications (Chisholm-Burns et al., 2019).

Absorption is the time needed for medications to enter the bloodstream. For drugs taken orally, a key factor is the time it takes for the medication to go from the stomach to the small intestine, where maximum absorption occurs. This transfer may take longer than expected in older adults, resulting in too little or too much absorption, depending on the drug. For example, if a drug takes longer to transfer from the stomach to the small intestine in older adults, too little of the drug may be left to be effective. However, once in the small intestine, absorption does not appear to differ among older, middle-aged, or younger adults (Chisholm-Burns et al., 2019).

Once in the bloodstream, the medication is distributed throughout the body. How well distribution occurs depends on the adequacy of the cardiovascular system. Maximal effectiveness of a drug depends on the balance between the portions of the drug that bind with plasma protein (and mostly become ineffective) and the portions that remain free (and are available to "do their thing"). As we grow older, more of the drug remains free. This means that toxic levels of a drug can build up more easily in older adults. Similarly, drugs that are soluble in water or fat tissue can also build up more easily in older adults because of age-related decreases in total body water or possible increases in fat tissue.

Because the effective dosage of a drug depends critically on the amount of free drug in the body, the age changes just summarized mean that medical professionals must monitor drug levels very closely to avoid overdose or toxicity. Knowing the age, gender, weight, and other metabolic factors is key to ensuring that the effective dose of each medication is provided (Chisholm-Burns et al., 2019).

Getting rid of medications in the bloodstream is partly the job of the liver, a process called **drug metabolism**. There is much evidence that this process is slower in older adults, meaning that drugs stay in the body longer as people grow older (Ruscin & Linnebur, 2021). Slower drug metabolism (i.e., taking longer for the drug to clear from the body) can also create the potential for toxicity if the medication schedule does not take this into account.

Sometimes drugs are decomposed into other compounds to help eliminate them. This happens through a process called drug excretion. **Drug excretion** occurs mainly through the kidneys in urine, although some elimination occurs through feces, sweat, and saliva. Changes in kidney function with age, related to lower total body water content, are common. This means that drugs often are not excreted as quickly by older adults, so they may built up in the body, again setting the stage for possible toxic effects (Ruscin & Linnebur, 2021).

What do these changes mean? Most important, there are multiple age-related changes in metabolism that affect how quickly and how well medications are absorbed into and excreted from the body. Each of these changes has the potential for creating toxic side effects from levels of medications that are too high or become ineffective by being too low. For all these reasons, the dosage of a drug needed to get a desired therapeutic effect may be different for older adults than for middle-aged or younger adults. In many cases, healthcare professionals recommend using one-third to one-half the usual adult dosage when the difference between the effective dosages and toxic dosages is small or there are high rates of side effects (Rascin & Lennebur, 2021). In addition, because of age-related physiological changes that result in dangerous toxicity potential, or unknown effective dosage levels, several drugs are not recommended for use by older adults. In general, a dosage strategy of "start low and go slow" is best.

Medication Side Effects and Interactions

As we noted, age-related increases in the frequency of chronic conditions means that older adults are likely to have more than one medical problem for which they take medications. In this regard, Lucy is fairly typical. But there is a major downside related to this. Because of their high rates of medication use, older adults also have the highest risk of adverse drug side effects (Chisholm-Burns et al., 2019; Rascin & Lennebur, 2021). In part, these problems result from physiological changes that occur with age in how drugs are absorbed into the body, how long they remain, and how well they work. But the main reason for the increase in medication side effects is the actual taking of various drugs for each chronic condition, as well as possibly additional medications for other concerns.

Treating multiple conditions results in **polypharmacy**, the use of multiple medications. Polypharmacy is potentially dangerous because many drugs do not interact well; the action of some drugs is enhanced in combination with others, whereas other drugs may not work at all in combination. Drug interactions may create secondary medical problems that in turn need to be treated, and the primary condition may not be treated as effectively. Moreover, drug interactions can produce symptoms that are very similar or identical to symptoms of other diseases; for example, one side effect may be confusion and memory loss that mimics that observed in dementia.

Healthcare professionals and family members need to monitor the situation closely. Lucy's daughter is correct in worrying about her mother taking her medications as prescribed. Analyzing a person's medication regimen, including both prescription and over-the-counter medications, and asking the patient or caregiver to describe how they are taken is important in diagnosing health problems. It is extremely important to know *all* the medications, including diet supplements and other over-the-counter drugs, a person is taking regardless of whether they are prescribed or not.

Given the typically higher level of medication use among older adults, what can be done to minimize drug interaction effects? Healthcare professionals play a key role, but others also must be alert because older adults who have access to healthcare typically go to more than one physician. Accurate medication histories including all types of medicines are essential. If a problem is detected, then careful consideration of the risks and benefits of each medication is necessary, and alternative approaches to intervention, such as behavioral interventions, should be explored. The goal should be to use medications only when absolutely necessary and to avoid creating additional problems through their use.

Adherence to Medication Regimens

For medications to be maximally effective, it is important that they be taken as directed. This means that there is a critical memory component to the safe and effective use of medications—one must remember to take them on time and correctly. This is much easier when one is taking only a few medications. However, as one is required to take more medications such as Lucy is doing, keeping track of them becomes a more difficult memory challenge. An example of having to keep track of six different medications—common among older adults—each of which has a different administration schedule, is presented in Table 4.3.

Even under the best of circumstances, medication adherence (taking medications on time and correctly) becomes less likely the more drugs people take and the more complicated the regimens are. Combined with sensory, physical, and cognitive changes in older adults, medication adherence is a significant challenge in this age group (Chisholm-Burns et al., 2019; Krousel-Wood et al., 2021). Prospective memory, remembering to take one's medication at a future time, is critical to good adherence to a medication regimen (Jones et al., 2021; Krousel-Wood et al., 2021). The oldest old (individuals over age 80) are especially at risk; the most common problem is that they simply forget to take the medication. (We consider ways to help people remember to take their medications in Chapter 7.) Yet adherence is crucial to treatment success. Christensen and Johnson (2002) present an interactive model that describes the context of patient adherence. This model is depicted in Figure 4.6.

Table 4.3 Example of a Complex Medication Regimen

	Morning	Dinner	Bedtime
Large yellow pill	Take 1 each day with food		
Small blue pill	Take 1 every other day		
Small white pill	Take 2 per day for two days, then 1 per day; repeat		
Round pink tablet		Take 1 every other day	
Oval white pill			Take 2 each night with plenty of water
Small yellow pill			Take one per week

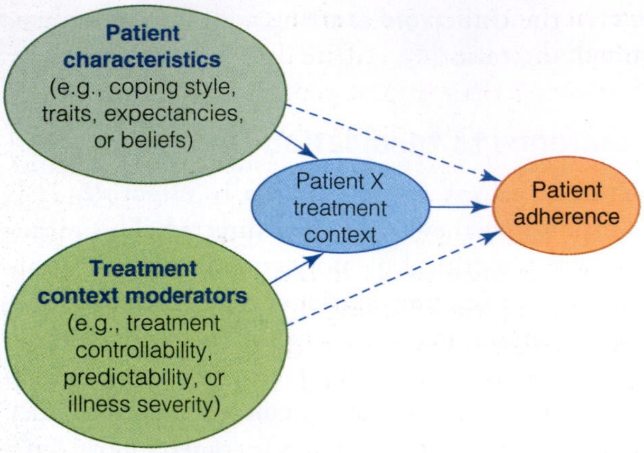

Figure 4.6 Conceptual representation of the patient-by-treatment context interactive framework. The dashed lines reflect the fact that research generally does not find that patient characteristics or contextual features have a significant effect on adherence.

Beyond basic adherence, another key issue is whether there are age-related differences in the ability of people to notice, remember, and report accurately adverse side effects from medications. Evidence suggests that when older adults are told to remember side effects that range from mild to severe, they recall the severe ones as well as younger adults. However, when told that certain side effects are critical to remember, they are less likely to differentiate the critical ones from other side effects than are younger adults, which may lead to a failure to contact their healthcare provider should those side effects occur (Friedman et al., 2015).

As noted in Chapter 7, one way to support medication adherence is via technology. Smartphone apps are available that monitor medication schedules as well as track several health indicators for compliance (Higgins, 2016; Li et al., 2021). These apps are increasingly used as part of a comprehensive telemedicine health and wellness approach to ensure that medications are taken, and other interventions and health monitoring are occurring as required.

The best approach, of course, is to keep the number of medications (and memory load) to a minimum if at all possible. If the use of drugs is determined to be essential, then periodic reevaluations should be conducted, and the medication discontinued when possible. In addition, the lowest effective dosage should be used. In general, medication use by older adults should get the same careful consideration as given to any other age group.

Adult Development in Actions

Given the higher frequency of chronic disease with age, what issues would you, as a professional human resources expert, need to include in creating support programs for employees?

Review questions

4.4 Pharmacology and Medication Adherence

- What is the typical pattern of medication use in older adults?
- What changes occur with age that influence how well medications work?
- What are the major risks for side effects and drug interactions?
- How can adherence to medication regimens be improved?

4.5 Functional Health and Disability

Key Questions

- What factors are important to include in a model of disability in late life?
- What is functional health?
- What causes functional limitations and disability in older adults?

Brian is a 68-year-old former welder who retired 3 years ago. He and his wife, Anita, had planned to spend more time with their grandchildren and maybe do some volunteer work at their church. But Brian's arthritis has been getting worse lately, and he is having increasing difficulty getting around and doing basic daily tasks. Brian and Anita wonder what the future holds for them.

Brian and Anita are not alone. Many couples plan to spend more time with family or to do other activities in later life, only to find health issues complicating the situation. To help find solutions, researchers have increasingly focused on how well people can function in their daily lives by managing the effects of chronic diseases to create the best level of functionality. In this section, we examine how functional health is determined and how disability occurs.

A Model of Disability in Late Life

As we learned earlier in this chapter, one defining characteristic of a chronic condition is that it lasts a long time. This means that for most adults, the time between the onset of a chronic condition and death is typically long, measured in years and even decades. Chronic diseases typically involve some level of discomfort and impact on one's functioning, and physical limitations are common, everyday issues for most people, as they are for Brian. Over the course of the disease, these problems usually increase, resulting in more efforts by patients and healthcare workers to try to slow the progress of the disease. In many cases, these efforts allow people to resume such activities as daily walks and shopping and to feel optimistic about the future (Verbrugge, 1994, 2020; Verbrugge et al., 2017; Verbrugge & Jette, 1994). This is especially true for the oldest old, people over age 80 (National Center for Health Statistics, 2021a). Social context also matters for older adults; a review of the research shows that disablement is associated with much higher feelings of loneliness (Dahlberg et al., 2022), and positive marital relationships, for instance, are associated with lower impairment (Warner & Adams, 2016).

In the context of chronic conditions, **disability** is the effects of chronic conditions on people's ability to engage in activities that are necessary, expected, and personally desired in their society (Verbrugge, 1994, 2020). When people are disabled because of a chronic condition, they may have difficulty doing daily tasks, such as household chores, personal care, job duties, active recreation, socializing with friends and family, and errands. One of the most important research efforts related to health and aging is seeking to understand how disability results from chronic conditions and what might be done to help prevent it. For these reasons, it is important to understand the changing context of disability in the United States.

Researchers point out that as the age at which disablement occurs in later life gets closer to the end of life, these changes may create what is called the compression of morbidity (Crimmins et al., 2021). **Compression of morbidity** refers to the situation in which the average age when one becomes disabled for the first time is postponed, causing the time between the onset of disability and death to be compressed into a shorter period of time. This implies that older adults in the United States are becoming disabled later in life than previously and are disabled a shorter time before dying than in past generations. Even though the idea is appealing, evidence for it is generally lacking (Crimmins et al., 2021). In fact, evidence shows that we have generally witnessed an increase in the prevalence and length of time with chronic disease because they are now diagnosed earlier in life, and chronic diseases are becoming less disabling due to better healthcare support systems and the use of technology.

Still, chronic disease and normative physiological changes do result in disability to various degrees. Verbrugge and Jette (1994; Verbrugge, 2020) originally proposed a comprehensive model of disability resulting from chronic conditions, a model that has greatly influenced research (depicted in Figure 4.7). The model consists of four main parts. The main pathway emphasizes the relations between pathology (the chronic conditions a person has), impairments of organ systems (such as muscular degeneration), functional limitations in the ability to perform activities (such as restrictions in one's mobility), and disability.

The model also includes risk factors and two types of intervention strategies: environmental and health care (*extraindividual factors*) and behavioral and personality (*intraindividual factors*). **Risk factors** are long-standing behaviors or conditions that increase one's chances of functional limitation or disability. Examples of risk factors include lower socioeconomic status, chronic health conditions, and unhealthy behaviors such as smoking. Extraindividual factors include interventions such as surgery, medications, social support services (e.g., Meals on Wheels), and physical environmental supports (e.g., wheelchair ramps). The presence of these factors often helps people maintain their independence and may make the difference between living at home and living in a long-term care facility. Intraindividual factors include such things as beginning an exercise program (such as walking), keeping a positive outlook, and taking advantage of transportation programs where they are available to increase mobility.

Extraindividual and intraindividual interventions are both aimed at reducing the restrictions and difficulties resulting from chronic conditions. Unfortunately, sometimes they do not work as intended and may even create problems of their own. For example, a prescribed medication may produce negative side effects that, instead of alleviating the condition, create a new problem. Or social service agencies may have inflexible policies about when a particular program is available, which may make it

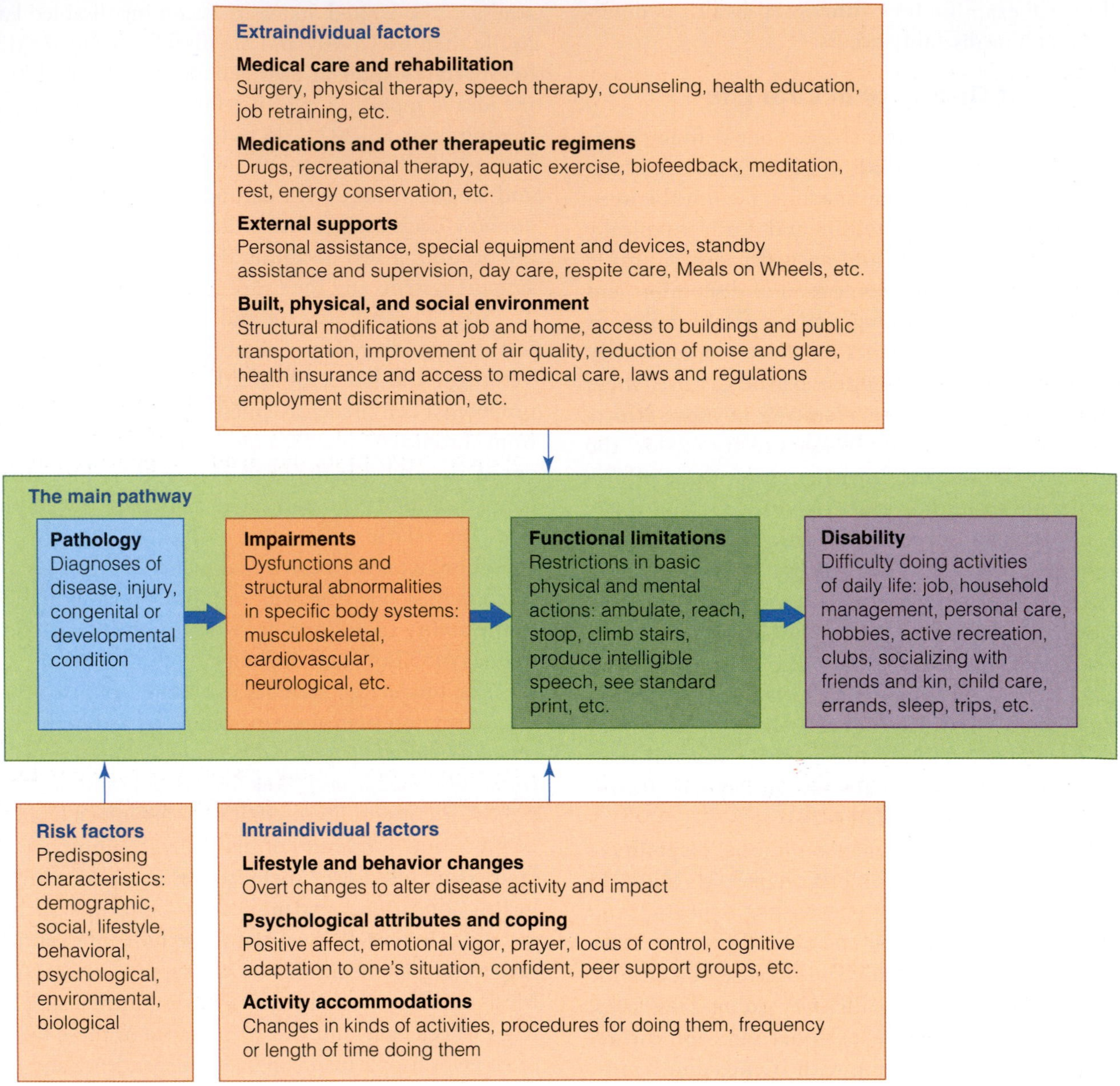

Extraindividual factors
Medical care and rehabilitation
Surgery, physical therapy, speech therapy, counseling, health education, job retraining, etc.
Medications and other therapeutic regimens
Drugs, recreational therapy, aquatic exercise, biofeedback, meditation, rest, energy conservation, etc.
External supports
Personal assistance, special equipment and devices, standby assistance and supervision, day care, respite care, Meals on Wheels, etc.
Built, physical, and social environment
Structural modifications at job and home, access to buildings and public transportation, improvement of air quality, reduction of noise and glare, health insurance and access to medical care, laws and regulations employment discrimination, etc.
The main pathway
Pathology
Diagnoses of disease, injury, congenital or developmental condition
Impairments
Dysfunctions and structural abnormalities in specific body systems: musculoskeletal, cardiovascular, neurological, etc.
Functional limitations
Restrictions in basic physical and mental actions: ambulate, reach, stoop, climb stairs, produce intelligible speech, see standard print, etc.
Disability
Difficulty doing activities of daily life: job, household management, personal care, hobbies, active recreation, clubs, socializing with friends and kin, child care, errands, sleep, trips, etc.
Risk factors
Predisposing characteristics: demographic, social, lifestyle, behavioral, psychological, environmental, biological
Intraindividual factors
Lifestyle and behavior changes
Overt changes to alter disease activity and impact
Psychological attributes and coping
Positive affect, emotional vigor, prayer, locus of control, cognitive adaptation to one's situation, confident, peer support groups, etc.
Activity accommodations
Changes in kinds of activities, procedures for doing them, frequency or length of time doing them

Figure 4.7 A model of the disablement process.

Source: Verbrugge, L. M., & Jette, A. M. (1994). The disablement process. *Social Science and Medicine, 38*(4). Reprinted with permission.

difficult for a person who needs the program to participate. Such situations are called **exacerbators**, because they make the situation worse than it was originally. Although they may be unintended, the results of exacerbators can be serious and necessitate additional forms of intervention, especially when the people who could benefit from them have do not have access.

One of the most important aspects of Verbrugge and Jette's (1994; Verbrugge, 2020) model is the emphasis on the fit between the person and the environment, a topic we explore in detail in Chapter 5. When a person's needs are met by the environment, the person's quality of life and adaptation are optimal; when they are not, the results can be quite stressful. We will also return to the issue of people with disabilities in the context of employment in Chapter 12, where we consider the role of the Americans with Disabilities Act and discrimination in the workplace.

Determining Functional Health Status

How can we determine where a person can be categorized along Verbrugge and Jette's continuum? The answer to this question describes a person's **functional health status**, that is, how well the person is functioning in daily life. Determining functional health status requires very careful assessment. Research indicates that loss of function tends not to occur randomly but rather follows certain sequences (Brown et al., 2022; Kingston et al., 2012; Levy et al., 2016). Generally, the first areas of difficulty involve tasks associated with strength, balance, and coordination, and the last areas with manual dexterity. This sequence of loss of function is referred to as the **hierarchy of loss.**

Verbrugge and Jette's model has provided a framework for understanding functional health status and the hierarchy of loss by explaining how disablement occurs in specific diseases such as osteoarthritis (Wang et al., 2005). The model informed the creation of the International Classification of Functioning, Disability and Health (ICF) that was endorsed by the World Health Organization in 2002 and is depicted in Figure 4.8. Among the most important contributions of ICF were the interacting and mediating roles of health, environmental, and personal factors that may result in disability that take sociocultural factors into account. The ICF has been an extremely valuable assessment tool and is widely used in Europe (Karlsson & Gustafsson, 2022).

Some older adults progress further along the disablement continuum such that their ability to function in their daily lives is impaired. They are officially termed **frail older adults**, individuals who have physical illnesses or conditions that create disabilities, are very ill, may have cognitive or psychological disorders, and need assistance with everyday tasks. Frail older adults constitute a minority of the population over age 65, but the size of this group increases considerably with age, as indicated in Figure 4.9.

Frail older adults are people whose competence (in terms of the competence–environmental press model discussed in Chapter 5) is declining. In the United States, frailty affects between 5% and 17% of all older adults depending on how it is defined. Frail older adults likely do not have one specific problem that differentiates them from their active, healthy counterparts; instead, they tend to experience multiple problems (Allison et al., 2021). The growing numbers and importance of frail older adults is a global problem, as gender inequality plays out differently across the world, traditional care-providing roles by adult children change, families are more dispersed geographically, and governmental policies regarding family size and health-care options have consequences (Dansereau et al., 2020; Lee et al., 2021).

To identify the areas in which people experience limited functioning, researchers have developed observational and self-report techniques to measure how well people can accomplish daily tasks. Everyday competence assessment consists of examining how well people can complete activities of daily living and instrumental activities of daily living, and whether they have other physical limitations (Verbrugge et al., 2017, 2020). **Activities of daily living (ADLs)** include basic self-care tasks such as eating, bathing, toileting,

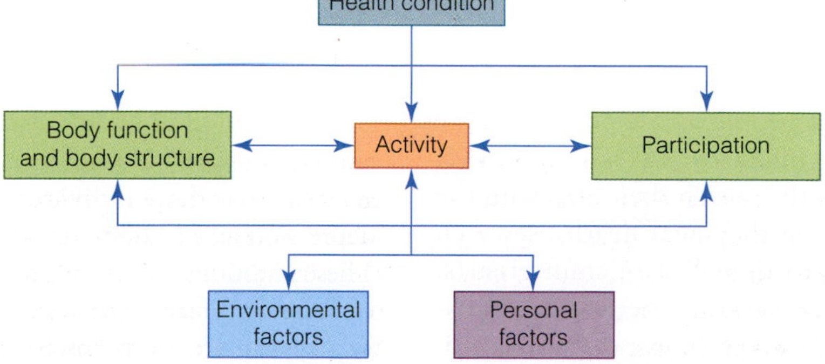

Figure 4.8 International classification of functioning, disability and health.
Source: World Health Organization. (2002). *Towards a common language for functioning, disability and health.* https://cdn.who.int/media/docs/default-source/classification/icf/icfbeginnersguide.pdf?sfvrsn=eead63d3_4

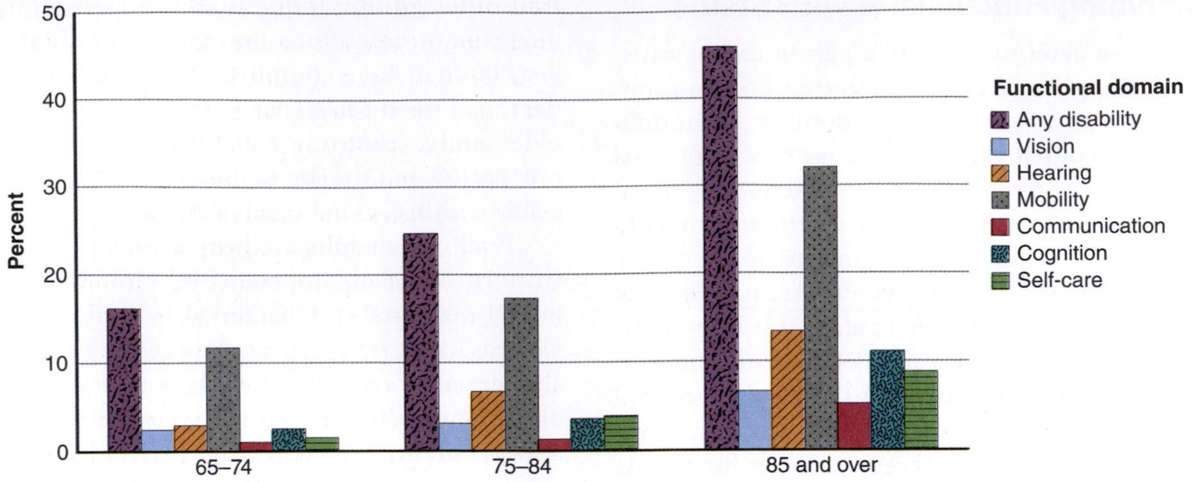

Note: Disability is defined as "a lot" or "cannot do/unable to do" when asked about difficulty with seeing, even if wearing glasses (vision); hearing, even if wearing hearing aids (hearing); walking or climbing steps (mobility); communicating, for example, understanding or being understood by others (communication); remembering or concentrating (cognition); and self-care, such as washing all over or dressing (self-care). Any disability is defined as having a lot of difficulty or being unable to do at least one of these activities. Reference population: These data refer to the civilian noninstitutionalized population.

Figure 4.9 Percentage of people aged 65 and over in the United States with a disability, by age group and functional domain, 2018.

Source: Federal Interagency Forum on Aging-Related Statistics. (2020). Older Americans 2020: Key indicators of well-being. U.S. Government Printing Office. https://agingstats.gov/docs/LatestReport/OA20_508_10142020.pdf. P. 107, Table 21b

walking, or dressing. A person can be considered frail if they need help with one or more of these tasks. **Instrumental activities of daily living (IADLs)** are actions that entail some intellectual competence and planning. Which activities constitute IADLs varies widely across cultures. For example, for most adults in Western cultures, IADLs would include shopping for personal items, paying bills, making telephone calls, taking medications appropriately, and keeping appointments. In other cultures, IADLs might include caring for animal herds, making bread, threshing grain, and tending crops. A third way of assessing competence is to focus on **physical limitations (PLIMs)**, activities that reflect functional limitations such as walking a block or sitting for about two hours.

The likelihood that people will experience some level of diminishment in ADLs, IADLs, or PLIMs increases a great deal as they reach their 80s, with the most rapid increase when they near death. Research shows that, compared to their White counterparts, Black and Latino/a older adults experience a multiplicative double disadvantage in the early stages of the disablement process in which they experience both (1) a more rapid onset and higher levels of functional limitations and (2) greater risk of functional limitation onset associated with chronic conditions (Kail et al., 2020). This double disadvantage was not reduced even at the highest levels of socioeconomic status. The implication is that disparities as a result of disablement that are based on race and ethnicity are not lessened by economic equity policies alone and are more strongly related to systemic issues including racism and discrimination. Thus, economic equity policies alone are unlikely to reduce the greater risk of functional limitations onset associated with chronic conditions encountered by persons of color.

In addition to basic assistance with ADLs, IADLs, and PLIMs, frail older adults have other needs. Research suggests that these individuals are also more prone to depression and anxiety disorders (Kojima et al., 2016). These additional outcomes may be related to feelings of isolation and fear of personal safety (e.g., fear of falling) that we explore more closely in Chapter 10.

How Does Disability in Older Adults Differ Globally?

Throughout this section, we have focused on how disablement is sometimes part of the aging process for many people in the United States. We have also noted important differences across gender, ethnic, racial, and socioeconomic groups. Do these patterns hold globally?

Not surprisingly, the answer is "yes." The United Nations (2021a) estimates that nearly half of the global older adult population has some form of disablement. Lee and colleagues (2021) documented widespread gender inequality in both the numbers of frail older adults and access to intervention. As the number of older adults rises around the world, the number of people with disabilities or functional limitations does, too. Also, the rates of disabilities are higher in low-income countries and among women. Early detection and treatment of chronic disease can lower these rates.

Globally, persons with disabilities of all ages face numerous obstacles including attitudinal, environmental, and institutional barriers preventing their full and equal participation in all aspects of life. Often older persons with disabilities are among the most adversely affected by discriminatory policies and practices, facing further age barriers in society.

The United Nations (UN) created the Convention on the Rights of Persons with Disabilities (CRPD) to outline the legal obligations of nations to promote and protect the rights of persons with disabilities. It draws attention to several intersectionalities between aging and disability: accessibility, living independently and being included in the community, personal mobility, and health. Promoting and protecting the rights and dignity of older persons and facilitating their full participation in society is an integral part of the UN's pursuit of the 2030 Agenda for Sustainable Development, which pledges that no one will be left behind. Specifically, the sustainable development goals of the 2030 agenda make explicit references to older persons and persons with disability regarding the need for ending poverty, good health and well-being, decent work and economic growth, and sustainable cities and communities. From the UN's perspective, sustainable development cannot be achieved without the conscious and intentional inclusion of the increasing number of older people with and without disabilities. It provides a critical platform for countries to address the intersection of aging and disability at global level.

As life expectancy in general increases, persons with disabilities who survive into old age can also be expected to contribute to the overall growth in the population of older persons with disabilities. This highlights the need for countries to take a longer-term approach to investment in the planning, design, and construction of their communities to ensure environmental inclusiveness and accessibility in moving toward the goal of creating a society that meets the needs and capacities of all people. It demonstrates a clear need to create policies and programs with regard to aging which take into consideration the intersections between aging and disability, and how society can ensure programs and facilities designed to meet the needs of an aging population are also successful in meeting the needs of older persons with disabilities.

Adult Development in Action

If you were a social policy leader, what national policies need to be addressed to best prepare the United States for the coming rapid increase in older adults and the resulting increase in functional limitations in this population?

Review Questions

4.5 Functional Health and Disability

- What are the key components in a model of disability in older adults?
- What are ADLs, IADLs, and PLIMs? How does the number of people needing assistance change with age?
- What conditions result in disability most often? How do socioeconomic status, race, ethnicity, and biological sex affect health and disability?

Social Policy Implications

Demographics Drive Decisions from Health to Wealth

As discussed in this chapter, two demographic trends will create the potential for significant worldwide change over the next few decades. First, increasing longevity in both developed and emerging economy countries will result in many more older adults. This means that societies and governments will have increased pressure to provide services tailored to older adults across gender, race, and ethnic groups. Such services are often much more expensive than those implemented for younger adults. For example, health care for older adults costs more because it involves treating more chronic diseases and more intensive intervention over time.

Second, the size of various generations will affect the scope of this change, as is clear in the population pyramids in Chapter 1. For instance, the large baby boomer generation, combined with increased longevity, will make the issue of more older adults acute. The future aging of the millennial generation will exacerbate these factors even more.

What does this mean? Through the middle of the 21st century there will be a great need for increased emphasis on social policies and services that directly benefit older adults, and older adults are likely to demand them. While they have the numbers, and the concomitant political power, such policies are likely to be adopted, perhaps to the detriment of younger generations.

This changing political climate plays out in elections. You may have noticed that in U.S. presidential election campaigns there is often great debate over changing the rules by which Medicare operates and the future of Social Security benefits. The commentary on both sides of the issue continues to be loud, even from older adults who would not be affected by some of the proposed changes.

As the baby boomers age and die, though, two further things will occur. First, there will be a tremendous transfer of wealth to a smaller generation (Gen X), with the likely outcome of concentrating wealth in fewer hands. Second, policies generally favorable to older adults may get changed even more as the next large generation (the millennials) continues entering middle age and grows ever more concerned with their own aging.

These shifts in policy could have major implications for everything from housing (e.g., more state and federal support for subsidized housing for older adults) to health care (e.g., substantially more expenditures for older adults' health care). If these policies are enacted, then pushback from even younger generations could force an unprecedented generational reckoning. Close attention to all these issues is necessary for the best policies to be enacted.

What do you think? What policies need to be changed? How?

In Review

In creating your summary for Chapter 4, you may want to create paragraphs for each of the major modules, as usual. In doing so, your first paragraph could be the story of different ways of measuring longevity, and how biological sex, race, and ethnicity influence those. Your framing of the influences could also serve as a template for understanding much of the effects of disparities in health care and other aspects of adult development that result in different outcomes as a function of demographic categories.

Your second paragraph should focus on differentiating health and illness, and how quality of life flows from that distinction. Additionally, you will want to describe how the immune system works and changes across adulthood, leading to increased experiences of chronic disease with age, and understanding how stress pervades nearly every aspect of adult life. Include evidence relating to disparities among racial, ethnic, and gender groups.

Your third paragraph will focus on the experience of cancer, diabetes, and incontinence in adulthood, and the issues relating to pain management. Related to this, your fourth paragraph will describe factors in ensuring that adults manage their medication regimens successfully, and how to help them do that. Finally, your final paragraph will focus on the disablement process and the ways in which we understand functional impairment and frailty in later life.

You may also consider using graphics to summarize some of these important points. For instance, a process chart might help you understand the disablement process. Use whatever graphic or table approach that helps your understanding of the key concepts.

Integrating Concepts in Development

- What physiological changes described in Chapter 2 are important in understanding health?
- Based on information in Chapters 2 and 3, how might a primary prevention program be designed to prevent cardiovascular disease? (Compare your answer with the intervention types described in Chapter 5.)
- How do the ethnic differences in average longevity and in health relate to the diversity issues we examined in Chapter 1?

Key Terms

absorption The time needed for a medication to enter a patient's bloodstream. 132

active life expectancy The age to which one can expect to live independently. 105

activities of daily living (ADLs) Basic self-care tasks such as eating, bathing, toileting, walking, and dressing. 137

acute diseases Conditions that develop over a short period of time and cause a rapid change in health. 117

autoimmunity The process by which the immune system begins attacking the body. 115

average longevity The length of time it takes for half of all people born in a certain year to die. 104

chronic diseases Conditions that last a longer period of time (at least 3 months) and may be accompanied by residual functional impairment that necessitates long-term management. 117

compression of morbidity The situation in which the average age when one becomes disabled for the first time is postponed, causing the time between the onset of disability and death to be compressed into a shorter period of time. 135

coping In the stress and coping paradigm, any attempt to deal with stress. 120

dependent life expectancy The age to which one can expect to live with assistance. 105

diabetes mellitus A disease that occurs when the pancreas produces insufficient insulin. 122

disability The effects of chronic conditions on people's ability to engage in activities that are necessary, expected, and personally desired in their society. 135

drug excretion The process of eliminating medications, usually through the kidneys in urine, but also through sweat, feces, and saliva. 132

drug metabolism The process of getting rid of medications in the bloodstream, partly in the liver. 132

emotion-focused coping A style of coping that involves dealing with one's feelings about the stressful event. 120

exacerbators Situations that makes a situation worse than it was originally. 136

frail older adults Older adults who have physical disabilities, are very ill, and may have cognitive or psychological disorders and need assistance with everyday tasks. 137

functional health status How well a person is functioning in daily life. 137

functional incontinence A type of incontinence usually caused when the urinary tract is intact but due to physical disability or cognitive impairment the person is unaware of the need to urinate. 129

health The absence of acute and chronic physical or mental disease and impairments. 111

health-related quality of life Includes all of the aspects of life that are affected by changes in one's health status. 113

hierarchy of loss Sequence of the loss of functional abilities. 137

illness The presence of a physical or mental disease or impairment. 111

incontinence The loss of the ability to control the elimination of urine and feces on an occasional or consistent basis. 128

instrumental activities of daily living (IADLs) Actions that entail some intellectual competence and planning. 138

maximum longevity The maximum length of time an organism can live—roughly 120 years for humans. 105

non-health-related quality of life Refers to things in the environment, such as entertainment, economic resources, arts, and so on that can affect our overall experience and enjoyment in life. 113

overflow incontinence A type of incontinence usually caused by improper contraction of the kidneys, causing the bladder to become overdistended. 129

physical limitations (PLIMs) Activities that reflect functional limitations such as walking a block or sitting for about 2 hours. 138

polypharmacy The use of multiple medications. 133

primary appraisal First step in the stress and coping paradigm in which events are categorized into three groups based on the significance they have for our well-being—irrelevant, benign or positive, and stressful. 119

problem-focused coping A style of coping that attempts to tackle a problem head-on. 120

psychoneuroimmunology The study of the relations between psychological, neurological, and immunological systems that raise or lower our susceptibility to and ability to recover from disease. 115

reappraisal In the stress and coping paradigm, this step involves making a new primary or secondary appraisal resulting from changes in the situation. 119

risk factors Long-standing behaviors or conditions that increase one's chances of functional limitation or disability. 135

secondary appraisal In the stress and coping paradigm, an assessment of our perceived ability to cope with harm, threat, or challenge. 119

stress and coping paradigm A model that views stress, not as an environmental stimulus or as a response, but as the interaction of a thinking person and an event. 119

stress incontinence A type of incontinence that happens when pressure in the abdomen exceeds the ability to resist urinary flow. 129

Type 1 diabetes A type of diabetes that tends to develop earlier in life and requires the use of insulin; also called insulin-dependent diabetes. 123

Type 2 diabetes A type of diabetes that tends to develop in adulthood and is effectively managed through diet. 123

urge incontinence A type of incontinence usually caused by a central nervous system problem after a stroke or urinary tract infection in which people feel the urge to urinate but cannot get to a toilet quickly enough. 129

Where People Live: Person–Environment Interactions

Chapter 5

Chapter Outline

Learning Objectives

After reading this chapter, you will be able to...

5.1. Describe the competence–environmental press and preventive and corrective proactivity models, as well as the resilience and stress-and-coping framework.

5.2. Describe aging in place and home modification strategies; compare and contrast adult day care, congregate housing, and assisted living.

5.3. Describe types of long-term care facilities, the major characteristics of nursing homes, how to effectively communicate with residents, how to determine whether residents are capable of making individual choices, and new directions for nursing homes.

Perhaps you have personally encountered them—home health organizations, communities designed for "active adults 55+," living facilities that provide varying levels of care, devices such as grip bars in bathrooms and chairlifts up staircases, and kitchen tools with easy-grip handles. Or you may be one of the millions of people who provide assistance for an older relative or friend. Or you may not have paid much attention to them and even take them for granted because you have yet to be confronted with these issues or needs. In any case, these organizations, communities, and environmental modifications have only become commonplace since the mid-20th century. However, in that time they have made a major difference between older adults being able to live independently and their living somewhere else. Supportive environments for adults, especially older adults with significant physical or cognitive impairment, are key to providing continuing quality of life.

Technology is also making it easier to be independent. Smartphones and smart watches make it possible to create reminders for medications and appointments and to keep track of key health indicators. Robots are increasingly being used to perform tasks around the house and to provide companionship. In development are a host of innovative devices, most notably self-driving cars. Within a generation or so, we will have gone from very challenging situations for many older adults to age in place, to having the option to age in place nearly anywhere.

All of these changes and innovations have resulted from research on how people deal with the settings where they reside and the psychological benefits (as well as challenges) they experience, which in turn has led to further research that has revolutionized the way we design houses and care facilities. The rapidly increasing need for alternatives to traditional nursing homes has resulted in the creation of a wide range of options for individuals and families. These changes began with the simple observation that behavior is a function of the interaction of environment in which it occurs and the individual's personal characteristics.

In this chapter, we explore how differences in the interaction between personal characteristics and living environments can have profound effects on our behavior and feelings about ourselves. Several theoretical frameworks are described that help us understand how to interpret person–environment interactions in a developmental context. Next, we consider the ecology of aging and discover how people can age in place, along with the support systems that underpin that goal. We consider the role of adult day care and several housing options that help people stay in the community as much as possible. Because some people need more intensive support, we examine skilled care facilities such as nursing homes. Sometimes we must consider the person separately from the environment, but keep in mind throughout the chapter that in the end it is the interaction of the two we want to understand.

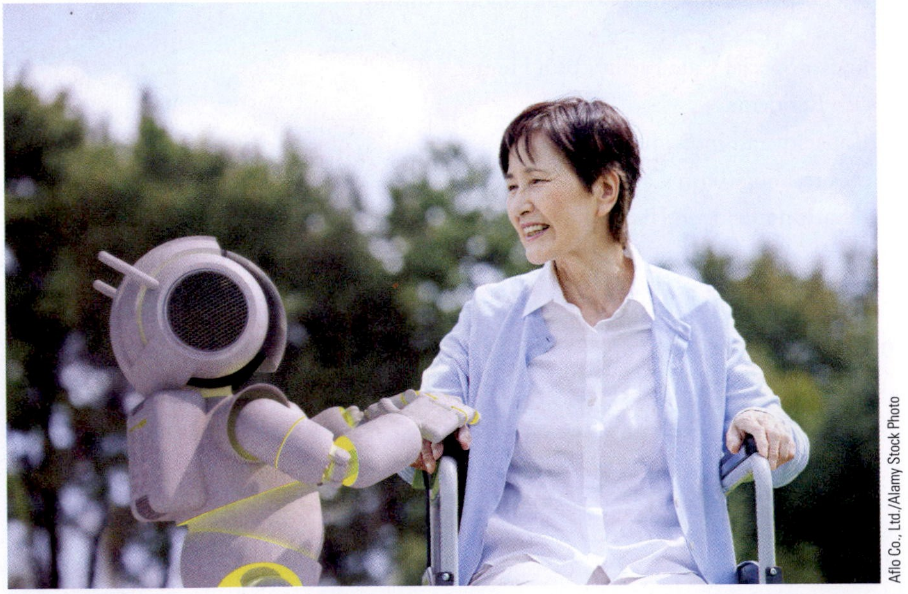

Home robots have much potential for helping adults age in place.

5.1 Describing Person–Environment Interactions

Key Questions

- What is the competence and environmental press model?
- What is the preventive and corrective proactivity model?
- What are the major aspects of stress and coping theory relating to person–environment interactions?
- What are the common themes in the theories of person–environment interactions?

Hank has lived in the same neighborhood all of his 75 years. He has lived alone for the past several months since his wife, Marilyn, had a stroke and was placed in a nursing home. Hank's oldest daughter expressed concern about her father and has been pressing him to move in with her. Hank is reluctant; he likes knowing his neighbors, shopping in familiar stores, and being able to do what he wants. He wonders how well he could adapt to living in a new neighborhood after all these years. He realizes it might be easier for him to cope if he lived with his daughter, but it's a tough decision.

To appreciate the roles different environments play in our lives, we need a framework for interpreting how people interact with them. Theories of person–environment interactions help us understand how people interpret and interact with their environments and how these may change as people age. These theories have been described since the 1930s and have significant impact on the study of adults (van Hoof & Marston, 2021; Pynoos et al., 2010). We consider four that help us understand adult development and aging: competence and environmental press, congruence, stress and coping, and everyday competence.

All these theories can be traced to a common beginning. Kurt Lewin (1936) was the first psychologist to conceptualize person–environment interactions as an interactive relationship, which he represented in the equation: $B = f(P, E)$. This relationship defining **person–environment interactions** means behavior (B) is a function of both the person (P) and the environment (E). More recent theorists took Lewin's equation and described the components in the equation in more detail. Specifically, their speculations concern the characteristics of people and environments that combine to form behavior.

Most of these models emphasize the importance of people's perceptions of their environments. Although objective aspects of environments (i.e., crime, housing quality, access to public transportation, neighborhood amenities) are important, personal choice plays a major role. For example, many people deliberately choose to live in Atlanta or Seattle for lifestyle reasons, even though traffic congestion and cost of living in those cities are much higher than in Selma or Des Moines. The importance of personal perception in environments is similar to the role of personal perception in social cognition (the focus of Chapter 8) and in concepts such as personal control (discussed in Chapter 9). As you will discover, these ideas, especially the notion of personal control, are included in many approaches to understanding person–environment interactions.

Competence and Environmental Press

Understanding psychosocial aging requires attention to individuals' needs rather than treating all older adults alike. One prominent method focuses on the dynamic relation between the person and the environment (Aldwin & Igarashi, 2012; Angevaare et al., 2020). Specifically, the *competence–environmental press approach* is a good example of a theory incorporating all the elements of the biopsychosocial model into the dynamic person–environment interaction (Lawton & Nahemow, 1973; Nahemow, 2000; Pynoos et al., 2010).

Competence is defined as the upper limit of a person's ability to function in five domains: physical health, sensory-perceptual skills, motor skills, cognitive skills, and ego strength. These domains are thought to underlie all other abilities and reflect biological and psychological forces. **Environmental press** refers to the physical, interpersonal, or social demands that environments put on people. Physical demands might include having to walk up three flights of stairs to your apartment due to the lack of an elevator. Interpersonal demands may require adjusting your behavior patterns to different types of people. Sociocultural demands involve dealing with laws or customs that place certain expectations and demands on people, often based on preconceived ideas or biases. These aspects of the theory reflect biological, psychological, and sociocultural forces.

Both competence and environmental press change as people move through the life span; what a person is capable of doing as a 5-year-old differs from what they are capable of doing as a 25-, 45-, 65-, or 85-year-old. Similarly, the demands put on people by the environment change over time. Thus, the competence–environmental press framework also reflects life-cycle factors.

The competence and environmental press model depicted in Figure 5.1 shows how the two are related. Low to high competence is represented on the vertical axis, and weak to strong environmental press is displayed on the horizontal axis. Points in the figure represent various combinations of the two. Most important, the shaded areas show adaptive behavior and positive affect can result from many different combinations of competence and environmental press levels. **Adaptation level** is the area where press level is average for a particular level of competence; this is where behavior and affect are normal. Slight increases in press tend to improve performance; this area on the figure is labeled the **zone of maximum performance potential**. Slight decreases in press create the **zone of maximum comfort**, in which people are able to live happily without worrying about environmental demands. Combinations of competence and environmental press that fall within either of these two zones result in adaptive behavior and positive emotion that translate into a high quality of life.

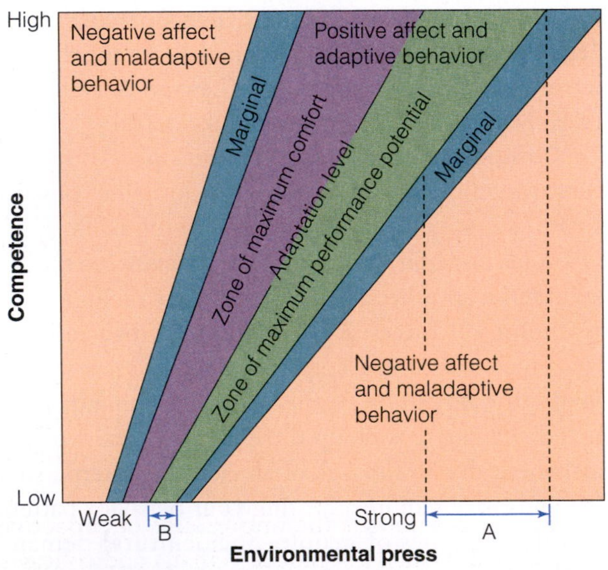

Figure 5.1 Behavioral and emotional outcomes of person–environment interactions are based on the competence and environmental press model. This figure indicates a person of high competence will show maximum performance over a larger range of environmental conditions than will a person with lower levels of competence. The range of optimal environments occurs at a higher level of environmental press (A) for the person with the most competence than it does for the person with the lowest level of competence (B).

Source: Lawton, M. P. & Nahemow, L. Ecology of the aging process. In C. Eisdorfer & M. P. Lawton (Eds.), *The Psychology of Adult Development and Aging*, p. 661.

As a person moves away from these zones, behavior becomes increasingly maladaptive and affect (feelings, emotions) becomes negative. Notice that these outcomes can result from several different combinations and for different reasons. For example, too many environmental demands on a person whose competence is low or too few demands on a person whose competence is high both result in maladaptive behaviors and negative emotion.

What does this mean with regard to later life? Is aging merely an equation relating levels of competence and environmental press? The important thing to realize about the competence–environmental press approach is that each person has the potential of being happily adapted to some living situations but not to others. Each situation is determined separately. Whether people function well depends on whether what they are able to do reasonably matches what the environment forces them to do. When their abilities match the demands, people adapt; when there is a mismatch, they don't. Thus, aging is more than an equation, because the best fit must be determined on an individual situation-by-situation basis.

How do people deal with changes in their particular combinations of environmental press (such as adjusting to a new living situation) and competence (perhaps reduced abilities due to illness)? People respond in two basic ways (Lawton, 1989; Nahemow, 2000). When people choose new behaviors to meet new desires or needs, they exhibit **proactivity** and exert control over their lives. In contrast, when people allow the situation to dictate the options they have, they demonstrate **docility** and have little control. Lawton (1989) argues that proactivity is more likely to occur in people with relatively high competence, and docility in people with relatively low competence. (Keep in mind that competence in this context does not equate to intelligence or related abilities—it focuses on the abilities the person has to have direct impact on their environment.)

The competence–environmental press model has considerable research support over a wide range of sociocultural groups. For example, the model accounts for why people choose the activities they do (Lawton, 1982), how well people adhere to medication regimens (LeRoux & Fisher, 2006), and how they adapt to changing conditions in their neighborhoods over time (Granbom et al., 2016; Sánchez-González et al., 2020). This model also helps us understand how well people adapt to various care settings, whether in their homes or in other facilities (Golant, 2012; van Hoof & Marston,

2021). In short, the model drives home the point that personal aging is a complex interaction between that person's competence level and environmental press regardless of setting, and it takes into account whether a person can exert choice or not.

Before leaving Lawton and Nahemow's model, we need to note an important implication. To the extent people experience declines in competence (such as those resulting from declines in health, sensory processes, motor skills, cognitive skills, or ego strength), they are less able to cope with a constant level of environmental demands. That is why the home modifications discussed later in the chapter, such as grab bars, smartphones, and other smart technologies, are important—they functionally increase competence and lower environmental press. Interventions based on artificial intelligence, such as robots and self-driving cars, will do even more to increase functional competence and enable people to remain in the community. City planners now incorporate aspects of the competence–environmental press model in designing and adapting housing and neighborhoods into age-friendly cities, with particular emphasis on such points as affordable housing and access to transportation (Oh, 2019; van Hoof & Marston, 2021).

Additionally, the competence and environmental press model has been the basis for evaluating and optimizing living situations with people who have severe cognitive impairments, such as those in dementia (Aljunaidy & Adi, 2021). To manage severe cognitive impairment effectively, care providers must identify the right level of environmental support based on the patient's level of competence. For example, people with mild cognitive impairment may be able to live independently, but as the impairment increases additional levels of support are needed. The model has provided the basis for designing special memory care units for people with dementia. In these units, environmental supports such as color-coded room doors help people with severe memory impairments identify where they reside.

Preventive and Corrective Proactivity Model

Maintaining a high quality of life is a key goal for adults of all ages. In the competence–environmental press approach, proactivity, exerting control over one's life, is central to achieving that goal. Because proactivity is so important, Kahana and Kahana (2003; Kahana et al., 2019; Midlarsky et al., 2015) created the preventive and corrective proactivity (PCP) model of successful aging, described in Figure 5.2.

The PCP model explains how life stressors (such as systematic trauma, discrimination, or chronic illnesses) and lack of good congruence in person–environment interactions (Component B in the figure), especially when the person has no buffer or protect against these things, result in poor life outcomes (Component F in the figure). The helpful buffers include external resources (Component E in the figure) such as friends or home modifications, internal resources or dispositions (Component C in the figure) such as a positive outlook on life, and specific proactive behaviors (Component D in the figure), such as physical exercise or an active prayer life, which work to lower the negative impact of the stressors and prepare people to cope better in the future. In brief, the PCP model proposes that proactive adaptations and helpful external resources reduce the effect of life stressors on quality-of-life outcomes.

What kinds of actions reflect proactive adaptations? Kahana and colleagues (2005) described two types of proactive adaptations: preventive and corrective. **Preventive adaptations** are actions that avoid stressors and increase or build social resources. An example of a preventive adaptation would be increasing one's social network by adding friends. **Corrective adaptations** are actions taken in response to stressors and can be facilitated by internal and external resources. An example of a corrective adaptation is stopping smoking after having a heart attack.

Older adults tend to engage in more corrective adaptations than preventive adaptations, at least initially. However, many actions that start as corrective adaptations turn into preventive adaptations. A great example of this is exercise. Many people begin an exercise program (such as walking) only after they are told to, perhaps as part of a recovery regimen after a health crisis. However, continued exercise becomes preventive by helping the person avoid future recurrences of the original health problem and avoid other problems altogether.

Research supports the importance of proactivity as described in the PCP model. Kahana and colleagues (2012, 2019) showed life stressors (such as ongoing trauma) can still have a negative effect on quality-of-life outcomes years after they occur, but proactive adaptations (such as exercise, and gathering support) significantly reduce this negative impact. Longitudinal research in China also showed the importance of proactivity and other external and internal resources in improving quality-of-life outcomes in residents over age 80 in the community and in long-term care facilities (Liu et al., 2012).

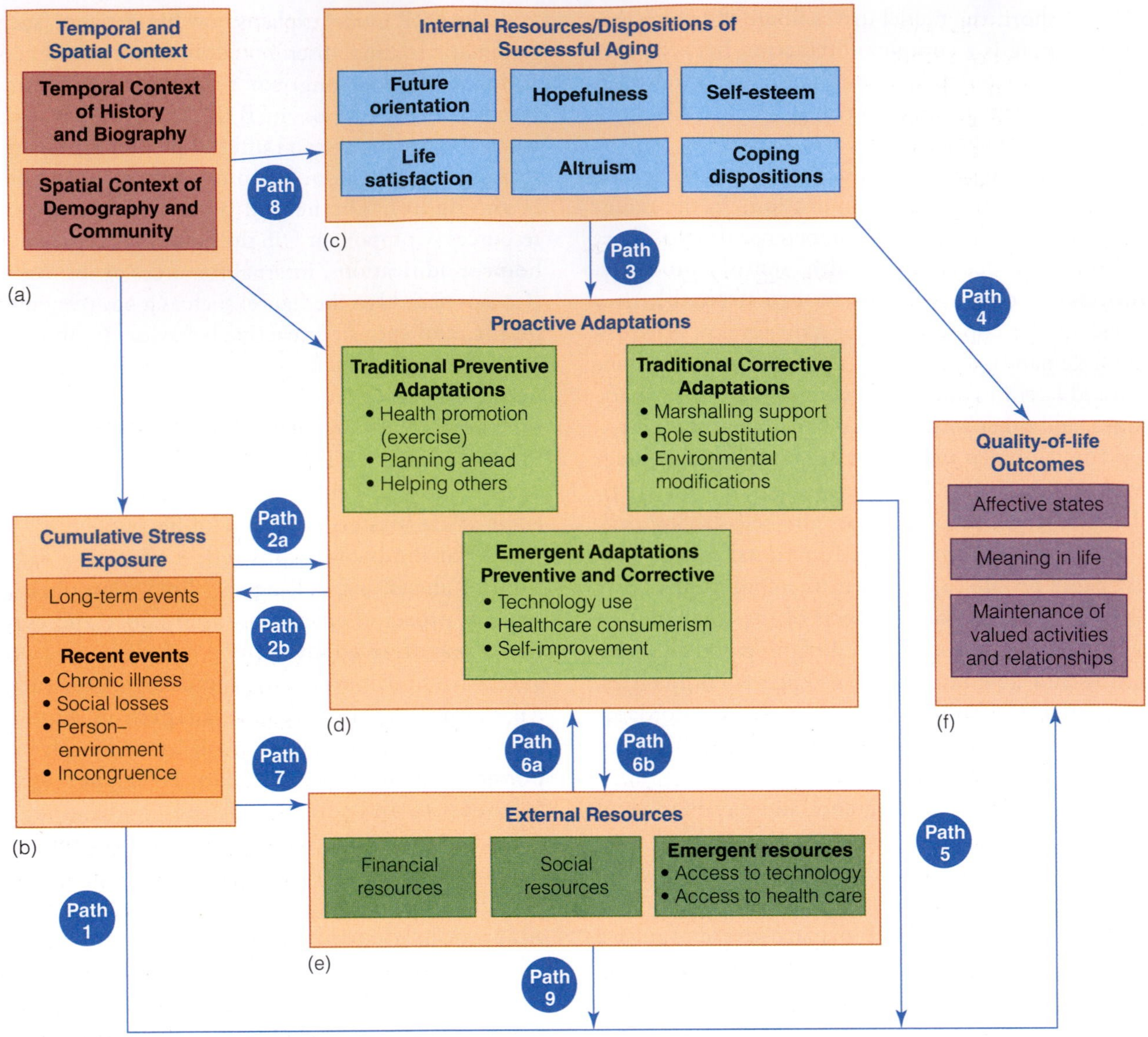

Figure 5.2 Model of emerging proactive options for successful aging.

Source: Kahana, E., Kahana, B., & Zhang, J. (2006). Motivational antecedents of preventive proactivity in late life: Linking future orientation and exercise. *Motivation and Emotion, 29*, 438–459 (Figure 1). thtps://doi.org/10.1007/s11031-006-9012-2

Resilience and the Stress and Coping Framework

As you may know from your own experience, sometimes your interaction with the environment is stressful. Schooler (1982) first applied Lazarus and Folkman's cognitive theory of stress and coping, described in Chapter 4, to the understanding of the older person's interaction with the environment. The basic premise of Lazarus and Folkman's theory is that people evaluate situations to assess their potential threat value. Situations can be evaluated as harmful/threatening, beneficial, or irrelevant. When situations are interpreted as harmful or threatening, people also establish the range of coping responses they have at their disposal for avoiding the situation. This process results in a coping response. Outcomes of coping may be positive or negative depending on many contextual factors; positive outcomes provide the foundation for resilience (Aldwin & Igarashi, 2012; Aldwin et al., 2021; Anstey & Dixon, 2021). **Resilience** consists of behaviors, thoughts, and actions that promote personal well-being and mental health.

Resilience is especially helpful in understanding older adults like Hank because of their greater vulnerability to social and physical hazards that can be mitigated by effective coping strategies (Aldwin et al., 2021; Anstey & Dixon, 2021). For example, in his classic study, Schooler (1982) evaluated retest data on a sample of 521 people drawn from a national sample of 4,000 older adults living in long-term care facilities. In particular, he examined the impact of three potential stressors (environmental change, residential mobility, and major life events) on health or morale. He also examined the buffering, or protective, effects of social support systems and ecological factors on the relations between the stressors and outcomes—essentially types of coping strategies. Consistent with the theory, Schooler argued that the presence of social support systems affected the likelihood that particular situations would be defined as harmful or threatening. For example, living alone is more likely to be interpreted as stressful when people have little social support than when they have many friends who live nearby.

Resilience as an aspect of the stress and coping framework provides an important theoretical addition because it deals with the relation between everyday environmental stressors and the adaptive responses of community-dwelling individuals. Resilience has provided insights into how older adults cope with many different situations, including challenges. Care providers of persons with dementia show resilience, for example, when they have effective ways of dealing with environmental stressors such as spending time with friends away from the care providing situation (Donnellan et al., 2015). The environmental stress caused by COVID-19 actually tapped many older adults' resilience through their lifelong accumulation of emotional coping strategies, such as staying busy, seeking social support, and having a positive mindset (Fuller & Huseth-Zosel, 2021). Research in Hong Kong suggested that designing communities in ways that promote a sense of resilience is associated with survival rates following stroke (Ho et al., 2022).

Common Theoretical Themes and Everyday Competence

The three theories we have considered have much in common. Most important, all agree the focus must be on the interaction between the person and the environment, not just on one or the other. Another important common theme is no single environment meets everyone's needs. Rather, a range of potential environments may be optimal.

Several researchers built on these ideas and focus on people's everyday competence (e.g., Cantarella et al., 2017; Gómez & Rodríguez, 2021; Hellström & Torres, 2021). **Everyday competence** is a person's potential ability to perform a wide range of activities considered essential for independent living; it is not the person's actual ability to perform the tasks. Everyday competence also involves a person's physical, psychological, and social functioning, which interact in complex ways to create the person's day-to-day behavior. Lou and Ng (2012) provided evidence that cognitive competence, closeness to family, and relationship-based coping help Chinese older adults who live alone cope effectively with loneliness. Additionally, an older person's competence in the psychological domain includes cognitive problem-solving abilities, beliefs about personal control and self-efficacy, and styles of coping, which can be trained successfully (Diehl et al., 2005, 2012; Gómez & Rodríguez, 2021).

Fstop123/E+/Getty Images

Older adults' ability to perform typical daily activities is essential for assessing everyday competence.

Although everyday competence is most often considered in the context of activities of daily living (ADLs) and instrumental activities of daily living (IADLs; discussed in Chapter 4), it can also be considered more broadly. The reason is a behavior must not be considered in isolation; behavior is expressed in a particular environmental context. In particular, researchers and clinicians need to be sensitive to cultural and contextual differences in everyday competence across different environments, including artificial intelligence platforms (Diehl et al., 2005, 2012; Papadopoulos et al., 2022).

Using these ideas, Willis (1991; Allaire, 2012; Allaire & Willis, 2006; Jones et al., 2013; Schaie & Willis, 2015; Willis & Belleville, 2016) developed a model of everyday competence incorporating all the key ideas discussed earlier. Willis distinguishes between antecedents, components, mechanisms, and outcomes of everyday competence. Antecedents include both individual (e.g., health, cognition) and sociocultural (e.g., cultural stereotypes, social policy, healthcare policy) factors. These influence the intraindividual and contextual components, that is, the particular domains and contexts of competence. Which components are most important or exert the most influence depend on the overall conditions under which the person lives. These elements of the model reflect the basic ideas in both the competence and environmental press model and the person–environment model we considered earlier. The mechanisms involve factors that moderate the way competence is actually expressed, such as whether one believes they are in control of the situation, influences how competent the person turns out to be. Finally, the model proposes the primary outcomes of everyday competence are psychological and physical well-being, two of the major components of successful aging.

Understanding the complexities of everyday competence is important as a basis for considering whether people, especially some older adults, are capable of making certain decisions for themselves. This issue often arises in terms of competence to make key healthcare and other decisions, a topic we consider in more detail later in this chapter. The model of everyday competence also points out the health outcomes of one episode of everyday competence are the antecedents of the next, illustrating how future competence is related to current competence. Research on cognitive training from this perspective shows that training on reasoning, maintained over time, can attenuate age-related change (Jones et al., 2013), and may last up to 10 years in certain areas, such as reasoning (Rebok et al., 2014). Finally, decline in older adults' ability to handle everyday problems predicts mortality, indicating everyday competence may be a reasonable indicator of health status (Allaire & Willis, 2006). Based on these findings, researchers are building predictive models of the likely benefits of training for specific types of interventions (Roheger et al., 2021).

All of this research supports the idea that older adults can age in place to the extent their everyday competence permits and the level of environmental press does not consistently exceed it. Aging in place requires whatever necessary services and supports an older adult needs to live in the community be provided or made available, which for many is a serious challenge—those services are simply unavailable, and the person ends up struggling. To address these gaps, the approach has been adopted by governments (e.g., Australia in relation to disability; Australian Government Department of Social Services, 2021) and is the goal for the implementation of much of the smart technology designed mainly for older adults, such as cognitive wellness systems (Chen et al., 2021; Meza-Kubo & Morán, 2013). We consider aging in place in more detail in the next section, and technological innovation in Chapter 14.

Adult Development in Action

How would a thorough understanding of competence and environmental press influence your work as a housing planner for older adults?

Review Questions

5.1 Describing Person–Environment Interactions

- What are person–environment interactions? Describe Lawton and Nahemow's theory of environmental press. In their theory, what is adaptation level?
- Describe the preventive and corrective proactivity or PCP model.
- Describe the application of the stress and coping model to person–environment interactions. What kinds of things buffer stress?
- What are the common themes expressed by the various theories of person–environment interactions?
- What are the key components of everyday competence?

5.2 The Ecology of Aging: Community Options

Key Questions

- What is aging in place? How do people decide the best option?
- How can a home be modified to provide a supportive environment?
- What options and services are provided in adult day care?
- What is congregate housing? What are the characteristics of assisted living?

Maria is a widow, living alone, who was diagnosed as having vascular dementia about six months ago. Because she now has difficulty remembering to turn off the gas stove, her daughter and son-in-law, who live several hours away, think it may be best for Maria to move into a supportive facility that her Medicaid would pay for. Maria's primary care physician agreed and indicated that for safety reasons a memory care facility is a good idea because Maria's daughter and son-in-law live so far away.

Most people go through young adulthood, middle age, and into later life performing routine daily tasks without much thought. As we grow older, the normative changes in physiological functioning, for instance (described in Chapters 3 and 4), often create challenges in dealing with these tasks. Even our homes, formerly a comfortable supportive place, can become problematic; the walk up the stairs to a bedroom may become the equivalent of climbing a mountain.

Maria is typical of a growing number of older adults in the United States and other countries—she experiences a significant decline in functioning, lives alone, and her adult child and family live in another city some distance away. As a result, Maria, like many older adults, needs a different living situation. Maria does not need full-time intensive nursing care at this point, but she does need a more supportive environment.

Changes in functional status and how these changes are helped or hurt by the environments in which we live are an important aspect of the experience of growing older for many people. These changes are studied in a field called the **ecology of aging or environmental psychology**, which seeks to understand the dynamic relations between older adults and the environments they inhabit (Greenfield, 2012; Greenfield et al., 2019; Scheidt & Schwarz, 2010; Schwarz, 2013). This perspective underlies the age-friendly approach to community design that supports older adults (Greenfield et al., 2022). An **age-friendly community** encourages active aging by optimizing opportunities for health, participation, and security in order to enhance quality of life as people age by adapting its structures and services to be accessible to and inclusive of older people with varying needs and capacities (World Health Organization, 2007). The Discovering Development feature dives deeper into the growing age-friendly community movement.

Discovering Development

Is Your Community Age-Friendly?

As the number of older adults increased rapidly during the latter part of the 20th century, communities around the world became concerned about how well they served their older residents. As a result, a global discussion began under the auspices of the World Health Organization (WHO) about the specific needs of older adults in communities and how to determine whether a community, city, or state met those needs. These discussions resulted in the creation of a set of guidelines for what became known as age-friendly communities, originally published in 2007 (World Health Organization, 2007).

The WHO identified eight dimensions that are key for communities to address in order to be friendly to residents of all ages: outdoor spaces and buildings, transportation, housing, social participation, respect and social inclusion, civic participation and employment, communication and information, and community support and health services. How each of these gets implemented in any given community will vary, of course. But each must be addressed in ways appropriate to the target age groups.

In the United States, AARP (2021) has created numerous resources to help cities and towns create livable communities for adults of all ages, but especially for adults over age 50. These resources provide ways to determine how age-friendly a particular community is, and what remains to be addressed to improve it. Importantly, these guidelines and resources do not only target affluent neighborhoods; they are designed to be implemented in all neighborhoods in both urban and rural areas by both building on existing resources and implementing supplemental resources as necessary.

Is your community age-friendly? Using the AARP or other toolkit, find out as much as you can about what your community has done to address the eight areas identified by the WHO. Keep in mind that there is not necessarily a strong link between community wealth and age-friendly aspects. Indeed, some of the communities that provide the best support for older adults, for example, are not the wealthiest, but are those that prioritize making sure that the needs of older people are addressed in community design and services available.

Share the information you gather about your own community with others in the class to gain better understanding of the range of communities and what makes age-friendly communities stand out.

It is important to understand how seemingly small changes in a person's environment can result in major changes in behavior, changes that can make the difference between a person being able to live independently or needing a more supportive situation. We explore how that happens in this section. We consider options for older adults that help them maintain as much independence as possible. First, we evaluate the concept of aging in place. Then we present three approaches to helping people live in the community as long as possible: home modification, and two living situations that provide various levels of support—congregate housing and assisted living. All of these approaches are making people rethink options for older adults not only in the United States but also in Canada, Europe, and Latin America (Sánchez-González & Rodríguez-Rodríguez, 2016).

To set the stage, meet Matthias Hollwich, an architect profiled in the Real People feature. Matthias is one of an emerging group of architects who are focusing on designing spaces in which people can grow old. As described in the feature, what's different about his approach is that it integrates smart technology with the biopsychosocial approach with the rethinking of physical space. It's intriguing, and a great mindset to use throughout the rest of this chapter.

Aging in Place

Where you live, and how you feel about it, is a critical aspect of personal identity. We experience this every time someone asks us, "Where do you live?" For most people, it is the sense of place that makes the difference. A **sense of place** refers to the cognitive and emotional attachments that a person puts on their place of residence, by which a "house" is made into a "home."

Throughout adulthood, people adapt to changes in the places where they live, sometimes severing connections with past settings (Rowles & Watkins, 2003; Wahl, 2015; Wahl et al., 2021). In each case, people work toward a higher goal of "being in place" that gives them a feeling of belonging, involvement, purpose, and meaningful connection (Finlay & Rowles, 2021). Having a sense of place results from the blending of two elements: personal place identification (the unique way in which people viscerally experience and react to an environment; Rowles, 2018) and the identity of places (the way in which environments are designed, inhabited, and modified over time). Together, they create emotional

Real People

Designing for a Reimagined Aging

Matthias Hollwich is an architect and cofounder of HWKN who thinks differently. He starts with the premise that society needs to reimagine how to serve the needs of older adults better, and that can only happen if we deliberately plan our own aging. For Hollwich, this means adopting a fundamentally different mindset about every aspect of our lives, from valuing growing old to strategically using smartphones as assistive devices to adapting living spaces as physical abilities change.

In his book *New Aging: Living Smarter Now to Live Better Forever* (Hollwich, 2016), Hollwich urges people to "love aging" and to adopt changes advocated by such organizations as Aging 2.0, a global group that fosters technology-based products and services for older adults. In his architecture practice, Hollwich helps clients rethink and reframe physical space to be readily adaptable as individual needs and competencies change. In that way, he strives for optimal competency–press balance so that people can maintain their independence.

Anthony Behar/Sipa USA/Newscom

Matthias Hollwich (on right)

Hollwich and other architects like him are challenging traditional notions of interior design and the use of physical space. By designing space today that anticipates future needs, they hope to change minds about the process of aging and to provide much better places in which that process occurs.

and cognitive attachments to a place, turning it into "my place" or "my home" (Finlay & Rowles, 2021). This process is presented in Figure 5.3.

It is this sense of place that makes relocation, especially having to psychologically disconnect with a place where they may have lived for many decades, difficult and traumatic. There is no question people develop attachments to place, develop a sense of place, and derive a major portion of their identity from it, usually no matter where that place is.

Rowles (2006, 2018; Finlay & Rowles, 2021) discusses the process of how a place becomes a home. Because of the psychological connections, the sense that one is "at home" becomes a major concern in relocation, especially if the relocation involves giving up one's home. This attachment to place appears to be a cross-cultural phenomenon (Felix et al., 2015).

Community Options. Imagine you are an older adult who has lived in the same home for decades, perhaps raising a family there, so there are many memories and a strong attachment to it. As you age, certain activities become a bit more difficult—perhaps cooking meals and getting around. If you had a choice of where you wanted to live, where would it be? To relocate to a new location that could provide better support, perhaps with your children? Or to stay where you are and create

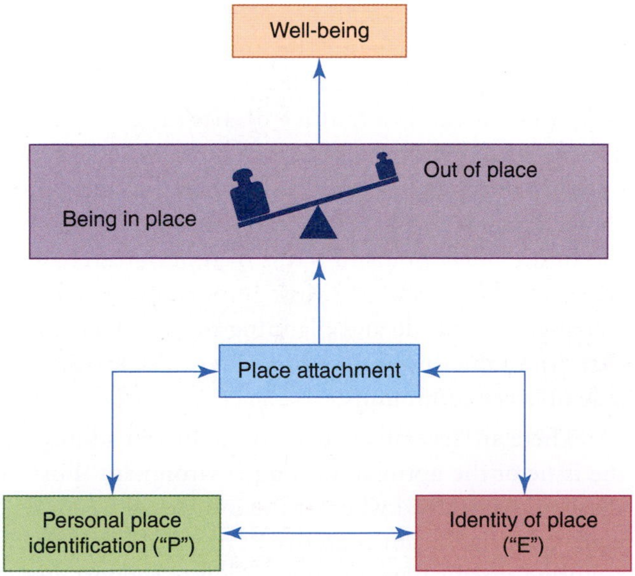

Figure 5.3 Conceptual approach to being in place.

Source: Rowles, G. D. (2018). Being in place: Identity and place attachment in late life. In M. Skinner, G. Andrews, & M. Cutchin (Eds.), *Geographical gerontology: Concepts and approaches* (pp. 203-15). Routledge.

compensations? Various family members may be urging one option or the other. For our consideration here, the most important issue is what the person in question wants to do.

Based on the competence–environmental press model described earlier, older adults may have options (Sánchez-González et al., 2020; Scheidt & Schwarz, 2010; Schwarz, 2013; Sumner et al., 2021). As the environment in which one lives becomes more restrictive due to an increasing mismatch between competence and environmental press, many older adults engage in selection and compensation to cope. They may select a different place to live, provided that option is available, that results in lower environmental press. Or they may adapt their behaviors in order to compensate for their limitations, such as not leaving their home as often or using voice-activated technology (e.g., Alexa or Siri on their devices) for many routine tasks, using microwaveable prepared foods instead of cooking meals from scratch, or relying on neighbors for help with errands.

The idea of aging in place reflects a balancing of environmental press and competence through selection and compensation. Being able to maintain one's independence in the community is often important for people, especially in terms of their self-esteem, well-being, and ability to continue engaging in meaningful ways with friends, family, and others, all of which maintains good quality of life. This is important psychologically (Fields & Dabelko-Schoeny, 2016). First, including a care partner in the process helps ensure the viability of aging in place (Fields et al., 2022). Second, older adults who age in place form strong emotional and cognitive attachment with their residences that help transform a "house" into a "home." Having a home provides a strong source of self-identity. Additionally, they form strong emotional connections with their neighborhood community to create a sense of place.

Throughout adulthood, people adapt to changes in the places where they live, sometimes severing connections with past settings (Wahl, 2015; Wahl et al., 2021). Making a change in where people live, and having to psychologically disconnect with a place where they may have lived for many decades, can be difficult and traumatic. There is no question people develop attachments to place, deriving a major portion of their identity from it and feeling they own it.

Feeling one is "at home" is a major aspect of aging in place. Providing older adults a place to call their own that supports the development of the psychological attachments necessary to convert the place to a home is

Aging in place is a major goal for the majority of older adults.

key for successful aging in place (Finlay & Rowles, 2021; Scheidt & Schwarz, 2010; Wahl, 2015; Wahl et al., 2021). Aging in place provides a way for older adults to continue finding aspects of self-identity in where they live and to take advantage of support systems that are established and familiar.

The growing understanding of the importance of aging in place has resulted in a rethinking of certain housing options that provide a way for frail older adults to stay in their communities. Such options are important for frail older adults who cannot afford more expensive formal assisted living or nursing home facilities (discussed later). One alternative is cluster housing that combines the aging in place philosophy with supportive services (Bigonnesse & Chadhury, 2020; Golant, 2008; Scharlach & Lehning, 2016).

There are several types of affordable cluster housing care (Golant, 2008, 2020; Scharlach & Lehning, 2016). A key feature of cluster housing is that it consists of residential-like settings that provide a range of care. Services might range from having only a case manager or public group transportation options to actually providing care assistance (e.g., meals, housekeeping), transportation, or health care, all of which may be based at a local community or senior center. The aging in place philosophy in these settings emphasizes individual choice on the part of residents in terms of what services to use. This approach is being adopted in other countries besides the United States, such as the Netherlands (de Jong, 2021).

One increasingly popular approach to cluster housing is active adult communities. Active adult communities are ones that cater to adults over age 55 and provide housing options that are rightsized, often on one level, require low maintenance, and have convenient amenities. These communities attract older adults who are capable of living independently or have the resources to contract for the services they need (e.g., housecleaning). For the most part, support services are limited. However, there are many opportunities to develop a social support network of similarly aged and situated people, an important consideration for quality of life and well-being that we will explore in more detail in Chapter 11.

Although cluster housing and other approaches to aging in place make sense as lower-cost alternatives to nursing homes that keep people in their communities, affording them is often difficult for many people. Unlike long-term care facilities, cluster housing developments are not currently covered by Medicaid or other insurance. Finding solutions to the funding issue will be an important aspect for keeping costs down and providing supporting environments for older adults who need support. For many, making modifications to their existing housing represents a more cost-effective option and provides a research-based way to remain in a familiar environment. We consider this approach later in this section.

Deciding on the Best Option. One of the most difficult decisions individuals and families have to make is where an older member who needs support should live (Wahl, 2015). Such decisions are never easy and can be quite wrenching. Figuring out the optimal "fit" where the individual's competence and the environmental press are in the best balance rests on the ability of all concerned to be objective about the individual's competence and the ability of the lived-in environment to provide the level of support necessary, and on the availability of affordable options. This balance requires a degree of honesty in communication with all family members that is sometimes challenging. It also requires an understanding of what the future likely holds in terms of functional changes (Koss & Ekerdt, 2017). Most important, it requires a change in attitude and planning regarding ensuring that affordable supportive housing options are available in every community.

There are several key decision points in addressing the issue of the optimal housing environment. First, it must be determined whether the individual has or will likely have significant cognitive or physical impairment requiring specific types of intervention or support. Next, an assessment of the ability of family members or friends to provide support or care must be made. Once that information is understood, a series of decisions can be made about the best way to provide the necessary environmental supports to create the optimal "fit." Assuming all information shows the need for some sort of intervention, the next critical decision is whether there is an option for providing that intervention in the current home situation or if other options need to be pursued. Later, we consider several living options for individuals needing support, ranging from minor modifications of the present home to skilled care nursing homes.

Throughout this process, the individual in question needs to be an integral part of decision making to the extent possible. This is especially important when the outcome is likely to be a placement that involves moving from the person's current residence. The degree the person actually understands the options available, why the options are being pursued, and the long-term meaning of the decision being considered is an integral part of the person's right to determine their own life outcome (a point considered in more detail later).

Individuals and families facing these decisions should consult with the person's physician after a thorough diagnostic evaluation. Additionally, objective information about available housing options can be obtained from local senior centers, offices on aging, and other nonprofit service providers.

Home Modification

Whenever you are in a public building, pay close attention to many of the deign details. As a result of the Americans with Disabilities Act of 1990, physical modifications in the environment were required to make buildings, public transit, and many other aspects of daily life more accessible. You are likely to encounter ramps rather than only stairs, height-adjusted counters and switches, grab bars in bathrooms, busses that kneel at stops, and other structural modifications. You may also use several technology based assistive modifications in your daily life—think of voice-activated remote controls or asking Siri for directions to the nearest coffee shop.

All of these environmental tweaks are grounded in the competence–environmental press model as ways to optimize people's competence at various levels of environmental press. These modifications reflect two options for people who experience challenges with the tasks of daily life. On one hand, people can increase their competence and develop better or new skills. To better remember where you put your car keys, you can learn to use your smartphone as a memory aid. On the other hand, you can lower the environmental press by modifying the environment to make the task easier; putting a hook for the car keys next to the door you exit so you see them on your way out is an example.

These two options represent applications of theory to real-world settings that also apply to helping people deal with the challenges they face in handling tasks of daily living in their homes. When it comes to certain kinds of issues, such as mobility and the risk of falling, the most frequent solutions involve modifying one's home (i.e., changing the environment by eliminating loose rugs and other tripping hazards) in order to create a new optimal balance or better "fit" between competence and environmental press (Pettersson et al., 2020; Scharlach & Lehning, 2016).

Many strategies are available for modifying a home to help a person accommodate changing competencies. Minor structural changes, such as installing assistive devices (e.g., handrails in bathrooms and door handles that are easier to grip), are common strategies. In other cases, more extensive modifications may be needed to make a home fully accessible, such as widening doorways, lowering countertops, adding power stairlifts, and constructing ramps.

Although minor alterations can often be done at low cost, more extensive modifications may be unaffordable. As a result, many older adults with functional impairments experience a mismatch between their competency and their environment that for financial reasons cannot be addressed (Granbom et al., 2016; Tsuchiya-Ito et al., 2019; Iwarsson et al., 2012; Wahl, 2015).

Research indicates home modifications done to address difficulties with accomplishing ADLs typically reduce disability-related outcomes (Choi, 2020; Wahl, 2015; Yuen & Vogtle, 2016). However, although home modification can help reduce falls in older adults, for instance (Ripp et al., 2016; M. E. Taylor et al., 2021), understanding the role of self-efficacy beliefs in falling and in other ADLs is also an important factor to address in successful interventions (Dadgari et al., 2015).

An increasingly popular approach to home modification is the accessory or auxiliary dwelling unit (ADU; AARP, 2019a). The ADU is a new spin on an old concept—create a separate living space either from existing spare space (e.g., a room over a garage) or a separate dwelling placed next to a family's main dwelling to give an older relative both privacy and proximity to family. More formally, an ADU is a smaller, independent residential dwelling unit located on the same lot as a single-family home. ADUs go by many different names throughout the United States, including accessory apartments and secondary suites. ADUs can be converted portions of existing homes (e.g., a basement apartment with separate entrance), additions to new or existing homes, or new stand-alone accessory structures or converted portions of existing stand-alone accessory structures (e.g., converting a separate garage to a separate living space) (AARP, 2019a). ADUs are growing in popularity in dense urban areas that have few opportunities for new, affordable housing.

To provide maximum support for older adults the ADU space frequently includes several design modifications (e.g., lower counter heights, grab bars) and especially the incorporation of "smart" devices that do everything from serving as a virtual companion to providing voice control over many household functions. A diagram of a typical stand-alone ADU that would house one or more persons is shown in Figure 5.4.

The advantage to ADUs is that they can be as temporary or permanent as needed, and they provide both independence and support for aging in place. As technology improves, it is likely solutions like ADUs will increase in popularity and decrease in cost. However, local building zoning codes vary a great deal, so the availability of ADUs depends on local rules, though the number of communities adopting favorable rules is increasing because of the flexibility and lower cost (AARP, 2019a).

Adult Day Care

In some cases, older adults need more support than is possible with just home modification but still do not need assistance on a full-time basis. For them, one possible option may be adult day care. **Adult day care is designed to provide support, companionship, and certain services during the day.** This situation arises most often when the primary caregiver is employed or has other obligations and is unavailable during the day.

The primary goal of adult day care is to delay placement into a more formal care setting. It achieves this goal by providing alternative care that enhances the client's self-esteem and encourages socialization. Three

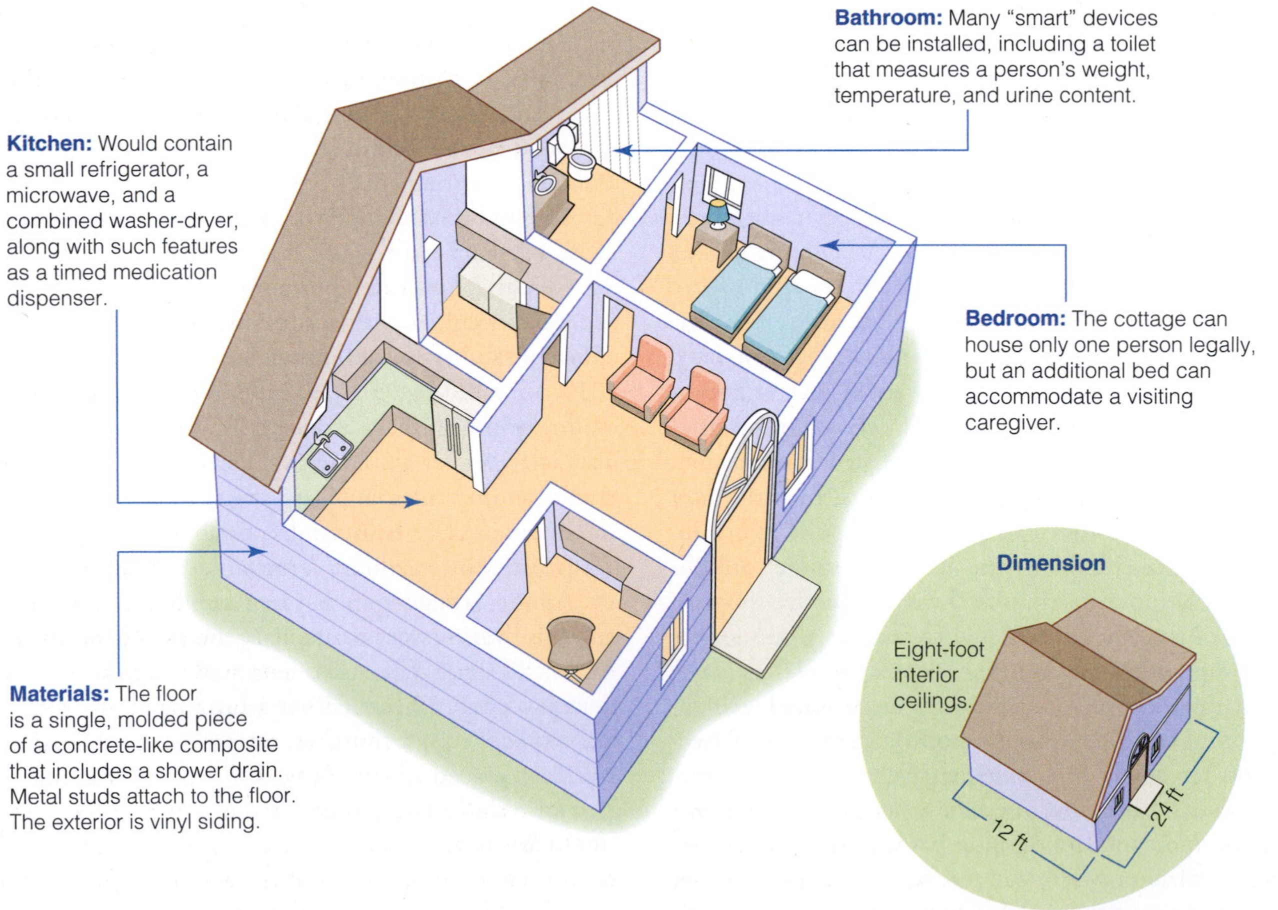
Bathroom: Many "smart" devices can be installed, including a toilet that measures a person's weight, temperature, and urine content.
Kitchen: Would contain a small refrigerator, a microwave, and a combined washer-dryer, along with such features as a timed medication dispenser.
Bedroom: The cottage can house only one person legally, but an additional bed can accommodate a visiting caregiver.
Dimension
Eight-foot interior ceilings.
12 ft
24 ft
Materials: The floor is a single, molded piece of a concrete-like composite that includes a shower drain. Metal studs attach to the floor. The exterior is vinyl siding.

Figure 5.4 An example of an auxiliary dwelling unit.

general types of adult day care are available (AARP, 2019b). The first provides only social activities, meals, and recreation, with minimal health services. The second type is adult day health care that provides more intensive health and therapy intervention and social services for people with more serious medical problems or who require intensive nursing care for a specific medical condition. The third provides specialized care to particular populations, such as people with dementia or developmental disabilities.

Adult day care centers can be independent or sponsored by for-profit (about 25%) or nonprofit (about 75%) organizations. Adult day care centers are often affiliated with local community or senior centers or other publicly funded agencies that provide services to older adults. They may provide transportation to and from the center. Depending on the services received, Medicaid, VA benefits, or other insurance may cover some of the expenses (traditional Medicare coverage does not). Because some states do not license adult day care centers, careful screening of a particular center is strongly advised (AARP, 2019b).

The average client at an adult day care center is over age 70, female, and living alone. About 35% of adult day care clients live with an adult child and 20% with a spouse or partner. Family members choosing adult day care (and who can afford it if it is private pay) typically do so because they need occasional assistance with caregiving, have safety concerns about the care recipient when the caregiver is not around, take increasing amounts of time off from work for caregiving, are experiencing problems in their relationship with the care recipient, or believe the care recipient could benefit from more contact with other older adults (AARP, 2019b). Most clients attend full-day programs and have significant physical impairments, chronic diseases, or cognitive impairments.

For people with cognitive impairments, changes in routine can result in confusion or disruptive behavior. It is especially important for them, as it is for all older adults who may become adult day care clients, to inform them of this care option and get their assent to participation. A good strategy is to engage in a few trials to find out how well the person acclimates to the different surroundings and activities, and how well they like the setting, staff, and activities.

Research demonstrates adult day care is a viable and important option for care providers. Care providers are interested in programs that meet the needs of their loved ones and are generally satisfied with the services provided, especially in giving them time to pursue necessary other activities such as employment (Neville et al., 2015). Family members clearly seek what is best for their loved one in searching for and helping make the transition to adult day care centers (Larson & Kao, 2016; Neville et al., 2015), and these findings are similar in other countries, such as China (Sun et al., 2021). However, as a study in Australia demonstrated, family care providers can be overwhelmed by the amount of information and confused by the process of placing their family member (Robinson et al., 2012). Furthermore, research in Ireland documented that a major cultural barrier for family members regarding use of day care or other respite services is the emotional barrier of asking for help (Ryan, 2021).

Evidence is clear that compared with keeping relatives with cognitive impairment at home, good adult day care programs can reduce problematic behaviors, lower the need for psychotropic medication in clients, and result in lower reports of burdens of caring among care providers (Larson & Kao, 2016). Positive benefits for family and other informal care providers are also well established (Lunt et al., 2021). However, a key factor in the success of day care programs is having culturally appropriate approaches and programs, as demonstrated in studies of Korean (Park, 2008) and Chinese (Wong & Yeung, 2015) clients who benefited most when programs took their cultural background into account.

Congregate Housing

Congregate housing includes a range of living options from those providing only housing to those providing some level of medical services (Howe et al., 2013). The most common form is an apartment complex of older adults (often with a minimum age of 62) where older adults live in private, individual units but share common spaces such as a dining room, kitchen, and other amenities with other residents. Some congregate facilities have a concierge who coordinates shared activities, repairs, and other tasks. Congregate housing is often the least expensive form of supported living for older adults, because the cost may be eligible to be subsidized by various government agencies and nonprofit organizations (U.S. Department of Housing and Urban Development, 2021). This is a form of housing often supported by local churches, especially in urban areas, due to the lack of affordable alternatives. Because of its relative affordability compared with assisted living or skilled nursing care, it is an especially important option for older adults who need some support with ADLs and IADLs, but not the level of care provided in other settings. However, there is a critical shortage of congregate housing in the United States (Joint Center for Housing Studies, 2016).

What distinguishes congregate living for older adults from other forms of housing is the hybrid approach to independent living and shared facilities. In many regards, it is very similar to modern residence facilities on college campuses that also combine independent living (e.g., private bedrooms) with spaces shared with suite mates (living rooms and kitchenettes) and larger shared spaces (e.g., dining halls). Congregate housing facilities do not provide 24-hour medical services on site but usually have physicians, physician assistants, and advanced practice nurses on call. Currently, newer congregate housing complexes are including higher levels of other social services, such as organized trips for shopping or entertainment, and onsite availability of certain medical services (e.g., vaccinations, hearing tests), so the distinction with assisted living (discussed next) is being blurred.

The service coordination provided in congregate living accomplishes several things: interface with housing officials, individual service plans for residents, coordination of shared activities (e.g., cleaning common spaces), and mediation of resident conflicts. Most congregate housing complexes require residents be capable of independent living and not require continual medical care, be medically stable, know where they are and be oriented to time (e.g., know today's date and other key time-related information), do not behave in a disruptive manner, be able to make independent decisions, and be able to follow any specific service plan developed for them. If at some point a resident no longer meets one of the criteria, they are usually required to move out.

The decision to move into congregate housing is usually done in conjunction with one's family or close friends and is typically a response to a significant decline in functioning or other health-related problem (Chaulagain et al., 2021; Koss & Ekerdt, 2017). The best decisions about where one should live in late life are those that lead to outcomes that are congruent with the person's needs and goals, so congregate living can work for those seeking specific types of social engagement.

Given the demand for congregate housing, it is clearly a popular choice for many older adults. Still, there are areas of concern driving innovations (Karp, 2021). As unearthed during the COVID-19 pandemic, large facilities have drawbacks. Thus, a move toward smaller facilities, including ones with pods, is an emerging trend. Designing interior and exterior spaces to promote health and safety will enable residents across the ability spectrum to make better use of facilities. Implementing technology-based assistance with communication (e.g., through videoconference-capable residences) would improve social interaction. And all of these innovations must be sensitive to and include ethnic, racially, and culturally appropriate programs and interventions.

Assisted Living

For many older adults, the levels of support provided by friends and family, or supplemented by those in a congregate facility, are enough to provide a good quality of life and personal independence. For others, though, the level of support they require goes beyond that. For example, a person may have mild cognitive impairment or be unable to perform multiple ADLs (e.g., may be unable to bathe oneself, prepare microwave meals, or take medication correctly) that are beyond the level of support available in one's home or in a congregate setting. As a result, they may consider relocating to an assisted living facility. **Assisted living facilities** are housing options for older adults that provide a supportive living arrangement for people needing assistance with personal care (such as bathing, meals, or taking medications) but who are not so impaired physically or cognitively that they need 24-hour care.

An ideal assisted living situation has three essential attributes (American Health Care Association and National Center for Assisted Living, 2021a, b). First, the physical environment where a person lives is designed to be as much like a single-family home as possible. That way, the setting has a personal residential feel, a small scale, and personal privacy that includes at a minimum a private room and a full bath that is not shared with

Assisted living facilities provide an intermediate level of support for residents.

other residents unless the resident explicitly requests that arrangement. The public spaces in the facility are designed to provide indoor and outdoor access, which enhances a resident's autonomy and independence.

Second, the philosophy of care at an ideal assisted living facility emphasizes personal control, choice, dignity, and autonomy and promotes a preferred lifestyle both residents and their families consider to be a typical, good quality of life. This philosophy is implemented by understanding residents' personal preferences and priorities and allowing residents to exert control over their lives, schedules, and private dwellings (e.g., by having the resident bring a few pieces of personal furniture for their room).

Third, ideal assisted living facilities should meet residents' routine services and special needs. Many assisted living facilities provide a range of in-facility services, such as physical therapy, exercise, and hair salons. It is important to keep in mind that assisted living facilities foster residents' autonomy, so the levels of support provided are not meant to deal with high-level, intensive nursing or other complex needs (Polivka & Rill, 2016; Thomas et al., 2011). For example, in North Carolina people who reside in assisted living facilities must not need supervision or care that reaches the level of nursing home care (e.g., require the use of a ventilator or 24/7 nursing care), may not have severe mental health or substance use issues or have a proven record of being a danger to themselves and others, must be able to comprehend and enter into a contract on their own, and may not be totally dependent on personal care to complete at least four ADLs per day (AssistedLiving.org, 2021).

Despite the fact assisted living facilities have existed for decades, there are serious gaps in service and in regulations (Polivka & Rill, 2016). For example, no national consensus or federal guidelines exist to govern the characteristics of the people who can and should be served in these facilities, the services provided, or minimum staffing standards. Despite the problems with precisely defining assisted living facilities, the number of them continues to grow. In the United States, there are about 30,000 assisted living facilities with nearly 1 million residents (most of whom are over age 80), and there will be strong continued demand for growth over the next few decades. One important reason for this growth is that assisted living offers a more supportive, intermediary, and cost-effective option beyond congregate living for those older adults who cannot live independently but do not need the level of nursing care provided in long-term care facilities.

A second major area of concern is staffing. In general, assisted living facilities are staffed by people of color, who are not well paid compared to other economic sectors; in the early 2020s, the average salary of people who provide most of the day-to-day care was less the $25,000/year (ZipRecruiter, 2022). Low pay and feeling that one is not valued turned out to be major reasons why people quit their jobs during and after the COVID-19 pandemic. (This issue is explored in more detail in Chapter 12.)

To help families choose the best option, the American Health Care Association and National Center for Assisted Living (2021) provides a *Consumer's Guide*. Before choosing an assisted living facility, you should consider several things:

- What are the resident's needs now, and what are they likely to be in the future? Will the facility meet those needs?
- Is the facility in a convenient location?
- What are the admission and retention policies?
- Does the facility permit residents to bring a few items from home?
- What level of support for personal care and what health services are provided?
- Does the facility provide a written statement of the philosophy of care and a statement of residents' rights?
- What do you notice on unannounced visits?
- How engaging and supportive are the staff? How is the food?
- What payment options are accepted by the facility?
- What social, recreational, and spiritual activities does the facility provide?
- What do other residents say about the facility?
- What types of training do staff receive, and how frequently do they receive it?
- What information is contained in state licensing and accreditation reports?

The average annual cost of assisted living in the United States was nearly $52,000 in 2021, with costs increasing each year (Genworth Financial, 2021). This is about half the cost of a nursing home. Medicare does not pay for either living costs or any of the services provided. In some cases, Medicaid or other specialized insurance may pay for services depending on the situation. Given that assisted living is usually less expensive than nursing homes, the lack of broad financial support for these programs means that the cost of care is not as low as it could be and is still well outside the ability of many people to afford it.

Research indicates that residents in assisted living facilities have higher well-being when the decision to live there was under their control and when the quality of relationships formed with co-residents is better (Mauldin et al., 2021; Street & Burge, 2012), as well as when they become attached to the place (Friesen et al., 2016). A key factor turns out to be how well the design of the facility, in combination with the services, optimizes the person–environment fit (discussed earlier in the chapter).

Adult Development in Action

As a gerontological social worker, what key factors would you consider when making recommendations about the best housing and living options for your older adult clients?

Review Questions

5.2 The Ecology of Aging: Community Options

- What is the ecology of aging?
- What is aging in place?
- What factors should people use to make decisions about the most supportive environment in which to live?
- How can homes be modified to support older adults? What is an auxiliary dwelling unit?
- What services are provided at adult day care centers?
- What is congregate housing? What services are provided at assisted living facilities?

5.3 Living in Skilled Nursing Facilities, Special Care Facilities, and Nursing Homes

Key Questions

- What is the difference between skilled nursing facilities and nursing homes?
- What are the major types of nursing homes?
- Who is most likely to live in nursing homes?
- What are the key characteristics of nursing homes?
- What are special care units?
- How can a nursing home be a home?
- How should people communicate with nursing home residents?
- How is decision-making capacity assessed?
- What are some new directions for nursing homes?

The last place Rosa thought she would end up was a bed in one of the local nursing homes. "That's a place where old people go to die," she used to say. "It's not gonna be for me." But here she is. Rosa, 87 and living alone, fell and broke her hip. Because she was already having problems with remembering to take her medications and with several ADLs, she was moved here from the hospital. She hates the food; "tasteless goo," she calls it. Her roommate, Arnetta, calls the place a "jail." Arnetta, 79, has extremely limited vision due to diabetic retinopathy and has early stage dementia.

Envisioning oneself as a nursing home resident is not something people tend to do. To be sure, you may have family members or acquaintances who are or were residents. Nevertheless, there are many people who must come to terms with their personal situation and decide where the best place for them to live may be. Long-term care facilities such as nursing homes are indeed places where people who have serious health problems may need to go, and for many it is their final address. Yet if you visit one, you will also find many inspiring people with extremely interesting life stories to tell.

Long-term care settings are different environments from those we have considered so far. The residents of such facilities differ in many respects from their community-dwelling counterparts. Likewise, the environment itself is dissimilar from neighborhood and community contexts. But because many aspects of the environment in these facilities are controlled, they offer a unique opportunity to examine person–environment interactions in more detail.

In this section we examine types of long-term care settings, the typical residents, the psychosocial environment, and residents' ability to make decisions for themselves.

Types of Long-Term Care Facilities and Resident Demographics

When people need more intense medical, psychosocial, and personal care support than is reasonably possible for aging in place or in assisted living, long-term care becomes the next option. As we will consider, whether this option is accessible depends critically on whether individuals have access to funding, either through self-pay or various types of insurance (e.g., Medicaid, private insurance). Note that Medicare provides very limited coverage (generally up to 20 days, with co-pays for days 21–100) for short-term stays that are medically necessary, such as for rehabilitation after a hip or pelvic fracture.

There are three major types of long-term care facilities based on the kinds of services and support they provide. These are as follows:

- *Skilled nursing facilities.* Skilled nursing and rehabilitation care consists of 24-hour medical monitoring under the direct supervision of a physician, with day-to-day services provided by a registered nurse or licensed practical nurse. This level of care is most often used up to 100 days for recovery from major illness (e.g., cerebrovascular accident), injury (e.g., broken pelvis or hip), or surgery (e.g., hip or knee replacement). In some cases, residents who need intensive nursing care (e.g., for monitoring of a ventilator or feeding tube) may remain in a skilled nursing facilities for much longer periods. Many skilled nursing facilities are subunits of nursing homes.
- *Special care facilities.* Special care facilities are organized around particular physical or mental health conditions such that all of the types of interventions and supports are geared specifically for that condition. With older adults, the most common example of a special care facility is a memory care center designed specifically for individuals who have serious cognitive impairment (e.g., Alzheimer's disease, traumatic brain injury). In many cases, special care facilities are established as sections of nursing homes (e.g., a wing or floor of the building), or are separate structures close by. Medical staff are available 24/7, and most have specialized training in the treatment and management of the specific conditions experienced by the residents.
- *Nursing homes.* Nursing homes constitute a broad category of facilities that provide long-term intensive care for residents. The nursing home residential care model includes nursing care, dietary needs, and environmental and maintenance services as well as activities to ensure active and engaged residents. As noted earlier, nursing homes may include other types of long-term care, thereby providing a comprehensive continuum of care.

Because of the overlap across the three major types of long-term care facilities, we will consider them together in much of the discussion in the remainder of this chapter. When the distinctions matter, especially in terms of specific approaches to intervention, we will carefully distinguish the types.

Who Is Likely to Live in Long-Term Care Facilities? Rosa, the 87-year-old we met in the vignette, reflects the typical resident. She is over age 85, a Hispanic White woman, recently admitted to a hospital (for her broken pelvis), who was living in the community, has problems with ADLs and IADLs, is widowed, and has no siblings or children living nearby. According to the most recent U.S. survey, about three-quarters of nursing home residents are White.

However, this profile is changing, especially in urban areas, as more older adults of color become residents of long-term care facilities (Centers for Medicare and Medicaid Services, 2016). As results from the 2020 U.S. Census verify, the population of the United States continues to diversify, so the increased diversity of nursing home residents reflects this overall trend (Jones et al., 2021). Given the rapid increase of adults of color, it is likely that these demographics will continue to change quickly over the coming decades. That said, a major limiting factor for this increased need for additional space for older adults of color is disparities in the ability to afford this type of care.

What are the health issues and functional impairments of typical nursing home residents? For the most part, the average nursing home resident has significant mental and physical problems. Nearly two-thirds of nursing home residents have significant impairments with at least four (of a possible five) ADLs, and roughly 60% have moderate or severe cognitive impairment (Centers for Medicare and Medicaid Services, 2016).

As you may surmise from the high level of impairment among nursing home residents, frail older people and their relatives do not consider nursing homes as the best option until other avenues have been explored. This may account for the numbers of

Maskot/DigitalVision/Getty Images

Physical activity is an important aspect of long-term care facilities for those able to participate.

Controversies

Financing Long-Term Care

The current system of financing long-term care in the United States is in serious trouble. With the average cost of a shared room in 2021 about $93,000 per year, increasing roughly 4% annually, long-term care is by far the leading catastrophic healthcare expense that most people will face (Genworth Financial, 2021). It is a source of legitimate fear for the havoc it can cause financially; few families have sufficient savings to afford nursing homes.

Payment options other than through one's personal funds are quite limited (Whitley, 2021). There are three federal and state options for those who qualify. As noted earlier, Medicare does not cover long-term nursing home care but does have limited coverage for people who need skilled nursing services for fewer than 100 days and who meet certain other criteria. Second, the U.S. Department of Veterans Affairs provides care to veterans who require long-term medical assistance depending on their specific needs. Veterans and their spouses must already be signed up for VA health care and meet enrollment and eligibility requirements based on income, disability level, and location. Third, Medicaid is a federal and state program that covers long-term care for individuals who have limited income and resources. Specific eligibility criteria vary by state, so check with local offices to determine whether you or someone you know would qualify.

Private insurance plans on average pay a relatively small portion of the costs. For those who do not qualify for VA or Medicaid benefits, the bulk of the costs are usually paid directly by nursing home residents. But most Americans do not have anywhere near the amount of personal savings (e.g., IRAs, investments, pensions) to cover the costs of long-term care, and most people over age 40 have done little financial planning for the possibility of needing long-term care. Given that about 70% of adults over age 65 will likely need some type of specialized care for at least some period of time, the funding gap is clearly a crisis.

There's more. The wealth disparity in the United States that is related to sociocultural factors including economic status, race, and ethnicity plays out in significant disparities in health care and access to long-term care. Consequently, older adults of color have, on average, significantly fewer resources and options at their disposal than do White individuals, other factors being equal. But even when they reside in nursing homes, the quality of care for Black residents is lower than it is for White residents (Gorges & Konetzka, 2021; Njoku, 2022).

Given these expenses, the lack of insurance coverage and personal planning, and significant disparities in access to quality care, how will we be able to provide and finance the long-term healthcare system? Sadly, the problem has been obvious for many years, but little action has been taken by the federal government. Several options proposed years ago remain viable, taking the Affordable Health Care Act into account (Pettinato, 2013). Four main strategies are possible:

- A strategy that promotes private long-term care insurance and keeps public financing as a safety net. This approach spreads the financial risk without expanding the demands on federal or state budgets and taxpayers to pay fully for long-term care. Still, a public safety net would be essential as a last resort.
- A strategy to expand the public safety net for people with low to moderate incomes, with people from higher-income brackets expected to provide for themselves through private financing. This approach is a needs-tested model that targets the people with the greatest need and the fewest resources for government assistance.
- A strategy to establish public catastrophic long-term care insurance and support complementary private insurance to fill the gap along with the public safety net. This approach spreads the risk and the burden on a greater number of people, reducing the cost of private insurance, but still pricing it beyond the means of many older adults.
- A strategy to establish universal public long-term care insurance supplemented with private financing and a public safety net. This approach spreads the burden over the greatest number of people, thereby addressing the problem of affordability of private insurance.

Despite the wide range of options, many of them still place the burden on individuals to devise ways of financing their own care. Given the cost, and the fact that millions of Americans do not have access to either adequate health insurance or personal savings, large subsidies from the government will still be needed for long-term care regardless of what the private sector does.

Given that government subsidies for long-term care will be needed for the foreseeable future, the question becomes how to finance them. Under the current federal systems, older adults are not always protected from becoming impoverished and in essence are required to have few assets in order to qualify. With the aging of the baby boom generation, many more people will spend down their assets to qualify, causing Medicaid costs to skyrocket. If we want to continue the program in its current form, additional revenues will be needed, either in the form of higher taxes or dramatic spending reductions in other areas of public budgets.

The questions facing us are whether we want to continue forcing older adults to become totally impoverished when they need long-term care, require the government to continue subsidy programs, and encourage those who can afford it to buy long-term care insurance, and if we are willing to pay higher taxes for better coverage. How we answer these questions will have a profound impact on the status of long-term care over the next few decades.

people with multiple serious impairments who live in nursing homes; the kinds and number of issues have made aging in place extremely difficult for them and their families, and also beyond the level of support provided by assisted living facilities. Still, the decision to place a family member in a nursing home is a very difficult one even when the family member in question has serious cognitive impairment (Koss & Ekerdt, 2017; Lord et al., 2016; Serrano-Gemes et al., 2021). Placement decisions are often delayed until there is a crisis, such as a person's impending discharge from a hospital or a near-catastrophic accident (e.g., leaving the stove on resulting in a fire). Most placement decisions are made by spouses/partners or adult children, a finding generalized across racial and ethnic groups such as White Americans, Mexican Americans, and Korean Americans, especially when there is evidence of cognitive impairment (Kwon & Tae, 2012; Ruiz et al., 2016; Serrano-Gemes et al., 2021).

Characteristics of Nursing Homes

Long-term care facilities in general, and nursing homes in particular, vary a great deal in the amount and quality of care they provide. One useful way of evaluating them is by applying the competence–environmental press model. When applied to nursing homes, the goal is to find the optimal level of environmental support for people who demonstrate relatively lower levels of competence due to serious physical, mental, or psychosocial difficulties.

Selecting a nursing home should be done carefully. They are governed by state and federal regulations that establish minimum standards of care. Across the United States, nursing homes offer a spectrum of levels of care, such as the skilled nursing care and special care discussed earlier, as well as intensive skilled nursing (for residents needing constant monitoring or complicated medical procedures that are usually provided by registered nurses), intermediate care (24-hour care including nursing supervision, but at a less intense level usually involving a chronic physical or emotional illness such as dementia or severe mobility impairment), and custodial care (covering all the nonmedical services a facility provides).

The cost of nursing home care in the United States is very high—an average of about $108,000 per year for a private room and about $93,000 annually for a two-person shared room (Genworth Financial, 2021). With the aging of the baby boom generation, how this cost will be met is an issue confronting millions of families. As noted in the Controversies feature, funding for nursing homes will be an increasingly important political issue in the coming decades.

How Do We Know the Quality of Nursing Homes? Making the decision to place a loved one in a nursing home is only the first step. Choosing the right placement is the next one. How do we know whether the facility we are considering provides quality care? To address that question and major concern for individuals and families, the Centers for Medicare and Medicaid Services (2021a) provides a detailed *Five-Star Quality Rating System* website that is a guide for choosing a nursing home based on several key quality factors. Among the most important things to consider are the following:

- Quality of life for residents (e.g., whether residents are well groomed, the food is tasty, and rooms contain comfortable furniture);
- Quality of care (whether staff respond quickly to calls, whether residents are receiving the appropriate levels and types of care; whether staff and family are involved in care decisions);

- Safety (whether there are enough staff, whether hallways are free of clutter); and
- Other issues (whether there are outdoor areas for residents to use).

These aspects of nursing homes reflect those dimensions considered by states in their inspections and licensing process.

Individuals and families should also keep several other things in mind:

- Skilled nursing care is usually available only for a short time following hospitalization, whereas
- Custodial care may be an option for a much longer period. If a facility offers both types, it may or may not be possible to shift level of care without relocating to another room.
- Nursing homes that only take Medicaid residents may offer longer term but less-intensive care levels. Nursing homes that do not accept Medicaid may force the resident to leave when Medicare or private funds run out.
- Ensure the facility and its administrator are fully licensed, and a full array of staff training is available on such topics as recognizing abuse and neglect, how to deal with difficult residents, and how to investigate and report your complaints.
- Ensure the resident's care plan is put together by a team of professionals, and residents have choices, can exert some control over their routines and care, and have appropriate assistance with ADLs and IADLs.
- Ask questions about staff educational levels (including continuing education) and turnover.

Based on the various theories of person–environment interaction discussed earlier in this chapter, the best nursing homes use what researchers recommend—a "person-centered care" approach to nursing home policies (Bhattacharyya et al., 2022; Morgan & Yoder, 2012). Although there is not yet complete consensus about the underlying characteristics of person-centered care (Bhattacharyya et al., 2022), this approach is based on promoting residents' well-being through engaging them in shared decision making and participation in their care and showing them respect. Person-centered planning focuses on the individual and does not use a one-size-fits-all approach. An example of this approach includes such things as residents getting to decorate their own rooms, choosing what they want to eat from a buffet or menu, being treated in a socioculturally appropriate and sensitive manner, and deciding whether they want to take a shower or a bath. Most important, this approach involves a team who knows and cares about the individual who work together with the person to create the best supportive environment possible.

Such policies are grounded in classic research showing that residents who have higher perceived personal control show significant improvement in well-being and activity level, and actually live longer (Langer & Rodin, 1976; Rodin & Langer, 1977). Nursing homes using the person-centered planning approach also note major decreases in the need for certain medications (e.g., sleep and antianxiety drugs) and soft restraints, as well as substantial declines in the number of residents who are incontinent (Wyatt, 2016). Feelings of self-efficacy are crucial to doing well and adjusting to life in a long-term care facility (Brandburg et al., 2013). As we will discover later, the benefits of person-centered care are crucial to residents' finding and experiencing joy in their life despite significant symptom severity (Rinnan et al., 2022).

Today, person-centered care is considered a best practice in nursing homes (Rinnan et al., 2022; Sharma et al., 2015; Wyatt, 2016). Including nursing home residents in the planning of their own care represents a major shift in culture from previous models based on convenience for staff and is an example of the application of research to practice.

Special Care Facilities. Many residents of nursing homes have some degree of cognitive impairment, and the majority of those individuals are in various stages of dementia. Providing a supportive environment for people with moderate to severe dementia requires certain specialized design and intervention features. This need has resulted in the development of special care units within or affiliated with many nursing homes.

Well-designed special care units for people with dementia provide a socioculturally appropriate supportive and therapeutic set of programs that help the person function at the highest level possible. Optimally, staff working in special care units receive specific training to work with persons with dementia. The best units have physical design elements that take functional limitations into account; for example, the hallways of some facilities are designed so if residents wander, they merely follow the interior halls or exterior path in a circle so they do not leave the building or the complex, and the decorating is done in a way to minimize confusion. Most facilities have residents with cognitive impairment wear wrist or ankle bands that trigger alarms if they wander beyond a certain point or exit the

How Do We Know?

Disparities in Quality of Life Among Nursing Home Residents

Who were the investigators, and what was the aim of the study? Research across different types of healthcare settings consistently shows that the quality of life of patients and residents matters for various outcomes. In nursing homes, quality of life matters not just for residents' satisfaction, but for their overall health and longevity. However, as we have encountered in several contexts in this text already, disparities in health care based especially on race and ethnicity are widespread. To determine the extent to which disparities are present in nursing homes, Tetyana Shippee and colleagues (2020) examined the role of individual residents' race/ethnicity, facility racial/ethnic composition, and the interaction of both for nursing home resident quality of life.

How did the investigator measure the topic of interest? The study used data from two sources. First, the minimum data set (MDS) is part of the federally mandated process for clinical assessment of all residents in Medicare and Medicaid certified nursing homes. The MDS provides a comprehensive assessment of each resident's functional capabilities and helps nursing home staff identify health problems. Care area assessments (CAAs) are part of this assessment and provide the foundation upon which a resident's individual care plan is formulated. All assessments are completed within specific guidelines and time frames. MDS information is transmitted electronically by nursing homes to the national MDS database.

Second, a validated quality of life instrument was used that has 31 items assessing six domains (environmental adaptations, negative mood, positive mood, social engagement, attention from staff, and meal enjoyment). Scores were calculated for each domain by adding individual items and standardizing the summed items to percentage points (i.e., 0 to 100) with higher values indicating better quality of life. A summary score was also calculated, which was the average of standardized scores on the six domains. Quality of life data were collected through interviews of residents.

Who were the participants in the study? 10,455 non-Hispanic White residents and 671 racial/ethnic minority residents (6.0% of sample) in 355 nursing homes in Minnesota participated. Of these, 415 were non-Hispanic Black residents, 101 were Native American residents, and 155 respondents were Asian American, Hispanic of any race, or any other race or ethnicity.

Because the threshold for what is considered high-non-White composition varies across states, the researchers defined a nursing home as high-non-White if it was above the 90th percentile for proportion of non-White residents in the state of Minnesota. For Minnesota, the 90th percentile facility had a non-White composition of more than 14%. Making facility the unit of analysis, the low-non-White nursing homes had 2.36% non-White residents. The high-minority facilities had 27.22% non-White residents on average. Of 355 nursing homes in the study, 118 had no non-White residents.

What was the design of the study? The study matched the clinical observation data from the MDS with the quality of life interview data.

Were there ethical concerns with the study? Because residents' identities were not included in the data, there were no ethical concerns.

What were the results? Shippee and colleagues found significant racial disparities in nursing home residents' quality of life. Non-White residents reported significantly lower quality of life scores than White residents, and nursing homes with higher proportions of non-White residents had significantly lower quality of life scores overall. Non-White residents had significantly lower adjusted quality of life than White residents, whether they were in low- or high-non-White facilities, indicating a remaining significant gap in individual care needs that remain unaddressed.

What did the investigators conclude? Shippee and colleagues argue that the results highlight system-level racial disparities in nursing home residents' quality of life, with residents who live in high-proportion non-White nursing homes facing the greatest threats to their quality of life. To reduce racial/ethnic disparities in quality of life, deliberate steps must be taken, including potential public reporting (similar to quality of care) and providing resources for and attention to culturally sensitive care in nursing homes to address residents' unique needs.

facility, another safe way to provide opportunities for residents to move about freely but safely. The best facilities also permit residents to bring a few personal items as reminders of their past in order to provide a more home-like environment. They also provide a private dining area in a family-like setting to minimize possible negative interactions between residents with dementia and residents without cognitive impairment.

Selecting the right special care unit for a person with dementia must be done carefully by the family with proper input from healthcare professionals, keeping in mind that such care units need to be grounded in basic principles of human rights (Charras et al., 2016; Verbeek et al., 2021). As noted in the competence–environmental press model, as competence declines the environment must provide more support for behavior to be optimized. Thus, the special care unit must have the right level of environmental support for each resident, as well as the availability of additional levels of support if the person's competence level continues to decline. Memory aids should be built into the design of the unit, such as color-coded halls. Staffing levels and training are key as is the range of intervention programs and activities available. Such programs should be research based, such as those based on the Montessori techniques discussed in Chapter 10.

The research-based staff training required at the best special care units includes several aspects of caring for older adults with moderate to severe cognitive impairment:

- Appropriate and effective communication techniques (as discussed later in this section)
- Behavioral management techniques to address aggressive or agitated behavior (a common symptom in dementia)
- Appropriate techniques for assisting with personal health and hygiene that protect residents' dignity
- Appropriate methods for dealing with incontinence
- Appropriate ways for handling sexuality in persons with dementia
- Effective techniques for controlling wandering (in addition to physical design aspects of the facility)
- Appropriate ways of supervising or assisting with eating
- Appropriate techniques and interventions to address memory failure and disorientation
- Appropriate techniques for assisting with mobility (e.g., walking, using a wheelchair).

Training in these areas will not guarantee high-quality care, but it increases the likelihood of it.

Research indicates that racial and ethnic disparities exist in access to quality special care units and nursing homes, with residents of color more likely to be in segregated, lower quality facilities (Rivera-Hernandez et al., 2019). Additionally, residents of color have significantly lower quality of life than White residents, whether they are in special care facilities or nursing homes with low or high proportions of residents of color, indicating a significant remaining gap exists in meeting individual care needs (Shippee et al., 2020). The process by which this disparity in quality of life was identified in nursing homes is explored more fully in the How Do We Know? feature.

The care residents of special care facilities receive is more the result of a difference in philosophy of care between nursing homes with and without special care units than it is due to the special care unit itself. The behavioral-based intervention preferred in well-designed special care units results in lower mortality and better functioning in residents, all other factors held constant, and is also likely to be used throughout the affiliated nursing home, improving quality overall (Khait et al., 2021; Yu, 2016).

Can a Nursing Home or Special Care Facility Be a Home?

Perhaps you know someone who has lived in a nursing home or special care facility for an extended period of time. If you had a chance to talk with them about their experience, what did they tell you? What do you think it is like living there? As you might imagine, one key aspect of living in a long-term care facility of any kind is what it is for anyone living anywhere: To what extent do residents consider a nursing home or special care facility to be *home*? This gets to the heart of what makes people feel the place where they live is more than just a dwelling, as we noted earlier in this chapter.

On the surface, it may seem that nursing homes and special care facilities are full of barriers to this feeling of home. After all, they may have regulations about the number and type of furnishings and other personal effects residents may bring, and residents are in an environment with plenty of structural reminders that it is not their former home. Not having their own stove, for example, means they can no longer invite friends over for a home-cooked meal. Thus, the culture of nursing homes and special care facilities makes a difference in residents' experiences (Killett et al., 2016). Increasingly, the traditional models of care are being questioned as advocates push for more basic human rights for residents that emphasize quality of life and personal dignity (Emmer De Albuquerque Green, 2022).

Can nursing home and special care facility residents move beyond these barriers and reminders and achieve a sense of home? The answer is yes, but with some important qualifications. In a groundbreaking series of studies, Groger (1995, 2002) proposed a nursing home can indeed be perceived as a home. She interviewed older African American adults, some who lived in nursing homes and others who were home care clients, along with a sample of the nursing home residents' care providers. Groger's analyses of her interviews revealed that nursing home residents can feel at home. The circumstances fostering this feeling include having the time to think about and participate in the placement decision, even if only minimally; having prior knowledge and positive experience with a specific facility; defining home predominantly in terms of family and social relationships rather than in terms of place, objects, or total autonomy; and being able to establish a kind of continuity between home and nursing home either through activities or similarities in living arrangements.

Groger (2002) points out that residents pull from their repertoire of coping strategies to help them come to terms with living in a nursing home. Groger (1995) also reports that getting nursing home residents to reminisce about home actually facilitates adjustment. Some residents concluded only after long and detailed reflection on their prior home that the nursing home they currently lived in was now home. In addition, it may be easier for nursing home residents to feel at home on some days than others and from one situation to another, depending on the events or stimuli at the time.

Miodrag ignjatovic/E+/Getty Images

Nursing home residents benefit from social activities and interaction with residents and staff in order to make it feel more like a "home."

Helping nursing home residents feel at home is an important issue that must be explored in more detail. Perhaps having people think about what constitutes a home, before and after placement, may make the transition from community to the facility easier to face. For those needing the care provided in a nursing home, anything done to ease the transition is a major benefit. Assessing the degree to which residents feel at home is possible and can be used to document functional changes after placement into a facility (Brandburg et al., 2013; Centers for Medicare and Medicaid Services, 2021a, c; Killett et al., 2016).

At a general level, nursing home and special care facility residents' satisfaction with their current living situation relates to several key variables: facility, staff, and resident factors, as shown in Figure 5.5 (Chou et al., 2003). Research indicates that staff satisfaction plays a crucial role in nursing home residents' satisfaction. In contrast, providing more care does not (Chou et al., 2003). Digging deeper, it turns out that whether the nursing assistants, the staff with whom residents interact with most, are satisfied with their jobs and have clearly defined roles and scope of practice are extremely important influencers of residents' quality of life (X. Li et al., 2021). In addition, when residents have a voice in determining the quality of care, irrespective of their functional abilities, their quality of life improves (Killett

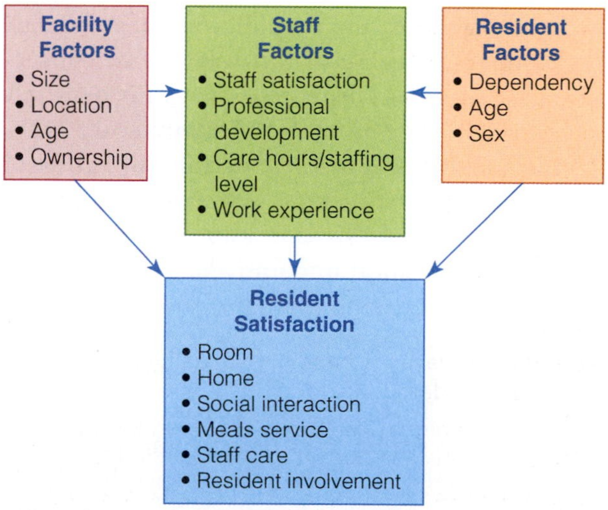

Figure 5.5 Major factors influencing resident satisfaction in nursing homes.

Source: Chou, S-C., Boldy, D. P., & Lee, A. H. (2003). Factors influencing residents' satisfaction in residential aged care. *The Gerontologist, 43*, 459–472. Copyright © Reprinted with permission from the Gerontological Society of America.

et al., 2016; Sharma et al., 2015). As we will learn next, how people communicate with residents is also key.

Communicating with Residents

Have you ever been to a nursing home or special care facility? If so, you may have been anxious the first time you visited, wondering how you should talk with the residents, especially when interacting with residents who are cognitively impaired. Unfortunately, this uneasiness often results from stereotypes of older adults in general and nursing home and special care facility residents in particular when speaking to them that can result in inappropriate communication styles.

The communication style most people use as a default is one in which they overaccommodate their speech based on their stereotyped expectations of dependence and incompetence. This style is described as a general "communication predicament" of older adults, and it reflects ageism (Friedman, 2020; Ryan et al., 1986, 1995). Such speech conveys a sense of declining abilities, loss of control, and helplessness, which, if continued, may cause older adults to lose self-esteem and withdraw from social interactions. As time goes on, older adults who are talked to in this way may even begin behaving in ways that reinforce the stereotypes.

Inappropriate speech to older adults that is based on stereotypes of incompetence and dependence is called **patronizing speech**. Patronizing speech is slower speech marked by exaggerated intonation, higher pitch, increased volume, repetitions, tag and closed-end questions, and simplification of vocabulary and grammar. Speaking in this way can be conceptualized as "secondary baby talk," which is baby talk inappropriately used with adults (Mohlman et al., 2012). Secondary baby talk, also called **infantilization or elderspeak**, also involves the unwarranted use of a person's first name, terms of endearment, simplified expressions, short imperatives, an assumption that the recipient has no memory, and cajoling as a way to demand compliance (Shaw & Gordon, 2021). Elderspeak appears to be a cross-cultural problem, too (Cavallaro et al., 2016; Leeuwen, 2016).

In a classic study, Whitbourne and colleagues (1995) established that infantilizing speech is interpreted extremely negatively by some older adults. They found community-dwelling older adults rated infantilizing speech especially negatively and were particularly resentful of its intonation aspects as indicative of a lack of respect. Nursing home residents were less harsh in their judgments, giving support to the idea that being exposed to infantilizing speech lowers one's awareness of its demeaning qualities. Whitbourne and colleagues also found no evidence that infantilizing speech is high in nurturance, as some previous authors had suggested. Shaw and Gordon (2021) summarized the history of research on elderspeak by pointing out that it was generally perceived as patronizing by older adults, and speakers were perceived as less respectful. Residents with dementia tend to be more resistive to care when they are the targets of elderspeak but show less resistance when elderspeak diminishes (Cavallaro et al., 2016; Shaw & Gordon, 2021; Williams et al., 2017).

Experience working with older residents is crucial to reducing patronizing speech (Marques et al., 2020). Younger adults' use of patronizing speech appears to be related to the amount of interaction they have had with unrelated older adults (i.e., older adults who are not their relatives or close friends), with less experience being related to higher use of patronizing speech.

It turns out there may be different types of elderspeak, with different effects on the targets of the communications. Chee (2011), as part of the overall research of Cavallaro and colleagues (2016), examined elderspeak in an eldercare facility in Singapore. Chee discovered there may be at least two types of elderspeak, what she terms "right" and "wrong." Chee also found elderspeak is a common approach used in a variety of settings, but that it is used toward older women most often.

Chee concluded elderspeak aimed at comprehension checking and encouragement, when no other elements of elderspeak are present, may enhance clients' performance. A subsequent review of related research confirmed this finding, but only if exaggerated forms of speaking are not used (Shaw & Gordon, 2021). In contrast, Chee found that all other forms of elderspeak tended to result in poorer performance of the task at hand.

So how should people talk to older adults, especially those needing services or living in long-term care facilities? Ryan and her colleagues (1995) initially proposed the communication enhancement model as a framework for appropriate exchange. This model is based on a health promotion model that seeks opportunities for healthcare providers to optimize outcomes for older adults through more appropriate and effective communication. As explained in Figure 5.6, this model emphasizes communication with older adults must be based on recognizing individualized cues, modifying communication to suit individual needs and situations, appropriately assessing health and social problems, and empowering both older adults and healthcare providers.

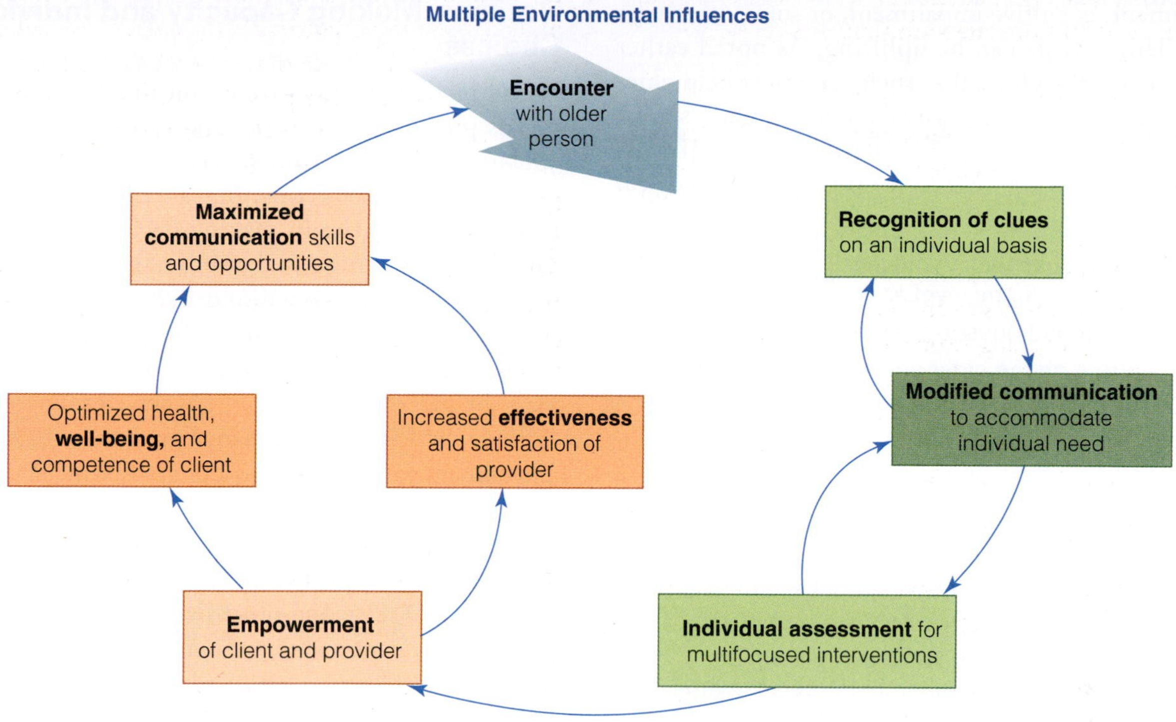

Figure 5.6 The communication enhancement model. Note that this model is dynamic in that there are opportunities to modify communication interactions and to have the outcomes of one interaction serve as input for another.
Source: Ryan, E. B., Meredith, S. D., MacLean, M. J., & Orange, J. B. (1995). Changing the way we talk with elders: Promoting health using the communication enhancement model. *International Journal of Aging and Human Development, 41*, 89–107. Reproduced by permission.

Combining the communication enhancement model with the person-centered care approach discussed earlier provides a way for paraprofessional staff in long-term care facilities in general to communicate more effectively with residents, including those living on dementia special care units (Lombard, 2021; Passalacqua & Harwood, 2012). For example, using personalized greetings with residents goes a long way in improving staff–resident relations (Lombard, 2021). Such strategies are important if the culture in long-term care facilities in general is to change.

The University of Queensland (Australia) has developed the *MESSAGE Communication Strategies in Dementia* training program based on this approach. MESSAGE stands for:

- ***M**aximize* attention.
- ***E**xpression* and body language.
- Keep it ***S**imple.*
- ***S**upport* their conversation.
- ***A**ssist* with visual **A***ids.*
- ***G**et* their message.
- ***E**ncourage* and ***E**ngage* in communication.

Research indicates that this training is effective and well-received by staff who care for individuals with dementia (Conway & Chenery, 2016).

In general, an approach to communication based on the communication enhancement model promotes mental, social, and physical well-being among older adults and counters the fostering of dependence that follows from the traditional medical model discussed earlier. When patronizing speech occurs in nursing homes, active steps should be taken to eliminate it (Cavallaro et al., 2016; Shaw & Gordon, 2021; Williams et al., 2017). Most important, this research reminds us we must speak to all older adults in a way that conveys the respect they deserve.

So, what should you do as a visitor? The first time most people visit a nursing home, they may be anxious about talking to family members or other residents who are frail, have trouble remembering, and cannot get around easily. The hardest part is trying to figure out *how* to speak to avoid patronizing speech. However, visiting residents of nursing homes is a way to maintain social contacts and provide a meaningful activity. Even if the person you are visiting is frail or has a sensory impairment, cognitive impairment, or some other type of challenge, visits can be uplifting. As noted earlier in the chapter, high-quality social contacts help older adults maintain their life satisfaction. Here are several suggestions for making visits more pleasant (Davis, 1985), along with guidance from the Gerontological Society of America (2012):

- Face older adults when you speak to them, with your lips at the same level as theirs.
- Ask open-ended questions and genuinely listen.
- Concentrate on the older adult's expertise and wisdom, as discussed in Chapter 7, by asking for advice on a life problem they know a lot about, such as dealing with friends, cooking, or crafts.
- Ask questions about an older adult's living situation and social contacts.
- Allow the older person to exert control over the visit: where to go (even inside the facility), what to wear, what to eat (if choices are possible).
- Listen attentively, even if the older person is repetitive. Avoid being judgmental, be sympathetic to complaints, and acknowledge feelings.
- Talk about things the person likes to remember, such as raising children, military service, growing up, work, courtship, and so on.
- Do a joint activity, such as putting a jigsaw puzzle together, arranging a photograph album, or doing arts and crafts.
- Record your visit if it is permitted. This is valuable for creating a family history you will be able to keep. The activity may facilitate a life review as well as provide an opportunity for the older person to leave something of value for future generations by describing important personal events and philosophies.
- Bring children when you visit, if possible. Grandchildren are especially important because many older adults are happy to include them in conversations. Such visits also give children the opportunity to see their grandparents and learn about the diversity of older adults.
- Stimulate as many senses as possible. Wearing bright clothes, singing songs, reading books, and sharing foods (as long as they have been checked and approved with the staff) help to keep residents involved with their environment. Above all, though, hold the resident's hands. There's nothing like a friendly touch.

Always remember your visits may be the only way the residents have of maintaining social contacts with friends and family. By following these guidelines, you will be able to avoid difficulties and make your visits more pleasurable.

Decision-Making Capacity and Individual Choices

Providing high-quality care for nursing home residents means putting into practice the various competence-enhancing interventions we have discussed relating to personal control and communication. Doing so means residents participate in making decisions about their care. But how can we make sure residents understand what they are being asked to decide, especially when a majority of them have cognitive impairment?

The need to address this question became apparent with the passage of the Patient Self-Determination Act (PSDA), which was passed by Congress in 1990 as an amendment to the Omnibus Budget Reconciliation Act of 1990. Effective on December 1, 1991, this legislation required many hospitals, nursing homes, home health agencies, hospice providers, health maintenance organizations (HMOs), and other healthcare institutions to provide information about advance healthcare directives (discussed in Chapter 13) to adult patients upon their admission to the facility. This law does not apply to individual physicians. The PSDA mandated that all affected facilities comply with five requirements regarding advance care planning, referred to as advance directives:

- Provide written information to people at the time of their admission about their right to make medical treatment decisions and to formulate advance directives (i.e., decisions about life-sustaining treatments and who can make medical decisions for them if they are incapacitated);
- Maintain written policies and procedures regarding advance directives;
- Document the completion of advance directives in the person's medical chart;
- Comply with state law regarding the implementation of advance directives; and
- Provide staff and community education about advance directives.

The PSDA mandates work well with most people. However, assessing a person's capacity to make medical decisions is a tremendous challenge for medical ethics (American Geriatrics Society Ethics Committee, 1996; Carney, 2016; Hoehner, 2018). In theory, advance directives enable people to choose the type of medical treatment they prefer in advance of a medical crisis (discussed in Chapter 13). However, numerous studies indicate the theory does not hold up well in practice: most people, especially older adults, consider such planning as a family process, especially when competence is in question (Finucane, 2016). They may engage in informal advance care planning, preferring to have informal discussions and to allow family members to make decisions for them when the need arises, and to give them and healthcare professionals leeway in interpreting advance directives even when they exist (Hoehner, 2018; Modra & Hilton, 2016). Thus, it is unlikely a typical person being admitted to any type of long-term care facility will have completed all of the formal advance directives before arriving.

Because placement in a nursing home or special care facility is already stressful and likely to occur in the context of a medical crisis, the new resident may not understand the information presented upon admission as mandated by the PSDA. To make matters worse, if new residents exhibit cognitive impairment, they may be thought to be unable to act in their own behalf in communicating treatment preferences and end-of-life wishes and understanding the consequences of their choices (Allen et al., 2003; Jones et al., 2019), although there still may be ways to assist them in expressing their preferences (Carney, 2016; Finucane, 2016; Hoehner, 2018). The degree to which cognitive impairment interferes with a person's ability to decide their treatment raises important ethical questions concerning whether physicians can trust any advance directive signed by such individuals after they move to a nursing home (Hoehner, 2018).

Assessing a nursing home resident's ability to make medical treatment decisions can be conceptualized as a problem involving the fit between the original intent of the PSDA law and the resident's cognitive capacity (Kepple et al., 2015). Several researchers have tackled the problem of how to assess decision-making capacity with varying results. Most important, a careful assessment of the resident's capacity to understand treatment and intervention options is necessary (Carney, 2016).

Still, many problems remain. No uniform approach to determining residents' cognitive competence exists, although progress is being made through the establishment of guidelines (American Bar Association/American Psychological Association, 2006, 2008, 2021). One barrier to a common approach is that each state sets the criteria needed to demonstrate cognitive competence (which is usually approached from the opposite side—what it takes to establish incompetence). To complicate matters further, research also shows lack of agreement between what nursing home and special care facility residents want and what their families think they would want, and this also varies with race and ethnicity (Connolly et al., 2012; Master et al., 2021; Winter & Parks, 2012). Resolving the problem involves using the various approaches we considered for determining person–environment interactions, combined with strong clinical assessment (discussed in Chapter 10), in the context of specific treatment goals and maintaining quality of life that is reflective of racial and ethnic contexts. Clearly, creating an optimal solution takes an interdisciplinary team of professionals, residents, and family members working together using clear and effective communication.

One solution may be to assess key members of the family (who serve as proxies in completing the forms) as to their beliefs as well as careful observation of the resident's capacity by the staff. Healthcare staff also need to sit down with family members and talk with them directly about treatment options so better and more concordant decisions are made between them and the resident (Lillyman & Bruce, 2017; Master et al., 2021).

Emerging Approaches to Long-Term Care

In response to the need to provide support for older adults who require assistance with ADLs and IADLs and their desire to age in place, new approaches to options for long-term care have emerged that provide both. These movements include programs that infuse a different culture into nursing homes, for example, as well as those approaches that create small-scale living (usually six to ten residents) in a community-based setting with an emphasis on living well rather than on receiving care (Coleman et al., 2020; Pfaff & Trentham, 2022).

The *Eden Alternative* (Eden Alternative, 2021) seeks to eliminate loneliness, helplessness, and boredom from the lives of those living in long-term care facilities and to create a community in which life is worth living. This can be achieved by rethinking how care is provided in the older person's own home or in long-term care facilities through training.

The *Green House Project* (The Green House Project, 2021) creates small neighborhood-integrated homes for six to ten residents in which older adults receive a high level of personal and professional care. The Green House Project takes the principles of the Eden Alternative and creates a different culture of care in the community.

The *Pioneer Network* (Pioneer Network, 2021) focuses on changing the culture of aging in America irrespective of where older adults live. Like the Eden Alternative, this approach focuses on respecting older adults and

Alternatives to traditional nursing homes, such as the Green House Project shown here, provide a person-centered approach to care based on small communal living.

providing maximally supportive environments for them. The Pioneer Network, as part of the larger cultural change in caring for older adults, advocates for a major emphasis on making nursing homes more like a home.

The *Hogeweyk*® (Dementia Village Associates, 2021) is a concept originating in the Netherlands to provide a normal life for people with severe dementia. The Hogeweyk® is just like any other neighborhood that is part of the broader society in the town of Weesp where people live together in houses based on similar lifestyles. Unlike assisted living or skilled care facilities, residents can visit the pub, restaurant, theater, the supermarket, or one of the many offered clubs. It focuses on possibilities, not on disabilities.

Biophilic design seeks to apply the innate and inherent connection people have with nature to the design of housing for older adults (Miller & Burton, 2020). The approach has influenced architecture; for example, the Singaporean–Italian firm Lanzavecchia + Wai used biophilic and other principles to create *Hack Care*, an innovative approach in design for dementia-friendly living (HackCare.org, 2021).

Various cohousing and cluster housing options provide additional alternative approaches. Cohousing is a planned community that is modest in size and is built around an open, walkable space designed to foster social interaction among neighbors (Klimczuk, 2017). Neighbors provide care for each other when it is needed as a way to foster personal autonomy, which combines aging in place with supportive services. A key feature is that services are provided to the residents by staff hired by the owner or by a service provider under contract. The aging-in-place philosophy in these settings emphasizes individual choice on the part of residents in terms of what services to use.

These alternatives to traditional long-term care options for older adults indicate that the choices for how one spends late life are becoming more varied and that appropriate support systems are in place. Such alternatives will be important as the baby boom generation enters the years in which support services will be needed even more. What they all have in common is a commitment to valuing older adults as worthwhile members of society regardless of their physical limitations. Treating all people with dignity is an important aspect in maintaining a person's quality of life. Everyone deserves that. Researchers need to focus their attention on documenting the types of advantages these alternatives offer and exploring their relative effectiveness.

Adult Development in Action

As a nursing home administrator, what changes would you predict in resident demographics, nursing home design, and the types of services offered based on what you know about the aging population?

Review Questions

5.3 Living in Nursing Homes

- What types of long-term care facilities are there? Who is most likely to live in a nursing home? Why? How have the characteristics of nursing homes been studied?
- Why do special care facilities often reflect better placement for people with significant physical or cognitive impairment?
- How is the quality of a nursing home assessed?
- How does a resident of a nursing home come to consider it as a home?
- What are the characteristics of inappropriate speech aimed at older adults? What is an alternative approach?
- How does the Patient Self-Determination Act relate to residents' decision-making capacity?
- What do the Eden Alternative, the Green House concept, the Pioneer Network, the Hogeweyk®, and biophilic design have in common?

Social Policy Implications

Evidence-Based Design of Healthcare Facilities

As noted in the chapter, considerable research has been done on understanding person–environment interactions and how the environment can be shaped to maximize individuals' competence and performance. More formally, evidence-based design is the process of constructing a building or physical environment based on scientific research to achieve the best possible outcomes. Evidence-based design is especially important in health care, where research indicates that environment design can affect patient

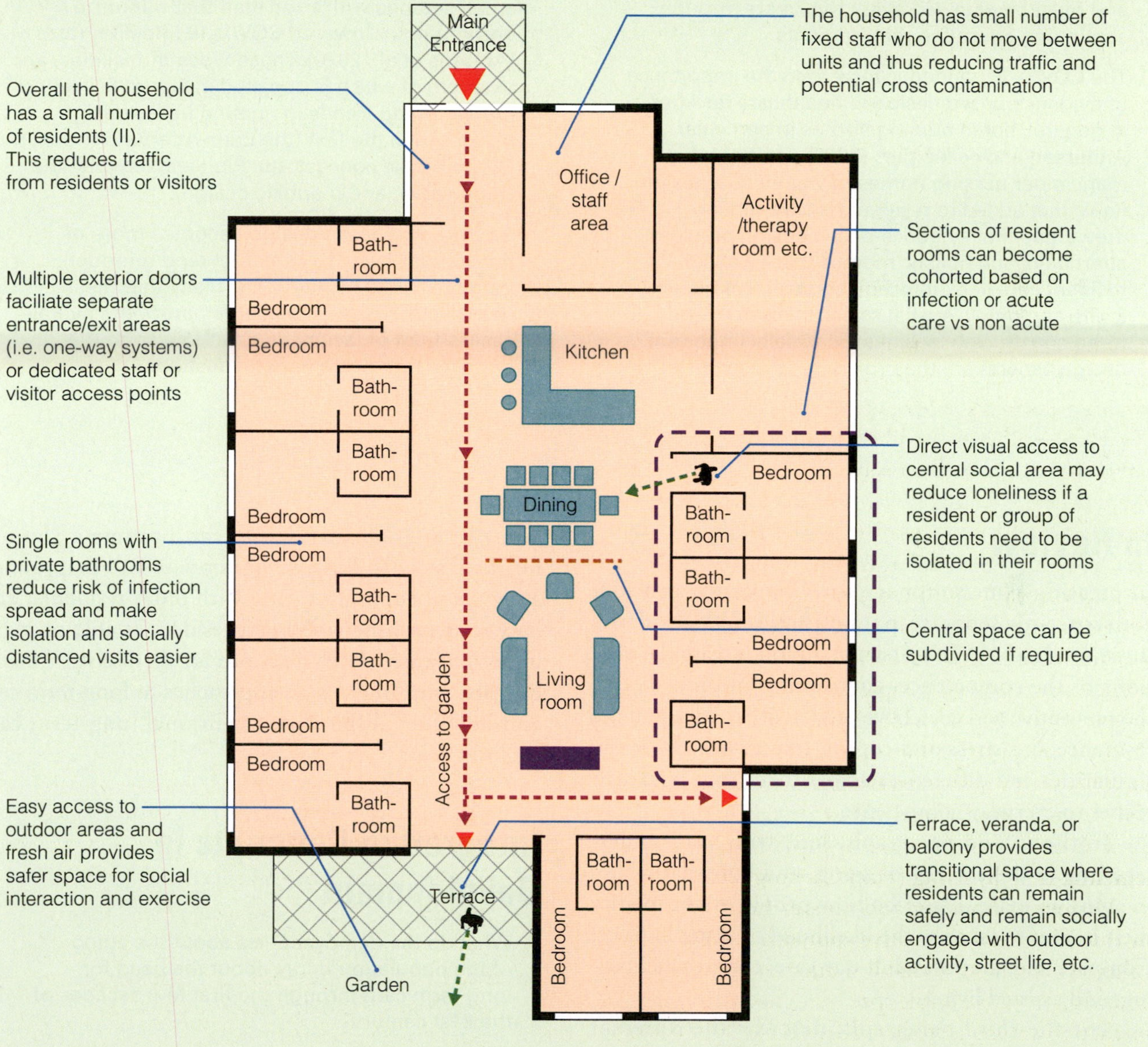

Figure 5.7 Example of evidence-based design of long-term care facility.

Source: Anderson, D. C., Grey, T., Kennelly, S., & O'Neill, D. (2020). Nursing home design and COVID-19: Balancing infection control, quality of life, and resilience. *Journal of the American Medical Directors Association, 21*, P1519–P1524 (Figure 2). https://doi.org/10.1016/j.jamda.2020.09.005, https://els-jbs-prod-cdn.jbs.elsevierhealth.com/cms/attachment/7ec3bdec-8ed6-4fca-bb58-7a50ff51775b/gr2_lrg.jpg

(Continued)

outcomes, patient and staff safety and stress, and quality of care. For instance, the presence of a window in a patient's room has a positive impact on their recovery (Ulrich et al., 2008).

In the healthcare field, the Center for Health Design oversees a process for Evidence-Based Design Accreditation and Certification (EDAC). The EDAC program awards a credential to professionals who demonstrate an understanding of how to apply an evidence-based process to the design and construction of all settings that contribute to health, safety, and well-being, including measuring and reporting results, and must be renewed every two years through continuing education requirements.

The COVID-19 pandemic increased the importance of evidence-based design in healthcare facilities in general, but in nursing homes in particular. Anderson and colleagues (2020) point out that many older nursing homes have inherent design flaws that added to resident risk. Moreover, they argue that evidence-based design provides alternative and holistic models that balance resident care (e.g., infection control) and quality of life at multiple spatial scales in existing and to-be-constructed facilities. Especially important design aspects are the proximity to a person's home community and the ability to be in contact with a familiar neighborhood; access to local services or shops for small purchases; support for ways of ensuring generativity and spiritual well-being; providing a home-like environment; and privacy. For those residents able to do so, the ability to visit each other's rooms, participation in meaningful activities, and opportunities to go outside the residence, including visiting family, going on organized tours, attending church, or experiencing nature, are ones frequently endorsed by residents.

Evidence-based design research indicates that small settings with fixed staff that minimize entry/re-entry lowered COVID-19 infection rates (Abrams et al., 2020). These types of facilities, an example of which is depicted in Figure 5.7, reflect the emerging trends in nursing home design discussed in the text (the Eden Alternative, the Green House concept, the Pioneer Network, the Hogeweyk®, and biophilic design).

As evidence-based design becomes more of the standard way to construct (and remodel) long-term care facilities, it is likely that these design principles will become part of the overall assessment of facility quality. How soon that happens remains an open question.

In Review

In creating your summary for Chapter 5, consider constructing separate paragraphs for each of the three modules. In the first paragraph, create descriptions of the competence–environmental press model, the preventive and corrective proactivity model, and the resilience and stress and coping framework. Note the similarities and differences across them, and how each relates to everyday competence.

In the second paragraph, start with your understanding of the ecology of aging, and how that relates to aging in place. Describe how people might modify their homes to increase the likelihood of aging in place. Compare and contrast adult day care, congregate housing, and assisted living.

For the third paragraph, describe the different types of long-term care facilities and the characteristics of the people who live in them. Go a bit deeper and describe what nursing homes are like, how their quality is assessed, and what special care facilities are and how they relate to nursing homes. Describe how a nursing home or special care facility can become a "home" for the residents. Discuss appropriate and inappropriate ways of communicating with older residents, and how to determine whether a resident is able to make important care-related decisions for themselves. Finally, describe emerging design approaches to long-term care and how they differ from traditional long-term care facilities.

Integrating Concepts in Development

- What do the demographics about the aging of the population imply about the need for long-term care through the first few decades of the 21st century?
- How do the theories of person–environment interaction include the basic developmental forces?
- How might a better financing arrangement for alternative living environments be designed?

Key Terms

adaptation level In Lawton and Nahemow's model, the point at which competence and environmental press are in balance. 146

adult day care Designed to provide support, companionship, and certain services during the day. 156

age-friendly community A community that encourages active aging by optimizing opportunities for health, participation, and security in order to enhance quality of life as people age by adapting its structures and services to be accessible to and inclusive of older people with varying needs and capacities. 151

assisted living facilities Housing options for older adults that provide a supportive living arrangement for people who need assistance with personal care (such as bathing or taking medications) but are not so impaired physically or cognitively they need 24-hour care. 158

competence In the Lawton and Nahemow model, the theoretical upper limit of a person's ability to function. 145

corrective adaptations Actions taken in response to stressors and that can be facilitated by internal and external resources. 147

docility When people allow the situation to dictate the options they have and exert little control. 146

ecology of aging Also called environmental psychology, a field of study that seeks to understand the dynamic relations between older adults and the environments they inhabit. 151

environmental press In the Lawton and Nahemow model, the demands put on a person by the environment. 145

everyday competence A person's potential ability to perform a wide range of activities considered essential for independent living. 149

infantilization or elderspeak Also called secondary baby talk, a type of speech that involves the unwarranted use of a person's first name, terms of endearment, simplified expressions, short imperatives, an assumption that the recipient has no memory, and cajoling as a means of demanding compliance. 168

patronizing speech Inappropriate speech to older adults based on stereotypes of incompetence and dependence. 168

person–environment interactions The interface between people and the world they live in that forms the basis for development, meaning behavior is a function of both the person and the environment. 145

preventive adaptations Actions that avoid stressors and increase or build social resources. 147

proactivity When people choose new behaviors to meet new desires or needs and exert control over their lives. 146

resilience Behaviors, thoughts, and actions that promote personal well-being and mental health. 148

sense of place Cognitive and emotional attachments that a person puts on their place of residence, by which a "house" is made into a "home". 152

zone of maximum comfort In competence–environmental press theory, the area where slight decreases in environmental press occur. 146

zone of maximum performance potential In competence–environmental press theory, the area where increases in press tend to improve performance. 146

Chapter

6

Attention and Memory

Learning Objectives

After studying this chapter, you will be able to...

6.1. Identify the major components of information processing and attention.

6.2. Describe the major types of memory processes.

6.3. Describe how memory operates in everyday life.

6.4. Describe how people self-evaluate their memory.

6.5. Define the differences between normative and nonnormative memory changes and how they are diagnosed.

Chapter Outline

Imagine waking up one day and having no memory of anything. You have no name, no past experiences, no information that you may have learned in school, no idea of what the things in the world are called, and no recognition of the people around you. Such situations make great plots for movies—the *Bourne Trilogy* and *Finding Nemo* come to mind. Occasionally, it actually happens to people who suffer brain injuries due to accidents or diseases and who experience various forms of amnesia, the inability to remember things.

There's no doubt about it, though—memory is the most important cognitive ability we have. It gives us our identity through the mental recordings of our past. It gets us through our lives by enabling us to find our way home, perform at our job or at school, recall the various rules of sports and games, and so much more. It enables us to recognize ourselves and loved ones and friends (and to know who we have never met). It provides our vast repertoire of information about everything. Memory really is the core of our being.

Perhaps that is why most people put so much value on maintaining a good memory throughout life, especially in old age. In fact, the ability to remember is a common measure of how well we are doing in late life, because older adults are stereotyped as people whose memory is on the decline, people for whom forgetting is not to be taken lightly. Many people think forgetting to buy a loaf of bread when they are 25 is annoying but otherwise all right, but forgetting it when they are 70 is cause for concern ("Do I have Alzheimer's disease?"). We will discover that forgetting is part of daily life, and the belief it only happens or matters in late life is wrong. In fact, older adults can be quite adept at using strategies in their everyday life contexts to remember what they need to know.

In this chapter, we focus on both attention and memory, since they are closely connected. We examine how people process information from the world around them and make sense out of it. We then discover cognition is a highly dynamic thing; lower-order processes such as attention create and influence higher-order thought, and higher-order thought determines where we focus our attention. People need to notice things in order to build knowledge and remember, because what we already know shapes what we notice. Thus, current research emphasizes changes in the different qualitative ways we process information and the quantitative differences in the amount of processing that occurs as we grow older. This research proves the traditional stereotype about memory and aging is wrong.

An important aspect of this research is that whether or not we observe age-related decline in cognitive processes such as memory and attention and depends on the type of task being experienced or the context wherein the memory operates. Some tasks, such as memorizing long lists of unrelated words, exhibit large declines in performance with age, whereas others, such as remembering emotionally charged or personally relevant information, demonstrate no decline, and at times, improvement with age.

Jordi Salas/Moment/Getty Images

Memory provides the ability to recognize friends and to share common life experiences as part of defining our identities.

These task-related differences bring us back to the life-span perspective. A key issue is the extent to which research on attention and memory reflects the everyday cognitive functioning of older adults. In other words, what are the practical implications of age-related changes in cognitive functioning in specific situations?

We use memory not only simply as a goal in itself, when the goal is what and how much we remember, but also as a means to a goal. For example, we use memory as an end when we summarize the most recent episode of our favorite television show. In other situations, we use memory as a means to an end—we tell other people about ourselves, or remember to make specific points in a discussion. In these situations, we use memory, but the point is not just what or how much we remember. In these and many other situations, memory is also a means to facilitate social exchange, allow other people to get to know us, or give ourselves a shared past with others. So memory is also a key tool for building relationships with others. We return to this idea when we examine memory in context later in the chapter.

Throughout this chapter, we consider results from experiments with responses made by people who are placed in contrived or simulated memory situations, often presented on computers. Such situations conform to the experimental research designs discussed in Chapter 1, but they don't usually reflect real-world situations very well. Additionally, we need to be mindful of cohort differences (also discussed in Chapter 1). Specifically, older adults may be less used to working on computers in testing situations than are younger adults, making the task less familiar to some older adults. Consequently, they may not perform up to their maximum. Because the vast majority of research on memory and attention is cross-sectional, keep in mind that age and cohort effects are confounded (discussed in Chapter 1), so researchers cannot discern for certain whether any performance differences between older and younger adults are due to age-related effects or to cohort effects.

Another key consideration is whether the patterns of age-related differences in memory reflect significant influences of sociocultural factors. In general, research suggests that the basic age-related patterns noted in this chapter transcend cultural, racial, ethnic, gender, and biological sex categories (Parisi et al., 2021; Saucedo et al., 2022). However, performance differences are noted under certain circumstances that reflect modifiable health-related variables (such as walking or fruit and vegetable consumption) that are related to socioeconomic barriers to access (Stinchcombe & Hammond, 2022) and to accumulated experiences of stress (Forrester et al., 2019). More research is needed to understand the complex dynamics of cognitive changes in later life experienced by people from different backgrounds.

We will begin our exploration of how information enters and is processed in the brain so that it can be eventually remembered by using the dominant theoretical model—information processing. We will uncover the major steps involved in getting information in, identifying which parts are relevant (and which ones aren't), and how that information gets put into storage in the brain.

Next, we will dive deeper into the different types and functions of memory, and various ways that information can be extracted out of storage. We'll discover ways that are available for people to help themselves remember, how we keep track of where we learned certain pieces of information, and how self-evaluations of memory influence how information is processed. We will conclude with a consideration of how memory is assessed when there are concerns about whether a person is experiencing normative or nonnormative changes in memory performance.

6.1 Information Processing and Attention

Key Questions

- What are the primary aspects of the information-processing model?
- What are the basic components of attention?
- How does speed of processing relate to cognitive aging?
- What types of processing resources relate to attention and memory?
- What is automatic and effortful processing?

> Trey strolled into a used car dealership and convinced the salesperson to let him take one of the sports cars on the lot for a drive around the block. When he climbed behind the wheel, his excitement almost got the better of him. As he started the engine, he became filled with anxiety because he had never driven a sports car before. He suddenly realized he must pay complete attention to what he was doing. Why? The car had—a clutch. He had not driven a car with manual transmission in at least a decade. Now he was faced with the need to filter out everything—people's conversations, the radio, and the sound of the wind whipping through his hair.

How can Trey filter everything out? More importantly, what abilities can he use to pay attention? If something happened on the road, how quickly could he respond? Would these abilities be any different in a younger adult than in an older adult? Have you ever had this experience? If so, how did you access this knowledge?

How do we learn, remember, and think about things? Psychologists do not know for sure. About the best they can do is create models or analogues of how they believe our cognitive processes work. In this section, we consider the most popular model: the information-processing model.

Information-Processing Model

The **information-processing model** uses a computer metaphor to explain how people process stimuli. As with a computer, information enters the system (people's brains) and is transformed, coded, and stored in various ways. Information enters storage temporarily, as in a computer's buffer or cache, until it becomes stored more permanently, as on a computer storage device (hard drive, cloud storage, etc.). At a later time, information can be retrieved in response to some cue, such as a command to open a file. Let's consider how this works more formally.

The information-processing model is based on three long-held assumptions (Neisser, 1976): (1) people are active participants; (2) both quantitative (how much information is remembered) and qualitative (what kinds of information are remembered) aspects of performance can be measured; and (3) information is processed through a series of steps. This basic model is depicted in Figure 6.1.

In terms of aging, researchers and theorists consider several aspects of information processing. First, incoming information is transformed based on what a person already knows about it. The more one knows, the more easily the information is incorporated. Thus, differences should be apparent with age, based on the fact that people continue to learn throughout their lives. Second, researchers look for specific patterns of age differences in both how much information is processed and what types of information are remembered best under various conditions. Third, researchers in adult development and aging focus on several specific aspects of information processing: early steps, including a brief sensory memory and attention; and later steps that transfer information into different memory storage areas (e.g., long-term memory).

Based on these three key aspects of information processing, researchers pose three fundamental questions regarding adult development and aging: (1) What aspects of information processing exhibit evidence of age differences? (2) How can we explain variability across people and tasks when we find age differences in information processing? (3) What are the practical implications of age-related changes in information processing?

We'll consider the various steps in information processing generally in the order in which they occur. Let's consider first the very earliest of these steps when information first arrives from the various senses.

Sensory Memory. All memories start as sensory stimuli—a song heard, a person seen, a hand felt. We need to experience these things for only a small fraction of a second in order to process the information. This ability is due to the earliest step in information processing, sensory memory, where new, incoming information is first registered. **Sensory memory** is a brief and almost identical representation of the stimuli that exist in the observable environment. Sensory memory takes in large amounts of information very rapidly and does not appear to have the capacity limits we will encounter in some later steps. Sensory memory exists as if the representation exists in your mind in the absence of the stimulus itself.

This very rapid and very large information uptake has a downside, though. Unless we pay attention to sensory information, the representation will also be lost quickly. To discover how this happens, do the following. Try drawing either side of a U.S. penny, or one dollar bill, in detail. (Those who are not from the United States can try drawing a common coin or paper money in their own country.) Most of us find this task difficult despite seeing the coins and paper money very frequently. Much detailed information about them has passed through our sensory memory repeatedly, but because we failed to pay attention to it, it was never processed to a longer lasting store. Importantly, age differences are not typically found in sensory memory—adults of all ages take in large amounts of information equally well, and lose it in equivalent ways when attention is not applied (Lustig & Lin, 2021; Park & Festini, 2017). But what happens if we do pay attention to at least some of the incoming information?

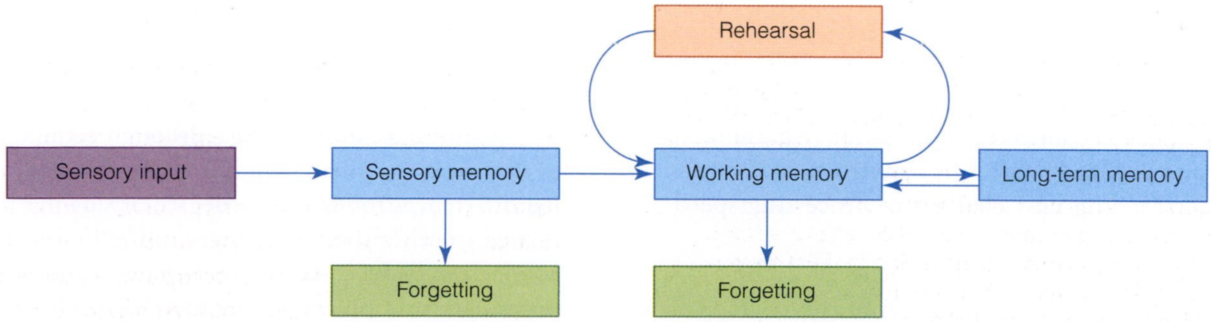

Figure 6.1 Information processing model of memory.

Source: Adapted from Atkinson, R. C., & Shiffrin, R. M. (1971). The control of short-term memory. *Scientific American, 225,* 82–90. https://doi.org/10.1038/scientificamerican0871-82

Attention: The Basics

Each of us has experienced being in a situation when our thoughts drift off and someone snaps at us, "Pay attention to me." We come back into focus and realize we had not been "paying attention"—and have missed potentially important information in the process.

But what exactly does it mean to "pay attention?" One way to consider it is to think of attention from a functional perspective (Bourke & Styles, 2017). From the functional perspective, attention is composed of several separate dimensions serving different functions. Let's consider an example. In Trey's case with the car, he must selectively attend to or focus on the clutch, shifting gears, the road and its obstacles, and at the same time filter out distracting information. Changing focus from one aspect to another is how we control attention and reflects the different dimensions of it. In addition, attentional processes are also influenced by our capacity to sustain our focus, as well as the speed with which we can handle the flood of incoming information by deciding what to pay attention to and what to ignore.

In the brain, attentional control is linked to the integration of processing in the parietal and frontal lobes (discussed in Chapter 2 as part of the P-FIT theory; Fischer et al., 2021). As we know, parieto-frontal integration processes undergo significant change with age. Not surprisingly, then, age differences emerge in various aspects of attention. Let's consider these in more detail, starting with the issue of speed of processing.

Monty Rakusen/Image Source/Getty Images

As adults grow older, how quickly and efficiently information processing occurs slows down.

Speed of Processing

Imagine you are crossing a busy street. Suddenly, a car turns the corner and comes speeding toward you. How quickly can you notice this car? That quick response refers to a concept in cognitive psychology known as speed of processing. **Speed of processing** is how quickly and efficiently the early steps in information processing are completed. Certainly, speed of processing matters in a great deal of the situations we face every day, such as crossing a busy street. Understanding how speed is connected to behavior (e.g., noticing the car and realizing it could be dangerous) is important for understanding how changes in processing speed play out across adulthood.

At one time, researchers believed decline in speed of processing explained the rest of age-related changes in cognitive functioning (e.g., Salthouse, 1996). After all, one belief about aging is that older people respond more slowly than young adults. However, this rather simple explanation fell out of favor because research indicated whether or not you find slower processing with age depends on what the task is. This is because all the components of processing do not slow down at the same rate, or at all.

Evidence from both laboratory simulations and neuroimaging studies indicates age-related slowing depends on what adults are being asked to do and how hard the task is (e.g., different levels of difficulty in choosing which response to make; Choi & Feng, 2016; Salthouse, 2021; Verhaeghen, 2022). These studies have allowed a deeper understanding of age-related differences in processing speed. Rather than pointing to some sort of general slowing, the results point to specific kinds of changes in the brain. For example, the amount of beta-amyloid protein found in the central nervous system, a biomarker linked with the possible subsequent development of dementia (discussed in Chapter 10), has been correlated with the degree to which processing speed slows (Almkvist et al., 2021; Jagust, 2016).

The discovery of both a pattern of overall slowing of processing speed, and a connection between the amount of slowing and certain biomarkers, has resulted in the refining of the role that processing speed plays in explaining cognitive aging. Although certain aspects of slowing are normative, it is the case that the individual differences found in the degree of slowing may be related to other specific changes in the brain. It is the connection between these other changes and how well people perform on cognitive tasks that underlies some of the assessments used to diagnose normative from nonnormative changes. We will return to this issue later in this chapter and in Chapter 10. For now, we conclude that slowing of processing speed alone does not provide an adequate explanation of age-related cognitive changes.

Processing Resources

Many theorists and researchers believe with increasing age comes a decline in the amount of cognitive "energy" one deploys on a task. This idea is described in terms of processing resources (Bourke & Styles, 2017). **Processing resources** refers to the total amount of attention one has to apply to a particular situation.

The idea of a decline in general processing resources is appealing because it would account for poorer performance not only on attention tasks but also on a host of others (Dirk & Schmiedek, 2012). The notion is that each person has a finite amount of attention that can be spread over the different parts of a task. Think about driving. Drivers are required to scan a wide visual field around them, monitor speed, keep their vehicle between the lane lines, and even participate in conversations with passengers (or sing along with the music). That's a lot to track and demands a large amount of processing resources.

However, there is a nagging problem about the processing resource construct: At this general level, it has never been clearly defined and is too broad. Cutting edge neuroscience research on how the brain is organized and interconnected (reviewed in Chapter 2) tells a much more complicated, nuanced, and increasingly precise story (Betzel, 2022). Changing patterns of interconnections and structural changes in the neurons and subsequently with entire brain structures and regions actually underlie the age-related changes formerly attributed simply to age-related decreases in "cognitive resources." Two more precise approaches at documenting these points behaviorally are inhibitory loss and attentional resources.

Inhibitory Loss. One popular hypothesis is older adults have reduced performance on attention tasks because they have difficulty inhibiting the processing of irrelevant information (Kliegl & Bäuml, 2021; Murayama et al., 2014; Radvansky, 2021). Evidence indicates people aged 85 or older have more task-irrelevant thoughts during processing and have trouble keeping them out of their minds. They report this effect as having difficulty focusing their attention, or as their mind wandering. This age-related difference could explain why these 85-year and older adults tend to have trouble with changing and dividing their attention.

The inhibition idea has long had a great deal of research support (Kimbler et al., 2012). Not only do older adults have difficulty inhibiting irrelevant information in laboratory tasks but they also have difficulty in matters with respect to everyday problem-solving. Kimbler and colleagues (2012) found that emotionally supportive messages reduce distracting thoughts and improve performance on everyday tasks for middle-aged and older adults.

Based on Kimbler and colleagues' work, several simple strategies to compensate for older adults' difficulties with inhibiting irrelevant information have been developed. For example, simply asking older adults to close their eyes or look away from irrelevant information improves performance, and evidence also indicates that older adults do not attend as much to faces or people as they navigate the world, a real-life example of this strategy (De Lillo et al., 2021). Better yet, this effect generalizes to young adults' performance on exams, an effect that is enhanced by supportive statements; together, these strategies mitigate interference by lowering test anxiety (Keller & Szakál, 2021). And older adults can dramatically improve their performance with practice, demonstrating that age-related declines in performance may have more to do with task familiarity than actual loss of ability to block out irrelevant information (Rienäcker et al., 2018).

Finally, researchers are asking whether there is a beneficial effect for the lack of inhibition of irrelevant information under the right circumstances. It turns out there is. When information that is initially distracting and irrelevant later becomes relevant, older adults perform better than young adults (Campbell & Hasher, 2018; Lourenço & Maylor, 2015; Thomas & Hasher, 2012). In such situations, the inability to inhibit distracting information turned into an advantage as the definition of relevant information changed.

Once again, we embrace a principle noted in Chapter 1: adult developmental changes in cognitive functioning are characterized by both gains and losses. It is important to consider inhibitory loss in both ways. Under certain conditions, it can be a hindrance, and in others it can be helpful. It all depends on the situation (Murayama et al., 2014). But inhibitory loss, on its own, does not account for age-related changes in cognitive performance.

Attentional Resources. Another way of looking at processing resource issues is through the lens of how well adults can perform more than one task at a time, such as talking on the phone and texting a friend. Such multitasking requires us to spread, or divide, our attention across all the tasks. **Divided attention** concerns how well people perform multiple tasks simultaneously. Driving a car is a classic divided attention task—you pay attention to other cars, the gauges in your car, pedestrians along the side of the street, and perhaps your passengers as you have a conversation with them.

Although it is widely believed older adults have more trouble than younger adults at dividing attention, it turns out the age differences observed are due to older adults' difficulties with the individual tasks and not to act of spreading their attention across them per se (Horwood & Beanland, 2016; R. Tunç & Ikier, 2021). For example, observations in the workplace indicate that older workers are just as able to multitask on simpler tasks but perform each task a bit more slowly than younger workers. Only when the tasks become complex do most older adults encounter difficulties dividing their attention, and their performance suffers as a result.

Age differences on divided-attention tasks can be minimized if older adults are given training on each task, thereby reducing the demands on attention. Such training is quite effective across several cognitive skills (selective attention, short-term memory, high level decision making) using computer games in the teaching process (Toril et al., 2016; Wang et al., 2021). These results imply that older adults may be able to learn through experience how to divide their attention effectively between tasks. Check out this idea by completing the Discovering Development feature.

So, you may ask, when do older adults have difficulty performing multiple tasks simultaneously in typical, everyday situations? You may have observed older adults having difficulty trying to remember something as they are walking down a staircase, or trying to simply walk and talk at the same time. Li and colleagues (Li et al., 2001) found older adults prioritize walking and maintaining balance at the expense of memory. In other words, older adults focused on the task most important to them: walking and balancing to prevent falls. This finding is supported by neurological research (Holtzer et al., 2016; O'Brien & Holtzer, 2021). Younger adults, on the other hand, optimized their memory performance and ignored walking and balancing. Thus, when older adults forget what they walked downstairs to get, it's likely because they paid more attention to safely walking down the stairs than to what they needed to get when they got there.

Discovering Development

How Good Are Your Notes?

Divided attention tasks are encountered all the time. You are undoubtedly familiar with one of them—taking notes during a lecture (either on video or live). An interesting developmental question is whether the quality of the notes differs with age. One way to find out informally is to compare the notes taken in the same class by younger and older students. If there are students of different ages in your class, ask them if you both could do this comparison. Or, perhaps you still have some of your notebooks from 9th or 10th grade that you could compare to the notes you take in this class. What predictions about the notes would you make based on the research evidence you have read thus far? What role would practice play in these differences? How could you decide whether notes are considered "good"? How would you design a training program on taking good notes?

Automatic and Effortful Processing

There are two other constructs that round out our understanding of attention and information processing: automatic and effortful processing (Eysenck & Keane, 2020). **Automatic processing** places minimal demands on attentional capacity and gets information into the system largely without us being aware of it. Some automatic processes appear to be "prewired" in the sense they never required attentional capacity and do not benefit from practice; others become automatic through experience and practice. These two types of automatic processes are mediated through different brain systems, thereby supporting the idea that they are truly different (Jeon & Friederici, 2015). A good example of a learned automatic process is stopping at a stop sign without really thinking about it. There's another aspect to automatic processing—it is extremely difficult to change. If you've played baseball or softball for a while, you know how difficult it is to change the way you swing the bat. The same is true with purely cognitive tasks—once you routinely use stereotypes in interacting with people, it is extremely difficult to stop. The reason is simple—the cognitive activity that goes into automatic processing is not at the level of consciousness, so people are not only unaware of the process, they have great difficulty even trying to describe the process while it is going on. Think again about swinging a bat—then try verbally describing exactly what you are doing at each step while you are doing it at full speed. It's exceedingly difficult. In general, performance on tasks that depend on automatic processes do not demonstrate significant age differences.

In contrast, **effortful processing** requires all of the available attentional capacity. Most of the tasks involving effortful processing are ones reflecting deliberate memory, such as learning the words on a list. In these cases, we are typically aware of what we are doing. Additionally, most learned automatic processing tasks start as tasks that require effortful processing. For instance, when we first learn how to drive a car with a clutch, we are aware of the information we process; in fact, most people report talking themselves through each step at this point in learning (e.g., how much to let up on the clutch versus how hard to press the accelerator pedal when starting on an incline). In general, age-related differences tend to emerge in effortful processing situations.

The distinction between automatic and effortful processing is extremely important—it helps explain a wide range of human behavior, from being able to do complex actions without conscious attention so that we can be "aware" of more important things (e.g., cooking a well-known recipe without thinking while we listen intently to our partner's retelling of the day's activities) to the intense and bitter ways that issues become polarized in society. As Ceci and Williams (2018) note in their thorough summary, there exist nine ways in which we process information automatically that result in what are termed *processing heuristics*. Processing heuristics are what enable us to make rapid judgments and decisions without much conscious reflection. Why do we think this way? Because it's faster and easier—imagine the work involved if every piece of information and every decision had to go through a thorough analysis in your conscious train of thought. Even brushing your teeth would become a laborious effort.

Ceci and Williams (2018) point out that all people (1) demonstrate selective perception, in which they perceive the same event differently; (2) consider the quality of argument made by people with whom they agree more positively and adopt more extreme positions as a result; (3) overestimate the depth of their understanding of controversial issues, termed the illusion of understanding bias; (4) consider the other side as more biased than their own side, termed the blind-spot bias; (5) tend to collect more evidence confirming their position and evaluating it positively, termed the myside bias; (6) consider their position on an issue as the basis for greater enlightenment, but view the opposite position of their opponents as a source of bias; (7) view their own position and arguments as based on what is "really out there," whereas their opponents' views are not, termed naïve realism; (8) consider arguments that are congruent with their position as more valid than alternative arguments, even when the validity of the arguments is controlled, resulting in increased polarization, termed motivated skepticism; and (9) are largely unaware of their own knowledge gaps and lack of competence.

Michael A. McCoy/Reuters

Political polarization occurs in part because of cognitive heuristics and biases that underlie automatic processes.

What does this mean in practical terms? Essentially, people even as young as preschoolers prefer to get information from like-minded people and to agree with them. For adolescents and adults, this plays out clearly in patterns on social media, such as "likes" on Facebook and "follow" on Twitter, and accounts for the "echo chambers" (Arguedas et al., 2022) in which we surround ourselves with people who "think" like us.

Decades of research point to a clear picture: People's brains are wired to take in information in ways that minimize the cognitive workload and that provide reasonable results most of the time (Ceci & Williams, 2018; Eysenck & Keane, 2020). In our normal daily routines, what we personally experience provides good enough information on which to base most of our decisions, so we make them using automatic processes, usually ones we have learned. For example, we typically do not need to worry whether this or that abstract concept will determine a better or worse outcome when we are cooking mac and cheese. We have evolved in a way that takes base probability rates into account, such that we "instinctively" know the right quantities of ingredients to make tasty mac and cheese. Of course, sometimes it matters that we are not engaged in effortful processing, as when a critical piece of information is glossed over by our heuristics (e.g., a child's ball rolls out into the street, but we "fail" to see it).

Finally, when considering attentional and processing resources, it is extremely important to ask the question: Is attention a fixed capacity that decreases with age? Researchers observe a decline in older adults' performance on laboratory tasks assessing memory. However, a different picture may emerge when we consider that functional capacity or the resources necessary in specific task contexts can be modified depending on the relevance, accessibility of knowledge, and expertise related to the cognitive processes required (Hertzog, 2008). Under conditions where the task requirement is to simply have a familiarity with the information, there are no age differences. However, when there is effort and deliberate processing needed to remember the exact information, age differences emerge. Because age differences are sensitive to the conditions under which they are measured, the key question for researchers is: When and under what circumstances will we observe age-related change in attention, and when does that change matter in everyday life?

Adult Development in Action

If you are an employee at an Apple store who shows people how to use the new device they bought, what principles would you apply from this section when instructing older adults?

Review Questions

6.1 Information Processing and Attention

- What is inhibition loss? What age differences have been found? What role do these processes play in understanding age differences in memory?
- What is sensory memory? How do processing speed and processing resources affect older adults' information processing?
- In what way do older adults have difficulty filtering out information?
- How do automatic and effortful processing contribute to age differences in information processing?
- What are heuristics and biases, and why are they important?
- Why are attentional resources important to our understanding of age differences in memory?

6.2 Memory Processes

Key Questions

- What is working memory?
- What age differences have been found in working memory?
- Within long-term memory, how do implicit and explicit memory, and episodic and semantic memory, performance differ across age?
- What age differences have been found in encoding versus retrieval?

Latifa is a 75-year-old who feels she does not remember recent events, such as if she took her medicine, as well as she used to. She also occasionally forgets to turn off the gas on her stove and sometimes does not recognize her friend's voice on the phone. However, she has no trouble remembering things from her 20s. Latifa wonders if this is typical or if she should be worried.

Memory researchers have long focused on three general steps in memory processing as potential sources of age differences: encoding, storage, and retrieval (Eysenck & Keane, 2020). **Encoding** is the process of getting information into the memory system. **Storage** involves the manner in which information is represented and kept in memory. Getting information back out of memory is termed **retrieval**. Because there is no evidence for age differences in how information is organized once it is in storage, most research has examined encoding and retrieval as sources of age-related differences (Lustig & Lin, 2021; Morcom, 2016).

Encoding and retrieval represent the input and output processes for information. Both are complicated and operate in many different ways, as we will discover. Both also can operate in or out of conscious awareness. In general, encoding involves getting information from early stages of information processing (e.g., information that has been attended to) transformed in such a way that it can connect to information that is already in storage in some manner. Retrieval has two main types. Recognition is the process in which a person makes a judgment as to whether a particular piece of information has been encountered before or is novel. Retrieval is the process in which a person pulls a specific piece of information out of storage. We'll dive much deeper into the nuances of both recognition and retrieval a bit later. First up is a closer examination of a key early and dynamic step in memory processing—working memory. Let's consider the role working memory plays in detail. Refer back to Figure 6.1 to remind yourself of the basic information processing model—we'll be focusing on the working memory and long-term memory aspects of it in this module.

Working Memory

Think about a time when you asked a friend for their mobile phone number so you could send them text messages. When you see your friend, they tell you their number, but you forgot your phone, so you will need to work to keep the phone number in your mind until you can write it down or type it in.

To successfully complete the task, you have to use working memory. **Working memory** is the active processes and structures involved in holding information in mind and simultaneously using that information, sometimes in conjunction with new incoming information, to solve a problem, make a decision, or learn new information.

Researchers typically consider working memory an umbrella term for many similar short-term holding and computational processes relating to a wide range of cognitive skills and knowledge domains (Eysenck & Keane, 2020). This places working memory right in the thick of things—it plays an active, dynamic, critical, and central role in encoding, storage, and retrieval.

Recall that sensory memory has a very large capacity to deal with incoming information. In contrast, researchers generally agree working memory has a relatively small capacity. This capacity limitation of working memory operates like a juggler who can only keep a small number of items in the air simultaneously.

Because working memory deals with information being processed right at this moment, it also acts as a kind of mental cache, like a computer cache. This means unless we take direct action to keep the information active, the "space" we are using will be used up quickly and some information tossed away to make room for more. For this reason, we need to have some way to keep information in working memory. That process is known as rehearsal. **Rehearsal** is the process that information is held in working memory, either by repeating items over and over or by making meaningful connections between the information in working memory and information already known.

Most evidence indicates there is significant age-related decline in working memory (Heathcote, 2016; Krinsky-McHale & Silverman, 2022), although the extent of the decline is still in doubt. These data are important because working memory is the key to understanding age differences in memory. The loss of some of the ability to hold items in working memory may limit older adults' overall cognitive functioning. If information becomes degraded or is only partially integrated into one's existing knowledge base due to problems in working memory, it will be difficult to remember it.

However, some evidence suggests age differences in working memory are not universal. Working memory performance appears to depend on the type of information in play and how it is presented, and may vary across different tasks (Jarjat et al., 2021; Loaiza et al., 2015). For example, age-related decline in spatial working memory (the ability to remember spatial locations) tends to be greater than that in verbal working memory, although there is decline in both types of working memory (Oosterman et al., 2011). Greater prior knowledge in older adults appears to counterbalance declines in working memory in some situations because it is easier to connect new information to a more extensive knowledge base (Jarjat et al., 2021; Loaiza et al., 2015).

Why does working memory ability decline with age? There are several reasons, including different levels of alertness at different times of the day, the order of the tasks, and task interference (Eysenck & Keane, 2020; Greene et al., 2020; Monteiro et al., 2022). Another idea is older adults simply have more trouble juggling all of the elements once they are accessed (McCabe & Loaiza, 2012).

Although the evidence for age-related decline in working memory indicates a general trend but is not entirely clear, there is compelling evidence for how age differences in working memory relate to performance on more complex cognitive tasks. For example, researchers include working memory as key to explaining the age differences in recall performance, which is more difficult than simply recognizing information (Cherry et al., 2021).

Long-Term Memory

When most people think about memory, they think about having to remember something over time, whether a few minutes or many days. Everyday life is full of examples—remembering routes, performing on an exam, summarizing a book or movie, remembering the names of family and friends, calling to mind numerous details at work, and remembering an appointment. These types of situations constitute what memory researchers call long-term memory (Rutherford et al., 2012). **Long-term memory** refers to the ability to remember extensive amounts of information from a few seconds to a few hours to decades. A diagram of the overall structure of long-term memory is depicted in Figure 6.2.

Memory researchers have created a wide variety of tasks requiring individuals to remember all sorts of information for varying lengths of time. Since the late 1800s, research has indicated that long-term memory represents a relatively large-capacity store where information can be kept for long periods. Mounting evidence in cognitive neuroscience suggests long-term memory is not a unitary construct or place in the brain, but consists of multiple distinct, functionally different systems that are served by different brain structures and pathways (discussed in Chapter 2). For example, Shimamura (2014) points to evidence indicating that memory for events involves interactions among the prefrontal cortex, medial temporal lobe, and ventral posterior parietal cortex. From Chapter 2, we also know that the hippocampus and amygdala, among other structures, are involved in other aspects of memory, especially emotion-based memories. In short, because memory is such an important part of us, it isn't surprising it involves numerous areas of our brain working together.

Implicit Versus Explicit Memory

At a general level, we can further divide long-term memory into two major types: implicit memory and explicit memory (Eysenck & Keane, 2020). **Implicit memory** (sometimes called automatic memory) involves retrieval of information without conscious or intentional recollection. **Explicit memory** (sometimes called declarative memory) is intentional and conscious remembering of information learned and remembered at a specific point in time.

Implicit memory is memory that is unconscious, much like getting into a routine—we do things from memory but we do not have to think about them. It reflects the content of automatic processes discussed earlier. The most common example of implicit memory, procedural memory, enables us to perform many everyday physical activities, such as walking, riding a bike, and brushing our teeth, without having to give them thought. Procedural memory primarily involves learning new motor skills and depends on the cerebellum and basal ganglia. Priming is a second, less common example of implicit memory. It involves using pictures, words, or other stimuli to help someone recognize another word or phrase in the future. Examples include using green to remember grass and red to remember apple.

Do younger, middle aged, and older adults differ in demonstrating implicit memory? As you might suspect by this point, whether age differences in implicit memory are observed depends on the specific kind of implicit memory task in question (Howard & Howard, 2012, 2013, 2016). Learning sequences of information tends to show age differences, whereas learning spatial contexts do not. Neuroimaging research backs this up. First, studies demonstrate the kind of overall brain activity in older adults that is typical in situations when older adults are compensating for declines (explained in Chapter 2). Additional neuroscience research reveals differences in how the specific parts of the brain in older adults involved in learning new information communicate and coordinate, revealing that the age differences are due to the type and stage of processing of various tasks, not age per se (Merenstein et al., 2022; Stillman et al., 2016).

By far, though, most research on long-term memory aging focuses on explicit memory. Two important

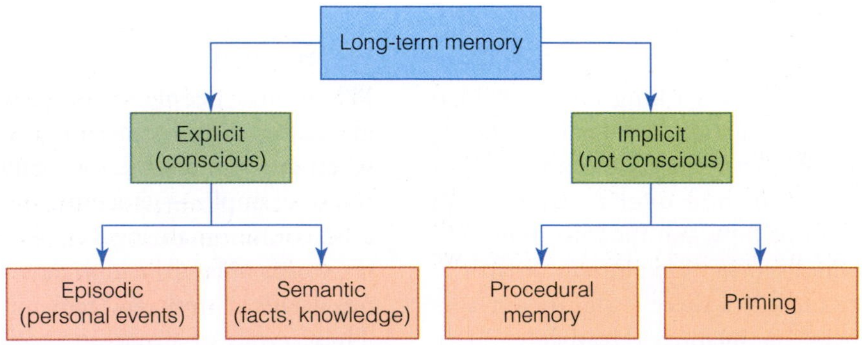

Figure 6.2 Structure of long-term memory.
Source: Cengage Learning

types explicit memory are semantic memory and episodic memory (Eysenck & Keane, 2020). **Semantic memory** concerns learning and remembering the meaning of words and concepts not tied to specific occurrences of events in time. Examples of semantic memory include knowing the definitions of words in order to converse and write, being able to translate this paragraph from English into Spanish, and understanding what symbols on traffic signs mean.

Episodic memory is the general class of memory having to do with the conscious recollection of information from a specific event or point in time. Examples of episodic memory include learning the material in this course so you will be able to reproduce it on an examination in the near future, remembering what you did on your summer vacation last year, and memorizing codes for various fruits and vegetables to help you perform as an efficient cashier at the supermarket.

Like implicit versus explicit memory, episodic and semantic memory appear to be impacted differently by aging (Dennis et al., 2020; Shimamura, 2014). Episodic memory typically stays fairly stable until around 55–60 years of age and then shows a precipitous decline beginning around age 65. In contrast, semantic memory tends to increase from 35 to 55 years of age and then levels off. Although semantic memory typically starts to decline around age 65, the decline is much less substantial than for episodic memory.

JGI/Tom Grill/Tetra images/Getty Images

Solving crossword puzzles is an example of using semantic memory.

Semantic Memory. As indicated previously, semantic memory is relatively spared in normative aging. Evidence suggests there are no meaningful age-related deficits in semantic memory processes such as language comprehension, the structure of knowledge, and the activation of general knowledge (Jarjat et al., 2021; Mohanty et al., 2016; Park & Festini, 2017). Semantic memory retrieval typically does not put stress on working memory, and thus older adults can draw upon experience in word meanings and/or general world knowledge quite easily (Jarjat et al., 2021; Loaiza et al., 2015). In addition, whereas retrieval of episodic memories is based on cues to the original experience, semantic memories are retrieved conceptually as part of our world knowledge. This connection between semantic memory and world knowledge will come up again in Chapter 7 when we consider certain types of intelligence that show little, if any, decline with age.

However, research also indicates age changes in semantic memory can happen if the knowledge becomes hard to access and retrieve. One reason for access problems is if the knowledge in semantic memory is not used on a regular basis (Hertzog, 2016). You may have experienced this already, if you learned another language in school but now have trouble with it if you didn't use it often. You may even have the feeling that you should know the word in the other language, but you simply cannot remember it.

A second reason that age differences are sometimes found in semantic memory tasks is simple momentary retrieval failure for information that is otherwise accessible. A common example is when adults have a "tip-of-the-tongue" or "feeling-of-knowing" experience (Thomas et al., 2016). A feeling-of-knowing (FOK) experience is when you try to retrieve a name or word you are certain you know, but it is not quite accessible at the moment. Imagine you are at a party and see someone familiar; you "know" that person's name, but you simply cannot retrieve it. Another aspect of this FOK experience is when you can retrieve partial information such as the number of syllables in word, or the initial sounds or letters.

Older adults not only tend to experience more FOKs, but also report less partial information about the target, both in the laboratory and in everyday life (Campos-Magdaleno et al., 2020; Facal et al., 2012). Such FOK problems indicate even highly familiar information can become more difficult to retrieve as we grow older. We'll dig a bit deeper into this later in our discussion of metamemory.

Episodic Memory. Because episodic memory includes so many of the day-to-day memory activities that adults perform, it has been the focus of more research than any other single topic in memory development (Dennis et al., 2020; Eysenck & Keane, 2020). Typically, researchers study episodic memory by having people learn information, such as a list of words, and then asking them to recall or recognize the items. In a **recall** test, people are asked to remember specific information without hints or cues. Everyday examples of recall include telling everything you can remember about a movie, remembering a grocery list, or taking an essay exam with no notes or access to materials. **Recognition**, on the other hand, involves selecting previously learned information from among several items. Everyday examples of recognition include taking multiple-choice tests and picking out the names of your high school friends from a complete list of your classmates.

Many factors influence adults' performance on episodic memory tests and whether age differences are found. Consider how the information to be learned is presented (organized into categories may be better than randomly), how fast it is presented (slower may be better), whether the material is familiar (familiar may be better), and how the test is given (recognition is usually better) all make a difference.

The results from hundreds of studies point to several conclusions. Overall, older adults perform worse than younger adults on recall tests of episodic memory because they omit more information, include more intrusions (e.g., items that are recalled but were never presented), and repeat more items that were recalled already (Dennis et al., 2020; Park & Festini, 2017). Why is that?

Research suggests that one reason older adults may demonstrate lower levels of recall performance on explicit memory tasks is due to what is terms a binding deficit (Dennis et al., 2020). A **binding deficit** is a deficit in the integration of the multiple elements of complex events within unified representations. In episodic memory, for example, binding is what happens when all the various pieces of an event are knit together to form a unified, coherent memory (a story of sorts) of that event. Researchers and theorists believe that one reason that older adults do not perform as well on episodic memory tests is that they have not sufficiently "bound" the elements of an event into an integrated episode, or memory. Episodic retrieval can involve accessing individual items, the retrieval of the context in which the item(s) were presented, or a combination of both. As a result, memory errors may occur because such individual pieces of a memory are not sufficiently integrated at encoding. Think about how your memory for a movie might work. Your ability to remember a specific detail might hinge on whether you can remember the context or part of the movie in which that detail appeared. If you didn't connect the detail to the context, then remembering the context won't help you remember the detail. That's how a problem in binding can lower a person's ability to remember details.

Memory errors can also occur when source information, or contextual detail, is similar across episodes making it hard to distinguish separate events. In these situations, retrieval results in remembering the incorrect source, or remembering details alongside an item which was not originally paired with those details at encoding. Older adults make these source errors more frequently than younger or middle-aged adults. For instance, an older person may recall a claim made by a contributor from a news show but mistakenly identify the contributor because that person is a frequent guest on the show.

On recognition tests, though, differences between older and younger adults are reduced. They may not be eliminated, though. For instance, in comparison with young adults, older adults are more likely to say they recognize items that were never-presented, especially if they share a conceptual meaning or perceptual resemblance to the items actually presented (Dennis et al., 2020; Park & Festini, 2017).

Numerous neuroimaging studies have examined the changes in brain activity associated with episodic memory. It turns out that identifying where changes are most profound maps reasonably well to normative versus memory aging due to disease. Specifically, a pattern of change that is located mainly in the prefrontal cortex

LightField Studios/Shutterstock.com

Similarity across events such as birthday parties can make it difficult to keep track of what specific event happened at which party.

is associated with normative aging, whereas significant changes and damage to the hippocampus relative to the prefrontal cortex are indicative of Alzheimer's disease or other form of dementia (Tromp et al., 2015). Research on the relation between biomarkers of dementia and episodic memory performance show no relation at middle age, but a correlation between level of biomarkers and memory performance is reported in otherwise healthy older adults (Rizzolo et al., 2021). We will return to these differential findings in Chapter 10 when we examine biomarkers and diagnosis of Alzheimer's disease and other forms of dementia in more detail.

One thing that helps people remember information in tests of episodic memory is using internal study strategies, such as rehearsal or organizing information into categories. Older adults tend to be less efficient at spontaneously using these strategies. But they can and do use them when instructed to do so, and show significant improvements in performance when they do. Moreover, adults of all ages benefit similarly from strategy instruction (Brehmer et al., 2016; Wenger et al., 2021). However, these improvements are not sufficient, in general, to eliminate age differences in recall, indicating that age differences in recall of episodic information are caused more by retrieval problems than poor encoding during study (Hertzog et al., 2013; Naveh-Benjamin & Mayr, 2018).

Age differences between older and younger adults can be reduced (but not eliminated) in several other ways: allowing older adults to practice or perform a similar task before learning a new list; using material more familiar to older adults; and using compensatory strategies to help themselves remember (we will examine this later in the chapter).

Although it would be easy to conclude episodic memory does nothing but decline with age, that would be wrong. First, instruction to use memory strategies improves performance and narrows the age differences. Second, it turns out there is one episodic memory process relatively spared with age: autobiographical memory, which we will consider a bit later.

Age Differences in Encoding Versus Retrieval

As we learned earlier, encoding is the process of getting information into memory, and retrieval is the process of getting that information out. What key changes occur in these processes with age?

Encoding. Researchers have known for many years that there is an age-related decrement in encoding processes (Craik & Rose, 2012). The most important reason for these changes is a decline in adults' spontaneous use of strategies during the learning of new information. A **strategy** is anything people do to make the task easier and increase the efficiency of encoding or retrieval. Examples of strategies include grouping related items together (e.g., listing all the vegetables or fruits together on your shopping list), associating mental images with the information (e.g., visualizing people's faces to help learn their names), and using knowledge to organize information (e.g., thinking of strings of numbers in patterns of 3-3-4 numbers to mimic U.S. phone numbers).

Many decades of research has documented that, compared to younger adults, older adults tend not to behave as strategically when studying to-be-remembered information in whatever way they choose (Dunlosky et al., 2011). However, when instructed to do so, older adults can use encoding strategies well, as we noted earlier. So, the age-related differences observed reflect more a decrease in the degree the strategies are used spontaneously, rather than a decrease in the ability to use strategies at all.

Cognitive neuroscience (discussed in Chapter 2) presents evidence explaining age differences in encoding. Neuroimaging studies indicate that during encoding several things change with age in how the brain works. In line with what we have noted in several other areas of cognitive functioning, older adults' prefrontal cortex shows overactivity during encoding, indicating the usual pattern of compensatory processes with age. Changes in the left lateral prefrontal cortex with age appear to underlie the decline in spontaneous strategy use, because stimulation of this area during learning improves performance (Huo et al., 2021; Indahlastari et al., 2021).

Certainly, if information does not get encoded well, it is less likely to be there or to be as accessible for remembering later. So, at least part of the reason older adults perform more poorly than younger adults on tests of memory recall is because of encoding difficulties.

Retrieval. We have already noted that one of the most consistent research findings is that older adults do more poorly than younger adults at recalling information. Besides potential encoding difficulties, what else might account for this difference?

Research evidence clearly points to the fact older adults tend to spontaneously use fewer retrieval strategies (Dennis et al., 2020; Hertzog et al., 2013; Park &

Festini, 2017). Moreover, even when encoding strategies are provided, and the opportunity to apply them during recall is allowed, older adults still do worse. This means that when encoding difficulties are largely eliminated, and retrieval strategies are available, older adults still recall less information than do younger adults. Thus, age-related memory declines in episodic memory appear to be due more to retrieval difficulties.

In terms of retrieval, neuroimaging studies show that another age-related difference lies in how the prefrontal cortex and hippocampus work together, and this change in communication may be a way to tease apart normative and nonnormative aging due to cognitive impairment (Sadeh et al., 2020; Wang & Giovanello, 2016). In younger adults, activity in these areas depends on the extent the retrieval task requires relations (i.e., binding) to be made between the information being remembered, whereas activity in these regions in older adults stayed equivalent irrespective of whether binding is a necessary part of the task.

Other neuroscience research indicates age-related compensatory brain activity for retrieval, similar to that seen in other cognitive processing (discussed in Chapter 2; Oedekoven et al., 2013). Specifically, younger adults have more extensive neural network connections in the parietal and frontal regions involved in retrieval than do older adults. However, older adults tend to show higher levels of brain activity overall in these regions, indicating a likely compensatory strategy for less extensive networks.

Shimamura (2014) took all of these findings and proposed a theory explaining declines in encoding and retrieval in episodic memory as the result of changes in how certain areas of the brain communicate and interact. This theory proposes that the prefrontal cortex drives retrieval, which is facilitated by the medial temporal lobe. The parietal lobe is where information from these regions converges. As we know from the discussions of three neuroscience-based theories of cognition in Chapter 2, the integration processes in these brain regions undergoes significant change with age.

Overall, much data support the view, also described in Chapter 2, that older adults process information in their brains differently than younger adults. These differences in part represent attempts at working around, or compensating for, the normal age-related changes occurring in information processing. In the area of memory, though, these compensation attempts are insufficient on their own to eliminate the effects of age-related changes.

In sum, the research on encoding and retrieval processes is important for three key reasons. First, it emphasizes that age-related decrements in memory are complex; they are not due to changes in a single process. Second, age-related decrements are not universal across types of remembering situations. Third, although older adults may use strategies to help themselves remember when instructed to do so, these strategies do not eliminate age differences, nor are they often maintained once instructions stop.

Adult Development in Action

Suppose you are a physician whose specialty is geriatric medicine (the branch of medicine that focuses on older adults). Based on what you learned in this section, what would be a good way to test for normative age-related changes in memory?

Review Questions

6.2 Memory Processes

- What are working memory processes, and how do they differ with increasing age?
- What is the difference between implicit and explicit memory? How do they change with age?
- What is a binding deficit?
- Why are there age-related differences in episodic but not semantic memory?
- What are the relative contributions of encoding and retrieval in understanding age differences in memory?

6.3 Memory in Context

Key Questions

- What age-related differences are there in prospective memory?
- How does autobiographical memory change across adulthood?
- How do source memory and processing of misinformation change across adulthood?
- What are some factors that preserve memory as we grow older?

Abdullah, who just turned 80, enjoys his role as a wise elder in the family. For many years, he has been the center of attention by telling stories from his life. The younger members of the family are especially interested in hearing about Abdullah's exploits. Over the years, family members have noticed that Abdullah tells more stories from his young adult years than from any other period. They wonder whether this is typical of older people.

As noted at the beginning of this chapter, memory is so integral to our everyday lives we often take it for granted. In the case of Abdullah, sharing his rich life experiences proved extremely important in connecting with the family. How memory operates in people's everyday lives has been the focus of much research (Eysenck & Groome, 2020; Groome, 2016).

This research is extremely important for three reasons. First, it may shed some insights that allow us to generalize findings based on laboratory tasks to everyday life. Second, new or alternative variables could be identified that affect performance in everyday life that do not operate in the lab. Third, research on memory in everyday contexts may force us to reconceptualize memory itself.

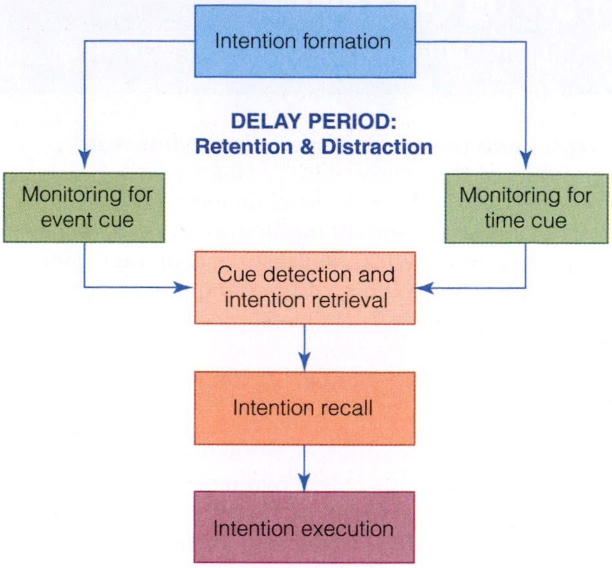

Figure 6.3 Conceptual model of the component processes of prospective memory.

Source: Zogg, J. B., Woods, S. P., Sauceda, J. A., Wiebe, J. S., & Simoni, J. M. (2012). The role of prospective memory in medication adherence: A review of an emerging literature. *Journal of Behavioral Medicine, 35*, 47–62. https://link.springer.com/article/10.1007/s10865-011-9341-9/figures/1

Prospective Memory

How well do you remember to do things such as complete an errand on your way home or show up for an appointment on time? **Prospective memory** involves remembering to remember something in the future, such as an action or event (Dismukes, 2012). Everyday life is full of examples, such as remembering you're meeting your friend this afternoon at 2:00 and remembering you have a health-related appointment next Friday morning.

A theoretical model of how prospective memory works is shown in Figure 6.3 (Zogg et al., 2012). Note the process starts with the intention to remember something in the future and depends critically on monitoring both event and time cues. This distinction between event and time monitoring, first introduced by Einstein and McDaniel (1990), is critical for understanding why people do and do not perform what it is they are attempting to remember to do.

In event-based tasks, an action is to be performed when a certain external event happens, such as getting a video call when a timer rings. A time-based task involves performing an action after a fixed amount of time, such as remembering to take the cookies out of the oven after 12 minutes of baking (with no alarm).

Researchers found time-based tasks showed more age differences as long as people used self-generated strategies to remember, as these tend to decline with age; the cues that typically accompany event-based tasks (such as buzzers on alarms) helped reduce or eliminate age differences (Jones et al., 2021). Adults of all ages benefit from the use of reminders, but older adults especially benefit from clear prioritization of tasks (i.e., ranking tasks from most to least important) (Kliegel et al., 2016).

Of course, it's clearly important to remember things one is supposed to do in the future. But once you have completed what you were supposed to do, it's equally important to remember that you have, indeed, done the task. Interestingly, relatively little research has been done examining age differences in people's ability to determine that all of the tasks they are supposed to remember to complete have been completed. This matters a great deal when it comes to taking medication, for instance. Forgetting that you've taken the proper dose could result in taking another, creating potentially serious medical complications. One intriguing example of this research, demonstrating important age differences, is described in the How Do We Know? feature.

How Do We Know?

Failing to Remember I Did What I Was Supposed to Do

Who were the investigators, and what was the aim of the study? Most research on prospective memory focuses on whether people remember to *do* something in the future. Scullin and colleagues (2012) realized it is also important for people to *stop* doing something once all of the tasks are done. They investigated whether there are age differences in people's ability to remember to stop doing an action when it is no longer necessary to do it.

How did the investigators measure the topic of interest? The study had two phases. In the first, younger and older adults were told to perform a task that they subsequently did. In Phase 2, participants were told the task was finished, yet still received the cue to perform the task, and measured whether they still did it despite being told not to.

Who were the participants in the study? Younger adult university students (average age = 19 years) and community-dwelling older adults (average age = 75 years) participated.

What was the design of the study? The experiment was a 2×3 between-subjects design that included age group (younger or older) and condition (nonsalient-cue/task-match, salient-cue/task-match, or salient-cue/task-mismatch). There were three conditions:

- The nonsalient-cue/task-match condition had a cue that did not signal the need to do the task.
- The salient-cue/task-match had a cue that was the signal to perform the task.
- The salient-cue/task-mismatch had the cue that formerly signaled the need to do the task but no longer indicated that.

Participants were randomly assigned to the three conditions.

Were there ethical concerns with the study? There were no ethical concerns because all of the participants were volunteers and had the experiment fully explained.

What were the results? In Phase 1, younger and older adults performed equivalently by correctly remembering to perform the task when cued. In Phase 2, though, older adults were more likely to continue attempting to perform the task when the cue occurred even though they had been told it was no longer necessary. Thus, older adults had more errors of commission.

What did the investigators conclude? Careful analyses of the results indicated older adults who made commission errors were less able to inhibit the task response than those who did not make commission errors. Inhibition is an important part of executive functioning, the higher-level cognitive processes that control decision making (in this case the decision to complete the task). Additionally, older adults who made commission errors were more likely to get stuck making the task response in ways that implied they might have had trouble stopping even if they wanted to.

Scullin et al.'s (2012) finding that older adults were more likely to continue to perform tasks even when they had been told it was no longer necessary has been supported by additional research (e.g., Anderson & Einstein, 2017; Jones et al., 2021; Matos & Albuquerque, 2021). Forgetting that one has completed a task can have both innocuous (triple checking that the door is locked) and harmful (forgetting to turn off the gas stove) consequences. Certain types of prospective memory are evaluated as indicators of nonnormative changes related to various types of conditions, which we will consider at the end of this chapter and in Chapter 10.

Autobiographical Memory

We noted earlier one main function of memory is to create one's sense of identity (Prebble et al., 2013). In fact, much of the information people learn and keep for a long time concerns information and events that happen to them. When we put all those incidents and information together, we create our autobiography. **Autobiographical memory** involves remembering information and events from our own life.

Testing autobiographical memory is tricky. To do it correctly requires having independent verification that a remembered event actually happened in the way claimed. That's fine if there is a video of the event, for instance. But much of our lives is not on video, making it difficult to validate event recall. Plus, just because a person doesn't remember something could be due to memory failure, certainly, or because they deliberately choose not to report it, or because they never actually learned it in the first place. Some ingenious researchers, though, have managed to circumvent these problems and figured out how to study autobiographical memory.

Autobiographical memory is primarily a form of episodic memory, although it can also involve semantic memory. The episodic component of autobiographical memory is the recollection of temporal and spatial events from one's past (e.g., birthday parties, vacations, graduations), so the binding of the various bits of information becomes crucial to forming the memory. The semantic component consists of knowledge and facts of one's past (e.g., personal characteristics, knowledge that an event occurred) without having to remember exactly what or when things occurred.

Autobiographical memories change over time for all adults, with certain specific episodic details (e.g., of details from specific conversations being put in the correct sequence with the correct conversation) being forgotten first, and other semantic information (e.g., the main points of the conversations) being remembered best (Meléndez & Satorres, 2021). Neuroscience research shows that these differences are due in part to how the hippocampus and related brain structures processes memories that are responsible for integrating different aspects of the memory (Andermane et al., 2021; Sadeh et al., 2014).

As you may have experienced yourself, what is remembered from autobiographical events changes over time. For instance, shortly after not getting a job you wanted very much, your recollection of the event may be much more negative than it is years later after being in a different job you like quite a lot. You reevaluate your initial negative recollection to be more positive under the notion that your current job satisfaction is perhaps due to the fact that you didn't get the initial job.

You might think details for events would get fuzzier or fewer over time. For many events, that's true. But, surprisingly, that's not what always happens. How memory for details of autobiographical events changes over time can only be studied when an independent record exists, made at the time the events happened. Biological and medical data, such as height or age at menarche (first menstruation), provide such a source. In a classic study, Casey and colleagues (1991) examined records available from the Harvard Longitudinal Studies of Child Health and Development on individuals from birth to age 50. Detailed information was collected over the years on such things as what childhood diseases the participants had, whether they smoked cigarettes, and what kinds and how much food they ate. At age 50, participants completed a lengthy questionnaire about these issues, and their responses were compared with similar reports made 10 and 20 years earlier, as well as with the official records. Casey and colleagues found half of the memories elicited at age 50 were more accurate than the memories for the same information elicited 10 years earlier at age 40. However, information about amounts of food consumed or individual episodes was not remembered well. Apparently, these events tend to get blended together and are not stored as separate incidents. Long-term accuracy for medical information has been validated by several other studies (e.g., Kyulo et al, 2012).

Although certain types of autobiographical information are recalled accurately over long periods of time, much is not. Researchers wondered whether autobiographical memory could be improved with the right intervention. It turns out they were right. Virtual reality, because of its immersive experience, is effective at increasing the amount and the accuracy of autobiographical memories, even for people who experience depression, a condition that usually suppresses such remembering (Fernandez-Alvarez et al., 2021; Kisker et al., 2021). As an adaptive research tool, virtual reality is likely to emerge as an important technological technique for autobiographical and other memory research (Preston & Pedala, 2022).

What distinguishes memorable autobiographical events from those that aren't? What makes a moment one we will remember the rest of our lives? Many people think highly traumatic or surprising and unexpected events are ones indelibly etched in our memories. Events such as September 11, 2001, or the death of George Floyd on May 25, 2020, or the birth of one's children, or an assault that occurs are examples. **Researchers label memories for personally traumatic or unexpected events flashbulb memories.**

Flashbulb memories tend to feel exceedingly real to people, who believe their recollections of these events are highly accurate down to small details (Neisser, 2012). It is the case that people do tend to remember some details about major news events, especially those with emotional aspects (Demiray & Freund, 2015). Additionally, people who are forced to evacuate during emergencies or natural disasters, such as in massive wildfires or hurricanes, not only remember details about those events, but how they affected them emotionally and changed their lives (Knez et al., 2021).

One type of autobiographical memory that has received a great deal of attention and research is memory for trauma (e.g., sexual abuse, physical abuse). Much of this attention has focused on the accuracy of people's memories for such events, and the debate as to whether recollections can be influenced by "false" or "planted" memories. The Controversies feature delves into these issues in more detail with respect to long-term recollections of these events and recollection of these events to support requests for asylum.

Controversies

Autobiographical Memory for Traumatic Events

Experiencing a highly traumatic event such as a sexual assault or an airplane crash or parental loss are autobiographical events that are both likely to be highly salient and have a long-lasting effect. Decades of research clearly show that experiencing very traumatic events in childhood or adolescence has potent, life-long effects on adults' mental health (McKay et al., 2021). We will consider some of these long-term effects in more detail in Chapter 10. These effects on mental health in adulthood have neurological underpinnings. For example, Li and colleagues (2022) reported that young adults who experienced childhood trauma showed differences in several brain structures and in communication networks among brain structures depending on the type of trauma. More specifically, Cross and colleagues (2017) found that the prefrontal cortex, hippocampus, and amygdala are especially sensitive to chronic interpersonal trauma during childhood.

When these traumatic events happen but are subsequently recalled much later, the accuracy of the recollections may be at issue. Such questions may be raised in many different contexts, from legal proceedings or hearings (e.g., criminal court cases, confirmation hearings for nominees to the U.S. Supreme Court) to sociocultural contexts (e.g., patriarchal values, reputational challenges). From the perspective of how memory works, what can we conclude about these situations?

Let's consider a view that was widely held at one time but is held in much lower regard now—that recollections of childhood trauma are easily manipulated, and false memories can be easily planted. Such arguments are unsupported by data, and research now provides behavioral and neurological evidence supporting dissociative identity disorder as the actual reality (Salter & Blizard, 2022).

Research strongly supports several points about remembering traumatic events from much earlier in life. One longitudinal study of diverse middle-aged and older adults in England found that memories of traumatic events early in life declined at the same rate as memories for other types of events (O'Shea et al., 2021). Another longitudinal study comparing remembrances of traumatic events in childhood or adolescence provided to investigators at the time of occurrence and again

Bloomberg/Getty Images

Requiring these refugees to remember traumatic events in detail may result in the person having gaps or memory difficulties due to that trauma.

20 years later revealed that age at occurrence and experience of psychological symptoms in adulthood were significant predictors of how much information was accurately recalled in adulthood (Wu et al., 2021). Specifically, trauma later in childhood or in adolescence was recalled better, and details from the occurrence were recalled better by those adults experiencing psychological symptoms.

Remembering personally experienced traumatic events is a challenge for individuals who are refugees fleeing dangerous environments and may also be seeking asylum (a status granted to people who have been persecuted or fear they will be persecuted on account of race, religion, nationality, and/or membership in a particular social group or political opinion [U.S. Citizenship & Immigration Services, 2015]). For example, the U.S. immigration system mandates that people seeking asylum prove their persecution claim is credible and their fear of returning home is well-founded. However, asylum seekers are a highly trauma-exposed group, and the neuropsychiatric symptoms they experience due to prior torture or maltreatment may interfere with cognitive functioning, such as their ability to recall details of their trauma. These effects can be compounded by language and cultural barriers to understanding and the long, dangerous journeys they may have taken to arrive at the point to apply for asylum. Memory lapses may be incorrectly perceived by officials who decide asylum cases as indicators of dishonesty, thereby jeopardizing the person's credibility and their asylum claim. Saadi and colleagues (2021) reported that asylum seekers with post-traumatic stress disorder (PTSD) or depression were more likely to experience memory loss for their trauma event than those with other conditions, such as head trauma. Thus, officials must be aware of the effects of trauma on memory and how the resultant memory loss might affect the outcome of immigration proceedings.

Khan and colleagues (2021) conducted a systematic review of research focusing on autobiographical memories of refugee people in the competing contexts of the unpleasantness of remembering their trauma and the need to satisfy authorities for asylum. They found that the recall of autobiographical memory by refugees and asylum seekers was often disrupted; they had difficulty both in describing their life experiences in detail and describing the same memory at a later point—sometimes simply being unable to recall it. However, refugees and asylum seekers in some situations were able to recall traumatic life experiences in enough detail to satisfy the legal requirement to defend their refugee status to authorities. In these cases, they did it without minimizing their recollections while still being able to minimize their distress. Apparently, the need for providing detailed recollections of traumatic life experiences outweighed the loss of re-experiencing those unpleasant events by having to retell them. The memories produced by refugees and asylum seekers frequently detailed their loss of physical and psychological resources and the challenges they faced in their resettlement environment. PTSD, depression, and feelings of hopelessness were common among refugees and asylum seekers.

In sum, traumatic events experienced in life can be remembered in detail when necessary by adults of all ages. The details of these events undergo the same age-related declines in recollection as other events, but unlike other events the traumatic experiences affect brain structures and connection patterns in nonnormative ways. Trauma has wide ranging life-long effects.

What if researchers can access recordings of an event as it happened and then compare it to sworn testimony? Such situations are possible under special circumstances, usually within the context of a special historical event or legal process. It turns out that when researchers compare what people claim they remember about events with concurrently recorded independent records of those events (e.g., videos, transcripts), the memories of the details are often wrong. For example, many people feel absolutely certain they remember exact details of the events on September 11, 2001. Former President George W. Bush often related his detailed recollection of how and what he heard about the terrorist attacks that day. However, comparison of his claims with actual historical records indicate his memory was inaccurate in important ways concerning the details (Greenberg, 2004). Other U.S. presidents have demonstrated the same types of memory failures.

Nevertheless, people tend to get the gist of the story correct, and highly emotional events do tend to be remembered better than unemotional ones (Neisser, 2012). The errors and influences on autobiographical memory help explain why eyewitness testimony is often unreliable (Berkowitz et al., 2015; Lackey, 2022).

Given autobiographical memory is the primary basis for a person's identity, what events do people remember, and when did they occur across the life span? Abdullah's more frequent telling of his life experiences from his young adulthood years is a typical pattern, noted in Figure 6.4. For both younger and older adults, when asked to remember life events, vivid memories

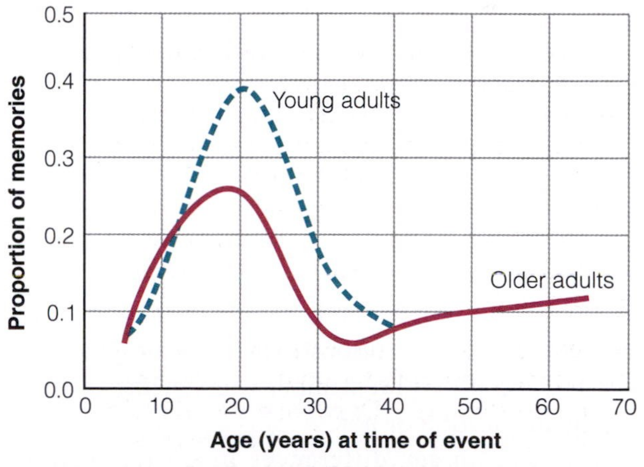

Figure 6.4 Both younger and older adults remember more life events from their teens and 20s than from any other period of life.

Source: Based on Fitzgerald, J. (1999). Autobiographical memory and social cognition. In T. M. Hess & F. Blanchard-Fields (Eds.), *Social Cognition and Aging* (pp. 147–171). Academic Press.

experienced earlier in life (between 10 and 30 years of age) are reported more often than those occurring during middle adulthood (between 30 and 50 years of age; Fitzgerald, 1999; Eysenck & Keane, 2020; Fuentes & Desrocher, 2012; Koppel & Berntsen, 2015). Events from less-remembered periods can be recalled if given additional context (such as news headlines from specific years) (Mace & Clevinger, 2013). Odors are especially powerful cues for autobiographical memories and increase the number of life events recalled even for people who have Alzheimer's disease and have difficulty with other forms of memory (Haj, 2022). It may be this earlier period of life contains more key events important in creating one's personal history (Koppel & Berntsen, 2015). Or not. The full reason why people focus more on this period of life remains a mystery.

Source Memory and Processing of Misinformation

Why are some autobiographical memories that seem so vivid for the person remembering them actually inaccurate at the detail level? Two main explanations have to do with how we remember the source of information and how susceptible we are to false information.

Think about a familiar event in your life. Now attempt to remember how you obtained your memory of it. Did you actually experience the event? Or, did you watch or listen to it live ? Are you sure?

Source memory refers to the ability to remember the source of a familiar event as well as the ability to determine if an event was imagined or actually experienced. Remembering the source of information is important in many contexts. It is important for people to be able to tell the difference between whether they actually remembered to take medication or only thought about doing it. The ability to discriminate between these two events requires one to retrieve information about the context in which the event in question originally occurred. By reconstructing the original event accurately, people will remember whether they actually took the medication or not.

Research on age differences in source memory reveals older adults are less accurate at a number of source-memory tasks (Mitchell & Hill, 2019; Spaniol, 2016). The difference appears to be that older and younger adults attend to different information (Mitchell & Hill, 2019). Younger adults are better than older adults at connecting (binding) the item to be remembered with the context in which it is learned (Boywitt et al., 2012; Kuhlmann & Boywitt, 2016). The main exception to these age differences is when the source memory information is emotional; in some cases both younger and older adults show identical patterns of performance, perhaps because emotional information is processed differently than the information in pure memory tasks and serves to enhance the memory (Kensinger & Ford, 2020). And it also could be that source memory is simply less important to older adults (Kuhlmann & Boywitt, 2016).

Neuroimaging research indicates older adults show overactivation of areas in the prefrontal cortex when confronted with source memory tasks (Giovanello & Schacter, 2012; Monge et al., 2018; Spaniol, 2016; Wang & Giovanello, 2016), a pattern we noted in Chapter 2 reflecting compensatory behavior. Some research supports the notion the brain regions in which source memory is processed may even change with increasing age (Dulas & Duarte, 2014).

We can relate these findings to the role retrieval cues play in older adults' memory functioning. Naveh-Benjamin and colleagues (Old & Naveh-Benjamin, 2008; Smyth & Naveh-Benjamin, 2016) suggest contextual details can serve as retrieval cues, and without access to them older adults may have more difficulty in remembering events. Furthermore, episodic memory is more highly dependent upon contextual information that could explain why older adults have difficulties with that kind of task.

False Memory. At times in our lives, we may be repeatedly told stories about us by relatives or friends that we could not have personally experienced. However, if we hear them enough, we may start believing the events are real and falsely incorporate them into our autobiographical memory. **False memory** is when one remembers items or events that did not occur.

The focus in false memory research is on memory errors (Groome, 2016), which are related to errors in autobiographical memory discussed earlier. One way to study false memory in the laboratory is to present participants with information (e.g., a list of related words, a video of an event) and test people's memory for both the information actually presented and information that was not (e.g., words related to those in the list but never studied, details that could plausibly have happened in the event but were not actually in the video).

People tend to falsely recall and incorrectly recognize such plausible information and feel quite confident about it (Groome, 2016; Johnson et al., 2012). Neuroimaging research has revealed a strange situation—it appears that accurate and false memories are processed through different neural pathways, and retrieval practice (repeatedly remembering the event) "steers" the memory into a pathway that accurately distinguishes actual from false memories (Zhuang et al., 2021).

What might be going on? The best explanation for this effect is older adults have more difficulty in correctly identifying information as false because they have trouble linking (binding) content information to its context, as noted earlier. Moreover, older adults have more difficulty separating misleading context from relevant context, which also explains why older adults are more susceptible to misleading information in general, and mishearing in particular (Colombel et al., 2016; Failes et al., 2020).

Factors That Influence Memory

As should be clear from our discussion thus far, older adults perform certain everyday memory tasks quite well. These findings imply there may be specific factors that help preserve memory performance, termed **cognitive reserve**. Let's investigate some of them.

Exercise. Global research over several decades has repeatedly demonstrated that aerobic exercise improves cognitive performance in older adults regardless of the training method or the older adults' personal characteristics (Colcombe & Kramer, 2003; Jardim et al., 2021). Neuroscience research also clearly demonstrates regular exercise has a wide range of effects on the brain, such as increased neural plasticity (i.e., flexibility and adaptability of brain functioning) and can be viewed as an intervention alternative for diseases such as Parkinson's, Alzheimer's, and stroke, and may also prevent some of the normative decline typically associated with aging (Marques-Aleixo et al., 2012, 2021). Additional evidence indicates that exercise, including household physical activity, increases gray matter volume in the frontal, temporal, and parietal lobes, and in the hippocampus, thalamus, and basal ganglia, as well as reduced brain atrophy in other regions (discussed in Chapter 2; Koblinsky et al., 2021; Raji et al., 2016). In short, physical exercise is great for the aging brain, a point we will explore further in Chapter 14.

Sirtravelalot/Shutterstock.com

Regular exercise has been shown to improve memory and overall cognitive functioning in older adults.

Multilingualism and Cognitive Functioning. In an intriguing study, Kavé and colleagues (2008) explored whether the number of languages a person speaks positively influences the cognitive state of older adults. In fact, older adults from 75 to 95 years of age who spoke four languages or more exhibited the best cognitive state. Other research has shown that bilingualism is associated with a 4.5 year delay in symptoms of Alzheimer's disease compared with monolinguists (Paulavicius et al., 2020), and should be pursued as a global public health policy (Mendis et al., 2021). Neuroscience research on the benefits of bilingualism shows that functional connectivity in the parietal-frontal control network is stronger (Grady et al., 2015; Tao et al., 2021). These findings suggest speaking multiple languages might be a protective factor for maintaining our cognitive abilities as we age.

Semantic Memory in Service of Episodic Memory. Given that semantic memory is relatively unimpaired as we grow older (as discussed earlier), it may have an enhancement or supportive effect on episodic memory for older adults. Several studies show older adults perform better when they can use previously learned semantic information to support episodic memory (Badham et al., 2016; Pitts et al., 2022). The more associations (more extensive bindings) are made, the stronger the effect and the more performance is improved.

Negative Stereotypes and Memory Performance. Older adults may not perform at optimal levels because they are aware of and threatened by negative, implicit stereotypes about aging, such as that aging inevitably results in declines in memory ability (Vailati Riboni & Pagnini, 2022). Specifically, negative or threatening stereotypes suppress older adults' controlled or conscious use of memory while increasing the likelihood they will use automatic response instead (Mazerolle et al., 2021; Popham & Hess, 2016). We will explore this psychosocial factor influencing cognition in more detail in Chapter 8.

Helping People Remember

The notion memory can be improved through acquiring skills and practicing them is old, dating to techniques to help people memorize long, epic poems long before these stories were written down (Yates, 1966). For example, the story related in *The Iliad* was told for generations through the use of mnemonic strategies before it was finally written down. Self-help books that teach readers how to improve their own memory have also been around for centuries (e.g., Grey, 1756).

Most adults benefit from training on how to remember information better, especially through the use of memory strategies. As you may have realized in our earlier discussion about memory strategies, most of the best strategies share several things in common. First, they require paying attention to the incoming information. Second, they rely on already-stored information to facilitate making new connections with the new material in semantic memory. Finally, in the process of encoding, strategies provide the basis for future retrieval cues. Additionally, putting training for memory strategies in the context of healthy lifestyles tends to enhance the positive outcomes. Research has generally shown well-designed memory training programs to be effective, and several studies show reasonably long-term positive effects (Brehmer et al., 2016; Jones et al., 2021; West & Strickland-Hughes, 2016). Memory improvement can also be an outcome of other forms of training that engage cognitive processes, such as training older adults to use tablet computers (Chan et al., 2016). Research in Korea also shows the utility of using tablet computers in cognitive training (Park, 2021).

Memory aids or strategies can be organized into meaningful groups. Among the most useful of these classifications is Camp and colleagues' (1993; Camp, 2005; Malone & Camp, 2007) E-I-E-I-O framework. The E-I-E-I-O framework combines two types of memory, explicit memory and implicit memory, with two types of memory aids: external aids and internal aids. (The "O" is the reaction on the part of the learner—"Oh!—when the strategy actually works.)

As discussed earlier, explicit memory involves the conscious and intentional recollection of information; remembering this definition on an exam is one example. Implicit memory involves effortless and unconscious recollection of information such as knowing stop signs are red octagons is usually not something people need to exert effort to remember when they see one on the road.

External aids are memory aids that rely on environmental resources, such as notebooks or calendars. **Internal aids** are memory aids that rely on mental processes, such as imagery. The Aha! or Oh! experience in the framework is the one that comes with suddenly remembering something. As depicted in Table 6.1, the E-I-E-I-O framework helps organize how different types of memory can be combined with different kinds of memory aids to provide a broad range of intervention options to help people remember.

We can use Camp and colleagues' approach to examine research on external and internal memory aids. In addition, we briefly review two alternatives, memory exercises and medications.

External Memory Aids. External memory aids are objects such as smartphones, smart watches, calendars, Post-It® notes, tablets, computers, and other devices commonly used to support memory in everyday situations like

Table 6.1 The E-I-E-I-O Model of Memory Helps Categorize Different Types of Memory Aids

Type of Memory	Type of Memory Aid	
	External	Internal
Explicit	Appointment book Grocery list	Mental imagery Rote rehearsal
Implicit	Color-coded maps Sandpaper letters	Spaced retrieval Conditioning

jotting down items you need to purchase at the supermarket (McGuire et al., 2000; Mercer, 2016; Richard et al., 2017). Devices such as smartphones are increasingly being used to assist memory through various built-in functions (e.g., video recording of medical visits) and apps (e.g., alarms and calendars). Other tried-and-true methods include setting objects in obvious locations (e.g., positioning the kitchen wastebasket by the door to help you remember to take out the trash).

In general, explicit-external interventions, especially those involving technology-based devices, are the most frequently used, because they are easy, widely available, and work well with adults affected by a wide variety of physical or mental disorders (Mercer, 2016; Schacter, 2022). Many of the apps on a smartphone are aimed at relieving us of memory burden (e.g., contacts, calendars, maps), and most social media use photos to help us link names and faces (presuming, of course, that the other user actually uses a self-photo). These explicit-external interventions have potential value for improving older adults' cognitive performance in real-world settings.

Interestingly, there is also growing evidence that using technology can also impair memory (Schacter, 2022). For instance, people have more trouble remembering a route after using a GPS-enabled app. Thus, the use of technology to assist memory should be done carefully, in a way that assures enhanced, rather than decremented, performance.

A good example of a situation in which technology really helps is remembering to take medication, an example of an explicit-external intervention. The most common device is a pillbox divided into compartments corresponding to days of the week and different times of the day, and some pillboxes include "smart apps" that sound alarms or have voice reminders. Smartphone apps and voice activated devices (e.g., Alexa) can also provide alarms with messages regarding what medication must be taken at what time. Access to such devices is crucial, so ensuring barriers to technology are overcome is crucial for providing these supports. Memory interventions like this can help older adults maintain their independence and age in place (as discussed in Chapter 5). Nursing homes and special memory care units also use explicit-external interventions, such as bulletin boards with the date and weather conditions, to help residents keep in touch with current events.

Advocating the use of external aids in memory intervention is popular as well as extensively grounded in research. Camp and colleagues (2011) advocate external aids either alone or in combination with other techniques (e.g., Montessori-based methods) in working with people with dementia. Research also indicates for external cues to be most effective, they should (1) be given close to the time action is required, (2) be active rather than passive, (3) be specific to the particular action, (4) be portable, (5) fit a wide range of situations, (6) store many cues for long periods, (7) be easy to use, and (8) not require a pen or pencil.

Rasstock/Shutterstock.com

Smartphones can serve as powerful external memory aids.

External-implicit combinations (e.g., pairing to-be-remembered information with colors or songs), widely used with children, have applicability with older adults in some situations. For example, special care memory units use different color schemes to designate different wings or sections of the building. Because people process the color-coded aspects of the building automatically, the implicit nature of this external cue makes it ideal for people who may otherwise have difficulty learning and remembering new information.

Internal Memory Aids. Camp and colleagues' examples of internal memory aids may trigger some personal experiences. Many people use rote rehearsal in preparing for an examination (e.g., repeating Camp—E-I-E-I-O over and over), or use mental imagery in remembering the location of their car in a parking lot (we're parked near the light post with the giraffe sign).

Most research on memory training discussed earlier concerns around improving people's use of these and other internal strategies that supply meaning and help organize incoming information. Classic examples of formal internal strategies include the method of loci (remembering items by mentally placing them in locations in a familiar environment), mental retracing (thinking about all the places you may have left your keys), turning letters into numbers, and forming acronyms out of initial letters (such as ICYMI for "in case you missed it" and ASAP for "as soon as possible").

Getting proficient at explicit-internal memory strategies is hard work. As noted earlier, explicit strategies require effortful processing that is more taxing on older adults. Thus, explicit memory intervention would most likely work best with older adults who are least likely to suffer memory failures or for young adults. In fact, healthy older adults are less willing to use effortful internal strategies. In addition, older adults with dementia are unlikely to benefit from these types of strategies (Camp et al., 2011). Thus, Camp argues older adults would benefit more from preserved implicit memory abilities.

One implicit-internal memory aid proven quite powerful is based on a technique called spaced retrieval. Research shows that this approach is highly successful across a wide spectrum of ability levels, including with people who have dementia (Bourgeois et al., 2003; Camp, 2005; Hunter et al., 2012; Oren et al., 2014; Small et al., 2020). Spaced retrieval is one of the few strategies effective with dementia or other serious cognitive impairment to remember new information by presenting to-be-remembered information (such as a person's name) and gradually increasing the time between retrieval attempts. This easy, almost magical technique has been used to teach names of staff members and other information, and it holds considerable potential for broad application. It is superior to other techniques, and combining spaced retrieval with additional memory encoding aids helps even more (Haslam et al., 2011; Jones et al., 2021; Small et al., 2020).

Does Memory Training Work? As is evident from the discussion, researchers are pretty successful in teaching older adults with a wide range of cognitive skills to improve their performance by using a selection of different techniques. So, in this sense memory training works—older adults can acquire new ways of learning information more efficiently and effectively.

The bigger question is how long the training effects last. The evidence here is much less favorable. A growing number of studies shows that training effects are generally restricted to the task(s) used in training and do not generalize to other tasks. Nor do the training effects last over the long run. These results are true for specific memory strategies and broader executive functioning skills (Anguera et al., 2021; Lindenberger et al., 2017; Nguyen et al., 2019). The lack of transfer to new tasks and the lack of long-term maintenance is the case even though there is some evidence of changes in brain activity and function during the training sessions.

In short, researchers have yet to find the magic that will eliminate age-related declines in certain types of memory or provide long-lasting interventions that would make older adults better memory processors. We will return to the issue of the efficacy of cognitive training in Chapter 7 when we consider other types of interventions.

Adult Development in Action

How might autobiographical memory be used in therapeutic settings?

Review Questions

6.3 Memory in Context

- What types of prospective memory have been distinguished? What age differences are there in prospective memory?
- What is autobiographical memory, and how does it differ with age?
- How do source memory and processing of misinformation change with age?
- What are factors preventing decline in memory functioning? How do they work?
- What is the E-I-E-I-O framework? How does it help organize memory training programs?
- How much do older adults benefit from each of the major types of memory training programs? How is technology used in memory training?
- What kinds of memory interventions work over time?

6.4 Self-Evaluations of Memory Abilities

Key Questions

- What are the major types of memory self-evaluations?
- What age differences have been found in metamemory and memory monitoring?

Paolo just reached his 70th birthday. However, he is greatly concerned. He believed since he was young this is the age when memory really goes downhill. He has a great fear of losing his memory completely. He asks people to repeat things to him over and over for fear he will forget them. This fear takes a toll on his self-concept. He doesn't feel he has control over his life the way he used to.

How good is your memory? Do you forget where you put your keys? People's names? Or are you like the proverbial elephant who never forgets anything? Like most people, you probably tend to be your own harshest critic when it comes to evaluating your memory performance. We analyze, scrutinize, nitpick, and castigate ourselves for the times we forget; we rarely praise ourselves for all the things we do remember, and continue to be on guard for more memory slips. The self-evaluations we make about memory may affect our daily life in ways that traditionally were unrecognized. This is exactly what is happening to Paolo. His negative evaluations of his memory ability are creating much undue stress in his life.

The self-evaluations we make about memory are complex but are key to understanding memory performance and how to improve it (Cavanaugh, 1996; Hertzog et al., 2021). They are based not only on memory and performance per se but also on how we view ourselves in general, our theories about how memory works, what we remember from past evaluations, and our attributions and judgments of our effectiveness.

Aspects of Memory Self-Evaluations

Researchers of memory self-evaluation have focused primarily on two types of awareness about memory (Tauber & Dunlosky, 2016). The first type involves knowledge about how memory works and what we believe to be true about it; this type of self-evaluation is referred to as **metamemory**. For instance, we may know recall is typically harder than recognition memory. We may also know that using strategies during encoding and retrieval is often helpful, and that working memory is not limitless. We may also believe memory declines with age, appointments are easier to remember than names, and anxiety impairs performance. Metamemory has several related notions, including memory self-efficacy (the belief that I have the ability to learn and remember things) and memory self-evaluation (the personal inventory one does regarding memory ability). Metamemory is most often assessed with questionnaires asking about these various facts and beliefs.

The second type of self-evaluation, called **memory monitoring**, refers to the awareness of what we are doing with our memory right now. We can be aware of the process of remembering in many ways. At times we know how we study, search for some particular fact, or keep track of time for an appointment. At other times we ask ourselves questions while doing a memory task. For example, when faced with having to remember an important appointment later in the day, we may consciously ask ourselves whether the steps we have taken (e.g., making a note in our smartphone) are sufficient.

Age Differences in Metamemory and Memory Monitoring

Researchers explored age differences in metamemory mainly by using questionnaires, the most common, as well as judgments of confidence in one's ability or performance (Dunlosky et al., 2016; Hertzog, 2016; McDonough et al., 2020). Questionnaires tap several dimensions of knowledge about memory and reflect the complexity of memory itself. It is well established that older adults seem to know less than younger adults about the internal workings of memory and its capacity, view memory as less stable, expect memory will deteriorate with age, and perceive they have less direct control over memory (Hertzog, 2016; Hertzog & Dunlosky, 2011). Importantly, though, people with symptoms of depression and with functional cognitive disorders tend to report poorer beliefs about memory, a key point we will examine later in this chapter and a key factor to consider in understanding the connections between metamemory and performance (Hülür et al., 2015; Larner, 2021).

Do these beliefs affect how well people actually remember information? Does what you believe about yourself matter?

The Role of Memory Self-Efficacy. Belief in one's ability to accomplish things is an old, pervasive theme in literature, religion, psychotherapy, and many other diverse arenas (Berry, 1989; Cavanaugh & Green, 1990). One of the most beloved children's books is *The Little Engine that Could.* The train engine keeps telling itself, "I think I can. I think I can." and, of course, it performs successfully.

As it applies to memory, belief in oneself is referred to as **memory self-efficacy**; it is the belief

one will be able to perform a specific task. This is an important construct in understanding how memory changes with age (Berry et al., 2016). Memory self-efficacy is an important type of memory belief distinct from general knowledge about memory; one may know a great deal about how memory works but still believe one's ability to perform in a specific situation is poor.

Memory self-efficacy emerged as one of the key aspects of metamemory because of its importance in accounting for performance in several different types of situations, as well as helping to explain how people make performance predictions in the absence of direct experience with tasks (Cavanaugh, 1996; Hertzog et al., 2021).

Overall, studies show older adults with lower memory self-efficacy perform worse on memory tasks. Longitudinal data from Australia show complicated patterns of interrelations in late life, but it is clear that knowledge about memory tasks is related to memory decline (Luszcz et al., 2015). Over the past few decades, researchers have documented that older adults with low memory self-efficacy compensate for poor memory performance by using people for assistance and compensatory strategies to aid in their memory performance (de Frias et al., 2003; Lachman & Agrigoroaei, 2012; Lin et al., 2020). Interestingly, several studies support the finding that how old (or young) a person feels is related to memory performance (Debreczeni & Bailey, 2021); for example, the younger one's subjective age, the better one's current performance and the slower one's decline is in immediate and delayed recall (Stephan et al., 2016).

Age Differences in Memory Monitoring. Memory monitoring involves knowing what you are doing with your memory right now. Research has demonstrated that there are two different components to making this determination: one occurring during initial presentation and one occurring at retrieval (McDonough et al., 2021). Overall, data indicate that the ability to monitor one's memory per se does not appear to decline with age (Hertzog & Dunlosky, 2011). This is important, as memory monitoring in general may provide a basis for compensating for real age-related declines in episodic memory through the use of memory strategies.

Older adults who are better at monitoring are more likely to use effective strategies, even if they have mild cognitive impairment (Hertzog et al., 2012; Lin et al., 2020), and apply strategies learned in training to other, appropriate situations (Hertzog & Dunlosky, 2012). Tapping into memory monitoring strategies may be an effective way to compensate for older adults' tendency to be more prone to false memories (Colombe et al., 2016; Shelton & Christopher, 2016; Zhuang et al., 2021).

Metamemory is important in understanding how people formulate predictions of how well they are likely to perform; monitoring and using data from one's performance may be more important for subsequent predictions on the same task. Both aspects are critical in maximizing the likelihood of successful memory strategy training, especially if the positive effects of training are to be maintained (West & Strickland-Hughes, 2016).

Hertzog and colleagues (2021) constructed an approach to memory training grounded on metamemory principles that also reflect several facts about people, such as being creatures of habit, being reactive rather than proactive, using strategies doesn't mean using them effectively, and needing to keep strategies simple. Their approach, called the Everyday Memory and Metacognitive Intervention (EMMI), entails building a memory skill and explicitly training how to use it in different contexts and individualizing the training appropriately. EMMI reflects the best of traditional memory skills training and metamemory skills training for better understanding of one's own memory system. In sum, building memory strategy interventions on skills that change little with age, such as metamemory and basic memory monitoring, can improve both performance and, by extension, quality of life.

Adult Development in Action

How might you use self-evaluations of memory in your job as a director of a senior center?

Review Questions

6.4 Self-Evaluations of Memory Abilities

- What major types of self-evaluations have been described?
- What age differences are there in metamemory and memory self-efficacy?
- What age differences have been found in memory monitoring?

6.5 Clinical Issues and Memory Testing

Key Questions

- What is the difference between normative and nonnormative memory aging?
- What are the connections between memory and physical and mental health?
- How is memory affected by nutrition?

Latarra's children are concerned. Latarra is 80 and is becoming more and more forgetful. With the scare of Alzheimer's disease so salient in our society, they are concerned Latarra is already showing symptoms. What should they do? A friend tells them memory decline is normal with aging. But to ease their concerns the children make an appointment for a clinical screening for Latarra. This would help them find out whether it is only normative aging causing Latarra's forgetfulness, or whether it may be Alzheimer's disease.

To this point we have been focusing on the changes that occur in normal memory with aging. But what about situations in which people have serious memory problems that interfere with their daily lives? How do we tell the difference between normative and nonnormative memory changes?

These are two of the issues clinicians face. Latarra's children face this critical issue. Clinicians are often confronted with relatives of clients, such as Latarra's children, who refer their loved one because of complaints of serious memory difficulties. Clinicians approach memory assessment by focusing systematically on several key questions: Has something gone wrong with memory? What makes the individual or the individual's family or friends believe that the problem goes beyond normative memory change with age? What are all the possible causes of the observed problem? What is the prognosis if something serious is occurring? What can be done to help the client compensate or recover? To address these questions, clinicians differentiate the individuals who have no real reason to be concerned from those who may have some sort of disease or other problem causing the apparent memory impairment. What criteria should be used to make this distinction? What diagnostic tests would be appropriate to evaluate adults of various ages?

Unfortunately, there are no easy answers to these questions. First, as we have learned, the exact nature of normative changes in memory with aging is not yet understood completely. This means we have few solid standards to use as a basis to evaluate all conceivable problems. Second, there are few comprehensive batteries of memory tests specifically designed to tap a wide variety of memory functions in older adults that are socioculturally appropriate (Castro & Smith, 2015). Third, interpreting performance data in the context of diagnostic categories such as mild cognitive impairment (MCI) remains controversial, an issue we will consider in more detail in Chapter 10. For our purposes here, it should be noted that although consensus is building regarding assessment tools for MCI and other diseases involving significant memory impairment, universal agreement has yet to be reached (Dunne et al., 2021; Zhuang et al., 2021).

In this section, we consider the efforts being made to bridge the gap between laboratory and clinic. We begin with a brief overview of the distinction between normative and nonnormative memory changes. Because nonnormative memory changes could be the result of a psychological or physical condition or both, or due to medication side effects or interactions, we consider links among memory, physical health, and mental health.

Normative Versus Nonnormative Memory Aging

Throughout this chapter, we have discussed many normative changes that take place in memory as people grow older. Still, many aspects of memory functioning do not change, such as the ability to remember the gist of a story. Forgetting names or what one needs at the supermarket, though annoying, are normative changes of aging. However, some people experience far greater changes, such as forgetting where they live or their spouse's name. Where is the line dividing normative memory changes from nonnormative ones?

From a functional perspective, one way to distinguish normal and nonnormative changes is to ask whether the changes disrupt a person's ability to perform daily living tasks. The normative changes we encountered in this chapter usually do not interfere with a person's ability to function in everyday life. When problems appear, however, it would be appropriate to find out what is the matter. A person who repeatedly forgets to turn off the stove or how to get home is clearly experiencing changes affecting personal safety and interfering with daily life. Such changes should be brought to the attention of a healthcare professional including a psychologist.

As indicated in Chapter 2, advances in neuroscience, especially the study of brain–behavior relations through neuroimaging, have led to an explosion in our knowledge of specific diseases and brain changes that can create nonnormative memory performance. Brain-imaging techniques also allow researchers to find tumors, strokes, and other types of damage or disease that could account for lower-than-expected memory performance.

Neuroimaging mapping of the normative age-related changes in memory is not easy, mainly because numerous parts of the brain are involved in processing information that eventually ends up in memory (Husain & Schott, 2016; Lowry et al., 2021). We know from Chapter 2 that the prefrontal cortex, parietal region, temporal lobe, amygdala, and hippocampus are intimately involved in memory. There are also structural changes in the white and gray matter that occur that affect memory (Coehlo et al., 2021; Lee et al., 2016). The specific changes observed depend upon whether there is or is not a presence of disease, and, in the latter case, which disease is occurring (discussed in more detail in Chapter 10).

The most important point to keep in mind in clinical memory assessment is that distinguishing between normative and nonnormative memory aging, and in turn, between memory and other cognitive problems, is often difficult. There is no magic number of times someone must forget something before there is reason for concern. Because serious memory problems can also be due to underlying mental or physical health problems, these must be thoroughly checked out in conjunction with obtaining a complete memory assessment. A good general rule about how to tell whether a memory problem is definitely worth a clinical evaluation, though, is this. Forgetting where you parked the car in a large parking lot is a typical memory problem. Forgetting that you drove is another matter.

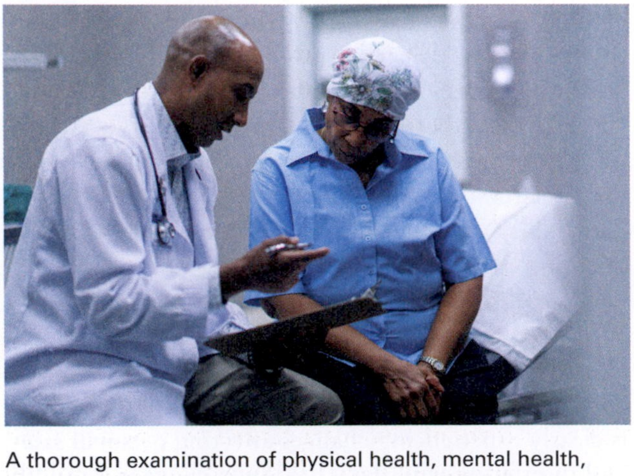

FatCamera/E+/Getty Images

A thorough examination of physical health, mental health, and cognitive functioning can determine whether memory concerns reflect normative or nonnormative issues.

Memory and Physical and Mental Health

Several disorders involve memory problems as one of the primary symptoms. Disorders that are the focus of much research are depression, anxiety, PTSD and related disorders, and the family of dementias (all of which are discussed in Chapter 10); but other diseases, such as COVID-19 and chronic obstructive pulmonary disease (COPD, described in Chapters 3 and 4) also have increased risk for memory impairment (Ranzini et al., 2020). In assessing memory function, it is very important to determine the cause of the impairment.

Damage to the brain resulting from various conditions can result in severe decrements in different types of memory. For example, severe seizures experienced in epilepsy can damage the hippocampus. This usually makes it difficult for people to learn and remember new facts and events, typically resulting in serious disruption of everyday life. Damage to the medial temporal lobe usually results in severe impairment of long-term memory (Warren et al., 2012). Stroke may occur in parts of the brain that result in significant memory loss.

Occasionally, people temporarily experience a complete loss of memory and are disoriented in time, a condition known as **transient global amnesia (TGA)**. The condition is most common in middle-aged adults who experience a sudden blackout accompanied by repetitive questions. Episodes may last a few minutes or hours, with the only long-term effect a gap in memory. The cause is unknown, although neuroimaging studies have shown significant disruption of the hippocampus neural circuitry (Park et al., 2016). TGA has been associated with migraines, temporal lobe epilepsy, a deficiency in a valve in the jugular vein in the neck, and especially transient ischemic attacks (TIAs) (Arena & Rabinstein, 2015).

Memory impairment as a result of concussion, or traumatic brain injury (TBI), is the focus of a great deal of research, especially following concussion injuries received playing sports. TBI, such as concussion, can happen in just about any sport, as well as in military combat injuries, exposure to explosions, automobile accidents, falls, or any other type of situation when one's head is hit hard. In TBI, the brain slams against the skull, resulting in various levels of at least temporary damage and impairment. In the United States, roughly 2.8 million TBIs occur annually, resulting in around 300,000 hospitalizations and over 60,000 deaths (Centers for Disease Control and Prevention, 2021f; Findley, 2021). It is the most common cause of long-term disability and death among young adults.

Two situations brought TBI to the forefront: military veterans and sports injuries (Rowson & Duma, 2021; Schulz-Heik et al., 2016). Estimates are nearly 500,000 U.S. military veterans were diagnosed with TBI between 2000 and 2021 (Traumatic Brain Injury Center of Excellence, 2021). Repeated TBI is a significant concern, as soldiers who have sustained a mild TBI are typically returned to duty within 7 to 10 days following a concussion. Regarding sports injuries, despite each state having legislation governing how soon athletes can return to playing after experiencing a concussion, there is little agreement on the diagnosis, treatment, and prognosis for athletes.

There are several approaches to the diagnosis of concussion or TBI in general. Globally, the Consensus Statement on Concussion in Sport, developed in Zurich in 2008 and updated regularly, governs the decision-making process (Herring et al., 2021). These criteria include the definition of concussion: Concussion is defined as a complex pathophysiological process affecting the brain, induced by traumatic biomechanical forces. Several common features can be described as follows:

- Caused either by a direct blow to the head, face, neck, or elsewhere on the body with an "impulsive" force transmitted to the head;
- Typically results in the rapid onset of short-lived impairment of neurologic function that resolves spontaneously;
- May result in neuropathological changes but the acute clinical symptoms largely reflect a functional disturbance rather than a structural injury;
- Results in a graded set of clinical symptoms that may or may not involve loss of consciousness. Resolution of the clinical and cognitive symptoms typically follow a sequential course; it is important to note in a small percentage of cases, post-concussive symptoms may be prolonged;
- No atypical findings on standard structural neuroimaging.

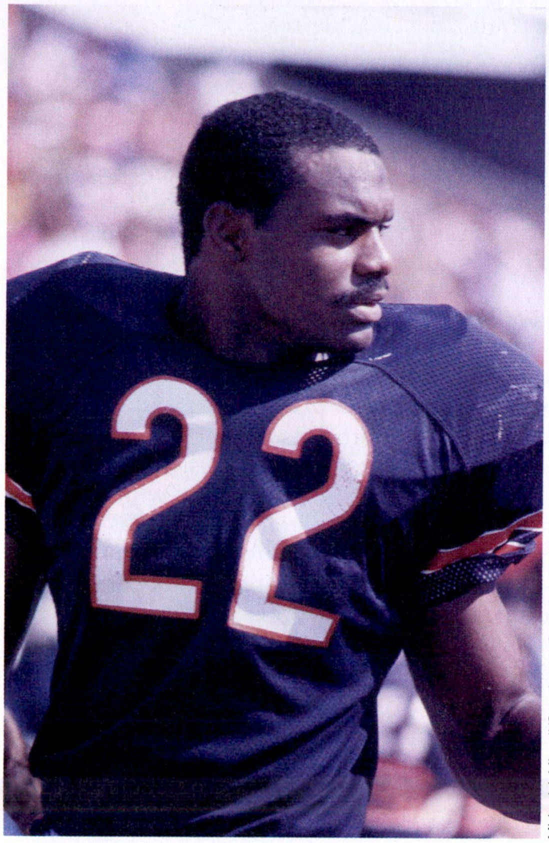

Michael J. Minardi/Getty Images Sport/Getty Images

Former NFL standout Dave Duerson suffered brain injury from repeated concussions. His death by suicide helped launch studies of CTE in professional athletes.

The difficulty with all of these criteria is that determining the seriousness of a TBI is often not easy. A significant percentage of people with a mild TBI based on the behavioral symptoms will show a significant lesion on a brain scan (Sharp et al., 2016). In contrast, individuals such as Natasha Richardson, who died after hitting her head in a fall on a ski slope in 2009, showed few immediate signs she was actually experiencing bleeding between her brain and her skull. Individuals who survive car accidents (in which air bags deploy) or falls may not be examined for brain trauma if they show no immediate symptoms, even though TBI may result.

Ignoring TBIs, especially repeated ones, can be deadly. A brain autopsy following the suicide at age 50 of former NFL player Dave Duerson in 2011 revealed he had chronic traumatic encephalopathy (CTE), a form of dementia caused by repeated head trauma. Duerson suffered 10 known concussions and reported symptoms well after he retired from football.

Real People

Dr. Ann McKee, Brain Injury Diagnostic Pioneer, and Najeh Davenport, Pro Player Who Took on the NFL

Dr. Ann McKee is a globally recognized bank director. But the type of banks she leads are probably not the kind you may be thinking about. Dr. McKee's banks consist of human brains, especially brains that were once in people who suffered known types of trauma injuries or had been diagnosed with various forms of cognitive disorders such as dementia. Ann wondered whether there could be a link between traumatic injuries and cognitive impairment. After a series of very carefully designed research projects, in 2013 she was one of the first to find and report significant connections—proof that individuals who had suffered repeated traumatic head injuries also showed significant indications of impairment and damage to areas of the brain that control important cognitive functions such as memory and executive functions. This research changed the way people view contact sports and earned Ann mention in 2018 as one of *Time*'s 100 most influential people.

Dr. Ann McKee

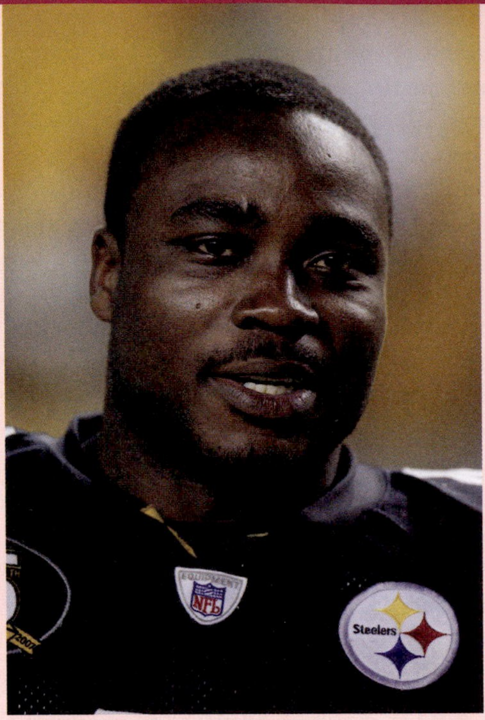

Najeh Davidson

Najeh Davenport earned a degree in theater from the University of Miami, but he was no actor as a running back in the NFL from 2002 to 2008. He ran hard; in fact, he was once hit so hard that not only did he sustain a concussion, but bones in his eye socket were broken. The cumulative effects of his 10 concussions resulted in a cognitive assessment in 2019 that indicated his executive functioning skills were sufficiently diminished that he qualified for compensation. Based on inappropriate use of race norming, the NFL denied his claim. So in 2020, Najeh and Kevin Henry, another retired Black NFL player, sued for equity. Evidence of race-based bias emerged, and Najeh and Henry won, reaching a settlement with the NFL on behalf of Black players.

His death started a movement within professional sports. Other former professional players who died relatively young have also had the disease. Dr. Ann McKee, one of the global experts on CTE, who is profiled in the Real People feature, has noted that we do not really know the extent of CTE among professional athletes who play contact sports (Smith, 2016). Due to evidence of racially biased norming that led to higher rejection of injury claims by Black players, in 2021 the NFL admitted that they had previously factored in race in their diagnosis of CTE, resulting in systematic discrimination against Black football team members who would have otherwise been diagnosed (NPR, 2021). Najeh Davenport, one of the plaintiffs in the suit and also profiled in the Real People feature, initially had his case denied even though he suffered 10 concussions.

Because of the concern over CTE, the National Institute of Neurological Disease and Stroke (NINDS) announced in 2021 the creation of evidence-informed, expert consensus research diagnostic criteria for traumatic encephalopathy syndrome (TES), the clinical disorder associated with neuropathologically diagnosed chronic traumatic encephalopathy (CTE). These criteria can be used to definitively diagnose cases of CTE (Katz et al., 2021).

Clearly, there is more awareness of the problems associated with repeated TBI. Whether sports, or at least certain sports involving physical contact, should now be considered dangerous remains to be seen. What is certain, though, is the effects of repeated TBI last well into adulthood and can cause serious cognitive impairment, and perhaps death, at a relatively early age.

Memory and Nutrition

Researchers and clinicians often overlook nutrition as a cause of memory failures in adulthood (Brown, 2020). Evidence points to several compounds in healthy diets essential for well-functioning memory. Considerable research indicates flavonoids, found in green tea and blueberries, among other foods, may reverse age-related deficits in spatial memory (Roodenrys, 2021). Dietary iron intake in midlife has also been associated with better verbal memory, even after other potential explanations for the data were taken into account (Rickard et al., 2012). Finally, several vitamins, especially B vitamins 6, 9 (folic acid), and 12, have been associated with memory and other cognitive functions (Rai et al., 2021).

These data indicate it is important to consider older adults' diets when assessing their memory performance. What may appear to be serious decrements in functioning may, in fact, be induced by poor nutrition or specific side effects or interactions of medications. However, many people cannot afford or do not have easy access to sources of brain-healthy foods. As a result, sociocultural disparities in disorders in which memory problems are found (discussed in Chapter 10) can be traced at least in part to these disparities. The worst part is that, in such cases, the memory problems can likely be eliminated with the provision of brain-healthy food.

Too often, researchers and clinicians fail to inquire about eating habits. Adequate assessment is essential to avoid diagnostic errors.

Adult Development in Action

As a family member with older relatives living in your home, how can you help them maintain good memory?

Review Questions

6.5 Clinical Issues and Memory Testing

- What criteria are used to determine the difference between normal and nonnormative changes in a person's memory?
- What physical and mental health conditions involve significant memory problems?
- What effect does nutrition have on memory?

Social Policy Implications

COVID-19 and Memory

COVID-19 has had many disparate effects on people. Not surprisingly, most of the focus has been on the physiological and health effects. We have noted many of these in other chapters, so we will focus here on specific effects on memory—possible long-term effects on the ability to encode, retain, and remember information. There are also other, less discussed effects regarding what people remember from their experience during the pandemic. We will note this interesting finding second.

From the early days of the COVID-19 pandemic, it was apparent that some people who recovered experienced cognitive aftereffects from the disease. Symptoms ranged from what was described as a general "brain fog" to difficulty remembering only certain kinds of information. These aftereffects were widely documented across the life span. However, data clearly indicate that older adults were the most affected age group in terms of seriousness of the immediate and long-term effects of COVID-19 (Iodice et al., 2021).

People who recovered from COVID-19 were more likely to be concerned about memory and other cognitive aftereffects than were people who never experienced (or did not know they had) COVID-19 (Winter & Braw, 2022). Such concern, seen also in people with regard to concern about ultimately experiencing dementia, can result in anxiety, which in turn can negatively affect memory, which was widely recognized as a common outcome of the pandemic (Qureshi, 2022). In brief, these people really had concerns about their memory self-efficacy.

What's the long-term prognosis for people who experience memory or other cognitive aftereffects of COVID-19? Neuroimaging research provides some insights. Follow-up studies at about 6 months post-COVID episode show evidence of significant recovery of brain function and accompanying cognitive functioning; however, residual aftereffects are still measurable in some individuals (Blazhenets et al., 2021). Why some people continue to experience difficulties long after they showed initial symptoms of COVID-19 and seemingly recovered is, at this point, unknown.

A second type of effect on memory from the pandemic has to do with what experiences people report they had during the pandemic. In a longitudinal study conducted during the first 6 months of the pandemic, Ford and colleagues (2021) surveyed Canadian and American adults between ages 18 and 90 years about what they remembered about their pandemic experiences. Even though the pandemic was clearly a shared, collective experience, older respondents emphasized more positive aspects of their pandemic experiences than did younger adults. This finding is similar to reports of other studies showing what is called the "positivity effect" in which older adults emphasize positive recollections, whether about their lives in general (e.g., spouse/partner) or pandemic experiences (discussed in Chapters 2 and 8).

Understanding the nature and extent of long-term aftereffects of COVID-19 on memory and other cognitive abilities will be crucial for designing and implementing appropriate follow-up care. The potential implications for public policy are clear—long-term memory problems, for instance, have implications for education, employment, and healthcare policies, as well as funding for the types of interventions and support people may need. Diagnostic and intervention strategies, especially for older adults, will be critical to accurately separate memory impairments due to COVID-19 aftereffects and other causes. As noted in the chapter, such supports at best combine aspects of basic memory skills training and metamemory, an approach also supported by research specifically focusing on individuals who experienced COVID-19 (Della Gatta et al., 2021).

Additionally, an emphasis on positive recollections may raise the question of the reliability of self-reports of memory and other personal aspects when people provide personal and medical histories. It is possible that the positivity effect could result in a glossing over of negative experiences or problems, resulting in an underestimate of actual need for assistance. Finding the balance will be a crucial aspect of differential diagnosis.

In Review

To create a summary for Chapter 6, include paragraphs about the basic processes underlying memory from the first two sections, and other paragraphs about how memory is used in various contexts, how we know what we know about our own memory, and how to tell the difference between normative and atypical memory changes with age.

Another approach would be to think of a way you use memory, then deconstruct all of the various processes involved in that memory experience. You could create charts or tables of them with definitions and descriptions of each. Then describe how you would know whether a specific example of a memory process or problem is an example of normative or nonnormative age-related change.

Integrating Concepts in Development

- Based on material in Chapter 2 on cognitive neuroscience and the material in this chapter, what are the major factors involved in understanding age-related differences in memory?
- What aspects of neurological functioning would be important to consider in designing memory training programs?
- How could you design a good set of observations for family members to help them tell whether a relative's memory failures were normal or nonnormative?
- Based on information in Chapters 3 and 4, what health-related behaviors might help preserve memory functioning?
- How would you design an informational brochure for older adults to maximize their ability to remember it?

Key Terms

autobiographical memory Remembering information and events from your own life. 192

automatic processing Processes that are fast, reliable, and insensitive to increased cognitive demands. 182

binding deficit A deficit in the integration of the multiple elements of complex events within unified representations. 188

cognitive reserve Factors that provide flexibility in responding and adapting to changes in the environment. 197

divided attention The ability to pay attention and successfully perform more than one task at a time. 182

effortful processing Cognitive processing that requires all of the available attentional capacity when processing information. 183

encoding The process of getting information into the memory system. 184

episodic memory The general class of memory having to do with the conscious recollection of information from a specific event or point in time. 187

explicit memory The conscious and intentional recollection of information. 186

external aids Memory aids that rely on environmental resources. 198

false memory When one remembers items or events that did not occur. 196

flashbulb memories Memories for personally traumatic or unexpected events. 193

implicit memory The effortless and unconscious recollection of information. 186

information-processing model The study of how people take in stimuli from their environment and transform them into memories; the approach is based on a computer metaphor. 178

internal aids Memory aids that rely on mental processes. 198

long-term memory The aspects of memory involved in remembering rather extensive amounts of information over relatively long periods of time. 185

memory monitoring The awareness of what we are doing in memory right now. 201

memory self-efficacy The belief in one's ability to perform a specific memory task. 201

metamemory Memory about how memory works and what one believes to be true about it. 201

processing resources The amount of attention one has to apply to a particular situation. 181

prospective memory Process involving remembering to remember something in the future. 191

recall Process of remembering information without the help of hints or cues. 188

recognition Process of remembering information by selecting previously learned information from among several items. 188

rehearsal Process by which information is held in working memory, either by repeating items over and over or by making meaningful connections between the information in working memory and information. 185

retrieval The process of getting information back out of memory. 184

semantic memory Learning and remembering the meaning of words and concepts that are not tied to specific occurrences of events in time. 187

sensory memory A very brief and almost identical representation of the stimuli that exists in the observable environment. 179

source memory The ability to remember the source of a familiar event as well as the ability to determine if an event was imagined or actually experienced. 196

speed of processing How quickly and efficiently the early steps in information processing are completed. 180

storage The manner in which information is represented and kept in memory. 184

strategies Various techniques that make learning or remembering easier and that increase the efficiency of storage. 189

transient global amnesia (TGA) Temporary experience of a complete memory loss and disorientation in time. 204

working memory Refers to the processes and structures involved in holding information in mind and simultaneously using that information, sometimes in conjunction with incoming information, to solve a problem, make a decision, or learn new information. 185

Intelligence, Reasoning, Creativity, and Wisdom

Chapter 7

Chapter Outline

Learning Objectives

After studying this chapter, you will be able to...

7.1. Define intelligence in the context of adult development and aging in everyday life.

7.2. Describe how psychometric intelligence is measured.

7.3. Describe primary and secondary abilities, and fluid and crystallized intelligence.

7.4. Describe the major modifiers of intelligence and how primary abilities can be trained.

7.5. Describe the qualitative changes in modes of thinking in adulthood and how emotion and logic become integrated in thought.

7.6. Describe decision making and problem solving in everyday life.

7.7. Describe expertise, creativity, and wisdom including the trajectory of each across adulthood.

7.8. Describe how culture influences wisdom.

The Dalai Lama, spiritual leader of the Tibetan people, was the recipient of the 1989 Nobel Peace Prize and remains recognized as a leader in Buddhist philosophy, human rights, and global environmental issues in his 80s. He reached this stature as a simple Buddhist monk and claims he is "no more, no less." To the world, the Dalai Lama is recognized for his great wisdom and insight into the human condition. A sample of this wisdom is

> A new way of thinking has become a necessary condition for responsible living and acting. If we maintain obsolete values and beliefs, a fragmented consciousness and a self-centered spirit, we will continue to hold to outdated goals and behaviors. Such an attitude by a large number of people would block the entire transition to an interdependent yet peaceful and cooperative global society. (Dalai Lama, 2000, p. 169)

He also states as a Buddhist monk, he tries to develop compassion, not simply as religious practice, but at a human level. "When we reach beyond the confines of narrow self-interest, our hearts become filled with strength. Peace and joy become our constant companion." (Dalai Lama, 1999)

Despite the Dalai Lama's and many others' long interest in wisdom, psychologists largely overlooked it for decades, perhaps because they were busy intensely studying a related topic—intelligence. Another reason for not researching wisdom was the widespread belief it would be a waste of effort. At one time, researchers and theorists were convinced all intellectual abilities, wisdom included, inevitably declined as people aged, because of biological deterioration. For instance, Wechsler (1958) wrote "nearly all studies have shown that most human abilities decline progressively after reaching a peak somewhere between ages 18 and 25" (p. 135).

Pallava Bagla/Getty Images News/Getty Images

The Dalai Lama.

Controversy about this belief raged for decades. Considering methodological comparisons between cross-sectional and longitudinal studies, Baltes and Schaie (1974) concluded "general intellectual decline is largely a myth" (p. 35). Botwinick (1977) countered with "decline in intellectual ability is clearly a part of the aging picture" (p. 580).

Who is right? Where do we stand now? Does intelligence decline, or is that a myth? Does wisdom come with age, or is it really something available to anyone at any age? Answering these questions will be our goal in this chapter. Such widely divergent conclusions about age-related changes in intelligence and related topics reflect different sets of assumptions about the nature of intelligence that are then translated into different theoretical and methodological approaches. We examine three avenues of research on intelligence and age: the psychometric approach, the life-span approach, and the cognitive-structural approach. Along the way we look at some attempts to modify intellectual abilities through training programs, but first we need to consider what intelligence is.

7.1 Defining Intelligence

Key Questions

- How do people define intelligence in everyday life?
- What are the major components of the life-span approach?
- What are the major research approaches for studying intelligence?

When Toni graduated from high school they decided to start their own pet-sitting business. Toni started small but ultimately cornered the market in the town. Toni now lives a comfortable lifestyle. Toni's high school classmate Stacey went to college and majored in math. Stacey pursued her doctorate and now also lives a comfortable lifestyle as a university professor. How should we assess their respective intellectual abilities?

In terms of intelligence, Toni and Stacey's different paths to success point to an important question: What do we mean by intelligence? Is intelligence the same as formal education? Is it being able to learn new things quickly? Being entrepreneurial and having a great sense of how to grow a business? Knowing a great deal of factual information? The ability to adapt to new situations or create new things or ideas? Having "street smarts?" The ability to make the most of what we have and to enjoy life? As we will discover, intelligence encompasses all these idea and more.

Intelligence in Everyday Life

Robert Sternberg has argued for decades that intelligence involves more than just a particular fixed set of characteristics (Sternberg, 1985, 2016, 2020). One intriguing way he investigated intelligence was based on a list of behaviors that laypeople at a train station, supermarket, or college library reported to be distinctly characteristic of exceptionally intelligent, academically intelligent, everyday intelligent, or unintelligent people. This list of behaviors was given to experts in the field of intelligence and to a new set of laypeople. They were asked to rate either how distinctively characteristic each behavior was, or how important each behavior was in defining the four types of intelligent people. Ratings were analyzed separately for the experts and the laypeople (Sternberg et al., 2010).

There is extremely high agreement between experts and laypeople on ratings of the importance of particular behaviors in defining intelligence. The two groups agreed intelligence consisted of three major clusters of related abilities: problem-solving ability, verbal ability, and social competence. Problem-solving ability consists of behaviors such as reasoning logically, identifying connections among ideas, recognizing all aspects of a problem, and making good decisions. Verbal ability comprises such things as speaking articulately, reading with high comprehension, and having a good vocabulary. Social competence includes behaviors such as accepting others for what they are, admitting mistakes, displaying interest in the world at large, and being on time for appointments.

In a classic study, Berg and Sternberg (1992) wanted to know how these conceptions of intelligence differed across the adult life span. To find out, people aged 22 to 85 were asked to rate 55 behaviors they considered as characteristic of exceptionally intelligent 30-, 50-, or 70-year-olds. Behaviors such as motivation, intellectual effort, and reading were said to be important indicators of intelligence for people of all ages. Other behaviors were specific to particular points in the life span. For example, for a 30-year-old, planning for the future and being open-minded were listed most often. The intelligent 50- and 70-year-olds were described as acting responsibly, adjusting to life situations, being verbally fluent, and displaying wisdom.

The remarkable result from all of these studies was that people really have a consistent sense of what intelligent behavior looks like at different ages. Whether this consistency maps onto systematic psychological research is a question to which we now turn.

The Big Picture: A Life-Span View

One thing is clear about the ways people view intelligence—everyone has an idea of what intelligence is, and everyone considers it a complex construct. In the big picture, then, intelligence consists of many different skills. Theories of intelligence, therefore, are **multidimensional**; that is, they specify many domains of intellectual abilities. Although people disagree on the number of dimensions, they agree no single generic type of intelligence is responsible for all the mental activities we perform.

Baltes (1993; Baltes et al., 2006) took a broad view of intellectual development. The life-span concepts discussed in Chapter 1 including multidirectionality, plasticity, and interindividual variability play an important role in this conceptualization of intellectual change. Overall, this perspective asserts intellectual decline may be seen with age but stability and growth in mental functioning also can be seen across adulthood. The life-span perspective emphasizes the role of intelligence in human adaptation and daily activity.

The first concept, **multidirectionality**, refers to the distinct patterns of change in abilities over the life span, with these patterns differing for different abilities. For example, developmental trajectories for specific abilities differ, meaning the directional change in intelligence depends on the skills in question. As we will discover later, everyday knowledge accumulates over time and thus increases with age. However, basic cognitive mechanisms underlying key intellectual skills show more declines, especially into older age.

The term **plasticity** refers to the range of functioning within an individual and the conditions under which a person's abilities can be modified within a specific age range. Plasticity implies what may appear to be declines in some skills may in part represent a lack of practice in using them. Current studies examining brain plasticity and behavior find experience alters the brain across the life span (discussed in Chapter 2). As we noted in Chapter 2, older adults activate areas in the brain that compensate for decline in their performance, resulting in better performance than would otherwise be the case. In other words, older adults activate new or additional areas in the brain to compensate for decline in other areas. Finally, the research on training cognitive abilities described later in this chapter supports this perspective because older adults who show decline in cognitive functioning can be trained to perform at a higher level, at least during the training sessions.

The last concept, **interindividual variability,** acknowledges adults differ in the direction of their intellectual development. Schaie's (2008; Willis & Schaie, 2021) sequential research indicates that within a given cohort or generation, some people show longitudinal decline in specific abilities, whereas other people show stability of functioning and display improvements in those same abilities. Consequently, a single representation of typical or average changes with age may not really represent how the various individuals in a group function.

Using these four concepts of multidimensionality, plasticity, multidirectionality, and interindividual variability, Baltes and colleagues proposed the dual-component model of intellectual functioning (Baltes et al., 2006). Two interrelated types of developmental processes are postulated. The first component, termed the **mechanics of intelligence,** concerns the neurophysiological architecture of the mind. This architecture provides the foundational bases for cognitive abilities, including basic forms of thinking associated with information processing and problem solving such as attention, reasoning, spatial orientation, or perceptual speed. Intellectual change in this first component is greatest during childhood and adolescence, as we acquire the brain interconnections responsible for the requisite skills to handle complex cognitive tasks such as those encountered in school.

The second component, **pragmatic intelligence,** concerns acquired bodies of knowledge available from and embedded within each culture. In other words, it includes everyday cognitive performance and human adaptation. Such abilities include verbal knowledge, wisdom, and practical problem solving. All of these abilities are grounded and interpreted within a specific sociocultural context. Pragmatic intellectual growth dominates adulthood.

These different trajectories of development are illustrated in Figure 7.1. As the figure suggests, different weightings of the forces of intelligence lead to specific predictions regarding the developmental pathway they take across the adult life span. The mechanics of intelligence are governed more by biological-genetic forces, so are subject to an overall downward trajectory across adulthood. However, the pragmatics of intelligence are governed more by environmental-cultural factors that accrue across adulthood, so an upward trajectory is maintained.

This broad view of intellectual development in adulthood we adopt in this chapter provides the

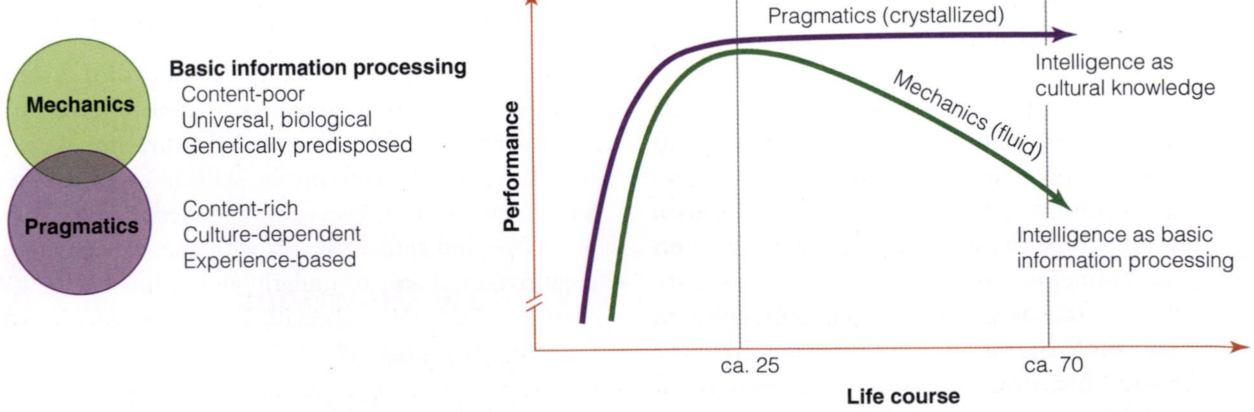

Figure 7.1 Life-span conceptualization of the mechanics and pragmatics of intelligence. The mechanics of intelligence correspond to fluid intelligence and the pragmatics to crystallized intelligence, as described later.

Source: Baltes, P. B. (1993). The aging mind: Potential and limits. *The Gerontologist, 33,* 580–594. The figure is Figure 1, p. 582.

background for asking more specific questions about particular aspects of intelligence. As we will discover, three primary research approaches have emerged.

Research Approaches to Intelligence

Sternberg's and Baltes and colleagues' work indicates that many different skills are involved in intelligence depending on one's point of view. Interestingly, the behaviors listed by Sternberg's participants and the organizational structure provided by Baltes fit nicely with the more formal attempts at defining intelligence we encounter later in this chapter. Researchers have studied these skills from many perspectives, depending on their theoretical orientation. For example, some investigators approach these skills from a statistical factor analysis approach and study them as separate pieces that can be added together to form intelligence. Others take a more holistic perspective and think of intelligence as a way or mode of thinking. These various theoretical orientations result in different means of studying intelligence.

Historically, psychological research on intelligence has focused on performance on standardized tests; this view represents the **psychometric approach**. For example, the problem-solving and verbal abilities in Sternberg and colleagues' study would be assessed by tests specifically designed to assess these skills. These tests focus on getting correct answers and tend to give less emphasis on the thought processes used to arrive at them. This is the approach you are likely to have experienced in school when you took standardized tests. It is also the approach most criticized for structural disparities in performance across cultural, racial, and ethnic groups.

Other researchers focus on information-processing mechanisms reviewed in Chapter 6. This approach aims at a detailed analysis of age-related changes in components of cognitive mechanisms and their interactions, such as attention and memory.

Finally, a number of researchers focus their efforts on reconceptualizing the very meaning and measurement of intelligence by taking a cognitive-structural approach. In the **cognitive-structural approach** researchers have been more concerned with the ways people conceptualize and solve problems than with scores on tests. Such approaches to intelligence emphasize developmental changes in the modes and styles of thinking, and how these ways of thinking play out in everyday life.

In this chapter, we consider these approaches and the research they stimulated. We discover that each approach has its merits, and whether age-related changes in intelligence are found depends on how intelligence is defined and measured. Before you continue, complete the exercise in the Discovering Development feature. The information you uncover will be useful as you read the rest of the chapter.

Discovering Development
Sociocultural Aspects of Intelligence

Before reading in detail about various approaches and components of intelligence, let's consider what might be examples of intelligence in daily life. As noted in Chapter 1, sociocultural forces are one source of differences across societal and cultural groups in defining and assessing intelligence. For example, what is considered intelligent behavior in one culture may (or may not) be considered an example in another.

With this in mind, think about a sociocultural group with which you identify. Ask yourself what some good examples of intelligent behavior would be within that group. Then talk to a few individuals who identify with different sociocultural groups to get a sense of similarities and differences in what is considered intelligent behavior. Bring all of those examples in class and have a group discussion about your findings. As you read the rest of the chapter, map your results into the different ways of organizing ideas reflected in research and theory within adult development and aging.

Adult Development in Action

If you were responsible for revising social policy regarding aging (say, criteria for living independently in the community), how would you approach that problem from the different perspectives of defining intelligence?

Review Questions

7.1 Defining Intelligence

- How do laypeople and researchers define intelligence?
- What are the two main ways intelligence has been studied? Define each.

7.2 Developmental Trends in Psychometric Intelligence

Key Questions

- What is intelligence in adulthood?
- What are primary and secondary mental abilities? How do they change?
- What are fluid and crystallized intelligence? How do they change?
- How has neuroscience research furthered our understanding of intelligence in adulthood?

Aaliyah, a 35-year-old woman recently laid off from her job as an administrative assistant, slides into her seat on her first day of classes at the community college. She is clearly nervous. "I'm worried I won't be able to compete with these younger students, that I may not be smart enough," she sighs. "Guess we'll find out soon enough, though, huh?"

Cognitive abilities are assessed across the life span using standardized tests.

Many returning adult students like Aaliyah worry they may not be "smart enough" to keep up with 18- or 19-year-olds. You may have felt this way yourself. Are these fears realistic? Let's find out.

As noted earlier, people naturally view intelligence as consisting of many components. One traditional way to measure intelligence, then, is to focus on individuals' performances on various tests of these component intellectual abilities and how these performances are interrelated. This approach to intelligence has a long history; the ancient Chinese and Greeks used this method to select people for certain jobs, such as master horse riders (Doyle, 1974; DuBois, 1968). Tests also served as the basis for Alfred Binet's (1903) pioneering work in developing standardized intelligence tests, as well as many modern theories of intelligence. Although problems with standardized tests relating to systematic sociocultural factors (e.g., certain types of knowledge on tests are culture-bound) were known from the beginning, they were usually either ignored or explained away as indicative of differences that supported prevailing stereotypes.

Because of this long history of research in psychometric intelligence, we probably know more about this area than any other area in cognitive aging except for episodic memory. Yet this still provided no definitive understanding of how intelligence changes with age—only consensus agreement on a few points. There is substantial agreement on descriptions of change in different intellectual abilities (as we discuss later) and agreement on the methodological issues needing to be addressed when studying intellectual change. There is also agreement that the psychometric approach is fraught with bias regarding people of color, even after other key personal characteristics are taken into account.

For these reasons, there is little consensus on the proper interpretation of the data. For example, what does it mean that changes in certain intellectual abilities are related to increasing age? Remember in Chapter 1 we noted age does not *cause* change, that the finding that age is *related to* decline in some intellectual abilities is not the same thing as "aging" per se. As we shall note, age-related intellectual change is also related to important variables such as health, activity level, and educational achievements. It is in this stew of complicated interrelationships that much of the controversy is still brewing.

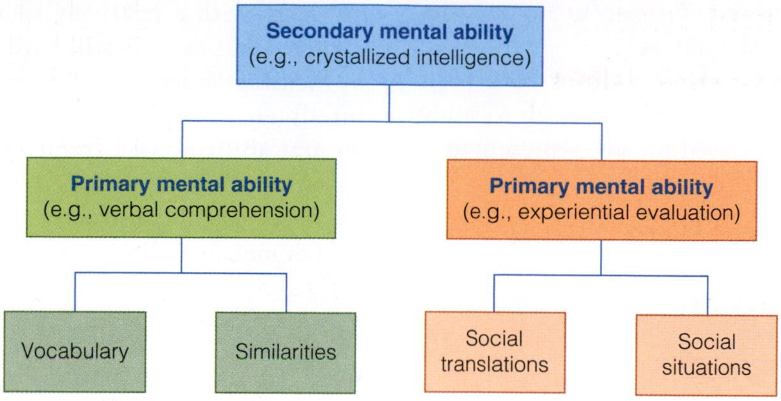

Figure 7.2 Secondary mental abilities reflect several primary mental abilities and their respective measurements. This figure shows those relations regarding crystallized intelligence.

The Measurement of Intelligence

Because the psychometric approach focuses on the interrelations among intellectual abilities, the major goal has long been to describe the ways these relationships are organized (Sternberg, 1985, 2020). This organization of interrelated intellectual abilities is termed the **structure of intelligence**. The most common way to describe the structure of intelligence is to think of it as a hierarchy such as denoted in Figure 7.2 (Cunningham, 1987).

Each successive level of this hierarchy represents a higher level of organizing the components of the level below. The lowest level consists of individual test questions—the specific items people answer on an intelligence test. These items or questions can be organized into intelligence tests, which constitute the second level.

The third level reflects interrelationships among scores on intelligence tests that assess similar abilities; these clusters of abilities are called primary mental abilities. Continuing to move up the hierarchy, the interrelationships existing among the primary mental abilities produce the secondary mental abilities at the fourth level. Finally, *general intelligence* at the top refers to the interrelationships among the secondary mental abilities.

Keep in mind that each time we move up the hierarchy we move away from people's actual performance. Each level above the first represents a theoretical description of how things fit together. Thus, there are no tests of primary abilities per se; primary abilities represent theoretical relationships among tests, which in turn represent theoretical relationships among actual performances (i.e., answers to test questions).

So exactly how do researchers construct this theoretical hierarchy? The structure of intelligence is uncovered through sophisticated statistical detective work using a technique called factor analysis. First, researchers obtain people's performances on many types of problems. Second, the results are examined to determine whether performance on one type of problem, such as filling in missing letters in a word, predicts performance on another type of problem, like unscrambling letters to form a word. If the performance on one test is highly related to the performance on another, the abilities measured by the two tests are interrelated and are called a **factor**.

Most psychometric theorists believe intelligence consists of several factors. However, we should note although factor analysis is a sophisticated statistical technique, it is not an exact technique. Thus, estimates of the exact number of factors vary from a few to over 100. Most researchers and theorists believe the number to be relatively small. We examine two factors: primary and secondary mental abilities.

Primary and Secondary Mental Abilities

Since the 1930s, researchers agreed intellectual abilities can be studied as groups of related skills (such as memory or spatial ability) organized into hypothetical constructs called **primary mental abilities**. In turn, related groups of primary mental abilities can be clustered into a half dozen or so broader skills termed **secondary mental abilities.**

Roughly 25 primary mental abilities have been identified (Horn, 1982). Because it is difficult to study all of them, researchers focused on five representative ones:

- *Number*: the basic skills underlying our mathematical reasoning
- *Word fluency*: how easily we produce verbal descriptions of things
- *Verbal meaning*: our vocabulary ability
- *Inductive reasoning*: our ability to extrapolate from particular facts to general concepts
- *Spatial orientation*: our ability to reason in the three-dimensional world

Even with a relatively small number of primary mental abilities, it is still hard to discuss intelligence by focusing on separate abilities. As a result, theories of intelligence emphasize clusters of related primary mental abilities as a framework for describing the structure of intelligence. Remember—because they are hypothetical constructs, secondary mental abilities are not measured directly.

Fluid and Crystallized Intelligence

As noted earlier, primary abilities are themselves organized into clusters of secondary mental abilities. A summary of the major secondary mental abilities is presented in Table 7.1. Two secondary mental abilities

Table 7.1 Descriptions of Major Secondary Mental Abilities

Crystallized Intelligence (Gc)

This form of intelligence is indicated by a very large number of performances indicating breadth of knowledge and experience, sophistication, comprehension of communications, judgment, understanding of conventions, and reasonable thinking. The factor that provides evidence of Gc is defined by primary abilities such as verbal comprehension, concept formation, logical reasoning, and general reasoning. Tests used to measure the ability include

- vocabulary (What is a word near in meaning to *temerity*?),
- esoteric analogies (Socrates is to Aristotle as Sophocles is to ___?),
- remote associations (What word is associated with *bathtub*, *prizefighting*, and *wedding*?), and
- judgment (Determine why a supervisor is not getting the best results from workers).

As measured, the factor is a fallible representation of the extent to which a person has incorporated, through the systematic influences of acculturation, the knowledge and sophistication that constitutes the intelligence of a culture.

Fluid Intelligence (Gf)

The broad set of abilities of this intelligence includes those of seeing relationships between stimulus patterns, drawing inferences from relationships, and comprehending implications. The primary abilities that best represent the factor, as identified in completed research, include induction, figural flexibility, integration, and, cooperatively with Gc, logical reasoning and general reasoning. Tasks that measure the factor include

- letter series (What letter comes next in the series *d f i m r x e*?),
- matrices (Discern the relationships between elements of 3-by-3 matrices), and
- topology (From among a set of figures in which circles, squares, and triangles overlap in different ways, select a figure that will enable one to put a dot within a circle and a square but outside a triangle).

The factor is a fallible representation of such fundamental features of mature human intelligence as reasoning, abstracting, and problem solving. In Gf these features are not imparted through the systematic influences of acculturation but instead are obtained through learning that is unique to an individual or is in other ways not organized by the culture.

Visual Organization (Gv)

This dimension is indicated by primary mental abilities such as visualization, spatial orientation, speed of closure, and flexibility of closure, measured by tests such as

- gestalt closure (Identify a figure in which parts have been omitted),
- form board (Show how cutout parts fit together to depict a particular figure), and
- embedded figures (Find a geometric figure within a set of intersecting lines).

To distinguish this factor from Gf, it is important that relationships between visual patterns be clearly manifest so performances reflect primarily fluency in perception of these patterns, not reasoning in inferring the process.

Auditory Organization (Ga)
This factor has been identified on the basis of several studies in which primary mental abilities of temporal tracking, auditory cognition of relations, and speech perception under distraction of distortion were first defined among other primary abilities and then found to indicate a broad dimension at the second order. Tasks that measure Ga include • repeated tones (Identify the first occurrence of a tone when it occurs several times), • tonal series (Indicate which tone comes next in an orderly series of tones), and • cafeteria noise (Identify a word amid a din of surrounding noise). Like Gv, this ability is best indicated when the relationships among stimuli are not such that one needs to reason for understanding but instead are such that one can fluently perceive patterns among the stimuli.
Short-Term Acquisition and Retrieval
This ability comprises processes of becoming aware and processes of retaining information long enough to do something with it. Almost all tasks that involve short-term memory have variance in this factor. Span memory, associative memory, and meaningful memory are primary abilities that define the factor, but measures of primary and secondary memory can also be used to indicate the dimension.
Long-Term Storage and Retrieval
Formerly this dimension was regarded as a broad factor among fluency tasks, such as those of the primary abilities called associational fluency, expressional fluency, and object flexibility. In recent work, however, these performances have been found to align with others indicating facility in storing information and retrieving information that was acquired in the distant past. It seems, therefore, that the dimension mainly represents processes for forming encoding associations for long-term storage and using these associations, or forming new ones, at the time of retrieval. These associations are not so much correct as they are possible and useful; to associate *teakettle* with *mother* is not to arrive at a truth so much as it is to regard both concepts as sharing common attributes (e.g., warmth).

Source: Horn, J. L. (1982). The aging of human abilities. In B. B. Wolman (Ed.), *Handbook of Developmental Psychology* (pp. 847–870). Englewood Cliffs, NJ: Prentice Hall. Reprinted with permission.

have received a great deal of attention in adult developmental research: fluid intelligence and crystallized intelligence (Horn, 1982).

Fluid intelligence consists of the abilities that make you a flexible and adaptive thinker, allow you to make inferences, and enable you to understand the relations among concepts. It includes the abilities you need to understand and respond to any situation, but especially new ones: inductive reasoning, integration, abstract thinking, and the like (Horn, 1982). An example of a question that taps fluid abilities is the following: What letter comes next in the series *d f i m r x e*?[1]

Crystallized intelligence is the knowledge you have acquired through life experience and education in a particular culture. Crystallized intelligence includes your breadth of knowledge, comprehension of communication, judgment, and sophistication with information (Horn, 1982). Many popular television game shows (such as *Jeopardy* and *Wheel of Fortune*) are based on contestants' accumulated crystallized intelligence.

Developmentally, fluid and crystallized intelligence follow two different paths, as depicted in Figure 7.3. Notice that fluid intelligence declines throughout adulthood, whereas crystallized intelligence improves. Although we do not yet fully understand why fluid intelligence (and its underlying primary abilities) declines, it likely is related to underlying changes in the brain (discussed in Chapter 2). In contrast, the increase in crystallized intelligence (and its underlying primary abilities, at least until late life) indicates most people continue adding knowledge every day.

What do these different developmental trends imply? First, they indicate that—although it continues through adulthood—performance or learning that depends on basic underlying skills becomes more difficult with age, whereas performance or learning that is based on what we already know continues to improve, at least until very late in life.

Second, intellectual development varies a great deal from one set of skills to another. Whereas individual

[1]The next letter is *m*. The rule is to increase the difference between adjacent letters in the series by one each time and use a continuous circle of the alphabet for counting. Thus, *f* is two letters from *d*, *i* is three letters from *f*, and *e* is seven letters from *x*.

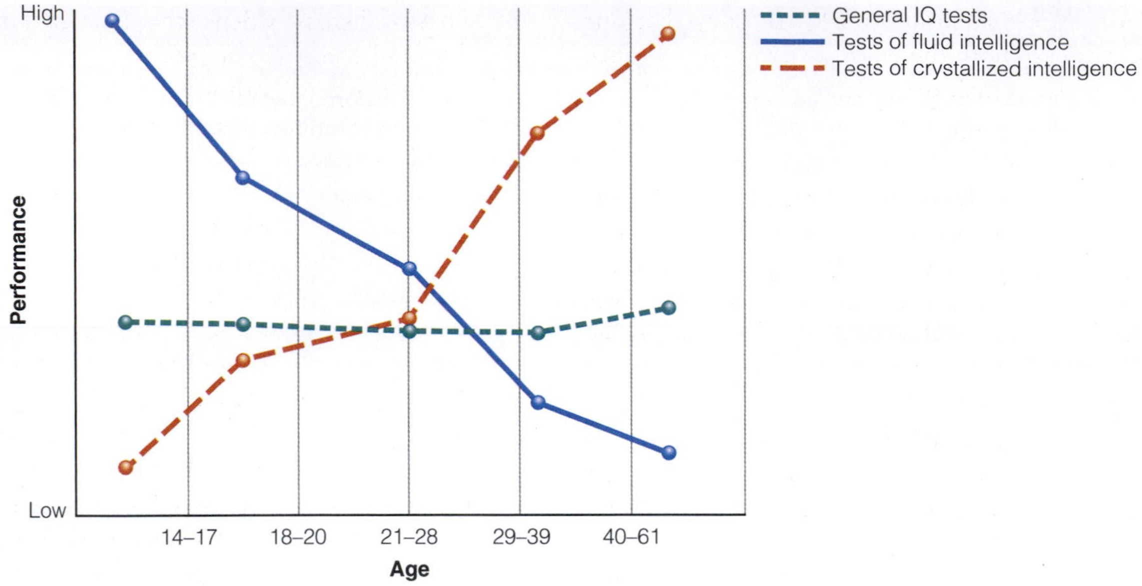

Figure 7.3 Performances on tests used to define fluid, crystallized, and general intelligence, as a function of age.

Source: Horn, J. L. (1970). Organization of data on life-span development of human abilities. In L. R. Goulet & P. B. Baltes (Eds.), *Life-span Development Psychology: Research and Theory* (p. 463). Copyright © 1970 by Academic Press, reproduced by permission of the publisher.

differences in fluid intelligence remain relatively uniform over time, individual differences in crystallized intelligence increase with age, mainly because maintaining crystallized intelligence depends on being in situations that require its use (Horn, 1982; Horn & Hofer, 1992). For example, few adults get much practice in solving complex letter series tasks such as the one on page 219, so individual difference tends to be minimal. But because people improve their vocabulary skills by reading and they vary considerably in how much they read, individual differences are likely to increase.

Neuroscience Research and Intelligence in Young and Middle Adulthood

As you might suspect from Chapters 2 and 6, considerable research shows specific areas in the brain are associated with intellectual abilities, and developmental changes in these areas are related to changes in performance. As described in Chapter 2, the parieto-frontal integration theory (P-FIT) proposes intelligence comes from a distributed and integrated network of neurons in the parietal and frontal lobes of the brain. In general, P-FIT accounts for individual differences in intelligence as having their origins in individual differences in brain structure and function. The P-FIT model has been tested in several studies. Results support the theory when measures of fluid and crystallized intelligence are mapped to brain structures. There are certain general processes and regions of the brain related to intelligence, but there is no specific area of the brain that corresponds to specific abilities, rather unlike the specializations of brain regions for each of our senses (e.g., vision, hearing, smell) (Basten & Fiebgach, 2021; Basten et al., 2015; Pineda-Pardo et al., 2016).

A second theory of intelligence grounded in neuroscience evidence is based on how efficiently the brain works (Di Domenico et al., 2015; Frith et al., 2021; Kievit et al., 2016; Langer et al., 2012; Zuo et al., 2020). The **neural efficiency hypothesis**, states intelligent people process information more efficiently, showing weaker neural activations in a smaller number of areas than less intelligent people. Research evidence is mounting that this idea holds merit: with greater intelligence does come demonstrably increased efficiency in neural processing. However, how this neural efficiency develops is not yet known, nor are its developmental pathways understood.

It is clear neuroscience and related research on intelligence will continue to provide many insights into the bases for both the development of fluid and crystallized intelligence as well as provide an understanding of individual differences in each. As neuroimaging and other techniques continue to improve, it is likely that our understanding of both the brain structure–intelligence relations as well as their development will improve.

Moderators of Intellectual Change

Based on the research considered thus far, two different general developmental trends: there are gains in experience-based processes but losses in information-processing abilities. The continued growth in some areas is viewed as a product of lifelong learning. The losses are viewed as an inevitable result of the decline of physiological processes with age.

Most researchers, though, emphasize individual differences in the rate of change in intellectual aging (Aron et al., 2022; Baltes et al., 2006; Schaie, 2008; Willis & Schaie, 2021). Their point is that each person has an individualized pattern of change in intellectual abilities over time. They argue there are many reasons besides age that explain performance differences. In this section, we explore some of the social and physiological factors proposed as modifiers of intellectual development. These include cohort differences, education level, social variables, personality, health and lifestyle, and relevancy and appropriateness of tasks.

Cohort Differences. Do the differences in intellectual performance obtained in some situations reflect true age-related change or mainly cohort, or generational, differences? This question gets right to the heart of the debate over interpreting developmental research on intelligence (Salthouse, 2019). On one hand, dozens of cross-sectional studies document significant differences in intellectual performance with age. On the other hand, several longitudinal investigations show either no decrement or even an increase in performance (Salthouse, 2014; Schaie, 2005, 2008, 2011; Zelinski et al., 2009).

A difficulty of figuring out whether cohort effects underlie differences in intelligence is ensuring that the contents of the tests transcend generations. For example, if a test included considerable information about how to use the latest social media platform or understanding emerging words or acronyms, younger generations would likely outperform older generations. But we should not conclude from those findings that intelligence declined significantly across generations because the skills or knowledge tested was biased in some way. This issue, of course, is the same as finding that one sociocultural group scores higher or lower than another—we cannot conclude anything about true differences if there is evidence that the tested material is biased toward one group or another.

If we are dealing with reasonable comparability in tests across generations, one reasonable hunch would be that people who are repeatedly tested in a longitudinal study build up practice over the sessions, so at least part of the explanation why longitudinal research provides more favorable assessments of performance could be related to practice effects. Salthouse (2019) argues that this is, indeed, the case, at least up to age 65.

Another way to resolve the discrepancy involves comparing data collected over long periods of time from several samples of people born in the same cohort but tested for the first time at different ages and analyzed simultaneously in both cross-sectional and longitudinal designs as discussed in Chapter 1 (Salthouse, 2014, 2019). When this is done, the results indicate part of the apparent decline with age in performance on intelligence tests may reflect generational differences rather than age differences (Salthouse, 2014; Schaie, 2005, 2011; Zelinski et al., 2009). These trends reflect better education opportunities, healthier lifestyles, better nutrition, and improved health care with more recently born cohorts overall.

The complex pattern of cohort differences indicates that interpreting data from cross-sectional studies is difficult. Recall from Chapter 1 cross-sectional studies confound age and cohort; and because there are both age- and cohort-related changes in intellectual abilities, drawing any meaningful conclusions is nearly impossible. Schaie (2005, 2008, 2011) argues the trends that indicate a leveling off of cohort differences may come to a halt in the 21st century. This conclusion is supported by a study of 531 adult parent–offspring pairs indicating generational (cohort) improvements were becoming smaller for more recently born pairs (Schaie et al., 1992, 2005, 2011).

Information Processing Factors. Several researchers suggest general processing constraints that occur with aging (discussed in Chapter 6) may underlie declines in fluid intelligence abilities with age (von Krause et al., 2020; Zimprich & Martin, 2002, 2009). For example, evidence suggests speed accounts for much of the age-related decline in both fluid and crystallized mental abilities beginning in middle age. Similarly, working memory decline with increasing age accounts for poor performance on the part of older adults when the tasks involve coordinating both new incoming information and stored information such as those found in the fluid and/or mechanic component of intelligence. Finally, evidence suggests the inability to inhibit actions and thoughts or to avoid interference typically found in older adults may also account for efficient functioning in fluid and/or mechanic abilities.

Sociocultural and Lifestyle Variables. Numerous sociocultural and lifestyle variables have been identified as important correlates of intellectual functioning. Think for a minute about the kind of job you currently have or would like to get. What kind of intellectual skills does it demand? What similarities or differences are there between your chosen job (e.g., school counselor) and a different one (say, accountant)?

An interesting line of research concerns how the differences in cognitive skills needed in different occupations make a difference in intellectual development (Bowlus et al., 2016; de Grip et al., 2008). To the extent a job requires you to use certain cognitive abilities a great deal, you may be less likely to show declines in them as you age.

Other social demographic variables implicated in slower rates of intellectual decline include a higher socioeconomic status, exposure to stimulating environments, access to and utilization of cultural and educational resources throughout adulthood, and not feeling lonely (Aron et al., 2022; Krinsky-McHale & Silverman, 2022). For example, research examining social relationships suggests that poor social relationships are associated with more rapid cognitive decline (Sharifian et al., 2022). We will explore this phenomenon in more detail in Chapter 11.

Shapecharge/E+/Getty Images

People in cognitively demanding jobs may be less likely to show noticeable declines in cognitive functioning with increasing age.

Although it would seem logical to suggest that years of formal education and other lifestyle factors should predict intellectual functioning, formal education, per se, does not, and clear conclusions on other lifestyle factors are elusive (Hertzog et al., 2009; Opdebeeck et al., 2016; Zahodne et al., 2011).

Personality. Several aspects of personality have been proposed as important for understanding intellectual change. Similar to research we examined in Chapter 6 on memory, one of these aspects concerns self-efficacy (Hayslip & Cooper, 2012; Šatienė, 2015). Older adults perceive what they do to help maintain their intellectual abilities can make a difference. Specifically, high initial levels of fluid abilities and a high sense of internal control led to positive changes in people's perceptions of their abilities; low initial levels led to decreases in perceptions of ability and behavior (Lachman & Andreoletti, 2006).

Positive beliefs and attitudes also have important indirect effects on cognitive enrichment. This indirect effect is reflected in the influence of these beliefs and attitudes on desirable behaviors such as exercise and mental stimulation known to be associated with enrichment effects on intelligence (Hertzog et al., 2009). Research indicates people with flexible attitudes at midlife tend to experience less decline in intellectual competence than people who are more rigid in middle age (Lachman, 2004; Willis & Boron, 2008).

Related to this idea connecting flexibility and intellectual competence is emerging evidence that being open to experiences, a key personality trait we will examine more closely in Chapter 9, helps buffer declines in fluid intelligence because people who are more open receive more environmental stimulation, which in turn helps develop crystallized intelligence (Ziegler et al., 2015). Ziegler and colleagues (2015) propose this as the Openness-Fluid-Crystallized-Intelligence (OFCI) model.

In Chapter 8, we will consider the concept of *emotional intelligence* and consider how people use their knowledge of their own and others' emotions to guide their thinking and behavior.

Health. The most obvious relationship between health and intelligence concerns the functioning of the brain itself. We noted in Chapter 2 several normative changes in brain structure with age affect functioning. We also noted in Chapter 6 how brain injuries, nutrition, and other factors can also affect functioning. Diseases such as dementia wreak havoc in the brain, and others, such as cardiovascular disease, cancer, and diabetes, can have serious negative effects directly and indirectly through medication side effects.

Cardiovascular disease and its implications for intellectual functioning have been studied extensively. These diseases are linked to a pattern of cognitive impairment that researchers suggest is related at least in part to vascular disease that selectively affects the prefrontal cortex (Spiro & Brady, 2008). An extensive longitudinal study of over 20,000 people (average age of 63 years) in the United Kingdom (Morys et al., 2021) showed that obesity in midlife and beyond is linked to increased inflammation, high levels of cholesterol and/or triglycerides (see Chapter 3), hypertension (see Chapter 3), and diabetes (see Chapter 4). In turn, hypertension and diabetes were related to cerebrovascular disease, which was associated with changes in brain structure and cognitive deficits.

As noted in Chapters 3, 6, and 14, physical exercise has considerable benefit. In this context, exercise helps maintain cognitive fitness as well as slow down cognitive decline once it has begun (Amoyal & Fallon, 2012; Aron et al., 2022; Hernandez et al., 2022; Law et al., 2014). In a study of 228 older adults (ages 60–80) who showed no signs of atypical cognitive performance, Burzynska and colleagues (2020) showed that time spent daily in moderate to vigorous physical activity was positively related with fluid abilities (i.e., perceptual speed and reasoning), a common finding in the research literature. These activities focus on overall fitness and health, and we know that basic brain functions respond well to aerobic exercise, for instance (refer to Chapter 2). Interestingly, they also found that people spending more time sedentary performed better on vocabulary knowledge and reasoning tasks. This finding is not as surprising as it seems; the types of cognitive activities associated with increasing one's vocabulary and reasoning skills are most often performed when reading, doing puzzles, and similar activities.

The relation between health and intellectual functioning is perhaps no clearer than in the concept of *terminal decline* (Cowl, 2016). **Terminal decline** is the gradual decline in cognitive function that occurs relatively near death. Even in the absence of dementia and other major physical and mental health factors, decline in intellectual abilities is a significant predictor of mortality (Connors et al., 2015; Karr et al., 2018). Yet, establishing broad connections between cognitive decline and death does not answer the next question of what, specifically, is going on? Answering that question was the aim of the research conducted by Aichele and colleagues (2016) that is highlighted in the How Do We Know? feature.

Modifying Primary Abilities

Older adults do not perform as well on tests of some primary abilities as younger adults, even after taking the moderators of performance into account (Schaie, 2005). In considering these results, investigators began asking whether there was a way to slow down or even reverse the declines. As we have reviewed, there has been much research examining the effects of lifestyle, health, and personality, among other variables, on intelligence.

Pursuing this issue further, we need to ask several questions regarding whether training can reduce any of the established age-related declines. Are the age-related differences remaining after cohort and other effects are removed indicators of real decline that cannot be reversed, or might these differences be reduced or even eliminated if older adults are given appropriate training? Can we really modify adults' intelligence? This again addresses the important issue of plasticity in intellectual functioning, one of the life-span tenets discussed in Chapter 1.

The most common training research focuses on those intellectual abilities that constitute primary mental abilities, especially those clustered into fluid intelligence. These are the intellectual abilities, such as speed of processing, most likely to decline with age. It turns out that middle-aged and older adults can be successfully taught to increase their speed of processing, and this training transfers to tasks not included in the training sessions (Cândea et al., 2015; Simpson et al., 2012). Additional discussion of memory-related training techniques is in Chapter 6. Research investigating whether brain stimulation might enhance the effects of cognitive training has shown mixed results, with brain stimulation having limited benefit in most studies (Brambilla et al., 2021). These results imply that cognitive training itself has positive benefits during the training sessions to reduce age differences.

Two large-scale projects examined training of primary abilities over extended periods of time. These projects adopt the view that aging in healthy adults has great potential for cognitive growth (Looi et al., 2016; Lövdén et al., 2012) and associated positive structural changes in the brain (Walhovd et al., 2016), with the research largely being conducted within the Selective

How Do We Know?

Think Fast, Feel Fine, Live Long

Who was the investigator and what was the aim of the study? Much research shows a relation between cognitive ability and the risk of dying. However, this connection is complicated because differences in cognitive ability and the risk of dying are both related to various physiological conditions, functional ability, psychological factors, and social support. To begin to unravel these complex relations, Stephen Aichele, Patrick Rabbitt, and Paolo Ghisletta (2016) examined a large set of health, well-being, and cognitive variables over a long period of time.

How did the investigator measure the topic of interest? Five areas of cognitive abilities were assessed:

- fluid intelligence (logic, arithmetic, number series, and verbal and visual object comparisons),
- crystallized intelligence (two vocabulary tests),
- verbal memory (free recall, cumulative recall, and delayed recall),
- visuospatial memory (picture recognition, memory for objects, and recall of shapes and their locations), and
- processing speed (visual search, alphabet coding, and semantic reasoning).

Participants gave subjective ratings of their general health status, the number of prescribed medications they took daily, sleep patterns, number of hobbies, hours per month in which they engaged in 14 different activities (e.g., housework, driving, exercise), degree of difficulty encountered in 12 different daily life activities (e.g., climbing stairs, cooking), and number of weekly social interactions. Medical status was also assessed through a comprehensive checklist of 195 total medical and psychiatric behaviors and symptoms. Mortality was measured through publicly available death records.

Who were the participants in the study? Data came from 6,203 participants in the Manchester Longitudinal Study of Cognition (MLSC) in the United Kingdom. At the time of their initial assessment, participants ranged in age from 41 to 96. All participants were screened for severe visual or auditory impairments; those with difficulties corrected by eyeglasses or hearing aids were allowed to participate. Information about participant mortality between 1983 (the beginning of the study) and 2012 (the most recent update on survival) was obtained through public records.

What was the design of the study? The study began in 1983. The cognitive assessments were administered four times, with each testing 4 years apart. Participants were followed over a 29-year span (1983–2012) in terms of their survival. Thus, the study was a longitudinal design.

Were there ethical concerns with the study? Participants were volunteers and were provided informed consent, so there were no ethical concerns. Mortality data were collected through public death records.

What were the results? The primary data analyses focused on predictors of mortality risk. In all, 65 predictor variables were considered: demographic variables (8), tobacco and alcohol use (5), slope and intercept of cognitive abilities (10), slope and intercept of daily life measures (16), and slope and intercept of health data (26). Two sets of survival analyses were conducted. Results showed that being female, having better subjective health, and having smaller declines in processing speed with age were most strongly related to lower mortality risk. More years smoking was the strongest prediction of high mortality risk.

What did the investigators conclude? Aichele, Rabbitt, and Ghisletta examined more variables in relation to mortality risk over a longer period of time than had ever been done previously. After carefully examining 65 predictors over 29 years, they showed that two psychological factors, subjective ratings of health and processing speed, were better indicators of mortality outcomes in middle-aged and older adults than almost any other predictors examined. Because both can be measured easily and are valid across cultures, Aichele and colleagues argue that they might form the basis of easy screening measures for increased mortality risk.

Optimization with Compensation (SOC) framework described in Chapter 1. Let's find out what researchers discovered in Project ACTIVE.

Project ACTIVE. Sherry Willis has revolutionized our understanding of how far researchers can go to investigate the impact of training primary mental abilities. She designed a longitudinal research project named Advanced Cognitive Training for Independent and Vital Elderly (ACTIVE) to provide answers to key questions about whether the age-related changes observed in intelligence research were inevitable or could be modified through training (Rebok et al., 2014; Schaie & Willis, 2015; Willis & Schaie, 2009).

Begun in the mid-1990s, the ACTIVE study was the largest multicenter, randomized, controlled clinical research project that investigated the long-term effectiveness of cognitive training on enhancing mental abilities (memory, reasoning, and attention) and preserving instrumental activities of daily living (managing finances, taking medication, using the telephone, and driving) in older adults. Six centers across the eastern United States enrolled nearly 3,000 people initially. Participants underwent detailed assessments of mental and functional ability on multiple occasions over a decade of follow-up. The design of Project ACTIVE is depicted in Figure 7.4.

The ACTIVE project findings show cognitive training interventions improved mental abilities and daily functioning in older independent living adults, with evidence that the improvements lasted at least 10 years (Rebok et al., 2014). These findings were specifically the case for training in reasoning and processing speed; memory training did not have the same effects, particularly when participants showed signs of even mild cognitive impairment. For example, Edwards

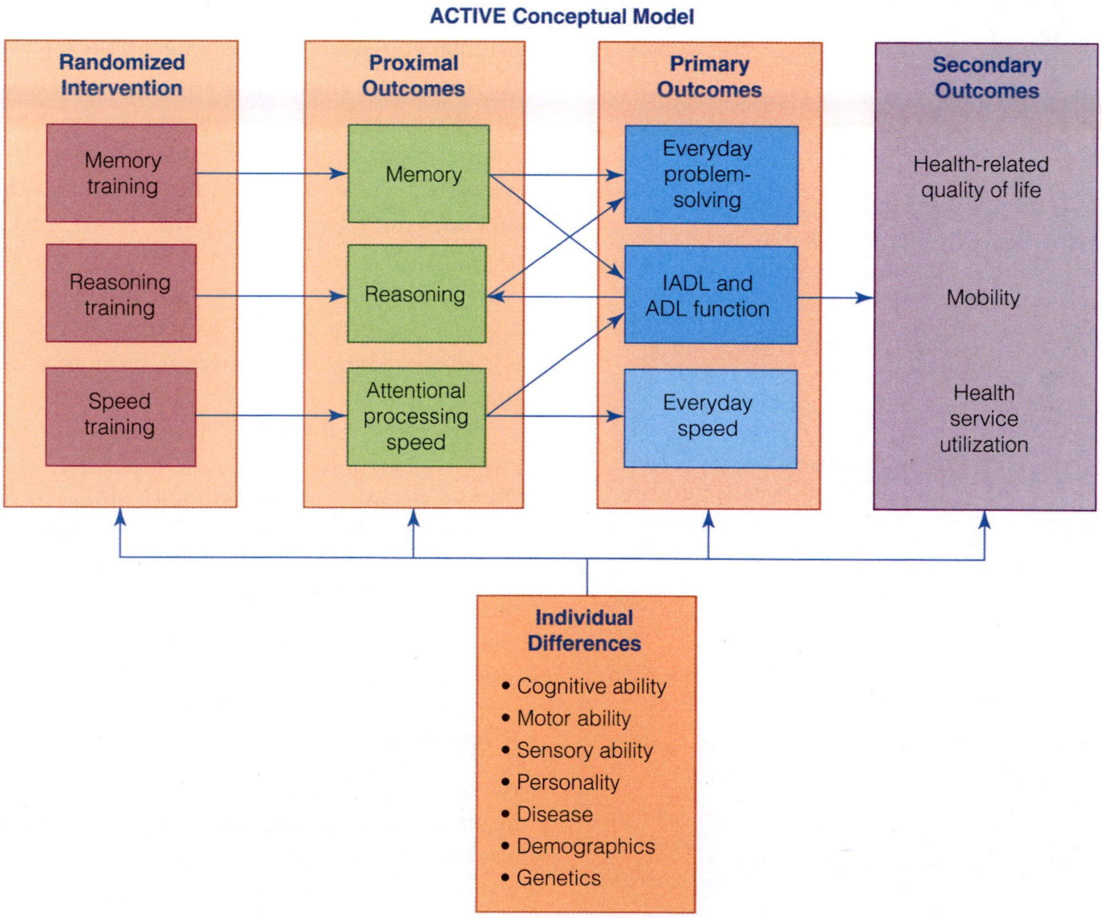

Figure 7.4 The design and conceptual model underlying Project ACTIVE.

Source: Unverzagt, F. W., Smith, D. M., Rebok, G. W., Marsiske, M., Morris, J. N., Jones, R., Willis, S. L., Ball, K., King, J. W., Koepke, K. M., Stoddard, A. & Tennstedt, S. L. (2009). The Indiana Alzheimer Disease Center's Symposium on Mild Cognitive Impairment. Cognitive training in older adults: Lessons from the ACTIVE Study. *Current Alzheimer Research, 6*, 375–383. https://www.ncbi.nlm.nih.gov/pmc/articles/PMC2729785/figure/F1/

and colleagues (2017) showed that speed of processing training (discussed in Chapter 6, and a process underlying fluid abilities) lowered the risk of dementia over a 10-year period by about 29%.

The results from Project ACTIVE indicate that declines in some fluid abilities may be modifiable to some extent. Perhaps the best news is the training effects of those abilities are relatively enduring. The less good news is that not all fluid abilities benefit from training, nor do the training effects generalize to nontrained abilities.

What do these findings mean? First, there is strong evidence in the typical course of aging that no one is too old to benefit from training, and that training reduces the rates of decline for some fluid abilities and may delay the onset of dementia. Second, transfer of training to abilities not trained is generally lacking unless training involves executive functioning and working memory, when the effects generalize to other tasks (Rebok et al., 2014). In sum, there is mixed news about the degree to which declines in fluid abilities can be slowed or reversed.

Adult Development in Action

If you were a director of a human resources department, how would the research on intelligence across adulthood influence your decisions about employee training programs?

Review Questions

7.2 Developmental Trends in Psychometric Intelligence

- What are primary mental abilities? Which ones have been studied most? How do they change with age?
- Define fluid and crystallized intelligence. How does each change with age?
- What factors moderate age changes in fluid and crystallized intelligence?
- What benefits do older people get from intervention programs aimed at improving fluid abilities? What training approaches have been used? How well do trained skills generalize?
- Are there any limitations on the extent to which older adults can improve their cognitive performance?

7.3 Qualitative Differences in Adults' Thinking

Key Questions

- What are the main points in Piaget's theory of cognitive development?
- What evidence is there for continued cognitive development beyond formal operations?
- What is the role of both emotion and cognition in cognitive maturity?

Eddie, a student at a local university, thought the test in the math course was unfair because the instructors simply marked the answers to complex problems right or wrong. Eddie complained that partial credit should be awarded for knowing how to set up the problem and being able to figure out some of the steps.

Although Eddie may not know it, this argument parallels one in the intelligence literature—the debate on whether we should pay attention mainly to whether an answer is right or wrong or to how the person reasons the problem through. The psychometric approach we considered earlier does not focus on the thinking processes underlying intelligence; rather, psychometrics concentrates on interrelationships among answers to test questions. In contrast, cognitive-structural approaches focus on the ways in which people think; whether a particular answer is right or wrong is not important.

We will consider theories that represent cognitive-structural approaches. First, we examine Piaget's theory as a foundation for this approach. Next, we explore the discussions concerning qualitative changes in thinking across adulthood, called postformal theory. These approaches postulate that intellectual changes are mainly qualitative, with the focus on the ways in which people think.

Piaget's Theory

According to Piaget (1970, 1980), intellectual development is adaptation through activity. We create the ways our knowledge is organized and, ultimately, how we think. Piaget believed development of intelligence stems from the emergence of increasingly complex cognitive structures. He organized his ideas into a theory of cognitive development that changed the way psychologists conceptualize intellectual development.

Basic Concepts. For Piaget, thought is governed by the principles of adaptation and organization. Adaptation is the process of adjusting thinking to the environment. Just as animals living in a forest eat food that is different from the food animals living in a desert eat, how we think changes from one developmental context to another. Adaptation occurs through organization; that is, how the organism is put together. Each component part has its own specialized function that is coordinated into the whole. In Piaget's theory, the organization of thought is reflected in cognitive structures that change over the life span. Cognitive structures determine how we think. It is the change in cognitive structures, the change in the fundamental ways we think, that Piaget tried to describe.

What processes underlie intellectual adaptation? Piaget defined two: assimilation and accommodation. **Assimilation** is the use of currently available knowledge to make sense out of incoming information. It is the application of cognitive structures to the world of experience that makes the world understandable. A child who knows only the word *dog* may use it for every animal encountered. So, when the child sees a cat and calls it a dog, the child is using available knowledge, the word *dog*, to make sense out of the world—in this case the cat walking across the living room. The process of assimilation sometimes leads to considerable distortion of incoming information, because we may have to force-fit it into our knowledge base. This is apparent in our tendency to forget information about a person that violates a stereotype.

Accommodation involves changing one's thought to make it a better approximation of the world of experience. The child in our example who thought cats were dogs eventually learns cats are cats. When this happens, the child accommodated their knowledge to incorporate a new category of animal.

The processes of assimilation and accommodation serve to link the structure of thought to observable behavior. Piaget believed most changes during development involved cognitive structures. His research led him to conclude there were four structures (i.e., four stages) in the development of mature thought: sensorimotor, preoperational, concrete operational, and formal operational. We consider the major characteristics of each stage briefly. Because we are most interested in Piaget's description of adult thought, we emphasize that.

Sensorimotor Period. In this first stage of cognitive development, intelligence is seen in infants' actions. Babies and infants gain knowledge by using their sensory and motor skills, beginning with basic reflexes (sucking and grasping) and eventually moving to purposeful, planned sequences of behavior (such as looking for a hidden toy). The most important thing infants learn during the sensorimotor period is that objects continue to exist even when they are out of sight; this ability is called object permanence.

Preoperational Period. Young children's thinking is best described as egocentric. This means young children believe all people and all inanimate objects experience the world just as they do. Young children believe dolls feel pain. Although young children can sometimes reason through situations, their thinking is not based on logic. A young child may believe that shaving causes the tap water to be turned on, because they always observe that shaving cream and the water being turned on always happen together.

Concrete Operational Period. Logical reasoning emerges in the concrete operational period. Children become capable of classifying objects into groups, such as fruits or vegetables, based on a logical principle; mentally reversing a series of events; realizing when changes occur in one perceptual dimension and they are compensated for in another, no net change occurs (termed conservation); and understanding the concept of transitivity (for instance, if $A > B$ and $B > C$, then $A > C$). However, children are still unable to deal with abstract concepts such as love; to children love is a set of concrete actions and not an ill-defined abstract concept.

Formal Operational Period. For Piaget, the acquisition of formal operational thought during adolescence marks the end of cognitive development. Because he argues formal operational thinking characterizes adult thought, we will consider this level in some detail. Piaget and other commentators (e.g., Lemieux, 2012) agree on four aspects of formal operational thought:

1. it takes a hypothesis-testing approach (termed hypothetico-deductive) to problem solving;
2. thinking is done in one framework at a time;
3. the goal is to arrive at one correct solution; and
4. it is unconstrained by reality.

Piaget describes the essence of formal operational thought as a way of conceiving abstract concepts and thinking about them in a systematic, step-by-step way. Formal operational thought is governed by a generalized logical structure that provides solutions to problems people have never seen and may never encounter. Hypothetico-deductive thought is similar to using the scientific method; it involves forming a hypothesis and testing it until the hypothesis is either confirmed or rejected. Just as scientists are systematic in testing experimental hypotheses, formal operational thinking allows people to approach problem solving in a logical, methodical way.

Consider the situation when your car breaks down. When you take it for repairs, the mechanic forms hypotheses about what may be wrong based on a description of the trouble. The mechanic then begins to test each hypothesis systematically. For instance, the compression of each cylinder may be checked, one cylinder at a time. This ability to hold other factors constant while testing a particular component is one of the hallmarks of formal operational thought. By isolating potential causes of the problem, the mechanic efficiently arrives at a correct solution.

When we use hypothetico-deductive thought, we do so to arrive at one unambiguous solution to the problem. Formal operational thought is aimed at resolving ambiguity; one and only one correct answer is the goal. When more than one solution occurs, there is a feeling of uneasiness and people begin a search for clarification. This situation can be observed in high school or college classes when students press their instructor to identify the "right" theory (from among several equally good ones) or believe there is only one "right" way to consider a social issue (such as equal justice). Moreover, when people arrive at an answer, they are quite certain about it because they believe they arrived at it through the use of logic. When answers are checked for "accuracy," the same logic and assumptions are typically used. That approach is fine, unless there is an error in the logic process which means the mistake is made repeatedly and never discovered.

Formal operational thinking knows no constraints (Piaget, 1970, 1980). It can be applied just as easily to real or imaginary situations. It is not bound by the limits of reality (Labouvie-Vief, 1980). Whether one can implement a solution is irrelevant; what matters is whether one can think about it. This is how people arrive at solutions to very complex problems, for example, such as eliminating the use of all fossil fuels within a short period of time. To the formal operational thinker, that this solution is impossible to implement quickly in the real world is no excuse—the solution is easily conceptualized, so it must be possible. The lack of reality constraints is not all bad, however. Creative innovation begins with reasoning from a "Why not?" perspective and may lead to the discovery of completely new ways to approach a problem or the invention of new solutions.

One serious problem for Piaget's theory is many adults apparently do not attain formal operations. Piaget (1972) himself admitted formal operations was probably not universal but tended to appear only in those areas in which individuals were highly trained or specialized. However, it also became evident that adults did not get stuck at the concrete operational level either. This inspired a search for figuring out how adults were thinking, and for the pathways of adult cognitive development.

Going Beyond Formal Operations: Thinking in Adulthood

Suppose you are faced with the following dilemma:

> You are a member of your college's or university's student judicial board and are currently hearing a case involving plagiarism. The student handbook states plagiarism is a serious offense resulting in expulsion. The student accused of plagiarizing in their paper admits copying verbatim from Wikipedia but says they have never been told they needed to use a formal citation and quotation marks. Do you vote to expel the student?

When this and similar real-world problems are presented to older adolescents and emerging and established adults, interesting differences emerge. Adolescents and younger emerging adults tend to approach the problem in formal-operational terms and point out the policy in the student handbook is clear and the student violated it, concluding the student should be expelled. Formal-operational thinkers are certain such solutions are right because they are based on their own experience and are logically driven (i.e., the policy states what plagiarism is and the penalty for it, the student plagiarized and admitted it, therefor the student must be expelled).

In contrast, many emerging and established adults (and most middle aged and older adults) are reluctant to draw conclusions based on the limited information in the problem, especially when the problem can be interpreted in different ways (Commons, 2016; Kallio, 2020; Sinnott, 2021). These adults point out there is much about the student we don't know: Have they ever

Kiattisakch/iStock/Getty Images

When confronted with real-world dilemmas, young adults think differently about them than middle-aged adults do.

been taught the proper procedure for using sources? Was the faculty member clear about what plagiarism is? For these adults, the problem is more ambiguous. They may eventually decide the student is (or is not) expelled, but they do so only after considering aspects of the situation that go beyond the information given in the problem.

Based on numerous investigations over many decades, researchers have concluded this different type of thinking represents qualitative changes beyond formal operations (King & Kitchener, 2015; Perry, 1970; Sinnott, 2014, 2021). Postformal thought is characterized by recognition that truth (the correct answer) may vary from situation to situation, solutions must be realistic to be reasonable, ambiguity and contradiction are the rule rather than the exception, emotion and subjective factors usually play a role in thinking, and principled thinking eventually results from careful analysis. In general, the research evidence indicates postformal thinking has its origins in young adulthood (King & Kitchener, 2015; Sinnott, 2014, 2021).

Several research-based descriptions of the development of thinking across adulthood have been offered. One of the best is the description of the development of reflective judgment, ways adults reason through real-life dilemmas such as life experiences, politics, identity issues, religion, science, personal relationships, and the like. Based on decades of longitudinal and cross-sectional research, King and Kitchener (2015) refined descriptions and identified a systematic progression of reflective judgment in young adulthood. A summary of these stages is discussed in Table 7.2.

The first three stages in the model represent prereflective thought. People in these stages typically believe that all problems have a clear and absolutely correct answer. For example, a student pressuring their instructor for the "right" theory to explain human development reflects this stage. People in these stages are also likely to hold firm positions on controversial issues and do so without acknowledging other people's ability (or right) to hold a different (but nevertheless equally logical) position.

Table 7.2 Description of the Stages of Reflective Judgment

Prereflective Reasoning (Stages 1–3): Belief that "knowledge is gained through the word of an authority figure or through firsthand observation, rather than, for example, through the evaluation of evidence. [People who hold these assumptions] believe that what they know is absolutely correct, and that they know with complete certainty. People who hold these assumptions treat all problems as though they were well-structured" (King & Kitchener, 2004, p. 39). *Example statements typical of Stages 1–3:* "I know it because I see it." "If it's on Fox News it must be true."
Quasi-Reflective Reasoning (Stages 4 and 5): Recognition "that knowledge—or more accurately, knowledge claims—contain elements of uncertainty, which [people who hold these assumptions] attribute to missing information or to methods of obtaining the evidence. Although they use evidence, they do not understand how evidence entails a conclusion (especially in light of the acknowledged uncertainty), and thus tend to view judgments as highly idiosyncratic" (King & Kitchener, 2004, p. 40). *Example statements typical of stages 4 and 5:* "I would believe in climate change if I could see the proof; how can you be sure the scientists aren't just making up the data?"
Reflective Reasoning (Stages 6 and 7): People who hold these assumptions accept "that knowledge claims cannot be made with certainty, but [they] are not immobilized by it; rather, [they] make judgments that are 'most reasonable' and about which they are 'relatively certain,' based on their evaluation of available data. They believe they must actively construct their decisions, and that knowledge claims must be evaluated in relationship to the context in which they were generated to determine their validity. They also readily admit their willingness to reevaluate the adequacy of their judgments as new data or new methodologies become available" (King & Kitchener, 2004, p. 40). *Example statements typical of stages 6 and 7:* "It is difficult to be certain about things in life, but you can draw your own conclusions about them based on how well an argument is put together based on the data used to support it."

Real People

Thích Nhất Hạnh

Thích Nhất Hạnh was born in central Vietnam in 1926. He entered Tù Hiếu Temple, in Hue city, as a novice monk at the age of 16. As a young bhikshu (monk) in the early 1950s he was actively engaged in the movement to renew Vietnamese Buddhism. He was one of the first bhikshus to study a secular subject at the university in Saigon, and one of the first six monks to ride a bicycle.

As his work to renew Vietnamese Buddhism progressed, Thích Nhất Hạnh began demonstrating that his typical mode of thought was at the highest level of reflective judgment. He rejected the traditional notion that one had to choose between a life of contemplative prayer and meditation and a life of work among the people. Instead, he saw a better, higher way when war enveloped Vietnam in the 1950s and 1960s. He led a movement that combined the contemplative life meditating in the monasteries with helping those suffering under the bombings and turmoil of war. This movement became "engaged Buddhism." At that time, he also founded the School of Youth and Social Service, a grassroots relief organization of 10,000 volunteers based on the Buddhist principles of nonviolence and compassionate action, along with Vạn Hạnh Buddhist University in Saigon, La Bọi publishing House, and an influential peace activist magazine. In 1966 he established the Order of Interbeing, a new order based on traditional Buddhist Bodhisattva precepts. During a visit to the United States in 1966, he met with Dr, Martin Luther King, Jr., who joined him in a call for an end to all hostilities in Vietnam. For that, both North and South Vietnam's governments denied him the right to return to his home country, an exile that lasted 39 years.

Thích Nhất Hạnh then moved to France, where he taught at the Sorbonne. Most important, he established Plum Village in 1982, now the largest Buddhist monastery in a Western country, with over 200 resident monks. Plum Village has enabled Thích Nhất Hạnh to spread his code of globalized ethics in daily life, which he terms "The Five Mindfulness Trainings" of Reverence for Life, True Happiness, True Love, Loving Speech and Deep Listening, and Nourishment and Healing (Hạnh, 2009). Based on the Buddha's teachings on the Four Noble Truths and the Noble Eightfold Path, the Five Mindfulness Trainings cultivate the insight of interbeing, or Right View, which can remove all discrimination, intolerance, anger, fear, and despair.

Reuters/Alamy Stock Photo

Thích Nhất Hạnh

From the 1980s, Thích Nhất Hạnh founded numerous monasteries and schools worldwide and taught hundreds of thousands of people how to live mindfully. He suffered a debilitating stroke in 2014 and moved permanently to Tù Hiếu Temple, bringing his mission full circle.

There is no doubt that Thích Nhất Hạnh embodied the essence of the highest level of reflective judgment. He guided his life on principles of doing the highest good for the most people and enacting the Golden Rule in all situations. Despite having been exiled from his home country for decades, he held no ill will, and returned when given the opportunity. His mission until his death in 2022 was to bring peace and awareness and to help people understand that how they behave has deep consequences on and for others.

About halfway through the developmental progression in the model, thinking shifts significantly again to reflect "quasi-reflective" thinking. In Stages 4 and 5, people are likely to say nothing can be known for certain and to base their conclusions on the current situation and the personally experienced evidence. In other words, knowledge is quite subjective; there is no universal "truth." People are also less persuasive about their positions on controversial issues; for instance, they might say, "Each person is entitled to their own view; I cannot force my opinions on anyone else."

As people continue their development into Stages 6 and 7, they shift again to show true reflective judgment. In these stages, there is clear evidence of understanding that people construct knowledge through careful analysis of the problem or situation using evidence and analysis of multiple perspectives. This allows them to once again hold firm convictions, but these are now reached only after careful consideration of several points of view, and they must continually reevaluate their beliefs as new evidence becomes available.

Even though people are able to think at complex levels, do they? Not usually (King & Kitchener, 2004, 2015; Sinnott, 2014, 2021). Why? Mostly because the environment rarely provides the supports necessary for using one's highest-level thinking, especially for issues concerning knowledge and experience you already have. People may not always purchase the product with the least impact on the environment, such as a fully electric car, even though philosophically they are strong environmentalists, because recharging stations are currently not widely available. However, if pushed and if given the necessary supports (e.g., easily available charging stations), people more readily demonstrate a higher level of thinking.

There are some people, though, who routinely demonstrate consistent thinking at the highest level. They typically take a nonviolent approach to life's challenges and use higher order understanding of collective good as the basis for making decisions—a principle similar to that noted by Mr. Spock and Captain James T. Kirk, that "the needs of the many outweigh the needs of the few, or of the one" (from the 1982 film *The Wrath of Khan*).

As noted in the Real People feature, Thích Nhất Hạnh (1926–2022) is one such person. Along with the Dalai Lama, Thích Nhất Hạnh is one of the most important Buddhist spiritual leaders of the 20th and 21st centuries. He founded what is known as the engaged Buddhism movement. Also known as socially engaged Buddhism, the engaged Buddhism movement refers to a Buddhist social movement that emerged in Asia in the 20th century, composed of Buddhists who are seeking ways to apply the Buddhist ethics, insights acquired from meditation practice, and the teachings of the Buddhist dharma to contemporary situations of social, political, environmental and economic suffering, and injustice. His life is a living example of Stage 7 in the reflective judgment model.

Integrating Emotion and Logic in Adult Thought

You may have noticed that a hallmark of postformal thinking is the movement from thinking "I'm right because I've experienced it" to thinking "I'm not sure who's right because your experience is different from mine" to thinking "I hold this position because I have carefully thought it through from different perspectives." Problem situations that seemed very clear-cut in adolescence appear more complicated to adults; the "right thing to do" is much tougher to figure out.

In addition to an increased understanding there is more than one "right" answer, adult thinking is characterized by the integration of emotion with logic (Kallio, 2020; Labouvie-Vief, 2015). Labouvie-Vief (2015; Labouvie-Vief et al., 2009) describes this emotional development as paralleling intellectual development, demonstrating both gains and losses with increasing age. These parallel processes between cognition and emotion create tension, resulting in the cognitive-emotional integration and interplay that middle-aged and older adults use to resolve real-life problems.

As they mature, adults tend to make decisions and analyze problems not so much on logical grounds alone as on combined pragmatic and emotional grounds. Rules and norms are viewed as relative, not absolute. Mature thinkers realize thinking is an inherently social enterprise that demands making compromises with other people and tolerating contradiction and ambiguity. Deciding what principles will guide one's life, then, is a result of these cognitive-emotional processes and involves careful analysis of multiple perspectives.

A good example of this developmental shift is the difference between how late adolescents or emerging adults view an emotionally charged issue—such as unethical behavior at work—compared to the views of established and middle-aged adults. Emerging adults may view such behavior as completely inexcusable, with firing of the employee an inescapable outcome. Established and middle-aged adults may take unstated contextual factors into account and consider what factors may account for the person's behavior. Some might argue this is because the topic is too emotionally charged for adolescents and emerging adults to deal with intellectually whereas established and middle-aged adults are better able to incorporate emotions into their thinking.

As people grow older, two things happen in terms of the integration of emotion and thought (Labouvie-Vief, 2015). First, the rich emotional experiences people have accumulated can be brought to bear in situations that are not too difficult in terms of cognitive demands, meaning that in these situations older adults have an easier time than other adults at integrating emotions and thought. In contrast, when the demands of the situation are great, the arousal that is created narrows their ability to bring emotions to bear.

Neuroimaging Evidence. We noted in Chapter 2 that important changes occur in the brain beginning in emerging adulthood. Evidence from neuroimaging research indicates emotion and logic processing become integrated in adults (Gu et al., 2013; Schurz et al., 2021). This integration occurs in the prefrontal cortex and the anterior insula (an area of the brain deep inside the cortex). Additional research indicates the amygdala (another structure deep in the middle of the brain) is also involved in processing emotion, which is also integrated with thought.

The existence of certain neural pathways associated with cognition-emotion integration can be used as a baseline for understanding what happens when the neural connections are altered or absent. Research evidence is now clear that these interconnections are different in some types of mental disorders (Anticevic et al., 2012; Hamilton et al., 2015, Vucurovic et al., 2020). This means intellectual and emotion processing pathways are similar in adults without mental disorders but display alternative pathways in adults who experience mental disorders.

The integration of emotion with logic that happens in adulthood provides the basis for decision making in the personal and sometimes difficult arenas of love and work that we examine in detail in Chapters 11 and 12, respectively. It also provides the basis for broader perspectives about life, and the ability to consider or understand positions on or interpretations of issues and ideas different from one's own.

Adult Development in Action

For what types of jobs would an assessment of psychometric intelligence be more appropriate than an assessment of reflective judgment? What about the other way around?

Review Questions

7.3 Qualitative Differences in Adults' Thinking

- What are the key concepts in Piaget's theory?
- What is reflective judgment? What are the stages in its development? What are absolutist, relativistic, and dialectical thinking?
- How do emotion and logic become integrated in adults' thought?

7.4 Decision Making and Everyday Cognition

Key Questions

- What are the characteristics of older adults' decision making in daily life?
- What age differences have been found in practical problem solving?

Kim is an 82-year-old in a quandary. On the table are the results of medical screenings indicating that her leg problems are now sufficiently severe that driving is not an option anymore. Because there is no public transportation available nearby, Kim realizes moving to a different place has to happen. But where? Lots of information and options have been offered. But how will the decision be made?

So far, our consideration of intellectual abilities includes examinations of how people's performance on standardized tests and their modes of thinking differ with age. But what we have not considered in detail is how people actually use their intellectual abilities in everyday life: dealing with multiple sources of input, balancing multiple tasks, solving everyday problems, making critical healthcare and related decisions, among other things. This situation is illustrated in Kim's quandary of what to do now that independent living isn't the best option.

What we discovered in this chapter to this point is people's fluid intelligence, the infrastructure on which many cognitive processes are built, shows several areas of decline; crystallized intelligence, reflecting life experience, continues to grow (or at least not decline) until much later in life; and some hallmarks of adults' thinking at an integrated level include going beyond the obvious information and integrating emotion and logic.

One might expect, then, the ability to make decisions and solve real-life problems may show a complicated developmental trajectory. Are these expectations correct? Let's find out.

A first step is to put several things into context. To be sure, there are many age-related declines in basic cognitive and sensory mechanisms. Yet there are age-related increases in experience that continue to build semantic memory and crystallized intelligence, as well as postformal thinking. These differing perspectives show why it is very important to consider the functional context of everyday life before we draw definitive conclusions about the developmental trajectory of cognition through adulthood. For one thing, even though older adults may experience declines in certain aspects of memory, they may have sufficient skills and knowledge adequate for tasks in their daily lives. Let's explore this distinction first in the area of everyday decision making.

Decision Making in Daily Life

People make hundreds of decisions every day. Most are rather mundane, such as whether to have jam on one's breakfast toast. Others are much more consequential, such as choosing a treatment option for a recently diagnosed cancer. How we make these decisions is grounded in the basic cognitive processes we considered in Chapter 6, including the various processing heuristics and biases that cause us to completely miss or fail to critically evaluate key pieces of information. Age differences on these underlying processes provide a preview of what happens in decision making across adulthood. On top of this, rapidly changing information presents profound challenges at simply keeping up, regardless of one's age. Whether the information one is attempting to sort through and understand is even reliable (i.e., from a trustworthy source) adds even more complexity.

We'll approach decision making first from a general processing perspective. We'll then go deeper by focusing on three areas of complex decision making: health care, financial matters, and quality of life. We'll then step back and consider how factors such as emotion and personal satisfaction with the decision options play important roles.

At first glance, research on decision making suggests older adults make less effective decisions (Bailey et al., 2021; Besedeš et al., 2012; Strough et al., 2015). For example, older adults use less optimal strategies when deciding what options to select to best meet their needs. When decision making involves a high degree of working memory capacity (e.g., lots of separate pieces of information must be held in memory simultaneously in order to make quick decisions), older adults do not perform as well (consult Chapter 6 regarding working memory). However, many everyday decision-making situations do not necessarily involve short time constraints. Real-world decisions often provide opportunities to seek advice from others, another way to bolster or compensate for changing aspects of cognitive processes. More time means that older adults have the possibility of using means that support working memory (e.g., writing down summaries of options to help keep track of information). This would help mitigate the age-related declines found in laboratory research. This is one example of why we must be cautious about immediately generalizing results from lab research to behavior in everyday life. Let's examine these factors in a few common decision-making situations to find out the circumstances that determine the presence or absence of age differences.

A common decision-making situation involves choosing one best option from a number of choices. These situations range from deciding which cereal option at the supermarket is best, to assessing automobiles for future purchase (Lambert-Pandraud et al., 2005), to choosing a treatment approach for breast cancer (Meyer et al., 2007), to financial planning (Hershey et al., 2015). Interestingly, research findings are quite comparable across numerous types of decisions involving these kinds of choices. Older adults search for less information in order to arrive at a decision, require less information to arrive at a decision, tend to avoid risk in decision making, and rely most on easily accessible information (Shivapour et al., 2012; Sunderaraman et al., 2021). Overall, adults of all ages tend to use gist information (the "bottom line") rather than verbatim information (the details), with this tendency increasing significantly with age (Nolte et al., 2022).

These tendencies help us understand how older adults make decisions. Let's consider this process in a situation that requires a complex and deeply personal decision—chronic renal (kidney) disease. Roughly 25% of patients whose disease has progressed to end stage renal disease (ESRD) are older adults. In ESRD, the kidneys have ceased to function, and patients must decide what to do next. The ultimate goal for ESRD patients is to minimize the complications including death and promote quality of life (Filho et al., 2022). Kidney transplantation as an option is limited by surgical suitability and is not widely available, so dialysis

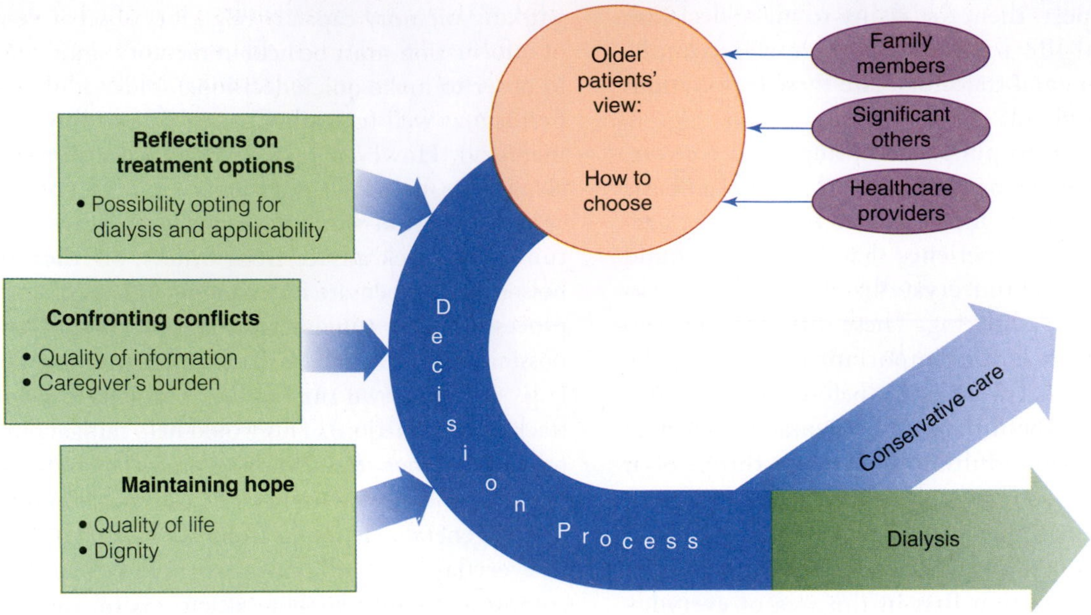

Figure 7.5 Conceptual model of older patients' decision-making process in choosing dialysis or conservative care using meta-ethnography.

Source: Kim, E. Y., & Son, Y.-J. (2022). Developing a conceptual model of older patients' decision-making process in choosing dialysis or conservative care using meta-ethnography. *Journal of Advanced Nursing, 78,* 1–13. https://doi.org/10.1111/jan.14945

may be the only realistic and suitable choice (Ladin et al., 2017; McClure et al., 2017). However, many older patients with ESRD have multiple other health problems, increased dependency, and lower life expectancy when compared with younger patients (Kim et al., 2015; Ladin et al., 2017). As a result, some older adults opt for conservative care rather than dialysis (McClure et al., 2017; Oestreich et al., 2020). How do older adults make this decision?

Kim and Son (2022) conducted a thorough analysis of qualitative research examining how older adults made treatment decisions regarding their ESRD. Their analysis revealed that factors besides underlying cognitive processes were key. The processes they uncovered are described in Figure 7.5.

Older adults with ESRD may feel uncertain and confused about choosing between dialysis and conservative care. Before choosing dialysis or conservative care, the decision process of older patients with ESRD can be influenced by three key factors: (1) reflection on treatment options, (2) confronting conflicts, and (3) expectation of maintaining hope in later life. Regarding the reflection on treatment option, older adults with ESRD realistically compare what treatment options are possible and applicable to their current situation and take into account various existing barriers such as their physical and mental health status, the pros and cons of treatment modalities, access to necessary health care, catheter accessibility and feasibility, and transportation to hospitals. Regarding confronting conflicts, older ESRD patients may face some problems with or resistance from their family care providers, including the care providers' health and quality of life and caregiving burden due to patients' dependency due to their being in ESRD. In addition, older patients often feel overwhelmed by the amount of available information on treatment options. During the decision process, these patients in particular expect social support from their significant others (friends or other individuals with ESRD), renal health professionals, and family care providers. Regarding the expectation of maintaining hope in everyday life, older ESRD patients feel fear of becoming dependent on others as a consequence of the treatment option chosen or worry about dying if they do not choose dialysis. Eventually, older persons with ESRD decide on their preferred treatment option on the basis of which one has the best odds of helping the person spend quality time with loved ones and maximize their own quality of life.

As this example of healthcare decision making indicates, factors beyond underlying cognitive processes are crucial for understanding how older adults make decisions about treating disease. Other situations, though, reflect different factors and ways of handling incoming and information and previous knowledge. One of the most important of these concerns financial exploitation of older adults, as older adults are the target of many scams and are the group most susceptible to them (Lichtenberg, 2015, 2016a, 2016b; Lichtenberg et al., 2020; Spreng et al., 2021). In this case, it helps to consider the decision process from a neuroscience perspective to gain insights into how decisions get made

Neuroscience research shows that people's financial and memory awareness (metamemory—discussed in Chapter 6) are associated with the thickness of the same right-hemisphere temporal lobe regions, pointing to a common brain structure related to multiple types of awareness (Sunderaraman et al., 2021). These results agree with the research on brain regions underlying financial exploitation (i.e., the right-hemisphere temporal regions). For example, research has found that for older adults who demonstrate no signs of dementia, changes in these brain regions were associated with susceptibility to financial scams (Han et al., 2016; Lamar et al., 2020; Spreng et al., 2017). Based on these findings, one can speculate that decreases in self-awareness, and financial awareness in particular, may be an important process by which vulnerability to exploitation arises, especially when the decision hinges on issues or topics about which the person has less knowledge or experience (Lichtenberg et al., 2020; Spreng et al., 2021). In contrast, when decision making taps into relevant experience or knowledge, older adults tend to be just as effective or better in making decisions as younger adults. Experience and knowledge tend to make older adults less susceptible to irrational biases in their decision making in comparison to younger adults, and these components can be trained (Hess et al., 2013; Lichtenberg, 2016a, b; Zaval et al., 2015).

The finding about the importance of prior knowledge or experience relates to fluid and crystallized intelligence. That is, to the extent that decision involves areas in which prior knowledge isn't extensive or readily accessible makes a person rely more heavily on basic mental processing (fluid intelligence), which show age differences. On the other hand, when decision making can be more reflective and relies on acquired knowledge and experience (crystallized intelligence), age differences are much less likely (Zaval et al., 2015). Additionally, it may be that when older adults are aware that decisions are personally relevant, that awareness bolsters their attentional focus on important cues so that they are less susceptible to fraud and exploitation (Meyer et al., 2007; Zaval et al., 2015). We will return to the issue of financial exploitation in a different context as an indicator of elder abuse in Chapter 11.

Emotion also plays an important role in age differences in decision making. Negative emotions such as anger and fear can sometimes be evoked when making a decision. This happens especially with decisions that involve threat and are high in personal relevance and importance to the individual (Löckenhoff & Carstensen, 2007). In support of the idea that older adults are motivated to reduce the experience of negativity and enhance the experience of positivity (Carstensen & Mikels, 2005), research shows older adults focus more on positive information when making a health decision, for example (English & Carstensen, 2016; Löckenhoff & Carstensen, 2007). As noted earlier with respect to ESRD, older adults place emphasis on options that increase quality of life and the ability to continue being with loved ones. Interestingly, older adults focus more on positive information than younger adults do when making a decision only when they were asked to explicitly evaluate their options before making a choice (Glass & Osman, 2017; Kim et al., 2008). If not asked to do so, there are no age differences in decision making.

Going one step further, Kim and colleagues (2008) asked participants how satisfied they were with their decisions. For the older adult group asked to evaluate their options, their focus on the positive and satisfaction with their decisions remained high over 2 weeks. In other words, older adults' high level of satisfaction with their decisions increased and persisted over 2 weeks by simply asking them to spend a few minutes evaluating their options. This did not happen for younger adults. Kim and colleagues (2008) note that advertisements or interventions having a positive impact on one age group may have a completely different impact on another.

Finally, we noted earlier that older adults are more likely to be susceptible to scams. Based on decision-making research, are there ways to reduce this susceptibility? Perhaps. Most people are aware of artificial intelligence (AI) based spam detectors that block out fraudulent email, for example. In general, spam reviews operate by focusing on either the content of the message (AI-text) or on the behavior the reader is asked to perform (AI-behavior).

For instance, an AI-text review would flag a message that is identified as containing fraudulent information (e.g., the sender is a long-lost relative of the reader) whereas an AI-behavior review would flag a message asking the reader to deposit $50,000 into an account in another country with the promise of then sharing a multimillion-dollar lottery prize.

Xiang and colleagues (2022) compared younger and older adults in terms of credibility judgments of the two types of spam reviews. They found three important results: (1) nearly all the older participants reported that they trust the predictions of which messages were spam by the AI tools, but 48.7% of them said they would abandon AI when the AI prediction differed from their own judgment; (2) younger adults showed a higher trust in the AI-behavior tool than in the AI-text tool, especially when the AI tool detected more spam than they did; and (3) regardless of age and type of AI tool, participants perceived AI tools as better when AI tools outperformed participants by detecting unexpected spam reviews.

In sum, research on decision making indicates that underlying cognitive processes matter, but factors beyond that matter more in many situations, especially for older adults. The roles of prior knowledge, emotion, satisfaction derived from the choice, and so forth must therefore be considered when creating choices from which older adults need to choose.

Everyday Problem Solving

One of the most important ways people use their intellectual abilities is to solve problems they face in their lives. Think for a minute about everyday life and the number of problem-solving situations you encounter in school, on the job, in relationships, driving a car, and so forth. Each of these settings requires you to analyze complex situations quickly, to apply knowledge, and to create solutions, sometimes in a matter of seconds.

Some people tend to be better at dealing with certain problems more than with others. Why is that? One possible explanation has to do with the kinds of abilities we use regularly versus the abilities we use only occasionally, which roughly maps onto the kinds of practical problems we encounter routinely and more abstract ones we face in specialized situations, such as research labs. We might expect that adults should perform better on practical problems than on abstract ones like those typically used on standardized intelligence tests. Tests of practical problem solving would use situations such as the following (Denney et al., 1982): "Let's say that a middle-aged [person] is frying chicken in her home when, all of a sudden, a grease fire breaks out on top of the stove. Flames begin to shoot up. What should [the person] do?" (p. 116).

One way to assess practical problem solving is to create measures with clearly identifiable dimensions that relate to specific types of problems (Allaire, 2012; Gamaldo & Allaire, 2016; Zhang, 2020). This is what Diehl and colleagues (1995) did by creating the Observed Tasks of Daily Living (OTDL) measure. The OTDL consists of three dimensions that reflect three specific problems in everyday life: food preparation, medication intake, and telephone use. Each of these dimensions also reflects important aspects of assessing whether people can live independently, a topic we explored in Chapter 5. Diehl and colleagues showed performance on the OTDL is directly influenced by age, fluid intelligence, and crystallized intelligence and indirectly by perceptual speed, memory, and several aspects of health. These results provide important links between practical problem solving and basic elements of psychometric intelligence and information processing.

Additional research indicates basic measures of cognitive processing (e.g., inductive reasoning, domain-specific knowledge, memory, working memory, cognitive strategies), and motivation are related to everyday assessments of each of these abilities as they underlie daily activities (Allaire, 2012; Frank et al., 2016; Gamaldo & Allaire, 2016; Romero-Ayuso et al., 2021). Allaire and Marsiske (1999, 2002) concluded that everyday problems that reflect well-structured challenges from activities of daily living show a strong relationship to traditional psychometric abilities.

The search for relations between psychometric intelligence and practical problem-solving abilities is only one way to examine the broader linkages with intellectual functioning. It focuses on the degree of how everyday problem solving is a manifestation of the cognitive processes that make up intellectual abilities (Berg, 2008). However, recall that postformal thinking is grounded in the ways people conceptualize situations, not necessarily solve them. Indeed, much of the research that led to the discovery of postformal thought involved presenting adults with lifelike problems. This approach enlarges the scope of what we consider everyday problem-solving skills to include not just cognitive abilities but also social, motivational, and sociocultural factors influencing how we solve problems (Berg, 2008; Zaval et al., 2015). As a result, we know that because the underlying modes of thinking evolve across adulthood, the ways that people approach and solve problems does as well. Examples of this developmental process include political behavior, identity, and life problems (Cavanaugh & Cavanaugh, 2021; King & Kitchener, 2004, 2015; Sinnott, 2014, 2021)

Another important factor that influences the way we solve everyday problems is the context in which the problem occurs. Do we use the same approach when solving a family conflict between two siblings as we do when solving a conflict over the leading role in a project at work? The answer is "not usually" when we look at this issue in middle-aged and older adults. Interestingly, however, younger adults are more likely to use a similar strategy across problem-solving contexts: they are much more likely to take it upon themselves to fix the problem rather than look for alternatives, such as waiting to find out whether the problem resolves itself, or find another approach other than a direct attempt to solve the problem. Older adults, on the other hand, are more likely to vary their strategy given the problem-solving context. For instance, in interpersonal conflict problems (e.g., family conflict) older adults use more emotion-regulating strategies (i.e., managing their emotions) whereas in instrumental situations (e.g., dealing with defective merchandise) they use self-action strategies (return the product) (Blanchard-Fields et al., 1997). As we grow older and accumulate more everyday experience, we become more sensitive to the problem context and use strategies accordingly.

There are also individual differences in the way the same problem situation is interpreted. How individuals represent problems differs across sociocultural groups, for example, and could also vary across the life span as developmental life goals change (Berg et al., 1998). Berg and colleagues (Berg et al., 1998; Strough et al., 1996) find there are age differences in how individuals define their own everyday problems. Overall, middle-aged older adults define problems more in terms of interpersonal goals (e.g., getting along with a person or spending more time with an individual), whereas adolescents and young adults focus more on competence goals (e.g., studying for an exam or becoming skilled at a sport).

Furthermore, problem-solving strategies fit the problem definitions. Older adults tend to define problems more in terms of interpersonal concerns and subsequently report strategies such as regulating others or including others to address problems, whereas competence concerns result in strategies that involve more self-action. Along these lines Artistico and colleagues (2003) found older adults were more confident and generated more effective solutions to problems typical of the life stage of older adults. Finally, Blanchard-Fields, Mienaltowski, and colleagues (2007) found older adults were rated as more effective in their everyday problem-solving strategy use than younger adults across all types of problem situations.

Tetra Images/Getty Images

Solving family-related problems requires different approaches than solving problems at work.

The research on problem-solving strategies raises and interesting question—Are there ways to teach people with declining capacity to improve their ability to solve everyday problems? It appears there may be. Law and colleagues (2022) conducted an experiment examining the effectiveness of functional task exercise (an occupational therapy task), exercise training (aerobic and whole-body exercise), and cognitive training (attention, memory, executive function, visual perceptual function) on everyday problem-solving performance. They randomly assigned participants who were experiencing mild cognitive impairment to either the experimental group or the waitlist control group (individuals who were waiting to participate in the training program). Results showed that the functional task exercise training had the largest effect on problem-solving performance immediately following training and at a 5-month follow up. Cognitive training had no significant effect immediately following training, but did lead to higher problem-solving performance compared to the wait-list control group at the 5-month follow up. Physical exercise improved functional status but not problem-solving performance. Law and colleagues (2022) noted that functional task exercise could be an effective intervention to improve everyday problem-solving ability and functional status in older adults with mild cognitive impairment, with effects lasting a reasonable length of time.

What can we conclude from the research on practical problem solving? First, practical problem-solving abilities are multidimensional and may not interrelate strongly with each other across contexts and types of problems. Second, the developmental functions of these abilities are complex and may differ to the extent that they are grounded in different underlying abilities. Third, the relations between practical problem-solving abilities and psychometric intelligence are equally complex. Finally, the close connection between solving practical problems and emotion and motivation may prove fruitful in furthering our understanding of individual differences in abilities. In short, solving practical problems offers an excellent way to discover how all the topics we have considered in this chapter come together to produce behavior in everyday life. In this sense, they track the trajectories of the qualitative aspects of thinking as demonstrated in postformal thought.

Adult Development in Action

If you were a financial advisor, how would you structure conversations with older adults to help them protect themselves from online financial scams?

Review Questions

7.4 Decision Making and Everyday Cognition

- How do older adults differ from younger adults in everyday decision making?
- What are the developmental trends in solving practical problems? How does the emotional salience of problems influence problem-solving style?

7.5 Expertise, Lifelong Learning, Creativity, and Wisdom

Key Questions

- What is expertise? How does expertise develop across adulthood?
- How does lifelong learning relate to cognitive development across adulthood?
- What is creativity? What is the developmental trajectory of creative expression and output?
- What is wisdom? How is wisdom influenced by sociocultural factors?

Sonequa is a highly respected member of her neighborhood community. Most days, you'll find Sonequa seated on a lawn chair under the front awning of her row house, along with a few of her close friends. Other community members of all ages stop, often making it appear that they are just passing by so as not to be teased, to seek advice and counsel. Although the young people who do that appreciate and need the relationship, they are amazed that Sonequa is so smart about so many things. They wonder how that happened.

Most of us have encountered people who we look up to as having deep and extensive life experience. Like Sonequa, they seem incredible insightful and have perspectives on really complicated issues of life that we just don't. In some cultural traditions, such people are considered leaders or shamans. In others, they make up the elders, the group of people who provide guidance and strategic insights; many religious congregations, for example, are headed by elders. We may not live in those situations, but we still may have people in our lives who have experienced and understand things in ways that are deeper. We often term such people "experts" or "wise."

Similarly, we may experience great music, or murals on a building, or an incredibly delicious dish, and wonder how the person who made it found the inspiration to do something that hadn't been done before. Such creativity seems incredible, especially if we sense that our talents lie elsewhere. (The author of this book is in awe of people who can visualize and draw a huge mural on a building because he has difficulty drawing a stick figure.)

In this module we will consider what expertise, creativity, and wisdom entail. We'll uncover the role that lifelong learning plays in building up knowledge for these, whether the knowledge is about living and what life brings or about a specific topic. We will find out how each of these develops across adulthood. Let's turn our attention first to expertise.

Expertise

We noted earlier in this chapter that aspects of intelligence grounded in experience (crystallized intelligence) tend to improve throughout most of adulthood. From a real-world experiential perspective, each of us becomes expert at something important to us, such as our work, interpersonal relationships, cooking, sports, photography, or auto repair. In this sense, an expert is someone who is much better at a task than people who have not put much effort into it. We tend to become selective experts in some areas while remaining amateurs or novices at others.

What makes experts better than novices? It's how experts handle the problem (Ericsson & Towne, 2010; Hambrick et al., 2016; Meyers & Bal, 2022). For novices, the goal for accomplishing the activity is to reach as rapidly as possible a satisfactory performance level that is stable and "autonomous." In contrast, experts build up a wealth of knowledge about alternative ways of solving problems or making decisions. These well-developed knowledge structures are the major difference between experts and novices, and they enable experts to bypass steps needed by novices (Chi, 2006).

Experts don't always follow the rules as novices do; they are more flexible, creative, and curious; and they have superior strategies grounded on superior knowledge for accomplishing a task (Ericsson & Towne, 2010). Even though experts may be slower in terms of raw speed because they spend more time planning, their ability to skip steps puts them at a decided advantage. In a way, this represents "the triumph of knowledge over reasoning" (Charness & Bosman, 1990).

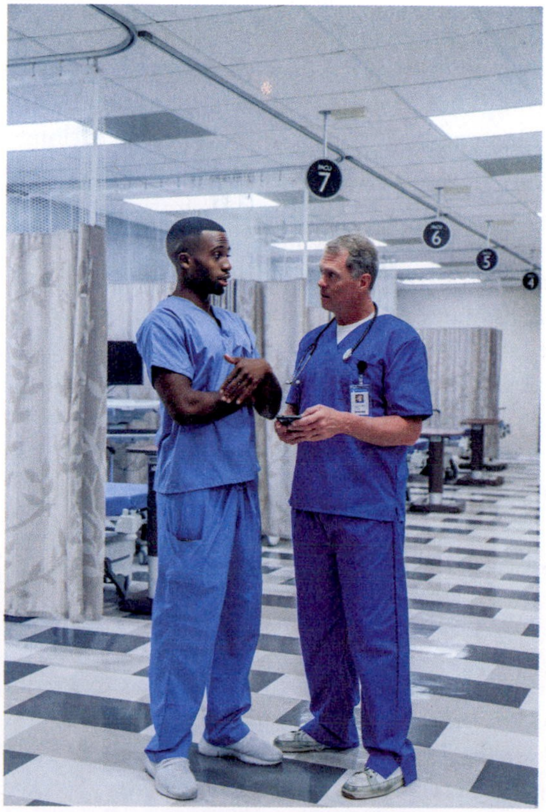

FS Productions/Tetra images/Getty Images

Experts in any field handle tasks in those fields differently than novices.

What happens to expertise over the adult life span? Research evidence indicates expert performance tends to peak by middle age and drops off slightly after that (Hertzog, 2020; Horn & Masunaga, 2006; Masunaga & Horn, 2001). However, the declines in expert performance are not nearly as great as they are for the abilities of information processing, memory, and fluid intelligence that underlie expertise, and expertise may sometimes compensate for declines in underlying cognitive abilities (Horn & Masunaga, 2006; Masunaga & Horn, 2001; Taylor et al., 2005).

Expertise serving to compensate for underlying declines in certain cognitive abilities is evident in a wide range of expert judgments, even in such things as how long certain figure skating maneuvers will take. Older people who were experts were as good as younger adults who were still skating at predicting the amount of time skating moves take (Diersch et al., 2012). Similarly, expert rock climbers were better than novices at accurately estimating whether they could perform certain actions (Whitaker et al., 2020).

These findings show that expertise provides ways to both process more complex information accurately and to compensate for a lack of raw cognitive speed and other age-related changes. Moreover, it appears knowledge based on experience is an important component of expertise. Indeed, researchers argue that people become "experts by experience" (Toikko, 2016). Expertise through experience is a frame used in numerous life situations, from medical expertise (Mazanderani et al., 2020) to being considered "streetwise" (Lindström & Rantanen, 2021). This research supports the selective optimization with compensation model (discussed in Chapter 1). That is, we decide (selective optimization) to become experts in some things and abandon the notion of becoming experts at other things (compensation). But this approach is predicated on the notion that people keep acquiring knowledge across adulthood. How do they do that?

Lifelong Learning

Many people work in occupations in which information and technology change rapidly. To keep up with these changes, many organizations and professions emphasize the importance of learning how to learn, rather than learning specific content that may become outdated in a couple of years. For most people, a college education will probably not be the last educational experience they have in their careers. Workers in many professions—such as medicine, nursing, social work, psychology, auto mechanics, and teaching—are required to obtain continuing education credits to stay current in their fields and maintain licensure. Online learning and the creation of microcredentials has made lifelong learning more accessible to professionals and interested adults alike (Council for Adult and Experiential Learning, 2021).

Lifelong learning is the way to approach the need for keeping active cognitively, and is viewed as critical part of cognitive fitness globally (Formosa, 2014; Molina & Schettini, 2021). In this sense, should lifelong learning be approached as merely an extension of earlier educational experiences? Knowles and colleagues (2020) argue teaching aimed at children and youth differs from teaching aimed at adults. Adult learners differ from their younger counterparts in several ways:

- Adults have a higher need to know why they should learn something before undertaking it.
- Adults enter a learning situation with more and different experience on which to build.
- Adults are most willing to learn those things they believe are necessary to deal with real-world problems rather than abstract, hypothetical situations.
- Most adults are more motivated to learn by internal factors (such as self-esteem or personal satisfaction) than by external factors (such as a job promotion or pay raise).

Lifelong learning is increasingly important, but educators need to keep in mind that people's preferred means of learning may change as people age. Effective lifelong learning requires smart decisions about how to keep knowledge updated and what approach works best among the many different learning options available (Knowles et al., 2020). Additionally, models of lifelong learning have incorporated research on age-related cognitive changes, ways in which artificial intelligence (AI) can tailor learning opportunities to the learner, and ways that online access to learning opportunities can help increase access to learners who have historically not had opportunities to reskill and upskill their knowledge (Fleming, 2021). We will return to the role of lifelong learning as a way to address people's employment needs in Chapter 12.

Based on the preceding discussion, you may have surmised that lifelong learning also plays a major role in the development of expertise. It does. For example, Johri (2022) points out that lifelong learning is central to developing expertise in engineering. Similarly, Jantzen (2022) argues the same point for nursing. Thus, expertise in every professional and technical area requires a process of lifelong learning in which the person is continually updating and refreshing their knowledge.

Lifelong learning can also be a powerful tool in addressing sociocultural issues in aging. For example, creating an age-friendly organization can be helped through lifelong learning that emphasizes the importance of multigenerational learning and transmission of knowledge (Heffernan et al., 2022). Additionally, the individuals' increasing transnational mobility and the multidimensional cultural representations and identities involved are leading to new paradigms such as the notion of transculturalism. **Transculturalism** involves exploring the impact of transnational migration on the mobile culture, identity, and integration of migrant populations spanning across several nations simultaneously (Guo & Maitra 2017).

Transculturalism represents a new way of being and learning where individuals interact with each other in a culturally dynamic environment. This requires the integration of new concepts and approaches in lifelong learning that promote active participation, adaptation and interaction. As a result, transcultural lifelong learning involves challenging our taken-for-granted frames of reference and expands our worldviews. Jurkova and Guo (2021) show how engaging in transcultural lifelong learning might serve as a catalyst for positive social change and transformation, and create a more inclusive environment for lifelong learning without opposing cultural, national, and ethnic binaries. This approach could open new horizons of cultural interaction and active participation in an increasingly diverse learning environment.

Creativity

What makes a person creative? Does creativity mean having accomplishments marked by precocity, innovation, and longevity? Is it connected to exceptional productivity?

It may surprise you to learn that there is no universally accepted definition of creativity. Some define creativity in adults as the ability to produce work that is novel, high in demand, and task appropriate; others

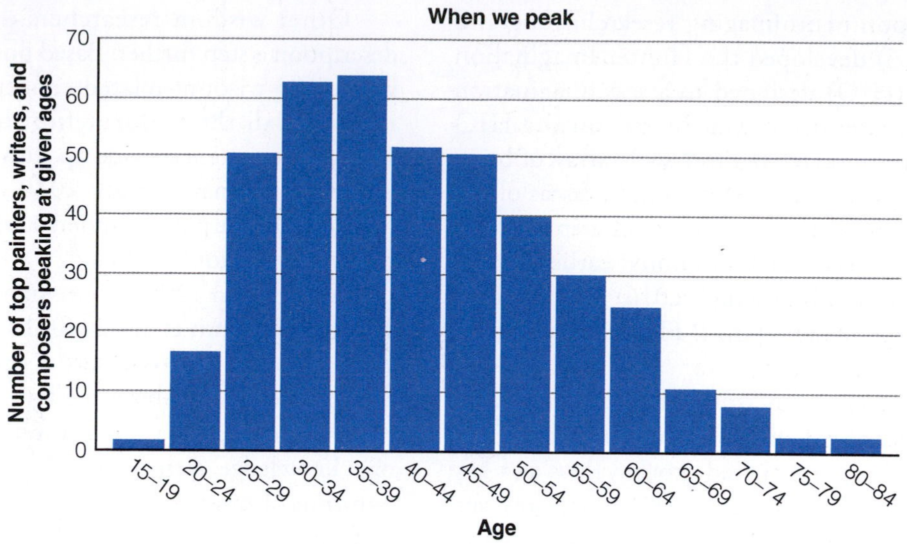

Figure 7.6 Age at which peak creative output was reached for painters, writers, and composers.

Source: https://img.washingtonpost.com/wp-apps/imrs.php?src=https://img.washingtonpost.com/blogs/wonkblog/files/2016/06/creative_age.png&w=1484

point to things that are potentially valuable improbable constructions; still others focus on the synergy of imagination, intention, and action (Brandt, 2021; Kaufman, 2016; Runco & Beghetto, 2019; Simonton, 2018). Creative output, in terms of the number of creative ideas a person has or the major contributions a person makes, varies across the adult life span and disciplines and shows a similar pattern across sociocultural groups (Fedyk & Xu, 2021; Franses, 2016; Hertzog, 2020; Kaufman, 2016; Kozbelt & Durmysheva, 2007; Simonton, 2018).

When considered as a function of age, if the primary criterion for "creativity" is the overall number of contributions a person makes that are generally considered "creative," that output tends to increase through one's 30s, peak in the late 30s to early 40s, and decline thereafter. A typical life-span trend is described for painters and composers in Figure 7.6.

The age-related decline from midlife on does *not* mean people stop being creative altogether, just that they produce fewer creative ideas than when they were younger (Damian & Simonton, 2015; Hertzog, 2020). For example, the age when people made major creative contributions, such as research that resulted in winning a Nobel Prize, increased throughout the 20th century (Jones, 2010), and the average age of winners of the Turing Award, the most prestigious and influential award in computer science, has risen from about 40 to about 70 (Jin et al., 2021). Even the average age at which entrepreneurs create successful companies, including in the tech industry, is at least 45 (Azoulay et al., 2020).

These data are clear. Creativity is not just about age—experience matters when it comes to innovation, whether in the form of realizing that the "old ways" are now insufficient or putting into perspective the knowledge gaps and knowing enough about how to fill them. Because creativity results from the interaction of cognitive abilities, personality, and developmental forces and is defined in ways other than the sheer number of "creative things" that people produce, creativity itself continues to operate throughout people's lives.

Exciting neuroimaging research is showing that creative people's brains work differently. For example, neuroimaging research indicates that creativity involves the static and dynamic reconfiguration of brain networks associated with complex cognitive processes (Heilman, 2016; Patil et al., 2021). This research supports the belief that creativity involves connecting disparate ideas in new ways, as different areas of the brain are responsible for processing different kinds of information. Because some of these brain structures tend to change with age, this finding also suggests there are underlying brain maturation reasons why different types of innovative thinking tends to occur at different points in adulthood.

Building upon neuroimaging research, Jung and colleagues (2016) developed the Hunter Imagination Questionnaire (HIQ) designed to assess imagination over time in a naturalistic way. Scores on the HIQ have been shown to be related to a wide array of brain volume in areas such as the hippocampus, areas of the frontal lobe, and other brain regions, and map onto the neuroimaging research outcomes noted earlier (Wertz et al., 2020). Jung and colleagues' (2016) research flows from the work that underlies the P-FIT model discussed in Chapter 2.

From a sociocultural perspective, creativity would seem to be a topic that lends itself to inclusivity in that the definition focuses on shared group values as a key factor in determining what is creative output. However, the field of creativity studies underrepresents—and often excludes—creators who have disabilities. The underrepresentation partly reflects an approach that pathologizes disability, which in turn results in the contributions of people with disabilities becoming invisible. People with disabilities participate in subcultures (e.g., deaf communities) and/or larger cultures (i.e., disability culture). Jones (2022) argues that creators with disabilities demonstrate that (a) members of disability culture experience the world in ways that generate creative expression; (b) encountering a world designed for abled bodies incites the creativity of disabled people; and (c) disabled and abled people collaboratively create. Similarly, Miron-Spektor and Paletz (2022, in press) point out that the increasing number of persons with multicultural backgrounds may require a rethinking of the meaning of creativity from a sociocultural perspective.

Wisdom

When you think about a "wise person," what special characteristics come to mind? Years of research using in-depth think-aloud interviews with young, middle-aged, and older adults about typical and unusual problems people face led Baltes and colleagues (Ardelt, 2010; Baltes & Staudinger, 2000; Scheibe et al., 2007) to describe four primary characteristics of wisdom:

- Wisdom deals with important or difficult matters of life and the human condition.
- Wisdom is truly "superior" knowledge, judgment, and advice.
- Wisdom is knowledge with extraordinary scope, depth, and balance that is applicable to specific situations.
- Wisdom, when used, is well intended and combines mind and virtue (character).

Other wisdom researchers decided to take this description a step further. Based on a survey of scientists who study wisdom-related concepts, and a thorough review of all the major definitions of wisdom over centuries, researchers came up with a consensus wisdom model (Grossmann et al., 2020.) The core aspect of wisdom, they argue, is understanding which action(s) fit which situation(s) at hand.

Grossmann (2017; Grossmann & Kung, 2019, 2020; Grossmann et al., 2020) has provided a detailed description of this consensus model. It emphasizes four characteristics about the knowledge that we use to reflect wisdom: (1) a recognition of the limits of one's own knowledge, termed "intellectual humility;" (2) recognition of others' perspectives and broader contexts than just the issue at hand; (3) uncertainty and change; and (4) the integration of different opinions and a preference for compromise. Taken together, these characteristics reflect *metacognition*, what we understand about our knowledge. In turn, metacognition helps implement our *moral aspirations*, which reflect our sense of fairness, justice, loyalty, and so forth. Grossmann and colleagues argue further that all of these characteristics are uniquely situated in each *culture*, and that there are few universally wise perspectives because situations calling for wisdom are all embedded in a particular cultural context. The basic model is also described in Figure 7.7.

Whether the understanding of what constitutes wisdom is the same across cultures is a matter of debate. There are some who would argue that wise people show similar characteristics across cultures; that is, they have insights about life and living that most people do not. Others disagree, and argue that the cultural context of wisdom matters a great deal. The Controversies feature delves into this issue in more detail.

As might be surmised from the Controversies feature, measuring wisdom turns out to be difficult (Glück, 2018). Current approaches emphasize the importance of real-life situations and giving people advice (reflecting a particular understanding of what "wisdom" represents). Interestingly, peer ratings of wisdom are better indicators of wisdom than self-ratings (Redzanowski & Glück, 2013). It appears people draw from a wide array of examples of wisdom (Weststrate et al., 2016) and are better at recognizing wisdom in others than they are in themselves. Perhaps it is better that way.

Sternberg and Karami (2021) combined all these threads of the various cultural understandings of wisdom and their measurement to create what they call the 6P model of wisdom. The model considers different

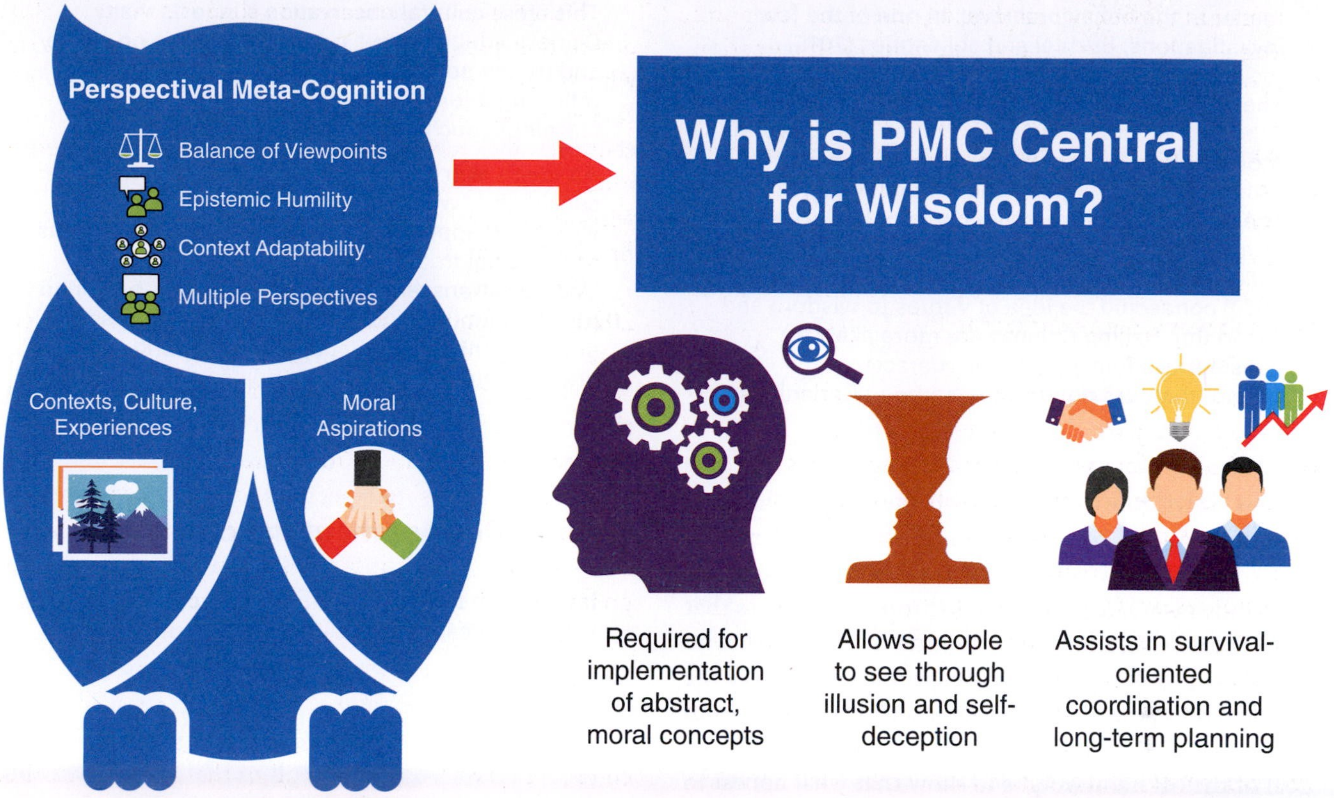

Figure 7.7 The common wisdom model, representing the consensus among empirical wisdom scientists. Central to wisdom are aspects of perspectival metacognition, which are grounded in moral aspirations and specific socio-cultural contexts and experiences.

Source: Grossmann, I., Weststrate, N. M., Ardelt, M., Brienza, J. P., Dong, M., Ferrari, M., Fournier, M. A., Hu, C. S., Nusbaum H. C., & Vervaeke, J. (2020). The science of wisdom in a polarized world: Knowns and unknowns. *Psychological Inquiry, 31,* 103–133, https://doi.org/10.1080/1047840X.2020.1750917. Figure 3, p. 110.

Controversies

Is Wisdom the Same Across Cultures?

"The concept of wisdom is ancient and deeply embedded in the cultural history of humanity" (Grossmann & Kung, 2019, 2020). Indeed, some of the oldest writings we have, as well as a significant proportion of texts considered sacred in many and varied religious traditions, are considered "wisdom literature." This widespread view of the centrality of wisdom as a desired virtue might lead to a conclusion that wisdom means the same thing across cultures. But is that so?

If we look carefully, we will discover that definitions of wisdom differ somewhat across cultures. For example, in Chinese, wisdom (智慧) concerns the integration of knowledge and intelligence, wit and brightness (Schroeter & Uecker, 2016a), whereas in Arabic, wisdom (حِكْمَة) implies prudence, insight, or a maxim (Schroeter & Uecker, 2016b). Western traditions emphasize the importance of intellectual humility which underlie two types of wisdom: sophia (σοφία)—the ultimate or divine knowledge about the true nature of things, and phronesis (φρόνησις)—the practical knowledge and rational thinking that promotes good character. In India, wisdom gives more emphasis to intuitive and personal experience, noninterference with the natural order of things, and benevolence or prosocial behavior (Grossmann & Kung, 2019, 2020).

Unfortunately, few cross-cultural studies have examined wisdom to gain insight about the extent to which these formal definitional differences

(Continued)

matter at the behavioral level. In one of the few investigations, Buchtel and colleagues (2015) focused on aspects of wisdom related to morality. They reported that, in comparison to Americans, Australians, and Canadians, Chinese adults were more likely to label behaviors that they perceived as harmless, yet highly "uncivilized" (e.g., to litter, to swear and curse loudly in public) to be immoral. In a subsequent study, Buchtel and colleagues (2017; cited in Grossmann & Kung, 2019, 2020) connected the idea of virtues to wisdom and found that Beijing Chinese are more likely to consider wisdom as virtuous character, a pattern that was not observed among Canadians. This cross-cultural observation suggests that Chinese adults place a greater emphasis on civility and proper social conduct as central to wisdom, reflecting a form of wisdom in Confucian teachings (Buchtel, 2020).

Although every culture has a concept of what is considered "wisdom," how that is demonstrated varies and appears related to deeply held religious and societal traditions. To the extent that these traditions transcend specific cultures, then overlap may be found in understandings of what wisdom entails. To the extent that the traditions and cultures are separate, those understandings will vary.

aspects of wisdom—starting with the *purpose* that wisdom is supposed to serve; the kinds of environmental *press* (discussed in Chapter 5) that instigate this purpose; the kinds of *problems* that arise through this press that require a wise solution; the attributes of the *persons* who face these problems; the *processes* people use to solve the problems; and the *products* or solutions that emerge from the application of these processes to the problem. The goal of the 6P framework is to show that what appear to be different and distinct models of wisdom are actually fairly consistent with each other. The 6P model suggests that different specific models of wisdom simply focus on different aspects of the phenomenon of wisdom. In some cases, they deal with different Ps within the 6P model, or they may deal with different foci of wisdom, such as personal versus general wisdom (Staudinger, 2019), or different kinds of wisdom.

Even with this blended model, though, Sternberg and Karami admit that the development course of wisdom remains unclear; about all that can be concluded is that wisdom increases through old age until disease processes intervene or cognitive decline becomes sufficiently significant.

Adult Development in Action

If you were the director of a senior center, how would you capitalize on the wisdom of your members?

Review Questions

7.5 Expertise, Lifelong Learning, Creativity, and Wisdom

- What is an expert? How is expertise related to age?
- How is lifelong learning related to expertise?
- What is meant by creativity? How does creativity change with age?
- How is wisdom defined? How is wisdom related to age?

Social Policy Implications

Is Cognitive Aging Preventable?

In the section discussing research on various types of cognitive training, evidence suggests that either a formal training program or a cognitively enriched lifestyle can positively influence intellectual change as we grow older. Additional evidence shows that the effects of this training may last as long as 10 years. Together, these findings show there is promise in developing long-term cognitive enrichment programs to reduce the rate of typical cognitive changes in older adults and to improve quality of life. For example, it may be the case we can defer the need for assisted living, improve well-being, and reduce healthcare costs as some of the collateral benefits of these training programs. As a result, projects aimed at training memory and other intellectual abilities in older adults have important public policy implications in terms of funding priorities and reducing the burden on public funding for the consequences of typical age-related cognitive changes. The long-term goals of projects such as ACTIVE are to increase the number of older adults who can age in place.

However, the level of concern over age-related cognitive decline, driven by stereotypes of aging, long-haul experiences of COVID-19 "brain fog," and personal factors, is quite high. These concerns have fueled the search for easier alternatives than weeks- or months-long training. The resulting market has fed the development of interventions that claim to delay or prevent these changes. However, close scrutiny of the claims reveals that at least some overstate the case. Two typical examples are Lumosity and Prevagen.

Lumosity was a very popular program focusing on memory and related cognitive abilities. It consisted of over 50 brain games that supposedly provide "exercise for your mind" if done for 15 minutes daily. The company could not show definitively that the program did what was promised. In 2016, Lumosity was found guilty in a U.S. District Court of making false claims. The Federal Trade Commission found that Lumosity's marketing "preyed on consumers' fears about age-related cognitive decline, suggesting their games could stave off memory loss, dementia, and even Alzheimer's disease" and settled for a $2 million fine and an agreement that customers would be notified about an easy way to cancel and avoid future billing (Federal Trade Commission, 2016).

Prevagen is a widely advertised over-the-counter (OTC) dietary supplement that claims to support brain health and boost memory. The most common version comes as once-daily oral capsules or chewable tablets. Each version contains 50 mcg (2,000 units) of vitamin D3 and either 10 mg, 20 mg, or 40 mg of apoaequorin, a protein found in certain types of jellyfish. Research on the actual efficacy in terms of rigorous clinical trials is lacking. Because the U.S. Food and Drug Administration does not evaluate dietary supplements, there is no official review. In laboratory experiments, apoaequorin acts similarly to a protein in our bodies called calmodulin, which is thought to play an important role in memory, although research evidence is limited.

One concern with placing apoaequorin in a capsule or tablet is that the protein may not be absorbed. That's because when you consume a protein by mouth, your stomach and pancreas quickly start working together to break it down and digest it. For apoaequorin to be absorbed effectively, it needs to get through this process without being digested. This is the reason why many actual protein medications are injectable only. The FTC also charged the makers of Prevagen with false advertising in 2012, but the case remains pending.

Hellmuth and colleagues (2019) made it clear what they thought of products like Lumosity and Prevagen that claim to ward off memory loss and even prevent dementia—they labeled it "pseudomedicine." They point out that "[p]atients and caregivers encounter sophisticated techniques that supply false "scientific" backing for brain health interventions" (Hellmuth et al., 2019, p. 543). To protect people from misleading claims and ineffective products, it will be critical for federal policy to be based on peer-reviewed, rigorous research including clinical trials examining the short- and long-term effects of well-designed cognitive training programs, dietary supplement, and other interventions. As we have learned, such research indicates that getting these outcomes is possible through regular exercise, healthy diet, and well-designed evidence-based cognitive training.

In Review

In creating your summary for Chapter 7, think of your paragraphs as moving from laying the foundation for understanding what intelligence is (the basic definitions of terms) and how researchers have studied it (e.g., the use of specific tests) to how people apply intelligence to everyday situations, act creatively, and appear wise.

Your first paragraph will focus on the basics: what intelligence is and how it is studied and measured. Your next paragraph will build on that—how the psychometric view of intelligence translates into how the pieces of intelligence are measured, what the different levels of intelligence are (primary abilities, secondary abilities), and what the issues are regarding fluid and crystallized intelligence. At each point, talk about the age-related trends and the factors that influence what those trends look like.

Your third paragraph will shift from the quantitative view of intelligence to a qualitative view in which *how* people think is the issue. What are the major theories and descriptions of the changes in modes of thinking across adulthood? How are logic and emotion integrated in adults' thinking?

For the fourth paragraph, summarize the various aspects of how decision making and everyday problem solving develop across adulthood. Include the interconnections of these with aspects of intelligence you summarized in the second paragraph.

The final paragraph should summarize what we know about expertise, lifelong learning, creativity, and wisdom. Include interconnections between expertise and lifelong learning. For creativity, point out concerns about the lack of focus on disability culture as an area of creative achievement. Especially for wisdom, include various definitions and the influence of culture.

Integrating Concepts in Development

- How are the primary and secondary mental abilities related to the aspects of information processing considered in Chapters 6 and 7?
- What do you think an integrated theory linking postformal thinking, practical problem solving, expertise, and wisdom would look like?
- What aspects of secondary mental abilities do you think would be most closely linked to expertise? Why?
- How does effective social cognitive functioning considered in Chapter 9 relate to wisdom-related behaviors?

Key Terms

accommodation Changing one's thought to better approximate the world of experience. 227

assimilation Using currently available knowledge to make sense out of incoming information. 227

cognitive-structural approach An approach to intelligence that emphasizes the ways people conceptualize problems and focuses on modes or styles of thinking. 215

crystallized intelligence Knowledge acquired through life experience and education in a particular culture. 219

factor The interrelations among performances on similar tests of psychometric intelligence. 217

fluid intelligence Abilities that make one a flexible and adaptive thinker, that allow one to draw inferences, and allow one to understand the relations among concepts independent of acquired knowledge and experience. 219

interindividual variability An acknowledgment adults differ in the direction of their intellectual development. 214

mechanics of intelligence The aspect of intelligence that concerns the neurophysiological architecture of the mind. 214

multidimensional The notion intelligence consists of many dimensions. 213

multidirectionality The distinct patterns of change in abilities over the life span, with these patterns being different for different abilities. 213

neural efficiency hypothesis States intelligent people process information more efficiently, showing weaker neural activations in a smaller number of areas than less intelligent people. 220

plasticity The range of functioning within an individual and the conditions under which a person's abilities can be modified within a specific age range. 213

pragmatic intelligence The component of intelligence that concerns acquired bodies of knowledge available from and embedded within culture. 214

primary mental abilities Independent abilities within psychometric intelligence based on different combinations of standardized intelligence tests. 217

psychometric approach An approach to intelligence involving defining it as performance on standardized tests. 215

secondary mental abilities Broad-ranging skills composed of several primary mental abilities. 218

structure of intelligence The organization of interrelated intellectual abilities. 217

terminal decline The gradual decline in cognitive function that occurs relatively near death. 223

transculturalism Involves exploring the impact of transnational migration on the mobile culture, identity, and integration of migrant populations spanning across several nations simultaneously. 240

Social Cognition

Chapter

8

Chapter Outline

Learning Objectives

After studying this chapter, you will be able to...

8.1. Describe age-related stereotypes and how they operate across adulthood.

8.2. Describe stereotype embodiment theory.

8.3. Describe age differences in social beliefs and how self-perception influences them.

8.4. Describe the primary components and processes in personal judgments.

8.5. Describe the components and processes involved in perceptions of personal control.

8.6. Describe the processes involved in emotional intelligence, impression formation, and social judgments.

8.7. Describe how attributional biases influence emotional intelligence, impression formation, and social judgments.

8.8. Describe the process of collaborative cognition and the social context of memory.

If there were any doubt that humans are social beings, the COVID-19 pandemic put an end to it. When lockdowns first occurred in March 2020, many assumed that introverts (people who tend to be shy and reticent, and who tend to need to be alone to recharge) would have an advantage over extraverts (people who prefer social interactions and engagements and get energized by them) in dealing with the social isolation. As logical as this may seem, the assumption turned out to be wrong. Research in Canada and Australia found that introverts actually had a harder time, and exhibited more mental health effects, with the lockdowns (Shokrkon & Nicoladis, 2021; Wei, 2020). This seemingly counterintuitive results were due to extraverts being better able to find alternative ways to connect, such as videoconference. The extraverts' advantage resulted in a more supportive activation of aspects of social cognition, the focus of this chapter.

The natural tendency of humans to seek social connections means that the social contexts in which we operate are intimately involved in our cognitive processes. This interaction is viewed in theory and research as social cognition. In short, **social cognition** involves how people process, store, and apply information about other people and social situations, and how cognition plays a role in social situations.

In this chapter, we take a deeper dive into how our basic cognitive abilities play out in our social cognitive processing. We examine how our past experiences and beliefs influence our social judgment processes such as how people make impressions and explain behavior (causal attributions). Finally, we examine four aspects of social cognition: the role of motivation and emotion as processing goals, the way stereotypes affect how we judge older adults' behavior, the amount of personal control people feel they have, and how cognition is affected when we communicate with others in a social context.

First, we need to highlight the importance of social-contextual aspects of cognition in terms of stereotypes. We will focus on stereotypes of older people as an example of how stereotypes operate. As noted in Chapter 1, we are confronted with images of older adults all the time through cartoons, advertisements for medical products, "jokes" on greeting cards, and art. Many of these images are ageist and negative (e.g., older adults are terribly forgetful, slow, and easily confused), but some are positive (e.g., older adults are wise). The impact of these stereotypes on our lives is more pervasive than you may think. We'll explore some of these influences.

Additionally, social cognition research raises important issues for research on aging more generally such as how our life experiences and emotions, as well as changes in our pragmatic knowledge, social expertise, and values, influence how we think and remember. To address these issues, we must consider both basic underlying cognitive abilities (identified in Chapters 6 and 7) and the functional applications of these processes in everyday cognition (discussed in Chapter 7). Even if basic underlying cognitive mechanisms decline (such as episodic memory recall or speed of processing), older adults still have the necessary social knowledge and skills that allow them to function effectively. In fact, by taking into consideration social and emotional factors, researchers find older adults' cognitive functioning often remains intact and may even improve across the life span (Blanchard-Fields et al., 2008; discussed in Chapters 6 and 7).

8.1 Stereotypes and Aging

Key Questions

- How does the content of stereotypes about aging differ across adulthood?
- How do younger and older adults perceive the competence of the elderly?
- How do stereotypes about aging unconsciously guide our behavior?

Manuel, aged 70, was getting ready to go home from a dominoes game at his friend's house. However, he could not find his keys. Down the street, Tomás, a 20-year-old college student, was ready to take his girlfriend home, but he could not find his keys. Each of their respective friends had different perceptions of Manuel and Tomás. Manuel's friends started to worry whether Manuel was showing signs of dementia, speculating it might be time for him to get a full medical evaluation. In contrast, Tomás' friends laughed and attributed his forgetfulness to being nervous with his girlfriend and being tired from long hours at work.

What accounts for these different explanations of losing one's keys for Manuel and Tomás? An explanation for the attributions Manuel's friends made involves a negative stereotype of aging, pervasive throughout our culture, that older adults are forgetful. Just peruse your local greeting card store and you will find supposedly "humorous" birthday cards capitalizing on our negative expectations about aging.

In contrast, the same behavior in Tomás, a young adult, holds very different meaning for most people; stress, preoccupation, lack of attention, anxiety, and other explanations are used. Rarely is the cause attributed to a young adult's potentially declining cognitive ability.

Fortunately, positive expectations about aging coexist with the negative ones, and stereotypes can be changed (Chonody, 2015; Levy et al., 2022). A complicating factor is that older adults are subjected to conflicting stereotypes. On one hand, older adults are portrayed stereotypically, for example, as grouchy, forgetful, and losing physical stamina and sexual abilities. On the other hand, older adults are also portrayed as wise, generous, and responsible. The important question researchers ask is what effect stereotypes of various sorts have on our social judgments and our behavior toward others, such as in Manuel's situation.

JGI/Tom Grill/Getty Images

Implicit stereotyping of people, such as of older adults, can have a profound effect on people's behavior.

Content of Stereotypes

Stereotypes are a special type of social knowledge structure or social belief that represent socially shared beliefs about characteristics and behaviors of a particular social group. We all have stereotypes of groups of people and beliefs about how they will act in certain situations, such as "Older adults are kind" or "Older adults repeat the same stories about their past."

These beliefs affect how we interpret new information about older adults. They are a type of cognitive heuristic or bias (discussed in Chapter 6). In other words, we use stereotypes to help us process information quickly and effortlessly when engaged in social interactions. In this case, we use stereotypes to size up people quickly when we first meet them. This categorizing helps us interpret why individuals behave the way they do and guides us in our behavior toward them. Remember, stereotypes are not inherently positive or negative. Stereotypes only become positive or negative when they take on these meanings because of the way they are used (e.g., as a slur or as a compliment) and influence our interpretation of incoming information. This will become more evident as we explore age-related stereotypes.

One area in which we use stereotypes is in judging how old we think someone is. For example, the ability to estimate the age of someone by seeing their face decreases as the age of the target face increases, but older adults are better than younger adults at judging older faces (Voelkle et al., 2012). In this context, a question arises: Does the ability to judge a person's age from their face differ culturally? It turns out it does, at least in judgments of a woman's age in various cultures. In a large cross-cultural study, Flament and colleagues (2021) photographed the faces of 1351 women, aged 18–80 years, from five countries (China, France, India, Japan, and South Africa). Fourteen to 24 facial signs (grouped under five clusters: wrinkles/texture, ptosis [drooping eyes]/sagging, pigmentation, vascular disorders, and cheeks/skin pores) were evaluated and rated by a panel of 15 experts and dermatologists using referential Skin Aging Atlases. Five nonexpert groups of 100 local women in each country rated the perceived age. Although perceived ages and actual ages were highly correlated, their differences varied according to country, particularly among Indian and South African women who were judged older than their actual age by about 5 and 7 years, respectively. Results also indicated that the clusters of wrinkles/texture and ptosis/sagging were predominant characteristics taken into account to varying degrees in almost all cultures, reaching nearly 100% in French women. Pigmentation was an important secondary factor in Japanese, South African, and Indian women. Regarding facial areas that drive aging perception, it seems the upper half of the face has prevalence for Chinese and Japanese women whereas the lower half of the face has major importance for South African women. Clearly, different cultures focus on different features when judging a person's age.

Much research has examined adult developmental changes in the content and structure of stereotypes. One focus of this research is on what happens when emerging adults are given the opportunity to actually interact with older adults (Levy et al., 2022; Obhi & Woodhead, 2016). From a developmental perspective, a key question is: Does the nature and strength of stereotypes typically change as we grow older, or does change require intentional intervention? Overall, the consensus is that adults of all ages have access to and use multiple stereotypes of older adults, even when they are self-referent, and that specific interventions are often necessary to change them (Levy, 2009; Levy et al., 2022; Tully-Wilson et al., 2021). Age-targeted stereotypes are pervasive and potent.

Other studies indicate that older adults identify more subcategories of age that fit under the superordinate category "older adult" than do younger and middle-aged adults, who tend to put everyone together in one category (Hayslip et al., 2013). Overall, these findings suggest that as we grow older, our ideas and age stereotypes become more elaborate and rich as we integrate our life experiences into our beliefs about aging (Baltes et al., 2006; O'Brien & Hummert, 2006).

Beyond the complexity of stereotypes, are there age differences in how negatively or positively people perceive older adults? Research indicates older adults in general have a more positive view of aging in comparison to younger adults (Tully-Wilson et al., 2021), a finding that holds cross-culturally, such as in Brazil (de Paula Couto & Koller, 2012).

But what if people believe the negative stereotypes and incorporate them into their personal belief structures about themselves? The outcomes are clear, and definitely not good. Much research indicates that believing negative stereotypes about age is a direct threat to cognitive performance and physical well-being and may exacerbate actual deterioration of key brain structures such as the hippocampus (B. R. Levy et al., 2016; Nelson, 2016a, 2016b). Specifically, believing aging stereotypes to be true reduces the will to live, impairs memory, reduces health promotion behaviors, lengthens the time it takes to recover from illness, increases cardiovascular reactivity to stress, and decreases longevity. How does this process of internalizing stereotypes happen? To answer this question, we turn to stereotype embodiment theory.

Stereotype Embodiment Theory

Stereotypes of older adults are presented to us our whole lives. It should not surprise you to learn that the more one is exposed to stereotypes, especially in the absence of information refuting them, the more likely it is that one will believe that the stereotypes are accurate. Thus, over a lifetime, it is highly likely that a person comes to believe as true at least some of the stereotypes of aging and of older adults that pervade society. As noted in the previous section, believing that the stereotypes of older adults apply to oneself has serious consequences that influence cognitive functioning and health.

At the point that age stereotypes become directed at oneself in old age, they are classified as self-perceptions of aging. People with more positive self-perceptions of aging have better functional health; some research found that they lived an average of 7.5 years longer than those with more negative self-perceptions of aging (Levy et al., 2002). Similar relations between age beliefs and long-term health have also been found in Europe and Asia.

To explain the process by which this pattern of findings regarding self-perceptions of aging, Levy (2009) proposed stereotype embodiment theory. **Stereotype embodiment theory** proposes that stereotypes in general, and aging stereotypes in the present case, become self-perceptions when they are assimilated from the surrounding culture into one's self-definitions that, in turn, influence functioning and health.

Stereotype embodiment theory has four components (Levy, 2009). The stereotypes (1) become internalized across the life span, (2) can operate unconsciously,

(3) gain salience by becoming self-relevant, and (4) utilize multiple cognitive pathways. Accordingly, these four components constitute a process that occurs in two directions: top-down (from culture and society to the individual) and over time (from childhood to old age).

Longitudinal research in the United States, Australia, Germany, Israel, and Switzerland all report the same outcomes regarding the consequences of self-perceptions (Tully-Wilson et al., 2021). More positive self-perceptions of aging were consistently associated with healthier longitudinal outcomes, including better self-rated health and less obesity, greater longevity, better performance of the activities of daily living, less depression, and better cognitive functioning (including reductions in cognitive decline and incidence of dementia). These were both direct and indirect effects and provide support for stereotype embodiment theory. Tully-Wilson and colleagues (2021) point out that the results have key public health implications about the benefits of positive self-perceptions of aging and in screening middle-aged adults with negative self-perceptions of aging to prevent future physical and psychological decline.

Stereotype embodiment theory is not limited to self-perceptions about aging. The same process can be used to understand how self-perceptions of race, ethnicity, gender, and other sociocultural characteristics can have very serious deleterious effects on individuals.

Stereotype Activation

From the preceding discussion we know that stereotypes about aging are pervasive, get incorporated into self-perceptions, and influence our judgments about our capacities, our health, and our future cognitive performance. However, it is not enough to know that stereotypes exist and the outcomes they create. We need to know under what conditions they are activated. How do negative stereotypes of older adults influence our behaviors (e.g., using inappropriate speech, as described in Chapter 5)? Considerable research in social cognition focuses on stereotype activation as a relatively unconscious and automatic process that guides our behaviors and social judgments in a wide variety of settings (e.g., Kunda & Spencer, 2003; Levy, 2009; Loe et al., 2016). We can use the topics of implicit stereotyping and perceived competence as examples of how the process works.

Implicit Stereotyping. Social psychologists suggest the reason stereotypes are automatically activated is they become overlearned and thus are spontaneously used when we encounter a member or members of a stereotyped group, such as older adults (Proctor, 2016; Stojnov, 2013). The activation of strong stereotypes, called **implicit stereotyping**, is not only automatic but also unconscious. Thus they usually influence our behavior without our being aware of it, and constitute a type of cognitive heuristic or bias (discussed in Chapter 6).

The effects of such implicit stereotyping are illustrated in a clever and classic study conducted by John Bargh and colleagues (Bargh et al., 1996). They demonstrated if you subliminally (outside of conscious awareness) prime young people with the image of an elderly person, the young people's actual behavior is influenced in an age-related manner (where age-related refers to the target person's age). In this case, the implicitly primed young adults walked down the hall more slowly after the experiment than did young adults who were not primed with the elderly image. This is a powerful demonstration of how our stereotypes of aging can influence our behavior without our being aware of it.

Measuring implicit aging stereotyping is a challenge because by definition it is inaccessible. However, research using a technique called the Implicit Association Test (IAT; Hummert et al., 2002; Teiga-Mocigemba et al., 2010) overcame this challenge. Let's consider how the IAT works when applied to aging (Crisp & Turner, 2012). Individuals are asked to categorize photographs of faces by indicating as fast as they can whether the photo is a younger or older person. They are asked to press a button with their right hand to indicate young and with their left hand to indicate old. Then they categorize other photographs as pleasant or unpleasant with the right hand indicating pleasant and the left hand indicating

Renate Wefers/EyeEm/Getty Images

How people judge the age of this person differs across several factors, as described in the text.

unpleasant. Next is the two-part test of implicit aging stereotypes. Part one consists of a combination of the young–old and pleasant–unpleasant categorization task using the same hands as just indicated. In this test, the right hand is associated with both young and pleasant, whereas the left hand is associated with both old and unpleasant. The second part reverses the hands for young–old. Now the right hand is associated with old and the left hand is associated with young. The right hand is still associated with pleasant, and the left hand with unpleasant. The logic is this: If you have a negative implicit stereotype regarding aging, you will be much slower in your response during the second test. It becomes difficult to use your right hand to indicate old because it is also associated with pleasant. This difficulty slows your response down.

Using this methodology, researchers (Crisp & Turner, 2012; Hummert et al., 2002) found people of all ages were faster to respond to young–pleasant and old–unpleasant trials than to old–pleasant and young–unpleasant trials. Furthermore, all individuals had implicit age attitudes that strongly favored the young over the old.

Based on these and related results, Crisp and Turner (2009) created an intervention strategy to help people change their implicit stereotypes—the imagined intergroup contact. The strategy is deceptively simple. Imagine yourself having a positive interaction with a member of a group about whom you hold negative stereotypes. There's more to it in actual practice, but essentially it is a focused, guided imagination strategy. Does it work?

A meta-analysis (a research technique discussed in Chapter 1) of the research using the imagined intergroup contact strategy focused on four indicators: attitudes, emotions, intentions, and behaviors (Miles & Crisp, 2014). The meta-analysis revealed significantly reduced bias across all four indicators. Two other findings were interesting: the more participants were asked to elaborate on the context in which their imagined interaction took place, the stronger the results, and the effects overall were greater for children than for adults. The results demonstrate clearly that even though we are unaware of them, implicit stereotypes can be changed if we imagine ourselves having different kinds of interactions with the target groups, though the older we get, the more cognitive effort this takes.

Age Stereotypes and Perceived Competence. Stereotypes are not simply reflected in our perceptions of what we think are the generally representative traits or characteristics of older adults. We also make appraisals or attributions of older adults' competence when we observe them perform tasks, and we assess whether we can count on them to perform important tasks. No area is more susceptible to negative stereotyped attributions of aging than memory competence, as the vignette at the beginning of the section describes. As noted in Chapter 6, people of all ages believe memory declines with age and that we have less and less control over current and future memory functioning as we grow older. We also know that this perception is not true as stated—but is believed anyway.

This raises an interesting question: How does this strong stereotypic belief in age-related loss of memory affect our attributions (explanations) about older adults' competencies? In an elegant and classic series of studies, Erber and Prager (1999) found an age-based double standard in judging the competence of old versus young adults. The **age-based double standard** operates when an individual attributes an older person's failure in memory as more serious than a memory failure observed in a young adult. If an older person, such as Manuel in the opening vignette, cannot find their keys, this is evaluated as a much more serious memory problem (e.g., possibly attributed to dementia) than if a younger person, such as Tomás, cannot find their keys. The age-based double standard is most evident when younger people are judging the memory failure.

In contrast, when older people observe the same memory failure, they tend to judge both young and old targets of the story more equally. In fact, most of the time older adults are more lenient toward memory failures in older adults. However, in other types of competence judgments, older adults also display the age-based double standard. When assessing the *cause* of a memory failure, both younger and older people felt the failure was due to greater mental difficulty in the case of an older adult, whereas the memory failure for a younger adult is attributed to a lack of effort or attention (Erber et al., 1990).

The research on the age-based double standard parallels works examining other aspects of aging stereotypes focused on competence. For example, considerable research indicates that older adults are stereotyped as warm and incompetent, based on perceptions of them as noncompetitive and of low social status (Cuddy et al., 2005). Such stereotypes are found across a wide range of cultures and reflect consistently held stereotypes that older adults are incompetent. When put into practice in various cultures, these perspectives result in a general social exclusion of older adults (Cuddy et al., 2005; Fiske & Taylor, 2021; Levy & Macdonald, 2016).

The widely held stereotypes of older adults as incompetent do not reflect the reality of a much more complicated picture, as we learned in Chapters 6 and 7. The social marginalization and the very serious individual effects that result from believing negative stereotypes have major consequences for societies that are aging, which nearly all economically developed and many emerging countries are (Levy & Macdonald, 2016; Nelson, 2016a, 2016b; Ng et al., 2021). We will revisit these negative outcomes in Chapter 14 when we explore broader societal issues; for now, we will focus more on how stereotypes operate in various ways.

Keep in mind, though, that stereotypes about older adults are not the only ones that reflect the processes we have just considered. All stereotypes about any sociocultural group follow the same pattern. Thus, stereotypes about various racial, ethnic, and gender groups also reflect automatic processes and double standards.

Stereotype Threat. Earlier in this chapter, and in Chapter 6, we learned that implicit negative stereotypes of aging influence the cognitive functioning of older adults. Here, we focus on the process by which this works—stereotype threat. **Stereotype threat** is an evoked fear of being judged in accordance with a negative stereotype about a group to which you belong. For example, if an individual is a member of a socially stigmatized group such as older adults or Black persons or Muslim individuals, that individual is vulnerable to cues in their environment that activate stereotype threat about their self-worth or ability, for example. In turn, people may perform more poorly on a task associated with that stereotype regardless of true high competence or good performance.

Substantial attention has focused on understanding the harmful effects of negative aging stereotypes on memory performance in older adults (B. R. Levy et al., 2012, 2016). Does that mean that older adults belong to a stigmatized group that is vulnerable to stereotype threat? Data indicate that the answer is yes (also refer to Chapter 6). The studies examining stereotype threat used techniques similar to those used in stereotype activation: assessing implicit stereotyping. Becca Levy's nearly two decades of research have caused some controversy in this area. Consider the Controversies feature. What do you think?

Controversies

Are Stereotypes of Aging Associated with Lower Cognitive Performance?

A major controversial issue in the cognitive aging literature is whether living in a society that equates old age with memory decline, dementia, and dependency produces what Langer (1989) calls a "premature cognitive commitment" early in life. As children, we acquire ideas of what it means to be old, ideas that are usually negative, that become implicit stereotypes guiding and influencing our behavior later in life. Thus, the question is the degree that negative societal beliefs, attitudes, and expectations actually create the cognitive decline we observe in older adults, which we learned in Chapters 6 and 7.

When Levy and Langer (1994) first compared memory performance and attitudes about aging of Chinese older adults, hearing American older adults, and deaf American older adults, they found the Chinese older adults outperformed both groups of American older adults on several memory tasks. In addition, the deaf American older adults outperformed their hearing American counterparts. Attitudes on aging held by the different cultures were related to memory performance (Chinese had more positive attitudes, whereas Americans had more negative attitudes). Levy and Langer concluded negative stereotypes in American culture accounted for this difference.

However, there were several concerns with this correlational study. Does enhanced memory performance lead to more positive attitudes, or do positive attitudes lead to enhanced memory performance? Are there educational differences between the two cultural groups? Are the memory tests really the same given that they had to be translated into Chinese?

To further test this notion, Levy (1996) subliminally primed younger and older adults with negative stereotypes of an older adult (e.g., the word *senile*, a term that at one time had a medical meaning but that is now considered perjorative) or positive stereotypes (e.g., the word *wise*). She found

(Continued)

when older adults were primed with negative aging stereotypes, their performance was worse on memory tests than older adults primed with positive stereotypes. Other researchers confirmed this result (e.g., Bouazzaoui et al., 2016; Stein et al., 2002; von Hippel & Henry, 2012).

Levy's most important and controversial finding goes well beyond results from laboratory task results in a one-time testing experience. She and her colleagues (Levy et al., 2012, 2016) found that adults over age 60 who held more negative age stereotypes demonstrated over 30% greater decline in memory performance over 38 years than those with fewer negative age stereotypes.

It is intriguing and intuitive to believe a self-fulfilling prophecy operates with respect to older adults' memory performance. If society portrays older adults as declining in cognitive capacity and a person is socialized to believe so at a young age, and if they believe these stereotypes, then it makes sense this will influence their memory performance as an older adult. Related evidence indicates clearly that holding such stereotypes does have very serious negative effects on health, brain structures, and other aspects of behavior, as noted earlier in this chapter.

However, it may not be as simple and straightforward as initially thought. Other research has raised questions about the nature of the stereotype threat effect. For instance, Brown and colleagues (2021) reported that *positive* self-perceptions about aging, but not negative ones, affected cognitive performance. Additionally, Fredriksen and colleagues (2020) found that even though stereotype threat was associated with lower memory self-efficacy in older adults, it did not suppress memory performance. Because the participants in Fredriksen and colleagues' (2020) study were highly educated, though, it is possible that the effects of stereotype threat on performance were offset by higher education.

What do we conclude about stereotype threat? Clearly, negative stereotypes of aging exist. They have an effect on health-related behaviors, and on cognitive performance under certain conditions. But results indicating that there are limits to this effect raise the possibility that the negative effects may be able to be mitigated. This hunch is supported by research demonstrating that interventions for improving attitudes and outlook on aging can improve the quality of performance (Calamia et al., 2016; Cherry et al., 2013, 2014; Reese-Melancon et al., 2021).

There is also evidence middle-aged adults are susceptible to negative age stereotypes (O'Brien & Hummert, 2006; Weiss, 2018). Middle-aged adults who identified with older adulthood demonstrated poorer memory performance if they were told their performance would be compared with other older adults. Middle-aged adults with more youthful identities did not demonstrate differences in memory performance regardless of whether they were told they would be compared to younger or older individuals. Additionally, people who believe that aging is fixed and inevitable demonstrate poorer memory performance. There may also be cohort effects (discussed in Chapter 1). Specifically, late middle-aged adults (aged 50–65) tend to reject age stereotypes more than older adults do, especially when they report that the stereotype threat felt is low to moderate (Strickland-Hughes & West, 2021). It may be the case that more recent generations of middle-aged adults do not view aging as stereotypically as older generations may have, so may be less susceptible to stereotype threat. This idea can be tested further as the millennial generation, which began to reach middle age (age 40) in 2021, continues to age.

Although most of the research in this area focused on the detrimental effects of negative stereotypes, some evidence also exists for the beneficial effects of positive stereotypes on older adults' cognitive performance. For example, compared to Italians who live in Milan, those who live on Sardinia hold more positive attitudes about memory aging and perform better on memory tasks (Cavallini et al., 2013). Positive aging stereotypes are also good for your health and social life. Several studies have found better health indicators in those with positive stereotypes (e.g., Ayalon, 2016; Nelson, 2016a, 2016b). Positive stereotypes are also related to having more new friends later in life (Menkin et al., 2017).

The preponderance of research evidence indicates that what you believe is true about aging has important consequences for what you actually experience. Believing that aging is inevitable and pretty much all decline results in decrements in cognitive performance, health, and social interactions. Believing that aging involves positive changes results in just the opposite, or at least a decrease in the speed and amount of decline. Which way you go is up to you.

Adult Development in Action

How would knowledge about the effects of negative stereotypes on older adult's cognition affect your approach to assessing them in a healthcare setting?

Review Questions

8.1 Stereotypes and Aging

- What are stereotypes? How is the content of stereotypes similar across age groups?
- What is stereotype embodiment theory?
- How does the content of stereotypes differ across age groups?
- What is the age-based double standard of perceived competence in younger and older adults?
- What do older and younger adults perceive as the cause of memory failure in older individuals?
- How does perceived competence influence the way tasks are assigned to older and younger targets?
- What other factors besides competence are taken into consideration when judging older adults' future performance?
- What evidence supports the notion that stereotypes can be automatically activated out of conscious awareness?
- What is implicit stereotyping? Under what conditions are stereotypes activated? How do negative stereotypes of aging influence young adults' behavior?

8.2 Social Knowledge Structures and Beliefs

Key Questions

- What are social knowledge structures?
- What are social beliefs, and how do they change with age?
- What are self-perceptions of aging, and what influences them across adulthood?

Anna has many years of success at being a facilitator of meetings, such as for team building in organizations. Before the COVID-19 pandemic, she had a set of well-honed skills (e.g., introductory exercises) and elements (e.g., scavenger hunts) that she had to give little thought to her actions during a session. But when the pandemic forced her work online, everything changed. She had difficulty coming up with new techniques because the previous ones were so well-ingrained.

Anna found out firsthand that well-learned social scripts or social knowledge, such as how to facilitate a team-building program, remain easily accessible even though it may not be optimal at the present time. These experiences have been likened to riding a bicycle—once you learn, you never really forget. Sometimes that is a good thing; sometimes not. Either way, it's this uncanny ability to remember social scripts automatically and how they drive behavior that greatly interests social cognitive researchers.

Social knowledge structures and social beliefs are defined in terms of how we represent and interpret the behavior of others in a social situation (Frith & Frith, 2012; Molenberghs et al., 2016; Schurz et al., 2021). In a real sense, social knowledge structures give us a way to read other people's minds. Social knowledge structures are part of the theory of mind concept examined in Chapter 2. They come in many different forms. We have scripted knowledge structures regarding everyday activities, such as what people should do when they go to a physician's office or a restaurant. We are socialized to adhere to and believe in social rules, or how to behave in specific social situations, such as how a person should act toward their partner. These structures enable us to create our Theory of Mind and interpret people's behaviors and figure out what we think their intentions are.

Understanding Age Differences in Social Beliefs

Two interesting developmental questions arise with respect to social knowledge structures. First, does the content of our social knowledge and beliefs change as we grow older? And second, do our knowledge structures and beliefs affect our social judgments, memory, problem solving, and more like stereotypes do?

There are many types of belief systems that differ in content across age groups and also influence behavior. Understanding age differences in social belief systems has three important aspects (Blanchard-Fields et al., 2012; Blanchard-Fields & Horhota, 2006; Greenwald & Lai, 2020; Phillips et al., 2014). First, we examine the specific content of social beliefs (i.e., the particular beliefs and knowledge individuals hold about rules, norms, and patterns of social behavior). Second, we consider the strength of these beliefs to know under what conditions they may influence behavior. Third, we need to know the likelihood that these beliefs will be automatically activated when a person is confronted with a situation when their beliefs are being violated or questioned. If these three aspects of the belief system are understood, it is possible to explain when and why age differences occur in social judgments.

Older adults may hold different beliefs than other age groups (e.g., different rules for appropriate social behavior). Such differences usually stem from cohort differences (discussed in Chapter 1). Such generational differences are found in a wide array of social behavior; we will return to this topic in Chapter 11 regarding interpersonal relationships.

On a related note, how strongly individuals hold their social beliefs may vary as a function of how particular generations were socialized. Although younger and older generations may both believe in free speech, for instance, the oldest generation may be more adamant about believing that under no circumstances should speech be restricted, even if it makes others uncomfortable, whereas the younger generation may support certain restrictions regarding speech that reflects bias. However, evidence of age differences in the content of social beliefs does not provide a sufficient basis for understanding age differences in how and when such beliefs are activated and how they influence behavior.

Social cognition researchers point out there are individual differences in the strength of social representations of rules, beliefs, and attitudes linked to specific situations (Frith & Frith, 2012; Greenwald & Lai, 2020). Such representations can be both cognitive (how we conceptualize the situation) and emotional (how we react to the situation). When encountering a specific situation, the individual's belief system predictably triggers an emotional reaction and related goals tied to the content of that situation. This in turn drives social judgments. These judgments reflect both a theory of mind and empathy. As discussed in Chapter 2, the theory of mind has to do with people's ability to judge what another is thinking, and the intent or motivation of that thought process. Does the person intend to be honest? Manipulative? Friendly? Theory of mind also concerns empathy, a person's ability to place oneself in the position of another emotionally—in essence to feel what they are feeling. Both matter in making social judgments about other people, especially about the principles (morals, ethics) that guide their behavior.

Let's take the rule "You should never live with a romantic partner before you are married." If you were socialized from childhood to believe in this rule, you would negatively evaluate anyone violating it. If you were told Allen was putting pressure on Tom to live with him before they were married, something that Tom believed was wrong, and they subsequently broke up, you might have a negative emotional response and blame Allen for the breakup of the relationship because he was pressuring Tom for cohabitation.

In a series of classic studies exploring social beliefs, age differences were found in the types of social rules related to marriage evoked in different types of situations (Blanchard-Fields, 1996, 1999). In the present context, these findings indicate the influence of cohort effects on how different generations are socialized with respect to important social rules, such as in marriage. The oldest generation was socialized differently from the current younger adult generation as to what is appropriate behavior. Such cohort differences could result in fundamental disagreements about what constitutes "correct" or "appropriate" behavior, potentially resulting in conflict and disrupted relationships. We will return to this scenario at the end of the chapter in our consideration of attributions about the cause(s) of behavior.

In summary, how social rules are invoked in making social judgments is a complex process. The process reflects generational differences, and it reflects current and cumulative life experiences. How these processes influence our judgments about personal responsibility for behavior is a topic we turn to next.

Self-Perception and Social Beliefs

An important facet for understanding the impact of social beliefs on people is to understand how we form impressions of ourselves. For instance, it's our personal answer to the question, "How old do you feel?" that creates our self-perception of aging. **Self-perception of aging** refers to individuals' perceptions of their own age and aging.

Researchers have been curious about how people see themselves on this dimension for many years. How we view ourselves is an important predictor of whether we age well (or not). We have already learned that holding positive views, or self-perceptions, are correlated with many good outcomes, such as better well-being, better health, and longer life (Nelson, 2016a, 2016b). We will return to this issue in Chapter 14 when we consider the different perspectives on aging well.

There are two major frameworks to explain how this influence works. **Labeling theory** argues when we confront an age-related stereotype, older adults are more likely to integrate it into their self-perception. Research on impression formation and priming of stereotypes supports this view. **Resilience theory** argues confronting a negative stereotype results in a rejection of that view in favor of a more positive self-perception. This perspective comes from people's tendency to want to distance themselves from the negative stereotype. Research indicates older adults dissociate themselves from their age group when negative stereotypes become relevant to them (e.g., Weiss, 2018; Weiss & Lang, 2012; D. Weiss et al., 2016).

A good example of this line of research is highlighted in the How Do We Know? feature. Ackerman and Chopik (2021) examined age bias and subjective age in nearly 1 million people from 68 different countries. Consider the feature and learn what they found.

What's so different about self-perceptions of age and aging as opposed to beliefs about age and aging in general is it is one of the few areas we go from looking at old people and aging as something that happens to someone else rather than something happening to us (Kornadt & Rothermund, 2012; Kornadt et al., 2018). Research on how people incorporate societal views of age and aging indicates the extent to which what happens depends critically on their own old age and aging in specific domains of life (e.g., health).

Evidence from Neuroscience

Given the importance of accuracy in figuring out what other people are thinking and feeling, researchers set out to find the brain pathways and regions that underlie our theory of mind and empathy. In Chapter 2, discussion on this topic focused on the brain changes involved in the executive processes underlying theory of mind. In this section, we examine this topic in more detail, starting with an overall model of social knowledge and beliefs and how that maps to brain structures and functions.

Schurz and colleagues (2020, 2021) have provided extensive analyses of nearly 200 studies neuroimaging and related studies involving over 4,000 participants, and have concluded that a hierarchical model, much like we encountered in our consideration of intelligence in Chapter 7, provides a good explanation of what is going on in our heads.

At the highest level, research evidence suggests that there are three distinct groups of neurocognitive processes: (1) predominantly cognitive processes, which are engaged when thinking requires self-generated cognition separated, or decoupled, from the physical world; (2) primarily affective/emotional processes, which are engaged when people observe emotions in others based on shared emotional, motor, and somatosensory representations (understandings of what the emotions "mean"); and (3) combined processes, which engage cognitive and affective functions in parallel (Schurz et al., 2021). It turns out that the combined processes may most closely describe the typical situations people are confronted with in everyday life.

Parallel to neuroimaging research are studies that examine situations and conditions under which people accurately understand others' behavior and intent. One such test is based on discerning a social faux pas, or embarrassing situation, and is called the Faux Pas Test. A faux pas is a situation in which "a speaker says something without considering if it is something that the listener might not want to hear or know, and which typically has negative consequences that the speaker never intended" (Baron-Cohen et al., 1999, p. 408). Examples include microaggressions, use of slurs, and other behaviors that stem mainly from automatic processing heuristics and biases. The recognition of a faux pas is considered an advanced test of a person's social knowledge ability because it requires subtle social reasoning within a specific sociocultural context. That is, a person must be able to appreciate (a) that two people might have different knowledge states and (b) the emotional impact a statement can have on a listener. Importantly, the Faux Pas Test is helpful in differentially diagnosing various clinically relevant issues, such as autism spectrum disorders, types of dementia, and schizophrenia, each of which are associated with specific disruptions in brain activity, which in turn is reflected in social behavior.

The most important aspect of Schurz and colleagues' research is that it demonstrates that the capacity to understand what other people think and feel remains a bit mysterious. It makes a great deal of sense that both thinking and feeling are involved, but we still do not have a simple explanation for why and how humans are so good at discerning the meaning of other people's moods and actions. Nor do we have a good understanding of how and why faux pas behaviors occur.

How Do We Know?

Cross-Cultural Aspects of Perceptions of Aging

Who were the investigators, and what was the aim of the study? As noted in the text, how people perceive themselves is an important aspect of social self-knowledge. A key question is whether self-perceptions of one's age vary across cultures. On the surface, cultures seem to vary in how well they view older adults and the roles they play in society. Are these views accurate, and do self-perceptions differ across cultures? Lindsay Ackerman and William Chopik (2021) decided to find out.

How did the investigators measure the topic of interest? Measures focused on three primary sets of issues: implicit judgments about younger and older adults, self-perceptions of age, and culture.

The Implicit Association Test is a reaction time task used to measure the strength of associations between two pairs of concepts to quantify implicit prejudice. Participants respond to pairings of face stimuli (i.e., young and old faces) with positively or negatively valued words (e.g., "fantastic" and "nasty"). The underlying assumption is that the more closely related a concept (e.g., a young face) with an evaluation (e.g., "happy"), the faster and easier participants are to associate that concept and evaluation, and the faster their reaction time. Participants were instructed what to do in two conditions: to pair both young stimuli with positive items (and old stimuli with negative items) in Condition 1, and old stimuli with positive items (and young stimuli with negative items) in Condition 2. Average response times in categorizing stimuli were compared between the two conditions: Participants who categorize items faster in Condition 1 compared with how fast they categorize items in Condition 2 are considered to have an implicit preference for young people compared with old people.

Participants' subjective age was assessed with an open-ended item, "How old do you feel?" Subjective age was calculated by subtracting this felt age from their actual, self-reported age. Subjective age was only available for a subset of the subjects (N = 344,141).

Country-level gross domestic product (GDP) per capita (N = 65 countries had available data) and Gini index of income inequality (N = 63 countries had available data) were gathered as country-level characteristics that measure the economic conditions of a country. Hofstede's dimensions of cultural variation were also included in the analysis. Hofstede and colleagues (2010) suggest that country-level differences in societal values can be characterized by six dimensions.

- Power Distance (PDI) measures the degree to which a culture is accepting of inequality.
- Individualism/Collectivism (IDV) refers to the degree to which people prefer loosely knit social networks and individuality (higher values) versus tightly knit social networks and interdependence with others (lower values).
- Masculinity/Femininity (MAS) assesses the degree to which a culture can be characterized by assertiveness and competitiveness (masculinity) or nurturance and cooperation (femininity).
- Uncertainty Avoidance (UAI) measures the degree to which a country's citizens are uncomfortable with uncertainty and ambiguity.
- Long-Term Orientation (LTO) assesses the outlook of a culture; countries with a long-term orientation place more importance on the future.
- Indulgence/Restraint (IVR) refers to the degree to which a society allows free gratification of basic and natural human drives related to enjoyment of life (relative to a suppression of gratification of needs by strict social norms).

Country-level scores on each of the dimensions were available for 64 countries in the current analyses.

Who were the participants in the study? The final analytic sample comprised 911,982 individuals (67.6% female) from 68 different countries. The overall sample ranged in age from 15 to 89 (M = 27.42, SD = 12.23) years; the median level of education was some college. The majority of respondents were from the United States (86.2%). The sample size for individual countries ranged widely, from 104 to 712,607.

Were there ethical concerns with the study? Participant were provided informed consent and could stop participation at any point, so there were no major concerns.

What were the results? Living in countries with greater long-term orientation, uncertainty avoidance, and individualism were all associated with greater implicit bias, explicit bias, and less warmth toward older adults. Women and people with lower levels of education reported less explicit bias and warmer feelings toward all groups. Younger adults felt warmer toward younger adults; older adults felt warmer toward older adults. Interestingly, there was a correlation between subjective age discrepancy and implicit bias. Additionally, living in countries with higher uncertainty avoidance was associated with a smaller subjective age discrepancy. Women, older adults, and people with lower levels of education reported a greater subjective age discrepancy (i.e., there was a larger gap between their chronological age and the age they felt, suggesting a type of distancing from the stigma of older adulthood).

What did the investigators conclude?
Ackerman and Chopik found that living in countries high in collectivism is associated with less implicit and explicit age bias (although bias still exists), as well as greater feelings of warmth toward older adults compared to individualistic countries. Greater uncertainty avoidance was associated with higher implicit and explicit bias, less warmth toward older adults, and was the only variable to predict reporting of a younger subjective age. This latter result is likely because, although people understand generally what to expect in old age, each individual's experience of aging is different, largely unpredictable, and cannot be controlled. This could be a source of discomfort for people living in a culture that prefers predictability over uncertainty. As a result, greater feelings of uncertainty result in negative affect and poorer evaluations of older adults.

Adult Development in Action

If you are a taking a poll on attitudes toward specific social issues, how would you design the survey to uncover the reasons for any age differences that were found?

Review Questions

8.2 Social Knowledge Structures and Beliefs

- What three important factors need to be considered to understand implicit social beliefs?
- Describe evidence for age differences in the content of social beliefs.
- What are labeling theory and resilience theory? What influences self-perceptions of aging across adulthood?

8.3 Individual Factors in Social Processing Goals

Key Questions

- How do goals influence the way we process information, and how does this change with age?
- How do emotions influence the way we process information, and how does this change with age?
- How does a need for closure influence the way we process information, and how does it change with age?

Chris and Eric are visiting their children and grandchildren. All are having a good time until their son, Eddie, raises the hot topic of the upcoming election. The debate among family members regarding the best candidate becomes heated. Chris and Eric are concerned about the negative feelings generated in the debate and encourage everyone to change the topic. However, Eddie is more interested in settling the issue on which candidate to support now rather than later. Chris and Eric cannot handle the negative energy and retire to bed early.

Why did Chris and Eric focus on the emotional side of the problem (the increase in negative feelings), whereas Eddie focused on the more instrumental side of the problem (e.g., whom to vote for)?

The different reactions of Chris and Eric in contrast to Eddie resulted in different problem-solving strategies. Much like the research on social rules and social judgments, there is a growing understanding that change in the relative importance of social goals and motivation across the life span profoundly influences how we interpret and use social information or direct attention and effort to certain aspects of the problem situation (Fernandes et al., 2021; Hess, 2006).

Social goals change with age as a function of experience and perceived time left in one's life span. This can influence the degree we observe age differences in social cognitive functioning, such as the desire to focus on preserving ones' resources or eliminating negative affect in problem situations. Let's explore these further.

Personal Social Processing Goals

Personal social processing goals play a major role in creating direction in our lives. They consist of underlying motivations for our behavior and how we perceive our own ever-changing environment. Across the life span, personal goals change to match our needs, with young adults striving mainly for achievement, such as earning a postsecondary credential or starting a job, and middle-aged and older adults seeking balance between functioning independently and sharing their lives with others (e.g., children, partners, work colleagues).

Selective optimization with compensation (SOC; discussed in Chapter 1) is an important theoretical model that suggests development occurs as we continuously update our personal goals to match our appraisal of available resources to obtain those goals (Baltes et al., 2006). We choose manageable and achievable goals based on our interests as well as physical and cognitive strengths and limitations. As we grow older, our limitations become more salient and require us to reevaluate. Therefore, in older adulthood, research suggests interests increasingly shift toward physical health and socio-emotional domains (Carstensen, 2021; Isaacowitz & Blanchard-Fields, 2012).

This shift in priorities means goals for the same event or outcome may be perceived differently by older, middle-aged, and younger adults. An example of the shift in goal selection is represented in research that examines how younger and older adults prioritize how they want to perform in a dual-task situation. In a classic study, younger and older adults were asked to memorize a list of words while simultaneously maintaining their balance as they walked through an obstacle course (Li et al., 2001). Although age differences in performing two tasks at the same time were larger for the memory task than the walking task, older adults chose to forgo using aids or strategies to improve their memory (e.g., organizing the list) and instead chose to use aids designed to optimize walking performance (e.g., holding onto a handrail). When deciding which was more important to them, memory performance versus balance, older adults displayed a preference for their physical safety even if it meant that choice would negatively affect performance on a cognitive test. From this example, we can infer that life-span shifts in personal goals can be both potentially helpful or harmful depending on one's perspective.

Goal selection requires us to choose carefully and thoughtfully where and how we invest our resources. In the research laboratory, younger adults are primarily motivated to achieve maximum performance on any cognitive task presented to them. Older adults usually take a different perspective. They prefer to maintain steady performance by optimizing their current resources rather than risking lower performance with an unknown strategy (Ebner et al., 2006; Hess et al., 2021; Napolitano & Freund, 2016).

Thus, although older adults are less willing than younger adults to invest energy into improving their cognitive performance, their strategy choice is more optimal for them because they are more interested in retaining their autonomy (and often their physical health and safety) by maintaining abilities at their current level. Although this does not directly translate into cognitive gains, it does help older adults optimize their cognitive performance in those domains they prioritize in their lives (Hess et al., 2021; Riediger et al., 2005). Although we cannot compensate for all of the resource limitations that come with advancing age, we can invest the resources we have into goals that maximize an independent lifestyle and a positive sense of well-being.

Along these lines, research by Carstensen and her colleagues suggests the pursuit of emotionally gratifying situations becomes a primary motivation that substantially influences cognition in the latter half of the life span (Carstensen, 2021; Carstensen et al., 2020). We therefore turn to the impact of emotional processing goals on cognition. Perhaps more important, these results reinforce the need to be cautious about interpreting age differences in task performance without also understanding underlying choices and motivation levels.

Emotion as a Social Processing Goal

Emotional goals become increasingly important and salient as we grow older (Carstensen, 2006; Carstensen & Fried, 2012; Carstensen et al., 2020). It is primarily a motivational model that posits the degree an individual construes time as limited or expansive that leads to the ranking of emotional or knowledge-seeking goals as higher in priority, respectively. Thus, given limited time left in the life span, older adults may be more motivated to emphasize emotional goals and emotion-related aspects of life. We examine this motivational factor in the context of maintaining and choosing intimate relationships in Chapter 11. However, it also can be applied in the context of social information processing.

Research suggests that older adults avoid negative information and focus more on positive information when making decisions and judgments and when remembering events, a

PeopleImages/iStock/Getty Images

Older adults tend to remember more positive than negative information, such as good traits of their spouse or partner rather than negative ones.

phenomenon called the **positivity effect** (Carstensen, 2021; Carstensen & Fried, 2012; Carstensen et al., 2006; English & Carstensen, 2016). For example, older adults remember positive images more than negative ones, whereas younger adults remember both positive and negative images equally well (Isaacowitz & Blanchard-Fields, 2012; Reed & Carstensen, 2012). When examining what types of stimuli younger and older adults initially attend to, older adults allocate less attention to negative stimuli (e.g., angry faces) than younger adults do. Older adults also remember more positive information when recalling their own autobiographical information and remember the positive aspects of their decisions more than the negative ones. There is much neuroscience research supporting the positivity effect in older adults (Petro et al., 2021).

An alternative perspective proposes that focusing on negative information is actually adaptive because it signals danger and vulnerability and thus is important for survival. This emphasis on negativity has been found in both the social and cognitive neuroscience literature for many years (Rozin & Royzman, 2001). Within the social cognitive aging literature, some studies demonstrate older adults spend more time viewing negative stimuli (Charles et al., 2003) and display a negativity effect, which can be overcome (Thomas & Hasher, 2006; Wood & Kisley, 2006).

Emotional goals appear to help older adults because they create a supportive context for their cognitive functioning. In Chapter 6, we noted the fact older adults create more false memories than younger adults do. Research on the interface between emotions and cognition suggests the distinctiveness of emotions helps older adults reduce the number of false memories produced (Mitchell, 2016).

However, it is important to recognize there are times when emotions may impede information processing. For example, highly arousing situations such as memories of trauma require a great amount of executive control processing (discussed in Chapter 6) that may lead older adults to be poorer at remembering and processing information (Kensinger & Corkin, 2004; Reed & Carstensen, 2012; Witherby et al., 2021). In addition, a focus on only positive information can interfere with decision making by leading older adults to miss out on important negative information necessary to make a quality decision (Reed & Carstensen, 2012).

As we have noted, emotion plays an increasingly important role as we grow older, and the brain mechanisms that underlie emotion change and become more central, as noted in Chapter 2. The power of the positivity effect also means that people intentionally use thoughts and behaviors to avoid negative emotional experiences.

Research demonstrates that it takes a lifetime to master this ability to focus on positive experiences. The aging process itself, accompanied as it is by an increased focus on time left to live rather than time lived to date, may hold a key to understanding how this happens. Charles and Luong (2013; Charles, 2010; Piazza et al., 2015) developed the Strength and Vulnerability Integration (SAVI) model to explain it. The SAVI model is described in Figure 8.1.

The SAVI model is based on the normative aging process in which physiological vulnerabilities that occur with increasing age make regulating high levels of emotional arousal harder (Sharifian et al., 2022). So, when older adults experience high levels of distress, the usual advantage they have in regulating emotion is interfered with (and even reversed). This results in older adults paying a higher price for sustained negative emotional arousal. Such experiences push them to focus on the positive.

The SAVI model, then, can explain the seemingly contradictory findings that some older adults have higher well-being whereas others personify the stereotype of "grumpy older people" (Charles & Luong, 2013). It all comes down to how sustained emotional experiences are processed.

Cognitive Style as a Social Processing Goal

Another type of motivational goal that influences our thinking comes from our **cognitive style**, or how we approach solving problems. For example, people

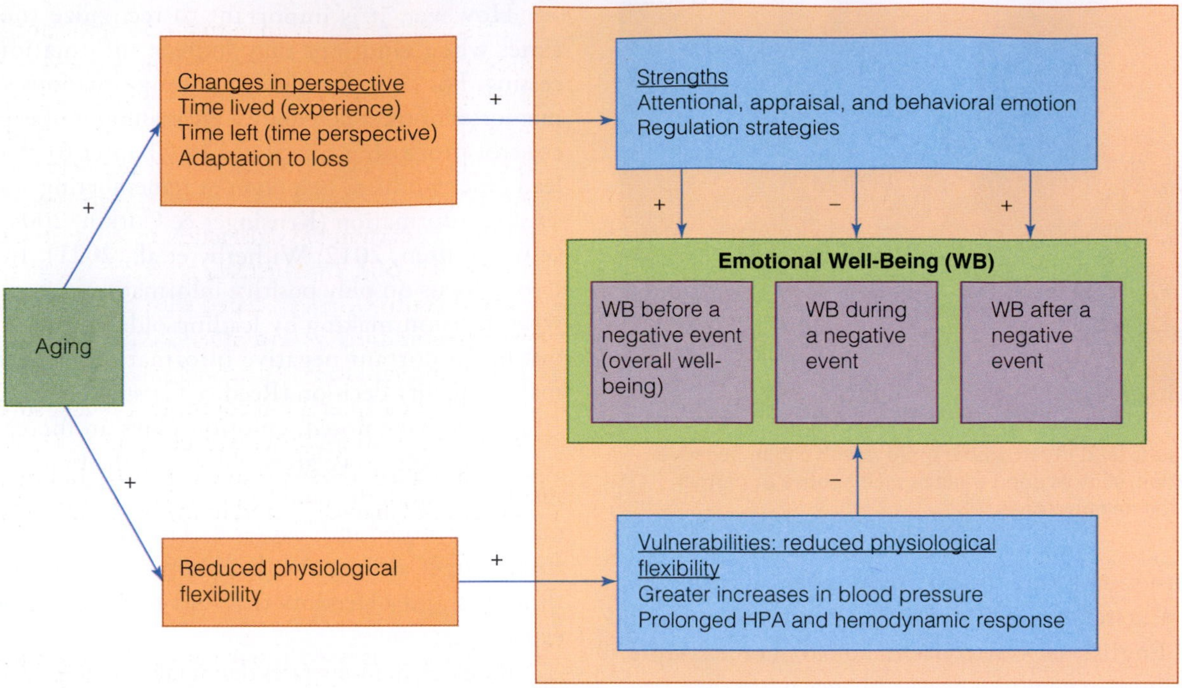

Figure 8.1 A model of strength and vulnerability integration.

Note: HPA=hypothalamic–pituitary–adrenal

Source: Charles, S. T. (2010). Strength and vulnerability integration: A model of emotional well-being across adulthood. *Psychological Bulletin, 136,* 1068–1091. Figure 1, p. 1069. https://doi.org/10.1037/a0021232.

with a cognitive style that reflects a high need for closure prefer order and predictability, are uncomfortable with ambiguity, and prefer quick and decisive answers (Bar-Tal et al., 2013).

How does cognitive style enter into social cognition? We know from previous discussions that situations requiring substantial cognitive resources (i.e., require a lot of effort such as processing information under time pressure) result in an increase in inaccuracies and biases in how we represent social information. But putting strains on cognitive resources isn't the only way to increase the odds that biases will occur. Cognitive style can do that, too. For instance, biased judgments can also be caused by high need for closure. In fact, research using Need for Closure assessments suggests that high need for closure and/or structure is related to attributional biases, the tendency to make stereotyped judgments, formation of spontaneous trait inferences, and the tendency to assimilate judgments to ideas that have been primed (e.g., Bar-Tal et al., 2013).

It may also be the case that cognitive resources and motivational differences are both age-related and influence social judgments in interaction with each other (English & Carstensen, 2016; Stanley & Isaacowitz, 2012). Researchers argue changes in cognitive resources with aging (such as the declines in working memory noted in Chapter 6) may lead to an increase in a need for closure with age. This leads to biases in the way older adults process social information.

Research documents that a high need for closure does not influence susceptibility to emotional priming influences on neutral stimuli in young and middle-aged adults. However, priming effects get stronger with higher levels of need for closure in older adults. In other words, older adults with a high need for closure could not inhibit the effects of an emotional prime (e.g., a subliminally presented negative word) on their subsequent behavior (e.g., whether they liked or disliked an abstract figure). Because of age-related changes in social and cognitive resources, motivational factors such as coming to quick and decisive answers to conserve those resources become more important to older adults.

Adult Development in Action

If you were designing an advertisement for adults of different ages, how would you approach the suggestion to use emotion in the ad?

Review Questions

8.3 Individual Factors in Social Processing Goals

- How do personal goals influence behavior? To what extent are there age differences in emotion as a processing goal in social cognitive functioning?
- What is need for closure? How does need for closure influence the processing of social information?
- Are there age differences in the degree to which need for closure influences social information processing?

8.4 Personal Control

Key Questions

- What is personal control?
- What is the multidimensionality of personal control?
- How do assimilation and accommodation influence behavior?
- What is primary and secondary control? What is the primacy of primary control over secondary control?

Daniel did not perform as well as they expected on their psychology exam. They then had the unhappy task of determining why they did poorly. Was it their fault? Was the exam too picky? They decided the exam was too picky and was not a good test of what they actually knew. This helped Daniel shake off the poor performance on this test and be motivated for the next exam.

How Daniel decided why they performed poorly on the exam sheds light on how we tend to explain, or attribute, our behavior to particular causes or reasons. Among the most important ways, we analyze the cause of events in our lives is in terms of who or what is in control in a specific situation. **Personal control** is the degree one believes one's performance in a situation depends on something that one personally does. A high sense of personal control implies a belief that performance is up to you and what you decide to do about it, whereas a low sense of personal control implies your performance is under the influence of forces other than your own.

Personal control is an extremely important idea in a wide variety of settings because of the way it guides behavior and relates to well-being (Brandtstädter, 1997; Curtis et al., 2018; Lachman, 2006). For example, Liao and colleagues (2021) found that greater perceived control over events remembered best from their young adult years predict current life satisfaction in adults in late midlife (ages 49–60). In contrast, greater present-focused perceived control was associated with higher life satisfaction in people aged 62 and older. Additionally, personal control is thought to play a central role in physical health (discussed in Chapter 4), in adjustment to and survival in different care settings (discussed in Chapter 5), in memory performance (discussed in Chapter 6), in intelligence (discussed in Chapter 7), and in mental health (discussed in Chapter 10).

Multidimensionality of Personal Control

The general consensus about personal control is that it is multidimensional (Hong et al., 2021; Infurna et al., 2020; Qian & Wu, 2022). Specifically, one's sense of control depends on which domain, such as intelligence or health, is being assessed. In a classic study, Lachman and colleagues (2009) found different patterns of changes in control beliefs depending on the domain being examined. Specifically, they found no changes in a sense of control over one's health up to participants' early 70s. However, when older adults transition from their early 70s to their mid-70s and 80s, their sense of control over their health declines. This makes sense given that people in these age groups typically experience accumulated losses in their reserve capacity to function. Thus, the shift in personal control may actually be very adaptive and accurate. In support of this point, Chipperfield and colleagues (2016) found that feelings of personal control can be maladaptive when it leads to a sense of invincibility even in the face of poor health. Such beliefs can result in the failure to seek medical help when it is actually needed.

The same is true for adults of any age in an academic context such as college, where attributions of control are particularly important in determining the causes of success and failure in school. Dweck and Yeager (2021) summarize research that has identified two main views of personal control in the domain of cognitive abilities: fixed and growth. A "fixed mindset" means you believe intelligence, talent, and other cognitive abilities are innate and unchangeable across the life span. Thus, you really have little control over them—if a person is not good at something, they typically think they will

Discovering Development

How Much Control Do You Have Over Your Cognitive Functioning?

As you progress through college, you perhaps are concerned with how much you will learn relating to your profession of choice and your performance on course and other types of exams.

As noted in the text, people tend to have either a fixed or growth mindset about cognitive abilities.

Are there age differences in these control beliefs? To find out, talk to students at your college or university who range from first-year students on up and differ in chronological age. Find out what they believe is the major cause of their successes and failures in school. Bring your results to class and pool them. Identify if there are differences in how long people have been in school and/or chronological age differences in perceptions of control over academic performance. Compare your findings to age differences reported in the text.

never be good at it no matter what they do. In contrast, a "growth mindset" means you believe intelligence, talent, and other cognitive abilities can be developed with practice and effort, so in this sense a person has control over how well they will ultimately perform. How do people in college consider themselves? Explore the notion of control in regard to class performance among older and younger students as described in the Discovering Development feature.

In sum, researchers find that, in general, maintaining a sense of personal control throughout adulthood is linked to better quality of social relationships, better health, and higher cognitive functioning. They suggest a sense of control may operate as a protective factor for one's well-being in the face of declining health and other losses that normatively come over age 80.

Control Strategies

The research just reviewed primarily examined control-related beliefs such as the belief that control is in one's own hands or lies externally. Building on these ideas, a number of theoretical approaches and research have examined control-related strategies.

Brandtstädter (1999) first proposed the preservation and stabilization of a positive view of the self and personal development in later life involve three interdependent processes. First, people engage in **assimilative activities** that prevent or alleviate losses in domains that are personally relevant for self-esteem and identity. People may use memory aids more if having a good memory is an important aspect of self-esteem and identity. Second, people make **accommodations** and readjust their goals and aspirations to lessen or neutralize the effects of negative self-evaluations in key domains. If a person notices the time it takes to walk a mile at a brisk pace increased, then the target time can be increased to help lessen the impact of feelings of failure. Third, people use **immunizing mechanisms** that alter the effects of self-discrepant evidence. In this case, a person who is confronted with evidence their memory performance has declined can look for alternative explanations or simply deny the evidence.

Taking a similar approach, Heckhausen and colleagues (2010, 2021; Barlow et al., 2017) view control as a motivational system that regulates individuals' abilities to control important outcomes over the life span. These researchers define control-related strategies in terms of primary control and secondary control. **Primary control** strategies involve bringing the environment in line with one's desires and goals. Much like in Brandtstädter's assimilative activities, action is directed toward changing the external world. So, for example, if you lost your job, and thus your income, primary control strategies would entail an active search for another job (changing the environment so you once again have a steady income). **Secondary control** strategies involve bringing oneself in line with the environment. Much like Brandtstädter's accommodative activities, it typically involves cognitive activities directed at the self. Secondary control strategies could involve appraising the situation in terms of how you really did not enjoy that particular job.

An important part of this theoretical perspective is that primary control has functional primacy over secondary control. In other words, primary control lets people shape their environment to fit their goals and developmental potential. Thus, primary control has more adaptive value to the individual. The major function of secondary control is to minimize losses or expand levels of primary control.

This relation is depicted in Figure 8.2. Notice that primary control striving is always high across the life span, but the capacity to achieve primary control peaks in midlife. As people continue to age, secondary control striving continues to increase, eventually approaching primary control striving.

Heckhausen and colleagues (2010, 2021; Barlow et al., 2017) believe this has important implications for aging. They find that in childhood much of development

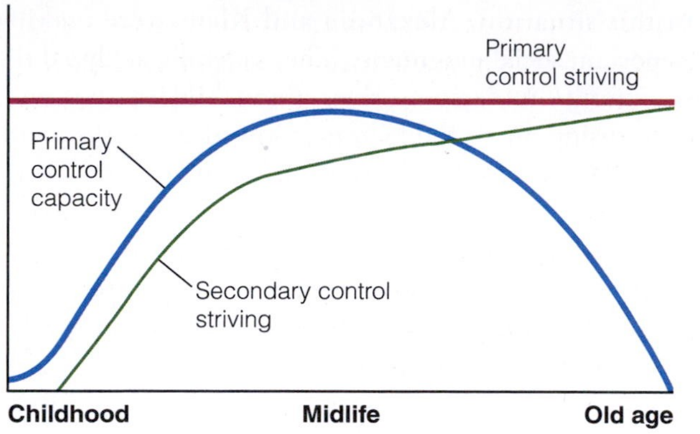

Figure 8.2 Hypothetical life-span trajectories for primary control potential and primary and secondary control striving.

Source: Heckhausen, J., Wrosch, C., & Schulz, R. (2010). A motivational theory of life-span development. *Psychological Review, 117*(1), 32–60 (at p. 36). https://www.ncbi.nlm.nih.gov/pmc/articles/PMC2820305/figure/F1/.

is directed at expanding the child's primary control potential, and they predict stability in primary control striving through most of adult life. However, as we enter old age, the maintenance of primary control increasingly depends on secondary control processes. This is because of threats to primary control as a function of biological decline that occurs as we grow older. Thus secondary control increases with age. Research supports this prediction (Heckhausen et al., 2021; Pfeiffer, 2013).

A particularly important question is how control strategies and beliefs affect emotional well-being. Research suggests control beliefs are important contributors to both positive and negative well-being. If someone perceives they have control over desirable outcomes, this control is associated with high emotional well-being (Barlow et al., 2017; Heckhausen et al., 2010, 2021; Pfeiffer, 2013). However, how adaptive control beliefs relate to well-being varies with life stage. For young and middle-aged adults, a strong sense of control relates to how people compensate for failure, for example, "We can overcome this momentary failure." In contrast, older adults focus a sense of control on how to master everyday demands (Barlow et al., 2017; Heckhausen et al., 2010, 2021). Finally, for all age groups, planning for the future enhances one's sense of perceived control, and this in turn relates to high life satisfaction (Lachman et al., 2009).

Evaluation of Personal Control Processes

The concept of personal control is extremely popular, as it seems to match people's everyday experience as well as numerous investigations. Nevertheless, the idea of increases in accommodative strategies (Brandtstädter, 1999) and secondary strategies (Barlow et al., 2017; Heckhausen et al., 2010, 2021) in older age are not without criticisms. Carstensen and Freund (1994; Freund & Ritter, 2009) question whether losses people experience, though real, actually threaten the self. In addition, these authors argue age-related changes in goals could also be the result of natural movement through the life cycle, not simply of coping with blocked goals.

Criticisms also can be leveled against these approaches to control by considering the globalization of so many aspects of our functioning. From a sociocultural perspective (e.g., cross-cultural research), there is much criticism regarding a bias toward Western cultures in the development of theories such as primary and secondary control, specifically the primacy of primary control over secondary control. A representative stance is expressed by Stephen J. Gould (1999) who suggested that in collectivist societies such as those found in Asia the emphasis is not on individualistic strategies such as those reflected in primary control. Instead, the goal is to establish interdependence with others, to be connected to them and bound to a larger social institution.

Although this view would seem to make sense, Hornsey and colleagues (2019) conducted two large studies comparing representative samples of residents of 38 countries on perceived control and 27 countries on desired control that included countries differing on numerous dimensions (such as collectivist–individualist, holistic–nonholistic). The results were clear—with the sole exception of Japan, no differences emerged based on culture. Rather, residents of all countries held similar positions on perceived and desired control. Residents of Japan, though, had lower levels of both than did residents of any other country studied, for reasons that were not clear.

Thus, one's sense of personal control is a complex, multidimensional aspect of the self that appears to transcend culture. Consequently, general normative age-related trends might not be found. Rather, changes in personal control may well depend on one's experiences in different domains and may differ widely from one domain to another.

Adult Development in Action

As a professional working with older adults, how would you combine your knowledge of the effects of stereotyping with your knowledge of the importance of personal control beliefs to create an intervention program?

Review Questions

8.4 Personal Control Processes

- What evidence is there of age differences in personal control beliefs?
- In what domains do older adults exhibit low perceived control, and in what domains do they exhibit higher levels of perceived control?
- How are assimilative and accommodative strategies adaptive in older adults' functioning?
- Why is primary control viewed as having more functional primacy than secondary control?
- What cross-cultural evidence challenges the notion of primary control as functionally more important?
- How does personal control influence older adults' emotional well-being?

8.5 Social Judgment Processes

Key Questions

- What is emotional intelligence and how does it develop across adulthood?
- What is the negativity bias in impression formation, and how does it influence older adults' thinking?
- Are there age differences in accessibility of social information?
- How does processing context influence social judgments?
- To what extent do processing capacity limitations influence social judgments in older adults?

Alexandra and Klaus were taking care of their grandchildren for the weekend. They took them to the zoo for an outing. When they passed the gift shop, the children would not stop whining that they wanted a present. This frustrated Alexandra and Klaus, and they both tried to come up with an explanation for this distressing behavior. At first, they were worried because it seemed the behavior of their grandchildren indicated they were, in essence, selfish children. But on further reflection, they considered other factors. The parents always bought the children a gift at the zoo, and so the children naturally expected it to happen again. The grandparents felt better about the situation after considering the parents' role in it and bought the gifts for the children.

In this situation, Alexandra and Klaus were making important social judgments. They carefully analyzed the situation to understand their grandchildren's behavior by focusing on all the factors involved in it. Alexandra and Klaus exemplify how we can correct our initial assessments of others' behavior if we take the time to reflect about all of the extenuating circumstances.

But what would have happened if they did not have the time to think about it, and instead had multiple distractions, such as dealing with the emotional outbursts of their grandchildren as well as their own emotional reactions, time constraints, the other tasks that needed to be completed that day, and so on? Their judgments could also have been influenced simply by strong beliefs (invoked automatically) about how children should behave in a social situation such as this one.

We consider the influence of both of these factors on making social judgments: the role played by applying cognitive capacity to have enough time to reflect on a situation, and underlying social knowledge and beliefs and how they operate. However, first, let us explore emotional intelligence and how it develops.

Emotional Intelligence

The increased integration of emotion and thought that begins in emerging and established adulthood and continues through late life (discussed in Chapter 7) provides a way of examining how cognitive abilities operate in social situations. The basic goal of the application of cognition to social situations is understanding how people make sense of themselves, others, and events in everyday life (Fiske & Taylor, 2021; Kornadt et al., 2018; R. Smith et al., 2018, 2020; Weiss & Perry, 2020).

Let's return to the case of Alexandra and Klaus and how they handled the zoo event. A key ability they demonstrated in dealing with their grandchildren's behavior in the social context of the zoo visit is emotional intelligence (Goleman, 1995; Salovey & Mayer, 1990). **Emotional intelligence (EI)** refers to people's ability to recognize their own and others' emotions, to correctly identify and appropriately tell the difference between emotions, and to use this information to guide their thinking and behavior. Emotional intelligence consists of two aspects. First, EI can be viewed as a trait that reflects a person's self-perceived dispositions and abilities. Second, EI can be viewed as an ability that reflects the person's success at processing emotional information and using it appropriately in social contexts. EI has been applied to a wide variety of situations, from everyday social cognition and problem solving to bullying to business to leadership.

EI has been mapped onto brain structures (Barbey et al., 2014; Smith et al., 2018; Yu et al., 2020). An example of a model of EI is in Figure 8.3.

Research indicates that emotional intelligence increases with age (Chen et al., 2016; Mankus et al., 2016), a finding that is supported in international studies (e.g., Delhom et al., 2022; Mikkelsen et al., 2020), and neuroscience research (C. Li et al., 2021). This evidence supports the view that increased emotional intelligence may be a source of older adults' higher subjective well-being. One practical application of this research is that perceiving others' emotions in the work context matters not only for getting along with coworkers but making good decisions (Cubrich & Petruzzelli, 2020; Doerwald et al., 2016).

EI is a key component of theory of mind, mainly because it provides a way to understand how many sources of complex information about others interacts with one's own physical, cognitive, and emotional states. EI is also increasingly considered a critical aspect of a fuller understanding of the concept of intelligence as being broader than merely a set of cognitive processes, as noted in Chapter 7.

Finally, EI is proving to be such an important aspect in understanding interpersonal interactions that it is being built into the artificial intelligence systems in social robots for use in older adults' homes (Abdollahi et al., 2022). Research suggests that older adults perceive robots that display empathy (based on their AI-based EI programming) more positively.

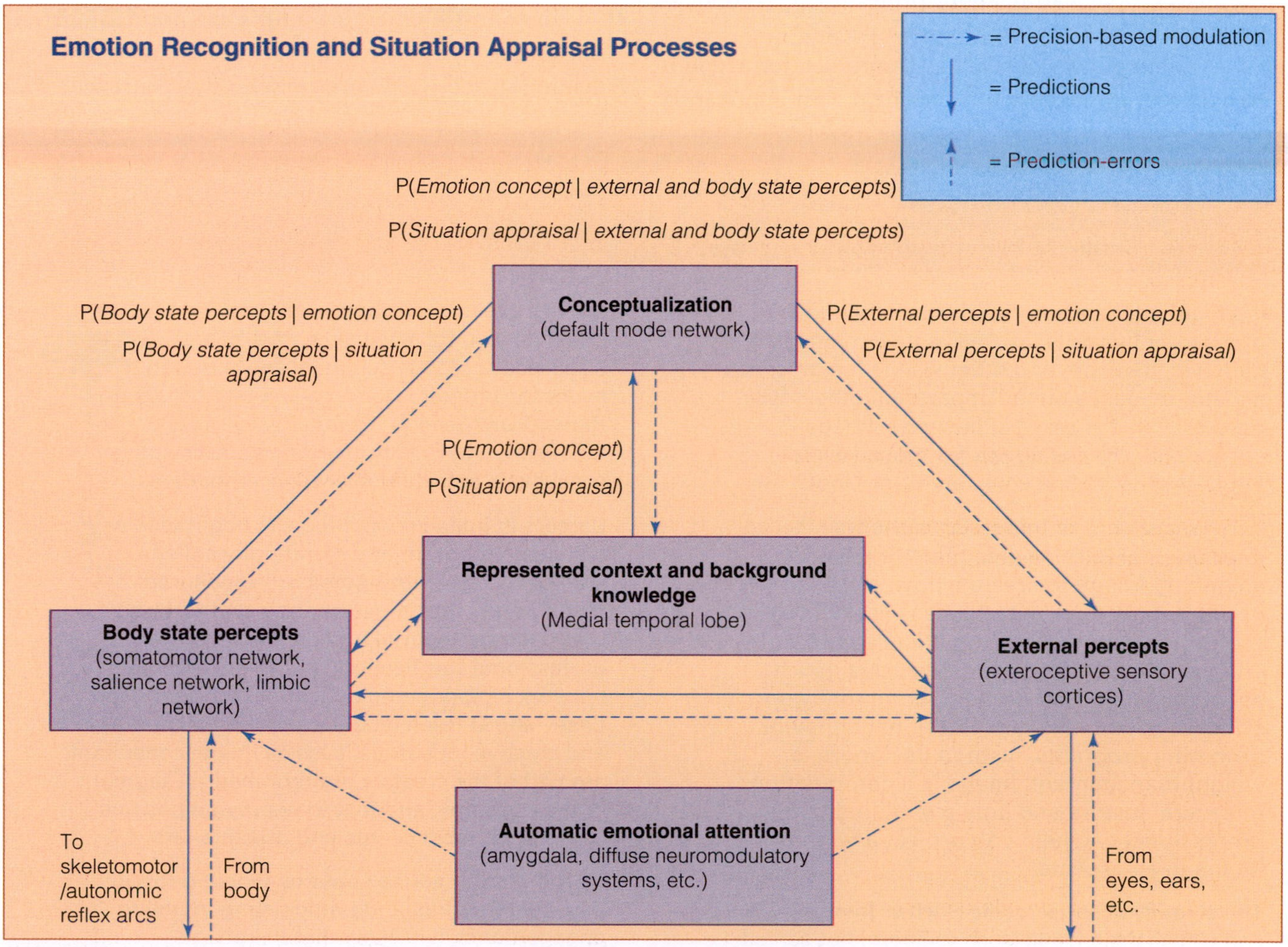

Figure 8.3 Schematic illustration of select emotion recognition and situation appraisal processes contributing to emotional intelligence.

Source: Smith, R., Kilgore, W. D. S., Alkozei, A., & Lane, R. D. (2018). A neuro-cognitive process model of emotional intelligence. *Biological Psychology, 139,* 131–151. Figure 1, p. 138. https://doi.org/10.1016/j.biopsycho.2018.10.012.

Impression Formation

When people meet each other, we tend to immediately come to conclusions about them on many dimensions. Researchers (e.g., Adams et al., 2012; Albohn & Adams, 2021; Leshikar et al., 2016) examine age differences in social judgments by examining impression formation. **Impression formation** is the way we form and revise first impressions about others. Researchers examine how people use diagnostic trait information (aspects about people that appear critical or unique) in making initial impressions of an individual, and how this process varies with age. Although we will be focusing mainly on personal traits such as personality, it is certainly the case that first impressions are also influenced by how one looks physically and by how one appears (clothing and hair style, for example), among other sociocultural factors. For more on one's "image," read the Real People feature about professionals who focus on creating the best image for each person.

A common way of studying impression formation is to have two groups of adults presented with information about a person, either through descriptions or inferences. One group gets positive information first, such as evidence of honesty. The other group is presented with negative information first, such as incidents of dishonest behavior. Each group then subsequently gets the opposite information about the person (e.g., the group that got positive information first then gets negative information).

What happens to people's first impressions as a function of age is a well-established finding. As is clear from Figure 8.4, Hess and Pullen (1994) found all study participants modified their impressions. When new negative information was presented after the initial positive portrayal of the target person, older adults modified their impression of the target from positive to negative. Interestingly, however, they modified their first impression *less* when the negative portrayal was followed by positive information. Older adults make impressions influenced by all the information they receive.

In contrast, emerging adults did not demonstrate this pattern. Instead, they were more concerned with making sure the new information was consistent with

Real People

Image Consultants and the Art of Impressions

It should not be a surprise to learn that how one looks physically, as well as one's clothes, hairstyle, body art, and other visible features, has a major influence on the impression others will have of you. It is *very* big business. Image consultants provide advice for those visible attributes that define your "style" or "look."

The Association of Image Consultants International (2021) notes that "Projecting a winning image to create a powerful first impression is the key to success in personal, professional, and social life. People try to enhance their image in various ways, [such as] personality development, communication skills, social behavior, professional behavior, grooming programs, fashion designers, or weight management. Image is a combination of several factors and only a qualified image professional can help you project a winning image in all aspects."

The ubiquity of social media (such as Instagram) and videoconferencing (such as Zoom) has served to put additional emphasis on how one appears. As a result of these platforms, many middle-aged and older people are turning to image consultants to get advice. Some AICI members, such as Ginger Burr, focus their work on these age groups. Since 1987, she has been providing private consultations for cisgender and transgender women clients. Ginger also leads corporate seminars and community education programs for organizations including Harvard Law School, Harvard Business School, the U.S. Army, and Fidelity Investments. Many other consultants provide similar services for men.

Careers in image consulting can begin with a certificate program at a community college, attendance at various seminars sponsored by AICI and other organizations, and through other entrepreneurial means. AICI provides professional certification, and offers a global network of continuing education opportunities. Casey and O'Brien (2020) point out that cultural and creative industries, such as image consultant, are part of the creative, entrepreneurial segment of the economy, and that they provide positive benefits for most clients and practitioners.

As more older adults continue working for pay, volunteering, and participating in online engagements, it is likely that the image consulting sector will become more focused on older adults. It will be interesting to track the degree to which image consultants adopt social stereotypes about aging, or whether they will work with clients to find their own styles.

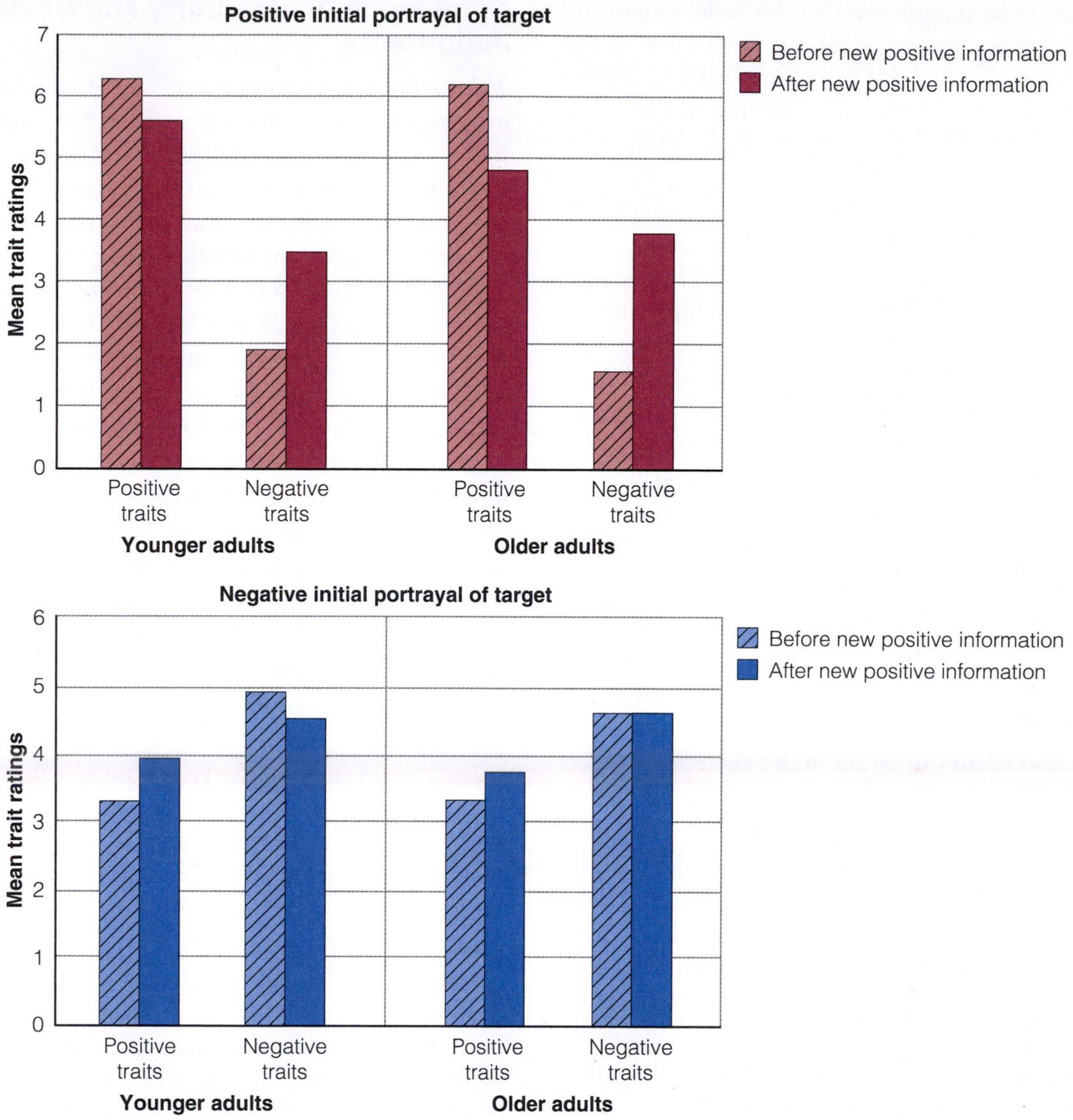

Figure 8.4 Mean trait ratings before and after presentation of new negative or positive information.

Source: A modified graph of the Hess, T. M., & Pullen, S. M. (1994). Adult age differences in impression change processes. *Psychology and Aging, 9*, p. 239.

their initial impressions. To do so, they modified their impressions to correspond with the new information regardless of whether it was positive or negative. Emerging adults, then, make their impression based on the most recent information they have.

Why do emerging and older adults differ? Hess and Pullen suggest older adults may rely more on life experiences and social rules of behavior when making their interpretations, whereas emerging adults may be more concerned with situational consistency of the new information presented. They also suggest older adults may be more subject to a negativity bias in impression formation. **Negativity bias** occurs when people allow their initial negative impressions to stand despite subsequent positive information because negative information was more striking to them and thus affected them more strongly.

Negativity bias corresponds well with other studies demonstrating older adults pay attention to and seek out emotional information more than younger people do (Isaacowitz & Blanchard-Fields, 2012; Kalokerinos et al., 2015). We discuss this further later in the chapter. Negativity bias also suggests that decline in underlying basic cognitive processes limits the ability of older adults to override the impact of their initial impressions, a result supported by neuroimaging research (Leshikar et al., 2016).

Further evidence indicates that the social judgments older adults make appear to be more sensitive to the diagnosticity of the available information (Hess, 2006). If emerging adults receive new information about a person that contradicts their original impression, they are likely to adjust the initial impression. However, older adults are more selective in the information they choose to use in forming their judgments. They focus more on the relevant details to make those judgments, and change their initial impression only if the new information is *diagnostic*, that is, relevant and informative (Hess & Emery, 2012; Hess et al., 2005). It appears that in order for older adults to invest information-processing resources in making a judgment, they need to be invested in the social situation that the judgment is made.

In some situations, older adults may be at a disadvantage when processing social information. Researchers have found although younger and older adults can process social information similarly, older adults are at a disadvantage when the social context is cognitively demanding (Hess & Emery, 2012; Kalokerinos et al., 2015). A cognitively demanding situation is similar to Alexandra and Klaus's situation in the vignette in which they were trying to understand their grandchildren's behavior under conditions of time pressure and multiple distractions. Researchers find when older adults take their time to make a social judgment, they process information similarly to younger adults and take into consideration all of the relevant information. However, when cognitive resources are stretched, they have difficulty remembering the information they need to make their social judgments (Coats & Blanchard-Fields, 2013; Ybarra et al., 2011).

Interestingly, there may be a positive interaction-cumulative benefit of personal control and impression formation in social relations that may help optimize cognitive aging. Zahodne (2021) speculates that despite the fact historically marginalized racial and ethnic groups face significant barriers to acquiring certain psychosocial protective factors (e.g., perceived control), these same groups also exhibit sources of psychosocial resilience (e.g., religious involvement—discussed in Chapter 9) that allow them to achieve better late-life cognitive health than would be otherwise expected. With regard to social relations, of which impression formation and emotional intelligence are crucial components, converging evidence indicates that fostering late-life social networks and social support (discussed in Chapter 11) in particular may have high potential for building cognitive reserve and promoting healthy cognitive aging.

Knowledge Accessibility and Social Judgments

Although we make judgments about people upon initial meeting and novel situations all the time, we tend not to be aware of exactly how those judgments are made. When we are faced with new situations, we draw on our previous experiences stored in memory, in other words, our **social knowledge**.

The stored knowledge about previous situations that might be similar and how easily we can retrieve it affects what types of social judgments we make and how we behave in social situations. If you are arriving on your first day of work, for example, in order to act appropriately you draw on social knowledge that tells you "how to behave in a job setting." This process includes having available stored representations of the social world or memories of past events, how to apply those memories to various situations, and easy access to the memories.

We draw on implicit theories of personality (our personal theories of how personality works) to make judgments. For example, we could draw on our social knowledge of how a supervisor should behave at work. If the supervisor's behavior is inconsistent with our implicit theory of how they should act, this affects the impression we form of the supervisor. If a supervisor dresses in shorts and a torn T-shirt and makes not-so-casual references about the wild party they attended last night at which everyone became highly intoxicated, this may violate our implicit theory that supervisors should dress and act professionally. Research supports that implicit personality theories we have about people, in general, influence the impressions we form about specific individuals (Kalokerinos et al., 2015; Uleman & Kressel, 2013).

However, the fact social information in memory is available does not necessarily imply it is always easy to access. The degree to which information in memory is easily accessible and remembered (discussed in Chapter 6) determines the extent that information will guide social judgments and/or behavior. Easy access to information will be influenced by several variables. First, accessibility depends on the strength of the information stored in memory. If a person has extensive past experience with people who are aggressive, retrieving and applying the specific personality trait "aggressive" will be a highly accessible social knowledge structure representing features of this particular personality trait (e.g., bullying, dominance in social situations, highly competitive, and so on). Thus, a person would judge a person as "aggressive" by interpreting the collection of behaviors you associate with "aggressive" as clearly diagnostic of aggressiveness.

In contrast, the personality trait construct "aggressive" would not be easily accessible for people who have little or no experience with aggressive people because the trait of aggressiveness may not have been retrieved often and the underlying knowledge base could be quite limited. These people would be likely to interpret the behavior differently (Uleman & Kressel, 2013). They may consider the bullying or aggressive behavior a person exhibits as indicative of positive leadership, for instance.

Age differences in the accessibility of social knowledge influence social judgments across adulthood. First, as we learned in the case of impression formation, older adults rely on easily accessible social knowledge structures such as the initial impression made about an individual. Second, **age differences in knowledge accessibility also depend on the extent people rely on source judgments, in other words, when they try to determine the source of a particular piece of information.** Suppose you were introduced to two new people last week. Jane is an athlete and Sereatha really enjoys reading and studying. Sereatha revealed to you a love of tennis. Today, you are asked whether it was Jane or Sereatha that loves to play tennis. This is a source judgment.

Mather and colleagues (Mather, 2012, 2016; Nashiro et al., 2013) found that when making source judgments, older adults rely more on easily accessible knowledge than younger adults. In the example of meeting Jane and Sereatha, older adults would be more likely to erroneously remember Jane loves to play tennis, as they would rely on an easily accessible stereotype of an athlete is more likely to love tennis than the bookworm.

Taiyou Nomachi/DigitalVision/Getty Images

Remembering how you learned information about this person is an example of source judgments.

Finally, older adults are more susceptible to social judgment biases because they have trouble distinguishing between true and false information (discussed in Chapter 6). This helps explain why older adults have more difficulty accurately updating judgments and are more likely to be susceptible to deceptive messages (e.g., phishing emails, false requests for personal information—discussed in Chapters 2 and 7; Marsh & Yang, 2021).

Neuroimaging research indicates damage to or age-related changes in certain parts of the prefrontal cortex may be responsible for increased susceptibility to false information (Asp et al., 2012; Marsh & Yang, 2021; Parris, 2016). We noted in Chapter 2 that this region of the brain is central to a host of complex cognitive and emotional processing. Therefore, there may be an age-related neurological reason why older adults are more likely to believe misleading information, such as that used in advertising or political campaigns.

A Processing Capacity Explanation for Age Differences in Social Judgments

Based on the research discussed so far, one could conclude that underlying processing resource limitations play an important role in understanding how older adults acquire and use social information. In fact, social cognitive researchers have long used information-processing models to describe how individuals make social judgments. In one of the best-known models, Gilbert and Malone (1995) established that the ability to make unbiased social judgments depends on the cognitive demands accompanying those judgments. We all make snap initial judgments, but then under some circumstances, we reconsider and evaluate possible extenuating circumstances that lead us to revise those judgments. This revision process is cognitively demanding, and if we are busy thinking about something else we may not be able to revise our initial judgments because we don't have enough cognitive resources remaining.

As is discussed in more depth in the later section on causal attributions, Blanchard-Fields and colleagues (Blanchard-Fields & Beatty, 2005; Blanchard-Fields et al., 2012) found that most older adults consistently hold to their initial judgments or conclusions (e.g., about why negative events occur) more often than younger adults. They appear not to adjust their initial judgments by considering other factors, as Alexandra and Klaus were able to do in the vignette when they revised their interpretation of their grandchildren's behavior.

Because older adults typically exhibit lower levels of underlying basic cognitive processing resources (discussed in Chapter 6), it is reasonable that this decline in resource capacity might impact social judgment processes. In the case of impression formation, older adults may have limited cognitive resources to process additional detailed information presented after the initial impression is formed. Such additional information overtaxes available processing resources. Similarly, source judgments and selectively attending to only certain "true" information also places demands on one's cognitive resources.

If processing resource capacity is the major explanation of age-related differences in social judgment biases, then it should affect all types of situations older people encounter. However, it also may be that to the extent social information is easily (and perhaps automatically) accessible, it operates independently of processing resource limitations to influence social judgments directly.

Attributional Biases

Consider the following scenario:

> Erin is cleaning up after her infant son who spilled his dinner all over the table and floor. At the same time, she is listening on the phone to a coworker, Brittany, describing the anxiety that occurred while making a marketing presentation in front of new clients earlier that day. Brittany is also describing how the supervisor said the company depended heavily on this presentation to obtain a contract from the new clients. Brittany did admit that giving presentations to prospective clients is part of the job, and that high anxiety accompanies every presentation. After the phone call, Erin reflected on Brittany's situation. Erin decided Brittany is an anxious person and should work on reducing anxiety in these types of situations.

Erin was interested in what caused Brittany's anxiety when presenting information at work. Was it something about Brittany, such as being an anxious person? Or was it because of the pressure placed on Brittany by her supervisor or even to just being in the wrong place at the wrong time?

Answers to these questions provide insights into particular types of social judgments people make to explain their behavior that are referred to as causal attributions. **Causal attributions** are explanations of why behaviors occur. There are two main types of attributions: dispositional and situational. A **dispositional attribution** is a causal attribution that concludes the cause resides within the actor. Erin's explanation that "Brittany is just an anxious person" would be a dispositional attribution of why Brittany is nervous. A **situational attribution** is an explanation that the cause resides outside the actor. An explanation such as, "Brittany is succumbing to pressures from the supervisor" would be a situational attribution.

In this section, we explore whether there are age differences in the tendency to rely more on dispositional attributions, situational attributions, or on a combination of both when making causal attributions.

One line of research on attributions and aging concerns attributional judgments made about the older adults in general, for instance, involving competence in some domain such as memory. In such situations, attributions about older persons' successes and failures are compared to attributions about similar successes and failures of younger adults. Results indicate that such attributions go hand-in-hand with the stereotyping of older adults; for example, older adults' memory failures are given more dispositional attributions whereas younger adults' memory failures are given more situational attributions.

A second focus of attribution and aging research examines changes in the nature of attributional processes, per se, in an adult developmental context as much of the research on attributions focuses on college students. Thus, the question can be asked whether findings typically discovered in social psychological attribution theory and research hold true beyond the college years (Blanchard-Fields et al., 2008).

For many years, we have known that emerging adults have a tendency to draw inferences about older people's dispositions from behavior that can be fully explained through situational factors, called **correspondence bias** (Gilbert & Malone, 1995). Ignoring critical situational information in determining the cause of another person's behavior can have important consequences in both individual and societal contexts.

Suppose you tried to contact your psychology professor yesterday regarding a question you had about course material. They did not acknowledge you. You might decide because your professor ignored your question that they are arrogant (a dispositional attribution). At the same time, you may have ignored important situational information, such as they were unavailable due to teaching another class or a personal appointment. Thus, you did not consider other potential pertinent information to make a more accurate attribution. This type of finding has been well documented with emerging adults. However, it may be the case the life experience accumulated by middle-aged and older adults causes them to make different attributions because they have learned to consider multiple types of information in explaining why things happen the way they do.

Age-related differences would reflect key differences we noted in modes of thinking that change across adulthood. As discussed in Chapter 7, the inclusion of situational factors, even when they are not obviously present, characterizes established, middle-aged, and older adults' default modes of thinking. These adults are much more likely to factor in context or situational factors in analyzing problems, such as why people behave or react in the ways they do. Is there evidence for this regarding attributions?

In a series of creative investigations, Blanchard-Fields (Blanchard-Fields & Beatty, 2005; Blanchard-Fields & Horhota, 2006; Blanchard-Fields et al., 2007; Blanchard-Fields et al., 2012) studied the differences in causal attributions across the adult life span. Blanchard-Fields and colleagues presented participants with different situations having positive or negative outcomes and asked them to decide whether something about the main character in the story (dispositional attributions), the situation (situational attributions), or a combination of both (interactive attributions) was responsible for the event. The vignettes represented situations such as that described earlier in the chapter describing how Allen was pressuring Tom to live with him before marriage. Suppose that Tom protested but Allen continued to pressure, and the relationship ended up falling apart. When the target events are ambiguous as to what was the specific cause of the outcome, as with Allen and Tom, all adults tend to make interactive attributions (i.e., say that it was a combination of dispositional and situational factors that drove the behavior), but older adults did so at a higher rate. However, as can be determined from Figure 8.5, older adults paradoxically also blamed the main character more (made dispositional attributions) than younger groups, especially in negative relationship situations.

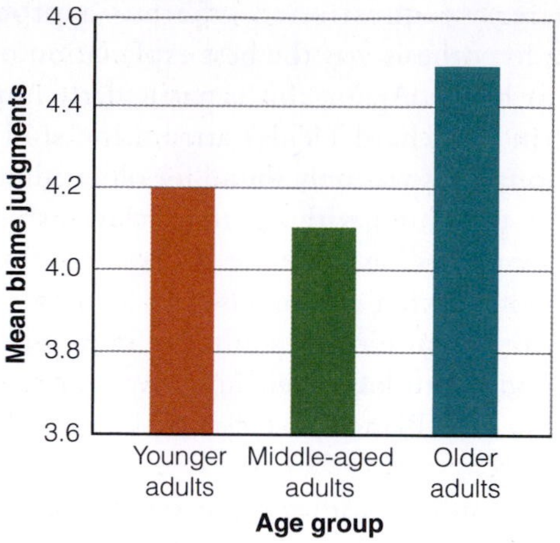

Figure 8.5 Dispositional attributions as a function of age.

In her research, Blanchard-Fields took a sociocultural perspective in explaining why older adults were more predisposed to making dispositional attributions and engaged in less postformal reasoning in negative relationship situations. She notes the correspondence bias in older adults only occurred in negative relationship situations. In this case, older adults appeared to apply specific social rules about relationships in making their attributional judgments, apparently because of their stage in life and the cohort in which they were socialized (such as rules about whether career or marriage is a higher priority). In these situations, strong beliefs about how one should act in relationship situations appeared to be violated for the older adults, particularly for older women. Therefore, these participants made snap judgments about the main character when that character violated their strong beliefs, and they did not engage in conscious, deliberate analyses. They simply "knew" the character was wrong.

The interesting question arises, however, as to whether these attributional biases in older adults are truly due to activated belief systems that strongly impact their judgments, or whether the older adults are simply failing to conduct a more thorough causal analysis. This failure to analyze could be the result of limited cognitive resources that would prevent them from processing all details of the situation (e.g., extenuating situational circumstances). The vignette involving Erin at the beginning of this module exemplifies how, on one hand, we can rely on our experience to guide us through uncomfortable situations; but on the other hand, a reduction in our capacity does not allow us to consider all the relevant information in this case to make an accurate judgment about Brittany's behavior.

Earlier we questioned whether a processing resource hypothesis was the best explanation of social judgment biases. Again, this is particularly important because in Blanchard-Fields's attribution studies, the dispositional bias was only found for older adults when they were presented with negative relationship situations. Researchers have found everyday reasoning biases in older adults occur not because of declining cognitive ability, but because older adults are more likely than younger adults to base their judgments on their own personal beliefs (Blanchard-Fields et al., 2012; Horhota et al., 2014).

These findings indicate the explanations people create to account for behavioral variances depending on the type of situation (e.g., relationship or achievement situations), the age of the person, and whether strongly held social beliefs have been violated by a person in the situation. What is also important is the sociocultural context in which people are socialized, since this appears to create different social rules that are then used to make causal attributions. Additional research supports this idea.

Blanchard-Fields, Chen, and colleagues (2007) examined causal attributions in younger and older Chinese adults in comparison to younger and older American adults. They found older Americans demonstrated a greater correspondence bias than younger Americans. However, both younger and older Chinese adults performed similarly and had less correspondence bias overall. Older Americans may focus their attributions on the individual due to a lifelong experience of an individualistic orientation; that is, American culture supports the right of each person to make up their own mind about social matters, whereas other cultures tend to support standards developed at the societal level and are more taken for granted by individuals.

In order to adjust this initial judgment, the contextual information must be made salient to people in a socially meaningful manner. Support for this idea comes from studies indicating that when there is a plausible motivation for the target person's behavior, older adults revise their judgments to be less biased than in a standard attitude attribution paradigm (Blanchard-Fields & Horhota, 2006). Additionally, mindfulness training has been found to reduce correspondence bias in emerging adults (Hopthrow et al., 2017).

For older Americans to revise their attributions, the situation itself needs to provide a meaningful reason why a person would contradict their own beliefs in making an attribution. For Chinese older adults, the meaningful nature of the situation does not need to be emphasized because to them situational influences and constraints represent the natural and usual manner to approach any judgment situation reflected in their lifelong experience of living within a collectivist orientation. More research is needed to shed additional light on how these age differences are created and under what circumstances they appear.

Adult Development in Action

How might older adults' impression formation behavior be important to you as a political candidate?

Review Questions

8.5 Social Judgment Processes

- What is emotional intelligence? How does it develop across adulthood?
- What are the stages in attributional processing? What is the negativity bias, and what are the age differences in its impact?
- Describe the age differences in the extent that trait information is used in forming an impression.
- How does processing capacity affect social cognitive processing?
- What influences the accessibility of social information?
- What is the status of processing resource limitations as an explanation for social judgment biases?
- What are causal attributions? What is a correspondence bias? Are there age differences in the correspondence bias? If so, under what conditions?
- What accounts for the age differences in the correspondence bias?

8.6 The Sociocultural Contexts of Cognition

Key Questions

- What is the social facilitation of cognitive functioning?
- What is collaborative cognition, and does it facilitate cognition and memory in older adults?
- How do sociocultural contexts influence cognition in older adults?

Tyrique and Venus's granddaughter asked them what happened when they first met. Venus recalled they met at a march for civil rights following the assassination of Dr. Martin Luther King, Jr. but couldn't remember the name of the person who introduced them; she could only describe him as tall and dark-haired. However, this cued Tyrique; he remembered the man's name was Samuel. This back-and-forth remembering continued until, to their own amazement, they successfully reconstructed the whole march. Their granddaughter was delighted and complimented them on how they made their story come alive.

When we typically think about the memories of older adults, we usually think of each individual's performance. Tyrique and Venus's reliance on each other to remember a past event exemplifies how our cognitive processes can work together to serve adaptive functions in social settings. In fact, how the social context can help compensate for memory difficulties and facilitate memory performance is an important focus for understanding the dynamics of long-term friends and couples, and for intervention research. In this section, we examine two approaches to this issue: collaborative cognition and facilitative sociocultural contexts.

Similar to practical intelligence, wisdom, and everyday problem solving discussed in Chapter 7, the social cognition perspective offers us an enriched understanding of cognitive competence in older adulthood. We are interested in how changes in social cognitive functioning both reflect the changing life contexts of the individual and affect adaptation to these changing contexts. In the previous modules in this chapter, we focused primarily on how developmental changes in representations of self or other (such as social beliefs and self-beliefs) influence social cognitive processes such as making attributional judgments. In this module, we focus on social cognition as it relates to the dynamic interplay among self, others, and context. A less researched but extremely important domain of social cognition and aging is how the particular types of social settings where we communicate with others influence our cognitive processing. This relates to a different aspect of social cognition and aging research: the sociocultural facilitation of cognitive functioning.

Collaborative Cognition

It is said that two heads are better than one. When it comes to cognition, it's usually true. In everyday life, it's often the case that we think about, analyze, and remember things with others. A key aspect of social cognition is understanding how cognition occurs when we are interacting with others, and not simply doing all the work alone. The central focus of this research is the benefits and costs of collaborative cognition on cognitive performance (e.g., memory and problem solving) (Bietti & Sutton, 2015; Dixon, 2011; Martens, 2020). **Collaborative cognition** *occurs when two or more people work together on a cognitive task.*

Collaborative cognition enhances adults' performance on a variety of memory and problem-solving tasks, thus serving an important adaptive function (Brennan & Enns, 2015). Researchers are interested in examining how this type of collaborative context could mitigate the normative performance declines in memory typically documented when assessing older adults in the laboratory (discussed in Chapter 6). Due to our social nature, humans are "wired" to seek efficient, effective strategies to address cognitive problems when the opportunity to work with others is available (Andrade-Lotero & Goldstone, 2021). How do we know?

Research suggests older adults collaborate on story recall as well as problem-solving performance, and their performance is better than the average performance of older adults in individual settings (Dixon, 2011). Memory knowledge and performance is also enhanced, not only in traditional situations in which collaboration is face-to-face and direct, but also when it is more indirect, technology-supported, and mediated (Michaelian & Arango-Muñoz, 2017). For example, by using a cognitive style of cooperation that minimizes working memory demands on a recall task, older married couples performed just as well as younger couples. There is also evidence of the positive outcomes of collaboration

Blend Images/Superstock

Older adults tend to use strategies such as collaborative cognition to compensate for declining memories by jointly remembering events with others.

when older adults tackle everyday problem-solving tasks such as errand running and planning a vacation (Allaire, 2012). Clearly, cognitive performance on many tasks improves with collaboration—when people decide to collaborate.

Interestingly, older adults prefer to collaborate on cognitive processing tasks when they perceive deficiencies in their own functioning and may prefer to work alone when they feel competent in the area (Strough et al., 2002). Collaborators of all ages report the benefits include optimizing the decision, enhancing the relationship, and compensating for individual weaknesses (Dixon, 2011; Kimbler et al., 2012; Michaelian & Arango-Muñoz, 2017). However, collaboration is not without its costs; people may act selfishly, withhold honest opinions, and not meet their partner's needs. It is also the case that enhanced remembering occurs most for collective recall of personal events; on standard laboratory tasks such as list learning, collaboration can even inhibit performance (Harris et al., 2017). The difference appears to be related to the opportunity to add personally relevant details to events that are not strictly necessary, but that serve to make the remembering process truly more personal to the people involved. As an example, you may have experienced situations in which people brought up an issue, but the discussion quickly turned to one involving personal reflections on the episode (the social context, who was there, what else happened, etc.), and not just the "facts" of the issue.

The composition of the group doing collaborative cognition also appears to matter. Pepe and colleagues (2021) report that in diverse groups of Asian American, White, and Black participants, Black members contributed less during collaboration and did not demonstrate post-collaborative recall benefits, and all-White groups exhibited the highest level of collaborative benefits. Such differences reflect prior experience; for example, Black or women members of a team may have experienced times when their contributions were downplayed or criticized, so they become reticent to add to the discussion.

What is it about collaboration that boosts performance in certain circumstances? Bietti and Sutton (2015) describe a succession of processes that occur as the time scale increases and the memory goes from personal to cultural: (a) faster, lower-level coordination processes of behavioral matching and interactional synchrony occurring at short timescale; (b) mid-range collaborative processes which re-evoke past experiences in groups, unfolding at longer timescales; (c) cooperative processes involved in the transmission of memories over even longer periods; and (d) cultural processes and practices operating within distributed sociocognitive networks over evolutionary and historical time frames. Thus, collaborative cognition can occur from the small scale of two people (e.g., a couple remembering a movie they saw together) up through entire societies (e.g., societal remembering of a major historical event such as a presidential election).

This approach can be taken to a more general explanatory approach to knowledge generated by a group called **transactive memory systems** (Liao et al., 2012; Palermos, 2020). These models share the view that each person (or group) brings certain experiences and expertise to the collaborative context. As noted in Figure 8.6, there is a recognition and acceptance of each person (or group's) contribution, and a presumption that the information or views contributed and shared are both reliable and valid. Thus, the combined views, expertise, and rememberings of each person (or group) serve to enhance what would have been produced by any one member (or group), resulting in better ideas and rememberings.

Because collaborative cognition is such a common experience and likely to be grounded in the nuances of the relationships people develop over time, it will be a rich area to learn more about the developmental trajectory of memory across adulthood. Most people do remembering in collaborative situations multiple times a day, whether with a spouse or partner or with other family or friends. As we will consider in Chapter 11, the quality of the relationship where this cognitive activity occurs probably has important influences on actual performance. Whether this is true, though, awaits more research.

Sociocultural Contexts of Memory

Another approach to identifying conditions when social facilitation of cognition in older adults occurs is in examining contextual variables, especially culture, that influence memory performance (Cerulo et al., 2021). Taking this approach puts a different spin on collective cognition, especially memory. This different perspective entails separating what is termed "collective memory" or "communicative memory" and its social basis from "cultural memory" and its cultural basis (A. Assmann, 2021; J. Assmann, 2011). **Collective or communicative memory** refers to the recent past, particularly personal and autobiographical memories, and is characterized by a typical span

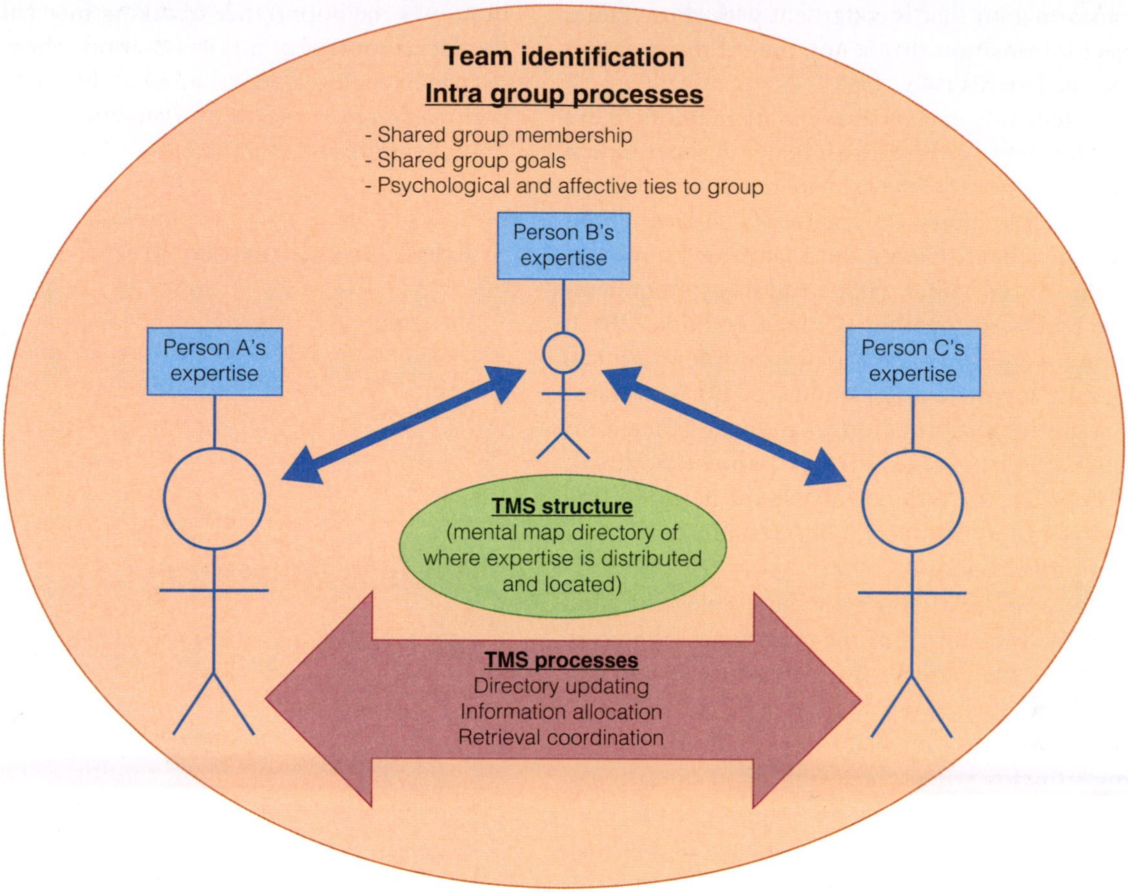

Figure 8.6 Model of transactive memory systems.

Source: Liao, J., Jimmieson, N., O'Brien, A., & Restubog, S. (2012). Developing transactive memory systems: Theoretical contributions from a social identity perspective. *Group & Organization Management, 37*, 204–240. Figure 1. https://doi.org/10.1177/1059601112443976.

of three to four generations (about 80 to 110 years). Due to its personal focus, special knowledge or expertise on the part of those who transmit it is not necessary. An example would be the stories and memories shared at a family or alumni reunion. Sharing these memories is a key role in most sociocultural groups; we will encounter the formal role of "kinkeeper" in Chapter 11 that assigns this role to particular family members.

In contrast, **cultural memory** is created through symbolic heritage. This may be embodied in texts, rites, art, music, monuments, celebrations, objects, sacred scriptures, and other media that serve as mnemonic triggers for remembering the meanings associated with something that has happened. Cultural memory can refer to the time of mythical origins, crystallize collective experiences of the past, and can last for millennia. Cultural memory's function, then, is to unify and stabilize a common identity that spans many generations, and it is not easy to change. For those reasons, cultural memory presupposes knowledge restricted to those who have been brought into the culture. An example is the ancient stories and myths about the founding of a country and what it's values are claimed to be that are used often in speeches by heads of state.

Both collective/communicative memory and cultural memory influence what individuals incorporate into their own personal memories of events. For instance, if you hear a story from older family members about something that occurred in your life when you were an infant enough times, there is a tendency to incorporate that event into your own autobiography as if the memory is actually yours. Similarly, the more you incorporate the shared story about the values that your home country claims, the more likely you will be to accept information that is congruent with those values and reject information that is not, even if the former is false and the latter is true.

How does this matter in everyday memory? Let's note that memory performance is better in sociocultural contexts when the task approximates a real-world learning and social memory experience (C. Adams et al., 2002). Others have pointed out that prior knowledge (Stein-Morrow & Miller, 2009) and how often memories are practiced together (Coman & Hirst, 2012) also influence performance. For example, a typical and relevant cognitive task for older adults is to transmit sociocultural information to younger generations (Birditt et al., 2012; Quéniart & Charpentier, 2013). In this context, the older adult would be motivated to communicate effectively, and transmit collective/communicative memories.

Storytelling situation is a good example. This kind of context is different from the traditional laboratory context, when the demand is to reproduce as much of the content of a text as possible. Adams and colleagues (2002) found when they placed older adults in a storytelling situation where they were asked to learn and retell a story from memory to a young child, their retellings of the story contained more detail and were more fluent than those of younger adults. Perhaps this superior performance stems from increased motivation in a social context where their concerns were directed at producing an interesting and coherent story for the child. This is a demonstration of how the social-communicative context or experience enhances what is most salient to the individual. Again, this finding illustrates the importance of taking into consideration the social context of a task situation when examining change in cognitive functioning as we grow older. This is also a common means of intergenerational transmission of culture and identity.

Adult Development in Action

How might the research on collaborative cognition be used in therapeutic situations you might design if you were working in a long-term care facility?

Review Questions

8.6 The Sociocultural Contexts of Cognition

- What is collaborative cognition? What evidence suggests collaborative cognition compensates for memory failures in older adults?
- How does collaborative cognition facilitate problem-solving behavior?
- What theories have been proposed to describe collaborative cognition?
- What are collective/communicative memory and cultural memory? How do they influence social cognition?
- What does it mean to say the social context facilitates cognitive performance?

Social Policy Implications

Polarization, Sociocultural Contexts of Cognition, and Aging

In the United States, the notion of "red states" and "blue states" is shorthand for an accepted view of the polarized nature of beliefs that is reflected best in elected politics and the so-called "culture wars." Although it is easily shown that neither "red" or "blue" states are as monochromatic as the labels imply (for example, there are plenty of people who ascribe to "red state" positions in "blue state New York" and proponents of "blue state ideas" in "red state Alabama"), the labels stick anyway.

Polarized beliefs have characterized societies since the beginning of historical record keeping. Examples in American history abound, from the 1796 presidential election, termed by many historians as perhaps the nastiest ever, to the Civil War, to the Vietnam and civil rights era marked with political assassinations, to the Black Lives Matter movement. How these are framed, though, reflect the influence of several factors: sociocultural aspects of cognition (e.g., collective/communicative memory and cultural memory), cognitive developmental level (discussed in Chapter 7), and socio-emotional processing (discussed in Chapters 2 and 6). Taken together, they provide a way to interpret the present experience of polarization and its consequences for what does (and does not) get done in federal and state legislatures. Let's go a bit deeper to find out how.

Jan Sinnott and Joan Rabin (2021) collected a series of papers that provides context, research, and theory on the forces that shape the various debates. For example, Cavanaugh and Cavanaugh (2021) explain how judgment and decision-making heuristics and biases (discussed in Chapter 6), cognitive developmental changes in default modes of thinking (discussed in Chapter 7), and sociocultural contexts of cognition help us understand how people become convinced of a specific set of "facts" and unable to incorporate contrary evidence. Joan Rabin (2021) applies the idea of cultural memory to our understanding of "national identity." Gizem and Burak (2021) apply ideas from impression formation to styles of leadership.

The importance of focusing on aspects of social cognition as a lens through which we can interpret polarization is ultimately played out in elections and in actions in legislatures. All of the factors we have considered in Chapters 2, 6, 7, and 8 interact in these contexts. How? Consider the ads for candidates during an election cycle. These ads tend to be short, focus on a specific message crafted to connect to already-held knowledge so as to trigger cognitive heuristics and biases, connect with strong emotions, and gloss over or omit information that might result in a deeper processing of the message. In legislatures, loud, frequent voices that are not demographically representative of a district are presumed to reflect "the will of the people." And the party out of power refuses to support anything proposed by the party in power much of the time, even if it would clearly benefit the people in their district, and even if something nearly identical had been proposed by their own party when they held the majority, and uses arguments to support this behavior that are also crafted to align with preconceived knowledge and ideas.

Based on the research reviewed in Chapters 2, 6, 7, and 8, change requires creating situations that support deeper thinking and analysis, and that connects with emotions that in turn are commonly held (e.g., support and service to others in need). We know from other discussions in Chapter 7 that logic alone will fail.

An interesting observation is that humans, by nature, seek social connection and social cognitive interactions. So it would seem that getting people "out of their respective bubbles" might be a way to find common ground. Perhaps. But as we learned from research on collaborative memory in diverse groups, it is not always as simple as creating new groups. But the evidence for seeking the solutions within the domain of social cognition is overwhelming. Performance, measured in many different ways, is usually better and more facets are explored when people come together and work for common cause.

In Review

Your summary should be based on six paragraphs. The first should focus on stereotypes of aging, and describe what those are and how they are understood within stereotype embodiment theory. You should also explain how stereotypes get activated.

The second paragraph should focus on what is known about age-related differences in social beliefs and self-perceptions. Note also whether these social perceptions and self-perceptions hold cross-culturally.

Your third paragraph should discuss the different types of social processing goals (personal, emotional, and cognitive style). What are the main drivers of each?

The fourth paragraph should define personal control, the different types of control, and age-related differences in them. How is personal control considered multidimensional? How do different personal control beliefs influence behavior and performance?

Your fifth paragraph should define and discuss what is meant by emotional intelligence, impression formation, social judgments, and attributional biases. What is the connection of these to processing capacity?

Your final paragraph should discuss the aspects underlying collaborative cognition and the sociocultural contexts of cognition. What processing models have been proposed to explain the sociocultural factors in cognition, especially in memory?

Integrating Concepts in Development

- To what degree are declines in processing resource capacity discussed in Chapter 6 as ubiquitous in their effects on social cognitive processes?
- What relations can be found among dispositional traits, personal concerns, and life narratives?

- How does emotion as a processing goal relate to socio-emotional selectivity theory in Chapter 10?
- How does social cognition relate to postformal thought as discussed in Chapter 7?
- How does personal control relate to concepts such as memory self-efficacy discussed in Chapter 6?

Key Terms

accommodations Readjustments of goals and aspirations as a way to lessen or neutralize the effects of negative self-evaluations in key domains. 264

age-based double standard When an individual attributes an older person's failure in memory as more serious than a memory failure observed in a young adult. 252

assimilative activities Exercises that prevent or alleviate losses in domains that are personally relevant for self-esteem and identity. 264

causal attributions Explanations people construct to explain their behavior, which can be situational, dispositional, or interactive. 272

cognitive style A traitlike pattern of behavior one uses when approaching a problem-solving situation. 261

collaborative cognition Cognitive performance that results from the interaction of two or more individuals. 275

collective or communicative memory Refers to the recent past, particularly personal and autobiographical memories, and is characterized by a typical span of three to four generations (about 80 to 110 years). 276

correspondence bias The tendency to draw inferences about older people's dispositions from behavior that can be fully explained through situational factors. 272

cultural memory Memory created through symbolic heritage. 277

dispositional attribution An explanation for someone's behavior that resides within the actor. 272

emotional intelligence (EI) People's ability to recognize their own and others' emotions, to correctly identify and appropriately tell the difference between emotions, and use this information to guide their thinking and behavior. 266

immunizing mechanisms Control strategies that alter the effects of self-discrepant evidence. 264

implicit stereotyping Stereotyped beliefs that affect your judgments of individuals without your being aware of it (i.e., the process is unconscious). 251

impression formation The way people combine the components of another person's personality and come up with an integrated perception of the person. 268

labeling theory Argues that when we confront an age-related stereotype, older adults are more likely to integrate it into their self-perception. 257

negativity bias Weighing negative information more heavily than positive information in a social judgment. 269

personal control The belief that what one does has an influence on the outcome of an event. 263

positivity effect The tendency to attend to and process positive information over negative information. 261

primary control The act of bringing the environment into line with one's own desires and goals, similar to Brandtstädter's assimilative activities. 264

resilience theory Argues that confronting a negative stereotype results in a rejection of that view in favor of a more positive self-perception. 257

secondary control The act of bringing oneself in line with the environment, similar to Brandtstädter's accommodative activities. 264

self-perception of aging Refers to individuals' perceptions of their own age and aging. 256

situational attribution An explanation for someone's behavior that is external to the actor. 272

social cognition Involves how people process, store, and apply information about other people and social situations, and how cognition plays a role in social situations. 248

social knowledge A cognitive structure that represents one's general knowledge about a given social concept or domain. 270

source judgments Process of accessing knowledge wherein one attempts to determine where one obtained a particular piece of information. 271

stereotype embodiment theory Proposes that stereotypes in general, and aging stereotypes in the present case, become self-perceptions when they are assimilated from the surrounding culture into one's self-definitions that, in turn, influence functioning and health. 250

stereotypes Beliefs about characteristics, attributes, and behaviors of members of certain groups. 249

stereotype threat An evoked fear of being judged in accordance with a negative stereotype about a group to which an individual belongs. 253

Personality

Chapter 9

Chapter Outline

Learning Objectives

After studying this chapter, you will be able to...

9.1. Describe the Five-Factor Model and the developmental trajectories of dispositional traits.

9.2. Describe Jung's and Erikson's theories and how personal concerns change across adulthood.

9.3. Describe McAdams' life-story model, Whitbourne's identity theory, and the Six-Foci Model.

9.4. Describe the importance of self-concept, gender identity, possible selves, and spirituality for adult personality.

Maya Angelou (1969) perhaps said it best: "There is no agony like bearing an untold story inside of you." True to her conviction, she spent a lifetime writing her story in numerous books, poems, and other literary works. She described an incredible developmental path of oppression, hatred, and hurt that ultimately resulted in self-awareness, understanding, and compassion. For example, in her later years she realized in confronting the atrocities of the world that if she accepted the fact of evil, she also had to accept the fact of good, thereby providing her with as little fear as possible for the anticipation of death. Another example involves integrating spirituality into her self-perception. Author Ken Kelley once asked her how spirituality fits into a way of life. She answered, "There is something more, the spirit, or the soul. I think that that quality encourages our courtesy, and care, and our minds. And mercy, and identity" (Kelley, 1995).

Maya Angelou's writings reflect some of the key issues involved in personality development we will examine in this chapter. First, we consider whether personality changes or remains stable across adulthood. We examine this from two perspectives: a dispositional trait perspective, as well as a personal concerns perspective. Then we consider how we construct life narratives and our identity and self.

AP Images/Lincoln Journal Star, Robert Becker

Maya Angelou

One of the oldest debates in psychology concerns whether personality development continues across the whole life span. From the earliest days, prominent people argued both sides. William James and Sigmund Freud believed personality was set by the time we reach adulthood. In contrast, Carl Jung asserted personality was continually shaped throughout our lives, with very important milestones occurring in middle age and late life.

Although we still have these two theoretical camps, one arguing for stability across adulthood and the other for change, there are ways to reconcile them. The data rarely converge neatly on only one perspective or another. Rather, results often depend on what specific measures researchers use and the aspect of personality investigated.

Why has the area of personality remained controversial for so long? The answer lies in how we use personality in daily life. At one level we all believe and base our interactions with people on the presumption their personality remains relatively constant over time. Imagine the chaos that would result if every week or so everyone woke up with a brand new personality: The once easy-going coworker is now a real tyrant, trusted friends become completely unpredictable, and our patterns of social interaction end up in shambles. Clearly, to survive in day-to-day life we must rely on a general consistency of personality. Abrupt and frequent changes are usually taken as indications that something is seriously amiss.

Still, we also believe quite strongly that people can change, especially with respect to undesirable aspects of their personalities. Imagine what it would be like if we could never change habits or tendencies that do us harm; if anxiety was a lifelong, incurable trait; or if our idiosyncratic tendencies causing others great annoyance could not be modified. The assumption of the modifiability of personality is strong indeed. The existence of psychotherapy and other forms of support (e.g., counseling, clinical social work, coaching) are formal verifications of that assumption.

Culture, Race, and Ethnicity in Personality Research

Our focus on personality in this chapter aims to help us understand what makes people the way they are—similar in some respects, different in others, combining in unique ways. To do so means we need to understand the broad kinds of forces that shape them, forces that include culture, race, and ethnicity. Although personality is one of the oldest topics in psychology, and has been the focus of tens of thousands of studies, few of them take these three forces into account to consider personality from perspectives other than the mainstream majority (Arshad & Chung, 2022; King, 2021).

Because social structures affect people (e.g., in terms of access to education and other resources that matter in shaping a person's personality), including samples of people who have been historically excluded in personality psychology is essential for understanding individual differences and personality processes. For example, some studies indicate that individuals' expression of their personality and self-views differ across different relationships and positions in society (Clifton, 2014). Findings also indicate geographical variations in personality traits, highlighting how contextual factors, such as racial diversity, community development, and crime rate, are associated with how people think, feel, and behave within and across countries (Rentfrow & Jokela, 2016).

Although relatively little research on personality has incorporated culture, race, and ethnicity, we will consider several of the studies that do as we proceed. We will examine work on dispositional traits, personal concerns, and life narratives that do include perspectives from various cultures and racial and ethnic groups. However, we must be cautious in generalizing from the mainstream work done mostly on White undergraduate students, and always keep in mind that it may or may not reflect results if other groups were included.

Levels of Analysis and Personality Research

Sorting out the various approaches to personality helps us understand what aspects of personality the various researchers describe. Drawing on the work of several theorists and researchers, McAdams (2015, 2021) describes three parallel levels of personality structure and function, each containing a wide range of personality constructs: dispositional traits, personal concerns, and life narrative.

- **Dispositional traits** consist of aspects of personality consistent across different contexts and can be compared across a group along a continuum representing high and low degrees of the characteristic. Dispositional traits are the level of personality most people think of first, and they include commonly used descriptors such as shy, talkative, authoritarian, and the like.
- **Personal concerns** consist of things important to people, their goals, and their major concerns in life. Personal concerns are usually described in motivational, developmental, or strategic terms; they reflect the stage of life a person is in at the time.
- **Life narrative** consists of the aspects of personality pulling everything together, those integrative aspects that give a person an identity or sense of self. The creation of one's identity is the goal of this level.

In an extension of McAdams's model of personality, Karen Hooker (Hooker, 2015; Hooker & McAdams, 2003; Ko et al., 2014) added three processes that act in tandem with the three structural components of personality proposed by McAdams:

- **State processes** act with dispositional traits to create transient, short-term changes in emotion, mood, hunger, anxiety, and so on.
- **Self-regulatory processes,** such as primary and secondary control (discussed in Chapter 8) and self-efficacy (discussed in Chapter 6), operate with personal concerns and are domain specific.
- **Cognitive processes** act jointly with life narratives to create natural interactions that occur between a storyteller and listener, processes central in organizing life stories.

Finally, as one moves from examining dispositional traits to personal concerns to life narrative (and their corresponding processes), it becomes more likely that observable change will take place (Debast et al., 2014; Hooker, 2015; Schultz & Schultz, 2017). In a sense, the level of dispositional traits can be viewed as the "raw stuff" of personality, whereas each of the next two successive levels must be constructed by the individual. In the following sections, we use McAdams's levels to organize our discussion of adulthood personality. Let's begin with the "raw stuff" and learn how dispositional traits are structured in adulthood.

9.1 Dispositional Traits Across Adulthood

Key Questions

- What is the Five-Factor Model of dispositional traits?
- What happens to dispositional traits across adulthood?
- What can we conclude from theory and research on dispositional traits?

Abby decided to attend her 20th high school reunion and hoped to see some of her friends from those days, especially Michelle. Abby remembered that in high school Michelle was always surrounded by a group of people. Michelle always walked up to people and initiated conversations, even with strangers, and was often described as the "life of the party." Abby wondered if Michelle would be the same outgoing person Abby remembered from high school.

Many people attend a high school reunion; perhaps you have been to one yourself. It is amusing, so it is said, to find out how our classmates changed over the years and whether we can recognize them. In addition to noticing physical changes, we also pay attention to personality characteristics. The questions that surfaced for Abby are similar to the ones we generate ourselves. For example, will Katy still be a fashion trendsetter? Will Kenan still be as concerned about social issues at 38 as they were at 18?

To learn as much about our friends as possible, we could make careful observations of our classmates' personalities over the course of several reunions. Then, at the gathering marking 60 years since graduation, we could examine the trends we observed. Did our classmates' personalities change substantially, or did they remain essentially the same as they were 60 years earlier?

How we think these questions will be answered provides clues to our personal beliefs concerning personality stability or change across adulthood. As we will uncover, beliefs about continuity and discontinuity shape and are shaped by our underlying beliefs about aging.

In addition to considering the old debate of whether Michelle's personality characteristics remained stable or have changed, Abby's description of Michelle suggests Michelle is an outgoing, or extroverted, person. How did Abby arrive at this judgment? She probably combined several aspects of Michelle's behavior into a concept that describes her rather concisely. What Abby has done is use the notion of a personality trait. Extending this same reasoning to many areas of behavior is the basis for trait theories of personality. More formally, people's characteristic behaviors can be understood through attributes that reflect underlying dispositional traits that are relatively enduring aspects of personality. We use the basic tenets of trait theory when we describe ourselves and others with such terms as calm, aggressive, independent, friendly, and so on.

Three assumptions are made about traits (Costa & McCrae, 2011). First, traits are based on comparisons of individuals, because there are no absolute quantitative standards for concepts such as friendliness. Second, the qualities or behaviors making up a particular trait must be distinctive enough to avoid confusion. Imagine the chaos if friendliness and aggressiveness had many behaviors in common and others were vastly different! Finally, the traits attributed to a specific person are assumed to be stable characteristics. We normally assume people who are friendly in several situations are going to be friendly the next time we see them.

These three assumptions are all captured in the classic definition of a trait: "A **trait** is any distinguishable, relatively enduring way that one individual differs from others" (Guilford, 1959, p. 6). Based on this definition, **trait theories** assume little change in personality occurs across adulthood.

Most trait theories have several common guiding principles. An important one for this discussion concerns the structure of traits. Like it does for intelligence (described in Chapter 7), structure concerns the way traits are organized hierarchically in the individual. This organization is usually inferred from the pattern of related and unrelated personality characteristics and is generally expressed in terms of dimensions (analogous to the "factors" in psychometric intelligence). Personality structures can be examined over time to see whether they change with age.

The Five-Factor Trait Model

One of the most important advances in research on adult development and aging has been the emergence of a personality theory aimed specifically at describing adults. Due mostly to the pioneering efforts of Robert McCrae and Paul Costa, Jr. (Costa & McCrae, 2011; McCrae, 2016, 2018; McCrae & Costa, 2003), we are now able to describe adults' personality traits using five dimensions: neuroticism, extraversion, openness to experience, agreeableness, and conscientiousness. These dimensions (the Five-Factor Model or the so-called Big Five traits) are strongly grounded in cross-sectional, longitudinal, and sequential research. First, though, let's consider each dimension. These descriptions are, necessarily, quite general. (You should consult the research by McCrae and Costa, cited earlier, for much more detail.) Within each dimension, several examples of common behavioral characteristics will be provided.

These examples may or may not all be present in any particular person displaying that dimension, nor are they the only characteristics, but are typical.

- People who are high on the **neuroticism** dimension tend to act anxious, hostile, self-conscious, depressed, impulsive, and vulnerable. They may exhibit negative emotions that interfere with their ability to get along with others or to handle problems in everyday life. People who are low on this dimension tend to be calm, even-tempered, self-content, comfortable, and hardy.
- Individuals who are high on the **extraversion** dimension thrive on social interaction, like to talk, take charge easily, readily express their opinions and feelings, like to keep busy, have boundless energy, and prefer stimulating and challenging environments. Such people tend to enjoy people-oriented jobs such as social work and sales. People who are low on this dimension tend to be reserved, quiet, and serious.
- People high on the **openness to experience** dimension tend to have a vivid imagination and dream life, an appreciation of art, and a strong desire to try anything once. These individuals tend to be naturally curious about things and to make decisions based on situational factors rather than absolute rules. People who are readily open to new experiences place a relatively low emphasis on personal economic gain. They tend to choose jobs such as the ministry or counseling, which offer wide varieties of experience rather than high pay. People who are low on this dimension tend to be down-to-earth, practical, conventional, less curious, and conservative.
- Scoring high on the **agreeableness** dimension is associated with being accepting, willing to work with others, and caring. People who score low on this dimension (i.e., demonstrate high levels of antagonism) tend to be more irritable and make say or do things intentionally that are offensive.
- People who characterized by high levels of **conscientiousness** tend to be hard-working, ambitious, energetic, scrupulous, and persevering. Such people have a strong desire to make something of themselves. People at the opposite end of this scale tend to not make and follow specific plans, may not always do what they promise, and may engage in riskier behavior.

Exciting neuroscience research suggests that each of the Big Five traits maps to a different part of the brain (Brooks et al., 2020). This is evident in Figure 9.1.

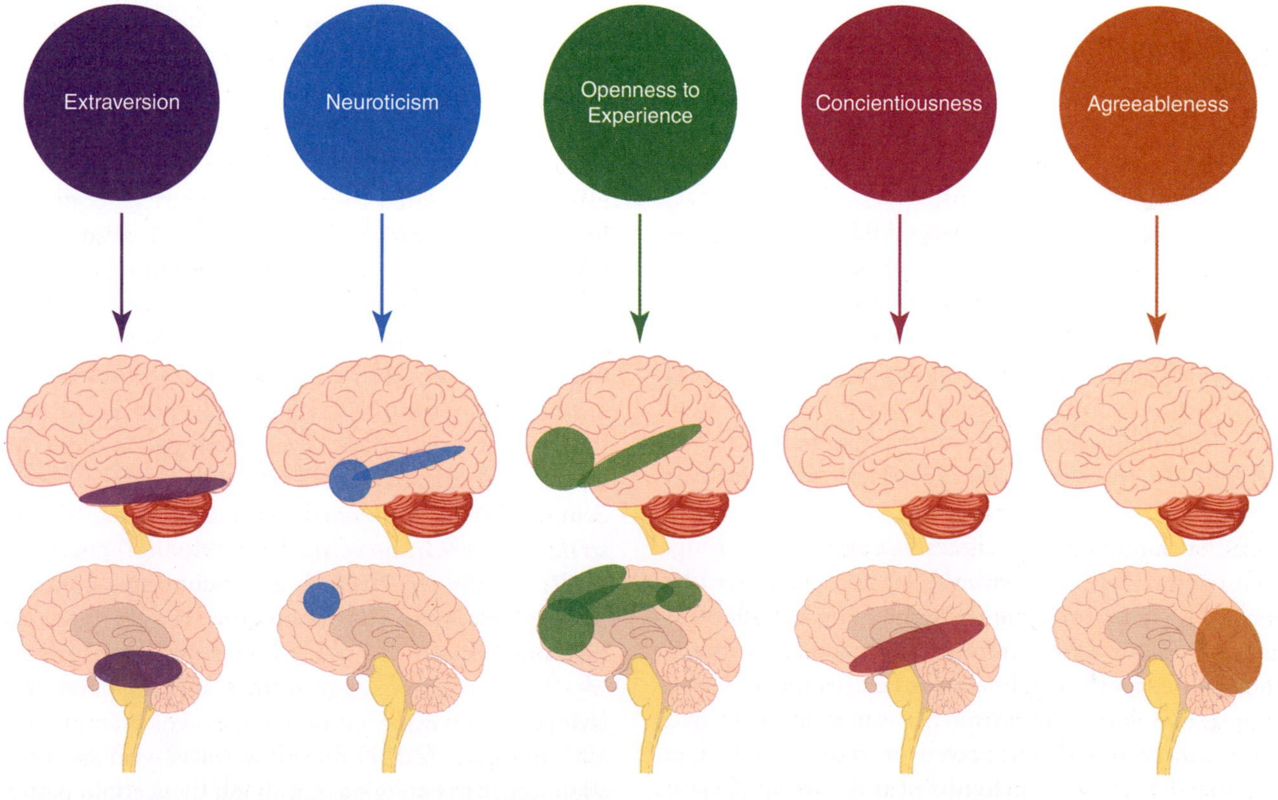

Figure 9.1 Schematic demonstration of the top-down approach to personality study denoting specific areas of the brain associated with each of the Big Five personality traits.

Source: Brooks, D., Hulst, H. E., de Bruin, L., Glas, G., Geurts, J. J. G., & Douw, L. (2020). The multilayer network approach in the study of personality neuroscience. *Brain Sciences, 10,* 915. Figure 1. https://doi.org/10.3390/brainsci10120915.

These findings help us understand why traumatic brain injuries and strokes, for instance, have very different effects on people's personality depending on where in the brain they occur. The personality-brain mapping may also help us understand the complicated patterns of change in traits in adulthood (as discussed in the next module) because different areas of the brain also change (or not) as we grow older (as noted in Chapter 2).

The Five-Factor Model has been examined cross-culturally (Church, 2016; McCrae, 2017). Research evidence generally indicates that the same five factors appear across at least 50 cultures, including understudied Arabic and Black African groups (McCrae, 2017; McCrae & Terracciano, 2005). Heine and Buchtel (2009) point out, though, that much of this research has been conducted by Westerners; it remains to be discovered whether similar studies conducted by local researchers will have the same outcomes. Additionally, Church (2016) points out that it is difficult to validate the Five-Factor Model in cultures that do not have written languages, such as some indigenous cultures; research suggests that measures developed specifically for indigenous populations do generalize across regions (Fetvadjiev et al., 2021).

What Happens to Dispositional Traits Across Adulthood?

Costa and McCrae investigated whether the general traits that make up their model remain stable across adulthood (e.g., Costa & McCrae, 2011; McCrae, 2016, 2018; McCrae & Costa, 2003). They suggest personality traits stop changing by age 30, after which they appear to be "set in plaster" (Costa & McCrae, 1994, p. 21). The data from the Costa, McCrae, and colleagues' studies came from the Baltimore Longitudinal Study of Aging for the 114 men who took the Guilford–Zimmerman Temperament Survey (GZTS) on three occasions, with each of the two follow-up tests about 6 years apart.

What Costa and colleagues found was surprising. Even over a 12-year period, the 10 traits measured by the GZTS remained highly stable; the correlations ranged from .68 to .85. In much of personality research we might expect to find this degree of stability over a week or two, but to see it over 12 years is noteworthy.

Stability was also observed in longitudinal data conducted over various lengths of time, from a 7-year period (Mõttus et al., 2012; Roberts & DelVecchio, 2000) to as long as a 30-year span (Leon et al., 1979). According to this evidence, it appears individuals change little in self-reported personality traits over periods of up to 30 years and over the age range of 20 to 90.

However, there is also substantial evidence that change, in addition to stability, can be detected in personality trait development across the adult life span. In a study that combined 16 longitudinal studies with a total of 60,000 participants, Graham and colleagues (2020) found complex trajectories of traits across adulthood. Across studies, they found linear declines in conscientiousness, extraversion, and openness. More complicated models suggested late-life increases in neuroticism. Clearly, the question of what happens to personality traits in adulthood is not a simple one to answer.

The consensus regarding change in the Five-Factor Model dispositional traits with increasing age is the decline of neuroticism and the presence of agreeableness and conscientiousness. These three traits are associated with personality adjustment, especially in terms of becoming emotionally less volatile and more attuned to social demands and social roles (Mühlig-Versen et al., 2012; Staudinger, 2015). These characteristics allow older adults to maintain or regain levels of well-being in the face of loss, threats, and challenges, all of which are common occurrences in late life.

Studies also found a decrease in openness to new experiences with increasing age (e.g., Graham & Lachman, 2012; Helson et al., 2002; Roberts et al., 2006; Srivastava et al., 2003). Staudinger argues openness to experience is related to personal maturity because it is highly correlated with ego development, wisdom, and emotional complexity. **Ego development** refers to fundamental changes in the ways our thoughts, values, morals, and goals are organized. Transitions from one stage to another depend on both internal biological changes and external social changes to which the person must adapt. Evidence suggests these three aspects of personality (ego level, wisdom, and emotional complexity) do not increase with age and may demonstrate decline (Grühn et al., 2013; Mühlig-Versen et al., 2012; Staudinger, 2015, 2020). Staudinger concludes personal growth in adulthood appears to be rare rather than normative.

Evidence also suggests that certain patterns of change predict important outcomes. For example, Hoff and colleagues (2021) found over a 12-year span from adolescence to emerging adulthood that certain patterns of personality growth predicted early career outcomes. Specifically, the strongest effects were found for growth in emotional stability (which predicted income and career satisfaction), conscientiousness (which predicted career satisfaction), and extraversion (which predicted career satisfaction and job satisfaction).

Making Sense of Stability and Change in Dispositional Traits. How do we make sense from the evidence that both stability and change occur? Ursula Staudinger and colleagues have a perspective that reconciles both stability and change in personality traits (Mühlig-Versen et al., 2012; Staudinger, 2015, 2020). They suggest personality takes on two forms: adjustment and growth. **Personality adjustment** involves developmental changes in terms of their adaptive value and functionality, such as functioning effectively within society, and how personality contributes to everyday life running smoothly. **Personality growth** refers to ideal end states such as increased self-transcendence, wisdom, and integrity.

Both of these personality dimensions interact because growth cannot occur without adjustment. However, Staudinger (2015, 2020) argues because growth in terms of ideal end states does not necessarily occur in everyone, strategies for adjustment develop across the latter half of the life span. This framework can be used to interpret stability and change in the Five-Factor Model personality dimensions.

Wrzus and Roberts (2017; Wrzus, 2021) propose a model that accounts for both developmental patterns. The **T**riggering situations, **E**xpectancy, **S**tates/**S**tate **E**xpressions, and **Rea**ctions (TESSERA) model, shown in Figure 9.2, describes a process by which long-term personality development is the product of repeated short-term, situational processes. These short-term processes repeat and create a feedback loop. These processes in turn can result in changes in personality characteristics and behavior over time, eventually emerging as changes in personality. That these short-term processes differ across people is why some people exhibit changes in personality traits and others do not. It can also explain why the life narratives of people also differ, a topic we will explore later in this chapter.

Wagner and colleagues (2020) take this a step further. They begin by pointing out sources of change

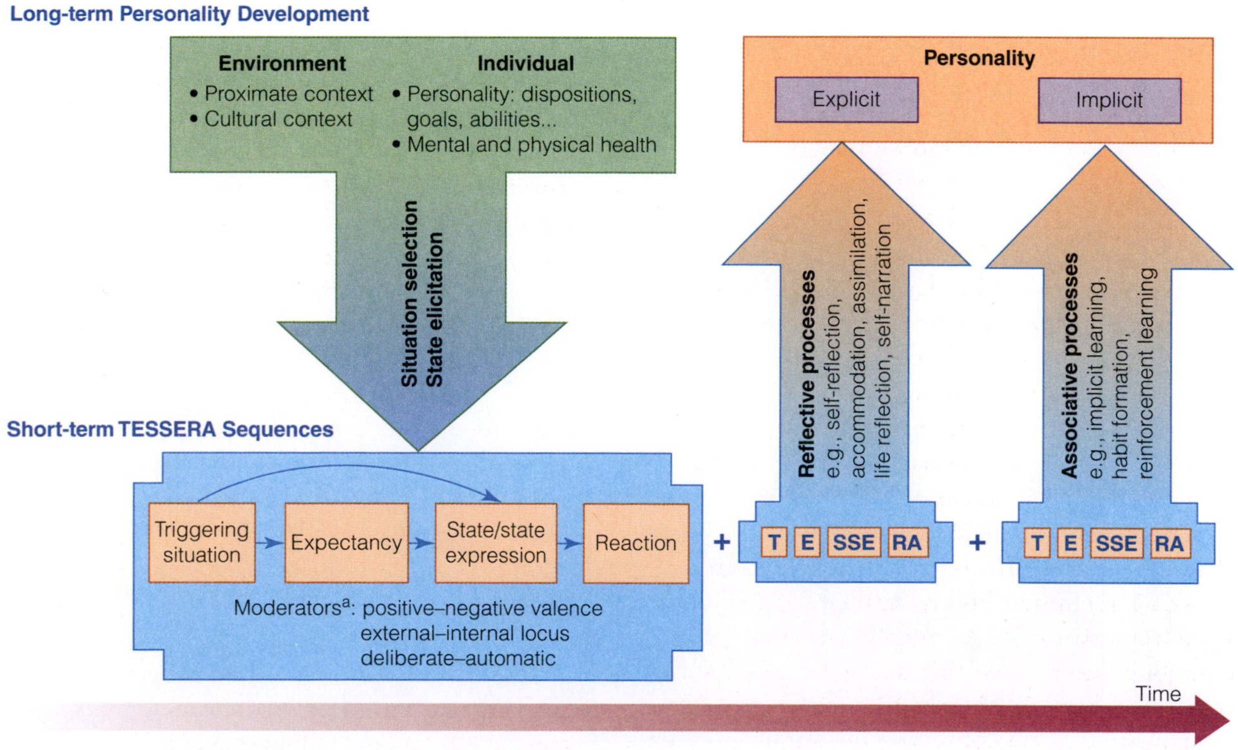

Figure 9.2 TESSERA framework of adult personality development.

Source: Wrzus, C., & Roberts, B. W. (2017). Processes of personality development in adulthood: The TESSERA framework. *Personality and Social Psychology Review, 21*, 253–277. doi:10.1177/1088868316652279.

regarding personality traits: (a) genetic and environmental, and (b) personal and situational-contextual. In the first instance, researchers using improved epigenetic and behavioral-genetic methods have found that genetic sources are intertwined with environmental factors in various ways. For example, environmental factors can alter how genes work and shape subsequent gene expression without changing genes. In the second instance, the distinction between personal and situational-contextual is fuzzy because personality is situational and contextual by definition (e.g., people who are extraverted understand that, in general, appropriate behaviors differ between birthday parties and courtrooms). Thus, Wagner and colleagues argue that a fully integrative approach to understanding personality stability and change is required.

Wagner and colleagues (2020) propose an evidence-based model that integrates various sources that might interact and transact synergistically and dynamically. A scheme denoting this kind of integrative model is depicted in Figure 9.3.

This model proposes that an individual can be characterized by relatively stable characteristics that give rise to individual differences in thoughts, feelings, strivings, and behaviors. Their genes can be expressed through both relatively stable traits and momentary, changeable situations. Through related cognitions, emotions, motivations, and behavior, genes can influence sources outside the person and thus guide the person through environmental conditions.

The environment reflects different external circumstances, which can also be regarded as more or less stable contexts and short-term situational fluctuations. Environmental influences interact and transact both with each other and with internal sources. Within external sources, sociocultural contexts might differentially exert pressure on social roles (e.g., parent, partner, employee) and thus affect the specific realization of relationships (e.g., between partners) as well as daily tasks (e.g., sharing of daily household chores).

The sources have a complex set of mutual interactions. Consequently, the affective states, motives, or trait levels of a person shape the experience of social roles, the realization of relationships, or the dealing with specific situations. The environment, in turn, provides opportunities and limits that reinforce or change personality characteristics.

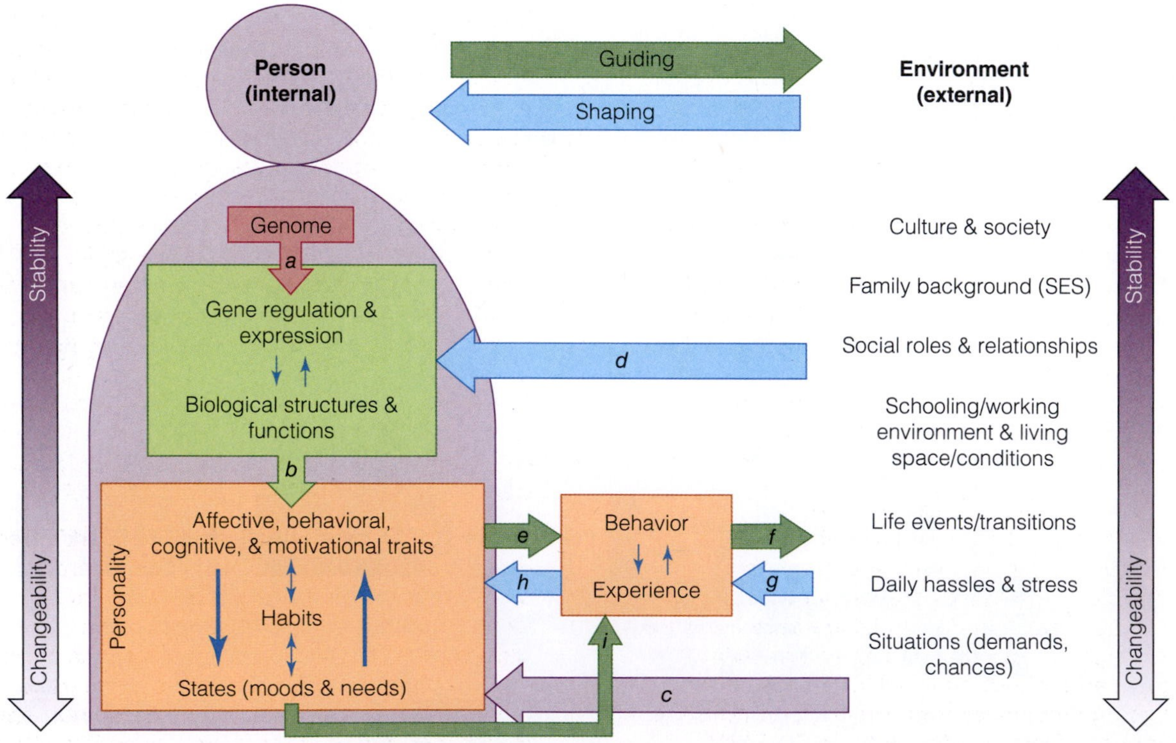

Figure 9.3 Integrative-source model illustrating the complex interplay between and within personal and environmental sources and resources that give rise to the stabilization and changeability of personality characteristics.

Source: Wagner, J., Orth, U., Bleidorn, W., Hopwood, C. J., & Kandler, C. (2020). Toward an integrative model of sources of personality stability and change. *Current Directions in Psychological Science, 29,* 438–444. Figure 1, p. 441. https://doi.org/10.1177/0963721420924751.

This is a complicated process. But it reflects the fact that personality is a complex issue. As a result, a comprehensive understanding of the factors that underlie personality stability and change requires an integration of these sources, which may be correlated and interact with each other.

Alternative Views of Dispositional Traits and Conclusions

Despite the dominance of the Five-Factor Model, it is clear that it does not capture all of the complexities of adults' personality. As discussed in the Controversies feature, important aspects of personality, left out of the

Controversies

Alternatives to the Five-Factor Model

As is clear from the discussion in this module, the Five-Factor Model has dominated theory and research on personality in adulthood. As important and powerful as this model is, however, research suggests that it does not capture all the facets of adults' personality and does not reflect aspects of personality as it is connected to cultures. To get a better understanding of what is not well represented in the Five-Factor Model, we'll consider some alternatives and some specific issues (Fehrer & Vernon, 2021).

Let's start with a cross-cultural perspective. The HEXACO model is a six-factor model of personality developed by applying the lexical approach to several languages around the world and how cultures describe dispositional traits (Ashton & Lee, 2007). Cross-cultural research reveals a sixth personality factor called Honesty–Humility, which taps into individual differences in fairness and modesty, along with five other dimensions that correlate with the Five-Factor Model: Emotionality, Extraversion, Agreeableness, Conscientiousness, and Openness to Experience. The HEXACO model expands cross-cultural descriptions of personality, mostly through stronger correlations between the Honesty–Humility dimension and such behaviors as risk-taking (Ashton et al., 2013), desire to have power (Lee et al., 2013), and materialism (Ashton & Lee, 2008).

A very different model, grounded in psychobiology, describes personality as a combination of seven facets (four temperaments and three character traits) (Cloninger et al., 1993). The temperaments in the model are based on neurobiological, developmental, and genetic research, and reflect inherited information processing differences connected with procedural memory and learning (discussed in Chapter 6). The four temperaments are novelty seeking, harm avoidance, reward dependence, and persistence. Character traits represent individual differences regarding aspects of self-concept. The three characters are cooperativeness, self-directedness, and self-transcendence.

A third approach examines personality from a quite negative perspective, which is clearly reflected in the name of the model: the Dark Tetrad. The Dark Tetrad encompasses broad constructs that embody a wide range of personality traits (Rogoza & Cieciuch, 2018, 2020). These include Machiavellianism (characterized by misanthropy and manipulation, whereby power, strategic planning, and deceit are inextricably intertwined), grandiose narcissism (characterized by entitled exploitation, inflated self-esteem, and a disproportionate need for power), vulnerable narcissism (characterized by hypersensitivity, low self-esteem, entitled resentment, and rage), primary psychopathy (characterized by callousness, deceit, manipulation, and a lack of remorse), and everyday sadism (characterized by tendencies to fantasize about, watch, or directly inflict psychological and/or physical pain and humiliation on others, while taking pleasure from their suffering). It's clear that these traits are different from those in the Five-Factor Model; the Dark Tetrad provides a complementary set of relations with behaviors that violate social norms. Katz and colleagues (2022) noted that measurement of the Dark Tetrad was invariant across biological sex.

The HEXACO, psychobiological, and Dark Tetrad models provide alternatives that complement the Five-Factor Model of dispositional traits. None should be viewed as replacing the others, but collectively they offer a richer, more complex understanding of dispositional traits. Mapping these various models to developmental trajectories and to brain structures and functions, with a need for understanding how these change with age, will be an important step forward.

Five-Factor Model, are built into alternative approaches. These traits include honesty, humility, risk-taking, religiosity, and more. Read the feature and learn about these intriguing alternatives.

To summarize all the work on dispositional traits, there appear to be increases in adjustment aspects of personality with increasing age, and these could be normative. At the same time, however, the basic indicators of personality growth tend to demonstrate stability or decline. You might ask, what's going on?

The most likely answer is personality growth or change across adulthood does not normally occur unless there are special circumstances that combine with an environmental push for it to occur. Thus, the personality-related adjustment that grows in adulthood does so in response to ever-changing developmental challenges and tasks, such as establishing a career, marriage, or family. This is what the competence–environmental press model, discussed in Chapter 5, would predict.

What about that high school reunion? On the basis of dispositional traits, then, we should have little difficulty knowing our high school classmates many years from now, even taking some degree of change into account.

Adult Development in Action

If you were a counselor, how would you use research on stability and dispositional traits to understand why it is difficult for people to change their behavior?

Review Questions

9.1 Dispositional Traits Across Adulthood

- What is a dispositional trait? Describe Costa and McCrae's Five-Factor Model of personality. What are the descriptors in each dimension? How do these dimensions change across adulthood?
- What evidence is there in other longitudinal research for change in personality traits in adulthood? Under what conditions is there stability or change?
- What are the specific criticisms raised concerning the Five-Factor Model?
- What are some alternative models to the Five-Factor Model?
- What does most of the evidence say about the stability of dispositional traits across adulthood?
- What is the TESSERA framework?

9.2 Personal Concerns and Qualitative Stages in Adulthood

Key Questions

- What are personal concerns?
- What are the main elements of Jung's theory?
- What are the stages in Erikson's theory? What types of clarifications and extensions of it have been offered? What research evidence is there to support his stages?
- What are the main points and problems with theories based on life transitions?
- What can we conclude about personal concerns?

Mayuri, a 52-year-old preschool teacher, thought carefully about what she believes is important in life. "I definitely feel differently about what I want to accomplish. When I was younger, I wanted to advance and be a great teacher. Now, although I still want to be good, I'm more concerned with providing help to the new teachers around here. I've got a lot of on-the-job experience that I can pass along."

Mayuri is not alone. Many people believe strongly middle age brings with it a different perspective about life compared to emerging and established adulthood. Some might label it as a "midlife crisis." Others may look at it differently. Are there such shifts in attitude about what matters in one's life? We'll find out in this module.

First we consider the evidence people's priorities and concerns change throughout adulthood, requiring adults to reassess themselves from time to time. This perspective of personality requires a different lens than the one used to understand dispositional traits. The lens we'll use here takes more of an experiential approach—it is what an individual experiences and interprets about their life that is the basis for understanding personality. From this perspective, personality cannot be deconstructed into a collection of dispositional traits. The difference between viewing personality more holistically as something that cannot be broken down into components and viewing personality as a collection of dispositional traits is analogous to the difference between viewing intelligence as modes or styles of thinking as opposed to a collection of underlying component skills.

This other lens of personality means that we must know a person well. What does that mean? McAdams and Olson (2010) believe to know another person well involves more than just knowing where they fall on the dimensions of dispositional traits. Rather, it means knowing what issues are important to them, that is, what the person wants, how they go about getting what they want, what their plans are for the future, how they interact with others who provide key personal relationships, and so forth. In short, we need to know something about a person's personal concerns. Personal concerns reflect what people want during particular times of their lives and within specific domains; they are the strategies, plans, and defenses people use to get what they want and avoid getting what they don't. One could say that personal concerns reflect the source of a person's meaning in life.

What's Different About Personal Concerns?

Many researchers study personality in ways explicitly contextual, in contrast to work on dispositional traits that largely ignores context. This work emphasizes the importance of sociocultural influences on development that shape people's wants and behaviors (Hooker, 2015; Hooker & McAdams, 2003). This research indicates, for example, that a person-centered approach focusing on personal control and social relationship quality is better than dispositional traits in understanding life satisfaction.

Focusing on personal concerns differs from research on dispositional traits (Hooker, 2015; McAdams, 2015, 2021). Most important, personality needs to be viewed as conscious descriptions of what people are trying to accomplish during a given period of life and what goals and goal-based concerns they have.

As Cantor (1990) initially noted, these constructs speak directly to the question of what people do and the goals they set for themselves in life. For this reason, we would expect to find considerable change in personality across adulthood, given the importance of sociocultural influences and the changing nature of life tasks as people mature. Accompanying these goals and motivations that define personal concerns are the self-regulation processes implemented to effect change in personal concerns. The transition from primary control to secondary control or from assimilative to accommodative coping (discussed in Chapter 8) enables people to recalibrate their goals and personal concerns in later life. This process serves the important function of maintaining satisfaction and meaningfulness in life (Hooker, 2015; McAdams, 2015).

We will consider various person-centered approaches in this module and Module 9.3. In this module, we focus on the idea that people's personality changes throughout the life span can be described as a series of qualitative stages that reflect the central concern of that period of life. Let's begin with Carl Jung's theory—the theory that started people thinking about personality change in midlife.

Jung's Theory

Jung represents a turning point in the history of psychoanalytic thought. Initially allied with Freud, he soon severed the tie and developed his own ideas that have elements of both Freudian theory and humanistic psychology. He was one of the first theorists to believe in personality development in adulthood; this marked a major break with Freudian thought that argued personality development ended in adolescence.

Jung's theory emphasizes each aspect of a person's personality must be in balance with all the others. This means each part of the personality will be expressed in some way, whether through normative means, neurotic symptoms, or in dreams. Jung asserts the parts of the personality are organized in such a way as to produce two basic orientations of the ego. One of these orientations is concerned with the external world; Jung labels it extraversion. The opposite orientation, toward the inner world of subjective experiences, is labeled introversion. To be psychologically healthy, both of these orientations must be present, and they must be balanced. Individuals must deal with the external world effectively and also be able to evaluate their inner feelings and values. When people emphasize one orientation over another, they are classified as extraverts or introverts.

Jung advocates two important age-related trends in personality development. The first relates to the introversion–extraversion distinction. Emerging and established adults tend to be more extraverted than older adults, perhaps because of their need to establish a number of things: relationships, career, and so forth. With increasing age, however, the need for balance creates a need to focus inward and explore personal feelings about aging and mortality (Cavanaugh, 2017). Thus, Jung argued that with age comes an increase in introversion.

The second age-related trend in Jung's theory involves what Jung termed the feminine and masculine aspects of our personalities. Each of us, according to Jung, has elements of both masculinity and femininity. In emerging adulthood, however, many people tend to express one of them while suppressing the other. In other words, many emerging adults tend to act in accordance with gender-role stereotypes appropriate to their culture. As they grow older, though, people begin to express the previously suppressed parts of their personality. For Jung, this means men begin to behave in ways that earlier in life they would have considered feminine, and women behave in ways that they formerly would have thought masculine. These changes achieve a better balance that allows people to deal more effectively with their individual needs rather than being driven by socially defined stereotypes. This balance, however, does not mean that Jung was implying a reversal of gender roles. On the contrary, it represents the expression of aspects of ourselves that have been there all along but that we have simply not revealed.

Jung's ideas that self and personality are organized by symbols and stories and the notion we transcend dualities such as femininity–masculinity and conscious–unconscious, among others, have been the focus of adult developmental research (Labouvie-Vief, 2015). However, as Labouvie-Vief points out, most empirical evidence suggests the reorganizations proposed by Jung are more indicative of advanced or exceptional development rather than being normative.

Jung stretched traditional psychoanalytic theory to new limits by postulating continued development across adulthood. Other theorists took Jung's lead and argued not only that personality development occurred in adulthood but also that it did so in an orderly, sequential fashion. We consider the sequences developed by Erik Erikson.

Erikson's Stages of Psychosocial Development

The best-known life-span theorist is Erik Erikson (1982), who called attention to sociocultural mechanisms involved in personality development. According to him, personality is determined by the interaction between an inner maturational plan and external societal-cultural demands. He proposes the life cycle has eight stages of development, summarized in Table 9.1. Erikson believed the sequence of stages is biologically fixed.

Each stage in Erikson's theory is marked by a struggle between two opposing tendencies and both are experienced by the person. The names of the stages reflect the issues that form the struggles. The struggles are resolved through an interactive process involving both the inner psychological and the outer sociocultural influences. Successful resolutions establish the basic areas of psychosocial strength; unsuccessful resolutions impair ego development in a particular area and adversely affect the resolution of future struggles.

Table 9.1 Summary of Erikson's Theory of Psychosocial Development, with Important Relationships and Psychosocial Strengths Acquired at Each Stage

	Psychosocial Crisis	Significant Relations	Basic Strengths
1. Infancy	Basic trust versus basic mistrust	Maternal person	Hope
2. Early childhood	Autonomy versus shame and doubt	Paternal people	Will
3. Play age	Initiative versus guilt	Basic family	Purpose
4. School age	Industry versus inferiority	Neighborhood, school	Competence
5. Adolescence	Identity versus identity confusion	Peer groups and outgroups; models of leadership	Love
6. Young adulthood	Intimacy versus isolation	Partners in friendship, sex competition, cooperation	Love
7. Adulthood	Generativity versus stagnation	Divided labor and shared household	Care
8. Old age	Integrity versus despair	Humankind, "my kind"	Wisdom

In that sense, each stage in Erikson's theory represents a kind of crisis.

The sequence of stages in Erikson's theory is based on the epigenetic principle, meaning each psychosocial strength has its own special time of ascendancy, or period of particular importance. The eight stages represent the order of this ascendancy. Because the stages extend across the whole life span, it takes a lifetime to acquire all of the psychosocial strengths. Moreover, Erikson realizes present and future behavior must have its roots in the past, such that later stages build on the foundations laid in previous ones. That is why the resolution (or lack of resolution) of each stage has consequences for the next stage(s).

Erikson believed the basic aspect of a healthy personality is a sense of trust toward oneself and others. Thus, the first stage in his theory involves *trust versus mistrust*, representing the conflict an infant faces in developing trust in a world it knows little about. With trust come feelings of security and comfort.

The second stage, *autonomy versus shame and doubt*, reflects children's budding understanding they are in charge of their own actions. This understanding changes them from totally reactive beings to ones who can act on the world intentionally. Their autonomy is threatened, however, by their inclinations to avoid responsibility for their actions and to go back to the security of the first stage.

In the third stage, the conflict is *initiative versus guilt*. Once children realize they can act on the world and are somebody, they begin to discover who they are. They take advantage of wider experience to explore the environment on their own, ask many questions about the world, and imagine possibilities about themselves.

The fourth stage is marked by children's increasing interests in interacting with peers, their need for acceptance, and their need to develop competencies. Erikson views these needs as representing *industry versus inferiority* manifested behaviorally in children's desire to accomplish tasks by working hard. Failure to succeed in developing self-perceived competencies results in feelings of inferiority.

During adolescence, Erikson believes we deal with the issue of *identity versus identity confusion*. The choice we make—the identity we form—is not so much who we are but who we can become. The struggle in adolescence is choosing from among a multitude of possible selves the one we will become. Identity confusion results when we are torn over the possibilities. The struggle involves trying to balance our need to choose a possible self and the desire to try out many possible selves.

During emerging adulthood, the major developmental task, achieving *intimacy versus isolation*, involves establishing a fully intimate relationship with another. Erikson (1968) argues intimacy means the sharing of all aspects of oneself without fearing the loss of identity. If intimacy is not achieved, isolation results. One way Erikson focused on to assist the development of intimacy is to choose a partner who represents the ideal of all one's past experiences. The psychosocial strength that emerges from the intimacy–isolation struggle is love.

With the advent of middle age, the focus shifts from intimacy to concern for the next generation, expressed as *generativity versus stagnation*. The struggle occurs between a sense of generativity (the feeling people must maintain and perpetuate culture and society) and a sense of stagnation (the feeling of self-absorption). Generativity is seen in such things as parenthood; teaching; or providing goods and services for the benefit of society. If the challenge of generativity is accepted, the development of trust in the next generation is facilitated, and the psychosocial strength of care is obtained. We examine generativity in more detail a bit later in this section, but for a preview, read the Real People feature.

In old age, individuals must resolve the struggle between *ego integrity and despair*. This last stage begins with a growing awareness of the nearness of the end of life, but it is actually completed by only a small number of people (Erikson, 1982). According to Erikson (1982), this struggle comes about as older adults try to understand and make sense of their lives in terms of the future of their family and community. Thoughts of a person's own death are balanced by the realization they live on through children, grandchildren, great-grandchildren, and their role in the community as a whole. This realization produces what Erikson calls a "life-affirming involvement" in the present.

To achieve integrity, a person must come to terms with the choices and events that made their life unique. There must also be an acceptance of the fact one's life is drawing to a close. Research indicates a connection between engaging in a life review and achieving integrity, so life review forms the basis for effective mental health interventions (Weiss et al., 2016).

Who reaches integrity? Erikson (1982) emphasizes people who demonstrate integrity made many different

Real People

Generativity Through Mentoring

Erikson made a big deal about the urge to ensure that culture and society are passed down from one generation to the next. Generally, this works through people taking the time to teach those in younger generations the key aspects of culture and society believed to be essential. These aspects can be simple things, such as treating people with respect, to more complex aspects such as how to collaborate with different types of people.

The key adults in people's lives (e.g., family, certain friends, identified "wise" individuals) may engage in this intergenerational transmission of values on an individual bases, and have a personal stake in it as a member of the family, for instance. In other cases, the key adult may be someone outside the family who is answering their internal call to engage in this effort.

Many organizations have been formed whose mission involves mentoring and this intergenerational transmission of values. For example, MENTOR: The National Mentoring Partnership, Communities in Schools, Big Brothers Big Sisters of America, and Junior Achievement are among the hundreds of local and national groups that provide opportunities for adults to mentor children and adolescents. All of them have in common the desire to provide the opportunities for bonds between adult mentors and youth as a way for young people to have another adult available for discussion and guidance who is not their parent or guardian. The ideal is that this relationship would provide a nonjudgmental source of advice as well as a way for adults to address their desire to mentor (and be generative).

In addition to national mentoring organizations, there are thousands of local ones. To learn more, explore those opportunities and find out the particular focus of a few of them. Share that information with the class to create a registry of volunteer opportunities in your community.

choices and follow different lifestyles; the point is everyone has this opportunity to achieve integrity if they strive for it. Those who reach integrity become self-affirming and self-accepting; they judge their lives to have been worthwhile and good. They are glad to have lived the lives they did. We will go deeper into the process of achieving integrity in Chapter 13 as part of our consideration of end-of-life issues and pondering our own death.

Aldomurillo/E+/Getty Images

Erikson's stage of integrity is achieved when older adults understand that they will live on through future generations of their family and community.

Clarifications and Expansions of Erikson's Theory. Erikson's theory made a major impact on thinking about life-span development. However, some aspects of his theory are unclear, poorly defined, unspecified, or tied to particular situations and beliefs in historical time. These problems often led critics to dismiss the theory as untestable and incomplete. However, closer reading in terms of the main points led other theorists to address these problems by identifying common themes, specifying underlying mental processes, and reinterpreting and integrating the theory with other ideas. These ideas are leading researchers to reassess the usefulness of Erikson's theory as a guide for research on adult personality development. For example, Gilleard (2020) argues that Erikson's theory can be viewed as a sequence of narrative themes in adults' character development.

Others approach Erikson from the perspective of much bigger thematic cycles. Logan (1986) points out Erikson's theory can be considered as a cycle that repeats: from basic trust to identity and from identity to integrity. In this approach the developmental progression is trust → achievement → wholeness. Throughout life, we first establish we can trust other people and ourselves. Initially, trust involves learning about ourselves and others, represented by the first two stages (trust vs. mistrust and autonomy vs. shame and doubt). The recapitulation of this idea in the second cycle is seen in our struggle to find a person with whom we can form a close relationship yet not lose our own sense of self (intimacy vs. isolation).

In addition, Logan notes how achievement—our need to accomplish and to be recognized for it—is a theme throughout Erikson's theory. During childhood this idea is reflected in the two stages initiative versus guilt and industry versus inferiority, whereas in adulthood it is represented by generativity versus stagnation. Finally, Logan points out the issue of understanding ourselves as worthwhile and whole is first encountered during adolescence (identity vs. identity confusion) and is re-experienced during old age (integrity vs. despair). Logan's analysis emphasizes that psychosocial development, although complicated on the surface, may actually reflect only a small number of issues. Moreover, Logan points out we do not come to a single resolution of these issues of trust, achievement, and wholeness. Rather, they are issues we struggle with our entire lives.

Slater (2003) expanded on Logan's reasoning, suggesting the central crisis of generativity versus stagnation includes struggles between pride and embarrassment, responsibility and ambivalence, career productivity and inadequacy, as well as parenthood and self-absorption. Each of these conflicts provides further knowledge about generativity as the intersection of society and the human life cycle.

Researchers focusing on emerging adulthood raised the possibility of an additional stage specific to this phase of life. Patterson (2012) speculates a fifth stage, labeled *incarnation versus impudence*, is needed between adolescence (identity vs. role confusion) and emerging adulthood (intimacy vs. isolation). For Patterson, this crisis is "resolved through experimental sexuality, temporal and spatial social and intimate relationships, interdependence and self-sufficiency and dependence and helplessness, and relativist and absolutist ideological experimentation."

Some critics argue Erikson's emphasis on struggles implies that life is a never-ending crisis, and that the conceptualizations of these struggles in terms of bipolar outcomes is simplistic. Kotre (1999, 2005) contends adult experience is richer than that; for example, adults have many opportunities to express generativity that are not equivalent and do not lead to a general state. Rather, Kotre considers generativity more as a set of impulses felt at different times and in different settings, such as at work or engaging in grandparenting behaviors. More formally, Kotre describes five types of generativity:

- biological and parental generativity, which concerns raising children (discussed in Chapter 11);
- technical generativity, relating to the passing of specific skills from one generation to another (discussed in Chapters 8 and 11);
- cultural generativity, referring to being a mentor (discussed in more detail in Chapter 12);
- agentic generativity, the desire to be or to do something that transcends death (discussed in Chapter 13); and
- communal generativity, manifesting as a person's participation in a mutual, interpersonal reality.

Only rarely, Kotre contends, is there a continuous state of a single understanding of generativity in adulthood. He asserts the struggles identified by Erikson are not fought constantly; rather, they probably come and go. We examine this idea in more detail in the next section that focuses on generativity.

What Are Generative People Like?—An Example of Erikson in Action. The central period in adulthood from an Eriksonian perspective is the stage of generativity versus stagnation. It is the adulthood stage that has been the focus of the most research. An example of the efforts to describe generativity is McAdams's model (McAdams, 2001, 2015, 2021; McAdams & Guo, 2015) depicted in Figure 9.4.

McAdams's multidimensional model describes how generativity results from the complex interconnections among sociocultural and inner psychological forces. The desire, for instance, to create a product or outcome that outlives oneself, or bestow one's wisdom or knowledge or resources as a gift to the next generation (reflecting a concern for what should be passed on to the future) through raising children or mentoring or financial bequest, results in a behavior toward the next generation and a belief in the goodness of the human enterprise. The positive resolution of this conflict finds middle-aged adults developing a generative commitment that produces generative actions. A person begins to derive personal meaning from being generative by constructing a new aspect to their life story or narration that helps create the person's identity.

The components of McAdams's model relate differently to personality traits. Generative *concern* is a general personality tendency of interest in caring for younger generations, and generative *action* is behaviors that promote the well-being of the next generation.

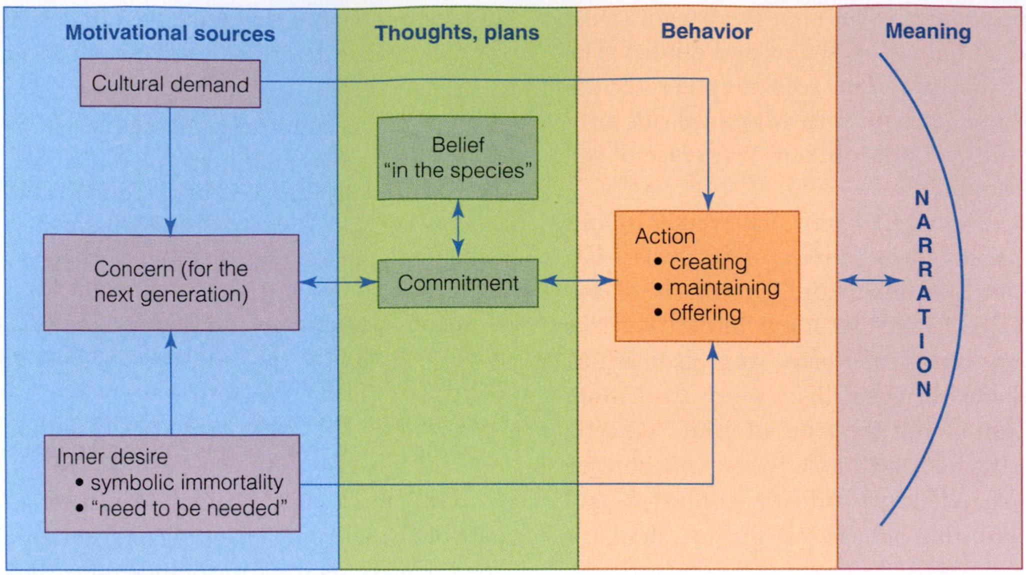

Figure 9.4 McAdams's model of generativity.

Source: McAdams, D. P., Hart, H. M., & Maruna, S. (1998). The anatomy of generativity. In D. P. McAdams & E. de St. Aubin (Eds.), *Generativity and Adult Development: How and Why We Care for the Next Generation* (p. 7). Washington, DC: American Psychological Association.

Generative concern relates to life satisfaction and overall happiness, whereas generative action does not. For example, new grandparents may derive satisfaction from their grandchildren and are greatly concerned with their well-being but may have little desire to engage in the daily behaviors of raising them if they are free to choose this option.

At a general level, generativity appears to be stable over time; for example, a longitudinal study examining adults ranging in age from their 40s through late 60s found no change in average generativity (Lodi-Smith et al., 2021). Although they can be expressed by adults of all ages, certain types of generativity are more common at some ages than others. For example, middle-aged adults demonstrate a greater preoccupation with generativity themes than do younger adults in their accounts of personally meaningful life experiences (McAdams, 2015, 2021; McAdams & Guo, 2015). Middle-aged adults make more generative commitments (e.g., "save enough money for my child to go to college"), reflecting a major difference in the inner and outer worlds of middle-aged and older adults as opposed to emerging adults. An important aspect of generativity is leaving a personal legacy, true regardless of gender (Newton & Jones, 2016; Newton et al., 2019, 2020). Leaving a legacy can involve such things as doing meaningful work or volunteer activities and donating money to support a worthy cause.

How well do these ideas generalize across sociocultural groups? Research has found that generativity matters and is present across cultures, including Indigenous Alaska Native elders (Lewis, 2020), Spain (Noriega et al., 2020), Cameroon, Costa Rica, and Germany (Hofer et al., 2008).

Likewise, concerns about the applicability of generativity in LGBTQIA+ communities have been raised within Kotre's (1999, 2005) and McAdams's (2015, 2021) emphases on sociocultural contextual factors. To find out, Rosati and colleagues (2021) studied evidence of generativity in Italian LGB adults over age 60. Their findings indicate that queer generativity is an integral part of the LGB aging process. The generative behaviors of LGB adults operate in a different context from those of the cis/heterosexual population because they are linked to a need to create a shared queer culture and recognize and strengthen one's oppressed status. Thus, queer generativity (Oswald & Masciadrelli, 2008) can be considered a series of behaviors performed by resilient LGB older adults (Landes et al., 2014), aimed at improving their own and other LGB people's life conditions and increasing their comfort with their sexual identity. Like other marginalized groups (e.g., people with disabilities), LGB youth experience a lack of continuity with their heterosexual parents in at least one fundamental aspect of their identity, as they are not heterosexual. Consequently, they are more likely to look for role models outside their families by identifying with other LGB adults or peers. Therefore, LGB generative people may represent a point of reference for other LGB people, regardless of their age. In these terms, queer generativity not only refers to an impulse of guiding next generations (social subdimension) but also to an impulse to take care of other potentially isolated people (relational subdimension), and to create a supportive context for the future (political subdimension). These behaviors are conceptually similar to the mentoring and related behaviors noted earlier as indicative of generativity.

These data collectively demonstrate that the personal concerns of middle-aged adults are fundamentally different from those of younger adults. In fact, generativity may be a stronger predictor of emotional and physical well-being in midlife and old age (Gruenewald et al., 2012; McAdams, 2015, 2021; McAdams & Guo, 2015; Newton et al., 2019). For example, across genders, generativity is associated with positive emotion and satisfaction with life and work, and it predicts physical health. Considered together, the data also indicate that generativity is more complex than Erikson originally proposed and, while peaking in middle age, may not diminish in late life.

Theories Based on Life Transitions

Jung's belief in a midlife crisis and Erikson's belief in stage-based psychosocial development laid the foundation for approaching personality development across adulthood from an experiential approach. From the perspective of everyday life, this makes intuitive sense. The idea adults go through a sequence of stages that includes changing crises, struggles, or changes in core personal issues and stability reflects their own experience. A universal assumption of these views is that people experience predictable age-related crises, along with periods of relative stability, sometimes simultaneously, sometimes not. Additionally, the ages at which particular crises are experienced are loose; generativity, for instance, continues beyond middle age well into later life. Much research data support these assumptions and views.

However, views of personality based on life transitions tightly tied to age are built on weak evidence. Some are based on small, highly selective samples (such as men who attended Harvard) or surveys completed by readers of particular magazines. Still, the intuitive appeal of these theories makes them worth examining.

An important question about life transition theories is the extent they are real and actually occur to everyone. Life transition theories typically present the transitions as if everyone universally experiences them at the same age (or narrowly defined age range). There is a caution, though. Given the popularity of some of the life transitions, the social pressure to "experience them" or to interpret what one is experiencing as "the transition" is powerful. Socialization, stereotypes, and personal expectations all come into play.

What actually happens demonstrates the difficulty in teasing apart facts from shared beliefs. We have known for a long time that a rigid version of life transitions was inaccurate. For example, Dunn and Merriam (1995) examined data from a large, diverse national sample and found less than 20% of people in their early 30s experienced an age-30 transition that forms a cornerstone of Levinson and colleagues' (1978) theory. Nevertheless, the belief in a transition in the late 20s persists. The experience of a midlife crisis, discussed next, is another excellent example.

Perhaps the most central idea in theories that consider the importance of life transitions is that middle-aged adults experience a personal crisis that results in major changes in how they consider themselves. During a midlife crisis, people are supposed to take a good hard look at themselves and, they hope, attain a much better understanding of who they are. Difficult issues such as one's own mortality and inevitable aging are supposed to be faced. Behavioral changes are supposed to occur, and stereotypic images of those abound. In support of this notion, Levinson and his colleagues (1978; Levinson & Levinson, 1996) write that middle-aged people in the research reported intense internal struggles much like depression. However, far more research fails to document the existence; in short, the midlife crisis is a myth (Infurna et al., 2020; Lachman, 2004). In fact, those who actually experience a crisis may be experiencing general problems of psychopathology (Goldstein, 2005; Infurna et al., 2020).

Midlife is considered a pivotal time in many theories relating to personal concerns as the key to personality in adulthood.

The myth of the midlife crisis did raise an important issue, though—what does happen during midlife? Is generativity all that is going on? Or is there more?

Midlife as a Pivotal Time. Although the "midlife crisis" has been found to be a myth, there is ample evidence that midlife is a pivotal time in the life span (Infurna et al., 2020; Lachman et al., 2015). The shifts that occur in midlife touch every aspect of a person's life, from family to work to social relations. The central position in the life course is captured by balancing gains and losses associated with the aging process, linking earlier and later periods of life, and bridging generations. The pivotal nature of midlife is articulated in Figure 9.5; the nature of development in midlife is affected by what occurred earlier in life.

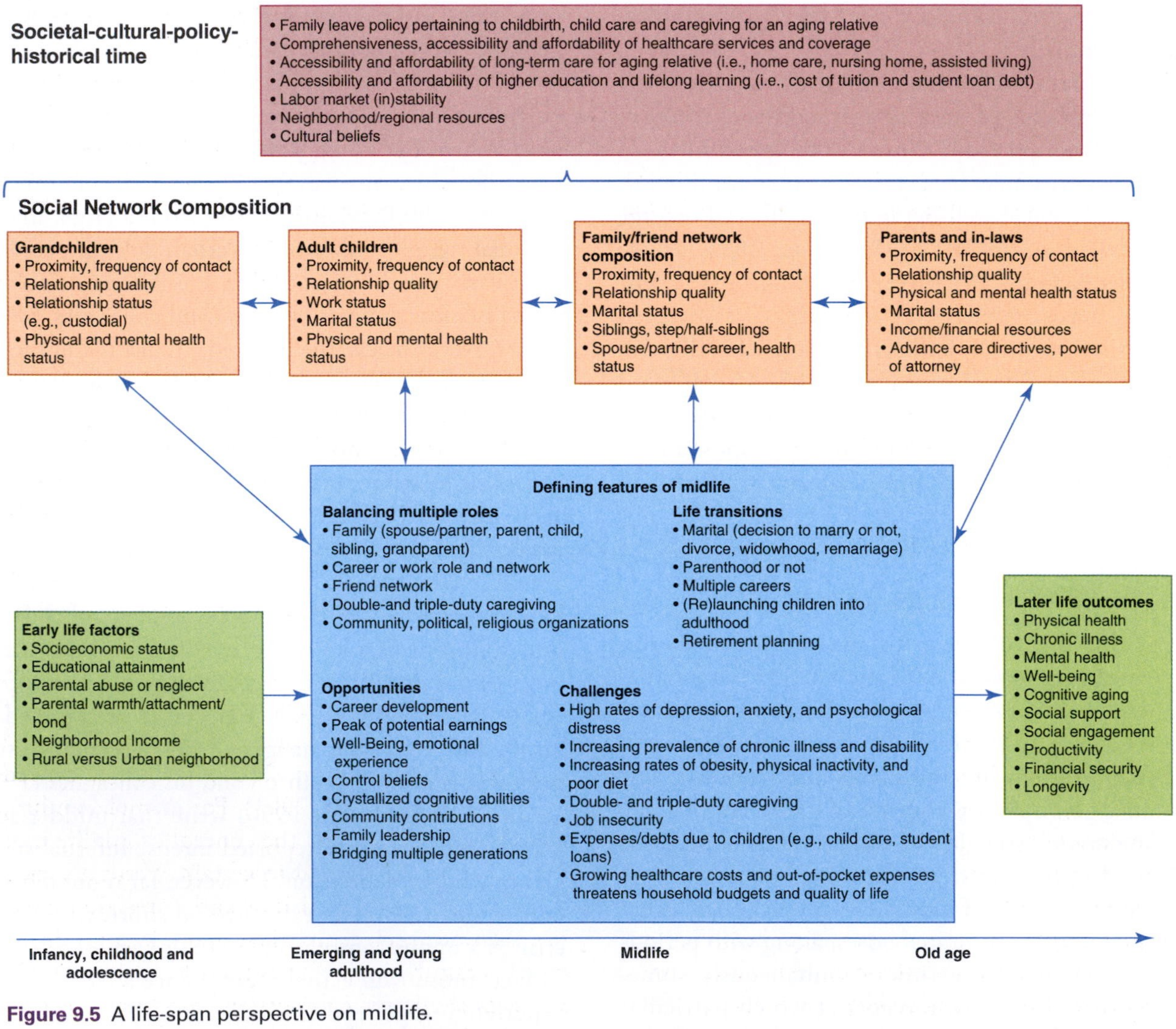

Figure 9.5 A life-span perspective on midlife.

Source: Infurna, F. J., Gerstorf, D., & Lachman, M. E. (2020). Midlife in the 2020s: Opportunities and challenges. *American Psychologist, 75*, 470–485. https://doi.org/10.1037/amp0000591.

Infurna and colleagues (2020) describe midlife this way:

> Midlife is best defined by balancing multiple roles, life transitions, opportunities, and challenges. These defining features of midlife transpire across the typically defined age periods of adulthood (i.e., young adulthood, midlife, and into old age). Early life factors, such as socioeconomic status (SES), parental relationships, and neighborhood factors, shape the nature of midlife, which in turn affects outcomes such as health and well-being in later life. Current cohorts of middle-aged adults are confronted with increases in the intensity, magnitude, or sheer load of concurrently balancing multiple roles and challenges while typically being responsible for those younger and older in the family and contending with increasing prevalence of chronic illness, disability, obesity, and mental health issues. The challenges of midlife are offset by opportunities, such as career development, peak of earnings, gains in well-being, control beliefs, and bridging multiple generations. Social network composition details the significance of middle-aged adults' connectedness with multiple generations, including their parents or in-laws, spouse or partner, adult children, and grandchildren. The form, function, and structure of social network composition across the multiple generations shown in Figure 9.5 is dependent on a variety of factors, such as the proximity, frequency of contact, and relationship quality with network members; their cognitive, mental, and physical health status; one's own and family members' marital status; and presence/number of children. The societal-cultural-policy-historical time context that middle-aged adults and their social network composition reside in carries great significance. Government policies and cultural beliefs have implications for development in midlife and connectedness with social network members. Important considerations for this component include family leave policy, health care services and coverage, and higher education. The timetable of midlife can be shifted for numerous reasons, including age of parents, the pursuit of higher education, timing and decision of having kids, and whether and when adult children have children. Targets for intervention can span multiple levels, including physical activity, social support and engagement, higher education, and workplace structure and organization and policy. Last, the life structure or the underlying pattern or design of a person's life at a given time will likely differ across race or ethnicity, gender, sexual orientation and SES. (p. 474)

How do middle-aged people reflect this pivotal role? There is evidence that people engage in self-reflection. Labouvie-Vief and colleagues (Grühn et al., 2013; Labouvie-Vief, 2015; Labouvie-Vief & Diehl, 1999; Labouvie-Vief et al., 2009) offer good evidence for a reorganization of self and values across the adult life span. They suggest the major dynamic that drives such changes may not be age dependent, but rather general cognitive changes.

Cavanaugh's (2017) application of this same self-reflection to the personal spiritual realm agrees that cognitive development is key. In this case, midlife is the time involving shifting from what Merton (1955, 1962), Rohr (2011, 2013), and others term the "False Self" (marked by striving for achievements that can be externally recognized, for instance) to what is termed the "True Self" (marked by internally defined achievement based more on values and helping others). We'll go deeper into this distinction a bit later in this chapter.

From a different perspective, Abigail Stewart (Newton & Stewart, 2012; Newton et al., 2019; Peterson & Stewart, 1996; Torges et al., 2008) found that women who have regrets about adopting traditional roles (e.g., wife/mother) but later pursue an education or career at midlife report higher well-being than either women who experience regret but do not make a change or women who never experienced regrets about their roles. Stewart suggests rather than a midlife crisis, such an adjustment may be more appropriately considered a **midlife correction**, reevaluating one's roles and dreams and making the necessary corrections.

Finally, we cannot overlook examining midlife from a cross-cultural perspective (Tanner & Arnett, 2009). Research results suggest midlife is a cultural invention (Jackson, 2020; Menon, 2001; Menon & Shweder, 1998; Sterns & Huyck, 2001). For example, anthropological evidence suggests the concept of midlife itself is limited to adults studied in certain Western societies. In other cultures, transitions and crises are linked to role relations such as marriage and relocation into the spouse's family. Major transitions are defined by such events as children's marriages and mothers-in-law moving into the older adult role of observer (Menon, 2001; Tanner & Arnett, 2009). Jackson (2020) argues that midlife is an important point of rethinking in many cultures, but also strongly argues that the notion of midlife as tied to crisis is a late 20th century invention of the Western perspective on things. Again, this is a good reminder that cultural context plays an important role in adult development.

Adult Development in Action

As a director of human resources at a major corporation, how would knowledge about generativity help you understand your middle-aged employees better?

Review Questions

9.2 Personal Concerns and Qualitative Stages in Adulthood

- What is meant by a personal concern? How does it differ from a dispositional trait?
- Describe Jung's theory. What important developmental changes did he describe?
- Describe Erikson's eight stages of psychosocial development. What cycles have been identified? How has his theory been clarified and expanded? What types of generativity have been proposed? What evidence is there for generativity? What modifications to Erikson's theory has this research suggested?
- What are the major assumptions of theories based on life transitions? What evidence is there regarding the developmental importance of midlife? How can midlife be viewed from a gain–loss perspective?

9.3 Life Narratives, Identity, and the Self

Key Questions

- What are the main aspects of McAdams's life-story model?
- What are the main points of Whitbourne's identity theory?
- How does the Six-Foci Model of adult personality account for development?
- How does self-concept come to take adult form? What is its development during adulthood?
- What are possible selves? Do they show differences during adulthood?
- What role does religion or spiritual support play in adult life?
- What conclusions can be drawn from research using life narratives?

Antje is a 19-year-old sophomore at a community college. She expects her study of early childhood education to be difficult but rewarding. Antje sees herself getting a good job teaching preschool children and someday owning her own day care center. Antje also sees herself in a special relationship at some point. But whether she will have children is not something she's thinking about at the moment.

Who are you? What are your hopes and dreams? What kind of person are you trying to become? These are the kinds of questions Antje is trying to answer. Answering these questions requires concepts of personality going beyond dispositional traits and personal concerns. These aspects of personality are important, but they lack a sense of integration, unity, coherence, and overall purpose (Hooker, 2015; McAdams, 2015, 2021). For example, understanding a person's goals from the perspective of personal concerns does not reveal who a person is trying to be or become. What is lacking in other levels of analysis is a sense of the person's lived experience as represented in their identity—a sense of self.

In contrast to Erikson's (1982) proposition that identity formation is the central task of adolescence, many researchers believe identity and the creation of the self continue to develop throughout adulthood (e.g., Grühn et al., 2013; Hooker, 2015; Infurna et al., 2020; McAdams, 2015, 2021; Newton et al., 2020). How adults continue constructing identity and the self relies on *life narratives*, or the internalized and evolving stories that integrate a person's reconstructed past, perceived present, and anticipated future into a coherent and vitalizing life myth (Curtin & Stewart, 2012; Hooker, 2015; McAdams, 2015, 2021; McAdams et al., 2021). Careful analysis of people's life narratives provides insight into their identity.

In this section, we consider three general theories of identity. Dan McAdams is concerned with understanding how people see themselves and how they fit into the adult world. Susan Krauss Whitbourne investigated people's own conceptions of the life course and

Discovering Development

Who Do You Want to Be When You "Grow Up"?

From the time you were a child, people have posed this question to you. In childhood, you probably answered by indicating some specific career, such as firefighter or teacher. But now that you are an adult, the question takes on new meaning. Rather than simply a matter of picking a profession, the question goes much deeper in to the kinds of values and the essence of the person you would like to become.

Take a few minutes and think about who you would like to be in another decade or two (or maybe even 50 years hence). What things will matter to you? What will you be doing? What experiences will you have had? What lies ahead?

This exercise can give you a sense of the way researchers try to understand people's sense of identity and self through the use of personal narrative. You might want to keep what you have written and check it when the appropriate number of years elapse.

how they differ from age norms and the expectations for society as a whole. Karen Hooker and McAdams jointly describe an interactive approach to personality and identity development.

To round out our understanding of identity and the self, we also examine several related constructs. Before beginning, though, take time to complete the exercise in the Discovering Development feature. This exercise will give you a sense of what a life narrative is and how it might be used to gain insight into identity and the sense of self.

McAdams's Life-Story Model

McAdams (2001, 2015, 2021, McAdams et al., 2021) argues a person's sense of identity cannot be understood using the language of dispositional traits or personal concerns. Identity is not just a collection of traits, nor is it a collection of resolutions of struggles and crises, strategies, or goals. Instead, it is based on a story of how the person came into being, where the person has been, where the person is going, and who the person wants to and will become, much like Antje's story. McAdams argues that people create a life story that is an internalized narrative with a beginning, middle, and an anticipated ending. The life story is created and revised throughout adulthood as people change and the changing environment places different demands on them. Importantly, the life story is much influenced by sociocultural forces.

McAdams's research indicates people in Western societies begin forming their life story during late adolescence and emerging adulthood, but its roots lie in one's earliest attachments in infancy. Indeed, attachment theory has had a major impact in framing the development of a wide range of topics, including personality, emotions, relationships, and love and loss (Fraley & Shaver, 2021). We know from Erikson's theory that adolescence marks the full initiation into forming an identity, and thus, a coherent life story begins. In emerging adulthood, it is continued and refined, and from midlife and beyond it is refashioned in the wake of major and minor life changes. Generativity marks the attempt to create a first draft of sorts of an appealing story "ending" that will generate new beginnings for future generations.

Paramount in these life stories is the changing personal identity reflected in the emotions conveyed in the story (from tragedy to optimism or through comic and romantic descriptions). In addition, motivations change and are reflected in the person repeatedly trying to attain their goals over time. The two most common goal themes are *agency* (reflecting power, achievement, and autonomy) and *communion* (reflecting love, intimacy, and a sense of belonging). Finally, life stories indicate one's beliefs and values, or the ideology a person uses to set the context for actions.

Every life story contains episodes that provide insight into perceived change and continuity in life. People prove to themselves and others they have either changed or remained the same by pointing to specific events supporting the appropriate claim. The main characters, representing the roles we play in our lives, represent idealizations of the self, such as "the dutiful parent" or "the reliable worker."

Integrating these various aspects of the self into a coherent whole is a major challenge of midlife and later adulthood (Infurna et al., 2020; Lachman et al., 2015; McAdams, 2015; McAdams et al., 2021). Finally, all life stories need an ending so the self can leave a legacy that creates new beginnings. Life stories in middle-aged and older adults have a clear quality of "giving birth to" a new generation, a notion essentially identical to generativity.

One of the more popular methods for examining the development of life stories is through autobiographical memory (Dunlop et al., 2016; Lilgendahl &

McAdams, 2011; McAdams et al., 2021; McLean, 2016; McLean & Pasupathi, 2012). When people tell their life stories to others, the stories are a joint product of the speaker and the audience, which includes other key people in a person's life, such as family (Pasupathi, 2013; McLean, 2016). This co-construction of identity is a good example of collaborative remembering (discussed in Chapter 8).

Overall, McAdams (2001, 2015, 2021; McAdams et al., 2021) believes the model for change in identity over time is a process of fashioning and refashioning one's life story. This process is strongly influenced by sociocultural forces. One's combination of cultural, racial, ethnic, sex, and gender backgrounds provides interpretive contexts and shaping influences on the creation of one's life story and how it is reformed across adulthood. At times, the reformulation may be at a conscious level, such as when people make explicit decisions about changing careers. At other times, the revision process is unconscious and implicit, growing out of everyday experiences. The goal each time, though, is to create a life story that is coherent, credible, open to new possibilities, richly differentiated, reconciles different and opposite aspects of oneself, and is integrated within one's sociocultural context.

Whitbourne's Identity Theory

Susan Krauss Whitbourne (Lodi-Smith et al., 2021; Mitchell et al., 2021; Whitbourne, 1986, 1987, 2010) believes that cognitive development plays a major role in how people create their identities. The result of this process is the **life-span construct**, the person's unified sense of the past, present, and future.

There are many influences on the development of a life-span construct: identity, values, and sociocultural context are a few. Together, they shape the life-span construct and the ways in which it is manifested. The life-span construct has two structural components, which in turn are the ways in which it is manifested. The first of these components is the *scenario*, which consists of expectations about the future. The scenario translates aspects of our identity that are particularly important at a specific point into a plan for the future. The scenario is strongly influenced by socioculturally based age norms that define key transition points (e.g., when one should marry, complete one's education, be established in a career, and so on). In short, a scenario is a GPS map for how we want our lives to go.

Tagging certain expected events with a particular age or time by which we expect to complete them creates a social clock. With each major life event, people check how they are doing against where their scenario says they should be. If they have achieved goals earlier than expected, they will be proud of being ahead of the game. If things work out more slowly than planned, they may chastise themself for being slow.

By experiencing events in the scenario, a person creates the second component of the life-span construct, the *life story*. The life story is a personal narrative history that organizes past events into a coherent sequence. The life story gives events personal meaning and a sense of continuity; it becomes our autobiography. Because the life story is what we tell others when they ask about our past, it eventually becomes somewhat over-rehearsed and stylized. An interesting aspect of the life story, and autobiographical memory in general, is that distortions occur with time and retelling (Lilgendahl & McAdams, 2011; Mace et al., 2021; Romano et al., 2020; Sotgiu, 2021). In life stories, distortions allow a person to have their life story come across as more "accurate" and positive than it actually was.

Whitbourne grounded her theory on a fascinating cross-sectional study of 94 adults ranging in age from 24 to 61 (Whitbourne, 1986). The participants came from diverse sociocultural backgrounds and represented a wide range of occupations and life situations. Using data from detailed interviews, Whitbourne was able to identify what she believes is the process of adult identity development based on equilibrium between identity and experience. Her model is presented in Figure 9.6. As the figure indicates, there is continuous feedback between identity and experience; this explains why we may evaluate ourselves positively at one point in time, yet appear defensive and self-protective at another.

The processes of equilibrium in the model are based on Piaget's concepts of assimilation and accommodation (described in Chapter 7). Whitbourne explicitly integrated concepts from cognitive development with identity development to better explain how identity is formed and revised across adulthood. The assimilation process involves using already existing aspects of identity to handle present situations. Overreliance on assimilation makes the person resistant to change. Accommodation, in contrast, reflects the willingness of the individual to let the situation determine what they will do. This often occurs when the person does not have a well-developed identity around a certain issue.

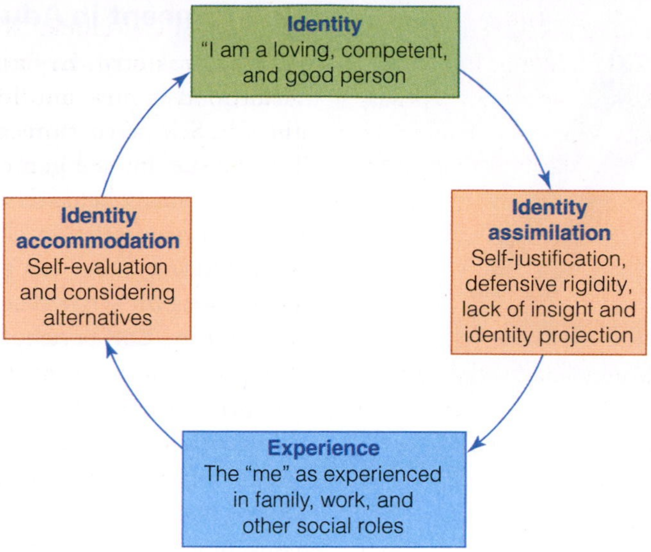

Figure 9.6 Whitbourne's model of adult identity processes.

Source: Whitbourne, S. K. (1986). The psychological construction of the life span. In J. E. Birren & K. W. Schaie (Eds.), *Handbook of the Psychology of Aging* (pp. 594-619). New York, NY: Van Nostrand Reinhold. All rights reserved. Reproduced by permission of the author.

Although Whitbourne found evidence of life transitions, overall she found little evidence that these transitions occurred in a "stage-like" fashion or were tied to specific ages. Rather, she found people tend to go through transitions when they feel they needed to and to do so on their own timeline. Her model has expanded to incorporate how people adapt more generally to middle age and the aging process (Whitbourne, 2010).

Several important ideas have emerged from Whitbourne's work. Most important, identity assimilation and identity accommodation change with age (Sneed & Whitbourne, 2003, 2005). Identity assimilation is higher in older adulthood, and identity accommodation is higher in emerging adulthood. Furthermore, identity assimilation in older adulthood is associated with maintaining and enhancing positive self-regard through the minimization of negativity. In contrast, a changing identity (e.g., through accommodation) in older adulthood is associated more with poor psychological health. The ability to integrate age-related changes into one's identity and maintain a positive conception of oneself is crucial to aging successfully (Whitbourne, 2010). This suggests people make behavioral adjustments to promote healthy adaptation to the aging process (discussed in Chapter 14).

Six Foci Model of Adult Personality

It should be clear at this point that personality in adulthood is a complicated matter. How each of us develops, indeed whether each of us experiences change in aspects of our personality, is a result of a complex set of forces. From this perspective, a more complete description of personality must include all of the forces discussed in Chapter 1, as well as cognitive development and underlying brain development. With these as the underlying infrastructure, we can integrate the dispositional traits, personal concerns, and life story conceptions of personality.

This is what Hooker and McAdams (2003; Hooker, 2015; McAdams, 2015, 2021) have done in creating the Six Foci Model of Personality, depicted in Figure 9.7. The Six Foci Model integrates both the structures of personality (e.g., traits) and processes of personality within a levels-of-analysis framework. Let's go deeper.

There are three levels of personality in the model. The first level is *traits*, the dispositional basis of personality. The corresponding personality process to trait is that of *states*, the intraindividual processes that offer the

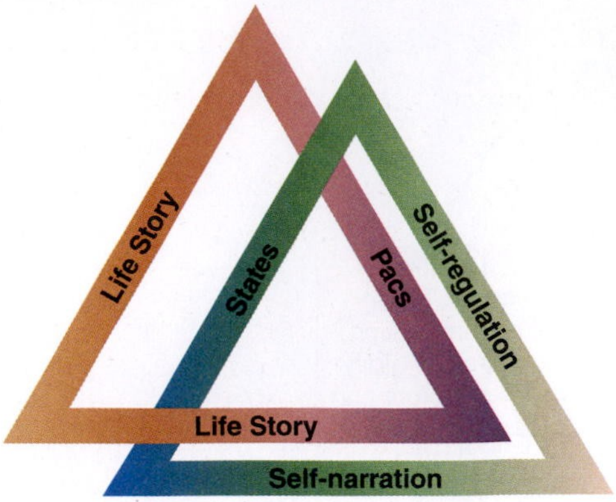

Figure 9.7 Six foci model of adult personality.
Source: Hooker, K., & McAdams, D. P. (2003). Personality reconsidered: A new agenda for aging research. *Journal of Gerontology: Psychological Sciences, 58B:* 297. https://doi.org/10.1093/geronb/58.6.P296.

potential of change, and include such things as moods, fatigue, and anxiety.

The second level of personality structures refer to personal concerns and are called *personal action constructs (PACs)*. PACs include goals, motivation, and developmental tasks, and reflect the "doing" of personality (Cantor, 1990). The parallel personality process to PACs is *self-regulatory processes*, such as self-efficacy and sense of control. Such self-regulatory processes place each PAC into specific domains and result in differences across domains in whether personal goals are actually achieved.

Finally, the third structural level is the life story each person creates to provide meaning and purpose to one's life. The process counterpoint to the life story is *self-narration*, which reflects the changes one makes in telling one's life story depending on the audience.

Hooker and McAdams are clear that the levels and processes are not hierarchical; that is, they all operate simultaneously and do not depend on each other. However, it is the case that life goals and life stories emerge later in development than do the other aspects.

What the Six Foci Model provides is a holistic framework in which to understand the complex ways that personality actually unfolds and operates. The model accounts for both stability and change and explains the conditions under which each may occur. Interestingly, the model also implies that it is not until late life that personality is most fully developed.

Now that we have a more complete understanding of personality at the general level, let's focus on some of the key concepts that enrich personality.

Self-Concept in Adulthood

As we have noted, an important aspect of identity in adulthood is how one integrates various aspects of the self. Self-perceptions and how they differ with age have been examined in a wide variety of studies and are related to many behaviors. Changes in self-perceptions are often manifested in changed beliefs, concerns, and expectations. One way to organize self-perceptions is to focus on what researchers and theorists term self-concept. **Self-concept** is the organized, coherent, integrated pattern of self-perceptions.

Self-concept is one of the most investigated topics in personality. Numerous theories have been proposed, especially describing how self-concept develops during childhood and adolescence (Harter, 2012). The concept is broad and often includes the notions of self-esteem and self-image. Our focus here will be on how self-concept connects with cognitive development.

Kegan's Theory of Self-Concept. Kegan (1982, 1994, 2009; Kegan & Lahey, 2010) integrated the development of self-concept and cognitive development. He postulated six stages of the development of self, corresponding to stages of cognitive development (described in Chapter 7). Kegan's first three stages—incorporative, impulsive, and imperial—correspond to Piaget's sensorimotor, preoperational, and concrete operational stages. During this time, Kegan believes children move from knowing themselves on the basis of reflexes to knowing themselves through needs and interests.

At the beginning of formal operational thought during early adolescence, a sense of interpersonal mutuality begins to develop; Kegan terms this period the interpersonal stage. By late adolescence or emerging adulthood, people move to a mature sense of identity based on taking control of their own life and developing an ideology; Kegan calls this period the institutional stage.

Finally, with the acquisition of postformal thought comes an understanding that the self is a complex system that takes into account other people; Kegan terms this period the interindividual stage.

Kegan's work emphasizes that personality development does not occur in a vacuum. Rather, we must remember a person is a complex integrated whole. Consequently, an understanding of the development of self-concept or any other aspect of personality is enhanced by an understanding of how it relates to other dimensions of development.

Labouvie-Vief's Dynamic Integration Theory. The integration of cognitive and personality development has also been a major focus of Gisela Labouvie-Vief (1997, 2003, 2005, 2015). She argues the self is a product of the integration of emotion and cognition, topics we explored in Chapters 7 and 8.

For Labouvie-Vief, the integration that creates a healthy self-concept in adulthood can be found in the optimization of happiness and the ability to tolerate tension and negativity to maintain objectivity. The ability to accomplish this integration increases from young through middle adulthood, but decreases in late life.

This point was clearly demonstrated by Labouvie-Vief and colleagues (1995). Working within a cognitive-developmental framework, they documented age differences in self-representation in people ranging in age from 11 to 85 years. Specifically, they found older adults move from representations of the self in emerging adulthood that are relatively poorly differentiated from others or from social conventions and expectations, to highly differentiated representations in middle age, to less differentiated representations in old age. An important finding was the degree of differentiation in self-representation (how many distinct aspects there are in a person's self-concept) was related to the level of cognitive development, thereby providing support for Kegan's position.

Other Research on Self-Concept. In addition to research integrating cognitive and emotional development, researchers also focus on other sources for creating the self across adulthood. For example, in Chapter 8, we s discussed the incorporation of aging stereotypes strongly influencing people's self-concept.

Some research documents how people organize the various facets of their self-concept. That research suggests older adults compartmentalize the different aspects of self-concept (e.g., various positive and negative aspects) more than either younger or middle-aged adults (Ready et al., 2012).

In general, research examining self-concept finds it is significantly related to a wide variety of variables such as health and longevity. Kotter-Grühn (2016) summarizes this work by concluding that self-concept does undergo some change across adulthood, but other aspects, such as self-perceptions of aging, remain fairly stable. Self-concept has also been studied in relation to well-being (considered later in this chapter) and life satisfaction (considered in more detail in Chapter 14).

Gender Identity in Adulthood

Gender identity constitutes an important aspect of one's self-concept and is one of the most rapidly evolving demographic categories globally. Gender identity is socially constructed and rooted in how people see themself and how others see them, contrasting with sex, a biological construct assigned at birth (Amaya, 2020). Within the LGBTQIA+ acronym, both sexual orientation and gender identity demographics are represented but should not be conflated (Meyer & Elias, 2022). This is not easy, because sexual orientation is closely linked to traditional gender identity norms. Sexual orientation typically centers around three areas: sexual attraction, sexual behavior, and sexual identity (Federal Interagency Working Group, 2016). Sexual attraction identifies who a person finds sexually interesting, while sexual behavior explores with whom a person currently or previously has had sexual relations, and sexual identity looks at a person's identity category, such as gay, straight, or bisexual.

A great deal of focus on the development of gender identity is in childhood and adolescence when awareness and exploration initially develop (Scroggs & Vennum, 2021). Although, on average, gender and sexual minority (GSM) individuals self-identify as GSM during middle to late adolescence, the average age of disclosure of that identity to peer groups is not until the very late teens or early twenties (Martos et al., 2015). Gender identity is fluid and should be understood as such, leading to complex, continued development and evolution in adulthood. Understanding a person's sex assignment at birth and their current gender identity provides a fuller picture of them at any given point in time (Meyer & Elias, 2022). Additionally, the place, time or generation, and sociocultural context in which a person lives affect gender identity and lived experiences. For example, the experience of a Black male who lives in a religiously conservative home in the U.S. south who comes out as gay is different than that of a White male who lives in a progressive community in an urban center who comes out as gay.

Increasingly, theorists are adopting an intersectional approach to our layers of identity. As discussed in Chapter 1, intersectionality involves understanding the lived experiences of individuals who occupy multiple sociocultural categories (e.g., Black, female, queer). In the case of gender identity, three theoretical and research approaches have been used in research on adults (Enno et al., 2022). First, an additive models approach operates under the assumption that LGBTQIA+ and racial and ethnic minority identities are understood cumulatively, and that individuals possessing these oppressed identities experience greater risk for adverse psychosocial outcomes (alternately referred to as the "double jeopardy" perspective; Huang et al., 2010). Second, a perspective of resilience proposes that possessing multiple oppressed identities fosters strength because coping resources developed to combat oppression in one domain can be utilized when faced with other forms of oppression (Ghabrial, 2017; Huang et al., 2010). Third, an intersectional model takes into account the impact of multiple oppressed identities (Balsam et al., 2011) with the underlying assumption that "people experience these facets of their identity simultaneously and in interaction with each other, just as they experience the self as a whole" (Enno, 2012, p. 2).

Enno and colleagues (2022) examined these issues from an intersectional perspective. They found that development of a multifaceted identity as a LGBTQIA+ racial–ethnic minority is a complicated process rich with nuanced self-identifications and

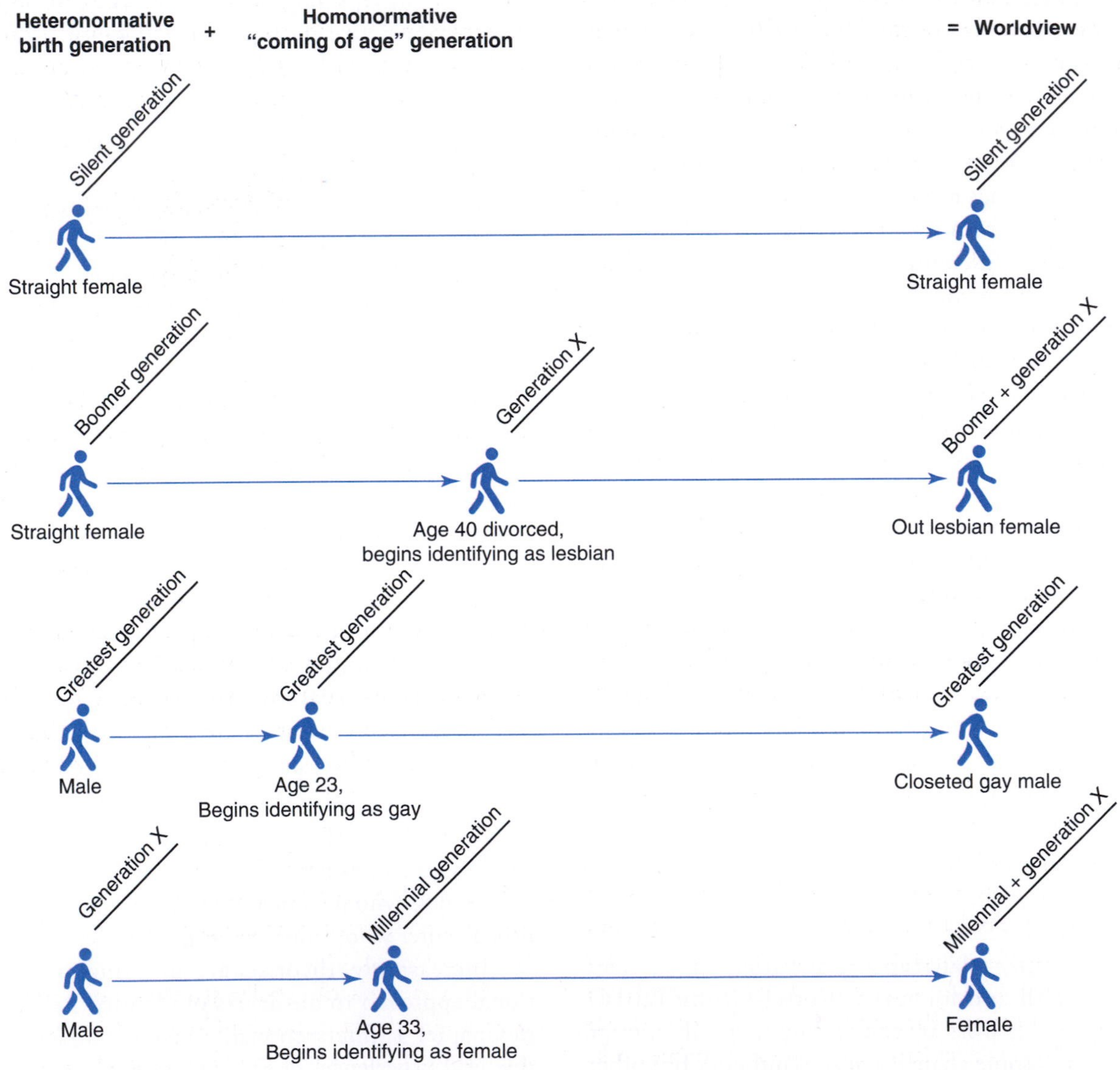

Figure 9.8 LGBTQIA+ individuals often identify with two generations: one defined by birth year and a second related to "coming of age" as a sexual minority. The birth generation worldview is overlain by an additional LGBTQIA+ generational worldview.

Source: Bitterman, A., & Hess, D. B. (2021). Understanding generation gaps in LGBTQ+ communities: Perspectives about gay neighborhoods among heteronormative and homonormative generational cohorts. In A. Bitterman & D. B. Hess (Eds.), The life and afterlife of gay neighborhoods: Renaissance and resurgence (pp. 307–338). Springer. Figure 14.3, p. 311.

impacted by a myriad of contextual influences. Participants agreed about the positive aspects of their LGBTQIA+ and their racial–ethnic minority identities. They were glad to be both and perceived that their unique constellations of identities made them particularly able to relate to people from a lot of different backgrounds. They also agreed that coming out was not necessary to be true to themselves.

Like everyone, LGBTQIA+ individuals belong to a generational cohort according to their birth year. However, Bitterman and Hess (2021) argue that some LGBTQIA+ individuals also identify with a second generational cohort corresponding to the time they identify as a member of the LGBTQIA+ communities, termed their coming of age. Birth year assignment to a generation assumes heteronormative behaviors across a person's lifespan, whereas coming of age (which can occur at any point over the lifespan) has sometimes greater importance than birth on how an LGBTQIA+ individual expresses sexual orientation and identity, given the social influences and societal norms of that specific point in time. Therefore, LGBTQIA+ individuals belong to a birth generation and may also belong to a separate parallel LGBTQIA+ generation based on the year the LGBTQIA+ individual began to identify as a sexual or gender minority. In that sense LGBTQIA+ generations can also be defined in historical time, distinct from broader heteronormative generational birth cohorts. As shown in Figure 9.8, the homonormative experience is shaped as a summation of the values, experiences, and events that shape a birth generation plus the values, experiences, and events that impact that person relative to their coming of age as an LGBTQIA+ individual. Because the coming of age or "coming out" moment may occur at any point along the continuum of the lifespan, the corresponding generational worldview most important to LGBTQIA+ people is better defined by their coming of age than only by their birth.

The importance of generation in understanding where people are regarding their gender identity is clear when the lives of older LGBTQIA+ individuals are considered. Hurd and colleagues (2022) interviewed older Canadian LGBTQIA+ adults about their experiences over their adult years. Participants reported that, earlier in life, they had lacked language or positive frameworks with which to make sense of their identities. Upon finding language and role models, all but one eventually came out or transitioned, often after consulting trusted others, experimenting in secret, leading double lives, and/or finding same-sex love. Many were fearful that as they aged, they might once again lose their abilities to openly claim their gender and sexual identities. These experiences reflect the times in which they came of age and the social attitudes that pervaded their environments.

These multiple ways of defining a person's generational identification means that it is difficult to categorize the meaning of gender identity for any given person based solely on their chronological age given that attitudes toward LGBTQIA+ individuals have changed over time. We will explore the importance of taking gender identity into account, in conjunction with sexual orientation, especially in Chapter 11 with respect to interpersonal relationships. We will consider how attitudes toward LGBTQIA+ persons make dealing with end-of-life issues even more complicated in Chapter 13.

Possible Selves in Adulthood

When we are asked questions like, "What do you think you'll be like a few years from now?" it requires us to imagine ourselves in the future. When we speculate like this, we create a possible self (Markus & Nurius, 1986). **Possible selves** represent what we could become, what we would like to become, and what we are afraid of becoming (Frazier & Hooker, 2006; Markus & Nurius, 1986; Oyserman, 2019; Stokes, 2021). Our possible selves are images that we mentally concoct of the person that we hypothetically imagine ourselves becoming as a result of following one path of behavior or another. Our possible selves are influenced by developmental, contextual, and cultural factors that create images of our future selves unique to each individual.

What we could or would like to become often reflects personal goals; we may see ourselves as leaders, as rich and famous, or in great physical shape. What we are afraid of becoming may be exhibited in our fear of being alone, or being injured, or being unsuccessful. Our possible selves are powerful motivators (Frazier et al., 2021); indeed, how we behave is largely an effort to achieve or avoid these various possible selves and protect the current conceptualization of the self (Baumeister, 2010).

In a rare set of similar studies conducted across time and research teams by Cross and Markus (1991) and Hooker and colleagues (Frazier et al., 2000, 2002; Hooker, 1999; Hooker et al., 1996; Morfei et al., 2001), people across the adult life span were asked to describe their hoped-for and feared possible selves. The responses were grouped into categories (e.g., family, personal, material, relationships, and occupation).

How Do We Know?

Possible Selves and Pursuing Social Goals

Who were the investigators, and what was the aim of the study? As we have discussed, personality development across adulthood involves the creation of life stories, which in turn involve setting and pursuing personal life goals. Han-Jung Ko, Shannon Mejía, and Karen Hooker (2014) wanted to understand one aspect of this process: how people make progress in achieving social goals that reflect their social possible selves over 100 days.

How did the investigators measure the topic of interest? Ko and colleagues used an initial questionnaire and 100 daily surveys. The initial survey focused on demographic information, a measure of hoped-for and feared social possible selves, the likelihood of each of the possible selves, and one social goal that was important to each participant that they intended to work on over the subsequent 100 days. The daily measures were an assessment of daily progress toward the selected social goal.

Who were the participants in the study? One hundred and five adults between ages 52 and 88 were recruited by emailing people on an existing list of potential research participants. 88% were women, 97% were White individuals, 93% said they were in good health, and 75% had earned at least a bachelor's degree.

Were there ethical concerns with the study? All participants were volunteers and provided written consent under a protocol approved by the Institutional Review Board.

What were the results? Twenty-two participants only had hoped-for, 13 only had feared-for, and 15 had balanced social possible selves; the remaining 49 participants had possible selves in other domains, but not in the social domain. People with balanced social possible selves made better overall daily progress toward their social goal than any other group. Additionally, those with higher self-regulatory beliefs made better overall goal progress, as did people who showed greater consistency in day-to-day progress.

What did the investigators conclude? Making consistent progress from day to day toward a goal that personally matters appears to be the best way to achieve it. Additionally, hope, rather than fear, is the better motivator. The notion of keeping one's eyes on the prize is borne out in research, especially when the prize matters to the person.

Several interesting age differences emerged. In terms of hoped-for selves, emerging adults listed family concerns—for instance, marrying the right person—as most important. In contrast, established adults listed family concerns last; their main issues involved personal concerns, such as being a more loving and caring person. By middle age, family issues again became most common—such as being a parent who can "let go" of the children. Reaching and maintaining satisfactory performance in one's occupational career as well as accepting and adjusting to the physiological changes of middle age were important to this age group.

For adults over 60, researchers find personal issues resurface, but differently—such as being active and healthy for at least another decade. The greatest amount of change for older adults occurred in the health domain, which predominated the hoped-for and feared-for selves. The health domain is the most sensitive and central to the self in the context of aging, and people's possible self with regard to health is quite resilient in the face of health challenges in later life.

Overall, emerging adults have multiple possible selves and believe they can actually become the hoped-for self and successfully avoid the feared self. Their outlook tends to be quite positive (Remedios et al., 2010). Life experience may dampen this outlook. By old age, both the number of possible selves and the strength of belief have decreased. Older adults are more likely to believe neither the hoped-for nor the feared-for self is under their personal control. These findings may reflect differences with age in personal motivation, beliefs in personal control, and the need to explore new options.

The emergence of online social media has created new opportunities for people to create possible selves in a traditional sense (Lefkowitz et al., 2012) or through the use of avatars (Freeman & Maloney, 2021). The flexibility and ubiquity of social media present many ways for people to speculate about themselves to others, and to gain feedback about those representations.

The connection between possible selves and how we construct meaning in our lives is important. The link is through the process of setting personal goals that derive from the possible selves we envision. The details of this link are explored in the How Do We Know? feature.

Spirituality and Identity in Adulthood

Humanity's oldest surviving literary work, the ancient Mesopotamian *Epic of Gilgamesh*, tells of Gilgamesh's search for the answer to one of life's great issues: the search for eternal life as an answer to the question "What happens after we die?" This is one of the big questions we all face, especially as part of Erikson's life review in service of achieving ego integrity: What is the meaning of life? Why do bad things happen to good people? Is there anything more than this life? Why is there so much suffering? Why am I here?

How people answer those questions derives from many aspects of their identity. Spirituality is a key aspect of identity through which many people find meaning and answers to these questions (Aldwin et al., 2014; Cavanaugh, 2017; Pargament, 2013; Wong et al., 2018). Spirituality "can inform all aspects of meaning, informing beliefs . . . and providing ultimate motivation and primary goals for living and guidelines for achieving those goals, along with a deep sense of purpose and mattering" (Park, 2013, p. 42).

Individuals' sense of spirituality develops across adulthood. Thomas Merton (1955, 1962) and Richard Rohr (2011, 2013) both describe this process as the progression from the *False Self* to the *True Self*. Essentially the distinction is between the superficial, external self that we mean when we use the first person singular pronoun "I," the self that Merton considers a prison from which we must escape, and the joy of dwelling in union with the essence of everything in the universe in the core of our soul, the self that Merton argues we must become.

Rohr writes that the False Self is rooted in a relative identity that each of us creates for ourselves, an identity that depends critically on external indicators of success (e.g., title, prestige, salary, status). The False Self is inherently fragile, tends to be dissatisfied because it depends on external definitions of achievement, and is felt as separate from others in the sense that we want to

Joseantona/iStock/Getty Images

Spiritual practice in all forms is evident throughout the latter half of the life span.

belong to the "in" group and define others selectively as members of the "out" group. Change is feared. Morality is defined in terms of adherence to rules. In short, the False Self is the result of building one's ego structure based on incorporating external messages regarding "values" and "success." There is a heavy emphasis on doing things "correctly" according to the rules of the group or society. In Rohr's view, achieving the True Self involves (re)discovering the universality and wholeness, an "authentic inner knowing," that has always been within but has gone unrecognized or unacknowledged. The True Self does not see anything with absolute certainty. The True Self is the fulfillment of the search for answers to the core existential questions. It entails a letting go and an acceptance of what is.

As noted earlier in this chapter, the developmental transition from False Self to True Self is a reflection of underlying cognitive (described in Chapters 6 and 7) and personality development. Other theorists (e.g., Fowler, 1981, 2000; McLaren, 2021) describe stages of faith development that closely mirror those in overall cognitive development. Cavanaugh (2017) argues that it is these underlying processes that permit the shifts in perspective reflected in the transition from False Self to True Self or through stages of faith development.

This change in perspective is also a key factor in how many older adults cope with life stresses. According to research, older adults in many countries and from many different backgrounds use their religious faith and spirituality as the basis for coping, often more than they use family or friends (Ai et al., 2010, 2013, 2017; Ardelt et al., 2013; Wink et al., 2021). For some older adults, especially African Americans, a strong attachment to

God is what they believe helps them deal with the challenges of life (Cosby, 2020; Pickard et al., 2018).

There is considerable evidence linking spirituality, religious-based coping, and health as applications of spiritual identity (Ai et al., 2010, 2017; Krause, 2012; Park, 2013; Wink et al., 2021). In general, older adults who are more involved with and committed to their faith have better physical and mental health than older adults who are not religious. For example, older Mexican Americans who pray to the saints and the Virgin Mary or attend religious services on a regular basis tend to have greater optimism and better health and a significant reduction in mortality from any cause (Hill et al., 2020; Krause & Bastida, 2011). Spirituality also helps improve psychological well-being (Ai et al., 2017; Hayward et al., 2016; Wink et al., 2021) and helps patients following cardiac surgery (Ai et al., 2010; Appel et al., 2020; Wink et al., 2021).

Researchers have increasingly focused on **spiritual support**—which includes seeking pastoral care, participating in organized and nonorganized religious activities, and expressing faith in a God who cares for people—as a key factor in understanding how older adults cope. Even when under high levels of stress, such as during critical illness or other major life trauma, people who have more highly developed spiritual identities and who rely on spiritual support report greater personal well-being (Ai et al., 2010, 2017; Hayward et al., 2016; Wink et al., 2021) and cope better with chronic health conditions (Lucette et al., 2016; Nienke, 2021).

Neuroscience research has shown a connection between certain spiritual mindfulness practices and brain activity (Dobkin & Hassed, 2016; Tang et al., 2020; Tang & Posner, 2012). For example, there is evidence that people who have practiced meditation show positive structural changes in areas of the brain related to attention and memory (Esch, 2014; Santaella, 2021). Thus, neurological evidence indicates that there may be changes in brain activity and in brain structure associated with spiritual practices that help people cope. An example of the changes that occur in brain activity between a normal resting state and a meditative state is in Figure 9.9. Notice the significant increase in activity during meditation.

This kind of positive structural change has led some researchers (Luders & Cherbuin, 2016; Manglani et al., 2020; Newberg et al., 2014) to argue that meditation might offer promise as a way to help slow down, and perhaps even prevent, the brain changes that underlie brain

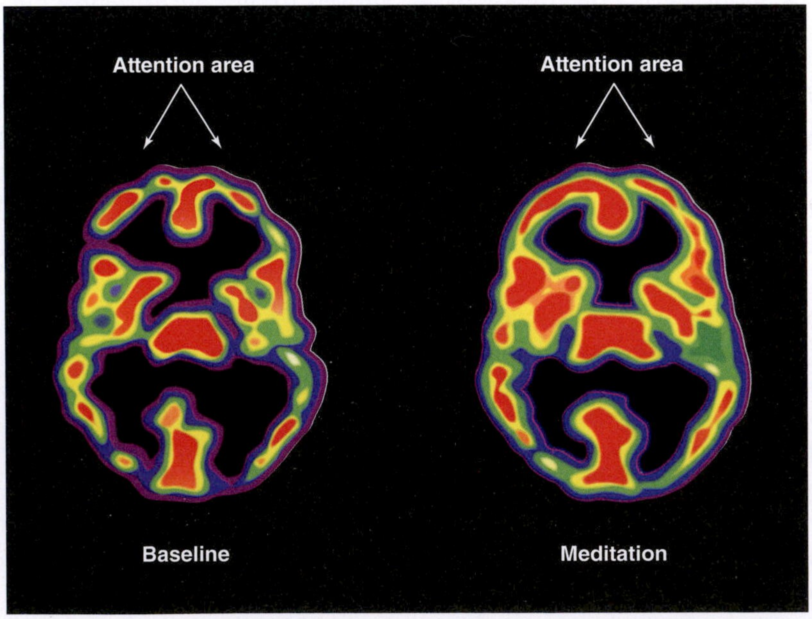

Figure 9.9 SPECT scans of a subject at rest and during peak meditation showing increased cerebral blood flow (arrows) during meditation.

diseases such as dementia. While it is still too early to tell for certain, the possibility that a practice done for centuries among all of the major world religions in one form or another, mindful meditation or contemplation, could prevent or reverse negative changes in the brain will undoubtedly be the focus of a great deal of research. It turns out that developing a spiritual aspect to one's identity may have wide-ranging positive benefits.

Conclusions About Narratives, Identity, and the Self

We have considered that to fully understand a person, we must consider how the individual integrates their life into a coherent structure. The life-narrative approach provides a way to learn how people accomplish this integration. The theoretical frameworks developed by McAdams and by Whitbourne offer excellent avenues for research. One of the most promising new areas of inquiry, possible selves, is already providing major insights into how people construct future elements of their life stories.

When combined with the data from the dispositional trait and personal concerns literature, research findings on identity and the self provide the capstone knowledge needed to understand what people are like. The complexity of personality is clear from this discussion; perhaps that is why it takes a lifetime to complete.

Adult Development in Action

If you were part of a multidisciplinary support team, how would you include spirituality as part of an overall plan to help your clients cope with life issues?

Review Questions

9.3 Life Narratives, Identity, and the Self

- What are the basic tenets of McAdams's life-story theory? What are the seven elements of a life story?
- What is Whitbourne's life-span construct? How does it relate to a scenario and a life story? How did Whitbourne incorporate Piagetian concepts into her theory of identity?
- What is the Six Foci Model of personality development?
- What is self-concept? What shapes it?
- What are possible selves? What developmental trends have been found in possible selves?
- How are spirituality aspects of identity important for adults?

Social Policy Implications

Adult Personality and the Curated World of Social Media

In this chapter, we focused on three main approaches to understanding personality in adulthood: dispositional traits, personal concerns, and life narratives. Each provided a lens through which various facets of personality were emphasized. Also in each we examined how personality remains sufficiently stable to permit us to recognize individuals as the same person over long periods of time, yet flexible enough to permit change in underlying conceptions of oneself and shifting priorities that define specific life situations.

All of these perspectives presume that there is dynamic interplay between the individual and the sociocultural environment in which that person is situated. We considered several of these, such as culture, race, ethnicity, and gender. These categories reflect both self- and socially defined (and imposed) categories for which there is ample evidence of strong influence on the person's ultimate personality and identity.

Increasingly, though, another context is being recognized as having very significant influence—social media. Such platforms present highly curated "ideals" of social norms, including personality and identity norms. Considerable evidence was reported in the early 2020s that certain social media platforms create very high levels of stress on adolescents, especially girls, and on emerging adults whose self-comparisons of their perceived selves failed to match the curated images presented in social media. The

(Continued)

practice of "canceling" individuals who transgress certain, often unclear and ill-defined, "norms" exacerbated the situations. Cyberbullying, many times done anonymously, added even more stress. Research also demonstrated that psychological distress and negative mental health outcomes were distressingly common.

As a result of these data, social media platforms are under scrutiny. For example, the U.S. Congress held hearings and debated various approaches to regulating social media platforms in order to mitigate the negative effects on adolescents and emerging adults, especially. Specific regulatory action became complicated, though, as a result of imprecise distinctions between speech that is protected (under the First Amendment) and speech that is not. It is also the case that such pressures for behavior and identity conforming are not new; for example, the Salem witch trials in Massachusetts also had their origins in rumor and pressure to conform, along with strongly held gender-based beliefs. How people are ultimately protected from the extreme pressures to conform that are easily transmitted via social media remains to be seen. Social policy will be a necessary part of the solution.

In Review

Your summary of Chapter 9 should be framed in three main paragraphs. The first should focus on dispositional traits. Create a description of the Five-Factor Model and define each of the trait dimensions. Then discuss the evidence for whether these dispositional traits remain stable or change. In cases in which change is evident, summarize the overall developmental trends. Close the paragraph with a description of alternative approaches to dispositional traits beyond the Big Five dimensions.

In your second paragraph, define personal concerns, then describe the main points of Jung's and Erikson's theories and how they relate to personal concerns. Discuss the various theories about life transitions, with special focus on midlife and the different views about that period in the adult life span.

In your third paragraph, begin with a discussion of life narratives, life stories, and scenarios. Summarize McAdams's life-story model, Whitbourne's identity theory, and the Six Foci Model. Discuss self-concept, gender identity, and possible selves, with special focus on the sources and importance of each. Conclude with a discussion of the role of spirituality in adult identity.

Integrating Concepts in Development

- What relations can be found among dispositional traits, personal concerns, and life narratives?
- How does personality development reflect the four basic forces of development discussed in Chapter 1?
- How does cognitive development relate to personality change?
- How does personality change relate to stages in occupational transition?

Key Terms

agreeableness Dimension of personality associated with being accepting, willing to work with others, and caring. 285

cognitive processes A structural component of personality that acts jointly with life narratives to create natural interactions between a storyteller and listener, processes central in organizing life stories. 283

conscientiousness Dimension of personality in which people tend to be hard-working, ambitious, energetic, scrupulous, and persevering. 285

dispositional trait A relatively stable, enduring aspect of personality. 283

ego development The fundamental changes in the ways our thoughts, values, morals, and goals are organized. Transitions from one stage to another depend on both internal biological changes and external social changes to which the person must adapt. 286

epigenetic principle In Erikson's theory, the notion that development is guided by an underlying plan in which certain issues have their own particular times of importance. 293

extraversion Personality trait dimension associated with the tendency to thrive on social interaction, to like to talk, to take charge easily, to readily express opinions and feelings, to keep busy, to have boundless energy, and to prefer stimulating and challenging environments. 285

life narrative The aspects of personality that pull everything together, those integrative aspects that give a person an identity or sense of self. 283

life-span construct In Whitbourne's theory of identity, the way people build a perspective of who they are. 302

midlife correction Reevaluating one's roles and dreams and making the necessary corrections. 299

neuroticism Personality trait dimension associated with the tendency to be anxious, hostile, self-conscious, depressed, impulsive, and vulnerable. 285

openness to experience Personality dimension that reflects a tendency to have a vivid imagination and dream life, an appreciation of art, and a strong desire to try anything once. 285

personal concerns Things that are important to people, their goals, and their major concerns in life. 283

personality adjustment Involves developmental changes in terms of their adaptive value and functionality such as functioning effectively within society and how personality contributes to everyday life running smoothly. 287

personality growth Refers to ideal end states such as increased self-transcendence, wisdom, and integrity. 287

possible selves Aspects of the self-concept involving oneself in the future in both positive and negative ways. 307

self-concept The organized, coherent, integrated pattern of self-perceptions. 304

self-regulatory processes Personality processes that work in conjunction with personal concerns to set expectations in various domains (e.g., memory). 283

spiritual support Includes seeking pastoral care, participating in organized and nonorganized religious activities, and expressing faith in a God who cares for people as a key factor in understanding how older adults cope. 310

state processes A structural component of personality that acts with dispositional traits to create transient, short-term changes in emotion, mood, hunger, anxiety, and the like. 283

trait Any distinguishable, relatively enduring way in which one individual differs from others. 284

trait theories Theories of personality that assume little change occurs across adulthood. 284

Chapter

10

Mental Health, Clinical Assessment, and Psychopathology

Learning Objectives

After studying this chapter you will be able to...

10.1. Define what mental health means and discuss how its meaning differs across sociocultural categories.

10.2. Discuss how assessment of psychopathology is approached with adults.

10.3. Discuss the symptoms, diagnosis, and treatment options for depression, anxiety disorders, post-traumatic stress disorder, and substance use disorders.

10.4. Discuss the symptoms, diagnosis, and treatment options for delirium, Alzheimer's disease, and other types of dementia.

Chapter Outline

March 2020 was a global turning point. That's when the world began shutting down due to the COVID-19 pandemic. In the beginning, very little about the virus was understood; that knowledge emerged over time, sometimes in seemingly contradictory and confusing ways. The uncertainty, sudden loss of physical contact with others, pivoting from working in an office to working remotely, challenging situations with children required to take classes online (providing that broadband and devices were available), and in so many cases having loved ones die without being able to be with them conspired to create a mental health crisis for many.

How people globally dealt with their own particular experiences differed widely (Graupensperger et al., 2022; McElroy-Heltzel et al., 2022; Mendez-Lopez et al., 2022; Pappa et al., 2022; Sterina et al., 2022). As discussed in the Controversies feature, some of these outcomes appear counterintuitive at first, others quite predictable. Many had never experienced the challenges to their mental health that COVID-19 presented; others had years of experience with major life stressors from numerous sources. And how people were affected depended critically on their background.

Controversies

COVID-19 and Mental Health as a Global Experience

The global lockdown in March 2020 due to the COVID-19 pandemic disrupted the lives of nearly everyone everywhere. There is no question that the drastic changes in daily routines set the stage for widespread challenges to people's physical and mental well-being. It also created one of the first opportunities for researchers to track the effects of a health pandemic on people's mental health globally. How did people fare?

A large number of studies showed convincingly that (1) the pandemic affected nearly everyone in some way, but (2) how those effects played out was influenced by a person's sociocultural background, where they live, prior experiences with stress and related coping resources, age, biology/physiology (e.g., genetics, physical health), and time into the pandemic. For example, Graupensperger and colleagues (2022) found in a longitudinal study that for emerging adults COVID-19-related stressors, especially social/relational stressors, had direct and time-varying associations with mental health and well-being that were generally stronger in earlier months and decreased linearly across the pandemic.

Research focused on older adults exhibited different patterns. For instance, on the basis of a meta-analysis of 20 studies Sterina and colleagues (2022) concluded that older adults consistently reported lower stress and fewer negative emotions than did emerging adults throughout the lockdowns. Even among U.S. homebound older adults living below the poverty line or who had chronic diseases, personal resilience and optimism buffered the effects of the pandemic (McElroy-Heltzel et al., 2022).

Evidence that where one lives mattered comes from meta-analyses of research in Southeast Asia, China, and Europe (Pappa et al., 2022). Individuals in Southeast Asia reported significantly lower levels of anxiety and depression than did comparable samples in Europe and China; the differences were especially large between Southeast Asia and southern European countries (France, Italy, Greece, Spain).

The COVID-19 pandemic also "brought age bias and the unmet mental health needs of older adults into bold relief" (Carpenter et al., 2022, p. 538). Given the growing numbers of older adults globally, changing views of aging, increased participation of persons in their own care, and geopolitical issues such as climate change and the sociocultural factors involved, increased attention needs to be paid to older adults' mental health needs.

What is clear from these studies is that results concerning mental health effects of the COVID-19 pandemic are particular to the group being studied. No sweeping generalities can be accurately applied—it all depends. For example, it would be natural for people to be anxious about a new disease which, at the outset, had no effective treatment, cure, or prevention.

In this chapter, we consider situations in which the adult developmental process does not follow a normative trajectory. Such outcomes happen in families every day. It happened twice in John Cavanaugh's family (the author of this book) with respect to family members who experienced dementia. Certainly, dementia is not part of normative aging, nor are the other conditions we consider.

This chapter is about the people who do not make it through adulthood and old age by only experiencing normative changes. Some adults develop mental health difficulties serious enough that they interfere to various degrees with daily life. In the first module we define mental health and how mental disorders, or psychopathology, are conceptualized across adulthood. Next, we consider how psychopathologies are assessed and treated in adults of different ages. Following that we focus on several specific disorders, including depression, delirium, dementia, anxiety disorders, psychotic disorders, and substance use. As we consider different types of psychopathology, we note how each is diagnosed, the known causes, and effective treatments that are available. Throughout, we will also note important differences across sociocultural groups.

10.1 Mental Health and the Adult Life Course

Key Questions

- How are mental health and psychopathology defined?
- What are the key dimensions used for categorizing psychopathology?
- Why are ethnicity and aging important variables to consider in understanding mental health?

Janet lives alone in a small apartment. Lately, some of her neighbors have noticed she doesn't come to church services as regularly as she used to. Betty, her friend and neighbor, noticed Janet cries a lot when she's asked whether anything is wrong and at times seems confused. Betty knows several of Janet's friends died recently but still wonders whether something more serious may be causing her problems.

Situations like Janet's are common. Like Betty, we might think Janet is trying to deal with the loss of friends and is simply experiencing grief, perhaps intensified by her living alone. Or there may be something more serious—could Janet's confusion indicate a physical or mental health problem? Janet's situation points out the difficulty in knowing exactly where normative behavior after the loss of people close to us (discussed in Chapter 13) that reflects good mental health ends and more serious mental disorders begin. What distinguishes the study of psychopathology in adulthood and aging is not so much the content of the behavior as its context, that is, whether it interferes with daily functioning. To understand psychopathology as manifested in adults of different ages, we must examine how it fits into the life-span developmental perspectives outlined in Chapter 1.

Defining Mental Health and Psychopathology

The precise difference between mental health and psychopathology has never been clear (Segal et al., 2017). Most scholars avoid the issue entirely or simply try to explain what mental health or psychopathology is not. Creating a bright line between normative and nonnormative behavior is hard to do precisely because expectations and standards for behavior change over time, situations, sociocultural groups, and age groups (Zarit & Zarit, 2007). Many researchers and practitioners invoke Birren and Renner's (1980) classic argument that mentally healthy people have the following characteristics: a positive attitude toward self, an accurate perception of reality, a mastery of the environment, autonomy, personality balance, and growth and self-actualization. Thus, all these characteristics must be evaluated when determining the mental health status of an individual.

There is a problem using the approach, though (Gopalkrishnan, 2018). Much of the theory and practice of mental health emerged from Western cultural traditions and Western understandings of humans. Separation of body and mind, positivism, and reductionism have been central to the development of mainstream mental health systems. While a Western-focused conceptualization of mental health has provided insights and frameworks for the treatment of psychopathologies, it has also been very problematic when applied to non-Western cultures without consideration of the complexity that working across cultures brings with it.

Based on their work in Southeast Asia, Hechanova and Waeldle (2017) propose that there are five key components of diverse cultures that have implications for mental health professionals. The first element that they identify is *emotional expression*—some cultures believe that talking about painful issues leads to further painful feelings, making them reluctant to engage in talk-based therapy. The second element is *shame*, an especially significant factor in cultures in which the family plays a central role in the lives of people with mental health issues. The third element is *power distance* or the large differences in power that may exist between a therapist and the person with a mental health issue, and which may have implications in terms of the autonomy or lack thereof in a therapeutic relationship. Fourth, the nature of *collectivism* (a focus on the group as the unit of analysis rather than the individual) and its impact as a supportive factor for resilience and coping is the case in many cultures. Finally, they discuss *spirituality and religion* from the point of view of attribution of the cause of mental health concerns as well as in terms of appropriate coping strategies. These cultural differences influence not only the definition of mental health but also how (and even whether) a diagnosis of a mental health issue is made and what (if any) treatment approaches should be taken.

As we proceed in our consideration of mental health and psychopathology in this chapter, keep in mind the need to be open to different approaches based on cultural context. We will return to this issue periodically throughout.

Alvarez/E+/Getty Images

The diagnosis of psychopathologies depends critically on understanding sociocultural differences in how behaviors are interpreted.

A Multidimensional Life-Span Approach to Psychopathology

Suppose two people, one younger adult and one older adult, came into your clinic, each complaining about a lack of sleep, changes in appetite, a lack of energy, and feeling down. What would you think about that and say to them?

If you respond to and evaluate them in identical ways, you might be headed for trouble. As we discussed in other chapters, older and younger adults may think or view themselves differently, so how they present their symptoms and complaints, and what they mean, may also differ, even though they appear to be the same. This point is often overlooked (Segal et al., 2017). Considering behavior from a life-span developmental forces perspective makes a big difference in how we understand psychopathology. Let's find out why.

Biological Forces. Various neurological changes, chronic diseases, functional limitations, and other ailments can change behavior. Changes in the structure and functioning of the brain can have important effects on behavior (discussed in Chapter 2). Because certain health problems increase with age (discussed in Chapters 3 and 4), as do certain memory performance declines (discussed in Chapters 6 and 7), we must be more sensitive to them when dealing with older adults. In addition, genetic factors (also in Chapter 3) often underlie important problems in old age. For example, several forms of dementia have a genetic component.

Physical problems may provide clues about underlying psychological difficulties, and physical problems may present themselves as psychological ones. For example, extreme irritability can be caused by thyroid problems, and memory loss can result from certain vitamin deficiencies. Physical health and genetic factors should be among the first avenues explored in a comprehensive diagnostic workup.

Psychological Forces. Psychological forces across adulthood are key to understanding psychopathology. As we discussed in Chapters 6, 7, 8, and 9, several important changes in memory, intelligence, social cognition, and personality must be considered carefully in interpreting behavior. Normative changes with age in these arenas can mimic certain mental disorders; likewise, these changes make it more difficult to tell when an older adult has a given type of psychopathology.

In addition, the nature of a person's relationships with other people, especially family members and friends, is a basic dimension in understanding how psychopathology is manifested in adults of different ages. Chapter 11 summarizes developmental changes in key relationships that may influence adults' interpretation of symptoms.

Sociocultural Forces. The social norms and cultural factors we all experience also play a key role in helping define psychopathology. They influence people's behaviors and affect our interpretation of them. Because customs differ across cultures, behaviors that may be normative in one culture may be regarded as indicating problems in another. In short, we must ask whether the behavior we observe is appropriate for a person in a particular setting and background, as we will explore in the next section.

Life-Cycle Factors. How people behave at any point in adulthood is strongly affected by their past experiences and the issues they faced. These life-cycle factors must be taken into account in evaluating adults' behaviors. Equally important, the meanings of particular symptoms change with age. For example, problems with early morning awakenings may indicate depression in an emerging adult but may simply be a result of normative aging in an older adult (reviewed in Chapter 3).

Race, Ethnicity, Gender, Aging, and Mental Health

As noted in the previous section, sociocultural factors provide key contexts for interpreting behaviors to determine whether they reflect mental health concerns. The role of intersectionality (discussed in Chapter 1) is especially important in this arena, as the social disparities associated with differing demographic groups are not equivalent, nor are they consistent across different types of mental health problems.

Mental health professionals have recognized that race and racial stereotypes have negatively influenced research and diagnosis of psychopathology (Bryant et al., 2022). Such bias, and concomitant barriers to obtaining mental health services, mean that we do not have an accurate understanding of true differences across racial groups regarding the incidence of mental health disorders (Muntaner et al., 2013). What is clear is that intersectionality creates complexity in understanding patterns across different groups.

For example, Dennis (2021) studied Black men and women in Detroit. Findings revealed correlations between higher total household income and lower levels of depression and anxiety, and between unemployment and increased depression and anxiety among working-age Black adults. Additionally, higher educational attainment was correlated with reduced anxiety, but not depression. Gender moderated these findings such that unemployment was associated with higher levels of depression and anxiety among women but not men.

In another study, Lacey and colleagues (2021) studied women who were either U.S.-born African American, U.S.-born Caribbean Black, or foreign-born Caribbean Black. They found that severe physical intimate partner violence (SPIPV) is a significant threat to the mental health of U.S.-born Black women. Analyses indicated that those with a history of SPIPV were at greater risk for mental disorders than women who did not experience violence by a spouse or partner. Racial discrimination was associated with higher odds of anxiety and substance disorders, whereas gender discrimination was associated with higher odds of mood disorders. Older age and being an Afro-Caribbean immigrant were associated with lower odds of mental disorders.

These and other studies point out the importance of carefully describing and differentiating groups of people who participate in research on mental health issues. Earlier we noted that neither mental health nor psychopathology has been adequately defined in any group in a way that takes sociocultural context into account. For example, although many explanations of problem behaviors are grounded in the oppressive life conditions that characterize many communities, the conceptualization of positive mental health for older ethnic groups does not take into account either the lifetime accumulation of such effects nor resilience factors (Delgado, 2015; Thomas Tobin et al., 2022) nor the effects of a lifetime of inadequate access to health care (Miranda et al., 2008; Thomas Tobin et al., 2022).

What little data we have consistently suggest more similarities than differences in the incidence of specific types of psychopathology across different racial and ethnic groups (Thomas Tobin et al., 2022). Based on stress theory (discussed in Chapter 4), it might be expected that people who face systematic discrimination, which is stressful, should consistently demonstrate higher levels of mental health issues. But that's not what the data tend to reveal. For example, the Black–White mental health epidemiological paradox (i.e., Black Americans' lower or similar rates of mental disorder relative to White Americans) characterizes the research on race and mental health over several decades. Thomas Tobin and colleagues (2022) expressed it this way: "The Black–White mental health paradox generally extends across lifetime mood, anxiety, and substance use disorders and is consistent across age and gender groups. We also found more similarity in mental disorders between older Blacks and Whites relative to their younger counterparts, suggesting that Black–White mental health differences are most pronounced among younger age groups" (p. 196). Note that the age pattern in these results points to age-related differences in mental health status—in other words, the Black–White mental health paradox may be an age-related phenomenon.

Sex and gender differences in the prevalence of certain mental disorders are well known and documented (Otten et al., 2021; Rosenfield & Mouzon, 2013; Smith et al., 2018). Studies in other cultures also find sex and gender differences. For instance, a community study in Korea, research in Germany, and a study of records in a day hospital in Italy found being female increased the risk of symptoms of depression (Luca et al., 2013; Oh et al., 2013; Otten et al., 2021).

Perhaps the most important conclusion to draw is that assumptions about the pattern of mental health issues and concerns are often not only wrong, but the facts are contrary to expectations based on other theories. Thus, interpreting data regarding how many people of a specific background have a mental disorder must be done quite carefully, taking into account all of the aspects of the biopsychosocial model.

Adult Development in Action

As an elected official, how would you put the data about mental health and aging into social policy?

Review Questions

10.1 Mental Health and the Adult Life Course

- How do definitions of mental health vary with age and sociocultural factors?
- How does the biopsychosocial model shape the understanding of mental health and psychopathology?
- How are race, ethnicity, sex, and gender, and aging factors reflected in understanding mental health?

10.2 Developmental Issues in Assessment and Therapy

Key Questions

- What key areas are included in a multidimensional approach to assessment?
- What factors influence the assessment of adults?
- How are mental health issues assessed?
- What are some major considerations for therapy across adulthood?

Juan is a 70-year-old retired plumber. Over the past year, his wife, Rocio, noticed Juan's memory isn't quite as sharp as it used to be. Juan also has less energy, stays home more, and does not have as much interest in playing dominos, a game at which he used to excel. Rocio wonders what might be wrong with Juan.

Many adults can relate to Rocio because they are concerned about someone they know. Whether the person is 25 or 85, it is important to be able to determine whether memory problems, energy loss, social withdrawal, or other areas of concern really indicate an underlying problem. In this module, we consider how assessment methods and therapies must be appropriate for people of different ages and backgrounds.

Areas of Multidimensional Assessment

What does it mean to assess someone's mental health status? Assessment makes it possible to describe the behavior or other characteristics of people in meaningful ways (Gallegos et al., 2018; Groth-Marnat & Wright, 2016; Samarina et al., 2021). Assessment is a formal process of measuring, understanding, and predicting behavior. It involves gathering medical, psychological, and sociocultural information about people through various means, such as interviews, observation, tests, and clinical interviews and examinations (Gallegos et al., 2018; Groth-Marnat & Wright, 2016).

A multidimensional assessment approach is essential (Gallegos et al., 2018; Groth-Marnat & Wright, 2016; Samarina et al., 2021). Multidimensional assessment is often done by a team of professionals: a physician may focus on physical health and medication regimen; a psychologist on cognitive, personality, and social functioning; a nurse on functional skills in daily life; and a social worker on the economic, social network, and environmental resources. Let's consider Juan's situation in the vignette as an example.

A thorough assessment of Juan's physical health is a critical, often first step. Many physical conditions can create (or hide) mental health problems, so it is important to identify any underlying issues. Laboratory tests or neuroimaging can also be ordered to provide additional clues to the presence or even to the cause of the problem.

Establishing Juan's cognitive abilities is also key. Complaints of cognitive problems increase across adulthood, so it is important to discriminate nonnormative changes from normative ones. Adults of all ages can be given intelligence tests, neuropsychological examinations, and mental status examinations to help make these determinations. **Mental status exams** are especially useful as quick screening measures of mental competence used to screen for cognitive impairment. Example items from one commonly used instrument, the Mini Mental Status Exam (MMSE), are in Table 10.1. If Juan's score on these brief measures indicated potential problems, more complete follow-up assessments would be used. It is important to remember that scales such as the MMSE are only used for general screening and not for final diagnosis.

Psychological functioning is typically assessed through interviews, observation, and tests or questionnaires. Usually a clinician begins with an interview of Juan and brief screening instruments and follows up, if necessary, with more thorough personality inventories, tests, or more detailed interviews.

How well Juan functions in his daily life is also assessed carefully. Usually this entails determining whether he has difficulty with activities of daily living and instrumental activities of daily living (see Chapter 4). Also assessed is the person's decision-making capacity; each state has legal standards guiding the competency assessment.

In general, it is important to assess the broad array of support resources (e.g., social networks, community resources) available to older adults. To be effective, these must be accessible and readily available.

Factors Influencing Assessment

Healthcare professionals' preconceived ideas about the people they assess may have negative effects on the assessment process (Chew-Graham & Ray, 2016; Gallegos et al., 2018; Groth-Marnat & Wright, 2016; Samarina et al., 2021). Two areas of concern are biases (negative or positive) and environmental conditions (where the assessment occurs, sensory or mobility problems, and health of the client).

Many types of bias have been documented as affecting the assessment process (Chew-Graham & Ray, 2016; Gallegos et al., 2018; Samarina et al., 2021). Negative biases about people are widespread and include racial, ethnic, gender, and age stereotypes. Clinicians may hold negative biases (discussed in Chapter 6) against adults from certain racial or ethnic groups and more readily "diagnose" problems that do not truly exist. Likewise, because of ageism (discussed in Chapter 1), older adults may be "diagnosed" with untreatable problems such as dementia rather than treatable problems such as depression. In contrast, positive biases about certain people also work against accurate assessment. A belief that older adults are often "eccentric" may mitigate against accurate assessment of abilities. Clearly, the best defense against bias is for clinicians to be fully educated about their prospective clients.

Table 10.1 A Sampling of Questions from the Mini Mental Status Exam

Cognitive Area	Activity
Orientation to time	"What is the date?"
Registration	"Listen carefully. I am going to say three words. You say them back after I say them. Ready? Here they are ... APPLE [pause], PENNY [pause], TABLE [pause]. Now repeat those words back to me." [Repeat up to 5 times, but score only the first trial.]
Naming	"What is this?" [Point to a pencil or pen.]
Reading stimulus form	"Please read this and do what it says." [Show examinee the words on the form.] CLOSE YOUR EYES

The environmental conditions where the assessment occurs can also work against accurate outcomes. Clinicians do not always have the option of selecting an ideal environment; rather, assessments sometimes occur with a bedridden patient or in a noisy emergency department. People with sensory or motor difficulties must be accommodated with alternative assessment formats. The patient's physical health may also complicate assessment; in many cases with older adults, health issues can also create a negative bias so mental health issues may be overlooked when a health problem is discovered (Gallegos et al., 2018; Samarina et al., 2021).

Assessment Methods

How are adults assessed? In terms of cognitive, psychological, and social assessments, there are six primary methods (American Psychological Association, 2014; Samarina et al., 2021): clinical interview, self-report, report by others, psychophysiological and neuroimaging assessment, direct observation, and performance-based assessment.

Clinical interviews are the most widely used assessment method (Groth-Marnat & Wright, 2016). They are useful because they provide both direct information in response to the questions and nonverbal information such as emotions. Interviews can be used to obtain historical information, determine appropriate follow-up procedures, build rapport with the client, obtain the client's informed consent to participate in the assessment, and evaluate the effects of treatment. All these tasks are important with adults of all ages. When interviewing older adults, though, it may be necessary to use somewhat shorter sessions and to be aware of sensory deficits and cognitive and medical conditions that may interfere with the interview.

Many commonly used formal assessment measures are presented in a self-report format, such as Likert scales. As noted in Chapter 1, a major concern is the reliability and validity of these measures with older adults.

Family members and friends are an important source of information. In some cases, such as dementia, discrepancies between the client's and others' descriptions of the problem can be diagnostic. Such sources also are valuable if the client is unlikely or unable to tell the whole story. Information from these other key informants can be obtained through interviews or self-report.

Psychophysiological assessment examines the relation between physical and psychological functioning. One common psychophysiological measure is the electroencephalogram (EEG), which measures brain wave activity. Other measures include heart rate, muscle activity, and skin temperature. Such measures provide a way to measure the body's reaction to certain stimuli, especially when the client gets anxious or fearful in response to them. Neuroimaging assessments (discussed in Chapter 2) may be used to help document the presence or absence of possible structural changes or individual variations in the brain that may be correlated with a particular symptom profile.

In some cases, it is possible to observe the client through systematic or naturalistic observation

Dann Tardif/The Image Bank Unreleased/Getty Images

A thorough assessment of physical health is an essential part of a comprehensive assessment for depression or any mental health problem.

(see Chapter 1). Direct observation is especially useful when the problem involves specific behaviors, such as acting out. A variety of techniques exist for making observations, especially webcams and other video tools, that can be used in a wide array of settings, from homes to healthcare facilities.

Finally, performance-based assessment involves giving clients a specific task to perform. This approach underlies much cognitive and neuropsychological assessment. A person's memory is assessed by giving the client a list of items to remember and then testing retention. Some neuropsychological tests involve drawing or copying pictures or solving picture puzzles.

Developmental Issues in Interventions

Assuming Juan is assessed properly and found to have a mental disorder, what happens next? How can he be helped?

Therapy for mental disorders generally involves two approaches (Chew-Graham & Ray, 2016; Gallegos et al., 2018; Groth-Marnat & Wright, 2016; Samarina et al., 2021): medical treatment and psychotherapy. Medical treatment most often involves the use of various medications based on the underlying physiological causes of the disorders. Psychotherapy usually involves talking to a clinician or participating in a group. In either case, it is essential to take into account developmental differences in people as they age.

As noted in Chapter 3, the ways medications work change with age. This means that medications administered to treat mental health disorders must be monitored very carefully, especially with older adults. Over- and under-medication not only can make a mental health problem worse but may also cause additional behavioral or health difficulties (Chew-Graham & Ray, 2016; Growth-Marnat & Wright, 2016).

In terms of psychotherapy, clinicians must adapt techniques to the unique needs of older adults (American Psychological Association, 2014). This led Jeste (Jeste, 2018; Jeste & Palmer, 2013, 2015) to propose a new, positive approach to geriatric psychiatry and geropsychology. This positive approach focuses "on recovery, promotion of successful ageing, neuroplasticity, prevention, and interventions to enhance positive psychological traits such as resilience, social engagement and wisdom" (Jeste & Palmer, 2013, p. 81).

Another major issue in psychotherapy is establishing whether a particular therapeutic approach is effective, based on research and clinical evidence. This move to evidence-based treatments has been a major step forward in ensuring that treatment options have a research base of demonstrated success. Major professional associations provide guidelines in their respective fields; the American Association of Family Physicians (2022) provides a tool kit for evidence-based approaches to medical therapy, and the American Psychological Association developed a set of criteria for evidence-based psychotherapy (American Psychological Association, 2014). The therapeutic approaches that meet the standard for adult therapy appear to be effective for a wide range of ages and are generally the therapies of choice. As we consider specific disorders, we will focus on evidence-based approaches to therapy.

Adult Development in Action

What factors must be considered in conducting a thorough clinical assessment for mental disorders?

Review Questions

10.2 Developmental Issues in Assessment and Therapy

- What is multidimensional assessment? How is it done?
- What major factors affect the accuracy of clinical assessment?
- How do the developmental forces influence assessment?
- What are the main developmental issues clinicians must consider in selecting treatments?

10.3 Depression, Anxiety Disorders, Psychotic Disorders, Substance Use Disorders

Key Questions

- What are the most common characteristics of people with depression? How is depression diagnosed? What causes depression? What is the relation between depression and age? How is depression treated?
- What are the types and symptoms of anxiety disorders? How are they treated?

- What are the characteristics of post-traumatic stress disorder (PTSD)? How is PTSD treated?
- What are the characteristics of psychotic disorders in adults?
- What are the major issues involved with alcohol use disorder (AUD)? How does AUD manifest itself in adults of different ages?

Imani has been having a difficult time lately. Feelings of sadness pop up for no apparent reason. Sleep is fitful. Nothing feels as exciting as it once did, and energy is down. Imani recently stepped out of a leadership position at a major financial institution after 35 years and can't find anything to fill that gap. Imani is wondering what is the matter.

On one level, Imani's struggles seem fairly common—everyone experiences happy and sad days. But on another level, Imani's experiences are nonnormative—the length of time the feelings have been around and the other things Imani is doing and feeling seem out of the ordinary.

In this module, we will examine some of the most common forms of psychopathologies adults of all ages experience: depression, anxiety disorders, psychotic disorders, and substance use disorders. Each of these can be quite disruptive in people's everyday lives and may manifest with symptoms that could be due to an underlying physical condition that is not due to a mental health issue. Keeping in mind the complexities we considered in the previous two modules, we will dive deeper into the signs and symptoms, causes, and interventions available for managing these conditions.

Depression Disorders

Most people feel down or sad from time to time, perhaps in reaction to a problem at work or in one's relationships or after the death of a loved one. But does this mean that most people exhibit signs of clinical depression? How is depression diagnosed? Are there age-related differences in the symptoms examined in diagnosis? How is depression treated?

First, let's dispense with a myth. Contrary to the popular belief that most older adults are depressed, for healthy people, the rate of severe depression declines by more than half from young adulthood to old age as explained in Figure 10.1 (National Institute of Mental Health, 2022a). Importantly, this downward age trend in prevalence does not hold in all cultures; for example, symptoms of depression among Chinese older adults rose over a 24-year period (1987–2010, inclusive) (Shao et al., 2013). For those people who do experience depression, let's focus on its diagnosis and treatment.

In the United States, the average age at diagnosis for depression is the early 30s (National Institute of Mental Health, 2022a). Less than 5% of older adults living in the community display signs of clinical depression, but the percentage rises to over 13% among those who require home health care (National Institute of

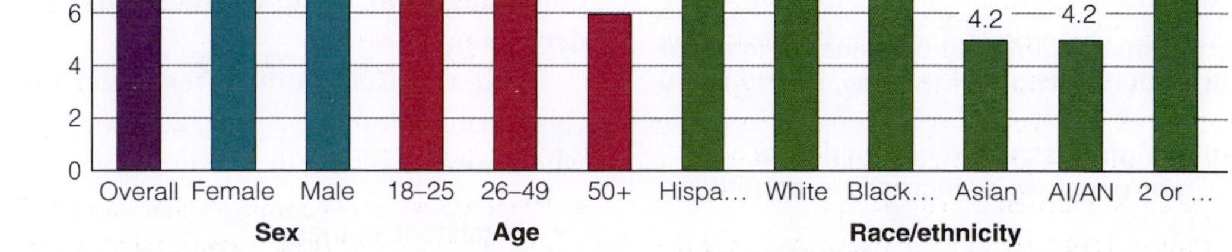

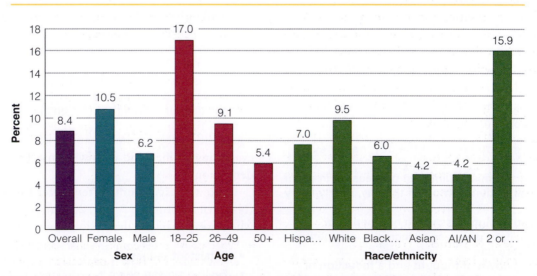

Figure 10.1 Past year prevalence of major depressive episode among U.S. adults (2020).

Source: Data Courtesy of SAMHSA. National Institute of Mental Health. (2022). *Major depression.* https://www.nimh.nih.gov/health/statistics/major-depression.shtml. Figure 1.

Mental Health, 2022). Subgroups of older adults who are at greater risk include those with chronic illnesses (such as diabetes, cancer, heart disease, and Parkinson's disease; up to half may have major depression), nursing home residents, and family care providers.

Rates of clinical depression vary across gender and racial and ethnic groups, although correct diagnosis is frequently a problem due to inadequate access to physical and mental health care and underlying diagnostic biases (Alegría et al., 2008; Garb, 2021). In the United States, rates of depression are about twice as high for women as for men (Gregory, 2021). In terms of race and ethnicity, rates for depression tend to be highest among individuals who report two or more races or ethnicities (National Institute of Mental Health, 2022a). Among individuals identifying as primarily one race or ethnicity, White adults have the highest rate, followed by Hispanic and Black adults. Bias issues also apply to immigrants (Ladin & Reinhold, 2013), who tend to have higher rates of symptoms of depression. The Controversies feature at the beginning of this chapter tells how rates of depression increased dramatically during the COVID-19 pandemic.

Recognizing these differences, clinicians developed culturally appropriate assessment and treatment guidelines (Kirmayer et al., 2015; Lewis-Fernández et al., 2015; Segal et al., 2017). Such guidelines take important contextual factors into account in the assessment process to help clinicians avoid making errors based simply on misunderstandings of culturally based behaviors.

General Symptoms and Characteristics of Depression. The *Diagnostic and Statistical Manual of Mental Disorders—5—Text Revision* (DSM-5-TR; American Psychiatric Association, 2022) outlines the following general criterion to make a diagnosis of depression in adults.

The individual must be experiencing five or more symptoms during the same 2-week period and at least one of the symptoms should be either (1) depressed mood or (2) loss of interest or pleasure.

1. Depressed mood most of the day, nearly every day.
2. Markedly diminished interest or pleasure in all, or almost all, activities most of the day, nearly every day.
3. Significant weight loss when not dieting or weight gain or decrease or increase in appetite nearly every day.
4. A slowing down of thought and a reduction of physical movement (observable by others, not merely subjective feelings of restlessness or being slowed down).
5. Fatigue or loss of energy nearly every day.
6. Feelings of worthlessness or excessive or inappropriate guilt nearly every day.
7. Diminished ability to think or concentrate, or indecisiveness, nearly every day.
8. Recurrent thoughts of death, recurrent suicidal ideation without a specific plan, or a suicide attempt or a specific plan for committing suicide.

To receive a diagnosis of depression, these symptoms must cause the individual clinically significant distress or impairment in social, occupational, or other important areas of functioning. The symptoms must also not be a result of substance abuse or another medical condition.

There are some important aspects of depression as experienced by women and by older adults that differ from the symptom pattern described earlier (American Psychiatric Association, 2022).

For women, Gregory (2021) notes that some of the distinguishing factors in how depression differs between women vs. men include:

- Women feel anxious and scared; men feel guarded.
- Women blame themselves for the depression; men blame others.
- Women commonly feel sad, worthless, and apathetic when depressed; men tend to feel irritable and angry.
- Women are more likely to avoid conflicts when depressed; men are more likely to create conflicts.
- Women turn to food and friends to self-medicate; men turn to alcohol, TV, sex, or sports to self-medicate.
- Women feel lethargic and nervous; men feel agitated and restless.
- Women easily talk about their feelings of self-doubt and despair; men hide feelings of self-doubt and despair-considering it a sign of weakness.

These differences are important to keep in mind when evaluating women and men who may be experiencing depression.

Likewise, symptoms often differ for older adults (National Institute on Aging, 2021a). Most older adults who are experiencing depression tend to exhibit:

- Persistent sadness
- Feeling slowed down
- Excessive worries about finances and health problems

- Frequent tearfulness
- Feeling worthless or helpless
- Weight changes
- Pacing or fidgeting
- Difficulty sleeping
- Difficulty concentrating
- Somatic complaints (unexplained physical pain or gastrointestinal problems)
- Withdrawal from social activities

Note that in some respects these symptoms are similar to those for other adults noted earlier (feeling worthless, weight changes). But others are more specific to older adults (pacing and fidgeting; difficulty sleeping, withdrawal form social activities). Careful evaluation is the best approach for accurate diagnosis.

Assessment Scales

Numerous scales are used to assess depression, but because most were developed on younger and middle-aged adults, they are most appropriate for these age groups. The most important difficulty in using these scales with older adults is they all include several items assessing physical symptoms. The Beck Depression Inventory (Beck, 1967) contains items that focus on feelings and physical symptoms. Although the presence of such symptoms usually is indicative of depression in younger adults, as we noted earlier, such symptoms may not be related to depression at all in older adults.

Scales such as the Geriatric Depression Scale (Yesavage et al., 1983) aimed specifically at older adults have been developed. Physical symptoms are omitted, and the response format is easier for older adults to follow. This approach reduces the age-related symptom bias and scale response problems with other self-report scales measuring depressive symptoms. A third screening inventory, the Center for Epidemiologic Studies–Depression Scale (CES-D; Radloff, 1977) is also frequently used in research.

An important point to keep in mind about these scales is that the diagnosis of depression should never be made on the basis of a single scale. As noted, the symptoms indicative of clinical depression could be indicative of other problems, and symptom patterns are complex. Only by assessing many aspects of physical and psychological functioning can a clinician make an accurate assessment.

Causes of Depression. There are two main schools of thought about the causes of depression (Nemeroff, 2020). The first of these focuses on genetic and physiological processes—genetic predispositions, imbalances of specific neurotransmitters, and changes in certain types of brain cells. Biological theories focus most on genetic predisposition, brain changes, and changes in neurotransmitters (Kendall et al., 2021). The genetic evidence is based on two sets of data: (1) several studies that find higher rates of depression in relatives of people diagnosed with depression than would be expected given base rates in the population and (2) genetically driven age-related changes in brain structures. Genetics overall accounts for about 40–50% of the risk of depression in adults (Kendall et al., 2021; H-Q. Wang et al., 2021). The first type of genetic link is stronger in early-onset depression than in late-onset depression, whereas the second type of evidence is thought to underlie much of late-life onset.

Neurobiological research indicates that the most likely cause of severe depression in later life is an imbalance in neurotransmitters such as low levels of serotonin and norepinephrine, and the action of brain-derived neurotrophic factor (BDNF), in part related to age-related changes in neurons and neurotransmitters (discussed in Chapter 2; Duman et al., 2021; H-Q. Wang et al., 2021). Low levels of serotonin are a likely result from high levels of stress experienced over a long period. The usual signs of low serotonin levels in general include waking up in the early morning (often around 4 a.m.), difficulty in concentrating and paying attention, feeling tired and listless, losing interest in activities such as sex or visiting friends, and racing of the mind with strong feelings of guilt and of reliving bad past experiences and creating negative thoughts. These effects of low serotonin are quite similar to those that characterize depression, which is why researchers believe that one possible cause is low serotonin. Low levels of another neurotransmitter, norepinephrine, that regulates arousal and alertness, may be responsible for the feelings of fatigue associated with depression. BDNF is a compound found in blood serum, and its level is negatively correlated with the severity of depression (i.e., lower levels of BDNF are correlated with more serious levels of depression). These neurochemical links are the basis for the medications developed to treat depression we will consider a bit later.

The second set of theories about the causes of depression focuses on psychosocial factors, such as stress, loss, and internal belief systems. Although several types of loss or negative events have been associated with depression—including loss of a spouse, a job, or one's health—it is how a person interprets a loss, rather than the event itself, that causes depression (Segal et al.,

Oliver Rossi/Stone/Getty Images

Depression is a form of psychopathology in adulthood that decreases in prevalence with age.

2017). In this approach, **internal belief systems**, or what one tells oneself about why certain things are happening, are emphasized as a cause of depression. For example, experiencing an unpredictable and uncontrollable event such as the death of a spouse may cause depression if you believe it happened because you are a bad person (Beck, 1967). This perspective underscores the appraisals people make about stressful events (discussed in Chapter 4) in conjunction with attributions, self-efficacy, and control judgments (discussed in Chapter 8). People who experience depression tend to believe that they are personally responsible for all the bad things that happen to them, that things are unlikely to get better, and that their whole life is a shambles. Therapies for depression based on these theories focus on changing a person's negative internal beliefs, as we will discover.

Treatments for Depression. Regardless of how severe depression is, people benefit from treatment, often through a combination of medication and psychotherapy (Rajput, 2022; Segal et al., 2017). Most medications used to treat depression work by altering the balance of specific neurotransmitters in the brain (Mischel, 2020; Rajput, 2022). For severe cases of major depression, the preferred medications include selective serotonin reuptake inhibitors (SSRIs; e.g., Prozac®, Paxil®, Zoloft®), serotonin and norepinephrine reuptake inhibitors (SNRIs; e.g., Cymbalta®, Effexor®), and norepinephrine–dopamine reuptake inhibitors (NDRIs; e.g., Wellbutrin® and Remeron®) because they have the fewest side effects overall. Older pharmaceutical treatments such as heterocyclic antidepressants (HCAs) and monoamine oxidase (MAO) inhibitors can be administered in situations where the preferred medications are ineffective, but they have serious, sometimes fatal side effects (Laban & Saadabadi, 2022). In certain situations, none of these medications is effective, or circumstances require a fast-acting medication (the usual medications usually take a few weeks to become effective). In these cases, the drug ketamine (e.g., the nasal spray Spravato®), or a derivative called esketamine, is used (Kasper et al., 2021; Lowe et al., 2020). However, ketamine has risks, including the potential for abuse.

In some cases, none of the medications is effective. In such situations, another group of medical interventions involving various ways of stimulating the brain (van Rooij et al., 2020) may be effective. The oldest and most researched of these is electroconvulsive therapy (ECT). Others include vagus nerve stimulation (VNS), repetitive transcranial magnetic stimulation (rTMS), magnetic seizure therapy (MST), and deep brain stimulation (DBS). Evidence suggests that all of these may be effective in treating depression in older adults when other medical therapies fail, but more research is needed to ensure their safety (van Rooij et al., 2020).

Either as an alternative to medication or brain stimulation methods, or in conjunction with them, psychotherapy is also a popular approach to treating depression. Two forms of psychotherapy have been demonstrated to have efficacy with adults of all ages. The basic idea in **behavior therapy** is that people with depression experience too few rewards or reinforcements from their environment. Thus, the goal of behavior therapy is to increase the rewards people derive from their environments by changing how they interpret those events (Lewinsohn, 1975). The net increase in positive events comes about through practice and homework assignments during the course of therapy, such as going out more or joining a club to meet new people.

A second effective approach is **cognitive therapy**, which is based on the idea that maladaptive beliefs or cognitions about oneself are responsible for depression. From this perspective, those who have depression consider themselves as unworthy and inadequate, the world as insensitive and ungratifying, and the future as bleak and unpromising (Beck et al., 1979). In a cognitive therapy session, a person is taught how to recognize these thoughts and to reevaluate the self, the world, and the future less negatively, resulting in a change in the underlying beliefs. Cognitive behavior therapy is especially effective for older adults (Carr & McNulty, 2016; Segal et al., 2017). This is good news, because medications may not be as effective or as tolerated by older adults because of age-related changes in metabolism.

Alternative approaches to treatment, such as yoga, have also demonstrated some success with older adults (Belam, 2020). Such alternatives are based on the idea that stress is a cause of depression, and these therapies have been demonstrated to be effective in lowering stress.

The most important fact to keep in mind about depression is that it is not a normal part of adulthood, especially of aging, and that it is treatable. Thus, if a person behaves in ways that raise concerns about depression, it is a good idea that they are evaluated by a mental health professional. Even if the situation turns out not to be depression, another underlying and possibly treatable condition may be uncovered. Unfortunately, many people of color and older adults never get the mental health and medical attention they need to figure it out.

Anxiety Disorders

Imagine you are about to give a speech before an audience of 500 people. In the last few minutes before your address, you begin to feel nervous, your heart starts to pound, and your palms get sweaty. These feelings, common even to veteran speakers, are similar to those experienced to a greater extent by people with anxiety disorders: a group of conditions based on fear or uneasiness.

Anxiety disorders constitute a cluster of six conditions that share feelings of intense uneasiness, panic, or terror (American Psychiatric Association, 2022). These include:

- **Generalized anxiety disorder**, which is a persistent and excessive worry that interferes with daily activities. This worry and tension may be accompanied by physical symptoms, such as restlessness, feeling on edge or easily fatigued, or difficulty concentrating or sleeping. The worries often focus on everyday things such as job responsibilities, family health chores, or appointments.
- **Panic disorder** is characterized by recurrent attacks of overwhelming combinations of physical and psychological distress. Because the symptoms are so severe, many people who experience a panic attack may believe they are having a heart attack or other life-threatening illness and go to a hospital emergency department. Panic attacks may be expected, such as a response to a feared object, or unexpected, apparently occurring for no reason. The mean age for onset is 20–24 years of age.
- A **phobia** is excessive and persistent fear of a specific object, situation, or activity that is generally not harmful. People know that their fear is excessive, but they can't overcome it. These fears cause such distress that some people go to extreme lengths to avoid what they fear. Examples are driving long distances due to phobia of flying or becoming extraordinarily fearful at seeing a spider.
- **Agoraphobia** is the fear of being in situations where escape may be difficult or embarrassing, or help might not be available in the event of panic symptoms. The fear is out of proportion to the actual situation and must last six months or more and cause problems in functioning. Common examples include fear of public transportation, elevators, and being in a crowd. The individual actively avoids the situation, requires a companion, or endures with intense fear or anxiety. Untreated agoraphobia can become so serious that a person may be unable to leave their residence.
- A person with **social anxiety disorder** has significant unease and discomfort about being embarrassed, humiliated, rejected, or looked down on in social interactions. People with this disorder will try to avoid the situation or endure it with great anxiety. Common examples are extreme fear of public speaking, meeting new people, or eating or drinking in public. The fear or anxiety must cause problems with daily functioning and have lasted at least six months.
- A person with **separation anxiety disorder** is excessively fearful or anxious about separation from those with whom they are attached. The feeling is beyond what is appropriate for the person's age, persists at least six months, and causes problems functioning. A person with separation anxiety disorder may be persistently worried about losing the person closest to them, may be reluctant or refuse to go out or sleep away from home or without that person, or may experience nightmares about separation. Physical symptoms may be present.

In any year, about 30% of adults in the United States report symptoms of anxiety disorders (American Psychiatric Association, 2021). Overall, women are 60% more likely than men to experience an anxiety disorder over their lifetime. The Controversies feature later in this chapter describes how anxiety disorders dramatically increased during the pandemic.

Symptoms and Diagnosis of Anxiety Disorders. An important issue concerning anxiety disorders in all adults, but especially in older adults, is that anxiety may be an appropriate response to the situation (Carr & McNulty, 2016; Segal et al., 2017). For example, helplessness anxiety is generated by a potential or actual loss of control or mastery, which as we know can decrease normatively with age (Varkal et al, 2013).

In addition, a series of negative life experiences may result in a person's appearing highly anxious. Many older adults who demonstrate symptoms of anxiety disorder have several underlying health problems that may be responsible for the symptoms. In all cases the anxious behavior should be investigated first as an appropriate response that may not warrant medical intervention. The important point is to evaluate the behavior in context.

These secondary causes of anxiety must be disentangled from the presenting anxiety symptoms so each may be dealt with appropriately. In short, the trick is to distinguish between the "worried" and the well. Zarit and Zarit (2007) report the key features of late-life anxiety disorder are distress and impairment, frequency and uncontrolled worry, muscle tension, and sleep disturbance.

Treating Anxiety Disorders. Anxiety disorders can be treated with medication and psychotherapy (American Psychiatric Association, 2021; Carr & McNulty, 2016; Segal et al., 2010). The most commonly used medications are benzodiazepine (e.g., Valium® and Librium®), paroxetine (an SSRI, e.g., Paxil®), buspirone, and beta-blockers. Though moderately effective, these drugs must be monitored carefully in older adults because the amount needed to treat the disorder is low and the potential for side effects is great. Obsessive-compulsive disorders are treated most often with serotonin reuptake inhibitors (SRIs) and SSRIs.

For older adults, the clear treatment of choice is psychotherapy, specifically cognitive behavioral or relaxation therapy, especially when anxiety disorders first occur in later life (Carr & McNulty, 2016; Ramos & Stanley, 2018). Relaxation therapy is exceptionally effective, easily learned, and presents a technique that is useful in many situations (Segal et al., 2017). The advantage of these psychotherapeutic techniques is they usually involve only a few sessions, have high rates of success, and offer clients procedures they can take with them.

Post-Traumatic Stress Disorder (PTSD)

Life experiences can sometimes be quite unpleasant, even brutal. It is natural to feel afraid during and after a shocking, scary, or dangerous traumatic situation. Fear triggers many split-second changes in the body to help defend against danger or to avoid it. The autonomic nervous system (described in Chapter 3) controls this "fight-or-flight" response—the typical reaction meant to protect a person from harm. Almost everyone experiences a range of reactions after trauma, yet most people recover from initial symptoms on their own. Some people, though, continue to experience problems, and their initial reactions of stress or fear do not diminish, such that they may even continue to feel they are endangered. Importantly, some people who experience these feelings did not themselves go through a traumatic event. Rather, they were deeply affected by traumatic events that happened to others (e.g., a friend or relative who was sexually assaulted, a school shooting that occurred in other city, a devastating war in another country). When these feelings last for a period of time, interfere with daily life, and are not caused by some other source or condition, then a person may be diagnosed as experiencing post-traumatic stress disorder (PTSD; National Institute of Mental Health, 2022b; National Institutes of Health, 2020a).

Symptoms and Diagnosis of PTSD. The American Psychiatric Association (2022) revised the criteria for diagnosing PTSD in the *DSM-5-TR™* published in 2022. These criteria are listed in Table 10.2. Note that the criteria include broad inclusion of different types of trauma and the fact that trauma may be experienced directly or indirectly to the person.

The diagnosis of PTSD must be done carefully and methodically in order to rule out other possible reasons why an individual is experiencing discomfort. In addition to determining whether the person's symptoms meet the clinical criteria for PTSD, clinicians must also determine whether the person experiences persistent or recurring symptoms of either of the following dissociative symptoms (American Psychiatric Association, 2022):

- **Depersonalization:** Persistent or recurrent experiences of feeling detached from, as if one were an outside observer of, one's mental processes or body (e.g., feeling as though one were in a dream; feeling a sense of unreality of self or body or of time moving slowly).
- **Derealization:** Persistent or recurrent symptoms of unreality of surroundings (e.g., the world around the individual is experienced as unreal, dreamlike, distant, or distorted). (p. 125)

Importantly, the dissociative symptoms must not be caused by the effects of substance use (e.g., blackouts) or other medical condition (e.g., complex seizures).

Treatments for PTSD. Providing assistance for individuals experiencing PTSD may be a multiphase process (American Psychological Association, 2020). The first step is to determine whether the person is in imminent danger, such as being in a situation that has a high

Table 10.2 *DSM-5-TR* Diagnostic Criteria for Post-Traumatic Stress Disorder (PTSD)

Posttraumatic Stress Disorder in Individuals Older Than 6 Years

A. Exposure to actual or threatened death, serious injury, or sexual violence in one (or more) of the following ways:
1. Directly experiencing the traumatic event(s).
2. Witnessing, in person, the event(s) as it occurred to others.
3. Learning that the traumatic event(s) occurred to a close family member or close friend. In cases of actual or threatened death of a family member or friend, the event(s) must have been violent or accidental.
4. Experiencing repeated or extreme exposure to aversive details of the traumatic event(s) (e.g., first responders collecting human remains; police officers repeatedly exposed to details of child abuse).

Note: Criterion A4 does not apply to exposure through electronic media, television, movies, or pictures, unless this exposure is work related.

B. Presence of one (or more) of the following intrusion symptoms associated with the traumatic event(s), beginning after the traumatic event(s) occurred:
1. Recurrent, involuntary, and intrusive distressing memories of the traumatic event(s).

Note: In children older than 6 years, repetitive play may occur in which themes or aspects of the traumatic event(s) are expressed.

2. Recurrent distressing dreams in which the content and/or affect of the dream are related to the traumatic event(s).

Note: In children, there may be frightening dreams without recognizable content.

3. Dissociative reactions (e.g., flashbacks) in which the individual feels or acts as if the traumatic event(s) were recurring. (Such reactions may occur on a continuum, with the most extreme expression being a complete loss of awareness of present surroundings.)

Note: In children, trauma-specific reenactment may occur in play.

4. Intense or prolonged psychological distress at exposure to internal or external cues that symbolize or resemble an aspect of the traumatic event(s).
5. Marked physiological reactions to internal or external cues that symbolize or resemble an aspect of the traumatic event(s).

C. Persistent avoidance of stimuli associated with the traumatic event(s), beginning after the traumatic event(s) occurred, as evidenced by one or both of the following:
1. Avoidance of or efforts to avoid distressing memories, thoughts, or feelings about or closely associated with the traumatic event(s).
2. Avoidance of or efforts to avoid external reminders (people, places, conversations, activities, objects, situations) that arouse distressing memories, thoughts, or feelings about or closely associated with the traumatic event(s).

D. Negative alterations in cognitions and mood associated with the traumatic event(s), beginning or worsening after the traumatic event(s) occurred, as evidenced by two (or more) of the following:
1. Inability to remember an important aspect of the traumatic event(s) (typically due to dissociative amnesia and not to other factors such as head injury, alcohol, or drugs).
2. Persistent and exaggerated negative beliefs or expectations about oneself, others, or the world (e.g., "I am bad," "No one can be trusted," "The world is completely dangerous," "My whole nervous system is permanently ruined").
3. Persistent, distorted cognitions about the cause or consequences of the traumatic event(s) that lead the individual to blame [themselves] or others.
4. Persistent negative emotional state (e.g., fear, horror, anger, guilt, or shame).
5. Markedly diminished interest or participation in significant activities.
6. Feelings of detachment or estrangement from others.
7. Persistent inability to experience positive emotions (e.g., inability to experience happiness, satisfaction, or loving feelings).

(Continued)

E. Marked alterations in arousal and reactivity associated with the traumatic event(s), beginning or worsening after the traumatic event(s) occurred, as evidenced by two (or more) of the following:
   1. Irritable behavior and angry outbursts (with little or no provocation) typically expressed as verbal or physical aggression toward people or objects.
   2. Reckless or self-destructive behavior.
   3. Hypervigilance.
   4. Exaggerated startle response.
   5. Problems with concentration.
   6. Sleep disturbance (e.g., difficulty falling or staying asleep or restless sleep).

F. Duration of disturbance (Criteria B, C, D, and E) is more than 1 month.

G. The disturbance causes clinically significant distress or impairment in social, occupational, or other important areas of functioning.

H. The disturbance is not attributable to the physiological effects of a substance (e.g., medication, alcohol) or other medical condition.

Source: American Psychiatric Association. (2022). *Desk reference to the Diagnostic Criteria from the diagnostic and statistical manual of mental disorders—5th Edition—Text Revision: (DSM-5-TRTM).* American Psychiatric Association. (pp. 123–125).

probability of ongoing abuse. In these cases, treatment is usually most effective when it addresses both the traumatic situation and the person's symptoms. Thus, mental health professionals may work closely with other professionals to find a safer environment for the person, for example at a facility for persons experiencing abuse.

People who have PTSD or who are exposed to trauma also may experience other mental health conditions, such as panic disorder, depression, substance use, or suicidal thoughts. Treatment for these conditions can help with recovery after trauma. Treatment for PTSD may also involve a person's support system. Research indicates that support from family and friends also can be an important part of recovery.

The typical approaches to therapy for PTSD are based on those used for depression, anxiety disorders, and substance use disorders discussed in this chapter (American Psychological Association, 2020; National Institute of Mental Health, 2022b). For example, two variations of cognitive behavior therapy used frequently with people experiencing PTSD are exposure therapy and cognitive restructuring. **Exposure therapy** helps people learn to manage their fear by gradually exposing them, in a safe way, to the trauma they experienced by thinking or writing about the trauma or visiting the place where it happened. **Cognitive restructuring** helps people make sense of the traumatic event. As noted in Chapter 6, people may remember an event differently than how it happened, or they may feel guilt or shame about something that is not their fault. Cognitive restructuring can help people with PTSD think about what happened in a realistic way. Similarly, the medications typically used to alleviate symptoms of PTSD are those used to treat depression and anxiety disorders.

If You Know Someone Experiencing Trauma. If you are concerned that someone you know may be experiencing PTSD, the most important thing you can do is to help that person get the correct diagnosis and treatment. Some people may need assistance scheduling an appointment with their healthcare provider, and others may benefit from having someone accompany them to their healthcare visits. If a close friend or relative is diagnosed with PTSD, you can encourage them to follow their treatment plan. You also can (National Institute of Mental Health, 2022b):

- Learn about PTSD so you can understand what your friend is experiencing.
- Offer emotional support, understanding, patience, and encouragement.
- Listen carefully. Pay attention to the person's feelings and the situations that may trigger PTSD symptoms.
- Share positive distractions, such as walks, outings, and other activities.

Substance Use Disorder

Although you might think substance use is primarily a problem of young and middle-aged adults, it's not—it

Table 10.3 Diagnosis of Alcohol Use Disorder (AUD) Based on DSM-5

Symptoms
In the past year, have you:
• Had times when you ended up drinking more, or longer, than you intended?
• More than once wanted to cut down or stop drinking, or tried to, but couldn't?
• Spent a lot of time drinking? Or being sick or getting over other aftereffects?
• Wanted a drink so badly you couldn't think of anything else?
• Found that drinking—or being sick from drinking—often interfered with taking care of your home or family? Or caused job troubles? Or school problems?
• Continued to drink even though it was causing trouble with your family or friends?
• Given up or cut back on activities that were important or interesting to you, or gave you pleasure, in order to drink?
• More than once gotten into situations while or after drinking that increased your chances of getting hurt (such as driving, swimming, using machinery, walking in a dangerous area, or having unsafe sex)?
• Continued to drink even though it was making you feel depressed or anxious or adding to another health problem? Or after having had a memory blackout?
• Had to drink much more than you once did to get the effect you want? Or found that your usual number of drinks had much less effect than before?
• Found that when the effects of alcohol were wearing off, you had withdrawal symptoms, such as trouble sleeping, shakiness, restlessness, nausea, sweating, a racing heart, or a seizure? Or sensed things that were not there?
Severity
The severity of the **AUD** is defined as:
• **Mild** The presence of two to three symptoms
• **Moderate** The presence of four to five symptoms
• **Severe** The presence of six or more symptoms

Source: Based on NIH Publication 13-7999. (2016). Alcohol Use Disorder: A Comparison Between DSM-IV and DSM-5. National Institutes of Health (NIH), National Institute on Alcohol Abuse and Alcoholism. Available at pubs.niaaa.nih.gov/publications/dsmfactsheet/dsmfact.pdf.

is also a concern of older adults (Substance Abuse and Mental Health Services Administration [SAMHSA], 2021). Because of the differences in the types of substances abused by adults of different ages (emerging adults are more likely to abuse illegal drugs than are middle-aged or older adults), alcohol provides a good basis for comparison across age groups. We considered another class of drugs that is most often abused by middle-aged adults, opioids, in Chapter 4.

What constitutes alcohol use disorder? **Alcohol use disorder (AUD)** is a drinking pattern that results in significant and recurrent consequences that reflect loss of reliable control over alcohol use. AUD is diagnosed whenever anyone meets any 2 of the 11 criteria listed in Table 10.3 during a 12-month period. If you or anyone you know meets these criteria, seek assistance.

Roughly 15 million adults in the United States are diagnosed with AUD (National Center for Drug Abuse Statistics, 2022). However, when data are examined more closely, there are biological sex and racial/ethnic group differences in alcohol abuse. The percentage of males who abuse alcohol ranges from about two times (ages 18–29) to six times (ages 65 and over) higher than those for females. In fact, 65% of older adults report high-risk drinking, and widowers over age 75 have the highest rate of AUD in the United States (Recovered.org, 2022). As is noted in Figure 10.2, across racial and ethnic groups, American Indians and Alaska Natives have the highest rates, followed by individuals who identify themselves with two or more races. Consumption of alcohol increased during the COVID-19 pandemic about 14% overall, with a 41% increase in self-reported heavy drinking by women (Pollard et al., 2020). Relatedly,

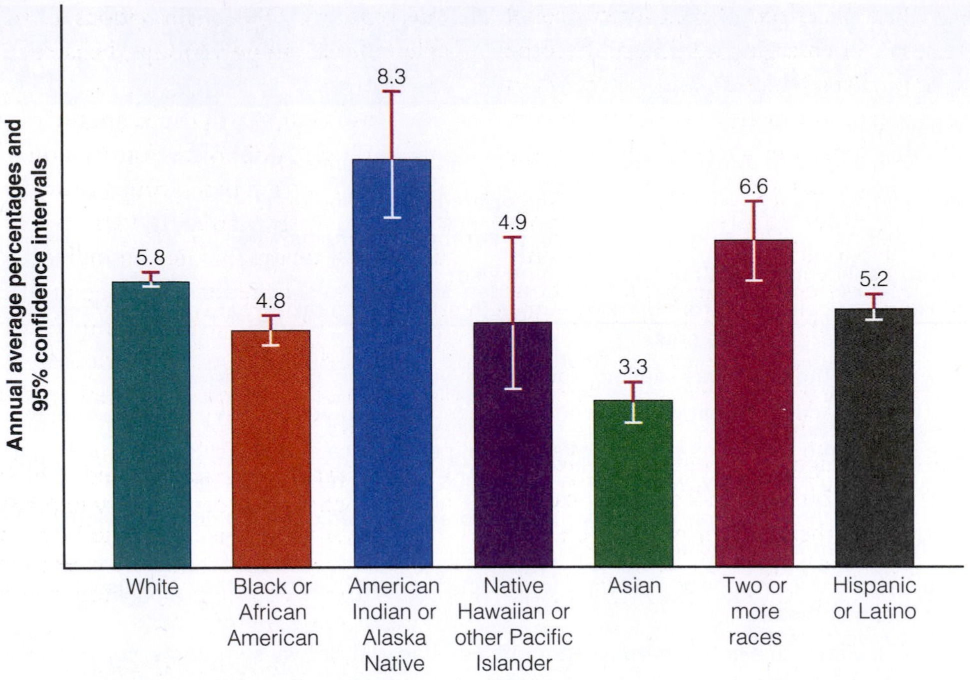

Figure 10.2 Alcohol use disorder in the past year among people aged 12 or older, by race/ethnicity: 2015–2019, annual averages.

Source: Substance Abuse and Mental Health Services Administration (SAMHSA). (2021). *National Survey on Drug Use and Health.* https://www.samhsa.gov/data/report/2019-nsduh-detailed-tables

the number and rate of alcohol-related deaths increased approximately 25% between 2019 and 2020, the first year of the COVID-19 pandemic (White et al., 2022).

Two age-related patterns of onset are evident with alcohol use disorder: early-onset in young adulthood or middle age often following a pattern of binge drinking, and late-onset often following a pattern of problem drinking, that is, exceeding the dietary recommendations of 2 drinks per day for males and 1 drink per day for females (Segal et al., 2017; Trevisan, 2014). People with an earlier onset AUD typically have a more severe course of illness. This group makes up about two-thirds of the older adults with AUD. They are predominantly male, less well-adjusted and demonstrate more antisocial traits, and have more alcohol-related medical and mental health problems.

Persons with later-onset AUD usually have fewer medical problems because of the shorter exposure to larger amounts of alcohol. They tend to be more affluent, include more women, and are likely to begin their increased alcohol use after a stressful event, such as retirement, loss of a spouse/partner, job, or home, or medical condition that causes pain.

Taking a life-span view of AUD provides insights into important differences in drinking patterns and outcomes (SAMHSA, 2021). Emerging adults are more likely to binge drink (a behavior that peaks around age 21), and consequently are more likely to experience problems such as alcohol poisoning, driving offenses, and assaults. The earlier drinking begins, especially if it starts in adolescence, the more likely brain damage occurs, and alcohol dependence develops. Emerging adult drinkers are less likely to feel the effects of alcohol, such as getting sleepy or losing motor coordination, that may result in their drinking more at one time ("binging"). However, emerging adults' cognitive performance is more impaired. Taken together, these effects create a dangerous situation—they do not feel the effects as easily, so tend to underestimate the degree they are impaired, and are worse at performing complex tasks such as driving, providing an explanation of why driving while intoxicated is more prevalent among emerging adults. It is usually the friends of such drinkers, who experience secondhand effects of drinking, who raise concerns about behavior.

Middle age is when the effects of continued alcohol dependence that began in emerging adulthood become evident. Diseases of the liver, pancreas, and various types of cancer and cardiovascular disease may occur. In part due to these health problems, middle-aged adults are the most likely group to seek treatment for their problem.

Drinking among older adults presents a more complicated picture. Even older adults who drink only modest amounts may experience dangerous interactions with medications they may be taking. Additionally, they metabolize alcohol much more slowly, meaning it remains in the bloodstream longer and it takes less alcohol to produce negative effects (e.g., intoxication). As a result, older adults are at higher risk for abusing alcohol if they simply continue habits of drinking from earlier points in their lives, even if their consumption when they were younger was only moderate. Diagnosing alcohol dependence in older women can be especially difficult given the higher likelihood that they live alone.

Treatment for AUD in all age groups focuses on three goals (National Institute on Alcohol Abuse and Alcoholism, 2021; Segal et al., 2017): stabilization and reduction of substance consumption, treatment of coexisting problems, and arrangement of appropriate social interventions. Three main options for treatment are available: mutual-support groups, behavioral treatments, and medications.

Mutual-support groups are the most widely known and include Alcoholics Anonymous (AA) and other 12-step groups. These groups provide peer support to help people stop abusing various drugs and alcohol. Behavioral treatments rely on individual or group counseling to stop or reduce drinking or drugging.

The U.S. Food and Drug Administration has approved three types of medications for use in treating alcohol use disorder (National Institute on Alcohol Abuse and Alcoholism, 2021):

- Disulfiram (Antabuse) is used to block alcohol metabolism and causes very unpleasant symptoms such as nausea to help people stop drinking. Disulfiram has been used for nearly a century, but some people stop taking it to stop the unpleasant effects.
- Naltrexone reduces the pleasure received from drinking and reduces the cravings that compel chronic drinking by blocking the endorphin receptors in the brain. Research evidence is mostly positive on the effectiveness of naltrexone, especially when combined with other treatments.

Discovering Development

What Substance Use Treatment Options Are Available in Your Area?

One of the most controversial topics regarding substance use disorders is how to deal with people who have a problem such as AUD. If a person uses a substance, should they be treated or jailed if the behavior is illegal? If treatment is the choice, should they be placed in inpatient facilities or in outpatient programs? Do we need to reconsider the criminality of certain substances?

These questions and decisions have become both political and sensitive. Many politicians built their careers on being perceived as "tough on drugs" and put offenders in jail, resulting in many people, predominantly of color, incarcerated for long periods of time and not receiving treatment. Budget pressures has also resulted in votes to reduce or eliminate treatment options for those seeking help for substance use disorders. The drive to lower healthcare costs has resulted in the near elimination of inpatient treatment facilities in favor of the less expensive outpatient programs and community treatment centers, many of which are significantly underfunded.

An enlightening exercise is to find out what treatment options are available in your area for people who have alcohol or other substance use disorders. Find out whether there are any inpatient programs, which outpatient programs and community treatment centers are available, and how long one must wait to receive treatment. Also, find out the costs of the various programs and whether health insurance policies cover the treatments.

Gather the information from several geographic regions, and compare program availability. Think about what you would do if you had no health insurance or were underinsured and needed help in your area. What do you think should be done to address the problem?

- Acamprosate (Campral®) reduces the unpleasant symptoms experienced from alcohol withdrawal by stabilizing the neurotransmitters in the brain. Research results on the effectiveness of acamprosate is mixed.

Perhaps the most important thing with people who have AUD is to encourage them to get treatment. Unfortunately, only a minority of people who need such treatment actually get it at any age, but especially later in life. In large part this is due to the lack of access to treatment programs, especially inpatient centers. The Discovering Development feature focuses on finding out what options are available in your local area.

Adult Development in Action

If you were a major employer, how could you provide support for workers with mental health concerns?

Review Questions

10.3 Depression, Anxiety Disorders, Post-Traumatic Stress Disorder, Substance Use Disorders

- How does the rate of depression vary with age, biological sex, race, and ethnicity? What symptoms are associated with depression and how do they vary with age? What causes depression? What treatments for depression have been developed?
- What are the types and symptoms of anxiety disorders? How are anxiety disorders treated?
- What are the symptoms of post-traumatic stress disorder (PTSD)? How is it diagnosed and treated?
- What is alcohol use disorder? What specific aspects differ with age? What treatments are effective?

10.4 Delirium and Dementia

Key Questions

- What is delirium? How is it assessed and treated?
- What is dementia? What are the major symptoms of Alzheimer's disease? How is it diagnosed? What causes it? What intervention options are there? What are some other major forms of dementia? What do family members caring for persons with dementia experience?

Ling has lived in the same neighborhood in New York City for all of her 74 years. Ling's son, who visits her every week, started noticing Ling's memory problems have gotten much worse, her kitchen pantry is often empty of her favorite foods (whereas it used to be full), and her refrigerator has lots of moldy leftovers. Ling acts unconcerned about all of that. When he investigated further, he found her bank accounts were in disarray. Ling's son wonders what might be going on with her; she used to be extremely well organized, with an excellent memory even for recent events.

Suppose Ling is a relative of yours. How would you deal with the situation? How would you decide whether her behavior is "typical for someone her age?" What information from Chapters 6 and 7 regarding memory and other cognitive skills might be relevant here? What would you do if you think there may be someone amiss?

Every day, families turn to healthcare and other professionals for help in dealing with behaviors they wonder about that they observe in their aging family and friends. Unfortunately, myths interfere with appropriate diagnoses and interventions, including those we considered in Chapters 6 and 7. When they observe older adults behaving in ways that invoke those stereotypes, especially those involving memory and decision making, they may take no action because they believe that nothing can be done.

In this module, we will learn that inaction is not the best approach. Accurate diagnosis is essential for sorting through all the options in dealing with two clusters of conditions that involve brain function directly: delirium and dementia.

Delirium

Suppose you encountered someone who seems very confused as to their surroundings, what is going on, maybe even their identity. Because of the way humans think, the first thing that most people do is attempt to make sense of the situation and make a guess as to what is going on and perhaps what is causing the person's distress. What we are likely witnessing is an episode of delirium.

Delirium is characterized by confused thinking and reduced awareness of one's environment that develop rapidly (Mayo Clinic, 2022a). The changes in cognition can include difficulties with attention, memory, orientation, and rambling speech. Delirium can also affect perception, the sleep–wake cycle, personality, and mood. The onset of delirium usually is rapid, and its course can vary a great deal over a day. Symptoms in older adults are generally more severe than in younger or middle-aged adults and may go undetected because of stereotypes and misconceptions about normative cognitive performance in older adults. With older adults, clinicians recommend systematic screening with assessments such as the Confusion Assessment Method (Kuczmarska et al., 2016).

Delirium can be caused by any of a number of medical conditions (such as stroke, cardiovascular disease, and metabolic condition), dehydration, medication side effects, substance intoxication or withdrawal, exposure to toxins, sleep deprivation, fever, or any combination of factors (Mayo Clinic, 2022). Because they take more medications on average than other age groups, older adults are particularly susceptible to delirium caused by medication interactions and side effects.

Once the presence of delirium and its likely cause have been identified, treatment focuses on removing the cause or mitigating its effects. Providing the cause of the delirium is correctly identified, treatment is usually successful. In general, the most important aspect of diagnosis is differentiating delirium from depression and dementia, and identifying the underlying cause.

About one-third of cases of delirium are preventable, such as cases due to medication and dehydration (Anand & MacLullich, 2021). If the cause of nonpreventable delirium can be identified and addressed, most cases of delirium can be cured. In some cases, however, delirium can be fatal or result in permanent brain damage.

Alzheimer's Disease

Probably no other condition associated with aging is more feared than the cluster of disorders known as dementia. **Dementia is not a specific disease but rather a cluster of diseases characterized by cognitive and behavioral deficits involving some form of permanent damage to the brain.** The most common and widely known type of dementia is Alzheimer's disease, but others are important as well: vascular dementia, Parkinson's disease, Huntington's disease, alcohol-related dementia, Lewy body dementia, and AIDS dementia complex.

Due to dementia individuals can lose their personal identity through the loss of autobiographical memory and the ability to recognize one's spouse or partner, children, or other family members. Dementias serious enough to impair independent functioning affect over 50 million people globally at present and are expected to triple by 2050 (World Health Organization, 2021a). The Alzheimer's Association (2022) reports that dementia costs the United States over $320 billion each year in actual paid healthcare costs, and over 11 million caregivers provide over 16 billion hours of unpaid care each year worth over $280 billion, more than 14 times the total revenue earned by McDonald's in 2020. The lifetime cost of care for a person with dementia is roughly $380,000.

The effects of the COVID-19 pandemic made this much worse. Families were not only barred from visiting their loved ones, but home care and other support became nearly impossible to find due to COVID-19 restrictions. Individuals with dementia who lived in long-term care facilities were at much higher risk of infection; deaths increased by 16%. The cumulative stress on families and care providers was often overwhelming.

Alzheimer's disease is the most common form of progressive, degenerative, and fatal dementia, accounting for between 60% and 80% of all cases of dementia (Alzheimer's Association, 2022). Because women live longer than men on average, the lifetime risk of Alzheimer's disease at age 45 is about 1 in 5 for women and 1 in 10 for men; both risks are slightly higher at age 65. The prevalence of Alzheimer's disease increases with age, rising from 5.3% of people ages 65 to 74 to about 35% of all people aged 85 and older. As the number of older adults increases rapidly over the next several decades, the number of cases is expected to roughly triple.

Older non-Hispanic Black and older Hispanic Americans are disproportionately more likely than older White Americans to have Alzheimer's or other dementias (Power et al., 2021; Steenland et al., 2015). Findings from the Chicago Health and Aging Project (CHAP) study indicate that 19% of Black and 14% of Latino/a adults age 65 and older have Alzheimer's dementia compared with 10% of White older adults (Rajan et al., 2021). These disparities have remained constant over time (Power et al., 2021). Research suggests the difference in risk for Alzheimer's and other dementias is explained by disparities produced by the historic and continued marginalization of Black and Latino/a people in the United States that are evident in life experiences, socioeconomic indicators, and ultimately health conditions (Bailey et al., 2021; Glymour & Manly, 2008).

What Are the Symptoms of Alzheimer's Disease? The major symptoms of Alzheimer's disease are gradual changes in cognitive and related functioning in 10 areas (Alzheimer's Association, 2022):

- memory loss that interferes with everyday life (e.g., asking the same question repeatedly due to failure to remember the answer),
- difficulty in dealing with everyday problems (e.g., trouble following a familiar recipe),
- difficulty completing familiar tasks (e.g., forgetting how to get to a familiar location),
- confusion with time or place,
- trouble understanding visual images (e.g., difficulty reading),
- new problems with words (e.g., trouble following or joining a conversation),
- misplacing things and having trouble retracing steps (which may result in accusations of stealing),
- poor judgment (e.g., giving large amounts of money to telemarketers),
- withdrawal from work or social activities, and
- changes in mood and personality.

These symptoms tend to be vague in the beginning, and mimic other psychological problems such as depression or stress reactions. For example, an executive may not be managing as well as they once did and may be missing deadlines more often. Slowly, the symptoms get worse. For instance, a financial officer who could easily handle millions of dollars can no longer add two small numbers. A person cannot set the table for a meal. A person who was previously outgoing is now quiet and withdrawn; a gentle person is now hostile and aggressive. Emotional problems become increasingly apparent, including depression, paranoia, and agitation, often accompanied by seemingly outlandish accusations of improper behavior with no real evidence (e.g., accusing a spouse/partner of infidelity or relatives of stealing items that have no basis in fact).

One common behavior exhibited by people with dementia is wandering. Wandering can become a serious problem, especially because the person may have no idea where they are or how to get home, thus posing a genuine safety concern. Neuroscience research indicates wandering likely results from damage to the specific parts of the brain that help us navigate through the world (the entorhinal cortex), an area usually damaged in the early stages of Alzheimer's disease (Igarashi, 2016). In general, the symptoms associated with Alzheimer's disease are worse in the evening than in the morning, a phenomenon care providers call **sundowning**.

In its advanced stages, Alzheimer's disease often causes **incontinence**, the loss of control of bladder or bowels. It may also result in a total loss of mobility. People with Alzheimer's disease eventually become completely dependent on others for care. When this milestone is reached, many care providers seek facilities such as adult day-care centers and other sources of help, such as family and friends, to provide a safe environment for the person with Alzheimer's disease while the primary care provider is at work or needs to attend to basic errands (e.g., grocery shopping, personal appointments).

The progression of Alzheimer's disease from brain changes that are unnoticeable to the person affected to brain changes that cause problems with memory and eventually physical disability is called the **Alzheimer's disease continuum**. This continuum reflects three broad phases: preclinical Alzheimer's disease, mild cognitive impairment (MCI) due to Alzheimer's disease, and dementia due to Alzheimer's disease. The Alzheimer's dementia (AD) phase is further subdivided into mild, moderate, and severe dementia. The Alzheimer's disease continuum is noted in Figure 10.3. It is important to note that individuals in the first two phases may or may not continue along the continuum to develop Alzheimer's dementia.

The main characteristics of each phase are (Alzheimer's Association, 2022):

- **Preclinical AD:** People may have measurable brain changes that indicate the earliest signs of Alzheimer's disease (biomarkers such as beta-amyloid and tau proteins, lower glucose metabolism), but they have not yet developed symptoms such as memory loss.
- **Mild Cognitive Impairment (MCI) Due to Alzheimer's Disease:** People with MCI due to Alzheimer's disease have biomarker evidence of Alzheimer's-related brain changes plus new but subtle cognitive symptoms such as problems with memory, language, and thinking. These cognitive problems may be noticeable to the individual, family members, and friends, but not to others, and they may not interfere with individuals' ability to carry out everyday activities.
- **Mild AD:** In the mild stage of Alzheimer's dementia, most people can function independently in several areas but are likely to require help with some activities to maintain independence and remain safe. Handling finances may be especially challenging, and more time may be needed to complete common daily tasks. They may still be able to drive, work, and participate in favorite activities.

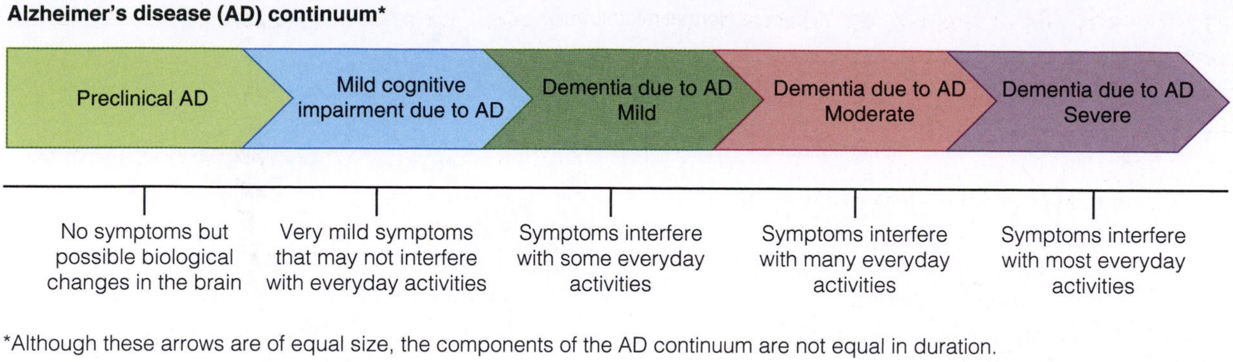
Alzheimer's disease (AD) continuum*
Preclinical AD
Mild cognitive impairment due to AD
Dementia due to AD Mild
Dementia due to AD Moderate
Dementia due to AD Severe
No symptoms but possible biological changes in the brain
Very mild symptoms that may not interfere with everyday activities
Symptoms interfere with some everyday activities
Symptoms interfere with many everyday activities
Symptoms interfere with most everyday activities
*Although these arrows are of equal size, the components of the AD continuum are not equal in duration.

Figure 10.3 Alzheimer's disease continuum of progression.

Source: Alzheimer's Association. (2022). *2022 Alzheimer's disease facts and figures.* https://www.alz.org/media/Documents/alzheimers-facts-and-figures.pdf. Figure 1, p. 9.

- **Moderate AD:** This is often the longest stage, during which people experience more problems with memory and language, become confused more often, and find it harder to complete multistep tasks such as bathing and dressing. They may become incontinent at times and may demonstrate personality and behavioral changes, including suspiciousness and agitation. Loved ones may no longer be recognized.
- **Severe AD:** The ability to communicate verbally is greatly diminished, and people are likely to require around-the-clock care. Because of damage to areas of the brain involved in movement, individuals become bed-bound, making them vulnerable to physical complications including blood clots, skin infections, and sepsis, which triggers body-wide inflammation that can result in organ failure. Damage to areas of the brain that control swallowing makes it difficult to eat and drink.

The rate of deterioration in Alzheimer's disease varies widely from one person to the next (Alzheimer's Association, 2022). Alzheimer's disease has an average duration of 9 years (but can range anywhere from 1 to over 20 years) from the onset of noticeable symptoms through death. The length of each part of the continuum is influenced by age, genetics, biological sex, and other factors.

What Neurological Changes Occur in Alzheimer's Disease? The changes in the brain that characterize Alzheimer's disease are microscopic. These changes are progressive, eventually causing so much brain destruction the person dies. The microscopic changes that define Alzheimer's disease are rapid cell death, neurofibrillary tangles, and neuritic plaques. Several changes in neurotransmitter levels also are observed, as is inflammation in brain structures. Rapid cell death occurs most in the hippocampus (a structure in the brain most closely involved in memory), the cortex (the outer layer of the brain where our higher-level cognitive abilities reside), and the basal forebrain (the lower portion of the front of the brain). This cell death occurs at a rate much greater and faster than what occurs in normative aging and results in dramatic brain shrinkage.

Each neuron has within it a set of tubules made of tau protein that act like railroad tracks to carry nutrients and information from the dendrites to the synapse. When too much phosphate binds with tau proteins, the aggregates cause the tubules to form neurofibrillary tangles (described in Chapter 2) that are accumulations of pairs of neurofilaments that become wrapped around each other. When the neurofibers become twisted, these tangles interfere with the transmission of the nutrients and information and kill the neurons. Neurofibrillary tangles occur in several areas of the brain, and the number of tangles is directly related to the severity of symptoms, specifically the severity of memory impairment (National Institute on Aging, 2017; Sala Frigerio & De Strooper, 2016). Figure 10.4 shows how this process works.

Neuritic or amyloid plaques are spherical structures consisting of a core of **beta amyloid**, a protein, surrounded by degenerated fragments of dying or dead neurons. The plaques are found in various parts of the brain, with the amount of beta amyloid moderately related to the severity of the disease (Alzheimer's Association, 2022; National Institute on Aging, 2017). A depiction of beta-amyloid plaques is also shown in Figure 10.4.

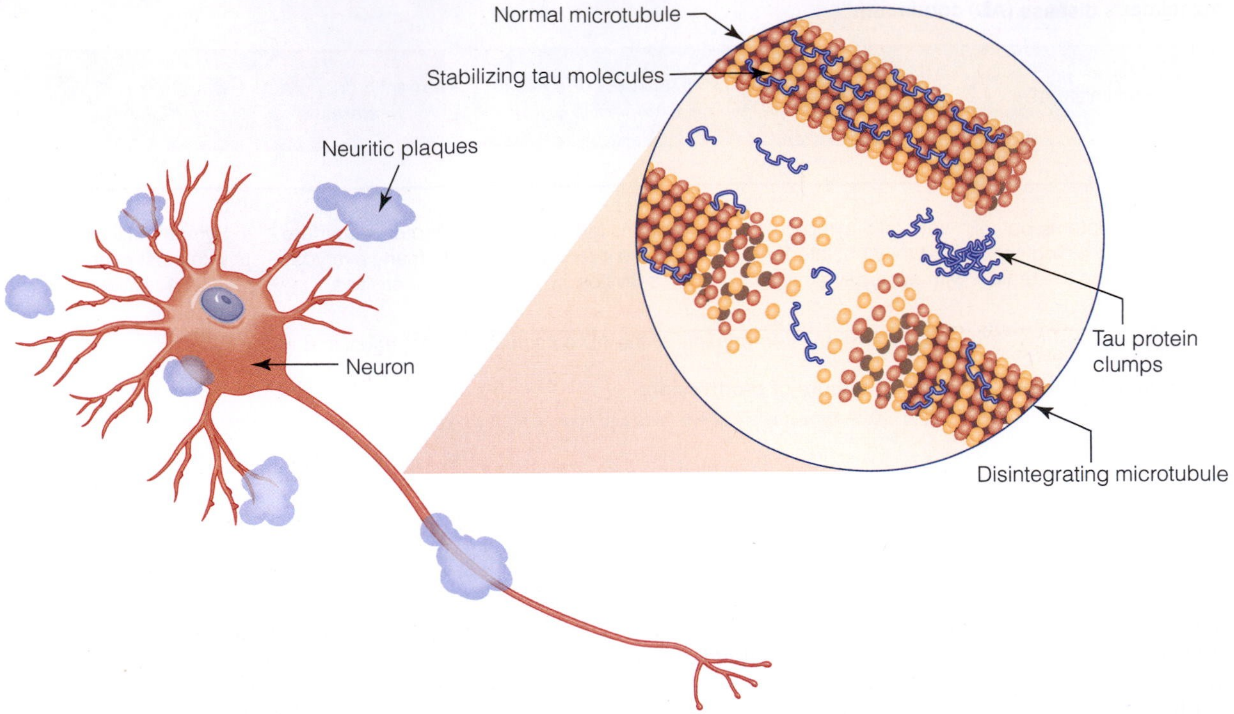

Figure 10.4 Action of beta-amyloid and tau proteins in relation to neurons. Each disrupts neurons, but in different ways.
Source: www.nytimes.com/interactive/2012/02/02/science/in-alzheimers-a-tangled-protein.html

Considerable research has focused on beta amyloid as a major factor in Alzheimer's disease, both in terms of being a possible cause and in representing possible avenues for treatment. The role of beta amyloid is controversial, though. Some researchers consider concentration of beta amyloid as a biomarker of Alzheimer's disease (Sala Frigerio & De Strooper, 2016). Others consider it an early warning of potential cognitive decline, even in the absence of any behavioral symptoms (Stevens et al., 2022). We will consider the controversy surrounding beta amyloid a bit later.

Although the structural changes occurring in the brains of people with Alzheimer's disease are substantial, we must use caution in assuming they represent qualitative differences from normative aging. They may not. All the changes seen in Alzheimer's disease, including the structural and neurotransmitter changes, are also found in normative aging. To be sure, the changes in Alzheimer's disease are much greater and, more importantly, happen much faster. But the important point is Alzheimer's disease may be merely an exaggeration of normal aging and not something qualitatively different from it. The locations and extent of changes in brain structures over the course of Alzheimer's disease are shown in Figure 10.5.

What's it like to live with Alzheimer's disease? Find out in the Real People feature what it was like for Kathy Collins, a resident of British Columbia, Canada. She and her sister Jean started "The Kathy Project" on TikTok to document it.

How Is Alzheimer's Disease Diagnosed? Given that the behavioral symptoms of Alzheimer's disease eventually become quite noticeable, one might assume that diagnosis would be straightforward. Quite the contrary. Accurate early diagnosis of Alzheimer's disease depends on a thorough assessment of the number and severity of neurological and behavioral changes, as well as assessment of other possible causes of the symptoms (Ismail et al., 2016, 2021).

A comprehensive and broad diagnostic process is essential. Figure 10.6 provides an overview of the process used to differentiate Alzheimer's disease from other conditions, such as mild cognitive impairment (Seixas et al., 2014). Note a great deal of the diagnostic effort goes into ruling out other possible causes for the observed cognitive deficits: any

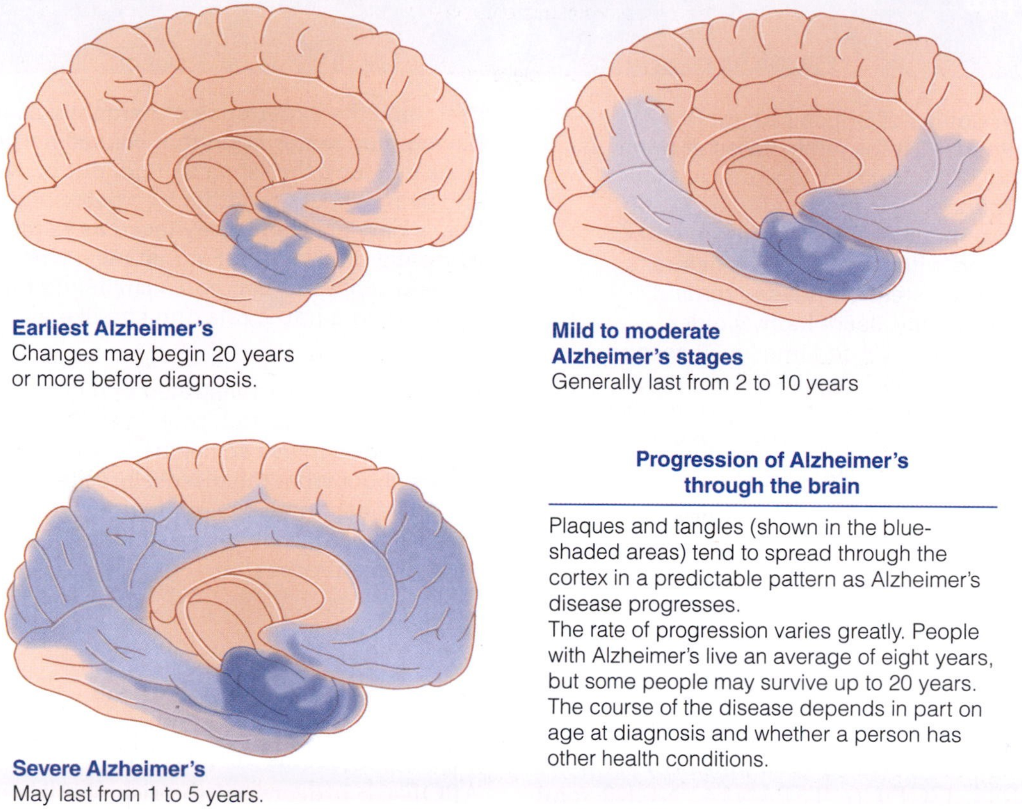
Earliest Alzheimer's
Changes may begin 20 years or more before diagnosis.
Mild to moderate Alzheimer's stages
Generally last from 2 to 10 years
Progression of Alzheimer's through the brain
Plaques and tangles (shown in the blue-shaded areas) tend to spread through the cortex in a predictable pattern as Alzheimer's disease progresses.
The rate of progression varies greatly. People with Alzheimer's live an average of eight years, but some people may survive up to 20 years. The course of the disease depends in part on age at diagnosis and whether a person has other health conditions.
Severe Alzheimer's
May last from 1 to 5 years.

Figure 10.5 Progression of Alzheimer's disease through the brain.
Source: Alzheimer's Association. (2022). *Inside the brain: Part 2: Alzheimer's effect.* https://www.alz.org/alzheimers-dementia/what-is-alzheimers/brain_tour_part_2

potentially treatable causes for the symptoms should be eliminated before a diagnosis of Alzheimer's disease is made. This ensures that if the person has a treatable condition, that condition is identified and, hopefully, treated successfully.

A great deal of attention has been given to the development of more definitive tests for Alzheimer's disease. Much of this work has focused on beta-amyloid and tau proteins that play important roles, as noted earlier, and on neuroinflammation (Mittal et al., 2021). Measures of these proteins in spinal fluid are associated with Alzheimer's disease; for example, higher concentrations of beta-amyloid protein are correlated with lower levels of cognitive functioning. Research is revealing that certain blood tests, much easier to do than tests of spinal fluid, may be just as good at detecting abnormal concentrations of these proteins and may offer an option for diagnosis (National Institutes of Health, 2020b; Thijssen et al., 2020).

What Causes Alzheimer's Disease? We do not know for sure what causes Alzheimer's disease in most people (Dujardin et al., 2022; Jellinger, 2020; Mehta & Schneider, 2021). What we do know is that early-onset (before age 65) forms of Alzheimer's disease are mostly caused by single-gene mutations related to beta-amyloid protein production (Boggula, 2021). Single-gene mutation forms of Alzheimer's disease usually involve mutations in the presenillin-1 (PSEN1), presenillin-2 (PSEN2), and amyloid (A4) precursor protein (APP) genes. As you might imagine, the genetic inheritance aspect of early-onset Alzheimer's disease is a major concern of families that have these mutations in their genetic histories.

Other genetic links to later-onset (after age 65) Alzheimer's disease involve the complex interaction of several genes, processes that are not yet fully documented or understood. Thus far, 37 risk sites on the human genome have been identified, and nine genes

Real People

The Kathy Project

Kathy and Jean Collins of British Columbia, Canada, downloaded TikTok while bored at home during the COVID-19 lockdown. One day in May of 2020, Jean found Kathy surrounded by Post-it Notes stuck to the bedroom wall. Kathy, in her late 50s, was living with early-onset Alzheimer's and developed the system of notes to remind her what to do each day. Jean, Kathy's older sister, took out her phone and filmed a 60-second video of Kathy, asking her what it's like to have early-onset Alzheimer's. They posted the video to TikTok — and it went viral, with their third video receiving more than 1.5 million views.

The sisters continued posting with the goal of educating people about early-onset Alzheimer's and showing that life is still lived. Kathy described the experience of dementia as like having mud in her brain that caused her to get stuck in a loop that she can't get out of. Kathy and Jean worked together to create solutions to any new problems they faced as Kathy's dementia progressed. For instance, when bathing started to become a challenge for Kathy, they turned it into a relaxing spa-like experience for her.

Kathy and Jean demonstrated that living with dementia provides both challenges but also opportunities to use social media to educate others about what the disease process really looks like and to help care providers learn some practical approaches to assisting their loved ones through the process.

have been proposed as most likely involved in later-onset Alzheimer's disease: BIN1, APH1B, PTK2B, PILRA, CASS4, CCDC6, TSPAN14, NCK2, and SPRED2 (Schwartzentruber et al., 2021). Additionally, multiple studies have found associations of rare variants in NOTCH3, TREM2, SORL1, ABCA7, BIN1, CLU, NCK2, AKAP9, UNC5C, PLCG2, and ABI3 with Alzheimer's disease, and suggested that they may influence disease via multiple mechanisms (Khani et al., 2022). These genes have reported functions related to the immune system, lipid metabolism, synaptic plasticity, and programmed cell death.

As noted earlier, other biomarkers of risk for Alzheimer's disease include beta-amyloid and tau proteins, and neuroinflammation. Genetic research here focuses on apolipoprotein ε4 (APOE-ε4), associated with chromosome 19, that may play a central role in creating neuritic plaques. People with the APOE-ε4 trait are more likely to get Alzheimer's disease than those with the more common APOE-ε3 trait (Flowers & Rebeck, 2020). There is some evidence that COVID-19 may increase the likelihood of developing Alzheimer's disease in individuals with this mutation (Manzo et al., 2021). Additionally, a related mutation (TREM2) may be involved with the brain's ability to respond to stress and to contain the buildup of beta amyloid and could be a genetic component underlying late-onset Alzheimer's disease (Ulland & Colonna, 2018).

Interestingly, another version of the mutation, APOE-ε2, seems to have the reverse effect from APOE-ε4: it decreases the risk of Alzheimer's disease (Vidal & Zhang, 2021). Despite the relation between APOE-ε4 and tau protein-based neuritic plaques and beta-amyloid buildup, researchers have yet to establish strong relations directly between apolipoprotein ε and general cognitive functioning (Granot-Hershkovitz, et al., 2021; Wu & Zhao, 2016). However, there is some evidence that the effects of the various APOE mutations differ across six Latino/a groups (Mexican, Puerto Rican, Dominican, Cuban, and Central and South American), and were further modified by continental genetic ancestry (European, African, and Amerindian). These findings point to very complex effects of genetic risk factors related to APOE mutations.

A mutation on the ABCA7 gene has been identified that roughly doubles the chances for Black persons to get late-onset Alzheimer's disease (Cukier et al., 2016). This mutation creates overproduction of cholesterol and lipids, which in turn are known to be risks for cardiovascular disease and strokes, both of which have higher rates in Black individuals. Evidence also suggests that other known genetic risks may work through different pathways in Black older adults (Kunkle et al., 2021).

Much of the genetics and related biomarker research focuses on beta amyloid and its proposed relation to Alzheimer's disease reviewed earlier. When considered as a cause of Alzheimer's disease,

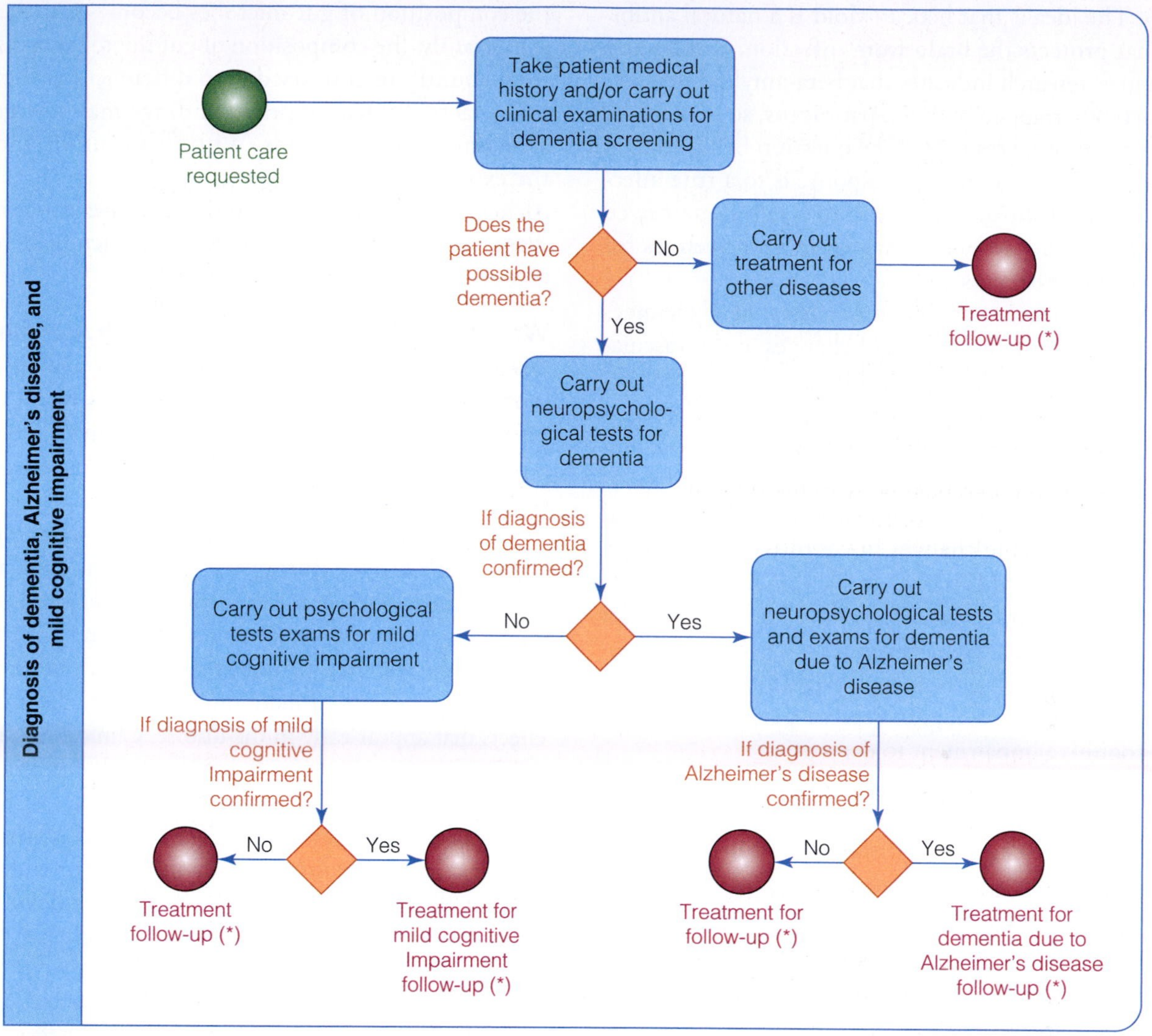

(*) A treatment should be defined by a physician

Figure 10.6 Diagnostic flowchart for Alzheimer's disease and mild cognitive impairment.

Source: Seixas, F. L., Zadrozny, B., Laks, J., Conci, A., & Saade, D. C. M. (2014). A Bayesian network decision model for supporting the diagnosis of dementia, Alzheimer's disease and mild cognitive impairment. *Computers in Biology and Medicine, 51,* 140–158. https://doi.org/10.1016/j.compbiomed.2014.04.010. Figure 5, p. 148.

researchers refer to the beta-amyloid cascade hypothesis as the process by which this occurs (Selkoe, 2016). The **beta-amyloid cascade hypothesis** refers to the hypothesis by which beta-amyloid deposits create neuritic plaques, that in turn lead to neurofibrillary tangles, that cause neuronal death and, when severe enough, Alzheimer's disease. Although this hypothesis has been popular since the early 1990s, due to the overall lack of definitive evidence that beta amyloid plays a causal role in Alzheimer's disease, and no medication based on reducing or preventing beta-amyloid deposits has demonstrated clear evidence of clinical efficacy, researchers argue that the beta-amyloid cascade hypothesis may not provide the main explanation of what causes Alzheimer's disease (Thomas et al., 2020).

One unsolved mystery is why beta-amyloid deposits occur in the first place. An intriguing line of research is providing hints that beta-amyloid deposits linked with Alzheimer's disease could be caused by the brain's natural response to infection, including ones that are too mild to cause symptoms (Kumar et al.,

2016). The idea is that beta amyloid is a natural antibiotic that protects the brain from infection. Kumar and colleagues' research indicates that beta-amyloid deposits have actually trapped bacterial pathogens, so may reflect a natural immune response. The question being studied is whether this beta-amyloid response is to a true infection or is an abnormal response to a falsely perceived infection. Either way, this may open new avenues for research on treatments.

Other research regarding the cause(s) of Alzheimer's disease is focusing on the role of changes in the vascular system in the brain. Beason–Held and colleagues (2012) discovered increased blood flow in the frontal cortex, combined with decreased blood flow in the parietal and temporal lobes, resulted in significant cognitive impairment. Interestingly, the changes in blood flow occurred prior to measurable changes in cognitive functioning. Other researchers (Falsetti et al., 2022; Hayakawa et al., 2015) reported that people who have vascular risk factors, such as hypertension or when blood pressure does not return to normal within 30 seconds of standing up, have a higher rate of progressing from mild cognitive impairment to dementia.

Other research focuses on different potential causes. Some researchers argue that Alzheimer's disease is caused at least in part by impairment in the brain's ability to use glucose and produce energy (De la Monte, 2012; Falsetti et al., 2022). For example, De la Monte (2012) found that processed foods containing nitrites and high fat may exacerbate cognitive decline. Support for this idea comes from research indicating that high blood sugar (glucose) levels are correlated with increased risk of Alzheimer's disease even in people without diabetes, which in turn is a risk factor (Crane et al., 2013; Vagelatos & Eslick, 2013).

Much attention is also focused on neuroinflammation as a possible cause (Fulop et al., 2022; Onyango et al., 2021). Increasing age is associated with an increase in low-grade chronic inflammation that may contribute to the degenerative brain processes in Alzheimer's disease. Related research indicates that gut microbes may play an important role in this process. There are thousands of microbes residing in the human gut, which is deeply involved in crucial functions for good health. Substantial evidence indicates that the gut and central nervous system interact. Changes in diversity and equilibrium of the gut microbes have attracted much attention due to their connection with many neurological and psychiatric disorders, including Alzheimer's disease (Hung et al., 2022). When the intestinal ecosystem is altered, the composition of gut microbes becomes imbalanced. Importantly, the composition of gut microbes is distinct from country to country due to differences in diet and other factors, meaning that findings may not generalize across global regions. With that caution, most of the existing literature suggests that older persons with Alzheimer's disease, but not mild cognitive impairment, demonstrate significantly reduced gut microbe diversity compared to healthy older adults.

What Can Be Done for Persons with Alzheimer's Disease? Most of the care provided to persons with Alzheimer's disease occurs in people's homes, the effects of which we will consider further in Chapter 11. Approaches to intervention fall into two categories: medication and behavioral.

Currently there is no effective medical treatment for Alzheimer's disease during the middle and late stages, and no way to prevent it (Alzheimer's Association, 2022). The best we can do is alleviate some of the symptoms. Most of the research is focused on medications aimed at improving cognitive functioning, especially the memory effects that appear early in the disease. Clinical research in 2022 on the drug lecanemab demonstrated some improvement in cognitive functioning in individuals with mild impairment. Unfortunately, the medications approved by the Food and Drug Administration to date provide little relief as the disease progresses, and few medications in development demonstrate consistently promising results in the later stages (Alexander et al., 2021).

The most effective interventions for Alzheimer's disease, especially in the middle and later stages of the disease, are behavioral strategies. These approaches are recommended over medications because they give better and more effective outcomes (Barton et al., 2016; Watt et al., 2021).

Toa55/iStock/Getty Images

Behavioral interventions with Alzheimer's disease is an effective intervention strategy.

These strategies can be used from the time of initial diagnosis throughout the duration of the disease.

Behavioral strategies range from simple interventions, such as large calendars to help with orientation to time, to the more complex, such as more elaborate memory interventions based on the E-I-E-I-O approach (discussed in Chapter 6). One behavioral intervention involves using an implicit-internal memory intervention called **spaced retrieval**. Developed by Camp and colleagues (Camp, 2001), spaced retrieval involves teaching persons with Alzheimer's disease to remember new information by gradually increasing the time between retrieval attempts. This easy, almost magical technique has been used to teach the names of staff members and other information; it holds considerable potential for broad application at home and in any residential care setting. It is easily taught to any care provider (Hunter et al., 2012). Research also suggests combining spaced retrieval with additional memory-encoding aids helps even more (Kinsella et al., 2007; Oren et al., 2014). Spaced retrieval also works in training nonmemory behaviors; it can be used with residents with dementia who have trouble swallowing to help them relearn how to swallow (Camp et al., 2012) and supporting people to eat (Leah, 2016).

Behavioral interventions work best when they are based on a broad support network of relatives and friends, healthcare professionals, and service providers. Of particular challenge for family and friends care providers is finding ways to balance their care responsibilities with their other roles. Once they find themselves caring for a person with Alzheimer's disease, care providers must rethink many behaviors and situations they otherwise take for granted. Dressing, bathing, and grooming may become more difficult or sometimes even aversive to the person receiving care. For example, it may be necessary to change to shoes and clothing with Velcro fasteners, or assist the person during a shower. Nutritional needs must be monitored because people with dementia may forget they have just eaten or may forget to eat. Sleeplessness can be addressed by establishing consistent bedtimes, giving warm milk before bedtime, and limiting caffeine intake. Wandering is especially worrisome because it is difficult to control; as a precaution, making sure the person with dementia has an identification bracelet with the nature of the individual's problem on it along with their home address, and making the home more difficult to exit are two preventive steps. Incontinence is an embarrassing issue for the person with dementia; using special undergarments or implementing any of a variety of behavioral interventions may help (Bochenska & Boller, 2016; Hsu et al., 2016).

Many care providers need to learn how to accomplish these tasks. Programs providing basic care information are available in multiple formats, including face-to-face and online. A comparison of in-person and online formats in Hong Kong found no differences in effectiveness (Lai et al., 2013). Burgio and colleagues (2003) reported that such skills training is equally effective for White and Black care providers and reduces the number of problem behaviors care providers experience from care recipients. Similarly, White and Latino/a care providers reported significant reductions in depressive symptoms, increased use of adaptive coping, and decreased use of negative coping strategies after training and practice in the use of specific cognitive and behavioral skills (Gallagher-Thompson et al., 2003). Additionally, home intervention strategies can result in care providers having more time to themselves and a decrease in the amount of assistance they need from external sources (Nichols et al., 2008).

One of the most difficult issues care providers face concerns taking tasks away from the affected person and restricting activity. For example, in many cases the person experiences problems handling finances relatively early in the process of dementia. It is not uncommon for individuals to spend hundreds or even thousands of dollars on strange items, to leave bank accounts in disarray and bills unpaid, and to lose money. Although they can be given some money to keep, someone else must handle the day-to-day accounts. That transition may be traumatic, and the care provider may be accused of trying to steal money.

Traveling alone is another difficult issue. Families of people with dementia who live in different parts of the country often do not recognize their loved one's deteriorating condition until a calamity occurs during travel by the affected person. Families may consider limiting solo excursions to places within walking distance; all other trips should be made with at least one other person along. Related to this, driving is often a contentious issue, especially if the person does not recognize their limitations. Once it is clear the individual cannot drive, the family must take whatever steps are necessary. In some cases, this entails simply taking the car keys, but in others it may become necessary to disable or remove the car. Suggesting the person could be driven by a shared ride service or a public transportation service is another alternative.

In general, how can family members and healthcare professionals deal with the behavioral and cognitive problems experienced by people with Alzheimer's disease? One successful approach for dealing with difficult behavior is a technique called *differential reinforcement of incompatible behavior* (DRI; Baker et al., 2015; Drossel et al., 2011). In DRI, care providers reduce the incidence of difficult behavior by rewarding the person with Alzheimer's disease for engaging in appropriate behaviors that cannot be done at the same time as the problem behaviors. For example, a person who throws food during dinner could be rewarded for sitting quietly and eating. One major advantage of DRI for care providers is the technique can be used in the home and provides a good way to deal with troublesome behaviors. Most important, the DRI technique is generally easily learned, has no side effects, and can be as effective as or more effective than medical treatments.

In designing behavioral interventions for those with Alzheimer's disease, the guiding principle is optimizing the person's functioning. Regardless of the level of impairment, attempts should be made to help the person cope as well as possible with the symptoms. The key is helping all individuals maintain their dignity as human beings. This can be achieved in some very creative ways. For example, Cameron Camp (1999) adapted the principles of Montessori methods of education to develop a series of interventions that are effective at decreasing medications, wandering, and agitation and improving overall functioning levels in persons with dementia who live in assisted living and skilled care facilities (De Witt-Hoblit et al., 2016). A major advantage of these therapies is that they are generally easily taught to family care providers who can implement them at home or when visiting the skilled-care facility (Mbakile-Mahlanza et al., 2020). The Spotlight on Research feature describes how the program works.

Ethics and Dementia. The How Do We Know? feature raised an important point about obtaining consent from persons with dementia prior to their participation in a research project. The point that was raised concerned the person's ability to understand the procedures sufficiently to make an informed decision. This concern goes well beyond research participation, though. The cognitive effects of dementia eventually impair a person's ability to make decisions about important issues, such as health care, financial, legal, and other matters. People with cognitive impairments are considered a vulnerable group whose ability to consent and right to participate must be carefully protected and monitored (National Institutes of Health, 2009). It is crucial to be able to decide when a person is no longer capable of making important decisions for themselves. As noted in Chapter 5, this determination involves a process to assess the person's competence to decide matters for themselves or their need to have someone be assigned by a court to provide assistance and act in the best interests of that individual.

Other Types of Dementia

As noted earlier, dementia reflects a cluster of diseases that have in common the progressive deterioration of the brain and cognitive functioning. Many other conditions fit this pattern. In this section, we will consider several of the more common ones in some detail: vascular dementia, Lewy body dementia, Parkinson's disease, Huntington's disease, alcohol-related dementia, and HIV-associated neurocognitive disorders. We considered chronic traumatic encephalopathy (CTE), a form of dementia caused by repeated head trauma, in Chapter 6. Other types that are extremely rare include Creutzfeldt–Jakob disease (which can be contracted from eating infected meat) and normal pressure hydrocephalus (caused by an accumulation of cerebrospinal fluid in the brain that damages and destroys brain tissue). Some other diseases, such as multiple sclerosis, may also cause dementia-like processes.

Vascular Dementia. Another reasonably common type of dementia results from cerebral atherosclerosis and its potential restriction of oxygen to the brain. As described in Chapter 3, atherosclerosis is a family of diseases that, if untreated, may result in heart attacks or strokes. For the present discussion it is the stroke, or cerebrovascular accident (CVA), that concerns us. CVAs result from a disruption of the blood flow called an infarct that may be caused by a blockage or hemorrhage.

A large CVA usually produces rapid, severe cognitive decline, but this loss is almost always limited to specific abilities. This pattern differs from the typical global, more gradual deterioration pattern in most types of dementia.

In contrast, if a person experiences numerous small CVAs, a disease termed **vascular dementia** may result. Vascular dementia is the second most common form of dementia. It may have either a sudden or gradual onset after a series of CVAs, depending on how quickly the CVAs occur in sequence, and its progression is described as stepwise and highly variable across people, especially early in the disease. Again, this contrasts with the pattern of cognitive decline in Alzheimer's disease that is similar across people and gradual.

Most people who have vascular dementia have a history of cerebrovascular or cardiovascular disease, and typical symptoms include hypertension, specific and extensive alterations on an MRI, and differential

How Do We Know?

Montessori-Based Activities Delivered by Family Carers to Nursing Home Residents with Dementia

Who were the investigators, and what was the aim of the study? One-on-one structured Montessori-based activities are effective with people with dementia and have been found to improve agitation and enhance engagement. However, staff at long-term care facilities may not always be available to implement them. Family members may present an untapped resource to do so. Lingani Mbakile-Mahlanza and colleagues (2020) set out to evaluate the impact of the Montessori activities implemented by family members when they visited with their loved ones who have dementia in long-term care facilities.

How did the investigators measure the topic of interest? The Montessori method is based on self-paced learning and developmentally appropriate activities. As Skrajner and Camp (2007) point out, many techniques used in rehabilitation (e.g., task breakdown, guided repetition, moving from simple to complex and concrete to abstract) and in intervention programs for people with dementia (e.g., use of external cues and implicit memory) are consistent with the Montessori method.

Who were the participants in the study? Mbakile-Mahlanza and colleagues recruited 20 persons who had been diagnosed as having dementia who were residents of a nursing home and 20 family care providers.

What was the design of the study? The study used an experimental design in which one group was taught the Montessori intervention and the other group served as a control (refer to Chapter 1). Halfway through the project, the process was switched so that the original control group received the intervention and the original intervention group became the control group.

Were there ethical concerns with the study? Having persons with dementia as research participants raises important issues regarding informed consent. Because of their serious cognitive impairments, these individuals may not fully understand the procedures. Thus, family care providers gave written informed consent on their own behalf and on behalf of the person with dementia prior to commencement of the project. People with dementia were only included if they also assented to participate in the study. The project protocol was approved by the ethics committees of Monash University (Australia) and Monash Health. Additionally, researchers must carefully monitor participants' emotions; if participants become agitated or frustrated, the training or testing session must be stopped. Mbakile-Mahlanza and colleagues took all these precautions.

What were the results? Relative to the control conditions, the intervention resulted in significantly more positive engagement and emotions from the persons with dementia, and higher levels of satisfaction from family care providers.

What did the investigators conclude? The study provided additional evidence of the effectiveness of Montessori-based intervention programs. Most important, it demonstrated that family care providers can be successful in learning and implementing these techniques. This is an important finding, as it means that family care providers can become key in an overall set of intervention strategies to improve the quality of life of people who have dementia.

impairment on neuropsychological tests (a pattern of scores indicating that some functions remain intact and others are significantly below average; Patel & Libman, 2022; Paul et al., 2013). Individuals' specific symptom patterns may vary a great deal, depending on which specific areas of the brain are damaged. In some cases, vascular dementia has a much faster course than Alzheimer's disease, resulting in death an average of 2 to 3 years after onset; in others, the disease may progress much more slowly with idiosyncratic symptom patterns, especially if no additional CVAs occur. It is common for people to have vascular brain changes as well as exhibit signs of other forms of dementia, such as Alzheimer's disease; such cases are referred to as *mixed dementia*.

Lewy Body Dementia. Lewy body dementia is the third most common form; this was the disease diagnosed in Robin Williams, the famous comedian.

The diagnosis of dementia with Lewy bodies depends on several specific things (National Institute on Aging, 2021b). The hallmark Lewy bodies are abnormal accumulations of alpha-synuclein protein that develops inside neurons and causes the loss of neurons that produce dopamine and acetylcholine (discussed in Chapter 2). It is this continued loss that causes the progressive dementia. Diagnosing Lewy body dementia is difficult, in that it is hard to separate specific symptoms from those found in other types of dementia. Key behavioral symptoms include recurring visual hallucinations (reported in about 80% of persons with Lewy body dementia); unpredictable episodes of illogical and disorganized thinking; severe loss of thinking abilities that interfere with daily life; muscle rigidity, balance problems, and repeated falls; sleep disturbances; and fear of being alone, agitation, delusions, and paranoia.

The movement difficulties manifested in Lewy body dementia are similar to those in Parkinson's disease, which is a risk factor for Lewy body disease. In fact, the diagnosis of Lewy body dementia has to do with the timing of symptom occurrence. For a diagnosis of Lewy body dementia, cognitive symptoms develop within a year of movement symptoms. In Parkinson's disease dementia (which we consider next), cognitive symptoms develop more than a year after the onset of movement symptoms (e.g., tremor or muscle stiffness).

Lewy body dementia is usually diagnosed in people over age 50 and is slightly more common in biological males. The disease lasts an average of 5 to 8 years from the time of diagnosis to death but can range from 2 to 20 years for some people. Interventions focus on alleviating the various symptoms, as there is no cure.

Parkinson's Disease. **Parkinson's disease** is known primarily for its characteristic motor symptoms—very slow walking, difficulty getting into and out of chairs, and a slow hand tremor—but it can develop into a form of dementia. These problems are caused by a deterioration of neurons in the midbrain that produce the neurotransmitter dopamine. Former boxing champion Muhammad Ali (who died in 2016); former NBA basketball star and community activist Brian Grant; Pope John Paul II (who died in 2005); civil rights leader Rev. Jesse Jackson; musicians Linda Ronstadt, Ozzy Osbourne, and Neil Diamond; and actor Michael J. Fox are some of the more famous individuals who have Parkinson's disease. Over one million people in the United States (over 10 million globally) have Parkinson's disease (Parkinson's Disease Foundation, 2022).

Parkinson's disease dementia starts as a movement disorder, with symptoms such as slowed movement, muscle stiffness, tremor, a shuffling walk, handwriting that gets significantly smaller, loss of smell, sleeping difficulties, constipation, soft or low voice, facial masking (looking angry when one is not), dizziness or fainting, and stooping or hunching over. Later, cognitive symptoms consistent with dementia and changes in mood and behavior may arise.

Although Parkinson's disease is incurable, symptoms are treated effectively with several medications (Parkinson's Disease Foundation, 2022). The most common are levodopa, which raises the functional level of dopamine in the brain; dopamine agonists that act like dopamine in the brain; MAO-B inhibitors that block the breakdown of dopamine; COMT-inhibitors that improve the effectiveness of levodopa; and amantadine that reduces tremors. Research also indicates a device called a neurostimulator, which acts like a brain pacemaker by regulating brain activity when implanted deep inside the brain, may be effective in significantly reducing the tremors, shaking, rigidity, stiffness, and walking problems when medications fail to do so.

For reasons we do not yet understand, some people with Parkinson's disease also develop severe cognitive impairment and eventually dementia (Oxtoby et al., 2021). Differentiating the dementia resulting from Parkinson's disease from other forms of dementia is crucial.

Huntington's Disease. Huntington's disease is a fatal autosomal dominant disorder (meaning that inheriting the gene from only one parent is necessary to have the disease) that usually begins between ages 30 and 45. The disease generally manifests itself through involuntary flicking movements of the arms and legs; the inability to sustain a motor act such as sticking out one's tongue; prominent psychiatric disturbances such as hallucinations, paranoia, and depression; and clear personality changes, such as swings from apathy to manic behavior (Huntington's Disease Society of America, 2022a, 2022b).

Huntington's disease affects the entire brain but begins with degeneration of the caudate nucleus and the small-cell population, as well as with substantial decreases in the neurotransmitters γ-aminobutyric acid (GABA) and substance P. A test is available to determine whether someone has the marker for the Huntington's disease gene (Huntington's Disease Society of America, 2022a, 2022b).

Cognitive impairments typically do not appear until late in the disease. The onset of these symptoms is gradual. The course of Huntington's disease is progressive; individuals ultimately lose the ability to care for themselves physically and mentally. Walking becomes impossible, swallowing is difficult, and cognitive loss becomes profound. Some people describe Huntington's disease as like having amyotrophic lateral sclerosis (ALS), Parkinson's disease, and Alzheimer's disease simultaneously; the rate of suicide is up to 10 times higher among persons with Huntington's disease compared to the rate in the general population (Huntington's Disease Society of America, 2022c).

Alcohol-Related Dementia. Alcohol use disorder that persists over time may result in significant cognitive decline, ranging from limited forms of amnesia or mild cognitive impairment to dementia (Davis et al., 2022; National Institute of Neurological Disorders and Stroke, 2019). There are two aspects to this condition: Wernicke's encephalopathy and Korsakoff syndrome.

Wernicke's encephalopathy is a degenerative brain disorder caused by the lack of thiamine (vitamin B1). It may result from prolonged high alcohol use, long-standing dietary deficiencies, prolonged vomiting, eating disorders, or the effects of chemotherapy. Vitamin B1 deficiency causes damage to the brain's thalamus and hypothalamus. Symptoms include mental confusion, vision problems, coma, hypothermia, low blood pressure, and lack of muscle coordination (ataxia).

Korsakoff syndrome is a memory disorder that also results from vitamin B1 deficiency and is associated with alcohol use disorder. Korsakoff's syndrome damages neurons and supporting cells in the brain and spinal cord, as well as the part of the brain involved with memory. Symptoms include amnesia, tremor, coma, disorientation, and vision problems, The disorder's main features are problems in acquiring new information or establishing new memories, and in retrieving previous memories.

Although Wernicke's and Korsakoff's are related disorders, some researchers believe them to be different stages of the same disorder, called Wernicke–Korsakoff syndrome. In this perspective, Wernicke's encephalopathy represents the "acute" phase of the disorder and Korsakoff's syndrome represents the disorder progressing to a "chronic" stage.

One key symptom of alcohol-related dementia that has progressed to the Korsakoff syndrome stage is confabulation, when the person makes up apparently believable, but completely fictitious, stories that cover the gaps in memory. Confabulation is often noted in a person's autobiographical memory.

Early in the course of the disease, the symptoms may be reduced or stopped if the person stops drinking alcohol, eats a well-balanced diet, and is given vitamin replacements. However, brain damage that has been experienced is usually permanent, and, without treatment, the disease continues to get worse and may result in death.

HIV-Associated Neurocognitive Disorders. HIV-associated encephalopathy occurs primarily in persons with more advanced HIV infection (Davis et al., 2022; Kopstein & Mohlman, 2022; Manji et al., 2013; Tauber et al., 2016). An aspect of HIV infection that is less well known is that it makes its way to the brain early in the disease process. *HIV encephalopathy* results, which is an infection that spreads throughout the brain. It is one cause of dementia in people infected with HIV. The wider the infection spreads in the brain, the worse the dementia symptoms become. The spectrum of progressively more severe neurologic and cognitive symptoms (previously known as AIDS dementia complex) are referred to as *HIV-associated neurocognitive disorders (HAND)*. Although up to 40% of HIV-infected individuals treated with antiretrovirals exhibit signs of some cognitive deficits, HAND is diagnosed in less than 15% and has become less common since the introduction of effective antiretroviral therapy (Davis et al., 2022; Johns Hopkins Medicine, 2022; Kopstein & Mohlman, 2022).

HIV does not appear to directly invade nerve cells, but it jeopardizes their health and function. The resulting inflammation may damage the brain and spinal cord and cause symptoms such as confusion and forgetfulness, behavioral changes (e.g., apathy, loss of spontaneity, depression, social withdrawal, and personality changes), severe headaches, progressive weakness, loss of sensation in the arms and legs, and stroke. Cognitive motor impairment or damage to the peripheral nerves is also common. HAND ranges in severity from asymptomatic neurocognitive impairment (ANI) to minor neurocognitive disorder (MND) and HIV-associated dementia (HAD).

The mainstay of prevention and treatment of HAND spectrum disorders is adherence to antiretroviral therapy. Appropriate treatment of HIV infection may result in improvement in cognitive function in patients diagnosed with severe deficits. Much of the evidence for the effectiveness of anti-HIV drugs against dementia relates to the drug AZT. Some of the more recently approved medications such as d4T, abacavir, nevirapine, indinavir, and efavirenz also reduce the amount of HIV as measured in the cerebrospinal fluid. When HIV infection is left untreated, HAD is fatal within about 6 months of diagnosis (Kopstein & Mohlman, 2022).

Review Questions

10.4 Delirium and Dementia

- What is delirium? What causes it? Why are older adults more susceptible?
- What is Alzheimer's disease? What are the major symptoms? How is it diagnosed? What causes Alzheimer's disease? What interventions are available?
- What other types of dementia have been identified? What are their characteristics?

Social Policy Implications

The Future of Dementia Care

As we have noted, dementia, especially Alzheimer's disease, takes a devastating toll on the people who have a form of it as well as on their family and friends. A significant problem facing the United States (as well as most other countries) is the prospect of a dramatic increase in the number of people with dementia over the next few decades with the continued aging of the world's population. The problem has many facets: the cost of caring for individuals with dementia, the lost income and productivity of family and friend care providers, and the lack of prospects for effective treatment or for a cure in the near future.

From the current estimate of 5 million people in the United States with Alzheimer's disease, the number is expected to nearly triple by 2050 to about 13 million. That would mean that someone would be diagnosed with Alzheimer's disease in 2015 every 33 seconds (Alzheimer's Association, 2022). The cost of care for these individuals will be staggering—roughly $1 trillion per year by 2050, or one of every three dollars spent in Medicare. The current model of funding cannot sustain this level of increase cost (discussed in Chapter 14). There is no proposed federal funding solution on the horizon.

Expecting family members to care for loved ones with dementia is not a good option either. Most adult child care providers and many spouse/partner care providers are still employed and may not have employers that will provide flexible schedules or paid leave especially in the United States. Lost productivity to organizations due to parent/spouse/partner care is equivalent to billions of dollars each year. Many insurance plans do not cover behavioral or in-home care options. Very few employers provide paid leave for employees to care for older parents. And the United States has no national policy for paid time off to care for a parent or spouse/partner.

The social policy implications of the coming wave of people who will develop dementia are clear. First, research funding aimed at finding an effective way to prevent or cure dementia is essential. Second, redesigning healthcare plans and service delivery to include behavioral and in-home care along with other more cost-effective alternatives needs to be undertaken and paid for. Third, employers must provide support for parent/spouse/partner care through paid leave programs.

The increase in the number of people with dementia is only one major aspect of the coming healthcare crisis resulting from the aging of the baby boomers. We revisit this issue in more detail in Chapter 14.

In Review

For this chapter, consider creating four major paragraphs. The first should summarize your understanding of what mental health is as distinct from psychopathology. Include a discussion of how the meanings of these concepts varies across sociocultural groups.

The second paragraph should concentrate on how psychopathology is assessed in adults of different ages. Include descriptions of the major steps in the process and the ways that symptoms that are causing a person distress are measured and evaluated.

The third paragraph should include discussions of the symptoms, diagnosis, causes, and treatment options relating to depression, anxiety disorders, PTSD, and substance use disorders. Be sure to include key age-related differences in these various aspects of the disorders.

The fourth paragraph should have your summaries of delirium and dementia. With respect to dementia, include discussions of the symptoms, diagnosis, causes, and treatment options for Alzheimer's disease as well as other forms of dementia. For Alzheimer's disease, discuss the varying approaches to behavior-based interventions.

Integrating Concepts in Development

- Why is it so difficult to diagnose mental disorders in older adults? What concepts from Chapters 2, 3, 4, 6, 7, and 8 provide major reasons?
- Why do you think people with Alzheimer's disease might experience hallucinations and delusions?
- Why is there a connection between depression and dementia?
- What would studying people with Alzheimer's disease tell us about normal memory changes with age?

Key Terms

agoraphobia Fear of being in situations where escape may be difficult or embarrassing, or help might not be available in the event of panic symptoms. 327

alcohol use disorder (AUD) A drinking pattern that results in significant and recurrent consequences that reflect loss of reliable control over alcohol use. 331

Alzheimer's disease An irreversible form of dementia characterized by progressive declines in cognitive and bodily functions, eventually resulting in death; it accounts for about 70% of all cases of dementia. 335

Alzheimer's disease continuum The progression of Alzheimer's disease from brain changes that are unnoticeable to the person affected to brain changes that cause problems with memory and eventually physical disability. 336

behavior therapy A type of psychotherapy that focuses on and attempts to alter current behavior. Underlying causes of the problem may not be addressed. 326

beta amyloid A type of protein involved in the formation of neuritic plaques both in normal aging and in Alzheimer's disease. 337

beta-amyloid cascade hypothesis The process in which beta-amyloid deposits create neuritic plaques, that in turn lead to neurofibrillary tangles, that cause neuronal death and, when severe enough, Alzheimer's disease. 341

cognitive therapy A type of psychotherapy aimed at altering the way people think as a cure for some forms of psychopathology, especially depression. 326

delirium A disorder characterized by a disturbance of consciousness and a change in cognition that develop over a short period of time. 334

dementia A cluster of diseases characterized by cognitive decline. Alzheimer's disease is the most common form. 335

generalized anxiety disorder Persistent and excessive worry that interferes with daily activities. 327

incontinence The loss of control of bladder or bowels. 336

internal belief systems What one tells oneself about why certain things are happening. 326

mental status exam A short screening test that assesses mental competence, usually used as a brief indicator of dementia or other serious cognitive impairment. 320

panic disorder Recurrent attacks of overwhelming combinations of physical and psychological distress. 327

Parkinson's disease A disease known primarily for its characteristic motor symptoms (very slow walking, difficulty getting into and out of chairs, and a slow hand tremor) but that can develop into a form of dementia. 346

phobia Excessive and persistent fear of a specific object, situation, or activity that is generally not harmful. 327

separation anxiety disorder Feeling excessively fearful or anxious about separation from those with whom a person is attached. 327

social anxiety disorder Feeling significant unease and discomfort about being embarrassed, humiliated, rejected, or looked down on in social interactions. 327

spaced retrieval A behavioral, implicit-internal memory intervention used in early- and middle-stage dementia. 343

sundowning The phenomenon when people with Alzheimer's disease exhibit an increase in symptoms later in the day. 336

vascular dementia A form of dementia caused by a series of small strokes. 344

Chapter

11

Relationships in Adulthood

Learning Objectives

After studying this chapter, you will be able to...

11.1. Describe characteristic patterns of friendship and adult love relationships.

11.2. Outline differences in adult relationship lifestyles.

11.3. Outline differences in family life, family forms, and parenting roles.

11.4. Describe trends and the social customs of divorce and remarriage.

Chapter Outline

One thing on which most people would agree about the year 2020 was that it was the Year of Not Being with Others. The behaviors needed to slow the spread of COVID-19 meant that we needed to keep physical distance and refrain from being in face-to-face groups, even with family and friends. It meant that people could not be with loved ones for birthday parties, weddings had to be postponed, and, sadly, people died alone. The COVID-19 pandemic really reminded us that being in the presence of others is a core personal need, and being blocked from it has major consequences. People coped as best they could through video chats; although better than nothing, those did not replace being able to hug one's loved ones. Humans have a very deep need for relationships that goes beyond texts and Facebook and Instagram posts.

That is what we'll explore in this chapter—the ways in which we share our lives with others. First, we consider what makes good friendships and love relationships. Because these relationships form the basis of our lifestyles, we examine these lifestyle patterns next. In the third module, we consider the complex dynamics of families, from the decision to become a parent to becoming a great-grandparent. Finally, we discover what happens when marriages or partnerships end and people decide to recouple.

11.1 Framing Interpersonal Relationships

Key Questions

- What role do friends play across adulthood? How do they develop?
- What characterizes love relationships? How do they vary across cultures?
- What is the nature of violence in some relationships?

Jamal and Kahlid have known each other all their lives. They grew up together in Dearborn, attended the same schools, and even married women who were sisters. Their business careers took them in different directions, but they and their families always got together on major holidays. Now as older men, they feel a special bond; many of their other friends have died.

Having other people in our lives we can count on is essential to our well-being. Just imagine how difficult life would be if you were totally alone, without even a Zoom or Facebook "friend" to communicate with. People need other people for their well-being. In this module we consider broadly the different types of relationships we have with other people and learn how these relationships help—and sometimes hurt—us.

First, we focus on how our lives are shaped by others and how we share the company of others. Friendships are the foundation of this and are the main component of our social convoy. The term **social convoy** is used to suggest how a group of people journeys with us in our lives, providing support in good and bad times. People form the convoy, and under ideal conditions, that convoy provides a protective, secure cushion that permits people to explore and learn about the world (English & Carstensen, 2016; Fuller et al., 2020; Sharifian et al., 2020). Especially for older adults, the social convoy provides a source of affirmation of who they are and what they mean to others, which leads to better mental health and well-being.

Several studies suggest that the size of one's social convoy and the amount of support it provides do not differ across generations. Clearly, friends and family are essential aspects of all adults' lives. In ethnic, racialized, and immigrant communities, these networks provide all sorts of informal assistance (Sharifian et al., 2020). Along these lines, a study of older Congolese refugees documented that they faced more challenges than younger refugees and relied on their networks more (Pachner et al., 2021).

Friendships

Jamal and Kahlid remind us that some of the most important people in our lives are our friends. They are often the people to whom we are closest and with whom we may have even life-long connections. They are often the ones we count on when we need validation and support.

What is a friend? Someone who is there when you need to share? Someone who's not afraid to tell you the truth? Someone you have fun with? Friends, of course, are all of these and more. Researchers define friendship as a mutual relationship in which those involved influence one another's behaviors and beliefs and define friendship quality as the satisfaction derived from the relationship (Blieszner, 2014; Blieszner & Roberto, 2012; Fiori et al., 2020).

The role and influence of friends is extremely important across adulthood (Blieszner et al., 2019; Fiori et al., 2020; Mehta et al., 2020; Nehamas, 2016). Friendships are predominantly based on feelings and grounded in reciprocity and choice. Friendships are different from love relationships (which we consider later in this module) mainly because friendships tend to be less emotionally intense and usually do not involve sexual activity (Nehamas, 2016). Having good friendships boosts self-esteem (Yu & Chang, 2021) and happiness (Fiori & Denckla, 2015; Y. T. Ng et al., 2021) across adulthood. Friendships also help us become socialized into new roles throughout adulthood.

Friendships Across Adulthood. What characterizes face-to-face and online adult friendships? Researchers have identified three key aspects (Adams et al., 2017; Frederick & Zhang, 2020; Wrzus et al., 2017):

- The *affective or emotional basis* of friendship refers to self-disclosure and expressions of intimacy, appreciation, affection, and support, which are all are based on trust, loyalty, and commitment.
- The *shared or communal nature* of friendship reflects how friends participate in or support activities of mutual interest.
- The *sociability and compatibility* dimension represents how our friends keep us entertained and are sources of amusement, fun, and recreation.

Having and maintaining good friendships is hard work. It takes a great deal of cognitive energy and effort, and time. Only if people are willing to do all that it takes will close friendships develop.

Because social media has become a core way that friendships begin and thrive for all generations, an important concern is the trustworthiness of connections that begin online, just as it was when friendships mainly happened through face-to-face encounters. In the case of online friendships, trust develops from four sources: (1) reputation; (2) performance, or what users do online; (3) precommitment, through personal self-disclosure; and (4) situational factors, especially the premium placed on closeness and the relationship (Håkansson & Witmer, 2015; Ledbetter, 2017).

Adult friendships tend to have a natural course to them (Blieszner et al., 2019; Wrzus et al., 2017). Most begin as a result of shared interests, and many never progress beyond that. However, some friendships move beyond sharing common activities to sharing more personal aspects of the self (Blieszner et al., 2019; Wrzus et al., 2017). These processes can be conceptualized as a dynamic interaction among three processes: formation, sustainment, and dissolution as noted in Figure 11.1.

Longitudinal research describes how friendships change across adulthood. As you may have experienced, some changes are predictable, such as life transitions (e.g., going away to college, moving, death), that result in fewer friends overall with increasing age and less contact with the friends you keep (Blieszner, 2014; Blieszner et al., 2019; Wrzus et al., 2017). People tend to have more friends and acquaintances during emerging adulthood than at any subsequent period, mostly because they have the desire, time, opportunities, and breadth of shared interests necessary to develop them (Demir et al., 2015).

Friendships are important throughout adulthood in part because life satisfaction is strongly related to the quantity and quality of contacts with friends (Yu & Chang, 2021). College students with strong friendship networks adjust better to stressful life events, such as those they faced during the COVID-19 pandemic, whether those networks are face-to-face or online (Antheunis, 2016; Murray & Arnett, 2019; Tibbetts et al., 2021; Wrzus et al., 2017).

The link between life satisfaction and friendships is supported by research on loneliness. It turns out

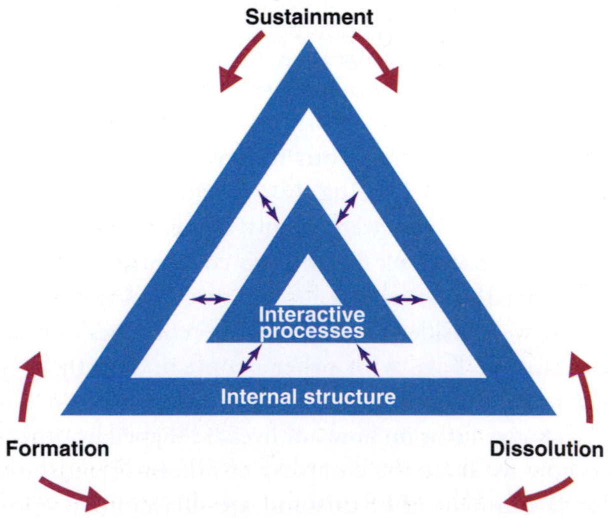

Figure 11.1 Friendship phases: changes over time in internal structure and interactive processes.

Source: Blieszner et al. (2019). p. 5, Figure 2.

that people are especially prone to feeling lonely at three different points in adulthood (Lee et al., 2019): in one's late 20s, mid 50s, and late 80s. For emerging adults, loneliness often stems from believing that one's peers have done a better job at managing the stresses of emerging adulthood. In midlife, feelings of loneliness tend to be connected to the physical and personal changes people experience. Losses of friends through death or other causes in later life create challenges for maintaining friendships, resulting in feelings of loneliness. However, Lee and colleagues (2019) also note that wisdom (explored in Chapter 7) dramatically reduces feelings of loneliness. That's good, because the health effects of loneliness are serious: feeling lonely has a similar negative health consequence as smoking about 15 cigarettes daily.

There are some important differences in later life friendships, though (Blieszner et al., 2019; Denworth, 2020; Fiori et al., 2020). Friends are sometimes even more important to older adults in part because older adults do not want to become burdens to their families, a feeling exacerbated by the COVID-19 pandemic (Adams & Taylor, 2015; Chen, 2020; Seidlein et al., 2019). As a result, friends help each other foster independence. Having friends also provides a buffer against the loss of roles and status that accompany later life, such as retirement or the death of a loved one, and can increase people's happiness and self-esteem. People who live alone especially benefit from friends in the neighborhood. And people who have ambivalent feelings about their social networks have shorter telomeres (discussed in Chapter 3) than people who have strong feelings about theirs (Kent de Grey & Uchino, 2020; Uchino et al., 2012).

Older adults do not limit their friendships to people who are roughly comparable in age. Rather, friendships are based on a number of factors. O'Dare and colleagues (2021) propose that an important factor for older adults is basing friendships on "doing-and-being" between adults who are of different generations. "Doing-and-being" based friendships have three components: being "friends in action" (pursuing shared interests and leisure activities, or simply spending time together), being "not only old" (sharing aspects of oneself beyond age), and sharing attitudes and approaches to friendship and life. Such friendships help broaden the opportunities for older adults to form and maintain strong networks for support.

Older adults tend to have fewer relationships with people in general and develop fewer new relationships than people do in midlife and particularly in emerging adulthood (Adams & Taylor, 2015; Blieszner et al., 2019; Fiori et al., 2020). Carstensen and colleagues (Carstensen, 2006, 2021; Charles & Carstensen, 2010; English & Carstensen, 2016; Reed & Carstensen, 2012; Shavit & Carstensen, 2020) have demonstrated that the changes in social behavior such as reducing the number of friends one interacts with in late life reflect a complicated and important process. They propose a life-span theory of **socioemotional selectivity**, which argues that social contact is motivated by a variety of goals, including information seeking, self-concept, and emotional regulation.

Each of these goals is differentially salient at different points of the adult life span and results in different social behaviors. When information seeking is the goal, such as when a person is exploring the world trying to figure out how they fit in, meeting many new people is an essential part of the process. However, when emotional regulation is the goal in later life, people become highly selective in their choice of social contacts and nearly always prefer people who are familiar or similar to them.

Carstensen and colleagues believe information seeking is the predominant goal for young adults, emotional regulation is the major goal for older people, and both goals are in balance in midlife. Their research supports this view; people become increasingly selective in whom they choose to have contact with as they age. Additionally, other evidence suggests there is an increase with age in emotional competency and regulation until very late life (e.g., Chen & Anderson, 2018; Doerwald et al., 2016; Le Vigouroux et al., 2022). Older adults appear to orient more toward emotional aspects of life and personal relationships as they grow older, and emotional expression and experience become more complex and nuanced. Carstensen's theory provides an explanation of why older adults tend not to replace, to any great extent, the friendships they lose on a one-for-one basis: older adults are more selective and have fewer opportunities to make new friends, especially in view of the emotional bonds involved in friendships.

Why does friendship have such overall positive benefits for us? Although researchers do not know for certain, there are insights from neuroscience research. Coan and colleagues (Beckes & Coan, 2013; Beckes et al., 2013; Coan & Sbarra, 2015) propose *social baseline theory*, a perspective that integrates the study of social relationships with principles of attachment, behavioral ecology, cognitive neuroscience, and perception science. Social baseline theory and its extensions (Gross & Medina-Villiers, 2020) suggest the human brain is wired to access social relationships that mitigate risk and diminish the level of effort needed to meet a variety of goals by incorporating friends and partners into our neural representations of the self. In short, each of us makes our friends part of our self-definition, and these reflect the way our brains are wired.

What's more, when we are faced with threatening situations, our brains process the situation differently when we face them alone compared to when we are with a close friend. Specifically, neuroimaging shows that the parts of the brain that respond to threat ("light up" on neuroimages) when facing threat alone differ from those that respond when facing the same threat with a close friend. In practical terms, what this means is a close friendship may change the way the brain functions, resulting in our perception of feeling safer. The trials we face are more manageable with friends than without them.

Siblings. A special type of friendship exists with one's siblings, who are often the friends people have the longest and who share the closest bonds. How important siblings are in one's life varies with age (Merz & De Jong Gierveld, 2016; Tanskanen & Danielsbacka, 2021). The centrality of siblings depends on several things, such as difference in age, proximity, health, prior relationship, and degree of relatedness (full, step-, or half-siblings). However, one event that often draws siblings together is the death of a parent (Hank, 2021). No clear pattern of emotional closeness emerges when viewing sibling relationships on the basis of gender identity in any combination.

laindiapiaroa/Tetra images/Getty Images

Sibling friendships are often the longest lasting friends people have.

When sibling relationships are close and one sibling dies, the surviving sibling often reports reflecting on the generational passing and can experience very significant grief (Carr & Mooney, 2021). What is also clear is that sibling relationships in later life are affected by events in the lives of the siblings that may have occurred decades earlier (Knipscheer & van Tilburg, 2013; Woolley & Greif, 2021). If there was no contact between the siblings over an extended period of time, it is unlikely that these relational rifts will be repaired. An important source for such tension is hard feelings stemming from perceived parental favoritism among siblings. This tension subsequently plays out when aging parents need care, and it may continue into the siblings' own late life (Gilligan et al., 2013, 2020; Woolley & Greif, 2021). In such situations, jealousies that have their roots in childhood fester for decades, only to resurface when siblings need to coordinate parental care.

Gender-Based and Interracial Friendships. Same-gender friendships reflect similarities and differences in adulthood (Adams et al., 2017; Blieszner & Roberto, 2012; Blieszner et al., 2019; Fiori et al., 2020; Mehta & Wilson, 2020; Wrzus et al., 2017). Four characteristics of same-gender friends do not appear to differ across cultures and age groups: geographic proximity, similarity of interests and values, inclusion, and symmetrical reciprocity (Hall, 2016). Three characteristics that distinguish women's same-gender friendships are communion and self-disclosure, greater effort and expectations from friends in general, and a greater risk of co-rumination (extensively discussing and re-visiting problems, and focusing on negative feelings). In contrast, men's same-gender friendships are typically based on shared activities or interests.

What about friendships between genders? These patterns of friendships were rare before the 20th century (Hart et al., 2016), and are particularly beneficial for men (Piquet, 2006). Cross-gender friendships help men have lower levels of dating anxiety and higher capacity for intimacy. These patterns hold across diverse racial and ethnic groups, too. Due to stereotypic beliefs, friendships among people of different genders may present challenges because of misperceptions. Misperception about one's own or one's partner's sexual attractiveness to others is a common area of contention, can be the basis for relationship difficulties, and is a major reason why such friendships usually constitute a small percentage of adult friendships (Hart et al., 2016; Mehta & Wilson, 2020). The #MeToo movement brought international attention to the issue of sexual harassment, abuse, and assault. In the #MeToo era, increased scrutiny on such friendships in organizations emerged especially when a power differential exists between the individuals (Green, 2018; Mehta & Wilson, 2020).

Very little research has examined interracial friendships distinct from relationships that involve romantic attraction. What seems clear is that developing contacts and friends across ethnic and racial groups turns out to affect attitudes. For example, research has long indicated that people who have diverse friendships (either in-person or virtual) have more positive attitudes toward people with different backgrounds (Aberson et al., 2004; Hermann et al., 2020; Vezzali & Stathi, 2021).

Love Relationships

Love is one of those things we feel but cannot describe adequately. (Test yourself: Can you explain fully what you mean when you look at someone special and say, "I love you"?) One way researchers try to understand love is to think about what components are essential. In an interesting series of studies, Sternberg (2006) argued love has three basic components: (1) *passion*, an intense physiological desire for someone; (2) *intimacy*, the feeling that you can share all your thoughts and actions with another; and (3) *commitment*, the willingness to stay with a person through good and bad times. Ideally, a true love relationship has all three components; when couples have equivalent amounts and types of love, they tend to be happier, even as the balance among these components shifts over time.

Love Through Adulthood. The different components of love help us understand how such relationships develop (Sternberg, 2006). Research is clear that the development of romantic relationships is a complex process influenced by attachments and relationships experienced in childhood and adolescence (Collins & van Dulmen, 2006; Oudekerk et al., 2015; Paquette et al., 2020).

In Sternberg's (2006) view, early in a romantic relationship, passion is usually high whereas intimacy and commitment tend to be low. This is infatuation: an intense, physically based relationship when the individuals have a high risk of jealousy and of misunderstanding the other's intent and the degree to which the other person is attracted to us. Indeed, during this time it is sometimes difficult to establish the boundaries between casual sex or hook-ups and dating in emerging adulthood (van de Bongardt & de Graaf, 2020). Research also suggests people who select a partner for a more permanent relationship (e.g., marriage) during the height of infatuation are likely to support the notion of "love at first sight" but are also more likely to divorce (Hansen, 2006; Robb, 2014).

It is also a time when misperceptions due to lack of clear communication may result in sexual assault (Simonson & Sarkis, 2018). Misperceptions occur, for instance, in interpreting and understanding whether each party has given affirmative consent for engaging in sexual relations. **Affirmative consent** requires the assurance that all parties engaging in a sexual encounter are informed, autonomous, and otherwise capable of making a valid choice regarding engaging in sexual activity. Lamb and colleagues (2021) argue that affirmative consent does not go far enough to clear up communication, though. They propose a *standard of mutuality* that is based on encountering the other with care and loving attention.

However, infatuation tends to be short-lived. Passion, as you may have experienced, can be taxing. As passion fades, either a relationship acquires emotional intimacy, or it will likely end. Trust, honesty, openness, and acceptance must be a part of any strong relationship; when they are present, romantic love can develop fully.

The intimacy phase is often exemplified by people spending much of their time together, making decisions together, caring for each other, sharing possessions, and developing ways to settle conflicts. These behaviors increase the chances that their relationship will last. Such people may show outward signs of commitment, such as wearing a lover's ring, having children together, cohabiting, or simply sharing the mundane details of daily life, from making toast at breakfast to following before-bed rituals. Intimacy tends to be a phase of stability for many people, and usually indicates a level of commitment.

Campbell and Kaufman (2017) surveyed 1,529 people across the United States in order to better understand the connections among love, personality, and creativity. They found that as time goes on, physical intimacy and passion decrease but emotional intimacy and commitment increase. This and related research indicate that good relationships tend to deepen as time goes on, even if intense physical passion decreases.

Falling in Love. In the book *The Prophet*, Kahlil Gibran (1923) points out love is two-sided: just as it can give you great ecstasy, so can it cause you great pain.

Yet most of us are willing to take the risk anyway. That willingness begs some questions: How do people fall in love? Is it more like people with very similar interests coming together? Or do opposites attract?

The best explanation of the process is the theory of **assortative mating**, which states people find partners based on their similarity to each other. Assortative mating occurs along many dimensions, including education, religious beliefs, physical traits, age, socioeconomic status, intelligence, and political ideology, among others (Conroy-Beam, 2021). Such nonrandom partnering occurs most often in societies that allow people to have more control over their own dating and pairing behaviors. Identifying what people have in common is the most popular way to sort through potential dating partners; if you've ever swiped through profiles on online dating sites, you will know how likely it is to be the basis for decisions—except, that is, in speed dating situations. In that case, it comes down mainly to physical attractiveness (Antheunis et al., 2020; Herrenbrueck et al., 2018; Luo & Zhang, 2009).

Does how people meet influence the likelihood they will "connect" on particular dimensions and form a couple? Kalmijn and Flap (2001) found that it does. Using data from more than 1,500 couples, they found meeting at school, for example, was most likely to result in *homogamy*—the degree to which people are similar. Not surprisingly, the pool of available people to meet is strongly shaped by the opportunities available.

Online matching services are increasingly the way of choice for adults of all ages to meet prospective dates (Rosenfield et al., 2019; Todd, 2021; Watson & Stelle, 2021). Research indicates virtual dating sites offer both possibilities, such as the number of people one could meet, and problems, such as the accuracy of personal descriptions. As in the offline world, physical attractiveness strongly influences initial selections online (Erevik et al., 2020; Sumter et al., 2017; Watson & Stelle, 2021).

One trend among emerging adults is the hookup culture of casual sex, often without even knowing the name of one's sexual partner (Kettrey & Johnson, 2021; Wade, 2017). Research indicates that people of many sexual orientations are interested in having hookup sex, but also prefer a more romantic relationship over the long run. However, ascribing the perception of "no strings attached" to hookup sex appears incorrect, as nearly three-fourths of those who engage in it eventually express some level of regret at having hookup sex (Kettrey & Johnson, 2021).

How do couple-forming behaviors compare cross-culturally? Researchers have examined the factors that attract people to each other in different cultures. In research described in the How Do We Know? feature, Schmitt and colleagues (2004; Schmitt, 2010) studied 62 cultural regions. They found that secure romantic attachment was the norm in nearly 80% of cultures, and what they termed "preoccupied" romantic attachment was particularly common in East Asian cultures. In general, multicultural studies suggest there are global patterns in partner selection and romantic relationships. The typical romantic attachment profiles reported in individual nations were correlated with sociocultural indicators in ways that supported evolutionary theories of romantic attachment and basic human partnering strategies.

Additional research exploring cultural differences has supported these earlier results. For example, Thomas and colleagues (2020) asked an international sample of nearly 2,500 people to design an ideal long-term partner. Clear cultural differences were again found on many dimensions, but traits fundamental for reproductive success were prioritized across all cultures, perhaps reflecting deeper evolutionary needs.

Clearly, culture and evolution are powerful forces shaping partner selection choices. Specifically, Buss (2016) argues that partner selection serves many deeply held, and deeply programmed, human needs. The kinds of partners we choose are driven by certain hardwired biological and psychological needs and desires that play out in many ways.

Traditional matchmaking remains a powerful tool to maintain certain cultural norms regarding partner selection (Al-Dawood et al., 2021; Chai, 2021). For example, pressure on unmarried adults in China and Saudi Arabia to base partner selection on traditional values even extends to how online dating services are used.

Little research has been conducted examining the development of transgender and gender nonconforming (TGNC) partner selection across adulthood (Bower et al., 2021; Porter et al., 2016; Witten, 2016). Research indicates that transgender older adults experience social isolation more than most other groups in large part due to discrimination in general and to rejection by family and friends (Harley et al., 2016). However, relationship stress patterns and outcomes among TGNC partners parallel those found in other types of partner relationships (Cooper et al., 2020; Randall & Bodenmann, 2017).

How Do We Know?

Patterns and Universals of Romantic Attachment Around the World

Who were the investigators and what was the aim of the study? One's attachment style may have a major influence on how one forms romantic relationships. In order to test this hypothesis, David Schmitt (2004, 2010) assembled a large international team of researchers.

How did the investigators measure the topic of interest? Great care was taken to ensure equivalent translation of the survey across the 62 cultural regions included. The survey was a two-dimension, four-category measure of adult romantic attachment (the Relationship Questionnaire) that measured models of self and others relative to each other:

- secure romantic attachment (high scores indicate positive models of self and others),
- dismissing romantic attachment (high scores indicate a positive model of self and a negative model of others),
- preoccupied romantic attachment (high scores indicate a negative model of self and a positive model of others), and
- fearful romantic attachment (high scores indicate negative models of self and others).

An overall score of model of self is computed by adding together the secure and dismissing scores and subtracting the combination of preoccupied and fearful scores. The overall model of others score is computed by adding together the secure and preoccupied scores and subtracting the combination of dismissing and fearful scores.

Additionally, there were measures of self-esteem, personality traits, and sociocultural correlates of romantic attachment (e.g., fertility rate, national profiles of individualism versus collectivism).

Who were the participants in the study? A total of 17,804 people (7,432 men and 10,372 women; no further information about the gender identities of the samples were noted) from 62 cultural regions around the world took part in the study. Such large and diverse samples are needed in developmental research.

What was the design of the study? Data for this cross-sectional, nonexperimental study were gathered by research teams in each country. The principal researchers asked the research collaborators to administer a nine-page survey to the participants that took 20 minutes to complete.

Were there ethical concerns with the study? Because the study involved volunteers, there were no ethical concerns. However, ensuring all participants' rights were protected was a challenge because of the number of countries and cultures involved.

What were the results? The researchers first demonstrated the model of self and others measures were valid across cultural regions, which provided general support for the independence of measures (i.e., they measure different things). Specific analyses indicated that 79% of the cultural groups studied demonstrated secure romantic attachments, but North American cultures tended to be high on dismissive and East Asian cultures tended to be high on preoccupied romantic attachment. These patterns are shown in Figure 11.2. Note all the cultural regions except East Asia reflected

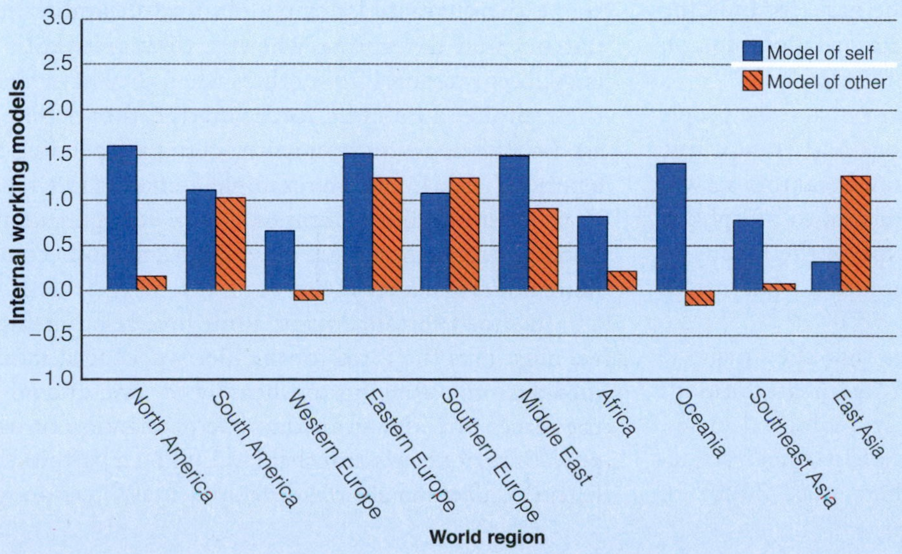

Figure 11.2 In research across 10 global regions, note that only in East Asian cultures were the "model of others" scores higher than the "model of self" scores.
Source: Data from Schmitt et al. (2004).

(Continued)

the pattern of model of self-scores higher than model of others scores.

What did the investigators conclude? Overall, Schmitt and colleagues concluded although the same attachment pattern holds across most cultures, no one pattern holds across all of them. East Asian cultures in particular tended to fit a pattern in which people report that others do not get as emotionally close as the respondent would like.

Developmental Forces, Neuroscience, and Love Relationships. As you may have experienced, finding a love relationship can be difficult. Many things must work just right: timing, meeting the right person, luck, and effort are but a few of the key factors. Centuries of romance stories describe this as a magical process and portray it as one of life's great mysteries.

Who chooses whom (and whether the feelings will be mutual) results from the interaction of developmental forces described in the biopsychosocial model presented in Chapter 1. Neuroscience research reveals how.

Many researchers and theorists consider love as one of three discrete, interrelated emotion systems (the sex drive and attachment are the other two; Fisher, 2016; refer also to Helen Fisher's series of TED Talks, and her website theanatomyoflove.com). In terms of passionate love, two areas of the brain are heavily involved: the ventral tegmental area (VTA), located near the base of the brain, and the caudate nucleus (a region of the striatum), a multi-part brain area located a bit higher. The caudate nucleus integrates your "rush" of romantic passion with your complex emotions and thoughts about your lover. Additionally, neurochemicals related to amphetamines come into play at this phase, providing a neurobiological explanation for the exhilaration of falling madly in love. Cacioppo and Cacioppo (2020) note that the interplay among brain structures and neurotransmitters provides the basis for building theories of social behavior, such as love relationships, on the basis of neurological research.

Once the relationship settles into what some people might call long-term commitment and tranquility, the brain processes switch from amphetamine-related neurotransmitters to substances related to morphine, a powerful narcotic. That may explain the feeling of comfort that usually comes in committed relationships (Cacioppo & Cacioppo, 2020).

Additional research indicates that the hormone oxytocin plays an important role in attachment (Cacioppo & Cacioppo, 2020). In biological males, it enhances their perception of their partner's attractiveness compared to others (Lieberz et al., 2020). In biological females, it enhances their orgasms, among other things (Cacioppo & Cacioppo, 2013), which has earned it the nickname of the "cuddle hormone" (Lee et al., 2009). Love really does a number on your brain!

And that's not all. The interactions among psychological aspects, neurological aspects, and hormonal aspects of romantic love help explain why partners tend to have exclusive relationships with each other. For biological females (but not biological males), blood levels of serotonin increase during periods of romantic love (Langeslag et al., 2012). In addition, among heterosexual biological females, the stronger the romantic bond with their biological male partner, the less likely they are to be able to identify the body odor of a different biological male friend or biological male stranger (Lundström & Jones-Gotman, 2009; Mahmut et al., 2019). That supports a view that heterosexual biological females' attention is deflected from other potential biological male partners the more they are romantically involved with one specific biological male.

Psychologically, an important developmental issue is intimacy (discussed in Chapter 9); according to Erikson, mature relationships are impossible without it. In addition, the kinds of relationships individuals witnessed and experienced as a child (and whether they involved violence) affect how they define and act in relationships they develop as adults. Sociocultural forces shape the characteristics people find desirable in a partner and determine whether they are likely to encounter resistance from others when they have made their choice. Life-cycle forces matter, too; different aspects of love are more or less important depending on a person's stage in life. For example, romantic love tends to be most prominent form of love in emerging adulthood, whereas the aspect of companionship becomes more important later in life.

In short, to understand adult love relationships, we must take the forces of the biopsychosocial model into account. Relying too heavily on one or two of the forces provides an incomplete description of why people are or are not successful in finding a partner or a friend. Unfortunately, the developmental forces do not influence only good relationships. As we will discover next, sometimes relationships turn violent.

Violence in Relationships

Up to this point, we have been considering relationships that are mainly healthy and positive. Unfortunately, this is not always the case. Sometimes relationships become violent; one person becomes aggressive toward the partner, creating an **abusive relationship**. Such relationships have received considerable attention since the early 1980s, when the U.S. criminal justice system ruled that, under some circumstances, abusive relationships can be used as an explanation for one's behavior (Walker, 1984). For example, **battered spouse syndrome** occurs when a spouse or partner believes they cannot leave the abusive situation and may even go so far as to kill their abuser. Battered spouse syndrome is recognized by U.S. courts as a defense for people on trial for taking violent action against an abusive partner (Holloway & Wiener, 2018).

Research suggests that there are several factors that increase the risk of experiencing relationship violence: being female; having more romantic partners; early onset of sexual activity; being in a relationship based on traditional power and gender roles; being alone in an unfamiliar environment; and being a survivor of child abuse (Centers for Disease Control and Prevention, 2021h). Although overall national rates of sexual violence have declined more than half since the early 1990s, acquaintance rape or date rape is still a major problem (Bureau of Justice Statistics, 2020). College women are more likely to be survivors of sexual assault than are people in other groups. The factors for this are many and varied, such as gender and racial stereotypes, power differentials, and sexism. Campus sexual assault has been a major focus for U.S. federal policy across multiple administrations, both Democrat and Republican.

What range of aggressive behaviors occurs in abusive relationships? What causes such abuse? Based on considerable research on abusive partners, O'Leary (1993) proposed a continuum of aggressive behaviors toward a partner that progresses as follows: verbally aggressive behaviors, physically aggressive behaviors, severe physically aggressive behaviors, and murder. This continuum is noted in Table 11.1. The causes of the abuse also vary with the type of abusive behavior being expressed.

Two points about the continuum should be noted. First, experiencing violence in a relationship is common. In the United States, the federal government reports that about 1 in 4 women and nearly 1 in 10 men have experienced contact sexual violence, physical violence, and/or stalking by an intimate partner during their lifetime and reported some form of intimate partner violence-related impact (Centers for Disease Control and Prevention, 2021h). Worldwide, between 10% and 69% of women report being physically assaulted or raped, making it one of the priority areas for the World Health Organization (World Health Organization, 2013).

The second point, reported in the table, is the suspected underlying causes of aggressive behaviors differ as the type of aggressive behaviors change (O'Leary, 1993; Sugimoto-Matsuda & Guerrero, 2016). Although anger and hostility in the perpetrator are associated with various forms of physical abuse, especially in emerging adulthood, the exact nature of this relationship remains elusive (Giordano et al., 2016).

Members of the LGBTQIA+ communities are also the survivors of violence from intimate partners, though accurate statistics are difficult to obtain (Lund et al., 2021; Scheer et al., 2021; Winstead et al., 2021). Members of these communities are frequently targeted based on stereotypes, attitudes, and beliefs, and research consistently indicates that they are reluctant to report such violence. All survivors need to be supported and provided safe ways for them to report assaults.

Because culture plays such a major role in the formation of relationships, it is also an important contextual factor in understanding partner abuse. In particular, violence against women worldwide often reflects cultural traditions, beliefs, and values of patriarchal societies. This is clear in the commonplace violent practices against women that include sexual slavery, female genital cutting, intimate partner violence, and "honor" killing (Ghanim, 2015; Samanta, 2021; World Health Organization, 2013).

International data indicate rates of violence are higher in cultures that emphasize female purity, virginity, male status, and family honor. A common cause of women's murders in some countries is brothers or other male relatives performing so-called "honor" killings, murdering the victim because she violated the family's honor (Ghanim, 2015; Solomon & Tausch, 2021; Sultan, 2021).

Alarmed by the seriousness of partner violence, many communities have established shelters for people who experience it. However, the legal system in many

Table 11.1 Continuum of Progressive Behaviors in Abusive Relationships

Verbal aggression →	Physical aggression →	Severe aggression →	Murder
Insults	Pushing	Beating	
Yelling	Slapping	Punching	
Name-calling	Shoving	Hitting with object	
Causes			
Need to control* →	→	→	→
Misuse of power* →	→	→	→
Jealousy* →	→	→	→
Marital discord →	→	→	→
	Accept violence as a means of control →	→	→
	Modeling of physical aggression →	→	→
	Abused as a child →	→	→
	Aggressive personality styles →	→	→
	Alcohol use disorders →	→	→
		Personality disorders →	→
		Emotional lability →	→
		Poor self-esteem →	→
Contributing factors			
Job stresses			
Unemployment			

Note: Need to control and other variables on the left are associated with all forms of aggression; acceptance of violence and other variables in the middle are associated with physical aggression, severe aggression, and murder. Personality disorders and the variables on the right are associated with severe aggression and murder.

*More relevant for males than for females.

Source: O'Leary, K. D. (1993). Through a psychological lens: Personality traits, personality disorders, and levels of violence. In R. J. Gelles & D. R. Loseke (Eds.), *Current Controversies on Family Violence* (pp. 7–30). Copyright © 1993 by Sage Publications. Reprinted by permission of the publisher.

localities is still not set up to deal with intimate partner violence; for example, women in some locations cannot sue their husbands for assault, and restraining orders all too often offer little real protection from additional violence. At the federal government level, much remains to be done to protect people from the fear and the reality of intimate partner violence.

Elder Abuse and Neglect. Relationship violence takes on a broader context with respect to older adults. Although elder abuse, neglect, and exploitation are difficult to define precisely, the following categories are commonly used (National Institute on Aging, 2020):

- **Physical abuse:** use of physical force that may result in bodily injury, physical pain, or impairment.
- **Sexual abuse:** nonconsensual sexual contact of any kind.
- **Emotional or psychological abuse:** infliction of anguish, pain, or distress.
- **Financial or material exploitation:** illegal or improper use of an older adult's funds, property, or assets.
- **Abandonment:** desertion of an older adult by an individual who had physical custody or otherwise had assumed responsibility for providing care for the older adult.
- **Neglect:** refusal or failure to fulfill any part of a person's obligation or duties to an older adult.
- **Self-neglect:** behaviors of an older person that threaten their health or safety, excluding those conscious and voluntary decisions made by a mentally competent and healthy adult.

Estimates are that 1 in 10 older adults living in the community experience some form of abuse, exploitation, or neglect (National Center on Elder Abuse, 2022a). However, it is also estimated that only about 1 in 24 cases of elder abuse, neglect, and exploitation are reported to authorities (Mars, 2022; Mercier et al.,

2020). Globally, researchers estimate that perhaps one in six older adults experience some type of abuse, neglect, or exploitation in a community setting (World Health Organization, 2021b).

Educating healthcare workers in how to spot elder abuse, neglect, and exploitation still needs significant improvement. Financial exploitation, particularly through scams perpetrated via email and phone calls, costs older adults billions of dollars annually (DeLiema et al., 2016; Segal et al., 2021). Because cognitive capacity and decline increase the likelihood of a person being duped by a scammer (as discussed in Chapters 6 and 7), such schemes are extremely common on email and social media that target older adults. Researchers and policy makers argue that prevention of financial exploitation can be greatly assisted by banks and other financial institutions, who can monitor account activity and question unusual withdrawals (Lichtenberg, 2016a, 2016b; Lichtenberg et al., 2015, 2020).

Researchers and professionals who focus on elder abuse, especially that perpetrated by adult children, conceptualize it not as an outcome of a stressful care providing situation, but as a development from the longer ongoing set of relationship issues between parent and child (Pickering & Phillips, 2014). Similarly, abuse by older intimate partners may also be tied to former existing relationship issues even if abuse had not been present previously (Band-Winterstein et al., 2021; Bows, 2018). Understanding, detecting, and addressing elder abuse requires culturally sensitive approaches that reflect the values of older adults in different cultures (Li et al., 2020). Although certain characteristics, such as a correlation with disability, occur across cultures, how those characteristics are manifested differ. Likewise, prevention and intervention strategies must take cultural differences into account.

As with relationship abuse at other points in the life span, identifying and reporting it is everyone's concern. The National Center on Elder Abuse (2022b) provides a guide for warning signs of elder abuse, neglect, or exploitation. If you suspect that an older adult is a victim of elder abuse, neglect, or exploitation, the best thing you can do is contact your local adult protective services office and report it.

Adult Development in Action

If you were a relationship counselor, what advice would you give to emerging adults who are seeking a love relationship?

Review Questions

11.1 Framing Interpersonal Relationships

- What are the major characteristics of friendships across adulthood?
- How does the nature of friendships change with age?
- What are the main characteristics of love relationships in adulthood? What phases do love relationships go through?
- How do love relationships vary across cultures?
- What are the main dynamics of violence in relationships?
- What are the main types of elder abuse, neglect, and exploitation?

11.2 Lifestyles and Relationships

Key Questions

- What are the challenges and advantages of being single?
- Why do people cohabit?
- What is marriage like across adulthood?

Kevin and Beth are ecstatic. They got married one month ago and have recently returned from their honeymoon. Everyone who encounters them can tell that they love each other a great deal. They are highly compatible and have much in common, sharing most of their values and even their leisure activities. Kevin and Beth wonder what lies ahead in their marriage.

Developing relationships is only part of the picture in understanding how adults live their lives with other people. Putting relationships such as Kevin and Beth's in context is important for us to understand how relationships come into existence and how they change over time. In the following sections, we explore different types and aspects of relationships: singlehood, cohabitation, and marriage.

Our discussion will focus on the most common forms of lifestyles and relationships. Within couples, we will mostly emphasize monogamy. However, there are several forms of consensual non-monogamy, such as polyamory (the practice of engaging in multiple romantic and typically sexual relationships, with the consent of all the people involved), swinging (the practice of engaging in group sex or the swapping of sexual partners within a group, especially on a habitual basis), and open relationships (a marriage or relationship in which both partners agree that each may have sexual relations with others). For some, celibacy (the practice of not having sex, and for some groups marriage as well) is also practiced.

Singlehood

Adults are single—defined as not living with an intimate partner—at multiple points in their lives, such as before marriage or other long-term commitment, following divorce, and in widowhood (Kislev, 2019). In the United States, roughly 50% of all households are headed by people who are not married (the U.S. government does not track the number of adults who live together in other forms of committed relationships in their living arrangements surveys; U.S. Census Bureau, 2020a). With so many people being single, we are witnessing some changes in attitudes, particularly since the demographics of singles increasingly reflects that of the United States as a whole (as well as many other countries). In this module, we focus on being single by choosing not to marry; elsewhere we return to living single in the context of divorce. We will consider being single due to the death of a spouse or partner in Chapter 13.

What's it like to be a single adult in the United States? It's tougher than you might think. Several researchers (e.g., Budgeon, 2016; Casper et al., 2016; Jamieson, 2020; Lahad, 2017) point out numerous stereotypes and biases against single people, especially women. For example, married people are perceived as kinder and more giving, and public policy also favors married couples. For instance, research indicates that singles face housing discrimination (Bhargava & Chilana, 2020; Goodsell, 2013; Kazis, 2021).

Why do people choose to remain single? Some do so to focus on establishing their careers. Others report they simply did not meet "the right person" or simply prefer singlehood, a factor especially important among people who express strong religious beliefs (Engelberg, 2016; Himawan, 2020; Ibrahim & Hassan, 2009; Yacovson et al., 2021).

An important distinction is between adults who are temporarily single (i.e., those who are single only until they find a suitable long-term partner) and those who choose to remain single permanently (Kislev, 2019). For most permanent singles, the decision to never marry is a gradual one. This transition is represented

FG Trade/iStock/Getty Images

More adults are choosing to remain single.

by a change in self-attributed status that occurs over time and is associated with a cultural timetable for marriage. It marks the experience of "becoming single" that occurs when an individual identifies more with singlehood than with marriage (Davies, 2003).

Choosing to remain single can also reflect an economic-based decision, and reflects decisions often made by people who choose to focus on their careers or for other related personal reasons (Çelik, 2018). Financial factors appear to be especially important for members of the millennial generation, who are less likely to think they are better off than their own parents and grandparents thought at the same age and who stay single at a higher rate than did previous generations (Kalish, 2016).

Having a strong friendship network is a major source of emotional and other support for singles (Kislev, 2019). Staying in touch, either face-to-face or virtually, is key. This proved to be essential for singles during the COVID-19 pandemic when physical distancing limited the ways people could interact in person (Kamin et al., 2021). Overall, people who choose to be single express good satisfaction with their lives (Kislev, 2019).

Cohabitation

Being unmarried does not necessarily mean living alone. People in committed, intimate relationships but who are not married may decide that living together, or **cohabitation**, provides a way to share daily life. Cohabitation is becoming an increasingly popular lifestyle choice in the United States as well as in Canada, Europe, Australia, and elsewhere, especially among those in the millennial generation and among older adults (Lamidi et al., 2019; Luxenberg, 2014; Manning et al., 2019; Martin et al., 2014).

It is important to note that people who cohabit are not necessarily in a committed relationship. For example, college students may cohabit in off-campus houses, and older adults may cohabit because it makes sense financially or because they simply desire the companionship.

There are generational differences in the frequency of cohabitation, especially among those who are in committed relationships. In the United States, evidence clearly indicates that cohabitation is more common and is now the most common form of committed living arrangement for the millennial generation (Lamidi et al., 2019; Manning et al., 2019). For example, the majority of emerging adult women cohabit with, rather than marry, a partner as a first committed relationship. But this is not just a millennial generation phenomenon. Cohabitation rates for adults 50 years of age and older are four times higher than in 1995 (Pew Research Center, 2019a). Evidence also indicates that the length of cohabiting relationships in the United States is 18 months, compared to 12 months in the 1980s (Lamidi et al., 2019).

Global cohabitation rates differ by culture (Ortiz-Ospina & Roser, 2020). In most European, South American, and Caribbean countries, cohabitation is a common alternative to marriage. For instance, cohabitation is extremely popular in the Netherlands, Norway, and Sweden, where this lifestyle is part of the culture; 99% of married couples in Sweden cohabited before they married, and one in four couples are not legally married. Decisions to marry in these countries are typically made to legalize the relationship after children are born—in contrast to Americans, who traditionally marry to confirm their love and commitment to each other.

The happiest cohabiting couples are those who look very much like happily married couples: they share financial responsibilities, household chores, and childcare. However, on average cohabiting couples in the United States are less satisfied with their relationship and less trusting of their partner (Pew Research Center, 2019a), perhaps due to the meaning attached to marriage as noted earlier.

Why do couples cohabit? Most married and cohabiting adults cite love and companionship as major reasons why they decided to move in with a partner. But about four-in-ten cohabiters also say finances and convenience were important factors in their decision: 38% say moving in with their partner made sense financially, and 37% say it was convenient. This is very different for married couples, who report that these reasons are far less important (Pew Research Center, 2019a).

Marriage

Many adults in the United States eventually want their love relationships to result in marriage. However, U.S. residents are in less of a hurry to achieve this goal; the median age at first marriage for adults in the United States has been rising for several decades. As the trends in Figure 11.3 make clear, between 1890 and 1960, average age at first marriage for men and women declined, but from 1970 on it has risen a little more than 7 years for both men and women (U.S. Census Bureau, 2020b). The U.S. trends mirror some global trends; Figure 11.4 presents global data on women's age at first marriage. Note that in developed countries, average age is increasing,

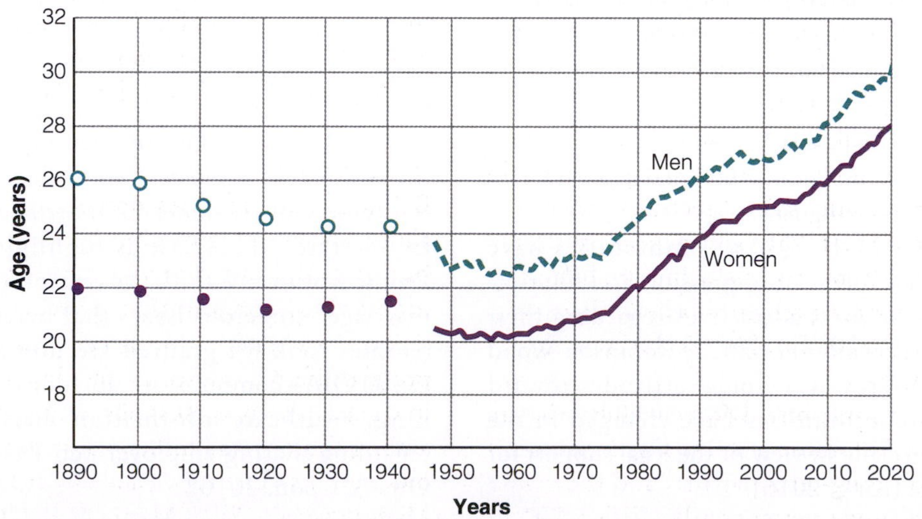

Figure 11.3 Median age at first marriage: 1890 to 2020.
Source: U.S. Census Bureau (2020b).

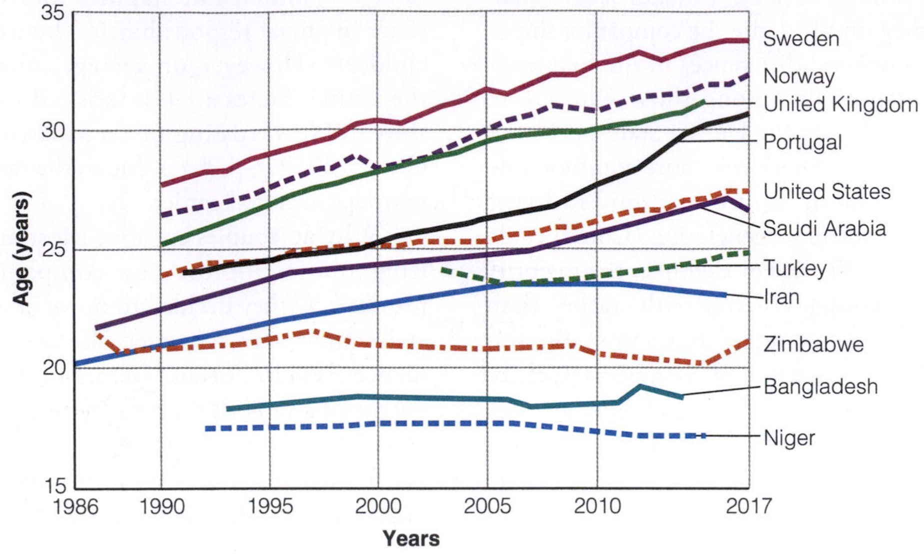

Figure 11.4 Median age of women at marriage in selected countries.
Source: https://ourworldindata.org/marriages-and-divorces#average-age-at-marriage

and that in countries in which cultural (e.g., arranged marriages) and religious traditions play larger roles, the average age has remained fairly stable.

The reasons for these increases in average age in the United States are mostly financial (e.g., student loan debt) and a desire to get one's career established. But there is more to it. As you may have surmised from the discussion about cohabitation, the popularity of marriage itself is on the decline in many countries. Couples are choosing to cohabit or to formalize their relationship in other ways first rather than marrying right away. The graphs in Figure 11.5 document this general downward global trend in rates of marriage; in the United States, for example, the rate of marriage since 2000 has been lower than at any other point in the past 100 years. Clearly, the central role that marriage once played in most countries, and the presumption that adults had marriage as a very high personal goal, is changing.

Adults in the LGBTQIA+ communities have experienced various forms of oppression and discrimination throughout their adult lives regarding their ability to marry (Bower et al., 2021; Robinson-Wood & Weber, 2016). However, social attitudes toward the LGBTQIA+ communities have changed in the United States, especially in view of the legal support for same-sex marriage (King, 2016).

Most research on relationships among members of the LGBTQIA+ communities has focused on gay and lesbian couples. These relationships are similar to those of heterosexual couples, although small differences favoring same-sex couples have been identified in terms of relationship satisfaction in some studies (Chonody et al., 2020; Kurdek, 2004). Most gay and lesbian couples are in dual-earner relationships, much like the majority of married heterosexual couples, and are likely to share household chores. However, gay and lesbian couples differ from heterosexual couples in the degree to which both partners are similar on demographic characteristics such as race, age, and education; gay and lesbian couples tend to be more dissimilar, except regarding education (Ciscato et al., 2020).

An important fact to keep in mind is that until the 2015 *Obergefell v. Hodges* decision in the U.S. Supreme Court, same-sex marriage was still illegal in 14 states. This case is highlighted in the Real People feature. With the advent of legalized same-sex marriage, numerous issues that heterosexual married couples took for granted are now extended to the LGBTQIA+ communities, including end-of-life planning, healthcare information sharing, and matters regarding sharing employer benefits (Godfrey, 2016; Orel & Coon, 2016).

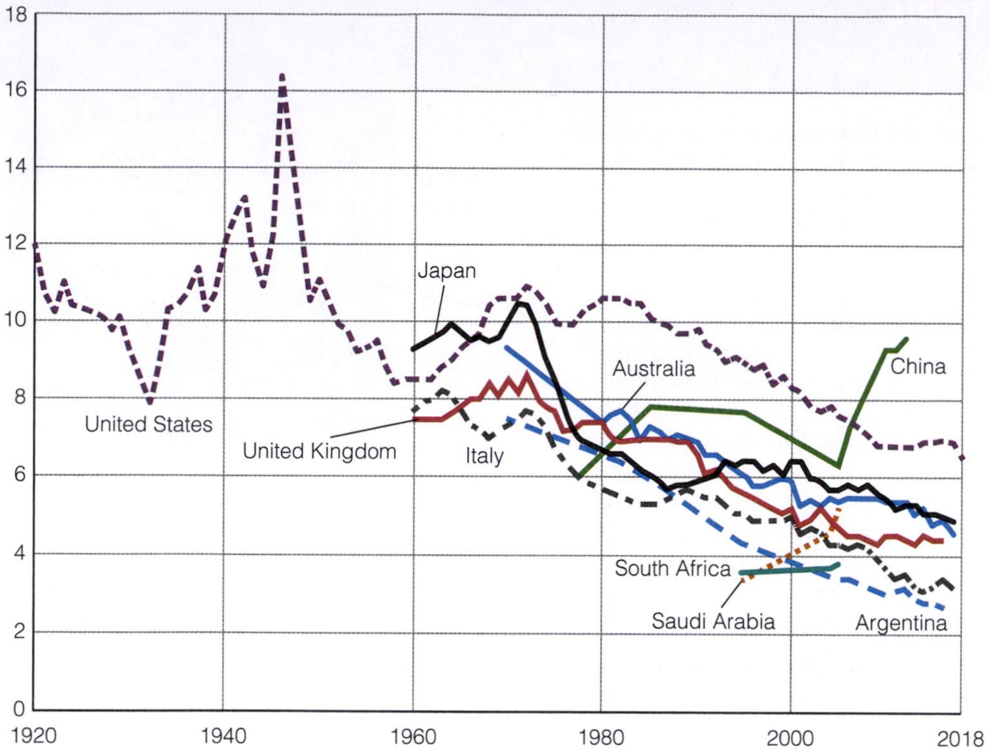

Figure 11.5 Marriages per 1,000 people in selected countries.
Source: https://ourworldindata.org/marriages-and-divorces#marriages-are-becoming-less-common

When compared to LGBTQIA+ individuals cohabiting with or married to partners, LGBTQIA+ individuals living alone or with others (but not in a relationship with them) report higher degrees of loneliness (Hsieh & Liu, 2021; Kim & Fredriksen-Goldsen, 2016). This finding parallels that found among heterosexual individuals in similar living arrangements.

What Is a Successful Marriage, and What Predicts It? You may know couples who appear to have a successful marriage. But what does that mean, really? Minnotte (2010) differentiates **marital success**, an umbrella term referring to any marital outcome (such as divorce rate); **marital quality**, a subjective evaluation of the couple's relationship on a number of different dimensions; **marital adjustment**, the degree spouses accommodate each other over a certain period of time; and **marital satisfaction**, a global assessment of one's marriage. Each of these provides a unique insight into the workings of a marriage.

An important predictor of successful marriage is **homogamy**, or the similarity of values and interests a couple shares. As we discussed in relation to choosing a partner, the extent the partners share similar age, values, goals, attitudes (especially the desire for children), socioeconomic status, certain behaviors (such as socializing), and ethnic background increases the likelihood their relationship will succeed (Chai, 2021; Karney, 2021; Kippen et al., 2013).

Another factor in predicting marital success is a feeling that the relationship is equal. According to **exchange theory**, marriage is based on each partner contributing something to the relationship the other would be hard pressed to provide. Satisfying and happy marriages result when both partners perceive there is a fair exchange, or equity, in all the dimensions of the relationship. Problems achieving equity arise because of the competing demands of work and family, an issue we take up again in Chapter 12.

Cross-cultural research supports these factors. For instance, couples in the United States and Iran say trust, consulting each other, honesty, making joint decisions, and commitment make the difference between a successful and an unsuccessful marriage (Asoodeh

Real People

James Obergefell and John Arthur Make History

When James (Jim) Obergefell met John Arthur in Cincinnati in 1992, there was no way they thought that their love relationship would make history. Neither one of them had ever been an activist, and it took tragedy and loss to set them on their mission.

After they fell in love, they lived and worked together as consultants. They were avid art collectors and had a large social network of friends and family. Nearly 20 years into their relationship, though, everything changed. Arthur, who had been experiencing severe mobility problems, was diagnosed with amyotrophic lateral sclerosis (ALS), also known as Lou Gehrig's disease. As the disease progressed, Jim became Arthur's primary care provider. By 2013, Arthur's condition had progressed very significantly.

What both of them wanted was to be married so that Jim could be recognized as Arthur's surviving spouse on Arthur's death certificate. Unfortunately for them, Ohio voters had passed a constitutional amendment banning same-sex marriage. However, such marriages were legal in Maryland. With support from friends, Jim hired a medical plane to fly them to Maryland, where Arthur's aunt officiated at their wedding on the tarmac at Baltimore-Washington International Thurgood Marshall Airport on July 11, 2013. Arthur died three months later.

James (Jim) Obergefell

Shortly before Arthur's death, they sued the state of Ohio in order for Jim to be listed as the surviving spouse on Arthur's death certificate. They lost the case but were granted a hearing by the U.S. Supreme Court. Their case was combined with several others for the hearing. By a 5 to 4 decision, the Court ruled that the U.S. Constitution supports same-sex marriage, thereby making these marriages legal in the entire country.

Together with the *Loving v. Virginia* (1967) decision (the basis for the movie *Loving*) that banned anti-miscegenation laws, the *Obergefell v. Hodges* decision opened marriage to all couples who had, in one way or another, been refused that right in the United States.

et al., 2010; Hall, 2006; Zaheri et al., 2020). Couples for whom religion is important also point to commonly held faith as a key factor.

So what really matters in predicting whether a relationship is likely to be successful? Dey and Ghosh (2016) found several key predictors: respect for emotion, attitude toward marriage, expression of love, regard for views and importance to the likings of the spouse, ignoring weaknesses of the spouse, sexual adjustment, temperament, value, taste, and interest. We will learn in the next few sections how these and other factors play out at specific times during the course of marriage across adulthood.

Do Married Couples Stay Happy? Few sights are happier than a couple on their wedding day. Newlyweds, like Kevin and Beth in the vignette, are at the peak of marital bliss. The beliefs people bring into a marriage influence how satisfied they will be as the marriage develops. But as you may have experienced, feelings change over time, sometimes getting better and stronger, sometimes not.

Research indicates for most couples, overall marital satisfaction is highest at the beginning of the marriage, may decline somewhat until the children begin leaving home, but is mainly stable overall; this pattern holds across demographic categories (Kulik, 2016; Williamson & Lavner, 2020). However, there is considerable variability across couples. For some couples, it declines more precipitously and the couple becomes, in essence or in fact, emotionally divorced (Proulx et al., 2017; Williamson & Lavner, 2020).

The pattern of a particular marriage over the years is determined by the nature of the dependence of each spouse on the other (Proulx et al., 2017; Williamson & Lavner, 2020). When dependence is mutual and about equal and both people hold similar values that form the basis for their commitment to each other, the marriage is strong and close (Givertz et al., 2009). When the dependence of one partner is much higher than that of the other, however, the marriage is likely to be characterized by stress and conflict. Learning how to deal with these changes is the secret to long and happy marriages.

The fact that marital satisfaction varies widely across couples led Karney and Bradbury (1995, 2020; Karney, 2021) to propose a vulnerability–stress–adaptation model of marriage, depicted in Figure 11.6. **The vulnerability–stress–adaptation model** considers marital quality as a dynamic process resulting from the couple's ability to handle stressful events in the context of their particular vulnerabilities and resources. As a couple's ability to adapt to stressful situations gets better over time, the quality of the marriage will probably improve. How well couples adapt to various stresses on the relationship determines whether the marriage continues or they get divorced. Let's explore how this works over time.

Setting the Stage: The Early Years of Marriage. Early in a marriage, couples tend to have global adoration for their spouse's qualities (Karney, 2010; Miller, 2020). For heterosexual married wives, but not for husbands, more accurate specific perceptions of what their spouses are really like were associated with more supportive behaviors, feelings of control in the marriage, and a decreased risk of divorce. Couples who are happiest in the early stage of their marriage focus on the good parts of their marriages, not the annoyances; nit-picking and nagging may not bode well for long-term wedded bliss (Miller, 2020).

Longitudinal research indicates disillusionment—as demonstrated by a decline in feeling in love, in demonstrations of affection, and in the feeling that one's spouse is responsive, as well as an increase in feelings of ambivalence—and other personality characteristics such as narcissism are key predictors of marital dissatisfaction (Lavner, Lamkin et al., 2016). Additional research since 2010 indicates two key trends (Karney & Bradbury, 2020): (1) Contrary to predictions of behavioral models of marriage, negative communication between spouses is not always a sign of trouble, can be difficult to change, and may not create more satisfying relationships if communication improves. (2) Processes between the couple that are reliably adaptive for middle-class and more affluent couples may operate differently in lower income couples, meaning that some models of marriage may not generalize to couples living in diverse environments.

During the early years of their marriage, many couples may spend significant amounts of time apart, especially those who are in the military (Zamir et al., 2020). Spouses who serve in combat areas on active-duty assignment and who have post-traumatic stress disorder (PTSD, discussed in Chapter 10) are particularly vulnerable, as they are at greater risk for other spouse-directed aggression. It is especially important to address the psychological consequences of deployment in order to minimize the effects on the couple.

What the nondeployed spouse believes turns out to be important. If the nondeployed spouse believes the deployment will have negative effects on the marriage, then problems are much more likely. In contrast, if the nondeployed spouse believes such challenges make the relationship stronger, then they typically can do so (Lewis et al., 2016; Moelker et al., 2019). Research indicates the effects of deployment may be greater on wives than on

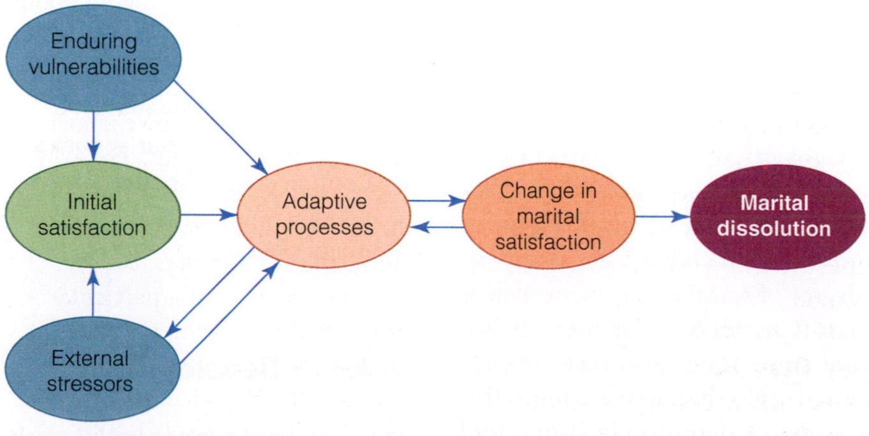

Figure 11.6 The vulnerability–stress–adaptation model illustrates how adapting to vulnerabilities and stress can result in either adaptation or dissolution of the marriage.
Source: Karney, B. R. (2010). Keeping marriages healthy, and why it's so difficult. Retrieved from www.apa.org/science/about/psa/2010/02/sci-brief.aspx.

husbands; divorce rates for female service members who are deployed is higher than for their male counterparts (Gribble et al., 2019; Karney & Crown, 2007).

Keeping Marriages Happy. The secret to long, happy marriages is seemingly simple: be flexible and adaptable. Couples who have been happily married for many years have an ability to "go with the flow" and adapt to changing circumstances in the relationship. For example, a serious problem of one spouse may not be detrimental to the relationship and may even make the bond stronger if the couple use good stress- and conflict-reduction strategies. Successful couples also find ways to keep romance in the relationship. Ensuring that couples continue to have "date night," and mutually agreeing on how to meet a partner's sexual needs are ways to keep romance alive (Birnbaum et al., 2016; Muise et al., 2013).

Sharing religious beliefs and spirituality with one's spouse is another good way to ensure higher quality marriages, and this holds true across diverse religious groups as well as atheists (Hwang et al., 2021; Lichter & Carmalt, 2009; Sorokowski et al., 2019). Religion and spirituality may also provide a framework for conflict resolution and a way to put one's marriage in a bigger, more significant context.

Overall, research indicates similarity among the developmental patterns of heterosexual, gay, lesbian, and bisexual older adult couples (Abela, 2020; King, 2016). Little research has been conducted examining the development of transgender and gender nonconforming (TGNC) couples across adulthood (Sloan & Benson, 2022; Witten, 2016).

Satisfaction in long-term relationships—that is, marriages or committed relationships of 40 years or more—is a complex issue. In general, satisfaction among older couples increases shortly after retirement but then decreases with health problems and advancing age, and is directly related to the level of perceived support each partner receives and the level of dependency of one's partner (Charles & Carstensen, 2020; Marini et al., 2020; Rauer & Proulx, 2020). The level of satisfaction appears to be unrelated to the amount of past or present sexual interest or sexual activity, but it is positively related to the degree of social engagement such as interaction with friends (Charles & Carstensen, 2020). One notable aspect of some long-term relationships is a detached, contented style that appears more like cohabitation or co-residence than deeply committed relationship (Lamanna et al., 2021; Proulx, 2016).

Older married couples show several specific characteristics (Charles & Carstensen, 2020; O'Rourke et al., 2010; Rauer & Proulx, 2020). Many older couples demonstrate a selective memory regarding the occurrence of negative events and perceptions of their partner. Older couples have a reduced potential for marital conflict and greater potential for pleasure, are more likely to be similar in terms of mental and physical health, and exhibit fewer gender differences in sources of pleasure. This is especially true if the couple have developed strong dyadic coping strategies, that is, coping strategies that rely on the interconnectedness of the couple (Berg et al., 2016; Schade et al., 2020). In short, older couples in long-term relationships developed adaptive ways to avoid conflict and grew more alike.

So how do long-term relationships change and develop from midlife through late life? Wickrama and colleagues (2013; Lee et al., 2020; Wickrama & O'Neal, 2021) developed a model accounting for the influences of genetic markers, personal characteristics, cumulative life experiences, and stressful events during the period from late midlife through later life. The model, presented in Figure 11.7, indicates how all these influences interact.

The key point in the model is that people bring their past with them when they enter late life, and those experiences, including their genetic makeup, work together to create the relationships that people experience. Although Wickrama et al. (2013) initially created the model to describe baby boomers' marriages as they experience retirement, subsequent work indicates that it applies to long-term relationships across generations.

What are the best ways to increase the chances of having a long, happy marriage? Based on research, do these:

- Make time for your relationship.
- Express your love to your spouse.
- Be there in times of need.
- Communicate constructively and positively about problems in the relationship.
- Be interested in your spouse's life.
- Confide in your spouse.
- Forgive minor offenses and try to understand major ones.

Adult Development in Action

If you were a relationship coach, what strategies would you recommend people use to maximize the odds that they will find a potential long-term partner(s) if they are seeking them?

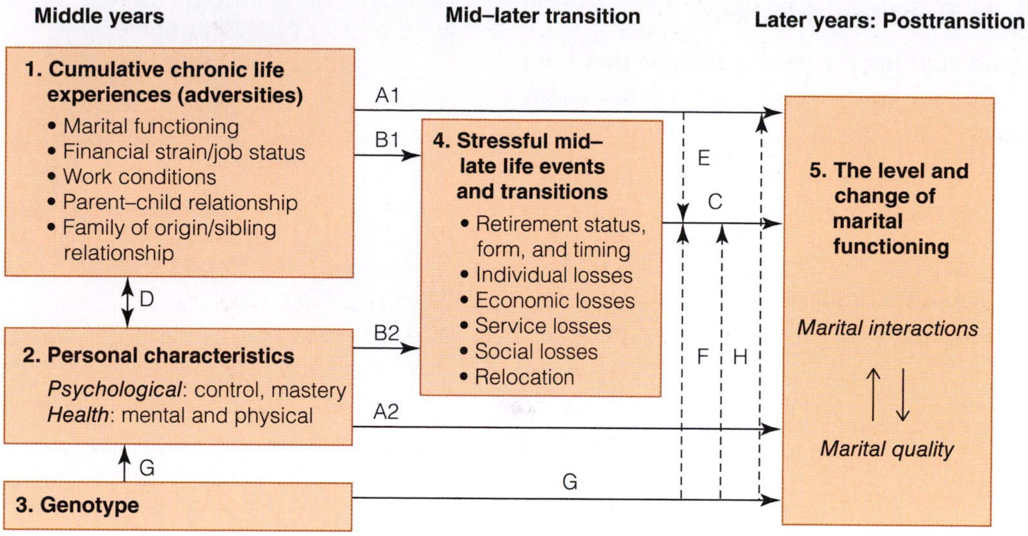

Figure 11.7 Marital functioning from middle to later years: A life course–stress process framework.
Source: Wickrama et al. (2013). p. 18, Figure 1.

Review Questions

11.2 Lifestyles and Relationships

- What are the major characteristics of people who choose to remain single? How do single people deal with the need to have relationships?
- Why do people cohabit? What characteristics describe people who cohabit?
- What are the most important factors in creating stable marriages?
- What factors are responsible for the success of long-term marriages?
- What are the major reasons people get divorced?
- What are the characteristics of grandparenthood and great-grandparenthood?
- What are the stresses and uplifts of caring for a family member?

11.3 Family Dynamics Across Adulthood

Key Questions

- What are the major factors involved in the decision to become a parent?
- How does the parental role affect most adults' lives?
- What are the similarities and differences across various structural forms of parenting?
- What are some major issues that confront middle-aged parents?

Tylawn, 32, and Denise, 33, just had their first child, D'Andre, after several years of trying. They've heard that having children in their 30s can have advantages, but Tylawn and Denise wonder whether people are just saying that to be nice to them. They are also concerned about the financial obligations they are likely to face.

Tylawn and Denise are increasingly typical of first-time parents, as more people than ever delay having children. As all parents discover, having a child changes everything. New parents are often overwhelmed with the responsibility.

In this module, we consider the dynamics of families, from deciding whether to have children through caring for aging parents and grandparenthood. As we do so, we must recognize the concept of "family" is undergoing change. Families are defined by the U.S. Census Bureau as a group of two or more people residing together related by birth, marriage, or adoption. Based on this definition, in 2020 there were 83.7 million families in the United States with an average size of about 3 people. In about 50 million families, there were no children under the age of 18, and about roughly 16 million were headed by a solo parent (Statista, 2021).

Deciding to Become a Parent

> "I'm afraid of losing my partner because they want kids, and I don't know what I want. I think I don't want them."
>
> "I'm afraid of losing my identity, career, freedom, and comfort if I have children. Afraid of regretting it if I don't."
>
> "I've always wanted to have a baby, but is it even ethical, knowing the environmental and political climate?"

You may have heard people ask (or perhaps asked yourself) these or similar questions as they confront one of the biggest decisions partnered people (and many singles) make—whether to have children. You would think that potential parents weigh the many benefits of child rearing—such as feeling personal satisfaction, fulfilling personal needs, continuing the family line, and enjoying companionship—with the many drawbacks—including expenses and lifestyle changes. But you would be wrong. This is not what most people actually do.

Rijken (2009; Rijken & Knijn, 2009) reports most potential parents actually don't think deliberately or deeply about when to have a child, and those who are career-oriented or like their freedom do not often deliberately postpone parenthood because of those factors. Rather, thoughts about having children are implicit and do not cross their minds in advance of actually having children, mainly because most societies take for granted the belief that everyone wants, or should want, to have children. Subsequent research supports these findings. In addition to thinking about the financial implications of having a child, people who are thinking about it talk with others who have children, apply their religious or spiritual beliefs, create a pros-and-cons list, and think about with whom they should have a child (Lorenzo-Echeverri, 2020).

It's more likely that individuals struggle mightily with this decision for many years (Davidman, 2021; Frizzell, 2021). Professionals who counsel people going through this decision process strongly emphasize that struggling with it is both very, very common and that ultimately, the decision is a highly personal one based on a complex set of interconnected factors. The most important step is taking the time to discern what one really wants (what their "heart's desire" is about the prospect of parenthood; Davidman, 2021) and what they intend to do about it (making the actual decision). Getting the desire and the decision in sync is the source of the struggle, a process that for some feels like panic (Frizzell, 2021).

Many first-time parents did not think systematically about the implications of having a child before they became parents.

Whether the pregnancy is planned or not (more than half of all U.S. pregnancies are unplanned), a first pregnancy is a milestone life event, with both benefits and stresses (Lavner & Bradbury, 2017; Lorenzo-Echeverri, 2020; Meijer & van den Wittenboer, 2007). Parents largely agree children add affection, improve family ties, and give parents a feeling of immortality and sense of accomplishment. Most parents willingly sacrifice a great deal for their children and hope they grow up to be happy and successful. In this way, children bring happiness to many parents' relationships.

Nevertheless, finances are of great concern to most parents because children are expensive. How expensive? According to U.S. average data adjusted for inflation, a typical middle-class family who had a child born in 2022 would spend about $275,000 for food, housing, and other necessities by the time the child turns 18 years old (Parker, 2022). College expenses would be additional. The actual total cost varies across socioeconomic status, with those at lower income levels spending somewhat less and those at the highest levels spending somewhat more. These costs do not differ significantly between two-parent and solo-parent households but clearly are a bigger financial burden for one-earner households. Annual costs vary across different types of expenses and with the age of the child. The main point is that having and raising a child is a very expensive proposition, and people are right to be concerned about it.

For many reasons that include personal choice, financial instability, and infertility, an increasing number of couples are choosing to be childfree. Social attitudes in many countries (Austria, Germany, Great Britain, Ireland, Netherlands, and United States) are improving toward childfree couples (Blackstone & Stewart, 2016; Gubernskaya, 2010; Smith et al., 2020; Stahnke et al., 2020).

Childfree couples have some advantages: more personal freedom and higher standards of living on average. Yet, they also must deal with societal expectations regarding having children and may feel defensive about their decision not to be a parent (e.g., Smith et al., 2020). A major international study of older adult couples without children in Australia, Finland, Germany, Japan, the Netherlands, the United Kingdom, and the United States revealed highly similar patterns across all countries except Japan (Koropeckyj-Cox & Call, 2007). In Japan, the cultural norm of children caring for older parents created difficulties for childfree older couples. In other countries, older adults make other arrangements if they need care, such as home health aides.

The factors that influence the decision to be childfree differ for women and men (Smith et al., 2020; Stahnke et al., 2020; Waren & Pals, 2013). For women, higher levels of education and economic factors increase the likelihood of remaining childfree, whereas holding traditional gender role beliefs decreases the chances of that decision. For men, though, neither education nor economic factors predict deciding to remain childfree, but traditional gender role beliefs lower the odds of that decision.

A trend that was exacerbated by the COVID-19 pandemic is that parents in the United States typically have fewer children and have their first child later than parents did in the past. The average age at the time of the birth of a first child is nearly 27 for women and 31 for men (Stahl, 2020). This average age has been increasing steadily since 1970 as a result of many women postponing having children because they marry later, they want to establish careers first, or they make a deliberate choice to delay childbearing for other reasons. Even though it has increased, the average age for women having a first child in the United States is actually lower than it is for women in other developed countries—the average in other developed countries is 31 years old (Stahl, 2020).

One result of delaying having children is a declining birth rate. The United States has been on a decades-long downward trend. In fact, the birthrate had hit an all-time low at 58.3 births per 1,000 women in 2019, before the COVID-19 pandemic (Barroso, 2021). That trend continued during the COVID-19 pandemic, declining further to 55.8 per 1,000 women in 2020 (Centers for Disease Control and Prevention, 2022d). The reasons for these continuing declines are complex and not easily explained, and have continued across multiple generations (Kearney et al., 2022).

Being older at the birth of one's first child is advantageous. Older mothers, like Denise in the vignette, tend to be more at ease being parents, spend more time with their babies and are more affectionate, sensitive, and supportive to them. In addition, there is usually a higher maternal investment in middle childhood and less child-perceived conflict in adolescence (Camberis et al., 2016; Helfrecht et al., 2020; Schlomer & Belsky, 2012). Fathers' age also makes a difference in how they interact with children (Cutler & Palkovitz, 2020; Palkovitz & Palm, 2009). Compared to men who become fathers in their 20s, men such as Tylawn who become fathers in their 30s are generally more invested in their paternal role and spend up to three times as much time caring for their preschool children as younger fathers do. Father involvement has increased significantly, due in part to social attitudes that support it (Fogarty & Evans, 2010; Palkovitz, 2020). Research clearly indicates that being a father is an important aspect of men's lives across adulthood (Marsiglio & Roy, 2013; Palkovitz, 2020).

Parenting skills do not come naturally, and they are arguably the most important skills that are not routinely taught in school. As a result, most people learn "on the job" and by talking with others (e.g., their own parents, friends, trusted mentors). Having a child changes all aspects of people's lives. Children place a great deal of stress on relationships. Parenthood requires major commitment and cooperation. Parenthood may create disagreements over division of household chores between partners, especially if both are employed outside the home (discussed in Chapter 12). Even when mothers are employed outside the home (and roughly 70% of women with children under age 18 in the United States are), they still perform most of the child-rearing tasks. Even when fathers take employment leave, although more likely to share tasks, they still do not spend more time with children than fathers who do not take leave (Seward & Stanley-Stevens, 2014).

The United States is the only major industrialized country not to require employers to provide paid leave for new parents (or for dependent or self-care in general). Although some states and cities have passed laws requiring paid parental leave, most have not. The Controversies feature explores the issue of paid parental leave in more detail.

Controversies

Paid Family Leave: Bulgaria Provides a Year; the United States Provides Nothing

Does your employer provide paid time off if you have a new child? In order to care for an ill child or older parent? If you have a serious illness or need to recover after surgery? If so, you are fortunate. One of the biggest needs for most employees is access to these types of benefits, especially employees in smaller organizations or employers that do not provide paid time off. In fact, the United States is the only developed country that has neither a national government program nor an employer mandate to provide such benefits (A Better Balance, 2021). Bulgaria provides a year of paid leave, and about 40 other developed nations provide at least several months.

The Family and Medical Leave Act of 1993 (FMLA) is the only national program in the United States. It requires employers to provide unpaid leave for up to 12 weeks for employees to care for a new child or seriously ill family member, to recover from one's own serious health condition, or to deal with certain obligations (including childcare and related activities) arising from a spouse, parent, or child being on, or called to, active duty in the military. The FMLA also provides up to 26 weeks of unpaid leave per year for workers whose spouse, child, parent, or next of kin is a seriously ill or injured member of the armed services (A Better Balance, 2021).

However, due to the specific provisions that create coverage gaps in the law, roughly 40% of employees are not covered. The unpaid nature of the law means that only those who can afford to lose their income take the leave.

A few states have taken the lead to create paid family leave programs. For example, California, Colorado, Connecticut, the District of Columbia, Massachusetts, New Jersey, New York, Oregon, Rhode Island, and Washington have some type of paid leave. (Find out what the policy is in your home state.) Many advocates and employees agree that paid leave for family reasons is important. Many businesses do as well. Evidence is strong that being able to care for one's family or oneself improves well-being and helps the employee be more productive.

But there are problems with most paid leave programs in the United States. Most important, they do not provide 100% of a person's income during the leave. For example, at the time it was implemented, the Washington, DC, program only provides a maximum of $1,000 per week, well below the median salary. Failure to provide full income means that some people who need the leave will be unable to afford it. Thus, even though these laws are well intentioned, they end up discriminating against people who are unable to afford the decrease in income to take the leave.

Can you think of other ways that such laws may not reflect the full diversity of U.S. adults who need paid leave programs? What do you think should be done?

The COVID-19 pandemic made parenting even more stressful than it usually is. Two areas provide examples. First, the pandemic widened gender differences in who performs childcare. As Kashen and colleagues (2020) note, the impact of the loss of the childcare infrastructure fell hardest on women, who ended up spending much more time on childcare tasks than did men, resulting in significant potential damage to women's careers.

Second, the pandemic added the role of "teacher" to most parents' already full to-do list. When schools closed in spring 2020 and classes shifted to online, parents immediately became at-home teachers to support their child's learning. Beyond the equity issues of differential access to broadband internet and devices required for online learning, the extra demands on parents' time were substantial. Bansak and Starr (2021) found that parents and children spent significantly more time in learning activities when their schools provided multiple types of learning activities, especially live contact time with teachers; live contact hours also helped children learn on their own. Perhaps the most interesting finding was that parents with secondary-level education spent no less time helping children than parents with a college education, although they faced significantly more problems with computer and internet access. Thus, all parents tried to help their children continue learning in the pandemic, even given wide differences in the resources they could supply to mitigate the loss of "normal" learning in school. But as we will document in Chapter 12, deciding to help one's child learn came at a cost to the parent's, usually mother's, career.

Diversity and Approaches to Parenting. Racial and ethnic background matters a great deal in terms of family structure and the parent–child relationship. Overall, most Black parents provide a parenting environment that exists within a context of strong religious beliefs (Murray & Hwang, 2020; Smith-Bynum, 2013; Teachman et al., 2013), interest in education, pride in cultural heritage, self-respect, and cooperation with the family (Coles, 2016; Riley, 2020). Within these contexts, generations of systemic racism have had a significant effect on Black parents. For example, Miller and Vittrup (2020) found that most of the participants in their study reported engaging in various forms of preparation for racial bias with their children. For many, this was done in order to ensure their children's survival. Despite the negative and sometimes traumatic experiences, participants indicated that they found strength primarily in their faith and their families. Other researchers have documented the need for and the difficulties Black parents report about having "The Talk," especially with their sons, about how to interact with the police (Anderson et al., 2020). These experiences were among the factors that led to the creation of the Black Lives Matter movement.

As a result of several generations of oppression, many Native American parents have not been taught the traditional parenting skills that were part of their culture: that children were valued, women were considered sacred and honored, and men cared for and provided for their families (Aisenstein & Rueda, 2019; Davis et al., 2014). Thus, restoring and retaining a strong sense of cultural identity is an important consideration for Native American families. Indeed, research suggests that Native American parents receive more support from extended family in child rearing than do White parents on average (Limb et al., 2014). Most important is that for Native Americans, extended family includes people who are related biologically as well as those who are not but are considered special, all of whom perform specific roles (Coser et al., 2020). This support helps with the transmission of cultural values.

Over 26% of all children under 18 in the United States are Latino/a, and most are at least second generation (Kids Count, 2020). This percentage has been growing steadily over many years. Latino/a families tend to demonstrate two key values: familism and the extended family. **Familism** **refers to the idea the well-being of the family takes precedence over the concerns of individual family members.** This value is a defining characteristic of Latino/a families (Gonzalez & Quinones, 2021). For example, Brazilian and Mexican families consider familism a cultural strength and one factor that holds them together (Carlo et al., 2007; Padilla et al., 2020). Indeed, familism is an important factor in why many Latino/a college students live at home (Desmond & López Turley, 2009). The extended family (relatives beyond parents and children living together) is also strong among Latino/a families and serves as the venue for a wide range of exchanges of goods and services, such as childcare and financial support, and discussions of difficult topics such as sexuality (Estrada-Martinez et al., 2021).

Asian Americans hold a complex racial position in the United States. Like other people of color, they have long been the target of explicit discrimination, such as the Chinese Exclusion Act of 1882, and Japanese Americans were the only group interred during World War II solely on racial fears. This history is complicated by an increased public focus on socioracial injustices in the United States experienced by racial groups (e.g., the Black Lives Matter movement). Research has found that discussions about race and ethnicity occur within Asian American families but often focus on cultural heritage rather than on an explicit awareness of discrimination and the historical roots of racism. Increasingly, younger members of Asian American families are teaching their parents about race, and express feeling left out of broader discussions about race (Young et al., 2021).

Asian American families also demonstrate the concept of familism, often through very high feelings of obligation to their families compared with White Americans. This is demonstrated typically in perceived obligatory care provision for older parents by their oldest son, although in fact, most care is

KaliI9/E+/Getty Images

Multiethnic families face special challenges in order to transmit cultural traditions.

done by daughters or daughters-in-law, not sons (Rodriguez-Galán, 2014). Contrary to commonly portrayed stereotypes, Asian American families do not represent the "model minority," but experience the same challenges with parenting as all other groups (Xia et al., 2013; Zhou & Bankston, 2020). In general, men enjoy higher status in traditional Asian families (Tsuno & Homma, 2009). Among recent immigrants, though, women are expanding their role by working outside the home, especially if they are the first in their family to arrive (He & Gerber, 2020).

Raising multiracial and multiethnic children presents social challenges not experienced by parents of same-race children (Colman, 2020; Sanchez et al., 2020). For example, parents of biracial children report feeling discrimination and being targets of prejudicial behavior from others (Franco et al., 2020). These parents also worry that their children may be rejected by members of both racial communities. Perhaps that is why parents of multiracial children tend to provide more economic and cultural resources to their children than do parents of single-race children (Cheng & Powell, 2007; Werum et al., 2018).

In multiethnic families, you might think that all parents help negotiate how to approach cultural and ethnic aspects of a multiracial child's upbringing. However, it is mothers who are key in most respects, regardless of racial and ethnic combinations of the parents (Harris et al., 2020; Schlabach, 2013). For example, a study of children of European mothers and Maori fathers in New Zealand found that the mothers played a major role in establishing the child's Maori identity, even though the mothers were not Maori (Kukutai, 2007). Race-based classification, and discriminatory behaviors resulting from it, has a long history in New Zealand and other countries (Didham & Rocha, 2020) that is part of the information transmitted to children. As multiracial and multiethnic families increase in the United States, research will be needed to document the experiences of both the parents and the children, and inquire about how those experiences are similar to or differ from those of same-race, same-ethnicity families.

Diverse Family Forms

The traditional family form of two married parents with their biological children does not reflect the wide diversity of family forms in U.S. society. You may be in, or know people who live in, one of these many forms. Let's consider several.

Solo Parents. About 40% of births in the United States currently are to unmarried individuals who give birth, a rate that has declined 14% since peaking in 2008 (National Center for Health Statistics, 2022a). Digging a bit deeper, there is considerable diversity in what is meant by an "unmarried" parent, as is documented in Figure 11.8. Among White and Black parents, the majority of unmarried mothers are in a cohabiting relationship, but fathers are about evenly split between solo parenting and cohabiting parenting. Unmarried Latino/a and Asian American parents are both roughly evenly split between solo and cohabiting. These trends reflect the increases in cohabitation discussed earlier.

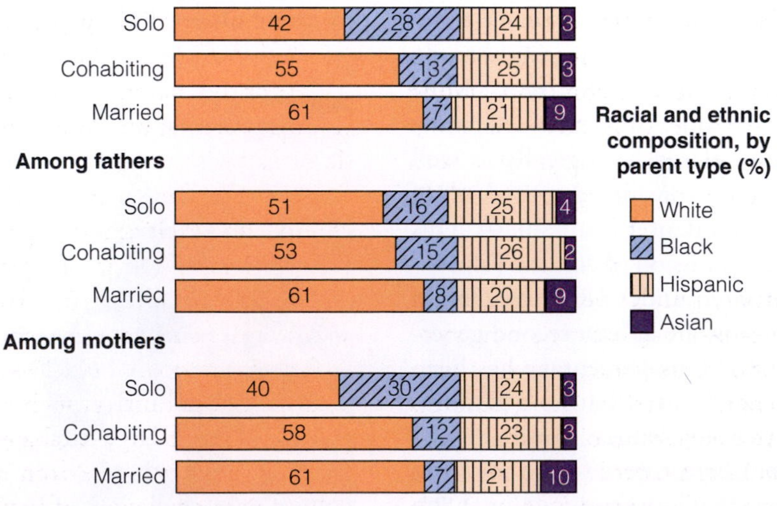

Figure 11.8 Characteristics of solo, cohabiting, and married parents.

Source: Pew Research Center (2018). The changing nature of unmarried parents: A growing share are living with a partner. https://www.pewsocialtrends.org/2018/04/25/the-changing-profile-of-unmarried-parents/.

Solo parents face considerable obstacles, but also experience many joys of parenting (Van Gasse & Mortelmans, 2020). Integrating the roles of work and parenthood are more difficult, as one person functionally does the work equivalent of two (or more). Loneliness among solo parents is a common feeling that was greatly exacerbated during the COVID-19 pandemic due to fewer options to get together with friends and family (Sharma et al., 2020). Loneliness is also a key issue when children grow up and leave or are visiting the noncustodial parent (Langlais et al., 2016). Financially, solo parents are usually less well-off than their married counterparts, especially solo mothers who also have to contend with gender-related wage discrimination (more about this in Chapter 12). Having only one source of income puts additional pressure on solo parents to provide all of the necessities. Because the United States does not have a subsidized system of childcare, many solo parents cannot afford it and rely on relatives and friends, and sometimes must forego career advancement as a result of the inability to find reliable, affordable childcare.

A particular concern for many solo parents is dating (Plumm et al., 2016). Several common questions are asked by solo parents about dating: "How do I become available (again)?" "How will my children react?" "How do I cope with my own sexual needs?" They have reason to be concerned. Research indicates that single parents tend to report that children may interfere with dating and romance (Sommer et al., 2013). They report feeling insecure about sexuality and wondering how they should behave around their children in terms of having partners stay overnight (Langlais et al., 2016; Lampkin-Hunter, 2010).

Military families experience unique aspects of temporary solo parenting. When one parent in a two-parent household deploys, the remaining parent becomes a solo parent. Separation anxiety is common among deployed parents, and the cycling of experience as a solo parent and partner in a two-parent household with both parents present can create stress (Mogil et al., 2019; Wadsworth et al., 2014).

Step-, Foster-, Adoptive, and Same-Sex Couple Parenting. Roughly one-third of parents become stepparents, foster parents, or adoptive parents at some time during their lives. In general, there are few differences among parents who have their own biological children or who become parents in some other way, but there are some unique challenges (Creating a Family, 2021; Ganong & Coleman, 2017).

A concern for foster parents, adoptive parents, and stepparents is how strongly the child will bond with them. Although infants less than 1 year old will probably bond well, children who are old enough to have formed attachments with their biological parents may have competing loyalties. For example, some stepchildren remain strongly attached to the noncustodial parent and actively resist attempts to integrate them into the new family ("My real mother wouldn't make me do that"), or they may exhibit behavioral problems. As a result, the dynamics in blended families can best be understood as a complex system (Kumar, 2017). Stepparents must often deal with continued visitation by the noncustodial parent, which may exacerbate any difficulties. These problems are a major reason that second marriages are at high risk for dissolution, as discussed later in this chapter. They are also a major reason why behavioral and emotional problems are more common among stepchildren (Ganong & Coleman, 2017).

In many cases, stepchildren, foster children, and adoptive children enter into families in which children are already present. This creates what is known as *transition days* in which the new family member arrives. Research indicates that the more preparation parents make for the transition among all current and future family members, the smoother the transition tends to go (Ganong et al., 2019; Perry & Fraser, 2020).

Still, many stepparents and stepchildren ultimately develop good relationships with each other (Coleman et al., 2013; Ganong et al., 2019). Stepparents must be sensitive to the relationship between the stepchild and their biological, noncustodial parent. Allowing stepchildren to develop a relationship with the stepparent at their own pace also helps. What style of stepparenting ultimately develops is influenced by the expectations of the stepparent, stepchild, spouse, and nonresidential parent (Ganong & Coleman, 2017; Ganong et al., 2019).

Adoptive parents also contend with attachment to birth parents, but in different ways. Adopted children may wish to locate and meet their birth parents. Such searches can strain the relationships between these children and their adoptive parents, who may interpret these actions as a form of rejection (Curtis & Pearson, 2010; Waterfield, 2020). An increasingly common approach is using genetic testing through such services such as Ancestry.com and 23 and Me (Lee et al., 2021). Though not definitive, such tests are inexpensive and provide access to large databases for potential matches.

Families with children adopted from another culture pose challenges of how to establish and maintain connection with the child's ethno-racial culture of origin (Darnell et al., 2017; Simon, 2020; Yngvesson, 2010). For mothers of transnationally adopted Chinese and Korean children, becoming connected to the appropriate Asian American community is a way to accomplish this (Johnston et al., 2007; Lecy, 2020). Research in the Netherlands found children adopted from Colombia, Sri Lanka, and Korea into Dutch homes struggled with looking different, and many expressed desires to be white (Juffer, 2006). Canadian parents who adopted children from China took several different approaches to introducing their children to Chinese culture, from not at all ("my child is simply Canadian") to deliberately blending both cultures to leaving it up to the child (Bian et al., 2015).

Foster parents have the most tenuous relationship with their children because the bond can be broken for any of a number of reasons having nothing to do with the quality of the care being provided. Dealing with attachment is difficult; foster parents want to provide secure homes, but they may not have the children long enough to establish continuity. Furthermore, because many children in foster care have found it difficult or have been unable to form attachments at all, they are less likely to form ones that will inevitably be broken. Despite the challenges, placement in good foster care results in the development of attachment between foster parents and children who were placed out of institutional settings (Alper & Howe, 2017; Smyke et al., 2010).

Finally, many in the LGBTQIA+ communities also want to be parents. Although changes in laws regarding same-sex couples and parenting have changed in important ways, legal and social barriers remain regarding adoption and foster parenting options (Frank, 2016; Levitt et al., 2020). Some have biological children themselves, whereas others choose adoption or foster parenting where that is possible.

Research indicates that children reared by gay or lesbian parents do not experience any more problems than children reared by heterosexual parents and are as psychologically healthy as children of heterosexual parents (Bos et al., 2016; Frank, 2016). Substantial evidence exists that children raised by gay or lesbian parents do not develop sexual identity problems or any other problems any more than children raised by heterosexual parents, disproving the myth that children of gay/lesbian parents would be more likely to have identity problems (Goldberg, 2009). Children of gay and lesbian parents were no more likely than children of heterosexual parents to identify as LGBTQIA+.

Adult children of gay or lesbian parents might be better adjusted than adult children of heterosexual parents in that they exhibit lower levels of homophobia and less fear of negative evaluation than do the adult children of heterosexual parents. Gay men are often especially concerned about being good and nurturing fathers, and they try hard to raise their children with nonsexist, egalitarian attitudes (Goldberg, 2009; Patterson, 2013). Evidence suggests that gay parents have more egalitarian sharing of child rearing than do fathers in heterosexual households (Biblarz & Savci, 2010).

Emerging research on transgender parents reveals the complexities of coming out, and of social perception and discrimination against transgender people (Pfeffer & Jones, 2020). Much more research is needed to better understand family dynamics in these, as well as queer, nonbinary, and other members of the LGBTQIA+ communities.

These data will not eliminate the controversy, much of which is based on long-held beliefs (often religion-based) and prejudices. In the United States, the topic of LGBTQIA+ couples' right to be parents is likely to continue to play out in political agendas for years to come.

Family Dynamics in Midlife

Family ties across the generations provide the context for socialization and for continuity in the family's identity. Families tend to have certain members of the middle generation who keep track of family history by doing such things as collecting pictures from different generations, important documents, and so on, as well as serve as the links between the older generation and their own maturing children (Chai et al., 2020; Deane et al., 2016; Fingerman et al., 2012; Infurna et al., 2020). Middle-aged women (more than men) tend to take on this role of **kinkeeper**, the person who gathers family members together across generations for celebrations and keeps them in touch with each other.

Think about the major issues confronting many middle-aged parents: maintaining good relationships with one's children, adjusting parenting responsibilities, dealing with children who are becoming adults themselves, handling job pressures and potential employment and financial insecurity, and worrying about aging parents, just to name a few. Middle-aged adults truly have a lot to deal with every day in balancing their responsibilities to themselves, as well as perhaps their spouse/partner, their children, and their aging parents (Boyczuk & Fletcher, 2016; Infurna et al., 2020). Indeed, middle-aged adults are sometimes referred to as the **sandwich generation** because they are caught between the competing demands of two generations: their children and their own aging parents. Add to these responsibilities those of taking care of oneself, and you get the situation—being middle-aged isn't always easy.

Letting Go: Middle-Aged Parents and Their Children. Sometime during middle age, most parents across numerous cultures experience two developments with regard to their children (Buhl, 2008; Vosylis, 2021): their children consider them in a new light that usually results in a better relationship, and the children leave home.

The extent to which parents support and approve of their children's attempts at being independent adults matters. Most parents across cultures manage the transition successfully (Koffer et al., 2022; Padmadas et al., 2021). That's not to say the transition is without challenges. When children leave home, emotional bonds are disrupted. Mothers across most ethnic groups report feeling sad at the time children leave but have positive feelings about the potential for growth in their relationships with their children (Feldman, 2010). Parents provide considerable emotional support (by staying in touch) and financial help (such as paying college tuition, providing a [sometimes free] place to live until the child finds employment) when possible (Farris, 2016; Pinsker, 2020).

A positive experience with adult children leaving home is strongly influenced by the extent the parents perceive a job well done and their children have turned out well (Farris, 2016; Padmadas et al., 2021; Vosylis, 2021). Children are regarded as successes when they meet parents' culturally based developmental expectations, and they are regarded as "good kids" when there is agreement between parents and children in basic values.

Maskot/Getty Images

Adult children moving back with their parents increased during the COVID-19 pandemic.

There are some key differences cross-culturally, though. In China, for example, parents in general report a smooth process, but those who do not may end up with no significant support from their child in later life (Padmadas et al., 2021).

Parents' experience with the empty nest (the name colloquially describing the time after the last child leaves home) is sometimes short-lived. Prior to the COVID-19 pandemic, roughly half of young adults in the United States returned to their parents' home at least once after moving out (Farris, 2016); that number grew by nearly 3 million in just the first three months of the COVID-19 pandemic (Pinsker, 2020). There is evidence these emerging adults, called "boomerang kids" (Farris, 2016; Mitchell, 2006; Pinsker, 2020), are increasingly viewing this as a necessary and acceptable living arrangement.

Why do children move back? The most important impetus is financial: the increased costs of living on their own when saddled with college debt, especially if the societal economic situation is bad and jobs are not available. This was especially true during both the Great Recession and during the COVID-19 pandemic. It also reflects the different kinds of relationships millennial and gen-Z adults have with their parents and a different attitude about living back at home compared with previous generations (Farris, 2016; Pinsker, 2020).

Grandparenthood and Great-Grandparenthood

Becoming a grandparent takes some help—it is your children's decisions and actions that determine whether you experience the transition to grandparenthood, making this role different from most others we experience throughout life.

Most people become grandparents in their 40s and 50s, though some are older, or perhaps as young as their late 20s or early 30s. For many middle-aged adults, becoming a grandparent is a peak experience (Hoffman et al., 2012; van de Goor et al., 2020). Although most research on grandparenting has been conducted with respect to heterosexual grandparents, attention to LGBTQIA+ grandparents is increasing as these family forms become more common and visible (Allen & Lavender-Stott, 2020; Allen & Roberto, 2016; Orel & Fruhauf, 2013).

How Do Grandparents Interact with Grandchildren? Grandparents have many different ways of interacting with their grandchildren. Categorizing these styles has been attempted over many decades (e.g., Neugarten & Weinstein, 1964), but none of these attempts has been particularly successful because grandparents use different styles with different grandchildren and styles change as grandparents and grandchildren age (Gardiner, 2020; Gonyea, 2013; Hoffman et al., 2012).

An alternative cross-cultural approach involves considering the many functions grandparents serve and the changing nature of families (Gardiner, 2020). The social dimension includes societal needs and expectations of what grandparents are to do, such as influencing emotional and cognitive growth and passing on family history to grandchildren. The personal dimension includes how well their individual needs are fulfilled by being a grandparent. Many grandparents pass on skills—as well as religious, social, and vocational values (social dimension)—through storytelling and advice, and may feel great pride and satisfaction (personal dimension) from working with grandchildren on joint projects.

Grandchildren give grandparents a great deal in return. Grandchildren keep grandparents in touch with youth and the latest trends. Sharing visits through video chat may be one way grandchildren keep grandparents updated about their lives.

Being a Grandparent Is Meaningful. Being a grandparent really matters. Most grandparents derive multiple meanings, and they are linked with generativity (Gardiner, 2020; Hayslip & Blumenthal, 2016). For some, grandparenting is the most important thing in their lives. For others, meaning comes from being considered wise, from spoiling grandchildren, from recalling the relationship they had with their own grandparents, or from taking pride in the fact they will be followed by not one but two generations.

Grandchildren also tend to highly value their relationships with grandparents, even when they are young adults (Alley, 2004; Bates & Taylor, 2016; Hayslip & Blumenthal, 2016; Wetzel & Hank, 2020). Grandparents can be valued as role models as well as for their personalities, the activities they share, and the attention they give to grandchildren. Emerging adult grandchildren (ages 21–29) derive both stress and rewards from caring for grandparents, much the same way middle-aged adults do when they care for their aging parents (D'Amen et al., 2021; Fruhauf et al., 2006; Wetzel & Hank, 2020).

Ethnic and Racial Differences in Grandparenting. How grandparents and grandchildren interact varies in different ethnic and racial groups (Gardiner, 2020), but researchers have known for decades that grandparents in families of color are viewed as responsible for cultural socialization, such as the transmission of language, cultural values, traditions, and activities to their grandchildren (Kataoka-Yahiro et al., 2004).

Black grandparents play an important role in many aspects of their grandchildren's lives, such as family storytelling (Fabius, 2016), hair styling (Mbilishaka et al., 2020), parenting information (Woods Barr et al., 2021), and religious education (King et al., 2006; Lewis et al., 2011). Similarly, Latino/a grandparents are more likely to emphasize a cultural core value of family (Burnette, 1999).

Native American grandparents are important in their grandchildren's lives, especially when the grandchildren live in urban settings and are reasonably close by (Limb et al., 2014). Research indicates Native American grandparents also use their own experiences of cultural disruption to reinvest in their grandchildren to ensure the continuity of culture (Thompson et al., 2013).

Asian American grandparents, particularly if they are immigrants, serve as a primary source of traditional culture for their grandchildren (Yoon, 2005). When these grandparents become heavily involved in caring for their grandchildren, they especially want and need services that are culturally and linguistically appropriate.

Gunter Marx/Alamy Stock Photo

How grandparents and grandchildren interact varies across cultures.

Beyond their role in transmitting general sociocultural norms to their grandchildren, some grandparents across ethnic groups may serve as gatekeepers of their own ethnicity and make it clear to grandchildren that they do not approve of a multiracial/multiethnic view (Jackson et al., 2020). Specifically, some grandparents may use microaggressions to send a message about the importance of maintaining the grandparent's own ethnic customs only, or make fun of grandchildren who do not become fluent in the grandparent's language of origin.

When Grandparents Care for Grandchildren. Grandparenthood today is more difficult than it used to be. Families are more mobile, which means grandparents are more often separated from their grandchildren by geographical distance. Grandparents also are more likely to have independent lives apart from their children and grandchildren. What being a grandparent entails in the 21st century is more ambiguous than it once was (Hayslip & Blumenthal, 2016; Hyer et al., 2017).

Perhaps the biggest change worldwide for grandparents is the increasing number serving as custodial parents or primary care providers for their grandchildren (Choi et al., 2016; McCarthy, 2021). Estimates are that nearly 3 million grandparents in the United States provide basic needs (food, shelter, clothing) for one or more of their grandchildren (Generations United, 2021). Families headed by a grandparent may be referred to as **grandfamilies**. Grandfamilies in the United States result from several factors (Choi et al., 2016): the parents are employed outside the home; the parents are deceased; the parents have substance use disorders, are incarcerated, or are unable to raise their children; or discipline or behavior problems are such that the grandchild is placed with a grandparent.

Grandfamilies are also found globally. In many parts of the world the reasons are similar to those in the United States. In some areas, though, other major reasons are the death of parents due to, for example, disease (e.g., HIV/AIDS, epidemics) or war. For example, in Uganda grandparents caring for grandchildren reported significant levels of physical, financial, emotional, and social stress while stating it was important for them to ensure their grandchildren received good care (Matovu & Wallhagen, 2020).

Because most grandparents in this situation do not always have legal custody of their grandchild, legal problems and challenges such as dealing with schools and obtaining school or health records are frequent. Typically, social service workers assist grandparents in navigating the many unresponsive policies and systems they encounter when trying to provide the best possible assistance to their grandchildren (Cox, 2007, 2019). Clearly, public policy changes are needed to address these issues, especially regarding grandparents' legal rights concerning schools and health care for their grandchildren (Grandfamilies.org, 2021).

Raising grandchildren is not easy. Financial stress, cramped living space, and social isolation are only some of the issues facing these grandparents (Choi et al, 2016; Generations United, 2021; Hayslip & Blumenthal, 2016). All of these stresses are reported cross-culturally; full-time grandmothers caring for grandchildren in Kenya and other sub-Saharan African countries reported higher levels of stress than part-time care providers (Mhaka-Mutepfa et al., 2017; Oburu & Palmérus, 2005).

Even custodial grandparents raising grandchildren without these problems report more stress and role disruption than noncustodial grandparents, though most grandparents are resilient and manage to cope (Hayslip & Blumenthal, 2016; Hayslip et al., 2013; Mendoza et al., 2020). Most custodial grandparents consider their situation better for their grandchild than any other alternative and report few negative effects on their marriages.

Great-Grandparenthood. With increasing numbers of people living to very old age, more people are experiencing great-grandparenthood. Age at first marriage and age at parenthood also play a critical role; people who reach these earlier milestones at relatively young ages are more likely to become great-grandparents.

Although surprisingly little research has been conducted on great-grandparents, their investment in their roles as parents, grandparents, and great-grandparents forms a single family identity (Castañeda-García et al., 2017; Even-Zohar & Garby, 2016). That is, great-grandparents experience a true continuity of the family through the passing on of genes as well as culture and traditions (Even-Zohar, 2019; Schuler & Brito Dias, 2021). However, their sources of satisfaction and meaning apparently differ from those of grandparents (Even-Zohar & Garby, 2016). Compared with grandparents, great-grandparents are more similar as a group in what they derive from the role, largely because they are less involved with the children than the grandparents are.

Three aspects of great-grandparenthood appear to be most important (Doka & Mertz, 1988; Schuler & Brito Dias, 2021). First, being a great-grandparent provides a sense of personal and family renewal—important components for achieving integrity. Their grandchildren have produced new life, renewing their own excitement for life and reaffirming the continuance of their lineage. Having their families stretch across four generations may also provide psychological support, through feelings of symbolic immortality, to help them face death. They take pride and comfort in knowing that their families will live many years beyond their own lifetime. Keeping the family together is a major source of meaning (Even-Zohar, 2019; Even-Zohar & Garby, 2016; Schuler & Brito Dias, 2021).

Second, great-grandchildren provide new diversions in great-grandparents' lives. There are now new people with whom they can share their experiences. Young children can learn from a person they perceive as "really old" (Mietkiewicz & Venditti, 2004).

Third, becoming a great-grandparent is a major milestone, a mark of longevity that most people never achieve. The sense that one has lived long enough to meet the fourth generation is perceived very positively (Schuler & Brito Dias, 2021).

As you might expect, people with at least one living grandparent and great-grandparent interact more with their grandparent, who is also perceived as more influential (Even-Zohar, 2019; Roberto & Skoglund, 1996). As more people live to very old age, it will be interesting to discover whether this pattern changes.

Caring for Family Members

Most middle-aged adults have parents who are in reasonably good health. But for nearly a quarter of adults, being a child of aging parents involves providing some level of care for them (Hyer et al., 2017; Infurna et al., 2020). How adult children become care providers varies, but the job of caring for older parents usually falls to a daughter or a daughter-in-law, mainly because of stereotypes of who should provide care (Barnett, 2013), especially in low income, low education situations (Waring, 2021). Sadly, data from surveys indicates that the primary care provider is unlikely to get much help from other family members (Northwestern Mutual, 2019). In Japan, even though the oldest son is culturally responsible for parental care, it is his wife who actually does the day-to-day caregiving for her own parents and her in-laws (Lee, 2010), though this traditional approach is changing (Umegaki-Constantini, 2017).

Across cultures, most adult children feel a sense of responsibility, termed **filial obligation**, to care for their parents if necessary. Most adult care providers express the feeling they "owe it to their parents" to care for them; after all, their parents provided for them for many years, and now the reverse is the case (Buchanan & Rotkirch, 2021; Gans, 2007; Nkimbeng & Parker, 2021). Adult children provide the majority of care when needed to their parents in all cultures studied (Barnett, 2013; Buchanan & Rotkirch, 2021; Haley, 2013; Lai, 2010; Nkimbeng & Parker, 2021). Almost none of the care provided in the United States is paid for by insurance or other means and very few care providers are compensated.

How many family members provide care to another family member or loved one? Roughly 53 million American adults care for someone with physical or mental disabilities, with 43 million providing unpaid care for people over age 50: older parents, in-laws, grandparents, and other older loved ones (National Alliance for Caregiving and AARP, 2020). Characteristics of care providers and changes from 2015 to 2020 are presented in Figure 11.9. Consider the typical care provider who is also a student. Reflecting the diversity of adults in post-secondary education, they are adults of color, 30.6 years old on average, and typically single. They usually care for a parent or grandparent (who is roughly 62 years old on average) who has a long-term physical condition and/or an emotional/mental health problem, and provide about 22 hours per week of care on top of their typical 32 hours per week of employment plus school.

Think for a moment about how extensive this informal care support is—and the fact that although many of us will be in this situation, very few of us have been taught even the basic aspects of caring for aging parents.

Stresses and Uplifts of Providing Care. Providing care is a major source of both stress and reward. Pearlin and colleagues (1990) provided a framework for understanding both. On the stress side, adult children and other family caregivers are especially vulnerable from two main sources:

- Adult children may have trouble coping with declines in their parents' functioning, especially those involving cognitive abilities and behaviors such as becoming physically violent, and with work overload, burnout, and the loss of the previous relationship characteristics with a parent.
- If the care situation is perceived as confining or seriously infringes on the adult child's other roles (spouse/partner, parent, employee, etc.), then the situation is likely to be perceived negatively, and that may lead to family or job conflicts, economic problems, loss of self-identity, and decreased sense of self-competence due to the number of "jobs" the person must balance.

When caring for an aging parent, even the most devoted adult child caregiver will at times feel depressed,

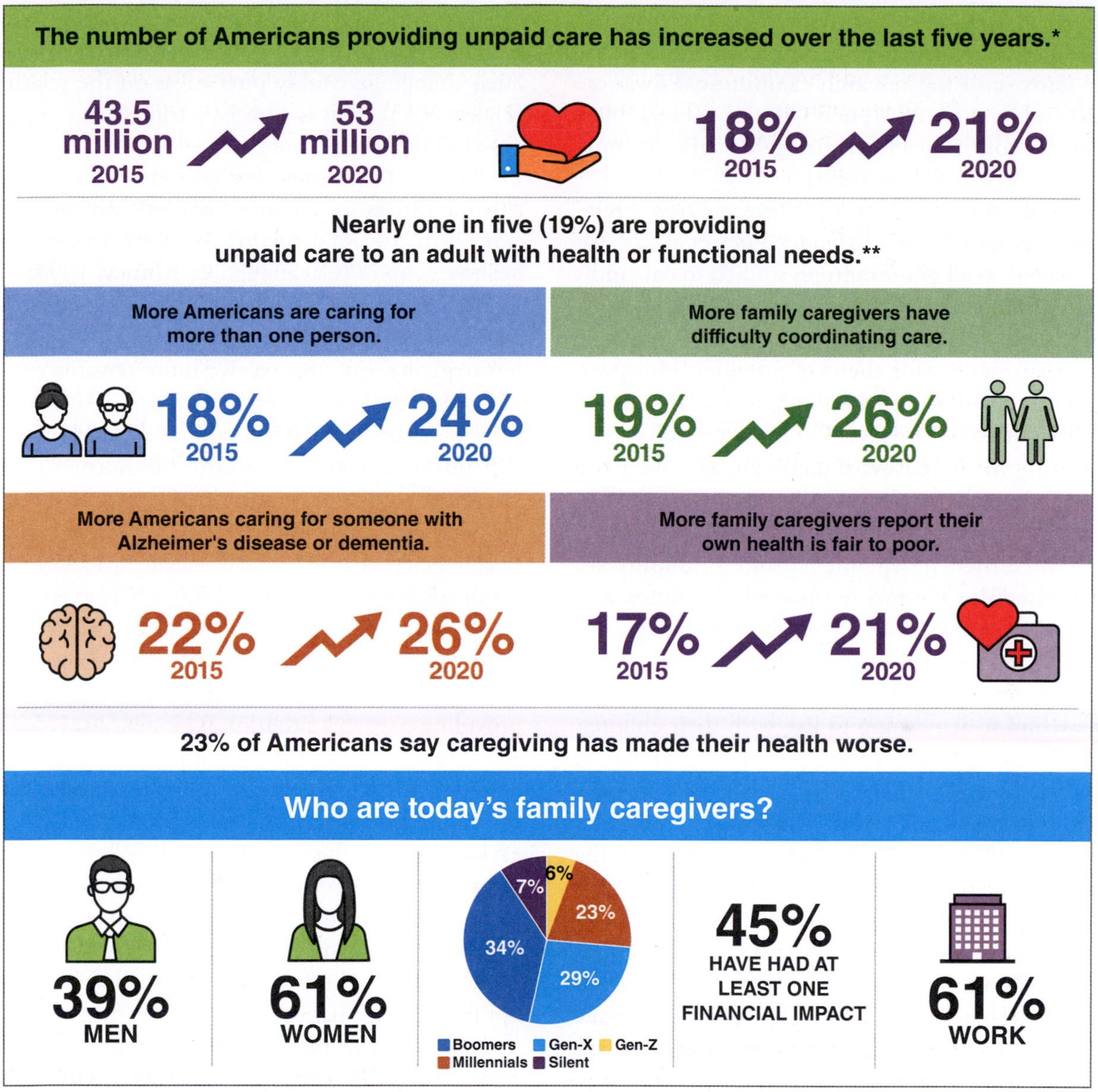

The number of Americans providing unpaid care has increased over the last five years.*
43.5 million 2015
53 million 2020
18% 2015
21% 2020
Nearly one in five (19%) are providing unpaid care to an adult with health or functional needs.**
More Americans are caring for more than one person.
18% 2015
24% 2020
More family caregivers have difficulty coordinating care.
19% 2015
26% 2020
More Americans caring for someone with Alzheimer's disease or dementia.
22% 2015
26% 2020
More family caregivers report their own health is fair to poor.
17% 2015
21% 2020
23% of Americans say caregiving has made their health worse.
Who are today's family caregivers?
39% MEN
61% WOMEN
7%
6%
23%
34%
29%
Boomers
Gen-X
Gen-Z
Millennials
Silent
45% HAVE HAD AT LEAST ONE FINANCIAL IMPACT
61% WORK

*Provided care to an adult or child with special needs.
**The remainder of this data is based on the 19% or 48 million caregivers caring for an adult.

Figure 11.9 Caregiving in the United States in 2020.
Source: National Alliance for Caregiving and AARP (2020).

resentful, angry, or guilty (Cavanaugh, 1999a; Haley, 2013; Hyer et al., 2017). Many middle-aged care providers are hard pressed financially: they may still be paying childcare or college tuition expenses, perhaps trying to save adequately for their own retirement, and having to work more than one job to do it. Financial pressures are especially serious for those caring for parents with chronic conditions, such as Alzheimer's disease, that require services, such as adult day care, not adequately covered by medical insurance. In some cases, adult children may quit their jobs to provide care if adequate alternatives, such as adult day care, are unavailable or unaffordable, usually creating even more financial stress.

The stresses of caring for a parent mean the care provider needs to carefully monitor their own health. Indeed, many professionals point out caring for the care provider is an important consideration to avoid care provider burnout (Ghosh et al., 2017; National Alliance for Caregiving, 2021; Tamayo et al., 2010).

On the plus side, caring for an aging parent also has rewards. Caring for aging parents can bring parents and their adult children closer together, provide a way for adult children to feel they are giving back, and provide a source of personal identity (Cooper, 2021; Miller et al., 2008). Cross-cultural research examining Taiwanese (Lee, 2007; Liu et al., 2021) and Chinese (Zhan, 2006) participants confirms adults caring for aging parents can find the experience rewarding.

Cultural values enter into the care providing relationship in an indirect way (Mendez-Luck et al., 2016). Care providers in all of the cultures studied to date indicate a common set of outcomes: care providers' stressors are appraised as burdensome, which creates negative health consequences for the care provider. However, cultural values influence the kinds of social support available to the care provider. For instance, cultures in which caring for parents is the norm may have more informal support services more widely available.

Things aren't always perfect from the parents' perspective, either. Independence and autonomy are important traditional values in some ethnic groups, and their loss is not taken lightly. Older adults in these groups are more likely to express the desire to pay a professional for assistance rather than ask a family member for help; they may find it demeaning to live with their children and express strong feelings about "not wanting to burden them" (Cahill et al., 2009). Most move in with their adult child only as a last resort. Many older adults who receive help with daily activities feel negatively about the situation, although cultural norms supporting the acceptance of help, such as in Japanese culture, significantly lessen those feelings (Park et al., 2013).

Determining whether older parents are satisfied with the help their children provide is a complex issue (Cahill et al., 2009; Park et al., 2013). Based on a critical review of the research, Newsom (1999) proposes a model of how certain aspects of care can produce negative perceptions of care directly or by affecting the interactions between care provider and care recipient (noted in Figure 11.10). The important thing to conclude from the model is even under the best circumstances, there is no guarantee the help adult children provide their parents will be well received. Misunderstandings can occur, and the frustration care providers feel may be translated directly into negative interactions.

When partners pledge their love to each other "in sickness and in health," most of them envision the sickness part to be no worse than an illness lasting a few weeks. That may be the case for many couples, but for others, the illness they experience severely tests their pledge. Caring for a chronically ill partner presents different challenges from caring for a chronically ill parent. The partner care provider assumes new roles, often without warning, after decades of a relationship based on a stable division of shared responsibilities. Such change inevitably puts stress on the relationship (Haley, 2013). This is especially true when one's partner has a debilitating chronic disease.

Studies of partner care providers of persons with chronic illness over many decades find that satisfaction with the relationship is much lower than for healthy couples (Cavanaugh & Kinney, 1994; Proulx, 2016; Thompson, 2021). Partner caregivers report a loss of companionship and intimacy over the course of caregiving, but also receive more rewards compared with adult child caregivers (Kimmel, 2014; Revenson et al., 2016; Shrestha et al., 2022). Marital satisfaction is also an important predictor of spousal caregivers' reports of symptoms of depression; the better the perceived quality of the marriage, the fewer symptoms caregivers report (Kinney & Cavanaugh, 1993), a finding that holds across racial/ethnic groups (Chiao et al., 2015).

Most partner care providers adopt the care role out of necessity. Interventions that help improve the functional level of the ill partner generally improve the care providing partner's situation (Cooper, 2021; Revenson et al., 2016). An important component of this is feeling competent as a partner care provider, which fits with the competence–environmental press model presented earlier in this chapter. Care providers attempt to balance their perceived competence with the environmental demands of caregiving. Perceived competence allows them to be proactive rather than merely reactive (and docile), which gives them a better chance to optimize their situation.

Even in the best of committed relationships, though, providing full-time care for a partner is both stressful and rewarding in terms of the relationship (Haley, 2013; Kimmel, 2014; Revenson et al., 2016; Shrestha et al., 2022). For example, coping with a wife who may not remember her partner's name, who may act strangely, and who has a chronic and fatal disease presents serious challenges even to the happiest of couples. Yet even in that situation, the care providing partner may experience no change in marital happiness despite the challenges presented by the disease.

Regardless of the relationship, providing care to a loved one is expensive in direct out-of-pocket cost and possible lost wages for having to cut back or quit one's job, and in the time it takes. AARP (2022a) estimates that the typical family care provider spends over $7,200 per year on household, medical, and other costs related to caring for a loved one, not counting any lost income.

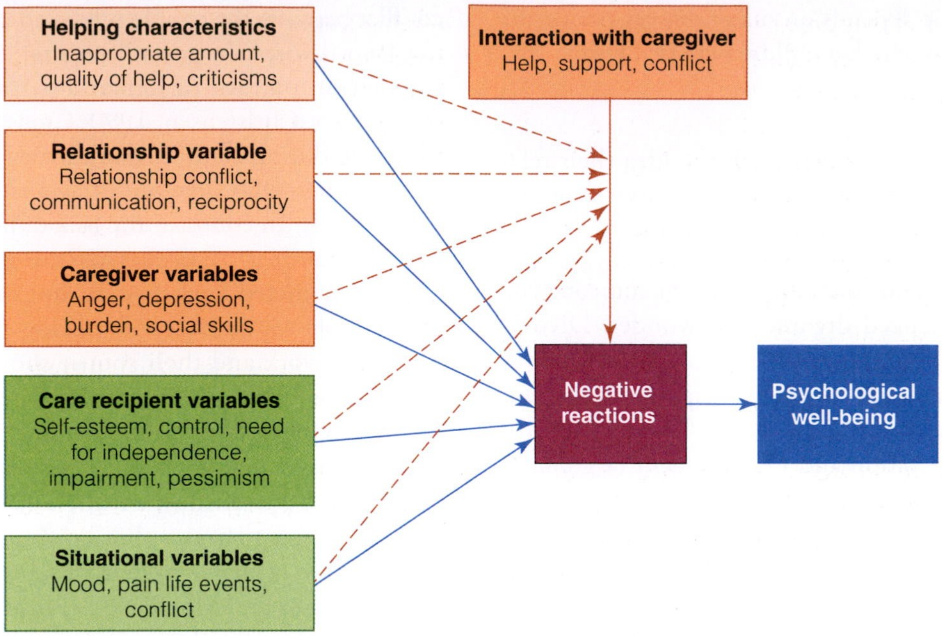

Figure 11.10 Whether a care recipient perceives care to be good depends on interactions with the care provider and whether those interactions are perceived negatively.

Source: Newsom, J. T. (1999). Another side to caregiving: Negative reactions to being helped. Current Directions in Psychological Science, 8, 185.

Adult Development in Action

Given the population demographics trends discussed in Chapter 1, what changes would you predict will happen in families by 2050?

Review Questions

11.3 Family Dynamics Across Adulthood

- What are the major factors involved in the decision to become a parent? How does parent age influence parenting?
- How does the parental role affect most adults' lives? How are child care responsibilities determined?
- What are the similarities and differences across various structural forms of parenting?
- What are some major issues that confront middle-aged parents?
- What are the characteristics of grandparenthood and great-grandparenthood? What special challenges confront grandparents raising grandchildren?
- What are the stresses and uplifts of caring for a family member?

11.4 Divorce and Remarriage

Key Questions

- Who gets divorced? Why? How does divorce affect parental relationships with children?
- What are remarriages like? How are they similar to and different from first marriages?

Frank and Marilyn, both in their late 40s, thought that their marriage would last forever. However, they weren't so lucky and have just been divorced. Although two of their children are married, their youngest daughter is still in high school. The financial pressures Marilyn feels now that she's living independently are beginning to take their toll. Marilyn wonders whether this financial situation is similar to that of other recently divorced people.

Despite what Frank and Marilyn pledged on their wedding day, their marriage did not last until death parted them; they dissolved their marriage through divorce. Many couples do, and are willing to experience the stress that divorce often brings. But even though divorce can be very stressful and difficult, thousands of people each year choose to try again. Most enter their second (or third or fourth) marriage with renewed expectations of success. Are these new dreams realistic?

As we'll discuss, it depends on many things; among the most important is whether children are involved.

Divorce

Most couples enter marriage with the idea their relationship will be permanent. Rather than growing together, though, many couples grow apart.

Who Gets Divorced and Why? You or someone you know has experienced divorce. No wonder. Divorce in the United States is common, and the divorce rate is substantially higher than in many other countries around the world. Within the Organisation for Economic Co-operation and Development (a group of 36 advanced and important emerging countries), only Russia has a higher divorce rate (OECD, 2018). American couples have roughly a 50–50 chance of remaining married for life; the odds of divorcing have been declining since 2000 and hit a 50-year low in 2020 (U.S. Census Bureau, 2020c). Data were mixed on what happened during the COVID-19 pandemic; some evidence indicated that rates jumped almost 35% in the first several months of the pandemic (Rosner, 2020), whereas other data showed a decline in several states (Manning & Payne, 2020).

Research indicates that couples tend to agree on the reasons for divorce (Braver & Lamb, 2013; Crowley, 2021). Not surprisingly, money, infidelity, lack of compatibility, partner abuse, and substance use are among the most commonly reported causes. An individual partner's specific reasons for divorcing vary with gender, social class, and life-course variables. Former husbands and wives are more likely to blame their ex-spouses than themselves for the problems that led to the divorce.

Why people divorce has been the focus of much research on intervention programs. Divorce touches every aspect of relationships: emotional, psychological, social, and economic (Coates, 2017). A great deal of attention has been devoted to the notion that success or failure of a marriage depends critically on how couples handle conflict. Although conflict management is important, it has become clear from research in couples therapy that the reasons couples split are complex (Galovan et al., 2022; Kayser, 2011).

Gottman and Levenson (2000; Gottman & Silver, 2015; Gottman et al., 2018) developed two models that predicted divorce early (within the first 7 years of marriage) and later (when the first child reaches age 14) with very high accuracy over the 14-year period of their study. The models are based on communication styles and habits between partners and how couples deal with conflict. Negative emotions displayed during conflict between the couple predicted early divorce, but not later divorce. In general, this reflects a destructive interaction pattern of demand–withdraw (Baucom et al., 2015; Christensen, 1990; Crenshaw et al., 2021) in which, during conflict, one partner places a demand on the other, who then withdraws either emotionally or physically. In contrast, the lack of positive emotions in a discussion of events-of-the-day and during conflict predicted later divorce, but not early divorce. An example would be a wife talking excitedly about a project at work and their spouse showing disinterest. Such "unrequited" interest and excitement in discussions likely carries over to the rest of the relationship.

Gottman's and other similar research (e.g., Baucom et al., 2015; Crenshaw et al., 2021) is important because it demonstrates that how couples communicate emotion is critical to marital success. Couples who divorce earlier typically do so because of high levels of negative feelings such as contempt, criticism, defensiveness, and stonewalling experienced as a result of intense marital conflict. But for many couples, such intense conflict is generally absent. Importantly, the mere absence of conflict does not mean the marriage is full of positive feelings. Although the absence of intense conflict makes it easier to stay in a marriage longer, the lack of positive emotions eventually takes its toll and results in later divorce. For a marriage to last, people need to be told regularly they are loved and that what they do and feel really matters to their partner.

We must be cautious about applying Gottman's model to all married couples. For lower-income and for culturally diverse couples, the variables Gottman says predict early divorce may not work as well (Friedlander et al., 2019; Kim et al., 2007). The priority given to couples' communication as the source of marital satisfaction is not always apparent (Lavner, Karney et al., 2016). For older, long-term married couples, the perception of the spouse's support is the most important predictor of remaining married (Landis et al., 2013).

The high divorce rate in the United States has led to many approaches to increase the likelihood that marriages will last. Most of these focus on teaching couples the skills necessary for maintaining strong relationships, such as good communication skills, joint problem-solving strategies, forgiveness, and compassion. Some U.S. states have legislated mandatory counseling for people contemplating divorce based on these ideas. Research related to these initiatives has found mixed results (Clyde et al., 2020).

Effects of Divorce on the Couple. Divorce takes a high toll on the couple, with nearly all reporting some degree of unhappiness at some point. Unlike the situation when one's spouse dies, divorce often means the person's ex-spouse is present to provide a reminder of outcome, especially of any unresolved negative issues. This situation reflects a type of ambiguous loss that we will consider in more detail in Chapter 13.

Global research in Ghana, Pakistan, Saudi Arabia, Spain, and the United States indicates great similarity in how both partners in a failed marriage feel: anxious, deeply disappointed, misunderstood, and rejected, along with anger in some cases (Doohan et al., 2010; Khan et al., 2019; Osafo et al., 2021; Rasheed et al., 2021; Yárnoz-Yaben, 2010). Divorced people experience negative health consequences as well (Lamela et al., 2016). Especially because of the financial consequences of divorce, the effects can even be traced to future generations due to long-term negative consequences on education and on quality of parenting (Friesen et al., 2017). Unlike the situation of a spouse dying, divorce, especially when children are involved, often means that one's ex-spouse is present to provide a reminder of the unpleasant aspects of the relationship and, in some cases, feelings of personal failure.

Divorced people sometimes find the transition difficult; researchers refer to these problems as "divorce hangover" (Walther, 1991). Divorce hangover reflects divorced partners' inability to let go, develop new friendships, or reorient themselves as single parents. Forgiving the ex-spouse is also important for eventual adjustment postdivorce (Sbarra, 2015; Sbarra & Coan, 2018). Both low preoccupation and forgiveness may be indicators ex-spouses are able to move on with their lives.

Divorce in middle age has some special characteristics. If wives initiate the divorce, they report self-focused growth and optimism; if they did not initiate the divorce, they tend to ruminate and feel vulnerable. Many middle-aged women who divorce also face significant financial challenges if their primary source of income was the ex-husband's earnings. However, many also identified positive aspects of their new lives, including higher levels of overall happiness, liberation from their ex-spouses, and enhanced independence and freedom (Crowley, 2019; Sakraida, 2005).

We must not overlook the financial problems that many divorced people who were not employed for pay face (Braver & Lamb, 2013). These problems are especially keen for the middle-aged divorced people who may have spent years raising children and who have few job skills that are currently in high demand. For them, divorce presents an especially difficult financial hardship, which is intensified if they have children in college and the former spouse provides little support.

Effects of Divorce on Children. When it involves children, divorce becomes a complicated matter, especially when viewed from an international perspective (Amato & Boyd, 2014). In most countries, mothers tend to obtain custody but often do not obtain sufficient financial resources to support the children. This puts an extreme financial burden on divorced mothers, whose standard of living is typically reduced.

In contrast, divorced fathers often pay a psychological price. Although many would like to remain active in their children's lives, few actually do. When mothers who have custody remarry, visits from noncustodial fathers usually decline (Anderson & Greene, 2013).

One hopeful direction that addresses the usually difficult custody situations following divorce is the Collaborative Divorce Project, based on collaborative law (Mosten, 2009; Pruett et al., 2005). **Collaborative divorce** is a voluntary, contractually based alternative dispute resolution process for couples who want to negotiate a resolution of their situation rather than have a ruling imposed on them by a court or an arbitrator (Ballard et al., 2014). Collaborative divorce is an intervention designed to assist the parents of children 6 years and younger as they begin the separation/divorce process.

Results from this approach are positive (DeLucia-Waack, 2011; McLeod, 2020). In addition to positive evaluations from both parents, couples benefited in terms of less conflict, greater father involvement, and better outcomes for children than in the control group. Attorneys and court records indicate that intervention families were more cooperative and were less likely to need custody evaluations and other costly services. The Collaborative Divorce Project is evidence that programs can be designed and implemented to benefit all members of the family.

What happens when the parents of adult children divorce? Are adult children affected, too? It certainly looks that way. Adults whose parents' divorce experience a great deal of emotional vulnerability and stress, and often feel that their "home" will never be the same (Hughes & Fredenburg, 2020). One young man put it this way:

> The difficult thing was that it was a time where, you know, [you're] making the transition from high school to college . . . your high school friends are dispersed . . . they're all over the place. . . . It's normally a very difficult transition [college], new atmosphere, new workload, meeting new

> people. You've got to start deciding what you want to do, you've got to sort of start getting more independent, and so forth. And then at the same time you find out about a divorce. You know, it's just that much more adjustment you have to make. (Cooney et al., 1986)

The effects of experiencing the divorce of one's parents while growing up can be quite long-lasting. College-age students report poorer relations with their parents if their parents are divorced (Pineda, 2020; Yu et al., 2010). Parental divorce also affects young adults' views on intimate relationships and marriage, often having negative effects on them (Ottaway, 2010; Pineda, 2020). Wallerstein and Lewis (2004) report the findings from a 25-year follow-up study of individuals whose parents divorced when they were between 3 and 18 years old. Results show an unexpected gulf between growing up in intact versus divorced families as well as the difficulties that children of divorce encounter in achieving love, sexual intimacy, and commitment to marriage and parenthood. Even when the length of time spent in the intact two-parent family was taken into account, negative effects of divorce on adult children were still found in a large Dutch study (Kalmijn, 2013). The "marriage protection" factor outweighed biological relatedness, especially for fathers. There is no doubt that divorce has significant effects regardless of when it occurs in a child's life.

What is the situation in your community? Complete the Discovering Development opportunity and find out.

Discovering Development

Divorce Realities in Your Community

What are the realities of divorce in your community? Are the rates higher, lower, or about the same as the national average? Are there opportunities for people to participate in Collaborative Divorce programs? Other programs? What is being done to help support couples and lower the local divorce rate?

Find out what the realities are in your community. Identify and talk with different professionals who deal with divorce—counselors, ministers, attorneys, and others. Research public records for the current number of divorces in the years just before, during, and after the COVID-19 pandemic to find out whether the pandemic affected the rates in your community. Gather the evidence, and discuss with your classmates. What conclusions can you draw?

Remarriage

The trauma of divorce does not always deter people from beginning new relationships that often lead to another marriage. However, the rate at which people remarry has dropped significantly since the mid-20th century, especially over the past 20 years (Reynolds, 2020). The decline in remarriage varies by age, however; between 1990 and 2018, the remarriage rate for divorced people aged 20 to 35 declined about 50%, whereas divorced people over age 55 remarried at about the same rate (Schweizer, 2020).

Cultural differences are apparent in the ability of women, in particular, to remarry; in Namibia, for example, widows are constrained in their options and typically must depend on others (Thomas, 2008). Among older adults, adult children may voice strong opposition to their parent remarrying that can put sufficient pressure on the parent that they remain single.

Adapting to new relationships in remarriage is stressful, which may account for the higher rate of divorce for remarriages. Partners may have unresolved issues from the previous marriage that may interfere with satisfaction with the new marriage (Faber, 2004; Gold, 2016; Martin-Uzzi & Duval-Tsioles, 2013). The challenges can include antagonism toward ex-spouses that interferes with child custody, differing loyalties among stepchildren, and financial difficulties. The effects of remarriage on children are complicated, at least for emerging adults (Collardeau & Ehrenberg, 2016; Gold, 2016). Parental divorce can have long-term consequences on children's attitudes toward marriage and divorce. The extent to which parental conflict was openly present and the religious affiliation of emerging adults influences their attitudes. For instance, those who were exposed to high levels of parental conflict have more positive views of divorce.

Remarriages tend to be less stable than first marriages and have become less so since the 1990s (Council on Contemporary Families, 2015). The typical first marriage lasts 13 years, whereas the typical remarriage lasts 10. These differences do not reflect relationship quality, which is equivalent; rather, pressures from complex family relationships, lower commitment, and financial pressures take a higher toll on remarriages.

Nevertheless, couples who are very committed to and work diligently at making the remarriage strong are usually successful.

Adult Development in Action

If you were a relationship counselor, what would you recommend to a couple who are considering divorcing?

Review Questions

11.4 Divorce and Remarriage

- What are the major reasons that people divorce?
- What interventions have been developed to assist couples who are divorcing, or to lower the overall rate of divorce?
- What are the characteristics of remarriage, and how to the compare to those of first marriages?

Social Policy Implications

Legal and Social Program Support for Grandfamilies

As noted in the chapter, grandfamilies may not have all of the legal or other societal supports that parents do to back them in raising grandchildren. Grandfamilies.org tracks these topics across the United States and provides summaries of existing laws and supports, as well as a wide variety of other topics, and where additional attention is needed.

A review of matters relating to the care and custody of grandchildren reveals the complexity of the issues. As noted in the text, many grandparents report that, "Without legal custody, I can't enroll my grandchild in school," or "I can't consent to my grandchild's annual medical examination, since I'm not the legal guardian." Obtaining legal authority requires going to court. For people who are unrelated to the child, this is usually straightforward (providing they have the resources to do so). In the case of a grandparent, however, there may be another very challenging emotional component—many grandparents find they may not want to sue their adult child (the grandchild's parent) to obtain legal custody of their grandchild.

The U.S. Supreme Court has ruled for many years that parents have a fundamental right to make decisions concerning their children's care, custody, and control. Because of this right, in order for a grandparent or other relative to be awarded legal custody, guardianship, or adoption of a child, the first step in a case is to prove that the parent (often the grandparent's own child) is unfit. This is a difficult emotional hurdle that can destroy families. To provide an alternative, some states have created legal relationship options such as standby or limited guardianship and de facto custody.

National advocacy efforts have been successful in gaining more rights for grandparents (Grandfamilies.org, 2022). Much work remains to be done, but states are moving in the right direction to provide the best environment possible for children. Through the creation of innovative options, states are also understanding that it is not always necessary to risk undermining family relationships that could well be needed later on.

In Review

For your review of this chapter, you may create four paragraphs. In the first paragraph, create three main subsections. First, summarize the various characteristics of friendships that are most important at different times in adulthood. Then talk about why friends matter during these different times. Second, describe what attracts people to each other, and the different phases of a relationship that turns into love. Include a description of how these processes vary across cultures. Third, discuss how violence can enter into a relationship, the various types of violence and their dynamics, and the main types of elder abuse, neglect, and exploitation.

Your second paragraph should focus on the three main lifestyles that were discussed: singlehood, cohabitation, and marriage. Describe the characteristics of each, why they are chosen, and what makes for long-term success in each.

Your third paragraph should concern the various aspects of families. In your first subsection, summarize the main factors that influence the decision to become a first-time parent. Your second subsection should focus on the various aspects of parenting and the effects that having a child (or children) have on parents' lives. Third, summarize the main aspects of the various structural family forms that characterize most U.S. households with children. Fourth, discuss some of the major issues that may confront middle-aged parents. Fifth, summarize the experiences of grandparents and great-grandparents and their grandchildren and great-grandchildren. Include a description of the main challenges faced by grandparents who are raising their grandchildren. In the sixth subsection, describe the major stresses and uplifts experienced by people providing care for family members.

In your fourth paragraph, summarize the main reasons people divorce and the factors that seem to predict divorce. Include notes about programs aimed at reducing the rate of divorce and at assisting divorcing couples. Also summarize the factors in why people remarry, and the factors that predict whether a remarriage will last.

Integrating Concepts in Development

- What components would a theory of adult relationships need to have?
- How do the four developmental forces (biological, psychological, sociocultural, and life-cycle) influence adult relationships?
- How are the changing populations demographics changing relationships and families?
- How do intergenerational relationships transcend generational differences?

Key Terms

abusive relationship A relationship that one partner displays aggressive behavior toward the other partner. 359

affirmative consent The assurance that all parties engaging in a sexual encounter are informed, autonomous, and otherwise capable of making a valid choice regarding engaging in sexual activity. 355

assortative mating A theory that people find partners based on their similarity to each other. 356

battered spouse syndrome A situation in which a woman believes she cannot leave an abusive relationship and where she may even go so far as to kill her abuser. 359

cohabitation Living with another person as part of a committed, intimate, sexual relationship. 362

collaborative divorce A voluntary, contractually based alternative dispute resolution process for couples who want to negotiate a resolution of their marriage rather than have a ruling imposed on them by a court or an arbitrator. 385

exchange theory A theory of relationships based on the idea each partner contributes something to the relationship the other would be hard-pressed to provide. 365

familism Refers to the idea the well-being of the family takes precedence over the concerns of individual family members. 373

filial obligation The feeling that, as an adult child, one must care for one's parents. 380

grandfamilies Families headed by a grandparent. 379

homogamy The similarity of values and interests a couple shares. 365

kinkeeper The person who gathers family members together for celebrations and keeps them in touch with each other. 376

marital adjustment The degree spouses accommodate each other over a certain period of time. 365

marital quality The subjective evaluation of the couple's relationship on a number of different dimensions. 365

marital satisfaction A global assessment of one's marriage. 365

marital success An umbrella term referring to any marital outcome. 365

sandwich generation Middle-aged adults caught between the competing demands of two generations: their parents and their children. 376

social convoy A group of people that journeys with us in our lives, providing support in good and bad times. 351

socioemotional selectivity A theory of relationships that argues social contact is motivated by a variety of goals, including information seeking, self-concept, and emotional regulation. 353

vulnerability–stress–adaptation model A model that considers marital quality as a dynamic process resulting from the couple's ability to handle stressful events in the context of their particular vulnerabilities and resources. 367

Work, Retirement, and Leisure

Chapter

12

Chapter Outline

Learning Objectives

After studying this chapter, you will be able to...

12.1. Describe the role of work in emerging, established, and midlife adulthood.

12.2. Describe the aspects of diversity, equity, and inclusion in the workplace.

12.3. Describe the effects of bias and discrimination in the workplace.

12.4. Describe occupational skill development, employment insecurity, and unemployment.

12.5. Describe challenges of balancing work and family life in adulthood.

12.6. Describe the meaning and experience of retirement.

12.7. Describe how people experience leisure time in adulthood.

When you were young, you were likely asked, "What do you want to be when you grow up?" Now that you are "grown up," the question has changed to "What do you do?"

Work is a central aspect of life and a defining characteristic of who we are. For some, work *is* life; for most, work is a prime source of identity in adulthood. But what, exactly, do we mean by **work**? In 2019, we might have said that work is usually something we do at a place other than our home. Only a year later, many of us might have said that work is usually something we do from home via videocalls and telecommuting. Just a decade or so ago, we might have said that work involves being an employee for an organization; these days, you might just as often be a so-called gig worker (independent contractor) and pursue several different ways to earn money. Clearly, the very concept of work has changed dramatically from a time when people expected to work for decades for the same organization and enjoy a wide range of benefits along with a decent (or better) salary. Today, the continuing replacement of jobs with technology (such as the use of robots and iPads in restaurants instead of human servers, the advent of driverless cars that eliminate taxi and ride share drivers, and artificial intelligence that replaces entry-level accountants) makes that view of a single-employer long-term work careers seem rather quaint.

In this chapter we will consider work and the contexts in which work happens. The rapid changes in where work occurs and whether people are actually employees are upending our understanding of the "workplace" and traditional employer–employee relationships. For example, gigs provide flexibility and work schedule options that help people accommodate personal needs and schedules. However, gigs mostly eliminate the availability of key benefits such as employer-paid health care, paid leave, retirement savings plan employer contributions, and many protections that make workplaces safe. We will learn that the demographics of workers has changed significantly, as have workers' expectations of employers, and what these mean for organizations and workers. All of this, and more, are shaped by the fundamental forces we encountered in Chapter 1, which means the situation continues to evolve. Let's get to work.

12.1 Occupational Selection and Development

Key Questions

- How do people view work?
- How do people choose their occupations?
- What factors influence occupational development?
- What is the relationship between job satisfaction and age?

Fatima, a 28-year-old senior communications major, wonders about career opportunities after graduation. Should they enter the broadcast field as a behind-the-scenes producer, or would they be better suited as a public relations spokesperson? They think their outgoing personality is a factor that should be considered in making this decision.

Choosing one's work is serious business, and involves more than scrolling through job posting websites such as *ZipRecruiter*, *Monster.com*, or *Indeed*. Like Fatima, we try to select a field that we find interesting, in which we are educated, and that maximizes the odds that we can achieve our goal of doing something meaningful. You may be taking this course as part of your preparation for a career in human development, social services, psychology, nursing, allied health, or another field, so in that sense it is career preparation. But work is more than that. Work is a source for friends and social engagement. People arrange personal activities around work schedules. People often choose where they live, as well as locations for services such as childcare, in terms of where they work.

The Meaning of Work

Studs Terkel, author of the fascinating classic book *Working* (1974), writes work is "a search for daily meaning as well as daily bread, for recognition as well as cash, for astonishment rather than torpor; in short, for a sort of life rather than a Monday through Friday sort of dying" (xiii). Kahlil Gibran (1923), in his mystical book *The Prophet*, put it this way: "Work is love made visible."

The meaning most of us derive from working includes both the money that can be exchanged for life's necessities (and perhaps a few luxuries) and the possibility of personal growth (Allan et al., 2020; Lips-Wiersma et al., 2016; Norcross & Farran, 2021). Schwartz (2015) says the belief that people only work for a paycheck is wrong; most people want to do something meaningful with people who they respect and who respect them. To achieve that true goal, Schwartz says most people would even be willing to make less money.

The upshot is that the specific tasks people perform or position a person holds appear to have no effect on their need to derive meaning from work. Finding meaning in one's work can mean the difference between experiencing work as a source of life problems or a source of fulfillment and contentment (Grawitch et al., 2010, 2020). Some workers tend to derive meaning most from finding unity with others and developing the inner self, whereas other workers place more emphasis on expressing their full potential. Even under the stress of the COVID-19 pandemic, workers across five countries (Canada, France, Germany, the United Kingdom, and the United States) found meaning and well-being; in fact, having dependents under 12, working more hours since the onset of the pandemic, and having essential worker status led to better well-being outcomes (Grawitch et al., 2020).

Contemporary business theory supports the idea that meaning matters. The concept called **meaning–mission fit** explains how organizations with a better alignment between their mission and their employees provide a richer, more supportive environment for their employees' happiness, job satisfaction, and emotional well-being (French-Holloway, 2020). This fit happens when people are encouraged to use their strengths, receive organizational support, and experience alignment between their personal values and those of the organization. Ensuring such fit is a major focus of talent management efforts in organizations.

Given the various meanings that people derive from work, what it is that people do at work, typically referred to as one's *occupation*, is clearly a key element of a person's sense of identity and self-efficacy (Lang & Lee, 2005; Schwartz, 2015; Sulphey, 2019). This can be readily observed when adults introduce themselves socially. You've probably noticed that when people are asked to tell something about themselves, they typically provide information about what they do for a living. Occupation affects your life in a host of ways and often influences where you live, what friends you make, and even what clothes you wear. In short, the impact of work cuts across all aspects of life. Work, then, is both a major social role you have and a powerful influence on your life. Work is an important anchor that complements the other major role of adulthood—love relationships—that we examined in Chapter 11. We will return to the issue of the meaning of work at the end of the chapter in the Social Policy Implications feature about the Great Resignation in the midst of the COVID-19 pandemic.

Because work plays such a key role in providing meaning for people, an important question is how people select an occupation. Let's turn our attention to two theories explaining how and why people choose the occupations they do.

Occupational Choice

It is not only that children use pretend play to imagine themselves in future occupations. By adolescence, there is evidence early occupational preferences are related to personality. But how does meaningful planning happen, and what are people preparing for? After all, we earlier acknowledged the rapidly changing nature of work and how people cannot assume they will have a stable career in which they work for the same organization throughout their working life. So how do people sort out their career options?

For one thing, it is more appropriate to consider a career as something you construct yourself rather than enter (Di Fabio, 2016; Hartung & Santilli, 2017; Savickas, 2013, 2020). **Career construction theory** posits people build careers through their own actions that result from the interface of their own personal characteristics and the social context. What people *do* in the world of work, then, results from how they adapt to their environment; in turn, that adaptation is a result of biopsychosocial processes grounded in the collection of experiences they have during their life. An important aspect of career construction theory is that it was specifically developed for multicultural societies in a global economy (Savickas, 2020).

Three specific theories about how people adapt themselves to their environment have influenced career construction theory (Savickas, 2020). First, Holland's (1997) personality-type theory proposes people choose occupations to optimize the fit between their individual traits (such as personality, intelligence, skills, and abilities) and their occupational interests. Second, the notion that career development occurs in stages owes its origins to Super's theory (1957, 1976, 1980; Super et al., 1996). Third, **social cognitive career theory (SCCT)** proposes career choice is a result of the application of Bandura's social cognitive theory, especially the concept of self-efficacy. Self-efficacy is an important aspect of how we construct our personal stories, one of which is about our work lives (Bandura, 2019). Let's consider these ideas in a bit more detail.

Holland categorizes occupations by the interpersonal settings in which people must function and by their associated lifestyles. He identifies six personality types that combine these factors—investigative, social, realistic, artistic, conventional, and enterprising—that he believes are optimally related to occupations.

How does Holland's theory help us understand the continued development of occupational interests in adulthood? Fatima, the college senior in the vignette, found a good match between their outgoing nature and their major, communications. Indeed, college students of all ages prefer courses and majors that fit well with their own personalities. You are likely to be one of them. Later, that translates into people's desire to choose occupations and careers they like. Complementarily, SCCT also proposes people's career choices are heavily influenced by their interests (Brown & Lent, 2016; Lent, 2013; Savvides & Stavrou, 2021). Such connections have longed been considered as a "calling," especially in careers related to religious ministry (Barnds, 2020).

How does SCCT explain occupational choice in practice? As explained in Figure 12.1, SCCT has two versions. The simplest includes four main factors: Self-Efficacy (your belief in your ability), Outcome Expectations (what you think will happen in a specific situation), Interests (what you like), and Choice Goals (what you want to achieve). The more complex version also includes Supports (environmental things that help you) and Barriers (environmental things that block or frustrate you). Several studies show support for the six-variable version of the model (Brown & Lent, 2016; Lent, 2020; Sheu & Phrasavath, 2019).

Over four decades, Donald Super (1957, 1976, 1980; Super et al., 1996) developed a theory of occupational development based on self-concept, first introduced in Chapter 9. He proposed a progression through five distinct stages during adulthood as a result of changes in individuals' self-concept and adaptation to an occupational role: implementation, establishment, maintenance, deceleration, and retirement (noted in Figure 12.2). People are located along a continuum of **vocational maturity** through their working years; the more congruent their occupational behaviors are with what is expected of them at different ages, the more vocationally mature they are.

Super also proposed five developmental tasks, the first two (crystallization and specification) occurring primarily in adolescence. The remaining three (implementation, stabilization, and consolidation) occur over the course of adulthood. Each of the tasks in adulthood has distinctive characteristics.

- The *implementation task* begins in the early 20s, when people take a series of temporary jobs to learn firsthand about work roles and to try out possible career choices. Summer internships that many students use to gain experience are one example.

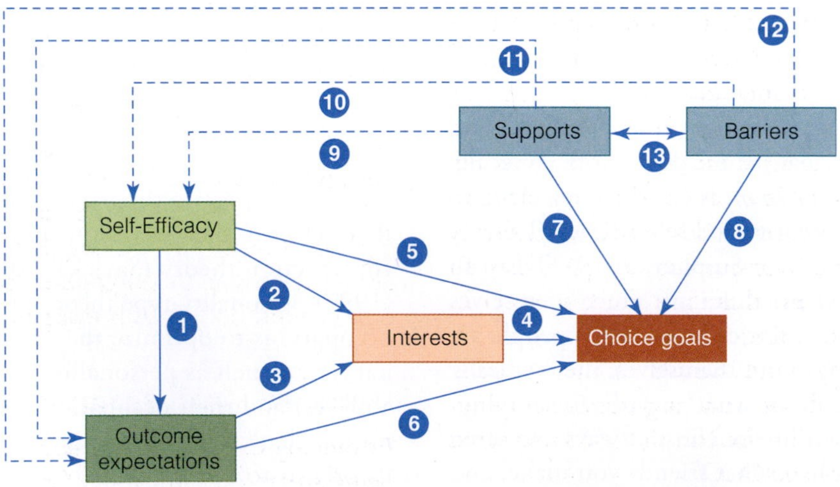

Figure 12.1 The four-variable (paths 1–6) and six-variable (paths 1–13) versions of the social cognitive career theory interest and choice models.

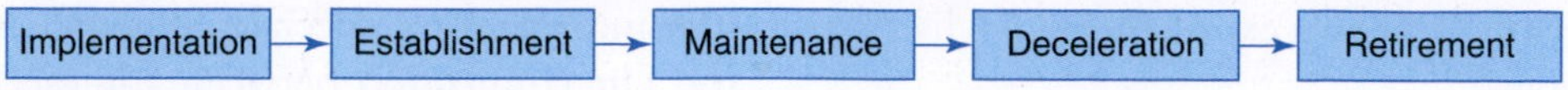

Figure 12.2 Super's occupational stages during adulthood.

- The *stabilization task* begins in the mid-20s with selecting a specific occupation during young adulthood. It continues until the mid-30s as the person confirms the occupational choice that was made.
- The *consolidation task* begins in the mid-30s and continues throughout the rest of the person's working life as they advance up the career ladder. Taking a position in a law firm and working one's way up from associate to partner or beginning as a server in a restaurant and moving up to front of the house manager are two examples.

Super also notes that these adult tasks overlap a sequence of developmental stages, beginning at birth and continuing during adulthood: exploratory (age 15 to 24), establishment (age 24 to 44), maintenance (age 45 to 64), and decline (age 65 and beyond). These stages reflect the overall occupational cycle from choosing what one wants to do through achieving the maximum possible in a career to the reduction in work in late adulthood.

Super's theory originally applied to people who enter and stay in a particular career their entire adult lives and to those who change occupations. Because it is now typical for Americans to have a series of careers, Super's notion is that we cycle and recycle through the tasks and stages as we adapt to changes in ourselves and the workplace (Super et al., 1996).

Perspectives on Theories of Career Development. How well do these theories work in actual practice, particularly in these times of rapid change in the nature, location, and stability of work careers? Certainly, the relations among occupation, personality, and demographic variables are complex (Brown & Lent, 2016; Lent, 2020; Hartung & Santilli, 2017). However, even given the lack of stable careers and the real need to change jobs frequently, there is still a strong tendency on people's part to find occupations in which they fit and feel comfortable, and that they like (Allan et al., 2020; Brown & Lent, 2016; French-Holloway, 2020; Hartung & Santilli, 2017). As we will note later, loss of self-efficacy through job loss and long-term unemployment provides support for the role the self-statements underlying self-efficacy and SCCT.

Super and colleagues' (1996) adaptation of traditional views of career to contemporary reality reflects a larger critique of career development theories. For example, McMahon and Arthur (2019; Arthur & McMahon, 2019) argue that context plays a very important role in what people choose to do for a living, and that these choices exist within interconnected, interactive systems.

SCCT and related theories are increasingly used as frameworks for career counselors and life coaches to help people identify and select initial occupations and navigate later occupational changes. The goal is to have people understand that the work world changes rapidly, that they need to develop coping and compensatory strategies to deal with that fact, and that they need to develop these strategies effectively within all of the levels of interactive systems in their lives. Increasingly, these approaches are using **employability skills mapping** as a way to help people identify job skills that are in demand with the skills they have and can demonstrate, and how to acquire them if they have gaps. Skills mapping is used to guide students toward in-demand careers as well as toward career advancement and career changes.

Of course, theory is one thing, and reality often differs. Selingo (2016) captured the reality of career selection when he described three general types of people. *Sprinters* are those who have seemingly always known what they wanted to be and do, and never vary from that path, sticking with a major, lining up internships in the field, and seeking employment that aligns with what they like and have done. *Wanderers* are less certain, are more likely to change majors or go back for additional degrees in a different field, and are more likely to delay entering into a specific field to start a career. *Stragglers* tend to drift after high school from job to job, may start and stop college more than once, and tend to find their optimal career option much later, if at all. One thing is clear, though—in the longer term, career success is always related to sorting oneself out and obtaining the type of education or skills that prepares you for a career.

Occupational Development

Advancing through one's career is not just a function of being smart and doing all of the explicit requirements of a job. It also depends on the socialization that occurs through learning the unwritten rules of an organization, in combination with one's own expectations of what the career should entail.

Certainly, the relations among occupation, personality, and demographic variables are complex (e.g., Barrick et al., 2013; Savvides & Stavrou, 2021). However, even given the real need for career flexibility and frequent job changes, there is still a strong tendency for people to find occupations in which they feel comfortable and that they like (Lent, 2013, 2020).

Although people may have underlying tendencies that relate to certain types of occupations, unless they believe they could be successful in those occupations and careers, they are unlikely to choose them. These beliefs can be influenced by external factors. For example, occupational prestige and gender-related factors need to be taken into account (Deng et al., 2007).

Occupational Expectations. Especially in adolescence, people begin to form opinions about what working in a particular occupation will be like based on what they learn in school and from their parents, peers, other adults, and online and other media. These expectations influence what occupation(s) they eventually pick, as well as implicit career pathways.

For college students, especially first-generation students, personal experiences in the workplace affect people's opinions of themselves as they continue to refine and update their occupational expectations and development (Fouad et al., 2016; Kezar et al., 2020; Stebleton et al., 2020). This usually involves identifying an occupational goal, monitoring progress toward it, and changing or even abandoning it as necessary. Modifying the goal happens for many reasons, such as realizing interests have changed, the occupation was not a good fit for them, they never got the chance to pursue the level of education necessary to achieve the goal, or they lack certain essential skills and do not have the opportunity to acquire them. Still other people modify their goals because of discrimination, a point we consider later in this chapter.

Research suggests that most people who know they have the talent, the confidence, and the opportunity to achieve their occupational and career goals often attain them. When high school students identified as academically talented were asked about their career expectations and outcomes, it turned out that 10 and even 20 years later they had been surprisingly accurate (Perrone et al., 2010).

In general, research suggests emerging adults modify their expectations at least once, usually on the basis of new information, especially about their academic ability. The connection between adolescent expectations and adult reality reinforces the developmental aspects of occupations and careers.

Many researchers believe occupational expectations also vary by generation. Nowhere has this belief been stronger than in the supposed differences among the baby boom generation (born between 1946 and 1964), Generation X (born between 1965 and 1980), the millennial generation (born between 1981 and 1996), and Generation Z (born between 1997 and 2012) (Deloitte, 2020; Pew Research Center, 2018). By the mid-2020s, the global workforce will be dominated by millennials (many of whom will be middle-aged by then) and Gen Z.

Perhaps the most important factor to keep in mind about millennials and Gen Z is that they have grown up and come of age during the worst economic and socio-health crises in more than a century—the Great Recession and the COVID-19 pandemic and related economic and employment challenges. Research and analysis (e.g., Deloitte, 2020; Pew Research Center, 2018; Porter & Yaffe-Bellany, 2020) indicate that both generations are less financially secure (e.g., less employment security, higher student debt) than were baby boomers and Gen Xers at the same age, and believe that success in life is more due to luck than to effort. Nearly half say they are stressed most of the time, and they agree that their loyalty to an organization increases the more the organization responds to worker needs (from diversity and inclusion to sustainability and reskilling).

The importance of occupational expectations is clearly evident in the transition from school to the workplace (Moen, 2016a, 2016b; Moen & Roehling,

Svetikd/E+/Getty Images

Reality shock typically hits younger workers soon after they begin an occupation.

2005). The 21st-century workplace is not one where hard work and long hours necessarily lead to a better outcome. It can be a place where you experience **reality shock**, a situation in which what you learn in the classroom does not always transfer directly into the real world and does not represent all you need to know. When reality shock sets in, things do not seem to happen the way we expect. Reality shock befalls most people who are new to a position. You can imagine how new teachers feel when their long hours preparing a lesson result in students who act bored and unappreciative of their efforts.

Many professions, such as nursing and teaching, have gone to great lengths to alleviate reality shock (Graf et al., 2020; Hinton & Chirgwin, 2010; Shayshon & Popper-Giveon, 2017). This problem is one best addressed through internship, apprenticeship, and practicum experiences for students under the careful guidance of experienced people in the field.

The Role of Mentors and Coaches. Entering an occupation involves more than the relatively short formal training a person receives. Instead, most people are oriented by a more experienced person who makes a specific effort to do this, taking on the role of a *mentor* or *coach*.

A **mentor** is part teacher, sponsor, model, and counselor who facilitates on-the job learning to help the new hire do the work required in their present role and to prepare for future career roles (Cavanaugh & Cavanaugh, 2018; Volpe et al., 2016). A **developmental or executive coach** is an individual who helps a person focus on their goals, motivations, and aspirations to help them achieve focus and apply them appropriately (Cavanaugh & Cavanaugh, 2018; Hunt & Weintraub, 2016). Mentoring and coaching are viewed as primary ways that organizations invest in developing their talent and future leadership (Cavanaugh & Cavanaugh, 2018; Smits & Bowden, 2013). Although mentors and coaches work with people at all career stages, mentoring is found most often with people new to a position, whereas coaching is used at all levels of experience.

The mentor helps a new worker avoid trouble by sharing invaluable information about the unwritten rules governing day-to-day activities in the workplace and be sensitive to the employment situation. A review of mentoring programs showed that good mentors make sure their mentees are noticed and receive credit from supervisors for good work, and mentoring programs generally improve the performance of mentees. Thus, occupational success often depends on the quality of the mentor–mentee relationship and the mentee's perceptions of its importance (Giacumo et al., 2020).

Image Source/Digital Vision/Getty Images

Mentoring is an important way new employees are onboarded into an organization.

What do mentors get from the relationship? Helping a younger employee learn the job is one way to achieve Erikson's phase of generativity (discussed in Chapter 9; Marcia & Josselson, 2013). Surprisingly, little research has been done regarding whether mentoring programs improve organizational performance (Giacumo et al., 2020).

Coaching is a process that helps people make fundamental changes in their lives by focusing on general skill development and performance improvement (Cavanaugh & Cavanaugh, 2018; Volpe et al., 2016). It tends not to focus on specific aspects of a job; rather, the intent is more general understanding of oneself and improvement of one's overall career success. Thus, coaching complements mentoring and helps people develop all of the key aspects of themselves. Consequently, coaching is a process that is applicable and useful at any point in one's adult life.

The need to adapt traditional models of mentoring and coaching to the needs of millennials and Gen Z'ers, as well as for women and historically marginalized groups, has resulted in creative new approaches such as *reverse mentoring* and *micro-mentoring* (Ainsworth, 2020; Blancero & Cotton-Nessler, 2017; Germain, 2020; Ortiz-Walters & Gilson, 2013). **Reverse mentoring** occurs when a more senior, experienced professional is paired with a colleague who may vary in experience, background, or perspective such that the senior professional becomes the mentee and the other professional serves as the mentor. A common example of reverse mentoring occurs when a member of Gen Z trains a Gen X-er on the latest social media app. A variation of this is **reciprocal mentoring** when each member of the pair switch roles from time to time depending on the situation. **Micro-mentoring** occurs when a more knowledgeable or experienced worker serves as a mentor on a specific task. A good example is when one worker helps another who is temporarily stuck on a problem, or introduces a coworker to a senior leader in the profession at a conference.

When paired with mentors and coaches, women and employees in historically marginalized groups show better career trajectories, both perceived and real (Adams-Harmon & Greer-Williams, 2021; Ransdell et al., 2021; Schulz & Enslin, 2014). It is also critical to adopt culturally conscious approaches to mentoring and coaching to maximize the benefits (Campinha-Bacote, 2010; Kochan & Freeman, 2020). Culturally conscious mentoring and coaching involves understanding how an organization's and employee's cultures mutually affect each other, and explicitly building those assumptions, interrelationships, and behaviors into the mentoring or coaching process.

Despite the evidence that having a mentor or coach has many positive effects on workers' occupational development, there is an important caveat: the quality of the mentor or coach really matters (Baran & Zarzycki, 2021; Tong & Kram, 2013; Volpe et al., 2016). Having a poor mentor or coach is worse than having no mentor at all. Consequently, people must be carefully matched. It is in the best interest of the organization to get the match correct. How can workers be matched more effectively? Some organizations have taken a page from dating and created speed mentoring as a way to create better matches (Ramani et al., 2020).

Job Satisfaction

What does it mean to be satisfied with one's job? **Job satisfaction** is the positive feeling that results from an appraisal of one's work. Research indicates that job satisfaction is a multifaceted concept in which certain characteristics—including hope, resilience, optimism, and self-efficacy—predict both job performance and job satisfaction. This research has resulted in the creation of **psychological capital theory**, the notion that having a positive outlook improves processes and outcomes (Luthans et al., 2007; Tefera & Hunsaker, 2021; Youssef-Morgan & Luthans, 2013).

Satisfaction with some aspects of one's job increases gradually with age, and successful aging includes a workplace component (Kooij et al., 2020). Why is this? Is it because people sort themselves out and end up in occupations they like? Is it that they simply learn to like the occupation they are in? What other factors matter?

How does job satisfaction evolve over young and middle adulthood? Research indicates, given sufficient time, most people eventually find a job in which they are reasonably happy (David, 2021; Hom & Kinicki, 2001). Optimistically, this indicates there is a job out there, somewhere, in which you will be happy. That's good, because research grounded in positive psychology theory indicates happiness fuels success (Achor, 2010; Chai, 2021).

It's also true that job satisfaction does not increase in all areas and job types with age. White-collar professionals show an increase in job satisfaction with age, whereas those in blue-collar positions generally do not, and these findings hold with both men and women (Aasland et al., 2010; Mooser et al., 2020). This is also true across cultures. A study of Filipino and Taiwanese workers in lower-level jobs in the long-term healthcare industry in Taiwan showed workers with 4 or 5 years' experience had lower job satisfaction than workers with less experience, but job satisfaction among physicians in Norway increases over time and with opportunities to expand the type of tasks one does (Aasland et al., 2010; Huang et al., 2020; Mooser et al., 2020; Tu, 2006). The decline over time may well reflect whether the organization is perceived to be supportive of its workers (Huang et al., 2020).

However, the changes in the labor market resulting in frequent job changes and a lower likelihood of having a long career with one organization have changed the traditional notions of job satisfaction (Bidwell, 2013; Murphy & Tierney, 2020). Specifically, the fact that companies may eliminate jobs and workers not based on performance, but on other grounds such as comments on social media, for instance, makes it more difficult for employees to develop a sense of organizational commitment, thereby making the relationship between worker age and job satisfaction more complicated (Abrams et al., 2016; Douglas & Roberts, 2020).

Also complicating traditional relations between job satisfaction and age is the fact that the type of job one has and the kinds of family responsibilities one has at different career stages—as well as the flexibility of work options such as telecommuting and family leave benefits to accommodate those responsibilities—influence the relationship between age and job satisfaction, but which are issues that human resource departments can address (Visser et al., 2021). For instance, family caregiving responsibilities may collide with work demands, resulting in lower job satisfaction, especially if the employer has no flexible work options nor paid family leave benefits to accommodate the employee's needs (Paulson et al., 2017). This suggests the accumulation of experience, changing context, and the stage of one's career development all influence job satisfaction over time. The general increase in job satisfaction, then, may reflect the reality of workers figuring out how to manage their lives, understanding the limited alternative options they have, or taking advantage of alternative work assignments, such as telecommuting.

Job Alienation and Burnout

Most jobs create a certain level of stress. For most workers, such negatives are merely annoyances, as the positive aspects of the job outweigh the negative. But for others, extremely stressful situations on the job, especially when they continue, may result in alienation and burnout.

When workers feel what they are doing is meaningless and their efforts are devalued, or when they do not connect what they do to the final product, a sense of **alienation** is likely to result. Terkel (1974) reported employees are most likely to feel alienated when they perform routine, repetitive actions. Alienation can also result from employees feeling abandoned by their employer, such as experiencing long periods without pay increases, without any positive feedback about performance, or without being told they matter.

To help their workers avoid feelings of alienation, it is essential for organizations to provide ways for people to feel connected to each other and to the organization (Jung et al., 2021). Research also indicates that leaders who show trust and behave ethically are key (Bachman, 2017; Bligh, 2017), as is a perception among employees that the employer deals with people fairly and impartially (Howard & Cordes, 2010; Palumbo & Manna, 2020). It is also helpful to involve employees in the decision-making process, create flexible work schedules, and institute employee development and enhancement programs.

Sometimes the pace and pressure of the occupation becomes more than a person can bear. **Burnout** is a state of emotional, physical, and mental exhaustion caused by excessive and prolonged stress. Burnout can make you feel emotionally and physically drained and unable to function in the context of many aspects of life, not just in your job. Burnout can lower your motivation and cause you to feel helpless, hopeless, and resentful (Queen & Harding, 2020).

Burnout is most common among people in the helping professions—such as teaching, social work, and health care (Bermejo-Toro et al., 2016; Lluch et al., 2022; Queen & Harding, 2020). During the COVID-19 pandemic, evidence of burnout in the helping professions was everywhere. Take a moment to reflect on the experiences described in the Real People feature to understand better how burnout can devastate entire professions.

Burnout has several bad effects on the brain such as weakened connections between the amygdala, anterior cingulate cortex, and prefrontal cortex (discussed in Chapters 2, 6, and 7; Golkar et al., 2014; Michel, 2016). These changes have been related to problematic behavior. For instance, burnout in physicians has been found to create changes in key areas of the brain connected to complex decision making, which in turn is connected to increased medical errors (Manji et al., 2021). The effects of burnout are clearly serious, with life-threatening consequences in certain circumstances. As noted in the Real People feature, one particularly troublesome aspect of pandemic-related burnout was that simple behaviors that could have significantly reduced the levels and extent of burnout—wearing a mask and keeping physical distance—were simply not done by many people for a variety of reasons. The consequences of such actions, which may not have been understood or considered, were nonetheless very real.

Interestingly, though, burnout does not affect everyone in a particular profession. Why? Vallerand (2015; Lavoie et al., 2021) proposes the difference relates to people feeling different types of passion (obsessive and harmonious) toward their jobs. A **passion** is a strong inclination toward an activity individuals like (or even love), they value (and thus find important), and where they invest time and energy (Vallerand, 2015). Vallerand's Passion Model proposes people develop a passion toward enjoyable activities that are incorporated into identity.

Vallerand's model differentiates between two kinds of passion: obsessive and harmonious. A critical aspect of obsessive passion is the internal urge to engage in the passionate activity, which makes it difficult for the person to fully disengage from thoughts about the activity, leading to conflict with other activities in the person's life (Vallerand, 2015). Such beliefs and an "all in" approach may also be detrimental to one's career. O'Keefe and colleagues (2018) and Lavoie and colleagues (2021) found that those who believe passion is something to discover rather than to develop, and were encouraged to find their passion, tend to put all of their effort or resources into one role and are more likely to abandon their career choice when the going gets tough.

In contrast, harmonious passion results when individuals do not feel compelled to engage in the enjoyable activity; rather, they freely choose to do so, and it is in harmony with other aspects of the person's life (Vallerand, 2015). These individuals seek balance in

Real People

Burnout on the Front Lines of Health Care

Early in the COVID-19 pandemic, healthcare workers were viewed with admiration as frontline heroes; many communities celebrated them each day with various types of demonstrations, such as ringing bells or banging on pots. But as those celebrations faded with time, the toll on healthcare workers began to be apparent. By August 2020, only about six months into the pandemic, 8% of physicians had already closed their practices due to burnout and related reasons (Physicians Foundation, 2020). What happened?

Andrew Jacobs (2021), a reporter for the *New York Times*, sought some answers. The stories he heard were all similar. After months of dealing with the nonstop onslaught of COVID patients, cuts in pay due to the loss of revenue from the stoppage of other medical procedures, and the frustration with people who disregarded mask-wearing and physical distancing, Dr. Sheetal Khedkar Rao, an internist from Chicago, closed her practice to spend more time with her young children as they switched to remote learning. Celia Nieto, an intensive care nurse in Las Vegas, said many Americans "had scant appreciation for the tribulations that she and her colleagues face day after day. There is the physical exhaustion of lifting and turning patients on their bellies so they might breathe easier, the never-ending scramble to adjust ventilators and pain medication, and the mental anguish of telling relatives she doesn't have the time to help them FaceTime with their loved ones."

Dr. Erica Bial, a pain specialist from suburban Boston who barely survived COVID-19, said, "We put on our masks and come to work every day because we don't have the luxury of working from home in our pajamas, but the apathy and ennui that's taken hold of society just makes our job feel thankless. It's so demoralizing."

These individuals, and thousands more, reflect the result of unrelenting pressure of life-and-death decisions, the helpless feelings of watching people die alone, and what appeared to them as an uncaring attitude on the part of people who disregarded preventive measures. As noted in the text, burnout has serious negative effects on brain function, health, and attitude; it can lead to stress-related physical and mental health problems.

As the pandemic continued, critical shortages in healthcare workers not only had implications for patient care in hospitals, but also for the rollout of vaccines. Despite the urgent need, none of the federal programs meant to provide assistance for those affected by the pandemic directly targeted healthcare workers or focused on ways to speed the credentialing process.

A key question emerging from these experiences is: How many people will still want to pursue a healthcare career knowing the potential consequences and the likelihood of another pandemic? Without specific programs that address the high risk of burnout, it may be difficult to meet the need for many more healthcare workers.

their lives and cycle through a number of enjoyable activities about which they are passionate.

Research in France and Canada indicates the Passion Model accurately predicts employees' feelings of burnout (Vallerand, 2008; Vallerand et al., 2010). As noted in Figure 12.3, obsessive passion predicts higher levels of conflict that in turn predict higher levels of burnout. In contrast, harmonious passion predicts higher levels of satisfaction at work and predicts lower levels of burnout.

The best ways to lower burnout are intervention programs that focus on both the organization and the employee (Bagnall et al., 2016; Cohen-Serrins, 2021) and foster an emphasis on developing (rather than seeking and finding) passion (Lavoie et al., 2021; O'Keefe et al., 2018; Vallerand, 2015). At the organizational level, job restructuring and employee-provided programs are important. For employees, prioritizing self-care (such as sleep and stress-reduction techniques), setting boundaries regarding other people's expectations, cognitive restructuring of the work situation, and finding alternative ways to enhance personal growth and identity are most effective (e.g., Allexandre et al., 2016).

Adult Development in Action

If you were a job recruiter, how would you encourage people to work for your organization?

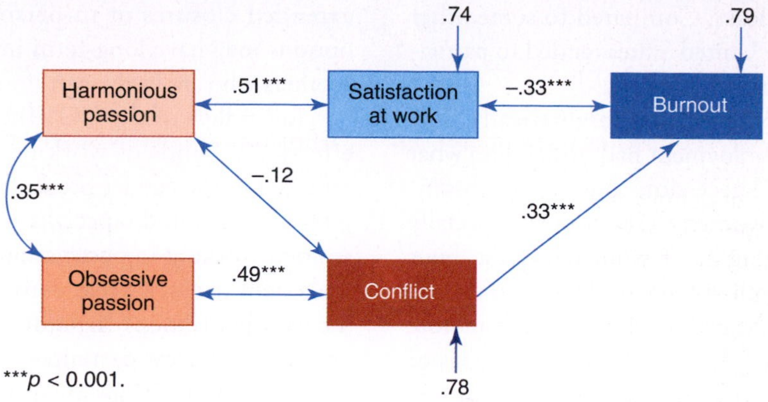

Figure 12.3 Model of the relations among passion, satisfaction at work, conflict, and burnout.

Note: Harmonious passion predicts higher levels of satisfaction at work that predict lower levels of burnout. In contrast, obsessive passion predicts higher levels of conflict that predict higher levels of burnout.

Source: Vallerand, R. J., Paquet, Y., Philippe, F. L., & Charest, J. (2010). On the role of passion for work in burnout: A process model. *Journal of Personality*, 78, 289–312. https://doi.org/10.1111/j.1467-6494.2009.00616.x

Review Questions

12.1 Occupational Selection and Development

- What does work mean for most people?
- How do people usually select their occupation? What factors influence this choice?
- What theories have been offered to explain occupational development? What are the main characteristics of each?
- What factors influence job satisfaction?
- What are the main reasons people experience alienation and burnout in their job?

12.2 Diversity, Equity, and Inclusion in the Workplace

Key Questions

- How do women's and men's occupational selection differ? How are people viewed when they enter occupations that are considered nontraditional?
- What types of bias and discrimination hinder occupational development?

Janice, a 35-year-old Black manager at a business consulting firm, is concerned because her career is not progressing as rapidly as she hoped. Janice works hard and has received excellent performance ratings every year. She has noticed there are few women overall, and even fewer women of color, in upper management positions in her company. Janice wonders whether she will ever be promoted.

Occupational choice and development are not equally available to all, as Janice is experiencing. Gender, race, ethnicity, age, and other sociocultural demographic categories may be used as barriers by organizations explicitly or implicitly to block people from achieving occupational goals. People in similar occupations may have had different life experiences and received different socialization as children and adolescents that made it easier or more difficult for them to pursue a particular career. Bias, harassment, and discrimination based solely on demographic characteristics create real barriers to occupational success.

Diversity and Occupational Development

Prior to the 2020 COVID-19 pandemic, roughly 60% of all women over age 16 in the United States participated in the labor force, which comprised about half of the total workforce (Borodovsky, 2019). Across racial and ethnic groups, Black women participated the most and Latina women the least. Compared to some other countries, women in the United States tended to participate in the labor force at a higher rate.

By 2021, that had all changed dramatically. The pandemic's impact on employment had turned into what Mason (2020) called a "shecession" due to its substantially greater impact on women than on men, especially Black women. By the end of 2020, women had lost about 1 million more jobs than had men, and also had to take on significantly more of the childcare tasks and remote learning responsibilities. This trend follows decades of increasing labor force participation rates for women, especially mothers of young children. The implications of such findings are particularly serious for mothers (Barua, 2022; Handwerker et al., 2020). The interaction of high rates of layoffs in occupations that employ women and extended closures of in-person school and childcare options may have long-term impacts on the number of mothers who are in the workforce.

Regardless of the COVID-19 pandemic's ultimate effects, the kinds of work people do has changed, as reflected in the gender breakdown of workers in specific jobs. This is found especially in the growing number of women working in occupations that were traditionally male dominated, such as construction and engineering. The skilled trades (carpenters, electricians) still have among the lowest participation rates of women. Data for several occupations are in Figure 12.4. Note the pay differentials between women and men; none of these occupations provide equal pay.

Despite the efforts to counteract gender stereotyping of occupations, male-dominated occupations

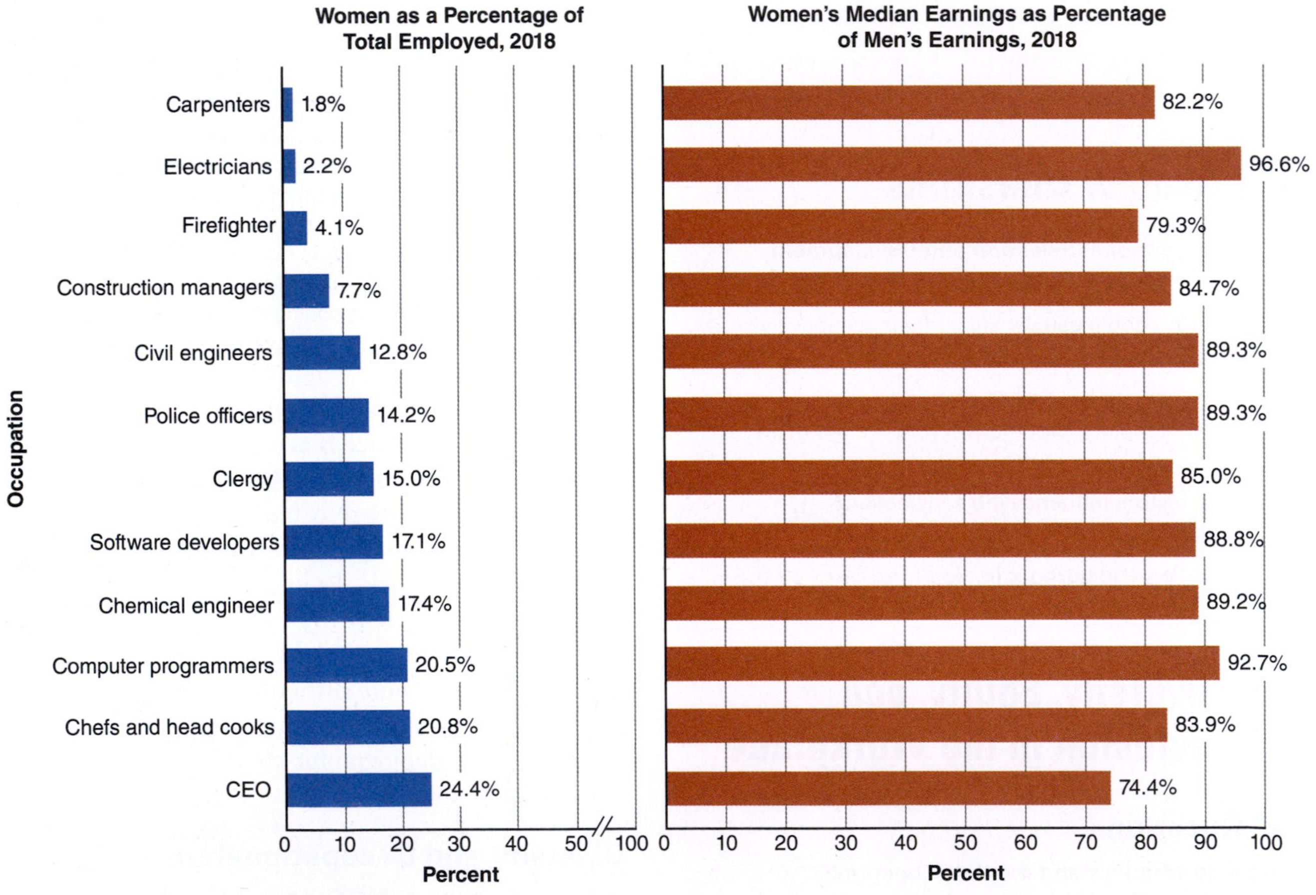

Notes:

*Nontraditional or male-dominated occupations are those in which women represent 25% or less of the total employed in occupations with at least 50,000 people employed.

*Median weekly earnings are 2018 annual averages based on full-time wage and salary workers only. The median for women across all occupations as a percentage of men's earnings is 81.1%.

Figure 12.4 Women's nontraditional occupations and median weekly earnings, 2019 annual averages.

Source: https://www.dol.gov/agencies/wb/data/occupations

tend to pay more than female-dominated occupations (Price, 2016). This differential occurs globally. We will return to pay discrimination a bit later in this chapter. Although the definition of nontraditional varies across cultures, the U.S. government bases data on occupations in which women are about 25% or less of the workforce in that occupation. Based on that, women who choose nontraditional occupations and are successful in them tend to be perceived negatively as compared with similarly successful men in those occupations. Additionally, sexual objectification of women is more frequent in nontraditional occupations and may result in higher rates of sexual objectification and harassment (Auzoult, 2020; Gervais et al., 2016).

One major change across the generations from the silent generation to Gen Z is the progressive increase in opportunities for employment choice regardless of gender. Still, that does not mean all things are equal. For instance, women entrepreneurs are starting small businesses but encounter structural barriers in gaining access to capital and are dissuaded from certain forms of entrepreneurship (BarNir, 2021; McLymont, 2016). As the last of the millennial generation and Gen Z continue to enter and advance in their chosen careers, it will be interesting to find out whether their high degree of technological sophistication, broader experience and background in entrepreneurship, and more egalitarian attitudes will provide more equitable opportunity (Parker & Grote, 2022; Wegman et al., 2018).

In the corporate world, unsupportive or insensitive work environments, organizational politics, and the lack of occupational development opportunities are the most important impediments for women working full-time. Greater empowerment of women is an essential element in ensuring they receive occupational development and remain in their jobs (Cornwall, 2016; Spark et al., 2021). Women professionals tend to leave their jobs for two main reasons. First, the organizations where they work are felt to idealize and reward masculine values of working—individuality, self-sufficiency, and individual contributions—while emphasizing tangible outputs, competitiveness, and rationality. Research indicates that most women prefer to work in organizations that highly value relationships, interdependence, and collaboration.

Second, many women may feel disconnected from the workplace because of these values mismatches. By midcareer, women may conclude they must leave unsupportive organizations in order to achieve satisfaction, growth, and development at work and be rewarded for the relational skills they consider essential for success. As we discover a bit later, whether women leave their careers or plateau before reaching their maximum potential in the organization because of lack of support and/or discrimination, or because of personal choice, is controversial.

Unfortunately, little research has been conducted from a developmental perspective related to occupational selection and development for people of color, especially women. Rather, most researchers have focused on the limited opportunities people of color have and on the structural barriers, such as discrimination, they face.

Women do not differ significantly in terms of participation in nontraditional occupations across ethnic groups (Hegewisch & Hartman, 2014). However, Black women who choose nontraditional occupations tend to plan for more formal education than necessary to achieve their goal. This is due to the discrimination in employment that forces them to achieve more than their White counterparts. This may actually make them overqualified for the jobs they get; a woman with a college degree may be working in a job that does not require that level of education.

Whether an organization is responsive to the needs of people of color makes a big difference for employees. Employees in several countries who work in a diverse organization report more positive feelings about their workplace when they perceive their organizations as responsive and communicative in supportive and transparent ways (Duchek et al., 2020; Fletcher & Beauregard, 2022; Hofhuis et al., 2016; Triana et al., 2021).

Bias, Harassment, and Discrimination

Since the 1960s, numerous laws have been enacted in the United States to prohibit various types of bias and discrimination in the workplace. Despite anti-discrimination laws, though, bias and discrimination still occur far too frequently. As evidenced by the #MeToo and #BlackLivesMatter movements, it may even seem that little progress has occurred. Let's consider the evidence for both progress and frustration.

Gender Bias, Glass Ceilings, and Glass Cliffs. More than half of all people employed in management, professional, and related occupations are women (U.S. Department of Labor Women's Bureau, 2022). However, women are still underrepresented at the top, as noted earlier. Janice's observation in the vignette that few women serve in the highest ranks of major corporations is accurate.

Why are there so few women in such positions? **The most important reason is gender discrimination: denying a job to someone solely on the basis of the person's gender.** Gender discrimination is still pervasive and gets worse the higher up the corporate ladder one looks (Thomas et al., 2020).

Women themselves refer to a glass ceiling, the level they may rise within an organization but beyond which they may not go. The glass ceiling is a major barrier for women (Northouse, 2022; Thomas et al., 2020), is a global phenomenon (Mohanty, 2021; Samii & West, 2021), and is one of the most important sources of loss of women leaders (Heppner, 2013; Thomas et al., 2020). Men are largely unaware or dismissive of the existence of the glass ceiling.

The glass ceiling is pervasive across higher management and professional workplace settings (Heppner, 2013; Thomas et al., 2020). Despite decades of attention to the issue, little overall progress is being made in the number of women, especially women of color, who lead major corporations; the situation is even worse in terms of the number of women who serve on the boards of directors of the top corporations (Azmat & Boring, 2020; Thomas et al., 2020). The glass ceiling also provides a framework for understanding limitations to women's careers in most countries around the world (Azmat & Boring, 2020; Mohanty, 2021; Samii & West, 2021; Thomas et al., 2020). The extent to which women have their careers limited compared with men is clearly evident in Figure 12.5, which indicates the talent pipeline in several occupations.

Research is indicating that the glass ceiling is not specific to women. The LGBTQIA+ communities have encountered this form of discrimination for decades, though for years it was neither studied nor discussed openly (Naylor, 2021). For example, it was not until 2021 that an openly gay person, Pete Buttigieg, served as the head of a federal agency and in the cabinet of

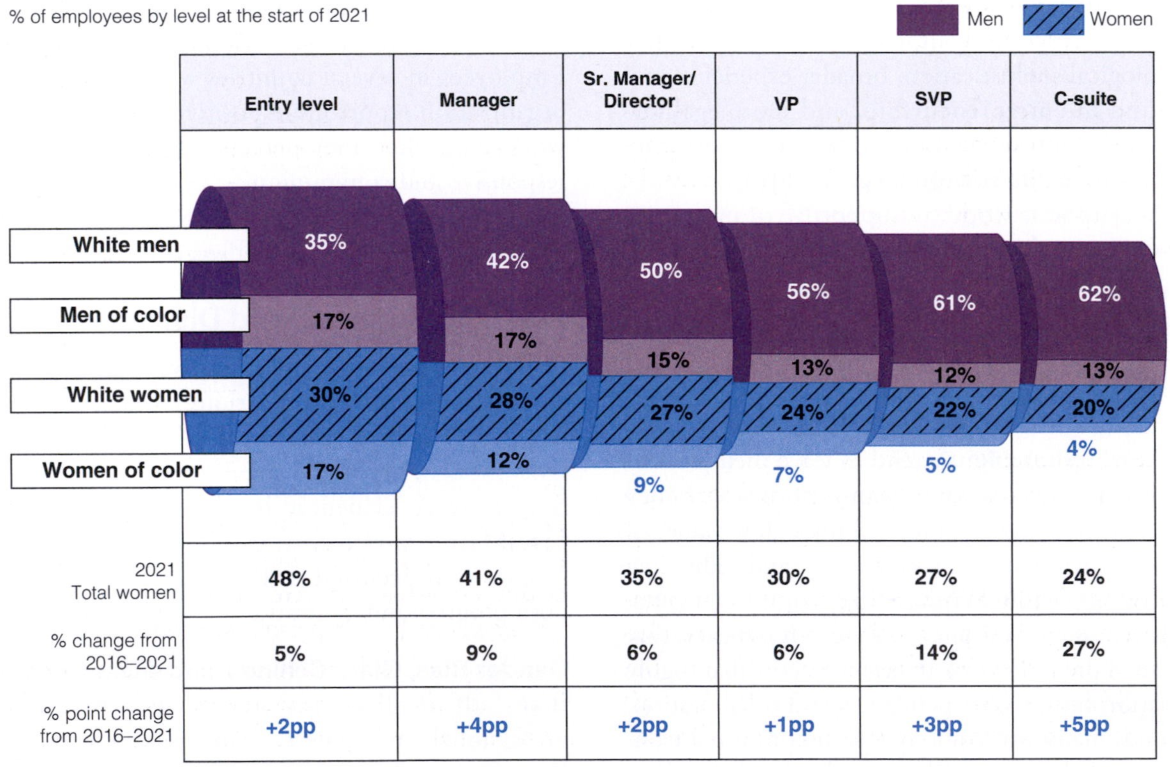

Figure 12.5 Representation in the corporate pipeline by gender and race.

Source: Thomas, R., Cooper, M., Urban, K., Cardazone, G., Bohrer, A., Mahajan, S., Yee, L., Krivkovich, A., Huang, J., Rambachan, I., Burns, T., & Trkulja, T. (2021). *Women in the workplace, 2021.* https://www.mckinsey.com/~/media/mckinsey/featured%20insights/diversity%20and%20inclusion/women%20in%20the%20workplace%202021/women-in-the-workplace-2021.pdf?shouldindex=false (Figure, p. 8).

the U.S. president. It is also the case that legal protections against discrimination do not extend to all groups equally; for example, such protections may not extend to members of LGBTQIA+ communities equally in all states or in the federal government.

A different trend emerges if one examines who is appointed to critical positions in organizations in times of crisis. Research demonstrates that women are more likely put in leadership positions when a company is in crisis. Consequently, women often confront a **glass cliff** where a woman is put into a leadership position because an organization is in a precarious situation. Evidence indicates companies are more likely to appoint a woman to their board of directors if their financial performance has been poor in the recent past, and women are more likely to be political candidates if the seat is a highly contested one (Ryan et al., 2010, 2016; Saridakis et al., 2022). This approach is more common in large organizations; in small and medium sized ones, men are given more responsibility during times of volatility, creating different forms of discrimination based on organization size (Saridakis et al., 2022). Most important, there is growing evidence that having a woman follow a man as CEO of a challenged organization generally lowers the organization's risk (Rigolini et al., 2021).

What can be done to eliminate the glass ceiling and the glass cliff? Most important, at the structural organizational level discrimination in the workplace must be eliminated so that every worker is protected equally. At the individual level, Shonk (2020) argues and Thomas and colleagues' (2020) research indicates women can and must be assertive in getting their rightful place at the table and improving their negotiation skills by focusing on several things: drilling deep into the organization so they can make informed decisions, taking advantage of training, getting critical support, getting the necessary resources, getting buy-in, and making a difference.

Equal Pay for Equal Work. In addition to discrimination in hiring and promotion, women are also subject to salary discrimination. According to the National Women's Law Center (2021), 97% of all occupations show a gender-based wage gap. Overall, the Institute for Women's Policy Research (2020) and the National Women's Law Center (2021) note that women who work full-time earn about 82% of men's median annual earnings. The Institute also noted that at the present rate of change, it will take until 2059 for women's overall median earnings to be equivalent to men's median earnings for the same occupations, though it will take much longer than that for Black women and Latina women to hit that mark. The wage gap is clear even when other factors are the same. For example, mothers are paid less than fathers, and women with disabilities are paid less than men with disabilities (National Women's Law Center, 2021).

Pay equity also does not exist for workers of color. For example, for every $1 earned by a White man, a Black man earns 88 cents, and a Black woman earns 76 cents (SHRM, 2021). Equating for education and experience does not eliminate this gap. A wage gap also exists for members of the LGBTQIA+ communities, but this is a bit more complicated. Although gay men earn less than straight men in the same occupation, they earn more than lesbians (National Women's Law Center, 2021). Note that the gender pay gap is still greater in all cases.

Many people have argued that there are legitimate reasons for the wage gap, such as women stepping out of their careers to raise children, or their taking lower paying jobs in the first place. Data do not support this view. Gender-based pay differentials still largely hold even when these other factors are considered. Most telling are data from situations in which the person is constant, but gender is not. Research indicates that average earnings for transgender women fall by about one-third (National Women's Law Center, 2021). The facts are clear—women are paid less simply because they are women.

Sexual Harassment. Suppose someone worked hard on a paper for a course and believes they've done a good job. When they receive an "A" for the paper, they are elated. When they discuss their paper (and their excitement) with their instructor, they receive a big hug. How do they feel? What if this situation involved a major project at work and the hug came from their boss? Their coworker? What if it were a kiss on their lips instead of a hug? What if it the person demanded sex?

Whether such behavior is acceptable, or whether it constitutes sexual harassment, has been the focus of changing attitudes and standards that reflect many situational factors, including the setting, people involved, and the relationship between them.

Sexual harassment is an extremely serious issue. How many people have been sexually harassed? That's a hard question to answer for several reasons: there is no universal definition of sexual harassment, people have different perceptions, and most survivors do not report it (Arekapudi & Recavarren, 2020; National Women's Law Center, 2022). The #MeToo movement makes clear that the number is far more than previously estimated. Global research by the World Bank indicates that in the European Union 55% of women overall and 75% in professional or top management positions report being sexually harassed at some point in their careers. After the #MeToo movement began in India, reports of sexual harassment increased by 80% (Arekapudi & Recavarren, 2020).

Formal complaints about sexual harassment are filed most often by women, but about 17% of workplace sexual harassment cases in the United States are filed by men (U.S. Equal Employment Opportunity Commission, 2021a). The number of formal workplace complaints in the United States has increased since 2015, but it is unclear whether this is because of increased sensitivity and training by employers that has resulted in individuals feeling more comfortable reporting incidents, an actual increase in the incidence of sexual harassment, or both. (It should be noted that sexual harassment in the workplace and sexual assault occurring to students are reported differently.)

What are the effects of being sexually harassed? As you might expect, research clearly reports negative job-related, psychological, and physical health outcomes (Cortina & Areguin, 2021; Holland & Cortina, 2016). Many people who have shared their stories as part of #MeToo and other platforms make these outcomes clear, and these stories show that the consequences can affect people for many years, even decades, after the harassment incident(s).

What can be done to provide people with safe work environments, free from sexual harassment? Training is a common approach that should have lowered incidents, but has not. Why has training failed? Zelin and Magley (2020) propose five main reasons why traditional organizational training sessions are ineffective at ending sexual harassment in the workplace: (1) training is only focused on legal compliance, (2) people expect immediate results after a single training session, (3) employees hold negative pretraining attitudes, (4) bystander training does not transfer as well to the workplace, and (5) there is no effective measurement to determine if training is working. Zelin and Magley argue that what is really needed to end sexual harassment in the workplace is culture and climate change.

Clearly, the #MeToo movement was a turning point. Whether the attention paid to sexual harassment as a result will result in genuine, permanent change in workplace culture and climate that are in turn grounded in attitudes and behaviors remains to be seen.

Discrimination in the Workplace. Beginning in 1963, the United States passed several laws making it illegal to use various demographic and other criteria as the primary basis for making hiring and promotion decisions in organizations. Among the more prominent laws are the Equal Pay Act of 1963 (making it "illegal to pay different wages to men and women if they perform equal work in the same workplace"), Title VII of the Civil Rights Act of 1964 (making it "illegal to discriminate against someone on the basis of race, color, religion, national origin, or sex" and later amended to include pregnancy, childbirth, or related medical condition), the Age Discrimination in Employment Act of 1967 (protecting people over age 40), and Title I of the Americans with Disabilities Act (ADA) of 1990 (making it "illegal to discriminate against a qualified person with a disability in the private sector and in state and local governments. The [ADA] law also requires that employers reasonably accommodate the known physical or mental limitations of an otherwise qualified individual with a disability who is an applicant or employee, unless doing so would impose an undue hardship on the operation of the employer's business"). This suggests the federal government desires to create the space for a diverse workforce. Reality, though, is another matter.

Discrimination on the basis of race and ethnicity has a very long history. Despite the laws prohibiting it, such discrimination continues and has proven to be very difficult to eradicate (Livingston, 2020). Research continues to document systematic underrepresentation of people of color in numerous occupational categories, especially those at the senior and executive levels and in professional categories (U.S. Equal Employment Opportunity Commission, 2021b). Livingston (2020) argues that there are five steps in moving toward equity: (1) problem awareness and (2) root-cause analysis that focus on understanding that discrimination aimed at people of color is a problem and where it comes from;

(3) empathy, relating to whether one cares about the problem and the people it harms; (4) strategies for addressing the problem; and (5) sacrifice, reflecting whether one is willing to do the work necessary to eliminate it.

Another structural barrier to occupational development is **age discrimination**, denying a job or promotion to someone solely on the basis of age. The U.S. Age Discrimination in Employment Act protects workers over age 40. (Consider that the oldest members of the millennial generation became covered under this law in 2021.) Very few other countries provide such protection; for instance, evidence reviewed by SHRM showed that age discrimination is common in India and China (Smith, 2019). One of the few exceptions is the Equality Act of 2010 in the United Kingdom that includes a prohibition against age discrimination, but the European Union as a whole has few protections against it (Equality and Human Rights Commission, 2018; Georgantzi, 2018). Age discrimination laws stipulate that applicants and employees must be evaluated based on their qualifications and performance, not their age, and that employers cannot segregate or classify workers or otherwise denote their status on the basis of age.

Age discrimination is difficult to document because employers can make such things as an applicant's earnings history or other variable appear to be a deciding factor in an employment decision. Or they can attempt to eliminate older workers by using retirement incentives. Or supervisors can let their stereotypes about aging interfere with their assessment of the quality of older workers' performance. As noted by the U.S. Equal Employment Opportunity Commission (2022), all of these actions are illegal.

Perfect Angle Images/Shutterstock.com

Employers cannot make a decision about promoting this person solely on the basis of age.

Employment prospects for middle-aged people around the world are lower than for their younger counterparts (Iparraguirre, 2020; Smith, 2019; Vansteenkiste et al., 2015). For example, age discrimination toward those over age 35 is common in China (Smith, 2019), resulting in longer periods of unemployment. Such practices may save companies money in the short run, but the loss of expertise and knowledge comes at a high price. Indeed, an emerging model of employment is **boomerang employees**, individuals who terminate employment at one point in time but return to work in the same organization at a future time. Boomerang employees sometimes return as employees on the company's payroll but increasingly are returning as contract workers who are not eligible for benefits, thereby meeting the company's needs for both expertise and lower costs (Gerhart & Feng, 2021; Shipp et al., 2014).

The Americans with Disabilities Act of 1990 was a major step to protect people with physical or mental conditions that had been used to screen people out of jobs (Hebl et al., 2020; Requero et al., 2020). Little research has focused specifically on this form of discrimination; most of the focus has been on the requirement to provide appropriate accommodations. Because a significant sector of individuals who are protected under this law are military veterans, more attention is being paid to hiring practices and the importance of including individuals with various abilities as part of a diverse workforce. Customized employment options are increasingly being used in organizations as one way to reduce discrimination and underemployment (Readhead & Owen, 2020).

This section has focused on attitudes and practices in organizations that are detrimental to supporting people's occupational and career aspirations. Not being hired or promoted because of a sociocultural category you are put into is frustrating, demeaning, and unfair. We each hope that hiring and promotion are based on knowledge, skills, and abilities, not what religious beliefs we have or our gender, for instance. The rise of the #MeToo, #BlackLivesMatter, and related movements; the reconceptualization of aging and later life by the baby boomers; and explicit efforts to diversify the talent pipelines from preschool onward

Controversies

Creating an Inclusive Workplace

Among the many findings and recommendations noted in research like the annual *Women in the Workplace* studies on organizational climate is what it takes to create a workplace environment that is truly inclusive and where everyone feels safe. Perhaps reflecting aspects of the broader culture, roughly 60% of the respondents in those studies indicated that they experience uncivil behavior at work, ranging from racial and ethnic slurs to sexual assault.

Though frustratingly slow, progress for women had been made—until the pandemic. As the *Women in the Workplace: 2020* (Thomas et al., 2020) and the *Women in the Workplace: 2021* (Thomas et al., 2021) studies noted, because of the differential impact of the pandemic on women, especially Black women, "All the progress we've seen [since 2015] would be erased" (Thomas et al., 2020, p. 9). The pandemic led to women leaving the workforce in record numbers, forcing a reckoning regarding the supports they need and how those are related to a diverse workforce.

Many organizations understand that they need to take important steps to address problems such as those noted in the *Women in the Workplace* studies. These include better paid leave options, support for child and other dependent care, and so forth.

But there is more to creating a diverse workforce than expanding worker benefits. Key steps include prioritizing diversity, not tolerating biased or disrespectful behavior, and encouraging inclusion. Mozilla (2020), the company that created the Firefox web browser and other apps, took these matters seriously. Through a series of employee focus groups and surveys, they created their *Community Participation Guidelines*, which serves as the code of conduct.

The *Guidelines* "aim to support a community where all people should feel safe to participate, introduce new ideas and inspire others, regardless of: background, family status, gender, gender identity or expression, marital status, sex, sexual orientation, native language, age, ability, race and/or ethnicity, caste, national origin, socioeconomic status, religion, geographic location, or any other dimension of diversity." Mozilla expects employees to be respectful, be direct but professional, be inclusive, understand different perspectives, appreciate and accommodate similarities and differences, and lead by example. Mozilla will not tolerate violence and threats of violence, personal attacks, derogatory language, unwelcome sexual attention or physical contact, or disruptive behavior. The consequences of these unacceptable behaviors are also clearly articulated.

When appropriately developed and implemented, policies such as Mozilla's *Guidelines* improve employee morale and retention. Do you know whether your workplace has similar policies? What do *you* think about them based on your experience and what you learned in this section?

represent important steps forward. One example of how a company takes inclusion seriously is provided in the Controversies feature. Many organizations are taking similar steps to create better, more supportive places to work.

Adult Development in Action

If you were the CEO of a major corporation, how would you ensure that your company treats all employees appropriately and fairly?

Review Questions

12.2 Diversity, Equity, and Inclusion in the Workplace

- What are the main concerns regarding diversity in the workplace?
- What are the main types of bias in the workplace?
- What forms of discrimination are specifically determined to be illegal?
- What are the main types of discrimination found in the workplace?

12.3 Occupational Transitions

Key Questions

- Why do people change occupations?
- Is worrying about potential job loss a major source of stress?
- How does job loss affect the amount of stress experienced?

Fred has 32 years of service for a vehicle manufacturer making pickup trucks. Over the years, more and more assembly-line jobs have been eliminated by new technology (including robots) and the export of manufacturing jobs to other countries. Although Fred has been assured by his employer that his job is safe, he isn't so sure. He worries he could be laid off at any time.

In the past, people like Fred commonly had the option of choosing an occupation during young adulthood that they could stay in throughout their working years. Today, however, not many people have that option. Corporations have restructured so often employees now assume occupational changes are part of the career process. This means people's conceptions of work and career are in flux and losing one's job no longer has only negative meanings (Biggs et al., 2017; Yu et al., 2021).

Several factors have been identified as important in determining who will remain in an occupation and who will not. Some factors—such as whether the person likes the occupation—lead to self-initiated occupation changes. However, other factors—such as obsolete skills and larger economic or social trends—may cause forced occupational changes. Continued improvement of robots has caused some manufacturing sector workers to lose their jobs; corporations send jobs overseas to increase profits; and economic recessions and pandemics usually result in large-scale layoffs and high levels of unemployment.

Reskilling and Upskilling Workers

When a person is hired into a specific job, they are selected because the employer believes they offer the best fit between the abilities they already have and those needed to perform the work. As most people can attest, though, the skills needed to perform a job usually change over time. Such changes may be based in the introduction of new technology, additional responsibilities, or promotion.

Unless a person's skills are kept up-to-date, the outcome is likely to be either job loss or a career plateau (da Costa & Oliveira, 2016; Jiang, 2016). **Career plateauing** occurs when there is a lack of challenge in one's job or promotional opportunity in the organization or when a person decides not to seek advancement. Research in Canada (De Clerq et al., 2020), Kenya (Gaturu & Njuguna, 2020), and China (P. Wang et al., 2021) indicates feeling one's career has plateaued usually results in less organizational commitment, lower job satisfaction, and a greater tendency to leave. But attitudes can remain positive if it is only the lack of challenge and not a lack of promotion opportunity responsible for the plateauing (da Costa & Oliveira, 2016; Jiang, 2016).

In cases of job loss or a career plateau, reskilling or upskilling may be an appropriate response. Around the world, large numbers of employees participate each year in programs and courses offered by their employer or by a college or university and aimed at improving existing skills (reskilling) or adding new job skills (upskilling). For mid-career employees, reskilling and upskilling might focus on how to advance in one's occupation or how to find new career opportunities—for example, through résumé preparation and career counseling. Increasingly, such programs are offered online in order to make them easier and more convenient for people to access. For people who were involuntarily separated from their employer, severance packages may provide a way to pay for these courses.

Alternatively, mid-career individuals may choose to change fields altogether. In this case, people may head back to a college or other educational provider and earn a credential in a completely different field. Increasingly, middle-aged adults are seeking career coaches to help them navigate through the decision to change careers (Stoltz, 2016).

The reskilling and upskilling of midcareer and older workers highlight the need for lifelong learning as a way to stay employable (Froehlich et al., 2016). If corporations are to meet the challenges of a global economy, it is imperative they include retraining in their employee development programs. Such programs will improve people's chances of advancement in their chosen occupations and also assist people in making successful transitions from one occupation to another.

Occupational Insecurity

Changing economic realities (e.g., increased competition in a global economy), changing demands for skills, continued advancements in technology, global recessions, a pandemic, and other factors force many people out of their jobs. Heavy manufacturing, resource extraction, and their support businesses, as well as family farming have been a few of the hard-hit sectors since the 1970s. The financial services sector was hard hit during the Great Recession. Service sector employment (e.g., hospitality, tourism, restaurants) was especially devastated in the COVID-19 pandemic. No one is immune anymore from layoff.

As a result, many people feel insecure about their jobs much of the time. Economic downturns create significant levels of stress, especially when such downturns create massive job loss (Niaz et al., 2021; Urbanaviciute et al., 2021). Continued shifts from in-person retail to online retail result in nearly constant retrenchment in retail jobs as traditional retailers declare bankruptcy or severely retrench. The advent of driverless cars even threatens the jobs of taxi and ride share drivers.

Like Fred, the autoworker in the vignette, many worried workers have several years of dedicated service to a company. Unfortunately, people who worry about their jobs tend to have poorer physical and psychological well-being (Gonza & Burger, 2017; Niaz et al., 2021). Anxiety about one's job may result in negative attitudes about one's employer or even about work in general, and in turn may result in diminished desire to be successful. Whether there is an actual basis for people's feelings of job insecurity may not matter; sometimes what people *think* is true about their work situation is more important than what is actually the case. Just the possibility of losing one's job can negatively affect physical and psychological health.

How does the possibility of losing one's job affect employees? Mantler and colleagues (2005) examined coping strategies for comparable samples of laid-off and employed high-technology workers. They found although unemployed participants reported higher levels of stress compared with employed participants, employment uncertainty mediated the association between employment status and perceived stress. That is, people who believe their job is in jeopardy—even if it is not—show levels of stress similar to unemployed participants. Perreault and colleagues (2020) found that such distress is long-lasting—and is lessened only if coping strategies are supported.

There are several ways people deal with stress; two of the more common are emotion-focused coping and problem-focused coping (discussed in Chapter 4). Some people focus on how the stressful situation makes them feel, so they cope by making themselves feel better about it. Others focus on the problem itself and do something to solve it. People who use emotional avoidance as a strategy report higher levels of stress, particularly when they are fairly certain of the outcome. Thus, even people whose jobs aren't really in jeopardy can report high levels of stress if they tend to use emotion-focused coping strategies.

Coping with Unemployment

Losing one's job can have enormous personal impact that can last a long time (Gonza & Burger, 2017; Norris, 2016) and even impact life expectancy (Bianchi et al., 2020). When the overall U.S. unemployment rates hit a post–World War II record 14.8% in April 2020 early into the COVID-19 pandemic, millions of people could relate. Years afterward, the psychological impact will remain (Bianchi et al., 2020; Gonza & Burger, 2017), even for people who found other jobs. When unemployment lasts and re-employment does not occur soon, unemployed people commonly experience a wide variety of negative effects (Norris, 2016) that range from a decline in health and immune system functioning (Altweck et al., 2021; Cohen et al., 2007; Rigby, 2021) to decreases in well-being (Gonza & Burger, 2017; Suppa, 2021).

In a comprehensive analysis of the effects of unemployment, McKee-Ryan and colleagues (2005) found several specific outcomes from losing one's job, all of which have been redocumented over the years, that tend to disappear eventually with reemployment. The elements underlying these effects are presented in Figure 12.6 (McKee-Ryan et al., 2005).

The effects of job loss vary with age, race, ethnicity, gender, and education (Norris, 2016). In the United States, middle-aged men are more vulnerable to negative effects than older or younger men—largely because they tend to have greater financial responsibilities than the other two groups and they derive more of their identity from work (Bambra, 2010; Norris, 2016). The higher one's education levels, the less stress one typically feels immediately after losing a job, probably because higher education levels usually result in faster re-employment (Mandemakers & Monden, 2013).

The pattern for women is more complicated. Longitudinal research in Germany showed that there is a

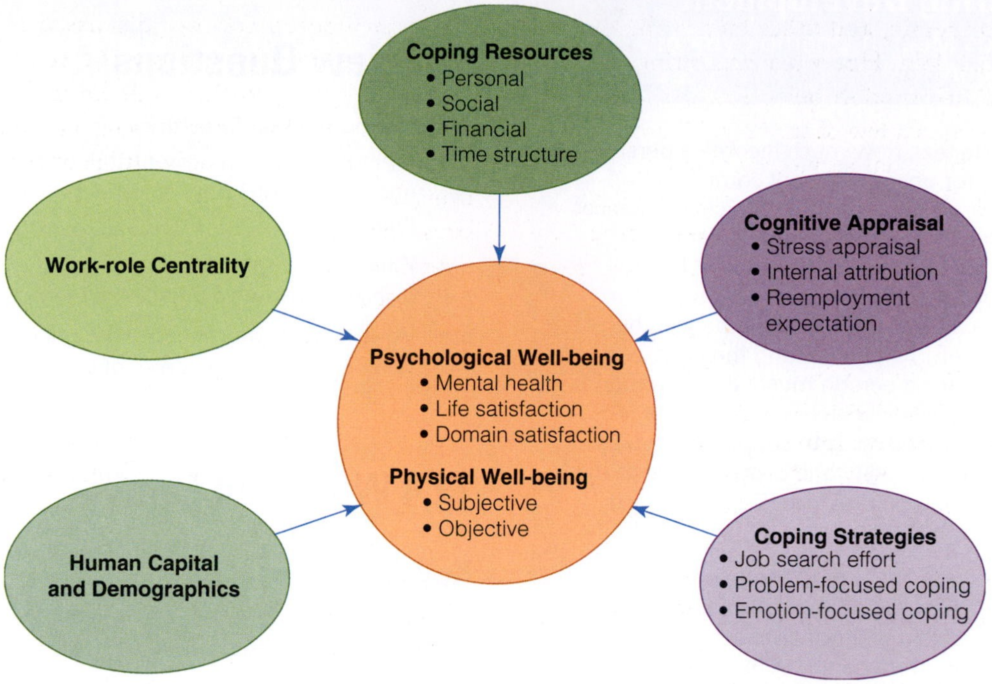

Figure 12.6 Psychological and physical well-being after losing one's job are affected by many variables.

Source: From McKee-Ryan, F., Song, Z., Wanberg, C. R.,& Kinicki, A. J. (2005). Psychological and physical well-being during unemployment: A meta-analytic study. *Journal of Applied Psychology,* 90(1), 53–76.

nonlinear trajectory in career recovery for women over time (Manzoni & Mooi-Reci, 2020). Over the first 6 years following unemployment, differences between women's and men's career quality narrow, but after that they diverge, with women experiencing significantly worse outcomes. Although some of this difference is due to multiple employment interruptions for planned reasons such as maternity, much of it reflects gender bias. For men, career quality takes 15 years on average to return to what it was right before unemployment; for most women, it never does.

Because unemployment rates are substantially higher for Black and Latino/a than for White individuals, differences that were exacerbated during the COVID-19 pandemic (Bureau of Labor Statistics, 2021a), the effects of unemployment are experienced by a greater proportion of people in these groups. Economic consequences of unemployment are often especially difficult for Black workers, particularly women. For example, compared to White workers, it usually takes workers of color significantly longer to find another job.

How long a person is unemployed also affects how they react. People who are unemployed for at least a year perceive their mental health significantly more negatively than either employed people or those who have removed themselves from the labor force (e.g., have stopped looking for work). For example, global evidence suggests that suicide risk increases the longer unemployment lasts (Gunnell & Chang, 2016; McIntyre & Lee, 2020) Those who lost their jobs involuntarily feel a loss of control over their work environment and feel less demand placed on them. Importantly, a reasonable amount of demand is critical to maintaining good health, whereas too little demand lowers health.

Coping with unemployment involves both financial and personal issues. The financial support people receive varies across states and situations. Unemployment compensation is typically much lower than one's original salary, often resulting in severe financial hardship and difficult choices for individuals. People risk losing their homes to foreclosure, for instance, as well as encountering difficulties with other everyday expenses such as food and medicine.

Discovering Development

Making Ends Meet in Unemployment Compensation

As noted in the text, how much income a person who qualifies for unemployment compensation will receive varies depending on the circumstances and where one lives. Do you know what those amounts would be in your community? Take the time to discover the basic benefits that your state provides, whether those are enhanced by the federal government, how long they last, and what other actions a person must take to remain qualified (e.g., actively searching for another job). Then consider what it costs to support the typical family in your community and compare that to the amount that would be provided. Do you think it would be enough?

Take your findings and share them with your classmates. If some of your classmates live in different states, you will notice that the amounts will differ. If not, perhaps some individuals in the class will be willing to research the data from other states. Gather all of the information together. Does any state, from all the sources available, provide sufficient income for a typical family to afford everything it needs?

Research also offers some advice for adults who are trying to manage occupational transitions (Ebberwein, 2008):

- Approach job loss with a healthy sense of urgency.
- Consider your next career move and what you must do to achieve it, even if there are no prospects for it in sight.
- Acknowledge and react to change as soon as it is evident.
- Be cautious of stopgap employment as a long-term alternative.
- Identify a realistic goal and then list the steps you must take to achieve it.

Additionally, the U.S. Department of Labor offers tips for job seekers, as do online services such as LinkedIn that also provides networking groups. These steps may not guarantee that a new job will be found quickly, but they will help create a better sense that a person is in control.

Adult Development in Action

If you headed the local Office of Unemployment Benefits, what would you recommend regarding helping to remove the stigma of losing one's job?

Review Questions

12.3 Occupational Transitions

- What are the main reasons that workers need to upskill or reskill? How do organizations address these needs?
- What are the main factors that create occupational insecurity? How do people tend to react?
- How do most people cope with unemployment? What are the main sources of stress?

12.4 Work and Family

Key Questions

- What are the issues faced by employed people who care for dependents?
- How do spouses/partners view the division of household chores? What is work–family conflict, and how does it affect couples' lives?

Jennifer, a 38-year-old auditor, feels her husband, Mustafa, doesn't do his share of the housework or child care. Mustafa says men don't do housework and he's really tired when he comes home from work. Jennifer thinks this isn't fair, especially because she works as many hours as Mustafa, sometimes more.

One of the most difficult challenges facing adults is trying to balance the demands of work with the demands of family. Over the past few decades, the rapid increase in the number of families where a solo parent or both parent-spouses/parent-partners are employed has fundamentally changed how we view the relationship between work and family. This can even mean taking a young child to work as a way to deal with the pushes and pulls of being an employed parent. For example, prior to the COVID-19 pandemic, in roughly half of married-couple families with children, both partners were employed; after the first year of the pandemic, these rates had dropped roughly 4% (Bureau of Labor Statistics, 2021b). Families mostly need the dual income to pay their bills and maintain a moderate standard of living.

In this module we will focus on dual-earner couples, as this will enable us to consider how gender roles and other aspects of a relationship factor into work–family balance. We will discover that dual-earner couples who are responsible for the care of dependent children or older parents experience both benefits and disadvantages. The stresses of living in this arrangement are substantial, and gender differences are clear—especially in the division of household chores.

The Dependent Care Dilemma

Many employed adults must also provide care for dependent children or other relatives (e.g., older parents). Deciding how to divide the chores is a major source of stress, as we will discover.

Employed Care Providers. Many parents have no option but to return to work after the birth or adoption of a child. As noted in Chapter 11, the United States is the only developed country that does not mandate paid parental leave. In fact, in 2021 about 65% of mothers with children under the age of 6 years and roughly 75% of those with children between 6 and 17 years old were in the labor force, which reflects a slight decline from rates prior to the COVID-19 pandemic (Bureau of Labor Statistics, 2021c).

Despite high participation rates, mothers grapple with the decision of whether they want to return to work. Surveys of mothers with preschool children reveal the motivation for returning to work is mainly financial need and how attached mothers are to their work. The amount of leave time a woman has matters, especially whether the leave is paid. The passage of the Family and Medical Leave Act (FMLA) in 1993 entitled workers to take unpaid time off to care for their dependents with the right to return to their jobs. The fact is, many employed parents cannot afford losing their income for an extended period.

The COVID-19 pandemic resulted in quick federal action regarding support for working parents. For example, the Families First Coronavirus Response Act (Congress.gov, 2020) addressed the emergency situations parents found themselves in and the degree to which the act provided the relief intended. For one thing, the extension of the child tax credit reached over 61 million households, and lowered monthly poverty rates among children by over 30% (Turner, 2022).

Another concern for many persons who give birth is whether stepping out of their occupations following childbirth will negatively affect their career paths. (Few men in the United States take paternal leave, making comparisons difficult.) Indeed, some evidence indicates it does (Evertsson et al., 2016; Thomas et al., 2020, 2021) whereas other research indicates that the effects depend on the type of employment (Wirth, 2020). In some employment situations, women in the United States are punished, even for short leaves. In contrast, the situation is different in other countries such as Sweden, where long leaves typically result in a negative effect on upward career movement, but shorter leaves do not.

Purestock/Getty Images

Dual-earner couples must figure out how to juggle all of their roles.

A more detailed look may provide some reasons for differing patterns. Wirth (2020) broke down level of employment into two categories: nonprofessional and professional. Wirth found that, overall, children reduce both mothers' and fathers' occupational status progressively more in the years following childbirth compared to the years preceding it, and that the negative effects accumulate over time. This is especially true for non-professional mothers' and fathers' occupational status, ultimately creating a downward trajectory. In contrast, for professional mothers and fathers, there is a slight upward trajectory for both. In male-dominated professional occupations, children have a positive effect on fathers' occupational status that increases over time and a small but significant negative effect on mothers' occupations status in the later years after first birth that persists.

Often overlooked is the increasing number of workers who must also care for a parent, spouse/partner, or other adult relative. Even fewer federal programs or employee benefits programs cover this type of need. As we noted in Chapter 11, providing this type of care takes a high toll through stress and has a generally negative impact on one's career. We turn to this issue in the next section.

Dependent Care and Effects on Workers. Being responsible for dependent care has significant negative effects on employed caregivers. Whether responsible for the care of an older parent or a child, those taking care of them report negative effects on their work, higher levels of stress, and problems with coping (Neal & Hammer, 2007). Roxburgh (2002) introduced the notion that parents dealing with time pressures feel much more stress. Subsequent research in the United States and Korea clearly indicates not only are stress levels higher, but "fast-forward families" (dual earner couples with a frenetic life style) also often deal with negative impacts on career advancement and physical and mental health consequences of this life style (Cha & Papastefanou, 2020; Ochs & Kremer-Sadlik, 2013). Unsurprisingly, women's careers are usually affected more negatively than men's.

How can these negative effects be lessened? When women's partners/spouses provide good support and women have average or high control over their jobs, employed mothers are significantly less distressed than employed nonmothers or mothers without support (Cram et al., 2016). One of the most important factors in this outcome is the realization that it is impossible for either mothers or fathers to "have it all" (Cram et al., 2016).

Like many other aspects of life, the COVID-19 pandemic made the usual stresses associated with being an employed parent worse. Most important, the need for parents to take on the role of teacher while their child attended remote schooling was extremely daunting. Because some states required parents to be online with their child during lesson times, figuring out how to fit that into already hectic work schedules became a major source of stress. Organizations such as Pandemic Parenting provided resources, including mental health support, and other help for parents who needed it (Pandemic Parenting, 2021). Even early in the pandemic, it was clear that the situation was a mental health crisis for parents, the extent of which had not been documented previously (Grose, 2020). Multiple surveys documented parents' fears of their inability to provide for their child's basic needs, and rates of depression and anxiety spiked (Davenport et al., 2020; UOregon CTN, 2020). It remains to be determined how long after the pandemic these mental health impacts on parents will last.

Employer Responses to Need for Dependent Care. Employed parents with small children or dependent adults (e.g., those need accommodations, who have certain health conditions such as dementia) are confronted with the difficult prospect of leaving them in the care of others for some portion of the day while they are working. This is especially problematic when the usual care arrangement is temporarily unavailable, such as due to weather-related closures of the school or the care facility. (Closures due to the pandemic were a different issue, as discussed earlier.) A growing need in the workplace is for **backup care** that provides emergency care for dependent children or adults so the employee does not need to lose a day of work.

Does providing a workplace care center or backup care make a difference in terms of an employee's feelings about work, absenteeism, and productivity? There is no simple answer. For example, making a childcare center available to employees does tend to reduce employee stress but does not necessarily reduce parents' work–family conflict or their absenteeism (Hipp et al., 2017; Masterson et al., 2021). A "family-friendly" company must also pay attention to the attitudes of their employees and make sure the company provides broad-based support beyond just providing a place for care (Aryee et al., 2013; Hill et al., 2016; Masterson et al., 2021). The keys are how supervisors act and the number and type of supportive benefits the company provides, such as flex-time work arrangements. Cross-cultural research in Korea confirms having a family-friendly supervisor matters (Aryee et al., 2013). The most important single thing a company can do is allow the employee to leave work without penalty to tend to family needs (Thomas et al., 2020, 2021).

Research also indicates there may not be differences for either mothers or their infants between work-based and nonwork-based childcare centers in terms of the mothers' ease in transitioning back to work or the infants' ability to settle into day care (Hill et al., 2016;

Hipp et al., 2016). Unfortunately, similar research focused on fathers is largely lacking.

It will be interesting to watch how these issues—especially paid family leave and flexible schedules—play out in the United States, where such practices are not yet common. A global study of family leave showed the more generous family leave policies are, the lower the infant mortality rates, clearly indicating parental leave policies are a good thing (Ferrarini & Norström, 2010).

Juggling Multiple Roles

When both members of a couple with dependents are employed, who cleans the house, cooks the meals, and takes care of the dependents when they are ill? This question goes to the heart of the core dilemma of modern, dual-earner couples: How are household chores divided? How are work and family role conflicts handled?

Dividing Household Chores. Despite much media attention and claims of increased sharing in the duties, in heterosexual couples, women still perform the majority of housework, regardless of employment status. As depicted in Figure 12.7, this is true globally (OECD, 2016). This unequal division of labor causes the most arguments and the most unhappiness for dual-earner couples. This is the case with Jennifer and Mustafa, the couple in the vignette; Jennifer does most of the housework.

The additional burden women carry with respect to household chores and dependent care is still reflected in millennial generation couples, in which about 60% say that tasks are divided roughly equally, though women still tend to do more of the child care (Pew Research Center, 2015, 2016, 2019b, 2020). Data also indicate that women are still more likely than men to say that parenting responsibilities interfere with career advancement.

Racial and ethnic differences in the division of household labor are also apparent. In Mexican American families, fathers are doing more of the housework and child care than was the case in earlier generations (Capistrant et al., 2020). Comparisons of Latino/a, Black, and White American men consistently show that how much men help at home depends on time availability, the resources that are available, and gender role beliefs (Capistrant et al., 2020; Davis & Wills, 2014).

Work–Family Conflict. When people have both occupations and dependents (e.g., children, aging parents), they must figure out how to balance the demands of each. These competing demands cause **work–family conflict**, the feeling of being pulled in multiple directions by incompatible demands from one's job and one's family.

Dual-earner couples must find a balance between their occupational and family roles. Many people believe work and family roles influence each other: When things go badly at work, the family suffers, and when there are troubles at home, work suffers. That's true, but the influence is not the same in each direction (Andreassi, 2011). Whether work influences family or vice versa is a complex function of personality, coping skills, support resources, type of job, and a host of other issues that interact—as was made clear during the pandemic (Grose, 2020; Queen & Harding, 2020; Repetti & Wang, 2017). One key but often overlooked factor is whether the work schedules of both partners/spouses allow them to coordinate activities such as child care or parent care (van Klaveren et al., 2013). Another is the ability of a spouse/partner to provide emotional and social support for the other spouse/partner when work stress increases (Repetti & Wang, 2017).

Understanding work–family conflict requires taking a life-stage approach to the issue (Blanchard-Fields et al., 2004). The availability of support for employed parents that takes the child's developmental age into account (e.g., day care for young children, flexible work schedules when children are older), and work-friendly schedules for parental day care goes a long way to helping employed couples balance work and family obligations.

The issues faced by dual-earner couples are global: burnout from the dual demands of work and caring for dependents is more likely to affect women across many cultures (Balogun & Afolabi, 2020; Bozzon & Murgia, 2021; Rashmi et al., 2021). Work–family conflicts are arguably worse for couples in the United States because Americans work more hours with fewer vacation days and with fewer family-friendly benefits than any other developed country (Thomas et al., 2020, 2021). You may be thinking that one obvious solution is to legislate shorter work schedules. Surprisingly, it's not that simple. It turns out that in the 32 countries Ruppanner and Maume (2016) studied, there is no reduction in work-to-family interference. In fact, the opposite occurs—there is an increase in such interference when work hours are reduced. Why? The most likely answer is that reduced work hours result in higher expectations of better work–family balance, so people become more sensitive to even little disruptions, thereby increasing feelings of unhappiness.

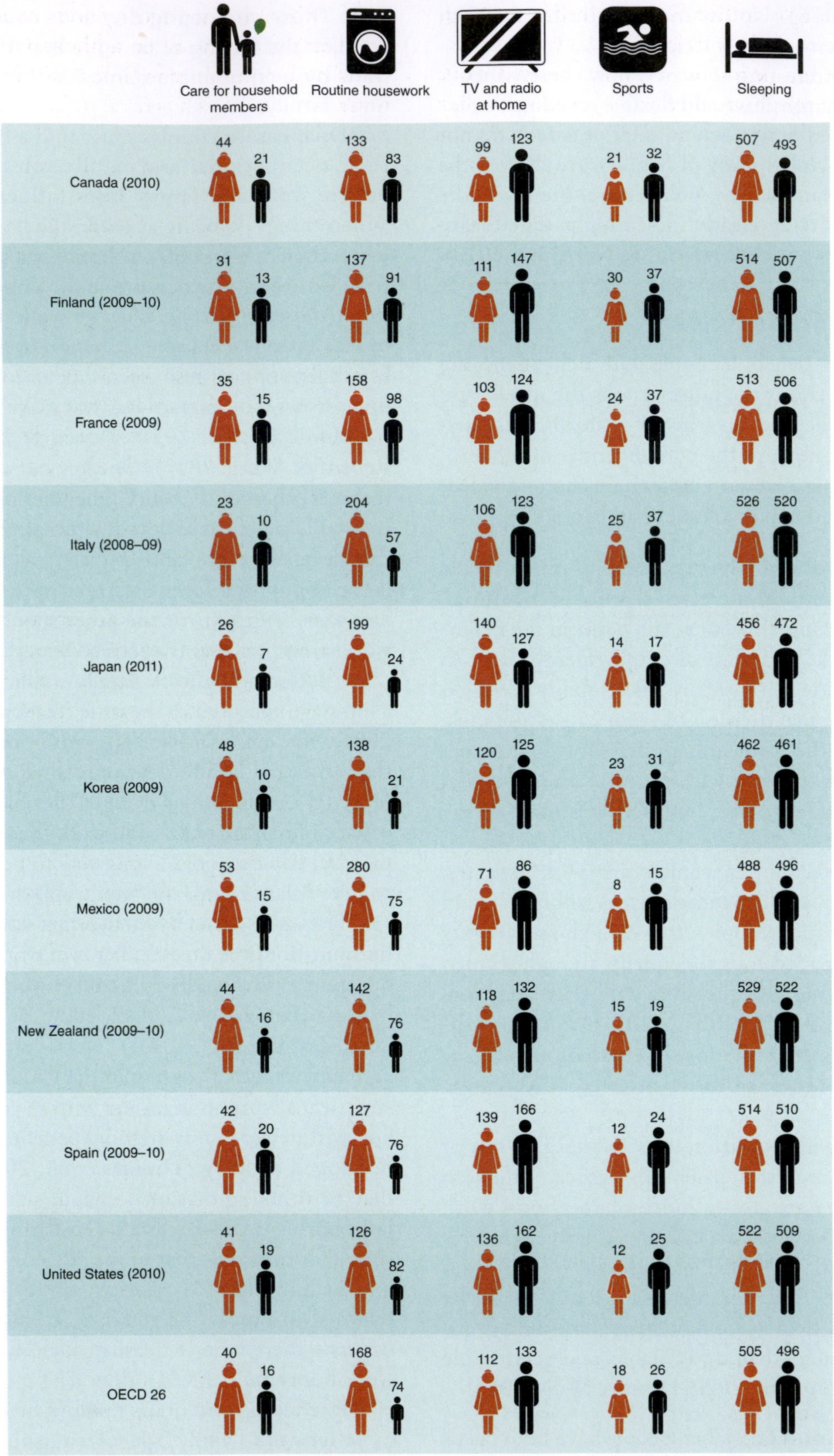

Figure 12.7 Average time spent in caregiving, housework, entertainment, and sleeping per day.

Source: OECD. (2016). Balancing paid work, unpaid work and leisure. https://www.oecd.org/gender/data/balancingpaidworkunpaidworkandleisure.htm

What is a couple to do? For one thing, they can work together to help mitigate the stress. Most important, they can negotiate schedules around work commitments throughout their careers, taking other factors such as child care and additional time demands into account (van Wanrooy, 2013). These negotiations should include discussion of such joint activities as meals and other family activities, too (Ochs & Kremer-Sadlik, 2013). In short, communicate about all of the demands and come to an understanding and compromise that provides an optimal solution for all concerned.

Adult Development in Action

If you were an elected official, what three things would you do to assist families?

Review Questions

12.4 Work and Families

- What is dependent care? How is dependent care a major issue in the workplace?
- How do dual-earner couples manage multiple roles?

12.5 I Used to Work at . . . : Living in Retirement

Key Questions

- What does being retired mean?
- Why do people retire?
- How do people adjust to retirement?
- What employment and volunteer opportunities are available for older adults?

Marcus is a 77-year-old retired construction supervisor who worked hard all of his life. He managed to save a little money, but he and his wife rely primarily on his monthly Social Security check. Although not rich, they have enough to pay the bills. For the most part, Marcus is happy with retirement, and he stays in touch with his friends. He thinks that maybe he's a little strange, though, because he has heard that retirees are supposed to be isolated and lonely.

Did you know that until the late 19th century retirement in the United States was rare, and until 1935, when Social Security was inaugurated, retirement was not considered a likely possibility by most Americans like Marcus (Iekel, 2018)? In a very real sense, retirement as a general practice is a 20th-century phenomenon.

The current generation of retirees tended to take retirement for granted as they navigated through their employment. However, because economic downturns have a major disruptive effect on people's retirement decisions and plans, such assumptions are not as widely held. Additionally, previous stereotypic views of retirement have changed as new views of aging and better health for the typical older adult have altered our very image of an older retired adult. These realities have, in turn, affected social policy. Living longer lives in retirement means longer payouts of benefits. A significant global social challenge is created regarding how to fund retiree benefits and support older adults (Cahill & Quinn, 2020; Quinn & Cahill, 2016; Wise, 2017).

After having one or several careers across adulthood, many older adults find themselves questioning whether they want to continue in that line of work anymore, or find themselves being forced to go through that questioning because they lost their jobs or have been offered buyouts. This period of questioning and potential exploration enables people to think about their options: retiring, searching for work in the same of a different field, volunteering, or some combination of all of these.

As we consider retirement and other options in late life, keep in mind that the changing nature of work will increase options and flexibility, including the likelihood that more older adults will continue in the labor force by choice and necessity.

Imtmphoto/Shutterstock.com

People in the baby boomer generation who retire are redefining what retirement means.

What Does Being Retired Mean?

Retirement means different things to men and women, and to people in different racial and ethnic groups and careers (Hou & Sanzenbacher, 2021; James et al., 2016; Silver, 2016; P. Taylor et al., 2021). These different meanings have been influenced by both the Great Recession in 2008 and the COVID-19 pandemic because of the abrupt changes in people's planning and expectations as a result of the loss of savings or pensions, changes in employer actions, and threats to personal health (Quinn & Cahill, 2016; Rappaport, 2021).

Part of the reason it is difficult to define retirement precisely is that the decision to retire involves the loss of occupational identity with no obvious replacement for that loss. Not having a specific job anymore means we either put that aspect of our lives in the past tense—"I used to work as a manager for Hilton"—or say nothing at all. Loss of this aspect of our identity can be difficult to face, so some look for a label other than "retired" to describe themselves (Grødem & Kitterød, 2021).

That's why researchers view retirement as another one of many transitions people experience in life (Kojola & Moen, 2016; Moen, 2016a; Phillipson, 2020). This view makes retirement a complex process where people withdraw from full-time participation in an occupation (Moen, 2016a; Phillipson, 2020), recognizing there are many pathways to this end.

Why Do People Retire?

Provided they have good health, more workers retire by choice than for any other reason (Cohen-Mansfield & Regev, 2018; Phillipson, 2020), as long they feel financially secure after considering projected income from Social Security, pensions and other structured retirement programs, and personal savings (Cahill & Quinn, 2020; Rappaport, 2021). Of course, some people are forced to retire because of health problems or because they lose their jobs. The COVID-19 pandemic also brought a large wave of retirements. As corporations downsize during economic downturns, pandemics, or after corporate mergers, some older workers accept buyout packages involving supplemental payments if they retire. Others are permanently furloughed, laid off, or fired.

The decision to retire voluntarily is influenced by one's occupational history and goal expectations (Moen, 2016a; Phillipson, 2020; P. Taylor et al., 2021). Whether people perceive they will achieve their personal goals through work or retirement influences the decision to retire and its connection with health and disability.

The rude awakening many people received during the Great Recession, for example, was that the best made plans are only as good as external factors allow them to be, especially when it comes to financial savings and pensions. Many people lost much of their investment savings and home equity as the value of stocks plummeted, companies eliminated pension plans, and the housing market collapsed. Consequently, many people were forced to delay their retirement until they had the financial resources to do so, or to continue working part time when they had not planned to do so to supplement their income. By comparison, although many people lost their job during the COVID-19 pandemic, financial investments did not collapse as was the case in the Great Recession.

Income security is now the primary driver of retirement decisions (Cahill & Quinn, 2020; Phillipson, 2020; Rappaport, 2021). How much do you need to have in savings to be comfortable in retirement? A decent rule of thumb is to save enough to generate between 70% and 80% of your current income, and to plan for about 25 years in retirement. This figure is based on typical living and medical expenses. The bottom line is longer life expectancies have added to the amount of money you will need in retirement—and that amount is usually much greater than you may think.

Gender, Racial, and Ethnic Differences. Women's experience of retiring can be quite different from men's (P. Taylor et al., 2021). Women's employment careers may have developed differently, such as having starts and stops related to dependent care responsibilities, or may reflect later entry into the workforce. Because of the pay gap and possible interruptions in work history, many women have fewer financial resources for retirement.

For women who were never employed outside the home, the process of retirement is especially unclear (P. Taylor et al., 2021), even though they are eligible for Social Security benefits. Because they were not paid for their work raising children and caring for the home, it is rare for them to have their own pensions or other sources of income in retirement beyond Social Security. Additionally, the work they have always done caring for the home continues, often nearly uninterrupted (Ciani, 2016).

There has been less research examining the process of retirement as a function of race or ethnicity. Black and Latino/a older adults are likely to continue working beyond age 65, mainly due to greater financial need on average and lower availability of employer-sponsored retirement savings plans (Angel & Angel, 2015; Hou & Sanzenbacher, 2021; Tamborini & Kim, 2020).

Adjustment to Retirement

How do people who go through the process of retirement adjust to it? Researchers agree on one point: new patterns of personal involvement and identity must be developed in the context of changing roles and lifestyles in retirement (Grødem & Kitterød, 2021; Phillipson, 2020; Rappaport, 2021; P. Taylor et al., 2021). People's adjustment to retirement evolves over time as a result of complex interrelations involving physical health, financial status, the degree their retirement was voluntary, and feelings of personal control.

How do most people fare? As long as people have financial security, health, a supportive network of relatives and friends, and an internally driven sense of motivation, they report feeling good about being retired (Moen, 2016a; Ng et al., 2016; Phillipson, 2020; P. Taylor et al., 2021). What motivates most people, though, is finding a sense of fulfillment in ways previously unavailable to them (James et al., 2016).

There is a stereotype that retirement has negative effects on health. Research describes the actual relation between health and retirement as complex. A study of over 9,300 retired U.S. residents showed that retirement for poor health reasons was related to worse health after retirement, but retirement due to non-health reasons was unrelated to health after retirement. Interestingly, health outcomes were worse if the person phased into partial retirement than if the person went from full-time work to complete retirement (Han, 2021). Regarding mental health, a study in the Netherlands showed that retirement of partnered men positively affects the mental health for the men and their partners, but retirement of partnered women or of single adults has no apparent effects on the mental health of either group (Picchio & van Ours, 2020).

Employment and Volunteering

Retirement is an important life transition, one best understood through a life-course perspective that takes other aspects of one's life, such as one's marital relationship, into account (Fye et al., 2020; Moen, 2016a). This life change means retirees must look for ways to adapt to new routines and patterns, while maintaining social integration and being active in various ways (e.g., friendship networks, community engagement).

Employment in Late Life. For an increasing number of people, especially for those whose retirement savings are insufficient, retirement involves working at least part-time. For one thing, many developed countries, including the United States, have increased the age at which people become fully eligible for benefits, such as Social Security, in retirement. Continued employment for them is likely a financial necessity to make ends meet, especially for those whose entire income would consist only of Social Security or other defined retirement benefits (Lain et al., 2020).

For others, the need to stay employed at least part-time represents a way to stay involved beyond an income supplement and a way for employers to continue benefiting from employees' experience. For example, even in the rapidly changing knowledge industry, employment of workers over age 65 has been demonstrated to benefit both older adults and companies (Bartkowiak, 2017).

The percentage of adults aged 65 and over who are in the workforce increased dramatically between 2000 and 2019. However, that trend ended abruptly in the COVID-19 pandemic (Johnson, 2021). Older adults were disproportionately affected by the job losses during the pandemic; more older adults left the U.S. workforce in 2020 than in any other year since record keeping began in 1948.

Workforce participation also fell most for older adults. Between February 2020 (just before the pandemic hit the United States) and February 2021, the participation rate fell 11.1% for people aged 65 and older but only 1.2% for those ages 55 to 64, 2.2% for those ages 25 to 54, and 2.9% for those ages 16 to 24. That's the largest 12-month drop in the participation rate for adults aged 65 and older in 60 years.

What the declines in older adults' participation rates mean is complicated. For one thing, by spring of 2022 nearly 2 million workers who had retired in 2021 were back in the workforce (AARP, 2022b). Most of them went back initially into part-time jobs, and their reasons were mainly financial (inflation, stock market volatility), the option of working remotely, and for social interaction. Thus, the actual impact of the COVID-19 pandemic on retirement decisions may never be known fully. Additionally, as we noted at the outset of this chapter, the meaning people derive from their work contributes a great deal to their sense of identity, making continued participation in work (however a person defines it for themselves) a key aspect of life satisfaction.

Whatever their motivation, though, older workers face many challenges globally, not the least of which are ageism and discrimination (World Health Organization, 2021c). Employers may believe older workers are less capable, and there is evidence this translates into lower likelihood of getting a job interview compared to younger or middle-aged workers, all other things being equal (Abrams et al., 2016; Kleissner & Jahn, 2021). As we noted earlier in this chapter, despite the fact that age discrimination laws in the United States protect people over age 40, such barriers are still widespread.

The relationship between age and job performance is extremely complex (Sterns & Spokus, 2020). This is because it depends a great deal on the kind of job one is considering, such as one that requires a great deal of physical exertion or one that involves a great deal of expertise and experience. In general, older workers show more reliability (e.g., showing up on time for work), organizational loyalty, and safety-related behavior.

Viewed globally, employers are facing the demographic changes described in Chapter 1, especially the aging of the available workforce. For example, countries in Europe are aging, so employers face critical decisions about how to accommodate older workers. How have companies done this? One example is BMW, a major automotive company that changed a number of things in its automobile assembly plants to better meet the needs of older workers (de Pommereau, 2012; Uţă, 2019). BMW provides physical trainers on the factory floor, has new, softer floors, offers chairs that rise up and down to make tasks easier, uses larger print fonts on computer screens, and provides special shoes. The interventions were so successful that within 10 years of its original test, BMW implemented the program globally.

Ariel Skelley/DigitalVision/Getty Images

Older adults often continue some level of employment to provide income during retirement.

The trend for companies to employ older workers, especially on a part-time basis, is likely to continue because it is a good option for many companies (Coleman, 2015; Sterns & Spokus, 2020). Some companies find they need the expertise older workers bring, and the flexibility of older workers in terms of hours and the type of benefits they need (or do not need) often make employing them less expensive. Consequently, "retirement" is likely to continue to evolve as a concept and is likely to include some aspect of employment well into late life.

Coleman (2015) argues that the benefits of hiring and retaining older workers could make companies stronger and more successful. However, a change in approach will require overcoming stereotypes of aging, as well as balancing the need to provide opportunities for younger workers with the need to retain the experience and knowledge of older workers.

Volunteering. Healthy, active retired adults often find meaning and explore things they always wished they had had a chance to do by volunteering (Ajrouch et al., 2014; Owen et al., 2022; Same et al., 2020). Older adults report they volunteer for many reasons that benefit their well-being such as to provide service to others, to maintain social interactions and improve their communities, and to keep active.

Why do so many people volunteer? Several factors are responsible (Ajrouch et al., 2015; Owen et al., 2022; Shen et al., 2020): changing characteristics of social networks, developing a new aspect of the self, finding a personal sense of purpose, desiring to share one's skills and expertise, redefining the nature and merits of volunteer work, and having a more highly educated and healthy population of older adults along with greatly expanded opportunities for people to become involved in volunteer work they enjoy. Research in New Zealand documents older adults who find volunteering enables them to give back to their local communities (Wiles & Jayasinha, 2013). Owen and colleagues (2022) argue volunteerism offers a way for society to tap into the vast resources older adults offer.

There is also evidence that the expectations of people who volunteer in retirement are changing. Women in the baby boom generation are interested in volunteering for personal rather than purely altruistic reasons and do so on their own terms (Seaman, 2012). They are not as willing as volunteers were in previous generations to serve on time-consuming boards and to engage in fundraising (Sheppard & Stanford, 2019; P. Taylor et al., 2021). As a result, organizations that rely on volunteers need to be in touch with the concerns and motivations of their pool of volunteers.

The U.S. government has been tapping into this pool of talented volunteers since President John F. Kennedy first proposed the idea. As part of the Corporation for National and Community Service, the AmericCorps Seniors consists of three major programs: Foster Grandparent Program, RSVP, and Senior Companion Program (Corporation for National and Community Service, 2021). These national organizations have programs and opportunities across the country, and interested people aged 55 and over are encouraged to explore them. These and other programs provide organized ways to get and stay active and to find meaningful forms of engagement.

Adult Development in Action

If you were the vice president for talent at a major corporation, how would you incorporate older adult workers?

Review Questions

12.5 I Used to Work at . . . : Living in Retirement

- What is the meaning of retirement? How has this meaning changed over time?
- What are the major reasons people give for retiring?
- How well do most people adjust to retirement? How is this demonstrated?
- What are the patterns of continued employment and volunteering among older adults?

12.6 Taking Time to Relax: Leisure Activities

Key Questions

- What activities are leisure activities? How do people choose among them?
- What changes in leisure activities occur with age?
- What do people derive from leisure activities?

Claude is a 55-year-old electrician who has enjoyed outdoor activities their whole life. From childhood they fished the trout rivers and snowshoed in the backcountry of Montana. Although snowshoeing the really rugged trails is now in the past, Claude still enjoys both sports every chance they get.

Adults do not work for pay every waking moment of their lives. As each of us knows, we need to disconnect from our smartphones, relax, and engage in leisure activities. Intuitively, leisure consists of activities not associated with work. **Leisure** is discretionary activity that includes simple relaxation, activities for enjoyment, and creative pursuits. Simply finding the time to fit leisure into an already busy schedule can be challenging. For too many people, leisure just becomes another scheduled component in our overall time management problem (Corbett & Hilty, 2006).

Types of Leisure Activities

Leisure can include virtually any activity. To organize the options, researchers classified leisure activities into several categories. Jopp and Hertzog (2010) developed an empirically based set of categories that includes a wide variety of activities:

- physical (e.g., lifting weights, backpacking, jogging),
- crafts (e.g., woodworking, household repairs),
- games (e.g., board/online games, puzzles, card games),
- watching TV,
- social–private (e.g., going out with a friend, visiting relatives, going out to dinner),
- social–public (e.g., attending a club meeting, volunteering),
- religious (e.g., attending a religious service, praying),
- travel (e.g., travel abroad, travel out of town),
- experiential (e.g., collect stamps, read for leisure, gardening, knitting),
- developmental (e.g., read as part of a job, study a foreign language, attend public lecture), and
- technology use (e.g., photography, use computer software, play an instrument).

More complete measures of leisure activities not only provide better understanding of how adults spend their time but can help in clinical settings. Declines in the frequency of leisure activities are associated with

Participating in leisure activities can improve one's well-being.

symptoms of depression (Schwerdtfeger & Friedrich-Mei, 2009), with lower well-being (Paggi et al., 2016), and with a later diagnosis of dementia (Hertzog et al., 2009). Monitoring changes in leisure activity levels during and after intervention programs can provide better outcomes assessments.

Given the wide range of options, how do people pick their leisure activities? Apparently, each of us has a leisure repertoire, a personal library of intrinsically motivated activities we do regularly and we take with us into retirement (Nimrod, 2007a, 2007b). The activities in our repertoire are determined by two things: perceived competence (how good we think we are at the activity compared to other people our age) and psychological comfort (how well we meet our personal goals for performance). As you might expect, men and women differ in their views of leisure, as do people in different ethnic and age groups (van der Pas & Koopman-Boyden, 2010).

Personality factors are related to one's choice of leisure activities (Gaudron & Vautier, 2007), and it is possible to construct interest profiles that map individuals to specific types of leisure activities, and to each other (Leuty et al., 2016). Other factors are important as well: income, health, abilities, transportation, education, and social characteristics. Some leisure activities, such as downhill skiing, are relatively expensive and require transportation and reasonably good health and physical coordination for maximum enjoyment. In contrast, reading requires minimal finances (if one uses a public library or other free sources) and is far less physically demanding.

As you may have experienced, the COVID-19 pandemic dramatically changed people's leisure time options (Lashua et al., 2021). Given that many options closed during various restrictions and lockdowns, many turned to online options such as social media and online gaming. All of these technology-mediated activities provide opportunities to create virtual friendship networks that provide the same types of support as traditional face-to-face networks. E-readers with built-in accommodation for visual impairments have increased access to books and other written materials, opening new opportunities for people to join local book clubs.

Developmental Changes in Leisure

Cross-sectional studies report age differences in leisure activities. Emerging adults participate in a greater range of high-energy activities than middle-aged or older adults. In later middle age, people spend more of their leisure in sedentary activities such as reading and watching television and in moderately strenuous activities such as scenic travel, tennis, and hiking (van der Pas & Koopman-Boyden, 2010). A key aspect is that when adults take leisure activities seriously (i.e., identify with and persevere in the activity) and make leisure activities different from what they do at work, their work-related self-efficacy increases (Kelly et al., 2020). Investing oneself in leisure is good for you.

Longitudinal studies of changes in individuals' leisure activities over time show considerable stability in leisure interests over reasonably long periods. For example, studies in the United States, Finland, Great Britain, and Japan show that level of activity in emerging adulthood predicts activity level later in life, and leisure physical activity in emerging adulthood bodes well for health later in life (Hillsdon et al., 2005; Lahti et al., 2016). Claude, the 55-year-old in the vignette who likes to fish and snowshoe, is a good example of this overall trend. As Claude demonstrates, frequent participation in particular leisure activities earlier in life tends to continue into adulthood. Similar findings hold for the pre- and postretirement years. Apparently, one's preferences for certain types of leisure activities are established early in life; they tend to change over the life span primarily in terms of how physically intense they are. Explore these findings in more detail in the How Do We Know? feature.

Consequences of Leisure Activities

What do people gain from participating in leisure activities? Researchers have long known involvement in leisure

How Do We Know?

Long-Term Effects of Leisure Activities

Who were the investigators and what was the aim of the study? It is well established that physical activity is related to better health at all ages in adulthood. However, much of the existing research has focused on more formal exercise programs, with much less attention paid to leisure forms of activity, and whether leisure time physical activity during emerging adulthood is related to subsequent health and well-being in midlife. To answer these questions, Jouni Lahti and colleagues (2016) followed adults in Finland, Great Britain, and Japan.

How did the investigators measure the topic of interest? The investigators used the Short Form-36 health questionnaire to assess physical and mental health. The eight subscales of the SF-36 include physical functioning, role limitations due to physical problems, bodily pain, general health perceptions, mental health, role limitations due to emotional problems, social functioning, and vitality. Scores can range from 0 to 100. Low scores imply poor health functioning, whereas high scores imply good health functioning. The SF-36 has very good reliability and validity.

Who were the participants in the study? Participants in the study were prospective employee cohorts originally recruited for the Finnish HHS study (2000–2002 and 2007, N=5958), British WHII I study (1997–1999 and 2003–2004, N=4142), and Japanese Civil Servants Study (JACS) (1998–1999 and 2003, N=1768). Across the three study samples, participants ranged in age from 20 to 60.

What was the design of the study? The research used a longitudinal design. As noted in Chapter 1, the strength of longitudinal designs is being able to measure a behavior over time in the same individual; the confound is the age of the person at the time of measurement.

Were there ethical concerns with the study? All participants were informed of the nature of the larger study and had given their consent to participate.

What were the results? Leisure physical activity was associated with better subsequent physical health functioning in all three cohorts. However, results varied somewhat across country and gender. Differences were the clearest among Finnish women (inactive: 46.0, active vigorous: 49.5) and men (inactive: 47.8, active vigorous: 51.1) and British women (inactive: 47.3, active vigorous: 50.4). For mental health functioning, the differences were generally smaller and not clearly related to the intensity of physical activity.

What did the investigators conclude? Lahti and colleagues concluded that vigorous physical activity was associated with better subsequent physical health functioning in all three cohorts, although with some differences in magnitude across countries. For mental health functioning, the intensity of physical activity was less important. Promoting leisure time physical activity may prove useful for the maintenance of health functioning among midlife employees.

activities is related to well-being (Paggi et al., 2016; Warr et al., 2004). This relation holds in other countries, such as China (Dai et al., 2013). Participating in leisure activities helps promote better mental health (e.g., Lahti et al., 2016). This is especially true for spouses/partners who use family-based leisure as a means to cope during their spouse/partner's military deployment (Werner & Shannon, 2013) and buffers the effects of stress and negative life events.

Studies show leisure activities provide an excellent forum for the interaction of the biopsychosocial forces discussed in Chapter 1 (Cheng & Pegg, 2016; Kleiber, 2013). Leisure activities are a good way to deal with stress, which—as we learned in Chapter 4—has significant biological effects. This is especially true for unforeseen negative events, such as cancer (Chun et al., 2016). Psychologically, leisure activities have been well documented as one of the primary coping mechanisms people use, such as providing a sense of purpose in life (Chun et al., 2016).

How people cope by using leisure varies across cultures depending on the various types of activities that are permissible and available. Likewise, leisure activities vary across socioeconomic status; basketball is one activity that is global because it is inexpensive, whereas scuba diving is more associated with people who can afford to travel to diving resorts and pay the high fees.

How do leisure activities provide protection against stress? Kleiber and colleagues (2002; Kleiber, 2013,

2020) offer four ways leisure activities serve as a buffer against negative life events:

- Leisure activities distract us from negative life events.
- Leisure activities generate optimism about the future because they are pleasant.
- Leisure activities connect us to our personal past by allowing us to participate in the same activities over much of our lives.
- Leisure activities can be used as vehicles for personal transformation.

Whether the negative life events we experience are personal, such as the loss of a loved one, or societal, such as a terrorist attack, leisure activities are a common and effective way to deal with them. They truly represent the confluence of biopsychosocial forces and are effective at any point in the life cycle.

Participating with others in leisure activities may also strengthen feelings of attachment to one's partner, friends, and family (Carnelley & Ruscher, 2000; Jakubiak & Tomlinson, 2020). Adults use leisure to explore interpersonal relationships or to seek social approval. In fact, research indicates marital satisfaction is linked with leisure time; marital satisfaction is even helped when couples spend some leisure time with others in addition to spending it just as a couple (Zabriskie & Kay, 2013). Couples who play together are happier (Johnson et al., 2006).

There is a second sense of attachment that can develop as a result of leisure activities: place attachment. Place attachment occurs when people derive a deep sense of personal satisfaction and identity from a particular place (Di Masso et al., 2017). Place attachment is an active process, bringing the individual a sense of belonging that might not be experienced elsewhere. As a result, place attachment generally drives people to return to the location over and over, and the meaning of being there continues to deepen over time.

One frequently overlooked outcome of leisure activity is social acceptance. For persons with disabilities, this is a particularly important consideration (Choi et al., 2013; Dysterheft et al., 2018). There is a positive connection between frequency of leisure activities and positive identity, social acceptance, friendship development, and acceptance of differences. These findings highlight the importance of designing inclusive leisure activity programs.

Adult Development in Action

If you were the director of an independent living center for older adults, how could you incorporate leisure activities into a wellness program?

Review Questions

12.6 Leisure Activities

- What is leisure? What are the main types of leisure activities?
- How are leisure activities age-related?
- What are the outcomes most people experience from leisure activities?

Social Policy Implications

The Great Resignation

No event in the 21st century has had a greater impact on the labor market than the COVID-19 pandemic. An unprecedented number of American workers quit their jobs at a rate unseen since the 1990s (Parker & Horowitz, 2022). Why?

Parker and Horowitz (2022) report findings from a Pew Research Center survey that noted that low pay, a lack of opportunities for advancement, and feeling disrespected at work were the top reasons why Americans quit their jobs in 2021; these and the remaining top 10 reasons are listed in Figure 12.8. The survey results also indicated that those who quit and are now employed elsewhere are more likely than not to say their current job has better pay, more opportunities for advancement, and more work–life balance and flexibility. Nevertheless, a significant number of respondents reported that things are either worse or unchanged in these areas compared with their former job. In fact, fewer than half of workers who quit a job in 2021 say they now have better benefits, such as health insurance and paid time off, while a similar number say it's comparable. Roughly a quarter now say their current benefits are worse than at their last job. Additionally, other reasons people quit reflected issues raised in the chapter relating

Among those who quit a job at any point in 2021, % saying each was a_____ why they did so

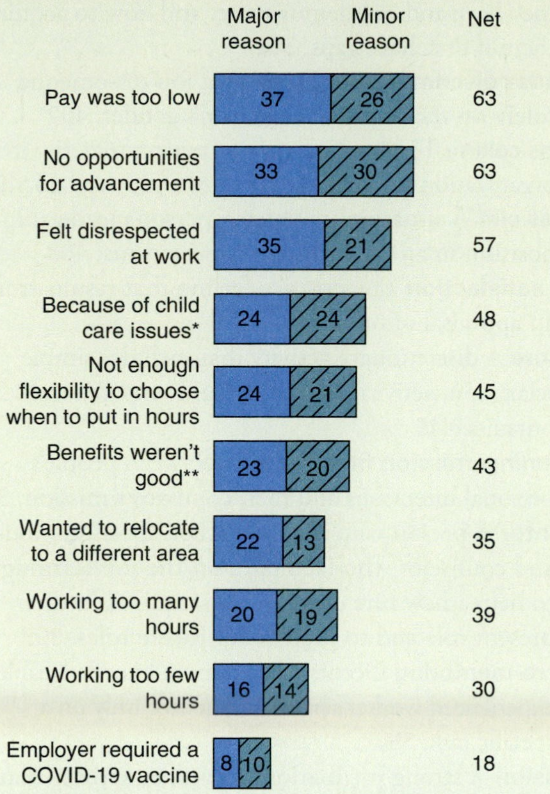

* Among those with children younger than 18 living in the household.

** Question provided health insurance and paid time off as examples.

Note: Figures may not add to subtotals due to rounding.

Source: Survey of U.S. adults conducted Feb. 7–13, 2022.

Figure 12.8 Top reasons why workers left a job in 2021.

Source: https://www.pewresearch.org/wp-content/uploads/2022/03/ft_2022.03.09_greatresignation_01.png

to work–family balance and the lack of paid leave. Interestingly, when asked separately from the main survey whether the COVID-19 pandemic itself was a significant factor, only about one-third of the respondents said it was. Those who were most likely to quit were emerging adults and people earning lower salaries.

What do these data mean for workplace policy? Researchers speculate that the Great Resignation will have a very significant impact on how people view work. At the beginning of the chapter, we noted that people work for many reasons beyond earning money. These are the factors that drove the massive quitting that occurred. Clearly, employers will need to adjust their views of employees and what organizations need to do to attract talent. Among the main trends that are foreseen are:

- A permanent switch to more flexible work schedules.
- Remote work will become a globally competitive talent market.
- Workers will demand more personally meaningful jobs.

Whether the Great Resignation will result in more perceived and real power by workers remains to be seen. But it is likely that work policies will change to provide people more control over schedules, as well as redesigned benefits that enable people to create the package that is best suited for them. Ultimately, it may result in better work–family balance. But it remains an open question whether any of these changes will close the pay equity gap or eliminate other bias and discrimination issues in the workplace.

In Review

For this chapter, you may want to organize your summary into six paragraphs. In the first paragraph, discuss the various meaning people derive from work, and the importance these play for people's identities. Also, describe the different factors that influence people's occupational choices, and the different theories that explain how occupations develop as people grow older. Make sure you describe the different issues that are important at different points in people's work lives. Describe the reasons that result in people being satisfied with their jobs, and the factors that result in alienation and burnout.

In the second paragraph, summarize the factors underlying diversity and the lack of inclusion in the workplace. Describe the various forms of bias in the workplace, especially pay equity, as well as sources of harassment. Discuss the various laws that prohibit different types of discrimination and describe the aims of each.

The third paragraph should summarize the reasons why workers need to upskill and reskill, and how organizations respond to those needs. Describe the reasons that workers feel insecure in their jobs, and how most people attempt to cope with being unemployed.

For the fourth paragraph, summarize the different types of dependent care and the challenges they present to dual-earner couples. Include a discussion of the barriers to support unique to the United States. Describe how most couples attempt to manage all the various roles they have.

Your fifth paragraph should focus on issues related to retirement. Include discussions of the meaning of retirement and how the meaning has changed over time. Discuss the main reasons why most people retire, and how well they adjust. Describe the patterns of employment and volunteering among older adults.

The final paragraph should summarize the meaning of leisure and the different types of leisure activities in which people engage. Include discussion about how these activities change with age. Describe the benefits most people get from engaging in leisure activities.

Integrating Concepts in Development

- What roles do personal relationships play in one's work, leisure, and retirement?
- How do cognitive development and personality influence work roles?
- How will the changing population demographics impact workplace bias, harassment, and discrimination?
- What implications are there for the lack of mandatory retirement in terms of normal cognitive changes with age, generativity, and opportunities for future generations?

Key Terms

age discrimination Denying a job or a promotion to a person solely on the basis of age. 405

alienation Situation in which workers feel what they are doing is meaningless and their efforts are devalued, or when they do not connect what they do and the final product. 397

backup care Emergency care for dependent children or adults so the employee does not need to lose a day of work. 412

boomerang employees Individuals who terminate employment at one point in time but return to work in the same organization at a future time. 405

burnout The depletion of a person's energy and motivation, the loss of occupational idealism, and the feeling of being exploited. 397

career construction theory Posits people build careers through their own actions that result from the interface of their own personal characteristics and the social context. 391

career plateauing Situation occurring when there is a lack of challenge in the job or promotional opportunity in the organization or when a person decides not to seek advancement. 407

developmental coach Individual who helps a person focus on their goals, motivations, and aspirations to help the person achieve focus and apply them appropriately. 395

employability skills mapping A way to help people identify job skills that are in demand with the skills they have and can demonstrate, and how to acquire them if they have gaps. 393

gender discrimination Denying a job to someone solely on the basis of the person's gender. 402

glass ceiling The level to which a person may rise in an organization but beyond which she may not go. 402

glass cliff A situation in which a person's leadership position in an organization is precarious. 403

job satisfaction The positive feeling that results from an appraisal of one's work. 396

leisure A discretionary activity that includes simple relaxation, activities for enjoyment, and creative pursuits. 419

meaning–mission fit Alignment between people's personal intentions and their company's mission. 391

mentor A person who is part teacher, sponsor, model, and counselor who facilitates on-the-job learning to help a new hire do the work required in their present role and to prepare for future roles. 395

micro-mentoring Occurs when a more knowledgeable or experienced worker serves as a mentor only on a specific task. 396

passion A strong inclination toward an activity that individuals like (or even love), that they value (and thus find important), and in which they invest time and energy. 397

psychological capital theory The notion that having a positive outlook improves processes and outcomes. 396

reality shock Situation in which what one learns in the classroom does not always transfer directly into the "real world" and does not represent all a person needs to know. 395

reciprocal mentoring When each member of the mentoring pair switch roles from time to time depending on the situation. 396

reverse mentoring Mentoring that occurs when a more senior, experienced professional is paired with a colleague who may vary in experience, background, or perspective such that the senior professional becomes the mentee and the other professional serves as the mentor. 395

social cognitive career theory (SCCT) Proposes career choice is a result of the application of Bandura's social cognitive theory, especially the concept of self-efficacy. 391

vocational maturity A continuum along which people move through their working years; the more congruent their occupational behaviors are with what is expected of them at different ages, the more vocationally mature they are. 392

work–family conflict The feeling of being pulled in multiple directions by incompatible demands from job and family. 413

Dying and Bereavement

Chapter

13

Chapter Outline

Learning Objectives

After studying this chapter, you will be able to...

13.1. Summarize how death is variably defined and the ethical issues that arise.

13.2. Describe how adults typically experience approaching death.

13.3. Describe ways in which people make and express decisions regarding their own death.

13.4. Define the process and types of grief.

13.5. Describe variation in patterns of experiencing bereavement across the life span.

When famous people such as actors Chadwick Boseman and Naya Rivera, or basketball player Kobe Bryant, die unexpectedly, people are confronted with the reality that death happens to everyone. Many of us may die from the same causes; the most likely ways people die across the life span are listed in Figure 13.1. Certainly, that was true during the COVID-19 pandemic, during which hundreds of thousands of people of all ages died from the virus and forced many more to face their own mortality. But the plain truth is that each of us eventually makes the transition from life to death.

We have a paradoxical relationship with death. Sometimes we are fascinated by it. As tourists, we may visit places where famous people died or are buried. We may watch newscasts showing scenes of devastation in natural disasters and war. But when it comes to pondering our own death or that of people close to us, we experience difficulty. As French writer and reformer La Rochefoucauld wrote over 300 years ago, "looking into the sun is easier than contemplating our death." When death is personal, we become uneasy. Looking at the sun is hard indeed.

In this chapter, we delve into thanatology. **Thanatology is the study of death, dying, grief, bereavement, and**

DFree/Shutterstock.com

Naya Rivera

DFree/Shutterstock.com

Chadwick Boseman

DFree/Shutterstock.com

Kobe Bryant

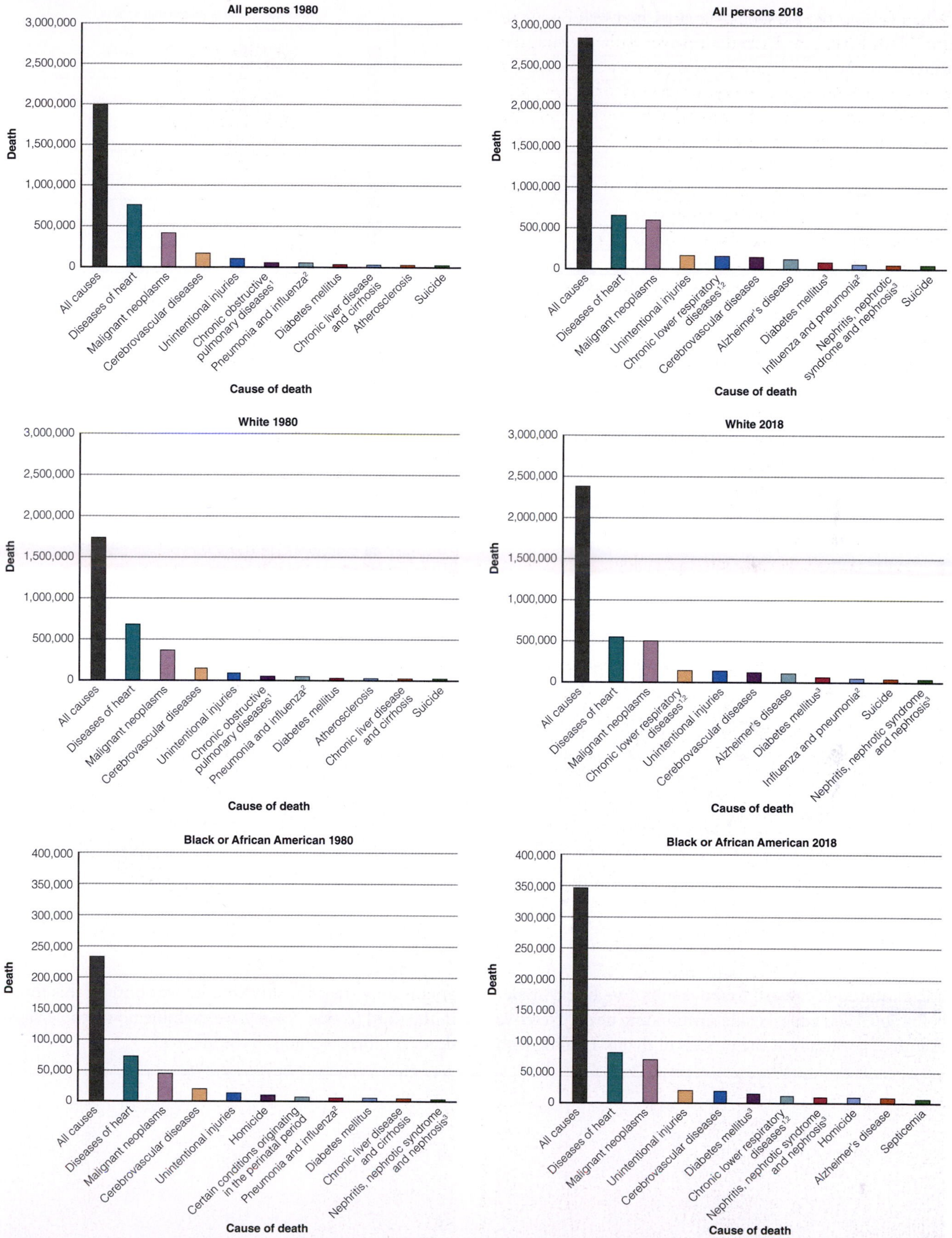

Figure 13.1 Age-adjusted death rates for selected causes of death for all ages, by sex: 1980 and 2018.

Source: National Center for Health Statistics. (2019). Health, United States, 2019. Table 6. https://www.cdc.gov/nchs/data/hus/hus19-508.pdf.

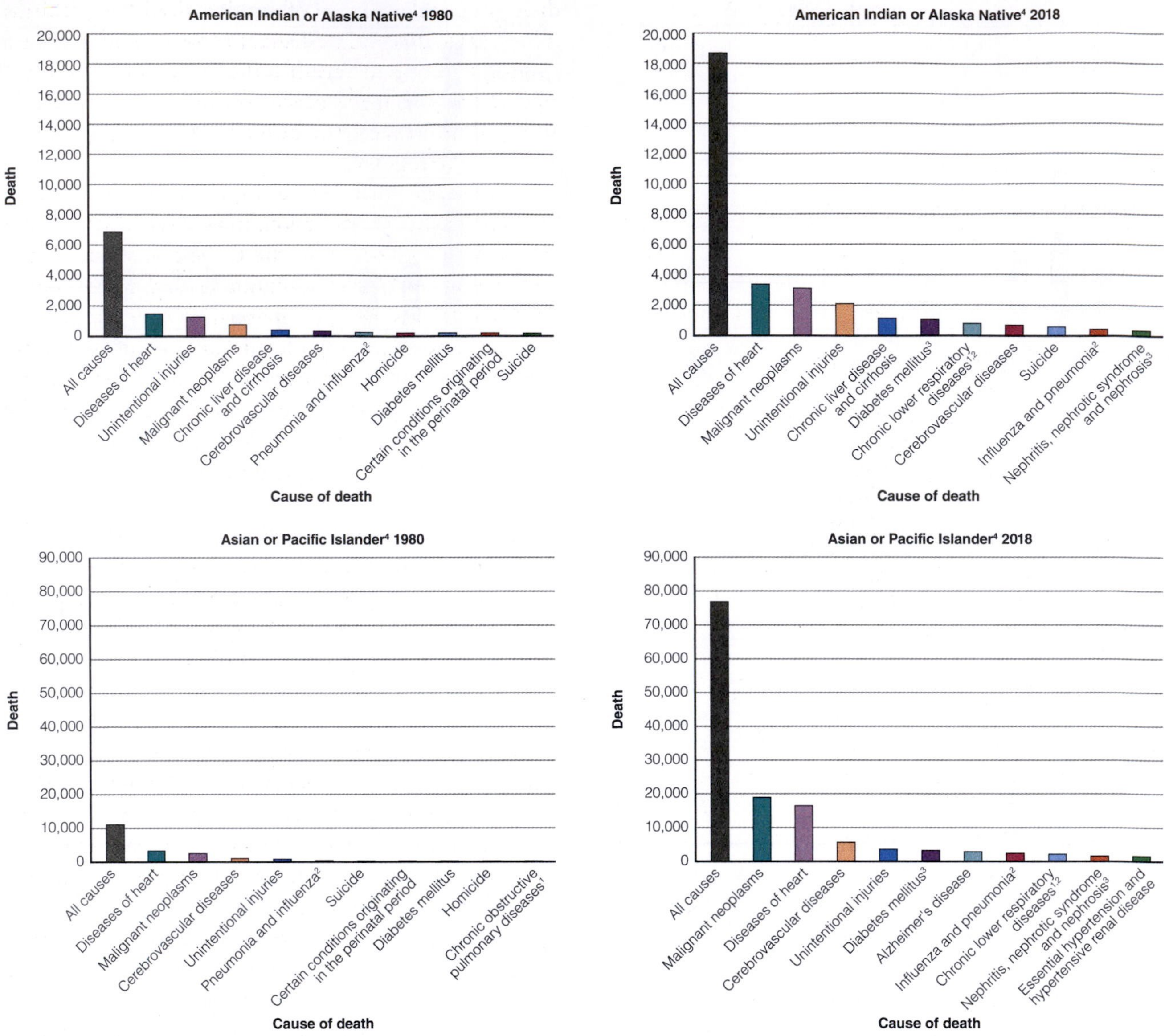

Figure 13.1 *(Continued)*

social attitudes toward these issues. We first consider definitional and ethical issues surrounding death. Next, we examine specifically at the process of dying. Dealing with grief is important for survivors, so we consider this topic in the third section. Finally, we examine how people view death at different points in the life span.

13.1 Definitions and Ethical Issues

Key Questions

- How is death defined?
- What legal and medical criteria are used to determine when death occurs?
- What are the ethical dilemmas surrounding euthanasia?
- What issues surround the costs of life-sustaining care?

Ernesto and Paulina had been married 48 years when Ernesto developed terminal pancreatic cancer. Ernesto was suffering terrible pain and begged Paulina to make it stop. He said she would not let their pet suffer this way, so why let him? Paulina heard about "mercy killing" that involved administering high dosages of certain medications, but she believed this was the same as murder. Yet, she could hardly bear to watch her beloved husband suffer. Paulina wondered what she should do.

When one first thinks about it, death seems a simple concept to define: it is the point when a person is no longer alive. Similarly, dying appears to be simply the process of making the transition from being alive to being dead. It all seems clear enough, doesn't it? But death and dying are actually far more complicated concepts.

As we will learn, there are many cultural and religious differences in the definition of death and the customs surrounding it. The meaning of death depends on the observer's perspective as well as the specific medical and biological criteria one uses.

Sociocultural Definitions of Death

Although death is one of the few truly universal experiences, each culture has its own ways of thinking about, defining, and ritualizing it (Bustos, 2007; Eyetsemitan, 2021; Gire, 2014, 2019; Stearns, 2021). Cultures have their own understandings of what death is and represents, that taken together create a diverse tapestry. For example, some cultures ritually pull their hair as a sign of grief (Lewis, 2013). Melanesians have a term, *mate*, that includes the extremely sick, the very old, and the dead; the term *toa* refers to all other living people (Nose, 2021). Some South Pacific cultures believe the life force leaves the body during sleep or illness, or involves reaching a certain age (Gire, 2014, 2019). Still other cultures view death as a transition to a different type of existence that still allows interaction with the living, and some believe there is a circular pattern of multiple deaths and rebirths (Gire, 2014, 2019). In Ghana, people are said to have a "peaceful" or "good" death if the dying person finished all business and made peace with others before death, which implies being at peace with their own death (van der Geest, 2004).

Mourning rituals, expressions of grief, and states of bereavement also vary across cultures (Eyetsemitan, 2021; Silverman et al., 2021). In the United States and many other countries, deaths of dignitaries and deaths due to tragedies, for instance, are marked by lowering flags to half-staff and declaring a formal period of mourning. Some cultures have formalized periods of time during which certain prayers or rituals are performed. After the death of a close relative, Orthodox Jews often recite ritual prayers and cover all the mirrors in the house. The men may slash their ties as a symbol of loss. In Papua New Guinea, there are accepted time periods for phases of grief (Hemer, 2010, 2021). The Muscogee Creek tribe's rituals include digging the grave by hand and giving a "farewell handshake" by throwing a handful of dirt into the grave before covering it (Walker, 2019). Ancestor veneration, a deep respectful feeling toward individuals from whom a family is descended or who are important to them, is an important part of customs of death in many Asian cultures (Kanai et al., 2020; Roszko, 2010). As we explore aspects of death, dying, and bereavement throughout this chapter, we must keep in mind that the experiences of any one culture or particular group may not generalize to other cultures or groups.

Death can also be a truly cross-cultural experience. The international outpouring of grief over the death of major world leaders (such as Queen Elizabeth II in 2022 and Nelson Mandela in 2013), victims of various wars around the world, and individuals killed in natural disasters draw much attention to the ways the deaths of people we do not know personally can still affect us. It is at these times we realize death happens to us all and death can simultaneously be personal and public.

The many meanings of death can be experienced in various funeral customs. You may have experienced a range of different types of funeral customs, from small, private services for the scattering of ashes to community-wide rituals, such as a homegoing service in the Black church. Variations in the customs surrounding death are reflected in some of the most iconic structures on earth, such as the pyramids in Egypt, and some of the most beautiful, such as the Taj Mahal in India. We even set these sites as lifetime travel destinations.

Ulrich Doering/Alamy Stock Photo

The symbols we use when people die, such as these elaborate caskets from Ghana, provide insights into how cultures think about death.

Legal and Medical Definitions

Sociocultural lenses help us understand the different ways people conceptualize and understand death, but they do not address a fundamental question: How do we determine someone has died? The medical and legal communities have grappled with this question for centuries. Let's focus on contemporary views.

Determining when death occurs has always been subjective. For hundreds of years, people accepted and applied the criteria that now define **clinical death**: lack of heartbeat and respiration. Today, however, the definition used in most countries is whole-brain death. In 2019, the American Academy of Neurology updated its guidelines for determining whole brain death (Russell et al., 2019). The goal in this revision of the criteria was to provide guidelines that were based on research and that helped physicians respond to objections regarding determining whether someone has died based on brain function. According to the guidelines, **whole-brain death** includes three aspects: (1) the person has an irreversible loss of all functions of the entire brain; (2) all brainstem reflexes have permanently stopped working; and (3) breathing has permanently stopped, so that a ventilator, or breathing machine, must be used to keep the body functioning.

The guidelines describe several complex steps physicians must follow to diagnose brain death. The guidelines also make clear that this complex determination of brain death must be completed by a physician who has been trained in diagnosing brain death.

Despite the existence of clear medical guidelines for at least 40 years, it is still the case that brain death definitions vary somewhat across the United States because each state can establish its own definition (Medical Justice, 2020). Brain death is also controversial from some religious perspectives. For example, although brain death is accepted as true death by a majority of Muslim scholars, it remains controversial among others (Abbasi et al., 2020; Sajjad et al., 2020). Roman Catholics focus on what they term "natural death" (Kassim & Alias, 2016). When these perspectives are considered, reaching consensus on the determination of death can be difficult.

It is possible for a person's cortical functioning to cease while brainstem activity continues; this is a **persistent vegetative state**, from which the person does not recover. This condition can occur following disruption of the blood flow to the brain, a severe head injury, or a drug overdose. Persistent vegetative state allows for spontaneous heartbeat and respiration but not for consciousness. The whole-brain standard does not permit a declaration of death for someone who is in a persistent vegetative state. Because of conditions like persistent vegetative state, family members sometimes face difficult ethical decisions concerning care for the individual. These issues are the focus of the next section.

Ethical Issues Concerning Death

An ambulance screeches to a halt and team of healthcare personnel rush a person into the emergency department. As a result of an accident at a swimming pool, the person being brought in has no pulse and no respiration. Working rapidly, the trauma team finally reestablishes a heartbeat through electric shock. A respirator is connected. An EEG and other tests reveal extensive and irreversible brain damage—the individual is in a persistent vegetative state. What should be done?

This is an example of the kinds of problems faced in the field of **bioethics**, the study of the interface between human values and technological advances in health and life sciences. Bioethics grew from two bases: respect for individual freedom and the impossibility of establishing any single version of morality by rational argument or common sense. In a healthcare situation, both of these factors are grounded in empirical evidence and sociocultural contexts, such as race, ethnicity, and ability (Priaulx, 2013; Reynolds & Wieseler, 2022; Russell, 2022).

In practice, bioethics emphasizes the importance of individual choice and the minimization of harm over the maximization of good. That is, bioethics requires people to weigh how much a patient will benefit from a treatment relative to the amount of suffering they will endure as a result of the treatment. Examples of the tough choices required are those facing cancer patients about aggressive treatment with serious side effects for a type of cancer that is quite likely to be fatal in any case, and those facing family members about whether to turn off a life-support machine attached to their loved one.

In the arena of death and dying, the most important bioethical issue is **euthanasia**—the practice of ending life for reasons of mercy. The ethical dilemma posed by euthanasia becomes apparent when trying to decide the circumstances in which a person's life should be ended that implicitly force us to place a value on the life of another (Conway, 2016; Karumathil & Tripathi, 2022; Kassim & Alias, 2016). It also makes us think about the difference between "killing" and "letting die" at the end of life (Dickens et al., 2008). In American society, this dilemma occurs most often when a person is being kept alive by machines or when someone is suffering from a terminal illness. This is the situation confronting Ernesto and Paulina in the opening vignette.

Euthanasia. Euthanasia can be carried out in two different ways: actively and passively (Moeller et al., 2010). **Active euthanasia** involves the deliberate ending of someone's life, that may be based on a clear statement of the person's wishes or be a decision made by someone else who has the legal authority to do so. Usually, this involves situations when people are in a persistent vegetative state or are at the end stages of a terminal disease. Examples of active euthanasia would be administering a drug overdose or ending a person's life through so-called mercy killing.

A second form of euthanasia, **passive euthanasia**, involves allowing a person to die by withholding available treatment. Examples of passive euthanasia include disconnecting a ventilator, ending chemotherapy for a person with terminal cancer, not performing a surgical procedure that is unlikely to save the person's life, or stopping nutrition.

The distinction between active and passive euthanasia was first made by Rachels (1975). There is still debate regarding the need to differentiate them, as to many the ultimate outcome is the same—an individual dies (e.g., Brassington, 2020; Garrard & Wilkinson, 2005; Strinic, 2015). Many argue the single label "euthanasia" suffices; others prefer to distinguish between the traditional labels. The main point is that a decision to continue or terminate a person's life is made.

Most Americans support disconnecting life support in situations involving persons in a persistent vegetative state, withholding treatment if a person agrees or has made their wishes about this known in advance, and the concept of assisted death. But feelings for many also run strongly against such actions for religious or other reasons (e.g., adamant opposition from a loved one; Meilaender, 2020; Strinic, 2015).

Globally, opinions about euthanasia vary (Inglehart et al., 2021; Karumathil & Tripathi, 2022). For example, residents of the Netherlands view euthanasia more positively as a result of lower levels of religious beliefs against euthanasia and more emphasis on it reflecting social welfare services. In contrast, residents of Jordan, who are more influenced by religious beliefs, do not tend to support such practices.

Disconnecting a life-support system is one thing; withholding nourishment from a terminally ill person is quite another issue for many people. Indeed, such cases often end up in court. The first high-profile legal case involving passive euthanasia in the United States was brought to the courts in 1990; the U.S. Supreme Court took up the case of Nancy Cruzan, whose family wanted to have her feeding tube removed. The Court ruled that unless clear and incontrovertible evidence is presented to indicate that an individual desires to have nourishment stopped, such as through a healthcare power of attorney or living will, a third party (such as a parent or partner) cannot decide to terminate nourishment. We will consider later in this chapter how to ensure that one's wishes about these matters are expressed clearly.

Physician-Assisted Suicide. Taking one's own life has never been popular in the United States because of religious and other prohibitions. In other cultures, such as Japan, suicide is viewed differently and has a long, honorable mythology connected to it (Kawashima et al., 2020).

Attitudes regarding suicide in certain situations are changing. Much of this change concerns the topic of **physician-assisted suicide**, in which a physician provides a dying person with a fatal dose of medication that the individual self-administers. Most Americans, as do people in other countries, favor having a choice regarding assisted suicide if they should ever be diagnosed with a terminal disease. However, many oppose it on moral or religious grounds; in some cases, family members object irrespective of the wishes of the dying person.

Physician-assisted suicide is legally available in parts of Australia, Belgium, Canada, Colombia,

Luxembourg, the Netherlands, Switzerland, and several U.S. States (California, Colorado, District of Columbia, Hawai'i, Maine, New Jersey, New Mexico, Oregon, Vermont, and Washington). Each of these laws sets clear guidelines for when this option is permitted. For example, in the Netherlands, five criteria must be met before a person who is experiencing "hopeless and unbearable suffering" can request physician-assisted suicide as an option:

1. The patient's condition is intolerable with no hope for improvement.
2. No relief is available.
3. The patient is competent.
4. The patient makes a request repeatedly over time.
5. Two physicians review the case and agree with the patient's request.

In the United States, voters in Oregon passed the Death with Dignity Act in 1994, the first physician-assisted suicide law in the country. Although the U.S. Supreme Court ruled in two cases in 1997 (*Vacco v. Quill* and *Washington v. Glucksberg*) there is no constitutional right to assisted suicide, the Court decided in 1998 not to overturn the Oregon law.

In general, all of these laws permit people to obtain and use prescriptions for self-administered lethal doses of medication. The laws often require a physician to inform the person that they are terminally ill and describe alternative options (e.g., hospice care, pain control). The person must be mentally competent and make multiple requests for the medication. Such provisions are included to ensure people making the request fully understand the issues and the request is not made hastily.

Attitudes toward assisted suicide tend to break along some expected lines. For example, in a survey in Switzerland (Vilpert et al., 2020), a large majority of older adults supported the right-to-die law. Preferences for control over the end of one's life and for maintaining essential capabilities at the end of life were positively associated with assisted suicide-related attitudes and behaviors, whereas preferences for feeling socially and spiritually connected, as well as for not being a burden on one's family displayed a negative association. Higher levels of trust in one's relative (who would be present at the time of death) were positively associated with potential use of assisted suicide. By contrast, trust in religious institutions has a negative association with all assisted suicide-related attitudes and behaviors.

A controversial case of assisted suicide involved Brittany Maynard, a 29-year-old woman who had terminal brain cancer and ended her life in 2014. As discussed in the Real People feature, such cases reveal the difficult legal, medical, and ethical issues as well as the high degree of emotion surrounding the topic of euthanasia and death with dignity.

There is no question the debate over physician-assisted suicide will continue. As the technology to keep people alive continues to improve, the ethical issues about active euthanasia in general and physician-assisted suicide in particular will continue to become more complex and will likely focus increasingly on quality of life and death with dignity. For example, some argue that physicians have an ethical obligation to inform individuals who would legally qualify about aid in dying in places where it is legal (Zhou & Shelton, 2020).

The Brittany Maynard case raises many serious personal, ethical, and moral issues. It also forces us to confront our anxieties about death, how we confront death as a society, and what we truly believe. Each of us must take the time to think through these issues and make our desires known, a topic we will explore later in the chapter.

The Price of Life-Sustaining Care. An intense debate in the United States concerns the financial, personal, ethical, and moral costs of keeping people alive on life-support machines and continuing aggressive care when people have terminal conditions. Debate continues on whether secondary health conditions in terminally ill people should be treated (e.g., whether a person who has advanced Alzheimer's disease should receive aggressive treatment for cancer). The argument is such care is very expensive, these people will die soon anyway, and needlessly prolonging life is a burden on society.

However, many others argue all means possible should be used, whether for an infant born prematurely or an older adult, to keep them alive regardless of the high cost and possible risk of negative side effects of a treatment or intervention. They argue life is precious, and humans should not "play God" and decide when it should end.

Evidence supports the opinion that extraordinary interventions are expensive. Healthcare costs can soar during the last year of a person's life. Data indicate that roughly 25% of all Medicare expenditures cover end-of-life care (Duncan et al., 2019). However, an analysis by Trella (2020) revealed that expenditures for end-of-life care are substantially less for those having

Real People

The Brittany Maynard Case

On November 2, 2014, Brittany Maynard took a lethal dose of medication prescribed by her physician and ended her life. She was 29 years old, a California resident for nearly all of her life, and had been diagnosed with terminal brain cancer, a diagnosis she received on New Year's Day 2014. She died in her bedroom in Portland, Oregon, surrounded by loved ones (Bever, 2014a, 2014b, 2014c).

Those are the basic facts of Brittany's case. The broader context and debate that her case created is much more complicated. Rather than keep her situation private, Brittany went public, conducting several interviews with media and making her thoughts widely known. From there, debate raged.

Brittany's disease progressed rapidly. Nine days after her diagnosis, surgeons removed part of her brain and performed a partial resection of her temporal lobe in an attempt to stop the tumor from growing. By April 2014, it was clear that this procedure did not work—the tumor was back, and it was even more aggressive. Brittany was given about 6 months to live.

Because of her diagnosis, Brittany qualified for physician-assisted suicide under the Oregon Death with Dignity Act discussed earlier in the chapter. At the time, though, Brittany and her husband, Dan Diaz, lived in San Francisco. After carefully considering the various treatment options, which would not cure her, as well as hospice options, she made her decision. Because California did not have a death with dignity law at the time, Brittany and her family moved to Portland, Oregon.

Brittany spent much of her remaining life working on behalf of the death with dignity movement, volunteering for Compassion & Choices. Because she was public and open about her dying process, her case has been a focal point for the right-to-die debate. Critics of death-with-dignity laws, such as National Right to Life, argue that terminal illness does not carry with it the "right" to be "assisted" in dying.

advance directives and receiving hospice or palliative care, especially at home, topics we will consider later in the chapter.

The biggest challenge in confronting these differences in approach and cost is the difficulty in deciding when to treat or not treat a disease a person has. There are no easy answers. Witness the loud criticism when research evidence overwhelmingly indicates various types of cancer screening (e.g., breast, prostate) should not be provided to everyone as early or as often as initially thought. Despite the lack of evidence to support and the cost of continuing traditional approaches, many patients and physicians do so anyway. Failure to base care on evidence has a price. Whether that is affordable in the long run is debatable.

Adult Development in Action

If you were the staff ethicist at a major medical center, how would you create a guidebook for ethical judgments regarding health care toward the end of life?

Review Questions

13.1 Definitions and Ethical Issues

- How does the meaning of death differ across cultures?
- What are the major legal-medical definitions of death?
- What are the types of euthanasia and how are they implemented? What ethical issues frame these actions?

13.2 Thinking About Death: Personal Aspects

Key Questions

- How do feelings about death change over adulthood?
- How do people deal with their own eventual death?
- What is death anxiety, and how do people show it?

Jean is a 49-year-old whose parents have both died in the past three years. Jean now realizes she is the oldest living member of her family (she has two younger siblings but no aunts, uncles, or older cousins). She started thinking about the fact that someday she too will die. Jean feels anxious when she thinks about her death and tries to block it out of her mind.

Like Jean, many people are uncomfortable thinking about their own death, especially if they think it will be unpleasant. Still, death is a paradox, as we noted at the beginning of the chapter. That is, many people feel afraid of or anxious about death, but also may be drawn to it, sometimes in public ways. We examine this paradox in this module. Specifically, we focus on two questions: How do people's feelings about death differ with age? What is it about death we fear or that makes us anxious?

Before we begin, let's take a moment and reflect on how people are remembered after death. One common way to remember people immediately after they die is through an obituary, an experience we may have with hundreds of people we know after they die but will never have after our own death. Here's a chance to think about your own death from that perspective. Take a few minutes and do the following exercise:

- In 200 words or less, write your own obituary. Be sure to include your age and cause of death. List your lifetime accomplishments. Don't forget to list your survivors.
- Think about all the things you will have done that are not listed in your obituary. List some of them.
- Think of all the friends you will have made and how you will have affected them.
- Reread your obituary. Would you make any changes to it based on your reflections on the other questions?

A Life-Course Approach to Dying

Suppose you learned today you had only a short time to live. How would you feel about dying? That's what many people face every day when they learn of a medical diagnosis, for instance, and what many healthcare workers feared during the COVID-19 pandemic. For many people, learning this news would be very distressing.

It probably doesn't surprise you to learn feelings about dying vary with age and cultures (Eyetsemitan, 2021; Leming & Dickinson, 2021). Each person comes to terms with death in an individual and an interpersonal way. When one knows that time left is short, these co-created understandings can be used to help meet personal goals about things a person wants to accomplish before dying (Bergdahl et al., 2013; Hemberg & Bergdahl, 2020).

Although not specifically addressed in research, the shift from formal operational thinking to postformal thinking (discussed in Chapter 7) could be important in adults' contemplation of death. Presumably, this shift in cognitive development is accompanied by a lessening of the feeling of immortality characterizing adolescence to one that integrates personal feelings and emotions with their thinking.

Midlife is the time when most people in developed countries experience the death of their parents. Until that point, people tend not to think much about their own death; the fact their parents are still alive buffers them from this reality. After all, in the normal course of events, our parents are supposed to die before we do.

Once their parents die, people realize they may now be the oldest generation of their family—the next in line to die. Reading the obituary notices over the ensuing years, they are reminded of this, as the ages of many of the people who died get closer and closer to their own.

Probably as a result of this growing realization of their own mortality, middle-aged adults' sense of time undergoes a subtle yet profound change. It changes from an emphasis on how long they have already lived to how long they have left to live, a shift that increases in importance into late life (Cicirelli, 2006; Cordella & Poiani, 2021; Golant, 2020). This shift in perspective may lead to occupational change (e.g., retirement) or other redirection such as improving relationships that deteriorated over the years. These decisions support socioemotional selectivity theory (discussed in Chapter 11) in terms of maximizing those outcomes that provide the greatest emotional benefit (Golant, 2020).

In general, older adults are less anxious about death and more accepting of it than any other age group. Still, because the discrepancy between desired and expected number of years left to live is greater for older adults 65–75 years old compared to those aged 85 and above, anxiety tends to be higher for the young-old adults (Cicirelli, 2006; Giasson et al., 2019; Liao & Carstensen, 2018). In part, the greater overall acceptance of death results from the achievement of ego integrity (described in Chapter 9).

For other older adults, the joy of living may be diminishing. More than any other age group, they may have experienced loss of family and friends, have more chronic diseases, and have come to terms with their own mortality. They may feel their most important life goals—their so-called bucket list—have been completed (Freund, 2020; Giasson et al., 2019; Kastenbaum, 1999; Liao & Carstensen, 2018).

Dealing with One's Own Death

Many authors have tried to describe the dying process, often using the metaphor of a trajectory that captures the duration of time between the diagnosis of a terminal disease or condition and death by describing the course of the dying process (Sadler et al., 2020). These dying trajectories vary a great deal across conditions, as illustrated in Figure 13.2. Some diseases, such as lung cancer, have a clear and rapid period of decline; this "terminal phase" is often used to determine eligibility for certain services (e.g., hospice, discussed later). Other diseases, such as congestive heart failure, have no clear terminal phase. The two approaches of describing the dying process we consider will try to account for various trajectories.

Kübler-Ross's Work. Elisabeth Kübler-Ross changed the way we approach dying. When she began her investigations into the dying process in the 1960s, such research was controversial; her physician colleagues initially were outraged and some even denied their patients were terminally ill. Still, she persisted. More than 200 interviews with terminally ill people convinced her most people experienced several emotional reactions. Using her experiences, she described five reactions that represented the ways people dealt with death: denial, anger, bargaining, depression, and acceptance (Kübler-Ross, 1969). Although they were first presented as a sequence, it was subsequently realized the emotions can overlap and be experienced in different orders.

Although she believed these five reactions or "stages" represent the typical range of emotional development in the dying, Kübler-Ross (1974, 1997) cautioned that not everyone experiences all of them or progresses through them at the same rate or in the same order. Research supports the view her "stages" should not be viewed as a sequence (Corr, 2020; Parkes, 2013). In fact, we could actually harm dying people by considering these stages as fixed and universal. Individual differences are great. Emotional responses may vary in intensity throughout the dying process. Thus, the goal in applying Kübler-Ross's ideas to real-world settings would be to help people achieve an appropriate death: one that meets the needs of the dying person, allowing them to work out each problem as it comes.

A Contextual Theory of Dying. Describing the process of dying is difficult. One reason for these problems is the realization there is no one right way to die, although there may be better or worse ways of coping (Corr, 1992, 2010a, 2010b, 2019; Corr et al., 2019). Corr identified four dimensions of the issues or tasks a

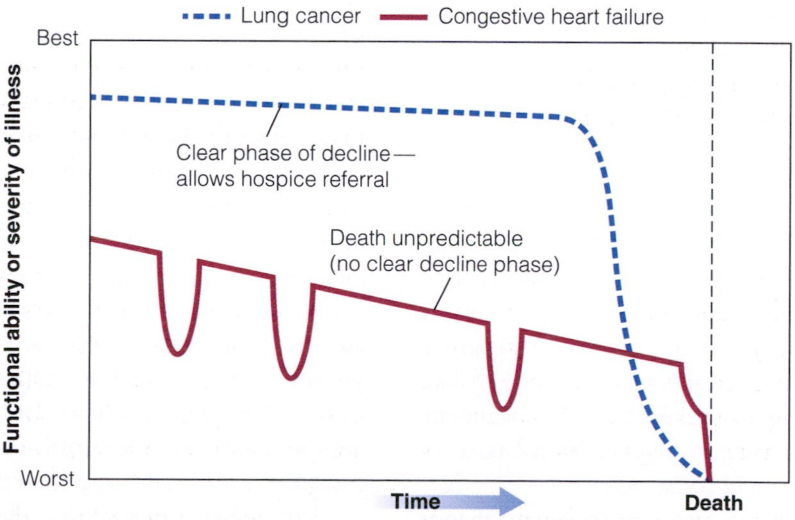

Figure 13.2 Some fatal diseases, such as lung cancer, have a clear decline phase, whereas others, such as congestive heart failure, do not.

Source: Adapted from Skolnick, A. A. (1998). MediCaring project to demonstrate and evaluate innovative end-of-life program for chronically ill. *Journal of the American Medical Association, 279*, 1511–1512.

dying person faces from their perspective: bodily needs, psychological security, interpersonal attachments, and spiritual energy and hope. This holistic approach acknowledges individual differences and rejects broad generalizations. Corr's task work approach also recognizes the importance of the coping efforts of family members, friends, and caregivers as well as those of the dying person.

Kastenbaum and Thuell (1995) argue what is needed is an even broader contextual approach that takes a more inclusive view of the dying process. They note that theories must be able to handle people who have a wide variety of terminal illnesses and be sensitive to dying people's own perspectives and values related to death. The socio-environmental context where dying occurs often changes over time and must be recognized. A person may begin the dying process living independently but end up in a long-term care facility. Such moves may have profound implications for how the person copes with dying. A contextual approach provides guidance for healthcare professionals and families for discussing how to protect the quality of life, provide better care, and prepare caregivers for dealing with the end of life. Such an approach would also provide research questions (e.g., How does one's acceptance of dying change across various stages?)

Because we do not yet have a comprehensive theory of dying, we can consider people's experiences as a narrative that can be written from many points of view (e.g., the patient, family members, care providers). What emerges is a rich description of a dynamically changing, individual process.

Death Anxiety

We have noted that people's view of death varies with age. In the process, we encountered the notion of feeling anxious about death. **Death anxiety** refers to people's anxiety or even fear of death and dying. Death anxiety is tough to pin down; indeed, it is the ethereal, unknown nature of death, rather than something about it in particular, that makes us feel so uncomfortable. Because of this, we must find indirect behavioral evidence to document death anxiety. Research findings suggest death anxiety is a complex, multidimensional construct.

Researchers have applied terror management theory as a framework to study death anxiety (Burke et al., 2010; Zuccala & Abbott, 2021). **Terror management theory** addresses the issue of why people engage in certain behaviors to achieve particular psychological states based on their deeply rooted concerns about mortality. The theory proposes that ensuring the continuation of one's life is the primary motive underlying behavior and that all other motives can be traced to this basic one. Much evidence of this was documented during the COVID-19 pandemic (Dimoff et al., 2021). An overview of the theory is provided in Figure 13.3 (Arndt & Goldenberg, 2017).

Essentially, terror management theory explains how health conditions affect the way we think about death. Basically, when mortality concerns are in our conscious thought, our health-related decisions are determined by our short-term goal of reducing our perceived vulnerability to the health threat and its related concerns about mortality. Terror management theory explains the health-related behaviors people did (or did not) engage in during the COVID-19 pandemic, for example, such as physical distancing and wearing a mask (Dimoff et al., 2021).

Additionally, some suggest older adults present an existential threat for the emerging, established, and middle-aged adults because they remind these younger groups that death is inescapable, the body is fallible, and the sources we use to manage death anxiety are transitory (Martens et al., 2005). That may be why some people seek cosmetic surgery as a way to deal with their death anxiety (Gire, 2019; Tam, 2013).

Neuroimaging research provides support that terror management theory provides a useful framework for studying brain activity related to death anxiety. Quirin and colleagues (2012) found brain activity in the right amygdala, left rostral anterior cingulate cortex, and right caudate nucleus was greater when male participants were answering questions about fear of death and dying than when they were answering questions about dental pain. Similarly, fMRI imaging and electrical activity in the brain indicate people defend themselves against emotions related to death (Klackl et al., 2013; Yanagisawa et al., 2021). Emerging adults exhibit greater brain responses to death-related terms than do older adults, indicating a fundamental shift in how adults process death-related concepts with age (Bluntschli et al., 2018). There is neurophysiological evidence that demonstrates Jean's attempts to block thoughts of her own death in the opening vignette are common.

On the basis of several studies using many different measures, researchers conclude death anxiety consists of several components. Each of these components is most easily described with terms that reflect areas of great concern (anxiety) but that cannot be tied to any one

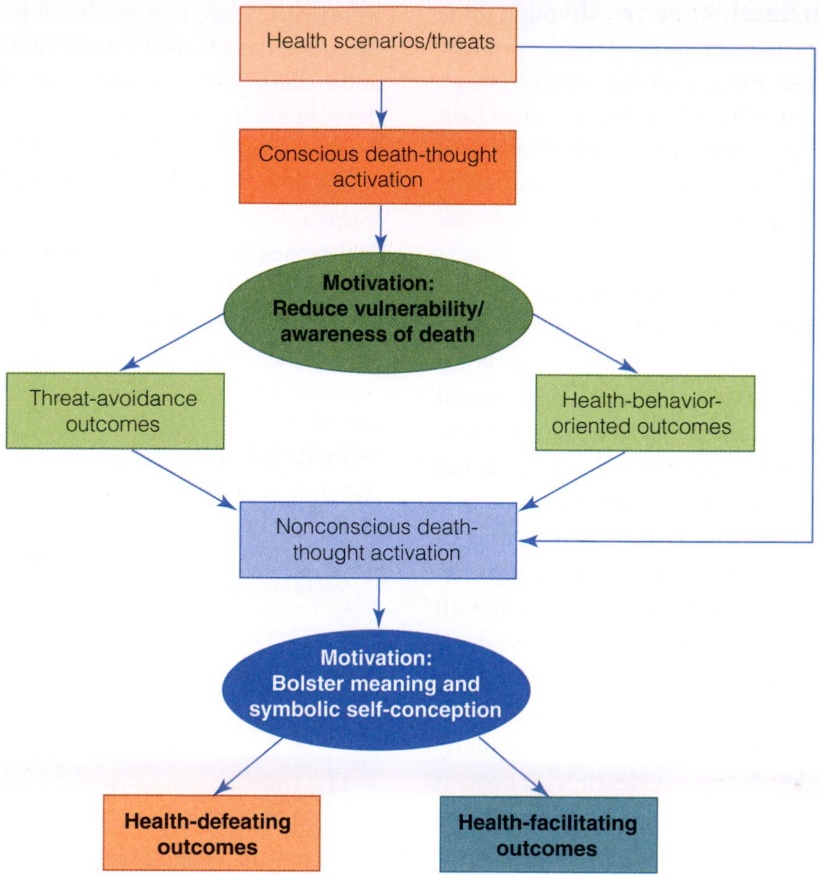

Figure 13.3 The terror management health model.

Source: Adapted from Arndt, J., & Goldenberg, J. L. (2017). Where health and death intersect: Insights from a terror management health model. *Current Directions in Psychological Science, 26,* 126–131. Figure 1, p. 127. https://doi.org/10.1177/0963721413689563.

specific focus. These components of death anxiety include pain, body malfunction, humiliation, rejection, nonbeing, punishment, interruption of goals, being destroyed, and negative impact on survivors (Power & Smith, 2008). To complicate matters further, each of these components can be assessed at any of three levels: public, private, and nonconscious. What we may admit feeling about death in public may differ greatly from what we feel when we are alone with our own thoughts from what we may be unaware of that still influences our behavior. In short, the measurement of death anxiety is complex, and researchers need to specify what aspects they are assessing.

Much research has been conducted to learn what demographic and personality variables are related to death anxiety. Although the results often are ambiguous, some patterns have emerged. Older adults tend to have lower death anxiety than younger adults, perhaps because of their tendency to engage in life review, have a different perspective about time, and their higher level of religious motivation (Henrie, 2010). Men generally show greater fear of the unknown than women, but women generally report more specific fear of the dying process (Cicirelli, 2001). Death anxiety varies across cultures in how it is (or is not) expressed (Park & Pyszczynski, 2016). In Taiwan, higher death anxiety among patients with cancer is associated with not having a purpose in life and level of fear of disease relapse (Tang et al., 2011).

Strange as it may seem, death anxiety may have a beneficial side. For one thing, being afraid to die means we often go to great lengths to make sure we stay alive, as argued by terror management theory (Arndt & Goldenberg, 2017; Burke et al., 2010; Park & Pyszczynski, 2016; Zuccala & Abbott, 2021). Because staying alive ensures the continuation and socialization of the species, fear of death serves as a motivation for some to have children and raise them properly.

Learning to Deal with Death Anxiety. Although some degree of death anxiety may be appropriate, we must guard against letting it become powerful enough to interfere with normal daily routines. Several ways exist to help us in this endeavor. Perhaps the one most often used is to live life to the fullest. Kalish (1984, 1987) argues people who do this enjoy what they have; although they may still fear death and feel cheated, they have few regrets.

Koestenbaum (1976) proposes several exercises and questions to increase one's death awareness. Some of these are to write your own obituary (as you did earlier in this chapter) and to plan your own death and funeral services. You can also ask yourself: "What circumstances would help make my death acceptable?" "Is death the sort of thing that could happen to me right now?"

These questions serve as a basis for a popular way to reduce anxiety: death education. Most death education programs combine factual information about death with issues aimed at reducing anxiety and fear to increase sensitivity to others' feelings. These programs vary widely in orientation; they include such topics as philosophy, ethics, psychology, drama, religion, medicine, art, and many others. Additionally, they focus on death, the process of dying, grief and bereavement, or any combination of those. In general, death education programs help primarily by increasing our awareness of the complex emotions felt and expressed by dying people and their families. It is important to make education programs reflect the diverse backgrounds of the participants (Fowler, 2008).

A novel way of confronting death anxiety is promoted by the Death Over Dinner organization (deathoverdinner.org, 2022). They have created the "Let's Have Dinner and Talk About Death" program to provide a safe context in which to ask questions and discuss all aspects of death, including rumors, myths, and beliefs that we may be aware of. The program was developed by medical and wellness leaders and has resulted in an experience many consider uplifting.

AlejandroCarnicero/Shutterstock.com

Facing death on a regular basis often forces people to confront their death anxiety.

Research indicates participating in experiential workshops and programs like Death Over Dinner significantly lowers death anxiety in people of all ages and across cultures and raises awareness about end-of-life issues to which we now turn (Friesen et al., 2020; Moeller et al., 2010; Phan et al., 2020).

Adult Development in Action

How might different approaches to lowering death anxiety be useful to you as a healthcare worker?

Review Questions

13.2 Thinking About Death: Personal Aspects

- What is the life-course approach to dying?
- How do people come to terms with the notion of their own eventual death?
- What is death anxiety? How is it manifested? How do people cope with death anxiety?

13.3 End-of-Life Issues

Key Questions

- What are end-of-life issues? What is a final scenario?
- What is palliative care? What are contexts in which palliative care is provided?
- How does one make end-of-life desires and decisions known?

Jorge is a 72-year-old recently diagnosed with advanced colon cancer. He has vivid memories of his father dying a long, protracted death in great pain. Jorge is afraid he will suffer the same fate. He heard the hospice in town emphasizes pain management and provides a lot of support for families. Jorge wonders whether that is something he should explore in the time he has left.

When people think about how they would like to die, virtually no one chooses a slow, painful process where medical intervention continues well beyond the point where it will increase quality of life. However, medical interventions such as life support or cardiopulmonary resuscitation (CPR) are common, often required by law, even in situations in which people would prefer them not to be used. How can people make their wishes known about how they want to experience the end of their life?

Creating a Final Scenario

When given the chance, many adults would like to discuss a variety of issues, collectively called **end-of-life issues**: management of the final phase of life, after-death disposition of their body, memorial services, and distribution of assets (Cordella & Poiani, 2021; Moeller et al., 2010). We are experiencing a major shift in how people handle end-of-life issues that is occurring across cultures (e.g., China; Li et al., 2021), religions (e.g., Sikhs; Camara & Rosengarten, 2021), and demographic groups (e.g., African Americans; Ahn et al., 2021; LGBTQIA+; Pecanac et al., 2021). Prior to the baby boom generation of older adults, people rarely planned ahead for or made their wishes known about medical care they did or did not want. Now, people want to manage the final part of their lives by thinking through the choices between traditional care (e.g., provided by hospitals and long-term care facilities) and alternatives (such as hospices, discussed in the next section), completing advance directives (e.g., healthcare power of attorney, living will), resolving key personal relationships, and perhaps choosing the alternative of ending one's life through assisted suicide.

Consider the issue of rituals surrounding the time immediately following death. What happens to one's body and how one is memorialized matters to most people. But decisions about these have to be made. Is a traditional burial preferred over cremation? A traditional funeral very soon after death over a memorial service at a later time? Such choices are often based in people's religious and cultural beliefs (Hidalgo et al., 2021).

Making sure one's estate and personal effects are passed on appropriately often is overlooked. Making a will is especially important to ensure one's wishes are carried out. Providing for the informal distribution of personal effects also helps prevent disputes between family members.

Whether people choose to address these issues formally or informally, it is important they be given the opportunity to do so. In many cases, family members are reluctant to discuss these matters with the dying relative because of their own anxiety about death. Making such choices known about how they do and do not want their lives to end constitutes a **final scenario**.

One of the most difficult and important parts of a final scenario for most people is the process of separation from family and friends (Corr et al., 2019; Wanzer & Glenmullen, 2007; Zahedi Bidgoli et al., 2020). The final days, weeks, and months of life provide opportunities to affirm love, resolve conflicts, and provide peace to dying people. The failure to complete this process often leaves survivors feeling they did not achieve closure in the relationship and can result in bitterness toward the deceased and mental health impacts due in part to a lack of closure. This situation became tragically apparent during the COVID-19 pandemic when family members were prohibited from visiting their loved ones in intensive care prior to their death (Montauk & Kuhl, 2020).

Healthcare workers realize the importance of giving dying patients the chance to create a final scenario and recognize the uniqueness of each person's final passage. A key part of their role is to ease this process through good communication with the family (Curtis et al., 2016; Scharf et al., 2021). Any given final scenario reflects the individual's personal past and their unique combination of the development forces. Primary attention is paid to how people's total life experiences prepared them to face end-of-life issues (Curtis et al., 2016).

One's final scenario helps family and friends interpret one's death, especially when the scenario is constructed jointly, such as between spouses/partners, and when communication is open and honest. The different perspectives of everyone involved are unlikely to converge without clear communication and discussion. Respecting each person's perspective is basic and greatly helps in creating a good final scenario.

Encouraging people to decide for themselves how the end of their lives should be handled helps people, even children, take control of their dying (Hains & Hulbert-Williams, 2013; Shih & Lu, 2021; Wijngaarde et al., 2021) and think through issues such as euthanasia (Feltz, 2015). Taking personal control over one's dying process is a trend occurring even in cultures such as Japan that traditionally defer to physician's opinions, and is promoted by the Japan Geriatrics Society (Alden et al., 2012; The Japan Geriatrics Society Subcommittee on End-of-Life Issues et al., 2020). The emergence of final scenarios as an important consideration fits well with the emphasis on addressing pain through palliative care, an approach underlying hospice.

Palliative Care

As we have noted, most people would prefer to die pain free among family and friends. An important barrier to this choice is the emphasis of healthcare systems on treatment to increase the quantity, but not necessarily the quality, of life, especially when a person has a terminal disease. This situation too often results in people thinking the best option is to go to a hospital or long-term care facility.

As noted earlier, though, there is an important difference between quantity and quality of life. In the case of a terminal illness, this important distinction becomes one between the mere prolongation of death (i.e., emphasizing the quantity of life) and the prolongation of a meaningful life (i.e., emphasizing the quality of life), a distinction important to Jorge, the person we met in the vignette. Emphasizing the quality of life puts the focus on maintaining a person's awareness and cognitive functions as long as possible and providing them with as pain-free a process as possible; it does not have attempting to cure the disease as a goal. An approach to care based on an ethic of controlling and relieving pain or other symptoms and not on attempting to cure disease is called **palliative care** (Emmerich et al., 2020; Prince-Paul & Daly, 2016).

The most well-known providers of palliative care are hospices, but palliative care can be adopted in other settings. **Hospice** is an approach to assist dying people emphasizing pain management, or palliative care, and death with dignity (Knee, 2010; National Hospice and Palliative Care Organization [NHPCO], 2019; Winslow & Meldrum, 2013). Hospice care focuses on the pain, symptoms, and stress of serious illness for an individual with a life expectancy of 6 months or less if the disease runs its natural course, and for their family (NHPCO, 2019). The emphasis in a hospice is on the dying person's quality of life. In a hospice the concern is to make the person as peaceful and as comfortable as possible, not to delay an inevitable death.

Modern hospices are modeled after St. Christopher's Hospice in England, founded in 1967 by Dr. Cicely Saunders. The differences between hospice and hospital care are evident in the principles that underlie hospice care (Knee, 2010):

- Clients and their families are viewed as a unit, clients should be kept free of pain, and emotional and social impoverishment must be minimal.
- Clients must be encouraged to maintain competencies.
- Conflict resolution and fulfillment of realistic desires must be assisted.
- Clients must be free to begin or end relationships.
- The interdisciplinary team and staff members deal with the client and their family holistically and seek to alleviate fear.

Two types of hospices exist: inpatient and outpatient. Inpatient hospices provide all care for clients and reflect a cross between skilled care and a home-like setting. Outpatient hospices provide services to clients who remain in their own homes. Having hospice services available to people at home is a preferable option for many people, especially since it provides a way for the person with a terminal illness to fulfill their wish to die at home (Newman et al., 2013). Home-based hospice services are particularly helpful for families of children who are terminally ill because of the holistic approach used and support provided to any siblings in the family (Boyden et al., 2021).

Because hospices use a palliative model of care, the role of the professional team in a hospice is not so much to treat the client as it is just to be with the client. A client's dignity, as defined by them, is always maintained; more attention is paid to appearance and personal grooming than to medical tests. Hospice professional team members also provide a great deal of emotional and other support to the client's family during the dying process and afterward as they grieve.

This support includes different ways of being present to and with the person who is dying. Many hospices have the option for death doulas who help ease the passage through death. **Death doula** is an umbrella term to identify lay people, primarily women, who provide a variety of nonmedical supports—social, emotional, practical, and spiritual—for people nearing the end of life, including individuals close to them (Krawczyk & Rush, 2020). For some dying individuals, the doula may simply hold their hand; for others, doulas may play special music and sit or meditate with them. The main role is to ensure that dying people are not alone, and that families, if present, have personal support. Indigenous people in Canada who live on their traditional territory, for example, have begun using doulas to help achieve their preference to enter the spirit world from their home rather than in a hospital (Gaspard et al., 2021).

Hospice and hospital patients differ in important ways (Knee, 2010). Inpatient hospice clients are more mobile, less anxious, and less depressed; partners visit hospice clients more often and participate more in their care; and hospice professional team members are perceived as more accessible. Research consistently demonstrates significant improvements in clients' quality of life occur after hospice placement or beginning palliative care (Blackhall et al., 2016; Perry et al., 2021).

Several studies have now documented that what appear to be racial and/or ethnic differences in use of hospice are actually explained by differences in the provision of consultations about palliative care approaches across hospitals. When comparing those who received consultations at the hospital about palliative care, no differences in use of hospice emerge across racial and/or ethnic lines (e.g., T. Johnson et al., 2020). African American faith leaders also support the use of hospice options for appropriate end-of-life care (T. Johnson et al., 2021).

How do people decide among various care options, such as hospice, home health, or skilled care? Families should ask several key questions (Hospice Foundation of America, 2021; Knee, 2010):

- *Is the hospice nationally accredited?* Hospices that meet rigorous national standards can generally be trusted to provide quality services. The Hospice Foundation of America provides excellent material for evaluating a hospice.
- *Is the person completely informed about the nature and prognosis of their condition?* Full knowledge and the ability to communicate with healthcare personnel are essential to understanding what hospice has to offer.
- *What are the person's expectations, fears, and hopes?* Some older adults, like Jorge, remember or have heard stories about people who suffered greatly at the end of their lives. This can produce anxiety about one's own death. Similarly, fears of becoming dependent play an important role in a person's decision making. Discovering and discussing these anxieties help clarify options.
- *How quickly will a care plan be developed and implemented?* The sooner a specific plan of care is developed and implemented, the sooner the client and support people around them can adjust to and take advantage of the services available. This eases the process of dealing with the pending death.
- *How well do people in the person's social network communicate with each other?* Talking about death is taboo in many families. In others, intergenerational communication is difficult or impossible. Even in families with good communication, the pending death of a loved relative is difficult. As a result, the dying person may have difficulty expressing their wishes. The decision to explore the hospice option is best made when it is discussed openly.
- *Are family members available to participate actively in terminal care?* Hospice relies on family members to provide much of the care that is supplemented by professionals and volunteers. We noted in Chapter 11 that being a primary care provider can be highly stressful. Having a family member who is willing to accept this responsibility is essential for the hospice option to work.
- *Does the hospice serve everyone?* Hospices have earned their reputation because they serve anyone medically eligible for its services. This first became evident decades ago when hospices overcame the fear and ignorance of HIV and compassionately served people dying from AIDS. Today, you should expect a hospice to routinely care for people in the LGBTIA+ community, those with intellectual or developmental disabilities, and those who do not speak English. Because these groups have been historically marginalized in the medical system (noted in Chapter 4), their inclusion in hospice services is especially noteworthy.
- *Is hospice covered by insurance?* Hospice services are reimbursable under Medicare in most cases, but any additional expenses may or may not be covered under other forms of insurance.

Hospice provides an important end-of-life option for many terminally ill people and their families. Moreover, the supportive follow-up services they provide, such as bereavement counseling, help surviving family and friends. Most important, the success of the hospice option has had important influences on traditional health care. For instance, medical education includes training in palliative care and hospice (e.g., Dyess et al., 2020), and demand for certified specialists is growing rapidly (Dingfield et al., 2020).

Despite the importance of the hospice option for end-of-life decisions, terminally ill persons face the barriers of family reluctance to face the reality of terminal illness and participate in the decision-making process, misperceptions about hospice care, language barriers in communicating with persons with terminal conditions, and healthcare providers who hinder access to hospice care (Dressler et al., 2021; Knee, 2010; Moon, 2017; Patel et al., 2020; Torres et al., 2016). As the end of life approaches, the most important thing to keep in mind is that the dying person has the right to state-of-the-art approaches to treatment and pain management. Irrespective of the choice of traditional health care or hospice, the wishes of the dying person should be honored, and family members and primary care providers must participate.

Making Your End-of-Life Intentions Known

End-of-life realities raise legal, political, and ethical issues that can be complex even in the best of circumstances. However, even routine medical surgical procedures, for instance, now require you to disclose whether you have designated certain care decisions (e.g., the use of life-sustaining interventions) and health decision-makers who can act on your behalf if necessary. In most jurisdictions, ending life through such means as euthanasia or assisted suicide is legal only when a person has made known their wishes concerning end-of-life intervention.

Unfortunately, many people fail to explicitly state their wishes, perhaps because it is difficult to think about such situations or because they do not know the options available to them. Without clear directions, though, medical personnel may be unable to take a patient's preferences into account. For instance, many states have laws requiring CPR or other attempts at resuscitation be used in the absence of clear evidence that the person does not want them used.

There are two ways to make one's intentions known. In a **living will**, a person simply states their wishes about life support and other treatments and interventions. In a **healthcare power of attorney**, an individual appoints someone to act as their agent for healthcare decisions (a sample is in Figure 13.4).

3. General statement of authority granted.

Except as indicated in section 4 below, I hereby grant to my healthcare agent named above full power and authority to make healthcare decisions on my behalf, including, but not limited to, the following:

A. To request, review, and receive any information, verbal or written, regarding my physical or mental health, including, but not limited to, medical and hospital records, and to consent to the disclosure of this information;

B. To employ or discharge my healthcare providers;

C. To consent to and authorize my admission to and discharge from a hospital, nursing or convalescent home, or other institution;

D. To give consent for, to withdraw consent for, or to withhold consent for, X ray, anesthesia, medication, surgery, and all other diagnostic and treatment procedures ordered by or under the authorization of a licensed physician, dentist, or podiatrist. This authorization specifically includes the power to consent to measures for relief of pain.

E. To authorize the withholding or withdrawal of life-sustaining procedures when and if my physician determines that I am terminally ill, permanently in a coma, suffer severe dementia, or am in a persistent vegetative state. Lifesustaining procedures are those forms of medical care that only serve to artificially prolong the dying process and may include mechanical ventilation, dialysis, antibiotics, artificial nutrition and hydration, and other forms of medical treatment which sustain, restore or supplant vital bodily functions. Life-sustaining procedures do not include care necessary to provide comfort or alleviate pain.

I DESIRE THAT MY LIFE NOT BE PROLONGED BY LIFE-SUSTAINING PROCEDURES IF I AM TERMINALLY ILL, PERMANENTLY IN A COMA, SUFFER SEVERE DEMENTIA, OR AM IN A PERSISTENT VEGETATIVE STATE.

F. To exercise any right I may have to make a disposition of any part or all of my body for medical purposes, to donate my organs, to authorize an autopsy, and to direct the disposition of my remains.

G. To take any lawful actions that may be necessary to carry out these decisions, including the granting of releases of liability to medical providers.

4. Special provisions and limitations.

(Notice: The above grant of power is intended to be as broad as possible so that your healthcare agent will have authority to make any decisions you could make to obtain or terminate any type of health care. If you wish to limit the scope of your healthcare agent's powers, you may do so in this section.)

In exercising the authority to make healthcare decisions on my behalf, the authority of my healthcare agent is subject to the following special provisions and limitations *(Here you may include any specific limitations you deem appropriate such as: your own definition of when life-sustaining treatment should be withheld or discontinued, or instructions to refuse any specific types of treatment that are inconsistent with your religious beliefs, or unacceptable to you for any other reason.)*:

____

____

____

____

5. Guardianship provision.

If it becomes necessary for a court to appoint a guardian of my person, I nominate my healthcare agent acting under this document to be the guardian of my person, to serve without bond or security.

6. Reliance of third parties on healthcare agent.

A. No person who relies in good faith upon the authority of or any representations by my healthcare agent shall be liable to me, my estate, my heirs, successors, assigns, or personal representatives, for actions or omissions by my healthcare agent.

Figure 13.4 Example of a healthcare power of attorney document.

Source: North Carolina State University, A&T State University Cooperative Extension.

A major purpose of both is to make one's wishes known about the use of life-support interventions in the event the person is unconscious or otherwise incapable of expressing them, along with other related end-of-life issues such as organ transplantation and other healthcare options. Without them, the considerations of life-sustaining intervention for terminally ill patients are fraught with ethical dilemmas (Awadi & Mrayyan, 2016; Portnoy et al., 2015; Rodrigues et al., 2018). A durable power of attorney for health care has an additional advantage: it names an individual who has the legal authority to speak and make decisions for the person if necessary.

A living will or a durable power of attorney for health care can be the basis for a do not resuscitate medical order. **A do not resuscitate (DNR) order means CPR is not started should one's heart and breathing stop.** In the normal course of events, a medical team will immediately try to restore normal heartbeat and respiration. With a DNR order, this intervention is not done. As with living wills and healthcare power of attorney, it is extremely important to let all appropriate medical personnel know a DNR order is in effect; this is why hospitals inquire about them at the point of admission.

Although there is considerable support for both living wills and healthcare power of attorney, there are several challenges as well (Alspach, 2016; Cordella, 2021). Historically, DNR orders were ignored in operating rooms, but that view is changing due to changes in law and in the healthcare profession's ethical positions on a person's right to determine the types of interventions they desire if the situation requires such decisions (Cordella, 2021). Still, significant barriers to implementing people's wishes exist. States vary in their laws relating to advance directives, so a document completed in one state may not be applicable in another. Many people fail to inform their relatives and physicians about their healthcare wishes, so even the person designated to make decisions may not be aware of preferences for intervention. Obviously, this puts relatives and other key individuals at a serious disadvantage if decisions concerning the use of life-support systems need to be made.

Fortunately, Medicare covers advance care planning as a separate service provided by physicians and other healthcare professionals such as nurse practitioners (Centers for Medicare and Medicaid Services, 2020). This makes it easier for patients to discuss their wishes with a healthcare professional and to learn about options. Ideally, these discussions result in the actual documentation of a person's specific wishes.

Patient Self-Determination and Competency Evaluation. Making your decisions about health care known presumes that you are competent and able to make those decisions for yourself. To aid healthcare providers in this process, the Patient Self-Determination Act, passed in 1990, requires most healthcare facilities to provide information to patients in writing that they have the right to:

- Make their own healthcare decisions.
- Accept or refuse medical treatment.
- Make an advance healthcare directive.

As noted earlier, patients must be asked if they have an advance directive, and, if so, it must be included in the medical record. Staff at the healthcare facility must receive training about advance directives and cannot make admissions or treatment decisions based on whether those directives exist.

One major concern regarding the appropriate implementation of the Patient Self-Determination Act is whether the person is cognitively or legally able to make the decisions about end-of-life care (Bejenaru & Ellison, 2021; Moye & Wood, 2020). There are two types of determination: the capacity to make decisions, which is a clinical determination, and a competency decision, made legally by the court (Moye & Wood, 2020; Wettstein, 2013). In terms of deciding about personal health matters, capacity determinations refer to whether the individual is able to make a decision about specific interventions, and the abilities necessary are subject to measurement (such abilities are discussed in Chapters 6 and 7). With competency determinations, the individual is being judged either with respect to a specific task or intervention in general, and the determination can be made subjectively by the court even in the absence of a formal assessment.

Case law is still emerging regarding whether a person who lacks the capacity to make healthcare decisions can still designate a surrogate to make decisions on their behalf. This situation is rather common, though, given the tendency for families to not discuss these issues, individuals' reluctance to face the potential need, and the politicization of the conversation in the healthcare arena. Guidelines for professionals regarding the assessment of competence are available, and they provide insight into both the psychological and legal

Discovering Development

What Options Are There for Burial in Your Community?

One aspect of death that many people consider difficult to discuss is what they would prefer to have happen with their remains after they die. Do they prefer a traditional burial following a viewing and funeral? Do they prefer green burial? Do they prefer cremation or aquamation with internment of their ashes in a columbarium? Do they prefer to have their ashes scattered in a location that was meaningful to them?

Take some time and discover what burial options are approved in your community. You might consider contacting a local funeral home or cemetery to inquire about traditional burial and cremation options they have. Also, check into local options for green burials, in which the body is not cremated, prepared with chemicals, or buried in a concrete vault, but is simply placed in a biodegradable container and interred in a gravesite to decompose fully and return to nature; organizations such as the Green Burial Council (https://www.greenburialcouncil.org/) can also provide information. Additionally, aquamation is a water-based process considered an eco-friendly alternative to traditional cremation; check to determine whether this option is available in your community. Bishop Desmond Tutu, the Nobel Peace Prize winner from South Africa, chose this method prior to his death in December 2021.

Knowing more about the burial options available in one's community may provide a place to begin a conversation about one's wishes. In any event, it will provide background knowledge for that conversation at an appropriate time.

issues surrounding such evaluations (Bejenaru & Ellison, 2021; Moye & Wood, 2020; Wettstein, 2013).

Research indicates family members and other surrogate decision-makers are often wrong about what loved ones, even spouses or partners, really want (Moorman & Inoue, 2013). This further emphasizes the critical need, especially for couples, to discuss end-of-life issues ahead of time and ensure the appropriate advance directives are in place and key individuals are aware of them (Siconolfi et al., 2021). One way to start this process is to complete the Discovering Development feature.

After reading this module and thinking about end-of-life issues, you may be wondering how COVID-19 impacted the way people dealt with them. The Social Policy Implications feature at the end of the chapter examines this in more detail.

As we conclude this module, an important question arises: Have *you* made your end-of-life wishes known?

Adult Development in Action

If you were a healthcare social worker, how would you raise the issue of making end-of-life wishes known with your clients?

Review Questions

13.3 End-of-Life Issues

- What is a final scenario? How does a person create one?
- What is palliative care? How does hospice practice that approach to health care?
- What are a living will, health care power of attorney, and a do-not-resuscitate order? How does a person make their end-of-life wishes known to others?

13.4 Surviving the Loss: The Grieving Process

Key Questions

- How do people experience the grief process?
- What feelings do grieving people have?
- How do people cope with grief?
- What are the types of ambiguous loss?
- What is the difference between typical and prolonged grief?
- What is disenfranchised grief?

After 45 years of marriage, Gracia's husband recently died. At 70, Gracia knew she and Luis had fewer years left than they had already lived, but the death was a shock just the same. Gracia thinks about him much of the time and often finds herself making decisions based on "what Luis would have done" in the same situation.

Each of us is likely to suffer many losses over a lifetime. Whenever we lose someone close to us through death or other separation, like Gracia we experience bereavement, grief, and mourning. **Bereavement** is the state or condition caused by loss through death. **Grief** is the sorrow, hurt, anger, guilt, confusion, and other feelings that arise after suffering a loss. **Mourning** concerns the ways we express our grief. Mourning is highly influenced by culture. You can tell people in some cultures are bereaved and in mourning because of the clothing they wear or the rituals they observe, as we noted earlier in this chapter. Grief corresponds to the emotional reactions following loss, whereas mourning is the culturally approved behavioral manifestations of those feelings. Even though mourning rituals may be fairly standard within a culture, how people grieve varies considerably across cultures, as we consider next. We will also discover how Gracia's reactions are fairly typical of most people.

The Grief Process

How do people grieve? What do they experience? Perhaps you already have a good idea about the answers to these questions from your own experience. If so, you already know the process of grieving is a complicated and personal one. Just as there is no right way to die, there is no right way to grieve. Recognizing there are plenty of individual differences, we consider these patterns in this section.

The grieving process reflects many themes and issues people confront that may be expressed through rituals, both in-person and digital (Anderson & De Souza, 2021; Beaunoyer et al., 2020; Gamba, 2018; Norton & Gino, 2014). Like the process of dying, grieving does not have clearly demarcated stages through which we pass in a neat sequence, although there are certain issues people must face similar to those faced by dying people. When someone close to us dies, we must reorganize our lives, establish new patterns of behavior, and redefine relationships with family and friends. Indeed, Attig (1996) provided one of the best descriptions of grief when he wrote that grief is the process by which we relearn the world.

Unlike bereavement, over which we have no control, grief is a process that involves choices in coping, from confronting the reality and emotions to using religion to ease one's pain (Anderson & De Souza, 2021; Norton & Gino, 2014). From this perspective, grief is an active process through which a person must do several things (Worden, 2018):

- *Acknowledge the reality of the loss.* We must overcome the temptation to deny the reality of our loss; we must fully and openly acknowledge it and realize it affects every aspect of our life.
- *Work through the emotional turmoil.* We must find effective ways to confront and express the complete range of emotions we feel after the loss and must not avoid or repress them.
- *Adjust to the environment where the deceased is absent.* We must define new patterns of living that adjust appropriately and meaningfully to the fact the deceased is not present.
- *Loosen ties to the deceased.* We must free ourselves from the bonds of the deceased in order to reengage with our social network. This means finding effective ways to say good-bye.

Grief is an active coping process (Bagbey Darian, 2014; Garos, 2021; Worden, 2018). In processing grief, survivors must come to terms with and integrate the physical world of things, places, and events as well as their spiritual place in the world; the interpersonal world of interactions with family and friends, the dead, and, in some cases, God; and aspects of our inner selves and our personal experiences. Gracia, the widow in the vignette, is in the middle of this process. Even the matter of deciding what to do with the deceased's personal effects can be part of this active coping process (Attig, 1996).

Standret/Shutterstock.com

Dealing with the death of a friend is often especially difficult for young adults.

To make sense of grief, we need to keep several things in mind. First, grieving is a highly individual experience (Bagbey Darian, 2014; Cummings, 2015; Garos, 2021; Worden, 2018). A process that works well for one person may not be the best for someone else. Second, we must not underestimate the amount of time people need to deal with the various issues. To a casual observer, it may appear a survivor is back to normal after a few weeks (Harris, 2016, 2019). Actually, what may look like a return to normal activities may reflect bereaved people feeling social pressure to get on with things. It takes most people much longer to resolve the complex emotional issues faced during bereavement. Researchers and therapists alike agree a person needs at least a year following the loss to begin recovery, and two years is not uncommon.

Finally, recovery may be a misleading term. It is probably more accurate to say we learn to live with our loss rather than we recover from it (Attig, 1996). The impact of the loss of a loved one lasts a long time, perhaps for the rest of one's life. Still, most people reach a point of moving on with their lives (Bagbey Darian, 2014; Bonanno, 2009; Bonanno & Malgaroli, 2020; Harris, 2016, 2019).

Recognizing these aspects of grief makes it easier to know what to say and do for bereaved people. Among the most useful things are simply to let the person know you are sorry for their loss, you are there for support, and mean what you say.

Risk Factors in Grief. Bereavement is a life experience people have many times, and most people eventually handle it, often better than we might suspect (Bonanno, 2009; Bonanno et al., 2011; Carr & Mooney, 2021; Cummings, 2015; Meichsner et al., 2020). However, there are some risk factors that can make bereavement more difficult. Several of the more important are the mode of death, personal factors (e.g., personality, religiosity, age, gender, income), and interpersonal context (availability of social support, kinship relationship to the deceased person).

Most people believe the circumstances of death affect the grief process. A person whose family member was killed in an automobile accident has a different situation to deal with than a person whose family member died after a long period of a terminal disease. It is believed when death is anticipated, people go through a period of **anticipatory grief** before the death that supposedly serves to buffer the impact of the loss when it does come and to facilitate recovery (Patinadan et al., 2022; Shore et al., 2016). Indicators of anticipatory grief may appear as pre-loss grief, and as depression, anxiety, or pain.

The research evidence for whether anticipatory grief helps people cope with loss better is mixed (Patinadan et al., 2022). Anticipating the loss of a loved one from cancer or other terminal disease, or after a stay in the intensive care unit, can provide a framework for understanding family members' reactions (Coombs, 2010; Shore et al., 2016; Singer & Papa, 2021; Walker & Trapani, 2018). However, anticipatory grief does not appear to alleviate the outcome of the bereavement; in fact, it may even make it more difficult to reach a positive outcome (Nielsen et al., 2016; Supiano et al., 2022).

The strength of attachment to the deceased person does make a difference in dealing with a sudden as opposed to an expected death. Attachment theory provides a framework for understanding different reactions (Captari et al., 2021; Hales, 2016; Stroebe & Archer, 2013). When the deceased person was one for whom the survivor had a strong and close attachment and the loss was sudden, the grief is greater. However, such secure attachment styles tend to result in less depression after the loss because of less guilt over unresolved issues (because there are fewer of them), things not provided (because more were likely provided), and so on.

Few studies of personal risk factors have been done, and few firm conclusions can be drawn. There are no consistent findings regarding personality traits that either help buffer people from the typical effects of bereavement or exacerbate them (Haley, 2013; Stroebe & Archer, 2013). Research also consistently indicates older adults experience the least health consequences following bereavement, with the impact perhaps being strongest for middle-aged adults, but strong social support networks, including virtual ones, lessen these effects to varying degrees (Chang et al., 2016; Papa & Litz, 2011). Evidence from China suggests that experiencing bereavement has more serious effects on men over 60 and on both men and women under the age of 60 (Yang et al., 2020).

Typical Grief Reactions

The feelings experienced during grieving are intense; these feelings not only make it difficult to cope but can also make a person question their own reactions. The feelings involved usually include sadness, denial, anger, loneliness, and guilt.

Many researchers and clinicians refer to the psychological side of coming to terms with bereavement as **grief work**. Whether the loss is ambiguous and lacking closure (e.g., waiting to learn the fate of a missing loved one) or certain (e.g., verification of death through a dead body), people need space and time to grieve (Berns, 2011; Worden, 2018). However, a major challenge in American society is that, as noted earlier, people feel pressured to move on quickly after a loss, especially if that loss is not of a spouse or child. That is not how most people really feel or want to deal with their grief; they want the opportunity to work through their feelings on their own terms and timeline.

Muller and Thompson (2003) examined people's experience of grief in a detailed interview study and found five themes. *Coping* concerns what people do to deal with their loss in terms of what helps them. *Affect* refers to people's emotional reactions to the death of their loved one, such as certain topics that serve as emotional triggers for memories of their loved one. *Change* involves the ways survivors' lives change as a result of the loss; personal growth (e.g., "I didn't think I could deal with something that painful, but I did") is a common experience. *Narrative* relates to the stories survivors tell about their deceased loved one, that sometimes include details about the process of the death. Finally, *relationship* reflects who the deceased person was and the nature of the ties between that person and the survivor. Collectively, these themes indicate the experience of grief is complex and involves dealing with one's feelings as a survivor as well as memories of the deceased person.

How people express their feelings of grief varies across racial, ethnic, and cultural groups (Gire, 2014, 2019; Rosenblatt, 2020). For example, families in KwaZulu-Natal, South Africa, have a strong desire for closure and need for dealing with the "loneliness of grief" (Brysiewicz, 2008). In many cultures the bereaved construct a relationship with the person who died, but how this happens differs widely, from ghosts to appearances in dreams to connection through prayer and ancestor veneration (Cacciatore & DeFrain, 2015). Differences in dealing with grief and bereavement can also be observed across different subgroups within ethnic groups. For instance, various Latino/a groups (e.g., Mexican, Puerto Rican, Central American) and Black persons from different cultural backgrounds (e.g., African Americans, Barbadians, Haitians, Trinidadians) differ from each other in ritual practices regarding grief (Moore et al., 2022; Schoulte, 2011).

In addition to psychological grief reactions, there are also physiological ones (McCoyd et al., 2021). Physical health may decline, illness may result, and use of healthcare services may increase. Some people report

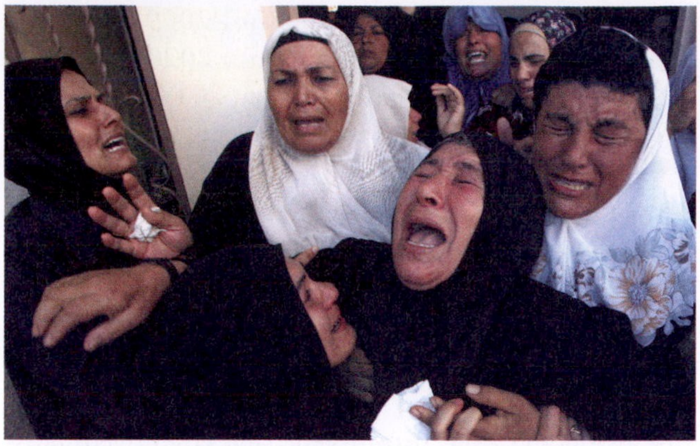

ZUMA Press, Inc./Alamy Stock Photo

How openly grief is expressed varies considerably across cultures.

sleep disturbances as well as neuroendocrine, neurological, and circulatory problems (Hopf et al., 2020; Lancel et al., 2020; Naef et al., 2013). In the time following the death of a loved one, dates having personal significance may reintroduce feelings of grief. Holidays such as Thanksgiving or birthdays that were spent with the deceased person may be difficult times. The actual anniversary of the death can be especially troublesome. The term **anniversary reaction** refers to changes in behavior related to feelings of sadness on this date. Personal experiences and research find recurring feelings of sadness or other examples of the anniversary reaction are common in normal grief (Glorioso et al., 2020; Rostila et al., 2015). Such feelings also accompany remembrances of major catastrophes across cultures, such as Thais remembering the victims of a tsunami and major flood (Assanangkornchai et al., 2007).

Researchers and clinicians agree that there is no standard timeline for grief work. Rather, people process loss in their own way at their own pace. The problem comes from social expectations that people are supposed to get over it in a reasonable amount of time, with the notion of reasonable somewhat related to the perceived closeness of the loss. It simply does not work that neatly. For example, research indicates that some widows demonstrate no sign of lessening of grief after 5 years (Kowalski & Bondmass, 2008). Rosenblatt (1996) reported people still felt the effects of the deaths of family members 50 years after the event. The depth of the emotions over the loss of loved ones sometimes never totally goes away, as people still cry and feel sad when discussing the loss despite the length of time that had passed (Edelman, 2020). Even though feelings of sadness pop up from time to time, most people find a way to move on with their lives and deal with their feelings reasonably well (Bonanno, 2009; Bonnano et al., 2011; Bonanno & Malgaroli, 2020; Edelman, 2020; Glorioso et al., 2020; Worden, 2018).

Coping with Grief

Thus far, we considered people's behaviors when they are dealing with grief. We have also reviewed how these behaviors change over time. How does this happen? How can we explain the grieving process?

Numerous theories have been proposed to account for the grieving process, such as general life-event theories, psychodynamic, attachment, and cognitive process theories (Corr, 2019, 2020; Stroebe & Archer, 2013). All of these approaches to grief are based on more general theories that result in none of them providing an adequate explanation of the grieving process. Three integrative approaches have been proposed specific to the grief process: the four-component model, the dual-process model of coping with bereavement, and the model of adaptive grieving dynamics.

The Four-Component Model. The **four-component model** proposes understanding grief is based on four things: (1) the context of the loss, referring to the risk factors such as whether the death was expected; (2) continuation of subjective meaning associated with loss, ranging from evaluations of everyday concerns to major questions about the meaning of life; (3) changing representations of the lost relationship over time; and (4) the role of coping and emotion regulation processes that cover all coping strategies used to deal with grief (Bonanno, 2009; Bonanno et al., 2011). The four-component model relies heavily on emotion theory, has much in common with the transactional model of stress, and has empirical support. According to the four-component model, dealing with grief is a complicated process only understood as a complex outcome that unfolds over time.

There are several important implications of this integrative approach. One of the most important in helping a grieving person involves helping them make meaning from the loss (Walsh, 2020; Wong, 2015, 2016, 2019). Second, this model implies that encouraging people to express their grief may actually not be helpful. An alternative view, called the **grief work as rumination hypothesis**, not only rejects the necessity of grief processing for recovery from loss but views extensive grief processing as a form of rumination that may actually increase distress (Bonanno et al., 2001; Eisma et al., 2020). Although it may seem people who think obsessively about their loss or who ruminate about it are confronting the loss, rumination is actually considered a form of avoidance because the person is not dealing with their real feelings and moving on (Bui et al., 2015; Eisma et al., 2015, 2020; Robinaugh & McNally, 2013).

One prospective study indicates, for instance, bereaved individuals who did not show symptoms of depression prior to their spouse's death but then developed chronically elevated depression through the first year and a half of bereavement (i.e., a chronic grief pattern) also tended to report more frequently thinking about and talking about their recent loss at the 6-month point in bereavement (Bonanno et al., 2004). Thus, it is the case that some bereaved individuals engage in minimal grief processing, whereas others are predisposed toward more extensive grief processing that shifts into rumination over time. Furthermore, the individuals who engage in minimal grief processing will likely exhibit a relatively favorable grief outcome, whereas those who are predisposed to more extensive grief processing tend toward ruminative preoccupation and, consequently, to a more prolonged grief course (Bonanno, 2009; Bonanno et al., 2011; Edelman, 2020; Eisma et al., 2020; Robinaugh & McNally, 2013).

In contrast to the traditional perspective that equates the absence of grief processing with grief avoidance, the grief work as rumination framework assumes resilient individuals are able to minimize processing of a loss through relatively automated processes, such as distraction or shifting attention toward more positive emotional experiences (Bonanno, 2009; Bonanno et al., 2011; Eisma et al., 2015, 2020).

The Dual Process Model. The **dual process model (DPM)** of coping with bereavement integrates existing ideas regarding stressors (Fiore, 2021; Stroebe & Archer, 2013; Utz & Pascoe, 2016). As indicated in Figure 13.5, the DPM defines two broad types of stressors. Loss-oriented stressors concern the loss itself, such as the grief work that needs to be done. Restoration-oriented stressors are those that involve adapting to the survivor's new life situation, such as building new relationships and finding new activities. The DPM proposes dealing with these stressors is a dynamic process, as indicated by the lines connecting them in the figure. This is a distinguishing feature of DPM. It describes how bereaved people cycle back and forth between dealing mostly with grief and trying to move on with life. At times the emphasis will be on grief; at other times on moving forward.

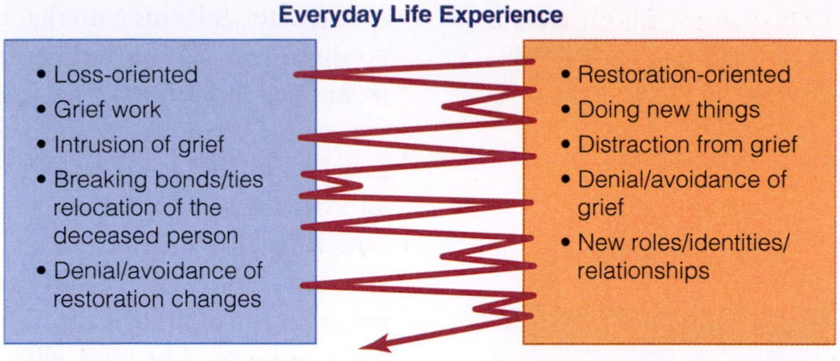

Figure 13.5 The dual process model of coping with bereavement describes the relation between dealing with the stresses of the loss itself (loss-oriented) and moving on with one's life (restoration-oriented).

Source: Stroebe, M., & Schut, H. (2001). Models of coping with bereavement: A review. In M. S. Stroebe, R. O. Hansson, W. Stroebe, & H. Schut (Eds.), *Handbook of bereavement research: Consequences, coping, and care* (pp. 375–403). American Psychological Association.

The DPM captures well the process bereaved people themselves report—at times they are nearly overcome with grief, while at other times they handle life well. The DPM also helps us understand how, over time, people come to a balance between the long-term effects of bereavement and the need to live life. Understanding how people handle grief requires understanding the various contexts in which people live and interact with others (Fiore, 2021; Ingram, 2020; Sandler et al., 2007, 2013).

The Model of Adaptive Grieving Dynamics. For anyone who has experienced the loss of a loved one, grieving can be an intense, personal, complicated process that does not follow a straight path through predictable stages (Edelman, 2020). Consequently, to understand grief is to understand that multiple responses to loss may each prove adaptive in different ways. Only when they are considered together and in their unique combination for each grieving person is a more complete understanding of grief possible.

The basic structure of the model of adaptive grieving dynamics is described in Figure 13.6. **The model of adaptive grieving dynamics (MAGD) is based on two sets of pairs of adaptive grieving dynamics**. One pair consists of lamenting and heartening responses to grief; the other pair consists of integrating and tempering responses to grief. These four interrelated dynamics are defined as follows (Bagbey Darian, 2014):

- *Lamenting*: experiencing and/or expressing grieving responses that are distressful, disheartening, and/or painful
- *Heartening*: experiencing and/or expressing grieving responses that are gratifying, uplifting, and/or pleasurable
- *Integrating*: assimilating internal and external changes catalyzed by a grief-inducing loss, and reconciling differences in past, present, and future realities in light of these changes
- *Tempering*: avoiding chronic attempts to integrate changed realities impacted by a grief-inducing loss that overwhelm a griever's and/or community's resources and capacities to integrate such changes

Bagbey Darian (2014) argues that although the pairs of dynamics appear to be contradictory, in processing grief they actually work together. For instance, grieving people often experience both joy and sorrow simultaneously when remembering a loved one. This simultaneity of experience is a key difference between MAGD and the dual process model, as the dual process model argues that grieving people oscillate between loss-oriented tasks and restoration-oriented tasks.

According to the MAGD, the outcome of grief is not "working things through," or necessarily finding meaning in the loss (Bagbey Darian, 2014; Garos, 2021). Rather, it aims at understanding how people continually negotiate and renegotiate their personal and interpersonal equilibrium over time. Grieving never really ends; how the person continues finding balance given that reality is the issue.

Ambiguous Loss

To this point we have been considering grief reactions to loss in which there is the possibility of closure. In these situations, there is proof of death, usually a

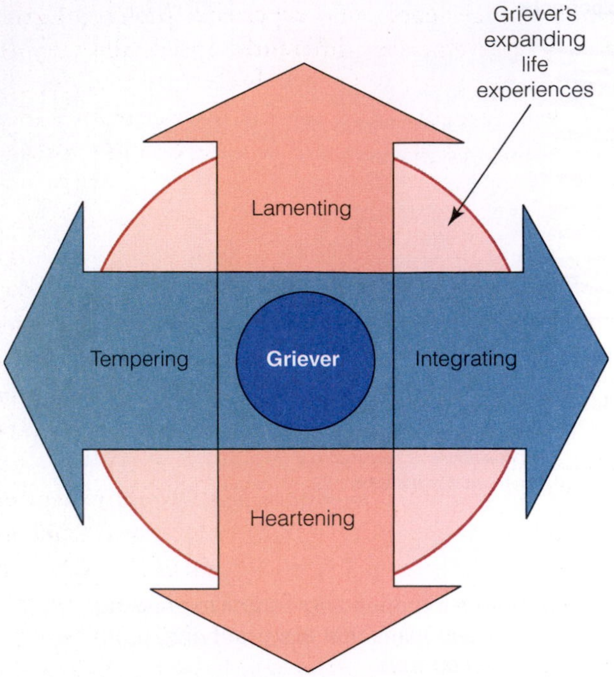

Figure 13.6 Model of adaptive grieving dynamics.

Source: Bagbey Darian, C. D. (2014). A new mourning: Synthesizing an interactive model of adaptive grieving dynamics. *Illness, Crisis & Loss, 22,* 195–235. https://doi.org/10.2190/IL.22.3.c (p. 203)

physical dead body, and the likelihood of a funeral or some other ritual for support of the survivors. But this is not always the case. Major natural disasters, such as tsunamis, or pandemics, major explosions, accidents, or repressive governments who kidnap or otherwise make people disappear are examples. In these cases, bodies are never recovered, so there is no possibility of tangible closure. But loss can occur in other ways, too. Consider divorce, in which a child, for instance, may lose connection with a parent, or in cases in which a family member with dementia no longer recognizes anyone.

Boss (2010, 2015; Dahl & Boss, 2020) coined the term *ambiguous loss* for these circumstances. **Ambiguous loss** refers to situations of loss in which there is no resolution or closure. Boss (2010, 2015; Dahl & Boss, 2020) describes two types of ambiguous loss.

The first type refers to a missing person who is physically absent but still very present psychologically to family and friends. Examples of this type include people missing after disasters, victims of kidnapping, and those never recovered from accidents. The primary challenge for the families and friends of the missing is the unending pain of not knowing for certain what happened, where their loved one is at present, and their specific fate. It is this pain that terrorists rely on to inflict constant pain and suffering. Typical grief reactions are postponed indefinitely, making it essentially impossible for people to move on with their lives, sometimes for generations (Boss, 2015). What motivates these families and friends is hope for an eventual return of the loved one (Boss, 2015; Wayland et al., 2016).

A second type of ambiguous loss involves a loved one who is psychologically absent but who is still physically present. They are what people term "here but gone," as is the case in certain diseases such as dementia. Families caring for loved ones with Alzheimer's disease, for instance, report going through grieving as their loved one loses more and more of what makes them who they are, ultimately coming to a point at which they think of their loved one as dead even though they are physically alive (Boss, 2010).

The common aspect of both types of ambiguous loss is that as long as certainty is not reached, closure is not possible in the usual sense. Families and friends report feeling pressure to stop holding out hope, on one hand, or are accused of being cold on the other. Either way, ambiguous loss is especially difficult to deal with.

Prolonged Grief

Not everyone is able to cope with grief well and begin rebuilding a life (Edelman, 2020). Sometimes the feelings of hurt, loneliness, and guilt are so overwhelming they become the focus of the survivor's life to such an extent there is never any psychological closure and the grief continues to interfere indefinitely with one's ability to function. When this occurs, individuals are viewed as experiencing **prolonged grief**, which is characterized by persistent and intrusive feelings of grief lasting beyond the expected period of adaptation to loss, and is associated with separation distress and traumatic distress (Eisma & Stroebe, 2021; Wilson et al., 2022).

Researchers and clinicians have long debated whether prolonged grief represents the complexity of grief and the fact that the time it takes to process grief varies a great deal across people, or whether prolonged grief represents a form of psychopathology. In 2022, the American Psychiatric Association (2022) reinstituted prolonged grief disorder as a separate diagnostic category. The diagnostic criteria for adults with prolonged grief disorder are:

A. The death, at least 12 months ago, of a person who was close to the bereaved individual.

B. Since the death, the development of a persistent grief response characterized by one or both of the following symptoms, which have been present most days to a clinically significant degree. In addition, the symptom(s) has occurred nearly every day for at least the last month:

1. Intense yearning/longing for the deceased person.
2. Preoccupation with thoughts or memories of the deceased person (in children and adolescents, preoccupation may focus on the circumstances of the death).

C. Since the death, at least three of the following symptoms have been present most days to a clinically significant degree. In addition, the symptoms have occurred nearly every day for at least the last month:

1. Identity disruption (e.g., feeling as though part of oneself has died) since the death.
2. Marked sense of disbelief about the death.
3. Avoidance of reminders that the person is dead.
4. Intense emotional pain (e.g., anger, bitterness, sorrow) related to the death.
5. Difficulty reintegrating into one's relationships and activities after the death (e.g., problems engaging with friends, pursuing interests, or planning for the future).
6. Emotional numbness (absence or marked reduction of emotional experience) as a result of the death.
7. Feeling that life is meaningless as a result of the death.
8. Intense loneliness as a result of the death.

D. The disturbance causes clinically significant distress or impairment: in social, occupational, or other important areas of functioning.

E. The duration and severity of the bereavement reaction clearly exceed expected social, cultural, or religious norms for the individual's culture and context.

F. The symptoms are not better explained by another mental disorder such as major depressive disorder or posttraumatic stress disorder, and are not attributable to the physiological effects of a substance (e.g., medication, alcohol) or another medical condition. (American Psychiatric Association, 2022, pp. 130–131)

Careful reading of each of the symptoms of prolonged grief disorder make it clear that most are typical grief reactions discussed earlier in this section. The primary difference is in the duration of these intense feelings. Neuroscience research provides some evidence that prolonged grief disorder may involve different brain processes that are found in typical emotional processing. Arizmendi and colleagues (2016) reported that people who experience prolonged grief process their emotions differently. Specifically, they do not engage those areas of the brain that are typically involved in regulating emotions, supporting the idea that prolonged grief involves avoidance and a disruption of emotion regulation.

Setting aside the issue of whether prolonged grief is a form of psychopathology, there is evidence of that prolonged grief transcends culture. For example, Li and Prigerson (2013) validated a measure of prolonged grief in a sample of Chinese adults. Likewise, prolonged grief was validated in a sample of Spanish adults in terms of how they respond to emotion (Fernández-Alcántara et al., 2016).

Some researchers believe that prolonged grief may be more likely with certain types of loss (such as sudden or unexpected deaths; Wilson et al., 2022). In addition, some also speculate that whether a person has a supportive social network may make a difference. However, too little research has been conducted for clear conclusions to be drawn.

Disenfranchised Grief

As we have noted repeatedly throughout this chapter, the experience of loss and the subsequent grief we feel is a highly personal matter. We have also noted that grief is heavily influenced by sociocultural factors, that in a sense provide rules for the types of loss for which grief is appropriate or not. Such rules govern who, what, when, and how one is supposed to grieve, thereby separating grief that is considered normative and legitimized from grief which is not (Attig, 2004; Doka, 2008). When losses happen that are outside of society's grieving norms, perhaps due to the kind of relationship the bereaved person had with the deceased, normative grief reactions are considered socially aberrant and inappropriate (Attig, 2004; Doka, 1989). In these cases, bereaved individuals are deprived of their desire to mourn their loss, despite their personal experience of intense feelings of grief and distress.

This experience was originally termed disenfranchised grief by Doka (1989) **Disenfranchised grief** is "the grief that persons experience when they incur a loss that is not or cannot be openly acknowledged, publicly mourned, or socially supported" (p. 4). Thus, the nature of disenfranchised grief is twofold: (1) the denial of one's grieving rights, which creates additional grief complications for the bereaved; and (2) the removal of sources of valuable social support.

Disenfranchised grief occurs most often in situations in which people in a relationship do not or cannot reveal the nature of that relationship, and in situations that involve the type of loss that many people do not consider valid for expressions of grief. The first situation is common among people who have a close, intimate relationship that is kept secret, an experience that historically has been true in the LGBTQIA+ community (Inventor et al., 2022). The second situation most commonly occurs in the context of the loss of a pet (Marr et al., 2022).

Disenfranchised grief stems from the social expectations we place on people to move on after loss (Harris, 2016; Pitcho-Prelorentzos & Mahat-Shamir, 2022). However, those expectations can result in failure to understand the personal impact that every loss has on someone and a failure to be empathetic to that person's experience. Such failure may also reflect certain stereotypes or bias regarding the value of various people's lives. Clinicians argue that the way to eliminate disenfranchised grief is to affirm individuals' right to grieve any loss they consider personally important.

In this context, it is good to keep in mind John Donne's passage from his *Devotions upon Emergent Occasions*, written in December 1323 as he recovered from a very serious illness:

No [one] is an island,
Entire of itself,
Every [one] is a piece of the continent,
A part of the main.
If a clod be washed away by the sea,
Europe is the less.
As well as if a promontory were.
As well as if a manor of thy friend's
Or of thine own were:
Any [person's] death diminishes me,
Because I am involved in mankind,
And therefore never send to know for whom the
bell tolls;
It tolls for thee.

Controversies

The Pain of Virtual Goodbyes

One of the most difficult and emotional experiences for healthcare workers during the COVID-19 pandemic was having to be a link between a dying person and their loved ones. Because no visitors were allowed, family and friends of the dying had no direct means of communicating with each other, even if the conversation could only be one-sided due to the dying person's condition. To help bridge this very challenging situation, healthcare workers would hold a phone, tablet, or computer so that communication could occur. In some cases, this was how religious priests and ministers provided final rites in their particular traditions.

U.S. data indicate that deaths from COVID-19 were roughly 2.4 times higher among non-Latino/a Native Americans and Alaska Native persons, and among Latino/a individuals, and 2 times higher among non-Latino/a Black individuals than among White individuals (Centers for Disease Control and Prevention, 2022e). This means that far more mediated conversations occurred among racially/ethnically marginalized families than among White families.

How did these conversations happen? It is emotionally difficult to tell a love one goodbye under optimal circumstances, let alone when it must be done virtually. The Center to Advance Palliative Care (2021) at the Icahn School of Medicine at Mount Sinai offered examples of scripts that healthcare workers could use to help facilitate these difficult conversations. In many cases, though, healthcare workers simply encouraged people to say what they thought needed to be said, to pray, and even to be silent and just be present.

Considered in the context of ethnic and racial disparities, though, additional challenges emerged. Healthcare disparities (discussed in Chapter 4) raised questions about differential care (Eligon & Burch, 2020). Differential access to health care (discussed in Chapter 4) meant that there may not be an opportunity for healthcare workers to assist families and friends even if they wanted to. The digital divide (Rainie, 2020) sometimes meant that key loved ones were unable to connect at all, or with considerable difficulty due to lack of broadband access or appropriate devices. The inability to engage in cultural practices created serious challenges for those whose beliefs about death rituals entail being able to perform specific prayers and actions.

Having to say goodbye to a loved one is difficult enough—and is only compounded by the racial/ethnic disparities in health care in the United States. The pandemic brought these to the fore.

Finally, our consideration of grief must include a consideration of how grieving is affected when family and friends are prevented from being present at the time of a loved one's death, as was the case during the COVID-19 pandemic. Hundreds of thousands of families in the United States alone had to say their final prayers and farewells via phones and computers. The Controversies feature explores these experiences and how the racial and ethnic disparities reflected in COVID-19 mortality rates played out in families' lives.

Adult Development in Action

If you were a grief counselor, how would you improve the ability of people to express their grief about the loss of their loved one?

Review Questions

13.4 Surviving the Loss: The Grieving Process

- What is the typical grief response following the loss of a loved one? How have typical grief responses been organized into theories and models?
- How do people usually cope with grief?
- What is ambiguous loss and how do people deal with it?
- What is prolonged grief, and how does it differ from typical grief responses? What is prolonged grief disorder?
- What is disenfranchised grief, and what are some examples of it?

13.5 Dying and Bereavement Experiences Across the Life Span

Key Questions

- What do children understand about death? How should adults help them deal with it?
- How do adolescents deal with death?
- How do adults deal with death? What special issues do they face concerning the death of a child or parent?
- How do older adults face the loss of a child, grandchild, or partner?

Hoa and Carl have a 6-year-old daughter, Jennie, whose grandmother just died. Jennie and her grandmother were very close, as the two saw each other almost every day. Other adults have told her parents not to take Jennie to the funeral. Hoa and Carl aren't sure what to do. They wonder whether Jennie will understand what happened to her grandmother, and they worry about how she will react.

Coming to grips with the reality of death may be one of the hardest things we have to do in life. American society does not help much either, as it tends to distance itself from death through euphemisms, such as "passed away" or "dearly departed," and by eliminating many rituals from the home (for example, viewings and wakes no longer take place there).

These trends make it difficult for people such as Hoa, Carl, and Jennie to learn about death in its natural context. Dying itself has been moved from the home to hospitals and other institutions such as nursing homes. The closest most people get to death is a quick glance inside a nicely lined casket at a corpse that has been made to look as if the person were still alive.

What should parents like Hoa and Carl do? How do the friends of Jennie's grandmother feel about the death? In this section, we consider how our understanding of death changes throughout the life span. To begin, we will consider what children and adolescents understand so that parents may have a better appreciation for how to discuss the death of a family member. We'll then move to how adults understand death.

Childhood

Some parents take their children to funerals of relatives and close friends. Others do not. Many adults, such as Hoa and Carl in the vignette, are conflicted and wonder whether young children really know what death means. Children's understanding of death must be understood in terms of their cultural background and the fact that it changes with their cognitive development (Menendez et al., 2020). Preschoolers tend to believe that death is temporary and magical, something dramatic that comes to get you in the middle of the night like a burglar or a ghost. Not until children are 5 to 7 years of age do they realize that death is permanent, that it eventually happens to everyone, and that dead people no longer have any biological functions.

Children's expressions of grief at the loss of a loved one also vary with age (Halliwell & Franken, 2016; Menendez et al., 2020). Several common manifestations of grief among children are listed in Figure 13.7. Typical

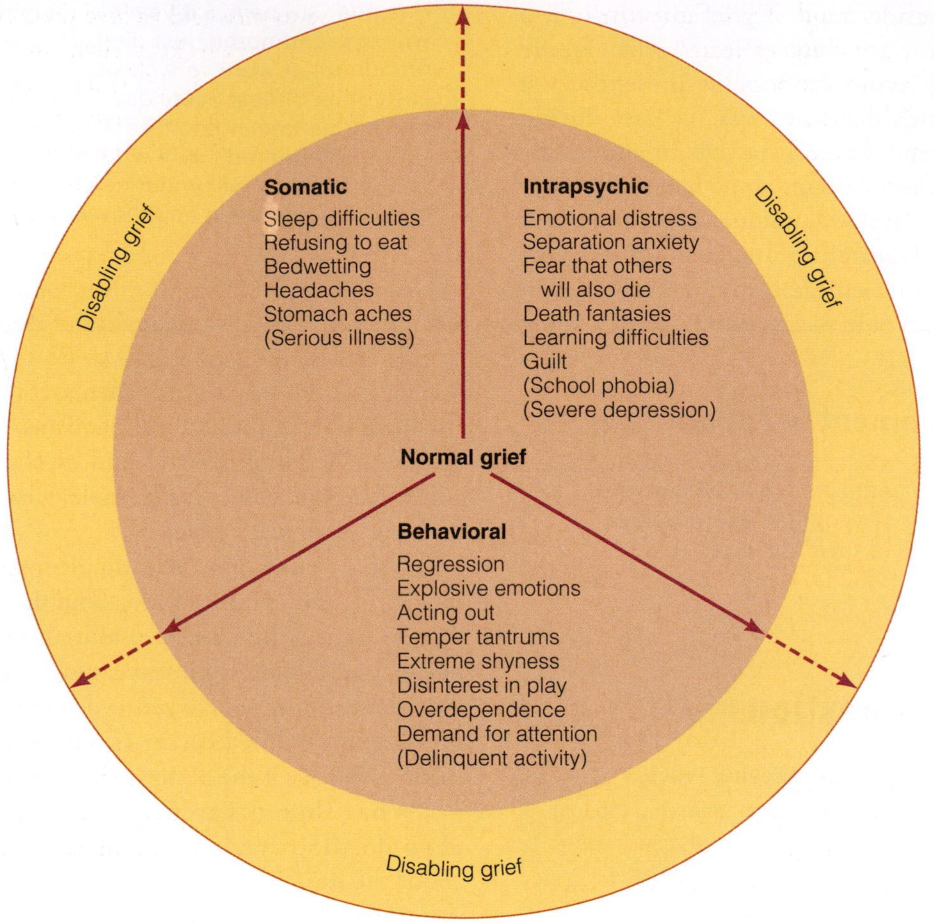

Figure 13.7 Children express their grief in many ways, including physiological (somatic), emotional (intrapsychic), and behavioral.

Source: Oltjenbruns, K. A. (2001). Developmental context of childhood: Grief and regrief phenomena. In M. S. Stroebe, R. O. Hansson, W. Stroebe, & H. Schut, (Eds.), *Handbook of Bereavement Research: Consequences, Coping, and Care* (Fig. 8–1, p. 177). American Psychological Association. Copyright © 2001 by the American Psychological Association.

reactions in early childhood include regression, guilt for causing the death, denial, displacement, repression, and wishful thinking that the deceased will return. In later childhood, common behaviors include problems at school, anger, and physical ailments. As children mature, they acquire more coping skills that permit a shift to problem-focused coping, which provides a better sense of personal control. Children will often flip between grief and normal activity, a pattern they may learn from adults (Duncan, 2020), and may be more likely to disclose their true feelings online (Halliwell & Franken, 2016). Sensitivity to these feelings and how they get expressed is essential so that the child can understand what happened and that they did not cause the death.

Research indicates that bereavement per se during childhood typically does not have long-lasting effects such as depression (Miller et al., 2014), but can have long-lasting grief triggers and impacts on attachment (Meyer-Lee et al., 2020), especially if children do not receive adequate care and attention following the death (Kentor & Kaplow, 2020).

Understanding death can be particularly difficult for children when adults are not open and honest with them, especially about the meaning of death (Ferow, 2019; Miller & Rosengren, 2014). Some adults believe that it is best to shield their children, especially younger children, from death. The use of euphemisms such as "Grandma has gone away" and "Mommy is only sleeping" reflects this belief, but is unwise. First, young children do not understand the deeper level of meaning in such statements and are likely to take them literally. Second, and more important, adults cannot fully shield children from the reality of death.

When explaining death to children, it is best to deal with them on their terms. Keep explanations simple, at a level they can understand. Try to allay their fears and reassure them that whatever reaction they have is okay. Providing loving support for the child will maximize the potential for a successful (albeit painful) introduction to one of life's realities. It is important for children to know that it is okay for them to feel sad, to cry, or to express their feelings in whatever way they want. Reassuring children that it's okay to feel this way helps them deal with their confusion at some adults' explanations of death. Young adults remember feeling uncomfortable as children around dead bodies, often fearing that the deceased person would come after them. Still, researchers believe it is very important for children to attend the funeral of a relative or to have a private viewing (Ferow, 2019; Hanna et al., 2022; McDermott, 2018). They will process the experience in age-appropriate ways, especially if they have understanding adults available to answer questions.

Adolescence

Adolescents have more personal experience with death and grief than many people realize (Balk, 2014; Revet et al., 2020). Surveys of college students indicate that between 40% and 70% of traditional-aged college students will experience the death of someone close to them during their college years, such as a parent, sibling, or friend.

Adolescence is a time of personal and physical change when one is trying to develop a theory of self. When teenagers experience the death of someone close to them, they may have considerable trouble making sense of the event, especially if this is their first experience (Oltjenbruns & Balk, 2007; Revet et al., 2020). The effects of bereavement in adolescence can be quite severe, especially when the death was unexpected, and can be expressed in many ways, such as chronic illness, enduring guilt, low self-esteem, poorer performance in school and on the job, substance abuse, problems in interpersonal relationships, and suicidal thinking (Kentor & Kaplow, 2020; Revet et al., 2020).

An important aspect of adolescent development is wanting to be perceived as part of the peer group. As a result, younger adolescents are particularly reluctant to discuss their grief (for instance, over the loss of a sibling), mainly because they do not want to appear different from their peers (Balk, 2014). This reluctance leaves them particularly vulnerable to psychosomatic symptoms such as headaches and stomach pains that signal underlying problems.

Adolescents often do not demonstrate a clear end point to their grief over the loss of a sibling or parent; they continue to miss and to love their dead loved ones and try to find ways to keep them in their lives, such as through social media (Barrera et al., 2013; Cope, 2020). However, few nonbereaved peers were willing to talk with the bereaved students about their experience or even felt comfortable being with them (Balk, 2014).

One approach to helping adolescents deal with grief is the Resilience Songwriting Program (Myers-Coffman et al., 2020a, 2020b). The Resilience Songwriting Program offers a way for adolescents to nurture strengths and inner resources while also processing grief alongside peers. Participants are assisted by music therapists. Research indicates that eight, 90-minute sessions are optimal, recruitment works best in a school setting, and it is best not to include participants' siblings. The sessions are aimed at enhancing self-esteem, coping, emotional expression, and meaning making. Essential elements of the protocol include participant agency and collaboration to enhance self-efficacy and self-esteem; use of cognitive behavior therapy strategies (i.e., psychoeducation, cognitive reframing, and positive appraisals) to enhance mood, coping, and emotional expression; and flexibility in the songwriting process to support emotional expression and meaning making based on group dynamics and musical aesthetics.

Adulthood

Adults accrue considerable experience with death as they continue through adulthood. We will focus on three specific types of loss adults experience in detail: the death of one's child, the death of one's parent, and the death of one's partner. These losses are not unique to adulthood, of course, but are experienced most commonly in adulthood.

For many people, it is not until adulthood that they experience the death of a family member or very close friend. For this reason, many adults are ill prepared for the emotional experiences they have. For instance, because emerging adults are just beginning to pursue the family, career, and personal goals they have set, they tend to be more intense in their feelings toward death. When asked how they feel about death, young adults report a strong sense that those who die at this point in their lives would be cheated out of their future (Attig, 1996). Prolonged grief and mental health problems are relatively common (Hoffman et al., 2020; Johnsen & Afgun, 2021).

Wrenn (1999) relates one of the challenges faced by bereaved college students is learning "how to respond to people who ignore their grief, or who tell them they need to get on with life and it's not good for them to continue to grieve" (p. 134). College students have a need to express their grief like other bereaved people do, so providing them the opportunity to do so is crucial (McCoyd et al., 2021). Social media is the usual outlet, and college students turn to peers most for support; however, peers may not know how to be maximally supportive (Tan & Andriessen, 2021).

The death of a person with whom one has a romantic relationship but to whom one is not married in young adulthood is often unacknowledged as bereavement. This may be the case in LGBTQIA+ relationships, which we explore more a bit later (Alasuutari, 2021). It is also a frequent situation in the military. For example, research has found that girlfriends of male soldiers killed in battle felt socially isolated and lonely in dealing with their loss (Hamama-Raz et al., 2021; Leichtentritt et al., 2013). Clearly, this is a missed opportunity to be sensitive to people's loss and to provide support.

As we consider some specific types of loss most often experienced by adults, we should keep the overall lack of broad experiences with death that most people bring as they enter adulthood. This situation has occurred as a result of the factors discussed in Chapter 4 that resulted in the rapid increase in average longevity, especially the lowering of infant mortality rates and the improvements in health care (such as antibiotics). Prior to that, individuals were likely to have direct experience with death from early childhood.

Death of One's Child

The death of one's child, for most parents, brings unimaginable grief (McCoyd et al., 2021; McQuaid, 2021; Worden 2018). Because children are not supposed to die before their parents, it is as if the natural order of things has been violated, shaking parents to their core (Aizenkot, 2022; Rubin & Malkinson, 2001). Mourning and relationship stress are always intense; some parents never recover or reconcile themselves to the death of their child and may terminate their relationship with each other, while others find solace and strength in each other (Albuquerque et al., 2016). The intensity of feelings is due to the strong parent–child bond that begins before birth and lasts a lifetime (Fernández-Sola et al., 2020; Maple et al., 2010, 2013).

Young parents who lose a child unexpectedly report high anxiety, a more negative view of the world, and much guilt, which result in a devastating experience (Fernández-Sola et al., 2020). The most overlooked losses of a child are those that happen through stillbirth, miscarriage, abortion, or neonatal death (McCoyd et al., 2021; Tian & Solomon, 2020). Attachment to the child begins before birth, especially for mothers, so the loss hurts deeply. For this reason, ritual is extremely important to acknowledge the death and validate parents' feelings of grief (Nuzum et al., 2015).

Yet parents who experience this type of loss are expected to recover quickly. The lived experience of parents tells a different story (Tian & Solomon, 2020). These parents talk about a life-changing event and report a deep sense of loss and hurt, especially when others do not understand their feelings. Worst of all, if societal expectations for quick recovery are not met, the parents may be subjected to unfeeling comments.

The loss of a young adult child for a middle-aged parent is experienced differently but is equally devastating (Maple et al., 2013; Schneider, 2013). This is especially so for parents of adult children who die from drug overdoses (Titlestad et al., 2021). Prolonged grief is more common among bereaved parents than in other groups, most likely due to the very different nature of the parent–child relationship (Zetumer et al., 2015).

The traumatic effects of experiencing the death of one's child are explored in more detail in the How Do We Know? feature. In it, we delve into the experiences of parents in Northern India who experience the loss of their child through stillbirth, perinatal, and childhood death.

Death of One's Parent

Most parents die after their children are grown. But whenever parental death occurs, it often hurts. Losing a parent in adulthood is a rite of passage as one is transformed from being a child to being without a parent, and for many, once their last parent dies they report feeling orphaned (Abrams, 2013; McCoyd et al., 2021). We, the children, are now next in line.

The loss of a parent is significant. For emerging adult women transitioning to parenthood, losing their own mother during this time raises many feelings, such as deep loss at not being able to share their pregnancies with their mothers and fear of dying young themselves (De Rosbo-Davies et al., 2022; Franceschi, 2005; Rowe & Harmon, 2014). Death of one's parent in adulthood has significant effects on adult children, such on the child's marriage, largely depending on the quality of the relationship with the deceased parent (Stokes, 2016).

The feelings accompanying the loss of an older parent reflect a sense of letting go, loss of a buffer against death, better acceptance of one's own eventual death, and a sense of relief the parent's suffering is over (Abrams, 2013; Igarashi et al., 2013; McCoyd

How Do We Know?

Impacts of Child Death and Stillbirth on Northern Indian Parents

Who were the investigators, and what was the aim of the study? When parents experience the loss of a child, they must cope with two main things: how to deal with one of the worst things imaginable with the death of their child and how to deal with each other. Surprisingly, little research has been done to examine how partners work through the grieving process alone and together. Das and colleagues (2021) wanted to document the grief and coping experiences of Northern Indian parents following stillbirth and child death.

How did the investigators measure the topic of interest? Individual interviews were conducted with bereaved mothers and fathers separately. The in-depth interviews for parents had open-ended questions that explored the issues including grief experience, interpersonal and family level challenges, coping mechanisms, support systems, and return to work/normalcy. The Perinatal Grief Scale was used to document the mother's grief severity after 6–9 months of loss. Additionally, in-depth interviews and eight focus group discussions were done with community members. The in-depth interviews for community and religious members and focus group discussions explored their broad perspectives about the grief and coping by parents in the society/community.

Who were the participants in the study? Two categories of participants were included: (1) parents who had child or neonate death and stillbirths at the hospital and their family members and (2) community representatives including influential community leaders, community health functionaries, and religious leaders. Out of these approached, 13 parents with child death, 12 parents with neonatal death, and 22 parents with stillbirth consented for in-depth interviews. The community representatives were purposively identified for interviews and focus groups. Four categories of community participants were identified: mothers, fathers, grandfathers, and grandmothers with a child under 5 years old but who had not experienced child death or stillbirth.

What was the design of the study? The study used an exploratory qualitative research design.

Were there ethical concerns in the study? There were no ethical concerns, as participants were carefully screened, were provided detailed information about the nature of the project, and were given the opportunity to stop their participation at any time.

What were the results? Four themes emerged from the interviews: grief anticipation and expression, impact of the bereavement, coping mechanisms, and sociocultural norms and practices. Both parents typically expressed various forms of disbelief, severe emotional pain, and helplessness. Mothers expressed severe grief openly, and some fainted. Fathers also felt severe grief but did not express it openly. Some parents expressed self-guilt and blamed the hospital/healthcare providers, themselves, or family for their loss. Most parents reported either no or positive change in their marital relationship, but a few reported increased marital disharmony. A majority of parents experienced sleep, eating, and psychological disturbances for several weeks. Mothers coped through engaging in household work, caring for other child(ren), and spiritual activities. Fathers coped through avoiding discussion of their grief and through work and professional engagement. Fathers resumed work after 5–20 days, and mothers took 2–6 weeks to resume household chores. Unanticipated loss, limited family support, and financial strain affected the severity and duration of grief. Nearly 60% of mothers who experienced perinatal or child death and 80% of mothers who experienced stillbirth reported severe grief after 6–9 months.

What did the investigators conclude? Stillbirth, perinatal, and child death have lasting psychosomatic, social, and economic impacts on Northern Indian parents, which are often ignored. Appropriate and broad-based interventions are needed to provide support.

et al., 2021). Yet, if the parent died from a cause such as Alzheimer's disease, which may involve the loss of the parent–child relationship along the way, then bodily death can feel like the second time the parent died (Shaw, 2007). Whether the adult child now tries to separate from the deceased parent's expectations or finds comfort in the memories, the impact of the loss is great.

Death of One's Partner

Experiencing the loss of one's partner is the type of loss in late life we know most about. The death of a partner differs from other losses. It clearly represents a deep personal loss, especially when the couple has had a long and close relationship (Lee, 2014; Lee et al., 2022). In a very real way, when one's partner dies, a part of oneself dies, too.

There is pressure from society to mourn the loss of one's partner for a period of time and then to move on (Jenkins, 2003). Typically, this pressure is manifested if the survivor begins to express interest in finding another partner before an acceptable period of mourning has passed. Although Americans no longer specify the length of the mourning period, many believe that about a year is appropriate. The fact that such pressure and negative commentary usually do not accompany other losses is another indication of the seriousness with which most people take the death of a partner.

Experiencing the loss of one's partner in young adulthood can be especially traumatic, not only because of the loss itself but also because such loss is unexpected. Very little research has examined this issue (Jones et al., 2019; Morris et al., 2021). As Trish Straine, a 32-year-old widow whose husband was killed in the World Trade Center attack, put it: "I suddenly thought, 'I'm a widow.' Then I said to myself, 'A widow? That's an older woman, who's dressed in black. It's certainly not a 32-year-old like me'" (Lieber, 2001). One of the most difficult aspects for young widows and widowers is they must deal with both their own and their young children's grief and provide the support their children need, and that can be extremely difficult. "Every time I look at my children, I'm reminded of Mark," said Stacey, a 35-year-old widow whose husband died of bone cancer. "And people don't want to hear you say you don't feel like moving on, even though there is great pressure from them to do that."

Monashee Frantz/OJO Images/Getty Images

Becoming a widow as a young adult can be especially traumatic.

Older bereaved spouses may grieve a great deal for a long time (Lee, 2014; Lee et al., 2022); research has indicated that grief can sometimes last for years (Lin & Brown, 2020; Naef et al., 2013). Given that, you might wonder whether having a supportive social network can help people cope. Research findings on this topic are mixed, however. Some studies find that social support plays a significant role in the outcome of the grieving process for older adults. For example, some data suggest that during the first two years after the death of a partner, the quality of the support system—rather than simply the number of friends—is especially important for the older grieving partner. Survivors who have confidants are better off than survivors who have many acquaintances (Hansson & Stroebe, 2007). In contrast, other studies find that having a supportive social network may play little role in helping people cope (DiGiacomo et al., 2013; Sekgobela et al., 2021). Still other research finds that social support networks increase in size over the first few years after bereavement but return to or end up somewhat smaller than they were prior to bereavement in about 7 years (Klaus, 2021). Issues may include whether there is a complex relationship involving the bereaved person, whether they want to have contact with others, who in the social network is willing to provide support, and whether that support is of high quality.

When one's partner dies, how they felt about the relationship can play a role in coping with bereavement. For instance, widowed older adults who felt worsening regret about unfinished aspects of their marriages over time had the hardest time dealing with grief (Holland et al., 2014, 2020).

Older bereaved spouses who can talk about their feelings concerning their loss exhibit reduced levels of depression and functional impairment (Johannsen et al., 2019; Pfoff et al., 2014). Cognitive-behavioral therapy is one especially effective intervention to help bereaved people make sense of the loss and deal with their other feelings and thoughts (Godzik et al., 2021; Lichtenthal & Sweeney, 2014). A key to this process is helping people make meaning from the death (Johannsen et al., 2019; Milman & Neimeyer, 2020). An extensive study of widowed adults in Scotland found the increased likelihood of dying lasted for at least 10 years (Boyle et al., 2011). Such loss is deeply personal. Lucy Kalanithi (2016) described how her marriage vows to love, to honor, and to be loyal to her husband did not end with his death at age 37 from cancer. For her, marriage did not end with her transition to being a widow.

Gay and lesbian couples may experience other feelings and reactions in addition to typical feelings of grief (Alasuutari, 2021; Valenti et al., 2021). For example, a partner may be discriminated against in the health-care system or feel disenfranchised by family members of the deceased at the funeral, making it hard for the partner to bring closure to the relationship (Candrian & Cloyes, 2021; McNutt & Yakushko, 2013). For gay partners who were also caregivers, the loss affects one's sense of identity in much the same way as the death of a spouse, and making sense of the death becomes the primary issue (Alasuutari, 2021; Nolan et al., 2021). Research is lacking on these experiences in queer and other relationships, so we do not know whether our current understandings apply in these situations.

Perhaps the main challenge in widowhood for all is loneliness. Widowed people may be left alone by family and friends who do not know how to deal with a bereaved person. As a result, widows and widowers may lose not only a partner, but also those friends and family who feel uncomfortable with including a single person rather than a couple in social functions (McCoyd et al., 2021).

Feelings of loss do not dissipate quickly. In general, those who had the most supportive relationships have the highest psychological distress; those with less supportive relationships have worse health outcomes but no additional increased distress (Lee et al., 2022). Those who were most dependent on their partners during the marriage report the highest increase in self-esteem in widowhood when they learn to do the tasks formerly done by their partners (Carr, 2004). For many women, widowhood results in difficult financial circumstances, especially for those lacking pensions or retirement savings particularly because they were not employed outside the home (Streeter, 2020).

For many reasons, including the need for companionship and greater financial security, some widowed people cohabit or remarry. One variation on repartnering is living alone together, an arrangement where two older adults form a romantic relationship but maintain separate living arrangements (Moorman & Greenfield, 2010; Wright, 2020). Repartnering in widowhood or due to late-life divorce can address the issue of loneliness, but can be difficult because of family objections (e.g., resistance from adult children), functional limitations (decreased mobility, poorer health), and social pressures to protect one's estate (Moorman & Greenfield, 2010; Wright et al., 2020).

Late Adulthood

It has long been accepted that older adults are less anxious about death and more accepting of it than any other age group (Jong, 2020; Kastenbaum, 1999). They may believe that their most important life tasks have been completed. However, that is not to say that older adults are unaffected by loss. Far from it.

The loss of a child can happen at any point over the adult life span. Older bereaved parents tend to reevaluate their grief as experienced shortly after the loss and years and decades later. Even more than 30 years after the death of a child, older adults still feel a keen sense of loss and have continued difficulty coming to terms with it (Malkinson & Bar-Tur, 2004–2005; Wright, 2022). The long-lasting effects of the loss of a child are often accompanied by a sense of guilt that the pain affected the parents' relationships with the surviving children. Loss of a child in young adulthood may also result in lower cognitive functioning in late life (Greene et al., 2014; Umberson et al., 2020). Because Black parents are more likely to experience the death of a child, for instance due to the lack of access to quality medical care (discussed in Chapter 4), this increased risk is compounded by race (Umberson et al., 2020).

The loss of a grandchild results in similar feelings: intense emotional upset, survivor guilt, regrets about the relationship with the deceased grandchild, and a need to restructure relationships with the surviving family. However, bereaved grandparents tend to control and hide their grief behavior in an attempt to shield their child (the bereaved parent) from the level of pain being felt. In cases in which older adults were the primary caregivers for grandchildren, feelings can be especially difficult. For example, custodial grandparents in South Africa whose grandchildren in their care died from AIDS go through emotionally difficult times due to the loss and to the social stigma regarding the disease (Boon et al., 2010).

Conclusion

Death is not as pleasant a topic as the formation of relationships or occupational development. It's not something we can go to college to master. What it represents to many people is the end of their existence, and that is a scary prospect. But because we all share in this fear at some level, each of us is equipped to provide support and comfort for grieving survivors.

Death is the last life-cycle force we encounter, the ultimate triumph of the biological forces that limit the length of life. Yet the same psychological and social forces so influential throughout life help us deal with death, either our own or someone else's. As we come to the end of our life journey, we understand death through an interaction of psychological forces—such as coping skills and intellectual and emotional understanding of death—and the sociocultural forces expressed in a particular society's traditions and rituals.

Learning about and dealing with death is clearly a developmental process across the life span that fits well in the biopsychosocial framework. Most apparent is that biological forces are essential to understanding death. The definition of death is based on whether certain biological functions are present; these same definitions create numerous ethical dilemmas that must be dealt with psychologically and socioculturally. Life-cycle forces also play a key role. We have noted, depending on a person's age, that the concept of death has varied meanings beyond the mere cessation of life.

How a person's understanding of death develops is also the result of psychological forces. As the ability to think and reflect undergoes fundamental change, the view of death changes from a mostly magical approach to one that can be transcendent and transforming. As we have noted, people who face their own imminent death experience certain feelings. Having gained experience through the deaths of friends and relatives, a person's level of comfort with their own death may increase. Such personal experience may also come about by sharing the rituals defined through sociocultural forces. People observe how others deal with death and how the culture sets the tone and prescribes behavior for survivors. The combined action of forces also determines how they cope with the grief that accompanies the loss of someone close. Psychologically, confronting grief depends on many things, including the quality of the support system we have.

We do not know for certain what the actual experience of dying is like. But consider these intriguing results from Vicente and colleagues' (2022) research on brain activity at the moment of death. They were in the process of recording brain activity by measuring brainwaves when the patient had a fatal heart attack. In the 30 seconds before and after the patient's heart stopped, the brainwaves followed the same patterns as in dreaming or remembering. The researchers suggest that this could be evidence of a "recall of life" during the person's last moments. Does it? It will likely remain a mystery for the foreseeable future.

Thus, just as the beginning of life represents a complex interaction of biological, psychological, sociocultural, and life-cycle factors, so does death. What people believe about happens during and what follows after death is also an interaction of these factors. What we experience in our lives cannot be understood from only a single perspective.

Adult Development in Action

If you were a family counselor, what advice would you provide to an extended family whose members of varying ages are dealing with the death of a loved family member?

Review Questions

13.5 Dying and Bereavement Experiences Across the Life Span

- What do children understand about death? What are the best ways to talk with children about death?
- How do adolescents confront and cope with death?
- How do adults cope with the death of a child?
- How is the death of a parent interpreted, and how do adults cope?
- What are the typical effects of the death of a partner?
- How do older adults interpret and experience the death of those close to them?

Social Policy Implications

COVID-19 and End-of-Life Issues

The discussion of end-of-life issues in this chapter is predicated on a very important assumption—that all of the parties involved have the gift of time to talk and think through all of the necessary issues and to have meaningful conversations about them in order to arrive at a set of clear decisions and directives. Unfortunately, this is not always the case. The COVID-19 pandemic denied millions of people globally the opportunity to go through these processes in a thoughtful, deliberative manner because of the rapid progression of the disease from onset to severe symptoms and death (Vahey et al., 2021; Wang et al., 2021). What did these families experience, and how did healthcare and other professionals provide support?

When people became severely ill from COVID-19, especially when breathlessness required the use of a respirator, palliative care became the approach of choice. As we know from our consideration of palliative care in this chapter, comfort becomes the overarching goal of medical intervention. Complicating the situation in COVID-19, though, was that the interventions used not only eased breathing but also kept the person alive. Further complicating matters, persons in the advanced stages of COVID-19 often experienced the malfunction of critical body systems and functions (e.g., kidney failure). Thus, in many cases, decisions needed to be made about whether to disconnect the person from the life-sustaining equipment. This was the point at which the lack of clear advance directives and the inability of family members to be present took already difficult discussions and decisions and made them extraordinarily gut-wrenching.

COVID-19 caught many families totally unprepared for death. For them, their loved one was in fine health just a few days earlier. Now they were on a ventilator, unresponsive, and tough decisions needed to be made. Dr. Mark Thomas Hughes, an internist and palliative care physician at Johns Hopkins Medicine and a core faculty member in the Berman Institute of Bioethics there, offered four key points in discussing options with patients and/or their families: (1) build a relationship in whatever way you can, whether face-to-face or on a video call; (2) be clear on the care options that are available and their limitations; (3) perform a life review with the patient and/or family to provide meaning to the patient's life; and (4) help the patient and/or family settle things and say what needs to be said, even if only by phone (Smith, 2020). Ting and colleagues (2020) also provided guidelines for conversations with patients and their families about the various aspects of palliative care and end-of-life decisions, especially how to support families that are confronting these issues for the first time.

The collective experience with severe cases of COVID-19 and the stresses under which patients and families had to make terribly difficult life-and-death decisions serve as a warning and an incentive to address end-of-life issues before a crisis arises and you are the one for whom the decisions are being made.

In Review

For your summary, you may want to consider organizing your material into five paragraphs. In the first, concentrate on summarizing the various definitions of death through both a sociocultural lens and a legal-medical lens. Note some of the differences across the definitions. End your paragraph with a description of the major ethical issues that confront people regarding death and the end of life.

Your second paragraph should include a description of the life-course approach to dying and how the biopsychosocial forces matter. Summarize the reasons why people have difficulty contemplating their own death, and how that manifests itself through death anxiety. Include a summary of some of the major factors in dealing with death anxiety.

In the third paragraph, describe the main aspects of creating a final scenario and other key end-of-life issues. Discuss palliative care and how this approach differs from traditional health care, especially as it is implemented in hospice. End with a discussion of how a person makes their end-of-life wishes and decisions known to others.

The fourth paragraph should focus on grief. Describe typical grief reactions and how people usually cope with it. Describe other situations such as ambiguous grief, prolonged grief, and disenfranchised grief, and discuss how they differ.

In the fifth paragraph, describe the various developmental phases and how people of different ages experience and understand loss and grief. In particular, describe the experiences of adults regarding the loss of one's child, one's parent, and one's partner and how the different types of loss are handled.

Integrating Concepts in Development

- What effect do you think being at different levels of cognitive development have on people's thinking about death?
- How can we use the study of death, dying, and bereavement to provide insights into other aspects of adult development and aging?
- How do the biopsychosocial forces influence people's approach to coping with death and loss?

Key Terms

active euthanasia The deliberate ending of someone's life. 431

ambiguous loss Refers to situations of loss in which there is no resolution or closure. 450

anniversary reaction Changes in behavior related to feelings of sadness on the anniversary date of a loss. 447

anticipatory grief Grief experienced during the period before an expected death occurs that supposedly serves to buffer the impact of the loss when it does come and to facilitate recovery. 446

bereavement The state or condition caused by loss through death. 445

bioethics Study of the interface between human values and technological advances in health and life sciences. 430

clinical death Lack of spontaneous heartbeat and respiration. 430

death anxiety People's anxiety or even fear of death and dying. 436

death doula An umbrella term to identify lay people, primarily women, who provide a variety of nonmedical supports—social, emotional, practical, and spiritual—for people nearing the end of life, including individuals close to them. 440

disenfranchised grief A loss that appears insignificant to others that is highly consequential to the person who suffers the loss. 451

do not resuscitate (DNR) order A medical order that means cardiopulmonary resuscitation (CPR) is not started should one's heart and breathing stop. 443

dual process model (DPM) View of coping with bereavement that integrates loss-oriented stressors and restoration-oriented stressors. 448

end-of-life issues Issues pertaining to the management of the final phase of life, after-death disposition of the body, memorial services, and distribution of assets. 439

euthanasia The practice of ending life for reasons of mercy. 431

final scenario Making choices known about how one does and does not want one's life to end. 439

four-component model Model of grief that understanding grief is based on (1) the context of the loss, (2) continuation of subjective meaning associated with loss, (3) changing representations of the lost relationship over time, and (4) the role of coping and emotion regulation processes. 448

grief The sorrow, hurt, anger, guilt, confusion, and other feelings that arise after suffering a loss. 445

grief work The psychological side of coming to terms with bereavement. 446

grief work as rumination hypothesis An approach that not only rejects the necessity of grief processing for recovery from loss but views extensive grief processing as a form of rumination that may actually increase distress. 448

healthcare power of attorney A document in which an individual appoints someone to act as their agent for healthcare decisions. 442

hospice An approach to assisting dying people that emphasizes pain management, or palliative care, and death with dignity. 440

living will A document in which a person states their wishes about life support and other treatments. 442

model of adaptive grieving dynamics (MAGD) A model of grief based on two pairs of adaptive grieving dynamics: lamenting/heartening, and integrating/tempering. 449

mourning The ways in which we express our grief. 445

palliative care Care that is focused on providing relief from pain and other symptoms of disease at any point during the disease process. 440

passive euthanasia Allowing a person to die by withholding available treatment. 431

persistent vegetative state Situation in which a person's cortical functioning ceases while brainstem activity continues. 430

physician-assisted suicide Process in which physicians provide dying patients with a fatal dose of medication the patient self-administers. 431

prolonged grief Persistent and intrusive feelings of grief lasting beyond the expected period of adaptation to loss that is associated with separation distress and traumatic distress. 450

terror management theory Addresses the issue of why people engage in certain behaviors to achieve particular psychological states based on their deeply rooted concerns about mortality. 436

thanatology The study of death, dying, grief, bereavement, and social attitudes toward these issues. 426

whole-brain death A definition of death that includes three aspects, (1) the person has an irreversible loss of all functions of the entire brain, (2) all brainstem reflexes have permanently stopped working, and (3) breathing has permanently stopped, so that a ventilator, or breathing machine, must be used to keep the body functioning. 430

Epilogue: Healthy Aging

Chapter

14

Chapter Outline

Learning Objectives

After studying this chapter, you will be able to...

14.1. Describe the demographic trends to 2030 and beyond, and relate these to the status of Social Security and Medicare.

14.2. Define healthy aging and how it relates to salutogenesis, positive psychology, uses of technology, and approaches to health promotion and disease prevention.

Welcome to your future. In this epilogue, we take a different perspective on aging. What does the future of aging hold? What lessons can and will we learn based on what we know now about older adults and the process of aging? How will we apply those lessons to improve our own experience?

In this final chapter, we consider key contexts and steps to make aging the best experience possible. First, we examine what population demographics portend, especially regarding the social safety net programs many people have come to rely on. Then we consider what each of us can do to keep ourselves in the best health possible to delay or even prevent some of the negative aspects of aging. We then take a closer examination of how the baby boomers are changing the realities of aging from how older adults are viewed to the coming enormous pressure on governmental resources. We also forecast a few decades ahead to preview what may be in store for Gen-Xers and millennials when they reach late life, and for Gen-Zers who will be the main financial supporters through Social Security and Medicare payroll taxes.

Aging today, and certainly aging in the future, is not what it was even a few years ago. Technological advances have and will continue to make commonplace what is only science fiction today. For example, aging in place will be the norm, as it is likely we will get our annual wellness medical examination remotely, arrive by driverless car for classes or meetings led by someone's interactive holographic projection so they can literally be in multiple places simultaneously, and use social and care providing robots as well as voice-activated controls at home for most routine chores. Medical research will make advances such as offering personalized genetic interventions that cure dementia and cancer, offering the possibility of much longer average life spans with improved quality of life. It is a future with a different understanding of support structures and systems for older adults. It will be an interesting experience, to say the least.

John C. Cavanaugh

We cannot always predict the path our lives will take.

Throughout this book we made predictions about this future and guessed how older people may fare. Some of these predictions are not so happy; as many people live to an old age, there will be greater need for long-term care until cures for terminal, chronic diseases are discovered. Whether we will be able to afford to provide the optimal care for them is much in doubt. Other aspects of the future may be more positive; for instance, when many more people live to older ages there will be a broader view of what late life can be. These predictions represent a best guess about what life will be like by mid-century, based on what we know now and what is likely to happen if there are no substantive changes in policy.

The purpose of this chapter is to consider several crucial issues facing society as we move through the 21st century and to suggest how we might set the best stage for aging in future generations. Threads first introduced in previous chapters will be woven with more speculative ideas to create a potential view of what may lie ahead.

14.1 Demographic Trends and Social Policy

Key Questions

- What key demographic changes will occur in the United States by 2030 and beyond?
- What are the challenges facing social safety net programs such as Social Security and Medicare?

Nancy, a 35-year-old new employee at a marketing and public relations firm, was flipping through the company's benefits package. When it came to the retirement plan, she commented to the human resources person, "I guess I better pay attention. I don't think Social Security and Medicare will be there for me when the time comes. So, it will be very important for me to save as much as I can."

Nancy isn't alone. Many emerging and established adults in the United States do not believe Social Security,

Medicare, or other government social support programs will be in existence by the time they get old enough to qualify for them. Demographic and financial trends support this pessimistic view. As we will discover, the baby boomer generation, coupled with structural problems in Social Security and Medicare, give emerging and established adults good reasons to be concerned.

Demographic Trends: 2030–2050 and Beyond

In Chapter 1, we noted several trends in the population of the United States and the rest of the world, and provided a brief peek at the shape of the population demographics in 2050. In the United States, several critical realities are evident. First, no demographic group will constitute a majority of the population. Second, the overall declining birthrate will continue to increase the average age of the population. In fact, by 2030, international migration to the United States will overtake the birthrate as the main source of population growth (Census Bureau, 2020d). Third, these changes in the composition of the population will make issues that are of concern now into full crises in the foreseeable future if left unaddressed.

It all comes down to numbers. Keep in mind the baby boomers represent the largest generation ever to reach older adulthood, and all of them will reach age 65 by 2030. Generation X, the group right behind them, is much smaller. But an even larger generation, the millennials, will still be feeling the economic and other effects of aging baby boomers when they themselves begin reaching age 65 in 2046. All of this pressure that began with the baby boomers creates the potential for intergenerational conflict over resources.

Because the resources (economic or otherwise) and roles in a society are never divided equally among different age groups or across different sociocultural groups within generations, the potential for inequity and conflict always exists. One well-known intergenerational conflict is between adolescents and their parents. Less well known is the potential for conflict between emerging/established/middle-aged adults and older adults. This type of conflict has not traditionally been a source of serious problems in society, for several reasons: older adults historically made up a small proportion of the population, family ties between adult children and their parents worked against conflict, and middle-aged people were hesitant to withdraw support from programs for older adults. Despite these potent forces protecting against conflict, the situation is changing. For example, controversies over the rate of growth of Medicare and Social Security and the proportion they represent of the federal budget would have been unthinkable just a few years earlier.

To understand more clearly how these changing demographics will have an enormous effect on society at large and on the programs that target older adults, let us project forward to the year 2050. Between now and 2050, the following changes will have set in:

- The proportion of older adults in the United States will nearly double.
- Older adults will be more educated, politically sophisticated, and organized than past generations. They will be familiar with life in a highly complex society where one must learn to deal with (and have little tolerance for) bureaucracies, and they will be proficient users of the internet and technology in general.
- Older adults will expect to keep their lifestyle, Social Security benefits, Medicare/health care benefits, and other benefits accrued throughout their adult life. A comfortable retirement will be viewed as a right, not a privilege. However, they will not, on average, have the financial savings necessary to support those expectations.
- Climate change will have major effects on resource distribution and health, meaning that the likelihood of new pandemics will increase, with older adults likely to be at increasing risk, especially in countries that do not have equitable distribution of health care.
- The increase in divorce that has occurred over the past few decades may result in a lowered sense of obligation on the part of middle-aged adults toward parents or stepparents who were not involved in their upbringing, or who the adult child feels disrespected the other parent. Should this lowered sense of obligation result, it is likely fewer older adults will have family members available to care for them, placing a significantly greater burden on social support systems.
- The rapid increase in the number of older adults of color compared to White older adults will force a reconsideration of issues such as health care disparities and access to goods and services, on one hand, as well as provide a much richer and broader understanding of the aging process on the other hand. At numerous points in the text we examined what these inequities have meant, and what is necessary to correct them.
- The dependency ratio will change. The **dependency ratio** reflects the number of people under age 15 and over age 64 in a country. The dependency ratio provides insight into the relative number of people who have to provide the financial support (in most countries those aged 16–64) for

others not as able to do so (in most countries, those under age 15 or 65 or older). The lower the number, the more workers are needed to pay taxes to provide the revenue for social support programs. As depicted in Figure 14.1, the overall global dependency ratio has been falling dramatically since the late 1960s (World Bank, 2022). This graph makes clear why the cost of providing such programs as Social Security has increased, as will be discussed next in detail. The data also provide good reason for Nancy to be concerned about the future viability of these programs.

Let's consider one example of the reason why dependency ratios matter—Social Security. The ratio of workers to retirees in the United States will fall from its level of roughly 2.7:1 in 2022 to 2.3:1 by 2035 (Social Security Administration, 2021). This means to maintain the level of benefits in Social Security, the working members of society will have to pay significantly higher taxes than workers do now. This is because Social Security is a pay-as-you-go system; the money collected from workers today is used to pay current retirees, not to create a personal account that will support you when you retire. (Your taxes only support the people who are receiving Social Security payments today.) Whether policy makers will make the necessary changes to maintain benefits that citizens have come to view as entitlements remains to be seen. We will examine both Social Security and Medicare later.

No one knows for certain what society will be like in the future. However, the changes we noted in demographic trends urge action now. Two federal social support systems facing the most challenge are Social Security and Medicare. Let's find out why many experts argue they face trouble. One point is certain: Members of the millennial and Gen-Z generations will be affected by the changing demographics as they continue their developmental journey through adulthood. The Real People feature provides a sense of their views of aging and the future.

Social Security and Medicare

The dramatic improvements in the everyday lives of older adults in developed countries that began in the 20th century have continued and picked up pace in the 21st century. Unprecedented gains for the average older person have occurred in nearly every aspect of life, changing the way they are viewed and the roles they play in society (Giele, 2013; James et al., 2016). For instance, since 1900, average longevity has increased about 30 years, older adults on average are significantly healthier (e.g., diseases such as typhoid are now rare), and the possibility of retirement is something to which many older adults aspire (Administration for Community Living, 2021).

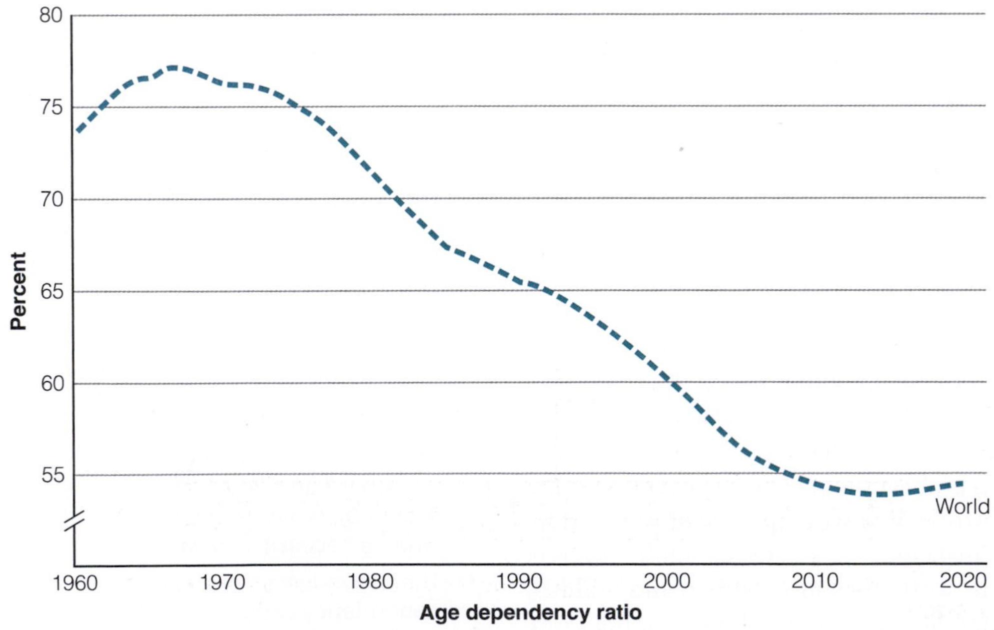

Figure 14.1 Age dependency ratio (% of working-age population).

Source: World Bank. (2022). *Age dependency ratio (% of working-age population).* https://data.worldbank.org/indicator/SP.POP.DPND?end=2020&start=1960

Real People

Millennials and Gen-Z—The Future from Their Perspectives

Much has been written about both millennials and Gen-Z in terms of their views of global issues (e.g., climate change) and well as personal values (e.g., volunteering for service groups). Now that the front wave of the millennial generation is over 40 years old, pollsters are more interested in their views about their own future.

For example, Deloitte (2020, 2021) notes that millennial respondents put health care and disease prevention at the top of their priority list of issues, perhaps reflecting both the experience of the pandemic but also a realization that midlife brings with it important changes that set the stage for healthy aging (discussed later in this chapter and in Chapters 3 and 4). Aperion Care (2019) found that millennial respondents expect to live about 4 years less than do members of the baby boomer generation (81 years versus 85 years). Although nearly 85% of millennial respondents predict they will be of average wealth or rich in retirement, a similar percentage think that they will need to save less than $1 million to achieve that goal.

Since it will be members of the millennial and Gen-Z generations that will eventually hold the majority of elected positions at the local, state, and national level, it is important to know their opinions and to understand their lived experience as major influences on their policy positions. With that in mind, it will be essential to ensure that knowledge about the realities of retirement costs as well as the emerging opportunities in later life are well instantiated. How people experience their future aging depends on it.

However, aspects of change are more complicated (Li & Dalaker, 2021). For example, on one hand, the percentage of adults over age 65 who are below the federal poverty level has declined since the late 1960s from nearly 30% in 1967 to 8.9% in 2020. But the number of older adults in poverty has only declined slightly, from about 5.5 million in 1967 to slightly less than 5 million in 2020. Figure 14.2 provides an overview of these trends.

These trends matter in terms of understanding the role that Social Security payments play in the lives of older adults. As of 2021, the U.S. government defined the poverty level for a person over age 65 living alone at roughly $13,000 per year, and for two people over age 65 at roughly $16,400 per year. Keep these number in mind. Compared to White older adults, poverty rates are about double for Latinos/as and

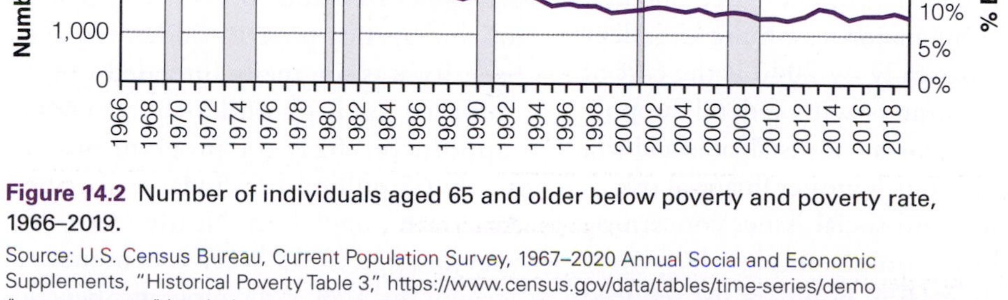

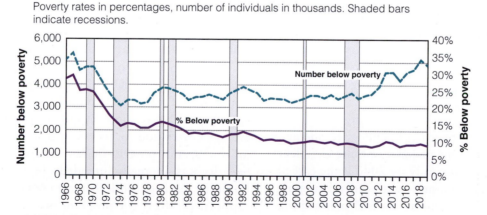

Figure 14.2 Number of individuals aged 65 and older below poverty and poverty rate, 1966–2019.

Source: U.S. Census Bureau, Current Population Survey, 1967–2020 Annual Social and Economic Supplements, "Historical Poverty Table 3," https://www.census.gov/data/tables/time-series/demo/income-poverty/historical-poverty-people.html. Recession dates obtained from National Bureau of Economic Research (NBER), "US Business Cycle Expansions and Contractions," http://www.nber.org/cycles/cyclesmain.html

Black older adults (Congressional Research Service, 2022). Poverty rates are also almost always higher for women regardless of marital status and whether there are children; the only exception is that never-married men who are child-free have a higher poverty rate than women in the same category (Congressional Research Service, 2022). Clearly, attention paid to income disparities must include older adults, and social policy needs to align with this reality.

The Political Landscape. Beginning in the 1970s, older adults began to be portrayed as scapegoats in the political debates concerning government resources. Part of the reason was due to the tremendous growth in the amount and proportion of federal dollars expended on benefits to them, such as through the increase of benefits paid from Social Security during the 1970s (Crown, 2001). At that time in history, older adults were also portrayed as highly politically active, fiscally conservative, and selfish (Fairlie, 1988; Smith, 1992). The healthcare reform debate of the early 1990s focused attention on the spiraling costs of care for older adults that were projected to bankrupt the federal budget if left uncontrolled (Binstock, 1999). This theme and warning continues today.

Rolf Bruderer/Blend Images/Alamy Stock Photo

The aging of the baby boomer generation will put severe strain on the federal budget in Social Security and Medicare.

It was in this context the U.S. Congress began making substantive changes in the benefits for older adults on the grounds of intergenerational fairness. Beginning in 1983, Congress has made several changes in Social Security, Medicare, the Older Americans Act, and other programs and policies. Some of these changes reduced benefits to wealthy older adults and changed some eligibility rules (e.g., age at which one is eligible for full benefits), whereas others provided targeted benefits for older adults below the poverty level, all of which had an effect on how older adults are viewed from a financial cost perspective (Binstock, 1999; Polivka, 2010). These changes also helped reduce the poverty rate, as noted earlier.

The aging of the baby boomers presents difficult and expensive problems (Elmendorf & Sheiner, 2017; Sheiner, 2021). One major reason the U.S. debt will likely increase dramatically by 2040 is the cost of providing older baby boomers with federal support programs. This growth in debt is not sustainable and will put younger generations at much greater financial risk.

Clearly, the political and social issues concerning benefits to older adults are quite complex. Driven by the eligibility of the first baby boomers for reduced Social Security benefits in 2008 (when the first members of the baby boomer generation reached age 62) and their eligibility for Medicare in 2011, the years through the early 2030s will feel the impact of previous congressional inaction and rapidly decreasing funds to use on discretionary programs such as education and infrastructure (e.g., mass transit, water pipes, power grids) There are no easy solutions, and it will be essential to discuss all aspects of the problem. Let's consider Social Security and Medicare more closely, how they work, and what they cost.

Social Security. Social Security, officially known as "Old Age, Survivors, and Disability Insurance" (OASDI) Program, had its beginnings in 1935 as an initiative by President Franklin Roosevelt to "frame a law which will give some measure of protection to the average citizen and to his family against the loss of a job and against poverty-ridden old age." Thus, Social Security was originally intended to provide a supplement to savings and other means of financial support. In 2021, the program provided benefits to nearly 65 million beneficiaries, or about 20% of the American population. Nearly 9 out of 10 individuals over the age of 65 receive benefits; retired workers account for 71% of the program's beneficiaries, disabled workers make up another 13%, and the remainder are the survivors of deceased workers as well as spouses and children of retired and disabled workers.

Social Security, along with Medicare, is paid through a payroll tax called the Federal Insurance Contributions Act (FICA). For Social Security, you and your employer each pay 6.2% of your gross wages (the amount of your wages before any taxes or other deductions are calculated) up to a certain maximum earning that is set each year (in 2022, this was $147,000) beyond which no tax is calculated.

Two key things have changed since Social Security was created. First, the proportion of people who reach age 65 has increased significantly. In 1940, only about 54% of men and 61% of women reached age 65. Today, that has increased to about 75% of men and 85% of women. Compared to 1940, men collect payments about 3 years longer, and women collect about 5 years longer. Both the increased percentages of people who collect payments and the length of time they collect them increase the cost of the program.

Second, revisions to the original law have changed Social Security so it now represents the primary source of financial support after retirement for most U.S. older adults, and the only source for many (Peter G. Peterson Foundation, 2022). For example, Social Security represents over 80% of the income for older adults whose total income is below about $25,000 per year. In 2022, the average monthly Social Security payment was $1,657, and the maximum amount for someone at full retirement age was $3,345.

With so many people benefitting from Social Security, the costs are quite high. Indeed, Social Security is the single biggest item in the federal budget. How big? In fiscal year 2020, total expenditures for all aspects of Social Security were over $1.1 trillion dollars (Social Security Administration, 2021). That constituted about 25% of the entire federal budget. Most of these costs are paid for by payroll taxes paid by employers and employees who participate in the Social Security system, a point we will return to in a bit.

Remember that Social Security was originally intended to be a supplement to a person's personal savings or other sources of income in retirement. Since the 1970s, more workers have been included in employer-sponsored defined contribution plans such as 401(k), 403(b), 457 plans, and mutual funds, as well as various types of individual retirement accounts (IRAs), but fewer defined benefit traditional pension plans (Kurshan, 2022; Polivka & Luo, 2015). A key difference in these plans is defined contribution plans rely a great deal on employee participation (i.e., workers saving money for retirement) whereas traditional pension programs did not require employee participation as they provided a monthly income for life paid completely by the employer. Pension plans were much more common in the early days of Social Security than were defined contribution plans; now, it is the reverse.

On the face of it, this inclusion of various retirement plans, especially savings options, may permit more future retirees to use Social Security as the supplemental financial source it was intended to be, thereby shifting retirement financial planning responsibility to the individual (Kurshan, 2022). But that's not an accurate way of considering it. What has actually happened is an erosion of the private retirement security system that guaranteed a certain income through company-provided pension plans (Polivka & Luo, 2015). Traditional pension plans were not subject to the ups and downs of the stock market like the typical contributory 401(k) or 403(b) plans are. Consequently, rather than lowering dependence on Social Security, the shift away from pensions to contributory plans is more likely to result in an increasing number of older adults relying on Social Security as their primary income source (Orlova et al., 2015; Polivka & Luo, 2015).

Over most of the history of Social Security, revenues were greater than payments because of the large number of people paying in compared to the lower number of people collecting benefits. Excess revenue was saved for the future. But that changed in 2010, when benefit payments first exceeded revenues, a situation that created a structural deficit that will remain until the funding rules change. Annual cash deficits are expected to total $2.9 trillion dollars between 2021 and 2034. As Social Security runs those cash deficits, the Treasury will have to borrow funds from the public to cover the shortfalls. The Social Security Trustees project that the trust funds will be fully depleted by 2034. Once the trust funds are exhausted, the Social Security Administration will be limited to spending only as much as incoming revenues. The 70 million beneficiaries could face an immediate 24% cut in their scheduled benefits (Peter G. Peterson Foundation, 2022). Despite knowing the fiscal realities for decades, Congress has not yet taken the actions necessary to ensure the long-term financial stability of Social Security.

Medicare. Over 65 million U.S. citizens depend on Medicare for their medical insurance at an annual cost of nearly $900 billion (Centers for Medicare and Medicaid Services, 2022). To be eligible, a person must meet one of the following criteria: be over age 65, be disabled, or have permanent kidney failure. Medicare consists of three parts (Centers for Medicare and Medicaid Services, 2021):

- Part A covers inpatient hospital services, skilled nursing facilities, home health services, and hospice care;
- Part B covers the cost of physician services, outpatient hospital services, medical equipment and supplies, and other health services and supplies; and
- Part D provides some coverage for prescription medications.

Expenses relating to most long-term care needs are funded by Medicaid, another major health care program funded by the U.S. government (and states) and aimed at people who meet financial eligibility requirements. Out-of-pocket expenses associated with co-payments and other charges are often paid by supplemental insurance policies, sometimes referred to as Medigap policies (Medicare.gov, 2021b). Note that there is no official Medicare Part C; this option is better known as Medicare Advantage Plans offered by private companies (HHS.gov, 2022). If you join a Medicare Advantage Plan, the plan will provide all of your Part A (Hospital Insurance) and Part B (Medical Insurance) coverage. Medicare Advantage Plans may offer extra coverage, such as vision, hearing, dental, and/or health and wellness programs. Most include Medicare prescription drug coverage (Part D; Medicare.gov, 2021a).

Like Social Security, Medicare is funded by a payroll tax paid by both the worker and the employer, which for Medicare is 1.45%. But unlike Social Security, where the earnings on which the tax is based has a cap, the tax supporting Medicare is paid on all of one's earnings. Still, the funding problems facing Medicare are worse than those facing Social Security and are grounded in the aging of the baby boomer generation in terms of numbers of recipients and sharp increases in health care costs in general (Centers for Medicare and Medicaid Services, 2021c). Estimates are that the annual expenditures for Medicare with double by 2030 to nearly $2 trillion per year. The level of federal taxation for Medicare in FICA (1.45% paid by both the worker and the employer) cannot cover this anticipated increase. This leads to estimates that the Medicare trust funds will be depleted by 2026, at the latest, and possibly as early as 2023 due to the healthcare cost effects of the COVID-19 pandemic (Committee for a Responsible Federal Budget, 2022).

Taken together, the challenges facing society concerning older adults' financial security and health insurance coverage will continue to be major political and economic issues throughout the first half of the 21st century at least. There are no easy answers and many political challenges, but open discussion of the various arguments and the stark budget realities will be essential for creating the optimal solution. Public misperceptions of how the programs actually work, and the tough choices that must be faced are discussed in more detail in the Controversies feature.

Controversies

What to Do About Social Security and Medicare

As pointed out in the text, the amount of benefits people collect in Social Security and Medicare is not directly connected to the amount they paid in taxes over their working careers. That's a point many people misunderstand—they think they are entitled to get out what they have put into their own personal account. As explained in the text, this is not the way either program works—the funds that come in each year, such as through the FICA payroll tax, go to pay the benefits for that year to those eligible to receive them. There are no personal accounts. This misperception makes it very difficult to make changes in the benefits structure (that drives the cost) of these programs.

The fact is the average person, if they live to become eligible for these programs, collects substantially more in lifetime Medicare benefits, for instance, than they paid in total taxes during their working career (Steuerle & Smith, 2021). This imbalance (and misperception) is a major reason why restructuring the benefits or raising co-payments to control costs is so difficult to do, and why the benefit structure described here is unsustainable given current FICA tax rates.

There's another aspect to the problem. To keep Medicare Part B and Part D premiums affordable, the typical older Americans only pays about

25% of the actual cost through premiums, deductibles, and co-insurance (higher income people pay a larger share, up to 80%). Where does the rest of the money come from? General revenue in the national budget pays for the rest and is why there is increasing pressure to allow Medicare to negotiate the prices of prescription medications and to cut reimbursements to healthcare providers.

Similar analyses can be done for Social Security, but with a different outcome depending on income level. Whereas nearly all Medicare recipients get much more out of the program than they paid in taxes, that's not true for many people regarding Social Security. For example, people in upper earnings brackets will pay more in taxes to support current beneficiaries (Steuerle & Smith, 2021).

The biggest challenge is controlling the costs of Medicare given the arrival of the baby boomers as beneficiaries and the continuing rapid increase in healthcare costs. But explaining this to those who are already receiving or are about to receive the benefit is a daunting task. That's why most proposals generally target individuals who are about 10 years or more away from receiving Medicare benefits.

Shoring up the financing of Social Security tends to focus on two sets of actions. First, many advocate increasing the age at which a person becomes fully eligible for benefits. This has already been done once, when the age was raised from the original age of 65 to age 67, which went into full effect in 2022. Second, others have suggested either instead of raising the age of full eligibility or in addition to it to raise or eliminate the cap on earnings subject to the payroll tax. One variation to those proposals is to keep the cap as it is, but open the tax again for those in very high earnings brackets (e.g., reinstitute the payroll tax for people earning over, say, $400,000).

The political debates around Social Security and Medicare will not end soon. What is clear, though, is the financial model for each is unsustainable, and action, especially with respect to Medicare, is needed immediately.

Adult Development in Action

If you were a professional demographer, what advice would you give to Congress about Social Security and Medicare policy in the United States?

Review Questions

14.1 Demographic Trends and Social Policy

- What are the main demographic changes that will occur by 2030 and beyond?
- What is the status and future projections of Social Security and Medicare?

14.2 Healthy Aging: Living Well in Later Life

Key Questions

- What is healthy aging?
- What are the key issues in health promotion and quality of life?
- How is technology used to maintain and enhance competence?
- What are the primary considerations in designing health promotion and disease prevention programs?
- What are the principal lifestyle factors that influence competence?

Jafar had long resisted buying a smartphone, saying that his flip phone was just fine. After years of urging form his friends and family, though, he finally concluded that he was missing a great deal by not being able to be online. So, after he purchased his first iPhone at age 75, he began surfing. He never stopped. Now he's an expert with a wide array of apps and bookmarked sites, especially those relating to health issues. Jafar also communicates by social media with his grandchildren and friends, and designed the online newsletter for his community.

Jafar is like many older adults—better educated and more technologically sophisticated (however reluctantly) than their predecessors. The coming demographic changes in the United States and the rest of the world present a challenge for improving the kind of lives older adults live. For this reason, promoting wellness and healthy lifestyles in all living settings (community, long-term care, etc.) is regarded as a top priority of the

Discovering Development
What Is Living Well?

What does it mean to live well in later life? Take some time to think about this question for yourself. Develop a thorough list of everything it would take for you to say you will have aged as well as you could have when the time comes. Then ask this question to several people of different ages and backgrounds. Compare their answers. Do the criteria differ as a function of age or background characteristics (e.g., age, ethnicity, race, personal experiences)? Discuss your findings with others in your class to discover whether your results were typical.

21st century (Parrella & Vormittag, 2017). Remaining healthy is the goal, and will be key for decelerating the rate of aging (Aldwin et al., 2018).

Before we plunge into an analysis of how to live well in later life, take a few minutes and reflect on the Discovering Development feature. What will constitute living well for you?

What Is Healthy Aging?

As you learned from completing the Discovering Development feature, what people list as criteria for living well have some commonalities as well as differences. Most people list something related to being healthy near the top. That notion of being healthy usually has lots of underlying meanings, some personal. Because it is so important to so many, it has become a focal point for theory and research about an appropriate goal for people to strive toward as they age. For many, it is considered a basic human right.

In fact, considering healthy aging as a human right led the United Nations in December 2020 to declare 2021–2030 as the Decade of Healthy Ageing (United Nations, 2021b). A major part of this effort is the creation of The Platform, (https://www.decadeofhealthyageing.org/) "an online space where all knowledge relevant for the Decade can be accessed, shared, and interacted with in one place by everyone around the world." Four major areas are emphasized under the United Nations work: combatting ageism, age-friendly environments, integrated care, and long-term care. Additionally, experiences from the COVID-19 pandemic led to the additional topic of social isolation and loneliness. From the United Nations' perspective, addressing these issues is the most important way to ensure that all people will have the opportunity to experience healthy aging.

Importantly, various global regions have created their own spinoffs from the United Nations Decade efforts. For example, the Pan American Health Organization (PAHO; 2022) launched its own work on the four major areas of emphasis. The PAHO has adopted a life course approach (discussed in Chapter 1) to provide a framework for all of its initiatives.

From the perspective of researchers and theorists, healthy aging concerns optimizing the individual outcome of the interplay of biopsychosocial forces and the individual over a lifetime (Aldwin et al., 2018; Hostetler & Paterson, 2017; National Institute on Aging, 2022). **Healthy aging** in this sense involves avoiding disease, being engaged with life, and maintaining high cognitive and physical functioning. Healthy aging is both measurable (e.g., in terms of specific health metrics, cognitive performance, other specific behaviors) and subjective (e.g., well-being). It is reached when a person achieves their desired goals with dignity and as independently as possible.

The life-span perspective (discussed in Chapter 1) can be used to create a formal model for healthy aging. Heckhausen and colleagues (2010, 2021; Barlow et al., 2017) developed a theory of life-span development based on motivation and control by applying core assumptions that recognize aging as a complex process that involves increasing specialization and is influenced by factors unrelated to age. The basic premises of healthy aging include keeping a balance between the various gains and losses that occur over time and minimizing the influence of factors unrelated to aging. In short, these premises involve paying attention to both internal and external factors impinging on the person. The antecedents include all the changes that happen to a person. The mechanisms in the model are the selection, optimization, and compensation processes that shape the course of development. Finally, the outcomes of the model denote that enhanced competence, quality of life, and future adaptation are the visible signs of healthy aging.

Using the selective optimization with compensation (SOC) model (discussed in Chapters 4, 7, 8, and 9) enhanced by Heckhausen and colleagues' (2010, 2021; Barlow et al., 2017) ideas of control and motivation, various types of interventions can be created to help people achieve healthy aging. In general, these interventions focus on the individual or on aspects of tasks and the physical and social environment that emphasize competence (Aldwin et al., 2018; Berezuk et al., 2022; Lindbergh et al., 2016). When designing interventions aimed primarily at the person, it is important to understand the target person's goals (rather than the goals of the researcher).

For example, in teaching older adults how to use technology, it is essential to understand the kinds of concerns and fears older adults have and ensure the training program addresses them (Ahmad et al., 2022). Ahmad and colleagues (2022) determined that various strategies are needed to ensure the effectiveness of teaching techniques for older adult learners. These include: (1) a collaborative learning strategy, which could involve small or large group discussions, activities that promote collective interaction, or training and workshop settings; (2) intergenerational learning, as it can reduce older adults' anxiety about technology and perhaps offer exchanges of insights across generations; (3) a collaborative learning environment; (4) an experience-based learning approach in an active environment; and (5) an informal learning setting with a personalized curriculum. We will return to the use of technology in a later section.

Salutogenesis and Healthy Aging

Let's consider the various components of healthy aging as noted by the United Nations as well as other key organizations, such as the National Institute on Aging. All of them agree on the basics: Many factors influence healthy aging. Some of these, such as genetics, are not things we can directly control. Others, such as exercise, a healthy diet, going to the doctor regularly, and taking care of our mental health, are things we can do something about personally, provided we solve the issues of ensuring that everyone has access to them. Still others, such as ageism and ensuring that the environments in which we live support older adults, are ones that we need to work together to address.

A challenge is that the tendency is to treat each of these various topics separately. That's great, but it fails to recognize that all of them interact with each other to create our quality of life (discussed in Chapter 4 and elsewhere). An increasingly important concept in the discussion of healthy aging is salutogenesis. **Salutogenesis** is an approach that emphasizes factors that support and promote health, rather than factors that cause disease. Introduced by Aaron Antonovsky (1979), salutogenesis has become a framework for creating wellness-based interventions in a wide range of settings, including school, work, and communities (Mittelmark & Bauer, 2017; Mittelmark et al., 2022). The various aspects that comprise salutogenesis are noted in Figure 14.3.

Mittelmark, Bauer, and colleagues (2017, 2022) point out that a salutogenesis framework emphasizes that life experiences help shape one's sense of coherence (a global orientation toward life). Life is more or less comprehensible, meaningful, and manageable. An extensive array of strengths, skills, and characteristics, noted in Figure 14.3, all interact to create salutogenesis, which in turn is the foundation of healthy aging.

A key idea in salutogenesis is sense of coherence. **Sense of coherence** reflects a coping capacity of people to deal with everyday life stressors and consists of three elements: comprehensibility, manageability, and meaningfulness. Sense of coherence helps us make sense out of a world filled with chaos and change. A second key point is that salutogenesis implies that health (which Antonovsky [1987] termed health-ease in contrast to its opposite, dis-ease) is a continuum. Third, taken together, salutogenesis is a complex process.

The salutogenic process model in Figure 14.4 documents the interactions among sense of coherence, life experiences, generalized resistance resources (GRRs), and the health-ease/dis-ease continuum (Antonovsky, 1987, 1996; Super et al., 2016). People can move along the health-ease/dis-ease continuum between the two extremes of "total absence of health" and "total health" (Antonovsky, 1987). Movement along the health-ease/dis-ease continuum is initiated by the stressors that people encounter in everyday life (theories of stress are discussed in Chapter 4). If people cope successfully with the stressors, they can maintain their health status (and movement toward "health-ease"), whereas unsuccessful coping with the stressors can lead to breakdown (and movement toward "dis-ease").

GRRs are resources within an individual (e.g., attitudes, self-efficacy beliefs, knowledge) or in their environment (e.g., social support, cultural stability) that can be used to counter the stressors of everyday life (Lindström and Eriksson, 2010). If the GRRs are applied successfully, this can prevent stress and, as a consequence, can lead to the maintenance of or movement towards 'health-ease' (Antonovsky, 1987). When the GRRs are not applied or are unsuccessful, stress may increase and result in breakdown and a movement towards dis-ease. As would be predicted by the stress and coping paradigm (discussed in Chapter 4),

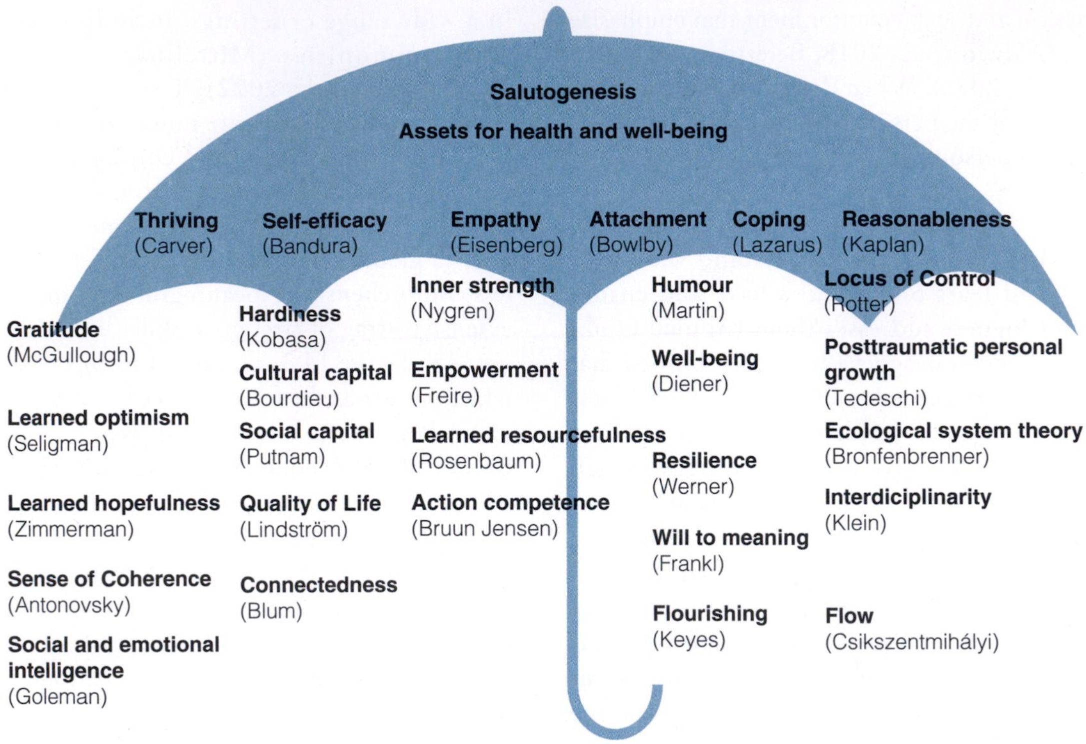

Figure 14.3 Salutogenesis component assets and primary theorist for each.

Source: Eriksson, M. (2014). Salutogenesis. In A. C. Michalos (Ed.), *Encyclopedia of quality of life and well-being research* (pp. 5623–5631). Dordrecht: Springer. https://doi.org/10.1007/978-94-007-0753-5_3445. Figure 3, p. 5627.

GRRs help people deal with stressors by (1) avoiding them, (2) defining them as nonstressors, or (3) managing the stressors.

Sense of coherence plays a vital role in orienting a person regarding a specific stressor and the GRRs that might be available to deal with everyday life stressors. People with a higher sense of coherence approach the world as more comprehensible, manageable, and meaningful, and are better able to understand the stressor, to identify GRRs to deal with the it, and to then actively deal with the stressor (Wainwright et al., 2007). Antonovsky (1987) hypothesized that sense of coherence develops in childhood and emerging adulthood under certain conditions when sufficient GRRs are present, as they provide a person with sets of meaningful and coherent life experiences (Eriksson, 2007; Lindström and Eriksson, 2010). The GRRs are, therefore, essential for the development of sense of coherence.

Thus, sense of coherence has a central position in the salutogenic model and strengthening people's sense of coherence would increase people's ability to impose structure on stressful situations and to search for resources that could help them to overcome these stressors. As a result, sense of coherence is key to healthy aging.

Salutogenesis shifts people's lifestyle emphasis to positive aspects that improve their existence. In this way, applying salutogenesis to various settings such as work (Jenny et al., 2022) and communities (Vaandrager & Kennedy, 2022) puts the focus on positive steps that can be taken to improve employees' performance in a healthy, less-stressed way, or the resources residents have at their disposal to address needs in daily life to make communities more age-friendly, for instance.

Adopting the framework of salutogenesis brings a more person-centered approach to healthy aging. Specifically, researchers argue that a salutogenic lens changes the focus to one that emphasizes people's ability to adapt and self-manage (Koelen & Eriksson, 2022; Stephens et al., 2015). Research indicates that a strong sense of coherence in older adults is related to good perceived health and quality of life, and mediates the relation between stress and depression (Koelen & Eriksson, 2022). From the perspective of an older person, healthy aging involves being independent,

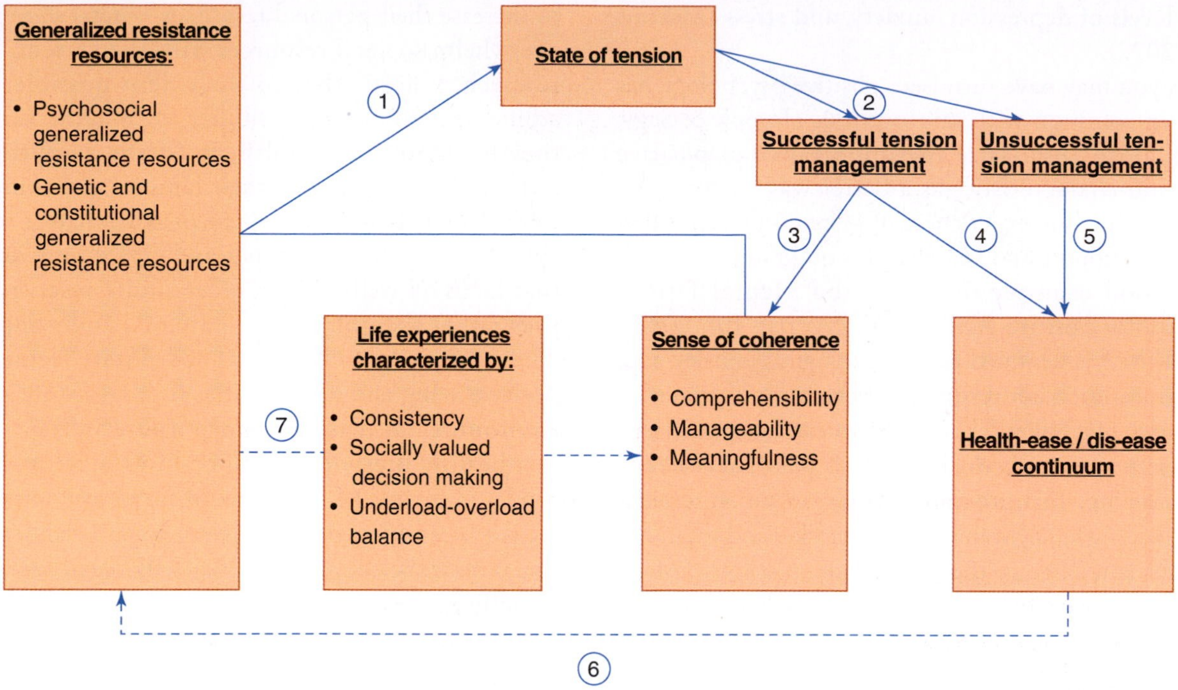

Figure 14.4 A simplified reproduction of the salutogenic model.

Source: Adapted from Antonovsky (1979, pp. 184–185) by Super, S., Wagemakers, M. A. E., Picavet, H. S. J., Verkooijen, K. T., & Koelen, M. A. (2016). Strengthening sense of coherence: opportunities for theory building in health promotion. *Health Promotion International*, 31, 869–878. https://doi.org/10.1093/heapro/dav071. Figure 1, p. 871

being connected, being able to use resources, and being able to make one's own decisions (Koelen & Eriksson, 2022). These four characteristics are embedded in the notion of aging in place (discussed in Chapter 5).

Positive Psychology and Healthy Aging

The late 1990s witnessed a major change in the focus of psychology. APA President Martin Seligman's presidential address in 1999 marked a shift from what he thought was a focus on people's problems to a focus that emphasized the positive aspects of people's experiences and behaviors. Seligman called this new approach positive psychology. As Seligman and Csikszentmihalyi (2000) described it:

> The aim of positive psychology is to begin to catalyze a change in the focus of psychology from preoccupation only with repairing the worst things in life to also building positive qualities (p. 5).

Emphasis on the positive qualities raised in positive psychology can be traced back to the origins of psychology itself. For instance, William James' wrote about "healthy mindedness" in the context of religious experiences (James, 1902), and it shares a common heritage with parts of humanistic psychology and the writings of Abraham Maslow and Carl Rogers, in particular (Robbins, 2015).

The positive psychology movement has produced new conceptual frameworks, instruments to measure human strengths and increased interest in topics such as optimism, hope, locus of control, creativity, self-esteem, emotional intelligence, empathy, humor, and gratitude (Joseph & Sagy, 2022). Positive psychologists have also worked to apply these topics to educational, health, and workplace contexts (Joseph, 2015). Perhaps most interestingly, positive psychology has also influenced the design of technology aimed at older adults so that their end-user experiences result in greater use (and reliance when appropriate) on technology and is the topic we examine in the next section (Pollini et al., 2022).

The influence of the positive psychology in the study of aging has been quite broad. For instance, we learned in Chapter 3 that telomere length is associated with biological aging. Research suggest that a core aspect of positive psychology, optimism, is associated with telomere length, especially in people who reported higher levels of stress (Schutte & Malouff, 2022). A longitudinal study in Brazil indicated that positive behaviors, attitudes, and values were associated with lower levels of depression, anxiety, and stress (Martins et al., 2022).

As you may have surmised, positive psychology has much in common with salutogenesis (Joseph & Sagy, 2022). Both emphasize the importance of positive assets and characteristics as a better way to approach understanding the experiences of older adults, as well as designing support and intervention programs.

A good example of this is the Mental Fitness Program for Positive Aging (MFPPA; Bar-Tur, 2022). The MFPPA is designed as a psychological journey with 12 stations, each addressing a different topic grounded in positive psychology. The program can be applied in a group setting or individually through personal coaching or counseling. The program focuses on assisting older adults plan how they want to live their lives and what they wish to experience in the near future. Various positive psychology strategies are introduced in each session (e.g., exploring personal strengths and practicing new ways to use them, learning how to invest in significant relationships, visualizing one's best self, keeping a gratitude diary or a list of good things occurring during the day, seeking out activities that create flow, practicing mindfulness and acts of kindness, or accessing stories from their own lives to hone their sense of hope). Homework assignments for practicing these strategies are included together with other assignments relevant to each session's topic and assignments that are addressed to maintaining a healthy lifestyle. Note that many of the strategies are ones that constitute salutogenesis assets depicted in Figure 14.3.

The MFPPA fits well within a salutogenesis approach to intervention based on a broad assessment of older adults' main areas of personal difficulty. It helps ascertain which components to positive well-being would benefit from enhancement, such as low self-esteem, unsatisfying relations with others, lack of emotional or social support, or difficulties in making decisions and taking the steps to fulfill personal needs. For persons who experience emotional problems or mental disorders, positive psychology interventions can be integrated into general treatment, such as positive psychotherapy, cognitive behavior therapy–rational emotive behavior therapy, or interpersonal psychotherapy.

Combining the salutogenesis and positive psychology perspectives provides an intriguing way to approach the pressures on resources that the demographic changes reviewed earlier in this chapter are creating (Bar-Tur, 2022; Joseph & Sagy, 2022). A challenge for older adults is to maintain and, if possible, to increase their personal resources (assets) so as not to overwhelm societal resources with their needs. Thus, researchers argue that to the extent possible, older adults have some responsibility for making sure that they maintain their health, maintain a healthy lifestyle, and are engaged in their families and communities. The challenge for helping professionals is to shift away from ageist stereotypes and create interventions that focus on wellness and older adults' reserve capacities rather than on illness, patients, and symptoms. These interventions should incorporate elements of positive aging and salutogenesis to increase autonomy, environmental mastery, and purpose in life, as well as a healthy lifestyle. As implied in the salutogenesis model in Figure 14.4, one main focus of intervention would be to identify the resources and facilitate the social network cooperation that will keep older adults socially and physically active and involved in their communities. That could be achieved in coordination with healthcare services across settings. Interventions should be adjusted to individual older adults' level of functioning, individual needs, and motivation.

The foundations for healthy aging are laid down early in life by adopting a healthy lifestyle that is maintained throughout the life cycle, to the extent possible with the individual's social and cultural contexts. The challenge to present and future societies is to remove structural barriers to these lifestyle factors and provide older persons with opportunities for self-realization, continued personal growth, and social engagements.

Technology and Healthy Aging

Like Jafar, the person introduced in the vignette, increasing numbers of older adults are discovering that smartphones, tablets, and computers are essential tools for everyday life. Many take advantage of the growing resources available on the web, including sites dedicated specifically to older adults. E-mail, social networking, and video-calling enable people of all ages to stay in touch with friends and family, and the growing success of e-commerce makes it easier for people with limited time or mobility to purchase goods and services. Smartphones are being used in more telemedicine applications and settings, and the fully networked and interactive home environment will soon be taken for granted (Desai et al., 2022; Thangavel et al., 2022).

The use of technology is one way to enhance the competence of older adults. In this section, we consider the general topic of how to maintain and enhance competence through a variety of interventions.

Geber86/E+/Getty Images

Older adults are increasingly using technology to stay in touch with family and to assist them in their lives.

Using technology to achieve the goals of healthy aging is a central aspect of the salutogenesis and positive psychology approaches.

The life-span perspective we considered in Chapter 1 is an excellent starting point for understanding how to maintain and enhance people's competence. In this perspective, the changes that occur with age result from multiple biological, psychological, sociocultural, and life-cycle forces. Mastering tasks of daily living and more complex tasks (such as personal finances) contributes to a person's overall sense of competence even if the person experiences dementia (Dawadi & Cook, 2017). How can this sense be optimized to achieve healthy aging?

The answer lies again in applying three key adaptive mechanisms for aging: the SOC framework (Baltes et al., 2006). This framework addresses what Bieman-Copland and colleagues (2002) call the "social facilitation of the nonuse of competence": the phenomenon of older people intentionally or unintentionally failing to perform up to their true level of ability because of social stereotypes that operate to limit what older adults are expected to do. Instead of behaving at their true ability level, older adults behave in ways they believe typical or characteristic of their age group (Lang, 2004). This phenomenon is the basis for the communication patterns we considered in Chapter 5.

Technology provides powerful ways to achieve healthy aging via all of the aspects of the SOC model, but compensation is the most apparent. For instance, several options are available for visually or cognitively impaired adults to compensate for these challenges and find their way from place to place (Bosch & Gharaveis, 2017). Smartphone mapping apps provide voice directions for people to guide them to their destination and provide a means to maintaining independence. Similarly, other apps can provide ways for care providers to monitor wandering behavior (Gordijn & Have, 2016; Zgonec, 2021). Technology is also revolutionizing the approach to health care. For example, telemedicine increased dramatically during the COVID-19 pandemic (Sano et al., 2022) but was not as popular with older adults for initial appointments (Frydman et al., 2022). In contrast, telemedicine is used extensively by older adults for pain management (Bhattarai & Phillips, 2017) and in increasing adherence to various types of medical therapies, from medication adherence to rehabilitation (Mertens et al., 2017).

The mixed results during the COVID-19 pandemic in the use and comfort level of older adults with technology-mediated physician visits raises the question of how to help individuals adopt broader uses of telemedicine. Desai and colleagues (2022) identified several specific ways to overcome barriers to technology use among older adults. They recommend: (1) design for product ecosystems with technologies and services well-coordinated and synchronized; (2) create awareness and information on privacy and security issues and explanations associated with it; (3) make anti-virus and anti-phishing software accessible to older adults in ways easy for them to use; (4) design technologies as tools that allow older adults to identify themselves in the community and family but protect privacy; and (5) ensure that technologies and services are affordable for older adults.

In addition to comfort and ability to use the technology are concerns about possible differences in outcomes for assessments conducted by telemedicine as compared with those conducted in-person. The How Do We Know? feature examines this concern in a study in Singapore by Hernandez and colleagues (2022).

At several points in the text, we have encountered the growing trend of using robots in various situations with older adults. These robots are not the same as voice activated systems such as Siri or Alexa. The type of robots being deployed include social companions, such as ElliQ, an artificial intelligence (AI)–based social companion. Social companion robots mainly offer encouragement, invitations to play games, gentle health prodding, music thoughts, and a friendly voice that learns a person's ways and provides a way to avoid the effects of loneliness (Zeitchik, 2022). Given that nearly 15 million people over age 65 live alone, social companion robots offer an innovative intervention grounded in positive psychology and salutogenic research.

How Do We Know?

Reliability Between Telemedicine and In-Person Assessments of Cognitive Functioning

Who were the investigators, and what was the aim of the study? In the text, we noted that telemedicine was very quickly adopted by healthcare professionals during the COVID-19 pandemic. However, in order for telemedicine to become maximally useful and beneficial, the reproducibility of face-to-face (F2F) versus online videoconference-based assessment remains to be established. Hernandez and colleagues (2022) decided to address this need by comparing videoconference-based assessment of older adults' cognitive functioning with F2F assessment using the same tests.

Who were the participants in the study? Participants were 60 community-dwelling older adults aged 65 years and older who presented to a hospital memory clinic with known or suspected cognitive impairment. All participants could understand English or Mandarin and could either independently use WhatsApp Messenger video calls (https://whatsapp.com), or had care providers to assist them. Most of the participants were female and of Chinese ethnicity. The mean education level was 8.38 ± 4.2 years, corresponding to a secondary school level. Almost half of the participants had a preexisting diagnosis of dementia, with Alzheimer's dementia (AD) the primary etiology in 21 participants (78%). Dementia was rated based on the CDR scale, with most cases of mild severity. Individuals with severe hearing or visual impairments or those with severe behavioral and psychological symptoms were excluded from the study.

How did the investigators measure the topic of interest? All participants completed two visits for cognitive assessment, a F2F visit followed 2–3 weeks afterward by a videoconference-based assessment. The Abbreviated Mental Test (AMT) and modified Chinese Mini Mental Status Exam (mCMMSE) were administered by trained nurses specializing in cognition and memory disorders, followed by an assessment of Chinese Frontal Assessment Battery (CFAB) by a physician from the memory clinic. For each participant, the same nurse and physician performed the F2F and remote assessments; all medical personnel were trained prior to the study in F2F and videoconference assessment techniques.

Various items on the cognitive tests were adapted for use on videoconference-based administration, such as clarifying the phrasing of questions and accommodating the different locations of the participants and assessors during remote assessment (Table 14.1 provides these modifications). Modifications were also made to any items on the mCMMSE that required the participants to perform an action to avoid participant responses outside of camera view. For the CFAB, the final item, "environmental autonomy," was omitted because it necessitates physical contact between the assessor and the participant. Thus, the final scores for both the F2F and remote CFAB excluded this item.

Table 14.1 Cognitive Tests Adapted for Videoconferencing

	Face-to-Face	Videoconference-Based
AMT	Where are we now?	Where are *you* now?
mCMMSE	What floor are we on now?	What floor are *you* on now?
	In which estate are we?	In which estate are *you now*?
	Three-stage command: "Take this piece of paper, fold it in half, and put it on the floor."	"Take this piece of paper, fold it in half, and *hold it in front of you*."
	"Read and obey: Raise your hands."	"Read and obey: *Close your eyes*."
CFAB	Question 6 "Prehension behavior: Do not take my hands?"	Removed Question 6.

AMT=Abbreviated Mental Test; mCMMSE=modified version of the Chinese Mini-Mental State Examination; CFAB=Chinese Frontal Assessment Battery.

Source: Hernandez, H. H. C., Ong, P. L., Anthony, P., Ang, S. L., Salim, N. B. M., Yew, P. Y. S., Ali, N. B., Lim, J. P., Lim, W. S., & Chew, J. (2022). Cognitive assessment by telemedicine: Reliability and agreement between face-to-face and remote videoconference-based cognitive tests in older adults attending a memory clinic. *Annals of Geriatric Medicine and Research, 26*, 42–48. Table 1. https://doi.org/10.4235/agmr.22.0005.

What was the design of the study? The design involved repeated measures of the cognitive assessments delivered through different modalities (F2F and videoconference). The lag between assessments was as short as practicable in order to avoid the possibility of natural changes in scores.

Were there ethical concerns with the study? All participants (and care providers if appropriate) were provided complete informed consent about the purposes of the study and the assessments that would be done. Participants could withdraw at any time without penalty. Upon consenting to the study, all participants and their care providers (if present) were informed about the conditions under which videoconferencing would occur. An information sheet was provided that described a standardized setting with adequate lighting; absence of visual orientation cues such as clocks, watches, or calendars; and a quiet environment.

What were the results? Of the 60 participants who consented to participate in this study, 56 (93.3%) completed both the F2F and remote assessments. Four participants were unable to complete the remote assessment—two due to a change of mind by the participant and family, one care provider unable to commit to assisting the participant, and one due to a dental condition. Thirty-eight participants (68%) required assistance from their care providers for the remote assessment.

On average, participants scored higher during videoconference-based testing than during F2F for AMT and mCMMSE. No significant differences were observed between F2F and videoconference-based CFAB mean scores. All three assessments demonstrated good to excellent levels of reliability.

What did the investigators conclude? Hernandez and colleagues concluded that remote videoconferencing-based administration of AMT, mCMMSE, and CFAB demonstrated good reliability but only fair agreement with the F2F assessment. The conclusion regarding agreement refers to a small but significant bias for AMT and mCMMSE with videoconference-based scores higher than those of the F2F-based assessment. One possible explanation for this discrepancy is practice effects, which cannot be eliminated entirely. A second, more likely, explanation for the higher scores found during the videoconference-based assessment may be attributed to cues or prompts provided by the care providers. For individuals with the largest discrepancies between the remote and F2F assessments, care providers were determined to be frequently prompting participants outside the camera field of view. In addition, the presence of environmental cues (e.g., clocks, calendars) may be another reason for the higher videoconference-based assessment scores, reflected in better performance in the orientation (e.g., to time, date) domain when administered remotely.

These findings underscore the need for an optimal environment with very close monitoring of others present in the testing environment for valid telehealth assessment. Such monitoring would be similar to that used for remote testing in courses in online academic programs.

Designers of social robots are careful not to go too deeply into human emotion, though. For example, ElliQ has no eyes, and uses robotic filters to the voice. It won't respond to "I love you" in kind; instead it will say it wishes it could understand emotion or joke that "you're making my processor overheat."

AI parameters (the variables it can be programmed for) have been scaling greatly in recent years, from very elementary interfaces to sophisticated systems that learn. ElliQ and other social robots rely on reinforcement learning, which strives to improve AI with repeated exposure (e.g., an older adult who talks about their regular bridge game) as well as cognitive AI (basically, humanlike thought patterns). (Such learning also underlies how streaming services hone in on your viewing or listening preferences, for example.)

ElliQ is only one of the many social robots that researchers are studying in terms of how to help older adults maintain social interactions, especially when they live alone, as well as how to assist older adults with basic tasks (e.g., monitoring medications, simple cleaning routines). Tobis and colleagues (2022) reported that implementation of robots is better if the eventual users have an opportunity to meet with robots in advance and become familiar with their technology and functionalities. Miller and McDaniel (2022) noted that older adults generally enjoy social robots, and about half of users considered Misty the Robot as a friend. In general, reviews of research on the use of robots with older adults, including those experiencing dementia, indicate therapeutic potential of using various types of robots with older adults, particularly for communication and mood, fall detection, daily reminders (e.g., medication reminders, prompts during meal time), cognitive stimulation, physical assistance, and reducing the burden for care providers (Kulpa et al., 2021; Moyle et al., 2022; Sekhon et al., 2022).

Perhaps the most anticipated goal for a technological boost to healthy aging is autonomous (so-called driverless) cars. Clearly, a fully autonomous vehicle would be a tremendous boost for aging in place (discussed in Chapter 5) and personal independence. The Society for Automotive Engineers (SAE) International published SAE J3216 Standard: Taxonomy and Definitions for Terms Related to Cooperative Driving Automation for On-Road Motor Vehicles (2021). The new standard provides clarity to support advancement of full automation.

In brief, SAE J3216 builds on earlier SAE J3016 standards that defined six levels of driving automation, from SAE Level Zero (no automation) to SAE Level 5 (full vehicle autonomy). The newly published J3216 standards go further, providing definitions and categories focused on cooperative driving automation (CDA), a key building block that supports all levels of automation. CDA involves various levels of interaction between human drivers and the autonomous vehicle.

Much research remains to be done with both robots and autonomous vehicles, to be sure. But advances as coming quickly, so it is likely that in the next decade we will experience broader implementation of robots in people's residences to support their autonomy and aging in place, as the initial options for vehicles to help them get around.

Healthy Aging, Health Promotion, and Disease Prevention

Given that we have frameworks for understanding healthy aging (e.g., National Institute on Aging, United Nations), along with a growing set of powerful, especially technology-based, tools, you may be wondering how best to promote healthy aging for others as well as for yourself. You may not be surprised to learn there is no one set of steps or magic potion you can take to guarantee you will have healthy aging. But research using traditional methods as well as cutting-edge neuroimaging is finding that there are some steps you can take to quality of life and the odds of aging well (Gatz et al., 2016; Stern, 2017). We'll examine these more closely later in this section.

At a general level, healthy aging is an excellent example of the emphasis on health promotion and disease prevention across the life span. In fact, the U.S. government's Center for Disease Control and Prevention is charged with leading efforts in both—their motto is "Saving lives, protecting people."

Because we've considered many aspects of health promotion throughout the text we'll focus first here on disease prevention. To provide an overall frame, we will expand on Verbrugge and Jette's disablement model that we first encountered in detail in Chapter 4 (Verbrugge, 1994, 2020; Verbrugge et al., 2017; Verbrugge & Jette, 1994).

Issues in Prevention. In Chapter 4, we discussed how Verbrugge and Jette's (Verbrugge, 1994, 2020; Verbrugge et al., 2017; Verbrugge & Jette, 1994) theoretical model offers a comprehensive account of disability resulting from chronic conditions and provides much guidance for research. Another benefit of the model is it also provides insight into ways to intervene so disablement can be prevented or its progress slowed. Prevention efforts can be implemented in many ways, including not only those that may come quickly to mind (e.g., vaccines) but also those that may not seem as obvious (e.g., furnishing transportation to cultural events so otherwise placebound people can get to and enjoy these activities).

Traditionally, three levels of prevention can be applied to aging: primary, secondary, and tertiary (Haber, 2020). Other researchers have introduced the concept of quaternary prevention (Jamoulle, 2015; Martins et al., 2018). A brief summary of these four levels of prevention is presented in Table 14.2.

Primary prevention is any intervention that prevents a disease or condition from occurring. Examples of primary prevention include immunizing against illnesses such as COVID-19 and influenza, or controlling significant health risk factors such as serum cholesterol levels and cigarette smoking in healthy people.

Secondary prevention is instituted early after a condition has begun (but may not yet have been diagnosed) and before significant impairments have occurred. Examples of secondary intervention include cancer and cardiovascular disease screening and routine medical testing for other conditions. These steps help identify diseases in their early stages, often reduce the severity of the condition, and may reduce mortality from it. In terms of the main pathway in Verbrugge and Jette's (1994) original model (on page 136), secondary prevention occurs between pathology and impairments.

Tertiary prevention involves efforts to avoid the development of complications or secondary chronic

Table 14.2 Types of Prevention Interventions

Type of Prevention	Description	Examples
Primary	Any intervention that prevents a disease or condition from occurring	Immunizations against diseases, healthy diet
Secondary	Program instituted early after a condition has begun (but may not have been diagnosed) and before significant impairment has occurred	Cancer screening, other medical tests
Tertiary	Efforts to avoid the development of complications or secondary chronic conditions, manage the panic associated with the primary chronic condition, and sustain life	Moving a person who is bedridden to avoid sores, getting medical intervention, getting a patient out of bed to improve mobility after surgery
Quaternary	Effort specifically aimed at improving the functional capacities of people who have chronic conditions	Cognitive interventions for people with Alzheimer's disease, rehabilitation programs after surgery

conditions, manage the pain associated with the primary chronic condition, and sustain life through medical intervention. Some chronic conditions have a high risk of creating additional medical problems; for example, being bedridden as a result of a chronic disease often is associated with contracting pneumonia due to fluid building up in the lungs from a lack of physical movement. Tertiary prevention involves taking steps such as raising the person up in bed to lower the risk of contracting pneumonia or other diseases. In terms of the model, tertiary interventions are aimed at minimizing functional limitations and disability.

Tertiary prevention efforts do not usually focus on functioning or quality of life, but rather on avoiding additional medical problems and sustaining life (Haber, 2020). Consequently, the notion of quaternary prevention has been developed to address functional issues, especially the avoidance of overmedication (Jamoulle, 2015; Martins et al., 2018). **Quaternary prevention** efforts are specifically aimed at improving the functional capacities of people who have chronic conditions and avoiding overmedication. Quaternary prevention strategies help healthcare professionals avoid unnecessary or excessive medical interventions, especially invasive ones. Some examples of quaternary prevention are cognitive interventions to help people experiencing Alzheimer's disease remember, or occupational therapy to help people maintain their functional independence. It would also include palliative care (discussed in Chapter 13) and other nonmedical actions to improve quality of life.

Although most efforts with older adults to date have focused on primary prevention, increasing attention is being paid to the other levels. For example, secondary prevention is more routinely used for screening and early diagnosis of diseases such as cancer and cardiovascular disease (discussed in Chapters 3 and 4), tertiary prevention is reflected in higher standards of care in long-term care facilities (reviewed in Chapter 5), and quaternary prevention strategies are increasingly being used with persons with dementia (discussed in Chapters 6 and 10).

The stakes are high. Because tertiary and quaternary prevention programs in particular are aimed at maintaining functional abilities and minimizing disablement, so by extension at maintaining or improving quality of life, they offer effective, lower-cost alternatives for addressing the needs of older adults with chronic conditions.

Lifestyle factors underlie many of these behavioral approaches that are clearly gaining favor in the healthcare professional community (Rippe, 2019). Achieving healthy aging requires more of these approaches. We now examine some of these.

Lifestyle Factors in Health Promotion. Most attention in health promotion and disease prevention programs is on tackling a handful of behaviors that have tremendous payoff in terms of health and quality of life. What do healthy aging practitioners recommend people do? Table 14.3 summarizes the best advice from the National Institute on Aging (2022).

To help more people achieve the goal of healthy aging as promoted by the United Nations, National Institute on Aging, and others, the U.S. government allocates funds appropriated by the Older Americans Act to the Administration on Aging (AoA) to provide a wide variety of direct service programs specifically aimed at improving the health and well-being of older adults. These programs include health risk assessments and screenings, nutrition screening and education, physical fitness, health promotion programs on chronic disabling conditions, home injury control services, counseling regarding social services, and follow-up health services. Most are provided free to the participant through local and regional offices.

One goal of these programs is to address the lack of awareness many people have about their own chronic health problems; as noted in Chapters 3 and 4, most people who experience chronic diseases such as hypertension and diabetes are unaware they have them. Health promotion and disease prevention programs such as those sponsored by the AoA could reduce the cost of treating and toll on people from the diseases through earlier diagnosis and better education. Getting people to participate and then engage in healthy behavior, though, remains elusive.

You may have noticed that the main health promotion topics in Table 14.3 have been discussed throughout the text. As a result, we will only focus on two of the most important ones in detail in this section—exercise and smart eating—and note that another powerful focus is smoking.

Smoking regular and e-cigarettes is the single biggest contributor to health problems. In the United States alone, roughly 480,000 people die each year from tobacco use and exposure to secondhand smoke (American Lung Association, 2020b), and the annual costs related to smoking exceeds $300 billion annually (American Lung Association, 2020c). The risks of smoking are many. Figure 14.5 documents the various forms of cancer and other chronic diseases that are caused by smoking. And smoking during one's lifetime has a significant negative impact on cognitive functioning in adults over age 50 (Deal et al., 2020).

Table 14.3 Strategies for Maximizing Successful Aging

- Get moving with exercise and physical activity
- Make smart food choices
- Get a good night's sleep
- Quit smoking
- Avoid drinking alcohol in excess
- Go to the doctor regularly
- Stay engaged with family and friends
- Manage stress levels
- Monitor overall mood
- Engage in leisure activities, hobbies, or other activities that give you meaning
- Stay active cognitively

Source: National Institute on Aging. (2022). *What do we know about healthy aging?* https://www.nia.nih.gov/health/what-do-we-know-about-healthy-aging

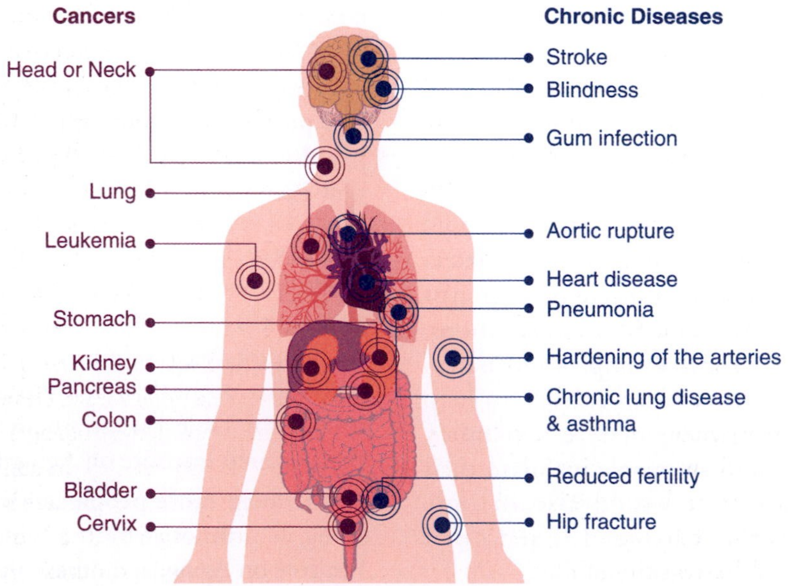

Figure 14.5 Smoking can damage every part of the body.

Source: Centers for Disease Control. www.cdc.gov/tobacco/basic_information/health_effects/cancer/index.htm

Most people begin to smoke (including vaping) by the time they are an emerging adult, so many first try to stop during their 20s and 30s. More than 90% of those who stop do so on their own. But quitting is not easy; most people who try to quit smoking relapse within 6 months. For most people, success is attained only after a long period of stopping and relapsing.

Regardless of how it happens, quitting smoking has enormous health benefits (American Lung Association, 2020d). For example, in less than a year after quitting, the lungs regain their normal ability to move mucus out. The risks of stroke and coronary heart disease return to normal after a period of roughly 15 years. Even people who do not quit until late life exhibit marked improvements in health. Refer to the American Lung Association's (2020e, 2020f) *Quit Smoking* websites for key information about how to quit and a quiz about whether you need help to quit.

Exercise. Since the ancient Greeks, physicians and researchers have known that exercise significantly slows the aging process. Indeed, evidence suggests a program of regular exercise, in conjunction with other aspects of a healthy lifestyle, is an almost magic preventive measure with numerous benefits, including slowing the physiological aging process and improving the immune system (Bartlett & Huffman, 2017; Parrella & Vormittag, 2017).

Adults benefit most from **aerobic exercise**, exercise that places moderate stress on the heart by maintaining a pulse rate between 60% and 90% of the person's maximum heart rate. You can calculate your maximum heart rate by subtracting your age from 220, then multiplying by .6 (for the minimum value in the range) and then by .9 (for the maximum value in the range). Thus, if you are 40 years old, your target range would be 108–162 beats per minute. The minimum time necessary for aerobic exercise to be of benefit depends on its intensity; at low heart rates, sessions may need to last an hour, whereas at high heart rates, 15 minutes may suffice. Examples of aerobic exercise include jogging, wheelchair aerobics, spinning, swimming, and vigorous cross-country skiing.

What happens when a person exercises aerobically (besides becoming tired and sweaty)? Physiologically, adults of all ages demonstrate improved cardiovascular functioning and maximum oxygen consumption; lower blood pressure; and better strength, endurance, flexibility, and coordination (Mayo Clinic, 2022b). Psychologically, people who exercise aerobically report lower levels of stress (noted in Chapter 4), better cardio functioning (noted in Chapter 3), and better cognitive functioning (noted in Chapters 6 and 7).

Kali9/E+/Getty Images

Exercise is a major way to help delay or prevent chronic disease and promote a healthy late life.

The best way to gain the benefits of aerobic exercise is to maintain physical fitness throughout the life span, beginning at least in middle age. In addition to those listed earlier, the benefits of various forms of exercise are numerous and include lowering the risk of osteoporosis if the exercise regimen includes a weight-bearing component. The Mayo Clinic's *Healthy Lifestyle* websites provide an excellent place to start, and include tips for adults of all ages and situations, including pregnancy. In planning an exercise program, three points should be remembered. First, check with a physician before beginning an aerobic exercise program. Second, bear in mind that moderation is important. Third, just because you intend to exercise doesn't mean you will; you must take the necessary steps to turn your intention into action (Kompf, 2018; Paech et al., 2016). If you do, and stick with it, you may feel much younger (Joyner & Barnes, 2013).

Without question, regular exercise is one of the most important behaviors you can do to promote healthy living and good aging. The Mayo Clinic (2022b) lists 10 top health benefits of aerobic exercise: improved immune system functioning, lower risks for many diseases (e.g., cancer, type 2 diabetes, cardiovascular disease), increased stamina, weight management, stronger heart, clearer arteries, better moods, stronger muscles, better management of chronic diseases, and longer life expectancy. In addition to the wide variety of positive effects on health there is also substantial evidence exercise is associated with a healthier brain: less cortical atrophy, better brain function overall and in the hippocampus specifically, a positive effect on the prefrontal cortex, increased gray matter, reversed progression of white matter hypersensitivities, and enhanced cognitive performance

(Bray et al., 2021; Eisenstein et al., 2022; Erickson et al., 2013; Huang et al., 2022).

What is clear from this research is that in normative aging, and likely in persons experiencing mild cognitive impairment, exercise can maintain brain functioning and perhaps slow any further changes. However, whether exercise can delay or prevent diseases such as Alzheimer's disease remains to be determined. Nevertheless, a better functioning brain may well be related to the mood improvements also found as another positive benefit of exercise, as noted in Figure 14.6.

In summary, if you want to maximize the odds of healthy aging, exercise. Guidelines state about 150 minutes of moderate aerobic exercise weekly with additional whole-body strength training and balance work is sufficient to produce positive effects (Laskowski, 2021). When you are done with your routine for the day, be mindful of what you eat, as discussed next.

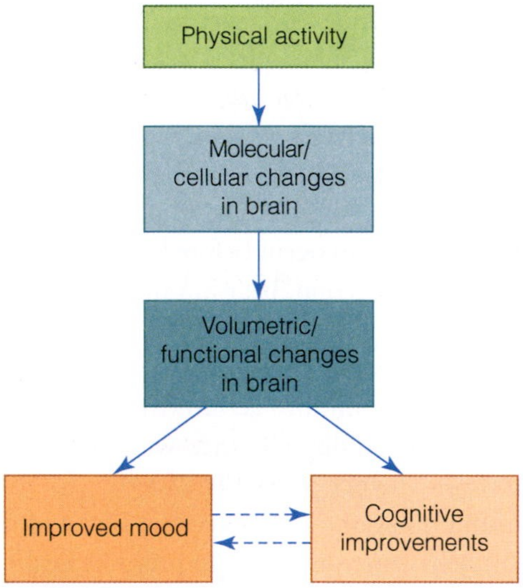

Figure 14.6 A schematic representation of the general path by which cognitive function and mood are improved by physical activity; it could be hypothesized that improvements in cognitive function mediate the improvements in mood or that improvements in mood mediate some of the improvements in cognitive function. The dotted lines represent these hypothesized paths.

Source: Erickson, K. I., Gildengers, A. G., & Butters, M. A. (2013). Physical activity and brain plasticity in late adulthood. *Dialogues in Clinical Neuroscience*, 15, 99–108. Open source. https://www.ncbi.nlm.nih.gov/pmc/articles/PMC3622473/ Image retrieved from www.ncbi.nlm.nih.gov/pmc/articles/PMC3622473/figure/DialoguesClinNeurosci-15-99-g001/

Nutrition. Experts agree nutrition directly affects one's mental, emotional, and physical functioning (Black & Bowman, 2020; Kahleova et al., 2021). Diet has been linked to cancer, cardiovascular disease, diabetes, anemia, and digestive disorders, among other conditions. To stay maximally healthy, though, we must recognize that nutritional requirements and eating habits change across the life span. This change is due mainly to differences in, or how much energy the body needs, termed **metabolism**. Body metabolism and the digestive process change with age; metabolism remains about the same from emerging adulthood through middle age but tends to decline in later life (Pontzer, 2021; Pontzer et al., 2021).

The U.S. Department of Agriculture publishes dietary guidelines based on research available at the time of publication. In its *Dietary Guidelines for Americans 2020–2025* (U.S. Department of Agriculture and U.S. Department of Health and Human Services, 2020), the USDA recommends we consume a variety of nutrient-dense foods and beverages across the basic food groups. The general guidelines for adults based on a 2,000 calories/day diet are listed in Figure 14.7.

The USDA approaches nutrition from the perspective of ensuring people eat a healthy plate of food at each meal, and the contents of that plate be appropriately balanced. Most important, we should choose foods that limit the intake of added sugar, saturated fats, sodium, and alcohol. And we need to keep our target calorie intake in mind. Read the full report and/or consult a dietician to obtain much more detail about the specific foods that are best for you and find out how you can design diets that are specific to you.

Of course, most people do not eat perfectly all the time. From time to time, each of us craves something—whether a triple-dip cone of premium ice cream or single source fair trade dark chocolate. If you feel even a tiny bit guilty after you enjoy that splurge, you are among the people who have taken to heart (literally) the link between diet and cardiovascular disease. The American Heart Association (2021a) makes it clear foods high in saturated fat (such as our beloved ice cream) should be eaten very sparingly or replaced with foods low in saturated fat (such as fat-free frozen yogurt). Refer to their website for the latest in advice on how to "Eat Smart."

Eating healthy foods is a special concern to communities who cannot access such food options. For example, the American Heart Association created the "Seeds of Native Health" campaign in partnership

Figure 14.7 Key Recommendations from Dietary Guidelines 2015–2020.
Source: https://health.gov/dietaryguidelines/2015/resources/2015-2020_Dietary_Guidelines.pdf p. xiii

with the Shakopee Mdewakanton Sioux Community to address the extreme poverty and lack of access to native foods that cause many Native Americans to experience widespread chronic diseases resulting from poor nutrition (American Heart Association, 2019). Additionally, food deserts in urban areas, where access to healthy food is limited due to a lack of grocery stores or their unaffordability or both, creates challenges for people living there. Without adequate access, it is difficult for people to eat the kind of healthy diet that will help them avoid chronic health conditions later in life.

Much of the focus of the various dietary guidelines and initiatives is to lower the risk of cardiovascular disease. To achieve this goal, it is important to understand the difference between two different types of lipoproteins. Lipoproteins are fatty chemicals attached to proteins carried in the blood. **Low-density lipoproteins (LDLs)** cause fatty deposits to accumulate in arteries, impeding blood flow; **very low-density lipoproteins (VLDLs)** are considered bad as well, but they mainly carry triglycerides, the most common type of fat in your body; and **high-density lipoproteins (HDLs)** help keep arteries clear and break down LDLs. Together, these three chemicals are types of cholesterol, which is a focus of screening during health checkups. It is not so much the overall cholesterol number but mainly the ratio of LDLs to HDLs and the level of VLDL that matter most in cholesterol screening (American Heart Association, 2021b). High levels of LDLs are a risk factor in cardiovascular disease, and high levels of HDLs are considered a protective factor.

Reducing LDL and VLDL levels, along with raising HLD levels, are effective in decreasing the risk of cardiovascular disease in adults of all ages. The National Heart,

Lung and Blood Institute updated their recommendations on target levels of LDL, VLDL, and HDL in 2019 (Grundy & Feingold, 2019). In healthy adults, LDL levels should optimally be kept below 100 mg/dL, VLDL levels below 150 mg/dL, and HDL above 60 mg/dL to help lower the risk of cardiovascular disease.

The revised diagnostic guidelines were followed by revised treatment guidelines from the American College of Cardiology and the American Heart Association (Arnett et al., 2019). LDL and VLDL levels can be lowered and HDL levels can be raised through various life style interventions including eating a heart-healthy diet, exercise, quitting smoking, and losing weight (American Heart Association, 2021c).

If diet and exercise are not effective in lowering cholesterol, numerous medications exist for treating cholesterol problems (American Heart Association, 2021d). The most popular of these drugs are from a family of medications called statins (e.g., Lipitor, Crestor). These medications lower LDL and moderately increase HDL. Before prescribing statins, healthcare professionals also assess a person's risk of cardiovascular disease from family history and lifestyle, among other factors. If statins are prescribed, their potential side effects on liver functioning should be monitored, and patients should consult with their physicians on a regular basis.

Adult Development in Action

If you were part of a healthy aging intervention team, how could the information about exercise and nutrition in this section be combined with the health information in Chapters 3 and 4 to create an education program for adults?

Review Questions

14.2 Healthy Aging: Living Well in Later Life

- What is meant by healthy aging?
- What is salutogenesis, and why is it important?
- What is positive psychology, and how does it relate to healthy aging?
- How can technology be used to improve older adults' lives?
- What are the four types of prevention strategies?
- Why are exercise and nutrition important for health promotion and disease prevention?

14.3 Epilogue

Marie Chen just celebrated her 100th birthday. During the daylong festivities, many people asked her whether she believed she had a good life. She answered everyone the same way, telling them she had her health, a roof over her head, and her family. What more could she want?

Marie gives every sign of having achieved healthy aging. She's 100 years old, with a loving family, good enough health to live in the community, and a place to live. But is there more to it than that?

From this book, you have a snapshot of what adult development and aging are like today. You learned about the complexities, myths, and realities of people's experience of growing old. But more than anything else, you have learned what we really know about the pioneers who blazed the trail.

In time, it will be your turn to lead the journey. When you do, you will make decisions about social policy, such as which interventions should be implemented and which ones should not. You will also make personal decisions about how you will prepare for later life. These decisions, along with so many others that you will make between now and when you reach late life will

AP Images/The Canadian Press/Chris Young

Reaching the goal of healthy aging is often visible on the face of those who reach it.

also have an enormous impact on those who will get there ahead of you: your parents, grandparents, and the people who taught and mentored you. These decisions will not be easy ones. But you have an advantage that the pioneers did not. You have the collected knowledge of gerontologists to apply in your decision making. With a continued concerted effort, you will be able to address the problems and meet the challenges that lie ahead. Then, when you yourself are old, you will be able to reminisce and conclude, "I lived long—and I prospered."

Social Policy Implications

Promoting Healthy Aging

In this chapter, we have focused on healthy aging as a way to maximize the likelihood that older adults will be able to age in place and enjoy a good quality of life. As was noted in the chapter, the basic principles are well established, and the benefits are equally well documented. So how is it that so many people do not have the opportunity to achieve healthy aging, and still others simply choose not to follow the guidelines?

It is true that the U.S. federal and state governments, along with most countries worldwide, provide substantial funding for a wide array of programs to educate people about healthy aging and to provide outreach and direct service. Local community groups and organizations such as senior centers are locations where people can learn more, perhaps obtain a healthy meal, and participate in many healthy aging type programs (e.g., movement classes, card games). Many religious organizations have these types of programs as part of their ministry.

Still, many people cannot participate. Why? For one thing, most of these programs require people to get to the place where the services are provided. If a person is placebound, though, or does not have access to transportation and cannot get there, they cannot participate and benefit.

Second, although many of the government programs are free, many are not. Individuals on very limited incomes may not have the financial resources to pay. This is especially the case with nutrition and eating healthily. As noted in the text, healthy food options are not universally available, especially in urban cores and rural areas. If healthy food options are unaffordable or inaccessible, people cannot implement healthy eating options. Related to affordability are the rules pertaining to eligibility for Supplemental Nutrition Assistance Program (SNAP, formerly called the Food Stamp Program), which have very low income and financial asset cutoffs (e.g., net income must be below the federal poverty line; Center on Budget and Policy Priorities, 2022).

Through the text, we have noted that structural barriers exist that restrict access to key goods and services, such as adequate health care. When these barriers, which are often based on sociocultural categories, operate, they have a direct effect on people's lives. If the goals of the United Nations and the United States regarding every person's basic right to healthy aging is to be achieved, governments and society at large will need to have the will to address these inequities. If they are willing to do so, the prospects of healthy aging for a world population that is itself aging will be bright.

In Review

Your summary of this final chapter should be organized into two paragraphs. In the first paragraph, summarize the various demographic changes that will occur by 2030, as well as those anticipated between 2030 and 2050 or so, in both the United States and globally. Discuss how those changes impact Social Security and Medicare.

Your second paragraph should focus on the various aspects of healthy aging. Define what healthy aging means. Define and discuss the idea of salutogenesis and how its components relate to healthy aging. Define and discuss the idea of positive psychology and how its aspects relate to healthy aging. Summarize the ways in which technology can be used to promote healthy aging and improve quality of life for older adults. Define the four levels of prevention and how they can help promote healthy aging. Describe the benefits of exercise and the components of healthy eating habits.

You may want to consider adding a general summary paragraph outlining what you consider are the most important things you learned in the course and how they will affect your life.

Integrating Concepts in Development

- Suppose you were brought in as a consultant on aging policy issues to your national government. Based on the demographic information in Chapter 1 and this chapter, what recommendations would you make?
- What trends in health care do you think will emerge based on information in this chapter and in Chapters 3, 4, and 10?
- How do you think older adults will define successful aging in the future?

Key Terms

aerobic exercise Exercise that places moderate stress on the heart by maintaining a pulse rate between 60% and 90% of the person's maximum heart rate. 483

dependency ratio The ratio of the number of people under age 15 and over age 64 in a country to the number of people between 15 and 64. 465

healthy aging Involves avoiding disease, being engaged with life, and maintaining high cognitive and physical functioning. 472

high-density lipoproteins (HDLs) Help keep arteries clear and break down LDLs. 485

low-density lipoproteins (LDLs) Cause fatty deposits to accumulate in arteries, impeding blood flow. 485

metabolism How much energy the body needs. 484

primary prevention Any intervention that prevents a disease or condition from occurring. 480

quaternary prevention Efforts specifically aimed at improving the functional capacities of people who have chronic conditions and avoiding overmedication. 481

salutogenesis An approach that emphasizes factors that support and promote health, rather than factors that cause disease. 473

secondary prevention Instituted early after a condition has begun (but may not yet have been diagnosed) and before significant impairments have occurred. 480

sense of coherence Core concept in salutogenesis that reflects a coping capacity of people to deal with everyday life stressors and consists of three elements: comprehensibility, manageability, and meaningfulness. 473

tertiary prevention Involves efforts to avoid the development of complications or secondary chronic conditions, manage the pain associated with the primary chronic condition, and sustain life through medical intervention. 480

very low-density lipoproteins (VLDLs) A type of lipoprotein that mainly carry triglycerides, the most common type of fat in the body. 485

References

A Better Balance. (2021). *Paid family and medical leave*. https://www.abetterbalance.org/our-issues/paid-family-medical-leave/

AARP. (1999). *AARP/Modern maturity sexuality survey*. http://assets.aarp.org/rgcenter/health/mmsexsurvey.pdf

AARP. (2005). *Sexuality at midlife and beyond: 2004 update of attitudes and behaviors*. http://assets.aarp.org/rgcenter/general/2004_sexuality.pdf

AARP. (2010). *Sex, romance, and relationships: AARP survey of midlife and older adults*. http://assets.aarp.org/rgcenter/general/srr_09.pdf

AARP. (2015). *Sex in the fifties*. https://www.aarp.org/relationships/love-sex/info-05-2010/2009-aarp-sex-survey.html

AARP. (2018). *Two-thirds of older adults are interested in sex, poll says*. https://www.aarp.org/health/healthy-living/info-2018/older-sex-sexual-health-survey.html

AARP. (2019a). *The ABCs of ADUs: A guide to accessory dwelling units and how they expand housing options for people of all ages*. https://www.aarp.org/content/dam/aarp/livable-communities/livable-documents/documents-2019/ADU-guide-web-singles-071619.pdf

AARP. (2019b). *Adult day care: What family caregivers need to know*. https://www.aarp.org/caregiving/home-care/info-2017/adult-day-care.html

AARP. (2021). *AARP livable communities*. https://www.aarp.org/livable-communities/

AARP. (2022a). *Tax tips for family caregivers*. https://www.aarp.org/caregiving/financial-legal/info-2017/tax-tips-family-caregivers.html.

AARP. (2022b). *5 unexpected reasons retirees are returning to work*. https://www.aarp.org/retirement/planning-for-retirement/info-2022/returning-to-work.html

Aasland, O. G., Rosta, J., & Nylenna, M. (2010). Healthcare reforms and job satisfaction among doctors in Norway. *Scandinavian Journal of Public Health, 38*, 253–258. https://doi.org/10.1177/1403494810364559

Abbasi, M., Amini, J., & Mahmoodian, N. (2020). Brain death according to the Sunni jurisprudence. *International Journal of Medical Toxicology and Forensic Medicine, 10*, 27388. https://doi.org/10.32598/ijmtfm.v10i4.27388

Abdollahi, H., Mahoor, M., Zandie, R., Sewierski, J., & Qualls, S. (2022). Artificial emotional intelligence in socially assistive robots for older adults: A pilot study. *IEEE Transactions on Affective Computing*. https://doi.org/10.1109/TAFFC.2022.3143803

Abela, A. (2020). The significance of the couple relationship in the twenty-first century. In A. Abela, S. Vella, & S. Piscopo (Eds.), *Couple relationships in a global context* (pp. 19–37). Springer, Cham. https://doi.org/10.1007/978-3-030-37712-0_2

Aberson, C. L., Shoemaker, C., & Tomolillo, C. (2004). Implicit bias and contact: The role of interethnic friendships. *Journal of Social Psychology, 144*, 335–347. https://doi.org/10.3200/SOCP.144.3.335–347

Abrams, D., Swift, H. J., & Drury, L. (2016). Old and unemployable? How age-based stereotypes affect willingness to hire job candidates. *Journal of Social Issues, 72*, 105–121. https://doi.org/10.1111/josi.12158

Abrams, H. R., Loomer, L., Gandhi, A., & Grabowski, D. C. (2020). Characteristics of U.S. nursing homes with COVID-19 cases. *Journal of the American Geriatric Society, 68*, 1653–1656. https://doi.org/10.1111/jgs.16661

Abrams, R. (2013). *When parents die: Learning to live with the loss of a parent* (3rd ed.). Routledge.

Achor, S. (2010). *The happiness advantage: The seven principles of positive psychology that fuel success and performance at work*. Random House.

Ackerman, L. S., & Chopik, W. J. (2021). Cross-cultural comparisons in implicit and explicit age bias. *Personality and Social Psychology Bulletin, 47*, 953–968. https://doi.org/10.1177%2F0146167220950070

Adams, C., Smith, M. C., Pasupathi, M., & Vitolo, L. (2002). Social context effects on story recall in older and younger women: Does the listener make a difference? *Journals of Gerontology: Psychological Sciences, 57B*, P28–P40. https://doi.org/10.1093/geronb/57.1. P28

Adams, R. B., Jr., Nelson, A. J., Soto, J. A., Hess, U., & Kleck, R. E. (2012). Emotion in the neutral face: A mechanism for impression formation? *Cognition and Emotion, 26*, 431–441. https://doi.org/10.1080/02699931.2012.666502

Adams, R. G., & Taylor, E. M. (2015). Friendship and happiness in the third age. In M. Demir (Ed.), *Friendship and happiness* (pp. 155–169). Springer.

Adams, R. G., Hahmann, J., & Blieszner, R. (2017). Interactive motifs and processes in old age friendship. In M. Hojjat & A. Moyer (Eds.), *The psychology of friendship* (pp. 39–55). Oxford University Press. https://doi.org/10.1093/acprof:oso/9780190222024.003.0003

Adams-Harmon, D., & Greer-Williams, N. (2021). Successful ascent of female leaders in the pharmaceutical industry: A qualitative, transcendental, and phenomenological study. *Equality, Diversity and Inclusion, 40*, 819–847. https://doi.org/10.1108/EDI-01-2019-0031

Adav, S. S., & Wang, Y. (2021). Metabolomics signatures of aging: Recent advances. *Aging and Disease*, 12, *646–661*. https://doi.org/10.14336%2FAD.2020.0909

Adeva-Andany, M. M., Adeva-Contreras, L., Fernández-Fernández, C., González-Lucán, M., & Funcasta-Calderón, R. (2021). Elastic tissue disruption is a major pathogenic factor to human vascular disease. *Molecular Biology Reports, 48*, 4865–4878. https://doi.org/10.1007/s11033-021-06478-8

Administration for Community Living. (2021). *2020 profile of older Americans*. https://acl.gov/sites/default/files/Profile%20of%20OA/2020ProfileOlderAmericans_RevisedFinal.pdf

Ahmad, N. A., Abd Rauf, M. F., Mohd Zaid, N. N., Zainal, A., Shahdan, T. S. T., & Razak, F. H. A. (2022). Effectiveness of instructional strategies designed for older adults in learning digital technologies: A systematic literature review. *SN Computer Science, 3*, 130. https://doi.org/10.1007/s42979-022-01016-0

Ahn, D., Williams, S., Stankus, N., & Saunders, M. (2021). Advance care planning among African American patients on haemodialysis and their end-of-life care preferences. *Journal of Renal Care, 47*, 265–278. https://doi.org/10.1111/jorc.12368

Ai, A. L., Richardson, R., Plummer, C., Ellison, C. G., Lemieux, C., Tice, T. N., & Huang, B. (2013). Character strength and deep connections following Hurricanes Katrina and Rita: Spiritual and secular pathways to resistance among volunteers. *Journal for the Scientific Study of Religion, 52*, 537–556. https://doi.org/10.1111/jssr.12043.

Ai, A. L., Wink, P., & Ardelt, M. (2010). Spirituality and aging: A journey for meaning through deep interconnection in humanity. In J. C. Cavanaugh & C. K. Cavanaugh (Eds.), *Aging in America: Vol. 3: Societal issues* (pp. 222–246). Praeger Perspectives.

Ai, A. L., Wink, P., Gall, T. L., Dillon, M., & Tice, T. N. (2017). Assessing reverence in contexts: A positive emotion related to psychological functioning. *Journal of Humanistic Psychology, 57*, 64–97. https://doi.org/10.1177/0022167815586657.

Aichele, S., Rabbitt, P., & Ghisletta, P. (2016). Think fast, feel fine, live long: A 29-year study of cognition, health, and survival in middle-aged and older adults. *Psychological Science, 27*, 518–529. https://doi.org/10.1177/0956797615626906

Ainsworth, C. (2020). Coaching and mentoring. In A. Viera, & R. Kramer (Eds.), *Management and leadership skills for medical faculty and healthcare executives* (pp. 171–182). Springer, Cham. https://doi.org/10.1007/978-3-030-45425-8_18

Aisenstein, C., Rueda, A. (2019). Working with Native American families during the perinatal stage and early childhood. In J. Maldonado-Duran, A. Jiménez-Gómez, M. Maldonado-Morales, & F. Lecannelier (Eds.), *Clinical handbook of transcultural infant mental health* (pp. 93–105). Springer, Cham. https://doi.org/10.1007/978-3-030-23440-9_8.

Aizenkot, D. (2022). Meaning-making to child loss: The coexistence of natural and supernatural explanations of death. *Journal of Constructivist Psychology, 35*, 318–343. https://doi.org/10.1080/10720537.2020.1819491

Ajrouch, K. J., Antonucci, T. C., & Webster, N. J. (2014). Volunteerism: Social network dynamics and education. *Journal of Gerontology: Social Sciences, 71*, 309–319. https://doi.org/10.1093/geronb/gbu166

Akincilar, S. C., Unal, B., & Tergaonkar, V. (2016). Reactivation of telomerase in cancer. *Cellular and Molecular Life Sciences, 73*, 1659–1670. https://doi.org/10.1007/s00018-016-2146-9. link.springer.com/article/10.1007/s00018-016-2146-9

Alasuutari, V. (2021). Tied together by death—Post-mortem forms of affective intimacy in LGBTQ people's stories of partner loss. *NORA—Nordic Journal of Feminist and Gender Research, 29*, 203–215. https://doi.org/10.1080/08038740.2021.1903554

Al-Attar, A., Presnell, S. R., Peterson, C. A., Thomas, D. T., & Lutz, C. T. (2016). The effect of sex on immune cells in healthy aging: Elderly women have more robust natural killer lymphocytes than do elderly men. *Mechanisms of Ageing and Development, 156*, 25–33. https://doi.org/10.1016/j.mad.2016.04.001

Alavi, M. V. (2016). Aging and vision. In C. B. Rickman, M. M. LaVail, R. E. Anderson, C. Grimm, J. Hollyfield, & J. Ash (Eds.), *Retinal degenerative diseases* (pp. 393–399). New York: Springer. https://doi.org/10.1007/978-3-319-17121-0_52

Albohn, D. N., & Adams, R. B., Jr. (2021). The expressive triad: Structure, color, and texture similarity of emotion expressions predict impressions of neutral faces. *Frontiers in Psychology, 12*. https://doi.org/10.3389/fpsyg.2021.612923

Albuquerque, S., Pereira, M., & Narciso, I. (2016). Couple's relationship after the death of a child: A systematic review. *Journal of Child and Family Studies, 25*, 30–53. https://doi.org/10.1007/s10826-015-0219-2

Al-Dawood, A., Alhajhussein, S., & Yarosh, S. (2021). Saudi Arabian parents' perception of online marital matchmaking technologies. *Proceedings of the ACM on Human-Computer Interaction, 4*, Article 211. https://doi.org/10.1145/3432910

Alden, D. L., Merz, M. Y., & Akashi, J. (2012). Young adult preference for physician decision-making style in Japan and the United States. *Asia-Pacific Journal of Public Health, 24*, 173–184. https://doi.org/10.1177/1010539510365098

Aldwin, C., & Igarashi, H. (2012). An ecological model of resilience in late life. *Annual Review of Gerontology and Geriatrics, 32*, 115–130. https://doi.org/10.1891/0198-8794.32.115

Aldwin, C., Yancura, L., & Lee, H. (2021). Stress, coping, and aging. In K. W. Schaie & S. L. Willis (Eds.), *Handbook of the psychology of aging* (9th ed., pp. 275–286). Academic Press. https://doi.org/10.1016/B978-0-12-816094-7.00016-7

Aldwin, C. M., Igarashi, H., Gilmer, D. F., & Levenson, M. R. (2018). *Health, illness, and optimal aging: Biological and psychosocial perspectives* (3rd ed.). Springer.

Aldwin, C. M., Park, C. L., Jeong, Y.-J., & Nath, R. (2014). Differing pathways between religiousness, spirituality, and health: A self-regulation perspective. *Psychology of Religion and Spirituality, 6*, 9–21. https://doi.org/10.1037/a0034416

Alegría, M., Chatterji, P., Wells, K., Cao, Z., Chen, C.-N., Takeuchi, D., Jackson, J., & Meng, X.-L. (2008). Disparity in depression treatment among racial and ethnic minority populations in the United States. *Psychiatric Services, 59*, 1264–1272. https://doi.org/10.1176/appi.ps.59.11.1264

Alexander, G. C., Emerson, S., & Kesselheim, A. S. (2021). Evaluation of aducanumab for Alzheimer disease: Scientific evidence and regulatory review involving efficacy, safety, and futility. *JAMA, 325*, 1717–1718. https://doi.org/10.1001/jama.2021.3854

Alhurani, R. E., Vassilaki, M., Aakre, J. A., Mielke, M. M., Kremers, W. K., Machulda, M. M. et al. (2016). Decline in weight and incident mild cognitive impairment: Mayo Clinic Study of Aging. *JAMA Neurology, 73*, 439–446. https://doi.org/10.1001/jamaneurol.2015.4756

Aljunaidy, M. M., & Adi, M. N. (2021). Architecture and mental disorders: A systematic study of peer-reviewed literature. *HERD: Health Environments Research & Design Journal, 14*, 320–330. https://doi.org/10.1177/1937586720973767

Allaire, J. C. (2012). Everyday cognition. In S. K. Whitbourne & M. J. Sliwinski (Eds.), *The Wiley-Blackwell handbook of adult development and aging* (pp. 190–207). New York: Wiley. https://doi.org/10.1002/9781118392966.ch10

Allaire, J. C., & Marsiske, M. (1999). Everyday cognition: Age and intellectual ability correlates. *Psychology and Aging, 14*, 627–644. https://doi.org/10.1037/0882-7974.14.4.627

Allaire, J. C., & Marsiske, M. (2002). Well- and ill-defined measures of everyday cognition: Relationship to older adults' intellectual ability and functional status. *Psychology and Aging, 17*, 101–115. https://doi.org/10.1037/0882-7974.17.1.101

Allaire, J. C., & Willis, S. L. (2006). Competence in everyday activities as a predictor of cognitive risk and morbidity. *Aging, Neuropsychology, and Cognition, 13*, 207–224. https://doi.org/10.1080/13825580490904228

Allan, B. A., Autin, K. L., Duffy, R. D., & Sterling, H. M. (2020). Decent and meaningful work: A longitudinal study. *Journal of Counseling Psychology, 67*, 669–679. https://doi.org/10.1037/cou0000432

Allen, K. R., & Lavender-Stott, E. S. (2020). The families of LGBTQ older adults: Theoretical approaches to creative family connections in the context of marginalization, social-historical change, and resilience. *Journal of Family Theory and Review, 12*, 200–219. https://doi.org/10.1111/jftr.12370

Allen, K. R., & Roberto, K. A. (2016). Family relationships of older LGBT adults. In D. A Harley & P. B. Teaster (Eds.), *Handbook of LGBT elders* (pp. 43–64). New York: Springer.

Allen, R. S., DeLaine, S. R., Chaplin, W. F., Marson, D. C., Bourgeois, M. S., Kijkstra, K., & Burgio, L. D. (2003). Advance care planning in nursing homes: Correlates of capacity and possession of advance directives. *The Gerontologist, 43*, 309–317. https://doi.org/10.1093/geront/43.3.309

Allexandre, D., Bernstein, A. M., Walker, E., Hunter, J., Roizen, M. F., & Morledge, T. J. (2016). A web-based mindfulness stress management program in a corporate call center. *Journal of Occupational and Environmental Medicine, 58*, 254–264. https://doi.org/10.1097/JOM.0000000000000680

Alley, J. L. (2004). The potential meaning of the grandparent-grandchild relationship as perceived by young adults: An exploratory study. *Dissertation Abstracts International. Section B. Sciences and Engineering, 65*(3-B), 1536.

Allison 2nd, R., Assadzandi, S., & Adelman, M. (2021). Frailty: Evaluation and management. *American Family Physician, 103*, 219–226. https://www.aafp.org/afp/2021/0215/p219.html

Almkvist, O., Brüggen, K., & Nordberg, A. (2021). Subcortical and cortical regions of amyloid-β pathology measured by ^{11}C-PiB pet are differentially associated with cognitive functions and stages of disease in memory clinic patients. *Journal of Alzheimer's Disease, 81*, 1613–1624. https://doi.org/10.3233/JAD-201612

Alper, J., & Howe, D. (2017). *Assessing adoptive parents, foster carers, and kinship carers* (2nd ed.). Jessica Kingsley Publishers.

Alspach, J. G. (2016). When it's your time, will it be your way? *Critical Care Nurse, 36*, 10–13. https://doi.org/10.4037/ccn2016452

Altweck, L., Hahm, S., Muehlan, H., Gfesser, T., Ulke, C., Speerforck, S., Schomerus, G., Beutel, M. E., Brähler, A., & Schmidt, S. (2021). The interplay of gender, social context, and long-term unemployment effects on subjective health trajectories. *BMC Public Health, 21*, Article 290. https://doi.org/10.1186/s12889-021-10324-8

Alzheimer's Association. (2022). *2022 Alzheimer's disease facts and figures.* https://www.alz.org/media/Documents/alzheimers-facts-and-figures.pdf

Amato, P. R., & Boyd, L. M. (2014). Children and divorce in world perspective. In A. Abela & J. Walker (Eds.), *Contemporary issues in family studies: Global perspectives on partnerships, parenting, and support in a changing world* (pp. 227–244). Wiley.

Amaya, A. (2020). *Adapting how we ask about the gender of our survey respondents.* https://medium.com/pew-research-center-decoded/adapting-how-we-ask-about-the-gender-of-our-survey-respondents-77b0cb7367c0

Ambrens, M., Stanners, M., Valenzuela, T., Razee, H., Chow, J., van Schooten, K. S., Close, J. C. T., Clemson, L., Zijlstra, G. A. R., Lord, S. R., Tiedemann, A., Alley, S. J., Vandelanotte, C., & Delbaere, K. (2021). Exploring older adults' experiences of a home-based, technology-driven balance training exercise program designed to reduce fall risk. *Journal of Geriatric Physical Therapy.* https://doi.org/10.1519/JPT.0000000000000321

American Academy of Dermatology. (2021a). *Anti-aging skin care.* https://www.aad.org/public/everyday-care/skin-care-secrets/anti-aging

American Academy of Dermatology. (2021b). *Skin care in your 40s and 50s.* https://www.aad.org/public/everyday-care/skin-care-basics/care/skin-care-in-your-40s-and-50s

American Academy of Dermatology. (2021c). *How to prevent premature skin aging.* https://www.aad.org/news/prevent-premature-skin-aging

American Association of Family Physicians. (2022). *Evidence-based medicine toolkit.* https://www.aafp.org/journals/afp/authors/ebm-toolkit.html

American Bar Association/American Psychological Association. (2006). *Judicial determination of capacity of older adults in guardianship proceedings.* https://www.apa.org/pi/aging/resources/guides/judges-diminished.pdf

American Bar Association/American Psychological Association. (2008). *Assessment of older adults with diminished capacity: A handbook for psychologists.* https://www.apa.org/pi/aging/programs/assessment/capacity-psychologist-handbook.pdf

American Bar Association/American Psychological Association. (2021). *Assessment of older adults with diminished capacity: A handbook for lawyers* (2nd ed.). https://www.apa.org/pi/aging/resources/guides/diminished-capacity.pdf

American Cancer Society. (2020). *Lifetime risk of developing or dying from cancer.* https://www.cancer.org/cancer/cancer-basics/lifetime-probability-of-developing-or-dying-from-cancer.html

American Cancer Society. (2021a). *About prostate cancer.* https://www.cancer.org/cancer/prostate-cancer/about.html

American Cancer Society. (2021b). *Stay healthy.* https://www.cancer.org/healthy.html

American College of Rheumatology. (2021). Rheumatoid arthritis guideline. https://www.rheumatology.org/Practice-Quality/Clinical-Support/Clinical-Practice-Guidelines/Rheumatoid-Arthritis

American Diabetes Association. (2021a). *Diabetes overview.* https://www.diabetes.org/diabetes

American Diabetes Association. (2021b). *Healthy living: You can live well with diabetes.* https://www.diabetes.org/healthy-living

American Farm Bureau Federation and National Farmers Union. (2021). *Rural opioid epidemic.* https://www.fb.org/issues/other/rural-opioid-epidemic/

American Geriatrics Society Ethics Committee. (1996). Making treatment decisions for incapacitated older adults without advance directives. *Journal of the American Geriatrics Society, 44*, 986–987. https://doi.org/10.1111/j.1532-5415.1996.tb01874.x

American Health Care Association and National Center for Assisted Living. (2021a). *What is assisted living?* https://www.ahcancal.org/Assisted-Living/Consumer-Resources/Pages/default.aspx

American Health Care Association and National Center for Assisted Living. (2021b). *Choosing an assisted living residence: A consumer's guide.* https://www.ahcancal.org/Assisted-Living/Consumer-Resources/Documents/Choosing%20An%20Assisted%20Living%20Residence%202013.pdf

American Heart Association. (2019). *Seeds of Native Health: A campaign for indigenous nutrition.* https://seedsofnativehealth.org/

American Heart Association. (2021a). *My life check: Life's simple 7.* https://www.heart.org/en/healthy-living/healthy-lifestyle/my-life-check--lifes-simple-7

American Heart Association. (2021b). *What your cholesterol levels mean.* https://www.heart.org/en/health-topics/cholesterol/about-cholesterol/what-your-cholesterol-levels-mean

American Heart Association. (2021c). *Prevention and treatment of high cholesterol (hyperlipidemia).* https://www.heart.org/en/health-topics/cholesterol/prevention-and-treatment-of-high-cholesterol-hyperlipidemia

American Heart Association. (2021d). *Cholesterol medications.* https://www.heart.org/en/health-topics/cholesterol/prevention-and-treatment-of-high-cholesterol-hyperlipidemia/cholesterol-medications

American Lung Association. (2020a). *Lung capacity and aging.* https://www.lung.org/lung-health-diseases/how-lungs-work/lung-capacity-and-aging

American Lung Association. (2020b). *Health effects.* https://www.lung.org/quit-smoking/smoking-facts/health-effects

American Lung Association. (2020c). *Smoking cessation: The economic benefits.* https://www.lung.org/policy-advocacy/tobacco/cessation/smoking-cessation-economic-benefits

American Lung Association. (2020d). *Benefits of quitting.* https://www.lung.org/quit-smoking/i-want-to-quit/benefits-of-quitting.

American Lung Association. (2020e). *Quit smoking.* https://www.lung.org/quit-smoking

American Lung Association. (2020f). *I want to quit smoking.* https://www.lung.org/quit-smoking/i-want-to-quit

American Lung Association. (2021a). *How lungs work.* https://www.lung.org/lung-health-diseases/how-lungs-work

American Lung Association. (2021b). *Chronic obstructive pulmonary disease (COPD).* https://www.lung.org/lung-health-diseases/lung-disease-lookup/copd

American Psychiatric Association. (2021). *What are anxiety disorders?* https://www.psychiatry.org/patients-families/anxiety-disorders/what-are-anxiety-disorders?_ga=2.51916457.1068855327.1647277212-1019003637.1647277212

American Psychiatric Association. (2022). *Desk reference to the Diagnostic Criteria from the diagnostic and statistical manual of mental disorders—5th Edition—Text Revision: (DSM-5-TR™).* American Psychiatric Association.

American Psychological Association. (2014). Guidelines for psychological practice with older adults. *American Psychologist, 69*, 34–65. https://doi.org/10.1037/a0035063

American Psychological Association. (2020). *PTSD Treatments.* https://www.apa.org/ptsd-guideline/treatments

American Stroke Association. (2018). *Ischemic stroke treatment.* https://www.stroke.org/en/about-stroke/types-of-stroke/ischemic-stroke-clots/ischemic-stroke-treatment

American Stroke Association. (2021). *Hemorrhagic stroke (bleeds).* https://www.stroke.org/en/about-stroke/types-of-stroke/hemorrhagic-strokes-bleeds

Amoyal, N., & Fallon, E. (2012). Physical exercise and cognitive training clinical interventions used in slowing degeneration associated with mild cognitive impairment: A review of the recent literature. *Topics in Geriatric Rehabilitation, 28*, 208–216. https://doi.org/10.1097/TGR.0b013e31825fc8d3

Anand, A., & MacLullich, A. M. J. (2021). Delirium in older adults. *Medicine, 49*, 26–31. https://doi.org/10.1016/j.mpmed.2020.10.002

Andermane, A., Joensen, B. H., & Horner, A. J. (2021). Forgetting across a hierarchy of episodic representations. *Current Opinion in Neurobiology, 67*, 50–57. https://doi.org/10.1016/j.conb.2020.08.004

Anderson, D. C., Grey, T., Kennelly, S., & O'Neill, D. (2020). Nursing home design and Covid-19: Balancing infection control, quality of life, and resilience. *Journal of the American Medical Directors Association, 21*, P1519–P1524. https://doi.org/10.1016/j.jamda.2020.09.005

Anderson, D., & De Souza, J. (2021). The importance and meaning of prayer rituals at the end of life. *British Journal of Nursing, 30*, 32–33. https://doi.org/10.12968/bjon.2021.30.1.34

Anderson, E. R., & Greene, S. M. (2013). Beyond divorce: Research on children in repartnered and remarried families. *Family Court Review, 51*, 119–130. https://doi.org/10.1111/fcre.12013

Anderson, F. T., & Einstein, G. O. (2017). The fate of completed intentions. *Memory, 25*, 467–480. https://doi.org/10.1080/09658211.2016.1187756

Anderson, R. E., Metzger, I., Applewhite, K., Sawyer, B., Jackson, W., Flores, S., Majors, A., McKenny, M. C., & Carter, R. (2020). Hands up, now what?: Black families' reactions to racial socialization interventions. *Journal of Youth Development, 15*. https://doi.org/10.5195/jyd.2020.755.

Andrade-Lotero, E., & Goldstone, R. L. (2021). Self-organized division of cognitive labor. *PLoS One*. https://doi.org/10.1371/journal.pone.0254532

Andreassi, J. K. (2011). What the person brings to the table: Personality, coping, and work–family conflict. *Journal of Family Issues, 32*, 1474–1499. https://doi.org/10.1177/0192513X11401815

Andrews-Hanna, J. R. (2012). The brain's default network and its adaptive role in internal mentation. *The Neuroscientist, 18*, 251–270. https://doi.org/10.1177/1073858411403316

Andrews-Hanna, J., Grilli, M., & Irish, M. (2019). A review and reappraisal of the default network in normal aging and dementia. *Oxford Research Encyclopedia of Psychology*. https://oxfordre.com/psychology/view/10.1093/acrefore/9780190236557.001.0001/acrefore-9780190236557-e-384

Angel, R. J., & Angel, J. L. (2015). *Latinos in an aging world: Social, psychological, and economic perspectives*. Routledge.

Angelou, M. (1969). *I know why the caged bird sings*. New York: Random House.

Angevaare, M. J., Roberts, J., van Hout, H. P. J., Joling, K. J., Smalbrugge, M., Schoonmade, L. J., Windle, G., & Hertogh, C. M. P. M. (2020). Resilience in older persons: A systematic review of the conceptual literature. *Ageing Research Reviews, 63*, 101144. https://doi.org/10.1016/j.arr.2020.101144

Anguera, J. A., Schachtner, J. N., Simon, A. J., Volponi, J., Javed, S., Gallen, C. L., & Gazzaley, A. (2021). Long-term maintenance of multitasking abilities following video game training in older adults. *Neurobiology of Aging, 103*, 22–30. https://doi.org/10.1016/j.neurobiolaging.2021.02.023

Anstey, K. J., & Dixon, R. A. (2021). Resilience in midlife and aging. In K. W. Schaie & S. L. Willis (Eds.), *Handbook of the psychology of aging* (9th ed., pp. 287–300). Academic Press. https://doi.org/10.1016/B978-0-12-816094-7.00007-6

Antheunis, M. L. (2016). Friendships and the internet. In C. R. Berger, M. E. Roloff, S. R. Wilson, J. P. Dillard, J. Caughlin, & D. Solomon (Eds.), *The international encyclopedia of interpersonal communication*. New York: Wiley. https://doi.org/10.1002/9781118540190.wbeic261

Antheunis, M. L., Schouten, A. P., & Walther, J. B. (2020). The hyperpersonal effect in online dating: Effects of text-based CMC vs. videoconferencing before meeting face-to-face. *Media Psychology, 23*, 820–839. https://doi.org/10.1080/15213269.2019.1648217

Anticevic, A., Repovs, G., & Barch, D. M. (2012). Emotion effects on attention, amygdala activation, and functional capacity in schizophrenia. *Schizophrenia Bulletin, 38*, 967–980. https://doi.org/10.1093/schbul/sbq168

Antonovsky, A. (1979). *Health, stress, and coping*. Jossey-Bass.

Antonovsky, A. (1987). *Unraveling the mystery of health: How people manage stress and stay well*. Jossey-Bass.

Antonovsky, A. (1996). The salutogenic model as a theory to guide health promotion. Health Promotion International, 11, 11–18. https://doi.org/10.1093/heapro/11.1.11

Aperion Care. (2019). *What millennials think about the future*. https://aperioncare.com/blog/millennials-on-aging/

Appel, H. B., Carretta, H., & Ai, A. L. (2020, October). *Character strengths and religious coping positive linked with anxiety in cardiac patients*. Paper presented at the annual meeting of the American Public Health Association. https://apha.confex.com/apha/2020/meetingapp.cgi/Paper/467794

Ardelt, M. (2010). Age, experience, and the beginning of wisdom. In D. Dannefer & C. Phillipson (Eds.), *The SAGE handbook of social gerontology* (pp. 306–316). SAGE Publications.

Ardelt, M., Landes, S. D., Gerlach, K. R., & Fox, L. P. (2013). Rediscovering internal strengths of the aged: The beneficial impact of wisdom, mastery, purpose in life, and spirituality on aging well. In J. D. Sinnott (Ed.), *Positive psychology* (pp. 97–119). Springer.

Arekapudi, N., & Recavarren, I. S. (2020). *Sexual harassment is serious business*. https://blogs.worldbank.org/developmenttalk/sexual-harassment-serious-business

Arena, J. E., & Rabinstein, A. A. (2015). Transient global amnesia. *Mayo Clinic Proceedings, 90*, 264–272. https://doi.org/10.1016/j.mayocp.2014.12.001

Arguedas, A. R., Robertson, C. T., Fletcher, R., & Nielsen, R. K. (2022). *Echo chambers, filter bubbles, and polarisation: A literature review*. https://reutersinstitute.politics.ox.ac.uk/echo-chambers-filter-bubbles-and-polarisation-literature-review

Arias, E., & Xu, J. (2020, November 17). United States life tables, 2018. *National Vital Statistics Reports, 69*. https://www.cdc.gov/nchs/data/nvsr/nvsr69/nvsr69-12-508.pdf

Arias, E., Tejada-Vera, B., Ahmad, F., & Kochanek, K. D. (2021). *Provisional life expectancy estimates for 2020*. https://www.cdc.gov/nchs/data/vsrr/vsrr015-508.pdf

Arizmendi, B., Kaszniak, A. W., & O'Connor, M.-F. (2016). Disrupted prefrontal activity during emotion processing in complicated grief: An fMRI investigation. *NeuroImage, 124 (Part A)*, 968–976. https://doi.org/10.1016/j.neuroimage.2015.09.054

Armento, A., Ueffing, M. & Clark, S. J. (2021). The complement system in age-related macular degeneration. *Cellular and Molecular Life Sciences, 78*, 4487–4505. https://doi.org/10.1007/s00018-021-03796-9

Arndt, J., & Goldenberg, J. L. (2017). Where health and death intersect: Insights from a Terror Management Health Model. *Current Directions in Psychological Science, 26*, 126–131. https://doi.org/10.1177/0963721416689563

Arnett, D. K., Blumenthal, R. S., Albert, M. A., Buroker, A. B., Goldberger, Z. D., Hahn, E. J., Himmelfarb, C. D., Khera, A., Lloyd-Jones, D., McEvoy, J. W., Michos, E. D., Miedema, M. D., Muñoz, D., Smith, S. C., Jr., Virani, S. S., Williams, K. A., Sr., Yeboah, J., & Ziaeian, B. (2019). 2019 ACC/AHA guideline on the primary prevention of cardiovascular disease: Executive summary: A report of the American College of Cardiology/American Heart Association Task Force on Clinical Practice Guidelines. *Circulation, 140*, e563–e595. https://doi.org/10.1161/CIR.0000000000000677

Arnett, J. J. (2015). *Emerging adulthood: The winding road from the late teens through the twenties* (2nd ed.). Oxford University Press.

Arnett, J. J. (2016). Introduction: Emerging adulthood theory and research: Where we are and where we should go. In J. J. Arnett (Ed.), *The Oxford handbook of emerging adulthood* (pp. 1–7). Oxford University Press.

Arnett, J. J., & Mitra, D. (2020). Are the features of emerging adulthood developmentally distinctive? A comparison of ages 18–80 in the United States. *Emerging Adulthood, 8*, 412–419. https://doi.org/10.1177%2F2167696818810073

Aron, L. Zullo, J., & Ynakner, B. A. (2022). The adaptive aging brain. *Current Opinion in Neurobiology, 72*, 91–100. https://doi.org/10.1016/j.conb.2021.09.009

Arshad, M., & Chung, J. M. (2022). Practical recommendations for considering culture, race, and ethnicity in personality psychology. *Social and Personality Psychology Compass, 16*, e12656. https://doi.org/10.1111/spc3.12656

Arthur, N., & McMahon, M. (2019). Contemporary career development theories: Expanding international perspectives. In N. Arthur & M. McMahon (Eds.), *Contemporary theories of career development: International perspectives* (pp. 241–257). Routledge.

Aryee, S., Chu, C. W. L., Kim, T.-Y., & Ryu, S. (2013). Family-supportive work environment and employee work behaviors: An investigation of mediating mechanisms. *Journal of Management, 39*, 792–813. https://doi.org/10.1177/0149206311435103

Ashton, M. C., & Lee, K. (2007). Empirical, theoretical, and practical advantages of the HEXACO model of personality structure. *Personality and Social Psychology Review, 11*, 150–166. https://doi.org/10.1177/1088868306294907

Ashton, M. C., & Lee, K. (2008). The prediction of Honesty–Humility-related criteria by the HEXACO and Five-Factor Models of personality. *Journal of Research in Personality, 42*, 1216–1228. https://doi.org/10.1016/j.jrp.2008.03.006

Ashton, M. C., Lee, K., Pozzebon, J. A., Visser, B. A., & Worth, N C. (2013). Status-driven risk taking and the major dimensions of personality. *Journal of Research in Personality, 44*, 734–737. https://doi.org/10.1016/j.jrp.2010.09.003

Asoodeh, M. H., Khalili, S., Daneshpour, N., & Lavasani, M. G. (2010). Factors of successful marriage: Accounts from self-described happy couples. *Procedia Social and Behavioral Sciences, 5*, 2042–2046. https://doi.org/10.1016/j.sbspro.2010.07.410

Asp, E., Manzel, K., Koestner, B., Cole, C. A., Denburg, N. L., & Tranel, D. (2012). A neuropsychological test of belief and doubt: Damage to ventromedial prefrontal cortex increases credulity for misleading advertising. *Frontiers in Neuroscience, 6*. https://doi.org/10.3389/fnins.2012.00100

Assanangkornchai, S., Tangboonngam, S., Samangsri, N., & Edwards, J. G. (2007). A Thai community's anniversary reaction to a major catastrophe. *Stress and Health, 23*, 43–50. https://doi.org/10.1002/smi.1118

AssistedLiving.org. (2021). *Assisted living in North Carolina*. https://www.assistedliving.org/north-carolina/#assisted_living_admission_requirements

Assmann, A. (2021). Cultural memory. In A. Hamburger, C. Hancheva, & V. D. Volkan (Eds.), *Social trauma: An interdisciplinary textbook* (pp. 25–36). Springer, Cham. https://doi.org/10.1007/978-3-030-47817-9_3

Assmann, J. (2011). Communicative and cultural memory. In P. Meusburger, M. Heffernan, & E. Wunder (Eds.), *Cultural memories* (pp. 15–27). Springer. https://doi.org/10.1007/978-90-481-8945-8_2

Association of American Medical Colleges. (2021). *Academic medicine's response to the opioid crisis*. https://www.aamc.org/news-insights/opioids

Association of Image Consultants International. (2021). *Our industry*. https://www.aici.org/page/our-industry

Attig, T. (1996). *How we grieve: Relearning the world*. Oxford University Press.

Attig, T. (2004). Disenfranchised grief revisited: Discounting hope and love. *OMEGA — Journal of Death and Dying, 49*, 197–215. https://doi.org/10.2190/P4TT-J3BF-KFDR-5JB1

Aundhia, C., Patel, S., Shah, N., Parmar, G., & Seth, A. (2020). Psychological effects and management of rheumatoid arthritis. *International Journal of Pharmaceutical Research, 12*, 2033–2039. https://doi.org/10.31838/ijpr/2020.12.02.273

Australian Government Department of Social Services. (2021). *Ageing and aged care*. https://www.health.gov.au/health-topics/aged-care?utm_source=health.gov.au&utm_medium=redirect&utm_campaign=digital_transformation&utm_content=agedcare

Auzoult, L. (2020). Can meaning at work guard against the consequences of objectification? *Psychological Reports, 123*, 872–884. https://doi.org/10.1177%2F0033294119826891

Awadi, M. A., & Mrayyan, M. T. (2016). Opponents and proponents views regarding palliative sedation at end of life. *Journal of Palliative Care & Medicine, 6*, 242. https://doi.org/10.4172/2165-7386.1000242

Ayalon, L. (2016). Satisfaction with aging results in reduced risk for falling. *International Psychogeriatrics, 28*, 741–747. https://doi.org/10.1017/S1041610215001969

Azmat, G., & Boring, A. (2020). *Gender diversity in firms.* http://ftp.iza.org/pp168.pdf

Azoulay, P., Jones, B. F., Kim, J. D., & Miranda, J. (2020). Age and high-growth entrepreneurship. *American Economic Review: Insights, 2*, 65–82. https://doi.org/10.1257/aeri.20180582

Babaei, P., Eyvani, K., & Kouhestani, S. (2021). Sex-independent cognition improvement in response to kaempferol in the model of sporadic Alzheimer's disease. *Neurochemical Research, 46*, 1480–1486. https://doi.org/10.1007/s11064-021-03289-y

Bachman, B. (2017). *Ethical leadership in organizations.* Springer.

Badham, S. R., Hay, M., Foxon, N., Kaur, K., & Maylor, E. A. (2016). When does prior knowledge disproportionately benefit older adults' memory? *Aging, Neuropsychology, and Cognition: A Journal on Normal and Dysfunctional Development, 23*, 338–365. https://doi.org/10.1080/13855585.2015.1099607

Bagbey Darian, C. D. (2014). A new mourning: Synthesizing an interactive model of adaptive grieving dynamics. *Illness, Crisis & Loss, 22*, 195–235. https://doi.org/10.2190/IL.22.3.c

Baggetta, P., & Alexander, P. A. (2016). Conceptualization and operationalization of executive function. *Mind, Brain, and Education, 10*, 10–33. https://doi.org/10.1111/mbe.12100

Bagnall, A.-M., Jones, R., Akter, H., & Woodall, J. (2016). *Interventions to prevent burnout in high risk individuals: Evidence review.* www.gov.uk/government/uploads/system/uploads/attachment_data/file/506777/25022016_Burnout_Rapid_Review_2015709.pdf

Bailey, Z. D., Feldman, J. M., & Bassett, M. T. (2021). How structural racism works: Racist policies as a root cause of U.S. racial health inequities. *New England Journal of Medicine, 384*, 768–773. https://doi.org/10.1056/NEJMms2025396

Baker, J. C., Fairchild, K. M., & Seefeldt, D. A. (2015). Behavioral gerontology: Research and clinical considerations. In H. S. Roane, J. E. Ringdahl, & T. S. Falcomata (Eds.), *Clinical and organizational applications of applied behavior analysis* (pp. 425–450). Academic Press.

Balistreri, C. R., Candore, G., Accardi, G., Bova, M., Buffa, S., Bulati, M., Forte, G. I., Listì, F., Marotrana, A., Palmeri, M., Pellicanò, M. V., Vaccarino, L., Scola, L., Lio, D., & Colanno-Romano, G. (2012). Genetics of longevity. Data from the studies on Sicilian centenarians. *Immunity and Ageing, 9*, 8. https://doi.org/10.1186/1742-4933-9-8 https://doi.org/10.1186/1742-4933-9-8

Balk, D. E. (2014). *Dealing with dying, death, and grief during adolescence.* Routledge.

Ballard, R. H., Rudd, B. N., Applegate, A. G., & Holtzworth-Munroe, A. (2014). Hearing the voice of the child in divorce. In M. K. Miller, J. Chamberlain, & T. Wingrove (Eds.), *Psychology, law, and the wellbeing of children* (pp. 121–137). Oxford University Press.

Balogun, A. G., & Afolabi, O. A. (2020). Do personal resources make a difference in the relation between work-family conflict and burnout among working mothers? *Covenant International Journal of Psychology, 5*, e. 2682–5368. https://journals.covenantuniversity.edu.ng/index.php/cijp/article/view/2435/1232

Balsam, K. F., Molina, Y., Beadnell, B., Simoni, J., & Walters, K. (2011). Measuring multiple minority stress: The LGBT People of Color Microaggressions Scale. *Cultural Diversity & Ethnic Minority Psychology, 17*, 163–174. https://doi.org/10.1037/a0023244

Baltes, P. B. (1987). Theoretical propositions of life-span developmental psychology: On the dynamics between growth and decline. *Developmental Psychology, 23*, 611–626. https://doi.org/10.1037/0012-1649.23.5.611

Baltes, P. B. (1993). The aging mind: Potential and limits. *The Gerontologist, 33*, 580–594. https://doi.org/10.1093/geront/33.5.580

Baltes, P. B., & Kliegl, R. (1992). Further testing of limits of cognitive plasticity: Negative age differences in mnemonic skill are robust. *Developmental Psychology, 28*, 121–125. https://doi.org/10.1037/0012-1649.28.1.121

Baltes, P. B., & Schaie, K. W. (1974). Aging and IQ: The myth of the twilight years. *Psychology Today, 7*, 35–40.

Baltes, P. B., & Staudinger, U. M. (2000). Wisdom: A metaheuristic (pragmatic) to orchestrate mind and virtue toward excellence. *American Psychologist, 55*, 122–136. https://doi.org/10.1037/0003-066X.55.1.122

Baltes, P. B., Lindenberger, U., & Staudinger, U. M. (2006). Life-span theory in developmental psychology. In R. M. Lerner & W. Damon (Eds.), *Handbook of child psychology: Vol. 1. Theoretical models of human development* (6th ed., pp. 569–664). Wiley.

Bambra, C. (2010). Yesterday once more? Unemployment and health in the 21st century. *Journal of Epidemiology and Community Health, 64*, 213–215. https://doi.org/10.1136/jech.2009.090621

Bandura, A. (2019). Applying theory for human betterment. *Perspectives on Psychological Science*, 14, 12–15. https://doi.org/10.1177/1745691618815165

Band-Winterstein, T., Goldblatt, H., & Lev, S. (2021). Breaking the taboo: Sexual assault in late life as a multifaceted phenomenon—toward an integrative theoretical framework. *Trauma, Violence, & Abuse, 22*, 112–124. https://doi.org/10.1177%2F1524838019832979

Banerjee, A., Pavane, M. S., Banu, L. H., Gopikar, S. R., Elizabth, K. R., & Pathak, S. (2021). Traditional medicine for aging-related disorders: Implications for drug discovery. In S. Pathak & A. Banerjee (Eds.), *Stem cells and aging* (pp. 281–297). Academic Press. https://doi.org/10.1016/B978-0-12-820071-1.00004-9

Bansak, C., & Starr, M. (2021). Covid-19 shocks to education supply: How 200,000 U.S. households dealt with the sudden shift to distance learning. *Review of Economics of the Household, 19*, 63–90. https://doi.org/10.1007/s11150-020-09540-9

Baran, M., & Zarzycki, R. (2021). Key effects of mentoring processes—multi-tool comparative analysis of the career paths of mentored employees with non-mentored employees. *Journal of Business Research, 124*, 1–11. https://doi.org/10.1016/j.jbusres.2020.11.032

Barbey, A. K., Colom, R., & Grafman, J. (2014). Distributed neural system for emotional intelligence revealed by lesion mapping. *Social Cognitive and Affective Neuroscience, 9*, 265–272. https://doi.org/10.1093/scan/nss124

Bargh, J. A., Chen, M., & Burrows, L. (1996). Automaticity of social behavior: Direct effects of trait construct and stereotype activation on action. *Journal of Personality and Social Psychology, 71*, 230–244. https://doi.org/10.1037/0022-3514.71.2.230

Barlow, M., Wrosch, C., Heckhausen, J., & Schulz, R. (2017). Control strategies for managing physical health problems in old age: Evidence for the motivational theory of lifespan development. In J. W. Reich & F. J. Infurna (Eds.), *Perceived control: Theory, research, and practice in the first 50 years* (pp. 281–308). Oxford University Press. https://doi.org/10.1093/acprof:oso/9780190257040.003.0012

Barnds, W. K. (2020). Called to the moment: A new vocation for Lutheran colleges. *Intersections, 2020*(52), Article 13. https://digitalcommons.augustana.edu/intersections/vol2020/iss52/13.

Barnett, A. E. (2013). Pathways of adult children providing care to older parents. *Journal of Marriage and the Family, 75*, 178–190. https://doi.org/10.1111/j.1741-3737.2012.01022.x

BarNir, A. (2021). To venture or not to venture? Gender stereotyping and women's entrepreneurial aspirations. *Sex Roles, 85*, 57–72. https://doi.org/10.1007/s11199-020-01204-3

Baron-Cohen, S., O'Riordan, M., Stone, V., Jones, R., & Plaisted, K. (1999). Recognition of faux pas by normally developing children and children with Asperger syndrome or high-functioning autism. *Journal of Autism and Developmental Disorders, 29*, 407–418. https://doi.org/10.1023/A:1023035012436

Barrera, M., Alam, R., D'Agostino, N. M., Nicholas, D. B., & Schneiderman, G. (2013). Parental perceptions of siblings' grieving after a childhood cancer death: A longitudinal study. *Death Studies, 37*, 25–46. https://doi.org/10.1080/07481187.2012.678262

Barrick, M. R., Mount, M. K., & Li, N. (2013). The theory of purposeful work behavior: The role of personality, higher order goals, and job characteristics. *Academy of Management Review, 38*, 132–153. https://doi.org/10.5465/amr.2010.0479.

Barroso, A. (2021). *With a potential 'baby bust' on the horizon, key facts about fertility in the U.S. before the pandemic.* https://www.pewresearch.org/fact-tank/2021/05/07/with-a-potential-baby-bust-on-the-horizon-key-facts-about-fertility-in-the-u-s-before-the-pandemic/

Bar-Tal, Y., Shrira, A., & Keinan, G. (2013). The effect of stress on cognitive structuring: A cognitive motivational model. *Personality and social Psychology Review, 17*, 87–99. https://doi.org/10.1177/1088868312461309

Bartkowiak, G. (2017). Best practices in the employment of knowledge workers 65 and over and the benefits of employing them (An empirical approach). In M. H. Bilgin, H. Danis, E. Demir, & U. Can (Eds.), *Financial environment and business development* (pp. 463–471). Springer.

Bartlett, D. B., & Huffman, K. M. (2017). Lifetime interventions to improve immunesenescence. In V. Bueno, J. M. Lord, & T. A. Jackson (Eds.), *The ageing immune system and health* (pp. 161–176). Springer.

Barton, C., Ketelle, R., Merrilees, J., & Miller, B. (2016). Non-pharmacological management of behavioral symptoms in frontotemporal and other dementias. *Current Neurology and Neuroscience Reports, 16*, 14. https://doi.org/10.1007/s11910-015-0618-1

Bar-Tur, L. (2022). Fostering well-being in the elderly: Translating theories on positive aging to practical approaches. *Frontiers in Medicine: Geriatric Medicine, 8*. https://doi.org/10.3389/fmed.2021.517226

Barua, A. (2022). *Gender equality, dealt a blow by COVID-19, still has much ground to cover.* https://www2.deloitte.com/us/en/insights/economy/impact-of-covid-on-women.html

Basten, U., & Fiebach, C. J. (2021). Functional brain imaging of intelligence. In A. K. Barbey, S. Karama, & R. J. Haier (Eds.), *The Cambridge handbook of intelligence and cognitive neuroscience* (pp. 235–260). Cambridge University Press. https://doi.org/10.1017/9781108635462.016

Basten, U., Hilger, K., & Fiebach, C. J. (2015). Where smart brains are different: A quantitative meta-analysis of functional and structural brain imaging studies on intelligence. *Intelligence, 51*, 10–27. https://doi.org/10.1016/j.intell.2015.04.009

Bates, J. S. and Taylor, A. C. (2016). Grandparent–grandchild relationships. In C. L. Shehan (Ed.), *Encyclopedia of family studies.* https://doi.org/10.1002/9781119085621.wbefs448

Battista, R. N., Blancquaert, I., Laberge, A.-M., van Schendel, N., & Leduc, N. (2012). Genetics in health care: An overview of current and emerging models. *Public Health Genomics, 15*, 34–45. https://doi.org/10.1159/000328846

Baucom, B. R., Dickenson, J. A., Atkins, D. C., Baucom, D. H., Fischer, M. S., Weusthoff, S., Hahlweg, K., & Zimmermann, T. (2015). The interpersonal process model of demand/withdraw behavior. *Journal of*

Family Psychology, 29, 80–90. https://doi.org/10.1037/fam0000044

Baumeister, R. F. (2010). The self. In R. F. Baumeister & E. J. Finkel (Eds.), *Advanced social psychology: The state of the science* (pp. 139–175). New York: Oxford University Press.

Beach, E. F., & Gilliver, M. (2019). Time to listen: Most regular patrons of music venues prefer lower volumes. *Frontiers in Psychology, 10*, 607. https://doi.org/10.3389/fpsyg.2019.00607

Beason-Held, L. L., Thambisetty, M., Deib, G., Sojkova, J., Landman, B. A., Zonderman, A. B., Ferrucci, L., Kraut, M. A., & Resnick, S. M. (2012). Baseline cardiovascular risk predicts subsequent changes in resting brain function. *Stroke, 43*, 1542–1547. https://doi.org/10.1161/STROKEAHA.111.638437

Beaty, R. E., Benedek, M., Silvia, P. J., & Schacter, D. L. (2016). Creative cognition and brain network dynamics. *Trends in Cognitive Sciences, 20*, 87–95. https://doi.org/10.1016/j.tics.2015.10.004

Beaunoyer, E., Torres, E. H., Maessen, L., & Guitton, M. J. (2020). Grieving in the digital era: Mapping online support for grief and bereavement. *Patient Education and Counseling, 103*, 2515–2524. https://doi.org/10.1016/j.pec.2020.06.013

Beck, A. T. (1967). *Depression: Clinical, experimental, and theoretical aspects*. Harper & Row.

Beck, A. T., Rush, J., Shaw, B., & Emery, G. (1979). *Cognitive therapy of depression*. Guilford.

Beckes, L., & Coan, J. A. (2013). Voodoo versus me–you correlations in relationship neuroscience. *Journal of Social and Personal Relationships, 30*, 189–197. https://doi.org/10.1177/0265407512454768

Beckes, L., Coan, J. A., & Hasselmo, K. (2013). Familiarity promotes the blurring of self and other in the neural perception of threat. *Social Cognitive and Affective Neuroscience, 8*, 670–677. https://doi.org/10.1093/scan/nss046

Bejenaru, A., & Ellison, J. M. (2021). Medicolegal implications of mild neurocognitive disorder. *Journal of Geriatric Psychiatry and Neurology, 34*, 513–527. https://doi.org/10.1177%2F0891988720957092

Belam, G. (2020). Yoga as an intervention for older peoples mental health: A literature review. *Working with Older People, 24*, 159–169. https://doi.org/10.1108/WWOP-05-2020-0017.

Bell, A. G. (1918). *The duration of life and conditions associated with longevity: A study of the Hyde genealogy*. Genealogical Records Office.

Belsky, G. (2007). *Over the hill and between the sheets: Sex, love and lust in middle age*. Springboard Press.

Benjamins, M. R., Hirschman, J., Hirschtick, J., & Whitman, S. (2012). Exploring differences in self-rated health among Blacks, Whites, Mexicans, and Puerto Ricans. *Ethnicity and Health, 17*, 463–476. https://doi.org/10.1080/13557858.2012.654769

Benjamins, M. R., Saiyed, N., Bunting, S., Lorenz, P., Hunt, B., Glick, N., & Silva, A. (2022). HIV mortality across the 30 largest U.S. cities: Assessing overall trends and racial inequities. *AIDS Care, 34*, 916-925. https://doi.org/10.1080/09540121.2021.1939849

Berboth, S., & Morawetz, C. (2021). Amygdala-prefrontal connectivity during emotion regulation: A meta-analysis of psychophysiological interactions. *Neuropsychologia, 153*, 107767. https://doi.org/10.1016/j.neuropsychologia.2021.107767

Berezuk, C., Scott, S. C., Black, S. E., & Zakzanis, K. K. (2022). Cognitive reserve, cognition, and real-world functioning in MCI: A systematic review and meta-analysis. *Journal of Clinical and Experimental Neuropsychology, 43*, 991–1005. https://doi.org/10.1080/13803395.2022.2047160

Berg, C. A. (2008). Everyday problem solving in context. In S. M. Hofer & D. F. Alwin (Eds.), *Handbook of cognitive aging: Interdisciplinary perspectives* (pp. 207–223). Sage.

Berg, C. A., & Sternberg, R. J. (1992). Adults' conceptions of intelligence across the adult life span. *Psychology and Aging, 7*, 221–231. https://doi.org/10.1037/0882-7974.7.2.221

Berg, C. A., Sewell, K. K., Hughes Lansing, A. E., Wilson, S. J., & Brewer, C. (2016). A developmental perspective to dyadic coping across adulthood. In J. Bookwala (Ed.), *Couple relationships in the middle and later years: Their nature, complexity, and role in health and illness* (pp. 259–280). American Psychological Association.

Berg, C. A., Strough, J., Calderone, K. S., Sansone, C., & Weir, C. (1998). The role of problem definitions in understanding age and context effects on strategies for solving every day problems. *Psychology and Aging, 13*, 29–44. https://doi.org/10.1037/0882-7974.13.1.29

Bergdahl, E., Benzein, E., Ternestedt, B.-M., Elmberger, E., & Andershed, B. (2013). Co-creating possibilities for patients in palliative care to reach vital goals—A multiple case study of home-care nursing encounters. *Nursing Inquiry, 20*, 341–351. https://doi.org/10.1111/nin.12022

Berkowitz, S. R., Enright, K., Bowman-Fowler, N. & Loftus, E. F. (2015). Eyewitness testimony. In A. Jamieson & A. Moenssens (Eds.), *Wiley encyclopedia of forensic science*. https://doi.org/10.1002/9780470061589.fsa264.pub2

Bermejo-Toro, L., Prieto-Ursúa, M., & Hernández, V. (2016). Towards a model of teacher well-being: Personal and job resources involved in teacher burnout and engagement. *Educational Psychology, 36*, 481–501. https://doi.org/10.1080/01443410.2015.1005006

Berns, N. (2011). *Closure: The rush to end grief and what it costs*. Temple University Press.

Berry, J. M. (1989). Cognitive efficacy across the life span: Introduction to the special series. *Developmental Psychology, 25*, 683–686. https://psycnet.apa.org/doi/10.1037/0012-1649.25.5.683

Berry, J. M., Cavanaugh, J. C., & West, R. L. (2016). *Self-efficacy and human agency: Implications for aging well*. Unpublished manuscript, Department of Psychology, University of Richmond.

Besedeš, T., Deck, C., Sarangi, S., & Shor, M. (2012). Age effects and heuristics in decision making. *The Review of Economics and Statistics, 94*, 580–595. https://doi.org/10.1162/REST_a_00174

Betzel, R. F. (2022). Network neuroscience and the connectomics revolution. In A. Horn (Ed.), *Connectomic deep brain stimulation* (pp. 25–58). Academic Press.

Bever, L. (2014a). Cancer patient Brittany Maynard, 29, has scheduled her death for Nov. 1. *Washington, Post*. https://www.washingtonpost.com/news/morning-mix/wp/2014/10/08/terminally-ill-brittany-maynard-29-has-scheduled-her-death-for-nov-1/

Bever, L. (2014b). Brittany Maynard, as promised, ends her life at 29. *Washington Post*. https://www.washingtonpost.com/news/morning-mix/wp/2014/11/02/brittany-maynard-as-promised-ends-her-life-at-29/

Bever, L. (2014c). How Brittany Maynard may change the right-do-die debate. *Washington Post*. https://www.washingtonpost.com/news/morning-mix/wp/2014/11/03/how-brittany-maynard-may-change-the-right-to-die-debate-after-death/

Bhargava, R., & Chilana, R. (2020). A flat of my own: Singlehood and rental housing. In D. Joshi & C. Brassard (Eds.), *Urban spaces and gender in Asia* (pp. 95–107). Springer, Cham. https://doi.org/10.1007/978-3-030-36494-6_6

Bhattacharyya, K. K., Craft Morgan, J., & Burgess, E. O. (2022). Person-centered care in nursing homes: Potential of complementary and alternative approaches and their challenges. *Journal of Applied Gerontology, 41*, 817–825. https://doi.org/10.1177/07334648211023661

Bhattarai, P., & Phillips, J. L. (2017). The role of digital health technologies in management of pain in older people: An integrative review. *Archives of Gerontology and Geriatrics, 68*, 14–24. https://doi.org/10.1016/j.archger.2016.08.008

Bian, F., Blachford, D., & Durst, D. (2015). The color purple: Perspectives of Canadian parents of adopted children from China. *Journal of Comparative Social Work, 10*, 107–137. https://doi.org/10.31265/jcsw.v10i2.129

Bianchi, F., Bianchi, G., & Song, D. (2020). *The long-term impact of the COVID-19 unemployment shock on life expectancy and mortality rates*. https://www.nber.org/papers/w28304

Biblarz, T. J., & Savci, E. (2010). Lesbian, gay, bisexual, and transgender families. *Journal of Marriage and Family, 72*, 480–497. https://doi.org/10.1111/j.1741-3737.2010.00714.x

Bidwell, M. (2013). What happened to long term employment? The role of worker power and environmental turbulence in explaining declines in worker tenure. *Organization Science, 24*, 1061–1082. https://doi.org/10.1287/orsc.1120.0816

Bieman-Copland, S., Ryan, E. B., & Cassano, J. (2002). Responding to the challenges of late life. In D. Pushkar, W. M. Bukowski, A. E. Schwartzman, D. M. Stack, & D. R. White (Eds.), *Improving competence across the lifespan* (pp. 141–157). Springer.

Bietti, L. M., & Sutton, J. (2015). Interacting to remember at multiple timescales: Coordination, collaboration, cooperation and culture in joint remembering. *Interaction Studies, 16*, vii–xii. https://doi.org/10.1075/is.16.3.001int

Biggs, S., McGann, M., Bowman, D., & Kimberley, H. (2017). Work, health and the commodification of life's time: Reframing work-life balance and the promise of a long life. *Ageing and Society, 37*, 1458–1483. https://doi.org/10.1017/S0144686X16000404

Bigonnesse, C., & Chadhury, H. (2020). The landscape of "aging in place" in gerontology literature: Emergence, theoretical perspectives, and influencing factors. *Journal of Aging and Environment, 34*, 233–251. https://doi.org/10.1080/02763893.2019.1638875

Binet, A. (1903). *Etude expérimentale de l'intelligence*. Schleicher Frères & Cie.

Binstock, R. H. (1999). Public policy issues. In J. C. Cavanaugh & S. K. Whitbourne (Eds.), *Gerontology: Interdisciplinary perspectives* (pp. 414–447). Oxford University Press.

Birditt, K. S., Tighe, L. A., Fingerman, K. L ., & Zarit, S. H. (2012). Intergenerational relationship quality across three generations. *Journals of Gerontology: Psychological Sciences, 67*, 627–638. https://doi.org/10.1093/geronb/gbs050

Birnbaum, G. E., Reis, H. T., Mizrahi, M., Kanat-Maymon, Y., Sass, O., Granovski-Milner, C. (2016). Intimately connected: The importance of partner responsiveness for experiencing sexual desire. *Journal of Personality and Social Psychology, 111*, 530–546. https://doi.org/10.1037/pspi0000069

Birren, J. E., & Renner, V. J. (1980). Concepts and issues of mental health and aging. In J. E. Birren & R. B. Sloane (Eds.), *Handbook of mental health and aging* (pp. 3–33). Prentice Hall.

Bitterman, A., & Hess, D. B. (2021). Understanding generation gaps in LGBTQ+ communities: Perspectives about gay neighborhoods among heteronormative and homonormative generational cohorts. In A. Bitterman & D. B. Hess (Eds.), *The life and afterlife of gay neighborhoods: Renaissance and resurgence* (pp. 307–338). Springer.

Black, M., & Bowman, M. (2020). Nutrition and healthy aging. *Clinics in Geriatric Medicine, 36*, P655–P669. https://doi.org/10.1016/j.cger.2020.06.008

Blackhall, L. J., Read, P., Stukenborg, G., Dillon, P., Barclay, J., Romano, A., & Harrison, J. (2016). CARE Track for advanced cancer: Impact and timing of an outpatient palliative clinic. *Journal of Palliative Medicine, 19*, 57–63. https://doi.org/10.1089/jpm.2015.0272

Blackstone, A., & Stewart, M. D. (2016). "There's more thinking to decide": How the childfree decide not to parent. *The Family Journal, 24*, 296–303. https://doi.org/10.1177/1066480716648676

Blancero, D. M., & Cotton-Nessler, N. C. (2017). Mentoring Latinos: An examination of cultural values through the lens of relational cultural theory. In A. J. Murrell & S. Blake-Beard (Eds.), *Mentoring diverse leaders: Creating change for people, processes, and paradigms* (pp. 44–64). Routledge/Taylor & Francis Group. https://doi.org/10.4324/9781315747569-3

Blanchard-Fields, F. (1996). Causal attributions across the adult life span: The influence of social schemas, life context, and domain specificity. *Applied Cognitive Psychology, 10* (Special Issue), 137–146. https://doi.org/10.1002/(SICI)1099-0720(199611)10:7<137::AID-ACP431>3.0.CO;2-Z

Blanchard-Fields, F. (1999). Social schematicity and causal attributions. In T. M. Hess & F. Blanchard-Fields (Eds.), *Social cognition and aging* (pp. 219–236). Academic Press.

Blanchard-Fields, F., Baldi, R. A., & Constantin, L. P. (2004). *Interrole conflict across the adult lifespan: The role of parenting stage, career stages and quality of experiences.* Unpublished manuscript, School of Psychology, Georgia Institute of Technology.

Blanchard-Fields, F., & Beatty, C. (2005). Age differences in blame attributions: The role of relationship outcome ambiguity and personal identification. *Journals of Gerontology: Psychological Sciences, 60*, P19–P26. https://doi.org/10.1093/geronb/60.1.P19

Blanchard-Fields, F., & Horhota, M. (2006). How can the study of aging inform research on social cognition? *Social Cognition, 24*, 207–217. https://doi.org/10.1521/soco.2006.24.3.207

Blanchard-Fields, F., Chen, Y., & Herbert, C. E. (1997). Interrole conflict as a function of life stage, gender, and gender-related personality attributes. *Sex Roles, 37*, 155–174. https://doi.org/10.1023/A:1025691626240

Blanchard-Fields, F., Chen, Y., Horhota, M., & Wang, M. (2007). Cultural differences in the relationship between aging and the correspondence bias. *Journals of Gerontology: Psychological Sciences, 62*, P362–P365. https://doi.org/10.1093/geronb/62.6.P362

Blanchard-Fields, F., Hertzog, C., & Horhota, M. (2012). Violate my beliefs? Then you're to blame! Belief content as an explanation for causal attribution biases. *Psychology and Aging, 27*, 324–337. https://doi.org/10.1037/a0024423

Blanchard-Fields, F., Horhota, M., & Mienaltowski, A. (2008). Social context and cognition. In S. M. Hofer & D. F. Alwin (Eds.), *Handbook of cognitive aging: Interdisciplinary perspectives* (pp. 614–628). Sage.

Blanchard-Fields, F., Mienaltowski, A., & Seay, R. (2007). Age differences in everyday problem-solving effectiveness: Older adults select more effective strategies for interpersonal problems. *Journals of Gerontology: Psychological Sciences, 62*, P61–P64. https://doi.org/10.1093/geronb/62.1.P61

Blatteis, C. M. (2012). Age-dependent changes in temperature regulation—A mini review. *Gerontology, 58*, 289–295. https://doi.org/10.1159/000333148

Blazer, D. G. (2008). How do you feel about…? Health outcomes in late life and self-perceptions of health and well-being. *The Gerontologist, 48*, 415–422. https://doi.org/10.1093/geront/48.4.415

Blazhenets, G., Schröter, N., Bormann, T., Thurow, J., Wagner, D., Frings, L., Weiller, C., Meyer, P. T., Dressing, A., & Hosp, J. A. (2021). Slow but evident recovery from neocortical dysfunction and cognitive impairment in a series of chronic COVID-19 patients. *Journal of Nuclear Medicine, 62*, 910–915. https://doi.org/10.2967/jnumed.121.262128

Blieszner, R. (2014). The worth of friendship: Can friends keep us happy and healthy? *Generations, 38*, 24–30. https://www.ingentaconnect.com/contentone/asag/gen/2014/00000038/00000001/art00005.

Blieszner, R., & Roberto, K. A. (2012). Partners and friends in adulthood. In S. K. Whitbourne & M. J. Sliwinski (Eds.), *The Wiley-Blackwell handbook of adulthood and aging* (pp. 381–398). Wiley-Blackwell.

Blieszner, R., Ogletree, A. M., & Adams, R. G. (2019). Friendship in later life: A research agenda, *Innovation in Aging, 3*, igz005. https://doi.org/10.1093/geroni/igz005

Bligh, M. C. (2017). Leadership and trust. In J. Marques & S. Dhiman (Eds.), *Leadership today* (pp. 21–42). Springer.

Blümel, J. E., Chedraui, P., Baron, G., Belzares, E., Bencosme, A., Calle, A., Danckers, L., Espinoza, M. T., Flores, D., Gomez, G., Hernandez-Bueno, J. A., Izaguirre, H., Leon-Leon, P., Lima, S., Mezones-Holguin, E., Monterrosa, A., Mostajo, D., Navarro, D., Ojeda, E., Onatra, W., et al. (2012). Menopausal symptoms appear before the menopause and persist 5 years beyond: A detailed analysis of a multinational study. *Climacteric, 15*, 542–551. https://doi.org/10.3109/13697137.2012.658462

Bluntschli, J. R., Maxfield, M. M., Grasso, R. L., & Kisley, M. A. (2018). The last word: A comparison of younger and older adults' brain responses to reminders of death. *Journals of Gerontology: Psychological Sciences and Social Sciences, 73*, 555–563. https://doi.org/10.1093/geronb/gbv115

Bochenska, K., & Boller, A.-M. (2016). Fecal incontinence: Epidemiology, impact, and treatment. *Clinics in Colon and Rectal Surgery, 29*, 264–270. https://doi.org/10.1055:/s-0036-1584504

Bodner, E., Bergman, Y. S., Shiloh-Levin, S., & Hoffman, Y. S. G. (2021). The interactive effect of aging anxiety and age awareness on meaning in life and psychological distress: A moderated mediation model. *Current Psychology*. https://doi.org/10.1007/s12144-021-02156-x

Boggula, V. R. (2021). Genetic aspects of early-onset Alzheimer's disease. In S. Kumar (Ed.), *The molecular immunology of neurological diseases* (pp. 29–39). Academic Press. https://doi.org/10.1016/B978-0-12-821974-4.00013-3.

Boisgontier, M. P., Cheval, B., van Ruitenbeek, P., Levin, O., Renaud, O., Chanal, J., & Swinnen, S. P. (2016). Whole-brain grey matter density predicts balance stability irrespective of age and protects older adults from falling. *Gait & Posture, 45*, 143–150. https://doi.org/10.1016/j.gaitpost.2016.01.019

Bonanno, G. A. (2009). *The other side of sadness: What the new science of bereavement tells us about life after loss.* Basic Books.

Bonanno, G. A., & Malgaroli, M. (2020). Trajectories of grief: Comparing symptoms from the DSM-5 and ICD-11 diagnoses. *Depression & Anxiety, 37*, 17–25. https://doi.org/10.1002/da.22902

Bonanno, G. A., Papa, A., & O'Neill, K. (2001). Loss and human resilience. *Applied and Preventive Psychology, 10*, 193–206. https://doi.org/10.1016/S0962-1849(01)80014-7

Bonanno, G. A., Westphal, M., & Mancini, A. D. (2011). Resilience to loss and trauma. *Annual Review of Clinical Psychology, 7*, 511–535. https://doi.org/10.1146/annurevclinpsy-032210-104526

Bonanno, G. A., Wortman, C. B., & Neese, R. M. (2004). Prospective patterns of resilience and maladjustment during widowhood. *Psychology and Aging, 19*, 260–271. https://doi.org/10.1037/0882-7974.19.2.260

Bonvillain, N. (2021). *Women and men: Cultural constructs of gender* (5th ed.). Rowman & Littlefield.

Boon, H., Ruiter, R. U. C., James, S., van den Borne, B., Williams, E., & Reddy, P. (2010). Correlates of grief among older adults caring for children and grandchildren as a consequence of HIV and AIDS in South Africa. *Journal of Aging and Health, 22*, 48–67. https://doi.org/10.1177/0898264309349165

Booth, A. L., & Carroll, N. (2008). Economic status and the indigenous/non-indigenous health gap. *Economic Letters, 99*, 604–606. https://doi.org/10.1016/j.econlet.2007.10.005

Borodovsky, L. (2019, January 7). The daily shot: Women driving growth in labor force participation. *Wall Street Journal*. https://blogs.wsj.com/dailyshot/2019/01/07/the-daily-shot-women-driving-growth-in-labor-force-participation/

Bos, H. M., Knox, J. R., van Rijn-van Gelderen, L., & Gartrell, N. K. (2016). Same-sex and different-sex parent households and child health outcomes: Findings from the National Survey of Children's Health. *Journal of Developmental & Behavioral Pediatrics, 37*, 179–187. https://doi.org/10.1097/DBP.0000000000000288

Bosch, S. J., & Gharaveis, A. (2017). Flying solo: A review of the literature on wayfinding for older adults experiencing visual or cognitive decline. *Applied Ergonomics, 58*, 327–333. https://doi.org/10.1016/j.apergo.2016.07.010

Boss, P. (2010). The trauma and complicated grief of ambiguous loss. *Pastoral Psychology, 59*, 137–145. https://doi.org/10.1007/s11089-009-0264-0

Boss, P. (2015). Coping with the suffering of ambiguous loss. In R. E. Anderson (Ed.), *World suffering and quality of life* (pp. 125–134). New York: Springer. https://doi.org/10.1007/978-94-017-9670-5_10

Boswell, J., Thai, J., & Brown, C. (2015). Older adults' sleep. In A. Green & C. Brown (Eds.), *An occupational therapist's guide to sleep and sleep problems* (pp. 185–206). Jessica Kingsley Publishers.

Botwinick, J. (1977). Intellectual abilities. In J. E. Birren & K. W. Schaie (Eds.), *Handbook of the psychology of aging* (pp. 580–605). Van Nostrand Reinhold.

Bouazzaoui, B., Follenfant, A., Ric, F., Fay, S., Croizet, J.-C., Atzeni, T. et al. (2016). Aging-related stereotypes in memory: When the beliefs come true. *Memory, 24*, 659–668. https://doi.org/10.1080/09658211.2015.1040802

Bourgeois, M. S., Camp, C., Rose, R., White, B., Malone, M., Carr, J., & Rovine, M. (2003). A comparison of training strategies to enhance use of external aids by persons with dementia. *Journal of Communication Disorders, 36*, 361–378. https://doi.org/10.1016/S0021-9924(03)00051-0

Bourke, P., & Styles, E. (2017). *The psychology of attention* (3rd ed.). New York: Psychology Press.

Bower, K. L., Lewis, D. C., Bermúdez, J. M., & Singh, A. A. (2021). Narratives of generativity and resilience among LGBT older adults: Leaving positive legacies despite social stigma and collective trauma. *Journal of Homosexuality, 68*, 231–251. https://doi.org/10.1080/00918369.2019.1648082

Bowlus, A. J., Mori, H., & Robinson, C. (2016). Ageing and the skill portfolio: Evidence from job based skill measures. *Journal of the Economics of Ageing, 7*, 89–103. https://doi.org/10.1016/j.jeoa.2016.02.003

Bows, H. (2018). Sexual violence against older people: A review of the empirical literature. *Trauma, Violence, & Abuse, 19*, 567–583. https://doi.org/10.1177/1524838016683455

Boyczuk, A. M., & Fletcher, P. C. (2016). The ebbs and flows: Stresses of sandwich generation caregivers. *Journal of Adult Development, 23*, 51–61. https://doi.org/10.1007/s10804-015-9221-6

Boyden, J. Y., Ersek, M., Deatrick, J. A., Widger, K., LaRagione, G., Lord, B., & Feudtner, C. (2021). What do parents value regarding pediatric palliative and hospice care in the home setting? *Journal of Pain and Symptom Management, 61*, 12–23. https://doi.org/10.1016/j.jpainsymman.2020.07.024

Boyle, P. J., Feng, Z., & Raab, G. M. (2011). Does widowhood increase mortality risk? Testing for selection effects by comparing causes of spousal death. *Epidemiology, 22*, 1–5. https://doi.org/10.1097/EDE.0b013e3181fdcc0b

Boywitt, C. D., Kuhlmann, B. G., & Meiser, T. (2012). The role of source memory in older adults' recollective experience. *Psychology and Aging, 27*, 484–497. https://doi.org/10.1037/a0024729

Bozzon, R., & Murgia, A. (2021). Work-family conflict in Europe: A focus on the heterogeneity of self-employment. *Community, Work & Family, 24*, 93–113. https://doi.org/10.1080/13668803.2020.1809995

Brambilla, M., Dinkelbach, L., Bigler, A., Williams, J., Zokaei, N., Kadosh, R. C., & Brem, A.-K. (2021). The effect of transcranial random noise stimulation on cognitive training outcome in healthy aging. *Frontiers in Neurology, 12*, 268. https://doi.org/10.3389/fneur.2021.625359

Brandburg, G. L., Symes, L., Mastel-Smith, B., Hersch, G., & Walsh, T. (2013). Resident strategies for making a life in a nursing home: A qualitative study. *Journal of Advanced Nursing, 69*, 862–874. https://doi.org/10.1111/j.1365-2648.2012.06075.x

Brandt, A. (2021). Defining creativity: A view from the arts. *Creativity Research Journal, 33*, 81–95. https://doi.org/10.1080/10400419.2020.1855905

Brandtstädter, J. (1997). Action culture and development: Points of convergence. *Culture and Psychology, 3*, 335–352. https://doi.org/10.1177/1354067X9733007

Brandtstädter, J. (1999). Sources of resilience in the aging self. In T. M. Hess & F. Blanchard-Fields (Eds.), *Social cognition and aging* (pp. 123–141). Academic Press.

Brannon, L., Updegraff, J. A., & Feist, J. (2022). *Health psychology: An introduction to behavior and health* (10th ed.). Cengage.

Brassington, I. (2020). What passive euthanasia is. *BMC Medical Ethics, 21*, 41. https://doi.org/10.1186/s12910-020-00481-7

Braver, S. L., & Lamb, M. E. (2013). Marital dissolution. In G. W. Peterson & K. R. Bush (Eds.), *Handbook of marriage and the family* (3rd ed., pp. 487–516). Springer.

Bray, N. W., Pieruccini-Faria, F., Bartha, R., Doherty, T. J., Nagamatsu, L. S., & Montero-Odasso, M. (2021). The effect of physical exercise on functional brain network connectivity in older adults with and without cognitive impairment. A systematic review. *Mechanisms of Ageing and Development, 196*, 111493. https://doi.org/10.1016/j.mad.2021.111493

BreastCancer.org. (2021). *Genetics*. https://www.breastcancer.org/risk/factors/genetics

Brehmer, Y., Shing, Y. L., Heekeren, H. R., Lindenberger, U., & Bäckman, L. (2016). Training-induced changes in subsequent-memory effects: No major differences among children, younger adults, and older adults. *NeuroImage, 131*, 214–225. https://doi.org/10.1016/j.neuroimage.2015.11.074

Brennan, A. A., & Enns, J. T. (2015). When two heads are better than one: Interactive versus independent benefits of collaborative cognition. *Psychonomic Bulletin & Review, 22*, 1076–1082. https://doi.org/10.3758/s13423-014-0765-4

Brett, C. E., Gow, A. J., Corley, J., Pattie, A., Starr, J. M., & Deary, I. J. (2012). Psychosocial factors and health as determinants of quality of life in community-dwelling older adults. *Quality of Life Research, 21*, 505–516. https://doi.org/10.1007/s11136-011-9951-2

Brody, J. E. (2018). The brain fog of menopause can burn off. *New York Times, December 18*, D5.

Brooks, D., Hulst, H. E., de Bruin, L., Glas, G., Geurts, J. J. G., & Douw, L. (2020). The multilayer network approach in the study of personality neuroscience. *Brain Sciences, 10*, 915. https://doi.org/10.3390/brainsci10120915

Brown, J. E. (2020). *Nutrition through the life cycle* (7th ed.). Boston: Cengage Learning.

Brown, K. E., Kim, J., Stewart, T., Fulton, E., & McCarrey, A. C. (2021). Positive, but not negative, self-perceptions of aging predict cognitive function among older adults. *The International Journal of Aging and Human Development, 93*, 543–561. https://doi.org/10.1177/0091415020917681

Brown, R. T., Diaz-Ramirez, L. G., Boscardin, W. J., Cappola, A. R., Lee, S. J., & Steinman, M. A. (2022). Changes in the hierarchy of functional impairment from middle age to older age. *Journals of Gerontology: Medical Sciences, 77*, 1577-1584. https://doi.org/10.1093/gerona/glab250

Brown, S. D., & Lent, R. W. (2016). Vocational psychology: Agency, equity, and well-being. *Annual Review of Psychology, 67*, 541–565. https://doi.org/10.1146/annurev-psych-122414-033237

Brunec, I. K., Robin, J., Olsen, R. K., Moscovitch, M., & Barense, M. D. (2020). Integration and differentiation of hippocampal memory traces. *Neuroscience & Biobehavioral Reviews, 118*, 196–208. https://doi.org/10.1016/j.neubiorev.2020.07.024

Bryant, B. E., Jordan, A., & Clark, U. S. (2022). Race as a social construct in psychiatry research and practice. *JAMA Psychiatry, 79*, 93–94. https://doi.org/10.1001/jamapsychiatry.2021.2877

Brysiewicz, P. (2008). The lived experience of losing a loved one to a sudden death in KwaZulu-Natal, South Africa. *Journal of Clinical Nursing, 17*, 224–231. https://doi.org/10.1111/j.1365-2702.2007.01972.x

Buchanan, A., & Rotkirch, A. (2021). The role of brothers and sisters in changing times. In A. Buchanan, & A. Rotkirch (Eds.), *Brothers and sisters* (pp. 3–21). Palgrave Macmillan, Cham. https://doi.org/10.1007/978-3-030-55985-4_1

Buchtel, E. E. (2020). The joy of obligation: Human cultural worldviews can enhance the rewards of meeting obligations. *Behavioral and Brain Sciences, 43*, e63. https://doi.org/10.1017/S0140525X19002607

Buchtel, E. E., Guan, Y., & Wang, N. (2017). *Chinese prototypes of moral character: Comparison and cognitive consequences of lay prototypes of moral character in Hong Kong and Beijing*. Unpublished manuscript, The Education University of Hong Kong.

Buchtel, E. E., Guan, Y., Peng, Q., Su, Y., Sang, B., Chen, S. X., & Bond, M. H. (2015). Immorality East and West: Are immoral behaviors especially harmful, or especially uncivilized? *Personality and Social Psychology Bulletin, 41*, 1382–1394. https://doi.org/10.1177/0146167215595606

Budgeon, S. (2016). The 'problem' with single women: Choice, accountability and social change. *Journal of Social and Personal Relationships, 33*, 401–418. https://doi.org/10.1177/0265407515607647

Buhl, H. (2008). Development of a model describing individuated adult child–parent relationships. *International Journal of Behavioral Development, 32*, 381–389. https://doi.org/10.1177/0165025408093656

Bui, E., Mauro, C., Robinaugh, D. J., Skritskaya, N. A., Wang, Y., Gribbin, C. et al. (2015). The Structured Clinical Interview for Complicated Grief: Reliability, validity, and explanatory factor analysis. *Depression and Anxiety, 32*, 485–492. https://doi.org/10.1002/da.22385

Bureau of Justice Statistics. (2020). *Criminal victimization, 2019*. https://www.bjs.gov/content/pub/pdf/cv19.pdf

Bureau of Labor Statistics. (2021a). *Unemployment rates by age, sex, race, and Hispanic or Latino ethnicity*. https://www.bls.gov/web/empsit/cpsee_e16.htm

Bureau of Labor Statistics. (2021b). *Families by presence and relationship of employed members and family type, 2019–2020 annual averages*. https://www.bls.gov/news.release/famee.t02.htm

Bureau of Labor Statistics. (2021c). *Employment status of the population by sex, marital status, and presence and age of own children under 18, 2019–2020 annual averages*. https://www.bls.gov/news.release/famee.t05.htm

Burgio, L., Stevens, A. Guy, D., Roth, D. L., & Haley, W. E. (2003). Impact of two psychosocial interventions on white and African American family caregivers of individuals with dementia. *The Gerontologist, 43*, 568–579. https://doi.org/10.1093/geront/43.4.568

Burke, B. L., Martens, A., & Faucher, E. H. (2010). Two decades of terror management theory: A meta-analysis of mortality salience research. *Personality and Social Psychology Review, 14*, 155–195. https://doi.org/10.1177/1088868309352321

Burnette, D. (1999). Social relationships of Latino grandparent caregivers: A role theory perspective. *The Gerontologist, 39*, 49–58. https://doi.org/10.1093/geront/39.1.49

Burzynska, A. Z., Voss, M. W., Fanning, J., Salerno, E. A., Gothe, N. P., McAuley, E., & Kramer, A. F. (2020). Sensor-measured sedentariness and physical activity are differentially related to fluid and crystallized abilities in aging. *Psychology and Aging, 35*, 1154–1169. https://doi.org/10.1037/pag0000580

Buss, D. (2016). *Evolutionary psychology: The new science of the mind* (5th ed.). Routledge.

Bustos, M. L. C. (2007). La muerte en la cultura occidental: Antropología de la muerte [Death in Western culture: Anthropology of death]. *Revista Colombiana de Psiquiatría, 36*, 332–339. https://www.redalyc.org/articulo.oa?id=80636212

Cabeza, R. (2002). Hemispheric asymmetry reduction in older adults: The HAROLD model. *Psychology and Aging, 17*, 85–100. https://doi.org/10.1037/0882-7974.17.1.85

Cabeza, R., & Dennis N. A. (2013). Frontal lobes and aging: Deterioration and compensation. In D. T. Stuss & R. T. Knight (Eds.), *Principles of frontal lobe function* (2nd ed., pp. 628–652). Oxford University Press.

Cabeza, R., Albert, M., Belleville, S., Craik, F. I. M., Duarte, A., Grady, C. L., & Rugg, M. D. (2018). Maintenance, reserve and compensation: The cognitive neuroscience of healthy ageing. *Nature Reviews Neuroscience, 19*, 701–710. https://doi.org/10.1038/s41583-018-0068-2

Cacciatore, J., & DeFrain, J. (2015). *The world of bereavement*. Springer.

Cacioppo, S., & Cacioppo, J. T. (2013). Lust for life. *Scientific American Mind, 24*(5), 56–63.

Cacioppo, S., & Cacioppo, J. T. (2020). *Introduction to social neuroscience*. Princeton University Press.

Cahill, E., Lewis, L. M., Barg, F. K., & Bogner, H. R. (2009). "You don't want to burden them": Older adults' views on family involvement in care. *Journal of Family Nursing, 27*, 295–317. https://doi.org/10.1177/1074840709337247

Cahill, K. E., & Quinn, J. F. (2020). The retirement income security outlook for older workers: Causes for concern and reasons for optimism. In S. Czaja, J. Sharit, & J. James (Eds.), *Current and emerging trends in aging and work* (pp. 121–140). Springer, Cham. https://doi.org/10.1007/978-3-030-24135-3_7

Calamia, M., Reese-Melancon, C., Cherry, K. E., Hawley, K. S., & Jazwinski, S. M. (2016). The Knowledge of Memory Aging Questionnaire: Factor structure and correlates in a lifespan sample. *Yale Journal of Biology and Medicine, 89*, 91–96. https://www.ncbi.nlm.nih.gov/pubmed/27505021

Camara, C., & Rosengarten, L. (2021). Faith-sensitive end of life care for children, young people and their families. *British Journal of Nursing, 30*, 276–279. https://doi.org/10.12968/bjon.2021.30.5.276

Camberis, A. L., McMahon, C. A., Gibson, F. L., & Bolvin, J. (2016). Maternal age, psychological maturity, parenting cognitions, and mother–infant interaction. *Infancy, 21*, 396–422. https://doi.org/10.1111/infa.12116

Campbell, K., & Kaufman, J. (2017). Do you pursue your heart or your art? Creativity, personality, and love. *Journal of Family Issues, 38*, 287–311. https://doi.org/10.1177/0192513X15570318

Campbell, K. L., & Hasher, L. (2018). Hyper-binding only apparent under fully implicit test conditions. *Psychology and Aging, 33*, 176–181. https://doi.org/10.1037/pag0000216

Campbell, K. L., Samu, D., Davis, S. W., Geerlings, L., Mustafa, A., Tyler, L. K., & Cambridge Centre for Aging and Neuroscience. (2016). Robust resilience of the frontotemporal syntax system to aging. *The Journal of Neuroscience, 36*, 5214–5227. https://doi.org/10.1523/JNEUROSCI.4561-15.2016

Camp, C. J. (1999). Memory interventions for normal and pathological older adults. In R. Schulz, M. P. Lawton, & G. Maddox (Eds.), *Annual review of gerontology and geriatrics* (Vol. 18, pp. 155–189). Springer.

Camp, C. J. (2001). From efficacy to effectiveness to diffusion: Making transitions in dementia intervention research. *Neuropsychological Rehabilitation, 11*, 495–517. https://doi.org/10.1080/09602010042000079

Camp, C. J. (2005). Spaced retrieval: A model for dissemination of a cognitive intervention for persons with dementia. In D. K. Attix & K. A. Velsh-Bohmer (Eds.), *Geriatric neuropsychology: Assessment and intervention* (pp. 275–292). Guilford Press.

Camp, C. J., Antenucci, V., Brush, J., & Slominski, T. (2012). Using spaced retrieval to effectively treat dysphagia in clients with dementia. *Perspectives on Swallowing and Swallowing Disorders (Dysphagia), 21*, 96–104. https://doi.org/10.1044/sasd21.3.96

Camp, C. J., Foss, J. W., Stevens, A. B., Reichard, C. C., McKitrick, L. A., & O'Hanlon, A. M. (1993). Memory training in normal and demented elderly populations: The E-I-E-I-O model. *Experimental Aging Research, 19*, 277–290. https://doi.org/10.1080/03610739308253938

Camp, C. J., Zeisel, J., & Antenucci, V. (2011). Implementing the "I'm Still Here"™ approach: Montessori-based methods for engaging persons with dementia. In P. E. Hartman-Stein & A. LaRue (Eds.), *Enhancing cognitive fitness in adults* (pp. 401–417). Springer.

Campinha-Bacote, J. (2010). A culturally conscious model of mentoring. *Nurse Educator, 35*, 130–135. https://doi.org/10.1097/NNE.0b013e3181d950bf

Campos-Magdaleno, M., Leiva, D., Pereiro, A. X., Lojo-Seoane, C., Mallo, S. C., Nieto-Vieites, A., Juncos-Rabadán, O., & Facal D. (2020, March 13). Longitudinal patterns of the tip-of-the-tongue phenomenon in people with subjective cognitive complaints and mild cognitive impairment. *Frontiers in Psychology*. https://doi.org/10.3389/fpsyg.2020.00425

Cancer Council of Australia. (2021). *Preventing skin cancer: How to protect your skin from the sun*. https://www.cancer.org.au/cancer-information/causes-and-prevention/sun-safety/preventing-skin-cancer

Cândea, D. M., Cotet, C. D., Stefan, S., Valenas, S. P., & Szentagotai-Tatar, A. (2015). Computerized training for working memory in older adults: A review. *Transylvanian Journal of Psychology, 16*, 141–161.

Candore, G., & Caruso, C. (2021). Aging and longevity: An evolutionary approach. In G. Candore & C. Caruso (Eds.), *Human aging: From cellular mechanisms to therapeutic strategies* (pp. 1–12). Academic Press. https://doi.org/10.1016/C2019-0-04856-X

Candrian, C., & Cloyes., K. G. (2021). "She's dying and I can't say we're married?": End-of-life care for LGBT older adults. *The Gerontologist, 61*, 1197–1201. https://doi.org/10.1093/geront/gnaa186

Cantarella, A., Borella, E., Carretti, B., Kliegel, M., & de Beni, R. (2017). Benefits in tasks related to everyday life competencies after a working memory training in older adults. *International Journal of Geriatric Psychiatry, 32*, 86–93. https://doi.org/10.1002/gps.4448

Cantor, N. (1990). From thought to behavior: "Having" and "doing" in the study of personality and cognition. *American Psychologist, 45*, 735–750. https://doi.org/10.1037/0003-066X.45.6.735

Capistrant, B. D., Kline Pruett, M., Rivera, S., Gilette, P., Cowan, C. P., & Cowan, P. A. (2020). Earner status, marital satisfaction, and division of childcare among Mexican American and Caucasian couples. *Smith College Studies in Social Work, 90*, 156–180. https://doi.org/10.1080/00377317.2020.1715750

Captari, L. E., Riggs, S. A., & Stephen, K. (2021). Attachment processes following traumatic loss: A mediation model examining identity distress, shattered assumptions, prolonged grief, and posttraumatic growth. *Psychological Trauma: Theory, Research, Practice, and Policy, 13*, 94–103. https://doi.org/10.1037/tra0000555

Cardoso, J., Apagueno, B., Lysne, P., Hoyos, L., Porges, E., Riley, J. L., Fillingim, R. B., Woods, A. J., Cohen, R., & Cruz-Almeida, Y. (2021). Pain and the Montreal Cognitive Assessment (MoCA) in aging, *Pain Medicine, 22*, 1776–1783. https://doi.org/10.1093/pm/pnab003

Carlo, G., Koller, S., Raffaelli, M., & de Guzman, M. R. T. (2007). Culture-related strengths among Latin American families: A case study of Brazil. *Marriage & Family Review, 41*, 335–360. https://doi.org/10.1300/J002v41n03_06

Carnelley, K., & Ruscher, J. B. (2000). Adult attachment and exploratory behavior in leisure. *Journal of Social Behavior and Personality, 15*, 153–165. https://www.proquest.com/docview/1292246523?pq-origsite=gscholar&fromopenview=true&imgSeq=1

Carney, K. O. (2016). Capacity assessments. In S. K. Whitbourne (Ed.), *The encyclopedia of adulthood and aging* (pp. 141–145). Wiley-Blackwell.

Carpenter, B. D., Gatz, M., & Smyer, M. A. (2022). Mental health and aging in the 2020s. *American Psychologist, 77*, 538–550. https://doi.org/10.1037/amp0000873

Carr, A., & McNulty, M. (2016). Cognitive behaviour therapy. In A. Carr & M. McNulty (Eds.), *The handbook of adult clinical psychology* (2nd ed.). Routledge.

Carr, D. (2004). Gender, preloss marital dependence, and older adults' adjustment to widowhood. *Journal of Marriage and Family, 66*, 220–235. https://doi.org/10.1111/j.0022-2445.2004.00016.x

Carr, D., & Mooney, H. (2021). Bereavement in later life. In K. F. Ferraro & D. Carr (Eds.), *Handbook of aging and the social sciences* (9th ed., pp. 239–254). Academic Press. https://doi.org/10.1016/B978-0-12-815970-5.00015-2

Carstensen, L. L. (2006). The influence of a sense of time on human development. *Science, 312*, 1913–1915. https://doi.org/10.1126/science.1127488

Carstensen, L. L. (2021). Socioemotional selectivity theory: The role of perceived endings in human motivation. *The Gerontologist, 61*, 1188–1196. https://doi.org/10.1093/geront/gnab116

Carstensen, L. L., & Freund, A. M. (1994). The resilience of the aging self. *Developmental Review, 14*, 81–92. https://doi.org/10.1006/drev.1994.1004

Carstensen, L. L., & Fried, L. P. (2012). The meaning of old age. In J. Beard, S. Biggs, D. Bloom, L. Fried, P. Hogan, A., Kalache, & S. J. Olshansky (Eds.), *Global population ageing: Peril or promise?* (pp. 15–17). Harvard University Program on the Global Demography of Aging.

Carstensen, L. L., & Mikels, J. A. (2005). At the intersection of emotion and cognition: Aging and the positivity effect. *Current Directions in Psychological Science, 14*, 117–121. https://doi.org/10.1111/j.0963-7214.2005.00348

Carstensen, L. L., Mikels, J. A., & Mather, M. (2006). Aging and the intersection of cognition, motivation, and emotion. In J. E. Birren & K. W. Schaie (Eds.), *Handbook of the psychology of aging* (6th ed., pp. 343–362). Elsevier.

Carstensen, L. L., Shavit, Y. Z., & Barnes, J. T. (2020). Age advantages in emotional experience persist even under threat from the COVID-19 pandemic. *Psychological Science, 31*, 1374–1385. https://doi.org/10.1177%2F0956797620967261

Caruso, C., & Puca, A. A. (2021). Special issue "Centenarians—A model to study the molecular basis of lifespan and healthspan." *International Journal of Molecular Sciences, 22*, 2044. https://doi.org/10.3390/ijms22042044

Casey, E., & O'Brien, D. (2020). Sociology, *Sociology* and the cultural and creative industries. *Sociology, 54*, 443–459. https://doi.org/10.1177/0038038520904712

Casey, V. A., Dwyer, J. T., Coleman, K. A., Krall, E. A., Gardner, J., & Valadian, I. (1991). Accuracy of recall by middle-aged participants in a longitudinal study of their body size and indices of maturation earlier in life. *Annals of Human Biology, 18*, 155–166. https://doi.org/10.1080/03014469100001492

Casper, W. J., Marquardt, D. J., Roberto, K. J., & Buss, C. (2016). The hidden family lives of single adults without dependent children. In T. D. Allen & L. T. Eby (Eds.), *The Oxford handbook of work and family* (pp. 182–195). Oxford University Press.

Castañeda-García, P. J., Valle-Sanz, C., & Gutiérrez-Barroso, J. (2017). From grandparenthood to great-grandparenthood: Exploring a family role. *Anuario de Psicología, 47*, 115–122. https://doi.org/10.1016/j.anpsic.2018.01.003

Castro, M., & Smith, G. E. (2015). Mild cognitive impairment and Alzheimer's disease. In P. A. Lichtenberg, B. T. Mast, B. D. Carpenter, & J. Loebach Wetherell (Eds.), *APA handbook of clinical geropsychology, Vol. 2: Assessment, treatment, and issues of later life* (pp. 173–207). American Psychological Association.

Cavallaro, F., Seilhamer, M. F., Chee, Y. T. F., & Ng, B. C. (2016). Overaccommodation in a Singapore eldercare facility. *Journal of Multilingual and Multicultural Development, 37*, 817–831. https://doi.org/10.1080/01434632.2016.1142553

Cavallini, E., Bottiroli, S., Fastame, M. C., & Hertzog, C. (2013). Age and subcultural differences on personal and general beliefs about memory. *Journal of Aging Studies, 27*, 71–81. https://doi.org/10.1016/j.jaging.2012.11.002

Cavanaugh, C. K., & Cavanaugh, J. C. (2018). The importance of executive coaching for academic administrators. *Journal of Higher Education Management, 33*, 22–31. https://aaua.org/wp-content/uploads/2019/03/JHEM_2018_33-1.pdf#page=28

Cavanaugh, J. C. (1996). Memory self-efficacy as a key to understanding memory change. In F. Blanchard-Fields & T. M. Hess (Eds.), *Perspectives on cognitive changes in adulthood and aging* (pp. 488–507). McGraw-Hill.

Cavanaugh, J. C. (1999a). Caregiving to adults: A life event challenge. In I. H. Nordhus, G. R. VandenBos, S. Berg, & P. Fromholt (Eds.), *Clinical geropsychology* (pp. 131–135). American Psychological Association.

Cavanaugh, J. C. (1999b). Theories of aging in the biological, behavioral, and social sciences. In J. C. Cavanaugh & S. K. Whitbourne (Eds.), *Gerontology: Interdisciplinary perspectives* (pp. 1–32). New York: Oxford University Press.

Cavanaugh, J. C. (2017). Spirituality as a framework for confronting life's existential questions. In J. D. Sinnott (Ed.), *Identity flexibility during adulthood: Perspectives on adult development* (pp. 115–127). Springer. https://doi.org/10.1007/978-3-319-55658-1_7

Cavanaugh, J. C., & Cavanaugh, C. K. (2021). Understanding polarization through a cognitive-developmental lens. In J. D. Sinnott & J. S. Rabin (Eds.), *The psychology of political behavior in a time of change: Identity in a changing world* (pp. 195–214). Springer Cham. https://doi.org/10.1007/978-3-030-38270-4_7.

Cavanaugh, J. C., & Green, E. E. (1990). I believe, therefore I can: Self-efficacy beliefs in memory aging. In E. A. Lovelace (Ed.), *Aging and cognition: Mental processes, self-awareness, and interventions* (pp. 189–230). North-Holland.

Cavanaugh, J. C., & Kinney, J. M. (1994, July). *Marital satisfaction as an important contextual factor in spousal caregiving*. Paper presented at the 7th International Conference on Personal Relationships, Groningen, The Netherlands.

Ceci, S. J., & Williams, W. M. (2018). Who decides what is acceptable speech on campus? Why restricting free speech is not the answer. *Perspectives on Psychological Science, 13*, 299–323. https://doi.org/10.1177/1745691618767324

Cederholm, T., & Barazzoni, R. (2021). A year with the GLIM diagnosis of malnutrition–Does it work for older persons? *Current Opinion in Clinical Nutrition and Metabolic Care, 24*, 4–9. https://doi.org/10.1097/MCO.0000000000000710

Cederholm, T., Jensen, G. L., Correia, M. I. T. D., Gonzalez, M. C., Fukushima, R., Higashiguchi, T., Baptista, G., Barazzoni, R., Blaauw, R., Coats, A. J. S., Crivelli, A. N., Evans, D. C., Gramlich, L., Fuchs-Tarlovsky, V., Keller, H., Llido, L., Malone, A., Mogensen, K. M., Morley, J. E., Muscaritoli, M., et al. (2019). GLIM criteria for the diagnosis of malnutrition—A consensus report from the global clinical nutrition community. *Journal Cachexia, Sarcopenia and Muscle, 10*, 207–217. https://doi.org/10.1002/jcsm.12383

Cedillo-Barrón, L., García-Cordero, J., Mendoza-Ramírez, N. J., & Martínez-Frías, S. P. (2022). Overview of the immune response against SARS-CoV-2. In S. Rosales-Mendoza, M. Comas-Garcia, & O. Gonzalez-Ortega (Eds.), *Biomedical innovations to combat COVID-19* (pp. 95–113). Academic Press. https://doi.org/10.1016/B978-0-323-90248-9.00004-8

Çelik, K. (2018). Unmarried women with closed "windows of opportunity": Professional women's reasons for not getting married. *Women's Studies International Forum, 66*, 48–55. https://doi.org/10.1016/j.wsif.2017.11.012

Census Bureau. (2020a). *America's families and living arrangements: 2020*. https://www2.census.gov/programs-surveys/demo/tables/families/2020/cps-2020/tabal-all.xls

Census Bureau. (2020b). *Historic marital status tables*. https://www.census.gov/content/dam/Census

/library/visualizations/time-series/demo/families-and-households/ms-2.pdf

Census Bureau. (2020c). *U.S. marriage and divorce rates by state: 2008 & 2018*. https://www.census.gov/library/visualizations/interactive/marriage-divorce-rates-by-state.html

Census Bureau. (2020d). *Demographic turning points for the United States: Population projections for 2020 to 2060*. https://www.census.gov/library/publications/2020/demo/p25-1144.html

Census Bureau. (2020e). *National demographic analysis tables: 2020*. https://www.census.gov/data/tables/2020/demo/popest/2020-demographic-analysis-tables.html

Census Bureau. (2021). *Educational attainment in the United States: 2019*. https://www.census.gov/content/census/en/data/tables/2019/demo/educational-attainment/cps-detailed-tables.html

Center on Budget and Policy Priorities. (2022). *A quick guide to SNAP eligibility and benefits*. https://www.cbpp.org/research/food-assistance/a-quick-guide-to-snap-eligibility-and-benefits

Center to Advance Palliative Care. (2021). *Saying goodbye to a dying family member over the phone: Conversation script*. https://www.capc.org/covid-19/saying-goodbye-dying-family-member-over-phone-conversation-script/

Centers for Disease Control and Prevention. (2020). *National diabetes statistical report, 2020: Estimates of diabetes and its burden in the United States*. https://www.cdc.gov/diabetes/data/statistics-report/

Centers for Disease Control and Prevention. (2021a). *Stroke*. https://www.cdc.gov/stroke/facts.htm

Centers for Disease Control and Prevention. (2021b). *STEADI: Stopping Elderly Accidents, Deaths, & Injuries*. https://www.cdc.gov/steadi/index.html

Centers for Disease Control and Prevention. (2021c). *HIV and older Americans*. https://www.cdc.gov/hiv/group/age/olderamericans/index.html

Centers for Disease Control and Prevention. (2021d). *Different types of flu vaccine*. https://www.cdc.gov/flu/prevent/different-flu-vaccines.htm

Centers for Disease Control and Prevention. (2021e). *Pneumococcal vaccines*. https://www.hhs.gov/immunization/diseases/pneumonia/index.html

Centers for Disease Control and Prevention. (2021f). *Traumatic brain injury and concussion*. https://www.cdc.gov/traumaticbraininjury/data/index.html

Centers for Disease Control and Prevention. (2021g). *HIV surveillance report, 2018 (Updated)*. https://www.cdc.gov/hiv/library/reports/hiv-surveillance/vol-32/index.html

Centers for Disease Control and Prevention. (2021h). *Intimate partner violence*. https://www.cdc.gov/violenceprevention/intimatepartnerviolence/index.html

Centers for Disease Control and Prevention. (2022a). *Laboratory-confirmed COVID-19-associated hospitalizations*. https://gis.cdc.gov/grasp/covidnet/covid19_5.html

Centers for Disease Control and Prevention. (2022b). *Rates of COVID-19-associated hospitalizations by vaccination and additional or booster dose status*. https://covid.cdc.gov/covid-data-tracker/#covidnet-hospitalizations-vaccination

Centers for Disease Control and Prevention. (2022c). *National diabetes statistics report*. https://www.cdc.gov/diabetes/data/statistics-report/index.html?CDC_AA_refVal=https%3A%2F%2Fwww.cdc.gov%2Fdiabetes%2Fdata%2Fstatistics%2Fstatistics-report.html

Centers for Disease Control and Prevention. (2022d). *Births and natality*. https://www.cdc.gov/nchs/fastats/births.htm

Centers for Disease Control and Prevention. (2022e). *Risk for COVID-19 infection, hospitalization, and death by race/ethnicity*. https://www.cdc.gov/coronavirus/2019-ncov/covid-data/investigations-discovery/hospitalization-death-by-race-ethnicity.html

Centers for Medicare and Medicaid Services. (2016). *Nursing home data compendium 2015*. https://www.cms.gov/Medicare/Provider-Enrollment-and-Certification/CertificationandComplianc/Downloads/nursinghomedatacompendium_508-2015.pdf

Centers for Medicare and Medicaid Services. (2020). *Advance care planning*. https://www.cms.gov/Outreach-and-Education/Medicare-Learning-Network-MLN/MLNProducts/Downloads/AdvanceCarePlanning.pdf

Centers for Medicare and Medicaid Services. (2021a). *Five-Star Quality Rating System*. https://www.cms.gov/medicare/provider-enrollment-and-certification/certificationandcomplianc/fsqrs

Centers for Medicare and Medicaid Services. (2021b). *Original Medicare (Part A and B) eligibility and enrollment*. https://www.cms.gov/Medicare/Eligibility-and-Enrollment/OrigMedicarePartABEligEnrol

Centers for Medicare and Medicaid Services. (2021c). 2021 Annual report of the boards of trustees of the federal hospital insurance and federal supplementary medical insurance trust funds. https://www.cms.gov/files/document/2021-medicare-trustees-report.pdf

Centers for Medicare and Medicaid Services. (2022). *CMS fast facts*. https://www.cms.gov/Research-Statistics-Data-and-Systems/Statistics-Trends-and-Reports/CMS-Fast-Facts/Downloads/CMS_Fast_Facts.zip

Cerulo, K. A., Leschziner, V., & Shepherd, H. (2021). Rethinking culture and cognition. *Annual Review of Sociology, 47*, 63–85. https://doi.org/10.1146/annurev-soc-072320-095202

Cha, A. E. (2022, March 27). How covid brain fog may overlap with "chemo brain" and Alzheimer's. *Washington Post*. https://www.washingtonpost.com/health/2022/03/27/covid-brain-fog-chemo-brain-alzheimers-disease/

Cha, H.-E., & Papastefanou, G. (2020). Understanding the time pressure of working parents: How parents' childcare time impacts the diurnal organization of activities and the sense of feeling rushed. *Journal of Comparative Family Studies, 51*, 110–130. https://doi.org/10.3138/jcfs.51.1.006

Chai, H. W., Zarit, S. H., & Fingerman, K. L. (2020). Revisiting intergenerational contact and relationship quality in later life: Parental characteristics matter. *Research on Aging, 42*,139–149. https://doi.org/10.1177/0164027519899576

Chai, J. (2021). A model of ambition, aspiration and happiness. *European Journal of Operational Research, 288*, 692–702. https://doi.org/10.1016/j.ejor.2020.06.009

Chai, X. (2021). Exploring the politics of sensibilities that promote marriage and reproduction among young Chinese adults residing in urban areas. In A. Scribano, M. Camarena Luhrs, & A. L. Cervio (Eds.), *Cities, capitalism and the politics of sensibilities* (pp. 157–176). Palgrave Macmillan. https://doi.org/10.1007/978-3-030-58035-3_9

Chan, M. Y., Haber, S., Drew, L. M., & Park, D. C. (2016). Training older adults to use tablet computers: Does it enhance cognitive function? *The Gerontologist, 56*, 475–484. https://doi.org/10.1093/geront/gnu057

Chang, J. E. Sequeira, A., McCord, C. E., & Garney, W. R. (2016). Videoconference grief group counseling in rural Texas: Outcomes, challenges, and lessons learned. *Journal for Specialists in Group Work, 41*, 140–160. https://doi.org/10.1080/01933922.2016.114376

Charles, S. T. (2010). Strength and vulnerability integration: A model of emotional well-being across adulthood. *Psychological Bulletin, 136*, 1068–1091. https://doi.org/10.1037/a0021232

Charles, S. T., & Carstensen, L. L. (2010). Social and emotional aging. *Annual Review of Psychology, 61*, 383–409. https://doi.org/10.1146/annurev.psych.093008.100448

Charles, S. T., & Carstensen, L. L. (2020). Marriage in old age. In M. Yalom & L. L. Carstensen (Eds.), *Inside the American Couple* (pp. 236–254). University of California Press. https://doi.org/10.1525/9780520927315-016

Charles, S. T., & Luong, G. (2013). Emotional experience across adulthood: The theoretical model of Strength and Vulnerability Integration. *Current Directions in Psychological Science, 22*, 443–448. https://doi.org/10.1177/0963721413497013

Charles, S. T., Mather, M., & Carstensen, L. L. (2003). Aging and emotional memory: The forgettable nature of negative images for older adults. *Journal of Experimental Psychology: General, 132*, 310–324. https://doi.org/10.1037/0096-3445.132.2.310

Charness, N., & Bosman, E. A. (1990). Expertise and aging: Life in the lab. In T. M. Hess (Ed.), *Aging and cognition: Knowledge organization and utilization* (pp. 343–385). North-Holland.

Charras, K., Eynard, C., & Viatour, G. (2016). Use of space and human rights: Planning dementia friendly settings. *Journal of Gerontological Social Work, 59*, 181–204. https://doi.org/10.1080/01634372.2016.1171268

Chaudhari, A., Gupta, R., Makwana, K., & Kondratov, R. (2017). Circadian clocks, diets, and aging. *Nutrition and Healthy Aging, 4*, 101–112. content.iospress.com/articles/nutrition-and-healthy-aging/nha160006

Chaulagain, S., Pizam, A., Wang, Y., Severt, D., & Oetjen, R. (2021). Factors affecting seniors' decision to relocate to senior living communities. *International Journal of Hospitality Management, 95*, 102920. https://doi.org/10.1016/j.ijhm.2021.102920

Chee, F. Y. T. (2011). *Elderspeak in Singapore: A case study*. https://hdl.handle.net/10356/93631

Chee, M. W. L., Zheng, H., Goh, J. O. S., Park, D., & Sutton, B. P. (2011). Brain structure in young and old East Asians and Westerners: Comparisons of structural volume and cortical thickness. *Journal of Cognitive Neuroscience, 23*, 1065–1079. https://doi.org/10.1162/jocn.2010.21513

Chen, C., Krieger, M. L., & Sundar, S. S. (2021). Smartphones, robots, and social media: Aging with communication technologies. In K. W. Schaie & S. L. Willis (Eds.), *Handbook of the psychology of aging* (9th ed., pp. 139–153). Academic Press. https://doi.org/10.1016/B978-0-12-816094-7.00014-3

Chen, J., & Wu, Z. (2008). Gender differences in the effects of self-rated health status on mortality among the oldest old in China. In Z. Yi, D. L. Poston, Jr., D. Asbaugh Vlosky, & D. Gu (Eds.), *Healthy longevity in China* (pp. 397–441). Springer.

Chen, K.-H. and Anderson, S. (2018). Emotional function during aging. In M. Rizzo, S. Anderson, & B. Fritzsch (Eds.), *The Wiley handbook on the aging mind and brain* (pp. 417–443). Wiley. https://doi.org/10.1002/9781118772034.ch20

Chen, L.-K. (2020). Older adults and COVID-19 pandemic: Resilience matters. *Archives of Gerontology and Geriatrics, 89*, 104124. https://doi.org/10.1016/j.archger.2020.104124

Chen, Y., & Li, Y. (2022). Metabolic reprogramming and immunity in cancer. In M. M. Amiji & Milane, L. S. (Eds.), *Cancer immunology and immunotherapy: Volume 1: Delivery strategies and engineering technologies in cancer immunotherapy* (pp. 137–196). Academic Press. https://doi.org/10.1016/B978-0-12-823397-9.00006-5

Chen, Y., Peng, Y., & Fang, P. (2016). Emotional intelligence mediates the relationship between age and subjective well-being. *International Journal of Aging and Human Development, 83*, 91–107. https://doi.org/10.1177/0091415016648705

Chen, Z., Ma, Y., Hua, J., Wang, Y., & Guo, H. (2021). Impacts from economic development and environmental factors on life expectancy: A comparative study based on data from both developed and developing countries from 2004 to 2016. *International Journal of Environmental Research and Public Health, 18*, 8559. https://doi.org/10.3390/ijerph18168559

Cheng, E., & Pegg, S. (2016). "If I'm not gardening, I'm not at my happiest": Exploring the positive subjective experiences derived from serious leisure gardening by older adults. *World Leisure Journal, 58*, 285–297. https://doi.org/10.1080/16078055.2016.1228219

Cheng, S., & Powell, B. (2007). Under and beyond constraints: Resource allocation to young children from biracial families. *American Journal of Sociology, 112*, 1044–1094. https://doi.org/10.1086/508793

Cherko, M., Hickson, L., & Bhutta, M. (2016). Auditory deprivation and health in the elderly. *Maturitas, 88*, 52–57. https://doi.org/10.1016/j.marturitas.2016.03.008

Cherry, K. E., Blanchard, B., Walker, E. J., Smitherman, E. A., & Lyon, B. A. (2014). Knowledge of memory aging across the lifespan. *The Journal of Genetic Psychology: Research and Theory on Human Development, 175*, 547–553. https://doi.org/10.1080/00221325.2014.982069

Cherry, K. E., Brigman, S., Reese-Melancon, C., Burton-Chase, A., & Holland, K. (2013). Memory aging knowledge and memory self-appraisal in younger and older adults. *Educational Gerontology, 39*, 168–178. https://doi.org/10.1080/03601277.20 12.699838

Cherry, K. E., Elliott, E. M., Golob, E. J., Brown, J. S., Kim, S., & Jazwinski, S. M. (2021). Strategic encoding and retrieval processes in verbal recall among middle-aged and older adults. *British Journal of Developmental Psychology, 39*, 252–268. https://doi.org/10.1111/bjdp.12349

Chevalley, T., & Rizzoli, R. (2022). Acquisition of peak bone mass. *Best Practice & Research Clinical Endocrinology & Metabolism, 36*, 101616. https://doi.org/10.1016/j.beem.2022.101616

Chew-Graham, C. A., & Ray, M. (Eds.). (2016). *Mental health and older people: A guide for primary care practitioners*. Springer.

Chi, M. T. H. (2006). Laboratory methods for assessing experts' and novices' knowledge. In K. A. Ericsson, N. Charness, P. J. Feltovich, & R. R. Hoffman (Eds.), *The Cambridge handbook of expertise and expert performance* (pp. 167–184). Cambridge University Press.

Chiao, C.-Y., Wu, H.-S., & Hsiao, C.-Y. (2015). Caregiver burden for informal caregivers of patients with dementia: A systematic review. *International Nursing Review, 62*, 340–350. https://doi.org/10.1111/inr.12194

Chipperfield, J. G., Perry, R. P., Pekrun, R., Barchfield, P., Lang, F. R., & Hamm, J. M. (2016). The paradoxical role of perceived control in late life health behavior. *PloS one*. https://doi.org/10.1371/journal.pone.0148921.

Chisholm-Burns, M. A., Schwinghammer, T. L., Malone, P. M., Kolesar, J. M., & Bookstaver, P. B. (2019). *Pharmacotherapy principles and practice* (5th ed.). McGraw-Hill Education.

Chmielewski, P. P. (2020). Human ageing as a dynamic, emergent and malleable process: From disease-oriented to health-oriented approaches. *Biogerontology, 21*, 125–130. https://doi.org/10.1007/s10522-019-09839-w

Choi, H. S., & Feng, J. (2016). General slowing hypothesis. In S. K. Whitbourne (Ed.), *The encyclopedia of adulthood and aging* (Vol. 2, pp. 556–559). Wiley. https://doi.org/10.1002/9781118521373.wbeaa198

Choi, H. S., Johnson, B., & Kriewitz, K. (2013). Benefits of inclusion and segregation for individuals with disabilities in leisure. *International Journal on Disability and Human Development, 12*, 15–23. https://doi.org/10.1515/ijdhd-2012-0120

Choi, M., Sprang, G., & Eslinger, J. G. (2016). Grandparents raising grandchildren: A synthetic review and theoretical model for interventions. *Family & Community Health, 39*, 120–128. https://doi.org/10.1097/0000000000000097

Choi, Y. J. (2020). Age-friendly features in home and community and the self-reported health and functional limitation of older adults: The role of supportive environments. *Journal of Urban Health, 97*, 471–485. https://doi.org/10.1007/s11524-020-00462-6

Chonody, J. M. (2015). Addressing ageism in students: A systematic review of the pedagogical intervention literature. *Educational Gerontology, 41*, 859–887. https://doi.org/10.1080/03601277.2015.1059139

Chonody, J. M., Killian, M., Gabb, J., & Dunk-West, P. (2020). Relationship quality and sexuality: A latent profile analysis of long-term heterosexual and LGB long-term partnerships. *Journal of Evidence-Based Social Work, 17*, 203–225. https://doi.org/10.1080/26408066.2020.1723769

Chou, R., Deyo, R., Devine, B., Hansen, R., Sullivan, S., Jarvik, J. G., Blazina, I., Dana, T., Bougatsos, C., & Turner, J. (2014). The effectiveness and risks of long-term opioid treatment of chronic pain. *AHRQ Publication No. 14-E005-EF*. Agency for Healthcare Research and Quality. https://doi.org/10.23970/AHRQEPCERTA218.

Chou, S.-C., Boldy, D. P., & Lee, A. H. (2003). Factors influencing residents' satisfaction in residential aged care. *The Gerontologist, 43*, 459–472. https://doi.org/10.1093/geront/43.4.459

Chow, S. K., Francis, B., Ng, Y. H., Naim, N., Beh, H. C., Ariffin, M. A. A., Yusuf, M. H. M., Lee, J. W., & Sulaiman, A. H. (2021). Religious coping, depression and anxiety among healthcare workers during the COVID-19 pandemic: A Malaysian perspective. *Healthcare, 9*, 79. https://doi.org/10.3390/healthcare9010079

Chowdhury-Paulino, I. M., Ericsson, C., Vince Jr., R., Spratt, D. E., George, D. J., & Mucci, L. A. (2022). Racial disparities in prostate cancer among black men: Epidemiology and outcomes. *Prostate Cancer and Prostatic Diseases, 25*, 397–402. https://doi.org/10.1038/s41391-021-00451-z

Christensen, A. (1990). Gender and social structure in the demand/withdrawal pattern of marital conflict. *Journal of Personality and Social Psychology, 59*, 73–81. https://doi.org/10.1037/0022-3514.59.1.73

Christensen, A. J., & Johnson, J. A. (2002). Patient adherence with medical treatment regimens: An interactive approach. *Current Directions in Psychological Science, 11*, 94–97. https://doi.org/10.1111/1467-8721.00176

Chun, S., Heo, J., Lee, S., & Kim, J. (2016). Leisure-related predictors on a sense of purpose in life among older adults with cancer. *Activities, Adaptation & Aging, 40*, 266–280. https://doi.org/10.1080/01924788.2016.1199517

Church, A. T. (2016). Personality traits across cultures. *Current Opinion in Psychology, 8*, 22–30. https://doi.org/10.1016/j.copsyc.2015.09.014

Ciani, E. (2016). Retirement, pension eligibility and home production. *Labour Economics, 38*, 106–120. https://doi.org/10.1016/j.labeco.2016.01.004

Ciarambino, T., Para, O., & Giordano, M. (2021). Immune system and COVID-19 by sex differences and age. *Women's Health, 17*. https://doi.org/10.1177%2F17455065211022262

Ciarmoli, D. (2022). Assistive technology for promoting the independence and the quality of life in persons with Alzheimer's disease: A selective review. In F. Stasolla (Ed.), *Assistive technologies for assessment and recovery of neurological impairments* (pp. 173–195). IGI Global. https://doi.org/10.4018/978-1-7998-7430-0.ch009

Cicirelli, V. G. (2001). Personal meaning of death in older adults and young adults in relation to their fears of death. *Death Studies, 25*, 663–683. https://doi.org/10.1080/713769896

Cicirelli, V. G. (2006). Fear of death in mid-old age. *Journals of Gerontology: Psychological Sciences, 61B*, P75–P81. https://doi.org/10.1093/geronb/61.2.P75

Ciscato, E., Galichon, A., & Goussé, M. (2020). Like attract like? A structural comparison of homogamy across same-sex and different-sex households. *Journal of Political Economy, 128*, 740–781. https://doi.org/10.1086/704611

Cleveland Clinic. (2019). *Women: Don't ignore these 3 subtle heart attack symptoms*. https://health.clevelandclinic.org/women-dont-ignore-3-subtle-heart-attack-symptoms/

Clifton, A. (2014). Variability in personality expression across contexts: A social network approach. *Journal of Personality, 82*, 103–115. https://doi.org/10.1111/jopy.12038

Cloninger, C. R., Svrakic, D. M., & Przybeck, T. R. (1993). A psychobiological model of temperament and character. *Archives of General Psychiatry, 50*, 975–990. https://doi.org/10.1001/archpsyc.1993.01820240059008

Clyde, T. L., Wikle, J. S., Hawkins, A. J., & James, S. L. (2020). The effects of premarital education promotion policies on U.S. divorce rates. *Psychology, Public Policy, and Law, 26*, 105–120. https://doi.org/10.1037/law0000218

Coan, J. A., & Sbarra, D. A. (2015). Social baseline theory: The social regulation of risk and effort. *Current Opinion in Psychology, 1*, 87–91. https://doi.org/10.1016/j.copsyc.2014.12.021

Coates, B. A. (2017). *Divorce with decency* (5th ed.). Latitude 20.

Coats, A. H., & Blanchard-Fields, F. (2013). Making judgments about other people: Impression formation and attributional processing in older adults. *International Journal of Ageing and Later Life, 8*, 97–110. https://doi.org/10.3384/ijal.1652-8670.12199

Coelho, A., Fernandes, H. M., Magalhães, R., Moreira, P. S., Marques, P., Soares, J. M., Amorim, L., Portugal-Nunes, C., Castanho, T., Santos, N. C., & Sousa, N. (2021). Signatures of white-matter microstructure degradation during aging and its association with cognitive status. *Scientific Reports, 11*, 4517. https://doi.org/10.1038/s41598-021-83983-7

Cohen, F., Kemeny, M. E., Zegans, L., Johnson, P., Kearney, K. A., & Sites, D. P. (2007). Immune function declines with unemployment and recovers after stressor termination. *Psychosomatic Medicine, 69*, 225–234. https://doi.org/10.1097/PSY.0b013e31803139a6

Cohen, S., & Janicki-Deverts, D. (2012). Who's stressed? Distributions of psychological stress in the United States in probability samples from 1983, 2006, and 2009. *Journal of Applied Social Psychology, 42*, 1320–1334. https://doi.org/10.1111/j.1559-1816.2012.00900.x

Cohen-Mansfield, J., & Regev, I. (2018). Retirement preparation programs: An examination of retirement perceptions, self-mastery, and well-being. *Research on Social Work Practice, 28*, 428–437. https://doi.org/10.1177/1049731516645194

Cohen-Serrins J. (2021). How COVID-19 exposed an inadequate approach to burnout: Moving beyond self-care. In C. Tosone (Ed.), *Shared trauma, shared resilience during a pandemic* (pp. 259–268). Springer, Cham. https://doi.org/10.1007/978-3-030-61442-3_27

Colcombe, S., & Kramer, A. F. (2003). Fitness effects on the cognitive function of older adults: A meta-analytic study. *Psychological Science, 14*, 125–130. https://doi.org/10.1111/1467-9280.t01-1-01430

Coleman, A., Goolsby, L., Lurvey, K., Von Achen, E., & Veverica, H. (2020). Older adults' perspectives on occupational supports in alternative housing communities. *Older Adult*, 10. https://scholarworks.gvsu.edu/ot_older_adult/10

Coleman, J. (2015). *Unfinished work: The struggle to build an aging American workforce*. Oxford University Press.

Coleman, M., Ganong, L., & Russell, L. T. (2013). Resilience in stepfamilies. In D. S. Becvar (Ed.), *Handbook of family resilience* (pp. 85–103). Springer.

Coles, R. L. (2016). *Race and family: A structural approach* (2nd ed.). Rowman & Littlefield.

Collardeau, F., & Ehrenberg, M. (2016). Parental divorce and attitudes and feelings toward marriage and divorce in emerging adulthood: New insights from a multiway-frequency analysis. *Journal of European Psychology Students*. https://doi.org/10.5334/jeps.341

Collins, P. H., & Bilge, S. (2020). *Intersectionality*. Wiley.

Collins, W. A., & van Dulmen, M. (2006). "The course of true love(s)…": Origins and pathways in the development of romantic relationships. In A. C. Crouter & A. Booth (Eds.), *Romance and sex in adolescence and emerging adulthood: Risks and opportunities* (pp. 63–86). Erlbaum.

Colman, B. E. (2020). *Through the lens of the parents: Navigating the intersectionalities of multiracial adoptive families*. Doctoral dissertation, University of Michigan. ProQuest Document 28148160.

Colombel, F., Tessoulin, M., Gilet, A.-L., & Corson, Y. (2016). False memories and normal aging: Links between inhibitory capacities and monitoring processes. *Psychology and Aging, 31*, 239–248. https://doi.org/10.1037/pag0000086

Coman, A., & Hirst, W. (2012). Cognition through a social network: The propagation of induced forgetting and practice effects. *Journal of Experimental Psychology: General, 141*, 321–336. https://doi.org/10.1037/a0025247

Cömert, E. D., & Gökmen, V. (2020). Physiological relevance of food antioxidants. In Fidel Toldrá (Ed.), *Advances in food and nutrition research* (Vol. 93, pp. 205–250). Academic Press. https://doi.org/10.1016/bs.afnr.2020.03.002

Committee for a Responsible Federal Budget. (2022). *Medicare hospital insurance trust fund*. https://www.crfb.org/our-work/projects/trust-fund-solutions/medicare-hospital-insurance-trust-fund

Commons, M. L. (2016). The fundamental issues with behavioral development. *Behavioral Development Bulletin, 21*, 1–12. https://doi.org/10.1037/bdb0000022

Congress.gov. (2020). *Families First Coronavirus Response Act; Public Law No. 116-127*. https://www.congress.gov/bill/116th-congress/house-bill/6201/text

Congressional Research Service. (2022). *Poverty in the United States in 2020*. https://crsreports.congress.gov/product/pdf/R/R47030

Connolly, A., Sampson, E. L., & Purandare, N. (2012). End-of-life care for people with dementia form ethnic minority groups: A systematic review. *Journal of the American Geriatrics Society, 60*, 351–360. https://doi.org/10.1111/j.1532-5415.2011.03754.x

Connors, M. H., Sachdev, P. S., Kochan, N. A., Xu, J., Draper, B., & Brodaty, H. (2015). Cognition and mortality in older people: The Sydney Memory and Aging Study. *Age and Ageing, 44*, 1049–1054. https://doi.org/10.1093/ageing/afv139

Conroy-Beam, D. (2021). Couple simulation: A novel approach for evaluating models of human mate choice. *Personality and Social Psychology Review, 25*, 191–228. https://doi.org/10.1177%2F1088868320971258

Constantinidis, C., & Klingberg, T. (2016). The neuroscience of working memory capacity and training. *Nature Reviews Neuroscience, 17*, 438–449. https://doi.org/10.1038/nrn.2016.43

Conway, E. R., & Chenery, H. J. (2016). Evaluating the MESSAGE Communication Strategies in Dementia training for use with community-based aged care staff working with people with dementia: A controlled pretest-post-test study. *Journal of Clinical Nursing, 25*, 1145–1155. https://doi.org/10.1111/jocn.13134

Conway, H. (2016). *The law and the dead*. Routledge.

Cools, R., & Arnsten, A. F. T. (2022). Neuromodulation of prefrontal cortex cognitive function in primates: The powerful roles of monoamines and acetylcholine. *Neuropsychopharmacology, 47*, 309–328. https://doi.org/10.1038/s41386-021-01100-8

Coombs, M. A. (2010). The mourning that comes before: Can anticipatory grief theory inform family care in adult intensive care? *International Journal of Palliative Nursing, 16*, 580–584. https://doi.org/10.12968/ijpn.2010.16.12.580

Cooney, T. M., Smyer, M. A., Hagestad, G. O., & Klock, R. (1986). Parental divorce in young adulthood: Some preliminary findings. *American Journal of Orthopsychiatry, 56*, 470–477. https://doi.org/10.1111/j.1939-0025.1986.tb03478.x

Cooper, A. N., Tao, C., Totenhagen, C. J., Randall, A. K., & Holley, S. R. (2020). Daily stress spillover and crossover: Moderating effects of difficulties in emotion regulation in same-sex couples. *Journal of Social and Personal Relationships, 37*, 1245–1267. https://doi.org/10.1177%2F0265407519891777

Cooper, R. A. (2021). "I am a caregiver": Sense-making and identity construction through online caregiving narratives. *Journal of Family Communication, 21*, 77–89. https://doi.org/10.1080/15267431.2021.1889554

Cope, L. (2020). *Grieving the death of a sibling on Facebook*. Doctoral dissertation, Alliant International University. ProQuest Document 28031514.

Corbett, B. A., & Hilty, D. M. (2006). Managing your time. In L. W. Roberts & D. M. Hilty (Eds.), *Handbook of career development in academic psychiatry and behavioral sciences* (pp. 83–91). American Psychiatric Publishing.

Cordella, C. (2021). Do-not-resuscitate orders in the operating room. *Professional Case Management, 26*, 162–165. https://doi.org/10.1097/NCM.0000000000000501

Cordella, M., & & Poiani, A. (2021). *Fulfilling aging: Psychosocial and communicative perspectives on ageing*. Springer, Cham.

Cornwall, A. (2016). Women's empowerment: What works? *Journal of International Development, 28*, 342–359. https://doi.org/10.1002/jid.3210

Corporation for National and Community Service. (2021). *Make giving back your second act*. https://americorps.gov/serve/americorps-seniors

Corr, C. A. (2010a). Children, development, and encounters with death, bereavement, and coping. In C. A. Corr & D. E. Balk (Eds.), *Children's encounters with death, bereavement, and coping* (pp. 3–19). Springer.

Corr, C. A. (2010b). Children's emerging awareness and understandings of loss and death. In C. A. Corr & D. E. Balk (Eds.), *Children's encounters with death, bereavement, and coping* (pp. 21–37). Springer.

Corr, C. A. (2019). The "five stages" in coping with dying and bereavement: Strengths, weaknesses and some alternatives. *Mortality, 24*, 405–419. https://doi.org/10.1080/13576275.2018.1527826

Corr, C. A. (2020). Elisabeth Kübler-Ross and the "Five Stages" model in a sampling of recent American textbooks. *OMEGA—Journal of Death and Dying, 82*, 294–322. https://doi.org/10.1177%2F0030222818809766

Corr, C. A., Corr, D. M., & Doka, K. J. (2019). *Death and dying: Life and living* (8th ed.). Cengage Learning.

Cortina, L. M., & Areguin, M. A. (2021). Putting people down and pushing them out: Sexual harassment in the workplace. *Annual Review of Organizational Psychology and Organizational Behavior, 8*, 285–309. https://doi.org/10.1146/annurev-orgpsych-012420-055606

Cosby, R. (2020). Older African American adults: Understanding the role of the Black Church's support in the community, *Journal of Religion & Spirituality in Social Work: Social Thought, 39*, 353–371. https://doi.org/10.1080/15426432.2020.1780183

Coser, A., Sullivan, M., & Espeleta, H. (2020). Beyond the nuclear family: A qualitative examination of extended family involvement among American Indian families. *Journal of Family Strengths, 20*. https://digitalcommons.library.tmc.edu/cgi/viewcontent.cgi?article=1425&context=jfs.

Cosh, S., Carrieere, I., Nael, V., Tzourio, C., Delcourt, C., Helmer, C., & the Sense-Cog Consortium. (2019). The association of vision loss and dimensions of depression over 12 years in older adults: Findings from the Three City study. *Journal of Affective Studies, 243*, 477–4848. https://doi.org/10.1016/j.jad.2018.09.071

Cosman, F., & Saag, K. G. (2021). Romosozumab for the treatment of postmenopausal osteoporosis. In D. W. Dempster, J. A. Cauley, M. L. Bouxsein, & F. Cosman (Eds.), *Marcus and Feldman's osteoporosis* (5th ed., Vol. 2, pp. 1827–1833). https://doi.org/10.1016/B978-0-12-813073-5.00080-0

Costa, P. T., Jr., & McCrae, R. R. (1994). Set like plaster? Evidence for the stability of adult personality. In T. F. Heatherton & J. L. Weinberger (Eds.), *Can personality change?* (pp. 21–40). American Psychological Association.

Costa, P. T., Jr., & McCrae, R. R. (2011). Five-factor theory, and interpersonal psychology. In L. M. Horowitz & S. Strack (Eds.), *Handbook of interpersonal psychology: Theory, research, assessment, and therapeutic interventions* (pp. 91–104). Wiley.

Coull, N. A., West, A. M., Hodder, S. G., Wheeler, P., & Havenith, G. (2021). Body mapping of regional sweat distribution in young and older males. *European Journal of Applied Physiology, 121*, 109–125. https://doi.org/10.1007/s00421-020-04503-5

Council for Adult and Experiential Learning. (2021). *What we do*. https://www.cael.org/what-we-do

Council on Contemporary Families. (2015). *Remarriage in the United States: If at first they don't succeed, do most Americans "try, try again"?* https://sites.utexas.edu/contemporaryfamilies/?s=remarriage

Cowl, A. (2016). Terminal decline. In S. K. Whitbourne (Ed.), *The encyclopedia of adulthood and aging* (Vol. 3, pp. 1398–1402). Wiley.

Cox, C. B. (2007). Grandparent-headed families: Needs and implications for social work interventions and advocacy. *Families in Society, 88*, 561–566. https://doi.org/10.1606/1044-3894.3678

Cox, C. B. (2019). Grandparents and social policy. In B. Hayslip, Jr., & C. A. Fruhauf (Eds.), *Grandparenting: Influences on the dynamics of family relationships* (pp. 301–312). Springer.

Craik, F. I. M., & Rose, N. S. (2012). Memory encoding and aging: A neurocognitive approach. *Neuroscience and Biobehavioral Reviews, 36*, 1729–1739. https://doi.org/10.1016/j.neubiorev.2011.11.007

Cram, B., Alkadry, M. G., & Tower, L. E. (2016). Social costs: The career–family tradeoff. In M. L. Connerley & J. Wu (Eds.), *Handbook of well-being of working women* (pp. 473–487). Springer.

Crane, P. K., Walker, R., Hubbard, R. A., Li, G., Nathan, D. M., Zhang, Z., Haneuse, S., Craft, S., Montine, T. J., Kahn, S. E., McCormick, W., McCurry, S. M., Bowen, J. D., & Larson, E. B. (2013). Glucose levels and risk of dementia. *New England Journal of Medicine, 369*, 540–548. https://doi.org/10.1056/NEJMoa1215740

Creating a Family. (2021). *Adoptive parenting*. https://creatingafamily.org/adoption/resources/adoptive-parenting/

Crenshaw, A. O., Leo, K., Christensen, A., Hogan, J. N., Baucom, K. J. W., & Baucom, B. R. W. (2021). Relative importance of conflict topics for within-couple tests: The case of demand/withdraw interaction. *Journal of Family Psychology, 35*, 377–387. https://doi.org/10.1037/fam0000782

Crimmins, E. M., Zhang, Y. S., Kim, J. K., & Levin, M. E. (2021). Trends in morbidity, healthy life expectancy, and the compression of morbidity. In N. Musie & P. J. Hornsby (Eds.), *Handbook of the biology of aging* (9th ed., pp. 405–414). Academic Press. https://doi.org/10.1016/B978-0-12-815962-0.00019-6

Crisp, R. J., & Turner, R. N. (2009). Can imagined interactions produce positive perceptions?: Reducing prejudice through simulated social contact. *American Psychologist, 64*, 231–240. https://doi.org/10.1037/a0014718

Crisp, R. J., & Turner, R. N. (2012). The imagined contact hypothesis. *Advances in Experimental Social Psychology, 46*, 125–182. https://doi.org/10.1016/B978-0-12-394281-4.00003-0

Cristina, T. J. N., Williams, J. A. S., Parkinson, L., Sibbritt, D. W., & Byles, J. E. (2016). Identification of diabetes, heart disease, hypertension and stroke in mid- and older-aged women: Comparing self-report and administrative hospital data records. *Geriatrics and Gerontology International, 16*, 95–102. https://doi.org/10.1111/ggi.12442

Crockett, R. A., Hsu, C. L., Dao, E., Tam, R., Alkeridy, A., Eng, J. J., Handy, T. C., & Liu-Ambrose, T. (2022). Mind the gaps: Functional networks disrupted by white matter hyperintensities are associated with greater falls risk. *Neurobiology of Aging, 109*, 166–175. https://doi.org/10.1016/j.neurobiolaging.2021.09.023

Cross, D., Fani, N., Powers, A., & Bradley, B. (2017). Neurobiological development in the context of childhood trauma. *Clinical Psychology: Science and Practice, 24*, 111–124. https://doi.org/10.1111/cpsp.12198

Crowley, J. (2021). *What are common reasons for divorce?* https://www.survivedivorce.com/common-reasons-for-divorce

Crowley, J. E. (2019). Does everything fall apart? Life assessments following a gray divorce. *Journal of Family Issues, 40*, 1438-1461. https://doi.org/10.1177%2F0192513X19839735

Crown, W. (2001). Economic status of the elderly. In R. H. Binstock & L. K. George (Eds.), *Handbook of aging and the social sciences* (5th ed., pp. 352–368). Academic Press.

Croy, I., Nordin, S., & Hummel, T. (2014). Olfactory disorders and quality of life—An updated review. *Chemical Senses, 39*, 185–194. https://doi .org/10.1093/chemse/bjt072

Cubrich, M., & Petruzzelli, A. (2020). Advancing our understanding of successful aging at work: A socioemotional selectivity theory perspective. *Industrial and Organizational Psychology, 13*, 369–373. https://doi.org/10.1017/iop.2020.71

Cuddy, A. J. C., Norton, M. I., & Fiske, S. T. (2005). The old stereotype: The pervasiveness and persistence of the elderly stereotype. *Journal of Social Issues, 61*, 267–285. https://doi. org/10.1111/j.1540-4560.2005.00405.x

Cukier, H. N., Kunkle, B. W., Vardarajan, B. N., Rolati, S., Hamilton-Nelson, K. L., Kohli, M. A., Whitehead, P. L., Dombroski, B. A., Van Booven, D., Lang, R., Dykxhoorn, D. M., Farrer, L. A., Cuccaro, M. L., Vance, J. M., Gilbert, J. R., Beecham, G. W., Martin, E. R., Carney, R. M., Mayeux, R., Schellenberg, G. D. et al. (2016). *ABCA7* frameshift deletion associated with Alzheimer disease in African Americans. *Neurology Genetics, 2*, e79. https://doi.org/10.1212 /NXG.0000000000000079

Cummings, K. (2015). *Coming to grips with loss: Normalizing the grief process*. Sense Publishers.

Cunningham, W. R. (1987). Intellectual abilities and age. In K. W. Schaie (Ed.), *Annual review of gerontology and geriatrics* (Vol. 7, pp. 117–134). Springer.

Curtin, N., & Stewart, A. J. (2012). Linking personal and social histories with collective identity narratives. In S. Wiley, G. Philogène, & T. A. Revenson (Eds.), *Social categories in everyday experience* (pp. 83–102). American Psychological Association.

Curtis, J. R., Treece, P. D., Nielsen, E. L., Gold, J., Ciechanowski, P. S., Shannon, S. E. et al. (2016). Randomized trial of communication facilitators to reduce family distress and intensity of end-of-life care. *Respiratory and Critical Care Medicine, 193*, 154–162. https://doi.org/10.1164 /rccm.201505-0900OC

Curtis, R. G., Huxhold, O., & Windsor, T. D. (2018). Perceived control and social activity in midlife and older age: A reciprocal association? Findings from the German Ageing Study. *Journals of Gerontology: Psychological Sciences, 73*, 807–815. https://doi .org/10.1093/geronb/gbw070

Curtis, R., & Pearson, F. (2010). Contact with birth parents: Differential psychological adjustment for adults adopted as infants. *Journal of Social Work, 10*, 347–367. https://doi .org/10.1177/1468017310369273

Cutler, L., & Palkovitz, R. (2020). Fathers' shared book reading experiences: Common behaviors, frequency, predictive factors, and developmental outcomes. *Marriage and Family Review, 56*, 144–173. https://doi .org/10.1080/01494929.2019.1683119

Cutler, V. J. (2021). The science and psychology of beauty. In E. A. Rieder & R. G. Fried (Eds.), *Essential psychiatry for the aesthetic practitioner*. Wiley Online Library. https://doi .org/10.1002/9781119680116.ch2

D'Amen, B., Socci, M., & Santini, S. (2021). Intergenerational caring: A systematic literature review on young and young adult caregivers of older people. *BMC Geriatrics, 21*, 105. https://doi.org/10.1186 /s12877-020-01976-z

da Costa, J. F., & Oliveira, T. C. (2016). Managing careers: Anchored, plateaued or drifting? In C. Machado & J. P. Davim (Eds.), *Organizational management* (pp. 31–62). Springer.

Dadgari, A., Hamid, T. A., Hakim, M. N., Mousavi, S. A., Dadvar, L., Mohammadi, M., & Amerian, N. (2015). The role of self-efficacy on fear of falls and fall among elderly community dwellers in Shahroud, Iran. *Nursing Practice Today, 2*, 112–120. https://npt.tums.ac.ir /index.php/npt/article/view/54

Dahl, C. M., & Boss, P. (2020). Ambiguous loss: Theory-based guidelines for therapy with individuals, families, and communities. In K. S. Wampler, M. Rastogi, & R. Singh (Eds.), *The handbook of systemic family therapy* (Vol. 4, pp. 127–151). Wiley. https://doi .org/10.1002/9781119438519.ch88

Dahlberg, L., McKee, K. J., Frank, A., & Naseer, M. (2022). A systematic review of longitudinal risk factors for loneliness in older adults. *Aging & Mental Health, 26*, 225–249. https://doi.org/10.1080/13607863.20 21.1876638

Dai, B., Zhang, B., & Li, J. (2013). Protective factors for subjective well-being in Chinese older adults: The roles of resources and activity. *Journal of Happiness Studies, 14*, 1225–1239. https://doi.org/10.1007 /s10902-012-9378-7

Dalai Lama (1999). *Ethics for the new millennium*. Riverhead Books.

Dalai Lama. (2000). The true source of political success. In S. Kaza & K. Kragt (Eds.), *Dharma rain: Sources of Buddhist environmentalism* (pp. 165–169). Shambhala.

Damian, R. I., & Simonton, D. K. (2015). Four psychological perspectives on creativity. In R. A. Scott & S. M. Kosslyn (Eds.), *Emerging trends in the social and behavioral sciences: An interdisciplinary, searchable, and linkable resource*. Wiley Online Library. https:// doi.org/10.1002/9781118900772.etrds0134

Dan, X., Wechter, N., Mohanty, J. G., Croteau, D. L., & Bohr, V. A., (2021). Olfactory dysfunction in aging and neurodegenerative diseases. *Aging Research Reviews, 70*, 101416. https://doi.org/10.1016/j.arr.2021.101416

Dansereau, A., Hunter, S. W., Gomez, F., Guralnik, J. M., DePaul, V. G., & Auais, M. (2020). Global cognition predicts the incidence of poor physical performance among older adults: A cross-national study. *Geriatrics and Gerontology International, 20*, 218–222. https:// doi.org/10.1111/ggi.13864

Darnell, F. J., Johansen, A. B., Tavakoli, S., & Brugnone, N. (2017). Adoption and identity experiences among adult transnational adoptees: A qualitative study. *Adoption Quarterly, 20*, 155–166. https://doi.org /10.1080/10926755.2016.1217574

Das, M. K., Arora, N. K., Gaikwad, H., Chellani, H., Debata, P., Rasaily, R., Meena, K. R., Kaur, G., Malik, P., Joshi, S., & Kumari, M. (2021). Grief reaction and psychosocial impacts of child death and stillbirth on bereaved North Indian parents: A qualitative study. *PLoS ONE, 16*, e0240270. https://doi.org/10.1371 /journal.pone.0240270

Davenport, M. H., Meyer, S., Meah, V. L., Strynadka, M. C., & Khurana, R. (2020). Moms are not OK: COVID-19 and maternal mental health. *Frontiers in Global Women's Health*. https://doi.org/10.3389 /fgwh.2020.00001

David, J. G. (2021). Recruiting passionate job seekers for better performance. *Evidence-Based HRM, 9*, 209–222. https://doi.org/10.1108/EBHRM-01-2020-0007

Davidman, A. (2021). *I help people decide if they want to have kids. Here's my advice*. https://www.vox.com/first -person/22370250/should-i-have-kids-a-baby-decide -start-family-parenthood-kids-childfree

Davies, L. (2003). Singlehood: Transitions within a gendered world. *Canadian Journal on Aging, 22*, 343–352. https://doi.org/10.1017/S0714980800004219

Davies, P. G. (2007). Between health and illness. *Perspectives in Biology and Medicine, 50*, 444–452. https://doi.org/10.1353/pbm.2007.0026

Davis, A., McMahon, C. M., Pichora-Fuller, K. M. Russ, S., Lin, F., Olusanya, B. O., Chadha, S., & Tremblay, K. L. (2016). Aging and hearing health: The life-course approach. *The Gerontologist, 56*, S256–S267. https://doi.org/10.1093/geront/gnw033

Davis, B. W. (1985). *Visits to remember: A handbook for visitors of nursing home residents*. Pennsylvania State University Cooperative Extension Service.

Davis, B., Dionne, R., Fortin, M. (2014). Parenting in two cultural worlds in the presence of one dominant worldview: The American Indian experience. In H. Selin (Ed.), *Parenting across cultures* (pp. 367–377). Springer.

Davis, L., Karim, Z., & Dening, T. (2022). Diagnostic, management and nursing challenges of less common dementias: Frontotemporal dementia, alcohol-related dementia, HIV dementia and prion diseases. *British Journal of Neuroscience Nursing, 18*. https://doi .org/10.12968/bjnn.2022.18.1.26

Davis, S. N., & Wills, J. B. (2014). Theoretical explanations amid social change: A content analysis of housework research (1975–2012). *Journal of Family Issues, 35*, 808–824. https://doi .org/10.1177%2F0192513X13513020

Dawadi, P. N., & Cook, D. J. (2017). Monitoring everyday abilities and cognitive health using pervasive technologies: Current state and prospect. In J. van Hoof, G. Demiris, & E. J. M. Wouters (Eds.), *Handbook of smart homes, health care and well-being* (pp. 365–385). Springer.

De Clerq, D., Haq, I. U., Azeem, M. U., & Hassan, A. (2020). How career plateau beliefs and leader interpersonal unfairness harm job performance in dysfunctional organizational settings. *Canadian Journal of Administrative Sciences, 37*, 197–210. https://doi.org/10.1002/cjas.1560

de Frias, C. M., Dixon, R. A., & Bäckman, L. (2003). Use of memory compensation strategies is related to psychosocial and health indicators. *Journals of Gerontology: Psychological Sciences, 58B*, P12–P22. https://doi.org/10.1093/geronb/58.1.P12

de Grip, A., Bosma, H., Willems, D., & van Boxtel, M. (2008). Job-worker mismatch and cognitive decline. *Oxford Economic Papers, 60*, 237–253. https://doi .org/10.1093/oep/gpm023

de Jong, P. (2021). *No place like home? Residential mobility and housing preferences of older adults in the Netherlands*. Dissertation, University of Gronigen. https://doi.org/10.33612/diss.178356380

De la Monte, S. (2012). Brain insulin resistance and deficiency as therapeutic targets in Alzheimer's disease. *Current Alzheimer's Research, 9*, 35–66. https://doi .org/10.2174/156720512799015037

De Lillo, M., Foley, R., Fysh, M. C., Stimson, A., Bradford, E. E. F., Woodrow-Hill, C., & Ferguson, H. J. (2021, May 13). Tracking developmental differences in real-world social attention across adolescence, young adulthood and older adulthood. *Nature Human Behaviour*. https://doi.org/10.1038 /s41562-021-01113-9

De Paula Couto, M. C. P., & Koller, S. H. (2012). Warmth and competence: Stereotypes of the elderly among young adults and older persons in Brazil. *International Perspectives in Psychology: Research, Practice, Consultation, 1*, 52–62. https://doi.org/10.1037/a0027118

de Pommereau, I. (2012). *How BMW reinvents the factory for older workers*. https://www .csmonitor.com/World/Europe/2012/0902 /How-BMW-reinvents-the-factory-for-older-workers

De Rosbo-Davies, C., Laletas, S., & Round, P. (2022). Daughters' experiences of maternal bereavement during adolescence: A scoping review. *Death Studies, 46*, 2156–2166. https://doi.org/10.1080/07481187 .2021.1900454

De Witt-Hoblit, I., Miller, M. N., & Camp, C. J. (2016). Effects of sustained, coordinated activities programming in long-term care: The Memory in Rhythm® program. *Advances in Aging Research, 5*. https://doi.org/10.4236/aar.2016.51001

Deal, J. A., Power, M. C., Palta, P., Alonso, A., Schneider, A. L. C., Perryman, K., Bandeen-Roche, K., Sharrett, A. R. (2020). Relationship of cigarette smoking and time of quitting with incident dementia and cognitive decline. *Journal of the American Geriatrics Society, 68*, 337–345. https://doi.org/10.1111/jgs.16228

Deane, G., Spitze, G. Ward, R. A., & Zhuo, Y. (2016). Close to you? How parent-adult child contact is influenced by family patterns. *Journals of Gerontology: Social Sciences, 71*, 344–357. https://doi.org/10.1093 /geronb/gbv036

deathoverdinner.org. (2022). *Let's have dinner and talk about death*. https://deathoverdinner.org/

Debast, I., van Alphen, S. P. J., Rossi, G., Tummers, J. H. A., Bolwerk, N., Derksen, J. J. L. et al. (2014).

Personality traits and personality disorders in late middle and old age: Do they remain stable? A literature review. *Clinical Gerontologist, 37*, 253–271. https://doi.org/10/1080/07317115.2014.885917

Debreczeni, F. A., & Bailey, P. E. (2021). A systematic review and meta-analysis of subjective age and the association with cognition, subjective well-being, and depression. *Journals of Gerontology: Psychological Sciences, 76*, 471–482. https://doi.org/10.1093/geronb/gbaa069

Delgado, M. (2015). *Baby boomers of color: Implications for social work policy and practice*. Columbia University Press.

Delhom, I., Satorres, E., & Meléndez, J. C. (2022). Emotional intelligence intervention in older adults to improve adaptation and reduce negative mood. *International Psychogeriatrics, 34*, 79–89. https://doi.org/10.1017/S1041610220003579

DeLiema, M., Yon, Y., & Wilber, K. H. (2016). Tricks of the trade: Motivating sales agents to con older adults. *The Gerontologist, 56*, 335–344. https://doi.org/10.1093/geront/gnu039

Della Gatta, F., Terribili, C., Fabrizi, E., & Moret-Tatay, C. (2021). Making older adults' cognitive health visible after Covid-19 outbreak. *Frontiers in Psychology, 12*, 648208. https://www.frontiersin.org/article/10.3389/fpsyg.2021.648208

Deloitte. (2020). *The Deloitte Global Millennial Survey 2020: Millennials and Gen Zs hold the key to creating a "better normal."* https://www2.deloitte.com/global/en/pages/about-deloitte/articles/millennialsurvey.html

Deloitte. (2021). *The Deloitte global 2021 millennial and gen Z survey*. https://www2.deloitte.com/global/en/pages/about-deloitte/articles/millennialsurvey.html

DeLucia-Waack, J. L. (2011). Children of divorce groups. In G. L. Greif & P. H. Ephross (Eds.), *Group work with populations at risk* (3rd ed., pp. 93–114). Oxford University Press.

Dementia Village Associates. (2021). *The Hogeweyk*. https://hogeweyk.dementiavillage.com/#NaN

Demir, M., Orthel-Clark, H., Özdemir, M., & Özdemir, S. B. (2015). Friendship and happiness among young adults. In M. Demir (Ed.), *Friendship and happiness* (pp. 117–135). New York: Springer.

Demiray, B., & Freund, A. M. (2015). Michael, Jackson, Bin Laden, and I: Functions of positive and negative, public and private flashbulb memories. *Memory, 23*, 487–506. https://doi.org/10.1080/09658211.2014.907428

Deng, C.-P., Armstrong, P. I., & Rounds, J. (2007). The fit of Holland's RIASEC model to US occupations. *Journal of Vocational Behavior, 71*, 1–22. https://doi.org/10.1016/j.jvb.2007.04.002

Deng, L., Stanley, M. L., Monge, Z. A., Wing, E. A., Geib, B. R., Davis, S. W., & Cabeza, R. (2021). Age-related compensatory reconfiguration of PFC connections during episodic memory retrieval. *Cerebral Cortex, 31*, 717–730. https://doi.org/10.1093/cercor/bhaa192

Denham, J., & Sellami, M. (2021). Exercise training increases telomerase reverse transcriptase gene expression and telomerase activity: A systematic review and meta-analysis. *Ageing Research Reviews, 70*, 101411. https://doi.org/10.1016/j.arr.2021.101411

Denney, N. W., Pearce, K. A., & Palmer, A. M. (1982). A developmental study of adults' performance on traditional and practical problem-solving tasks. *Experimental Aging Research, 8*, 115–118. https://doi.org/10.1080/03610738208258407

Dennis, A. (2021). Those left behind: Socioeconomic predictors and social mediators of psychological distress among working-age African Americans in a post-industrial city. *Du Bois Review: Social Science Research on Race, 18*, 119–151. https://doi.org/10.1017/S1742058X21000011

Dennis, N., Gutchess, A., & Thomas, A. (2020). Overview of models of cognitive aging. In A. Thomas & A. Gutchess (Eds.), *The Cambridge handbook of cognitive aging: A life course perspective* (pp. 5–31). Cambridge University Press. https://doi.org/10.1017/9781108552684.002

Denworth, L. (2020). *Friendship is a lifesaver*. https://lydiadenworth.com/articles/friendship-is-a-lifesaver/

Desai, S., McGrath, C., McNeil, H., Sveistrup, H., McMurray, J., & Astell, A. (2022). Experiential value of technologies: A qualitative study with older adults. *International Journal of Environmental Research and Public Health, 19*, 2235. https://doi.org/10.3390/ijerph19042235

Desmond, N., & López Turley, R. N. (2009). The role of familism in explaining the Hispanic–white college application gap. *Social Problems, 56*, 311–334. https://doi.org/10.1525/sp.2009.56.2.311

Dey, S., & Ghosh, J. (2016). Factors in the distribution of successful marriage. *International Journal of Social Sciences and Management, 3*, 60–64. https://doi.org/10.3126/ijssm.v3i1.14315

Di Domenico, S., Rodrigo, A. H., Ayaz, H., Fournier, M. A., & Ruocco, A. C. (2015). Decision-making conflict and the neural efficiency hypothesis of intelligence: A functional near-infrared spectroscopy investigation. *NeuroImage, 109*, 307–317. https://doi.org/10.1016/j.neuroimage.2015.01.039

Di Fabio, A. (2016). Life design and career counseling innovative outcomes. *The Career Development Quarterly, 64*, 35–48. https://doi.org/10.1002/cdq.12039

Di Masso, A., Dixon, J., & Hernández, B. (2017). Place attachment, sense of belonging and the micro-politics of place satisfaction. In G. Fleury-Bahi, E. Pol, & O. Navarro (Eds.), *Handbook of environmental psychology and quality of life research* (pp. 85–104). Springer.

Diab, D. L., Watts, N. B., & Miller, P. D. (2021). Bisphosphonates pharmacology and use in the treatment of osteoporosis. In D. W. Dempster, J. A. Cauley, M. L. Bouxsein, & F. Cosman (Eds.), *Marcus and Feldman's osteoporosis* (5th ed., Vol. 2, pp. 1721–1736). https://doi.org/10.1016/B978-0-12-813073-5.00074-5

Dickens, B. M., Boyle, J. M., Jr., & Ganzini, L. (2008). Euthanasia and assisted suicide. In P. A. Singer & A. M. Viens (Eds.), *The Cambridge textbook of bioethics* (pp. 72–77). Cambridge University Press.

Didham, R., & Rocha, Z. L. (2020). Where you feel you belong: Classifying ethnicity and mixedness in New Zealand. In Z. Rocha & P. Aspinall (Eds.), *The Palgrave International Handbook of Mixed Racial and Ethnic Classification* (pp. 587–604). Palgrave Macmillan, Cham. https://doi.org/10.1007/978-3-030-22874-3_31

Diehl, M., Hay, E. L., & Chui, H. (2012). Personal risk and resilience factors in the context of daily stress. *Annual Review of Gerontology and Geriatrics, 32*, 251–274. https://doi.org/10.1891/0198-8794.32.251

Diehl, M., Marsiske, M., Horgas, A. L., Rosenberg, A., Saczynski, J. S., & Willis, S. L. (2005). The Revised Observed Tasks of Daily Living: A performance-based assessment of everyday problem solving in older adults. *Journal of Applied Gerontology, 24*, 211–230. https://doi.org/10.1177/0733464804273772

Diehl, M., Willis, S. L., & Schaie, K. W. (1995). Everyday problem solving in older adults: Observational assessment and cognitive correlates. *Psychology and Aging, 10*, 478–491. https://doi.org/10.1037/0882-7974.10.3.478

Diersch, N., Cross, E. S., Stadler, W., Schütz-Bosbach, S., & Rieger, M. (2012). Representing others' actions: The role of expertise in the aging mind. *Psychological Research, 76*, 525–541. https://doi.org/10.1007/s00426-011-0404-x

DiGiacomo, M., Davidson, P. M., Byles, J., & Nolan, M. T. (2013). An integrative and socio-cultural perspective of health, wealth, and adjustment in widowhood. *Health Care for Women International, 34*, 1067–1083. https://doi.org/10.1080/07399332.2012.712171

Dillaway, H., Byrnes, M., Miller, S., & Rehnan, S. (2008). Talking "among *us*": How women from different racial–ethnic groups define and discuss menopause. *Health Care for Women International, 29*, 766–781. https://doi.org/10.1080/07399330802179247

Dimoff, J. D., Dao, A. N., Mitchell, J. & Olson, A. (2021). Live free and die: Expanding the terror management health model for pandemics to account for psychological reactance. *Social and Personality Psychology Compass, 15*, e12585. https://doi.org/10.1111/spc3.12585

Dingfield, L. E., Jackson, V. A., deLima Thomas, J., Doyle, K. P., Ferris, F., & Radwany, S. M. (2020). Looking back, and ahead: A call to action for increasing the hospice and palliative medicine specialty pipeline. *Journal of Palliative Medicine, 23*, 895–899. https://doi.org/10.1089/jpm.2020.0008

Dirk, J., & Schmiedek, F. (2012). Processing speed. In S. K. Whitbourne & M. J. Sliwinski (Eds.), *The Wiley-Blackwell handbook of adulthood and aging* (pp. 133–153). Oxford, UK: Wiley-Blackwell.

DiSalvio, N. L., Rosano, C., Aizenstein, H. J., Redfern, M. S., Furman, J. M., Jennings, J. R., Whitney, S. L., & Sparto, P. J. (2020). Gray matter regions associated with functional mobility in community-dwelling older adults. *Journal of the American Geriatrics Society, 68*, 1023–1028. https://doi.org/10.1111/jgs.16309

Dismukes, R. K. (2012). Prospective memory in workplace and everyday situations. *Current Directions in Psychological Science, 21*, 215–220. https://doi.org/10.1177/0963721412447621

Dixon, R. A. (2011). Evaluating everyday competence in older adult couples: Epidemiological considerations. *Gerontology, 57*, 173–179. https://doi.org/10.1159/000320325

Dobkin, P. L., & Hassed, C. S. (2016). Scientific underpinings and evidence pertaining to mindfulness. In P. L. Dobkin & C. S. Hassed (Eds.), *Mindful medical practitioners: A guide for clinicians and educators* (pp. 9–31). Springer.

Doerwald, F., Scheibe, S., Zacher, H., & Van Yperen, N. W. (2016). Emotional competencies across adulthood: State of knowledge and implications for the work context. *Work, Aging and Retirement, 2*, 159–216. https://doi.org/10.1093/worker/waw013

Doets, E. L., & Kremer, S. (2016). The silvery sensory experience—A review of senior consumers' food perception, liking and intake. *Food Quality and Preference, 48*, 316–332. https://doi.org/10.1016/j.foodqual.2015.08.010

Doka, K. J. (2008). Disenfranchised grief in historical perspective. In M. S. Stroebe, R. O. Hansson, H. Schut, & W. Stroebe (Eds.), *Handbook of bereavement research and practice: Advances in theory and intervention* (pp. 223–240). American Psychological Association.

Doka, K. J. (Ed.). (1989). *Disenfranchised grief: Recognizing hidden sorrow*. Lexington Books.

Doka, K. J., & Mertz, M. E. (1988). The meaning and significance of great-grandparenthood. *The Gerontologist, 28*, 192–197. https://doi.org/10.1093/geront/28.2.192

Donnellan, W. J., Bennett, K. M., & Soulsby, L. K. (2015). What are the factors that facilitate or hinder resilience in older spousal dementia carers? A qualitative study. *Aging & Mental Health, 19*, 932–939. https://doi.org/10.1080/13607863.2014.977771

Doohan, E.-A. M., Carrère, S., & Riggs, M. L. (2010). Using relational stories to predict the trajectory toward marital dissolution: The oral history interview and spousal feelings of flooding, loneliness, and depression. *Journal of Family Communication, 10*, 57–77. https://doi.org/10.1080/15267430903396401

Doornenbal, B. M., & Bakx, R. (2021). Self-rated health trajectories: A dynamic time warp analysis. *Preventive Medicine Reports, 24*, 101510. https://doi.org/10.1016/j.pmedr.2021.101510

Doubeni, C. A., Schootman, M., Major, J. M., Torres Stone, R. A., Laiyemo, A. O., Park, Y., Lian, M., Messer, L., Graubard, B. I., Sinha, R., Hollenbeck, A. R., & Schatzkin, A. (2012). Health status, neighborhood socioeconomic context, and premature mortality in the United States: The National Institutes of Health—AARP Diet and Health Study. *American Journal of Public Health, 102*, 680–688. https://doi.org/10.2105/AJPH.2011.300158

Douglas, S. and Roberts, R. (2020). Employee age and the impact on work engagement. *Strategic HR Review, 19*,

209–213. https://doi.org/10.1108/SHR-05-2020-0049

Doyle, K. O., Jr. (1974). Theory and practice of ability testing in ancient Greece. *Journal of the History of the Behavioral Sciences, 10*, 202–212. https://doi.org/10.1002/1520-6696(197404)10:2<202:AIDJHBS2300100208>3.0.CO;2-Q

Dressler, G., Cicolello, K., & Anandarajah, G. (2021). "Are they saying it how I'm saying it?" A qualitative study of language barriers and disparities in hospice enrollment. *Journal of Pain and Symptom Management, 61*, 504–512. https://doi.org/10.1016/j.jpainsymman.2020.08.019

Drossel, C., Fisher, J., & Mercer, V. (2011). A DBT training group for family caregivers of persons with dementia. *Behavior Therapy, 42*, 109–119. https://doi.org/10.1016/j.beth.2010.06.001

DuBois, P. H. (1968). A test-dominated society: China 1115 B.C.–1905 A.D. In J. L. Barnette (Ed.), *Readings in psychological tests and measurements* (pp. 249–255). Dorsey Press.

Duchek, S., Raetze, S. & Scheuch, I. (2020). The role of diversity in organizational resilience: A theoretical framework. *Business Research, 13*, 387–423. https://doi.org/10.1007/s40685-019-0084-8

Dujardin, P., Vandenbroucke, R. E., & Van Hoecke, L. (2022). Fighting fire with fire: The immune system might be key in our fight against Alzheimer's disease. *Drug Discovery Today, 27*, 1261–1283. https://doi.org/10.1016/j.drudis.2022.01.004

Dulas, M. R., & Duarte, A. (2014). Aging affects the interaction between attentional control and source memory: An fMRI study. *Journal of Cognitive Neuroscience, 26*, 2653–2669. https://doi.org/10.1162/jocn_a_00663

Duman, R. S., Deyama, S., & Fogaça, M. V. (2021). Role of BDNF in the pathophysiology and treatment of depression: Activity-dependent effects distinguish rapid-acting antidepressants. *European Journal of Neuroscience, 53*, 126–139. https://doi.org/10.1111/ejn.14630.

Duncan, D. A. (2020). Death and dying: A systematic review into approaches used to support bereaved children. *Review of Education, 8*, 452–479. https://doi.org/10.1002/rev3.3193

Duncan, I., Ahmed, T., Dove, H., & Maxwell, T. L. (2019). Medicare cost at end of life. *American Journal of Hospice and Palliative Medicine, 36*, 705–710. https://doi.org/10.1177%2F1049909119836204

Duncan, J. J. (2022). *The geriatric neuropsychology casebook*. Routledge.

Dunlop, W. L., Guo, J., & McAdams, D. P. (2016). The autobiographical author through time: Examining the degree of stability and change in redemptive and contaminated personal narratives. *Social Psychological and Personality Science, 7*, 428–436. https://doi.org/10.1177/1948550616644654

Dunlosky, J., Bailey, H., & Hertzog, C. (2011). Memory enhancement strategies: What works best for obtaining memory goals? In P. E. Hartman-Stein & A. La Rue (Eds.), *Enhancing cognitive fitness in adults* (pp. 3–23). Springer.

Dunlosky, J., Mueller, M. L., & Thiede, K. W. (2016). Methodology for investigating human metamemory: Problems and pitfalls. In J. Dunlosky & S. K. Tauber (Eds.), *The Oxford handbook of metamemory* (pp. 23–38). Oxford University Press.

Dunn, T. R., & Merriam, S. B. (1995). Levinson's age thirty transition: Does it exist? *Journal of Adult Development, 2*, 113–124. https://doi.org/10.1007/BF02251259

Dunne, R. A., Aarsland, D., O'Brien, J. T., Ballard, C., Banerjee, S., Fox, N. C., Isaacs, J. D., Underwood, B. R., Perry, R. J., Chan, D., Dening, T., Thomas, A. J., Schryer, J., Jones, A.-M., Evans, A. R., Alessi, C., Coulthard, E. J., Pickett, J., Elton, P., Jones, R. W., Mitchell, S., Hooper, N., Kalafatis, C., Rasmussen, J. G. C., Martin, H., Schott, J. M., & Burns, A. (2021). Mild cognitive impairment: The Manchester consensus. *Age and Ageing, 50*, 72–80. https://doi.org/10.1093/ageing/afaa228

Dweck, C. S., & Yeager, D. S. (2021). A growth mindset about intelligence. In G. M. Walton & A. J. Crum (Eds.), *Handbook of wise interventions: How social psychology can help people change* (pp. 9–35). Guilford.

Dyess, S. M., Prestia, A. S., Levene, R., & Gonzalez, F. (2020). An interdisciplinary framework for palliative and hospice education and practice. *Journal of Holistic Nursing, 38*, 320–330. https://doi.org/10.1177%2F0898010119899496

Dysterheft, J., Chaparro, G., Rice, L., & Rice, I. (2018). Benefits of inclusion and segregation for individuals with disabilities in leisure. *Journal of Postsecondary Education and Disability, 31*, 41–56. http://files.eric.ed.gov/fulltext/EJ1182344.pdf

Ebberwein, C. A. (2008). Career flexibility for a lifetime of work. In S. J. Lopez (Ed.), *Positive psychology: Exploring the best in people, volume 3: Growing in the face of adversity* (pp. 123–144). Praeger.

Ebner, N. C., Freund, A. M., & Baltes, P. B. (2006). Developmental changes in personal goal orientation from young to late adulthood: From striving for gains to maintenance and prevention of losses. *Psychology and Aging, 21*, 664–678. https://doi.org/10.1037/0882-7974.21.4.664

Edelman, H. (2020). *The afterGrief: Finding your way along the long arc of loss*. Ballantine Books.

Eden Alternative. (2021). *Mission, vision, values, principles*. http://www.edenalt.org/about-the-eden-alternative/mission-vision-values/

Edwards, J. D., Xu, H., Clark, D. O., Guey, L. T., Ross, L. A., & Unverzagt, F. W. (2017). Speed of processing training results in lower risk of dementia. *Alzheimer's & Dementia: Translational Research & Clinical Interventions, 3*, 603–611. https://doi.org/10.1016/j.trci.2017.09.002

Einstein, G. O., & McDaniel, M. A. (1990). Normal aging and prospective memory. *Journal of Experimental Psychology: Learning, Memory, and Cognition, 16*, 717–726. https://doi.org/10.1037/0278-7394.16.4.717

Eisenstein, T., Giladi, N., Hendler, T., Havakuk, O., & Lerner, Y. (2022). Hippocampal and non-hippocampal correlates of physically active lifestyle and their relation to episodic memory in older adults. *Neurobiology of Aging, 109*, 100–112. https://doi.org/10.1016/j.neurobiolaging.2021.08.017

Eisma, M. C., & Stroebe, M. S. (2021). Emotion regulatory strategies in complicated grief: A systematic review. *Behavior Therapy, 52*, 234–249. https://doi.org/10.1016/j.beth.2020.04.004

Eisma, M. C., de Lang, T. A., & Boelen, P. A. (2020). How thinking hurts: Rumination, worry, and avoidance processes in adjustment to bereavement. *Clinical Psychology and Psychotherapy, 27*, 548–558. https://doi.org/10.1002/cpp.2440

Eisma, M. C., Schut, H. A. W., Stroebe, M. S., Voerman, K., van den Bout, J., Stroebe, W., & Boelen, P. A. (2015). Psychopathology symptoms, rumination and autobiographical memory specificity: Do associations hold after bereavement? *Applied Cognitive Psychology, 29*, 478–484. https://doi.org/10.1002/acp.3120

Elam, J. S., Glasser, M. F., Harms, M. P., Sotiropoulos, S. N., Andersson, J. L. R., Burgess, G. C., Curtiss, S. W., Oostenveld, R., Larson-Prior, L. J., Schoffelen, J.-M., Hodge, M. R., Cler, E. A., Marcus, D. M., Barch, D. M., Yacoub, E., Smith, S. M., Ugurbil, K., & Van Essen, D. C. (2021). The Human Connectome Project: A retrospective. *NeuroImage, 244*, 118543. https://doi.org/10.1016/j.neuroimage.2021.118543

Eligon, J., & Burch, A. D. S. (2020, May 20). Questions of bias in Covid-19 treatment add to the mourning for black families. *New York Times*. https://www.nytimes.com/2020/05/10/us/coronavirus-african-americans-bias.html

Emmer De Albuquerque Green, C., Tinker, A., & Manthorpe, J. (2022). Human rights and care homes for older people: A typology of approaches from academic literature as a starting point for activist scholarship in human rights and institutional care. *International Journal of Human Rights, 26*, 717–739. https://doi.org/10.1080/13642987.2021.1961753

Emmerich, N., Mallia, P., Gordijn, B., & Pistoia, F. (Eds.). (2020). *Contemporary European perspectives on the ethics of end-of-life care*. Springer Nature.

Emsell, L., Van Hecke, W., & Tournier, J.-D. (2016). Introduction to diffusion tensor imaging. In W. Van Hecke, L. Emsell, & S. Sunaert (Eds.), *Diffusion tensor imaging* (pp. 7–19). Springer.

Engelberg, A. (2016). Religious Zionist singles: Caught between "family values" and "young adulthood." *Journal for the Scientific Study of Religion, 55*, 349–364. https://doi.org/10.1111/jssr.12259

English, T., & Carstensen L. L. (2016). Socioemotional selectivity theory. In N. A Pachana (Ed.), *Encyclopedia of geropsychology*. Springer. https://doi.org/10.1007/978-287-080-3_110-1

Enno, A. M. (2012). *The intersection of multiple oppressed identities: Implications for identity development* (Order No. 1510090). Masters thesis. Utah State University. ProQuest Dissertations & Theses Global (1015170039).

Enno, A. M., Galliher, R. V., Parmenter, J. G., & Domenech Rodríguez, M. M. (2022). Sexual, gender, and ethnic identity intersectionality among LGBTQ+ people of color. *Journal of LGBTQ Issues in Counseling, 16*, 2–27. https://doi.org/10.1080/15538605.2021.1972894

Equality and Human Rights Commission. (2018). *Equality Act 2010*. https://www.equalityhumanrights.com/en/equality-act/equality-act-2010

Erber, J. T., & Prager, I. G. (1999). Perceptions of forgetful young and older adults. In T. M. Hess & F. Blanchard-Fields (Eds.), *Social cognition and aging* (pp. 197–217). Academic Press.

Erber, J. T., Szuchman, L. T., & Rothberg, S. T. (1990). Everyday memory failure: Age differences in appraisal and attribution. *Psychology and Aging, 5*, 236–241. https://doi.org/10.1037/0882-7974.5.2.236

Erevik, E. K., Kristensen, J. H., Torsheim, T., Vendaa, Ø., & Pallesen, S. (2020). Tinder use and romantic relationship formations: A large-scale longitudinal study. *Frontiers in Psychology, 11*, Article 1757. https://doi.org/10.3389/fpsyg.2020.01757

Ericsson, K. A., & Towne, T. J. (2010). Expertise. *Wiley Interdisciplinary Reviews: Cognitive Science, 1*, 404–416. https://doi.org/10.1002/wcs.47

Erikson, E. H. (1968). *Identity: Youth and crisis*. Norton.

Erikson, E. H. (1982). *The life cycle completed: Review*. Norton.

Eriksson, M. (2007). *Unravelling the mystery of salutogenesis: The evidence base of the salutogenic research as measured by Antonovsky's Sense of Coherence Scale*. Åbo Akademi.

Erving, C. L., & Zajdel, R. (2022). Assessing the validity of self-rated health across ethnic groups: Implications for health disparities research. *Journal of Racial and Ethnic Health Disparities, 9*, 462–477. https://doi.org/10.1007/s40615-021-00977-x

Esch, T. (2014). The neurobiology of meditation and mindfulness. In S. Schmidt & H. Walach (Eds.), *Meditation—Neuroscientific approaches and philosophical implication* (pp. 153–173). Springer.

Espinola, M., DeVinney, H., & Steinberg, A. (l.). (2017). Women at midlife. In K. A. Kendall-Tackett & L. M. Ruglass (Eds.), *Women's mental health across the lifespan: Challenges, vulnerabilities, and strengths* (pp. 41–58). Routledge. https://doi.org/10.4324/9781315641928-3

Estrada-Martinez, L. M., Grossman, J. M., & Richer, A. M. (2021). Sex behaviours and family sexuality communication among Hispanic adolescents. *Sex Education, 21*, 59–74. https://doi.org/10.1080/14681811.2020.1749042

Etzel, L. C., & Shalev, I., (2021). Effects of psychological stress on telomeres as genome regulators. In G. Fink (Ed.), *Stress: Genetics, epigenetics, and genomics* (pp. 109–117). Academic Press. https://doi.org/10.1016/B978-0-12-813156-5.00009-1

Evans, D. G. R., Barwell, J., Eccles, D. M., Collins, A., Izatt, L., Jacobs, C., Donaldson, A., Brady, A. F., Cuthbert, A., Harrison, R., Thomas, S., Howell, A., The FH02 Study Group, RGC teams, Miedzybrodzka, Z., & Murray, A. (2014). The Angelina Jolie effect:

How high celebrity profile can have a major impact on provision of cancer related services. *Breast Cancer Research, 16*, 442. https://doi.org/10.1186/s13058-014-0442-6

Even-Zohar, A. (2019). Great-grandparenting in Israel. In B. Hayslip, Jr., & C. A. Fruhauf (Eds.), *Grandparenting: Influences on the dynamics of family relationships* (pp. 95–109). Springer Publishing Company. https://doi.org/10.1891/9780826149855.0006

Even-Zohar, A., & Garby, A. (2016). Great-grandparents' role perception and its contribution to their quality of life. *Journal of Intergenerational Relationships, 14*, 197–219. https://doi.org/10.1080/15350770.2016.1195246

Evertsson, M., Grunow, D., & Aisenbrey, S. (2016). Work interruptions and young women's career prospects in Germany, Sweden, and the US. *Work, Employment and Society, 30*, 291–308. https://doi.org/10.1177/0950017015598283

Eyetsemitan, F. E. (2021). *Understanding death and dying: Encountering death, dying, and the afterlife*. Sage Publications.

Eysenck, M. W., & Groome, D. (Eds.). (2020). *Forgetting: Explaining memory failure*. Sage Publications Ltd.

Eysenck, M. W., & Keane, M. T. (2020). *Cognitive psychology* (8th ed.). Psychology Press.

Faber, A. J. (2004). Examining remarried couples through a Bowenian family systems lens. *Journal of Divorce & Remarriage, 40*, 121–133. https://doi.org/10.1300/J087v40n03_08

Fabius, C. D. (2016). Toward an integration of narrative identity, generativity, and storytelling in African American elders. *Journal of Black Studies, 47*, 423–434. https://doi.org/10.1177/0021934716638801

Facal, D., Juncos-Rabadán, O., Rodriguez, M. S., & Pereiro, A. X. (2012). Tip-of-the-tongue in aging: Influence of vocabulary, working memory and processing speed. *Aging Clinical Experimental Research, 24*, 647–656. https://doi.org/10.3275/8586

Failes, E., Sommers, M. S. & Jacoby, L. L. (2020). Blurring past and present: Using false memory to better understand false hearing in young and older adults. *Memory and Cognition, 48*, 1403–1416. https://doi.org/10.3758/s13421-020-01068-8

Fairlie, H. (1988). Talkin' bout my generation. *New Republic, 198*, 19–22.

Falsetti, L., Viticchi, G., Zaccone, V., Guerrieri, E., Moroncini, G., Luzzi, S., & Silvestrini, M. (2022). Shared molecular mechanisms among Alzheimer's disease, neurovascular unit dysfunction and vascular risk factors: A narrative review. *Biomedicines, 10*, 439. https://doi.org/10.3390/biomedicines10020439

Faour, S., & Ashok, A. (2021). An overview of stem cell therapies for Parkinson's disease. *Journal of Natural Sciences, 2*, 35890. https://doi.org/10.33137/jns.v2i1.35890

Farris, D. N. (2016). *Boomerang kids: The demography of previously launched adults*. Springer.

Federal Interagency Working Group on Improving Measurement of Sexual Orientation and Gender Identity in Federal Surveys. (2016). *Current measures of sexual orientation and gender identity in federal surveys*. https://nces.ed.gov/FCSM/pdf/current_measures_20160812.pdf

Federal Trade Commission. (2016). *Lumosity to pay $2 million to settle FTC deceptive advertising charges for its "brain training" program*. https://www.ftc.gov/news-events/press-releases/2016/01/lumosity-pay-2-million-settle-ftc-deceptive-advertising-charges

Fedyk, M., & Xu, F. (2021). Creativity as potentially valuable improbable constructions. *European Journal for Philosophy of Science, 11*, 27. https://doi.org/10.1007/s13194-020-00343-4

Feehan, J., Tripodi, N., & Apostolopoulos, V. (2021). The twilight of the immune system: The impact of immunosenescence in aging. *Maturitas, 147*, 7–13. https://doi.org/10.1016/j.maturitas.2021.02.006

Fehrer, A., & Vernon, P. A. (2021). Looking beyond the Big Five: A selective review of alternatives to the Big Five model of personality. *Personality and Individual Differences, 169*, 110002. https://doi.org/10.1016/j.paid.2020.110002

Feldman, K. (2010). *Post parenthood redefined: Race, class, and family structure differences in the experience of launching children*. Doctoral dissertation, Case Western Reserve University. http://rave.ohiolink.edu/etdc/view?acc_num=case1267730564

Felix, E., De Haan, H., Vaandrager, L., & Koelen, M. (2015). Beyond thresholds: The everyday lived experience of the house by older people. *Journal of Housing for the Elderly, 29*, 329–347. https://doi.org/10.1080/027633893.2015.1055027

Feltz, A. (2015). Everyday attitudes about euthanasia and the slippery slope argument. In M. Cholbi & J. Varelius (Eds.), *New directions in the ethics of assisted suicide and euthanasia* (pp. 217–237). Springer. https://doi.org/10.1007/978-3-319-22050-55_13

Fernandes, C., Barbosa, F., Martins, I. P., & Marques-Teixeira, J. (2021). Aging and social cognition: A comprehensive review of the literature. *Psychology & Neuroscience, 14*, 1–15. https://doi.org/10.1037/pne0000251

Fernández-Alcántara, M., Cruz-Quintana, Pérez-Marfil, M. N., Catena-Martinez, A., Pérez-Garcia, M., & Turnbull, O. H. (2016). Assessment of emotional and emotional recognition in complicated grief. *Frontiers in Psychology, 7*. https://doi.org/10.3389/fpsyg.2016.00126

Fernandez-Alvarez, J., Colombo, D., Suso-Ribera, C., Chirico, A., Serino, S., Di Lernia, D., Palacios, A. G., Riva, G., & Botella, C. (2021). Using virtual reality to target positive autobiographical memory in individuals with moderate-to-moderately severe depressive symptoms: A single case experimental design. *Internet Interventions, 25*, 100407. https://doi.org/10.1016/j.invent.2021.100407.

Fernández-Ríos, M., Redolat, R., Serra, E., & González-Alcaide, G. (2021). A systematic review of facial emotion recognition in Alzheimer's disease: A developmental and gender perspective. *Anales de Psicología / Annals of Psychology, 37*, 478–492. https://doi.org/10.6018/analesps.439141

Fernández-Sola, C., Camacho-Ávila, M., Hernández-Padilla, J. M., Fernández-Medina, I. M., Jiménez-López, F. R., Hernández-Sánchez, E., Conesa-Ferrer, M. B., & Granero-Molina, J. (2020). Impact of perinatal death on the social and family context of the parents. *International Journal of Environmental Research and Public Health, 17*, 3421. https://doi.org/10.3390/ijerph17103421

Ferow, A. (2019). Childhood grief and loss. *European Journal of Educational Sciences, Special Edition*, 1–13. https://doi.org/10.19044/ejes.s.v6a1

Ferrarini, T., & Norström, T. (2010). Family policy, economic development, and infant mortality: A longitudinal comparative analysis. *International Journal of Social Welfare, 19*, S89–S102. https://doi.org/10.1111/j.1468–2397.2010.00736.x

Ferré, P., Jarret, J., Brambati, S. M., Bellec, P., & Joanette, Y. (2020). Task-induced functional connectivity of picture naming in healthy aging: The impacts of age and task complexity. *Neurobiology of Language, 1*, 161–184. https://doi.org/10.1162/nol_a_00007

Fetvadjiev, V. H., Neha, T., van de Vijver, F. J. R., McManus, M., & Meiring, D. (2021). The cross-cultural relevance of indigenous measures: The South African Personality Inventory (SAPI), family orientation, and well-being in New Zealand. *Journal of Cross-Cultural Psychology, 52*, 3–21. https://doi.org/10.1177%2F0022022120969979

Fields, B., Yanes, C., Ennis, M., & Toto, P. (2022). Community Aging in Place, Advancing Better Living for Elders (CAPABLE) program: Understanding the potential involvement of care partners. *Health & Social Care in the Community, 30*, e1212–e1219. https://doi.org/10.1111/hsc.13529

Filho, J., Rocha, L. P., Cavalcanti, F. C., & Marinho, P. E. (2022). Relevant functioning aspects and environmental factors for adults and seniors undergoing hemodialysis: A qualitative study. *Chronic Illness, 18*, 206–217. https://doi.org/10.1177/1742395320945200

Findley, C. (2021). *Brain injury awareness month 2021*. https://www.asbmb.org/asbmb-today/science/030121/brain-injury-awareness-month-2021

Fingerman, K. L., Pillemer, K. A., Silverstein, M., & Suitor, J. J. (2012). The baby boomers' intergenerational relationships. *The Gerontologist, 52*, 199–209. https://doi.org/10.1093/geront/gnr139

Finlay, J. M., & Rowles, G. D. (2021). Clinical geography: A proposal to embrace space, place, and wellbeing through person-centered practice. *Wellbeing, Space and Society, 2*, 100035. https://doi.org/10.1016/j.wss.2021.100035

Finucane, T. E. (2016). Social and ethical issues in home-based medical care. In J. L. Hayashi & B. Leff (Eds.), *Geriatric home-based medical care* (pp. 237–249). Springer. https://doi.org/10.1007/978-3-319-23365-9_11

Fiore, J. (2021). A systematic review of the dual process model of coping with bereavement (1999–2016). *OMEGA—Journal of Death and Dying, 84*, 414–458. https://doi.org/10.1177%2F0030222819893139

Fiori, K. L., & Denckla, C. A. (2015). Friendship and happiness among middle-aged adults. In M. Demir (Ed.), *Friendship and happiness* (pp. 137–154). Springer.

Fiori, K. L., Windsor, T. D., & Huxhold, O. (2020). The increasing importance of friendship in late life: Understanding the role of sociohistorical context in social development. *Gerontology, 66*, 286–294. https://doi.org/10.1159/000505547.

Fischer, M., Moscovitch, M., & Alain, C. (2021). A systematic review and meta-analysis of memory-guided attention: Frontal and parietal activation suggests involvement of fronto- parietal networks. *WIREs Cognitive Science, 12*, e1546. https://doi.org/10.1002/wcs.1546

Fisher, H. (2016). *Anatomy of love: A natural history of mating, marriage, and why we stray* (revised and updated). W. W. Norton.

Fisher, J. S., Rezk, A., Nwefo, E., Masterson, J., & Ramasamy, R. (2020). Sexual health in the elderly population. *Current Sexual Health Reports, 12*, 381–388. https://doi.org/10.1007/s11930-020-00278-0

Fiske, S. T., & Taylor, S. E. (2021). *Social cognition: From brains to culture* (4th ed.). SAGE Publications.

Fitzgerald, J. M. (1999). Autobiographical memory and social cognition: Development of the remembered self in adulthood. In T. M. Hess & F. Blanchard-Fields, *Social cognition in aging* (pp. 147–171). Academic Press.

Fjell, A. M., Sneve, M. H., Grydeland, H., Storsve, A. B., & Walhovd, K. B. (2017). The disconnected brain and executive function decline in aging. *Cerebral Cortex, 27*, 2303–2317. https://doi.org/10.1093/cercor?bhw082

Flament, F., Abric, A., & Adam, A.-S. (2021). Evaluating the respective weights of some facial signs on perceived ages in differently aged women of five ethnic origins. *Journal of Cosmetic Dermatology, 20*, 842–853. https://doi.org/10.1111/jocd.13612

Fleming, T. (2021). Models of lifelong learning: An overview. In M. London (Ed.), *The Oxford handbook of lifelong learning* (2nd ed., pp. 35–55). Oxford University Press.

Fletcher, L., & Beauregard, T. A. (2022). The psychology of diversity and its implications for workplace (in) equality: Looking back at the last decade and forward to the next. *Journal of Occupational and Organizational Psychology, 95*, 577–594. https://doi.org/10.1111/joop.12388

Flowers, S. A., & Rebeck, G. W. (2020). APOE in the normal brain. *Neurobiology of Disease, 136*, 104724. https://doi.org/10.1016/j.nbd.2019.104724

Flynn, E., Pine, K., & Lewis, C. (2006). The microgenetic method: Time for change? *The Psychologist, 19*, 152–155. https://www.thepsychologist.org.uk/archive/archive_home.cfm/volumeID_19-editionID_133-ArticleID_997-getfile_getPDF/thepsychologist/0306flyn.pdf

Fogarty, K., & Evans, G. D. (2010). Being an involved father: What does it mean? https://ufdcimages.uflib.ufl.edu/IR/00/00/33/64/00001/HE14100.pdf

Ford, J. H., Garcia, S. M., Fields, E. C., Cunningham, T. J., & Kensinger, E. A. (2021). Older adults remember more positive aspects of the COVID-19 pandemic. *Psychology and Aging, 36*, 694-699. https://doi.org/10.1037/pag0000636

Formosa, M. (2014). Four decades of universities of the Third Age: Past, present, future. *Ageing and Society, 34*, 42–66. https://doi.org/10.1017/S0144686X12000797

Forrester, S. N., Gallo, J. J., Whitfield, K. E., & Thorpe, Jr., R. J. (2019). A framework of minority stress: From physiological manifestations to cognitive outcomes. *The Gerontologist, 59*, 1017–1023. https://doi.org/10.1093/geront/gny104

Foscolou, A., D'Cunha, N. M., Naumovski, N., Tyrovolas, S., Rallidis, L., Matalas, A.-L., Polychronopoulos, E., Sidossis, L. S., & Panagiotakos, D. (2021). Midday napping and successful aging in older people living in the mediterranean region: The Epidemiological Mediterranean Islands Study (MEDIS). *Brain Sciences, 10*, 14. https://doi.org/10.3390/brainsci10010014

Fossati, P. (2012). Neural correlates of emotion processing: From emotional to social brain. *European Neuropsychopharmacology, 22*(Suppl. 3), S487–S491. https://doi.org/10.1016/j. euroneuro.2012.07.008

Fouad, N., Ghosh, A., Chang, W-h., Figueiredo, C., & Bachhuber, T. (2016). Career exploration among college students. *Journal of College Student Development, 57*, 460–464. https://doi.org/10.1353/csd.2016.0047

Fowler, J. W. (1981). *Stags of faith: The psychology of human development and the quest for meaning*. HarperCollins.

Fowler, J. W. (2000). *Becoming adult, becoming Christian: Adult development and Christian faith* (rev. ed.). Jossey-Bass.

Fowler, K. L. (2008). "The wholeness of things": Infusing diversity and social justice into death education. *Omega: Journal of Death and Dying, 57*, 53–91. https://doi.org/10.2190/OM.57.1.d

Fraenz, C., Schlüter, C., Friedrich, P., Jung, R. E., Güntürkün, O., & Genç, E. (2021). Interindividual differences in matrix reasoning are linked to functional connectivity between brain regions nominated by Parieto-Frontal Integration Theory. *Intelligence, 87*, 101545. https://doi.org/10.1016/j.intell.2021.101545

Fraley, R. C., & Shaver, P. R. (2021). Attachment theory and its place in contemporary personality theory and research. In O. P. John & R. W. Robins (Eds.), *Handbook of personality: Theory and research* (pp. 642–666). Guilford Press.

Franceschi, K. A. (2005). The experience of the transition to motherhood in women who have suffered maternal loss in adolescence. *Dissertation Abstracts International: Section B: The Sciences and Engineering, 65*(8-B), 4282.

Franco, M., Katz, R., Pickens, J., & Brunsma, D. L. (2020). From my own flesh and blood: An exploratory examination of discrimination from family for Black/White Multiracial people. *Qualitative Social Work, 19*, 246–266. https://doi.org/10.1177%2F1473325018815734

Frank, D. J., Jordano, M. L., Browne, K., & Touron, D. R. (2016). Older adults' use of retrieval strategies in everyday life. *Gerontology, 62*, 624–635. https://doi.org/10.1159/000446277

Frank, M. G., Weber, M. D., Watkins, L. R., & Maier, S. F. (2016). Stress-induced neuroinflammatory priming: A liability factor in the etiology of psychiatric disorders. *Neurobiology of Stress, 66*, 82–90. https://doi.org/10.1016/j.ynstr.2015.12.004

Frank, N. (2016). Moving beyond anti-LGBT politics: Commentary on "Same-sex and different-sex parent households and child health outcomes: Findings from the National Survey of Children's Health." *Journal of Developmental & Behavioral Pediatrics, 37*, 245–247. https://doi.org/10.1097/DBP.0000000000000295

Franses, P. H. (2016). When did classic composers make their best work? *Creativity Research Journal, 28*, 219–221. https://doi.org/10.1080/10400419.2016.1162489

Frazier, L. D., & Hooker, K. (2006). Possible selves in adult development: Linking theory and research. In C. Dunkel & J. Kerpelman (Eds.), *Possible selves: Theory, research and applications* (pp. 41–59). Nova Publishers.

Frazier, L. D., Hooker, K., Johnson, P. M., & Kaus, C. R. (2000). Continuity and change in possible selves in later life: A 5-year longitudinal study. *Basic and Applied Social Psychology, 22*, 237–243. https://doi.org/10.1207/S15324834BASP2203_10

Frazier, L. D., Johnson, P. M., Gonzalez, G. K., & Kafka, C. L. (2002). Psychosocial influences on possible selves: A comparison of three cohorts of older adults. *International Journal of Behavioral Development, 26*, 308–317. https://doi.org/10.1080/01650250143000184

Frazier, L. D., Schwartz, B. L. & Metcalfe, J. (2021). The MAPS model of self-regulation: Integrating metacognition, agency, and possible selves. *Metacognition Learning, 16*, 297–318. https://doi.org/10.1007/s11409-020-09255-3

Frederick, C. M., & Zhang, T. (2020). *Examining the qualities of online and offline friendships: A comparison between groups*. Manuscript, Embry-Riddle Aeronautical University. https://commons.erau.edu/publication/1413.

Fredriksen, L., Zucchero, R., Partlow, B., Infante, R., Taylor, J., & Washburn, H. (2020). The impact of memory stereotype threat on memory and memory self-efficacy in older adults. *Innovation in Aging, 4*, 326–327. https://doi.org/10.1093/geroni/igaa057.1047

Freeman, G., & Maloney, D. (2021). Body, avatar, and me: The presentation and perception of self in social virtual reality. *Proceedings of the ACM on Human-Computer Interaction*. Article No. 239. https://doi.org/10.1145/3432938.

French-Holloway, M. (2020). *A new meaning-mission fit: Aligning life and work in business*. Springer.

Freund, A. M. (2020). The bucket list effect: Why leisure goals are often deferred until retirement. *American Psychologist, 75*, 499–510. https://doi.org/10.1037/amp0000617

Freund, A. M., & Ritter, J. O. (2009). Midlife crisis: A debate. *Gerontology, 55*, 582–591. https://doi.org/10.1159/000227322

Friedlander, M. L., Lee, M., & Escudero, V. (2019). What we do and do not know about the nature and analysis of couple interaction. *Couple and Family Psychology: Research and Practice, 8*, 24–44. https://doi.org/10.1037/cfp0000114

Friedman, D. B. (2020). Do words really matter? A focus on communication and aging, *Journal of Women & Aging, 32*, 361–364. https://doi.org/10.1080/08952841.2020.1764298

Friedman, M. C., McGillivray, S., Murayama, K., & Castel, A. D. (2015). Memory for medication side effects in younger and older adults: The role of subjective and objective importance. *Cognitive Psychology, 43*, 206–215. https://doi.org/10.3758/s13421-014-0476-0

Friesen, H., Harrison, J., Peters, M., Epp, D., & McPherson, N. (2020). Death education for children and young people in public schools. *International Journal of Palliative Nursing, 26*, 332–335. https://doi.org/10.12968/ijpn.2020.26.7.332

Friesen, M. D., Horwood, L. J., Fergusson, D. M., & Woodward, L. J. (2017). Exposure to parental separation in childhood and later parenting quality as an adult: Evidence from a 30-year longitudinal study. *Journal of Child Psychology and Psychiatry, 58*, 30–37. https://doi.org/10.1111/jcpp.12610

Friesen, S., Brémault-Phillips, S., Rudrum, L., & Rogers, L. G. (2016). Environmental design that supports health aging: Evaluating a new supportive living facility. *Journal of Housing for the Elderly, 30*, 18–34. https://doi.org/10.1080/02763893.2015.1129380

Frith, C. D., & Frith, U. (2012). Mechanisms of social cognition. *Annual Review of Psychology, 63*, 287–313. https://doi.org/10.1146/annurev-psych-120710-100449

Frith, E., Elbich, D. B., Christensen, A. P., Rosenberg, M. D., Chen, Q., Kane, M. J., Silvia, P. J., Seli, P., & Beaty, R. E. (2021). Intelligence and creativity share a common cognitive and neural basis. *Journal of Experimental Psychology: General, 150*, 609–632. https://doi.org/10.1037/xge0000958

Frizzell, N., (2021). *The panic years: Dates, doubts, and the mother of all decisions*. Flatiron Books.

Froehlich, D. E., Beausaert, S., & Segers, M. (2016). Aging and the motivation to stay employable. *Journal of Managerial Psychology, 31*, 756–770. https://doi.org/10.1108/JMP-08-2014-0224

Fruhauf, C. A., Jarrott, S. E., & Allen, K. R. (2006). Grandchildren's perceptions of caring for grandparents. *Journal of Family Issues, 27*, 887–911. https://doi.org/10.1177/0192513X05286019

Frydman, J. L., Li, W., Gelfman, L. P., & Liu, B. (2022). Telemedicine uptake among older adults during the COVID-19 pandemic. *Annals of Internal Medicine, 175*, 145–148. https://doi.org/10.7326/M21-2972

Fuentes, A., & Desrocher, M. (2012). Autobiographical memory in emerging adulthood: Relationship with self-concept clarity. *Journal of Adult Development, 19*, 28–39. https://doi.org/10.1007/s10804-011-9131-1

Fuller, H. R., & Huseth-Zosel, A. (2021). Lessons in resilience: Initial coping among older adults during the COVID-19 pandemic. *The Gerontologist, 61*, 114–125. https://doi.org/10.1093/geront/gnaa170

Fuller, H. R., Ajrouch, K. J., & Antonucci, T. C. (2020). The convoy model and later-life family relationships. *Journal of Family Theory and Review, 12*, 126–146. https://doi.org/10.1111/jftr.12376.

Fulop, T., Larbi, A., Khalil, A., Plotka, A., Laurent, B., Ramassamy, C., Bosco, N., Hirokama, K., Frost, E. H., & Witkowski, J. M. (2022). Immunosenescence and Alzheimer's disease. In V. Bueno & G. Pawelec (Eds.), *Healthy longevity and immune system* (pp. 177–199). Springer, Cham. https://doi.org/10.1007/978-3-030-87532-9_9

Fye, M. A., Chasek, C. T., Mims, G. A., Sandman, J., & Hinrichsen, A. (2020). Marital satisfaction during retirement. *Family Journal, 28*, 313–318. https://doi.org/10.1177%2F1066480720929689

Gallagher-Thompson, D., Coon, D. W., Solano, N., Ambler, C., Rabinowitz, Y., & Thompson, L. W. (2003). Change in indices of distress among Latino and Anglo female caregivers of elderly relatives with dementia: Site-specific results from the REACH national collaborative study. *The Gerontologist, 43*, 580–591. https://doi.org/10.1093/geront/43.4.580

Gallegos, J. Lutz, J., Katz, E., & Edelstein, B. (2018). Psychological assessment of older persons. *Oxford Research Encyclopedias: Psychology*. https://doi.org/10.1093/acrefore/9780190236557.013.408

Gallen, C. L., Turner, G. R., Adnan, A., & D'Esposito, M. (2016). Reconfiguration of brain network architecture to support executive control in aging. *Neurobiology of Aging, 44*, 42–52. https://doi.org/10.1016/j.neurobiolaging.2016.04.003

Galovan, A. M., Hawkins, A. J., Harris, S. M., & Simpson, D. M. (2022). What are they doing? A national survey of help-seeking and relationship-repair behavior of individuals who are thinking about divorce. *Journal of Marital and Family Therapy, 48*, 371–390. https://doi.org/10.1111/jmft.12480.

Gamaldo, A. A., & Allaire, J. C. (2016). Daily fluctuations in everyday cognition: Is it meaningful? *Journal of Aging and Health, 28*, 834–849. https://doi.org/10.1177/0898264315611669

Gamba, F. (2018). Coping with loss: Mapping digital rituals for the expression of grief. *Health Communication, 33*, 78–84. https://doi.org/10.1080/10410236.2016.1242038

Ganong, L., & Coleman, M. (2017). *Stepfamily relationships: Development, dynamics, and interventions* (2nd ed.). Springer.

Ganong, L., Jensen, T., Sanner, C., Russell, L., & Coleman, M. (2019). Stepfathers' affinity-seeking with stepchildren, stepfather-stepchild relationship quality, marital quality, and stepfamily cohesion among stepfathers and mothers. *Journal of Family Psychology, 33*, 521-531. https://doi.org/10.1037/fam0000518

Gans, D. (2007). Normative obligations and parental care in social context. *Dissertation Abstracts International. Section A. Humanities and Social Sciences, 68*(5-A), 2115.

Garb, H. N. (2021). Race bias and gender bias in the diagnosis of psychological disorders. *Clinical Psychology Review, 90*, 102087. https://doi.org/10.1016/j.cpr.2021.102087

Gardiner, H.W. (2020). Grandparenting across cultures. In B. Ashdown & A. Faherty (Eds.), *Parents and caregivers across cultures* (pp. 273–281). Springer, Cham. https://doi.org/10.1007/978-3-030-35590-6_19

Garos, S. (2021). Goodbye is just the beginning. *Journal of Loss and Trauma, 26*, 303–308. https://doi.org/10.1080/15325024.2020.1721726

Garrard, E., & Wilkinson, S. (2005). Passive euthanasia. *Journal of Medical Ethics, 31*, 64–68. https://doi.org/10.1136/jme.2003.005777

Gaspard, G., Gadsby, C., & Mallmes, J. (2021). Indigenous end-of-life doula course: Bringing the culture home. *International Journal of Indigenous Health, 16*, 33230. https://doi.org/10.32799/ijih.v16i2.33230

Gaturu, M., & Njuguna, F. W. (2020). Career plateauing and its relationship with secondary school teachers' pursuit of post-graduate studies in Nyandarua and Murang'a counties, Kenya. *Journal of Educational Research in Developing Areas, 1*, 153–166. https://doi.org/10.47434/JEREDA/1.2.2020.153

Gatz, M., Smyer, M. A., & DiGilio, D. A. (2016). Psychology's contribution to the well-being of older Americans. *American Psychologist, 71*, 257–267. https://doi.org/10.1037/a0040251

Gaudron, J.-P., & Vautier, S. (2007). Analyzing individual differences in vocational, leisure, and family interests: A multitrait-multimethod approach. *Journal of Vocational Behavior, 70*, 561–573. https://doi.org/10.1016/j. jvb.2007.01.004

Gawas, M., Bains, A., Janghu, S., Kamat, P., & Chawla, P. (2022). A comprehensive review on varicose veins: Preventive measures and different treatments. *Journal of the American College of Nutrition, 41*, 499–510. https://doi.org/10.1080/07315724.2021.1909510

Gayatri, D. (2018). Menopause-related cognitive impairment. *Obstetrics & Gynecology, 132*, 1325–1327. https://doi.org/10.1097/AOG.0000000000002963

Generations United. (2021). *Grandfamilies*. https://www.gu.org/explore-our-topics/grandfamilies/

Genworth Financial. (2021). *Cost of care survey*. https://www.genworth.com/aging-and-you/finances/cost-of-care.html

Georgantzi, N. (2018). The European Union's approach towards ageism. In L. Ayalon & C. Tesch-Römer (Eds.), *Contemporary perspectives on ageism* (pp. 341–368). Springer, Cham. https://doi.org/10.1007/978-3-319-73820-8_21

Gerhart, B., & Feng, J. (2021). The resource-based view of the firm, human resources, and human capital: Progress and prospects. *Journal of Management, 47*, 1796–1819. https://doi.org/10.1177%2F0149206320978799

Germain, M.-L. (2020). How millennial mentors can help upskill, reskill, and retain mature workers. In C. Hughes (Ed.), *Strategies for attracting, maintaining, and balancing a mature workforce* (pp. 179–207). IGI Global. https://doi.org/10.4018/978-1-7998-2277-6

Gerontological Society of America. (2012). *Communicating with older adults: An evidence-based review of what really works*. Author.

Gervais, S. J., Wiener, R. L., Allen, J., Farnum, K. S., & Kimble, K. (2016). Do you see what I see? The consequences of objectification in work settings for experiencers and third party predictors. *Analyses of Social Issues and Public Policy, 16*, 143–174. https://doi.org/10.1111/asap.12118

Ghabrial, M. A. (2017). "Trying to figure out where we belong": Narratives of racialized sexual minorities on community, identity, discrimination, and health. *Sexuality Research and Social Policy, 14*, 42–55. https://doi.org/10.1007/s13178-016-0229-x

Ghanim, D. (2015). *The virginity trap in the Middle East*. Springer.

Ghosh, S., Capistrant, B., & Friedemann-Sánchez, G. (2017). Who will care for the elder caregiver? Outlining theoretical approaches and future research questions. In T. Samanta (Ed.), *Cross-cultural and cross-disciplinary perspectives in social gerontology* (pp. 23–43). Springer.

Giacumo, L. A., Chen, J., & Seguinot-Croz, A. (2020). Evidence on the use of mentoring programs and practices to support workplace learning: A systematic multiple-studies review. *Performance Improvement Quarterly, 33*, 259–303. https://doi.org/10.1002/piq.21324

Gianotten, W. L. (2021). The (mental) health benefits of sexual expression. In M. Lew-Starowicz, A. Giraldi, & T. Krüger (Eds.), *Psychiatry and sexual medicine* (pp. 57–70). Springer, Cham. https://doi.org/10.1007/978-3-030-52298-8_6

Giasson, H. L., Liao, H.-W., & Carstensen, L. L. (2019). Counting down while time flies: Implications of age-related time acceleration for goal pursuit across adulthood. *Current Opinion in Psychology, 26*, 85–89. https://doi.org/10.1016/j.copsyc.2018.07.001

Gibran, K. (1923). *The prophet*. Knopf.

Giele, J. Z. (2013). *Family policy and the American safety net*. Sage Publications.

Gilbert, D. T., & Malone, P. S. (1995). The correspondence bias. *Psychological Bulletin, 117*, 21–38. https://doi.org/10.1037/0033-2909.117.1.21

Gilleard, C. (2020). The final stage of human development? Erikson's view of integrity and old age. *International Journal of Ageing and Later Life, 14*, 139–162. https://doi.org/10.3384/ijal.1652-8670.1471

Gilligan, M., Stocker, C. M., & Jewsbury Conger, K. (2020). Sibling relationships in adulthood: Research findings and new frontiers. *Journal of Family Theory & Review, 12*, 305–320. https://doi.org/10.1111/jftr.12385

Gilligan, M., Suitor, J. J., Kim, S., & Pillemer, K. (2013). Differential effects of perceptions of mothers' and fathers' favoritism on sibling tension in adulthood. *Journals of Gerontology: Social Sciences, 68B*, S593–S598. https://doi.org/10.1093/geronb/gbt039

Gilliver, M., Carter, L., Macoun, D., Rosen, J., & Williams, W. (2012). Music to whose ears? The effect of social norms on young people's risk perceptions of hearing damage resulting from their music listening behavior. *Noise and Health, 14*, 47–51. https://www.noiseandhealth.org/text.asp?2012/14/57/47/95131

Giordano, P. C., Copp, J. E., Longmore, M. A., & Manning, W. D. (2016). Anger, control, and intimate partner violence in young adulthood. *Journal of Family Violence, 31*, 1–13. https://doi.org/10.1007/s10896-015-9753-3

Giovanello, K. S., & Schacter, D. L. (2012). Reduced specificity of hippocampal and posterior ventrolateral prefrontal activity during relational retrieval in normal aging. *Journal of Cognitive Neuroscience, 24*, 159–170. https://doi.org/10.1162/jocn_a_00113

Gire, J. (2014). How death imitates life: Cultural influences on conceptions of death and dying. *Online Readings in Psychology and Culture, 6*(2). https://doi.org/10.9707/2307-0919.1120

Gire, J. T. (2019). Cultural variations in perceptions of aging. In K. D. Keith (Ed.), *Cross-cultural psychology; Contemporary themes and perspectives* (2nd ed., pp. 216–240). Wiley. https://doi.org/10.1002/9781119519348.ch10

Gitlin, L. N., Parisi, J., Huang, J., Winter, L., & Roth, D. L. (2016). Attachment to life: Psychometric analyses of the Valuation of Life Scale and differences among adults. *The gerontologist, 56*, e21-e31. https://doi.org/10.1093/geront/gnv696

Givertz, M., Segrin, C., & Hansal, A. (2009). The association between satisfaction and commitment differs across marital couple types. *Communication Research, 36*, 561–584. https://doi.org/10.1177/0093650209333035

Gizem, E., & Burak, D. (2021). Facial appearance and dominance in leadership. In J. D. Sinnott & J. S. Rabin (Eds.), *The psychology of political behavior in a time of change: Identity in a changing world* (pp. 335–347). Springer Cham.

Glass, B. D., & Osman, M. (2017). Positive explorers: Modeling dynamic control in normal aging. *Aging, Neuropsychology, and Cognition: A Journal on Normal and Dysfunctional Development, 24*, 62–79. https://doi.org/10.1080/13825585.2016.1171290

Glasser, M. F., Coalson, T. S., Robinson, E. C., Hacker, C. D., Harwell, J., Yacoub, E., Ugurbil, K., Andersson, J., Beckmann, C. F., Jenkinson, M., Smith, S. M., & Van Essen, D. C. (2016). A multi-modal parcellation of human cerebral cortex. *Nature, 536*, 171–178. https://doi.org/10.1038/nature18933

Global Industry Analysts. (2021, May 12). *Global anti-aging products market to reach $47.8 billion by 2027*. https://www.prnewswire.com/news-releases/global-anti-aging-products-market-to-reach-47-8-billion-by-2027--301287461.html

Glorioso, D. K., Iglewicz, A., & Zisook, S. (2020). Bereavement and grief. In N. Hartke, A. Etkin, & R. O'Hara (Eds.), *Handbook of mental health and aging* (3rd ed., pp. 245–256). Academic Press. https://doi.org/10.1016/B978-0-12-800136-3.00018-1

Glück, J. (2018). Measuring wisdom: Existing approaches, continuing challenges, and new developments. *Journals of Gerontology: Psychological Sciences, 73*, 1393–1403. https://doi.org/10.1093/geronb/gbx140

Glymour, M. M., & Manly, J. J. (2008). Lifecourse social conditions and racial and ethnic patterns of cognitive aging. *Neuropsychology Review, 18*, 223–254. https://doi.org/10.1007/s11065-008-9064-z

Godfrey, D. (2016). End-of-life issues for LGBT elders. In D. A. Harley & P. B. Teaster (Eds.), *Handbook of LGBT elders* (pp. 439–454). Springer.

Godzik, C., Crawford, S., & Ryan, E. (2021). Feasibility of an online cognitive behavioral therapy program to improve insomnia, mood, and quality of life in bereaved adults ages 55 and older. *Geriatric Nursing, 42*, 99–106. https://doi.org/10.1016/j.gerinurse.2020.12.006

Golant, S. M. (2008). Affordable clustered housing-care: A category of long-term care options for the elderly poor. *Journal of Housing for the Elderly, 22*, 3–44. https://doi.org/10.1080/027638908802096906

Golant, S. M. (2012). Out of their residential comfort and mastery zones: Toward a more relevant environmental gerontology. *Journal of Housing for the Elderly, 26*, 26–43. https://doi.org/10.108 0/027663893.2012.655654

Golant, S. M. (2020). The distance to death perceptions of older adults explain why they age in place: A theoretical examination. *Journal of Aging Studies, 54*, 100863. https://doi.org/10.1016/j.jaging.2020.100863

Gold, J. M. (2016). *Stepping in, stepping out: Creating stepfamily rhythm*. American Counseling Association.

Goldberg, A. E. (2009). *Lesbian and gay parents and their children: Research on the family life cycle*. American Psychological Association.

Goldfarb, E. V., Rosenberg, M. D., Seo, D., Constable, R. T., & Sinha, R. (2020). Hippocampal seed connectome-based modeling predicts the feeling of stress. *Nature Communications, 11*, 2650. https://doi.org/10.1038/s41467-020-16492-2

Goldstein, E. G. (2005). *When the bubble bursts: Clinical perspectives on midlife issues*. Routledge.

Goleman, D. (1995). *Emotional intelligence*. Bantam Books.

Golkar, A., Johansson, E., Kasahara, M., Osika, W., Perski, A., & Savic, I. (2014). The influence of work-related chronic stress on the regulation of emotion and on functional connectivity in the brain. *PLOS ONE 9*, e104550. https://doi.org/10.1371/journal.pone.0104550

Gómez, C. S., & Rodríguez, E. J. F. (2021). The effectiveness of a training programme in everyday cognition in healthy older adults: A randomised controlled trial. *BMC Geriatrics, 21*, 79. https://doi.org/10.1186/s12877-020-01998-7

Gonyea, J. G. (2013). Midlife, multigenerational bonds, and caregiving. In R. C. Talley & R. J. V. Montgomery (Eds.), *Caregiving across the lifespan* (pp. 105–130). Springer.

Gonza, G., & Burger, A. (2017). Subjective well-being during the 2008 economic crisis: Identification of mediating and moderating factors. *Journal of Happiness Studies, 18*, 1763–1797. https://doi.org/10.1007/s10902-016-9797-y

Gonzalez, A., & Quinones, M. C. (2021). People of Puerto Rican heritage. In L. Purnell & E. Fenkl (Eds.), *Textbook for transcultural health care: A population approach* (pp. 637–668). Springer, Cham. https://doi.org/10.1007/978-3-030-51399-3_25

Goodsell, T. L. (2013). Familification: Family, neighborhood change, and housing policy. *Housing Studies, 28*, 845–868. https://doi.org/10.1080/02673037.2013.768334

Gopalkrishnan, N. (2018). Cultural diversity and mental health: Considerations for policy and practice. *Frontiers in Public Health, 6*. https://doi.org/10.3389/fpubh.2018.00179

Gordijn, B., Have, H. t. (2016). Technology and dementia. *Medicine, Health Care and Philosophy, 19*, 339–340. https://doi.org/10.1007/s11019-016-9715-4

Gorges, R. J., & Konetzka, R. T. (2021). Factors associated with racial differences in deaths among nursing home residents with COVID-19 infection in the US. *JAMA Network Open*, 4, e2037431. https://doi.org/10.1001/jamanetworkopen.2020.37431

Gorgoni, M., & De Gennaro, L. (2021). Sleep in the aging brain. *Brain Sciences, 11*, 229. https://doi.org/10.3390/brainsci11020229

Gottman, J. M., & Levenson, R. W. (2000). The timing of divorce: Predicting when a couple will divorce over a 14-year period. *Journal of Marriage and the Family, 62*, 737–745. https://doi.org/10.1111/j.1741-3737.2000.00737.x

Gottman, J. M., & Silver, N. (2015). *The seven principles for making marriage work* (Rev. ed.). Harmony Books.

Gottman, J. M., Gottman, J. S., Abrams, D., & Abrams, R. C. (2018). *Eight dates: Essential conversations for a lifetime of love*. Workman Publishing.

Goukasian, N., Porat, S., Blanken, A., Avila, D., Zlatev, D., Hurtz, S., Hwang, K. S., Pierce, J., Joshi, S. H., Woo, E., & Apostolova, L. G. (2019). Cognitive correlates of hippocampal atrophy and ventricular enlargement in adults with or without mild cognitive impairment. *Dementia and Geriatric Cognitive Disorders Extra, 9*, 281–293. https://doi.org/10.1159/000490044

Gould, S. J. (1999). A critique of Heckhausen and Schulz's (1995) life-span theory of control from a cross-cultural perspective. *Psychological Review, 106*, 597–604. https://doi.org/10.1037/033-295X.106.3.597

Grady, C. (2012). The cognitive neuroscience of ageing. *Nature Reviews Neuroscience, 13*, 491–505. https://doi.org/10.1038/nrn3256

Grady, C. Luk, G., Craik, F. I. M., & Bialystok, E. (2015). Brain network activity in monolingual and bilingual older adults. *Neuropsychologia, 66*, 170–181. https://doi.org/10.1016/j.neuropsychologia.2014.10.042

Grady, C., Sarral, S., Saverino, C., & Campbell, K. (2016). Age differences in the functional interactions among the default, frontoparietal control, and dorsal attention networks. *Neurobiology of Aging, 41*, 159–172. https://doi.org/10.1016/j.neurobiolaging.2016.02.020

Graf, A. C., Jacob, E., Twigg, D., & Nattabi, B. (2020). Contemporary nursing graduates' transition to practice: A critical review of transition models. *Journal of Clinical Nursing, 29*, 3097–3107. https://doi.org/10.1111/jocn.15234

Graham, E. K., & Lachman, M. E. (2012). Personality and aging. In S. K. Whitbourne & M. J. Sliwinski (Eds.), *The Wiley-Blackwell handbook of adulthood and aging* (pp. 254–272). Wiley-Blackwell.

Graham, E. K., Weston, S. J., Gerstorf, D., Yoneda, T. B., Booth, T., Beam, C. R., Petkus, A. J., Drewelies, J., Hall, A. N., Bastarache, E. D., Estabrook, R., Katz, M. J., Turiano, N. A., Lindenberger, U., Smith, J., Wagner, G. G., Pedersen, N. L., Allemand, M., Spiro, A., III, ... Mroczek, D. K. (2020). Trajectories of Big Five personality traits: A coordinated analysis of 16 longitudinal samples. *European Journal of Personality, 34*, 301–321. https://doi.org/10.1002/per.2259

Granacher, U., Muehlbauer, T., & Gruber, M. (2012). A qualitative review of balance and strength performance in healthy older adults: Impact for testing and training. *Journal of Aging Research, 2012*, 708905. https://doi.org/10.1155/2012/708905

Granbom, M., Slaug, B., Löfqvist, C., Oswald, F., & Iwarsson, S. (2016). Community relocation in very old age: Changes in housing accessibility. *American Journal of Occupational Therapy, 70*, 7002270020p1–7002270020p9. https://doi.org/10.5014/ajot.2016.016147

Grandfamilies.org. (2021). *Resources*. https://www.grandfamilies.org/Resources

Grandfamilies.org. (2022). *State fact sheets*. https://grandfamilies.org/State-Fact-Sheets

Granot-Hershkovitz, E., Tarraf, W., Kurniansyah, N., Daviglus, M., Isasi, C. R., Kaplan, R., Lamar, M., Perreira, K. M., Wassertheil-Smoller, S., Stickel, A., Thyagarajan, B., Zeng, D., Fornage, M., DeCarli, C. S., González, H. M., & Sofer, T. (2021). *APOE* alleles' association with cognitive function differs across Hispanic/Latino groups and genetic ancestry in the study of Latinos-investigation of neurocognitive aging (HCHS/SOL). *Alzheimer's & Dementia, 17*, 466–474. https://doi.org/10.1002/alz.12205

Graupensperger, S., Calhoun, B. H., Patrick, M. E., & Lee, C. M. (2022). Longitudinal effects of COVID-19-related stressors on young adults' mental health and wellbeing. *Applied Psychology: Health and Well-Being, 14*, 734-756. https://doi.org/10.1111/aphw.12344

Grau-Rivera, O., Navalpotro-Gomez, I., Sánchez-Benavides, G., Suárez-Calvet, M., Milà-Alomà, M., Arenaza-Urquijo, E. M., Salvadó, G., Sala-Vila, A., Shekari, M., González-de-Echávarri, J. M., Minguillón, C., Niñerola-Baizán, A., Perissinotti, A., Simon, M., Kollmorgen, G., Zetterberg, H., Blennow, K., Gispert, J. D., & Molinuevo, J. L. for the ALFA Study. (2021). Association of weight change with cerebrospinal fluid biomarkers and amyloid positron emission tomography in preclinical Alzheimer's disease. *Alzheimer's Research and Therapy, 13*, Article 46. https://doi.org/10.1186/s13195-021-00781-z

Grawitch, M. J., Barber, L. K., & Justice, L. (2010). Rethinking the work–life interface: It's not about balance, it's about resource allocation. *Health and Well-Being, 2*, 127–159. https://doi.org/10.1111/j.1758-0854.2009.01023.x

Grawitch, M. J., Lavigne, K., Cornelius, A., Gill, R., & Winton, S. (2020). *COVID-19 and well-being: Demographics, individual differences, and leadership help explain pandemic impact*. https://doi.org/10.31234/osf.io/ce84n

Green, K. C. (2018). Creating sustainable workplace environments: An exploratory study of social energy expenditure in cross-sex, heterosexual organizational friendships. Master's thesis, Illinois State University. https://ir.library.illinoisstate.edu/etd/858/.

Greenberg, D. L. (2004). President Bush's false [flashbulb] memory of 9/11/01. *Applied Cognitive Psychology, 18*, 363–370. https://doi.org/10.1002/acp.1016

Greene, D., Tschanz, J. T., Smith, K. R., Østbye, T., Corcoran, C., Welsh-Bohmer, K. A., Norton, M. C. & Cache County Investigators. (2014). Impact of offspring death on cognitive health in late life: The Cache County study. *American Journal of Geriatric Psychiatry, 22, 1307–1315*. https://doi.org/10.1016/j.jagp.2013.05.002

Greene, N. R., Naveh-Benjamin, M., & Cowan, N. (2020). Adult age differences in working memory capacity: Spared central storage but deficits in ability to maximize peripheral storage. *Psychology and Aging, 35*, 866–880. https://doi.org/10.1037/pag0000476

Greenfield, E. A. (2012). Using ecological frameworks to advance a field of research, practice, and policy on aging-in-place initiatives. *The Gerontologist, 52*, 1–12. https://doi.org/10.1093/geront/gnr108

Greenfield, E. A., Black, K., Buffel, T., & Yeh, J. (2019) Community gerontology: A framework for research, policy, and practice on communities and ageing. *The Gerontologist, 59*, 803–810. https://doi.org/10.1093/geront/gny089

Greenfield, E. A., Black, K., Oh, P., & Stevens, A. P. (2022). Theories of community collaboration to advance age-friendly community change. *The Gerontologist, 62*, 36–45. https://doi.org/10.1093/geront/gnab136

Greenwald, A. G., & Lai, C. K. (2020). Implicit social cognition. *Annual Review of Psychology, 71*, 419–445. https://doi.org/10.1146/annurev-psych-010419-050837

Gregory, C. (2021). *Depression in women: Types, causes, symptoms, and treatments*. https://www.psycom.net/depression.central.women.html

Grey, R. (1756). *Memoria technica* (4th ed.). Hinton.

Gribble, R., Goodwin, L., Oram, S., & Fear, N. (2019). "Happy wife, happy soldier": How the relationship between military spouses and the military institution influences spouse well-being. In R. Moelker, M. Andres, & N. Rones (Eds.), *The politics of military families: State, work organizations, and the rise of the negotiation household*. Routledge.

Grødem, A., & Kitterød, R. (2021). Older workers imagining retirement: The collapse of agency, or freedom at last? *Ageing and Society*, 1–19. https://doi.org/10.1017/S0144686X20002044

Groger, L. (1995). A nursing home can be a home. *Journal of Aging Studies, 9*, 137–153. https://doi.org/10.1016/0890-4065(95)90008-X

Groger, L. (2002). Coming to terms: African-Americans' complex ways of coping with life in a nursing home. *The International Journal of Aging and Human Development, 55*, 183–205. https://doi.org/10.2190/MDLP-UDE7-P376-QXE3

Groome, D. (2016). Everyday memory. In D. Groome & M. W. Eysenck (Eds.), *An introduction to applied cognitive psychology* (2nd ed., pp. 153–173). Routledge.

Grose, J. (2020, September 9). The pandemic is a "mental health crisis" for parents. *New York Times*. https://www.nytimes.com/2020/09/09/parenting/mental-health-parents-coronavirus.html?smid=url-share

Gross, E. B., & Medina-Villiers, S. E. (2020). Cognitive processes unfold in a social context: A review and extension of social baseline theory. *Frontiers in Psychology, 11*. https://doi.org/10.3389/fpsyg.2020.00378

Grossmann, I. (2017). Wisdom in context. *Perspectives on Psychological Science, 12*, 233–257. https://doi.org/10.1177/1745691616672066

Grossmann, I., & Kung, F. (2019). Wisdom and culture. In S. Kitayama & D. Cohen (Eds.), *Handbook of cultural psychology* (2nd ed., pp. 343–364). Guilford Press.

Grossmann, I., & Kung, F. (2020). Wisdom across cultures. In O. Braddock (Ed.), *Oxford research encyclopedia of psychology*. https://doi.org/10.1093/acrefore/9780190236557.013.586

Grossmann, I., Weststrate, N. M., Ardelt, M., Brienza, J. P., Dong, M., Ferrari, M., Fournier, M. A., Hu, C. S., Nusbaum H. C., & Vervaeke, J. (2020). The science of wisdom in a polarized world: Knowns and unknowns. *Psychological Inquiry, 31*, 103–133. https://doi.org/10.1080/1047840X.2020.1750917

Groth-Marnat, G., & Wright, A. J. (2016). *Handbook of psychological assessment* (6th ed.). Wiley.

Gruenewald, T. L., Liao, D. H., & Seeman, T. E. (2012). Contributing to others, contributing to oneself: Perceptions of generativity and health in later life. *Journals of Gerontology: Psychological Sciences, 67*, 660–665. https://doi.org/10.1093/geronb/gbs034

Grühn, D., Lumley, M. A., Diehl, M., Labouvie-Vief, G. (2013). Time-based indicators of emotional complexity: Interrelations and correlates. *Emotion, 13*, 226–237. https://doi.org/10.1037/a0030363

Grundy, S. M., & Feingold, K. R. (2019). *Guidelines for the management of high blood cholesterol*. https://www.ncbi.nlm.nih.gov/books/NBK305897/

Gu, X., Liu, X., Van Dam, N. T., Hof, P. R., & Fan, J. (2013). Cognition-emotion integration in the anterior insular cortex. *Cerebral Cortex, 23*, 20–27. https://doi.org/10.1093/cercor/bhr367

Gubernskaya, Z. (2010). Changing attitudes toward marriage and children in six countries. *Sociological Perspectives, 53*, 179–200. https://doi.org/10.1525/sop.2010.53.2.179

Guergova, S., & Dufour, A. (2011). Thermal sensitivity in the elderly: A review. *Ageing Research Reviews, 10*, 80–92. https://doi.org/10.1016/j.arr.2010.04.009

Guilford, J. P. (1959). *Personality*. McGraw-Hill.

Gunnell, D., & Chang, S.-S. (2016). Economic recession, unemployment, and suicide. In R. C. O'Connor & J. Pirkis (Eds.), *The international handbook of suicide prevention* (2nd ed., pp. 284–300). Wiley.

Guo, S., & Maitra, S. (2017). Revisioning curriculum in the age of transnational mobility: Towards a transnational and transcultural framework. *Curriculum Inquiry, 47*, 80–91. https://doi.org/10.1080/03626784.2016.1254504

Gurguryan, L., Rioux, M., & Sheldon, S. (2021). Reduced anterior hippocampal and ventromedial prefrontal activity when repeatedly retrieving autobiographical memories. *Hippocampus, 31*, 869–880. https://doi.org/10.1002/hipo.23330

Gutchess, A., Mukadam, N., Zhang, W., & Zhang, X. (2021). Influence of aging on memory across cultures. In J. Y. Chiao, S.-C. Li, R. Turner, S. Y. Lee-Tauler, & B. A. Pringle (Eds.), *The Oxford handbook of clinical neuroscience and global mental health* (pp. 262–287). Oxford University Press.

Haber, D. (2020). *Health promotion and aging: Practical applications for health professionals* (8th ed.). Springer.

Habes, M., Erus, G., Toledo, J. B., Zhang, T., Bryan, N., Launer, L. J., Rosseel, Y., Janowitz, D., Doshi, J., Van der Auwera, S., von Sarnowski, B., Hegenscheid, K., Hosten, N., Homuth, G., Völzke, H., Schminke, U., Hoffmann, W., Grabe, H. J., Davatzikos, C. (2016). White matter hyperintensities and imaging patterns of brain ageing in the general population. *Brain: A Journal of Neurology, 139*, 1164–1179. https://doi.org/10.1093/brain/aww008

HackCare.org. (2021). *Hack care: Tips and tricks for a dementia-friendly home*. https://hackcare.org/download-book.php

Haier, R. J., & Jung, R. E. (2018). The parieto-frontal integration theory: Assessing intelligence from brain images. In D. Flanagan & E. M. McDonough (Eds.), *Contemporary intellectual assessment: Theories, tests, and issues* (4th ed., pp. 219–224). Guilford.

Hains, C.-A. M., & Hulbert-Williams, N. J. (2013). Attitudes toward euthanasia and physician-assisted suicide: A study of the multivariate effects of healthcare training, patient characteristics, religion and locus of control. *Journal of Medical Ethics, 39*, 713–716. https://doi.org/10.1136/medethics-2012-100729

Haj, M. E. (2022). Odor-evoked autobiographical memory in Alzheimer's disease? *Archives of Clinical Neuropsychology, 37*, 513–520. https://doi.org/10.1093/arclin/acab074

Hajek, A., Wolfram, C., Spitzer, M., & König, H.-H. (2021). Association of vision problems with psychosocial factors among middle-aged and older individuals: Findings from a nationally representative study. *Aging & Mental Health, 25*, 946–953. https://doi.org/10.1080/13607863.2020.1725806

Håkansson, P., & Witmer, H. (2015). Social media and trust: A systematic literature review. *Journal of Business and Economics, 6*, 517–524. https://doi.org/10.15341/jbe(2155-7950)/03.06.2015/010

Hales, S. (2016). Attachment and the end of life experience. In J. Hunter & R. Maunder (Eds.), *Improving patient treatment with attachment theory* (pp. 93–103). Springer. https://doi.org/10.1007/978-3-319-233000-0_7

Haley, W. E. (2013). Family caregiving at the end-of-life: Current status and future directions. In R. C. Talley & R. J. V Montgomery (Eds.), *Caregiving across the lifespan* (pp. 157–175). Springer.

Halfmann, K., Hedgcock, W., & Denburg, N. L. (2021) Neural correlates of cognitive reappraisal of positive and negative affect in older adults. *Aging & Mental Health, 25*, 126–133. https://doi.org/10.1080/13607863.2019.1693970

Hall, J. A. (2016). Same-sex friendships. In C. R. Berger, M. E. Roloff, S. R. Wilson, J. P. Dillard, J. Caughlin, & D. Solomon (Eds.), *The international encyclopedia of interpersonal communication*. Wiley. https://doi.org/10.1002/9781118540190.wbeic138

Hall, S. S. (2006). Marital meaning: Exploring young adult's belief systems about marriage. *Journal of Family Issues, 27*, 1437–1458. https://doi.org/10.1177/0192513X06290036

Halliwell, D., & Franken, N. (2016). "He was supposed to be with me for the rest of my life": Meaning-making in bereaved siblings' online stories. *Journal of Family Communication, 16*, 337–354. https://doi.org/10.1080/15267431.2016.1194841

Halvarsson, A., Roaldsen, K. S., Nilsen, P., Dohrn, I.-M., & Ståhle, A. (2021). StayBalanced: Implementation of evidence-based fall prevention balance training for older adults—Cluster randomized controlled and hybrid type 3 trial. *Trials, 22*, 166. https://doi.org/10.1186/s13063-021-05091-1

Hamama-Raz, Y., Shir, S., & Mahat-Shamir, M. (2021). Meanings attributed by bereaved unmarried intimate partners of fallen soldiers to their loss. *Death Studies, 45*, 380–389. https://doi.org/10.1080/07481187.2019.1648332

Hambrick, D. Z., Macnamara, B. N., Campitelli, G., Ullén, F., & Mosing, M. A. (2016). Beyond born versus made: A new look at expertise. *Psychology of Learning and Motivation, 64*, 1–55. https://doi.org/10.1016/bs.plm.2015.09.001

Hamilton, R. K. B., Hiatt Racer, K., & Newman, J. P. (2015). Impaired integration in psychopathology: A unified theory of psychopathic dysfunction. *Psychological Review, 122*, 770–791. https://doi.org/10.1037/a0039703

Hampstead, B. M., Khoshnoodi, M., Yan, W., Deshpande, G., & Sathian, K. (2016). Patterns of effective connectivity during memory encoding and retrieval differ between patients with mild cognitive impairment and healthy older adults. *NeuroImage, 124 (Part A)*, 997–1008. https://doi.org/10.1016/j.neuroimage.2015.10.002

Han, S. D., Boyle, P. A., Yu, L., Arfanakis, K., James, B. D., Fleischman, D. A., & Bennett, D. A. (2016). Grey matter correlates of susceptibility to scams in community-dwelling older adults. *Brain Imaging and Behavior, 10*, 524–532. https://doi.org/10.1007/s11682-015-9422-4

Han, S. H. (2021). Health consequences of retirement due to non-health reasons or poor health. *Social Science & Medicine, 273*, 113767. https://doi.org/10.1016/j.socscimed.2021.113767

Handler, A., & Ginty, D. D. (2021). The mechanosensory neurons of touch and their mechanisms of activation. *Nature Reviews Neuroscience, 22*, 521–537. https://doi.org/10.1038/s41583-021-00489-x

Handwerker, E. W., Meyer, P. B., Piacentini, J., Schultz, M., & Sveikauskas, L. (2020). Employment recovery in the wake of the COVID-19 pandemic. *Monthly Labor Review, December*. https://doi.org/10.21916/mlr.2020.27

Hanh, T. N. (2009). *Happiness: Essential mindfulness practices*. Parallax Press.

Hank, K., (2021). Linked in life and death: A note on the effect of parental death on sibling relations in young and middle adulthood. *Journal of Family Issues, 42*, 2679–2690. https://doi.org/10.1177%2F0192513X20985566

Hanna, J. R., McCaughan, E., & Semple, C. J. (2022). Immediate bereavement experiences when a parent of dependent children has died of cancer: Funeral directors' perspectives, *Death Studies, 46*, 969–978. https://doi.org/10.1080/07481187.2020.1793433

Hansen, S. R. (2006). Courtship duration as a correlate of marital satisfaction and stability. *Dissertation Abstracts International: Section B: The Sciences and Engineering, 67*(4-B), 2279.

Hansson, R. O., & Stroebe, M. S. (2007). *Bereavement in late life: Coping, adaptation, and developmental influences*. American Psychological Association.

Harley, D. A., Gassaway, L., & Dunkley, L. (2016). Isolation, socialization, recreation, and inclusion of LGBT elders. In D. A. Harley & P. B. Teaster (Eds.), *Handbook of LGBT elders* (pp. 563–581). Springer.

Harris, C. B., Barnier, A. J., Sutton, J., Keil, P. G., & Dixon, R. A. (2017). "Going episodic": Collaborative inhibition and facilitation when long-married couples remember together. *Memory, 25*, 1148–1159. https://doi.org/10.1080/09658211.2016.1274405

Harris, D. L. (2016). Social expectations of the bereaved. In D. L. Harris & T. C. Bordere (Eds.), *Handbook of social justice in loss and grief: Exploring diversity, equity, and inclusion* (pp. 165–174). Routledge.

Harris, D. L. (2019). Supporting people through living losses. In D. L. Harris (Ed.), *Non-death loss and grief* (pp. 311–323). Routledge.

Harris, T. M., Youn-Heil, F., & Duong, H. T. (2020). Negotiating and communicating about identity within multi-ethnic/multi-racial families. In J. Soliz & C. W. Colaner (Eds.), *Navigating relationships in the modern family: Communication, identity, and difference* (pp. 19–32). Peter Lang.

Hart, W., Adams, J., & Tullett, A. (2016). "It's complicated"—Sex differences in perceptions of cross-sex friendships. *Journal of Social Psychology, 156*, 190–201. https://doi.org/10.1080/00224545.2015.1076762

Harter, S. (2012). *The construction of the self: Developmental and sociocultural foundations* (2nd ed.). Guilford Press.

Hartung, P. J., & Santilli, S. (2017). The theory and practice of career construction. In M. McMahon (Ed.), *Career counselling: Constructivist approaches* (2nd ed., pp. 174–184). Routledge.

Haslam, C., Hodder, K. I., & Yates, P. J. (2011). Errorless learning and spaced retrieval: How do these methods fare in healthy and clinical populations? *Journal of Clinical and Experimental Neuropsychology, 33*, 1–16. https://doi.org/10.10 80/13803395.2010.533155

Hayakawa, T., McGarrigle, C. A., Coen, R. F., Soraghan, C. J., Foran, T., Lawlor, B. A., & Kenny, R. A. (2015). Orthostatic blood pressure behavior in people with mild cognitive impairment predicts conversion to dementia. *Journal of the American Geriatrics Society, 63*, 1868–1873. https://doi.org/10.1111/jgs.13596

Hayflick, L. (1996). *How and why we age* (2nd ed.). New York: Ballantine.

Hayslip Jr, B., & Blumenthal, H. (2016). Grandparenthood: A developmental perspective. In M. H. Meyer & E. A. Daniele (Eds.), *Gerontology: Changes, challenges, and solutions* (Vol. 1, pp. 271–298). Praeger.

Hayslip Jr., B., & Cooper, A. M. (2012). Subjective and objective intellectual change in older adults. *Educational Gerontology, 38*, 190–200. https://doi.org/10.108 0/03601277.2010.532069

Hayslip Jr., B., Davis, S. R., Neumann, C. S., Goodman, C., Smith, G. C., Maiden, R. J., & Carr, G. F. (2013). The role of resilience in mediating stressor outcome relationships among grandparents raising their grandchildren. In B. Hayslip, Jr., & G. C. Smith (Eds.), *Resilient grandparent caregivers: A strengths-based perspective* (pp. 48–69). Routledge.

Hayward, R. D., Krause, N., Ironson, G., Hill, P. C., & Emmons, R. (2016). Health and well-being among the non-religious: Atheists, agnostics, and no preference compared with the religious group members. *Journal of Religion and Health, 55*, 1024–1037. https://doi.org/10.1007/s10943-015-0179-2

He, Q., & Gerber, T. P. (2020). Origin-country culture, migration sequencing, and female employment: Variations among immigrant women in the United States. *International Migration Review, 54*, 233–261. https://doi.org/10.1177%2F0197918318821651

He, X., Liu, J., Liu, B., & Shi, J. (2021). The use of DNA methylation clock in aging research. *Experimental Biology and Medicine, 246*, 436–446. https://doi.org/10.1177/1535370220968802

Healey, M. L., & Grossman, M. (2016). Social coordination in older adulthood: A dual-process model. *Experimental Aging Research, 42*, 112–127. https://doi.org/10.1080/0361073X.2015.1108691

Health and Human Services. (2021). *COVID-19 (Coronavirus)*. https://www.hhs.gov/immunization/diseases/covid/index.html.

Heathcote, D. (2016). Working memory and performance limitations. In D. Groome & M. W. Eysenck (Eds.), *An introduction to applied cognitive psychology* (2nd ed., pp. 99–123). Routledge.

Hebl, M., Cheng, S. K., & Ng, L. C. (2020). Modern discrimination in organizations. *Annual Review of Organizational Psychology and Organizational Behavior, 7*, 257–282. https://doi.org/10.1146/annurev-orgpsych-012119-044948

Hechanova, R., Waelde, L. (2017). The influence of culture on disaster mental health and psychosocial support interventions in Southeast Asia. *Mental Health Religion and Culture, 20*, 31–44. https://doi.org/10.1080/13674676.2017.1322048

Heckhausen, J., Brandtstätter, V., Fishbach, A., Freund, A. M., Lachman, M. E., & Robert, P. (2021). Goal changes and healthy aging. *Journals of Gerontology: Psychological Sciences, 76*, S105–S114. https://doi.org/10.1093/geronb/gbab038

Heckhausen, J., Wrosch, C., & Schulz, R. (2010). A motivational theory of life-span development. *Psychological Review, 117*, 32–60. https://doi.org/10.1037/a0017668

Heffernan, K., Hazzan, A. A., & Dauenhauer, J. (2022). Promoting age-friendly organizational culture through lifelong learning programs in higher education: Experience and insights from faculty. *Educational Gerontology, 48*, 260–272. https://doi.org/10.1080/03601277.2022.2033929

Hegewisch, A., & Hartman, H. (2014). *Occupational segregation and the gender wage gap: A job half done*. https://iwpr.org/wp-content/uploads/2020/08/C419.pdf

Heilman, K. M. (2016). Possible brain mechanisms of creativity. *Archives of Clinical Neuropsychology, 31*, 285–296. https://doi.org/10.1093/arclin/acw009

Heine, S. J., & Buchtel, E. E. (2009). Personality: The universal and the culturally specific. *Annual Review of Psychology, 60*, 369–394. https://doi.org/10.1146/annurev.psych.60.110707.163655

Helfrecht, C., Roulette, J. W., Lane, A., Sintayehu, B., & Meehan, C. L. (2020). Life history and socioecology of infancy. *American Journal of Physical Anthropology, 173*, 619–629. https://doi.org/10.1002/ajpa.24145

Hellmuth, J., Rabinovici, G. D., & Miller, B. L. (2019). The rise of pseudomedicine for dementia and brain health. *JAMA, 321*, 543–544. https://doi.org/10.1001/jama.2018.21560

Helson, R., Kwan, V. S. Y., John, O. P., & Jones, C. (2002). The growing evidence for personality change in adulthood: Findings from research with personality inventories. *Journal of Research in Personality, 36*, 287–306. https://doi.org/10.1016/S0092-6566(02)00010-7

Hemberg, J., & Bergdahl, E. (2020). Dealing with ethical and existential issues at end of life through co-creation. *Nursing Ethics, 27*, 1012–1031. https://doi.org/10.1177%2F0969733019874496

Hemer, S. R. (2010). Grief as social experience: Death and bereavement in Lahir, Papua, New Guinea. *TAJA: The Australian Journal of Anthropology, 21*, 281–297. https://doi.org/10.1111/j.1757-6547.2010.00097.x

Hemer, S. R. (2021). Shock, anger and bad deaths in Lihir: A reanalysis of grieving in Papua New Guinea. *Death Studies, 45*, 40–50. https://doi.org/10.1080/07481187.2020.1851884

Henderson, T. A., van Lierop, M. J., McLean, M., Uszler, J. M., Thornton, J. F., Siow, Y.-H., Pavel, D. G., Cardaci, J., & Cohen, P. (2020). Functional neuroimaging in psychiatry—Aiding in diagnosis and guiding treatment. What the American Psychiatric Association does not know. *Frontiers in Psychiatry, 11*. https://doi.org/10.3389/fpsyt.2020.00276

Henrie, J. A. (2010). *Religiousness, future time perspective, and death anxiety among adults*. Dissertation submitted to West Virginia University.

Heppner, R. S. (2013). *The lost leaders: How corporate America loses women leaders*. Palgrave Macmillan.

Hermann, E., Eisend, M., & Bayón, T. (2020). Facebook and the cultivation of ethnic diversity perceptions and attitudes. *Internet Research, 30*, 1123–1141. https://doi.org/10.1108/INTR-10-2019-0423

Hernandez, A. R., Hoffman, J. M., Hernandez, C. M., Cortes, C. J., Jumbo-Lucioni, P., Baxter, M. G., Esser, K. A., Liu, A. C., McMahon, L. L., Bizon, J. L., Burke, S. N., Buford, T. W., & Carter, C. C. (2022). Reuniting the body "neck up and neck down" to understand cognitive aging: The nexus of geroscience and neuroscience. *Journals of Gerontology: Biological Sciences, 77*, e1–e9. https://doi.org/10.1093/gerona/glab215

Hernandez, H. H. C., Ong, P. L., Anthony, P., Ang, S. L., Salim, N. B. M., Yew, P. Y. S., Ali, N. B., Lim, J. P., Lim, W. S., & Chew, J. (2022). Cognitive assessment by telemedicine: Reliability and agreement between face-to-face and remote videoconference-based cognitive tests in older adults attending a memory clinic. *Annals of Geriatric Medicine and Research, 26*, 42–48. https://doi.org/10.4235/agmr.22.0005

Herrenbrueck, L., Xia, X., Eastwick, P., Finkel, E., & Hui, C. M. (2018). Smart-dating in speed-dating: How a simple search model can explain matching decisions. *European Economic Review, 106*, 54–76. https://doi.org/10.1016/j.euroecorev.2018.04.001

Herring, S., Kibler, W. B., Putukian, M., Solomon, G. S., Boyajian-O'Neill, L., Dec, K. L., Franks, R. R., Indelicato, P. A., LaBella, C. R., Leddy, J. J., Matuszak, J., McDonough, E. B., O'Connor, F., & Sutton, K. M. (2021). Selected issues in sport-related concussion (SRC|mild traumatic brain injury) for the team physician: A consensus statement. *British Journal of Sports Medicine, 55*, 1251–1261. http://doi.org/10.1136/bjsports-2021-104235

Hershey, D. A., Austin, J. T., & Gutierrez, H. C. (2015). Financial decision making across the adult life span: Dynamic cognitive capacities and real-world competence. In T. M. Hess, J. Strough, and C. E. Lockenhoff (Eds.), *Aging and decision making: Empirical and applied perspectives* (pp. 329–349). Academic Press.

Hertzog, C. (2008). Theoretical approaches to the study of cognitive aging: An individual differences perspective. In S. M. Hofer & D. F. Alwin (Eds.), *Handbook of cognitive aging: Interdisciplinary perspectives* (pp. 34–49). SAGE.

Hertzog, C. (2016). Aging and metacognitive control. In J. Dunlosky & S. K. Tauber (Eds.), *The Oxford handbook of metamemory* (pp. 537–558). Oxford University Press.

Hertzog, C. (2020). Aging and peak human performance: A glance back. *Journals of Gerontology: Psychological Sciences, 75*, 1621–1624. https://doi.org/10.1093/geronb/gbaa057

Hertzog, C., & Dunlosky, J. (2011). Metacognition in later adulthood: Spared monitoring can benefit older adults' self-regulation. *Current Directions in Psychological Science, 20*, 167–173. https://doi.org/10.1177/0963721411409026

Hertzog, C., Fulton, E. K., Mandviwala, L., & Dunlosky, J. (2013). Older adults show deficits in retrieving and decoding associative mediators generated at study. *Developmental Psychology, 49*, 1127–1131. https://doi.org/10.1037/a0029414

Hertzog, C., Kramer, A. F., Wilson, R. S., & Lindenberger, U. (2009). Fit body, fit mind? *Scientific American Mind, 20*, 24–31. https://doi.org/10.1038/scientificamericanmind0709-24

Hertzog, C., Pearman, A., Lustig, E., & Hughes, M. (2021). Fostering self-management of everyday memory in older adults: A new intervention approach. *Frontiers in psychology, 11*, 560056. https://doi.org/10.3389/fpsyg.2020.560056

Hertzog, C., Price, J., & Dunlosky, J. (2012). Age differences in the effects of experimenter-instructed versus self-generated strategy use. *Experimental Aging Research, 38*, 42–62. https://doi.org/10.1080/0361073X.2012.637005

Hervey-Jumper, S. L., & Monje, M. (2021). Unravelling the mechanisms of cancer-related cognitive dysfunction in non–central nervous system cancer. *JAMA Oncology, 7*, 1311–1312. https://doi.org/10.1001/jamaoncol.2021.1900

Hess, T. M. (2006). Adaptive aspects of social cognitive functioning in adulthood: Age-related goal and knowledge influences. *Social Cognition, 24*, 279–309. https://doi.org/10.1521/soco.2006.24.3.279

Hess, T. M., & Emery, L. (2012). Memory in context: The impact of age-related goals on performance. In M. Naveh-Benjamin & N. Ohta (Eds.), *Memory and aging: Current issues and future directions* (pp. 183–214). Psychology Press.

Hess, T. M., & Pullen, S. M. (1994). Adult age differences in impression change processes. *Psychology and Aging, 9*, 237–250. https://doi.org/10.1037/0882-7974.9.2.237

Hess, T. M., Freund, A. M., & Tobler, P. N. (2021). Effort mobilization and healthy aging. *The Journals of Gerontology: Psychological Sciences, 76*, S135–S144. https://doi.org/10.1093/geronb/gbab030

Hess, T. M., Germain, C. M., Rosenberg, D. C., Leclerc, C. M., & Hodges, E. A. (2005). Aging-related selectivity and susceptibility to irrelevant affective information in the construction of attitudes. *Aging, Neuropsychology, and Cognition, 12*, 149–174. https://doi.org/10.1080/13825580590925170

Hess, T. M., Queen, T. L., & Ennis, G. E. (2013). Age and self-relevance effects on information search during decision making. *Journals of Gerontology: Psychological Sciences, 68*, 703–711. https://doi.org/10.1093/geronb/gbs108

HHS.gov. (2022). *What is Medicare Part C?* https://www.hhs.gov/answers/medicare-and-medicaid/what-is-medicare-part-c/index.html

Hidalgo, I., Brooten, D., Youngblut, J. M., Roche, R., Li, J., & Hinds, A. M. (2021). Practices following the death of a loved one reported by adults from 14 countries or cultural/ethnic group. *Nursing Open, 8*, 453–462. https://doi.org/10.1002/nop2.646

Higgins, J. P. (2016). Smartphone applications for patients' health and fitness. *The American Journal of Medicine, 129*, 11–19. https://doi.org/10.1016/j.amjmed.2015.05.038

Hill, R. T., Thomas, C., English, L., & Callaway, K. (2016). The importance and impact of child care on a woman's transition to motherhood. In C. Spitzmueller & R. A. Matthews (Eds.), *Research perspectives on work and the transition to motherhood* (pp. 241–265). Springer.

Hill, T. D., Saenz, J. L., & Rote, S. M. (2020). Religious participation and mortality risk in Mexico. *Journals of Gerontology: Social Sciences, 75*, 1053–1061. https://doi.org/10.1093/geronb/gby152.

Hillsdon, M., Brunner, E., Guralnik, J., & Marmot, M. (2005). Prospective study of physical activity and physical function in early old age. *American Journal of Preventive Medicine, 28*, 245–250. https://doi.org/10.1016/j.amepre.2004.12.008

Himawan, K. K. (2020). Singleness, sex, and spirituality: How religion affects the experience of being single in Indonesia. *Mental Health, Religion, and Culture, 23*, 204–215. https://doi.org/10.1080/13674676.2020.1767555

Hinton, A., & Chirgwin, S. (2010). Nursing education: Reducing reality shock for graduate indigenous nurses—It's all about time. *Australian Journal of Advanced Nursing, 28*, 60–66. https://search.informit.com.au/documentSummary;dn=053211061337305;res=IELHEA

Hipp, L., Morrissey, T. W., & Warner, M. E. (2017). Who participates and who benefits from employer-provided child-care assistance? *Journal of Marriage and Family, 79*, 614–635. https://doi.org/10.1111/momf.12359

Hirve, S., Juvekar, S., Sambhudas, S., Lele, P., Blomstedt, Y., Wall, S. et al. (2012). Does self-rated health predict death in adults aged 50 years and above in India? Evidence from a rural population under health and demographic surveillance. *International Journal of Epidemiology, 41*, 1719–1727. https://doi.org/10.1093/ije/dys163

Ho, H. C., Guo, H., Chan, T.-C., Shi, Y., Webster, C., & Fong, K. N. K. (2022). Community planning for a "healthy built environment" via a human-environment nexus? A multifactorial assessment of environmental characteristics and age-specific stroke mortality in Hong Kong. *Chemosphere, 287*, 132043. https://doi.org/10.1016/j.chemosphere.2021.132043

Ho, N. T. T., Kutzner, A., & Heese, K. (2018). Brain plasticity, cognitive functions and neural stem cells: A pivotal role for the brain-specific neural master gene |-SRGAP2–FAM72-|. *Biological Chemistry, 399*, 55–61. https://doi.org/10.1515/hsz-2017-0190

Hoehner, P. J. (2018). Ethical and legal issues of geriatrics. In J. Reves, S. Barnett, J. McSwain, & G. Rooke. (Eds.), *Geriatric anesthesiology* (pp. 27–51). Springer, Cham. https://doi.org/10.1007/978-3-319-66878-9_3

Hofer, J., Busch, H., Chasiotis, A., Kärtner, J., & Campos, D. (2008). Concern for generativity and its relation to implicit pro-social power motivation, generative goals, and satisfaction with life: A cross-cultural investigation. *Journal of Personality, 76*, 1–30. https://doi.org/10.1111/j.1467-6494.2007.00478.x

Hoff, K. A., Einarsdóttir, S., Chu, C., Briley, D. A., & Rounds, J. (2021). Personality changes predict early career outcomes: Discovery and replication in 12-year longitudinal studies. *Psychological Science, 32*, 64–79. https://doi.org/10.1177%2F0956797620957998

Hoffman, B. L., Shensa, A., Escobar-Viera, C. G., Sidani, J. E., Miller, E., & Primack, B. A. (2021). "Their page is still up": Social media and coping with loss. *Journal of Loss and Trauma, 26*, 451–468. https://doi.org/10.1080/15325024.2020.1820227

Hoffman, E., Kaneshiro, S., & Compton, W. C. (2012). Peak-experiences among Americans in midlife. *Journal of Humanistic Psychology, 52*, 479–503. https://doi.org/10.1177/0022167811433851

Hofhuis, J., van der Rijt, P. G. A., & Vlug, M. (2016). Diversity climate enhances work outcomes through trust and openness in workgroup communication. *SpringerPlus, 5*, 714. https://doi.org/s40064-016-2499-4

Hofstede, G. H., Hofstede, G. J., & Minkov, M. (2010). *Cultures and organizations: Software of the mind.* McGraw-Hill.

Holland, J. M. (1997). *Making vocational choices: A theory of vocational personalities and work environments* (3rd ed.). Johns Hopkins University Press.

Holland, J. M., Plant, C. P., Klingspon, K. L., & Neimeyer, R. A. (2020). Bereavement-related regrets and unfinished business with the deceased. *Death Studies, 44*, 42–47. https://doi.org/10.1080/07481187.2018.1521106

Holland, J. M., Thompson, K. L., Rozalski, V., & Lichtenthal, W. G. (2014). Bereavement-related regret trajectories among widowed older adults. *Journals of Gerontology: Psychological Sciences and Social Sciences, 69B*, 40–47. https://doi.org/10.1093/geronb/gbt050

Holland, K. J., & Cortina, L. M. (2016). Sexual harassment: Undermining the wellbeing of working women. In M. L. Connerley & J. Wu (Eds.), *Handbook on well-being of working women* (pp. 83–101). Springer.

Holloway, C. P., & Wiener, R. L. (2018). Abuse history and culpability judgments: Implications for battered spouse syndrome. *Psychology, Public Policy, and Law, 24*, 279–291. https://doi.org/10.1037/law0000167

Hollwich, M. (2016). *New aging: Living smarter now to live better forever.* Penguin Books.

Holmes, M. L., Manor, B., Hsieh, W-h., Hu, K., Lipsitz, L. A., & Li, L. (2016). Tai Chi training reduced coupling between respiration and posture control. *Neuroscience Letters, 610*, 60–65. https://doi.org/10.1016/j.neulet.2015.10.053

Holtzer, R., Verghese, J., Allali, G., Izzetoglu, M., Wang, C., & Mahoney, J. R. (2016). Neurological gait abnormalities moderate the functional brain signature of the posture first hypothesis. *Brain Topography, 29*, 334–343. https://doi.org/10.1007/s10548-015-0465-z

Hom, P. W., & Kinicki, A. J. (2001). Toward a greater understanding of how dissatisfaction drives employee turnover. *Academy of Management Journal, 44*, 975–987. https://doi.org/10.2307/3069441

Hong, J. H., Lachman, M. E., Charles, S. T., Chen, Y., Wilson, C. L., Nakamura, J. S., VanderWeele, T. J., & Kim, E. S. (2021). The positive influence of sense of control on physical, behavioral, and psychosocial health in older adults: An outcome-wide approach. *Preventive Medicine, 149*, 106612. https://doi.org/10.1016/j.ypmed.2021.106612

Hooker, K. (1999). Possible selves in adulthood. In T. M. Hess & F. Blanchard-Fields (Eds.), *Social cognition and aging* (pp. 97–122). Academic Press.

Hooker, K. (2015). Towards a new synthesis for development in adulthood. *Research in Human Development, 12*, 229–236. https://doi.org/10.1080/15427609.2015.1068036

Hooker, K., & McAdams, D. P. (2003). Personality reconsidered: A new agenda for aging research. *Journals of Gerontology: Psychological Sciences, 58*, P296–P304. https://doi.org/10.1093/geronb/58.6.P296

Hooker, K., Fiese, B. H., Jenkins, L., Morfei, M. Z., & Schwagler, J. (1996). Possible selves among parents of infants and preschoolers. *Developmental Psychology, 32*, 542–550. https://doi.org/10.1037/0012-1649.32.3.542

Hopf, D., Eckstein, M., Aguilar-Raab, C., Warth, M., & Ditzen, B. (2020). Neuroendocrine mechanisms of grief and bereavement: A systematic review and implications for future interventions. *Journal of Neuroendocrinology, 32*, e12887. https://doi.org/10.1111/jne.12887

Hopthrow, T., Hooper, N., Mahmood, L., Meier, B. P., & Weger, U. (2017). Mindfulness reduces the correspondence bias. *Quarterly Journal of Experimental Psychology, 70*, 351–360. https://doi.org/10.1080/17470218.2016.1149498

Horhota, M., Mienaltowski, A., & Chen, Y. (2014). Causal attributions across the adult lifespan. In P. Verhaeghen & C. Hertzog (Eds.), *The Oxford handbook of emotion, social cognition, and problem solving in adulthood* (pp. 288–301). Oxford University Press.

Horn, J. L. (1982). The aging of human abilities. In B. B. Wolman (Ed.), *Handbook of developmental psychology* (pp. 847–870). Prentice Hall.

Horn, J. L., & Hofer, S. M. (1992). Major abilities and development in the adult period. In R. J. Sternberg & C. A. Berg (Eds.), *Intellectual development* (pp. 44–99). Cambridge University Press.

Horn, J., & Masunaga, H. (2006). A merging theory of expertise and intelligence. In K. A. Ericsson, N. Charness, P. J. Feltovich, & R. R. Hoffman (Eds.), *The Cambridge handbook of expertise and expert performance* (pp. 587–611). Cambridge University Press. https://doi.org/10.1017/CBO9780511816796.034

Horne, E. D., de Chastelaine, M., & Rugg, M. D. (2021). Neural correlates of post-retrieval monitoring in older adults are preserved under divided attention, but are decoupled from memory performance. *Neurobiology of Aging, 97*, 106–119. https://doi.org/10.1016/j.neurobiolaging.2020.10.010

Hornsey, M. J., Greenaway, K. H., Harris, E. A., & Bain, P. G. (2019). Exploring cultural differences in the extent to which people perceive and desire control. *Personality and Social Psychology Bulletin, 45*, 81–92. https://doi.org/10.1177%2F0146167218780692

Horwood, S., & Beanland, V. (2016). Inattentional blindness in older adults: Effects of attentional set and to-be-ignored distractors. *Attention, Perception, & Psychophysics, 78*, 818–828. https://doi.org/10.3758/s13414-015-1057-4

Hospice Foundation of America. (2021). *How to choose a hospice provider*. http://hospicefoundation.org/End-of-Life-Support-and-Resources/Coping-with-Terminal-Illness/Hospice-Services

Hostetler, A. J., & Paterson, S. E. (2017). Toward a community psychology of aging: A lifespan perspective. In M. A. Bond, I. Serrano-Garcia, C. B. Keys, & M. Shinn (Eds.), *APA handbook of community psychology: Methods for community research and action for diverse groups and issues* (Vol. 5, pp. 605–622). American Psychological Association.

Hou, W., & Sanzenbacher, G. T. (2021). Measuring racial/ethnic retirement wealth inequality. *Journal of Retirement, 8*, 12–28. https://doi.org/10.3905/jor.2020.1.079

Howard, D. V., & Howard, J. H., Jr. (2012). Dissociable forms of implicit learning in aging. In M. Naveh-Benjamin & N. Ohta (Eds.), *Memory and aging: Current issues and future directions* (pp. 125–151). Psychology Press.

Howard, D. V., & Howard, J. H., Jr. (2016). Implicit learning and memory. In S. K. Whitbourne (Ed.), *The encyclopedia of adulthood and aging* (pp. 631–635). Wiley.

Howard, J. H., Jr., & Howard, D. V. (2013, November 7). Aging mind and brain: Is Implicit learning spared in healthy aging? *Frontiers in Psychology*. https://doi.org/10.3389/fpsyg.2013.00817

Howard, L. W., & Cordes, C. L. (2010). Flight from unfairness: Effects of perceived injustice on emotional exhaustion and employee withdrawal. *Journal of Business and Psychology, 25*, 409–428. https://doi.org/10.1007/s10869-010-9158-5

Howe, A. L., Jones, A. E., & Tilse, C. (2013). What's in a name? Similarities and differences in international terms and meanings for older peoples' housing with services. *Ageing and Society, 33*, 547–578. https://doi.org/10.1017/S0144686X12000086

Howe, M. (2020). *A user's manual for the aging voice.* Compton Publishing.

Hsieh, N., & Liu, H. (2021). Social relationships and loneliness in late adulthood: Disparities by sexual orientation. *Journal of Marriage and Family, 83*, 57–74. https://doi.org/10.1111/jomf.12681

Hsu, A., Suskind, A. M., & Huang, A. J. (2016). Urinary incontinence among older adults. In L. A. Lindquist (Ed.), *New directions in geriatric medicine* (pp. 49–69). Springer. https://doi.org/10.1007/978-3-319-28137-7_4

Huang, C.-Y., Weng, R.-H., Wu, T.-C., Hsu, C.-T., Hung, C.-H., & Tsai, Y.-C. (2020). The impact of person-centred care on job productivity, job satisfaction and organisational commitment among employees in long-term care facilities. *Journal of Clinical Nursing, 29*, 2967–2978. https://doi.org/10.1111/jocn.15342

Huang, X., Zhao, X., Cai, Y., & Wan, Q. (2022). The cerebral changes induced by exercise interventions in people with mild cognitive impairment and Alzheimer's disease: A systematic review. *Archives of Gerontology and Geriatrics, 98*, 104547. https://doi.org/10.1016/j.archger.2021.104547

Huang, Y.-P., Brewster, M. E., Moradi, B., Goodman, M. B., Wiseman, M. C., & Martin, A. (2010). Content analysis of literature about LGB people of color: 1998–2007. The *Counseling Psychologist, 38*, 363–396. https://doi.org/10.1177/0011000009335255

Hughes, C. R., & Fredenburg, B. R. (2020). *Home will never be the same again: A guide for adult children of gray divorce.* Rowman & Littlefield.

Hülür, G., Hertzog, C., Pearman, A. M., & Gerstof, D. (2015). Correlates and moderators of change in subjective memory and memory performance: Findings from the Health and Retirement Study. *Gerontology, 61*, 232–240. https://doi.org/10.1159/000369010

Hummert, M. L., Garstka, T. A., O'Brien, L. T., Greenwald, A. G., & Mellott, D. S. (2002). Using the implicit association test to measure age differences in implicit social cognitions. *Psychology and Aging, 17*, 482–495. https://doi.org/10.1037/0882-7974.17.3.482

Hung, C. C., Chang, C. C., Huang, C. W., Nouchi, R., & Cheng, C. H. (2022). Gut microbiota in patients with Alzheimer's disease spectrum: A systematic review and meta-analysis. *Aging, 14*, 477–496. https://doi.org/10.18632/aging.203826

Hunt, J. M., & Weintraub, J. R. (2016). *The coaching manager: Developing top talent* (3rd ed.). Sage Publications.

Hunter, C. E. A., Ward, L., & Camp, C. J. (2012). Transitioning spaced retrieval training to care staff in an Australian residential aged care setting for older adults with dementia: A case study approach. *Clinical Gerontologist, 35*, 1–14. https://doi.org/10.1080/07317115.2011.626513

Huntington's Disease Society of America. (2022a). *History and genetics of Huntington's disease.*

https://hdsa.org/what-is-hd/history-and-genetics-of-huntingtons-disease/

Huntington's Disease Society of America. (2022b). *Huntington's disease symptoms*. https://hdsa.org/what-is-hd/huntingtons-disease-symptoms/

Huntington's Disease Society of America. (2022c). *Suicide prevention*. https://hdsa.org/find-help/clinical-care-services/suicide-prevention/

Huo, L., Zhu, X., Zheng, Z., Ma, J., Ma, Z., Gui, W., & Li, J. (2021). Effects of transcranial direct current stimulation on episodic memory in older adults: A meta-analysis. *Journals of Gerontology: Psychological Sciences, 76*, 692–702. https://doi.org/10.1093/geronb/gbz130

Hurd, L., Mahal, R., Wardell, V., & Liang, J. (2022). "There were no words": Older LGBTQ+ persons' experiences of finding and claiming their gender and sexual identities. *Journal of Aging Studies, 60*, 100999. https://doi.org/10.1016/j.jaging.2022.100999

Hurley, R. A., Masters, S. C., & Taber, K. H. (2020). Functional neuroimaging in neuropsychiatry. In N. Agrawal, R. Faruqui, & M. Bodani (Eds.), *Oxford textbook of neuropsychiatry* (pp. 95–103). Oxford University Press.

Husain, M., & Schott, J. M. (2016). *Oxford textbook of cognitive neurology and dementia*. Oxford University Press.

Hwang, W., Cakirsoy-Aslan, A. D., Brown, M. T. and Silverstein, M. (2021). Husband–wife religious denomination homogamy and marital satisfaction over time: The moderating role of religious intensity. *Family Relations, 70*, 1498–1513. https://doi.org/10.1111/fare.12521

Hyer, L., Mullen, C. M., & Jackson, K. (2017). The unfolding of unique problems in later life families. In G. L. Welch & A. W. Harris (Eds.), *Family resilience and chronic illness: Interdisciplinary and translational perspectives* (pp. 197–224). Springer.

Ibrahim, R., & Hassan, Z. (2009). Understanding singlehood from the experiences of never-married Malay Muslim women in Malaysia: Some preliminary findings. *European Journal of Social Sciences, 8*, 395–405. https://www.researchgate.net/profile/Rozita-Ibrahim/publication/242190636_Understanding_Singlehood_from_the_Experiences_of_Never-Married_Malay_Muslim_Women_in_Malaysia_Some_Preliminary_Findings/links/5642c13d08aebaaea1f92726/Understanding-Singlehood-from-the-Experiences-of-Never-Married-Malay-Muslim-Women-in-Malaysia-Some-Preliminary-Findings.pdf

Iekel, J. (2018). *Retirement: An historical perspective*. https://www.asppa.org/news/browse-topics/retirement-historical-perspective/

Igarashi, H., Hooker, K. Coehlo, D. P., & Manoogian, M. M. (2013). "My nest is full:" Intergenerational relationships at midlife. *Journal of Aging Studies, 27*, 102–112. https://doi.org/10.1016/j.jaging.2012.12.004

Igarashi, K. M. (2016). The entorhinal map of space. *Brain Research, 1637*, 177–187. https://doi.org/10.1016/j.brainres.2015.10.041

Imoscopi, A., Inelmen, E. M., Sergi, G., Miotto, F., & Manzato, E. (2012). Taste loss in the elderly: Epidemiology, causes and consequences. *Aging Clinical and Experimental Research, 24*, 570–579. https://doi.org/10.3275/8520

Indahlastari, A., Hardcastle, C., Albizu, A., Alvarez-Alvarado, S., Boutzoukas, E. M., Evangelista, N. D., Hausman, H. K., Kraft, J., Langer, K., & Woods, A. J. (2021). A systematic review and meta-analysis of transcranial direct current stimulation to remediate age-related cognitive decline in healthy older adults. *Neuropsychiatric Disease and Treatment, 17*, 971–990. https://doi.org/10.2147/ndt.s259499

Infurna, F. J., Gerstorf, D., & Lachman, M. E. (2020). Midlife in the 2020s: Opportunities and challenges. *American Psychologist, 75*, 470–485. https://doi.org/10.1037/amp0000591

Inglehart, R. C., Nash, R., Hassan, Q. N., & Schwartzbaum, J. (2021). Attitudes toward euthanasia: A longitudinal analysis of the role of economic, cultural, and health-related factors. *Journal of Pain and Symptom Management, 62*, P559–P569. https://doi.org/10.1016/j.jpainsymman.2021.01.009

Ingram, A. M. (2020). *Cascading effects of the Family Bereavement Program preventive intervention on competence in emerging and young adults*. Doctoral Dissertation, Arizona State University. ProQuest Document 28151390.

Institute for Women's Policy Research. (2021). *Same gap, different year. The gender wage gap: 2019 earnings differences by gender, race, and ethnicity*. https://iwpr.org/iwpr-issues/employment-and-earnings/same-gap-different-year-the-gender-wage-gap-2019-earnings-differences-by-gender-race-and-ethnicity/

Inventor, B. R., Paun, O., & McIntosh, E. (2022). Mental health of LGBTQ older adults. *Journal of Psychosocial Nursing and Mental Health Services, 62*, 7–10. https://doi.org/10.3928/02793695-20220303-01

Iodice, F., Cassano, V. & Rossini, P. M. (2021). Direct and indirect neurological, cognitive, and behavioral effects of COVID-19 on the healthy elderly, mild-cognitive-impairment, and Alzheimer's disease populations. *Neurological Sciences, 42*, 455–465. https://doi.org/10.1007/s10072-020-04902-8

Iparraguirre, J. L. (2020). *Economics and ageing*. Palgrave Macmillan, Cham. https://doi.org/10.1007/978-3-030-29019-1_3

Isaacowitz, D. M., & Blanchard-Fields, F. (2012). Linking process and outcome in the study of emotion and aging. *Perspectives on Psychological Science, 7*, 3–16. https://doi.org/10.1177/1745691611424750

Ismail, Z., McGirr, A., Gill, S., Hu, S., Forkert, N. D., & Smith, E. E. (2021). Mild behavioral impairment and subjective cognitive decline predict cognitive and functional decline. *Journal of Alzheimer's Disease, 80*, 459–469. https://doi.org/10.3233/JAD-201184

Ismail, Z., Smith, E. E., Geda, Y., Sultzer, D., Brodaty, H., Smith, G., Agüera-Ortiz, L., Sweet, R., Miller, D., & Lyketsos, C. G. (2016). Neuropsychiatric symptoms as early manifestations of emergent dementia: Provisional diagnostic criteria for mild behavioral impairment. *Alzheimer's & Dementia, 12*, 195–202. https://doi.org/10.1016/j.jalz.2015.05.017

Iwarsson, S., Slaug, B., & Fänge, A. M. (2012). The Housing Enabler Screening Tool: Feasibility and interrater agreement in a real estate company practice context. *Journal of Applied Gerontology, 31*, 641–660. https://doi.org/10.1177/0733464810397354

Jackson, K. F., Mitchell, F. M., Snyder, C. R., & Miranda Samuels, G. E. (2020). Salience of ethnic minority grandparents in the ethnic-racial socialization and identity development of multiracial grandchildren. *Identity, 20*, 73–91. https://doi-org.proxy.library.nd.edu/10.1080/15283488.2020.1728535

Jackson, M. (2020). Life begins at 40: The demographic and cultural roots of the midlife crisis. *The Royal Society Journal of the History of Science, 74*, 345–364. https://doi.org/10.1098/rsnr.2020.0008

Jacobs, A. (2021, February 4). A parallel pandemic hits health care workers: Trauma and exhaustion. *New York Times*. https://www.nytimes.com/2021/02/04/health/health-care-workers-burned-out-quitting.html

Jagust, W. (2016). Is amyloid-β harmful to the brain? Insights from human imaging studies. *Brain, 139*, 23–30. https://doi.org/10.1093/brain/awv326

Jain, U., & Ma, M. (2020). Height shrinkage, health and mortality among older adults: Evidence from Indonesia. *Economics & Human Biology, 37*, 100863. https://doi.org/10.1016/j.ehb.2020.100863

Jakubiak, B. K., & Tomlinson, J. M. (2020). The role of social support in promoting self-development. In B. Mattingly, K. McIntyre, & G. Lewandowski, Jr. (Eds.), *Interpersonal relationships and the self-concept* (pp. 125–143). Springer, Cham. https://doi.org/10.1007/978-3-030-43747-3_8

James, J. B., Matz-Costa, C., & Smyer, M. A. (2016). Retirement security: It's not just about the money. *American Psychologist, 71*, 334–344. https://doi.org/10.1037/a0040220

James, W. (1902). *The varieties of religious experience: A study in human nature*. Longman, Green.

Jamieson, L. (2020). Between the couple and living alone. In A. Abela, S. Vella, & S. Piscopo (Eds.), *Couple relationships in a global context* (pp. 329–344). Springer, Cham. https://doi.org/10.1007/978-3-030-37712-0_20

Jamoulle, M. (2015). Quaternary prevention, an answer of family doctors to overmedicalization. *International Journal of Health Policy and Management, 4*, 61–64. https://doi.org/10.15171/ijhpm.2015.24

Jantzen, D. (2022). Getting grounded: Educational foundations for nurses' lifelong learning. *Journal of Professional Nursing, 39*, 34–40. https://doi.org/10.1016/j.profnurs.2021.12.009

Jardim, N. Y. V., Bento-Torres, N. V. O., Costa, V. O., Carvalho, J. P. R., Pontes, H. T. S., Tomás, A. M., Sosthenes, M. C. K., Erickson, K. I., Bento-Torres, J., & Diniz, C. W. P. (2021). Dual-task exercise to improve cognition and functional capacity of healthy older adults. *Frontiers in Aging Neuroscience, 13*. https://doi.org/10.3389/fnagi.2021.589299

Jarjat, G., Ward, G., Hot, P., Portrat, S., & Loaiza, V. M. (2021). Distinguishing the impact of age on semantic and nonsemantic associations in episodic memory. *Journals of Gerontology: Psychological Sciences, 76*, 722–731. https://doi.org/10.1093/geronb/gbaa010

Jaspal, R. (2015). Migration and identity processes among first-generation British South Asians. *South Asian Diaspora, 7*, 79–96. https://doi.org/10.1080/19438192.2015.1007634

Jaspal, R., & Cinnirella, M. (2012). The construction of ethnic identity: Insights from identity process theory. *Ethnicities, 12*, 503–530. https://doi.org/10.1177/1468796811432689

Jellinger, K. A. (2020). Neuropathological assessment of the Alzheimer spectrum. *Journal of Neural Transmission, 127*, 1229–1256. https://doi.org/10.1007/s00702-020-02232-9

Jenkins, C. L. (Ed.). (2003). *Widows and divorcees in later life: On their own again*. Haworth Press.

Jenny, G. J., Bauer, G. F., Vinje, H. F., Brauchli, R., Vogt, K., & Torp, S. (2022). Applying salutogenesis in the workplace. In M. B. Mittelmark, G. F. Bauer, L. Vaandrager, J. M. Pelikan, S. Sagy, M. Eriksson, B. Lindström, & C. M. Magistretti (Eds.), *The handbook of salutogenesis* (2nd ed., pp. 321–336). Springer.

Jeon, H.-A., & Friederici, A. D. (2015). Degree of automaticity and the prefrontal cortex. *Trends in Cognitive Sciences, 19*, 244–250. https://doi.org/10.1016/j.tics.2015.03.003

Jeste, D. (2018). Positive psychiatry comes of age. *International Psychogeriatrics, 30*, 1735–1738. https://doi.org/10.1017/S1041610218002211

Jeste, D. V., & Palmer, B. W. (2013). A call for a new positive psychiatry of ageing. *British Journal of Psychiatry, 202*, 81–83. https://doi.org/10.1192/bjp. bp.112.110643

Jeste, D. V., & Palmer, B. W. (2015). Introduction: What is positive psychiatry? In D. V. Jeste & B. W. Palmer (Eds.), *Positive psychiatry: A clinical handbook* (pp. 1–16). American Psychiatric Publishing.

Jiang, X., Randhawa, S. B., & Kagan, R. (2021). Estrogen and estrogen analogs for prevention and treatment of osteoporosis. In D. W. Dempster, J. A. Cauley, M. L. Bouxsein, & F. Cosman (Eds.), *Marcus and Feldman's osteoporosis* (5th ed., 1711–1719). https://doi.org/10.1016/B978-0-12-813073-5.00073-3

Jiang, Z. (2016). The relationship between career adaptability and job content plateau: The mediating roles of fit perceptions. *Journal of Vocational Behavior, 95*, 1–10. https://doi.org/10.1016/j.jvb.2016.06.001

Jin, Y., Yuan, S., Shao, Z., Hall, W., & Tang, J. (2021). Turing Award elites revisited: Patterns of productivity, collaboration, authorship and impact. *Scientometrics, 126*, 2329–2348. https://doi.org/10.1007/s11192-020-03860-4

Johannsen, M., Damholdt, M. F., Zachariae, R., Lundorff, M., Farver-Vestergaard, I., & O'Connor, M. (2019). Psychological interventions for grief in adults: A systematic review and meta-analysis of randomized controlled trials. *Journal of Affective Disorders, 253*, 69–86. https://doi.org/10.1016/j.jad.2019.04.065

Johns Hopkins Medicine. (2021). *Radiation oncology and molecular radiation sciences.* https://www.hopkinsmedicine.org/radiation_oncology/

Johns Hopkins Medicine. (2022). *HIV and dementia.* https://www.hopkinsmedicine.org/health/conditions-and-diseases/hiv-and-aids/hiv-and-dementia

Johnsen, I., & Afgun, K. (2021). Complicated grief and post-traumatic growth in traumatically bereaved siblings and close friends. *Journal of Loss and Trauma, 26*, 246–259. https://doi.org/10.1080/15325024.2020.1762972

Johnson, C., Hallemans, A., Verbecque, E., Vestel, C., Herssens, N., & Vereeck, L. (2020). Aging and the relationship between balance performance, vestibular function and somatosensory thresholds. *The Journal of International Advanced Otology, 16*, 328–337. https://doi.org/10.5152/iao.2020.8287

Johnson, H. A., Zabriskie, R. B., & Hill, B. (2006). The contribution of couple leisure involvement, leisure time, and leisure satisfaction to marital satisfaction. *Marriage & Family Review, 40*, 69–91. https://doi.org/10.1300/J002v40n01_05

Johnson, M. K., Raye, C. L., Mitchell, K. J., & Ankudowich, E. (2012). The cognitive neuroscience of true and false memories. *Nebraska Symposium on Motivation, 58*, 15–52. https://doi.org/10.1007/978-1-4614-1195-6_2

Johnson, R. W. (2021). *Will older adults return to the workforce?* https://www.urban.org/urban-wire/will-older-adults-return-workforce

Johnson, T., Walton, S., Levine, S., Fister, E., Baron, A., & O'Mahony, S. (2020). Racial and ethnic disparity in palliative care and hospice use. *American Journal of Managed Care, 26*, e36–e40. http://ajmc.s3.amazonaws.com/_media/_pdf/AJMC_02_2020_Johnson%20final.pdf

Johnston, K. E., Swim, J. K., Saltsman, B. M., Deater-Deckard, K., & Petrill, S. A. (2007). Mothers' racial, ethnic, and cultural socialization of transracially adopted Asian children. *Family Relations, 56*, 390–402. https://doi.org/10.1111/j.1741-3729.2007.00468.x

Johri, A. (2022). Lifelong and lifewide learning for the perpetual development of expertise in engineering. *European Journal of Engineering Education, 47*, 70–84. https://doi.org/10.1080/03043797.2021.1944064

Joint Center for Housing Studies. (2016). Projections & implications for housing a growing population: Older households 2015–2035. https://www.jchs.harvard.edu/research-areas/reports/projections-and-implications-housing-growing-population-older-households

Jolie, A. (2013, May 14). *My medical choice.* https://www.nytimes.com/2013/05/14/opinion/my-medical-choice.html

Jolie, A. (2015, March 24). *Diary of a surgery.* https://www.nytimes.com/2015/03/24/opinion/angelina-jolie-pitt-diary-of-a-surgery.html?referrer=&_r=0

Jones, B. F. (2010). Age and great invention. *Review of Economics and Statistics, 92*, 1–14. https://doi.org/10.1162/rest.2009.11724

Jones, D. R. (2022). Reclaiming disabled creativity: How cultural models make legible the creativity of people with disabilities. *Culture & Psychology, 28*, 491–505. https://doi.org/10.1177/1354067X211066816

Jones, E., Oka, M., Clark, J., Gardner, H., Hunt, R., & Dutson, S. (2019). Lived experience of young widowed individuals: A qualitative study. *Death Studies, 43*, 183–192. https://doi.org/10.1080/07481187.2018.1445137

Jones, K., Birchley, G., Huxtable, R., Clare, L., Walter, T., & Dixon, J. (2019). End of life care: A scoping review of experiences of advance care planning for people with dementia. *Dementia, 18*, 825–845. https://doi.org/10.1177%2F1471301216676121

Jones, M. R., Ehrhardt, K. P., Ripoll, J. G., Sharma, B., Padnos, I. W., Kaye, R. J., & Kaye, A. D. (2016). Pain in the elderly. *Current Pain and Headache Reports, 20*, 23. https://doi.org/10.1007/s11916-016-0551-2

Jones, N., Marks, R., Ramirez, R., & Ríos-Vargas, M. (2021). *2020 Census illuminates racial and ethnic composition of the country.* https://www.census.gov/library/stories/2021/08/improved-race-ethnicity-measures-reveal-united-states-population-much-more-multiracial.html

Jones, R. N., Marsiske, M., Ball, K., Rebok, G., Willis, S. L., Morris, J. N., & Tennstedt, S. L. (2013). The ACTIVE cognitive training interventions and trajectories of performance among older adults. *Journal of Aging and Health, 25*(suppl.), 186S–208S. https://doi.org/10.1177/0898264312461938

Jones, W. E., Benge, J. F., & Scullin, M. K. (2021). Preserving prospective memory in daily life: A systematic review and meta-analysis of mnemonic strategy, cognitive training, external memory aid, and combination interventions. *Neuropsychology, 35*, 123–140. https://doi.org/10.1037/neu0000704

Jong, J. (2020). Death anxiety and religious belief: A critical review. In K. E. Vail, III, & C. Routledge (Eds.), *The science of religion, spirituality, and existentialism* (pp. 21–35). Academic Press. https://doi.org/10.1016/B978-0-12-817204-9.00003-2

Jopp, D. S., & Hertzog, C. (2010). Assessing adult leisure activities: An extension of a self-report activity questionnaire. *Psychological Assessment, 22*, 108–120. https://doi.org/10.1037/a0017662

Joseph, S. (Ed.). (2015). *Positive psychology in practice: Promoting human flourishing in work, health, education, and everyday life.* Wiley.

Joseph, S., & Sagy, S. (2022). Positive psychology and its relation to salutogenesis. In M. B. Mittelmark, G. F. Bauer, L. Vaandrager, J. M. Pelikan, S. Sagy, M. Eriksson, B. Lindström, & C. M. Magistretti (Eds.), *The handbook of salutogenesis* (2nd ed., pp. 233–238). Springer.

Joyner, M. J., & Barnes, J. N. (2013). I am 80 going on 18: Exercise and the fountain of youth. *Journal of Applied Physiology, 114*, 1–2. https://doi.org/10.1152/japplphysiol.01313.2012

Ju, Y., & Tam, Y. P. (2022). Pathological mechanisms and therapeutic strategies for Alzheimer's disease. *Neural Regeneration Research, 17*, 543–549. https://doi.org/10.4103%2F1673-5374.320970

Juffer, F. (2006). Children's awareness of adoption and their problem behavior in families with 7-year-old internationally adopted children. *Adoption Quarterly, 9*, 1–22. https://doi.org/10.1300/J145v09n02_01

Jung, H. S., Song, M. K., & Yoon, H. H. (2021). The effects of workplace loneliness on work engagement and organizational commitment: Moderating roles of leader-member exchange and coworker exchange. *Sustainability, 13*, 948. https://doi.org/10.3390/su13020948

Jung, R. E., & Haier, R. J. (2007). The parieto-frontal integration theory (P-FIT) of intelligence: Converging neuroimaging evidence. *Behavioral and Brain Sciences, 30*, 135–154. https://doi.org/10.1017/S0140525X07001185

Jung, R. E., Flores, R. A., & Hunter, D. (2016). A new measure of imagination ability: Anatomical brain imaging correlates. *Frontiers in Psychology, 7*, 496. https://doi.org/10.3389/fpsyq.2016.00496

Jurkova, S., & Guo, S. (2021). Conceptualising a holistic model of transcultural lifelong learning. *International Review of Education, 67*, 791–810. https://doi.org/10.1007/s11159-021-09930-w

Kahana, E., & Kahana, B. (2003). Patient proactivity enhancing doctor-patient-family communication in cancer prevention and care among the aged. *Patient Education and Counseling, 50*, 67–73. https://doi.org/10.1016/S0738-3991(03)00083-1

Kahana, E., Kahana, B., & Zhang, J. (2005). Motivational antecedents of preventive proactivity in late life: Linking future orientation and exercise. *Motivation and Emotion, 29*, 438–459. https://doi.org/10.1007/s11031-006-9012-2

Kahana, E., Kahana, J. S., Kahana, B., & Ermoshkina, P. (2019). Meeting challenges of late life disability proactively. *Innovation in Aging, 3*, igz023. https://doi.org/10.1093/geroni/igz023

Kahana, E., Kelley-Moore, J., & Kahana, B. (2012). Proactive aging: A longitudinal study of stress, resources, and well-being in late life. *Aging and Mental Health, 16*, 438–451. https://doi.org/10.1080/13607863.20 11.644519

Kahleova, H., Levin, S., Barnard, N. D. (2021). Plant-based diets for healthy aging. *Journal of the American College of Nutrition, 40*, 478–479. https://doi.org/10.1080/07315724.2020.1790442

Kail, B. L., Taylor, M. G., & Rogers, N. (2020). Double disadvantage in the process of disablement: Race as a moderator in the association between chronic conditions and functional limitations. *Journals of Gerontology: Social Sciences, 75*, 448–458. https://doi.org/10.1093/geronb/gby027

Kaiser Family Foundation. (2021). *Opioid overdose deaths by race/ethnicity.* https://www.kff.org/other/state-indicator/opioid-overdose-deaths-by-raceethnicity/?currentTimeframe=0&sortModel=%7B%22colId%22:%22Location%22,%22sort%22:%22asc%22%7D

Kakimoto, Y., Okada, C., Kawabe, N., Sasaki, A., Tsukamoto, H., Nagao, R., & Osawa, M. (2019). Myocardial lipofuscin accumulation in ageing and sudden cardiac death. *Scientific Reports, 9*, 3304. https://doi.org/10.1038/s41598-019-40250-0

Kalanithi, L. (2016). *My marriage didn't end when I became a widow.* https://opinionator.blogs.nytimes.com/2016/01/06/my-marriage-didnt-end-when-i-became-a-widow/

Kalish, E. (2016). *Millennials are the least wealthy, but most optimistic, generation.* https://www.urban.org/research/publication/millennials-are-least-wealthy-most-optimistic-generation

Kalish, R. A. (1984). *Death, grief, and caring relationships* (2nd ed.). Brooks/Cole.

Kalish, R. A. (1987). Death and dying. In P. Silverman (Ed.), *The elderly as modern pioneers* (pp. 320–334). Indiana University Press.

Kallio, E. K. (2020). From multiperspective to contextual integrative thinking in adulthood: Considerations on theorisation of adult thinking and its place as a component of wisdom. In E. K. Kallio (Ed.), *Development of adult thinking: Interdisciplinary perspectives on cognitive development and adult learning* (pp. 9–32). Routledge. https://doi.org/10.4324/9781315187464-2

Kalmijn, M. (2013). Adult children's relationships with married parents, divorced parents, and stepparents: Biology, marriage, or residence? *Journal of Marriage and Family, 75*, 1181–1193. https://doi.org/10.1111/jomf.12057

Kalmijn, M., & Flap, H. (2001). Assortative meeting and mating: Unintended consequences of organized settings for partner choices. *Social Forces, 79*, 1289–1312. https://doi.org/10.1353/sof.2001.0044

Kalokerinos, E. K., von Hippel, W., & Henry, J. D. (2015). Social cognition and aging. In N. A. Pachana (Ed.), *Encyclopedia of geropsychology*. New York: Springer. https://doi.org/10.1007/978-981-287-080-3_2-1

Kamin, T., Perger, N., Debevec, L., & Tivadar, B. (2021). Alone in a time of pandemic: Solo-living women coping with physical isolation. *Qualitative Health Research, 31*, 203–217. https://doi.org/10.1177%2F1049732320971603

Kanai, M., Shimane, K., & Dang, T. V. P. (2020). Ancestor worship and quality of life: Transforming bonds with the deceased in contemporary Japan. In M. C. Tsai & N. Iwai (Eds.), *Quality of life in Japan: Contemporary perspectives on happiness* (pp. 151–169). Springer, Singapore. https://doi.org/10.1007/978-981-13-8910-8_7

Karalija, N., Papenberg, G., Wåhlin, A., Johansson, J., Andersson, M., Axelsson, J., Riklund, K., Lindenberger, U., Nyberg, L., & Bäckman, L. (2021). Sex differences in dopamine integrity and brain structure among healthy older adults: Relationships to episodic memory. *Neurobiology of Aging, 105*, 272–279. https://doi.org/10.1016/j.neurobiolaging.2021.04.022

Karanikas, E., Daskalakis, N. P., & Agorastos, A. (2021). Oxidative dysregulation in early life stress and

posttraumatic stress disorder: A comprehensive review. *Brain Sciences, 11*, 723. https://doi.org/10.3390/brainsci11060723
Karim, S. S., Ramanna, G., Petit, T., Doward, L., & Burns, A. (2008). Development of the Dementia Quality of Life questionnaire (D-QOL): UK version. *Aging and Mental Health, 12*, 144–148. https://doi.org/10.1080/13607860701616341
Karlsson, E., & Gustafsson, J. (2022). Validation of the international classification of functioning, disability and health (ICF) core sets from 2001 to 2019: A scoping review. *Disability and Rehabilitation, 44*, 3736–3748. https://doi.org/10.1080/09638288.2021.1878562
Karney, B. R. (2010). *Keeping marriages healthy, and why it's so difficult.* https://www.apa.org/science/about/psa/2010/02/sci-brief.aspx
Karney, B. R. (2021). Socioeconomic status and intimate relationships. *Annual Review of Psychology, 72*, 391–414. https://doi.org/10.1146/annurev-psych-051920-013658
Karney, B. R., & Bradbury, T. N. (1995). The longitudinal course of marital quality and stability: A review of theory, method, and research. *Psychological Bulletin, 118*, 3–34. https://doi.org/10.1037/0033-2909.1881.1.3
Karney, B. R., & Bradbury, T. N. (2020). Research on marital satisfaction and stability in the 2010s: Challenging conventional wisdom. *Journal of Marriage and Family, 82*, 100–116. https://doi.org/10.1111/jomf.12635
Karney, B. R., & Crown, J. S. (2007). *Families under stress: An assessment of data, theory, and research on marriage and divorce in the military* (MG-599-OSD). RAND Corporation.
Karp, N. (2021). *Fixing congregate living for older adults.* https://longevity.stanford.edu/fixing-congregate-living-for-older-adults/
Karr, J. E., Graham, R. B., Hofer, S. M., & Muniz-Terrera, G. (2018). When does cognitive decline begin? A systematic review of change point studies on accelerated decline in cognitive and neurological outcomes preceding mild cognitive impairment, dementia, and death. *Psychology and Aging, 33*, 195–218. https://doi.org/10.1037/pag0000236
Karumathil, A. A., & Tripathi, R. (2022). Culture and attitudes towards euthanasia: An integrative review. *OMEGA—Journal of Death and Dying, 86*, 688–720. https://doi.org/10.1177%2F0030222820984655
Karyotaki, E., Cuijpers, P., Albor, Y., Alonso, J., Auerbach, R. P., Bantjes, J., Bruffaerts, R., Ebert, D. D., Hasking, P., Kiekens, G., Lee, S., McLafferty, M., Mak, A., Mortier, P., Sampson, N. A., Stein, D. J., Vilagut, G., & Kessler, R. C. (2020). Sources of stress and their associations with mental disorders among college students: Results of the World Health Organization World Mental Health Surveys International College Student Initiative. *Frontiers in Psychology, 11*, 1759. https://doi.org/10.3389/fpsyg.2020.01759
Kashen, J., Glynn, S. J., & Novello, A. (2020). *How COVID-19 sent women's workforce progress backward.* https://www.americanprogress.org/issues/women/reports/2020/10/30/492582/covid-19-sent-womens-workforce-progress-backward/.
Kasper, S., Cubała, W. J., Fagiolini, A., Ramos-Quiroga, J. A., Souery, D., & Young, A. H. (2021). Practical recommendations for the management of treatment-resistant depression with esketamine nasal spray therapy: Basic science, evidence-based knowledge and expert guidance. *The World Journal of Biological Psychiatry, 22*, 468–482. https://doi.org/10.1080/15622975.2020.1836399.
Kassim, P. N. J., & Alias, F. (2016). Religious, ethical and legal considerations in end-of-life issues: Fundamental requisites for medical decision making. *Journal of Religion and Health, 55*, 119–134. https://doi.org/10.1007/210943-014-9995-z
Kastenbaum, R. (1999). Dying and bereavement. In J. C. Cavanaugh & S. K. Whitbourne (Eds.), *Gerontology: An interdisciplinary perspective.* New York: Oxford University Press.
Kastenbaum, R., & Thuell, S. (1995). Cookies baking, coffee brewing: Toward a contextual theory of dying. *Omega: The Journal of Death and Dying, 31*, 175–187. https://doi.org/10.2190/LQPX-71DE-V5AA-EPFT
Kasuya, H., Yoshida, H., Mori, H., & Kido, H. (2008). A longitudinal study of vocal aging: Changes in F0, jitter, shimmer, and glottal noise. *Journal of the Acoustical Society of America, 123*, 3428–3428. https://doi.org/10.1121/1.2934194
Kataoka-Yahiro, M., Ceria, C., & Caulfield, R. (2004). Grandparent caregiving role in ethnically diverse families. *Journal of Pediatric Nursing, 19*, 315–328. https://doi.org/10.1016/j.pedn.2004.05.010
Katz, D. I., Bernick, C., Dodick, D. W., Mez, J., Mariani, M. L., Adler, C. H., Alosco, M. L., Balcer, L. J., Banks, S. J., Barr, W. B., Brody, D. L., Cantu, R. C., Dams-O'Connor, K., Geda, Y. E., Jordan, B. D., McAllister, T. W., Peskind, E. R., Petersen, R. C., Wethe, J. V., Zafonte, R. D … Stern, R. A. (2021). National Institute of Neurological Disorders and Stroke consensus diagnostic criteria for traumatic encephalopathy syndrome. *Neurology, 96*, 848–863. https://doi.org/10.1212/WNL.0000000000011850
Katz, L., Harvey, C., Baker, I. S., & Howard, C. (2022). The Dark Side of Humanity Scale: A reconstruction of the Dark Tetrad constructs. *Acta Psychologica, 222*, 103461. https://doi.org/10.1016/j.actpsy.2021.103461
Kaufman, J. C. (2016). *Creativity 101* (2nd ed.). Springer.
Kavé, G., Eyal, N., Shorek, A., Cohen-Mansfield, J. (2008). Multilingualism and cognitive state in the oldest old. *Psychology and Aging, 23*, 70–78. https://doi.org/10.1037/0882-7974.23.1.70
Kawashima, D., Kawamoto, S., Shiragawa, K., & Kawano, K. (2020). Is suicide beautiful? *Crisis, 41*, 114–120. https://doi.org/10.1027/0227-5910/a000612
Kayser, K. (2011). Couple therapy. In J. R. Brandell (Ed.), *Theory and practice in clinical social work* (2nd ed., pp. 259–288). Sage Publications.
Kazanis, I. (2012). Can adult neural stem cells create new brains? Plasticity in the adult mammalian neurogenic niches: Realities and expectations in the era of regenerative biology. *Neuroscientist, 18*, 15–27. https://doi.org/10.1177/1073858410390379
Kazis, N. (2021). Fair housing for a non-sexist city. *Harvard Law Review, 134*, 1683. https://doi.org/10.2139/ssrn.3552190
Kearney, M., Levine, P., & Purdue, L. (2022). *The mystery of the declining U.S. birth rate.* https://econofact.org/the-mystery-of-the-declining-u-s-birth-rate
Kegan, R. (1982). *The evolving self.* Harvard University Press.
Kegan, R. (1994). *In over our heads: The mental demands of modern life.* Harvard University Press.
Kegan, R. (2009). What "form" transforms?: A constructive-developmental approach to transformative learning. In K. Illeris (Ed.), *Contemporary theories of learning: Learning theorists … in their own words* (2nd ed., pp. 35–52). Routledge.
Kegan, R., & Lahey, L. L. (2010). From subject to object: A constructive-developmental approach to reflective practice. In N. Lyons (Ed.), *Handbook of reflection and reflective inquiry* (pp. 433–449). Springer. https://doi.org/10.1007/978-0-387-85744-2_22
Keller, T., & Szakál, P. (2021). Not just words! Effects of a light-touch randomized encouragement intervention on students' exam grades, self-efficacy, motivation, and test anxiety. *PLoS ONE, 16*, e0256960. https://doi.org/10.1371/journal.pone.0256960
Kelley, K. (1995, May/June). Visions: Maya Angelou. *Mother Jones.* https://www.motherjones.com/media/1995/05/visions-maya-angelou
Kelly, C. M., Strauss, K., Arnold, J., & Stride, C. (2020). The relationship between leisure activities and psychological resources that support a sustainable career: The role of leisure seriousness and work-leisure similarity. *Journal of Vocational Behavior, 117*, Article 103340. https://doi.org/10.1016/j.jvb.2019.103340
Kendall, K., Van Assche, E., Andlauer, T., Choi, K., Luykx, J., Schulte, E., & Lu, Y. (2021). The genetic basis of major depression. *Psychological Medicine, 51*, 2217–2230. https://doi.org/10.1017/S0033291721000441
Kensinger, E. A. (2012). Emotion–memory interactions in older adulthood. In M. Naveh-Benjamin & N. Ohta (Eds.), *Memory and aging: Current issues and future directions* (pp. 215–244). Psychology Press.
Kensinger, E. A., & Corkin, S. (2004). The effects of emotional content and aging on false memories. *Cognitive, Affective and Behavioral Neuroscience, 4*, 1–9. https://doi.org/10.3758/CABN.4.1.1
Kensinger, E. A., & Ford, J. H. (2020). Retrieval of emotional events from memory. *Annual Review of Psychology, 871*, 251–272. https://doi.org/10.1146/annurev-psych-010419-051123
Kensinger, E. A., & Ford, J. H. (2021). Guiding the emotion in emotional memories: The role of the dorsomedial prefrontal cortex. *Current Directions in Psychological Science, 30*, 111–119. https://doi.org/10.1177%2F0963721421990081
Kensinger, E. A., & Gutchess, A. H. (2017). Cognitive aging in a social and affective context: Advances over the past 50 years. *Journals of Gerontology: Psychological Sciences, 72*, 61–70. https://doi.org/10.1093/geronb/gbw056
Kent de Grey, R. G., & Uchino, B. N. (2020). The health correlates and consequences of friendship. In K. Sweeny, M. L. Robbins, & L. M. Cohen (Eds.), *The Wiley encyclopedia of health psychology* (pp. 239–245). Wiley Blackwell. https://doi.org/10.1002/9781119057840.ch72
Kentor, R. A., & Kaplow, J. B. (2020). Supporting children and adolescents following parental bereavement: Guidance for health-care professionals. *The Lancet Child & Adolescent Health, 4*, 889–898. https://doi.org/10.1016/S2352-4642(20)30184-X
Kepple, A. L., Azzam, P. N., Gopalan, P., & Arnold, R. M. (2015). Decision-making capacity at the end of life. *Progress in Palliative Care: Science and the Art of Caring, 23*, 133–136. https://doi.org/10.1179/1743291X14Y.0000000109
Kettrey, H. H., & Johnson, A. D. (2021). Hooking up and pairing off: Correlates of college students' interest in subsequent hookups and romantic relationships with other-sex and same-sex hookup partners. *The Journal of Sex Research, 58*, 915–942. https://doi.org/10.1080/00224499.2020.1766403.
Kezar, A., Hypolite, L., & Kitchen, J. A. (2020). Career self-efficacy: A mixed-methods study of an underexplored research area for first-generation, low-income, and underrepresented college students in a comprehensive college transition program. *American Behavioral Scientist, 64*, 298–324. https://doi.org/10.1177%2F0002764219869409
Khait, A. A., Reagan, L., & Shellman, J., (2021). Uses of reminiscence intervention to address the behavioral and psychosocial problems associated with dementia: An integrative review. *Geriatric Nursing, 42*, 756–766. https://doi.org/10.1016/j.gerinurse.2021.03.021
Khalil, D. N., Smith, E. L., Brentjens, R. J., & Wolchok, J. D. (2016). The future of cancer treatment: Immunomodulation, CARs, and combination immunotherapy. *Nature Reviews Clinical Oncology, 13*, 273–290. https://doi.org/10.1038/nrclinonc.2016.25
Khan, G., Sikander, P., & Akhlaq, A. (2019). Factors pertaining to rising divorce rate and its consequences on the family culture of Pakistan: A qualitative study. *IBT—Journal of Business Studies, 15*, 199–210. http://jms.ilmauniversity.edu.pk/index.php/IBTJBS/article/download/323/269
Khan, S., Kuhn, S. K., & Haque, S. (2021). A systematic review of autobiographical memory and mental health research on refugees and asylum seekers. *Frontiers in Psychiatry, 12*, 658700. https://doi.org/10.3389/fpsyt.2021.658700
Khanal, P., He, L., Stebbings, G. K., Onambele-Pearson, G. L., Degens, H., Williams, A. G., Thomis, M., & Morse, C. I. (2021). Static one-leg standing balance test as a screening tool for low muscle mass in healthy elderly women. *Aging Clinical and Experimental Research, 33*, 1831–1839. https://doi.org/10.1007/s40520-021-01818-x

Khani, M., Gibbons, E., Bras, J., & Guerreiro, R. (2022). Challenge accepted: Uncovering the role of rare genetic variants in Alzheimer's disease. *Molecular Neurodegeneration 17*, 3. https://doi.org/10.1186/s13024-021-00505-9

Kids Count. (2020). *Child population by race in the United States*. https://datacenter.kidscount.org/data/tables/103-child-population-by-race#detailed/1/any/false/1729,37,871,870,573,869,36,868,867,133/68,69,67,12,70,66,71,72/423,424.

Kievit, R. A., Scholte, H. S., Waldorp, L. J., & Borsboom, D. (2016). Inter- and intra-individual differences in fluid reasoning show distinct cortical responses. *bioRxiv*. https://doi.org/10.1101/039412

Killett, A., Burns, D., Kelly, F., Brooker, D., Bowes, A., La Fontaine, J., Latham, I., Wilson, M., & O'Neill, M. (2016). Digging deep: How organizational culture affects care home residents' experiences. *Ageing and Society, 36*, 160–188. https://doi.org/10.1017/S0144686X14001111

Kim, E. Y., & Son, Y.-J. (2022). Developing a conceptual model of older patients' decision-making process in choosing dialysis or conservative care using meta-ethnography. *Journal of Advanced Nursing, 78*, 1–13. https://doi.org/10.1111/jan.14945

Kim, H. K., Capaldi, D. M., & Crosby, L. (2007). Generalizability of Gottman and Colleagues' affective process models of couples' relationship outcomes. *Journal of Marriage and Family, 69*, 55–72. https://doi.org/10.1111/j.1741-3737.2006.00343.x

Kim, H., An, J. N., Kim, D. K., Kim, M.-H., Kim, H. O., Kim, Y.-L., Park, K. S., Oh, Y. K., Lim, C. S., Kim, Y. S., & Lee, J. P. (2015). Elderly peritoneal dialysis compared with elderly hemodialysis patients and younger peritoneal dialysis patients: Competing risk analysis of a Korean prospective cohort study. *PLoS One, 10*, e0131393. https://doi.org/10.1371/journal.pone.0131393

Kim, H.-J., & Fredriksen-Goldsen, K. I. (2016). Living arrangement and loneliness among lesbian, gay, and bisexual older adults. *The Gerontologist, 56*, 548–558. https://doi.org/10.1093/geront/gnu083

Kim, P., Strathearn, L., & Swain, J. E. (2016). The maternal brain and its plasticity in humans. *Hormones and Behavior, 77*, 113–123. https://doi.org/10.1016/j.yhbeh.2015.08.001

Kim, S., Healey, M. K., Goldstein, D., Hasher, L., & Wiprzycka, U. J. (2008). Age differences in choice satisfaction: A positivity effect in decision making. *Psychology and Aging, 23*, 33–38. https://doi.org/10.1037/0882-7974.23.1.33

Kimbler, K. J., Margrett, J. A., & Johnson, T. L. (2012). The role of supportive messages and distracting thoughts on everyday problem-solving performance. *Experimental Aging Research, 38*, 537–558. https://doi.org/10.1 080/0361073X.2012.726158

Kimmel, D. (2014). Lesbian, gay, bisexual, and transgender aging concerns. *Clinical Gerontologist, 37*, 49–63. https://doi.org/10.1080/07317115.2014.847310

King, A. (2016). *Older lesbian, gay, and bisexual adults: Identities, intersections, and institutions*. Routledge.

King, L. (2021, July 9, 16, 23). *Discussion on personality psychology and marginalized communities* [Conference Presentation]. ARP 2021 Convention. https://www.tinyurl.com/ARP2021KingBooker

King, P. M., & Kitchener, K. S. (2004). Reflective judgment: Theory and research on the development of epistemic assumptions through adulthood. *Educational Psychologist, 39*, 5–18. https://doi.org/10.1207/s15326985ep3901_2

King, P. M., & Kitchener, K. S. (2015). Cognitive development in the emerging adult: The emergence of complex cognitive skills. In J. J. Arnett (Ed.), *The Oxford handbook of emerging adulthood* (pp. 105–125). Oxford University Press.

King, S. V., Burgess, E. O., Akinyela, M., Counts-Spriggs, M., & Parker, N. (2006). The religious dimensions of the grandparent role in three-generation African American households. *Journal of Religion, Spirituality & Aging, 19*, 75–96. https://doi.org/10.1300/J496v19n01_06

Kingston, A., Collerton, J., Davies, K., Bond, J., Robinson, L., & Jagger, C. (2012). Losing the ability in activities of daily living in the oldest old: A hierarchic disability scale from the Newcastle 85+ study. *PLOS ONE, 7*, e31665. https://doi.org/10.1371/journal.pone.0031665

Kinney, J. M., & Cavanaugh, J. C. (1993, November). *Until death do us part: Striving to find meaning while caring for a spouse with dementia*. Paper presented at the meeting of the Gerontological Society of America, New Orleans.

Kinney, J. M., Ishler, K. J., Pargament, K. I., & Cavanaugh, J. C. (2003). Coping with the uncontrollable: The use of general and religious coping by caregivers to spouses with dementia. *Journal of Religious Gerontology, 14*, 171–188. https://doi.org/10.1300/J078v14n02_06

Kinsella, G. J., Ong, B., Storey, E., Wallace, J., & Hester, R. (2007). Elaborated spaced-retrieval and prospective memory in mild Alzheimer's disease. *Neuropsychological Rehabilitation, 17*, 688–706. https://doi.org/10.1080/09602010600892824

Kinsella, K., & Phillips, D. (2005). The challenge of global aging. *Population Bulletin, 60*, 5-41.

Kippen, R., Chapman, B., & Yu, P. (2013). What's love got to do with it? Homogamy and dyadic approaches to understanding marital instability. *Journal of Population Research, 30*, 213–247. https://doi.org/10.1007/s12546-013-9108-y

Kirmayer, L. J., Rousseau, C., Eric Jarvis, G., & Guzder, J. (2015). The cultural context of clinical assessment. In A. Tasman, J. Kay, J. A. Lieberman, M. B. First, & M. B. Riba (Eds.), *Psychiatry* (4th ed., pp. 56–70). Wiley.

Kisker, J., Gruber, T. & Schöne, B. (2021). Virtual reality experiences promote autobiographical retrieval mechanisms: Electrophysiological correlates of laboratory and virtual experiences. *Psychological Research, 85*, 2485–2501. https://doi.org/10.1007/s00426-020-01417-x

Kislev, E. (2019). *Happy singlehood: The rising acceptance and celebration of solo living*. University of California Press.

Kite, E., & Davy, C. (2015). Using Indigenist and Indigenous methodologies to connect to deeper understandings of Aboriginal and Torres Strait Islander peoples' quality of life. *Health Promotion Journal of Australia, 26*, 191–194. https://doi.org/10.1071/HE15064

Klackl, J., Jonas, E., & Kronbichler, M. (2013). Existential neuroscience: Neurophysiological correlates of proximal defenses against death-related thoughts. *Social Cognitive and Affective Neuroscience, 8*, 333–340. https://doi.org/10.1093/scan/nss003

Klaus, D. (2021). Differential effects of widowhood on network and support. *Journal of Family Issues, 42*, 2755–2781. https://doi.org/10.1177%2F0192513X20988068

Kleiber, D. A. (2013). Redeeming leisure in later life. In T. Freire (Ed.), *Positive leisure science* (pp. 21–38). Springer.

Kleiber, D. A. (2020). Toward an applied social psychology of leisure. *Journal of Leisure Research, 51*, 618–625. https://doi.org/10.1080/00222216.2020.1807843

Kleiber, D. A., Hutchinson, S. L., & Williams, R. (2002). Leisure as a resource in transcending negative life events: Self-protection, self-restoration, and personal transformation. *Leisure Sciences, 24*, 219–235. https://doi.org/10.1080/01490400252900167

Kleissner, V., & Jahn, G. (2021). Implicit and explicit age cues influence the evaluation of job applications. *Journal of Applied Social Psychology, 85*, 107–120. https://doi.org/10.1111/jasp.12720

Kliegel, M., Ballhausen, N., Hering, A., Ihle, A., Schnitzspahn, K. M., & Zuber, S. (2016). Prospective memory in older adults: Where we are now and what is next. *Gerontology, 62*, 459–466. https://doi.org/10.1159/000443698

Kliegl, O., & Bäuml, K.-H. T. (2021). The mechanisms underlying interference and inhibition: A review of current behavioral and neuroimaging research. *Brain Sciences, 11*, 1246. https://doi.org/10.3390/brainsci11091246

Klimczuk, A. (2017). *Economic foundations for creative ageing policy: Putting theory into practice* (Vol. II). Springer.

Klingberg, S., Mehlig, K., Dangol, R., Björkelund, C., Heitmann, B. L., & Lissner, L. (2021). Loss of height predicts total and cardiovascular mortality: A cohort study of northern European women. *BMJ Open, 11*, e049122. http://doi.org/10.1136/bmjopen-2021-049122

Knee, D. O. (2010). Hospice care for the aging population in the United States. In J. C. Cavanaugh & C. K. Cavanaugh (Eds.), *Aging in America: Vol. 3: Societal issues* (pp. 203–221). Praeger Perspectives.

Knez, I., Willander, J., Butler, A., Sang, Å. O., Sarlöv-Herlin, I., & Åkerskog, A. (2021). I can still see, hear and smell the fire: Cognitive, emotional and personal consequences of a natural disaster, and the impact of evacuation. *Journal of Environmental Psychology, 74*, 101554. https://doi.org/10.1016/j.jenvp.2021.101554

Knipscheer, K., & van Tilburg, T. (2013). Generational contact and support among late adult siblings within a verticalized family. In M. Silverstein & R. Giarusso (Eds.), *Kinship and cohort in an aging society: From generation to generation* (pp. 59–76). Johns Hopkins University Press.

Knowles, M. S., Holton, E. F., III, Swanson, R. A., & Robinson, P. A. (2020). *The adult learner* (9th ed.). Routledge.

Ko, H.-J., Mejia, S., & Hooker, K. (2014). Social possible selves, self-regulation, and social goal progress in older adulthood. *International Journal of Behavioral Development, 38*, 219–227. https://doi.org/10.1177/0165025413512063

Koblinsky, N. D., Meusel, L. A. C., Greenwood, C. E., & Anderson, N. D. (2021). Household physical activity is positively associated with gray matter volume in older adults. *BMC Geriatrics, 21*, 104. https://doi.org/10.1186/s12877-021-02054-8

Kochan, F., & Freeman, S., Jr. (2020). Mentoring across race, gender, and generation in higher education: A cross-cultural analysis. In B. J. Irby, J. N. Boswell, L. J. Searby, F. Kochan, R. Garza, & N. Abdelrahman (Eds.), *The Wiley international handbook of mentoring: Paradigms, practices, programs, and possibilities* (471-486). Wiley.

Koelen, M., & Eriksson, M. (2022). Older people, sense of coherence and community. In M. B. Mittelmark, G. F. Bauer, L. Vaandrager, J. M. Pelikan, S. Sagy, M. Eriksson, B. Lindström, & C. M. Magistretti (Eds.), *The handbook of salutogenesis* (2nd ed., pp. 185–199). Springer.

Koestenbaum, P. (1976). *Is there an answer to death?* Prentice Hall.

Koffer, R. E., Thurston, R. C., Bromberger, J. T., & Matthews, K. A. (2022). Racial/ethnic differences in women's life event exposure across midlife. *The Journals of Gerontology: Psychological Sciences, 77*, 272–283. https://doi.org/10.1093/geronb/gbab024

Kojima, G., Iliffe, S., Jivraj, S., & Walters, K. (2016). Association between frailty and quality of life among community-dwelling older people: A systematic review and meta-analysis. *Journal of Epidemiology & Community Health, 70*, 716–721. https://doi.org/10.1136/jech-2015-206717

Kojola, E., & Moen, P. (2016). No more lock-step retirement: Boomers' shifting meanings of work and retirement. *Journal of Aging Studies, 36*, 59–70. https://doi.org/10.1016/j.jaging.2015.12.003

Kompf, J. (2018). Implementation intentions for exercise and physical activity: Who do they work for? A systematic review. *Journal of Physical Activity and Health, 17*, 349–359. https://doi.org/10.1123/jpah.2018-0720

Kooij, D., Zacher, H., Wang, M., & Heckhausen, J. (2020). Successful aging at work: A process model to guide future research and practice. *Industrial and Organizational Psychology, 13*, 345–365. https://doi.org/10.1017/iop.2020.1

Koppel, J., & Berntsen, D. (2015). The peaks of life: The differential temporal locations of the reminiscence bump across disparate cueing methods. *Journal of Applied Research in Memory and Cognition, 4*, 66–80. https://doi.org/10.1016/j.jarmac.2014.11.004

Kopstein, M., & Mohlman, D. J. (2022). *HIV-1 Encephalopathy and Aids dementia complex*. StatPearls Publishing. https://www.ncbi.nlm.nih.gov/books/NBK507700/

Kornadt, A. E., & Rothermund, K. (2012). Internalization of age stereotypes into the self-concept via future self-views: A general model and domain-specific differences. *Psychology and Aging, 27*, 164–172. https://doi.org/10.1037/a0025110

Kornadt, A. E., Hess, T. M., Voss, P., & Rothermund, K. (2018). Subjective age across the life span: A differentiated, longitudinal approach. *Journals of Gerontology: Psychological Sciences, 73*, 767–777. https://doi.org/10.1093/geronb/gbw072

Koropeckyj-Cox, T., & Call, V. R. A. (2007). Characteristics of older childless persons and parents: Cross-national comparisons. *Journal of Family Issues, 28*, 1362–1414. https://doi.org/10.1177/0192513X07303837

Koss, C., & Ekerdt, D. J. (2017). Residential reasoning and the tug of the Fourth Age. *The Gerontologist, 57*, 921–929. https://doi.org/10.1093/geront/gnw010

Kotre, J. N. (1999). *Make it count: How to generate a legacy that gives meaning to your life*. Free Press.

Kotre, J. N. (2005, September). Generativity: Reshaping the past into the future. *Science and Theology News*, 42–43.

Kotter-Grühn, D. (2016). Aging self. In S. K. Whitbourne (Ed.), *The encyclopedia of adulthood and aging* (pp. 55–59). Wiley.

Kowalski, S. D., & Bondmass, M. D. (2008). Physiological and psychological symptoms of grief in widows. *Research in Nursing & Health, 31*, 23–30. https://doi.org/10.1002/nur.20228

Kozbelt, A., & Durmysheva, Y. (2007). Lifespan creativity in a non-Western artistic tradition: A study of Japanese Ukiyo-e printmakers. *International Journal of Aging & Human Development, 65*, 23–51. https://doi.org/10.2190/166N-6470-1325-T341

Krause, N. (2012). Feelings of gratitude toward God among older whites, older African Americans, and older Mexican Americans. *Research on Aging, 34*, 156–173. https://doi.org/10.1177/0164027511417884

Krause, N., & Bastida, E. (2011). Prayer to the saints or the Virgin and health among older Mexican Americans. *Hispanic Journal of Behavioral Sciences, 33*, 71–87. https://doi.org/10.1177/0739986310393628

Krawczyk, M., & Rush, M. (2020). Describing the end-of-life doula role and practices of care: Perspectives from four countries. *Palliative Care and Social Practice,14*, 1–15. https://doi.org/10.1177%2F2632352420973226

Krinsky-McHale, S. J., & Silverman, W. (2022). Cognitive profile of aging and dementia. In E. Head & I. Lott (Eds.), The neurobiology of aging and Alzheimer disease in Down syndrome (pp. 289–305). Academic Press. https://doi.org/10.1016/B978-0-12-818845-3.00005-0

Kristof, N. (2021). What are sperm telling us? *New York Times, February 20*. https://www.nytimes.com/2021/02/20/opinion/sunday/endocrine-disruptors-sperm.html?referringSource=articleShare

Krousel-Wood, M., Craig, L. S., Peacock, E., Zlotnick, E., O'Connell, S., Bradford, D., Shi, L., & Petty, R. (2021). Medication adherence: Expanding the conceptual framework. *American Journal of Hypertension, 34*, 895–909. https://doi.org/10.1093/ajh/hpab046

Kübler-Ross, E. (1969). *On death and dying*. Macmillan.

Kübler-Ross, E. (1974). *Questions and answers on death and dying*. Macmillan.

Kübler-Ross, E. (1997). *The wheel of life: A memoir of living and dying*. Touchstone.

Kuczmarska, A., Ngo, L. H., Guess, J., O'Connor, M. A., Branford-White, L., Palihnich, K., Gallagher, J., & Marcantonio, E. R. (2016). Detection of delirium in hospitalized older general medicine patients: A comparison of the 3D-CAM and CAM-ICU. *Journal of General Internal Medicine, 31*, 297–303. https://doi.org/10.1007/s11606-015-3514-0

Kuhlmann, B. G., & Boywitt, C. D. (2016). Aging, source memory, and the experience of "remembering." *Aging, Neuropsychology, and Cognition: A Journal on Normal and Dysfunctional Development, 23*, 477–498. https://doi.org/10.1080/13825585.2015.1120270

Kukutai, T. H. (2007). White mothers, brown children: Ethnic identification of Maori–European children in New Zealand. *Journal of Marriage and Family, 69*, 1150–1161. https://doi.org/10.1111/j.1741-3737.2007.00438.x

Kulik, L. (2016). Long-term marriages. In S. K. Whitbourne (Ed.), *The encyclopedia of adulthood and aging* (pp. 820–823). Wiley.

Kulpa, E., Rahman, A. T., & Vahia, I. V. (2021). Approaches to assessing the impact of robotics in geriatric mental health care: A scoping review. *International Review of Psychiatry, 33*, 424–434. https://doi.org/10.1080/09540261.2020.1839391

Kumar, D. K. V., Choi, S. H., Washicosky, K. J., Eimer, W. A., Tucker, S., Ghofrani, J., Lefkowitz, A., McColl, G., Goldstein, L. E., Tanzi, R. E., & Moir, R. D. (2016). Amyloid-β peptide protects against microbial infection in mouse and worm models of Alzheimer's disease. *Science Translational Medicine, 8*, 340ra72. https://doi.org/10.1126/scitranslmed.aaf1059

Kumar, K. (2017). The blended family life cycle. *The Journal of Divorce and Remarriage, 58*, 110–125. https://doi.org/10.1080/10502556.2016.1268019

Kunda, Z., & Spencer, S. J. (2003). When do stereotypes come to mind and when do they color judgment? A goal-based theoretical framework for stereotype activation and application. *Psychological Bulletin, 129*, 522–544. https://doi.org/10.1037/0033-2909.129.4.522

Kunkle, B. W., Schmidt, M., Klein, H.-U., Naj, A. C., Hamilton-Nelson, K. L., Larson, E. B., Evans, D. A., De Jager, P. L., Crane, P. K., Buxbaum, J. D., Ertekin-Taner, N., Barnes, L. L., Fallin, M. D., Manly, J. J., Go, R. C. P., Obisesan, T. O., Kamboh, M. I., Bennett, D. A., Hall, H. S., … Kukull, W. A. (2021). Novel Alzheimer disease risk loci and pathways in African American individuals using the African genome resources panel: A meta-analysis. *JAMA Neurology, 78*, 102–113. https://doi.org/10.1001/jamaneurol.2020.3536

Kurdek, L. A. (2004). Are gay and lesbian cohabiting couples really different from heterosexual married couples? *Journal of Marriage and Family, 66*, 880–900. https://doi.org/10.1111/j.0022-2445.2004.00060.x

Kurpiers, L. A., Schulte-Herbrüggen, Ejotre, I., & Reeder, D. M. (2016). Bushmeat and emerging infectious diseases: Lessons from Africa. In F. M. Angelici (Ed.), *Problematic Wildlife* (pp. 507–551). Springer. https://doi.org/10.1007/978-3-319-22246-2_24

Kurshan, R. P. (2022). *Investment industry claims debunked*. Springer.

Kwon, S., & Tae, Y.-S. (2012). Nursing home placement: The process of decision making and adaptation among adult children caregivers of demented parents in Korea. *Asian Nursing Research, 6*, 143–151. https://doi.org/10.1016/j.anr.2012.10.006

Kyulo, N. L., Knutsen, S. F., Tonstad, S., Fraser, G. E., & Singh, P. N. (2012). Validation of recall of body weight over a 26-year period in cohort members of the Adventist Health Study 2. *Annals of Epidemiology, 22*, 744–746. https://doi.org/10.1016/j.annepidem.2012.06.106

Laban, T. S., & Saadabadi, A. (2022). *Monoamine oxidase inhibitors (MAOI)*. StatPearls Publishing.

Labouvie-Vief, G. (1980). Beyond formal operations: Uses and limits of pure logic in life-span development. *Human Development, 23*, 141–161. https://doi.org/10.1159/000272546

Labouvie-Vief, G. (1997). Cognitive-emotional integration in adulthood. In K. W. Schaie & M. P. Lawton (Eds.), *Annual review of gerontology and geriatrics: Focus on emotion and adult development* (Vol. 17. pp. 206–237). Springer.

Labouvie-Vief, G. (2003). Dynamic integration: Affect, cognition, and the self in adulthood. *Current Directions in Psychological Science, 12*, 201–206. https://doi.org/10.1046/j.0963-7214.2003.01262.x

Labouvie-Vief, G. (2005). Self-with-other representations and the organization of the self. *Journal of Research in Personality, 39*, 185–205. https://doi.org/10.1016/j.jrp.2004.09.007

Labouvie-Vief, G. (2015). *Integrating emotions and cognition throughout the lifespan*. Springer.

Labouvie-Vief, G., Chiodo, L. M., Goguen, L. A., Diehl, M., & Orwoll, L. (1995). Representations of self across the life span. *Psychology and Aging, 10*, 404–415. https://doi.org/10.1037/0882-7974.10.3.404

Labouvie-Vief, G., & Diehl, M. (1999). Self and personality development. In J. C. Cavanaugh & S. K. Whitbourne (Eds.), *Gerontology: An interdisciplinary perspective* (pp. 238–268). Oxford University Press.

Labouvie-Vief, G., Grühn, D., & Mouras, H. (2009). Dynamic emotion–cognition interactions in development: Arousal, stress, and the processing of affect. In H. B. Bosworth & C. Hertzog (Eds.), *Aging and cognition: Research methodologies and empirical advances* (pp. 181–196). American Psychological Association.

Lacey, K. K., Mouzon, D. M., Parnell, R. N., & Laws, T. (2021). Severe intimate partner violence, sources of stress and the mental health of U.S. Black women. *Journal of Women's Health, 30*, 17–28. https://doi.org/10.1089/jwh.2019.8215

Lachman, M. E. (2004). Development in midlife. *Annual Review of Psychology, 55*, 305–331. https://doi.org/10.1146/annurev.psych.55.090902.141521

Lachman, M. E. (2006). Perceived control over aging-related declines: Adaptive beliefs and behaviors. *Current Directions in Psychological Science, 15*(6), 282–286. https://doi.org/10.1111/j.1467-8721.2006.00453.x

Lachman, M. E., & Agrigoroaei, S. (2012). Low perceived control as a risk factor for episodic memory: The mediational role of anxiety and task interference. *Memory and Cognition, 40*, 287–296. https://doi.org/10.3758/s13421-011-0140-x

Lachman, M. E., & Andreoletti, C. (2006). Strategy use mediates the relationship between control beliefs and memory performance for middle-aged and older adults. *Journals of Gerontology: Psychological Sciences, 61*, P88–P94. https://doi.org/10.1093/geronb/61.2.P88

Lachman, M. E., Rosnick, C., & Röcke, C. (2009). The rise and fall of control beliefs in adulthood: Cognitive and biopsychosocial antecedents of stability and change over nine years. In H. Bosworth & C. Hertzog (Eds.), *Aging and cognition: Research methodologies and empirical advances* (pp. 143–160). American Psychological Association.

Lachman, M. E., Teshale, S., & Agrigoroaei, S. (2015). Midlife as a pivotal period in the life course: Balancing growth and decline at the crossroads of youth and old age. *International Journal of Behavioral Development, 39*, 20–31. http://doi.org/10.1177/0165025414533223

Lackey, J. (2022). Eyewitness testimony and epistemic agency. *Noûs, 56*, 696–715. https://doi.org/10.1111/nous.12380

Ladin, K., & Reinhold, S. (2013). Mental health of aging immigrants and native-born men across 11 European countries. *Journals of Gerontology: Social Sciences, 68*, 298–309. https://doi.org/10.1093/geronb/gbs163

Ladin, K., Lin, N., Hahn, E., Zhang, G., Koch-Weser, S., & Weiner, D. E. (2017). Engagement in decision-making and patient satisfaction: A qualitative study of older patients' perceptions of dialysis initiation and modality decisions. *Nephrology, Dialysis, Transplantation, 32*, 1394–1401. https://doi.org/10.1093/ndt/gfw307

Lahad, K. (2017). *A table for one: A critical reading on singlehood, gender, and time*. Manchester University Press.

Lahti, J., Sabia, S., Singh-Manoux, A., Kivimäki, M., Tatsuse, T., Yamada, M., Sekine, M., & Lallukka, T. (2016). Leisure time physical activity and subsequent physical and mental health functioning among midlife Finnish, British, and Japanese employees: A follow-up study in three occupational cohorts. *BMJ Open, 6*, e009788. https://doi.org/10.1136/bmjopen-2015-009788

Lai, C. K. Y., Wong, L. F., Liu, K.-H., Lui, W., Chan, M. F., & Yap, L. S. Y. (2013). Online and onsite training for family caregivers of people with dementia: Results form a pilot study. *International Journal of Geriatric Psychiatry, 28*, 107–108. https://doi.org/10.1002/gps.3798

Lai, D. W. L. (2010). Filial piety, caregiving appraisal, and caregiving burden. *Research on Aging, 32*, 200–223. https://doi.org/10.1177/0164027509351475

Lain, D., van der Horst, M., & Vickerstaff S. (2020). Extended working lives: Feasible and desirable for all? In S. Czaja, J. Sharit, & J. James (Eds.), *Current and emerging trends in aging and work* (pp. 101–119). Springer, Cham. https://doi.org/10.1007/978-3-030-24135-3_6

Lamanna, M. A., Riedmann, A., & Stewart, S. D. (2021). *Marriages, families, and relationships: Making choices in a diverse society* (14th ed.). Cengage Learning.

Lamar, M., Arfanakis, K., Yu, L., Zhang, S., Han, S. D., Fleischman, D. A., Bennett, D. A., & Boyle, P. A. (2020). White matter correlates of scam susceptibility in community-dwelling older adults. *Brain Imaging and Behavior, 14*, 1521–1530. https://doi.org/10.1007/s11682-019-00079-7

Lamb, S., Gable, S., & de Ruyter, D. (2021). Mutuality in sexual relationships: A standard of ethical sex? *Ethical Theory and Moral Practice, 24*, 271–284. https://doi.org/10.1007/s10677-020-10150-8

Lambert-Pandraud, E., Laurent, G., & Lapersonne (2005). Repeat purchasing of new automobiles by older consumers: Empirical evidence and interpretations. *Journal of Marketing, 69*, 97–113. https://doi.org/1509/jmkg.69.2.97.60757

Lamela, D., Figueiredo, B., Bastos, A., & Feinberg, M. (2016). Typologies of post-divorce coparenting and parental well-being, parenting quality and children's psychological adjustment. *Child Psychiatry & Human Development, 47*, 716–728. https://doi.org/10.1007/s10578-015-0604-5

Lamidi, E. O., Manning, W. D., & Brown, S. L. (2019). Change in the stability of first premarital cohabitation among women in the United States, 1983–2013. *Demography, 56*, 427–450. https://doi.org/10.1007/s13524-019-00765-7

Lampkin-Hunter, T. (2010). *Single parenting*. Xlibris.

Lancel, M., Stroebe, M., & Elsma, M. C. (2020). Sleep disturbances in bereavement: A systematic review. *Sleep Medicine Reviews, 53*, 101331. https://doi.org/10.1016/j.smrv.2020.101331

Landes, S. D., Ardelt, M., Vaillant, G. E., & Waldinger, R. J. (2014). Childhood adversity, midlife generativity, and later life well-being. *Journals of Gerontology: Social Sciences, 69*, 942–952. https://doi.org/10.1093/geronb/gbu055

Landis, M., Peter-Wright, M., Martin, M., & Bodenmann, G. (2013). Dyadic coping and marital satisfaction of older spouses in long-term marriages. *GeroPsych: The Journal of Gerontopsychology and Geriatric Psychiatry, 26*, 39–47. https://doi.org/10.1024/1662-9647/a000077

Landrine, H., Corral, I., Hall, M. B., Bess, J. J., & Efird, J. (2016). Self-rated health, objective health, and racial discrimination among African-Americans: Explaining inconsistent findings and testing health pessimism. *Journal of Health Psychology, 21*, 2514–2524. https://doi.org/10.1177/1359105315580465

Lang, F. R. (2004). Social motivation across the life span. In F. R. Land & K. L. Fingerman (Eds.), *Growing together: Personal relationships across the life span* (pp. 341–367). Cambridge University Press.

Lang, J. C., & Lee, C. H. (2005). Identity accumulation, others' acceptance, job-search self-efficacy, and stress. *Journal of Organizational Behavior, 26*, 293–312. https://doi.org/10.1002/job.309

Langer, E. J. (1989). *Mindfulness*. Addison-Wesley.

Langer, E. J., & Rodin, J. (1976). The effects of choice and enhanced personal responsibility for the aged: A field experiment in an institutional setting. *Journal of Personality and Social Psychology, 34*, 191–198. https://psycnet.apa.org/doi/10.1037/0022-3514.34.2.191

Langer, N., Pedroni, A., Gianotti, L. R. R., Hänggi, J., Knoch, D., & Jäncke, L. (2012). Functional brain network efficiency predicts intelligence. *Human Brain Mapping, 33*, 1393–1406. https://doi.org/10.1002/hbm.21297

Langeslag, S. J. E., van der Veen, F. M., & Fekkes, D. (2012). Blood levels of serotonin are differentially affected by romantic love in men and women. *Journal of Psychophysiology, 26*, 92–98. https://doi.org/10.1027/0269-8803/a000071

Langlais, M. R., Anderson, E. R., & Greene, S. M. (2016). Consequences of dating for post-divorce maternal well-being. *Journal of Marriage and Family, 78*, 1032–1046. https://doi.org/10.1111/jomf.12319

Larner, A. J. (2021). Functional cognitive disorders (FCD): How is metacognition involved? *Brain Sciences, 11*, 1082. https://doi.org/10.3390/brainsci11081082

Larson, C., & Kao, H. (2016). Caregiving. In J. L. Hayashi & B. Leff (Eds.), *Geriatric home-based medical care* (pp. 269–290). Springer. https://doi.org/10.1007/978-3-319-23365-9_13

Lashua, B., Johnson, C. W., & Parry, D. C. (2021). Leisure in the time of coronavirus: A rapid response special issue. *Leisure Sciences, 43*, 6–11. https://doi.org/10.1080/01490400.2020.1774827.

Laskowski, E. R. (2021). *How much should the average adult exercise every day?* https://www.mayoclinic.org/healthy-lifestyle/fitness/expert-answers/exercise/faq-20057916

Laurent, H. K., Lucas, T., Pierce, J., Goetz, S., & Granger, D. A. (2016). Coordination of cortisol response to social evaluative threat with autonomic and inflammatory responses is moderated by stress appraisals and affect. *Biological Psychology, 118*, 17–24. https://doi.org/10.1016/j.biopsycho.2016.04.066

Lavner, J. A., & Bradbury, T. N. (2017). Protecting relationships from stress. *Current Opinion in Psychology, 13*, 11–14. https://doi.org/10.1016/j.copsyc.2016.03.003

Lavner, J. A., Karney, B. R., & Bradbury, T. N. (2016). Does couples' communication predict marital satisfaction, or does marital satisfaction predict communication? *Journal of Marriage and Family, 78*, 680–694. https://doi.org/10.1111/jomf.12301

Lavner, J. A., Lamkin, J., Miller, J. D., Campbell, W. K., & Karney, B. R. (2016). Narcissism and newlywed marriage: Partner characteristics and marital trajectories. *Personality Disorders: Theory, Research, and Treatment, 7*, 169–179. https://doi.org/10.1037/per0000137

Lavoie, C.-E., Vallerand, R. J., & Verner-Filion, J. (2021). Passion and emotions: The mediating role of cognitive appraisals. *Psychology of Sport and Exercise, 54*, 101907. https://doi.org/10.1016/j.psychsport.2021.101907

Law, L. L. F., Mok, V. C. T., Yau, M. K. S., & Fong, K. N. K. (2022). Effects of functional task exercise on everyday problem-solving ability and functional status in older adults with mild cognitive impairment—A randomised controlled trial. *Age and Ageing, 51*, afab210. https://doi.org/10.1093/ageing/afab210

Lawton, M. P. (1982). Competence, environmental press, and the adaptation of old people. In M. P. Lawton, P. G. Windley, & T. O. Byerts (Eds.), *Aging and the environment: Theoretical approaches* (pp. 33–59). New York: Springer.

Lawton, M. P. (1989). Environmental proactivity in older people. In V. L. Bengtson & K. W. Schaie (Eds.), *The course of later life: Research and reflections* (pp. 15–23). Springer.

Lawton, M. P., & Nahemow, L. (1973). Ecology of the aging process. In C. Eisdorfer & M. P. Lawton (Eds.), *The psychology of adult development and aging* (pp. 619–674). American Psychological Association.

Lawton, M. P., Moss, M., Hoffman, C., Grant, R., Have, T. T., & Kleban, M. H. (1999). Health, valuation of life, and the wish to live. *The Gerontologist, 39*, 406–416. https://doi.org/10.1093/geront/39.4.406

Lazarus, R. S. (1984). Puzzles in the study of daily hassles. *Journal of Behavioral Medicine, 7*, 375–389. https://doi.org/10.1007/BF00845271

Lazarus, R. S., & Folkman, S. (1984). *Stress, appraisal, and coping*. Springer.

Lazarus, R. S., DeLongis, A., Folkman, S., & Gruen, R. (1985). Stress and adaptational outcomes: The problem of confounded measures. *American Psychologist, 40*, 770–779. https://doi.org/10.1037/0003-066X.40.7.770

Le Vigouroux, S., Dauvier, B., & Congard, A. (2022). Development of affect and affective stability in adulthood: Nonlinear age-related differences in daily life. *Current Psychology, 41*, 2277–2286. https://doi.org/10.1007/s12144-020-00743-y

Leah, V. (2016). Supporting people with dementia to eat. *Nursing Older People, 28*, 33–39. https://doi.org/10.7748/nop.2016.e811

Lebo, P. B., Quehenberger, F., Kamolz, L.-P., & Lumenta, D. B. (2015). The Angelina Jolie effect revisited: Exploring a media-related impact on public awareness. *Cancer, 121*, 3959–3964. https://doi.org/10.1002/cncr.29461

Lecy, N. (2020). *Ethno-racial factors identity development factors of Chinese American adoptees*. Master's thesis, South Dakota State University. ProQuest Document 27834572.

Ledbetter, A. M. (2017). Friendship and social media. In M. Hojjat & A. Moyer (Eds.), *The psychology of friendship* (pp. 93–108). Oxford University Press. https://doi.org/10.1093/acprof:oso/9780190222024.003.0006.

Lee, B. T., Tana, M. M., Kahn, J. A., & Dara, L. (2021). We are not immune: Racial and ethnic disparities in autoimmune liver diseases. *Hepatology, 74*, 2876–2887. https://doi.org/10.1002/hep.31985

Lee, E. E., Depp, C., Palmer, B. W., Glorioso, D., Daly, R., Liu, J., Tu, X. M., Kim, H.-C., Tarr, P., Yamada, Y., & Jeste, D. V. (2019). High prevalence and adverse health effects of loneliness in community-dwelling adults across the lifespan: Role of wisdom as a protective factor. *International Psychogeriatrics, 31*, 1447–1462. https://doi.org/10.1017/S1041610218002120

Lee, G. R. (2014). Current research on widowhood: Devastation and human resilience. *Journals of Gerontology: Psychological Sciences and Social Sciences, 69B*, 2–3. https://doi.org/10.1093/geronb/gbt111

Lee, H. J., Han, S. H., & Boerner, K. (2022). Psychological and physical health in widowhood: Does marital quality make a difference? *Research on Aging, 44*, 54–64. https://doi.org/10.1177%2F0164027521989083.

Lee, H. J., Macbeth, A. H., Pagani, J. H., & Young, W. S. (2009). Oxytocin: The great facilitator of life. *Progress in Neurobiology, 88*, 127–151. https://doi.org/10.1016/j.pneurobio.2009.04.001

Lee, H., Vogel, R. I., LeRoy, B., & Zierhut, H. A. (2021). Adult adoptees and their use of direct-to-consumer genetic testing: Searching for family, searching for health. *Journal of Genetic Counseling, 30*, 144–157. https://doi.org/10.1002/jgc4.1304

Lee, J., Meijer, E., Phillips, D., & Hu, P. (2021). Disability incidence rates for men and women in 23 countries: Evidence on health effects of gender inequality. *Journals of Gerontology: Medical Sciences, 76*, 328–338. https://doi.org/10.1093/gerona/glaa288

Lee, K. H., & Siegle, G. J. (2012). Common and distinct brain networks underlying explicit emotional evaluation: A meta-analytic study. *Social Cognitive and Affective Neuroscience, 7*, 521–534. https://doi.org/10.1093/scan/nsp001

Lee, K. S. (2010). Gender, care work, and the complexity of family membership in Japan. *Gender & Society, 24*, 647–671. https://doi.org/10.1177/0891243210382903

Lee, K., Ashton, M. C., Wiltshire, J., Bourdage, J. S., Visser, B. A., & Gallucci, A. (2013). Sex, power, and money: Prediction from the Dark Triad and Honesty–Humility. *European Journal of Personality, 27*, 169–184. https://doi.org/10.1002/per.1860

Lee, M.-D. (2007). Correlates of consequences of intergenerational caregiving in Taiwan. *Journal of Advanced Nursing, 59*, 47–56. https://doi.org/10.1111/j.1365-2648.2007.04274.x

Lee, R. E., Hitchcock, R., & Biesele, M. (2002). Foragers to first peoples: The Kalahari San today. *Cultural Survival Quarterly, 26*, 22–26.

Lee, S., King, V., Wickrama, K. K. A. S., & O'Neal, C. W. (2020). Psychological resources, constructive conflict management behaviors, and depressive symptoms: A dyadic analysis. *Family Processes, 59*, 1293–1307. https://doi.org/10.1111/famp.12486

Lee, Y.-M., Ha, J.-K., Park, J.-M., Lee, B.-D., Moon, E., Chung, Y-I., Kim, J.-H., Kim, H.-J., Mun, C.-W., Kim, T.-H., & Kim, Y.-H. (2016). Impact of apolipoprotein E4 polymorphism on the gray matter volume and the white matter integrity in subjective memory impairment without white matter hyperintensities: Voxel-based morphometry and tract-based spatial statistics study under 3-Tesla MRI. *Journal of NeuroImaging, 26*, 144–149. https://doi.org/10.1111/jon.12207

Leeuwen, K. van. (2016). *Treating grandparents as grandchildren: An overview of elderspeak and the perception of elderspeak in Dutch nursing home.* Unpublished bachelor's thesis, Faculty of Humanities, University of Leiden. https://openaccess.leidenuniv.nl/handle/1887/37514

Lefkowitz, E. S., Vukman, S. N., & Loken, E. (2012). Young adults in a wireless world. In A. Booth, S. L. Brown, N. S. Landale, W. D. Manning, & S. M. McHale (Eds.), *Early adulthood in a family context* (pp. 45–56). Springer.

Leichtentritt, R. D., Leichtentritt, J., Barzllal, Y., & Pedatsur-Sukenik, N. (2013). Unanticipated death of a partner: The loss experience of bereaved girlfriends of fallen Israeli soldiers. *Death Studies, 37*, 803–829. https://doi.org/10.1080/07481187.2012.699907

Lemaire, P. (2022). *Emotion and cognition: An introduction.* Routledge.

Lemaître, J.-F., Garratt, M., & Gaillard, J. M. (2020a). Going beyond lifespan in comparative biology of aging. *Advances in Geriatric Medicine and Research, 2*, e200011. https://doi.org/10.20900/agmr20200011

Lemaître, J.-F., Ronget, V., Tidière, M., Allainé, D., Berger, V., Cohas, A., Colchero, F., Conde, D. A., Garratt, M., Liker, A., Marais, G. A. B., Scheuerlein, A., Székely, T., & Gaillard, J. M. (2020b). Sex differences in adult lifespan and aging rates of mortality across wild mammals. *Proceedings of the National Academy of Sciences, 117*, 8546–8553. https://doi.org/10.1073/pnas.1911999117

Lemieux, A. (2012). Post-formal thought in gerontagogy or beyond Piaget. *Journal of Behavioral and Brain Science, 2*, 399–406. https://doi.org/10.4236/jbbs.2012.23046

Leming, M. R., & Dickinson, G. E. (2021). *Understanding dying, death, and bereavement* (9th ed.). Cengage Learning.

Lent, R. W. (2013). Career-life preparedness: Revisiting career planning and adjustment in the new workplace. *Career Development Quarterly, 61*, 2–14. https://doi.org/10.1002/j.2161-0045.2013.00031.x

Lent, R. W. (2020). Career development and counseling: A social cognitive framework. In S. D. Brown & R. W. Lent (Eds.), *Career development and counseling: Putting theory and research to work* (pp. 129–163). Wiley.

Leon, G. R., Gillum, B., Gillum, R., & Gouze, M. (1979). Personality stability and change over a 30-year period: Middle to old age. *Journal of Consulting and Clinical Psychology, 47*, 517–524. https://doi.org/10.1037/0022-006X.47.3.517

LeRoux, H., & Fisher, J. E. (2006). Strategies for enhancing medication adherence in the elderly. In W. T. O'Donohue & E. R. Levensky (Eds.), *Promoting treatment adherence: A practical handbook for health care providers* (pp. 353–362). Sage.

Leshikar, E. D., Cassidy, B. S., & Gutchess, A. H. (2016). Similarity to the self influences cortical recruitment during impression formation. *Cognitive, Affective, & Behavioral Neuroscience, 16*, 302–314. https://doi.org/10.3758/s13415-015-0390-3

Letsiou, S. (2021). Tracing skin aging process: A mini-review of in vitro approaches. *Biogerontology 22*, 261–272. https://doi.org/10.1007/s10522-021-09916-z

Leuty, M. E., Hansen, J.-I. C., & Speaks, S. Z. (2016). Vocational and leisure interests: A profile-level approach to examining interests. *Journal of Career Assessment, 24*, 215–239. https://doi.org/10.1177/1069072715580321

Levinson, D. J., Darrow, C., Kline, E., Levinson, M., & McKee, B. (1978). *The seasons of a man's life.* Knopf.

Levinson, D., & Levinson, J. D. (1996). *The seasons of a woman's life.* Knopf.

Levitin, D. J. (2020). *Successful aging: A neuroscientist explores the power and potential of our lives.* Dutton.

Levitt, H. M., Schuyler, S. W., Chickerella, R., Elber, A., White, L., Troeger, R. L., Karter, J. M., Preston, J. M., & Collins, K. M. (2020). How discrimination in adoptive, foster, and medical systems harms LGBTQ+ families: Research on the experiences of prospective parents. *Journal of Gay & Lesbian Social Services, 32*, 261-282. https://doi.org/10.1080/10538720.2020.1728461

Levy, B. (1996). Improving memory in old age through implicit stereotyping. *Journal of Personality and Social Psychology, 71*, 1092–1107. https://doi.org/10.1037/0022-3514.71.6.1092

Levy, B. (2009). Stereotype embodiment: A psychosocial approach to aging. *Current Directions in Psychological Science, 18*, 332–336. https://doi.org/10.1111/j.1467-8721.2009.01662.x

Levy, B. R., & Bavishi, A. (2018). Survival advantage mechanism: Inflammation as a mediator of positive self-perceptions of aging on longevity. *Journals of Gerontology: Psychological Sciences, 75*, 409–412. https://doi.org/10.1093/geronb/gbw035

Levy, B. R., Ferrucci, L., Zonderman, A. B., Slade, M. D., Troncoso, J., & Resnick, S. M. (2016). A culture–brain link: Negative age stereotypes predict Alzheimer's disease biomarkers. *Psychology and Aging, 31*, 82–88. https://doi.org/10.1037/pag0000062

Levy, B. R., Slade, M. D., & Kasl, S. V. (2002). Longitudinal benefit of positive self-perceptions of aging on functional health. *Journals of Gerontology: Psychological Sciences, 57B*, P409–P417. https://doi.org/10.1093/geronb/57.5.P409

Levy, B. R., Zonderman, A. B., Slade, M. D., & Ferrucci, L. (2012). Memory shaped by age stereotypes over time. *Journals of Gerontology: Psychological Sciences, 67*, 432–436. https://doi.org/10.1093/geronb/gbr120

Levy, B., & Langer, E. (1994). Aging free from negative stereotypes: Successful memory in China and among the American deaf. *Journal of Personality and Social Psychology, 66*, 989–997. https://doi.org/10.1037/0022-3514.66.6.989

Levy, C. R., Zargoush, M., Williams, A. E., Williams, A. R., Giang, P. Wojtusiak, J., Kheirbek, R. E., & Alemi, F. (2016). Sequence of functional loss and recovery in nursing homes. *The Gerontologist, 56*, 52–61. https://doi.org/10.1093/geront/gnv099

Levy, S. R., & Macdonald, J. L. (2016). Progress on understanding ageism. *Journal of Social Issues, 72*, 5–25. https://doi.org/10.1111/josi.12153

Levy, S. R., Lytle, A., Monahan, C., Macdonald, J., & Apriceno, M. (2022). Ageism-reduction programs. In A. H. Nordstrom & W. Goodfriend (Eds.), *Innovative stigma and discrimination reduction programs across the world.* Routledge. https://doi.org/10.4324/9781003042464-12

Lewin, K. (1936). *Principles of topological psychology.* McGraw-Hill.

Lewinsohn, P. M. (1975). The behavioral study and treatment of depression. In M. Hersen, R. M. Eisler, & P. M. Miller (Eds.), *Progress in behavior modification* (Vol. 1, pp. 19–64). Academic Press.

Lewis, D. C., Seponski, D. M., & Camp, T. G. (2011). Religious and spiritual values transactions: A constant-comparison analysis of grandmothers and adult-granddaughters. *Journal of Religion, Spirituality & Aging, 23*, 184–205. https://doi.org/10.1080/15528030.2011.533407

Lewis, H. (2021, October 26). Why I'll keep saying "pregnant women." *The Atlantic.* https://www.theatlantic.com/ideas/archive/2021/10/pregnant-women-people-feminism-language/620468/

Lewis, J. P. (2020). Alaska natives in recovery and indigenous cultural generativity: Sharing redemptive narratives to increase quality of life. In B. R. Nikku (Ed.), *Global social work: Cutting edge issues and critical reflections* (pp. 149–161). IntechOpen.

Lewis, J. R. (2013). Hair-pulling, culture, and unmourned death. *International Journal of Psychoanalytic Self Psychology, 8*, 202–217. https://doi.org/10.1080/15551024.2013.768749

Lewis, M., Lamson, A., & White, M. (2016). The state of dyadic methodology: An analysis of the literature on interventions for military couples. *Journal of Couple & Relationship Therapy, 15*, 135–157. https://doi.org/10.1080/15332691.2015.1106998

Lewis-Fernández, R., Aggarwal, N. K., Hinton, L., Hinton, D. E., & Kirmayer, L. J. (2015). *DSM-5®: Handbook on the cultural formulation interview.* American Psychiatric Publishing.

Li, A., Del Olmo, M. G., Fong, M., Sim, K., Lymer, S. J., Cunich, M., & Caterson, I. (2021). Effect of a smartphone application (Perx) on medication adherence and clinical outcomes: A 12-month randomised controlled trial. *BMJ Open, 11*, e047041. https://doi.org/10.1136/bmjopen-2020-047041

Li, C., Qiao, K., Mu, Y., & Jiang, L. (2021). Large-scale morphological network efficiency of human brain: Cognitive intelligence and emotional intelligence. *Frontiers in Aging Neuroscience, 13*. https://doi.org/10.3389/fnagi.2021.605158

Li, J., & Prigerson, H. G. (2016). Assessment and associated features of prolonged grief disorder among Chinese bereaved individuals. *Comprehensive Psychiatry, 66*, 9–16. https://doi.org/10.1016/j.comppsych.2015.12.001

Li, J., Zhang, G., Wang, J., Liu, D., Wan, C., Fang, J., Wu, D., Zhou, Y., Tian, T., Zhu, W. (2022). Experience-dependent associations between distinct subtypes of childhood trauma and brain function and architecture. *Quantitative Imaging in Medicine and Surgery, 12*. https://qims.amegroups.com/article/view/79579

Li, K. Z. H., Lindenberger, U., Freund, A. M., & Baltes, P. B. (2001). Walking while memorizing: Age-related differences in compensatory behavior. *Psychological Science, 12*, 230–237. https://doi.org/10.1111/1467-9280.00341

Li, M., Chen, R., & Dong, X. (2020). Elder mistreatment across diverse cultures. *Generations, 44*, 20–25. https://www.ingentaconnect.com/content/asag/gen/2020/00000044/00000001/art00006.

Li, T., Pei, X., Chen, X., & Zhang, S. (2021). Identifying end-of-life preferences among Chinese patients with cancer using the Heart to Heart Card Game. *American Journal of Hospice and Palliative Medicine, 38*, 62–67. https://doi.org/10.1177%2F1049909120917361

Li, X., Dorstyn, D., Mpofu, E., O'Neill, L., Li, Q., Zhang, C., & Ingman, S. (2021). Nursing assistants and resident satisfaction in long-term care: A systematic review. *Geriatric Nursing, 42*, 1323-1331. https://doi.org/10.1016/j.gerinurse.2021.08.006

Li, Z., & Dalaker, J. (2021). *Poverty among the population aged 65 and older.* https://crsreports.congress.gov/product/pdf/R/R45791

Liao, F., & Jan, Y.-K. (2016). Using modified entropy to characterize aging-associated microvascular dysfunction. *Frontiers in Physiology, 7*, 126. https://doi.org/10.3389/fphys.2016.00126

Liao, H.-W., & Carstensen, L. L. (2018). Future time perspective. *GeroPsych, 31*, 163–167. https://doi.org/10.1024/1662-9647/a000194

Liao, H.-W., Bluck, S., & Glück, J. (2021). Recalling youth: Control over reminiscence bump events predicts life satisfaction in midlife. *Psychology and Aging, 36*, 232–240. https://doi.org/10.1037/pag0000592

Liao, J., Jimmieson, N., O'Brien, A., & Restubog, S. (2012). Developing transactive memory systems: Theoretical contributions from a social identity perspective. *Group & Organization Management, 37*, 204–240. https://doi.org/10.1177/1059601112443976

Lichtenberg, P. A. (2016a). Financial exploitation, financial capacity, and Alzheimer's disease. *American Psychologist, 71*, 312–320. https://doi.org/10.1037/a0040192

Lichtenberg, P. A. (2016b). New approaches to preventing financial exploitation: A focus on the banks. *Public Policy & Aging Report, 26*, 15–17. https://doi.org/10.1093/ppar/prv032

Lichtenberg, P. A., Campbell, R., Hall, L., & Gross, E. Z. (2020). Context matters: Financial, psychological, and relationship insecurity around personal finance is associated with financial exploitation. *The Gerontologist, 60*, 1040–1049. https://doi.org/10.1093/geront/gnaa020

Lichtenberg, P. A., Stoltman, J., Ficker, L. J., Iris, M., & Mast, B. (2015). A person-centered approach to financial capacity assessment: Preliminary development of a new rating scale. *Clinical Gerontologist, 38*, 49–67. https://doi.org/10.1080/07317115.2014.970318

Lichtenthal, W. G., & Sweeney, C. (2014). Families "at risk" of complicated bereavement. In D. W. Kissane & F. Parnes (Eds.), *Bereavement care for families* (pp. 249–265). Routledge.

Lichter, D. T., & Carmalt, J. H. (2009). Religion and marital quality among low-income couples. *Social Science Research, 38*, 168–187. https://doi.org/10.1016/j.ssresearch.2008.07.003

Lieber, J. (2001, October 10). Widows of tower disaster cope, but with quiet fury. *USA Today*, pp. A1–A2.

Lieberman, M. D., Gaunt, R., Gilbert, D. T., & Trope, Y. (2002). Reflexion and reflection: A social cognitive neuroscience approach to attributional inference. *Advances in Experimental Social Psychology, 34*, 199–249. https://doi.org/10.1016/S0065-2601(02)80006-5

Lieberz, J., Scheele, D., Spengler, F. B., Matheisen, T., Schneider, L., Stoffel-Wagner, B., Kinfe T. M., & Hurlemann, R. (2020). Kinetics of oxytocin effects on amygdala and striatal reactivity vary between women and men. *Neuropsychopharmacology, 45*, 1134–1140. https://doi.org/10.1038/s41386-019-0582-6

Liem, F., Geerligs, L., Damoiseaux, J. S., & Margulies, D. S. (2021). Functional connectivity in aging. In K. W. Schaie & S. L. Willis (Eds.), *Handbook of the psychology of aging* (9th ed., pp. 37–51). Academic Press. https://doi.org/10.1016/B978-0-12-816094-7.00010-6

Ligotti, M. E., Aiello, A., Accardi, G., Aprile, S., Bonura, F., Bulati, M., Gervasi, F., Giammanco, G. M., Pojero, F., Zareian, N., Caruso, C., Farzaneh, F., & Candore, G. (2021). Analysis of T and NK cell subsets in the Sicilian population from young to supercentenarian: The role of age and gender. *Clinical and Experimental Immunology, 205*, 198–212. https://doi.org/10.1111/cei.13606

Li-Korotky, H.-S. (2012). Age-related hearing loss: Quality of care for quality of life. *The Gerontologist, 52*, 265–271. https://doi.org/10.1093/geront/gnr159

Lilgendahl, J. P., & McAdams, D. P. (2011). Constructing stories of self-growth: How individual differences in patterns of autobiographical reasoning relate to well-being in midlife. *Journal of Personality, 79*, 391–428. https://doi.org/10.1111/j.1467-6494.2010.00688.x

Lillyman, S., & Bruce, M. (2017). Palliative care for people with dementia: A literature review. *International Journal of Palliative Nursing, 22*, 76–81. https://doi.org/10.12968/ijpn.2016.22.2.76

Lilomaiava Silulu, F. M. (2021). *Samoan elders' perceptions of wellness*. Doctoral dissertation, Auckland University of Technology. http://156.62.60.45/bitstream/handle/10292/14338/LilomaiavaSiluluF.pdf?sequence=3&isAllowed=y

Lim, S., Nzegwu, D., & Wright, M. L. (2022). The impact of psychosocial stress from life trauma and racial discrimination on epigenetic aging—A systematic review. *Biological Research for Nursing, 24*, 202–215. https://doi.org/10.1177/10998004211060561

Limb, G. E., Shafer, K., & Sandoval, K. (2014). The impact of kin support on urban American Indian families. *Child & Family Social Work, 19*, 423–442. https://doi.org/10.1111/cfs.12041

Lin, I.-F., & Brown, S. L. (2020). Consequences of later-life divorce and widowhood for adult well-being: A call for the convalescence model. *Journal of Family Theory & Review, 12*, 264–277. https://doi.org/10.1111/jftr.12366

Lin, P., LaMonica, H., Naismith, S., & Mowszowski, L. (2020). Memory compensation strategies in older people with mild cognitive impairment. *Journal of the International Neuropsychological Society, 26*, 86–96. https://doi.org/10.1017/S1355617719000912

Lindbergh, C. A., Dishman, R. K., & Miller, L. S. (2016). Functional disability in mild cognitive impairment: A systematic review and meta-analysis. *Neuropsychology Review, 26*, 129–159. https://doi.org/10.1007/s11065-016-9321-5

Lindenberger, U., Wenger, E. & Lövdén, M. (2017). Towards a stronger science of human plasticity. *Nature Reviews Neuroscience, 18*, 261–262. https://doi.org/10.1038/nrn.2017.44

Lindgren, L., Bergdahl, J., & Nyberg, L. (2016). Longitudinal evidence for smaller hippocampus volume as a vulnerability factor for perceived stress. *Cerebral Cortex, 26*, 3527–3533. https://doi.org/10.1093/cercor/bhw154

Lindström, B., & Eriksson, M. (2010). *The hitchhiker's guide to salutogenesis: Salutogenic pathways to health promotion*. Tuo-kinprint Oy. https://www.diva-portal.org/smash/record.jsf?pid=diva2%3A400361&dswid=44

Lindström, J., & Rantanen, T. (2021). Experts of the streets: The thoughts of experts by experience with a history of crime and substance abuse on working as a team with professionals. *European Journal of Probation, 13*, 226–241. https://doi.org/10.1177/20662203211028250

Ling, K. H., Ning, W. H., & Hoon, T. C. (2016). *Ginseng and ginseng products 101: What are you buying?* World Scientific.

Lips-Wiersma, M., Wright, S., & Dik. B. (2016). Meaningful work: Differences among blue-, pink-, and white-collar occupations. *Career Development International, 21*, 534–551. https://doi.org/10.1108/DCI-04-2016-0052

Liu, C-j., Chang, P.-S., Griffith, C. F., Hanley, S. I., & Lu, Y. (2022). The nexus of sensory loss, cognitive impairment, and functional decline in older adults: A scoping review. *The Gerontologist, 62*, e457–e467. https://doi.org/10.1093/geront/gnab082

Liu, G., Dupre, M. E., Gu, D., Mair, C. A., & Chen, F. (2012). Psychological well-being of the institutionalized and community-residing oldest old in China: The role of children. *Social Science and Medicine, 75*, 1874–1882. https://doi.org/10.1016/j.socscimed.2012.07.019

Liu, H.-Y., Hsu, W.-C., Shyu, Y. L., Wang, Y.-N., Huang, T.-H., Lin, Y.-E., & Huang, C.-H. (2021). Finding a balance in family caregiving for people with dementia: A correlational longitudinal study. *Journal of Advanced Nursing, 77*, 2278–2292. https://doi.org/10.1111/jan.14747.

Livingston, R. (2020, September–October). How to promote racial equity in the workplace: A five-step plan. *Harvard Business Review*. https://hbr.org/2020/09/how-to-promote-racial-equity-in-the-workplace.

Lluch, C., Galiana, L., Doménech, P., & Sansó, N. (2022). The impact of the COVID-19 pandemic on burnout, compassion fatigue, and compassion satisfaction in healthcare personnel: A systematic review of the literature published during the first year of the pandemic. *Healthcare, 10*, 364. https://doi.org/10.3390/healthcare10020364

Loaiza, V., Rhodes, M. G., & Anglin, J. (2015). The influence of age-related differences in prior knowledge and attentional refreshing opportunities on episodic memory. *Journals of Gerontology: Psychological Sciences, 70*, 729–736. https://doi.org/10.1093/geronb/gbt119

Löckenhoff, C. E., & Carstensen, L. L. (2007). Aging, emotion, and health-related decision strategies: Motivational manipulations can reduce age differences. *Psychology and Aging, 22*, 134–146. https://doi.org/10.1037/0882-7974.22.1.134

Lodi-Smith, J., Ponterio, E. J., Newton, N. J., Poulin, M. J., Baranski, E., & Whitbourne, S. K. (2021). The codevelopment of generativity and well-being into early late life. *Psychology and Aging, 36*, 299–308. https://doi.org/10.1037/pag0000446

Loe, M., Sherry, A., & Chartier, E. (2016). Ageism: Stereotypes, causes, effect, and countermovements. In M. H. Meyer & E. A. Daniele (Eds.), *Gerontology: Changes, challenges, and solutions* (Vol. 1, pp. 57–82). ABC-CLIO.

Logan, R. D. (1986). A reconceptualization of Erikson's theory: The repetition of existential and instrumental themes. *Human Development, 29*, 125–136. https://doi.org/10.1159/000273036

Lombard, D. (2021). Person-centred communication in long-term care with older people: A scoping review. *Journal of Integrated Care, 29*, 306–333. https://doi.org/10.1108/JICA-10-2020-0070

Looi, C. Y., Duta, M., Brem, A.-K., Huber, S., Nuerk, H.-C., & Kadosh, R. C. (2016). Combining brain stimulation and video game to promote long-term transfer of learning and cognitive enhancement. *Scientific Reports, 6*, 22003. https://doi.org/10.1038/srep22003

Lord, K., Livingston, G., Robertson, S., & Cooper, C. (2016). How people with dementia and their families decide about moving to a care home and support their needs: Development of a decision aid, a qualitative study. *BMC Geriatrics, 16*, 68. https://doi.org/10.1186/s12877-016-0242-1.

Lorenzo-Echeverri, L. N. (2020). *Exploring the experience of married couples making the decision of whether or not to have a first child*. Doctoral dissertation, Nova Southeastern University. ProQuest Document 27958715. https://search.proquest.com/openview/524fe14d155ab3137045bb4872b9a0bc/1?pq-origsite=gscholar&cbl=18750&diss=y.

Lou, V. W. Q., & Ng, J. W. (2012). Chinese older adults' resilience to the loneliness of living alone: A qualitative study. *Aging and Mental Health, 16*, 1039–1046. https://doi.org/10.1080/1360786 3.2012.692764

Lourenço, J. S., & Maylor, E. A. (2015). When distraction holds relevance: A prospective memory benefit for older adults. *International Journal of Environmental Research and Public Health, 12*, 6523–6541. https://doi.org/10.3390/ijerph120606523

Lövdén, M., Brehmer, Y., Li, S.-C., & Lindenberger, U. (2012). Training-induced compensation versus magnification of individual differences in memory performance. *Frontiers in Human Neuroscience, 6*, 141. https://doi.org/10.3389/fnhum.2012.00141.

Lowe, D. J. E., Müller, D. J., & George, T. P. (2020). Ketamine treatment in depression: A systematic review of clinical characteristics predicting symptom improvement. *Current Topics in Medicinal Chemistry, 20*, 1398–1414. https://doi.org/10.2174/1568026620666200423094423.

Lowry, E., Puthusseryppady, V., Johnen, A.-K., Renoult, L., & Hornberger, M. (2021). Cognitive and neuroimaging markers for preclinical vascular cognitive impairment. *Cerebral Circulation - Cognition and Behavior, 2*, 100029. https://doi.org/10.1016/j.cccb.2021.100029

Luca, M., Prossimo, G., Messina, V., Luca, A., Romeo, S., & Calandra, C. (2013). Epidemiology and treatment of mood disorders in a day hospital setting from 1996 to 2007: An Italian study. *Neuropsychiatric Disease and Treatment, 9*, 169–176. https://doi.org/10.2147/NDT.S39227

Lucette, A., Ironson, G., Pargament, K. I., & Krause, N. (2016). Spirituality and religiousness are associated with fewer depressive symptoms in individuals with medical conditions. *Psychosomatics, 57*, 505–513. https://doi.org/10.1016/j.psym.2016.03.005

Luders, E., & Cherbuin, N. (2016). Searching for the philosopher's stone: Promising links between meditation and brain preservation. *Annals of the New York Academy of Sciences, 1373*, 38–44. https://doi.org/10.1111/nyas.13082.

Lund, E. M., Burgess, C., & Johnson, A. J. (2021). Queer violence: Confronting diverse forms of violence against LGBTQ+ persons and communities. In E. M. Lund, C. Burgess, & A. J. Johnson (Eds.), *Violence against*

LGBTQ+ persons: Research, policy, and advocacy (pp. 1–4). Springer. https://doi.org/10.1007/978-3-030-52612-2_1

Lundström, J. N., & Jones-Gotman, M. (2009). Romantic love modulates women's identification of men's body odors. *Hormones and Behavior, 55*, 280–284. https://doi.org/10.1016/j.yhbeh.2008.11.009

Lunt, C., Dowrick, C., & Lloyd-Williams, M. (2021). What is the impact of day care on older people with long-term conditions: A systematic review. *Health and Social Care in the Community, 29*, 1201–1221. https://doi.org/10.1111/hsc.13245

Luo, S., & Zhang, G. (2009). What leads to romantic attraction: Similarity, reciprocity, security, or beauty? Evidence from a speed-dating study. *Journal of Personality, 77*, 933–964. https://doi.org/10.1111/j.1467-6494.2009.00570.x

Lustig, C., & Lin, Z. (2021). Memory: Behavioral and neural basis. In K. W. Schaie & S. L. Willis (Eds.), *Handbook of the psychology of aging* (9th ed., pp. 53–66). Academic Press. https://doi.org/10.1016/B978-0-12-816094-7.00018-0

Luszcz, M. A., Anstey, K. J., & Ghisletta, P. (2015). Subjective beliefs, memory and functional health: Change and associations over 12 years in the Australian Longitudinal Study of Ageing. *Gerontology, 61*, 241–250. https://doi.org/10.1159/000369800

Luthans, F., Avolio, B. J., Avey, J. B., & Norman, S. M. (2007). Positive psychological capital: Measurement and relationship with performance and satisfaction. *Personnel Psychology, 60*, 541–572. https://doi.org/10.1111/j.1744-6570.2007.00083.x

Luxenberg, S. (2014, April 25). Welcoming love at an older age, but not necessarily marriage. *New York Times*. https://www.nytimes.com/2014/04/26/your-money/welcoming-love-at-an-older-age-but-not-necessarily-marriage.html?_r=0

Mace, J. H., & Clevinger, A. M. (2013). Priming voluntary autobiographical memories: Implications for the organization of autobiographical memory and voluntary recall processes. *Memory, 21*, 524–536. https://doi.org/10. 1080/09658211.2012.744422

Mace, J. H., Staley, B. J. A., & Sopoci, M. K. (2021). When trying to recall our past, all roads lead to Rome: More evidence for the multi-process retrieval theory of autobiographical memory. *Memory & Cognition, 49*, 438–450. https://doi.org/10.3758/s13421-020-01099-1

Mahady, G. B., Locklear, T. D., Doyle, B. J., Huang, Y., Perez, A. L., & Caceres, A. (2008). Menopause, a universal female experience: Lessons from Mexico and Central America. *Current Women's Health Reviews, 4*, 3–8. https://doi.org/10.2174/157340408783572033

Mahal, B. A., Gerke, T., Awasthi, S., Soule, H. R., Simons, J. W., Miyahira, A., Halabi, S., George, D., Platz, E. A., Mucci, L., & Yamoah, K. (2022). Prostate cancer racial disparities: A systematic review by the Prostate Cancer Foundation Panel. *European Urology Oncology, 5*, 18–29. https://doi.org/10.1016/j.euo.2021.07.006.

Mahamid, F. A., & Bdier, D. (2021). The association between positive religious coping, perceived stress, and depressive symptoms during the spread of coronavirus (COVID-19) among a sample of adults in Palestine: A cross sectional study. *Journal of Religion and Health, 60*, 34–49. https://doi.org/10.1007/s10943-020-01121-5

Mahendiratta, S., Sarma, P., Kaur, H., Kaur, S., Kaur, H., Bansal, S., Prasad, D., Prajapat, M., Upadhay, S., Kumar, S., Kumar, H., Singh, R., Singh, A., Mishra, A., Prakash, A., & Medhi, B. (2020). Premature graying of hair: Risk factors, co-morbid conditions, pharmacotherapy and reversal—A systematic review and meta-analysis. *Dermatologic Therapy, 33*, e13990. https://doi.org/10.1111/dth.13990

Mahmut, M. K., Stevenson, R. J., & Stephen, I. (2019). Do women love their partner's smell? Exploring women's preferences for and identification of male partner and non-partner body odor. *Physiology & Behavior, 210*, Article 112517. https://doi.org/10.1016/j.physbeh.2019.04.006

Maiorano, E., Calastri, A., Robotti, C., Cassaniti, I., Baldanti, F., Zuccaro, V., Stellin, E., Ferretti, V. V., Klersy, C., & Benazzo, M. (2022). Clinical, virological and immunological evolution of the olfactory and gustatory dysfunction in COVID-19. *American Journal of Otolaryngology, 43*, 103170. https://doi.org/10.1016/j.amjoto.2021.103170

Malec, M., & Shega, J. W. (2015). Pain management in the elderly. *Medical Clinics, 99*, P337–350. https://doi.org/10.1016/j.mcna.2014.11.007

Malkinson, R., & Bar-Tur, L. (2004–2005). Long term bereavement processes of older parents: The three phases of grief. *Omega: The Journal of Death and Dying, 50*, 103–129. https://doi.org/10.2190/W346-UP8T-RER6-BBD1

Malone, M. L., & Camp, C. J. (2007). Montessori-Based Dementia Programming®: Providing tools for engagement. *Dementia: The International Journal of Social Research and Practice, 6*, 150–157. https://doi.org/10.1177/1471301207079099

Mandemakers, J. J., & Monden, C. W. S. (2013). Does the effect of job loss on psychological distress differ by educational level? *Work, Employment and Society, 27*, 73–93. https://doi.org/10.1177/0950017012460312

Manglani, H. R., Samimy, S., Schirda, B., Nicholas, J. A., & Prakash, R. S. (2020). Effects of 4-week mindfulness training versus adaptive cognitive training on processing speed and working memory in multiple sclerosis. *Neuropsychology, 34*, 591–604. https://doi.org/10.1037/neu0000633

Manji, H., Jäger, H. R., & Winston, A. (2013). HIV, dementia and antiretroviral drugs: 30 years of an epidemic. *Journal of Neurology, Neurosurgery, and Psychiatry, 84*, 1126–1137. https://doi.org/10.1136/jnnp-2012-304022

Manji, R. A., Manji, J. S., & Arora, A. S. (2021). Are maladaptive brain changes the reason for burnout and medical error? *Journal of Thoracic and Cardiovascular Surgery, 162*, 1136–1140. https://doi.org/10.1016/j.jtcvs.2020.06.146

Mankus, A. M., Boden, M. T., & Thompson, R. J. (2016). Sources of variation in emotional awareness: Age, gender, and socioeconomic status. *Personality and Individual Differences, 89*, 28–33. https://doi.org/10.1016/j.paid.2015.09.043

Manning, W. D., Smock, P. J., & Fettro, M. N. (2019). Cohabitation and marital expectations among single millennials in the U.S. *Population Research and Policy Review, 38*, 327–346. https://doi.org/10.1007/s11113-018-09509-8

Manning, W., & Payne, K. (2020). *Marriage and divorce decline during the COVID-19 pandemic: A case study of five states*. https://doi.org/10.31235/osf.io/tdfvc

Manson, J. E., Aragaki, A. K., Rossouw, J. E., Anderson, G. L., Prentice, R. L., LaCroix, A. Z., Chlebowski, R. T., Howard, B. V., Thomson, C. A., Margolis, K. L., Lewis, C. E., Stefanik, M. L., Jackson, R. D., Johnson, K. C., Martin, L. W., Shumaker, S. A., Espeland, M. A., Wactawski-Wende, J., for the WHI investigators. (2017). Menopausal hormone therapy and long-term all-cause and cause-specific mortality: The Women's Health Initiative Randomized Trials. *JAMA, 318*, 927–938. https://doi.org/10.1001/jama.2017.11217

Mantler, J., Matejicek, A., Matheson, K., & Anisman, H. (2005). Coping with employment uncertainty: A comparison of employed and unemployed workers. *Journal of Occupational Health Psychology, 10*, 200–209. https://doi.org/10.1037/1076-8998.10.3.200

Manzo, C., Serra-Mestres, J., Isetta, M., & Castagna, A. (2021). Could COVID-19 anosmia and olfactory dysfunction trigger an increased risk of future dementia in patients with ApoE4? *Medical Hypotheses, 147*, 110479. https://doi.org/10.1016/j.mehy.2020.110479

Manzoni, A., & Mooi-Reci, I. (2020). The cumulative disadvantage of unemployment: Longitudinal evidence across gender and age at first unemployment in Germany. *PLoS ONE, 15*, e0234786. https://doi.org/10.1371/journal.pone.0234786

Maple, M., Edwards, H. E., Minichiello, V., & Plummer, D. (2013). Still part of the family: The importance of physical, emotional and spiritual memorial places and spaces for parents bereaved through the suicide death of their son or daughter. *Mortality, 18*, 54–71. https://doi.org/10.1080/13576275.2012.755158

Maple, M., Edwards, H., Plummer, D., & Minichiello, V. (2010). Silenced voices: Hearing the stories of parents bereaved through the suicide death of a young adult child. *Health and Social Care in the Community, 18*, 241–248. https://doi.org/10.1111/j.1365-2524.2009.00886.x

Marcia, J., & Josselson, R. (2013). Eriksonian personality research and its implications for psychotherapy. *Journal of Personality, 81*, 617–629. https://doi.org/10.1111/jopy.12014

Marcotte, T. D., Schmitter-Edgecombe, M., & Grant, I. (2022). *Neuropsychology of everyday functioning* (2nd ed.). Guilford Press.

Marini C. M., Ermer, A. E., Fiori, K. L., Rauer, A. J., & Proulx, C. M. (2020). Marital quality, loneliness, and depressive symptoms later in life: The moderating role of own and spousal functional limitations. *Research in Human Development, 17*, 211–234. https://doi.org/10.1080/15427609.2020.1837598

Markland, A. D., Vaughan, C. P., Johnson, T. M., Burgio, K. L., & Goode, P. S. (2012). Incontinence. *The Medical Clinics of North America, 95*, 539–554. https://doi.org/10.1016/j.mcna.2011.02.006

Markus, H., & Nurius, P. (1986). Possible selves. *American Psychologist, 41*, 954–969. https://doi.org/10.1037/0003-066X.41.9.954

Marques, S., Mariano, J., Mendonça, J., De Tavernier, W., Hess, M., Naegele, L., Peixeiro, F., & Martins, D. (2020). Determinants of ageism against older adults: A systematic review. *International Journal of Environmental Research and Public Health, 17*, 2560. https://doi.org/10.3390/ijerph17072560

Marques-Aleixo, I., Beleza, J., Sampaio, A., Stevanović, J., Coxito, P., Gonçalves, I., Ascensão, A., & Magalhães, J. (2021). Preventive and therapeutic potential of physical exercise in neurodegenerative diseases. *Antioxidants & Redox Signaling, 34*, 674–693. https://doi.org/10.1089/ars.2020.8075

Marques-Aleixo, I., Oliveira, P. J., Moreira, P. I., Magalhães, J., & Ascensão, A. (2012). Physical exercise as a possible strategy for brain protection: Evidence from mitochondrial-mediated mechanisms. *Progress in Neurobiology, 99*, 149–162. https://doi.org/10.1016/j.pneurobio.2012.08.002

Marr, C. T., Kaufman, S. V. A., & Craig, E. A. (2022). Communication and disenfranchised grief: Managing the unrecognized grief of pet loss. In G. D. Luurs (Ed.), *Handbook of research on communication strategies for taboo topics* (pp. 459–481). IGI Global.

Mars, L. (2022). *The untold stories of elder mistreatment*. https://ncea.acl.gov/NCEA-Blog/Jan-5-2022.aspx

Marsh, E. J., & Yang, B. W. (2021). Believing things that are not true: A cognitive science perspective on misinformation. In B. G. Southwell, E. A. Thorson, & L. Sheble (Eds.), *Misinformation and mass audiences* (pp. 15–34). University of Texas Press. https://doi.org/10.7560/314555

Marshall, J. C. (1986, March 2). In the region of lost minds. *New York Times*, C7. https://www.nytimes.com/books/98/12/06/specials/sacks-mistook.html.

Marsiglio, W., & Roy, K. (2013). Fathers' nurturance of children over the life course. In G. W. Peterson & K. R. Bush (Eds.), *Handbook of marriage and the family* (3rd ed., pp. 353–376). Springer.

Martens, A., Goldenberg, J. L., & Greenberg, J. (2005). A terror management perspective on ageism. *Journal of Social Issues, 61*, 223–239. https://doi.org/10.1111/j.1540-4560.2005.00403.x

Martens, J. (2020). *Doing things together: A theory of skillful joint action*. De Gruyter. https://doi.org/10.1515/9783110671315

Martin, S. P., Astone, N. M., & Peters, H. E. (2014). *Fewer marriages, more divergence: Marriage projections for millennials to age 40*. https://www.urban.org/research/publication/fewer-marriages-more-divergence-marriage-projections-millennials-age-40/view/full_report

Martinez-Lage, M., Torres-Ruiz, R., Puig-Serra, P., Moreno-Gaona, P., Martin, M. C., Moya, F. J., Quintana-Bustamonte, O., Garcia-Silva, S., Carcaboso, A. M., Petazzi, P., Bueno, C., Mora, J., Peinado, H., Segovia, J. C., Menendez, P., & Rodriguez-Perales, S. (2020). In vivo CRISPR/Cas9 targeting of fusion oncogenes for selective elimination of cancer cells. *Nature Communications, 11*, 5060. https://doi.org/10.1038/s41467-020-18875-x

Martins, C., Godycki-Cwirko, M., Heleno, B., & Brodersen, J. (2018). Quaternary prevention: Reviewing the concept. *European Journal of General Practice, 24*, 106–111. https://doi.org/10.1080/13814788.2017.1422177

Martins, E. L. M., Salamene, L. C., Lucchetti, A. L. G., & Lucchetti, G. (2022). The role of positive behaviors, attitudes and virtues in the mental health of community-dwelling older adults: A 1-year follow-up study. *Journal of Psychosomatic Research, 154*, 110721. https://doi.org/10.1016/j.jpsychores.2022.110721

Martin-Uzzi, M., & Duval-Tsioles, D. (2013). The experience of remarried couples in blended families. *Journal of Divorce & Remarriage, 54*, 43–57. https://doi.org/10.1080/10502556.2012.743828

Martos, A., Nezhad, S., & Meyer, I. H. (2015). Variations in sexual identity milestones among lesbians, gay men and bisexuals. *Sexuality Research and Social Policy, 12*, 24–33. https://doi.org/10.1007/s13178-014-0167-4

Mason, C. N. (2020). *Build(ing) the future: Bold policies for a gender-equitable recovery*. https://iwpr.org/wp-content/uploads/2020/11/Policies-for-a-Gender-Equitable-Recovery-Finalsm2.pdf

Master, J. F., Wu, B., Ni, P., & Mao, J. (2021). The compliance of end-of-life care preferences among older adults and its facilitators and barriers: A scoping review. *Journal of the American Medical Directors Association, 22*, P2273–2280.E2. https://doi.org/10.1016/j.jamda.2021.05.007

Masterson, C., Suglyama, K., & Ladge, J. (2021). The value of 21st century work–family supports: Review and cross-level path forward. *Journal of Organizational Behavior, 42*, 118–138. https://doi.org/10.1002/job.2442

Mastrangelo, A., Bonato, M., & Cinque, P. (2021). Smell and taste disorders in COVID-19: From pathogenesis to clinical features and outcomes. *Neuroscience Letters, 748*, 135694. https://doi.org/10.1016/j.neulet.2021.135694

Masunaga, H., & Horn, J. (2001). Expertise and age-related changes in components of intelligence. *Psychology and Aging, 16*, 293–311. https://doi.org/10.1037/0882-7974.16.2.293

Masunari, N., Fujiwara, S., Kasagi, F., Takahashi, I., Yamada, M., & Nakamura, T. (2012). Height loss starting in middle age predicts increased mortality in the elderly. *Journal of Bone and Mineral Research, 27*, 138–145. https://10.1002/jbmr.513

Masunari, N., Fujiwara, S., Kasagi, F., Takahashi, I., Yamada, M., & Nakamura, T. (2012). Height loss starting in middle age predicts increased mortality in the elderly. *Journal of Bone and Mineral Research, 27*, 138–145. https://doi.org/10.1002/jbmr.513

Mather, M. (2012). The emotion paradox in the aging brain. *Annals of the New York Academy of Sciences, 1251*, 33–49. https://doi.org/10.1111/j.1749-6632.2012.06471.x

Mather, M. (2016). The affective neuroscience of aging. *Annual Review of Psychology, 67*, 213–238. https://doi.org/10.1146/annurev-psych-122414-033540

Matos, P., & Albuquerque, P. B. (2021). From retrospective to prospective memory research: A framework for investigating the deactivation of intentions. *Cognitive Processing, 22*, 411–434. https://doi.org/10.1007/s10339-021-01016-7

Matovu, S. N., & Wallhagen, M. I. (2020). Perceived caregiver stress, coping, and quality of life of older Ugandan grandparent-caregivers. *Journal of Cross-Cultural Gerontology, 35*, 311–328 (2020). https://doi.org/10.1007/s10823-020-09403-x

Matsumoto, D., & Juang, L. (2017). *Culture and psychology* (6th ed.). Cengage Learning.

Mauldin, R. L., Fujimoto, K., Wong, C., Herrera, S., & Anderson, A. (2021). Social networks in an assisted living community: Correlates of acquaintance and companionship ties among residents. *Journals of Gerontology: Social Sciences, 76*, 1463–1474. https://doi.org/10.1093/geronb/gbab079

Mayo Clinic. (2020a). *Menopause*. https://www.mayoclinic.org/diseases-conditions/menopause/symptoms-causes/syc-20353397

Mayo Clinic. (2020b). *Peyronie's disease*. https://www.mayoclinic.org/diseases-conditions/peyronies-disease/symptoms-causes/syc-20353468

Mayo Clinic. (2020c). *Back pain: Diagnosis and treatment*. https://www.mayoclinic.org/diseases-conditions/back-pain/diagnosis-treatment/drc-20369911

Mayo Clinic. (2021a). *Angina*. https://www.mayoclinic.org/diseases-conditions/angina/symptoms-causes/syc-20369373

Mayo Clinic. (2021b). *Urinary incontinence*. https://www.mayoclinic.org/diseases-conditions/urinary-incontinence/symptoms-causes/syc-20352808

Mayo Clinic. (2022a). *Delirium*. https://www.mayoclinic.org/diseases-conditions/delirium/symptoms-causes/syc-20371386

Mayo Clinic. (2022b). *Aerobic exercise: Top 10 reasons to get physical*. https://www.mayoclinic.org/healthy-lifestyle/fitness/in-depth/aerobic-exercise/art-20045541

Mazanderani, F., Noorani, T., Dudhwala, F., & Kamwendo, Z. (2020). Knowledge, evidence, expertise? The epistemics of experience in contemporary healthcare. *Evidence & Policy: A Journal of Research, Debate and Practice, 16*, 267–284. https://doi.org/10.1332/174426420X15808912561112

Mazerolle, M., Smith, A. M., Torrance, M., & Thomas, A. K. (2021). Understanding older adults' memory distortion in the light of stereotype threat. *Frontiers in Psychology, 12*. https://doi.org/10.3389/fpsyg.2021.628696

Mbakile-Mahlanza, L., van der Ploeg, E. S., Busija, L., Camp, C. J., Walker, H., & O'Connor, D. W. (2020). A cluster-randomized crossover trial of Montessori activities delivered by family carers to nursing home residents with behavioral and psychological symptoms of dementia. *International Psychogeriatrics, 32*, 347–358. https://doi.org/10.1017/S1041610219001819

Mbilishaka, A. M., Mitchell, D. S. B., & Conyers, C. (2020). Grandma's hands: Memories of hair styling interaction with African American grandmothers. *Journal of Intergenerational Relationships, 18*, 139–155. https://doi.org/10.1080/15350770.2019.1658008

McAdams, D. P. (2001). The psychology of life stories. *Review of General Psychology, 5*, 100–122. https://doi.org/10.1037/1089-2680.5.2.100

McAdams, D. P. (2015). *The art and science of personality development*. Guilford.

McAdams, D. P. (2021). Narrative identity and the life story. In O. P. John & R. W. Robins (Eds.), *Handbook of personality: Theory and research* (4th ed., pp. 122–141). Guilford Press.

McAdams, D. P., & Guo, J. (2015). Narrating the generative life. *Psychological Science, 26*, 475–483. https://doi.org/10.1177/0956797614568318

McAdams, D. P., & Olson, B. D. (2010). Personality development: Continuity and change over the life course. *Annual Review of Psychology, 61*, 517–542. https://doi.org/10.1146/annurev.psych.093008.100507

McAdams, D. P., Trzesniewski, K., Lilgendahl, J., Benet-Martinez, V., & Robins, R. W. (2021). Self and identity in personality psychology. *Personality Science, 2*, e6035. https://doi.org/10.5964/ps.6035

McCabe, D. P., & Loaiza, V. M. (2012). Working memory. In S. K. Whitbourne & M. J. Sliwinski (Eds.), *The Wiley-Blackwell handbook of adulthood and aging* (pp. 154–173). Wiley-Blackwell.

McCarthy, C. E. (2021). Sleep disturbance, sleep disorders and co-morbidities in the care of the older person. *Medical Sciences, 9*, 31. https://doi.org/10.3390/medsci9020031

McCarthy, L. P. (2021). Attention to gender and race in interventions for custodial grandparents: A scoping review. *Journal of Feminist Family Therapy, 33*, 295–314. https://doi.org/10.1080/08952833.2021.1880186

McCloskey, M. S., Phan, K. L., Angstadt, M., Fettich, K. C., Keedy, S., & Coccaro, E. F. (2016). Amygdala hyperactivation to angry faces in intermittent explosive disorder. *Journal of Psychiatric Research, 79*, 34–41. https://doi.org/10.1016/j.jpsychires.2016.04.006

McClung, M. R. (2021). Denosumab for the treatment of osteoporosis. In D. W. Dempster, J. A. Cauley, M. L. Bouxsein, & F. Cosman (Eds.), *Marcus and Feldman's osteoporosis* (5th ed., Vol. 2, pp. 1737–1755). https://doi.org/10.1016/B978-0-12-813073-5.00075-7

McClure, M., Jorna, T., Wilkinson, L., & Taylor, J. (2017). Elderly patients with chronic kidney disease: Do they really need referral to the nephrology clinic? *Clinical Kidney Journal, 10*(5), 698–702. https://doi.org/10.1093/ckj/sfx034

McCoyd, J. L. M., Koller, J. M., & Walter, C. A. (2021). *Grief and loss across the lifespan: A biopsychosocial perspective* (3rd ed.). Springer.

McCrae, R. R. (2016). Integrating trait and process approaches to personality: A sketch of an agenda. In U. Kumar (Ed.), *The Wiley handbook of personality assessment* (pp. 3–18). Wiley.

McCrae, R. R. (2018). Defining traits. In V. Zeigler-Hill & T. K. Shackelford (Eds.), *The SAGE handbook of personality and individual differences: The science of personality and individual differences* (pp. 3–22). Sage Reference. https://doi.org/10.4135/9781526451163.n1

McCrae, R. R., & Costa, P. T., Jr. (2003). *Personality in adulthood: A five-factor theory perspective* (2nd ed.). Guilford.

McCrae, R. R., & Terracciano, A. (2005). Universal features of personality traits from the observer's perspective: Data from 50 cultures. *Journal of Personality & Social Psychology, 88*, 547–561. https://doi.org/10.1037/0022-3514.88.3.547

McCrae, R. R., (2017). The five-factor model across cultures. In A. T. Church (Ed.), *The Praeger handbook of personality across cultures* (pp. 47–72). Praeger.

McDermott, S. (2018). *Children and loss: Caring for yourself and others*. Redemptorist Publications.

McDonough, I. M., Enam, T., Kraemer, K. R., Eakin, D. K., & Kim, M. (2021). Is there more to metamemory? An argument for two specialized monitoring abilities. *Psychonomic Bulletin & Review, 28*, 1657–1667. https://doi.org/10.3758/s13423-021-01930-z

McDonough, I. M., McDougall, G. J., LaRocca, M., Dalmida, S. G., & Arheart, K. L. (2020). Refining the metamemory in adulthood questionnaire: A 20-item version of change and capacity designed for research and clinical settings. *Aging & Mental Health, 24*, 1054–1063. https://doi.org/10.1080/13607863.2019.1594160

McElroy-Heltzel, S. E., Shannonhouse, L. R., Davis, E. B., Lemke, A. W., Mize, M. C., Aten, J., Fullen, M. C., Hook, J. N., Van Tongeren, D. R., Davis, D. E., & Miskis, C. (2022). Resource loss and mental health during COVID-19: Psychosocial protective factors among U.S. older adults and those with chronic disease. *International Journal of Psychology, 57*, 127–135. https://doi.org/10.1002/ijop.12798

McEwen, B. S. (2017). Neurobiological and systemic effects of chronic stress. *Chronic Stress, 1*, 2470547017692328. https://doi.org/10.1177/0734242X14545374

McEwen, B. S., Nasca, C., & Gray, J. D. (2016). Stress effects on neuronal structure: Hippocampus, amygdala, and prefrontal cortex. *Neuropsychopharmacology, 41*, 3–23. https://doi.org/10.1038/npp.2015.171

McGonigle, K., (2021). *Now isn't the time to ignore the opioid crisis*. https://www.medpagetoday.com/primarycare/opioids/91490

McGuire, L. C., Morian, A., Codding, R., & Smyer, M. A. (2000). Older adults' memory for medical information: Influence of elderspeak and note taking. *International Journal of Rehabilitation and Health, 5*, 117–128. https://doi.org/10.1023/A:1012906222395

McIntyre, R. S., & Lee, Y. (2020). Preventing suicide in the context of the COVID-19 pandemic. *World Psychiatry, 19*, 250–251. https://doi.org/10.1002/wps.20767

McKay, B. (2016, February 9). A cholesterol conundrum. *Wall Street Journal*, D1–D2.

McKay, M. T., Cannon, M., Chambers, D., Conroy, R. M., Coughlan, H., Dodd, P., Healy, C., O'Donnell, L., & Clarke, M. C. (2021). Childhood trauma and adult mental disorder: A systematic review and meta-analysis of longitudinal cohort studies. *Acta Psychiatrica Scandinavica, 143*, 189–205. https://doi .org/10.1111/acps.13268

McKee-Ryan, F., Song, Z., Wanberg, C. R., & Kinicki, A. J. (2005). Psychological and physical well-being during unemployment: A meta-analytic study. *Journal of Applied Psychology, 90*, 53–76. https://doi .org/10.1037/0021-9010.90.1.53

McLaren, B. (2021). *Faith after doubt: Why your beliefs stopped working and what to do about it.* St. Martin's Press.

McLean, K. C. (2016). *The co-authored self: Family stories and the construction of personal identity.* Oxford University Press.

McLean, K. C., & Pasupathi, M. (2012). Processes of identity development: Where I am and how I got there. *Identity, 12*, 8–28. https://doi .org/10.1080/15283 488.2011.632363

McLeod, E. D. (2020). *An exploratory study of the collaborative divorce process from the perspective of collaborative professionals.* Master's thesis, University of Regina. http://hdl.handle.net/10294/9351

McLymont, R. (2016, Spring). State of women-owned businesses. *The Network Journal*, 18–19.

McMahon, M., & Arthur, N. (2019). Career development theory: Origins and history. In M. McMahon & N. Arthur (Eds.), *Contemporary theories of career development: International perspectives* (pp. 3–19). Routledge.

McNutt, B., & Yakushko, O. (2013). Disenfranchised grief among lesbian and gay bereaved individuals. *Journal of LGBT Issues in Counseling, 7*, 87–116. https://doi.org /10.1080/15538605.2013.758345

McQuaid, C. (2021). *Understanding bereaved parents and siblings: A handbook for professionals, families, and friends.* Routledge.

Medical Justice. (2020). *Every state determines brain death differently. Really: An interview with Thaddeus Pope, M.D.* https://medicaljustice.com /every-state-determines-brain-death-differently-really/

Medicare.gov. (2021a). *Drug coverage (Part D)*. https:// www.medicare.gov/drug-coverage-part-d

Medicare.gov. (2021b). *What's Medicare supplemental insurance (Medigap)?* https://www .medicare.gov/supplements-other-insurance/ whats-medicare-supplement-insurance-medigap

Mehta, C. M., Arnett, J. J., Palmer, C. G., & Nelson, L. J. (2020). Established adulthood: A new conception of ages 30 to 45. *American Psychologist, 75*, 431–444. https://doi.org/10.1037/amp0000600

Mehta, C. M., & Wilson, J. (2020). Gender segregation and its correlates in established adulthood. *Sex Roles, 83*, 240–253. https://doi.org/10.1007/ s11199-019-01099-9

Mehta, R. I., & Schneider, J. A. (2021). What is "Alzheimer's disease"? The neuropathological heterogeneity of clinically defined Alzheimer's dementia. *Current Opinion in Neurology, 34*, 237–245. https://doi.org/10.1097 /WCO.0000000000000912

Meichsner, F., O'Connor, M., Skritskaya, N., & Shear, M. K. (2020). Grief before and after bereavement in the elderly: An approach to care. *American Journal of Geriatric Psychiatry, 28*, 560–569. https://doi .org/10.1016/j.jagp.2019.12.010

Meijer, A. M., & van den Wittenboer, G. L. H. (2007). Contribution of infants' sleep and crying to marital relationship of first-time parent couples in the 1st year after childbirth. *Journal of Family Psychology, 21*, 49–57. https://doi.org/10.1037/0893-3200.21.1.49

Meilaender, G. (2020). *Bioethics: A primer for Christians* (4th ed.). Eerdmans Publishing.

Meléndez, J. C., & Satorres, E. (2021). Autobiographical memory as a diagnostic tool in aging. In C. R. Martin, V. R. Preedy, & R. Rajendram (Eds.), *Assessments, treatments and modeling in aging and neurological disease: The neuroscience of aging* (pp. 306–314). Academic Press. https://doi.org/10.1016 /B978-0-12-818000-6.00028-7

Mendez-Lopez, A., Stuckler, D., McKee, M., Semenza, J. C., & Lazarus, J. V. (2022). The mental health crisis during the COVID-19 pandemic in older adults and the role of physical distancing interventions and social protection measures in 26 European countries. *SSM-Population Health, 17*, 101017. https://doi .org/10.1016/j.ssmph.2021.101017

Mendez-Luck, C. A., Geldhof, G. J., Anthony, K. P., Steers, W. N., Mangione, C. M., & Hays, R. D. (2016). Orientation to the caregiver role among Latinas of Mexican origin. *The Gerontologist, 56*, e99–e108. https://doi.org/10.1093/geront/gnw087

Mendis, S. B., Raymont, V., & Tabet, N. (2021). Bilingualism: A global public health strategy for healthy cognitive aging. *Frontiers in Neurology, 12*. https://doi.org/10.3389/fneur.2021.628368

Mendoza, A. N., Fruhauf, C. A., & MacPhee, D. (2020). Grandparent caregivers' resilience: Stress, support, and coping predict life satisfaction. *The International Journal of Aging and Human Development, 91*, 3–20. https://doi.org/10.1177/0091415019843459

Menendez, D., Hernandez, I. G., & Rosengren, K. S. (2020). Children's emerging understanding of death. *Child Development Perspectives, 14*, 55–60. https://doi .org/10.1111/cdep.12357

Mengelkoch, S., Gassen, J., Corrigan, E. K., & Hill, S. E. (2022). Exploring the links between personality and immune function. *Personality and Individual Differences, 184*, 111179. https://doi.org/10.1016/j .paid.2021.111179

Menkin, J. A., Robles, T. F., Gruenewald, T. L., Tanner, E. K., & Seeman, T. E. (2017). Positive expectations regarding aging linked to more new friends in later life. *Journals of Gerontology: Social Sciences, 72*, 771–781. https://doi.org/10.1093/geronb/gbv118

Menon, U. (2001). Middle adulthood in cultural perspective: The imagined and the experienced in three cultures. In M. E. Lachman (Ed.), *Handbook of midlife development* (pp. 40–74). Wiley.

Menon, U., & Shweder, R. A. (1998). The return of the "White man's burden": The moral discourse of anthropology and the domestic life of Hindu women. In R. A. Shweder (Ed.), *Welcome to the middle age (and other cultural fictions)* (pp. 139–188). University of Chicago Press.

Mercer, T. (2016). Technology-assisted memory. In A. Attrill & C. Fullwood (Eds.), *Applied cyberpsychology* (pp. 74–88). Springer. https://doi .org/10.1057/9781137517036_5

Mercier, E., Nadeau, A., Brousseau, A.-A., Émond, M., Lowthian, J., Berthelot, S., Costa, A. P., Mowbray, F., Melady, D., Yadav, K., Nickel, C., & Cameron, P. A. (2020). Elder abuse in the out-of-hospital and emergency department settings: A scoping review. *Annals of Emergency Medicine, 75*, 181–191. https:// doi.org/10.1016/j.annemergmed.2019.12.011

Merenstein, J. L., Petok, J. R., & Bennett, I. J. (2022). Age group differences in learning-related activity reflect task stage, not learning stage. *Behavioural Brain Research, 416*, 113570. https://doi.org/10.1016/j.bbr.2021.113570

Mertens, A., Becker, S., Theis, S., Rasche, P., Wille, M., Bröhl, C. et al. (2017). Mobile technology improves therapy-adherence rates in elderly patients undergoing rehabilitation—A crossover design study. In V. G. Duffy & N. Lightner (Eds.), *Advances in human factors and ergonomics in healthcare* (pp. 295–308). Springer.

Merton, T., OSCO. (1955). *No man is an island.* Houghton Mifflin.

Merton, T., OSCO. (1962). *New seeds of contemplation.* New Directions.

Merz, E.-M., & De Jong Gierveld, J. (2016). Childhood memories, family ties, sibling support and loneliness in ever-widowed older adults: Quantitative and qualitative results. *Ageing and Society, 36*, 534–561. https://doi.org/10.1017/S0144686X14001329

Meyer, B. J. F., Talbot, A. P., & Ranalli, C. (2007). Why older adults make more immediate treatment decisions about cancer than younger adults. *Psychology and Aging, 22*, 505–524. https://doi .org/10.1037/0882-7974.22.3.505

Meyer, S. J., Elias, N. M. (2022). Rainbow research: Challenges and recommendations for sexual orientation and gender identity and expression (SOGIE) survey design. *Voluntas*. https://doi .org/10.1007/s11266-021-00436-5

Meyer-Lee, C. B., Jackson, J. B., & Gutierrez, N. S. (2020). Long-term experiencing of parental death during childhood: A qualitative analysis. *The Family Journal, 28*, 247–256. https://doi .org/10.1177%2F1066480720926582

Meyers, M. C., & Bal, A. (2022). Hard work or hard wired? The nature-nurture debate on talent. In I. Tarique (Ed.), *The Routledge companion to talent management* (pp. 229–240). Routledge. https://doi .org/10.4324/9781315474687-18

Meza-Kubo, V., & Morán, A. L. (2013). UCSA: A design framework for usable cognitive systems for the worried well. *Personal and Ubiquitous Computing, 17*, 1135–1145. https://doi.org/10.1007/s00779-012-0554-x

Mhaka-Mutepfa, M., Mpofu, E., Moore, A., & Ingman, S. (2017). Carer grandparents of sub-Saharan Africa. In D. W. Shwalb & Z. Hossain (Eds.), *Grandparents in Cultural Context.* Routledge.

Michaelian, K., & Arango-Muñoz, S. (2017). Collaborative memory knowledge: A distributed reliabilist perspective. In M. L. Meade, C. B. Harris, P. Van Bergen, J. Sutton, & A. J. Barnier (Eds.), *Collaborative remembering: Theories, research, and applications.* Oxford University Press. https://doi.org/10.1093 /oso/9780198737865.003.0013

Michalska, J., Kamieniarz, A., Sobota, G., Stania, M., Juras, G., & Slomka, K. J. (2021). Age-related changes in postural control in older women: Transitional tasks in step initiation. *BMC Geriatrics, 21*, Article 17. https://doi.org/10.1186/s12877-020-01985-y

Michel, A. (2016, February). Burnout and the brain. *Observer, 29*. https://www.psychologicalscience.org /index.php/publications/observer/2016/february-16 /burnout-and-the-brain.html

Midlarsky, E., Kahana, E., & Belser, A. (2015). Prosocial behavior in late life. In D. A Schroeder & W. G. Graziano (Eds.), *The Oxford handbook of prosocial behavior* (pp. 415–432). Oxford University Press.

Mietkiewicz, M.-C., & Venditti, L. (2004). Les arrière-grands-pères le point de vue de leurs arrière-petits-enfants [Great-grandfathers from their great-grandchildren's point of view]. *Psychologie & NeuroPsychiatrie du Vieillissement, 2*, 275–283.

Mikkelsen, M. B., O'Toole, M. S., & Mehlsen, M. (2020). Comparing negative emotion differentiation in young and older individuals: A picture-based study. *Scandinavian Journal of Psychology, 61*, 513–517. https://doi.org/10.1111/sjop.12615

Miles, E., & Crisp, R. J. (2014). A meta-analytic test of the imagined contact hypothesis. *Group Processes & Intergroup Relations, 17*, 3–26. https://doi .org/10.1177/1368430213510573

Miller, B., Rocks, S., Catalina, S., Zemaitis, N., Daniels, K., & Londono, J. (2019). The missing link in contemporary health disparities research: A profile of the mental and self-rated health of multiracial young adults. *Health Sociology Review, 28*, 209–227. https://doi.org/10.1080/14461242. 2019.1607524

Miller, C., & Vittrup, B. (2020). The indirect effects of police racial violence on African American families. *Journal of Family Issues, 41*, 1699–1722. https://doi .org/10.1177%2F0192513X20929068

Miller, E., & Burton, L. O. (2020). Redesigning aged care with a biophilic lens: A call to action. *Cities & Health*. https://doi.org/10.1080/23748834.2020.1772557

Miller, J., & McDaniel, T. (2022). I enjoyed the chance to meet you and I will always remember you: Healthy older adults' conversations with Misty the Robot. *Proceedings of the 2022 ACM/IEEE International Conference on Human–Robot Interaction*, 914–918. https://dl.acm.org/doi/abs/10.5555/3523760.3523904
Miller, K. D. (2020). *Marriage psychology and therapy: The science of successful relationships*. https://positivepsychology.com/marriage-fulfillment-lifelong-relationship/
Miller, K. I., Shoemaker, M. M., Willyard, J., & Addison, P. (2008). Providing care for elderly parents: A structurational approach to family caregiver identity. *Journal of Family Communication, 8*, 19–43. https://doi.org/10.1080/15267430701389947
Miller, P. J., & Rosengren, K. S. (2014). Final thoughts. *Monographs of the Society for Research in Child Development, 79*, 113–124. https://doi.org/10.1111/mono.12082
Miller, P. J., Rosengren, K. S., & Gutiérrez, I. T. (2014). Children's understanding of death: Toward a contextualized and integrated account: Introduction. *Monographs of the Society for Research in Child Development, 79*, 1–18. https://doi.org/10.1111/mono.12076
Milman, E., & Neimeyer, R. A. (2020). Meaning-making in bereavement transitions: Review and clinical relevance. In E. M. Altmaier (Ed.), *Navigating life transitions for meaning* (pp. 69–89). Academic Press. https://doi.org/10.1016/B978-0-12-818849-1.00005-9
Minasi, S., Baldi, C., Gianno, F., Antonelli, M., Buccoliero, A. M., Pietsch, T., Massimino, M., & Buttarelli, F. R. (2021). Alternative lengthening of telomeres in molecular subgroups of paediatric high-grade glioma. *Child's Nervous System, 37*, 809–818. https://doi.org/10.1007/s00381-020-04933-8
Minnotte, K. L. (2010). *Methodologies of assessing marital success*. https://wfrn.org/wp-content/uploads/2018/09/Marital_Success-encyclopedia.pdf
Miranda, J., McGuire, T. G., Williams, D. R., & Wang, P. (2008). Mental health in the context of health disparities. *American Journal of Psychiatry, 165*, 1102–1108. https://doi.org/10.1176/appi.ajp.2008.08030333
Miron-Spektor, E., & Paletz, S., (2022, in press). Culture and creativity in organization: New directions and discoveries. In M. Gelfand & M. Erez (Eds.), *The Oxford handbook of culture and organizations*. Oxford University Press.
Mischel, N. (2020, December 21). New antidepressants can lift depression and suicidal thoughts fast, but don't expect magic cures. *The Conversation*. https://theconversation.com/new-antidepressants-can-lift-depression-and-suicidal-thoughts-fast-but-dont-expect-magic-cures-148721.
Mitchell, B. A. (2006). *The boomerang age: Transitions to adulthood in families*. Aldine Transaction.
Mitchell, K. J. (2016). The cognitive neuroscience of source monitoring. In J. Dunlosky & S. K. Tauber (Eds.), *The Oxford handbook of metamemory* (pp. 425–450). Oxford University Press.
Mitchell, K. J., & Hill, E. M. (2019). The impact of focusing on different features during encoding on young and older adults' source memory. *Open Psychology, 1*, 106–118. https://doi.org/10.1515/psych-2018-0008
Mitchell, L. L., Lodi-Smith, J., Baranski, E. N., & Whitbourne, S. K. (2021). Implications of identity resolution in emerging adulthood for intimacy, generativity, and integrity across the adult lifespan. *Psychology and Aging, 36*, 545–556. https://doi.org/10.1037/pag0000537
Mittal, P., Singh, N., Chaturvedi, S., Jyoti, A., Mishra, A. K., & Hazari, P. P. (2021). Comprehensive review on design perspective of PET ligands based on β-amyloids, tau and neuroinflammation for diagnostic intervention of Alzheimer's disease. *Clinical and Translational Imaging, 9*, 153–175. https://doi.org/10.1007/s40336-021-00410-7
Mittelmark, M. B., & Bauer, G. F. (2017). The meanings of salutogenesis. In M. B. Mittelmark, S. Sagy, M. Eriksson, G. F. Bauer, J. M. Pelikan, B. Lindström et al. (Eds.), *The handbook of salutogenesis* (pp. 7–13). Springer.
Mittelmark, M. B., Bauer, G. F., Vaandrager, L., Pelikan, J. M., Sagy, S., Eriksson, M., Lindström, B., & Magistretti, C. M. (Eds.). (2022). *The handbook of salutogenesis* (2nd ed.). Springer.
Modra, L., & Hilton, A. (2016). Ethical issues in resuscitation and intensive care medicine. *Anaesthesia & Intensive Care Medicine, 17*, 35–37. https://doi.org/10.1016/j.mpaic.2015.10.006
Moelker, R., Andres, M., & Rones, N. (2019). The politics of military families: State, work organizations, and the rise of the negotiation household—Tensions between state, work, and families. In R. Moelker, M. Andres, & N. Rones (Eds.), *The politics of military families: State, work organizations, and the rise of the negotiation household*. Routledge.
Moeller, J. R., Lewis, M. M., & Werth, J. L., Jr. (2010). End of life issues. In J. C. Cavanaugh & C. K. Cavanaugh (Eds.), *Aging in America: Vol. 1: Psychological aspects* (pp. 202–231). Praeger Perspectives.
Moen, P. (2016a). *Encore adulthood: Boomers on the edge of risk, renewal, & purpose*. Oxford University Press.
Moen, P. (2016b). Work over the gendered life course. In M. J. Shanahan, J. T. Mortimer, & M. K. Johnson (Eds.), *Handbook of the life course* (pp. 249–275). Springer.
Moen, P., & Roehling, P. (2005). *The career mystique: Cracks in the American dream*. Rowman & Littlefield.
Mogil, C., Heiselberg, H., Clement, A., & Sternhagen Nielsen, A. B. (2019). Programs for children in military families. *Journal of Military, Veteran and Family Health, 5*, 97–115. https://doi.org/10.3138/jmvfh.2019-0011
Mohanty, P., Naveh-Benjamin, M., & Ratneshwar, S. (2016). Beneficial effects of semantic memory support on older adults' episodic memory: Differential patterns of support of item and associative information. *Psychology and Aging, 31*, 25–36. https://doi.org/10.1037/pag0000059
Mohanty, S. (2021). A distributional analysis of the gender wage gap among technical degree and diploma holders in urban India. *International Journal of Educational Development, 80*, 102322. https://doi.org/10.1016/j.ijedudev.2020.102322
Mohlman, J., Sirota, K. G., Papp, L. A., Staples, A. M., King, A., & Gorenstein, E. E. (2012). Clinical interviewing with older adults. *Cognitive and Behavioral Practice, 19*, 89–100. https://doi.org/10.1016/j. cbpra.2010.10.001
Mojon-Azzi, S. M., Sousa-Poza, A., & Mojon, D. S. (2008). Impact of low vision on well-being in 10 European countries. *Ophthalmologica, 222*, 205–212. https://doi.org/10.1159/000126085
Molenberghs, P., Johnson, H., Henry, J. D., & Mattingley, J. B. (2016). Unertanding the minds of others: A neuroimaging meta-analysis. *Neuroscience and Biobehavioral Reviews, 65*, 276–291. https://doi.org/10.1016/j.neurobiorev.2016.03.020
Molina M. Á., & Schettini R. (2021). Lifelong learning and quality of life. In F. Rojo-Pérez & G. Fernández-Mayoralas (Eds.), *Handbook of active ageing and quality of life* (pp. 111–119). Springer Cham. https://doi.org/10.1007/978-3-030-58031-5_6
Monge, A. Z., Stanley, M. L., Geib, B. R., Davis, S. W., & Cabeza, R. (2018). Functional networks underlying item and source memory: Shared and distinct network components and age-related differences. *Neurobiology of Aging, 69*, 140–150. https://doi.org/10.1016/j.neurobiolaging.2018.05.016
Montauk, T. R., & Kuhl, E. A. (2020). COVID-related family separation and trauma in the intensive care unit. *Psychological Trauma: Theory, Research, Practice, and Policy, 12*, S96–S97. https://doi.org/10.1037/tra0000839
Monteiro, F., Rodrigues, P., Nascimento, C. S., Simões, F., & Miguel, M. (2022). The daily rhythms of working memory and their methodological constraints: A critical overview. *Biological Rhythm Research, 53*, 1116–1143. https://doi.org/10.1080/09291016.2021.1907511
Moon, P. J., (2017). Hospice admission assessment: A narrative view. *American Journal of Hospice & Palliative Care, 34*, 201–204. https://doi.org/10.1177/1049909115624375
Moore, S. E., Jones-Eversley, S. D., Tolliver W. F., Wilson, B., & Harmon, D. K. (2022). Cultural responses to loss and grief among Black Americans: Theory and practice implications for clinicians. *Death Studies, 46*, 189–199. https://doi.org/10.1080/07481187.2020.1725930
Moorman, S. M., & Greenfield, E. A. (2010). Personal relationships in later life. In J. C. Cavanaugh & C. K. Cavanaugh (Eds.), *Aging in America: Vol. 3: Societal Issues* (pp. 20–52). ABC-CLIO.
Moorman, S. M., & Inoue, M. (2013). Persistent problems in end-of-life planning among young- and middle-aged American couples. *Journals of Gerontology: Social Sciences, 68*, 97–106. https://doi.org/10.1093/geronb/gbs103
Mooser, B., Senn, N. Heritier, F., & Cohidon, C. (2020). Exploring whether teaching activity is a way to improve GPs' satisfaction and wellbeing: A cross-sectional study. *BJGP Open, 4*. https://doi.org/10.3399/bjgpopen20X101038
Morcom, A. M. (2016). Mind over memory: Cuing the aging brain. *Current Directions in Psychological Science, 25*, 143–150. https://doi.org/10.1177/0963721416645536
Morfei, M. Z., Hooker, K., Fiese, B. H., & Cordeiro, A. M. (2001). Continuity and change in parenting possible selves: A longitudinal follow-up. *Basic and Applied Social Psychology, 23*, 217–223. https://doi.org/10.1207/153248301750433777
Morgan, S., & Yoder, L. H. (2012). A concept analysis of person-centered care. *Journal of Holistic Nursing, 30*, 6–15. https://doi.org/10.1177/0898010111412189
Morris, S. E., Souza, P. M., & Fasciano, K. M. (2021). The development of a bereavement support group curriculum for young adults dealing with the death of a partner: A quality improvement project. *Journal of Adolescent and Young Adult Oncology, 10*, 260–265. https://doi.org/10.1089/jayao.2020.0131
Morton, K. R., Tanzini, L., & Lee, J. W. (2019). Adult life satisfaction and the role of forgiveness after childhood sexual abuse: Evidence from a Seventh-Day Adventist cohort. *Journal for the Scientific Study of Religion, 58*, 138–152. https://doi.org/10.1111/jssr.12575
Morys, F., Dadar, M., & Dagher, A. (2021). Association between midlife obesity and its metabolic consequences, cerebrovascular disease, and cognitive decline. *Journal of Clinical Endocrinology & Metabolism, 106*, e4260–e4274. https://doi.org/10.1210/clinem/dgab135
Mosten, F. S. (2009). *Collaborative divorce handbook: Helping families without going to court*. Jossey-Bass.
Mõttus, R., Johnson, W., & Deary, I. J. (2012). Personality traits in old age: Measurement and rank-order stability and some mean-level change. *Psychology and Aging, 27*(1), 243–249. https://doi.org/10.1037/a0023690
Moye, J., & Wood, E. (2020). Understanding legal and clinical capacities. In J. Moye (Ed.), *Assessing capacities of older adults: A casebook to guide difficult decisions* (pp. 9–23). American Psychological Association. https://doi.org/10.1037/0000184-002
Moyle, W., Murfield, J., & Lion, K. (2022). Therapeutic use of the humanoid robot, Telenoid, with older adults: A critical interpretive synthesis review. *Assistive Technology*. https://doi.org/10.1080/10400435.2022.2060375
Mozilla. (2020). *Mozilla community participation guidelines* (Version 3.1). https://www.mozilla.org/en-US/about/governance/policies/participation/
Mühlig-Versen, A., Bowen, C. E., & Staudinger, U. M. (2012). Personality plasticity in later adulthood: Contextual and personal resources are needed to increase openness to new experiences. *Psychology and*

Aging, 27, 855–866. https://doi.org/10.1037/a0029357

Muise, A., Impett, E. A., Kogan, A., & Desmarais, S. (2013). Keeping the spark alive: Being motivated to meet a partner's sexual needs sustains sexual desire in long-term romantic relationships. *Social Psychological and Personality Science, 4*, 267–273. https://doi.org/10.1177/1948550612457185

Muller, E. D., & Thompson, C. L. (2003). The experience of grief after bereavement: A phenomenological study with implications for mental health counseling. *Journal of Mental Health Counseling, 25*, 183–203. https://doi.org/10.17744/mehc.25.3.wu4n7dljyekuh4ef

Muntaner, C., Ng, E., Vanroelen, C., Christ, S., & Eaton, W. W. (2013). Social stratification, social closure, and social class as determinants of mental health disparities. In C. S. Aneshensel, J. C. Phelan, & A. Bieman (Eds.), *Handbook of the sociology of mental health* (pp. 206–227). Springer.

Murayama, K., Toshiya, B., Storm, D., & Benjamin, C. (2014). Forgetting as a consequence of retrieval: A meta-analytic review of retrieval-induced forgetting. *Psychological Bulletin, 140*, 1383–1409. https://doi.org/10.1037/a0037505

Murphy, K. M., & Weaver, C. (2022). *Janeway's immunobiology* (10th ed.). Norton.

Murphy, K. R., & Tierney, W. (2020). What has changed and what has not? In B. J. Hoffman, M. K. Shoss, & L. A. Wegman (Eds.), *The Cambridge handbook of the changing nature of work* (pp. 42–66). Cambridge University Press.

Murray, F. L., & Hwang, S. H. (2020). Exploring parenting influences: Married African American fathers' perspectives. *The Qualitative Report, 25*, 553–568. https://search.proquest.com/openview/5d3e4b839ca74972108501434dbef531/1?pq-origsite=gscholar&cbl=55152

Murray, J. L., & Arnett, J. J. (2019). Introduction. In J. L. Murray & J. J. Arnett (Eds.), *Emerging adulthood and higher education: A new student development paradigm* (pp. 1–10). Routledge.

Myers-Coffman, K., Baker, F. A., & Bradt, J. (2020). The Resilience Songwriting Program: A working theoretical model and intervention protocol for adolescent bereavement. *Nordic Journal of Music Therapy, 29*, 132–149. https://doi.org/10.1080/08098131.2019.1642373

Myers-Coffman, K., Krater, C., Shanine, M., & Bradt, J. (2020). Feasibility and acceptability of the resilience songwriting program for adolescent bereavement. *The Arts in Psychotherapy, 71*, 101724. https://doi.org/10.1016/j.aip.2020.101724

Naef, R., Ward, R., Mahrer-Imhof, R., & Grande, G. (2013). Characteristics of the bereavement experience of older persons after spousal loss: An integrative review. *International Journal of Nursing Studies, 50*, 1108–1121. https://doi.org/10.1016/j.ijnurstu.2012.11.026

Nagaratnam, N., Nagaratnam, K., & Cheuk, G. (2016). Ear-related problems in the elderly. In N. Nagaratnam, K. Nagaratnam, & G. Cheuk (Eds.), *Diseases in the elderly* (pp. 357–371). Springer. https://doi.org/10.1007/978-3-319-25787-7_17

Nahemow, L. (2000). The ecological theory of aging: Powell Lawton's legacy. In R. L. Rubinstein & M. Moss (Eds.), *The many dimensions of aging* (pp. 22–40). Springer.

Napolitano, C. M., & Freund, A. M. (2016). On the use and usefulness of backup plans. *Perspectives on Psychological Science, 11*, 56–73. https://doi.org/10.1177/1745691615596991

Nash, J. F., & Tanner, P. R. (2016). The controversy of sunscreen product exposure: Too little, too much, or just right. In S. Q. Wang & H. W. Lin (Eds.), *Principles and practice of photoprotection* (pp. 125–139). New York: Springer. https://doi.org/10.1007/978-3-319-29382-0_8

Nashiro, K., Sakaki, M., Huffman, D., & Mather, M. (2013). Both younger and older adults have difficulty updating emotional memories. *Journals of Gerontology: Psychological Sciences, 68*, 224–227. https://doi.org/10.1093/geronb/gbs039

National Alliance for Caregiving and AARP. (2020). *Caregiving in the U.S.: 2020 report*. https://www.caregiving.org/caregiving-in-the-us-2020/

National Alliance for Caregiving. (2021). *Caring for the caregiver*. https://www.caregiving.org/resources/caregiver-health/

National Cancer Institute. (2021a). *Targeted cancer therapies*. https://www.cancer.gov/about-cancer/treatment/types/targeted-therapies/targeted-therapies-fact-sheet

National Cancer Institute. (2021b). *Genetics of prostate cancer (PDQ®)–Health professional version*. https://www.cancer.gov/types/prostate/hp/prostate-genetics-pdq

National Center for Drug Abuse Statistics. (2022). *Drug abuse statistics*. https://drugabusestatistics.org/

National Center for Health Statistics. (2021a). *Health, United States 2019*. https://www.cdc.gov/nchs/data/hus/hus19-508.pdf

National Center for Health Statistics. (2021b). *Provisional drug overdose death counts*. https://www.cdc.gov/nchs/nvss/vsrr/drug-overdose-data.htm

National Center for Health Statistics. (2022). *Percentage of births to unmarried mothers by state*. https://www.cdc.gov/nchs/pressroom/sosmap/unmarried/unmarried.htm.

National Center on Elder Abuse. (2022a). *Research, statistics, and data*. https://ncea.acl.gov/What-We-Do/Research/Statistics-and-Data.aspx#prevalence

National Center on Elder Abuse. (2022b). *Signs of elder abuse*. https://ncea.acl.gov/NCEA/media/publications/NCEA_SignsEA_508.pdf

National Council on Aging. (2015). *Falls Free® National Falls Prevention Action Plan*. https://www.ncoa.org/article/2015-falls-free-national-falls-prevention-action-plan

National Council on Aging. (2021). *Get the facts on falls prevention*. https://www.ncoa.org/article/get-the-facts-on-falls-prevention

National Deaf Center on Postsecondary Outcomes. (2019). *The deaf community: An introduction*. https://www.nationaldeafcenter.org/resource/deaf-community-introduction

National Eye Institute. (2022). *Diabetic retinopathy*. https://www.nei.nih.gov/learn-about-eye-health/eye-conditions-and-diseases/diabetic-retinopathy

National Heart, Lung, and Blood Institute. (2020). *High blood pressure: Also known as hypertension*. https://www.nhlbi.nih.gov/health-topics/high-blood-pressure

National Heart, Lung, and Blood Institute. (2021a). *What is atherosclerosis?* https://www.nhlbi.nih.gov/health-topics/atherosclerosis

National Heart, Lung, and Blood Institute. (2021b). *Low blood pressure: Also known as hypotension*. https://www.nhlbi.nih.gov/health-topics/low-blood-pressure

National Hospice and Palliative Care Organization. (2019). *Palliative care or hospice?* https://www.nhpco.org/wp-content/uploads/2019/04/PalliativeCare_VS_Hospice.pdf

National Institute of Arthritis and Musculoskeletal and Skin Diseases. (2019a). *What is osteoarthritis?* https://www.niams.nih.gov/health-topics/osteoarthritis

National Institute of Arthritis and Musculoskeletal and Skin Diseases. (2019b). *What is rheumatoid arthritis?* https://www.niams.nih.gov/health-topics/rheumatoid-arthritis/advanced

National Institute of Mental Health. (2022a). *Major depression*. https://www.nimh.nih.gov/health/statistics/major-depression.shtml

National Institute of Mental Health. (2022b). *Post-traumatic stress disorder*. https://www.nimh.nih.gov/health/topics/post-traumatic-stress-disorder-ptsd

National Institute of Neurological Disorders and Stroke. (2019). *Wernicke–Korsakoff syndrome information page*. https://www.ninds.nih.gov/Disorders/All-Disorders/Wernicke-Korsakoff-Syndrome-Information-Page

National Institute on Aging. (2017). *What happens to the brain in Alzheimer's disease?* https://www.nia.nih.gov/health/what-happens-brain-alzheimers-disease

National Institute on Aging. (2018). *Aging hearts and arteries: A scientific quest*. https://www.nia.nih.gov/health/heart-health-and-aging#changes

National Institute on Aging. (2020). *Elder abuse*. https://www.nia.nih.gov/health/elder-abuse

National Institute on Aging. (2021a). *Depression and older adults*. https://www.nia.nih.gov/health/depression-and-older-adults

National Institute on Aging. (2021b). *What is Lewy body dementia? Causes, symptoms, and treatments*. https://www.nia.nih.gov/health/what-lewy-body-dementia-causes-symptoms-and-treatments

National Institute on Aging. (2022). *What do we know about healthy aging?* https://www.nia.nih.gov/health/what-do-we-know-about-healthy-aging

National Institute on Alcohol Abuse and Alcoholism. (2021). *Treatment for alcohol problems: Finding and getting help*. https://www.niaaa.nih.gov/publications/brochures-and-fact-sheets/treatment-alcohol-problems-finding-and-getting-help

National Institute on Drug Abuse. (2021). *Opioid overdose crisis*. https://www.drugabuse.gov/drug-topics/opioids/opioid-overdose-crisis

National Institutes of Health. (2009). *Research involving individuals with questionable capacity to consent: Points to consider*. https://grants.nih.gov/grants/policy/questionablecapacity.htm

National Institutes of Health. (2020a). *Posttraumatic stress disorder*. https://www.nimh.nih.gov/health/publications/post-traumatic-stress-disorder-ptsd

National Institutes of Health. (2020b). *New blood test method may predict Alzheimer's disease*. https://www.nih.gov/news-events/nih-research-matters/new-blood-test-method-may-predict-alzheimers-disease

National Osteoporosis Foundation. (2021a). *Bone health basics: Get the facts*. https://www.nof.org/prevention/general-facts

National Osteoporosis Foundation. (2021b). *Food and your bones: Osteoporosis nutrition guidelines*. https://www.nof.org/patients/treatment/nutrition

National Osteoporosis Foundation. (2021c). *Calcium and vitamin D*. https://www.nof.org/patients/treatment/calciumvitamin-d

National Women's Law Center. (2021). *The wage gap: The who, how, why, and what to do*. https://nwlc.org/resource/the-wage-gap-the-who-how-why-and-what-to-do/

National Women's Law Center. (2022). *Sexual harassment in the workplace*. https://nwlc.org/issue/sexual-harassment-in-the-workplace/

Naveh-Benjamin, M., & Mayr, U. (2018). Age-related differences in associative memory: Empirical evidence and theoretical perspectives. *Psychology and Aging, 33*, 1–6. http://doi.org/10.1037/pag0000235

Naylor, L. A. (2021). *Social equity and LGBTQ rights: Dismantling discrimination and expanding civil rights*. Routledge.

Neal, M. B., & Hammer, L. B. (2007). *Working couples caring for children and aging parents: Effects on work and well-being*. Erlbaum.

Neff, L. S., & Bradshaw, A. D. (2021). Cross your heart? Collagen cross-links in cardiac health and disease. *Cellular Signalling, 79*, 109889. https://doi.org/10.1016/j.cellsig.2020.109889

Nehamas, A. (2016). *On friendship*. Basic Books.

Neisser, U. (1976). *Cognition and reality*. W. H. Freeman.

Neisser, U. (2012). Flashbulb memories. In S. R. R. Schmidt (Ed.), *Extraordinary memories for exceptional events* (pp. 45–66). Psychology Press.

Nelson, T. D. (2016a). Promoting healthy aging by confronting ageism. *American Psychologist, 71*, 276–282. https://doi.org/10.1037/a0040221

Nelson, T. D. (2016b). The age of ageism. *Journal of Social Issues, 72*, 191–198. https://doi.org/10.1111/josi.12162

Nemeroff, C. B. (2020). The state of our understanding of the pathophysiology and optimal treatment of depression: Glass half full or half empty? *American Journal of Psychiatry, 177*, 671–685. https://doi.org/10.1176/appi.ajp.2020.20060845

Nenclares, P., & Harrington, K. J. (2020). The biology of cancer. *Medicine, 48*, 67–72. https://doi.org/10.1016/j.mpmed.2019.11.001

Neubeck, M., Karbach, J., & Könen, T. (2022). Network models of cognitive abilities in younger and older adults. *Intelligence, 90*, 101601. https://doi.org/10.1016/j.intell.2021.101601

Neugarten, B. L., & Weinstein, K. K. (1964). The changing American grandparent. *Journal of Marriage and Family, 26*, 299–304. https://doi.org/10.2307/349727

Nevalainen, N., Riklund, K., Andersson, M., Axelsson, J., Ögren, M., Lövden, M., Lindenberger, U., Bäckman, L., & Nyberg, L. (2015). COBRA: A prospective multimodal imaging study of dopamine, brain structure and function, and cognition. *Brain Research, 1612*, 83–103. https://doi.org/10.1016/j.brainres.2014.09.010

Neville, C., Beattie, E., Fielding, E., & MacAndrew, M. (2015). Literature review: Use of respite by carers of people with dementia. *Health and Social Care in the Community, 23*, 51–63. https://doi.org/10.1111/hsc.12095

Newberg, A. B., Serruya, M., Wintering, N., Moss, A. S., Reibel, D. & Monti, D. A. (2014). Meditation and neurodegenerative diseases. *Annals of the New York Academy of Sciences, 1307*, 112–123. https://doi.org/10.1111/nyas.12187

Newman, A., Thompson, J., & Chandler, E. M. (2013). Continuous care: A home hospice benefit. *Clinical Journal of Oncology Nursing, 17*, 19–20. https://doi.org/10.1188/13.CJON.19-20

Newman, B. M., & Newman, P. R. (2016). *Theories of human development* (2nd ed.). Psychology Press.

Newsom, J. T. (1999). Another side to caregiving: Negative reactions to being helped. *Current Directions in Psychological Science, 8*, 183–187. https://doi.org/10.1111/1467-8721.00043

Newton, N. J., & Jones, B. K. (2016). Passing on: Personal attributes associated with midlife expressions of intended legacies. *Developmental Psychology, 52*, 341–353. https://doi.org/10.1037/a0039905

Newton, N. J., & Stewart, A. J. (2012). Personality development in adulthood. In S. K. Whitbourne & M. J. Sliwinski (Eds.), *The Wiley-Blackwell handbook of adulthood and aging* (pp. 209–235). Wiley-Blackwell.

Newton, N. J., Chauhan, P. K., & Pates, J. L. (2020). Facing the future: Generativity, stagnation, intended legacies, and well-being in later life. *Journal of Adult Development, 27*, 70–80. https://doi.org/10.1007/s10804-019-09330-3

Newton, N. J., Stewart, A. J., & Vandewater, E. A. (2019). "Age is opportunity": Women's personality trajectories from mid- to later-life. *Journal of Research in Personality, 80*, 43–54. https://doi.org/10.1016/j.jrp.2019.04.005

Ng, R., Allore, H. G., Monin, J. K., & Levy, B. R. (2016). Retirement as meaningful: Positive retirement stereotypes associated with longevity. *Journal of Social Issues, 72*, 69-85. https://doi.org/10.1111/josi.12156

Ng, R., Yu, T., & Chow, J. (2021). Aging narratives over 210 years (1810–2019). *The Journals of Gerontology: Social Sciences, 76*, 1799–1807. https://doi.org/10.1093/geronb/gbaa222

Ng, Y. T., Huo, M., Gleason, M. E., Neff, L. A., Charles, S. T., & Fingerman, K. L. (2021). Friendships in old age: Daily encounters and emotional well-being. *The Journals of Gerontology: Psychological Sciences, 76*, 551–562. https://doi.org/10.1093/geronb/gbaa007

Nguyen, L., Murphy, K., & Andrews, G. (2019). Cognitive and neural plasticity in old age: A systematic review of evidence from executive functions cognitive training. *Ageing Research Reviews, 53*, 100912. https://doi.org/10.1016/j.arr.2019.100912

Niaz, S. A., Hameed, W. U., Saleem, M., Bibi, S., Anwer, B., & Razzaq, S. (2021). Fourth industrial revolution: A way forward to technological revolution, disruptive innovation, and their effects on employees. In E. N. Abe (Ed.), *Future of work, work-family satisfaction, and employee well-being in the fourth industrial revolution* (pp. 297–312). IGI Global. https://doi.org/10.4018/978-1-7998-3347-5.ch020

Nichols, L. O., Chang, C., Lummus, A., Burns, R., Martindale-Adams, J., Graney, M. J., Coon, D. W., & Czaja, S. (2008). The cost-effectiveness of a behavioral intervention with caregivers of patients with Alzheimer's disease. *Journal of the American Geriatrics Society*, 56, 413–420. https://doi.org/10.1111/j.1532-5415.2007.01569.x

Nicolini, C., Fahnestock, M., Gibala, M. J., & Nelson, A. J. (2021). Understanding the neurophysiological and molecular mechanisms of exercise-induced neuroplasticity in cortical and descending motor pathways: Where do we stand? *Neuroscience, 457*, 259–282. https://doi.org/10.1016/j.neuroscience.2020.12.013

Nielsen, M. K., Neergaard, M. A., Jensen, A. B., Bro, F., & Guldin, M.-B. (2016). Do we need to change our understanding of anticipatory grief in caregivers? A systematic review of caregiver studies during end-of-life caregiving and bereavement. *Clinical Psychology Review, 44*, 75–93. https://doi.org/10.1016/j.cpr.2016.01.002

Nienke, F. (2021). Religion, health and well-being in later life: Storying our lives in the face of death. *NTT Journal for Theology and the Study of Religion, 75*, 95–119. https://doi.org/10.5117/NTT2021.1.006.FORT

Nikolaidis, A., Baniqued, P. L., Kranz, M. B., Scavuzzo, C. J., Barbey, A. K., Kramer, A. F., & Larsen, R. J. (2017). Multivariate associations of fluid intelligence and NAA. *Cerebral Cortex, 27*, 2607–2616. https://doi.org/10.1093/cercor/bhw070

Nimrod, G. (2007a). Retirees' leisure: Activities, benefits, and their contribution to life satisfaction. *Leisure Studies, 26*, 65–80. https://doi.org/10.1080/02614360500333937

Nimrod, G. (2007b). Expanding, reducing, concentrating and diffusing: Post retirement leisure behavior and life satisfaction. *Leisure Sciences, 29*, 91–111. https://doi.org/10.1080/01490400600983446

Njoku, A. (2022). COVID-19 and health disparities opportunities for public health curriculum enhancement. In R. Ammigan, R. Y. Chan, & K. Bista (Eds.), *COVID-19 and higher education in the global context: Exploring contemporary issues and challenges* (pp. 139–153). STAR Scholars. https://starscholars.org/product/covid-19-and-higed/

Nkimbeng, M. J., & Parker, L. J. (2021). Diverse, culturally rich approaches to family care in the United States. In J. E. Gaugler (Ed.), *Bridging the family care gap* (pp. 43–69). Academic Press. https://doi.org/10.1016/B978-0-12-813898-4.00002-6

Noel, S. E., Santos, M. P., & Wright, N. C. (2021). Racial and ethnic disparities in bone health and outcomes in the United States. *Journal of Bone and Mineral Research, 36*, 1881–1905. https://doi.org/10.1002/jbmr.4417

Nolan, R., Kirkland, C., & Davis, R. (2021). LGBT* after loss: A mixed-method analysis on the effect of partner bereavement on interpersonal relationships and subsequent partnerships. *OMEGA—Journal of Death and Dying, 82*, 646–667. https://doi.org/10.1177%2F0030222819831524

Nolte, J., Löckenhoff, C. E., & Reyna, V. F. (2022). The influence of verbatim versus gist formatting on younger and older adults' information acquisition and decision-making. *Psychology and Aging, 37*, 197–209. https://doi.org/10.1037/pag0000676

Norcross M. A., & Farran P. (2021). Improving engagement during times of change. In S. K. Dhiman (Ed.) *The Palgrave handbook of workplace well-being* (pp. 819–842). Palgrave Macmillan, Cham. https://doi.org/10.1007/978-3-030-30025-8_70

Noriega, C., Velasco, C., & López, J. (2020). Perceptions of grandparents' generativity and personal growth in supplementary care providers of middle-aged grandchildren. *Journal of Social and Personal Relationships, 37*, 1114–1135. https://doi.org/10.1177%2F0265407519886661

Norris, D. R. (2016). *Job loss, identity, and mental health.* Rutgers University Press.

North American Menopause Society. (2021). *The experts do agree about hormone therapy.* http://www.menopause.org/for-women/menopauseflashes/menopause-symptoms-and-treatments/the-experts-do-agree-about-hormone-therapy

Northouse, P. G. (2022). *Leadership: Theory and practice* (9th ed.). Sage Publications.

Northwestern Mutual. (2019). *Northwestern Mutual study: Caring for aging parents is not a family affair.* https://news.northwesternmutual.com/2019-04-03-Northwestern-Mutual-Study-Caring-for-Aging-Parents-is-Not-a-Family-Affair

Norton, M. I., & Gino, F. (2014). Rituals alleviate grieving for loved ones, lovers, and lotteries. *Journal of Experimental Psychology: General, 143*, 266–272. https://doi.org/10.1037/a0031772

Nose, M. (2021). Persons and address terms in Melanesia. In T. Okamura & M. Kai (Eds.), *Indigenous language acquisition, maintenance, and loss and current language policies* (pp. 179–205). IGI Global.

NPR. (2021, June 2). *The NFL will stop assuming racial differences when assessing brain injuries.* https://www.npr.org/2021/06/02/1002627309/nfl-says-it-will-halt-race-norming-and-review-brain-injury-claims

Nunes, L. (2021). Totally wired: Where could we go with a map of the brain? *APS Observer, 34*. https://www.psychologicalscience.org/observer/totally-wired

Nurk, S., Koren, S., Rhie, A., Rautiainen, M., Bzikadze, A. V., Mikheenko, A., Vollger, M. R., Altemose, N., Uralsky, L., Gershman, A., Aganezov, S., Hoyt, S. J., Diekhans, M., Logsdon, G. A., Alonge, M., Antonarakis, S. E., Borchers, M., Bouffard, G. G., Brooks, S. Y., … Phillippy, A. M.(2022). The complete sequence of a human genome. *Science, 376*, 44–53. https://doi.org/10.1126/science.abj6987

Nuzum, D., Meaney, S., O'Donoghue, K., & Morris, H. (2015). The spiritual and theological issues raised in stillbirth for healthcare chaplains. *Journal of Pastoral Care & Counseling, 69*, 163–170. https://doi.org/10.1177/1542305015602714

O'Brien, C., & Holtzer, R. (2021). Cognitive reserve moderates associations between walking performance under single- and dual-task conditions and incident mobility impairment in older adults. *Journals of Gerontology: Medical Sciences, 76*, e314–e320. https://doi.org/10.1093/gerona/glab178

O'Brien, L. T., & Hummert, M. L. (2006). Memory performance of late middle-aged adults: Contrasting self-stereotyping and stereotype threat accounts of assimilation to age stereotypes. *Social Cognition, 24*, 338–358. https://doi.org/10.1521/soco.2006.24.3.338

O'Dare, C., Timonen, V., & Conlon, C. (2021). "Doing" intergenerational friendship: Challenging the dominance of age homophily in friendship. *Canadian Journal on Aging/La Revue Canadienne Du Vieillissement, 40*, 68–81. https://doi.org/10.1017/S0714980819000618

O'Keefe, P. A., Dweck, C. S., & Walton, G. M. (2018). Implicit theories of interest: Finding your passion or developing it? *Psychological Science, 29*, 1653–1664. https://doi.org/10.1177%2F0956797618780643

O'Leary, K. D. (1993). Through a psychological lens: Personality traits, personality disorders, and levels of violence. In R. J. Gelles & D. R. Loseke (Eds.), *Current controversies on family violence* (pp. 7–30). Sage.

O'Rourke, N., Neufeld, E., Claxton, A., & Smith, J. Z. (2010). Knowing me-knowing you: Reported personality and trait discrepancies as predictors of marital idealization between long-wed spouses. *Psychology and Aging, 25*(2), 412–421. https://psycnet.apa.org/doi/10.1037/a0017873

O'Shea, B. Q., Demakakos, P., Cadar, D., & Kobayashi, L. C. (2021). Adverse childhood experiences and rate of memory decline from mid to later life: Evidence from the English Longitudinal Study of Ageing. *American Journal of Epidemiology, 190*, 1294–1305. https://doi.org/10.1093/aje/kwab019

Obhi, H. K., & Woodhead, E. L. (2016). Attitudes and experiences with older adults: A case for service learning for undergraduates. *Gerontology and Geriatrics Education, 37*, 108–122. https://doi.org/10.1080/02701960.2015.1079704

Oburu, P. O., & Palmérus, K. (2005). Stress-related factors among primary and part-time caregiving grandmothers of Kenyan grandchildren. *International Journal of Aging & Human Development, 60*, 273–282. https://doi.org/10.2190/XLQ2-UJEMTAQR-4944

Ochs, E., & Kremer-Sadlik, T. (2013). *Fast-forward family: Home, work, and relationships in middle-class America.* University of California Press.

OECD. (2016). *Balancing paid work, unpaid work and leisure.* https://www.oecd.org/gender/data/balancingpaidworkunpaidworkandleisure.htm

OECD. (2018). *Marriage and divorce rates.* https://www.oecd.org/els/family/SF_3_1_Marriage_and_divorce_rates.pdf

Oedekoven, C. S. H., Jansen, A., Kircher, T. T., & Leube, D. T. (2013). Age-related changes in parietal lobe activation during an episodic memory retrieval task. *Journal of Neural Transmission, 120,* 799–806. https://doi.org/10.1007/s00702-012-0904-x

Oestreich, T., Sayre, G., O'Hare, A. M., Curtis, J. R., & Wong, S. (2020). Perspectives on conservative care in advanced kidney disease: A qualitative study of US patients and family members. *American Journal of Kidney Diseases, 77,* 355–364. https://doi.org/10.1053/j.ajkd.2020.07.026

Ogrodnik, M. (2021). Cellular aging beyond cellular senescence: Markers of senescence prior to cell cycle arrest in vitro and in vivo. *Aging Cell, 20,* e13338. https://doi.org/10.1111/acel.13338

Oh, D. H., Kim, S. A., Lee, H. Y., Seo, J. Y., Choi, B.-Y., & Nam, J. H. (2013). Prevalence and correlates of depressive symptoms in Korean adults: Results of a 2009 Korean community health survey. *Journal of Korean Medical Science, 28,* 128–135. https://doi.org/10.3346/jkms.2013.28.1.128

Oh, P. A. (2019). Developing age-friendly communities: Evidence from multiple case studies, *Innovation in Aging, 3,* S183. https://doi.org/10.1093/geroni/igz038.654

Oh, S., Chun, S., Hwang, S., Kim, J., Cho, Y., Lee, J., Kwack, K. B., & Choi, S.-W. (2021). Vitamin D and exercise are major determinants of natural killer cell activity, which is age- and gender-specific. *Frontiers in Immunology, 12,* 2488. https://doi.org/10.3389/fimmu.2021.594356

Olajubu, A. O., Olowokere, A. E., Amujo, D. O., & Olajubu, T. O. (2017). Influence of menopausal symptoms on perceived work ability among women in a Nigerian University. *Climacteric, 20,* 558–563. https://doi.org/10.1080/13697137.2017.1373336

Old, S., & Naveh-Benjamin, M. (2008). Memory for people and their actions: Further evidence for an age-related associative deficit. *Psychology and Aging,* 23, 467–472. https://doi.org/10.1037/0882-7974.23.2.467

Oliveira, B. S., Zunzunegui, M. V., Quinlan, J., Fahmi, H., Tu, M. T., & Guerra, R. O. (2016). Systematic review of the association between chronic social stress and telomere length: A life course perspective. *Aging Research Reviews, 26,* 37–52. https://doi.org/10.1016/j.arr.2015.12.006

Oltjenbruns, K. A., & Balk, D. E. (2007). Life span issues and loss, grief, and mourning: Part 1. The importance of a developmental context: Childhood and adolescence as an example; Part 2. Adulthood. In D. Balk, C. Wogrin, G. Thornton, & D. Meagher (Eds.), *Handbook of thanatology: The essential body of knowledge for the study of death, dying, and bereavement* (pp. 143–163). Routledge/Taylor & Francis.

Onuora, S. (2021). New insights into RA genetics from GWAS meta-analysis. *Nature Reviews Rheumatology, 17,* 128. https://doi.org/10.1038/s41584-021-00580-8

Onyango, I. G., Jauregui, G. V., Čarná, M., Bennett, J. P., Jr., & Stokin, G. B. (2021). Neuroinflammation in Alzheimer's disease. *Biomedicines, 9,* 524. https://doi.org/10.3390/biomedicines9050524

Oosterman, J. M., Morel, S., Meijer, L., Buvens, C., Kessels, R. P. C., & Postma, A. (2011). Differential age effects on spatial and visual working memory. *International Journal of Aging and Human Development, 73,* 195–208. https://doi.org/10.2190/AG.73.3.a

Opdebeeck, C., Martyr, A., & Clare, L. (2016). Cognitive reserve and cognitive function in healthy older people: A meta-analysis. *Aging, Neuropsychology, and Cognition: A Journal on Normal and Dysfunctional Development, 23,* 40–60. https://doi.org/10.1080/13825585.2015.1041450

Orel, N. A., & Coon, D. W. (2016). The challenges of change: How can we meet the care needs of the ever-evolving LGBT family? *Generations, 40,* 41–45.

Orel, N. A., & Fruhauf, C. A. (2013). Lesbian, gay, bisexual, and transgender grandparents. In A. E. Goldberg & K. R. Allen (Eds.), *LGBT-parent families* (pp. 177–192). Springer.

Oren, S., Willerton, C., & Small, J. (2014). Effects of spaced retrieval training on semantic memory in Alzheimer's disease: A systematic review. *Journal of Speech, Language, and Hearing Research, 57,* 247–270. https://doi.org/10.1044/1092-4388(2013/12-0352)

Orlova, N. S., Rutledge, M. S., & Wu, A. Y. (2015). *The transition from defined benefit to defined contribution pensions: Does it influence elderly poverty?* https://crr.bc.edu/working-papers/the-transition-from-defined-benefit-to-defined-contribution-pensions-does-it-influence-elderly-poverty/

Ortaliza, J., Orgera, K., Amin, K., & Cox, C. (2021, August 27). *COVID-19 continues to be a leading cause of death in the U.S. in August 2021.* https://www.healthsystemtracker.org/brief/covid-19-continues-to-be-a-leading-cause-of-death-in-the-u-s-in-august-2021/

Ortiz-Ospina, E., & Roser, M. (2020). Marriages and divorces. https://ourworldindata.org/marriages-and-divorces

Ortiz-Walters, R., & Gilson, L. L. (2013). Mentoring programs for under-represented groups. In J. Passmore, D. B. Peterson, & T. Freire (Eds.), *The Wiley-Blackwell handbook of coaching and mentoring* (pp. 266–282). Wiley-Blackwell.

Osafo, J., Oppong Asante, J., Asantewaa Ampomah, C., & Osei-Tutu, A. (2021). Factors contributing to divorce in Ghana: An exploratory analysis of evidence from court suits. *Journal of Divorce & Remarriage, 62,* 312–326. https://doi.org/10.1080/10502556.2021.1871839

Oswald, R. F., & Masciadrelli, B. P. (2008). Generative ritual among nonmetropolitan lesbians and gay men: Promoting social inclusion. *Journal of Marriage and Family, 70,* 1060–1073. https://doi.org/10.1111/j.1741-3737.2008.00546.x

Ottaway, A. J. (2010). The impact of parental divorce on the intimate relationships of adult offspring: A review of the literature. *Graduate Journal of Counseling Psychology, 2*(1), Article 5. http://epublications.marquette.edu/cgi/viewcontent.cgi?article=1037&context=gjcp.

Otten, D., Tibubos, A. N., Schomerus, G., Brähler, E., Binder, H., Kruse, J., Ladwig, K.-H., Wild, P. S., Grabe, H. J., & Beutel, M. E. (2021). Similarities and differences of mental health in women and men: a systematic review of findings in three large German cohorts. *Frontiers in Public Health, 9.* https://www.frontiersin.org/article/10.3389/fpubh.2021.553071

Oudekerk, B. A., Allen, J. P., Hessel, E. T., & Molloy, L. E. (2015). The cascading development of autonomy and relatedness from adolescence to adulthood. *Child Development, 86,* 472–485. https://doi.org/10.1111/cdev.12313

Owen, R., Berry, K., & Brown, L. J. E. (2022). Enhancing older adults' well-being and quality of life through purposeful activity: A systematic review of intervention studies. *The Gerontologist, 62,* e317–e327. https://doi.org/10.1093/geront/gnab017

Oxtoby, N. P., Leyland, L.-A., Aksman, L. M., Thomas, G. E. C., Bunting, E. L., Wijeratne, P. A., Young, A. L., Zarkali, A., Tan, M. M. X., Bremner, F. D., Keane, P. A., Morris, H. R., Schrag, A. E., Alexander, D. C., & Weil, R. S. (2021). Sequence of clinical and neurodegeneration events in Parkinson's disease progression. *Brain, 144,* 975–988. https://doi.org/10.1093/brain/awaa461

Oyserman, D. (2019). The essentialized self: Implications for motivation and self-regulation. *Journal of Consumer Psychology, 29,* 336–343. https://doi.org/10.1002/jcpy.1093

Pachner, T. M., Schuman, D. L., & Parekh, R. M. (2021). Older Congolese refugees' resettlement challenges in the U.S.: A bioecological convoy model. *Journal of Immigrant & Refugee Studies, 19,* 393–406. https://doi.org/10.1080/15562948.2020.1821420

Padilla, J., Jager, J., Updegraff, K. A., McHale, S. M., & Umaña-Taylor, A. J. (2020). Mexican-origin family members' unique and shared family perspectives of familism values and their links with parent–youth relationship quality. *Developmental Psychology, 56,* 993–1008. https://doi.org/10.1037/dev0000913

Padmadas, S. S., Zheng, Z. & Gu, B. (2021). New developments in family demography. *China Population and Development Studies, 4,* 339–343. https://doi.org/10.1007/s42379-020-00073-3

Paech, J., Luszczynska, A., & Lippke, S. (2016). A rolling stone gathers no moss—The long way from good intentions to physical activity mediated by planning, social support, and self-regulation. *Frontiers in Psychology, 7,* 1024. https://doi.org/10.3389/fpsyg.2016.01024

Paggi, M. E., Jopp, D., & Hertzog, C. (2016). The importance of leisure activities in the relationship between physical health and well-being in a life span sample. *Gerontology, 62,* 450–458. https://doi.org/10.1159/000444415

Palacios, S. (2022). Medical treatment of osteoporosis. *Climacteric, 25,* 43–49. https://doi.org/10.1080/13697137.2021.1951697

Palermos, S. O. (2020). Epistemic collaborations: Distributed cognition and virtue reliabilism. *Erkenntnis.* https://doi.org/10.1007/s10670-020-00258-9

Palkovitz R. (2020). Fathering and being fathered: Developmental interdependence. In H. E. Fitzgerald, K. von Klitzing, N. J. Cabrera, J. Scarano de Mendonça, & T. Skjøthaug (Eds.), *Handbook of fathers and child development* (pp. 29–46). Springer, Cham. https://doi.org/10.1007/978-3-030-51027-5_3

Palkovitz, R., & Palm, G. (2009). Transitions within fathering. *Fathering, 7,* 3–22. https://doi.org/10.3149/fth.0701.3

Palumbo, R. and Manna, R. (2020). For better or for worse? Handling the side effects of organizational change on workplace discrimination. *Journal of Organizational Change Management, 33,* 1181–1200. https://doi.org/10.1108/JOCM-05-2020-0147

Pan American Health Organization. (2022). *Healthy aging.* https://www.paho.org/en/healthy-aging

Pandemic Parenting. (2021). *Resources & recordings.* https://www.pandemic-parent.org/resources

Papa, A., & Litz, B. (2011). Grief. In W. T. O'Donohue & C. Draper (Eds.), *Stepped care and e-health: Practical applications to behavioral disorders* (pp. 223–245). Springer.

Papadopoulos, C., Castro, N., Nigath, A., Davidson, R., Faulkes, N., Menicatti, R., Khaliq, A. A., Recchiuto, C., Battistuzzi, L., Randhawa, G., Merton, L., Kanoria, S., Chong, N.-Y., Kamide, H., Hewson, D., & Sgorbissa, A. (2022). The CARESSES randomised controlled trial: Exploring the health-related impact of culturally competent artificial intelligence embedded into socially assistive robots and tested in older adult care homes. *International Journal of Social Robotics, 14,* 245–256. https://doi.org/10.1007/s12369-021-00781-x

Papapoulos, S. E. (2019). New bone-forming agents. In S. L. Ferrari & C. Roux (Eds.), *Pocket reference to osteoporosis* (pp. 85–93). Springer.

Pappa, S., Chen, J., Barnett, J., Chang, A., Dong, R. K., Xu, W., Yin, A., Chen, B. Z., Delios, A. Y., Chen, R. Z., Miller, S., Wan, X., & Zhang, S. X. (2022). A systematic review and meta-analysis of the mental health symptoms during the Covid-19 pandemic in Southeast Asia. *Psychiatry and Clinical Neurosciences, 76,* 41–50. https://doi.org/10.1111/pcn.13306

Paquette, V., Rapaport, M., St-Louis, A. C., & Vallerand, R. J. (2020). Why are you passionately in love? Attachment styles as determinants of romantic passion and conflict resolution strategies. *Motivation and Emotion, 44,* 621–639. https://doi.org/10.1007/s11031-020-09821-x

Pardal, R., & Barneo, J. L. (2016). Mature neurons modulate neurogenesis through chemical signals acting on neural stem cells. *Development, Growth & Differentiation, 58*, 456–462. https://doi.org/10.1111/dgd.12283

Pargament, K. I. (2013). Searching for the sacred: Toward a nonreductionistic theory of spirituality. In K. I., Pargament, J. J. Exline, & J. W. Jones (Eds.), *APA handbook of psychology, religion, and spirituality (Vol. 1): Context, theory, and research* (pp. 257–273). American Psychological Association.

Parisi, J. M., Sharifian, N., Rebok, G. W., Aiken-Morgan, A. T., Gross, A. L., & Zahodne, L. B. (2021). Subjective memory, objective memory, and race over a 10-year period: Findings from the ACTIVE study. *Psychology and Aging, 36*, 572–583. https://doi.org/10.1037/pag0000622

Park, C. L. (2013). The Meaning Making Model: A framework for understanding meaning, spirituality, and stress-related growth in health psychology. *The European Health Psychologist, 15*, 40–47. http://openhealthpsychology.net/ehp/issues/2013/v15iss2_June2013/EHP_June_2013.pdf#page=13

Park, D. C., & Festini, S. B. (2017). Theories of memory and aging: A look at the past and a glimpse of the future. *Journals of Gerontology: Psychological Sciences, 72*, 82–90. https://doi.org/10.1093/geronb/gbw066

Park, D. C., & Reuter-Lorenz, P. (2009). The adaptive brain: Aging and neurocognitive scaffolding. *Annual Review of Psychology, 60*, 173–196. https://doi.org/10.1146/annurev. psych.59.103006.093656

Park, J., Kitayama, S., Karasawa, M., Curhan, K., Markus, H. R., Kawakami, N., Miyamoto, Y., Love, G. D., Coe, C. L., Ryff, C. D. (2013). Clarifying the links between social support and health: Culture, stress, and neuroticism matter. *Journal of Health Psychology, 18*, 226–235. https://doi.org/10.1177/1359105312439731

Park, J.-H. (2021). Can cognitive training using a tablet computer enhance cognitive function of healthy older adults? An alternating treatment design. *Journal of Mechanics in Medicine and Biology, 21*, 2140044. https://doi.org/10.1142/S0219519421400443

Park, Y. C., & Pyszczynski, T. (2016). Cultural universals and differences in dealing with death. In L. A. Harvell & G. S. Nisbett (Eds.), *Denying death: An interdisciplinary approach to terror management theory* (pp. 193–214). Routledge.

Park, Y. H., Jeong, H.-Y., Jang, J.-W., Park, S. Y., Lim, J.-S., Kim, J.-Y., Im, C.-H., Ahn, S., Park, S.-H., & Kim, S. Y. (2016). Disruption of the posterior medial network during the acute stage of transient global amnesia. *Clinical EEG and Neuroscience, 47*, 69–74. https://doi.org/10.1177/1550059414543684

Park, Y.-H. (2008). Day healthcare services for family caregivers of older people with stroke: Needs and satisfaction. *Journal of Advanced Nursing, 61*, 619–630. https://doi.org/10.1111/j.1365-2648.2007.04545.x

Parker, K., & Horowitz, J. M. (2022). *Majority of workers who quit a job in 2021 cite low pay, no opportunities for advancement, feeling disrespected.* https://www.pewresearch.org/fact-tank/2022/03/09/majority-of-workers-who-quit-a-job-in-2021-cite-low-pay-no-opportunities-for-advancement-feeling-disrespected/

Parker, S. K., & Grote, G. (2022). Automation, algorithms, and beyond: Why work design matters more than ever in a digital world. *Applied Psychology: An International Review, 71*, 1171–1204. https://doi.org/10.1111/apps.12241

Parker, T. (2022). *The cost of raising a child in the United States: A lot more than you think.* https://www.investopedia.com/articles/personal-finance/090415/cost-raising-child-america.asp

Parkes, C. M. (2013). Elisabeth Kübler-Ross, *On death and dying:* A reappraisal. *Mortality, 18*, 94–97. https://doi.org/10.1 080/13576275.2012.758629

Parkinson's Disease Foundation. (2022). *Understanding Parkinson's.* https://www.parkinson.org/understanding-parkinsons

Parrella, N., & Vormittag, K. (2017). Health promotion and wellness. In A. A. Paulman & L. S. Nasir (Eds.), *Family medicine* (pp. 99–111). Springer.

Parris, B. A. (2016). The prefrontal cortex and suggestion: Hypnosis vs. placebo effects. *Frontiers in Psychology, 7*, 415. https://doi.org/10.3389/fpsyg.2016.00415

Pascale, A., & Govoni, S. (2016). Cerebral aging: Implications for the heart autonomic nervous system regulation. In E. Gronda, E. Vanoli, & A. Costea (Eds.), *Heart failure management: The neural pathways* (pp. 115–127). Springer. https://doi.org/10.1007/978-3-319-24993-3_9

Passalacqua, S. A., & Harwood, J. (2012). VIPS communications skill straining for paraprofessional dementia caregivers: An intervention to increase person-centered dementia care. *Clinical Gerontologist, 35*, 425–445. https://doi.org/10.1080/07317115.2012.702655

Passarino, G., De Rango, F., & Montesanto, A. (2016). Human longevity: Genetics or lifestyle? It takes two to tango. *Immunity & Ageing, 13*, 12. https://doi.org/10.1186/s12979-016-0066-z

Pasupathi, M. (2013). Making meaning for the good life: A commentary on the special issue. *Memory, 21*, 143–149. https://doi.org/10.1080/09658211.20 12.744843

Patel, A. V., & Libman, R. B. (2022). Vascular cognitive impairment. In A. M. Franceschi & D. Franceschi (Eds.), *Hybrid PET/MR neuroimaging* (pp. 441–458). Springer, Cham. https://doi.org/10.1007/978-3-030-82367-2_37

Patel, M. N., Nicolla, J. M., Friedman, F. A. P., Ritz, M. R., & Kamal, A. H. (2020). Hospice use among patients with cancer: Trends, barriers, and future directions. *JCO Oncology Practice, 16*, 803–809. https://doi.org/10.1200/OP.20.00309

Patil, A. U., Ghate, S., Madathil, D., Tzeng, O. J. L., Huang, H.-W., & Huang, C.-M. (2021). Static and dynamic functional connectivity supports the configuration of brain networks associated with creative cognition. *Nature: Scientific Reports, 11*, 165. https://doi.org/10.1038/s41598-020-80293-2

Patinadan, P. V., Tan-Ho, G., Choo, P. Y., & Ho, A. H. Y. (2022). Resolving anticipatory grief and enhancing dignity at the end of life: A systematic review of palliative interventions. *Death Studies, 46*, 337–350. https://doi.org/10.1080/07481187.2020.1728426

Patterson, A. V. (2012). *Emerging adulthood as a unique stage in Erikson's psychosocial development theory: Incarnation v. impudence.* Doctoral dissertation, University of Texas at Arlington. https://rc.library.uta.edu/uta-ir/handle/10106/11059

Patterson, C. J. (2013). Family lives of lesbian and gay adults. In G. W. Peterson & K. R. Bush (Eds.), *Handbook of marriage and the family* (3rd ed., pp. 659–681). Springer.

Paul, R., Lane, E., & Jefferson, A. (2013). Vascular cognitive impairment. In L. D. Ravdin & H. L. Katzen (Eds.), *Handbook of the neuropsychology of aging and dementia* (pp. 281–294). Springer.

Paulavicius, A. M., Mizzaci, C. C., Tavares, D. R. B., Rocha, A. P., Civile, V. T., Schultz, R. R., Pinto, A. C. P. N., & Trevisani, V. F. M. (2020). Bilingualism for delaying the onset of Alzheimer's disease: A systematic review and meta-analysis. *European Geriatric Medicine, 11*, 651–658. https://10.1007/s41999-020-00326-x

Paulson, D., Bassett, R., Kitsmiller, E., Luther, K., & Conner, N. (2017). When employment and caregiving collide: Predictors of labor force participation in prospective and current caregivers. *Clinical Gerontologist, 40*, 401–412. https://doi.org/10.1080/07317115.2016.1198856

Pearlin, L. I., Mullan, J. T., Semple, S. J., & Skaff, M. M. (1990). Caregiving and the stress process: An overview of concepts and their measures. *The Gerontologist, 30*, 583–594. https://doi.org/10.1093/geront/30.5.583

Pecanac, K. E., Hill, M. V., & Borkowski, E. (2021). "It made me feel like I didn't know my own body": Patient-provider relationships, LGBTQ+ identity, and end-of-life discussions. *American Journal of Hospice and Palliative Medicine, 38*, 644–649. https://doi.org/10.1177%2F1049909121996276

Pepe, N. W., Wang, Q., & Rajaram, S. (2021). Collaborative remembering in ethnically uniform and diverse group settings. *Journal of Applied Research in Memory and Cognition, 10*, 95–103. https://doi.org/10.1016/j.jarmac.2020.08.001

Perkins, J. M., Subramanian, S. V., Smith, G. G., & Özaltin, E. (2016). Adult height, nutrition, and population health. *Nutrition Reviews, 74*, 149–165. https://doi.org/10.1093/nutrit/nuv105

Perreault, M., Power, N., Touré, E. H., & Caron, J. (2020). Transitional employment and psychological distress: A longitudinal study. *Psychiatric Quarterly, 91*, 735–747. https://doi.org/10.1007/s11126-020-09739-0

Perrone, K. M., Tschopp, K. M., Snyder, E. R., Boo, J. N., & Hyatt, C. (2010). A longitudinal examination of career expectations and outcomes of academically talented students 10 and 20 years post-high school graduation. *Journal of Career Development, 36*, 291–309. https://doi.org/10.1177/0894845309359347

Perry, C., & Fraser, R. (2020). A qualitative analysis of new norms on transition days in blended families. *Sociology Mind, 10*. https://doi.org/10.4236/sm.2020.102005

Perry, L. M., Sartor, O., Malhotra, S., Alonzi, S., Kim, S., Voss, H. M., Rogers, J. L., Robinson, W., Harris, K., Shank, J., Morrison, D. G., Lewson, A. B., Fuloria, J., Miele, L., Lewis, B., Mossman, B., & Hoerger, M. (2021). Increasing readiness for early integrated palliative oncology care: Development and initial evaluation of the Empower 2 intervention. *Journal of Pain and Symptom Management, 62*, P987–P986. https://doi.org/10.1016/j.jpainsymman.2021.03.027

Perry, W. I. (1970). *Forms of intellectual and ethical development in the college years.* Holt, Rinehart & Winston.

Peter G. Peterson Foundation. (2022). *Budget basics: How does Social Security work?* https://www.pgpf.org/budget-basics/how-does-social-security-work

Peterson, B. E., & Stewart, A. J. (1996). Antecedents and contexts of generativity motivation at midlife. *Psychology and Aging, 11*, 21–33. https://doi.org/10.1037/0882-7974.11.1.21

Petro, N. M., Basyouni, R., & Neta, M. (2021). Positivity effect in aging: Evidence for the primacy of positive responses to emotional ambiguity. *Neurobiology of Aging, 106*, 232–240. https://doi.org/10.1016/j.neurobiolaging.2021.06.015

Pettersson, C. Malmqvist, I., Gromark, S., & Wijk, H. (2020). Enablers and barriers in the physical environment of care for older people in ordinary housing: A scoping review. *Journal of Aging and Environment, 34*, 332–350. https://doi.org/10.1080/02763893.2019.1683671

Pettinato, J. (2013). Financing long-term care. In A. E. McDonnell (Ed.), *Managing geriatric health services* (pp. 147–172). Jones & Bartlett Learning.

Pew Research Center. (2015). *Raising kids and running a household: How working parents share the load.* https://www.pewsocialtrends.org/2015/11/04/raising-kids-and-running-a-household-how-working-parents-share-the-load/

Pew Research Center. (2016). *Sharing chores a key to good marriage, say majority of married adults.* https://www.pewresearch.org/fact-tank/2016/11/30/sharing-chores-a-key-to-good-marriage-say-majority-of-married-adults/

Pew Research Center. (2018). *Defining generations: Where millennials end and Generation Z begins.* https://www.pewresearch.org/fact-tank/2019/01/17/where-millennials-end-and-generation-z-begins/

Pew Research Center. (2019a). *Marriage and cohabitation in the U.S.* https://www.pewsocialtrends.org/2019/11/06/marriage-and-cohabitation-in-the-u-s/

Pew Research Center. (2019b). *Among U.S. couples, women do more cooking and grocery shopping than men.* https://www.pewresearch.org/fact-tank/2019/09/24/among

-u-s-couples-women-do-more-cooking-and-grocery -shopping-than-men/
Pew Research Center. (2020). *As millennials near 40, they're approaching family life differently than previous generations*. https://www.pewresearch.org /social-trends/2020/05/27/as-millennials-near-40 -theyre-approaching-family-life-differently-than -previous-generations/
Pfaff, R., & Trentham, B. (2022). Rethinking home: Exploring older adults' occupational engagement in senior cohousing. *Journal of Occupational Science, 29*, 562–576. https://doi.org/10.1080/14427591.2020 .1821755
Pfeffer, C. A., Jones, K. B. (2020). Transgender-parent families. In A. Goldberg, & K. Allen (Eds.), *LGBTQ-parent families* (pp. 199–214). Springer, Cham. https://doi.org/10.1007/978-3-030-35610-1_12
Pfeiffer, E. (2013). *Winning strategies for successful aging*. Yale University Press.
Pfoff, M. K., Zarotney, J. R., & Monk, T. H. (2014). Can a function-based therapy for spousally bereaved seniors accrue benefits in both functional and emotional domains? *Death Studies, 38*, 381–386. https://doi.org /10.1080/07481187.2013.766658
Phan, H. P., Ngu, B. H., Chen, S. C., Wu, L., Lin, W.-W., & Hsu, C.-S. (2020). Introducing the study of life and death education to support the importance of positive psychology: An integrated model of philosophical beliefs, religious faith, and spirituality. *Frontiers in Psychology, 11*, 5801106. https://doi.org/10.3389 /fpsyg.2020.580186
Phillips, L. H., Slessor, G., Bailey, P. E., & Henry, J. D. (2014). Older adults' perception of social and emotional cues. In P. Verhaeghen & C. Hertzog (Eds.), *The Oxford handbook of emotion, social cognition, and problem solving in adulthood* (pp. 9–25). Oxford University Press.
Phillipson, C. (2020). Reconstructing work and retirement. *Annual Review of Gerontology and Geriatrics, 40*, 1–21. https://doi.org/10.1891/0198-8794.40.1
Physicians Foundation. (2020). *2020 Survey of America's physicians: COVID-19 impact edition*. https:// physiciansfoundation.org/wp-content /uploads/2020/08/20-1278-Merritt-Hawkins-2020 -Physicians-Foundation-Survey.6.pdf
Piaget, J. (1970). Piaget's theory. In P. H. Mussen (Ed.), *Carmichael's manual of child psychology* (3rd ed., Vol. 1, pp. 703–732). Wiley.
Piaget, J. (1972). Intellectual evolution from adolescence to adulthood. *Human Development, 15*, 1–12. https:// doi.org/10.1159/000271225
Piaget, J. (1980). *Les formes élémentaires de la dialectique*. Gallimard.
Piazza, J. R., Charles, S. T., & Luong, G. (2015). One size fits all? Applying theoretical predictions about age and emotional experiences to people with functional disabilities. *Psychology and Aging, 30*, 930–939. https:// doi.org/10.1037/pag0000045
Picchio, M., & van Ours, J. C. (2020). Mental health effects of retirement. *De Economist, 168*, 419–452. https://doi.org/10.1007/s10645-020-09369-8
Pickard, J. G., Witt, J-P. R., & Aitch, G. T. (2018) Resilience and faith of African American caregivers. In B. Resnick, L. Gwyther, & K. Roberto (Eds.), *Resilience in aging* (pp. 281–295). Springer, Cham. https://doi.org/10.1007/978-3-030-04555-5_15
Pickering, C. E. Z., & Phillips, L. R. (2014). Development of a causal model for elder mistreatment. *Public Health Nursing, 31*, 363–372. https://doi.org/10.1111 /phn.12108
Pienkowski, M. (2021). Loud music and leisure noise is a common cause of hearing loss, tinnitus and hyperacusis. *International Journal of Environmental Research and Public Health, 18*, 4236. https://doi .org/10.3390/ijerph18084236
Pignolo, R. J., Law, S. F., & Chandra, A. (2021). Bone aging, cellular senescence, and osteoporosis. *JMBR Plus, 5*, e10488. https://doi.org/10.1002/jbm4.10488
Pineda, A. M., Jr. (2020). *Parental divorce and its effects on the emerging adult*. Doctoral dissertation, Alliant International University. ProQuest Document 28093574.
Pineda-Pardo, J. A., Martinez, K., Román, F. J., & Colom, R. (2016). Structural efficiencies within a parieto-frontal network and cognitive differences. *Intelligence, 54*, 105–116. https://doi.org/10.1016/j .intell.2015.12.002
Pini, L., Pievani, M., Bocchetta, M., Altomare, D., Bosco, P., Cavedo, E., Galluzzi, S., Marizzoni, M., & Frisoni, G. B. (2016). Brain atrophy in Alzheimer's disease and aging. *Ageing Research Reviews, 30*, 25–48. https://doi .org/10.1016/j.arr.2016.01.002
Pinsker, J. (2020, July 3). The new boomerang kids could change American views of living at home. *The Atlantic*. https://www.theatlantic.com/family/archive/2020/07 /pandemic-young-adults-living-with-parents/613723/
Pinto, M., Camargo, C., Marrero, M., & Baumel, B. (2021). Stem cell therapy in Alzheimer's disease. In A. Birbrair (Ed.), *Recent advances in iPSCs for therapy* (Vol. 3, pp. 97–132). Academic Press. https://doi .org/10.1016/B978-0-12-822229-4.00008-5
Pioneer Network. (2021). *Our vision and mission*. https:// www.pioneernetwork.net/about-us /mission-vision-values/
Piquet, B. J. (2006). That's what friends are for. Doctoral dissertation, Alliant International University, San Diego. ProQuestLLC, Publication 3227678. https:// search.proquest.com/openview/ea487b4e262d2c783 6dd26061af6b1a8/1?pq-origsite=gscholar&cbl=187 50&diss=y.
Pitcho-Prelorentzos, S., & Mahat-Shamir, M. (2022). "Empty chairs at empty tables": Disenfranchisement by association. *OMEGA—Journal of Death and Dying, 84*, 998–1010. https://doi .org/10.1177/0030222820925365
Pitts, B. L., Smith, M. E., Newberry, K. M., & Bailey, H. R. (2022). Semantic knowledge attenuates age-related differences in event segmentation and episodic memory. *Memory and Cognition, 50*, 586–600. https:// doi.org/10.3758/s13421-021-01220-y
Pizzagalli, D. A., & Roberts, A. C. (2022). Prefrontal cortex and depression. *Neuropsychopharmacology 47*, 225–246. https://doi.org/10.1038 /s41386-021-01101-7
Platt, M. L., Seyfarth, R. M., & Cheyney, D. L. (2016). Adaptations for social cognition in the primate brain. *Philosophical Transactions of the Royal Society B, 371*. https://doi.org/10.1098/rstb.2015.0096
Plumm, K. M., Sommer, S., Uhl, C., & Stone, K. (2016). Single parent seeking single parent? The effects of parental and previous relationship status on perceptions of online dating profiles. *Journal of Relationships Research, 7*. https://doi/org/10.1017 /jrr.2016.10
Polivka, L. (2010). Neoliberalism and the new politics of aging and retirement security. In J. C. Cavanaugh & C. K. Cavanaugh (Eds.), *Aging in America: Vol. 3: Societal Issues* (pp. 161–202). ABC-CLIO.
Polivka, L., & Luo, B. (2015). The neoliberal political economy and erosion of retirement security. *The Gerontologist, 55*, 183–190. https://doi.org/10.1083 /geront/gnv006
Polivka, L., & Rill, L. (2016). Assisted living. In S. K. Whitbourne (Ed.), *Encyclopedia of adulthood and aging* (Vol. 1, pp. 90–95). Wiley-Blackwell. https://doi .org/10.1002/9781118521373.wbeaa109
Pollard, M. S., Tucker, J. S., & Green, H. D. (2020). Changes in adult alcohol use and consequences during the COVID-19 pandemic in the US. *JAMA Network Open, 3*, e2022942. https://10.1001 /jamanetworkopen.2020.22942
Pollini, A., Giacobone, G. A., & Zannoni, M. (2022). Aging and interaction: Designing for active living experiences. In S. Scataglini, S. Imbesi, & G. Marques (Eds.), *Internet of things for human-centered design* (pp. 39–61). Springer. https://doi .org/10.1007/978-981-16-8488-3_3
Pontzer, H. (2021). Metabolism myths. *NewScientist, 249*(3323), 32–36. https://doi.org/10.1016 /S0262-4079(21)00332-8
Pontzer, H., Yamada, Y., Sagayama, H., Ainslie, P. N., Andersen, L. F., Anderson, L. J., Arab, L., Baddou, I., Bedu-Addo, K., Blaak, E. E., Blanc, S., Bonomi, A. G., Bouten, C. V. C., Bovet, P., Buchowski, M. S., Butte, N. F., Camps, S. G., Close, G. L., Cooper, J. A., ... IAEA DLW Database Consortium. (2021). Daily energy expenditure through the human life course. *Science, 373*, 808–812. https://doi.org/10.1126 /science.abe5017
Popham, L. E., & Hess, T. M. (2016). Stereotype threat. In S. K. Whitbourne (Ed.), *The encyclopedia of adulthood and aging* (pp. 1354–1358). Wiley.
Population Reference Bureau. (2020). *The U.S. population is growing older, and the gender gap in life expectancy is narrowing*. https://www.prb.org/the-u-s-population-is -growing-older-and-the-gender-gap-in-life-expectancy -is-narrowing/
Porter, E., & Yaffe-Bellany, D. (2020, May 19). Facing adulthood with an economic disaster's lasting scars. *New York Times*. https://nyti.ms/2WLoF02
Porter, K. E., Brennan-Ing, M., Chang, S. C., dickey, l. m., Singh, A. A., Bower, K. L., & Witten, T. M. (2016). Providing competent and affirming services for transgender and gender nonconforming older adults. *Clinical Gerontologist, 39*, 366–388. https://doi.org/10 .1080/07317115.2016.1203383
Portnoy, A., Rana, P., Zimmerman, C., & Rodin, G. (2015). The use of palliative sedation to treat existential suffering: A reconsideration. In P. Taboada (Ed.), *Sedation at the end-of-life: An interdisciplinary approach* (pp. 41–54). Springer. https://doi .org/10.1007/978-94-017-9106-9_4
Powell, A. L., Hinger, C., Marshall-Lee, E. D., Miller-Roberts, T., & Phillips, K. (2021). Implementing coordinated specialty care for first episode psychosis: A review of barriers and solutions. *Community Mental Health Journal, 57*, 268–276. https://doi.org/10.1007 /s10597-020-00644-1
Power, M. C., Bennett, E. E., Turner, R. W., Dowling, N. M., Ciarleglio, A., Glymour, M. M., & Gianattasio, K. Z. (2021). Trends in relative incidence and prevalence of dementia across non-Hispanic black and white individuals in the United States, 2000–2016. *JAMA Neurology, 78*, 275–284. https://doi.org/10.1001 /jamaneurol.2020.4471
Power, T. L., & Smith, S. M. (2008). Predictors of fear of death and self-mortality: An Atlantic Canadian perspective. *Death Studies, 32*, 252–272. https://doi .org/10.1080/07481180701880935
Prebble, S. C., Addis, D. R., & Tippett, L. J. (2013). Autobiographical memory and sense of self. *Psychological Bulletin, 139*, 815–840. https://doi .org/10.1037/a0030146
Preston, A., & Padala, P. (2022). Virtual reality on the verge of becoming a reality for geriatric research. *International Psychogeriatrics, 34*, 97–99. https://doi .org/10.1017/S1041610221000867
Priaulx, N. (2013). The troubled identity of the bioethicist. *Health Care Analysis, 21*, 6–19. https://doi .org/10.1007/s10728-012-0229-9
Price, V. (2016). Women in non-traditional work fields. In N. A. Naples, R. C. Hoogland, M. Wickramasing, & W. C. A. Wong (Eds.), *The Wiley Blackwell encyclopedia of gender and sexuality studies*. Wiley. https://doi.org/10.1002/9781118663219.wbegss546
Prince-Paul, M., & Daly, B. J. (2016). Ethical considerations in palliative care. In N. Coyle (Ed.), *Legal and ethical aspects of care* (pp. 1–28). Oxford University Press.
Proctor, H. (2016). Personal construct psychology, society, and culture: A review. In D. A. Winter & N. Reed (Eds.), *The Wiley handbook of personal construct psychology* (pp. 139–153). Wiley.
Proulx, C. M. (2016). Marital trajectories. In S. K. Whitbourne (Ed.), *The encyclopedia of adulthood and aging* (pp. 842–845). Wiley.
Proulx, C. M., Ermer, A. E., & Kanter, J. B. (2017). Group-based trajectory modeling of marital quality: A critical review. *Journal of Family Theory and Review, 9*, 307–327. https://doi.org/10.1111/jftr.12201
Pruett, M. K., Insabella, G. M., & Gustafson, K. (2005). The collaborative divorce project: A court-based

intervention for separating parents with young children. *Family Court Review*, *43*, 38–51. https://doi.org/10.1111/j.1744-1617.2005.00006.x

Pynoos, J., Caraviello, R., & Cicero, C. (2010). Housing in an aging America. In J. C. Cavanaugh & C. K. Cavanaugh (Eds.), *Aging in America: Vol. 3: Societal issues* (pp. 129–159). Praeger Perspectives.

Pyrkov, T. V., Avchaciov, K., Tarkhov, A. E., Menshikov, L. I., Gudkov, A. V., & Fedichev, P. O. (2021). Longitudinal analysis of blood markers reveals progressive loss of resilience and predicts human lifespan limit. *Nature Communications*, *12*, 2765. https://doi.org/10.1038/s41467-021-23014-1

Qian, H., & Wu, H. (2022). Research progress on influencing factors of sense of control in the elderly and its effects on successful aging. In X. S. Yang, S. Sherratt, N. Dey, & A. Joshi. (Eds.), *Proceedings of Sixth International Congress on Information and Communication Technology* (pp. 953–960). Springer. https://doi.org/10.1007/978-981-16-2380-6_84

Queen, D., & Harding, K. (2020). Societal pandemic burnout: A COVID legacy. *International Wound Journal*, *17*, 873–874. https://doi.org/10.1111/iwj.13441

Quéniart, A., & Charpentier, M. (2013). Initiate, bequeath, and remember: Older women's transmission role within the family. *Journal of Women and Aging*, *25*, 45–65. https://doi.org/10.1080/08952841.2012.720181

Quinn, J. F., & Cahill, K. E. (2016). The new world of retirement income security in America. *American Psychologist*, *71*, 321–333. https://doi.org/10.1037/a0040276

Quirin, M., Loktyushin, A., Arndt, J., Küstermann, E., Lo, Y.-Y., Kuhl, J., & Eggert, L. (2012). Existential neuroscience: A functional magnetic resonance imaging investigation of neural responses to reminders of one's mortality. *Social Cognitive and Affective Neuroscience*, *7*, 193–198. https://doi.org/10.1093/scan/nsq106

Qureshi, I. (2022). Psychological and social implications of COVID-19. In A. I. Qureshi, O. Saeed, & U. Syed (Eds.), *Coronavirus disease: From origin to outbreak* (pp. 187–205). Academic Press. https://doi.org/10.1016/B978-0-12-824409-8.00003-5

Rab, S. L., & Admon, R. (2021). Parsing inter- and intra-individual variability in key nervous system mechanisms of stress responsivity and across functional domains. *Neuroscience and Biobehavioral Reviews*, *20*, 550–564. https://doi.org/10.1016/j.neubiorev.2020.09.007

Rabin, J. (2021). American national identity: Issues of race, culture, social class, gender and politics affected by social change. In J. D. Sinnott & J. S. Rabin (Eds.), *The psychology of political behavior in a time of change: Identity in a changing world* (pp. 385–421). Springer Cham.

Rachels, J. A. (1975). Active and passive euthanasia. *New England Journal of Medicine*, *292*, 78–80. https://doi.org/10.1056/NEJM197501092920206

Radloff, L. S. (1977). The CES-D scale: A self-report depression scale for research in the general population. *Applied Psychological Measurement*, *1*, 385–401. https://doi.org/10.1177/014662167700100306

Radvansky, G. A. (2021). *Human memory* (4th ed.). Routledge.

Rai, S. N., Singh, P., Steinbusch, H. W. M., Vamanu, E., Ashraf, G., & Singh, M. P. (2021). The role of vitamins in neurogenerative disease: An update. *Biomedicine*, *9*, 1284. https://doi.org/10.3390/biomedicines9101284

Rainie, L. (2020). *American life in the midst of crisis: How people are using technology as their lives are upended.* https://www.pewresearch.org/internet/2020/11/13/american-life-in-the-midst-of-crisis-how-people-are-using-technology-as-their-lives-are-upended/

Rajan, K. B., Weuve, J., Barnes, L. L., McAninch, E. A., Wilson, R. S., & Evans, D. A. (2021). Population estimate of people with clinical Alzheimer's disease and mild cognitive impairment in the United States (2020–2060). *Alzheimer's and Dementia*, *17*, 1966–1975. https://doi.org/10.1002/alz.12362

Raji, C. A., Merrill, D. A., Eyre, H., Mallam, S., Torosyan, N., Erickson, K. I., Lopez, O. L., Becker, J. T., Carmichael, O. T., Gach, H. M., Thompson, P. M., Longstreth, Jr., W. T., & Kuller, L. H. (2016). Longitudinal relationships between caloric expenditure and gray matter in the Cardiovascular Health Study. *Journal of Alzheimer's Disease*, *52*, 719–729. https://doi.org/10.3233/JAD-160057

Rajput, K. (2022). *A psychiatrist explains common treatment options including medication and therapy for people who are depressed.* https://www.psycom.net/depression/depression-treatment

Ramani, S., Thampy, H., McKimm, J., Rogers, G. D., Hays, R., Kusurkar, R. A., Schumacher, D. J., Kachur, E. K., Fornari, A., Chisolm, M. S., Filipe, H. P., Turner, T. L., & Wilson, K. W. (2020). Twelve tips for organising speed mentoring events for healthcare professionals at small or large-scale venues. *Medical Teacher*, *42*, 1322–1329. https://doi.org/10.1080/0142159X.2020.1737323

Ramos, K., & Stanley, M. A. (2018). Anxiety disorders in late life. *Psychiatric Clinics*, *41*, 55–64. https://doi.org/10.1016/j.psc.2017.10.005

Ramos-Zúñiga, R. (2015). Challenge of the translational neuroscience. *World Journal of Neurology*, *5*, 102–106. https://doi.org/10.5316/wjn.v5.i4.102

Randall, A. K., & Bodenmann, G. (2017). Stress and its associations with relationship satisfaction. *Current Opinion in Psychology*, *13*, 96–106. https://doi.org/10.1016/j.copsyc.2016.05.010

Rango, M., & Bresolin, N. (2018). Brain mitochondria, aging, and Parkinson's disease. *Genes*, *9*, 250. https://doi.org/10.3390/genes9050250

Ransdell, L. B., Lane, T. S., Schwartz, A. S., Wayment, H. A., & Baldwin, J. A. (2021). Mentoring new and early-stage investigators and underrepresented minority faculty for research success in health-related fields: An integrative literature review (2010–2020). *International Journal of Environmental Research and Public Health*, *18*, 432. https://doi.org/10.3390/ijerph18020432

Ranzini, L., Schiavi, M., Pierobon, A., Granata, N., & Giardini, A. (2020). From mild cognitive impairment (MCI) to dementia in chronic obstructive pulmonary disease. Implications for clinical practice and disease management: A mini-review. *Frontiers in Psychology*, *11*. https://doi.org/10.3389/fpsyg.2020.00337

Rappaport, A. M. (2021). Retirement risks and planning: What did COVID-19 teach us? *Benefits Quarterly*, *37*, 23–35. https://www.proquest.com/docview/2489775308?pq-origsite=gscholar&fromopenview=true

Rasheed, A., Amr, A., & Fahad, N. (2021). Investigating the relationship between emotional divorce, marital expectations, and self-efficacy among wives in Saudi Arabia. *Journal of Divorce & Remarriage*, *62*, 19–40. https://doi.org/10.1080/10502556.2020.1833290

Rashmi, K., Kataria, A., & Singh, R. (2021). Work–life balance: A review and future research agenda. *Prabandhan: Indian Journal of Management*, *14*, 8–25. https://doi.org/10.17010/pijom%2F2021%2Fv14i2%2F157690

Rattan, S. I. S. (2020). Biological health and homeodynamic space. In J. Sholl, & S. I. S. Rattan (Eds,), *Explaining health across the sciences: Healthy ageing and longevity* (Vol. 12, pp. 43–51). Springer, Cham. https://doi.org/10.1007/978-3-030-52663-4_4

Rauer, A. J., & Proulx, C. M. (2020). A social perspective on couples across the lifespan: Challenges and opportunities. *Research in Human Development*, *17*, 191–194. https://doi.org/10.1080/15427609.2021.1878000

Razgonova, M. P., Zakharenko, A. M., Golokhvast, K. S., Thanasoula, M., Sarandi, E., Nikolouzakis, K., Fragkiadaki, P., Tsoukalas, D., Spandidos, D. A., & Tsatsakis, A. (2020). Telomerase and telomeres in aging theory and chronographic aging theory (Review). *Molecular Medicine Reports*, *22*, 1679–1694. https://doi.org/10.3892/mmr.2020.11274

Readhead, A., & Owen, F. (2020). Employment supports and outcomes for persons with intellectual and/or developmental disabilities: A review of recent findings. *Current Developmental Disorders Report 7*, 155–162. https://doi.org/10.1007/s40474-020-00202-0

Ready, R. E., Carvalho, J. O., & Åkerstedt, A. M. (2012). Evaluative organization of the self-concept in younger, midlife, and older adults. *Research on Aging*, *34*, 56–79. https://doi.org/10.1177/0164027511415244

Rebok, G., W., Ball, K., Guey, L. T., Jones, R. N., Kim, H.-Y., King, J. W., Marsiske, M., Morris, J. N., Tennstedt, S. L., Unverzagt, F. W., & Willis, S. W. (2014). Ten-year effects of the ACTIVE cognitive training trial on cognition and everyday functioning in older adults. *Journal of the American Geriatrics Society*, *62*, 16–24. https://doi.org/10.1111/jgs.12607

Recovered.org. (2022). *Alcohol and drug abuse in seniors*. https://recovered.org/addiction/alcohol-and-drug-abuse-in-seniors

Redzanowski, U., & Glück, J. (2013). Who knows who is wise? Self and peer ratings of wisdom. *Journals of Gerontology: Psychological Sciences*, *68*, 391–394. https://doi.org/10.1093/geronb/gbs079

Reed, A. E., & Carstensen, L. L. (2012). The theory behind the age-related positivity effect. *Frontiers in Psychology*. https://doi.org/10.3389/fpsyg.2012.00339

Reed, R. G., & Raison, C. L. (2016). Stress and the immune system. In C. Esser (Ed.), *Environmental influences on the immune system* (pp. 97–126). Springer. https://doi.org/10.1007/978-3-7091-1890-0_5

Reese-Melancon, C., Cherry, K. E., & Harrington, E. E. (2021). The knowledge of memory aging questionnaire. In C. R. Martin, V. R. Preedy, & Rajendram, R. (Eds.), *Assessments, treatments and modeling in aging and neurological disease: The neuroscience of aging* (pp. 329–339). Academic Press. https://doi.org/10.1016/B978-0-12-818000-6.00030-5

Remedios, J. D., Chasteen, A. L., & Packer, D. J. (2010). Sunny side up: The reliance on positive age stereotypes in descriptions of future older selves. *Self and Identity*, *9*, 257–275. https://doi.org/10.1080/15298860903054175

Rentfrow, P. J., & Jokela, M. (2016). Geographical psychology: The spatial organization of psychological phenomena. *Current Directions in Psychological Science*, *25*, 393–398. https://doi.org/10.1177/0963721416658446

Repetti, R., & Wang, S-w. (2017). Effects of job stress on family relationships. *Current Opinion in Psychology*, *13*, 15–18. https://doi.org/10.1016/j.copsyc.2016.03.010

Requero, B., Santos, D., Paredes, B., Briñol, P., & Petty, R. E. (2020). Attitudes toward hiring people with disabilities: A meta-cognitive approach to persuasion. *Journal of Applied Social Psychology*, *50*, 276–288. https://doi.org/10.1111/jasp.12658

Reuter-Lorenz, P. A. (2002). New visions of the aging mind and brain. *Trends in Cognitive Sciences*, *6*(9), 394–400. https://doi.org/10.1016/S1364-6613(02)01957-5

Reuter-Lorenz, P. A., & Cappell, K. A. (2008). Neurocognitive aging and the compensation hypothesis. *Current Directions in Psychological Science*, *17*, 177–182. https://doi.org/10.1111/j.1467-8721.2008.00570.x

Reuter-Lorenz, P. A., & Mikels, J. A. (2006). The aging mind and brain: Implications of enduring plasticity for behavioral and cultural change. In P. B. Baltes, P. A. Reuter-Lorenz, & F. Rösler (Eds.), *Lifespan development and the brain: The perspective of biocultural co-constructivism* (pp. 255–276). Cambridge University Press.

Reuter-Lorenz, P. A., & Park, D. C. (2014). How does it STAC up? Revisiting the scaffolding theory of aging and cognition. *Neuropsychology Review*, *24*, 355–370. https://doi.org/10.1007/s11065-014-9270-9

Reuter-Lorenz, P. A., Festini, S. B., & Jantz, T. K. (2021). Executive functions and neurocognitive aging. In K. W. Chaie & S. L. Willis (Eds.), *Handbook of the psychology of aging* (9th ed., pp. 67–81). Academic Press. https://doi.org/10.1016/B978-0-12-816094-7.00019-2

Revenson, T. A., Griva, K., Luszczynska, A., Morrison, V., Panagopoulou, E., Vilchinsky, N., & Hagedoorn, M. (2016). *Caregiving in the illness context*. Palgrave Macmillan.

Revet, A., Bui, E., Benvegnu, G., Suc, A., Mesquida, L., & Raynaud, J.-P. (2020). Bereavement and reactions of grief among children and adolescents: Present data and perspectives. *L'Encéphale*, *46*, 356–363. https://doi.org/10.1016/j.encep.2020.05.007

Reynard, L. N., & Barter, M. J. (2020). Osteoarthritis year in review 2019: Genetics, genomics and epigenetics. *Osteoarthritis and Cartilage*, *28*, 275–284. https://doi.org/10.1016/j.joca.2019.11.010

Reynolds, J. M., & Wieseler, C. (Eds.). (2022). *The disability bioethics reader*. Routledge.

Reynolds, L. (2020). *Ten years of change in remarriage*. https://www.bgsu.edu/ncfmr/resources/data/family-profiles/reynolds-ten-years-change-remarriage-fp-20-20.html

Richard, C., Glaser, E. & Lussier, M.-T. (2017). Communication and patient participation influencing patient recall of treatment discussions. *Health Expectations*, *20*, 760–770. https://doi.org/10.1111/hex.12515

Rickard, A. P., Chatfield, M. D., Powell, J. J., Stephen, A. M., & Richards, M. (2012). Dietary iron is associated with memory in midlife: Longitudinal cohort study. *Journal of Pharmacy and Nutritional Sciences*, *2*, 57–62. http://www.lifescienceglobal.com/pms/index.php/jpans/article/view/238

Rieck, J. R., Baracchini, G., Nichol, D., Abdi, H., & Grady, C. L. (2021). Reconfiguration and dedifferentiation of functional networks during cognitive control across the adult lifespan. *Neurobiology of Aging*, *106*, 80–94. https://doi.org/10.1016/j.neurobiolaging.2021.03.019

Riediger, M., Freund, A. M., & Baltes, P. B. (2005). Managing life through personal goals: Intergoal facilitation and intensity of goal pursuit in younger and older adulthood. *Journals of Gerontology: Psychological Sciences*, *60B*, P84–P91. https://doi.org/10.1093/geronb/60.2.P84

Rienäcker, F., Jacobs, H. I. L., Van Heugten, C. M., & Van Gerven, P. W. M. (2018). Practice makes perfect: High performance gains in older adults engaged in selective attention within and across sensory modalities. *Acta Psychologica*, *191*, 101–111. https://doi.org/10.1016/j.actpsy.2018.09.005

Rigby, E. (2021). The COVID-19 economy, unemployment insurance, and population health. *JAMA Network Open*, *4*, e2035955. https://doi.org/10.1001/jamanetworkopen.2020.35955

Rigolini, A., Gabaldon, P., & Goldeng, G. B. (2021). CEO succession with gender change in troubled companies: The effect of a new woman CEO on firm risk and firm risk perceived. *Scandinavian Journal of Management*, *37*, Article 101138. https://doi.org/10.1016/j.scaman.2020.101138

Rijken, A. J. (2009). *Happy families, high fertility?: Childbearing choices in the context of family and partner relationships*. Dissertation submitted in partial fulfillment of the Doctor of Philosophy degree, University of Utrecht.

Rijken, A. J., & Knijn, T. (2009). Couples' decisions to have a first child: Comparing pathways to early and late parenthood. *Demographic Research*, *21*, 765–802. https://doi.org/10.4054/DemRes.2009.21.26

Riley, G. (2020). *Unschooling*. Palgrave Macmillan, Cham. https://doi.org/10.1007/978-3-030-49292-2_4.

Rinnan, E., André, B., Espnes, G. A., Drageset, J., Garåsen, H., & Haugan, G. (2022). Despite symptom severity, do nursing home residents experience joy-of-life? The associations between joy-of-life and symptom severity in Norwegian nursing home residents. *Journal of Holistic Nursing*, *40*, 84–96. https://doi.org/10.1177/08980101211021219

Ripp, J., Jones, E., & Zhang, M. (2016). Common functional problems. In J. L. Hayashi & B. Leff (Eds.), *Geriatric home-based medical care* (pp. 151–172). Springer. https://doi.org/10.1007/978-3-319-23365-9_8

Rippe, J. M. (2019). *Lifestyle medicine* (3rd ed.). CRC Press.

Rivera-Hernandez, M., Kumar, A., Epstein-Lubow, G., & Thomas, K. S. (2019). Disparities in nursing home use and quality among African American, Hispanic, and White Medicare residents with Alzheimer's disease and related dementias. *Journal of Aging and Health*, *31*, 1259–1277. https://doi.org/10.1177%2F0898264318767778

Rizzolo, L., Narbutas, J., Van Egroo, M., Chylinski, D., Besson, G., Baillet, M., Bahri, M. A., Salmon, E., Maquet, P., Vandewalle, G., Bastin, C., & Collette, F. (2021). Relationship between brain AD biomarkers and episodic memory performance in healthy aging. *Brain and Cognition*, *148*, 10568. https://doi.org/10.1016/j.bandc.2020.105680

Robb, A. (2014). Shirley Temple only dated her husband for 12 days. *The New Republic*. https://newrepublic.com/article/116571/unless-youre-shirley-temple-longer-courtship-means-happier-marriage

Robbins, B. D. (2015). Building bridges between humanistic and positive psychology. In S. Joseph (Ed.), *Positive psychology in practice: Promoting human flourishing in work, health, education, and everyday life* (pp. 31–46). Wiley.

Roberto, K. A., & Skoglund, R. R. (1996). Interactions with grandparents and great-grandparents: A comparison of activities, influences, and relationships. *International Journal of Aging & Human Development*, *43*, 107–117. https://doi.org/10.2190/8F1D-9A4D-h)QY-W9DD

Roberts, B. W., & DelVecchio, W. F. (2000). The rank-order consistency of personality traits from childhood to old age: A quantitative review of longitudinal studies. *Psychological Bulletin*, *126*, 3–25. https://doi.org/10.1037/0033-2909.126.1.3

Roberts, B. W., Walton, K., Bogg, T., & Caspi, A. (2006). De-investment in work and non-normative personality trait change in young adulthood. *European Journal of Personality*, *20*, 461–474. https://doi.org/10.1002/per.607

Robinaugh, D. J., & McNally, R. J. (2013). Remembering the past and envisioning the future in bereaved adults with and without complicated grief. *Clinical Psychological Science*, *1*, 290–300. https://doi.org/10.1177/2167702613476027

Robinson-Wood, T., & Weber, A. (2016). Deconstructing multiple oppressions among LGBT older adults. In D. A. Harley & P. B. Teaster (Eds.), *Handbook of LGBT elders* (pp. 65–81). Springer.

Roca, M. (2016). The relationship between executive functions and theory of mind: A long and winding road. *Journal of Neurology, Neurosurgery & Psychiatry*, *87*, 229. http://doi.org/10.1136/jnnp-2015-312568

Rodin, J., & Langer, E. J. (1977). Long-term effects of a control-relevant intervention with the institutionalized aged. *Journal of Personality and Social Psychology*, *35*, 897–902. https://psycnet.apa.org/doi/10.1037/0022-3514.35.12.897

Rodrigues, P., Crokaert, J., & Gastmans, C. (2018). Palliative sedation for existential suffering: A systematic review of argument-based ethics literature. *Journal of Pain and Symptom Management*, *55*, 1577–1590. https://doi.org/10.1016/j.jpainsymman.2018.01.013

Rodriguez, J. J., Noristani, H. N., & Verkhratsky, A. (2012). The serotonergic system in ageing and Alzheimer's disease. *Progress in Neurobiology*, *99*, 15–41. https://doi.org/10.1016/j.pneurobio.2012.06.010

Rodriguez-Galán, M. B. (2014). The ethnography of ethnic minority families and aging: Familism and beyond. In K. E. Whitfield & T. A. Baker (Eds.), *Handbook of minority aging* (pp. 435–453). Springer.

Rogoza, R., & Cieciuch, J. (2018). Dark Triad traits and their structure: An empirical approach. *Current Psychology*, *39*, 1287–1302. https://doi.org/10.1007/s12144-018-9834-6

Rogoza, R., & Cieciuch, J. (2020). Dark Triad traits and their structure: An empirical approach. *Current Psychology*, *39*, 1287–1302. https://doi.org/10.1007/s12144-018-9834-6

Roheger, M., Folkerts, A.-K., Krohm, F., Skoetz, N., & Kalbe, E. (2021). Prognostic models for changes in memory performance after memory training in healthy older adults: A systematic review. *Journal of Cognitive Enhancement*, *5*, 372–385. https://doi.org/10.1007/s41465-020-00194-0

Rohr, R., OFM. (2011). *Falling upward: A spirituality for the two halves of life*. Jossey-Bass.

Rohr, R., OFM. (2013). *Immortal diamond: The search for our true self*. Jossey-Bass.

Roigk, P., & Graeb, F. (2021). Malnutrition prevention. In Ó. G. Geirsdóttir & J. J. Bell (Eds.), *Interdisciplinary nutritional management and care for older adults: Perspectives in nursing management and care for older adults* (pp. 51–64). Springer, Cham. https://doi.org/10.1007/978-3-030-63892-4_4

Romano, M., Ma, R., Moscovitch, M., & Moscovitch, D. A. (2020). Autobiographical memory bias. In J. S. Abramowitz & S. M. Blakey (Eds.), *Clinical handbook of fear and anxiety: Maintenance processes and treatment mechanisms* (pp. 183–202). American Psychological Association. https://doi.org/10.1037/0000150-011

Romero-Ayuso, D., Castillero-Perea, Á., González, P., Navarro, E., Molina-Massó, J. P., Funes, M. J., Ariza-Vega, P., Toledano-González, A., & Triviño-Juárez, J. M. (2021). Assessment of cognitive instrumental activities of daily living: A systematic review. *Disability and Rehabilitation*, *43*, 1342–1358. https://doi.org/10.1080/09638288.2019.1665720

Roodenrys, S. (2021). Nutritional interventions to improve cognitive function. In M. Hall, M. Forshaw, & C. Montgomery. (Eds.), *Chemically modified minds* (pp. 59–79). Palgrave Macmillan. https://doi.org/10.1007/978-981-15-6771-1_4

Rosati, F., Pistella, J., Giovanardi, G., & Baiocco, R. (2021). Queer generativity in lesbian, gay, and bisexual older adults: Personal, relational, and political/social behaviours. *Journal of Community & Applied Social Psychology*, *31*, 673–689. https://doi.org/10.1002/casp.2529

Rosenblatt, P. C. (1996). Grief that does not end. In D. Klass, P. R. Silverman, & S. L. Nickman (Eds.), *Continuing bonds: New understandings of grief* (pp. 45–58). Taylor & Francis.

Rosenblatt, P. C. (2020). Challenges to cultural outsiders from the culture of grief counseling/therapy. *Journal of Loss and Trauma*, *25*, 207–223. https://doi.org/10.1080/15325024.2019.1672936

Rosenfield, M. J., Thomas, R. J., & Hausen, S. (2019). Disintermediating your friends: How online dating in the United States displaces other ways of meeting. *PNAS*, *116*, 17753–17758. https://doi.org/10.1073/pnas.1908630116

Rosenfield, S., & Mouzon, D. (2013). Gender and mental health. In C. S. Aneshensel, J. C. Phelan, & A. Bieman (Eds.), *Handbook of the sociology of mental health* (pp. 277–296). Springer.

Rosner, E. (2020, September 1). *US divorce rates skyrocket amid COVID-19 pandemic*. https://nypost.com/2020/09/01/divorce-rates-skyrocket-in-u-s-amid-covid-19/

Rostila, M., Saarela, J., Kawachi, I., & Hjern, A. (2015). Testing the anniversary reaction: Causal effects of bereavement in a nationwide follow-up study from Sweden. *Psychiatric Epidemiology*, *30*, 239–247. https://doi.org/10.1007/s10654-015-9989-5

Roszko, E. (2010). Commemoration and the state: Memory and legitimacy in Vietnam. *Sojourn: Journal of Social Issues in Southeast Asia*, *25*, 1–28. https://doi.org/10.1353/soj.0.0041

Rowe, B., & Harman, B. A. (2014). Motherless mothers: Maternally bereaved women in their everyday roles as mothers. *Journal of Family Studies*, *20*, 28–38. https://doi.org/10.5172/jfs.2014.20.1.28

Rowles, G. D. (2006). Commentary: A house is not a home: But can it become one? In H.-W. Wahl, H. Brenner, Mollenkopf, H., Rothenbacher, D., & Rott, C. (Eds.), *The many faces of health, competence and well-being in old age* (pp. 25–32). Springer.

Rowles, G. D. (2018). Being in place: Identity and place attachment in late life. In M. Skinner, G. Andrews, & M. Cutchin (Eds.), *Geographical gerontology: Concepts and approaches* (pp. 203–215). Routledge.

Rowles, G. D., & Watkins, J. F. (2003). History, habit, heart, and hearth: On making spaces into places. In K. W. Schaie, H.-W. Wahl, H. Mollenkopf, & F. Oswald (Eds.), *Aging independently: Living arrangements and mobility* (pp. 77–96). Springer.

Rowson, B., & Duma, S. M. (2021). Special issue on concussions in sports. *Annals of Biomedical Engineering, 49*, 2673–2676. https://doi.org/10.1007/s10439-021-02847-3

Roxburgh, S. (2002). Racing through life. The distribution of time pressures by roles and roles resources among full-time workers. *Journal of Family and Economic Issues, 23*, 121–145. https://doi.org/10.1023/A:1015734516575

Rozin, P., & Royzman, E. B. (2001). Negativity bias, negativity dominance, and contagion. *Personality and Social Psychology Review, 5*, 296–320. https://doi.org/10.1207/S15327957PSPR0504_2

Rubin, S. S., & Malkinson, R. (2001). Parental response to child loss across the life cycle: Clinical and research perspectives. In M. S. Stroebe, R. O. Hansson, W. Stroebe, & H. Schut (Eds.), *Handbook of bereavement research: Consequences, coping, and care* (pp. 169–197). American Psychological Association.

Rubio, J., Dumitrache, C., Cordon-Pozo, E., & Rubio-Herrara, R. (2016). Coping: Impact of gender and stressful life events in middle and old age. *Clinical Gerontologist, 39*, 468–488. https://doi.org/10.1080/07317115.2015.1132290

Rudy, J. W. (2020). *The neurobiology of learning and memory*. Oxford University Press.

Ruiz, M. E., Phillips, L. R., Kim, H., & Woods, D. L. (2016). Older Latinos: Applying the ethnocultural gerontological nursing model. *Journal of Transcultural Nursing, 27*, 8–17. https://doi.org/10.1177/1043695615569539

Runco, M. A., & Beghetto, R. A. (2019). Primary and secondary creativity. *Current Opinion in Behavioral Sciences, 27*, 7–10. https://doi.org/10.1016/j.cobeha.2018.08.011

Ruppanner, L., & Maume, D. J. (2016). Shorter work hours and work-to-family interference: Surprising findings from 32 countries. *Social Forces, 95*, 693–720. https://doi.org/10.1093/sf/sow057

Ruscin, J. M., & Linnebur, S. A. (2021). Pharmacokinetics in older adults. In *Merck manual for the professional*. https://www.merckmanuals.com/professional/geriatrics/drug-therapy-in-older-adults/pharmacokinetics-in-older-adults

Russell, C. (2022). Meeting the moment: Bioethics in the time of Black Lives Matter. *The American Journal of Bioethics, 22*, 9–21. https://doi.org/10.1080/15265161.2021.2001093

Russell, J. A., Epstein, L. G., Greer, D. M., Kirschen, M., Rubin, M. A., & Lewis, A. (2019). Brain death, the determination of brain death, and member guidance for brain death accommodation requests: AAN position statement. *Neurology, 92*, 228–232. https://doi.org/10.1212/WNL.0000000000006750

Rutherford, A., Markopoulos, G., Bruno, D., & Brady-Van den Bos, M. (2012). Long-term memory: Encoding to retrieval. In N. Braisby & A. Gellatly (Eds.), *Cognitive psychology* (pp. 229–265). Oxford University Press.

Ryan, E. B., Giles, H., Bartolucci, G., & Henwood, K. (1986). Psycholinguistic and social psychological components of communication by and with the elderly. *Language and Communication, 6*, 1–24. https://doi.org/10.1016/0271-5309(86)90002-9

Ryan, E. B., Meredith, S. D., MacLean, M. J., & Orange, J. B. (1995). Changing the way we talk with elders: Promoting health using the communication enhancement model. *International Journal of Aging and Human Development, 41*, 89–107. https://doi.org/10.2190/FP05-FM8V-0Y9F-53FX

Ryan, L. (2021). Accessing community dementia care services in Ireland: Emotional barriers for caregivers. *Health and Social Care in the Community, 29*, 1980–1989. https://doi.org/10.1111/hsc.13342

Ryan, M. K., Haslam, S. A., & Kulich, C. (2010). Politics and the glass cliff: Evidence that women are preferentially selected to contest hard-to-win seats. *Psychology of Women Quarterly, 34*, 56–64. https://doi.org/10.1111/j.1471-6402.2009.01541.x

Ryan, M. K., Haslam, S. A., Morgenroth, T., Rink, F., Stoker, J., & Peters, K. (2016). Getting on top of the glass cliff: Reviewing a decade of evidence, explanations, and impact. *The Leadership Quarterly, 27*, 446–455. https://doi.org/10.1016/j.leaqua.2015.10.008

Saadi, A., Hampton, K., de Assis, M. V., Mishori, R., Habbach, H., & Haar, R. J. (2021). Associations between memory loss and trauma in US asylum seekers: A retrospective review of medico-legal affidavits. *PLoS One, 16*, e0247033. https://doi.org/10.1371/journal.pone.0247033

Sacks, O. (2015, February 19). My own life: Oliver Sacks on learning he has terminal cancer. *New York Times*, A25. www.nytimes.com/2015/02/19/opinion/oliver-sacks-on-learning-he-has-terminal-cancer.html?_r=0.

Sadeghi, H., Jehu, D. A., Daneshjoo, A., Shakoor, E., Razeghi, M., Amani, A., Hakim, M. N., & Yusof, A. (2021). Effects of 8 weeks of balance training, virtual reality training, and combined exercise on lower limb muscle strength, balance, and functional mobility among older men: A randomized controlled trial. *Sports Health, 13*, 606–612. https://doi.org/10.1177/1941738120986803

Sadeh, T., Dang, C., Gat-Lazer, S., & Moscovitch, M. (2020). Recalling the firedog: Individual differences in associative memory for unitized and nonunitized associations among older adults. *Hippocampus, 30*, 130–142. https://doi.org/10.1002/hipo.23142

Sadeh, T., Ozubko, J. D., Winocur, G., & Moscovitch, M. (2014). How we forget may depend on how we remember. *Trends in Cognitive Sciences, 18*, 26–36. https://doi.org/10.1016/j.tics.2013.10.008

Sadler, K., Abudari, G., Aljawi, D., & Snelling, D. (2020). Deaths in the emergency department: An assessment of patient's end-of-life trajectory and quality of care. *Indian Journal of Palliative Care, 26*, 352-357. https://doi.org/10.4103/IJPC.IJPC_206_19

Sajjad, F., Shahid, R., Ahmed, M., Saleh, Z., Dr, A., Ali, S., Akmal, M., & Khan, K., (2020). Brain death Islamic perspective. *Pakistan Journal of Neurological Surgery, 24*, 2–7. http://www.pakjns.org/index.php/pjns/article/view/395/412

Sakraida, T. J. (2005). Divorce transition differences of midlife women. *Issues in Mental Health Nursing, 26*, 225–249. https://doi.org/10.1080/01612840590901699

Sala Frigerio, C., & De Strooper, B. (2016). Alzheimer's disease mechanisms and emerging roads to novel therapeutics. *Annual Review of Neuroscience, 39*, 57–79. https://doi.org/10.1146/annurev-neuro-070815-014015

Salmond, S., & Allread, V. (2019). A population health approach to America's opioid epidemic. *Orthopaedic Nursing, 38*, 95–108. https://doi.org/10.1097/NOR.0000000000000521

Salovey, P., & Mayer, J. D. (1990). Emotional intelligence. *Imagination, Cognition, and Personality, 9*, 185–211. https://doi.org/10.2190/DUGG-P24E-52WK-6CDG

Salter, M., & Blizard, R. (2022). False memories and the science of credibility: Who gets to be heard? *Journal of Trauma & Dissociation, 23*, 141-147. https://doi.org/10.1080/15299732.2022.2028219

Salthouse, T. A. (1996). The processing speed theory of adult age differences in cognition. *Psychological Review, 103*, 403–428. https://doi.org/10.1037/0033-295X.103.3.403

Salthouse, T. A. (2014). Why are there different age relations in cross-sectional and longitudinal comparisons of cognitive functioning? *Current Directions in Psychological Science, 23*, 252–256. https://doi.org/10.1177/0963721414535212

Salthouse, T. A. (2019). Trajectories of normal cognitive aging. *Psychology and Aging, 34*, 17–24. https://doi.org/10.1037/pag0000288

Salthouse, T. A. (2021). Individual differences in working memory and aging. In J. Rummel (Ed.), *Current issues in memory: Memory research in the public interest*. Routledge. https://doi.org/10.4324/9781003106715

Samanta, T. (2021). Hymen interrupted: Negotiating body, markets, and consumerist modernity in India. *Indian Journal of Medical Ethics, 6*, 1–14. https://doi.org/10.20529/ijme.2021.001

Samarina, V., Suresh, M., Picchiello, M., Lutz, J., Carpenter, B. D., & Beaudreau, S. A. (2021). Assessment approaches for psychiatric and cognitive syndromes. In N. A. Prachana, V. Molinari, L. W. Thompson, & D. Gallagher-Thompson (Eds.), *Psychological assessment and treatment of older adults* (pp. 13–42). Hogrefe.

Same, A., McBride, H., Liddelow, C., Mullan, B., & Harris, C. (2020). Motivations for volunteering time with older adults: A qualitative study. *PLoS ONE, 15*, e0232718. https://doi.org/10.1371/journal.pone.0232718

Samii, C., & West, E. (2021). Repressed productive potential and revolt: Insights from an insurgency in Burundi. *Political Science Research and Methods, 9*, 106–121. https://doi.org/10.1017/psrm.2019.28

Sanchez, D. T., Gaither, S. E., Albuja, A. F., & Eddy, Z. (2020). How policies can address multiracial stigma. *Policy Insights from the Brain and Behavioral Sciences, 7*, 115–122. https://doi.org/10.1177%2F2372732220943906

Sanchez, M., Hidalgo, B., Rosario, A., Artiles, L., Stewart, A. L., & Nápoles, A. M. (2021). Applying self-report measures in minority health and health disparities research. In I. Dankwa-Mullan, E. J. Pérez-Stable, K. L. Gardner, X. Zhang, and A. M. Rosario (Eds.), *The science of health disparities research* (pp. 153–169). Wiley. https://doi.org/10.1002/9781119374855.ch10

Sánchez-González, D., & Rodríguez-Rodríguez, V. (2016). Introduction to environmental gerontology in Latin America and Europe. In D. Sánchez-González & V. Rodríguez-Rodríguez (Eds.), *Environmental gerontology in Latin America and Europe* (pp. 1–7). Springer. https://doi.org/10.1007/978-3-319-21419-1_1

Sánchez-González, D., Rojo-Pérez, F., Rodríguez-Rodríguez, V., & Fernández-Mayoralas, G. (2020). Environmental and psychosocial interventions in age-friendly communities and active ageing: A systematic review. *International Journal of Environmental Research and Public Health, 17*, 8305. https://doi.org/10.3390/ijerph17228305

Sandalu, A. (2020). *How do COVID-19 vaccines compare with other existing vaccines?* https://www.medicalnewstoday.com/articles/how-do-covid-19-vaccines-compare-with-other-existing-vaccines

Sandler, I. N., Wolchik, S. A. Ayers, T. S., Tein, J.-Y., & Luecken, L. (2013). Family bereavement program (FBP) approach to promoting resilience following the death of a parent. *Family Science, 4*, 87–94. https://doi.org/10.1080/19424620.2013.821763

Sandler, I. N., Wolchik, S. A., & Ayers, T. S. (2007). Resilience rather than recovery: A contextual framework on adaptation following bereavement. *Death Studies, 32*, 59–73. https://doi.org/10.1080/07481180701741343

Sano, E., Benton, E., Kenny, J., Olsen, E., Heravian, A., & Truong, J. (2022). Telemedicine use by older adults in a COVID-19 epicenter. *Journal of Emergency Medicine*. https://doi.org/10.1016/j.jemermed.2022.01.024

Santaella, D. F. (2021). Neurobiology of meditation. In S. Telles & R. K. Gupta (Eds.), *Handbook of research on evidence-based perspectives on the psychophysiology of yoga and its applications* (pp. 61–71). IGI Global. https://doi.org/10.4018/978-1-7998-3254-6.ch004

Santoro, N., Roeca, C., Peters, B. A., & Neal-Perry, G. (2021). The menopause transition: Signs, symptoms, and management options. *The Journal of Clinical Endocrinology & Metabolism, 106*, 1–15. https://doi.org/10.1210/clinem/dgaa764

Santos-Lozano, A., Valenzuela, P. L., Llavero, F., Lista, S., Carrera-Bastos, P., Hampel, H., Pareja-Galeano, H., Gálvez, B. G., López, J. A., Vázquez, J., Emanuele, E., Zugaza, J. L., & Lucia, A. (2020). Successful aging: Insights from proteome analyses of healthy centenarians. *Aging*, *12*, 3502–3515. https://doi.org/10.18632/aging.102826

Saridakis, G., Ferreira, P., Mohammed, A.-M. and Marlow, S. (2022). The relationship between gender and promotion over the business cycle: Does firm size matter? *British Journal of Management*, *33*, 806–827. https://doi.org/10.1111/1467-8551.12458

Šatienė, S. (2015). Learning in later life: The perspective of successful aging. *Applied Research in Health and Social Sciences: Interface and Interaction*, *12*, 11–23. https://doi.org/10.1515/arhss-2015-0003

Saucedo, H. H., Whitmer, R. A., Glymour, M., DeCarli, C., Mayeda, E.-R., Gilsanz, P., Miles, S. Q., Bhulani, N., Farias, S. T., Olichney, J., & Mungas, D., (2022). Measuring cognitive health in ethnically diverse older adults. *Journals of Gerontology: Psychological Sciences*, *77*, 261–271. https://doi.org/10.1093/geronb/gbab062

Savickas, M. L. (2013). Career construction theory and practice. In S. D. Brown & R. W. Lent (Eds.), *Career development and counseling: Putting theory and research to work* (pp. 147–183). Wiley.

Savickas, M. L. (2020). Career construction theory and counseling model. In S. D. Brown & R. W. Lent (Eds.), *Career development and counseling: Putting theory and research to work* (pp. 165–199). Wiley.

Savvides, E., & Stavrou, E. (2021). Purpose, meaning, and well-being at work. In S. K. Dhiman (Ed.), *The Palgrave handbook of workplace well-being* (pp. 897–923). Palgrave Macmillan, Cham. https://doi.org/10.1007/978-3-030-30025-8_36

Sbarra, D. A. (2015). Divorce and health: Current trends and future directions. *Psychosomatic Medicine*, *77*, 227–236. https://doi.org/10.1097/0000000000000168

Sbarra, D. A., & Coan, J. A. (2018). Relationships and health: The critical role of affective science. *Emotion Review*, *10*, 40–54. https://doi.org/10.1177%2F1754073917696584

Schacter, D. (2022). Media, technology, and the sins of memory. *Memory, Mind & Media*, *1*, E1. https://doi.org/10.1017/mem.2021.3

Schade, H. M., Drewelies, J., Hülür, G., Hoppmann, C. A., Ram, N., & Gerstorf, D. (2020). I feel you, we can do this: Partner similarity in emotional experience and dyadic mastery in older couples. *GeroPsych: The Journal of Gerontopsychology and Geriatric Psychiatry*, *33*, 125–137. https://doi.org/10.1024/1662-9647/a000228

Schaie, K. W. (1994). The course of adult intellectual development. *American Psychologist*, *49*, 304–313. https://doi.org/10.1037/0003-066X.49.4.304

Schaie, K. W. (2005). *Developmental influences on adult intelligence: The Seattle longitudinal study*. Oxford University Press.

Schaie, K. W. (2008). A lifespan developmental perspective of psychological aging. In K. Laidlaw & B. G. Knight (Eds.), *Handbook of emotional disorders in late life: Assessment and treatment* (pp. 3–32). Oxford University Press.

Schaie, K. W. (2011). Historical influences on aging and behavior. In K. W. Schaie & S. L. Willis (Eds.), *Handbook of the psychology of aging* (7th ed., pp. 41–55). Academic Press.

Schaie, K. W., Maitland, S. B., Willis, S. L., & Intrieri, R. L. (1998). Longitudinal invariance of adult psychometric ability factor structures across seven years. *Psychology and Aging*, *13*, 8–20. https://doi.org/0.1037/0882-7974.13.1.8

Schaie, K. W., Plomin, R., Willis, S. L., Gruber-Baldini, A., & Dutta, R. (1992). Natural cohorts: Family similarity in adult cognition. In T. Sonderegger (Ed.), *Psychology and aging: Nebraska symposium on motivation, 1991* (pp. 205–243). University of Nebraska Press.

Schaie, K. W., & Willis, S. L. (2015). History of cognitive aging research. In N. A. Prachana (Ed.), *Encyclopedia of geropsychology* (pp. 1–19). Springer Singapore.

Schaie, K. W., & Zanjani, F. (2006). Intellectual development across adulthood. In C. Hoare (Ed.), *Oxford handbook of adult development and learning* (pp. 99–122). Oxford University Press.

Scharf, B., Zhu, S., Tomlin, S., Cheon, J., Mooney-Doyle, K., Baggs, J. G., & Weigand, D. (2021). Feasibility of an intervention study to support families when their loved one has life-sustaining therapy withdrawn. *Journal of Hospice & Palliative Nursing*, *23*, 89–97. https://doi.org/10.1097/NJH.0000000000000717

Scharlach, A. E., & Lehning, A. J. (2016). *Creating aging-friendly communities*. Oxford University Press.

Scheer, J. R., Breslow, A. S., Esposito, J., Price, M. A., & Katz, J. (2021). Violence against gay men. In E. M. Lund, C. Burgess, & A. J. Johnson (Eds.), *Violence against LGBTQ+ persons: Research, policy, and advocacy* (pp. 135–148). Springer. https://doi.org/10.1007/978-3-030-52612-2_10

Scheibe, S., Kunzmann, U., & Baltes, P. B. (2007). Wisdom, life longings, and optimal development. In J. A. Blackburn & C. N. Dulmus (Eds.), *Handbook of gerontology: Evidence-based approaches to theory, practice, and policy* (pp. 117–142). Wiley.

Scheidt, R. J., & Schwarz, B. (2010). Environmental gerontology: A sampler of issues and application. In J. C. Cavanaugh & C. K. Cavanaugh (Eds.), *Aging in America: Vol. 1: Psychological aspects* (pp. 156–176). Praeger Perspectives.

Schlabach, S. (2013). The importance of family, race, and gender for multiracial adolescent well-being. *Family Relations*, *62*, 154–174. https://doi.org/10.1111/j.1741-3729.2012.—758.x

Schlomer, G. L., & Belsky, J. (2012). Maternal age, investment, and parent–child conflict: A mediational test of the terminal investment hypothesis. *Journal of Family Psychology*, *26*, 443–452. https://doi.org/10.1037/a0027859

Schmidt, F. L., & Hunter, J. E. (2015). *Methods of meta-analysis: Correcting error and bias in research findings* (3rd ed.). SAGE.

Schmidt, S., Gull, S., Herrmann, K.-H., Boehme, M., Irintchev, A., Urbach, A., Reichenbach, J. R., Klingner, C. M., Gaser, C., & Witte, O. W. (2021). Experience-dependent structural plasticity in the adult brain: How the learning brain grows. *NeuroImage*, *225*, 117502. https://doi.org/10.1016/j.neuroimage.2020.117502

Schmitt, D. P. (2010). Romantic attachment from Argentina to Zimbabwe: Patterns of adaptive variation across contexts, cultures, and local ecologies. In P. Erdman & K.-M. Ng (Eds.), *Family therapy and counseling series. Attachment: Expanding the cultural connections* (pp. 211–226). Routledge/Taylor & Francis Group.

Schmitt, D. P., Alcalay, L., Allensworth, M., Allik, J., Ault, L., Austers, I., Bennett, K. L., Bianchi, G., Boholst, F., Cunen, M. A. B., Braeckman, J., Brainard, E. G., Jr., Caral, L. G. A., Caron, G., Casullo, M. M., Cunningham, M., Daibo, I., De Backer, C., De Souza, E., ... Zupanèiè, A. (2004). Patterns and universals of adult romantic attachment across 62 cultural regions: Are models of self and of other pancultural constructs? *Journal of Cross-Cultural Psychology*, *35*, 367–402. https://doi.org/10.1177/0022022104266105

Schneider, J. (2013). The death of an adult child: Contemporary psychoanalytic models of mourning. In S. Arbiser & G. Saragnano (Eds.), *On Freud's inhibitions, symptoms, and anxiety* (pp. 219–230). Karnac Books.

Schneider, J. L., Rowe, J. H., Garcia-de-Alba, C., Kim, C. F., Sharpe, A. H., & Haigis, M. C. (2021). The aging lung: Physiology, disease, and immunity. *Cell*, *184*, 1990–2019. https://doi.org/10.1016/j.cell.2021.03.005

Schooler, K. K. (1982). Response of the elderly to environment: A stress-theoretical perspective. In M. P. Lawton, P. G. Windley, & T. O. Byerts (Eds.), *Aging and the environment: Theoretical approaches* (pp. 80–96). Springer.

Schoulte, J. (2011). Bereavement among African Americans and Latino/a Americans. *Journal of Mental Health Counseling*, *33*, 11–20. https://doi.org/10.17744/mehc.33.1.r4971657p7176307

Schroeter, A., & Uecker, P. (2016a). *Arabic-English translation for* حكمة. http://en.bab.la/dictionary/arabic-english/حكمة

Schroeter, A., & Uecker, P. (2016b). *Chinese-English translation for* 智慧. http://en.bab.la/dictionary/chinese-english/智慧

Schuler, E., & Brito Dias, C. M. D. (2021). Legacies from great-grandparents to their descendants. *Journal of Intergenerational Relationships*. https://doi.org/10.1080/15350770.2021.1913275

Schultz, D. P., & Schultz, S. E. (2017). *Theories of personality* (11th ed.). Cengage Learning.

Schulz, D. J., & Enslin, C. (2014). The female executive's perspective on career planning and advancement in organizations. *Sage Open*. https://doi.org/10.1172/2158244014558040

Schulz-Heik, R. J., Poole, J. H., Dahdah, M. N., Sullivan, C., Date, E. S., Salerno, R. M., Schwab, K., & Harris, O. (2016). Long-term outcomes after moderate-to-severe traumatic brain injury among military veterans: Success and challenges. *Brain Injury*, *30*, 271–279. https://doi.org/10.3109/02699052.2015.1113567

Schurz, M., Maliske, L., & Kanske, P. (2020). Cross-network interactions in social cognition: A review of findings on task related brain activation and connectivity. *Cortex: A Journal Devoted to the Study of the Nervous System and Behavior*, *130*, 142–157. https://doi.org/10.1016/j.cortex.2020.05.006

Schurz, M., Radua, J., Tholen, M. G., Maliske, L., Margulies, D. S., Mars, R. B., Sallet, J., & Kanske, P. (2021). Toward a hierarchical model of social cognition: A neuroimaging meta-analysis and integrative review of empathy and theory of mind. *Psychological Bulletin*, *147*, 293–327. http://doi.org/10.1037/bul0000303

Schutte, N., & Malouff, J. M. (2022). The association between optimism and telomere length: A meta-analysis. *Journal of Positive Psychology*, *17*, 82–88. https://doi.org/10.1080/17439760.2020.1832249

Schwartz, B. (2015). *Why we work*. TED Books.

Schwartzentruber, J., Cooper, S., Liu, J. Z., Barrio-Hernandez, I., Bello, E., Kumasaka, N., Young, A. M. H., Franklin, R. J. M., Johnson, T., Estrada, K., Gaffney, D. J., Beltrao, P., & Bassett, A. (2021). Genome-wide meta-analysis, fine-mapping and integrative prioritization implicate new Alzheimer's disease risk genes. *Nature Genetics*, *53*, 392–402. https://doi.org/10.1038/s41588-020-00776-w

Schwarz, B. (2013). Environmental gerontology: What now? In R. J. Scheidt & B. Schwarz (Eds.), *Environmental gerontology: What next?* (pp. 7–22). Routledge.

Schweizer, V. (2020). *Age variation in the remarriage rate, 1990 & 2018*. https://core.ac.uk/download/pdf/327170606.pdf

Schwerdtfeger, A., & Friedrich-Mai, P. (2009). Social interaction moderates the relationship between depressive mood and heart rate variability: Evidence from an ambulatory monitoring study. *Health Psychology*, *28*, 501–509. https://doi.org/10.1037/a0014664

Scroggs, B., & Vennum, A. (2021). Gender and sexual minority group identification as a process of identity development during emerging adulthood. *Journal of LGBT Youth*, *18*, 287–304. https://doi.org/10.1080/19361653.2020.1722780

Scullin, M. K., Bugg, J. M., & McDaniel, M. A. (2012). Whoops, I did it again: Commission errors in prospective memory. *Psychology and Aging*, *27*, 46–53. https://doi.org/10.1037/a0026112

Seaman, P. M. (2012). Time for my life now: Early boomer women's anticipation of volunteering in retirement. *The Gerontologist*, *52*, 245–254. https://doi.org/10.1093/geront/gns001

Seene, T., & Kaasik, P. (2015). Age-associated changes in skeletal muscle regeneration: Effect of exercise. *Advances in Aging Research*, 4, 230–241. https://doi.org/10.4236/aar.2015.46025

Segal, D. L., Qualls, S. H., & Smyer, M. A. (2017). *Aging and mental health* (3rd ed.). Wiley-Blackwell.

Segal, M., Doron, I., & Mor, S. (2021). Consumer fraud: Older people's perceptions and experiences. *Journal of Aging & Social Policy, 33*, 1–21. https://doi.org/10.1080/08959420.2019.1589896

Seidlein, A.-H., Buchholz, I., Buchholz, M., & Salloch, S. (2019). Relationships and burden: An empirical-ethical investigation of lived experience in home nursing arrangements. *Bioethics, 33*, 448–456. https://doi.org/10.1111/bioe.12586

Seixas, F. L., Zadrozny, B., Laks, J., Conci, A., & Saade, D. C. M. (2014). A Bayesian network decision model for supporting the diagnosis of dementia, Alzheimer's disease and mild cognitive impairment. *Computers in Biology and Medicine, 51*, 140–158. https://doi.org/10.1016/j.compbiomed.2014.04.010

Sekgobela, G., Peu, M., & van der Wath, A. (2021). "They brought my smile back": A phenomenological description of widows' experiences of psychosocial support. *Death Studies, 45*, 603–612. https://doi.org/10.1080/07481187.2019.1671542

Sekhon, H., Cray, H. V., & Vahia, I. V. (2022). Robots in geriatric mental health: Pipe dream or viable solution? *American Journal of Geriatric Psychiatry, 30*, P246–P248. https://doi.org/10.1016/j.jagp.2021.08.013

Seligman, M. E. P., & Csikszentmihalyi, M. (2000). Positive psychology: An introduction. *American Psychologist, 55*, 5–14. https://doi.org/10.1037/0003-066X.55.1.5

Selingo, J. J. (2016). *There is life after college: What parents and students should know about navigating school to prepare for the jobs of tomorrow*. HarperCollins.

Selkoe, D. J. (2016). The amyloid hypothesis of Alzheimer's disease at 25 years. *EMBO Molecular Medicine, 8*, 595–608. https://doi.org/10.15252/emmm.201606210

Sergi, G., Bano, G., Pizzato, S., Veronese, N., & Manzato, E. (2017). Taste loss in the elderly: Possible implications for dietary habits. *Critical Reviews in Food Science and Nutrition, 57*, 3684–3689. https://doi.org/10.1080/10408398.2016.1160208

Serrano-Gemes, G., Serrano-del-Rosal, R., & Rich-Ruiz, M. (2021). Experiences in the decision-making regarding the place of care of the elderly: A systematic review. *Behavioral Sciences, 11*, 14. https://doi.org/10.3390/bs11020014

Seward, R. R., & Stanley-Stevens, L. (2014). Fathers, fathering, and fatherhood across cultures. In H. Selin (Ed.), *Parenting across cultures* (pp. 459–474). Springer.

Shafrir, A. L., Wise, L. A., Palmer, J. R., Shuaib, Z. O., Katuska, L. M., Vinayak, P., Kvaskoff, M., Terry, K. L., & Missmer, S. A. (2021). Validity of self-reported endometriosis: A comparison across four cohorts. *Human Reproduction, 36*, 1268–1278. https://doi.org/10.1093/humrep/deab012

Shakir, H. J., & Levy, E. I. (2022). Acute ischemic stroke. In M. L. Dryjski & L. M. Harris (Eds.), *Complications in endovascular surgery: Peri-procedural prevention and treatment* (pp. 335–338). Elsevier. https://doi.org/10.1016/B978-0-323-55448-0.00053-X

Shao, J., Li, D., Zhang, D., Zhang, L., Zhang, Q., & Qi, X. (2013). Birth cohort changes in the depressive symptoms of Chinese older adults: A cross-temporal meta-analysis. *International Journal of Geriatric Psychiatry, 28*, 1101–1108. https://doi.org/10.1002/gps.3942

Sharifian, N., Sol, K., Zahodne, L. B., & Antonucci, T. C. (2022). Social relationships and adaptation in later life. *Reference Module in Neuroscience and Biobehavioral Psychology*. https://doi.org/10.1016/B978-0-12-818697-8.00016-9

Sharma, R. (2021). Perspectives on the dynamic implications of cellular senescence and immunosenescence on macrophage aging biology. *Biogerontology, 22*, 571–587. https://doi.org/10.1007/s10522-021-09936-9

Sharma, R. A., Maheshwari, S., & Bronsther, R. (2020). COVID-19 in the era of loneliness. *Current Psychiatry, 19*. https://www.researchgate.net/profile/Rachel_Bronsther2/publication/342877509_COVID-19_in_the_era_of_loneliness_Current_Psychiatry_2020_May19531-33/links/5f0ae20e4585155050a020f7/COVID-19-in-the-era-of-loneliness-Current-Psychiatry-2020-May19531-33.pdf.

Sharma, T., Bamford, M., & Dodman, D. (2015). Person-centered care: An overview of reviews. *Contemporary Nurse, 51*, 107–120. https://doi.org/10.1080/10376178.2016.1150192

Sharp, D. J., Fleminger, S., & Powell, J. (2016). Traumatic brain injury. In M. Husain & J. M. Schott (Eds.), *Oxford textbook of cognitive neurology and dementia* (pp. 435–452). Oxford University Press.

Sharpe, D., & Poets, S. (2020). Meta-analysis as a response to the replication crisis. *Canadian Psychology/Psychologie canadienne, 61*, 377–387. https://doi.org/10.1037/cap0000215

Shavit, Y., & Carstensen, L. (2020). Age associated with preference for more and emotionally meaningful information in time-use decisions. *Innovation in Aging, 4*, 502. https://doi.org/10.1093/geroni/igaa057.1621

Shaw, C. A., & Gordon, J. K. (2021). Understanding elderspeak: An evolutionary concept analysis. *Innovation in Aging, 5*, igab023. https://doi.org/10.1093/geroni/igab023

Shaw, S. S. (2007). Losing a parent twice. *American Journal of Alzheimer's Disease and Other Dementias, 21*, 389–390. https://doi.org/10.1177/1533317506292860

Shayshon, B., & Popper-Giveon, A. (2017). "These are not the realities I imagined": An inquiry into the lost hopes and aspirations of beginning teachers. *Cambridge Journal of Education, 47*, 533–549. https://doi.org/10.1080/0305764X.2016.1214238

Sheiner, L. (2021). The long-term impact of aging on the federal budget. In R. L. Clark, YW. Lee, & A. Mason (Eds.), *Fiscal accountability and population aging: New responses to new challenges* (pp. 93–117). Edward Elgar Publishing. https://doi.org/10.4337/9781800370470.00013

Sheldon, S., & Levine, B. (2016). The role of the hippocampus in memory and mental construction. *Annals of the New York Academy of Sciences, 1369*, 76–92. https://doi.org/10.1111/nyas.13006

Shelton, J. T., & Christopher, E. A. (2016). A fresh pair of eyes on prospective memory monitoring. *Cognitive Psychology, 44*, 837–845. https://doi.org/10.3758/s13421-016-0601-3

Shen, H. W., Wang, Y., Wong, R., & Amano, T. (2020). Resource and network predictors of multiple volunteering cessations: Implications for social policy and practice. *Clinical Social Work Journal, 48*, 189–195. https://doi.org/10.1007/s10615-020-00748-x

Sheppard, F. H., & Stanford, D. (2019). Women's perceptions of retirement. *Journal of Gerontological Nursing, 45*, 31–39. https://doi.org/10.3928/00989134-20190221-01

Sheu, H.-B., & Phrasavath, L. (2019). Social cognitive career theory: Empirical evidence and cross-cultural applications. In N. Arthur & M. McMahon (Eds.), *Contemporary theories of career development: International perspectives* (pp. 47–60). Routledge.

Shih, Y. A., & Lu, Q. (2021). Decision making of artificial nutrition and hydration for cancer patients at terminal stage—A systematic review of the views from patients, families and healthcare professionals. *Journal of Pain and Symptom Management, 62*, P1065–1078. https://doi.org/10.1016/j.jpainsymman.2021.04.013

Shimamura, A. P. (2014). Remembering the past: Neural substrates underlying episodic encoding and retrieval. *Current Directions in Psychological Science, 23*, 257–263. https://doi.org/10.3758/s13415-016-0427-2

Shipp, A. J., Furst-Holloway, S., Harris, T. B., & Rosen, B. (2014). Gone today but here tomorrow: Extending the unfolding model of turnover to consider boomerang employees. *Personnel Psychology. 67*, 421–462. https://doi.org/10.1111/peps.12039

Shippee, T. P., Ng, W., & Bowblis, J. R. (2020). Does living in a higher proportion minority facility improve quality of life for racial/ethnic minority residents in nursing homes? *Innovation in Aging, 4*, iga0014. https://doi.org/10.1093/geroni/igaa014

Shivapour, S. K., Nguyen, C. M., Cole, C. A., & Denburg, N. L. (2012). Effects of age, sex, and neuropsychological performance on financial decision-making. *Frontiers in Neuroscience, 6*. https://doi.org/10.3389/fnins.2012.00082

Shokrkon, A., & Nicoladis, E. (2021). How personality traits of neuroticism and extroversion predict the effects of the COVID-19 on the mental health of Canadians. *PLoS ONE, 16*, e0251097. https://doi.org/10.1371/journal.pone.0251097

Shonk, K. (2020). *Women and negotiation: Narrowing the gender gap in negotiation*. https://www.pon.harvard.edu/daily/business-negotiations/women-and-negotiation-narrowing-the-gender-gap/

Shore, J. C., Gelber, M. W., Koch, L. M., & Sower, E. (2016). Anticipatory grief: An evidence-based approach. *Journal of Hospice & Palliative Nursing, 18*, 15–19. https://doi.org/10.1097/NJH.0000000000000208

Shrestha, S., Richey, S., Lipovac-Dew, M., Kunik, M. E., Stanley, M. A., Ramsey, D., & Amspoker, A. B. (2022). An examination of positive and negative dementia caregiving experiences. *Clinical Gerontologist, 45*, 1263–1272. https://doi.org/10.1080/07317115.2020.1868033

SHRM. (2021). *How to ensure pay equity for people of color*. https://www.shrm.org/hr-today/news/hr-magazine/spring2021/pages/pay-equity-for-people-of-color.aspx

Shukla, A., Cudjoe, T. K. M., Lin, F. R., & Reed, N. S. (2021). Functional hearing loss and social engagement among Medicare recipients. *Journals of Gerontology: Social Sciences, 76*, 195–200. https://doi.org/10.1093/geronb/gbz094

Siconolfi, D., Bandini, J., & Chen, E. (2021). Individual, interpersonal, and health care factors associated with informal and formal advance care planning in a nationally representative sample of midlife and older adults. *Patient Education and Counseling, 104*, 1806–1813. https://doi.org/10.1016/j.pec.2020.12.023

Silulu, F. M. L. (2021). *Samoan elders' perceptions of wellness: A New Zealand case study*. Dissertation, Auckland University of Technology. http://156.62.60.45/bitstream/handle/10292/14338/LilomaiavaSiluluF.pdf?sequence=3&isAllowed=y

Silva, A. R. (2016). HIV prevention and screening in older adults. In G. Guaraldi, J. Falutz, C. Mussi, & A. R. Silva (Eds.), *Managing the older adult patient with HIV* (pp. 117–122). Springer. https://doi.org/10.1007/978-3-319-20131-3_8

Silver, M. P. (2016). An inquiry into self-identification with retirement. *Journal of Women & Aging, 28*, 477–488. https://doi.org/10.1080/08952841.2015.1018068

Silverman, G. S., Baroiller, A., & Hemer, S. R. (2021). Culture and grief: Ethnographic perspectives on ritual, relationships and remembering, *Death Studies, 45*, 1–8. https://doi.org/10.1080/07481187.2020.1851885

Simon, C. (2020). The role of race and ethnicity in parental ethnic-racial socialization: A scoping review of research. *Journal of Child and Family Studies, 30*, 182–195. https://doi.org/10.1007/s10826-020-01854-7

Simonson, L., & Sarkis, M. (2018). You and I and anyone: Misperceptions of sexual intent and implications for prevention strategies. *International Development, Community and Environment (IDCE)*, 194. https://commons.clarku.edu/idce_masters_papers/194

Simonton, D. K. (2018). Defining creativity: Don't we also need to define what is *not* creative? *Journal of Creative Behavior, 52*, 80–90. https://doi.org/10.1002/jocb.137

Simpson, T., Camfield, D., Pipingas, A., Macpherson, H., & Stough, C. (2012). Improved processing speed: Online computer-based cognitive training in older adults. *Educational Gerontology, 38*, 445–458. https://doi.org/10.1080/03601277.2011.559858

Singer, J., & Papa, A. (2021). Preparedness for the death of an elderly family member: A possible protective factor for pre-loss grief in informal caregivers. *Archives of Gerontology and Geriatrics, 94*, 104353. https://doi.org/10.1016/j.archger.2021.104353

Sinnott, J. D. (2014). *Adult development: Cognitive aspects of thriving close relationships*. Oxford University Press.

Sinnott, J. D. (2021). Psychology, politics, and complex thought: A time for postformal thought in politics. In J. D. Sinnott & J. S. Rabin (Eds.), *The psychology of political behavior in a time of change: Identity in a changing world* (pp. 147–176). Springer. https://doi.org/10.1007/978-3-030-38270-4_5

Sinnott, J. D., & Rabin, J. S. (Eds.). (2021). *The psychology of political behavior in a time of change: Identity in a changing world.* Springer Cham.

Skin Cancer Foundation. (2021). *Melanoma warning signs: What you need to know about early detection.* https://www.skincancer.org/skin-cancer-information/melanoma/melanoma-warning-signs-and-images/

Skrajner, M. J., & Camp, C. J. (2007). Resident-Assisted Montessori Programming (RAMPTM): Use of a small group reading activity run by persons with dementia in adult health care and long-term care settings. *American Journal of Alzheimer's Disease and Other Dementias, 22,* 27–36. https://doi.org/10.1177%2F1533317506297895

Slater, C. L. (2003). Generativity versus stagnation: An elaboration of Erikson's adult stage of human development. *Journal of Adult Development, 10,* 53–65. https://doi.org/10.1023/A:1020790820868

Sloan, S., & Benson, J. J. (2022). Toward a conceptual model for successful transgender aging. *Qualitative Social Work, 21,* 455–471. https://doi.org/10.1177/1473325021994666

Small, J. A., & Cochrane, D. (2020). Spaced retrieval and episodic memory training in Alzheimer's disease. *Clinical Interventions in Aging, 15,* 519–536. https://doi.org/10.2147/CIA.S242113

Smith, A. (2019). *Workers around the globe face age discrimination.* https://www.shrm.org/resourcesandtools/legal-and-compliance/employment-law/pages/global-age-discrimination.aspx

Smith, D. T., Mouzon, D. M., & Elliott, M. (2018). Reviewing the assumptions about men's mental health: An exploration of the gender binary. *American Journal of Men's Health, 12,* 78–89. https://doi.org/10.1177/1557988316630953

Smith, I., Knight, T., Fletcher, R., & Macdonald, J. A. (2020). When men choose to be childless: An interpretative phenomenological analysis. *Journal of Social and Personal Relationships, 37,* 325–344. https://doi.org/10.1177%2F0265407519864444

Smith, L. (1992). The tyranny of America's old. *Fortune, 125*(1), 68–72.

Smith, M. D. (2016). *Dr. Ann McKee: We have no idea what percentage of NFL players develop CTE.* https://profootballtalk.nbcsports.com/2016/03/28/dr-ann-mckee-we-have-no-idea-what-percentage-of-nfl-players-develop-cte/

Smith, R., Kilgore, W. D. S., Alkozei, A., & Lane, R. D. (2018). A neuro-cognitive process model of emotional intelligence. *Biological Psychology, 139,* 131–151. https://doi.org/10.1016/j.biopsycho.2018.10.012

Smith, R., Steklis, H. D., Steklis, N. G., Weihs, K. L., & Lane, R. D. (2020). The evolution and development of the uniquely human capacity for emotional awareness: A synthesis of comparative anatomical, cognitive, neurocomputational, and evolutionary psychological perspectives. *Biological Psychology, 154,* 107925. https://doi.org/10.1016/j.biopsycho.2020.107925

Smith, T. M. (2020). *4 touchstones for end-of-life conversations during COVID-19.* https://www.ama-assn.org/delivering-care/ethics/4-touchstones-end-life-conversations-during-covid-19

Smith-Bynum, M. A. (2013). African American families: Research progress and potential in the age of Obama. In G. W. Peterson & K. R. Bush (Eds.), *Handbook of marriage and the family* (3rd ed., pp. 683–704). Springer.

Smits, S. J., & Bowden, D. E. (2013). Leveraging psychological assets from the development and maintenance of leadership capabilities. *International Leadership Journal, 5,* 3–26. http://internationalleadershipjournal.com/wp-content/uploads/2019/07/Winter-2013-Vol.-5-No.-1.pdf#page=4

Smyke, A. T., Zeanah, C. H. Fox, N. A., Nelson, C. A., & Guthrie, D. (2010). Placement in foster care enhances quality of attachment among young institutionalized children. *Child Development, 81,* 212–223. https://doi.org/10.1111/j.1467-8624.2009.01390.x

Smyth, A. C., & Naveh-Benjamin, M. (2016). Can DRYAD explain age-related associative memory deficits? *Psychology and Aging, 31,* 1–13. https://doi.org/10.1037/a0039071

Sneed, J. R., & Whitbourne, S. K. (2003). Identity processing and self-consciousness in middle and later adulthood. *Journals of Gerontology: Psychological Sciences, 58B,* P313–P319. https://doi.org/10.1093/geronb/58.6.P313

Sneed, J. R., & Whitbourne, S. K. (2005). Models of the aging self. *Journal of Social Issues, 61,* 375–388. https://doi.org/10.1111/j.1540-4560.2005.00411.x

Social Security Administration. (2021). The 2021 annual report of the Board of Trustees of the Federal Old-Age and Survivors Insurance and Federal Disability Insurance Trust Funds. https://www.ssa.gov/OACT/TR/2021/trTOC.html

Society for Automotive Engineers International. (2021). *Taxonomy and definitions for terms related to cooperative driving automation for on-road motor vehicles: J3216-Revised.* https://www.sae.org/standards/content/j3216_202107/

Solomon, H., & Tausch, A. (2021). Beyond patriarchy: Gender, Islam, and the MENA region. In H. Solomon & A. Tausch. *Arab MENA countries: Vulnerabilities and constraints against democracy on the eve of the global COVID-19 crisis. Perspectives on development in the Middle East and North Africa (MENA) region* (pp. 153–166). Springer. https://doi.org/10.1007/978-981-15-7047-6_5

Someya, S., & Ikeda, A. (2021). Aging of the sensory systems: Hearing and vision disorders. In N. Musi & P. J. Hornsby (Eds.), *Handbook of the biology of aging* (9th ed., pp. 297–321). Academic Press. https://doi.org/10.1016/B978-0-12-815962-0.00014-7

Sommer, S., Plumm, K. M., Terrance, C. A., & Tubré, T. (2013). Perceptions of younger single adults as a function of their gender and number of children. *Journal of General Psychology, 140,* 87–109. https://doi.org/10.1080/00221309.2013.769931

Sorokowski, P., Kowal, M., & Sorokowska, A. (2019). Religious affiliation and marital satisfaction: Commonalities among Christians, Muslims, and atheists. *Frontiers in Psychology: Gender, Sex and Sexualities, 10.* https://doi.org/10.3389/fpsyg.2019.02798

Sotgiu, I. (2021). *The psychology of autobiographical memory: History, theory, research.* Palgrave Macmillan, Cham. https://doi.org/10.1007/978-3-030-69571-2_4

Spaniol, J. (2016). Item and source memory. In S. K. Whitbourne (Ed.), *The encyclopedia of adulthood and aging* (pp. 694–699). Wiley.

Spark, C., Sharp, T. L. M., & Koczberski, G. (2021). Relationality and economic empowerment: The role of men in supporting and undermining women's pathways. *Journal of Development Studies, 57,* 1138–1153. https://doi.org/10.1080/00220388.2020.1850697

Spence, C., & Youssef, J. (2021). Aging and the (chemical) senses: Implications for food behaviour amongst elderly consumers. *Foods, 10,* 168. https://doi.org/10.3390/foods10010168

Spiro, A., III, & Brady, C. B. (2008). Integrating health into cognitive aging research and theory: Quo vadis? In S. M. Hofer & D. F. Alwin (Eds.), *Handbook of cognitive aging: Interdisciplinary perspectives* (pp. 260–283). Sage.

Spreckley, M., Macleod, D., González Trampe, B., Smith, A., & Kuper, H. (2020). Impact of hearing aids on poverty, quality of life and mental health in Guatemala: Results of a before and after study. *International Journal of Environmental Research and Public Health, 17,* 3470. https://doi.org/10.3390/ijerph17103470

Spreng, R. N., Cassidy, B. N., Darboh, B. S., DuPre, E., Lockrow, A. W., Setton, R., & Turner, G. (2017). Financial exploitation is associated with structural and functional brain differences in healthy older adults. *Journals of Gerontology: Medical Sciences, 72,* 1365–1368. https://doi.org/10.1093/gerona/glx051

Spreng, R. N., Ebner, N. C., Levin, B. E., & Turner, G. R. (2021). Aging and financial exploitation risk. In R. M. Factora (Ed.), *Reducing risk of financial exploitation and protecting financial resources* (2nd ed., pp. 55–73). Springer Nature. https://doi.org/10.31219/osf.io/w2bfz

Srivastava, S., John, O. P., Gosling, S. D., & Potter, J. (2003). Development of personality in early and middle adulthood: Set like plaster or persistent change? *Journal of Personality and Social Psychology, 84,* 1041–1053. https://doi.org/10.1037/0022-3514.84.5.1041

St. Fleur, N., Williams, C., & Wood, C. (2021, August 27). Can we live to 200? *New York Times.* https://www.nytimes.com/interactive/2021/04/27/magazine/longevity-timeline.html?searchResultPosition=1

Stahl, A. (2020, May 1). New study: Millennial women are delaying having children due to their careers. *Forbes.* https://www.forbes.com/sites/ashleystahl/2020/05/01/new-study-millennial-women-are-delaying-having-children-due-to-their-careers/?sh=36f6b3bc276a.

Stahnke, B., Blackstone, A., & Howard, H. (2020). Lived experiences and life satisfaction of childfree women in late life. *The Family Journal, 28,* 159–167. https://doi.org/10.1177%2F1066480720911611

Stanley, J. T., & Isaacowitz, D. M. (2012). Socioemotional perspectives on adult development. In S. K. Whitbourne & M. J. Sliwinski (Eds.), *The Wiley-Blackwell handbook of adulthood and aging* (pp. 237–253). Wiley-Blackwell.

Statista. (2021). *Families in the United States—statistics & facts.* https://www.statista.com/topics/1484/families/#dossierKeyfigures

Staudinger, U. M. (2015). Images of aging: Outside and inside perspectives. *Annual Review of Gerontology and Geriatrics, 35,* 187–209. https://doi.org/10.1891/0198-8794.35.187

Staudinger, U. M. (2019). The distinction between personal and general wisdom: How far have we come? In R. J. Sternberg & J. Glück (Eds.), *Cambridge handbook of wisdom* (pp. 182–201). Cambridge University Press. https://doi.org/10.1017/9781108568272.010

Staudinger, U. M. (2020). The positive plasticity of adult development: Potential for the 21st century. *American Psychologist, 75,* 540–553. https://doi.org/10.1037/amp0000612

Stearns, P. N. (2021). Introduction. In P. N. Stearns (Ed.), *The Routledge history of death since 1800.* Routledge.

Stebleton, M. J., Kaler, L. S., Diamond, K. K., & Lee, C. (2020). Examining career readiness in a liberal arts undergraduate career planning course. *Journal of Employment Counseling, 57,* 14–26. https://doi.org/10.1002/joec.12135

Steele, T. A., St Louis, E. K., Videnovic, A., & Auger, R. R. (2021). Circadian rhythm sleep–wake disorders: A contemporary review of neurobiology, treatment, and dysregulation in neurodegenerative disease. *Neurotherapeutics, 18,* 53–74. https://doi.org/10.1007/s13311-021-01031-8

Steenland, K., Goldstein, F. C., Levey, A., & Wharton, W. (2015). A meta-analysis of Alzheimer's disease incidence and prevalence comparing African-Americans and Caucasians. *Journal of Alzheimer's Disease, 50,* 71–76. https://psycnet.apa.org/doi/10.3233/JAD-150778

Stein, R., Blanchard-Fields, F., & Hertzog, C. (2002). The effects of age-stereotype priming on the memory performance of older adults. *Experimental Aging Research, 28,* 169–191. https://doi.org/10.1080/03610730252800184

Stein-Morrow, E. L., & Miller, L. M. S. (2009). Aging, self-regulation, and learning from text. *Psychology of Learning and Motivation, 51,* 255–296. https://doi.org/10.1016/S0079-7421(09)1008-0

Stephan, Y., Sutin, A. R., Caudroit, J., & Terracciano, A. (2016). Subjective age and changes in memory in older adults. *Journals of Gerontology: Psychological Sciences, 71,* 675–683. https://doi.org/10.1093/geronb/gbv010

Stephens, C., Breheny, M., & Mansvelt, J. (2015). Healthy ageing from the perspective of older people: A capability approach to resilience. *Psychology and Health, 30*, 715–731. https://doi.org/10.1080/08870446.2014.904862

Sterina, E., Hermida, A. P., Gerberi, D. J., & Lapid, M. I. (2022). Emotional resilience of older adults during COVID-19: A systematic review of studies of stress and well-being. *Clinical Gerontologist, 45*, 4–19. https://doi.org/10.1080/07317115.2021.1928355

Stern, Y. (2017). An approach to studying the neural correlates of reserve. *Brain Imaging and Behavior, 11*, 410–416. https://doi.org/10.1007/s11682-016-9566-x

Sternberg, R. J. (1985). *Beyond IQ: A triarchic theory of human intelligence*. Cambridge University Press.

Sternberg, R. J. (2006). A duplex theory of love. In R. J. Sternberg & K. Weis (Eds.), *The new psychology of love* (pp. 184–199). Yale University Press.

Sternberg, R. J. (2016). The gift that keeps on giving—But for how long? *Journal of Intelligence, 4*, 4. https://doi.org/10.3390/jintelligence4010004

Sternberg, R. J. (2020). Rethinking what we mean by intelligence. *Phi Delta Kappan, 102*, 36–41. https://doi.org/10.1177/0031721720970700

Sternberg, R. J., Jarvin, L., & Grigorenko, E. L. (2010). *Explorations in giftedness*. Cambridge University Press.

Sternberg, R. J., & Karami, S. (2021). What is wisdom? A unified 6P framework. *Review of General Psychology, 25*, 134–151. https://doi.org/10.1177/1089268020985509

Sterns, H. L., & Huyck, M. H. (2001). The role of work in midlife. In M. E. Lachman (Ed.), *Handbook of midlife development* (pp. 447–486). Wiley.

Sterns, H. L., & Spokus, D. M. (2020). Training the older workers: Pathways and pitfalls. In S. Czaja, J. Sharit, & J. James (Eds.), *Current and emerging trends in aging and work* (pp. 259–278). Springer, Cham. https://doi.org/10.1007/978-3-030-24135-3_13

Steuerle, C. E., & Smith, K. E. (2021). *Social Security and Medicare lifetime benefits and taxes: 2021*. https://www.urban.org/research/publication/social-security-medicare-lifetime-benefits-and-taxes-2021

Stevens, D. A., Workman, C. I., Kuwabara, H., Butters, M. A., Savonenko, A., Nassery, N., Gould, N., Kraut, M., Joo, J. H., Kilgore, J., Kamath, V., Holt, D. P., Dannals, R. F., Nandi, A., Onyike, C. U., & Smith, G. S. (2022). Regional amyloid correlates of cognitive performance in ageing and mild cognitive impairment. *Brain Communications, 4*, fcac016. https://doi.org/10.1093/braincomms/fcac016

Stillman, C. M., You, X., Seaman, K. L., Vaidya, C. J., Howard, J. H., Jr., & Howard, D. V. (2016). Task-related functional connectivity of the caudate mediates the association between trait mindfulness and implicit learning in older adults. *Cognitive, Affective, & Behavioral Neuroscience, 16*, 736–753. https://doi.org/10.3758/s13415-016-0427-2

Stinchcombe, A., & Hammond, N. G. (2022). Correlates of memory and executive function in middle-aged and older adults in the CLSA: A minority stress approach. *Journals of Gerontology: Psychological Sciences, 77*, 1105–1117. https://doi.org/10.1093/geronb/gbab084

Stojnov, D. (2013). Stereotypes that help define who we are. *Journal of Constructivist Psychology, 26*, 21–29. https://doi.org/10.1080/10720537.201 3.732530

Stokes, J. (2016). The influence of intergenerational relationships on marital quality following the death of a parent in adulthood. *Journal of Social and Personal Relationships, 33*, 3–22. https://doi.org/10.1177/0265407514558962

Stokes, V. (2021). Self-efficacy and the future selves construct: Strategies in support of adult learners' academic performance. In Information Resources Management Association (Ed.), *Research anthology on adult education and the development of lifelong learners* (pp. 988–1009). IGI Global.

Stoltz, K. B. (2016). Midlife adults: At 40, the eyes had it, now at 50, the career does! When career vision begins to blur. In W. K. Killam, S. Degges-White, & R. E. Michel (Eds.), *Career counseling interventions: Practice with diverse clients* (pp. 59–66). Springer.

Štrac, D. Š., Pivac, N., & Mück-Šeler, D. (2016). The serotonergic system and cognitive function. Translational Neuroscience, 7, 35–49. https://doi.org/10.1515/tnsci-2016-0007

Street, D., & Burge, S. W. (2012). Residential context, social relationships, and subjective well-being in assisted living. *Research on Aging, 34*, 365–394. https://doi.org/10.1177/0164027511423928

Streeter, J. L. (2020). Gender differences in widowhood in the short-run and long-run: Financial, emotional, and mental wellbeing. *Journal of the Economics of Aging, 17*, 100258. https://doi.org/10.1016/j.jeoa.2020.100258

Strickland-Hughes, C., & West, R. L. (2021). The impact of naturalistic age stereotype activation. *Frontiers in Psychology, 12*. https://doi.org/10.3389/fpsyg.2021.685448

Strinic, V. (2015). Arguments in support and against euthanasia. *British Journal of Medicine & Medical Research, 9*, 1–12. https://doi.org/10.9734/BJMMR/2015/19151

Stroebe, M. S., & Archer, J. (2013). Origins of modern ideas on love and loss: Contrasting forerunners of attachment theory. *Review of General Psychology, 17*, 28–39. https://doi.org/10.1037/a0030030

Strough, J., Berg, C. A., & Sansone, C. (1996). Goals for solving everyday problems across the interpersonal concerns. *Developmental Psychology, 32*, 1106–1115. https://doi.org/10.1037/0012-1649.32.6.1106

Strough, J., Cheng, S., & Swenson, L. M. (2002). Preferences for collaborative and individual everyday problem solving in later adulthood. *International Journal of Behavioral Development, 26*, 26–35. https://doi.org/10.1080/01650250143000337

Strough, J., de Bruin, W. B., & Peters, E. (2015). New perspectives for motivating better decisions in older adults. *Frontiers in Psychology, 6*. https://doi.org/10.3389/fpsyg.2015.00783

Substance Abuse and Mental Health Services Administration (SAMHSA). (2021). *2020 National Survey on Drug Use and Health*. https://www.samhsa.gov/data/release/2020-national-survey-drug-use-and-health-nsduh-releases

Sugimoto-Matsuda, J. J., & Guerrero, A. P. S. (2016). Violence and abuse. In D. Alicata, N. Jacobs, A. Guerrero, & M. Piasecki (Eds.), *Problem-based behavioral science and psychiatry* (pp. 113–133). Springer.

Sugiura, M. (2016). Functional neuroimaging of normal aging: Declining brain, adapting brain. *Ageing Research Reviews, 30*, 61–72. https://doi.org/10.1016/j.arr.2016.006

Suja, C., Shuhaib, B., Khathoom, H., & Simi, K. (2016). A review on dietary antioxidants. *Research Journal of Pharmacy and Technology, 9*(2), 196–202. https://doi.org/10.5958/0974-360X.2016.00035.4

Sulphey, M. M. (2019). The concept of workplace identity, its evolution, antecedents and development. *International Journal of Environment, Workplace and Employment, 5*, 151–168. https://doi.org/10.1504/IJEWE.2019.103022

Sultan, T. (2021). Burning brides in south Asia. *Pakistan Journal of Medical Sciences, 37*, 608. https://doi.org/10.12669/pjms.37.2.4053.

Sumner, J., Chong, L. S., Bundele, A., & Lim, Y. W. (2021). Co-designing technology for aging in place: A systematic review. *The Gerontologist, 61*, e395–e409. https://doi.org/10.1093/geront/gnaa064

Sumowski, J. F., Rocca, M. A., Leavitt, V. M., Riccitelli, G., Sandry, J., DeLuca, J., Comi, G., & Filippi, M. (2016). Searching for the neural bases of reserve against memory decline: Intellectual enrichment linked to larger hippocampal volume in multiple sclerosis. *European Journal of Neurology, 23*, 39–44. https://doi.org/10.1111/ene.12662

Sumter, S. R., Vandenbosch, L., & Ligtenberg, L. (2017). Love me Tinder: Untangling emerging adults' motivations for using the dating application Tinder. *Telematics and Informatics, 34*, 67–78.

Sun, Q., Lu, N., Jiang, N., & Lou, V. (2021). Intention to use respite services among informal care-givers of frail older adults in China: The role of care needs change. *Ageing and Society, 41*, 101–120. https://doi.org/10.1017/S0144686X20000628

Sunderaraman, P., Lee, S., Varangis, E., Habeck, C., Chapman, S., Joyce, J. L., Hartstone, W., Brickman, A., Stern, Y., & Cosentino, S. (2021, February 15). Self-awareness for financial decision making abilities is linked to right temporal cortical thickness in older adults. *Research Square*. https://orcid.org/0000-0001-6011-8412

Super, D. E. (1957). *The psychology of careers*. Harper & Row.

Super, D. E. (1976). *Career education and the meanings of work*. U.S. Offices of Education.

Super, D. E. (1980). A life-span, life-space approach to career development. *Journal of Vocational Behavior, 16*, 282–298. https://doi.org/10.1016/0001-8791(80)90056-1

Super, D., Savickas, M., & Super, C. (1996). The life-span, life-space approach to careers. In D. Brown, L. Brooks, & Associates (Eds.), *Career choice & development* (3rd ed., pp. 121–178). Jossey-Bass.

Super, S., Wagemakers, M. A. E., Picavet, H. S. J., Verkooijen, K. T., & Koelen, M. A. (2016). Strengthening sense of coherence: Opportunities for theory building in health promotion. *Health Promotion International, 31*, 869–878. https://doi.org/10.1093/heapro/dav071

Supiano, K. P., Luptak, M., Andersen, T., Beynon, C., Iacob, E., & Wong, B. (2022). If we knew then what we know now: The preparedness experience of pre-loss and post-loss dementia caregivers. *Death Studies, 46*, 369-380. https://doi.org/10.1080/07481187.2020.1731014

Suppa, N. (2021). Unemployment and subjective well-being. *Global Labor Organization (GLO) Discussion Paper No. 760*. https://www.econstor.eu/bitstream/10419/228706/1/GLO-DP-0760.pdf

Swanson, D. A. & Tedrow, L. M. (2018). A bio-demographic perspective on inequality and life expectancy: An analysis of 159 countries for the periods 1970–90 and 1990–2010. In A. S. R. Srinivasa Rao & C. R. Rao (Eds.), *Handbook of statistics: Integrated population biology and modeling, Part A* (pp. 577–613). North-Holland. https://doi.org/10.1016/bs.host.2018.04.001

Swanson, D. A., & Sanford, D. A. (2012). Socio-economic status and life expectancy in the United States, 1990–2010: Are we reaching the limits of human longevity? *Population Review*, 51. https://muse.jhu.edu/article/485100

Swenor, B. K., Lee, M. J., Varadaraj, V., Whitson, H. E., & Ramulu, P. Y. (2020). Aging with vision loss: A framework for assessing the impact of visual impairment on older adults. *The Gerontologist, 60*, 989–995. https://doi.org/10.1093/geront/gnz117

Tabibzadeh, S. (2021). Cell-centric hypotheses of aging. *Frontiers in Bioscience-Landmark, 26*, 1–49. https://fbscience.com/Landmark/articles/10.2741/4888

Takamatsu, K., Ideno, Y., Kikuchi, M., Yasui, T., Maruoka, N., Nagai, K., & Hayashi, K. (2021). Validity of self-reported diagnoses of gynaecological and breast cancers in a prospective cohort study: The Japan Nurses' Health Study. *BMJ Open, 11*, e045491. https://doi.org/10.1136/bmjopen-2020-045491

Tam, K.-P. (2013). Existential motive underlying cosmetic surgery: A terror management analysis. *Journal of Applied Social Psychology, 43*, 947–955. https://doi.org/10.1111/jasp.12059

Tamayo, G. J., Broxson, A., Munsell, M., & Cohen, M. Z. (2010). Caring for the caregiver. *Oncology Nursing Forum, 37*, E50–E57. https://doi.org/10.1188/10.ONF.E50-E57

Tamborini, C. R., & Kim, C. (2020). Are you saving for retirement? Racial/ethnic differentials in contributory retirement savings plans. *Journals of Gerontology: Social Sciences, 75*, 837–848. https://doi.org/10.1093/geronb/gbz131

Tan, A., Morton, K. R., Lee, J. W., Hartman, R., & Lee, G. (2020). Adverse childhood experiences and depressive symptoms: Protective effects of dietary flavonoids. *Journal of Psychosomatic Research, 131*, 109957. https://doi.org/10.1016/j.jpsychores.2020.109957

Tan, J., & Andriessen, K. (2021). The experiences of grief and personal growth in university students: A qualitative study. *International Journal of Environmental Research and Public Health, 18*, 1899. https://doi.org/10.3390/ijerph18041899

Tang, P.-L., Chiou, C.-P., Lin, H.-S., Wang, C., & Liand, S.-L. (2011). Correlates of death anxiety among Taiwanese cancer patients. *Cancer Nursing, 34*, 286–292. https://doi.org/10.1097/NCC.0b013e31820254c6

Tang, R., Friston, K. J., & Tang, Y.-Y. (2020). Brief mindfulness meditation induces gray matter changes in a brain hub. *Neural Plasticity, 2020*, 8830005. https://doi.org/10.1155/2020/8830005

Tang, Y.-Y., & Posner, M. I. (2012). Tools of the trade: Theory and method in mindfulness neuroscience. *Social Cognitive and Affective Neuroscience, 8*, 118–120. https://doi.org/10.1093/scan/nss112

Tanner, J. L., & J. J. Arnett (2009). The emergence of emerging adulthood: The new life stage between adolescence and young adulthood. In A. Furlong (Ed.), *Handbook of youth and young adulthood: New perspectives and agendas* (pp. 39–45). Routledge.

Tanskanen, A. O., & Danielsbacka, M. (2021). Brothers and sisters across the life course: Eleven factors shaping relationship quality in adult siblings. In A. Buchanan & A. Rotkirch (Eds.), *Brothers and sisters* (pp. 25–40). Palgrave Macmillan. https://doi.org/10/1007/978-3-030-55985-4_2

Tao, L., Wang, G., Zhu, M., & Cai, Q. (2021). Bilingualism and domain-general cognitive functions from a neural perspective: A systematic review. *Neuroscience & Biobehavioral Reviews, 125*, 264–295. https://doi.org/10.1016/j.neubiorev.2021.02.029

Tauber, S. C., Staszewski, O., Prinz, M., Nolte, K., & Bunkowski, S. (2016). HIV encephalopathy: Glial activation and hippocampal neuronal apoptosis, but limited neural repair. *HIV Medicine, 17*, 143–151. https://doi.org/10.1111/hiv.12288

Tauber, S. K., & Dunlosky, J. (2016). A brief history of metamemory research and handbook overview. In J. Dunlosky & S. K. Tauber (Eds.), *The Oxford handbook of metamemory* (pp. 7–21). Oxford University Press.

Taylor, J. L., O'Hara, R., Mumenthaler, M. S., Rosen, A. C., & Yesavage, J. A. (2005). Cognitive ability, expertise, and age differences in following air-traffic control instructions. *Psychology and Aging, 20*, 117–133. https://doi.org/10.1037/0882-7974.20.1.117

Taylor, M. E., Wesson, J., Sherrington, C., Hill, K. D., Kurrle, S., Lord, S. R., Brodaty, H., Howard, K., O'Rourke, S. D., Clemson, L., Payne, N., Toson, B., Webster, L., Savage, R., Zelma, G., Koch, C., John, B., Lockwood, K., & Close, J. C. T. (2021). Tailored exercise and home hazard reduction program for fall prevention in older people with cognitive impairment: The i-FOCIS randomized controlled trial. *The Journals of Gerontology: Medical Sciences, 76*, 655–665. https://doi.org/10.1093/gerona/glaa241

Taylor, P., Earl, C., Brooke, E., & McLoughlin, C. (2021). *Retiring women: Work and post-work transitions*. Edward Elgar Publishing.

Teachman, J., Tedrow, L., & Kim, G. (2013). The demography of families. In G. W. Peterson & K. R. Bush (Eds.), *Handbook of marriage and the family* (3rd ed., pp. 39–63). Springer.

Tefera, C. A. and Hunsaker, W.D. (2021). Using psychological capital at organizational levels of study. *Journal of Advances in Management Research, 18*, 548–567. https://doi.org/10.1108/JAMR-08-2020-0179

Teiga-Mocigemba, S., Klauer, K. C., & Sherman, J. W. (2010). A practical guide to implicit association tests and related tasks. In B. Gawronski & B. K. Payne (Eds.), *Handbook of implicit social cognition: Measurement, theory, and applications* (pp. 117–139). Guilford.

Terkel, S. (1974). *Working*. Pantheon.

Testard, C., Tremblay, S., & Platt, M. (2021). From the field to the lab and back: Neuroethology of primate social behavior. *Current Opinion in Neurobiology, 68*, 76–83. https://doi.org/10.1016/j.conb.2021.01.005

Thangavel, G., Memedi, M., & Hedström, K. (2022). Customized information and communication technology for reducing social isolation and loneliness among older adults: Scoping review. *JMIR Mental Health, 9*, e34221. https://doi.org/10.2196/34221

The Green House Project. (2021). *Who we are*. https://www.thegreenhouseproject.org/about/visionmission

The Japan Geriatrics Society Subcommittee on End-of-Life Issues, Kuzuya, M., Aita, K., Katayama, Y., Katsuya, T., Nishikawa, M., Hirahara, S., Miura, H., Rakugi, H., & Akishita, M. (2020). Japan Geriatrics Society "Recommendations for the Promotion of Advance Care Planning": End-of-Life Issues Subcommittee consensus statement. *Geriatrics Gerontology International*, 20, 1024–1028. https://doi.org/10.1111/ggi.14042

Thijssen, E. H., Verberk, I. M., Stoops, E., Boxer, A. L., & Teunissen, C. E. (2020). Amyloid, pTau, NfL, and GFAP as biomarkers for Alzheimer's disease. *Alzheimer's & Dementia, 16*, e038179. https://doi.org/10.1002/alz.038179

Thomas Tobin, C. S., Erving, C. L., Hargrove, T. W., & Satcher, L. A. (2022). Is the Black-White mental health paradox consistent across age, gender, and psychiatric disorders? *Aging & Mental Health, 26*, 196–204. https://doi.org/10.1080/13607863.2020.1855627

Thomas, A. G., Jonason, P. K., Blackburn, J. D., Kennair, L. E. O., Lowe, R., Malouff, J., Stewart-Williams, S., Sulikowski, D., & Li, N. P. (2020). Mate preference priorities in the East and West: A cross-cultural test of the mate preference priority model. *Journal of Personality, 88*, 606–620. https://doi.org/10.1111/jopy.12514

Thomas, A. K., Lee, M., & Hughes, G. (2016). Introspecting on the elusive: The uncanny state of the feeling of knowing. In J. Dunlosky & S. K. Tauber (Eds.), *The Oxford handbook of metamemory* (pp. 81–94). Oxford University Press.

Thomas, F. (2008). Remarriage after spousal death: Options facing widows and implications for livelihood security. *Gender and Development, 16*, 73–83. https://doi.org/10.1080/13552070701876235

Thomas, K. R., Bangen, K. J., Weigand, A. J., Edmonds, A. C., Wong, C. G., Cooper, S., Delano-Wood, L., & Bondi, M. W. for the Alzheimer's Disease Neuroimaging Initiative. (2020). Objective subtle cognitive difficulties predict future amyloid accumulation and neurodegeneration. *Neurology, 94*, e397–e406. https://doi.org/10.1212/WNL.0000000000008838

Thomas, M. D., Guihan, M., & Mambourg, F. (2011). What do potential residents need to know about assisted living facility type? The trade-off between autonomy and help with more complex needs. *Journal of Housing for the Elderly, 25*, 109–124. https://doi.org/10.1080/02763893.2011.571108

Thomas, R. C., & Hasher, L. (2006). The influence of emotional valence on age differences in early processing and memory. *Psychology and Aging, 21*, 821–825. https://doi.org/10.1037/0882-7974.21.4.821

Thomas, R. C., & Hasher, L. (2012). Reflections of distraction in memory: Transfer of previous distraction improves recall in younger and older adults. *Journal of Experimental Psychology: Learning, Memory, and Cognition, 38*, 30–39. https://doi.org/10.1037/a0024882

Thomas, R., Cooper, M., Cardazone, G., Urban, K., Bohrer, A., Long, M., Yee, L., Krivkovich, A., Huang, J., Prince, S., Kumar, A., & Coury, S. (2020). *Women in the workplace, 2020*. https://womenintheworkplace.com/Women_in_the_Workplace_2020.pdf

Thomas, R., Cooper, M., Urban, K., Cardazone, G., Bohrer, A., Mahajan, S., Yee, L., Krivkovich, A., Huang, J., Rambachan, I., Burns, T., & Trkulja, T. (2021). *Women in the workplace, 2021*. https://www.mckinsey.com/~/media/mckinsey/featured%20insights/diversity%20and%20inclusion/women%20in%20the%20workplace%202021/women-in-the-workplace-2021.pdf?shouldindex=false

Thompson, B. (2021). Marital satisfaction in older adults. In P. N. Claster & S. L. Blair (Eds.), *Aging and the family: Understanding changes in structural and relationship dynamics* (pp. 267–291). Emerald Publishing Limited. https://doi.org/10.1108/S1530-353520210000017014.

Thompson, G. E., Cameron, R. E., & Fuller-Thompson, E. (2013). Walking the red road: The role of First Nations grandparents in promoting cultural well-being. *International Journal of Aging and Human Development, 76*, 55–78. https://doi.org/10.2190/AG.76.1.c

Tian, X., & Solomon, D. H. (2020). Grief and post-traumatic growth following miscarriage: The role of meaning reconstruction and partner supportive communication. *Death Studies, 44*, 237–247. https://doi.org/10.1080/07481187.2018.1539051

Tibbetts, M., Esptein-Shuman, A., & Kushlev, K. (2021). A week during COVID-19: Online social interactions are associated with greater connection and more stress. *Computers in Human Behavior Reports, 4*, 100133. https://doi.org/10.1016/j.chbr.2021.100133

Ting, R., Edmonds, P., Higginson, I. J., & Sleeman, K. E. (2020). Palliative care for patients with severe covid-19. *BMJ, 370*, m2710. https://doi.org/10.1136/bmj.m2710

Tinnirello, A., Mazzoleni, S., & Santi, C. (2021). Chronic pain in the elderly: Mechanisms and distinctive features. *Biomolecules, 11*, 1256. https://doi.org/10.3390/biom11081256

Titlestad, K. B., Mellingen, S., Stroebe. M., & Dyregrov, K. (2021). Sounds of silence. The "special grief" of drug-death bereaved parents: A qualitative study. *Addiction Research & Theory, 29*, 155–165. https://doi.org/10.1080/16066359.2020.1751827

Tobin, D. J. (2017). Introduction to skin aging. *Journal of Tissue Viability, 26*, 37–46. https://doi.org/10.1016/j.jtv.2016.03.022

Tobis, S., Piasek, J., Cylkowska-Nowak, M., & Suwalska, A. (2022). Robots in eldercare: How does a real-world interaction with the machine influence the perceptions of older people? *Sensors, 22*, 1717. https://doi.org/10.3390/s22051717

Todd, M. (2021). In and out, on and off: LGBT+ online experiences. In T. Owen & J. Marshall (Eds.), *Rethinking cybercrime* (pp. 169–189). Palgrave Macmillan. https://doi.org/10.1007/978-3-030-55841-3_9

Toikko, T. (2016). Becoming an expert by experience: An analysis of service users' learning process. *Social Work in Mental Health, 14*, 292–312. https://doi.org/10.1080/15332985.2015.1038411

Tong, C., & Kram, K. E. (2013). The efficacy of mentoring—the benefits for mentees, mentors, and organizations. In J. Passmore, D. B. Peterson, & T. Freire (Eds.), *The Wiley-Blackwell handbook of coaching and mentoring* (pp. 217–242). Wiley-Blackwell.

Torges, C. M., Stewart, A. J., & Duncan, L. E. (2008). Achieving ego integrity: Personality development in late midlife. *Journal of Research in Personality, 42*, 1004–1019. https://doi.org/10.1016/j.jrp.2008.02.006

Toril, P., Reales, J. M., Mayas, J., & Ballesteros, S. (2016). Video game training enhances visuospatial working memory and episodic memory in older adults. *Frontiers in Human Neuroscience, 10*, 206. https://doi.org/10.3389/fnhum.2016.00206

Torres, L., Lindstrom, K., Hannah, L., & Webb, F. (2016). Exploring barriers among primary care providers in referring patients to hospice. *Journal of Hospice & Palliative Nursing, 18*, 167–172. https://doi.org/10.1097/NJH.0000000000000233

Traumatic Brain Injury Center of Excellence. (2021). *DOD TBI worldwide numbers*. https://health.mil/About-MHS/OASDHA/Defense-Health-Agency/Research-and-Development/Traumatic-Brain-Injury-Center-of-Excellence/DOD-TBI-Worldwide-Numbers

Trella. (2020). *Quantifying hospice's end-of-life impact*. https://www.trellahealth.com/portfolio_page/quantifying-hospices-end-of-life-impact/

Tremblay, F., & Master, S. (2016). Touch in aging. In T. Prescott, E. Ahissar, & E. Izhikevich (Eds.), *Scholarpedia of touch* (pp. 351–361). Springer. https://doi.org/10.2991/978-94-6239-133-8_29

Trevisan, L. A. (2014). Elderly alcohol use disorders: Epidemiology, screening, and assessment issues. *Psychiatric Times*. https://www.psychiatrictimes.com/alcohol-abuse/elderly-alcohol-use-disorders-epidemiology-screening-and-assessment-issues

Triana, M. C., Gu, P., Chapa, O., Richard, O., & Colella, A. (2021). Sixty years of discrimination and diversity research in human resource management: A review with suggestions for future research directions. *Human Resource Management, 60*, 145–204. https://doi.org/10.1002/hrm.22052

Tromp, D., Dufour, A., Lithfous, S., Pebayle, T., & Després, O. (2015). Episodic memory in normal aging and Alzheimer's disease: Insights from imaging and behavioral studies. *Aging Research Reviews, 24(Part B)*, 232–262. https://doi.org/10.1016/j.arr.2015.08.066

Tsimpida, D., Kontopantelis, E., Ashcroft, D. M., Panagioti, M. (2022). The dynamic relationship between hearing loss, quality of life, socioeconomic position and depression and the impact of hearing aids: Answers from the English Longitudinal Study of Ageing (ELSA). *Social Psychiatry and Psychiatric Epidemiology, 57*, 353–362. https://doi.org/10.1007/s00127-021-02155-0

Tsourdi, E., Makras, P., Rachner, T. D., Polyzos, S., Rauner, M., Mandanas, S., Hobbauer, L. C., & Anastasilakis, A. D. (2019). Denosumab effects on bone density and turnover in postmenopausal women with low bone mass with or without previous treatment. *Bone, 120*, 44–49. https://doi.org/10.1016/j.bone.2018.10.001

Tsuchiya-Ito, R., Iwarsson, S. & Slaug, B. (2019). Environmental challenges in the home for ageing societies: A comparison of Sweden and Japan. *Journal of Cross-Cultural Gerontology, 34*, 265–289. https://doi.org/10.1007/s10823-019-09384-6

Tsuno, N., & Homma, A. (2009). Aging in Asia—The Japan experience. *Ageing International, 34*, 1–14. https://doi.org/10.1007/s12126-009-9032-9

Tu, M. C.-H. (2006). *Culture and job satisfaction: A comparative study between Taiwanese and Filipino caregivers working in Taiwan's long-term care industry.* Unpublished dissertation, Nova Southeastern University.

Tubi, M. A., Feingold, F. W., Kothapalli, D., Hare, E. T., King, K. S., Thompson, P. M., & Braskie, M. N. (2020). White matter hyperintensities and their relationship to cognition: Effects of segmentation algorithm. *NeuroImage, 206*, 116327. https://doi.org/10.1016/j.neuroimage.2019.116327

Tully-Wilson, C., Bojack, R., Millear, P. M., Stallman, H. M., Allen, A., & Mason, J. (2021). Self-perceptions of aging: A systematic review of longitudinal studies. *Psychology and Aging, 36*, 773–789. https://doi.org/10.1037/pag0000638

Tumasian, R. A., III, Harish, A., Kundu, G., Yang, J.-H., Ubaida-Mohien, C., Gonzalez-Freire, M., Kaileh, M., Zukley, L. M., Chia, C. W., Lyashkov, A., Wood. W. H., III, Piao, Y., Coletta, C., Ding, J., Gorospe, M., Sen, R., De, S., & Ferrucci, L. (2021). Skeletal muscle transcriptome in healthy aging. *Nature Communications, 12*, Article 2014. https://doi.org/10.1038/s41467-021-22168-2

Tunç, R., & Ikier, S. (2021, August 8). Age differences in inattentional blindness to emotional stimulus. *Current Psychology*. https://doi.org/10.1007/s12144-021-02159-8

Turner, C. (2022). *The expanded child tax credit briefly slashed child poverty. Here's what else it did.* https://www.npr.org/2022/01/27/1075299510/the-expanded-child-tax-credit-briefly-slashed-child-poverty-heres-what-else-it-d

U.S. Citizenship & Immigration Services. (2015). *Refugees and asylum*. https://www.uscis.gov/humanitarian/refugees-asylum

U.S. Department of Agriculture and U.S. Department of Health and Human Services. (2020). *Dietary guidelines for Americans: 2020–2025* (9th ed.). https://www.dietaryguidelines.gov/.

U.S. Department of Housing and Urban Development. (2021). *Congregate housing services program (CHSP)*. https://www.hud.gov/program_offices/housing/mfh/progdesc/chsp

U.S. Department of Labor Women's Bureau. (2022a). *Women of working age*. https://www.dol.gov/agencies/wb/data/latest-annual-data/working-women#Percent-Distribution-of-the-Labor-Force-by-Age-and-Sex

U.S. Equal Employment Opportunity Commission. (2021a). *Data visualizations: Sexual harassment charge data*. https://www.eeoc.gov/statistics/data-visualizations-sexual-harassment-charge-data

U.S. Equal Employment Opportunity Commission. (2021b). *Job patterns for minorities and women in private industry (EEO-1)*. https://www.eeoc.gov/statistics/employment/jobpatterns/eeo1

U.S. Equal Employment Opportunity Commission. (2022). *Age discrimination*. https://www.eeoc.gov/age-discrimination

U.S. Food and Drug Administration. (2021a). *Opioid medications*. https://www.fda.gov/drugs/information-drug-class/opioid-medications

U.S. Food and Drug Administration. (2021b). *Medicines and you: A guide for older adults*. https://www.fda.gov/drugs/resources-you-drugs/medicines-and-you-guide-older-adults

Uchino, B. N., Cawthon, R. M., Smith, T. W., Light, K. C., McKenzie, J., Carlisle, M., Gunn, H., Birmingham, W., & Bowen, K. (2012). Social relationships and health: Is feeling positive, negative, or both (ambivalent) about your social ties related to telomeres? *Health Psychology, 31*, 789–796. https://doi.org/10.1037/a0026836.

Uleman, J. S., & Kressel, L. M. (2013). A brief history of theory and research on impression formation. In D. E. Carlston (Ed.), *The Oxford handbook of social cognition* (pp. 53–73). Oxford University Press.

Ulland, T. K., & Colonna, M. (2018). TREM2—A key player in microglial biology and Alzheimer's disease. *Nature Reviews Neurology, 14*, 667–675. https://doi.org/10.1038/s41582-018-0072-1.

Ulrich, R. S., Zimring, C., Zhu, X., DuBose, J., Seo, H.-B., Choi, Y.-S., Quan, X., & Joseph, A. (2008). A review of the research literature on evidence-based healthcare design. *HERD: Health Environments Research & Design Journal, 1*, 61–125. https://doi.org/10.1177%2F193758670800100306

Umberson, D., Donnelly, R., Xu, M., Farina, M., & Garcia, M. A. (2020). Death of a child prior to midlife, dementia risk, and racial disparities. *Journals of Gerontology: Social Sciences, 75*, 1983–1995. https://doi.org/10.1093/geronb/gbz154

Umegaki-Constantini, H. (2017). Caring for my wife's parents?: Reconciling practices, masculinity and family relations. *Intersections: Gender and Sexuality in Asia and the Pacific, Issue 41*. http://intersections.anu.edu.au/issue41/umegaki-hiroko.pdf

United Nations. (2019). *World population prospects 2019*. Department of Economic and Social Affairs, Population Dynamics. https://population.un.org/wpp/DataQuery/

United Nations. (2020). *World population ageing 2020 highlights*. https://www.un.org/development/desa/pd/sites/www.un.org.development.desa.pd/files/files/documents/2020/Nov/undesa_pd-2020_world_population_ageing_highlights.pdf

United Nations. (2021a). *Ageing and disability*. https://www.un.org/development/desa/disabilities/disability-and-ageing.html

United Nations. (2021b). *UN resolution 75/131: United Nations Decade of Health Ageing (2021–2030)*. https://undocs.org/en/A/RES/75/131

UOregon CTN. (2020). *Something's gotta give*. https://medium.com/rapid-ec-project/somethings-gotta-give-6766c5a88d18

Urbanaviciute, I., Christina Roll, L., Tomas, J. & de Witte, H. (2021). Proactive strategies for countering the detrimental outcomes of qualitative job insecurity in academia. *Stress and Health, 37*, 557–571. https://doi.org/10.1002/smi.3023

Uţă, I.-C. (2019). *BMW is riding the ageing workforce trend*. https://brandminds.live/bmw-is-riding-the-ageing-workforce-trend/

Utz, R. L., & Pascoe, A. (2016). Bereavement/widowhood. In S. K. Whitbourne (Ed.), *Encyclopedia of adulthood and aging* (Vol. 1, pp. 118–121). Wiley-Blackwell.

Vaandrager, L., & Kennedy, L. (2022). The application of salutogenesis in communities and neighborhoods. In M. B. Mittelmark, G. F. Bauer, L. Vaandrager, J. M. Pelikan, S. Sagy, M. Eriksson, B. Lindström, & C. M. Magistretti (Eds.), *The handbook of salutogenesis* (2nd ed., pp. 349–359). Springer.

Vagelatos, N. T., & Eslick, G. D. (2013). Type 2 diabetes as a risk factor for Alzheimer's disease: The confounders, interactions, and neuropathology associated with this relationship. *Epidemiologic Reviews, 35*, 152–160. https://doi.org/10.1093/epirev/mxs012

Vahey, G. M., Marshall, K. E., McDonald, E., Martin, S. W., Tate, J. E., Midgley, C. M., Killerby, M. E., Kawasaki, B., Herlihy, R. K., Alden, N. B., & Staples, J. (2021). Symptom profiles and progression in hospitalized and nonhospitalized patients with coronavirus disease. *Emerging Infectious Diseases, 27*, 385–395. https://doi.org/10.3201/eid2702.203729

Vailati Riboni, F., & Pagnini, F. (2022). Age-based stereotype threat: A scoping review of stereotype priming techniques and their effects on the aging process. *Aging & Mental Health, 26*, 1444–1450. https://doi.org/10.1080/13607863.2021.1932741

Valenti, K. G., Janssen, L. M., Enguidanos, S., & de Medeiros, K. (2021). We speak a different language: End-of-life and bereavement experiences of older lesbian, gay, and bisexual women who have lost a spouse or partner. *Qualitative Health Research, 31*, 1670–1679. https://doi.org/10.1177%2F10497323211002823

Valiathan, R., Ashman, M., & Asthana, D. (2016). Effects of ageing on the immune system: Infants to elderly. *Scandinavian Journal of Immunology, 83*, 255–266. https://doi.org/10.1111/sji.12413

Vallerand, R. J. (2008). On the psychology of passion: In search of what makes people's lives most worth living. *Canadian Psychology, 49*, 1–13. https://doi.org/10.1037/0708-5591.49.1.1

Vallerand, R. J. (2015). *The psychology of passion: A dualistic model.* Oxford University Press.

Vallerand, R. J., Paquet, Y., Philippe, F. L., & Charest, J. (2010). On the role of passion for work in burnout: A process model. *Journal of Personality, 78*, 289–312. https://doi.org/10.1111/j.1467-6494.2009.00616.x

van de Bongardt, D., & de Graaf, H. (2020). Youth's socio-sexual competences with romantic and casual sexual partners. *The Journal of Sex Research, 57*, 1166–1179. https://doi.org/10.1080/00224499.2020.1743226

Van de Goor, J., Sools, A. M., & Westerhof, G. J. (2020). The emergence of meaning from meaningful moments in life. *Journal of Humanistic Psychology*. https://doi.org/10.1177%2F0022167820967779

van der Geest, S. (2004). Dying peacefully: Considering good death and bad death in Kwahu-Tafo, Ghana. *Social Science and Medicine, 58*, 899–911. https://doi.org/10.1016/j.socscimed.2003.10.041

van der Pas, S., & Koopman-Boyden, P. (2010). Leisure and recreation activities and wellbeing among midlife New Zealanders. In C. Waldegrave & P. Koopman-Boyden (Eds.), *Midlife New Zealanders aged 40–64 in 2008: Enhancing well-being in an aging society* (pp. 111–128). Family Centre Social Policy Research Unit, Lower Hutt, Wellington and the Population Studies Centre, University of Waikato. https://familycentre.org.nz/wp-content/uploads/2019/04/EWAS_M2.pdf

Van Gasse, D., & Mortelmans, D. (2020). With or without you—Starting single-parent families: A qualitative study on how single parents by choice reorganise their lives to facilitate single parenthood from a life course perspective. *Journal of Family Issues, 41*, 2223–2248. https://doi.org/10.1177%2F0192513X20911971

van Hoof, J., & Marston, H. R. (2021). Age-friendly cities & communities: State of the art and future perspectives. *International Journal of Environmental Research and Public Health, 18*, 1644. https://doi.org/10.3390/ijerph18041644

van Klaveren, C., van den Brink, H. M., & van Praag, B. (2013). Intrahousehold work timing: The effect on joint activities and the demand for child care. *European Sociological Review, 29*, 1–18. https://doi.org/10.1093/esr/jcr035

van Rooij, S. J. H., Riva-Posse, P., & McDonald, W. M. (2020). The efficacy and safety of neuromodulation treatments in late-life depression. *Current Treatment Options in Psychiatry, 7*, 337–348. https://doi.org/10.1007/s40501-020-00216-w

van Wanrooy, B. (2013). Couple strategies: Negotiating working time over the life course. In A. Evans, & J. Baxter (Eds.), *Negotiating the life course: Stability and change in life pathways* (pp. 175–190). Springer.

Van Wicklin, S. A. (2020). Changes as the body ages. *Plastic Surgical Nursing, 40*, 189–192. https://doi.org/10.1097/PSN.0000000000000339

Vansteenkiste, S., Deschacht, N., & Sels, L. (2015). Why are unemployed aged fifty and over less likely to find a job? A decomposition analysis. *Journal of Vocational Behavior, 90*, 55–65. https://doi.org/10.1016/j.jvb.2015.07.004

Varkal, M. D., Yalvac, D., Tufan, F., Turan, S., Cengiz, M., & Emul, M. (2013). Metacognitive differences between elderly and adult outpatients with generalized anxiety disorder. *European Geriatric Medicine, 4*, 150–153. https://doi.org/10.1016/j.eurger.2012.12.001

Verbeek, H., Peisah, C., de Mendonca Lima, C. A., Rabheru, K., & Ayalon, L. (2021). Human rights to inclusive living and care for older people with mental health conditions. *American Journal of Geriatric Psychiatry, 29*, 1015–1020. https://doi.org/10.1016/j.jagp.2021.05.023

Verbrugge, L. M. (1994). Disability in late life. In R. P. Abeles, H. C. Gift, & M. G. Ory (Eds.), *Aging and quality of life* (pp. 79–98). Springer.

Verbrugge, L. M. (2020). Revisiting the disablement process. In C. Jagger, E. Crimmins, Y. Saito, R. De Carvalho Yokota, H. Van Oyen, & J. M. Robine (Eds.), *International handbook of health expectancies* (pp. 275–285). Springer, Cham. https://doi.org/10.1007/978-3-030-37668-0_20

Verbrugge, L. M., & Jette, A. M. (1994). The disablement process. *Social Science and Medicine, 38*, 1–14. https://doi.org/10.1016/0277-9536(94)90294-1

Verbrugge, L. M., Brown, D. C., Zajacova, A. (2017). Disability rises gradually for a cohort of older Americans, *Journals of Gerontology: Psychological Sciences, 72*, 151–161. https://doi.org/10.1093/geronb/gbw002

Verhaeghen, P. (2022). There is nothing wrong with cognitive aging, and here is what to do about it. In G. Sedek, T. M. Hess, & D. R. Touron (Eds.), *Multiple pathways of cognitive aging: Motivational and contextual influences* (pp. 309–339). Oxford University Press.

Vezzali, L., & Stathi, S. (2021). *Using intergroup contact to fight prejudice and negative attitudes*. Routledge.

Vicente, R., Mausset-Bonnefont, A. L., Jorgensen, C., Louis-Plence, P., & Brondello, J. M. (2016). Cellular senescence impact on immune cell fate and function. *Aging Cell, 15*, 400–406. https://doi.org/10.1111/acel.12455

Vicente, R., Rizzuto, M., Sarica, C., Yamamoto, K., Sadr, M., Khajuria, T., Fatehi, M., Moien-Afshari, F., Haw. C. S., Llinas, R. R., Lozano, A. M., Neimat, J. S., & Zemmar, A. (2022). Enhanced interplay of neuronal coherence and coupling in the dying human brain. *Frontiers in Aging Neuroscience, 14*, 813531. https://www.frontiersin.org/articles/10.3389/fnagi.2022.813531

Vidal, C., & Zhang, L. (2021). An analysis of the neurological and molecular alterations underlying the pathogenesis Alzheimer's disease. *Cells, 10*, 546. https://doi.org/10.3390/cells10030546.

Vilpert, S., Borrat-Besson, C., Domenico Borasio, G., & Maurer, J. (2020). Correction: Associations of end-of-life preferences and trust in institutions with public support for assisted suicide: Evidence from nationally representative survey data of older adults in Switzerland. *PLoS ONE, 15*, e0234954. https://doi.org/10.1371/journal.pone.0234954

Virani, S. S., Alonso, A., Aparicio, H. J., Benjamin, E. J., Bittencourt, M. S., Callaway, C. W., Carson, A. P., Chamberlain, A. M., Cheng, S., Delling, F. N., Elkind, M. S. V., Evenson, K. R., Ferguson, J. F., Gupta, D. K., Khan, S. S., Kissela, B. M., Knutson, K. L., Lee, C. D., Lewis, T. T., … American Heart Association Council on Epidemiology and Prevention Statistics Committee and Stroke Statistics Subcommittee. (2021). Heart disease and stroke statistics—2021 update: A report from the American Heart Association. *Circulation, 143*, e254–e743. https://doi.org/10.1161/CIR.0000000000000950

Visser, M., Lössbroek, J., & van der Lippe, T. (2021). The use of HR policies and job satisfaction of older workers. *Work, Aging and Retirement, 7*, 303–321. https://doi.org/10.1093/workar/waaa023

Voelkle, M. C., Ebner, N. C., Lindenberger, U., & Riediger, M. (2012). Let me guess how old you are: Effects of age, gender, and facial expression on perceptions of age. *Psychology and Aging, 27*, 265–277. https://doi.org/10.1037/a0025065

Volpe, U., Fiorillo, A., Jovanovic, N., & Bhugra, D. (2016). Mentoring and career coaching. In A. Fiorillo, U. Volpe, & D. Bhugra (Eds.), *Psychiatry in practice: Education, experience, and expertise* (pp. 83–95). Oxford University Press.

von Hippel, W., & Henry, J. D. (2012). Social cognitive aging. In S. T. Fiske & C. N. Macrae (Eds.), *The SAGE handbook of social cognition* (pp. 390–410). SAGE Publications.

von Krause, M., Lerche, V., Schubert, A.-L., & Voss, A. (2020). Do non-decision times mediate the association between age and intelligence across different content and process domains? *Journal of Intelligence, 8*, 33. https://doi.org/10.3390/jintelligence8030033

Vosylis, R. (2021). Linking holistic pathways to adult roles with resolution of tasks and features of emerging adulthood: A person-oriented approach. *Emerging Adulthood, 9*, 35–52. https://doi.org/10.1177%2F2167696818808149

Vucurovic, K., Caillies, S., & Kaladjian, A. (2020). Neural correlates of theory of mind and empathy in schizophrenia: An activation likelihood estimation meta-analysis. *Journal of Psychiatric Research, 120*, 163–174. https://doi.org/10.1016/j.jpsychires.2019.10.018

Wade, L. (2017). *American hookup: The new culture of sex on campus*. Norton.

Wadsworth, S. M., Hughes-Kirchubel, L., & Riggs, D. S. (2014). Research and training about military families: Where are we? In S. M. Wadsworth & D. S. Riggs (Eds.), *Military deployment and its consequences for families* (pp. 1–17). Springer.

Wagner, J., Orth, U., Bleidorn, W., Hopwood, C. J., & Kandler, C. (2020). Toward an integrative model of sources of personality stability and change. *Current Directions in Psychological Science, 29*, 438–444. https://doi.org/10.1177/0963721420924751

Wahl, H.-W. (2015). Theories of environmental influences on aging and behavior. In N. A. Pachana (Ed.), *Encyclopedia of geropsychology* (pp. 1–8). Springer. https://doi.org/10.1007/978-981-287-080-3_132-1

Wahl, H.-W., Hoppmann, C. A., Ram, N., & Gerstorf, D. (2021). Healthy aging-relevant goals: The role of person–context co-construction. *Journals of Gerontology: Psychological Sciences, 76*, S181–S190. https://doi.org/10.1093/geronb/gbab089

Wainwright, N. W. J., Surtees, P. G., Welch, A. A., Luben, R. N., Khaw, K.-T., & Bingham, S. A. (2007). Healthy lifestyle choices: Could sense of coherence aid health promotion? *Journal of Epidemiology & Community Health, 61*, 871–876. http://doi.org/10.1136/jech.2006.056275

Wakelin, S. H. (2021). Benign skin lesions. *Medicine, 49*, 443–446. https://doi.org/10.1016/j.mpmed.2021.04.009

Walhovd, K. B., Westerhausen, R., de Lange, A.-M. G., Bråthen, A. C. S., Grydeland, H., Engvig, A., & Fjell, A. M. (2016). Premises of plasticity—And the loneliness of the medial temporal lobe. *NeuroImage, 131*, 48–54. https://doi.org/10.1016/j.neuroimage.2015.10.060

Walker, A.C. (2019). Death and dying in American Indian cultures. In H. Selin & R. Rakoff (Eds.), *Death across cultures: Death and dying in non-Western cultures* (pp. 335–349). Springer, Cham. https://doi.org/10.1007/978-3-030-18826-9_20

Walker, L. E. A. (1984). *The battered woman syndrome*. Springer.

Walker, W., & Trapani, J. (2018). Spotlight on bereavement care. *Nursing in Critical Care, 23*, 169–171. https://doi.org/10.1111/nicc.12362

Wallerstein, J. S., & Lewis, J. M. (2004). The unexpected legacy of divorce: Report of a 25-year study. *Psychoanalytic Psychology, 21*, 353–370. https://doi.org/10.1037/0736-9735.21.3.353

Walsh, F. (2020). Loss and resilience in the time of COVID-19: Meaning making, hope, and transcendence. *Family Process, 59*, 898–911. https://doi.org/10.1111/famp.12588

Walther, A. N. (1991). *Divorce hangover*. Pocket Books.

Wang, G., Zhao, M., Yang, F., Cheng, L. J., & Lau, Y. (2021). Game-based brain training for improving cognitive function in community-dwelling older adults: A systematic review and meta-regression. *Archives of Gerontology and Geriatrics, 92*, 104260. https://doi.org/10.1016/j.archger.2020.104260

Wang, H.-Q., Wang, Z.-Z., & Chen, N.-H. (2021). The receptor hypothesis and the pathogenesis of depression: Genetic bases and biological correlates. *Pharmacological Research, 167*, 105542. https://doi.org/10.1016/j.phrs.2021.105542

Wang, J., Zheng, X., & Chen, J. (2021). Clinical progression and outcomes of 260 patients with severe COVID-19: An observational study. *Scientific Reports, 11*, 3166. https://doi.org/10.1038/s41598-021-82943-5

Wang, L-C., Ye, M-Z., Xiong, J., Wang, X-Q., Wu, J-W., Zheng, G-H. (2021). Optimal exercise parameters of tai chi for balance performance in older adults: A meta-analysis. *Journal of the American Geriatrics Society, 69*, 2000–2010. https://doi.org/10.1111/jgs.17094

Wang, P., Zhang, B., & Huang, H. (2021). Research on the influence mechanism of career insecurity on individual career dynamics. *SHS Web of Conferences, 96*, 02001. https://doi.org/10.1051/shsconf/20219602001

Wang, T., Maden, S. K., Luebeck, G. E., Li, C. I., Newcomb, P. A., Ulrich, C. M., Joo, J. E., Buchanan, D. D., Milne, R. L., Southey, M. C., Carter, K. T., Willbanks, A. R., Luo, Y., Yu, M., & Grady, W. M. (2020). Dysfunctional epigenetic aging of the normal colon and colorectal cancer risk. *Clinical Epigenetics, 12*, 5. https://doi.org/10.1186/s13148-019-0801-3

Wang, W.-C., & Giovanello, K. S. (2016). The role of medial temporal lobe regions in incidental and intentional retrieval of item and relational information in aging. *Hippocampus, 26*, 693–699. https://doi.org/10.1002/hipo.22578

Wanzer, S. H., & Glenmullen, J. (2007). *To die well: Your right to comfort, calm, and choice in the last days of life*. Da Capo Press.

Waren, W., & Pals, H. (2013). Comparing characteristics of voluntarily childless men and women. *Journal of Population Research, 30*, 151–170. https://doi.org/10.1007/s12546-012-9103-8

Waring, M. K. (2021). The costs of unpaid care: Is there an education gradient in women's time transfers to their parents? *International Journal of Care and Caring, 5*, 85–104. https://doi.org/10.1332/239788220X15784101935186

Warner, D. F., & Adams, S. A. (2016). Physical disability and increased loneliness among married older adults: The role of changing social norms. *Society and Mental Health, 6*, 106–128. https://doi.org/10.1177/2156869315616257

Warner, S. C., & Valdes, A. M. (2016). The genetics of osteoarthritis: A review. *Journal of Functional Morphology and Kinesiology, 1*, 140–153. https://doi.org/10.3390/jfmk1010140

Warr, P., Butcher, V., & Robertson, I. (2004). Activity and psychological well-being in older people. *Aging & Mental Health*, 8, 172–183. https://doi.org/10.1080/13607860410001649662

Warren, D. E., Duff, M., Magnotta, V., Capizzano, A. A., Cassell, M. D., & Tranel, D. (2012). Long-term neuropsychological, neuroanatomical, and life outcome in hippocampal amnesia. *The Clinical*

Neuropsychologist, 26, 335–369. https://doi.org/10.1080/13854046. 2012.655781

Waterfield, R. (2020). *Non-adoptive siblings search-and-reunion experiences*. Doctoral thesis, Open University. https://ethos.bl.uk/OrderDetails.do?uin=uk.bl.ethos.817610

Watson, W., & Stelle, C. (2021). Love in cyberspace: Self presentation and partner seeking in online dating advertisements of older adults. *Journal of Family Issues, 42*, 2438–2463. https://doi.org/10.1177%2F0192513X20982024

Watt, J. A., Goodarzi, Z., Veroniki, A. A., Nincic, V., Khan, P. A., Ghassemi, M., Treister, V., Schneider, R., Tricco, A. C., & Straus, S. E. (2021). Comparative efficacy of interventions for reducing symptoms of depression in people with dementia: Systematic review and network meta-analysis. *BMJ, 372*, 532. https://doi.org/10.1136/bmj.n532

Wayland, S., Maple, M., McKay, K., & Glassock, G. (2016). Holding onto hope: A review of the literature exploring missing persons, hope and ambiguous loss. *Death Studies, 40*, 54–60. https://doi.org/10.1080/07481187.2015.1068245

Wechsler, D. (1958). *The measurement and appraisal of adult intelligence* (4th ed.). Williams & Wilkins.

Wegman, L. A., Hoffman, B. J., Carter, N. T., Twenge, J. M., & Guenole, N. (2018). Placing job characteristics in context: Cross-temporal meta-analysis of changes in job characteristics since 1975. *Journal of Management, 44*, 352–386. https://doi.org/10.1177/149206316654545

Wei, M., (2020). Social distancing and lockdown—An introvert's paradise? An empirical investigation on the association between introversion and the psychological impact of COVID-19-related circumstantial changes. *Frontiers in Psychology, 11*, 2440. https://doi.org/10.3389/fpsyg.2020.561609

Weigard, A. S., Sathian, K., & Hampstead, B. M. (2020). Model-based assessment and neural correlates of spatial memory deficits in mild cognitive impairment. *Neuropsychologia, 136*, 107251. https://doi.org/10.1016/j.neuropsychologia.2019.107251

Weiss, D. (2018). On the inevitability of aging: Essentialist beliefs moderate the impact of negative age stereotypes on older adults' memory performance and physiological reactivity. *Journals of Gerontology: Psychological Sciences, 73*, 925–933. https://doi.org/10.1093/geronb/gbw087

Weiss, D., & Lang, F. R. (2012). "They" are old but "I" feel younger: Age-group dissociation as a self-protective strategy in old age. *Psychology and Aging, 27*, 153–163. https://doi.org/10.1037/a0024887

Weiss, D., & Perry, E. L. (2020). Implications of generational and age metastereotypes for older adults at work: The role of agency, stereotype threat, and job search self-efficacy. *Work, Aging, and Retirement, 6*, 15–27. https://doi.org/10.1093/workar/waz010

Weiss, D., Job, V., Mathias, M., Grah, S., & Freund, A. M. (2016). The end (is not) near: Aging, essentialism, and future time perspective. *Developmental Psychology, 52*, 996–1009. https://doi.org/10.1037/dev0000115

Weiss, L. A., Westerhof, G. J., & Bohlmeijer, E. T. (2016). Can we increase psychological well-being? The effects of interventions on psychological well-being: A meta-analysis of randomized controlled trials. *PLoS ONE 11*, e0158092. https://doi.org/10.1371/journal.pone.0158092

Wenger, E., Fandakova, Y., & Shing, Y. L. (2021). Episodic memory training. In T. Strobach & J. Karbach (Eds.), *Cognitive training* (pp. 169–184). Springer, Cham. https://doi.org/10.1007/978-3-030-39292-5_12

Werner, T. L., & Shannon C. S. (2013). Doing more with less: Women's leisure during their partners' military deployment. *Leisure Sciences, 35*, 63–80. https://doi.org/10.1080/01490400.201 3.739897

Wertz, C. J., Chohan, M. O., Flores, R. A., & Jung, R. E. (2020). Neuroanatomy of creative achievement. *NeuroImage, 209*, 116487. https://doi.org/10.1016/j.neuroimage.2019.116487

Werum, R., Davis, T., Cheng, S., & Browne, I. (2018). Adoption context, parental investment, and children's educational outcomes. *Journal of Family Issues, 39*, 720–746. https://doi.org/10.1177%2F0192513X16680010

West, R. L., & Strickland-Hughes, C. M. (2016). Memory training for older adults: A review with recommendations for clinicians. In D. Bruno (Ed.), *The preservation of memory* (pp. 152–168). Routledge.

Weststrate, N. M., Ferrari, M., & Ardelt, M. (2016). The many faces of wisdom: An investigation of cultural-historical wisdom exemplars reveals practical, philosophical, and benevolent prototypes. *Personality and Social Psychology Bulletin, 42*, 662–676. https://doi.org/10.1177/0146167216638075

Wettstein, R. M. (2013). Legal issues geriatric psychiatrists should understand. In M. D. Miller & L. K. Salai (Eds.), *Geriatric psychiatry* (pp. 55–77). Oxford University Press.

Wetzel, M., & Hank, K. (2020). Grandparents' relationship to grandchildren in the transition to adulthood. *Journal of Family Issues, 41*, 1885–1904. https://doi.org/10.1177/0192513X19894355

Wexler, A., & Sullivan, L. S. (2021). Translational neuroethics: A vision for a more integrated, inclusive, and impactful field. *AJOB Neuroscience*. https://doi.org/10.1080/21507740.2021.2001078

Whalley, L. J. (2015). *Understanding brain aging and dementia: A lifecourse approach*. Columbia University Press.

Whitaker, M. M., Pointon, G. D., Tarampi, M. R., & Rand, K. M. (2020). Expertise effects on the perceptual and cognitive tasks of indoor rock climbing. *Memory and Cognition, 48*, 494–510. https://doi.org/10.3758/s13421-019-00985-7

Whitbourne, S. K. (1986). The psychological construction of the life span. In J. E. Birren & K. W. Schaie (Eds.), *Handbook of the psychology of aging* (pp. 594–618). Van Nostrand Reinhold.

Whitbourne, S. K. (1987). Personality development in adulthood and old age: Relationships among identity style, health, and well-being. In K. W. Schaie (Ed.), *Annual review of gerontology and geriatrics* (Vol. *7*, pp. 189–216). Springer.

Whitbourne, S. K. (2010). *The search for fulfillment: Revolutionary new research that reveals the secret to long-term happiness*. Ballantine Books.

Whitbourne, S. K., Culgin, S., & Cassidy, E. (1995). Evaluation of infantilizing intonation and content of speech directed at the aged. *International Journal of Aging and Human Development, 41*, 109–116. https://doi.org/10.2190/J9XE-2GB6-H49GMR7V

White, A. M., Castle, I. P., Powell, P. A., Hingson, R. W., & Koob, G. F. (2022). Alcohol-related deaths during the COVID-19 pandemic. *JAMA, 327*, 1704–1706. https://doi.org/10.1001/jama.2022.4308

Whited, C., Keeler, J., Scearce, L., & Cohen, S. (2016). The aging voice. In M. S. Benninger, T. Murry, & M. M. Johns III (Eds.), *The performer's voice* (2nd ed., pp. 89–102). Plural Publishing.

Whitley, M. (2021). *How to pay for a nursing home: Resources and advice*. https://www.aplaceformom.com/caregiver-resources/articles/pay-for-nursing-home-care

Wickrama, K. A. S., O'Neal, C. W., & Lorenz, F. O. (2013). Marital functioning form middle to later years: A life course-stress process framework. *Journal of Family Theory and Review, 5*, 15–34. https://doi.org/10.1111/jftr.12000

Wickrama, K. K. A. S., & O'Neal, C. W. (2021). Mastery and marital processes: Mechanisms linking midlife economic adversity and later-life loneliness for husbands and wives in enduring marriages. *Family Process, 60*, 836–852. https://doi.org/10.1111/famp.12611.

Wiepjes, C. M., de Blok, C. J., Staphorsius, A. S., Nota, N. M., Vlot, M. C., de Jongh, R. T., & den Heijer, M. (2020). Fracture risk in trans women and trans men using long-term gender-affirming hormonal treatment: A nationwide cohort study. *Journal of Bone and Mineral Research, 35*, 64–70. https://doi.org/10.1002/jbmr.3862

Wijngaarde, R. O., Hein, I., Daams, J., Van Goudoever, J. B., & Ubbink, D. T. (2021). Chronically ill children's participation and health outcomes in shared decision-making: A scoping review. *European Journal of Pediatrics, 180*, 2345–2357. https://doi.org/10.1007/s00431-021-04055-6

Wiles, J. L., & Jayasinha, R. (2013). Care for place: The contributions older people make to their communities. *Journal of Aging Studies, 27*, 93–101. https://doi.org/10.1016/j.jaging.2012.12.001

Williams, C. N., Perkhounkova, Y., Herman, R., & Bossen, A. (2017). A communication intervention to reduce resistiveness in dementia care: A cluster randomized controlled trial. *The Gerontologist, 57*, 707–718. https://doi.org/10.1093/geront/gnw047

Williamson, H. C., & Lavner, J. A. (2020). Trajectories of marital satisfaction in diverse newlywed couples. *Social Psychological and Personality Science, 11*, 597–604. https://doi.org/10.1177%2F1948550619865056

Willis, S. L. (1991). Cognition and everyday competence. In K. W. Schaie (Ed.), *Annual review of gerontology and geriatrics* (Vol. 11, pp. 80–109). Springer.

Willis, S. L., & Belleville, S. (2016). Cognitive training in later adulthood. In K. W. Schaie & L. Willis (Eds.), *Handbook of the psychology of aging* (8th ed., pp. 219–243). Academic Press. https://doi.org/10.1016/B978-0-12-411469-2.00012-1

Willis, S. L., Blieszner, R., & Baltes, P. B. (1981). Intellectual training research in aging: Modification of performance on the fluid ability of figural relations. *Journal of Educational Psychology, 73*, 41–50. https://doi.org/10.1016/0193-3973(81)90005-8

Willis, S. L., & Boron, J. B. (2008). Midlife cognition: The association of personality with cognition and risk of cognitive impairment. In S. M. Hofer & D. F. Alwin (Eds.), *Handbook of cognitive aging: Interdisciplinary perspectives* (pp. 647–660). Sage.

Willis, S. L., & Schaie, K. W. (2009). Cognitive training and plasticity: Theoretical perspective and methodological consequences. *Restorative Neurology and Neuroscience, 27*, 375–389. https://doi.org/10.3233/RNN-2009-0527

Willis, S. L., & Schaie, K. W. (2021). Cognitive functioning and dementia prevalence in baby boomers and adjacent cohorts: Longitudinal and cohort effects. In K. W. Schaie & S. L. Willis (Eds.), *Handbook of the psychology of aging* (9th ed., pp. 319–337). Academic Press. https://doi.org/10.1016/B978-0-12-816094-7.00021-0

Wilson, D. M., Darko, E. M., Kusi-Appiah, E., Roh, S. J., Ramic, A., & Erasti-Ibarrondo, B. (2022). What exactly is "complicated" grief? A scoping research literature review to understand its risk factors and prevalence. *OMEGA—Journal of Death and Dying, 86*, 471–487. https://doi.org/10.1177%2F0030222820977305

Winecoff, A., LaBar, K. S. Madden, D. J., Cabeza, R., & Huettel, S. A. (2011). Cognitive and neural contributions to emotion regulation in aging. *Social Cognitive and Affective Neuroscience, 6*, 165–176. https://doi.org/10.1093/scan/nsq030

Wink, P., Ai, A. L., & Paloutzian, R. F. (2021). Diverse spirituality revisited: Lessons learned. In A. L. Ai, P. Wink, R. F. Paloutzian, & K. A. Harris (Eds.), *Assessing spirituality in a diverse world* (pp. 577–594). Springer, Cham. https://doi.org/10.1007/978-3-030-52140-0_23

Winslow, M., & Meldrum, M. (2013). A history of hospice and palliative care. In S. Lutz, E. Chow, & P. Hoskin (Eds.), *Radiation oncology in palliative cancer care* (pp. 63–71). Wiley.

Winstead, B. A., Shappie, A. T., & Dawson, C. A. (2021). Intimate partner violence in women's same-sex relationships. In E. M. Lund, C. Burgess, & A. J. Johnson (Eds.), *Violence against LGBTQ+ persons: Research, policy, and advocacy* (pp. 117–133). Springer. https://doi.org/10.1007/978-3-030-52612-2_9

Winter, D., & Braw, Y. (2022). COVID-19: Impact of diagnosis threat and suggestibility on subjective cognitive complaints. *International Journal of Clinical and Health Psychology, 22*, 100253. https://doi.org/10.1016/j.ijchp.2021.100253

Winter, L., & Parks, S. M. (2012). Elders' preferences for life-prolonging treatment and their proxies' substituted judgment: Influence of the elders' current health. *Journal of Aging and Health, 24*, 1157–1178. https://doi.org/10.1177/0898264312454572

Wirth, K. P. (2020). *The career cost of children: A life course perspective of the gender gap in occupational status*. Doctoral dissertation, North Carolina State University. https://repository.lib.ncsu.edu/bitstream/handle/1840.20/37499/etd.pdf?sequence=1

Wise, D. (2017). *Social security programs and retirement around the world*. University of Chicago Press.

Witten, T. M. (2016). The intersectional challenges of aging and of being a gender non-conforming adult. *Generations, 40*, 63–70.

WomensHealth.gov. (2019). *Menopause basics*. https://www.womenshealth.gov/menopause/menopause-basics/

Wong, F. K. Y., & Yeung, S. M. (2015). Effects of a 4-week transitional care programme for discharged stroke survivors in Hong Kong: A randomised controlled trial. *Health and Social Care in the Community, 23*, 619–631. https://doi.org/10.1111/hsc.12177

Wong, P. T. P. (2015). *The meaning hypothesis of living a good life: Virtue, happiness and meaning*. http://www.drpaulwong.com/the-meaning-hypothesis-of-living-a-good-life-virtue-happiness-and-meaning/

Wong, P. T. P. (2016). Meaning-seeking, self-transcendence, and well-being. In A. Batthyany (Ed.), *Logotherapy and existential analysis: Proceedings of the Viktor Frankl Institute* (Vol. 1, pp. 311–322). Springer.

Wong, P. T. P. (2019). Second wave positive psychology's (PP 2.0) contribution to counselling psychology. *Counselling Psychology Quarterly, 32*, 275–284. https://doi.org/10.1080/09515070.2019.1671320

Wong, S., Pargament, K. I., & Faigin, C. A. (2018) Sustained by the sacred: Religious and spiritual factors for resilience in adulthood and aging. In B. Resnick, L. Gwyther, & K. Roberto (Eds.), *Resilience in aging* (pp. 191–214). Springer, Cham. https://doi.org/10.1007/978-3-030-04555-5_10

Woo, H., Hong, C. J., Jung, S., Choe, S., & Yu, S.-W. (2018). Chronic restraint stress induces hippocampal memory deficits by impairing insulin signaling. *Molecular Brain, 11*, 37. https://doi.org/10.1186/s13041-018-0381-8

Wood, S., & Kisley, M. A. (2006). The negativity bias is eliminated in older adults: Age-related reduction in event-related brain potentials associated with evaluative categorization. *Psychology and Aging, 21*, 815–820. https://doi.org/10.1037/0882-7974.21.4.815

Woods Barr, A. L., Miller, E., Smith, J. L., Cummings, S. M., & Schafer, E. J. (2021). #EveryGenerationMatters: Intergenerational perceptions of infant feeding information and communication among African American women. *Breastfeeding Medicine, 16*, 131–139. http://doi.org/10.1089/bfm.2020.0308

Woolley, M. E., & Greif, G. L. (2021). Adult sibling relationships in the United States: Mostly close, occasionally contentious, and caring for ageing parents. In A. Buchanan & A. Rotkirch (Eds.), *Brothers and sisters* (pp. 205–221). Palgrave Macmillan, Cham. https://doi.org/10.1007/978-3-030-55985-4_12

Worden, J. W. (2018). *Grief counseling and grief therapy: A handbook for the mental health practitioner* (5th ed.). Springer.

World Bank. (2021). *Life expectancy at birth, total (years)*. https://data.worldbank.org/indicator/SP.DYN.LE00.IN?most_recent_value_desc=true

World Bank. (2022). *Age dependency ratio (% of working-age population)*. https://data.worldbank.org/indicator/SP.POP.DPND?end=2020&start=1960

World Health Organization. (1946). *Constitution of the World Health Organization*. https://apps.who.int/gb/bd/pdf_files/BD_49th-en.pdf#page=6

World Health Organization. (2002). Towards a common language for functioning, disability and health. https://cdn.who.int/media/docs/default-source/classification/icf/icfbeginnersguide.pdf?sfvrsn=eead63d3_4

World Health Organization. (2007). *Global age-friendly cities: A guide*. https://www.who.int/ageing/publications/Global_age_friendly_cities_Guide_English.pdf

World Health Organization. (2013). *Responding to intimate partner violence and sexual violence against women*. https://www.who.int/reproductivehealth/publications/violence/9789241548595/en/

World Health Organization. (2021a). *World report on hearing*. https://apps.who.int/iris/bitstream/handle/10665/339913/9789240020481-eng.pdf?sequence=1

World Health Organization. (2021b). *Elder abuse*. https://www.who.int/news-room/fact-sheets/detail/elder-abuse

World Health Organization. (2021c). *Global report on ageism*. https://www.who.int/publications/i/item/9789240016866.

Wrenn, R. L. (1999). The grieving college student. In J. D. Davidson & K. J. Doka (Eds.), *Living with grief: At work, at school, at worship* (pp. 131–141). Brunner/Mazel.

Wright, M. R. (2020). Relationship quality among older cohabitors: A comparison to remarrieds. *Journals of Gerontology: Social Sciences, 75*, 1808–1817. https://doi.org/10.1093/geronb/gbz069

Wright, M. R., Hammersmith, A. M., Brown, S. I., & Lin, I.-F. (2020). The roles of marital dissolution and subsequent repartnering on loneliness in later life. *Journals of Gerontology: Social Sciences, 75*, 1796–1807. https://doi.org/10.1093/geronb/gbz121

Wright, P. M. (2022). Parental bereavement in older age: A scoping review. *Illness, Crisis & Loss, 30*, 531–571. https://doi.org/10.1177%2F1054137321995811

Wrzus, C. (2021). Processes of personality development: An update of the TESSERA framework. In J. F. Rauthmann (Ed.), *The handbook of personality dynamics and processes* (pp. 101–123). Academic Press. https://doi.org/10.1016/B978-0-12-813995-0.00005-4

Wrzus, C., & Roberts, B. W. (2017). Processes of personality development in adulthood: The TESSERA framework. *Personality and Social Psychology Review, 21*, 253–277. https://doi.org/10.1177/1088868316652279

Wrzus, C., Zimmermann, J., Mund, M., & Neyer, F. J. (2017). Friendships in young and middle adulthood: Normative patterns and personality differences. In M. Hojjat & A. Moyer (Eds.), *The psychology of friendship* (pp. 21–38). Oxford University Press.

Wu, L., & Zhao, L. (2016). ApoE2 and Alzheimer's disease: Time to take a closer look. *Neural Regeneration Research, 11*, 412–413. https://doi.org/10.4103/1673-5374.179044

Wu, Y., Goodman, G. S., Goldfarb, D., Wang, Y., Vidales, D., Brown, L., Eisen, M. L., & Qin, J. (2021). Memory accuracy after 20 years for interviews about child maltreatment. *Child Maltreatment*. https://doi.org/10.1177/10775595211055184

Wu, Z., Phyo, A. Z. Z., Al-harbi, T., Woods, R. L., & Ryan, J. (2020). Distinct cognitive trajectories in late life and associated predictors and outcomes: A systematic review. *Journal of Alzheimer's Disease Reports, 4*, 459–478. https://doi.org/10.3233/ADR-200232

Wyatt, A. (2016). Resident advocates, diversity, and resident-centered care. In R. Perley (Ed.), *Managing the long-term care facility: Practical approaches to providing quality care* (pp. 69–97). Jossey-Bass.

Xia, Y. R., Do, K. A., & Xie, X. (2013). The adjustment of Asian American families to the U.S. context: The ecology of strengths and stress. In G. W. Peterson & K. R. Bush (Eds.), *Handbook of marriage and the family* (3rd ed., pp. 723–747). Springer.

Xiang, H., Zhou, J., & Xie, B. (2022). AI tools for debunking online spam reviews? Trust of younger and older adults in AI detection criteria. *Behaviour & Information Technology*. https://doi.org/10.1080/0144929X.2021.2024252

Xu, Y. (2020, October 25). China expected to have 300 million senior residents in five years. *Global Times*. https://www.globaltimes.cn/content/1204581.shtml

Yacovson, A., Shadach, E., & Levy, S. (2021). Attachment style and prolonged singlehood in the ultra-Orthodox community in Israel. *Current Psychology, 41*, 1311–1322. https://doi.org/10.1007/s12144-020-00654-y

Yamasaki, T. (2021). Use of VEPs as electrodiagnostic biomarkers of mild cognitive impairment. *Neurology and Clinical Neuroscience, 9*, 3–9. https://doi.org/10.1111/ncn3.12387

Yan, M., Sun, S., Xu, K., Huang, X., Dou, L., Pang, J., Tang, W., Shen, T., & Li, J. (2021). Cardiac aging: From basic research to therapeutics. *Oxidative Medicine and Cellular Longevity, 2021*, Article 9570325. https://doi.org/10.1155/2021/9570325

Yanagisawa, K., Kashima, E. S., Shigemune, Y., Nakai, R., & Abe, N. (2021). Neural representations of death in the cortical midline structures promote temporal discounting. *Cerebral Cortex Communications, 2*, tgab013. https://doi.org/10.1093/texcom/tgab013

Yang, L., Weng, X., & Subramanian, S. V. (2020). Associations between older adults' parental bereavement and their health and well-being: Evidence from the China health and retirement longitudinal study. *Journal of Affective Disorders, 272*, 207–214. https://doi.org/10.1016/j.jad.2020.03.136

Yang, Z., Bishai, D., & Harman, J. (2008). Convergence of body mass with aging: The longitudinal interrelationship of health, weight, and survival. *Economics & Human Biology, 6*, 469–481. https://doi.org/10.1016/j. ehb.2008.06.006

Yárnoz-Yaben, S. (2010). Attachment style and adjustment to divorce. *Spanish Journal of Psychology, 13*, 210–219. https://doi.org/10.1017/S1138741600003796

Yarwood, A., Huizinga, T. W. J., & Worthington, J. (2016). The genetics of rheumatoid arthritis: Risk and protection in different stages of the evolution of RA. *Rheumatology, 55*, 1990209. https://doi.org/10.1093/rheumatology/keu323

Yassi, N., & Campbell, B. C. V. (2021). White matter hyperintensities: How much (and what shape) is too much? *Neurology, 96*, 781–782. https://doi.org/10.1212/WNL.0000000000011829

Yates, F. A. (1966). *The art of memory*. University of Chicago Press.

Yazdkhasti, M., Negarandeh, R., & Moghadam, Z. B. (2019). An empowerment model of Iranian women for the management of menopause: A grounded theory study. *International Journal of Qualitative Studies on Health and Well-being, 14*, Article 1665958. https://doi.org/10.1080/17482631.2019.1665958

Ybarra, O., Winkielman, P., Yeh, I., Burnstein, E., & Kavanagh, L. (2011). Friends (and sometimes enemies) with cognitive benefits: What types of social interactions boost executive functioning? *Social Psychological and Personality Science, 2*, 253–261. https://doi.org/10.1177/1948550610386808

Yesavage, J. A., Brink, T. L., Rose, T. L., Lum, O., Huang, V., Adey, M., & Leirer, V. O.(1983). Development and validation of a geriatric depression screening scale: A preliminary report. *Journal of Psychiatric Research, 17*, 37–49. https://doi.org/10.1016/0022-3956(82)90033-4

Yin, D. (2016). The essential mechanisms of aging: What have we learnt in ten years? *Current Topics in Medicinal Chemistry, 16*, 503–510.

Yin, X., & Wang, R. (2016). Simulation of dopamine modulation-based memory model. *Neurocomputing, 194*, 241–245. https://doi.org/10.1016/j.neucom.2016.01.077

Yngvesson, B. (2010). *Belonging in an adopted world: Race, identity, and transnational adoption*. University of Chicago Press.

Yoon, S. M. (2005). The characteristics and needs of Asian-American grandparent caregivers: A study of Chinese-American and Korean-American grandparents in New York City. *Journal of Gerontological Social Work, 44*, 75–94. https://doi.org/10.1300/J083v44n03_06

Young, J. L., Kim, HD., & Golojuch, L. (2021). "Race was something we didn't talk about": Racial socialization in Asian American families. *Family Relations, 70*, 1027–1039. https://doi.org/10.1111/fare.12495

Youssef-Morgan, C. M., & Luthans, F. (2013). Psychological capital theory: Toward a positive holistic model. In A. B. Bakker (Ed.), *Advances in positive organizational psychology* (Vol. 1, pp. 145–166). Emerald Group Publishing.

Yu, E. A., & Chang, E. C. (2021). Relational meaning in life as a predictor of interpersonal well-being: A prospective analysis. *Personality and Individual Differences, 168*, Article 110377. https://doi.org/10.1016/j.paid.2020.110377

Yu, F. (2016). Behavioral management in long-term care. In S. K. Whitbourne (Ed.), *The encyclopedia of adulthood and aging* (pp. 113–118). Wiley-Blackwell.

Yu, H., Lee, L., Popa, J., & Madera, J. M. (2021). Should I leave this industry? The role of stress and negative emotions in response to an industry negative work event. *International Journal of Hospitality Management, 94*, Article 102843. https://doi.org/10.1016/j.ijhm.2020.102843

Yu, L. Q., Kan, I. P., & Kable, J. W. (2020). Beyond a rod through the skull: A systematic review of lesion studies of the human ventromedial frontal lobe. *Cognitive Neuropsychology, 37*, 97–141. https://doi.org/10.1080/02643294.2019.1690981

Yu, T., Pettit, G. S., Lansford, J. E., Dodge, K. A., & Bates, J. E. (2010). The interactive effects of marital conflict and divorce on parent–adult children's relationships. *Journal of Marriage and Family, 72*, 282–292. https://doi.org/10.1111/j.1741-3737.2010.00699.x

Yuen, H. K., & Vogtle, L. K. (2016). Multi-morbidity, disability and adaptation strategies among community-dwelling adults aged 75 years and older. *Disability and Health Journal, 9*, 593–599. https://doi.org/10.1016/j.dhjo.2016.03.004

Zabriskie, R. B., & Kay, T. (2013). Positive leisure science: Leisure in family contexts. In T. Freire (Ed.), *Positive leisure science* (pp. 81–99). Springer.

Zahedi Bidgoli, Z., Tagharrobi, Z., Sooki, Z., & Sharifi, K. H. (2020). Death anxiety and its predictors among older adults. *Journal of Holistic Nursing and Midwifery, 30*, 101–110. https://doi.org/10.32598/jhnm.30.2.101

Zaheri, F., Dolatian, M., Shariati, M., Simbar, M., Ebadi, A., & Azghadi, S. B. H. (2020). The concept and aspects of a successful marriage as stated by successful Iranian couples and experts: A qualitative study. *Crescent Journal of Medical and Biological Sciences, 7*, 159–169. http://www.cjmb.org/uploads/pdf/pdf_CJMB_353.pdf

Zahodne, L. B. (2021). Psychosocial protective factors in cognitive aging: A targeted review. *Archives of Clinical Neuropsychology, 36*, 1266–1273. https://doi.org/10.1093/arclin/acab051

Zahodne, L. B., Glymour, M. M., Sparks, C., Bontempo, D., Dixon, R. A., MacDonald, S. W. S., & Manly, J. J. (2011). Education does not slow cognitive decline with aging: 12-year evidence form the Victoria Longitudinal Study. *Journal of the International Neuropsychological Society, 17*, 1039–1046. https://doi.org/10.1017/S1355617711001044

Zamir, O., Gewirtz, A. H., Cheng, C. H., Zhang, N., & Lavee, Y. (2020). Psychological distress and communication quality in military couples after deployment to war. *Journal of Family Psychology, 34*, 383–391. https://doi.org/10.1037/fam0000589

Zarit, S. H., & Zarit, J. M. (2007). *Mental disorders in older adults: Fundamentals of assessment and treatment* (2nd ed.). Guilford.

Zaval, L., Li, Y., Johnson, E. J., & Weber, E. U. (2015). Complementary contributions of fluid and crystallized intelligence to decision making across the life span. In T. M. Hess, J. Strough, & C. E. Lockenhoff (Eds.), *Aging and decision making: Empirical and applied perspectives* (pp. 149–168). Academic Press.

Zeitchik, S. (2022, March 16). Meet ElliQ, the robot who wants to keep grandma company. *Washington Post*. https://www.washingtonpost.com/technology/2022/03/16/lonely-elderly-companion-ai-device/

Zelin, A. I., Magley V. J. (2020). Sexual harassment training: Why it (currently) doesn't work and what can be done. In R. Geffner, V. Vieth, V. Vaughan-Eden, A. Rosenbaum, L. Hamberger, & J. White (Eds.), *Handbook of interpersonal violence across the lifespan* (pp. 1–21). Springer, Cham. https://doi.org/10.1007/978-3-319-62122-7_276-1

Zelinski, E. M., & Kennison. R. F., Watts, A., & Lewis, K. L. (2009). Convergence between longitudinal and cross-sectional studies: Cohort matters. In C. Hertzog & H. Bosworth (Eds.), *Aging and cognition: Research methodologies and empirical advances* (pp. 101–118). American Psychological Association.

Zetumer, S., Young, I., Shear, M. K., Skritskaya, N., Lebowitz, B., Simon, N., Reynolds, C., Mauro, C., & Zisook, S. (2015). The impact of losing a child on the clinical presentation of complicated grief. *Journal of Affective Disorders, 170*, 15–21. https://doi.org/10.1016/j.jad.2014.08.021

Zgonec, S. (2021). Mobile apps supporting people with dementia and their carers: Literature review and research agenda. *IFAC—PapersOnLine, 54*, 663-668. https://doi.org/10.1016/j.ifacol.2021.10.527

Zhan, H. J. (2006). Joy and sorrow: Explaining Chinese caregivers' reward and stress. *Journal of Aging Studies, 20*, 27–38. https://doi.org/10.1016/j.aging.2005.01.002

Zhang, S. (2020). *The role of basic cognition and domain-specific knowledge on everyday cognition across the adult life-span*. Dissertation, North Carolina State University Proquest Dissertations, 28122839.

Zhou, M., & Bankston, C. L., III. (2020). The model minority stereotype and the national identity question: The challenges facing Asian immigrants and their children. *Ethnic and Racial Studies, 43*, 233–253. https://doi.org/10.1080/01419870.2019.1667511

Zhou, Y. M. J., & Shelton, W. (2020). Physicians' end of life discussions with patients: Is there an ethical obligation to discuss aid in dying? *HEC Forum, 32*, 227–238. https://doi.org/10.1007/s10730-020-09402-y

Zhuang, L., Wang, J., Xiong, B., Bian, C., Hao, L., Bayley, P. J., & Qin, S. (2021). Rapid neural reorganization during retrieval practice predicts subsequent long-term retention and false memory. *Nature Human Behaviour*. https://doi.org/10.1038/s41562-021-01188-4

Zhuang, L., Yang, Y., & Gao, J. (2021). Cognitive assessment tools for mild cognitive impairment screening. *Journal of Neurology, 268*, 1615–1622. https://doi.org/10.1007/s00415-019-09506-7

Ziaei, M., & Fisher, H. (2016). Emotion and aging: The impact of emotion on attention, memory, and face recognition in late adulthood. In J. R. Absher & J. Cloutier (Eds.), *Neuroimaging personality, social cognition, and character* (pp. 259–278). Elsevier.

Ziegler, M., Cengia, A., Mussel, P., & Gerstorf, D. (2015). Openness as a buffer against cognitive decline: The Openness-Fluid-Crystallized-Intelligence (OFCI) model applied to late adulthood. *Psychology and Aging, 30*, 573–588. https://doi.org/10.1037/a0039493

Zimprich, D., & Martin, M. (2002). Can longitudinal changes in processing speed explain longitudinal age change in fluid intelligence? *Psychology and Aging, 17*, 690–695. https://doi.org/10.1037/0882-7974.17.4.690

Zimprich, D., & Martin, M. (2009). A multilevel factor analysis perspective on intellectual development in old age. In C. Hertzog & H. Bosworth (Eds.), *Aging and cognition: Research methodologies and empirical advances* (pp. 53–76). American Psychological Association.

ZipRecruiter. (2022). *Caregiver assisted living salary*. https://www.ziprecruiter.com/Salaries/Caregiver-Assisted-Living-Salary

Zogg, J. B., Woods, S. P., Sauceda, J. A., Wiebe, J. S., & Simoni, J. M. (2012). The role of prospective memory in medication adherence: A review of an emerging literature. *Journal of Behavioral Medicine, 35*, 47–62. https://doi.org/10.1007/s10865-011-9341-9

Zuccala, M., & Abbott, M. J. (2021). Social anxiety disorder and the fear of death: An empirical investigation of the terror management approach towards understanding clinical anxiety. *Cognitive Therapy and Research, 45*, 628–641. https://doi.org/10.1007/s10608-020-10187-0

Zuo, N., Salami, A., Liu, H., Yang, Z., & Jiang, T. (2020). Functional maintenance in the multiple demand network characterizes superior fluid intelligence in aging. *Neurobiology of Aging, 85*, 145–153. https://doi.org/10.1016/j.neurobiolaging.2019.09.006

Name Index

Subject Index

Note: Page numbers in bold indicate key terms, those with f indicate figures, and those with t indicate tables.